Official
BASEBALL
RECORD BOOK

1984 EDITION

Editor/Baseball Record Book
CRAIG CARTER

President-Chief Executive Officer
RICHARD WATERS

Editor
DICK KAEGEL

Director of Books and Periodicals
RON SMITH

Published by

The Sporting News

1212 North Lindbergh Boulevard
P.O. Box 56 — St. Louis, Mo. 63166

Copyright © 1984
The Sporting News Publishing Company
a Times Mirror company

ISBN 0-89204-150-1   ISSN 0162-5438

Table of Contents

On the Cover:
Kansas City bullpen ace Dan Quisenberry put together an amazing season in 1983, recording a major league-record 45 saves for a team that finished four games under .500. Quisenberry, who also recorded five victories and a 1.94 earned-run average, broke John Hiller's record of 38 saves for Detroit in 1973.

—Photograph by Richard Pilling

Cobb, Lajoie Records in Dispute

The April 18, 1981, issue of THE SPORTING NEWS carried a story by Associate Editor Paul Mac Farlane detailing record-keeping discrepancies in the playing records of Tyrus Cobb and Napoleon Lajoie. The discrepancies were uncovered during research for the 1981 edition of Daguerreotypes, a book that contains the records of baseball's greatest players.

The Key issue was the 1910 batting championship. At the time, Lajoie was thought to be the winner but, after a review, American League President Ban Johnson ruled that Cobb had won. Therefore, for 70 years, Cobb was listed as the 1910 leader with a .385 average, one point higher than Lajoie's .384. Mac Farlane's findings, corroborated by other researchers, showed that Lajoie actually batted .383 and Cobb .382.

Research revealed that in 1910 Cobb was erroneously credited with an extra 2-for-3 game and was not credited with two additional hitless at-bats. This made Cobb's corrected average for that year .382 (194-for-508). Also, one additional hitless at-bat was discovered in Lajoie's record, making his corrected average .383 (227-for-592).

Furthermore, research showed that in 1906, two games in which Cobb was 1-for-8 were omitted from his record. The 1906 and 1910 corrections dropped Cobb's career hits total by one, to 4,190, and his lifetime average by a point, to .366.

THE SPORTING NEWS believes the evidence is irrefutable. However, on December 16, 1981, the Official Records Committee met at the commissioner's office in New York and rejected the findings of this research, supporting Commissioner Bowie Kuhn's earlier decision that Ban Johnson's 1910 decision should not be overturned. As a result, the Baseball Record Book lists Cobb as the 1910 batting leader and his career totals as .367 with 4,191 hits and 12 American League batting championships (including nine in succession), but with the appropriate notations that these records are in dispute.

AMERICAN LEAGUE

PENNANT WINNERS

Year	Club	Manager	W.	L.	Pct.	*G.A.
1901—Chicago		Clark Griffith	83	53	.610	4
1902—Philadelphia		Connie Mack	83	53	.610	5
1903—Boston		James Collins	91	47	.659	14½
1904—Boston		James Collins	95	59	.617	1½
1905—Philadelphia		Connie Mack	92	56	.622	2
1906—Chicago		Fielder Jones	93	58	.616	3
1907—Detroit		Hugh Jennings	92	58	.613	1½
1908—Detroit		Hugh Jennings	90	63	.588	½
1909—Detroit		Hugh Jennings	98	54	.645	3½
1910—Philadelphia		Connie Mack	102	48	.680	14½
1911—Philadelphia		Connie Mack	101	50	.669	13½
1912—Boston		Garland Stahl	105	47	.691	14
1913—Philadelphia		Connie Mack	96	57	.627	6½
1914—Philadelphia		Connie Mack	99	53	.651	8½
1915—Boston		William Carrigan	101	50	.669	2½
1916—Boston		William Carrigan	91	63	.591	2
1917—Chicago		Clarence Rowland	100	54	.649	9
1918—Boston		Edward Barrow	75	51	.595	2½
1919—Chicago		William Gleason	88	52	.629	3½
1920—Cleveland		Tristram Speaker	98	56	.636	2
1921—New York		Miller Huggins	98	55	.641	4½
1922—New York		Miller Huggins	94	60	.610	1
1923—New York		Miller Huggins	98	54	.645	16
1924—Washington		Stanley (Bucky) Harris	92	62	.597	2
1925—Washington		Stanley (Bucky) Harris	96	55	.636	8½

PENNANT WINNERS—Continued

Year Club	Manager	W.	L.	Pct.	*G.A.
1926—New York	Miller Huggins	91	63	.591	3
1927—New York	Miller Huggins	110	44	.714	19
1928—New York	Miller Huggins	101	53	.656	2½
1929—Philadelphia	Connie Mack	104	46	.693	18
1930—Philadelphia	Connie Mack	102	52	.662	8
1931—Philadelphia	Connie Mack	107	45	.704	13½
1932—New York	Joseph McCarthy	107	47	.695	13
1933—Washington	Joseph Cronin	99	53	.651	7
1934—Detroit	Gordon (Mickey) Cochrane	101	53	.656	7
1935—Detroit	Gordon (Mickey) Cochrane	93	58	.616	3
1936—New York	Joseph McCarthy	102	51	.667	19½
1937—New York	Joseph McCarthy	102	52	.662	13
1938—New York	Joseph McCarthy	99	53	.651	9½
1939—New York	Joseph McCarthy	106	45	.702	17
1940—Detroit	Delmer Baker	90	64	.584	1
1941—New York	Joseph McCarthy	101	53	.656	17
1942—New York	Joseph McCarthy	103	51	.669	9
1943—New York	Joseph McCarthy	98	56	.636	13½
1944—St. Louis	J. Luther Sewell	89	65	.578	1
1945—Detroit	Stephen O'Neill	88	65	.575	1½
1946—Boston	Joseph Cronin	104	50	.675	12
1947—New York	Stanley (Bucky) Harris	97	57	.630	12
1948—Cleveland†	Louis Boudreau	97	58	.626	1
1949—New York	Charles (Casey) Stengel	97	57	.630	1
1950—New York	Charles (Casey) Stengel	98	56	.636	3
1951—New York	Charles (Casey) Stengel	98	56	.636	5
1952—New York	Charles (Casey) Stengel	95	59	.617	2
1953—New York	Charles (Casey) Stengel	99	52	.656	8½
1954—Cleveland	Alfonso Lopez	111	43	.721	8
1955—New York	Charles (Casey) Stengel	96	58	.623	3
1956—New York	Charles (Casey) Stengel	97	57	.630	9
1957—New York	Charles (Casey) Stengel	98	56	.636	8
1958—New York	Charles (Casey) Stengel	92	62	.597	10
1959—Chicago	Alfonso Lopez	94	60	.610	5
1960—New York	Charles (Casey) Stengel	97	57	.630	8
1961—New York	Ralph Houk	109	53	.673	8
1962—New York	Ralph Houk	96	66	.593	5
1963—New York	Ralph Houk	104	57	.646	10½
1964—New York	Lawrence (Yogi) Berra	99	63	.611	1
1965—Minnesota	Sabath (Sam) Mele	102	60	.630	7
1966—Baltimore	Henry A. Bauer	97	63	.606	9
1967—Boston	Richard H. Williams	92	70	.568	1
1968—Detroit	E. Mayo Smith	103	59	.636	12
1969—Baltimore (E)**	Earl S. Weaver	109	53	.673	19
1970—Baltimore (E)**	Earl S. Weaver	108	54	.667	15
1971—Baltimore (E)**	Earl S. Weaver	101	57	.639	12
1972—Oakland (W)**	Richard H. Williams	93	62	.600	5½
1973—Oakland (W)**	Richard H. Williams	94	68	.580	6
1974—Oakland (W)**	Alvin Ralph Dark	90	72	.556	5
1975—Boston (E)**	Darrell D. Johnson	95	65	.594	4½
1976—New York (E)**	Alfred M. Martin	97	62	.610	10½
1977—New York (E)**	Alfred M. Martin	100	62	.617	2½
1978—New York (E)†**	Alfred M. Martin, Robert G. Lemon	100	63	.613	1
1979—Baltimore (E)**	Earl S. Weaver	102	57	.642	8
1980—Kansas City (W)**	James G. Frey	97	65	.599	14
1981—New York (E)**	Eugene R. Michael, Robert G. Lemon...	59	48	.551	‡
1982—Milwaukee (E)**	Robert L. Rodgers, Harvey E. Kuenn ...	95	67	.586	1
1983—Baltimore (E)**	Joseph S. Altobelli	98	64	.605	6

*Games ahead of second-place club.   †Defeated Boston in one-game playoff.   ‡First half 34-22; second 25-26.   **Won Championship Series.

YEARLY FINISHES

Year	Balt.	Bos.	Calif.	Chi.	Cleve.	Det.	Minn.	N.Y.	Oak.	Wash.
1901	a8	2	....	1	7	3	§6	z5	‡4	....
1902	†2	3	....	4	5	7	§6	z8	‡1	....
1903	†6	1	....	7	3	5	§8	4	‡2	....
1904	†6	1	....	3	4	7	§8	2	‡5	....
1905	†8	4	....	2	5	3	§7	6	‡1	....

Year	Balt.	Bos.	Calif.	Chi.	Cleve.	Det.	Minn.	N.Y.	Oak.	Wash.
1906	†5	8	....	1	3	6	§7	2	‡4	....
1907	†6	7	....	3	4	1	§8	5	‡2	....
1908	†4	5	....	3	2	1	§7	8	‡6	....
1909	†7	3	....	4	6	1	§8	5	‡2	....
1910	†8	4	....	6	5	3	§7	2	‡1	....
1911	†8	5	....	4	3	2	§7	6	‡1	....
1912	†7	1	....	4	5	6	§2	8	‡3	....
1913	†8	4	....	5	3	6	§2	7	‡1	....
1914	†5	2	....	*6	8	4	§3	*6	‡1	....
1915	†6	1	....	3	7	2	§4	5	‡8	....
1916	†5	1	....	2	6	3	§7	4	‡8	....
1917	†7	2	....	1	3	4	§5	6	‡8	....
1918	†5	1	....	6	2	7	§3	4	‡8	....
1919	†5	6	....	1	2	4	§7	3	‡8	....
1920	†4	5	....	2	1	7	§6	3	‡8	....
1921	†3	5	....	7	2	6	§4	1	‡8	....
1922	†2	8	....	5	4	3	§6	1	‡7	....
1923	†5	8	....	7	3	2	§4	1	‡6	....
1924	†4	7	....	8	6	3	§1	2	‡5	....
1925	†3	8	....	5	6	4	§1	7	‡2	....
1926	†7	8	....	5	2	6	§4	1	‡3	....
1927	†7	8	....	5	6	4	§3	1	‡2	....
1928	†3	8	....	5	7	6	§4	1	‡2	....
1929	†4	8	....	7	3	6	§5	2	‡1	....
1930	†6	8	....	7	4	5	§2	3	‡1	....
1931	†5	6	....	8	4	7	§3	2	‡1	....
1932	†6	8	....	7	4	5	§3	1	‡2	....
1933	†8	7	....	6	4	5	§1	2	‡3	....
1934	†6	4	....	8	3	1	§7	2	‡5	....
1935	†7	4	....	5	3	1	§6	2	‡8	....
1936	†7	6	....	3	5	2	§4	1	‡8	....
1937	†8	5	....	3	4	2	§6	1	‡7	....
1938	†7	2	....	6	3	4	§5	1	‡8	....
1939	†8	2	....	4	3	5	§6	1	‡7	....
1940	†6	*4	....	*4	2	1	§7	3	‡8	....
1941	*†6	2	....	3	*4	*4	*§6	1	‡8	....
1942	†3	2	....	6	4	5	§7	1	‡8	....
1943	†6	7	....	4	3	5	§2	1	‡8	....
1944	†1	4	....	7	*5	2	§8	3	*‡5	....
1945	†3	7	....	6	5	1	§2	4	‡8	....
1946	†7	1	....	5	6	2	§4	3	‡8	....
1947	†8	3	....	6	4	2	§7	1	‡5	....
1948	†6	2	....	8	1	5	§7	3	‡4	....
1949	†7	2	....	6	3	4	§8	1	‡5	....
1950	†7	3	....	6	4	2	§5	1	‡8	....
1951	†8	3	....	4	2	5	§7	1	‡6	....
1952	†7	6	....	3	2	8	§5	1	‡4	....
1953	†8	4	....	3	2	6	§5	1	‡7	....
1954	7	4	....	3	1	5	§6	2	‡8	....
1955	7	4	....	3	2	5	§8	1	‡6	....
1956	6	4	....	3	2	5	§7	1	‡8	....
1957	5	3	....	2	6	4	§8	1	‡7	....
1958	6	3	....	2	4	5	§8	1	‡7	....
1959	6	5	....	1	2	4	§8	3	‡7	....
1960	2	7	....	3	4	6	§5	1	‡8	....
1961	3	6	x8	4	5	2	7	1	*‡9	*9
1962	7	8	x3	5	6	4	2	1	‡9	10
1963	4	7	x9	2	*5	*5	3	1	‡8	10
1964	3	8	x5	2	*6	4	*6	1	‡10	9
1965	3	9	x7	2	5	4	1	6	‡10	8
1966	1	9	6	4	5	3	2	10	‡7	8
1967	*6	1	5	4	8	*2	*2	9	‡10	*6
1968	2	4	*8	*8	3	1	7	5	6	10

EAST DIVISION / WEST DIVISION

	EAST DIVISION							WEST DIVISION						
Year	Balt.	Bos.	Cleve.	Det.	N.Y.	Wash.	Mil.	Calif.	Chi.	K.C.	Mil.	Minn.	Oak.	Tex.
1969	1	3	6	2	5	4	....	3	5	4	y6	1	2	....
1970	1	3	5	4	2	6	....	3	5	*4	*4	1	2	....
1971	1	3	6	2	4	5	....	4	3	3	6	5	1	....
1972	3	2	5	1	4	....	6	5	2	4	....	3	1	6
1973	1	2	6	3	4	....	5	4	5	2	....	3	1	6
1974	1	3	4	6	2	....	5	6	4	5	....	3	1	2

YEARLY FINISHES—Continued

	EAST DIVISION							WEST DIVISION						
Year	Balt.	Bos.	Cleve.	Det.	Mil.	N.Y.	Tor.	Calif.	Chi.	K.C.	Minn.	Oak.	Sea.	Tex.
1975	2	1	4	6	3	....	5	6	5	2	....	4	1	3
1976	2	3	4	5	1	....	6	*4	6	1	....	3	2	*4
1977	*2	*2	5	4	6	1	7	5	3	1	4	7	6	2
1978	4	2	6	5	3	1	7	*2	5	1	4	6	7	*2
1979	1	3	6	5	2	4	7	1	5	2	4	7	6	3
1980	2	4	6	5	3	1	7	6	5	1	3	2	7	4
1981b	2	5	6	4	3	1	7	4	3	5	7	1	6	2
c	3	*2	*4	*2	1	*4	5	7	6	1	4	2	5	3
1982	2	3	*6	4	1	5	*6	1	3	2	7	5	4	6
1983	1	6	7	2	5	3	4	*5	1	2	*5	4	7	3

*Tied for position. †Record of predecessor St. Louis club. ‡Predecessor Philadelphia (1901-54), Kansas City (1955-67). §Predecessor Washington club. xKnown as Los Angeles Angels from 1961 to September 2, 1965. yPredecessor Seattle club. zPredecessor Baltimore club. aPredecessor Milwaukee club. bStandings for first half of split season. cStandings for second half of split season.

LEADING BATSMEN

Year	Player and Club	G.	AB.	R.	H.	TB.	2B.	3B.	HR.	RBI.	B.A.
1901—	Napoleon Lajoie, Philadelphia	131	543	145	229	345	48	13	14	....	.422
1902—	Edward Delahanty, Washington	123	474	103	178	279	41	15	10	....	.376
1903—	Napoleon Lajoie, Cleveland	126	488	90	173	260	40	13	7	....	.355
1904—	Napoleon Lajoie, Cleveland	140	554	92	211	304	50	14	5	....	.381
1905—	Elmer Flick, Cleveland	131	500	72	154	233	29	19	4	....	.308
1906—	George Stone, St. Louis	154	581	91	208	288	24	19	6	....	.358
1907—	Tyrus Cobb, Detroit	150	605	97	212	286	29	15	5	116	.350
1908—	Tyrus Cobb, Detroit	150	581	88	188	276	36	20	4	101	.324
1909—	Tyrus Cobb, Detroit	156	573	116	216	296	33	10	9	115	.377
1910—	*Tyrus Cobb, Detroit	140	509	106	196	282	36	13	8	88	.385
1911—	Tyrus Cobb, Detroit	146	591	147	248	367	47	24	8	144	.420
1912—	Tyrus Cobb, Detroit	140	553	119	227	324	30	23	7	90	.410
1913—	Tyrus Cobb, Detroit	122	428	70	167	229	18	16	4	65	.390
1914—	Tyrus Cobb, Detroit	97	345	69	127	177	22	11	2	57	.368
1915—	Tyrus Cobb, Detroit	156	563	114	208	274	31	13	3	95	.369
1916—	Tristram Speaker, Cleveland	151	546	102	211	274	41	8	2	83	.386
1917—	Tyrus Cobb, Detroit	152	588	107	225	336	44	24	6	108	.383
1918—	Tyrus Cobb, Detroit	111	421	83	161	217	19	14	3	64	.382
1919—	Tyrus Cobb, Detroit	124	497	92	191	256	36	13	1	69	.384
1920—	George Sisler, St. Louis	154	631	137	257	399	49	18	19	122	.407
1921—	Harry Heilmann, Detroit	149	602	114	237	365	43	14	19	139	.394
1922—	George Sisler, St. Louis	142	586	134	246	348	42	18	8	105	.420
1923—	Harry Heilmann, Detroit	144	524	121	211	331	44	11	18	115	.403
1924—	George (Babe) Ruth, New York	153	529	143	200	391	39	7	46	121	.378
1925—	Harry Heilmann, Detroit	150	573	97	225	326	40	11	13	133	.393
1926—	Henry Manush, Detroit	136	498	95	188	281	35	8	14	86	.378
1927—	Harry Heilmann, Detroit	141	505	106	201	311	50	9	14	120	.398
1928—	Leon (Goose) Goslin, Washington	135	456	80	173	280	36	10	17	102	.379
1929—	Lew Fonseca, Cleveland	148	566	97	209	301	44	15	6	103	.369
1930—	Aloysius Simmons, Philadelphia	138	554	152	211	392	41	16	36	165	.381
1931—	Aloysius Simmons, Philadelphia	128	513	105	200	329	37	13	22	128	.390
1932—	Dale Alexander, Detroit-Boston	124	392	58	144	201	27	3	8	60	.367
1933—	James Foxx, Philadelphia	149	573	125	204	403	37	9	48	163	.356
1934—	H. Louis Gehrig, New York	154	579	128	210	409	40	6	49	165	.363
1935—	Chas. (Buddy) Myer, Washington	151	616	115	215	288	36	11	5	100	.349
1936—	Lucius Appling, Chicago	138	526	111	204	267	31	7	6	128	.388
1937—	Charles Gehringer, Detroit	144	564	133	209	293	40	1	14	96	.371
1938—	James Foxx, Boston	149	565	139	197	398	33	9	50	175	.349
1939—	Joseph DiMaggio, New York	120	462	108	176	310	32	6	30	126	.381
1940—	Joseph DiMaggio, New York	132	508	93	179	318	28	9	31	133	.352
1941—	Theodore Williams, Boston	143	456	135	185	335	33	3	37	120	.406
1942—	Theodore Williams, Boston	150	522	141	186	338	34	5	36	137	.356
1943—	Lucius Appling, Chicago	155	585	63	192	238	33	2	3	80	.328
1944—	Louis Boudreau, Cleveland	150	584	91	191	255	45	5	3	67	.327
1945—	George Stirnweiss, New York	152	632	107	195	301	32	22	10	64	.309
1946—	Jas. (Mickey) Vernon, Wash.	148	587	88	207	298	51	8	8	85	.353
1947—	Theodore Williams, Boston	156	528	125	181	335	40	9	32	114	.343
1948—	Theodore Williams, Boston	137	509	124	188	313	44	3	25	127	.369
1949—	George Kell, Detroit	134	522	97	179	244	38	9	3	59	.343

Year	Player and Club	G.	AB.	R.	H.	TB.	2B.	3B.	HR.	RBI.	B.A.
1950—	William Goodman, Boston	110	424	91	150	193	25	3	4	68	.354
1951—	Ferris Fain, Philadelphia	117	425	63	146	200	30	3	6	57	.344
1952—	Ferris Fain, Philadelphia	145	538	82	176	231	43	3	2	59	.327
1953—	Jas. (Mickey) Vernon, Wash.	152	608	101	205	315	43	11	15	115	.337
1954—	Roberto Avila, Cleveland	143	555	112	189	265	27	2	15	67	.341
1955—	Albert Kaline, Detroit	152	588	121	200	321	24	8	27	102	.340
1956—	Mickey Mantle, New York	150	533	132	188	376	22	5	52	130	.353
1957—	Theodore Williams, Boston	132	420	96	163	307	28	1	38	87	.388
1958—	Theodore Williams, Boston	129	411	81	135	240	23	2	26	85	.328
1959—	Harvey Kuenn, Detroit	139	561	99	198	281	42	7	9	71	.353
1960—	James (Pete) Runnels, Boston	143	528	80	169	208	29	2	2	35	.320
1961—	Norman Cash, Detroit	159	535	119	193	354	22	8	41	132	.361
1962—	James (Pete) Runnels, Boston	152	562	80	183	256	33	5	10	60	.326
1963—	Carl Yastrzemski, Boston	151	570	91	183	271	40	3	14	68	.321
1964—	Pedro (Tony) Oliva, Minnesota	161	672	109	217	374	43	9	32	94	.323
1965—	Pedro (Tony) Oliva, Minnesota	149	576	107	185	283	40	5	16	98	.321
1966—	Frank Robinson, Baltimore	155	576	122	182	367	34	2	49	122	.316
1967—	Carl Yastrzemski, Boston	161	579	112	189	360	31	4	44	121	.326
1968—	Carl Yastrzemski, Boston	157	539	90	162	267	32	2	23	74	.301
1969—	Rodney Carew, Minnesota	123	458	79	152	214	30	4	8	56	.332
1970—	Alexander Johnson, California	156	614	85	202	282	26	6	14	86	.329
1971—	Pedro (Tony) Oliva, Minnesota	126	487	73	164	266	30	3	22	81	.337
1972—	Rodney Carew, Minnesota	142	535	61	170	203	21	6	0	51	.318
1973—	Rodney Carew, Minnesota	149	580	98	203	273	30	11	6	62	.350
1974—	Rodney Carew, Minnesota	153	599	86	218	267	30	5	3	55	.364
1975—	Rodney Carew, Minnesota	143	535	89	192	266	24	4	14	80	.359
1976—	George H. Brett, Kansas City	159	645	94	215	298	34	14	7	67	.333
1977—	Rodney Carew, Minnesota	155	616	128	239	351	38	16	14	100	.388
1978—	Rodney Carew, Minnesota	152	564	85	188	249	26	10	5	70	.333
1979—	Fredric Lynn, Boston	147	531	116	177	338	42	1	39	122	.333
1980—	George H. Brett, Kansas City	117	449	87	175	298	33	9	24	118	.390
1981—	Carney R. Lansford, Boston	102	399	61	134	175	23	3	4	52	.336
1982—	Willie J. Wilson, Kansas City	136	585	87	194	252	19	15	3	46	.332
1983—	Wade A. Boggs, Boston	153	582	100	210	283	44	7	5	74	.361

*Cobb's 1910 title in dispute. See explanation on Page 3.

LEADERS IN RUNS SCORED

Year	Player and Club	Runs	Year	Player and Club	Runs
1900—	(Not classed as major)		1927—	George (Babe) Ruth, New York	158
1901—	Napoleon Lajoie, Philadelphia	145	1928—	George (Babe) Ruth, New York	163
1902—	David Fultz, Philadelphia	110	1929—	Charles Gehringer, Detroit	131
1903—	Patrick Dougherty, Boston	108	1930—	Aloysius Simmons, Philadelphia	152
1904—	Patrick Dougherty, Boston-N.Y.	113	1931—	H. Louis Gehrig, New York	163
1905—	Harry Davis, Philadelphia	92	1932—	James Foxx, Philadelphia	151
1906—	Elmer Flick, Cleveland	98	1933—	H. Louis Gehrig, New York	138
1907—	Samuel Crawford, Detroit	102	1934—	Charles Gehringer, Detroit	134
1908—	Matthew McIntyre, Detroit	105	1935—	H. Louis Gehrig, New York	125
1909—	Tyrus Cobb, Detroit	116	1936—	H. Louis Gehrig, New York	167
1910—	Tyrus Cobb, Detroit	106	1937—	Joseph DiMaggio, New York	151
1911—	Tyrus Cobb, Detroit	147	1938—	Henry Greenberg, Detroit	144
1912—	Edward Collins, Philadelphia	137	1939—	Robert (Red) Rolfe, New York	139
1913—	Edward Collins, Philadelphia	125	1940—	Theodore Williams, Boston	134
1914—	Edward Collins, Philadelphia	122	1941—	Theodore Williams, Boston	135
1915—	Tyrus Cobb, Detroit	144	1942—	Theodore Williams, Boston	141
1916—	Tyrus Cobb, Detroit	113	1943—	George Case, Washington	102
1917—	Owen (Donie) Bush, Detroit	112	1944—	George Stirnweiss, New York	125
1918—	Raymond Chapman, Cleveland	84	1945—	George Stirnweiss, New York	107
1919—	George (Babe) Ruth, Boston	103	1946—	Theodore Williams, Boston	142
1920—	George (Babe) Ruth, New York	158	1947—	Theodore Williams, Boston	125
1921—	George (Babe) Ruth, New York	177	1948—	Thomas Henrich, New York	138
1922—	George Sisler, St. Louis	134	1949—	Theodore Williams, Boston	150
1923—	George (Babe) Ruth, New York	151	1950—	Dominic DiMaggio, Boston	131
1924—	George (Babe) Ruth, New York	143	1951—	Dominic DiMaggio, Boston	113
1925—	John Mostil, Chicago	135	1952—	Lawrence Doby, Cleveland	104
1926—	George (Babe) Ruth, New York	139	1953—	Albert Rosen, Cleveland	115

LEADERS IN RUNS SCORED—Continued

Year	Player and Club	Runs	Year	Player and Club	Runs
1954—	Mickey Mantle, New York	129	1969—	Reginald Jackson, Oakland	123
1955—	Alphonse Smith, Cleveland	123	1970—	Carl Yastrzemski, Boston	125
1956—	Mickey Mantle, New York	132	1971—	Donald Buford, Baltimore	99
1957—	Mickey Mantle, New York	121	1972—	Bobby Murcer, New York	102
1958—	Mickey Mantle, New York	127	1973—	Reginald Jackson, Oakland	99
1959—	Edward Yost, Detroit	115	1974—	Carl Yastrzemski, Boston	93
1960—	Mickey Mantle, New York	119	1975—	Fredric Lynn, Boston	103
1961—	Mantle, New York-Maris, New York.	132	1976—	Roy White, New York	104
1962—	Albert G. Pearson, Los Angeles	115	1977—	Rodney Carew, Minnesota	128
1963—	W. Robert Allison, Minnesota	99	1978—	Ronald LeFlore, Detroit	126
1964—	Pedro (Tony) Oliva, Minnesota	109	1979—	Donald Baylor, California	120
1965—	Zoilo Versalles, Minnesota	126	1980—	Willie Wilson, Kansas City	133
1966—	Frank Robinson, Baltimore	122	1981—	Rickey Henderson, Oakland	89
1967—	Carl Yastrzemski, Boston	112	1982—	Paul Molitor, Milwaukee	136
1968—	Richard McAuliffe, Detroit	95	1983—	Calvin Ripken, Baltimore	121

LEADERS IN HITS

Year	Player and Club	Hits	Year	Player and Club	Hits
1900—	(Not classed as major)		1941—	Cecil Travis, Washington	218
1901—	Napoleon Lajoie, Philadelphia	229	1942—	John Pesky, Boston	205
1902—	Charles Hickman, Cleveland	194	1943—	Richard Wakefield, Detroit	200
1903—	Patrick Dougherty, Boston	195	1944—	George Stirnweiss, New York	205
1904—	Napoleon Lajoie, Cleveland	211	1945—	George Stirnweiss, New York	195
1905—	George Stone, St. Louis	187	1946—	John Pesky, Boston	208
1906—	Napoleon Lajoie, Cleveland	214	1947—	John Pesky, Boston	207
1907—	Tyrus Cobb, Detroit	212	1948—	Robert Dillinger, St. Louis	207
1908—	Tyrus Cobb, Detroit	188	1949—	L. Dale Mitchell, Cleveland	203
1909—	Tyrus Cobb, Detroit	216	1950—	George Kell, Detroit	218
1910—	Napoleon Lajoie, Cleveland	227	1951—	George Kell, Detroit	191
1911—	Tyrus Cobb, Detroit	248	1952—	J. Nelson Fox, Chicago	192
1912—	Tyrus Cobb, Detroit	227	1953—	Harvey Kuenn, Detroit	209
1913—	Joseph Jackson, Cleveland	197	1954—	Fox, Chicago-Kuenn, Detroit	201
1914—	Tristram Speaker, Boston	193	1955—	Albert Kaline, Detroit	200
1915—	Tyrus Cobb, Detroit	208	1956—	Harvey Kuenn, Detroit	196
1916—	Tristram Speaker, Cleveland	211	1957—	J. Nelson Fox, Chicago	196
1917—	Tyrus Cobb, Detroit	225	1958—	J. Nelson Fox, Chicago	187
1918—	George Burns, Philadelphia	178	1959—	Harvey Kuenn, Detroit	198
1919—	Tyrus Cobb, Detroit	191	1960—	Orestes (Minnie) Minoso, Chicago	184
	Robert Veach, Detroit	191	1961—	Norman Cash, Detroit	193
1920—	George Sisler, St. Louis	257	1962—	Robert Richardson, New York	209
1921—	Harry Heilmann, Detroit	237	1963—	Carl Yastrzemski, Boston	183
1922—	George Sisler, St. Louis	246	1964—	Pedro (Tony) Oliva, Minnesota	217
1923—	Charles Jamieson, Cleveland	222	1965—	Pedro (Tony) Oliva, Minnesota	185
1924—	Edgar (Sam) Rice, Washington	216	1966—	Pedro (Tony) Oliva, Minnesota	191
1925—	Aloysius Simmons, Philadelphia	253	1967—	Carl Yastrzemski, Boston	189
1926—	George Burns, Cleveland	216	1968—	Dagoberto Campaneris, Oakland	177
	Edgar (Sam) Rice, Washington	216	1969—	Pedro (Tony) Oliva, Minnesota	197
1927—	Earle Combs, New York	231	1970—	Pedro (Tony) Oliva, Minnesota	204
1928—	Henry Manush, St. Louis	241	1971—	Cesar Tovar, Minnesota	204
1929—	Dale Alexander, Detroit	215	1972—	Joseph Rudi, Oakland	181
	Charles Gehringer, Detroit	215	1973—	Rodney Carew, Minnesota	203
1930—	U. John Hodapp, Cleveland	225	1974—	Rodney Carew, Minnesota	218
1931—	H. Louis Gehrig, New York	211	1975—	George Brett, Kansas City	195
1932—	Aloysius Simmons, Philadelphia	216	1976—	George Brett, Kansas City	215
1933—	Henry Manush, Washington	221	1977—	Rodney Carew, Minnesota	239
1934—	Charles Gehringer, Detroit	214	1978—	James Rice, Boston	213
1935—	Joseph Vosmik, Cleveland	216	1979—	George Brett, Kansas City	212
1936—	H. Earl Averill, Cleveland	232	1980—	Willie Wilson, Kansas City	230
1937—	Roy (Beau) Bell, St. Louis	218	1981—	Rickey Henderson, Oakland	135
1938—	Joseph Vosmik, Boston	201	1982—	Robin Yount, Milwaukee	210
1939—	Robert (Red) Rolfe, New York	213	1983—	Calvin Ripken, Baltimore	211
1940—	Raymond (Rip) Radcliff, St. Louis	200			
	W. Barney McCosky, Detroit	200			
	Roger (Doc) Cramer, Boston	200			

ONE-BASE HIT LEADERS

Year	Player and Club	1B.
1900—	(Not classed as major)	
1901—	Napoleon Lajoie, Philadelphia	154
1902—	Fielder A. Jones, Chicago	148
1903—	Patrick H. Dougherty, Boston	161
1904—	William H. Keeler, New York	164
1905—	William H. Keeler, New York	147
1906—	William H. Keeler, New York	166
1907—	Tyrus R. Cobb, Detroit	163
1908—	Matthew W. McIntyre, Detroit	131
	George R. Stone, St. Louis	131
1909—	Tyrus R. Cobb, Detroit	164
1910—	Napoleon Lajoie, Cleveland	165
1911—	Tyrus R. Cobb, Detroit	169
1912—	Tyrus R. Cobb, Detroit	167
1913—	Edward T. Collins, Philadelphia	145
1914—	John P. McInnis, Philadelphia	160
1915—	Tyrus R. Cobb, Detroit	161
1916—	Tristram Speaker, Cleveland	160
1917—	Tyrus R. Cobb, Detroit	151
	J. Clyde Milan, Washington	151
1918—	George H. Burns, Philadelphia	141
1919—	Edgar C. Rice, Washington	144
1920—	George H. Sisler, St. Louis	171
1921—	John T. Tobin, St. Louis	179
1922—	George Sisler, St. Louis	178
1923—	Charles D. Jamieson, Cleveland	172
1924—	Charles D. Jamieson, Cleveland	168
1925—	Edgar C. Rice, Washington	182
1926—	Edgar C. Rice, Washington	167
1927—	Earle B. Combs, New York	166
1928—	Henry E. Manush, St. Louis	161
1929—	Earle B. Combs, New York	151
1930—	Edgar C. Rice, Washington	158
1931—	Oscar D. Melillo, St. Louis	142
	Jonathan T. Stone, Detroit	142
1932—	Henry E. Manush, Washington	145
1933—	Henry E. Manush, Washington	167
1934—	Roger M. Cramer, Philadelphia	158
1935—	Roger M. Cramer, Philadelphia	170
1936—	Raymond A. Radcliff, Chicago	161
1937—	John K. Lewis, Washington	162
1938—	Melo B. Almada, Wash.-St. Louis	158
1939—	Roger M. Cramer, Boston	147
1940—	Roger M. Cramer, Boston	160
1941—	Cecil H. Travis, Washington	153
1942—	John M. Pesky, Boston	165
1943—	Roger M. Cramer, Detroit	159
1944—	George H. Stirnweiss, New York	146
1945—	Irvin G. Hall, Philadelphia	139
1946—	John M. Pesky, Boston	159
1947—	John M. Pesky, Boston	172
1948—	L. Dale Mitchell, Cleveland	162
1949—	L. Dale Mitchell, Cleveland	161
1950—	Philip F. Rizzuto, New York	150
1951—	George C. Kell, Detroit	150
1952—	J. Nelson Fox, Chicago	157
1953—	Harvey E. Kuenn, Detroit	167
1954—	J. Nelson Fox, Chicago	167
1955—	J. Nelson Fox, Chicago	157
1956—	J. Nelson Fox, Chicago	158
1957—	J. Nelson Fox, Chicago	155
1958—	J. Nelson Fox, Chicago	160
1959—	J. Nelson Fox, Chicago	149
1960—	J. Nelson Fox, Chicago	139
1961—	Robert C. Richardson, New York	148
1962—	Robert C. Richardson, New York	158
1963—	Albert G. Pearson, Los Angeles	139
1964—	Robert C. Richardson, New York	148
1965—	Donald A. Buford, Chicago	129
1966—	Luis E. Aparicio, Baltimore	143
1967—	Horace M. Clarke, New York	140
1968—	Dagoberto B. Campaneris, Oakland	139
1969—	Horace M. Clarke, New York	146
1970—	Alexander Johnson, California	156
1971—	Cesar L. Tovar, Minnesota	171
1972—	Rodney C. Carew, Minnesota	143
1973—	Rodney C. Carew, Minnesota	156
1974-	Rodney C. Carew, Minnesota	180
1975—	Thurman Munson, New York	151
1976—	George Brett, Kansas City	160
1977—	Rodney Carew, Minnesota	171
1978—	Ronald LeFlore, Detroit	153
1979—	Willie Wilson, Kansas City	148
1980—	Willie Wilson, Kansas City	184
1981—	Willie Wilson, Kansas City	115
1982—	Willie Wilson, Kansas City	157
1983—	Wade Boggs, Boston	154

TWO-BASE HIT LEADERS

Year	Player and Club	2B.
1900—	(Not classed as major)	
1901—	Napoleon Lajoie, Philadelphia	48
1902—	Harry Davis, Philadelphia	43
1903—	Ralph Seybold, Philadelphia	43
1904—	Napoleon Lajoie, Cleveland	50
1905—	Harry Davis, Philadelphia	47
1906—	Napoleon Lajoie, Cleveland	49
1907—	Harry Davis, Philadelphia	37
1908—	Tyrus Cobb, Detroit	36
1909—	Samuel Crawford, Detroit	35
1910—	Napoleon Lajoie, Cleveland	53
1911—	Tyrus Cobb, Detroit	47
1912—	Tristram Speaker, Boston	53
1913—	Joseph Jackson, Cleveland	39
1914—	Tristram Speaker, Boston	46
1915—	Robert Veach, Detroit	40
1916—	Graney, Cleveland-Speaker, Cleve.	41
1917—	Tyrus Cobb, Detroit	44
1918—	Tristram Speaker, Cleveland	33
1919—	Robert Veach, Detroit	45
1920—	Tristram Speaker, Cleveland	50
1921—	Tristram Speaker, Cleveland	52
1922—	Tristram Speaker, Cleveland	48
1923—	Tristram Speaker, Cleveland	59
1924—	J. Sewell, Cleveland-Heilmann, Det.	45
1925—	Martin McManus, St. Louis	44
1926—	George Burns, Cleveland	64
1927—	H. Louis Gehrig, New York	52
1928—	Manush, St. Louis-Gehrig, New York	47
1929—	Manush, St. Louis	45
	R. Johnson, Detroit	45
	Gehringer, Detroit	45
1930—	U. John Hodapp, Cleveland	51
1931—	Earl Webb, Boston	67
1932—	Eric McNair, Philadelphia	47
1933—	Joseph Cronin, Washington	45
1934—	Henry Greenberg, Detroit	63
1935—	Joseph Vosmik, Cleveland	47
1936—	Charles Gehringer, Detroit	60
1937—	Roy (Beau) Bell, St. Louis	51
1938—	Joseph Cronin, Boston	51
1939—	Robert (Red) Rolfe, New York	46

TWO-BASE HIT LEADERS—Continued

Year	Player and Club	2B.	Year	Player and Club	2B.
1940—	Henry Greenberg, Detroit	50	1965—	Zoilo Versalles, Minnesota	45
1941—	Louis Boudreau, Cleveland	45		Carl Yastrzemski, Boston	45
1942—	Donald Kolloway, Chicago	40	1966—	Carl Yastrzemski, Boston	39
1943—	Richard Wakefield, Detroit	38	1967—	Pedro (Tony) Oliva, Minnesota	34
1944—	Louis Boudreau, Cleveland	45	1968—	C. Reginald Smith, Boston	37
1945—	Wallace Moses, Chicago	35	1969—	Pedro (Tony) Oliva, Minnesota	39
1946—	Jas. (Mickey) Vernon, Washington	51	1970—	Pedro (Tony) Oliva, Minnesota	36
1947—	Louis Boudreau, Cleveland	45		Amos Otis, Kansas City	36
1948—	Theodore Williams, Boston	44		Cesar Tovar, Minnesota	36
1949—	Theodore Williams, Boston	39	1971—	C. Reginald Smith, Boston	33
1950—	George Kell, Detroit	56	1972—	Louis Piniella, Kansas City	33
1951—	Kell, Det.-Yost, Wash.-Mele, Wash.	36	1973—	Salvatore Bando, Oakland	32
1952—	Ferris Fain, Philadelphia	43		Pedro Garcia, Milwaukee	32
1953—	Jas. (Mickey) Vernon, Washington	43	1974—	Joseph Rudi, Oakland	39
1954—	Jas. (Mickey) Vernon, Washington	33	1975—	Fredric Lynn, Boston	47
1955—	Harvey Kuenn, Detroit	38	1976—	Amos Otis, Kansas City	40
1956—	James Piersall, Boston	40	1977—	Harold McRae, Kansas City	54
1957—	Minoso, Chicago-Gardner, Baltimore	36	1978—	George Brett, Kansas City	45
1958—	Harvey Kuenn, Detroit	39	1979—	Chester Lemon, Chicago	44
1959—	Harvey Kuenn, Detroit	42		Cecil Cooper, Milwaukee	44
1960—	John (Tito) Francona, Cleveland	36	1980—	Robin Yount, Milwaukee	49
1961—	Albert Kaline, Detroit	41	1981—	Cecil Cooper, Milwaukee	35
1962—	Floyd Robinson, Chicago	45	1982—	Harold McRae, Kansas City	46
1963—	Carl Yastrzemski, Boston	40		Robin Yount, Milwaukee	46
1964—	Pedro (Tony) Oliva, Minnesota	43	1983—	Calvin Ripken, Baltimore	47

THREE-BASE HIT LEADERS

Year	Player and Club	3B.	Year	Player and Club	3B.
1900—	(Not classed as major)		1937—	F. Walker, Chicago	16
1901—	James Williams, Baltimore	22		Kreevich, Chicago	16
1902—	James Williams, Baltimore	23	1938—	J. Geoffrey Heath, Cleveland	18
1903—	Samuel Crawford, Detroit	25	1939—	John (Buddy) Lewis, Washington	16
1904—	Charles (Chick) Stahl, Boston	22	1940—	Barney McCosky, Detroit	19
1905—	Elmer Flick, Cleveland	19	1941—	J. Geoffrey Heath, Cleveland	20
1906—	Elmer Flick, Cleveland	22	1942—	Stanley Spence, Washington	15
1907—	Elmer Flick, Cleveland	18	1943—	John Lindell, New York	12
1908—	Tyrus Cobb, Detroit	20		Wallace Moses, Chicago	12
1909—	J. Franklin Baker, Philadelphia	19	1944—	John Lindell, New York	16
1910—	Samuel Crawford, Detroit	19		George Stirnweiss, New York	16
1911—	Tyrus Cobb, Detroit	24	1945—	George Stirnweiss, New York	22
1912—	Joseph Jackson, Cleveland	26	1946—	Henry Edwards, Cleveland	16
1913—	Samuel Crawford, Detroit	23	1947—	Thomas Henrich, New York	13
1914—	Samuel Crawford, Detroit	26	1948—	Thomas Henrich, New York	14
1915—	Samuel Crawford, Detroit	19	1949—	L. Dale Mitchell, Cleveland	23
1916—	Joseph Jackson, Chicago	21	1950—	Dom DiMaggio, Boston	11
1917—	Tyrus Cobb, Detroit	24		Robert Doerr, Boston	11
1918—	Tyrus Cobb, Detroit	14		Walter (Hoot) Evers, Detroit	11
1919—	Robert Veach, Detroit	17	1951—	Orestes (Minnie) Minoso, Clev.-Chi.	14
1920—	Joseph Jackson, Chicago	20	1952—	Roberto Avila, Cleveland	11
1921—	Howard Shanks, Washington	19	1953—	Manuel (Jim) Rivera, Chicago	16
1922—	George Sisler, St. Louis	18	1954—	Orestes (Minnie) Minoso, Chicago	18
1923—	Sam Rice, Washington	18	1955—	Mickey Mantle, New York	11
	Leon (Goose) Goslin, Washington	18		Max Carey, New York	11
1924—	Walter Pipp, New York	19	1956—	Minoso, Chicago-Jensen, Boston-	
1925—	Leon (Goose) Goslin, Washington	20		Simpson, Kansas City-Lemon, Wash.	11
1926—	H. Louis Gehrig, New York	20	1957—	McDougald, Bauer, Simpson, N.Y.	9
1927—	Earle Combs, New York	23	1958—	Victor Power, Kansas City-Cleveland	10
1928—	Earle Combs, New York	21	1959—	W. Robert Allison, Washington	9
1929—	Charles Gehringer, Detroit	19	1960—	J. Nelson Fox, Chicago	10
1930—	Earle Combs, New York	22	1961—	Jacob Wood, Detroit	14
1931—	Roy Johnson, Detroit	19	1962—	Gino Cimoli, Kansas City	15
1932—	Joseph Cronin, Washington	18	1963—	Zoilo Versalles, Minnesota	13
1933—	Henry Manush, Washington	17	1964—	Richard Rollins, Minnesota	10
1934—	W. Benjamin Chapman, New York	13		Zoilo Versalles, Minnesota	10
1935—	Joseph Vosmik, Cleveland	20	1965—	Dagoberto Campaneris, Kansas City	12
1936—	Earl Averill, Cleveland	15		Zoilo Versalles, Minnesota	12
	Joe DiMaggio, New York	15	1966—	Robert Knoop, California	11
	Robert (Red) Rolfe, New York	15	1967—	Paul L. Blair, Baltimore	12

Year	Player and Club	3B.	Year	Player and Club	3B.
1968—James Fregosi, California		13	1976—George Brett, Kansas City		14
1969—Delbert Unser, Washington		8	1977—Rodney Carew, Minnesota		16
1970—Cesar Tovar, Minnesota		13	1978—James Rice, Boston		15
1971—Freddie Patek, Kansas City		11	1979—George Brett, Kansas City		20
1972—Carlton Fisk, Boston		9	1980—Alfredo Griffin, Toronto		15
Joseph Rudi, Oakland		9	Willie Wilson, Kansas City		15
1973—Alonza Bumbry, Baltimore		11	1981—John Castino, Minnesota		9
Rodney Carew, Minnesota		11	1982—Willie Wilson, Kansas City		15
1974—John (Mickey) Rivers, California		11	1983—Robin Yount, Milwaukee		10
1975—George Brett, Kansas City		13			
John (Mickey) Rivers, California		13			

HOME RUN LEADERS

Year	Player and Club	HR.	Year	Player and Club	HR.
1900—(Not classed as major)			1944—Nicholas Etten, New York		22
1901—Napoleon Lajoie, Philadelphia		14	1945—Vernon Stephens, St. Louis		24
1902—Ralph (Socks) Seybold, Philadelphia..		16	1946—Henry Greenberg, Detroit		44
1903—John (Buck) Freeman, Boston		13	1947—Theodore Williams, Boston		32
1904—Harry Davis, Philadelphia		10	1948—Joseph DiMaggio, New York		39
1905—Harry Davis, Philadelphia		8	1949—Theodore Williams, Boston		43
1906—Harry Davis, Philadelphia		12	1950—Albert Rosen, Cleveland		37
1907—Harry Davis, Philadelphia		8	1951—Gus Zernial, Chicago-Philadelphia		33
1908—Samuel Crawford, Detroit		7	1952—Lawrence Doby, Cleveland		32
1909—Tyrus Cobb, Detroit		9	1953—Albert Rosen, Cleveland		43
1910—J. Garland (Jake) Stahl, Boston		10	1954—Lawrence Doby, Cleveland		32
1911—J. Franklin Baker, Philadelphia		11	1955—Mickey Mantle, New York		37
1912—J. Franklin Baker, Philadelphia		10	1956—Mickey Mantle, New York		52
Tristram Speaker, Boston		10	1957—Roy Sievers, Washington		42
1913—J. Franklin Baker, Philadelphia		12	1958—Mickey Mantle, New York		42
1914—J. Franklin Baker, Philadelphia		9	1959—Rocco Colavito, Cleveland		42
1915—Robert Roth, Chicago-Cleveland		7	Harmon Killebrew, Washington		42
1916—Walter Pipp, New York		12	1960—Mickey Mantle, New York		40
1917—Walter Pipp, New York		9	1961—Roger Maris, New York		61
1918—George (Babe) Ruth, Boston		11	1962—Harmon Killebrew, Minnesota		48
Tilly Walker, Philadelphia		11	1963—Harmon Killebrew, Minnesota		45
1919—George (Babe) Ruth, Boston		29	1964—Harmon Killebrew, Minnesota		49
1920—George (Babe) Ruth, New York		54	1965—Anthony Conigilaro, Boston		32
1921—George (Babe) Ruth, New York		59	1966—Frank Robinson, Baltimore		49
1922—Kenneth Williams, St. Louis		39	1967—Harmon Killebrew, Minnesota		44
1923—George (Babe) Ruth, New York		41	Carl Yastrzemski, Boston		44
1924—George (Babe) Ruth, New York		46	1968—Frank Howard, Washington		44
1925—Robert Meusel, New York		33	1969—Harmon Killebrew, Minnesota		49
1926—George (Babe) Ruth, New York		47	1970—Frank Howard, Washington		44
1927—George (Babe) Ruth, New York		60	1971—William E. Melton, Chicago		33
1928—George (Babe) Ruth, New York		54	1972—Richard Allen, Chicago		37
1929—George (Babe) Ruth, New York		46	1973—Reginald Jackson, Oakland		32
1930—George (Babe) Ruth, New York		49	1974—Richard Allen, Chicago		32
1931—George (Babe) Ruth, New York		46	1975—Reginald Jackson, Oakland		36
H. Louis Gehrig, New York		46	George Scott, Milwaukee		36
1932—James Foxx, Philadelphia		58	1976—Graig Nettles, New York		32
1933—James Foxx, Philadelphia		48	1977—James Rice, Boston		39
1934—H. Louis Gehrig, New York		49	1978—James Rice, Boston		46
1935—James Foxx, Philadelphia		36	1979—J. Gorman Thomas, Milwaukee		45
Henry Greenberg, Detroit		36	1980—Reginald Jackson, New York		41
1936—H. Louis Gehrig, New York		49	Benjamin Oglivie, Milwaukee		41
1937—Joseph DiMaggio, New York		46	1981—Antonio Armas, Oakland		22
1938—Henry Greenberg, Detroit		58	Dwight Evans, Boston		22
1939—James Foxx, Boston		35	Robert Grich, California		22
1940—Henry Greenberg, Detroit		41	Eddie Murray, Baltimore		22
1941—Theodore Williams, Boston		37	1982—Reginald Jackson, California		39
1942—Theodore Williams, Boston		36	J. Gorman Thomas, Milwaukee		39
1943—Rudolph York, Detroit		34	1983—James Rice, Boston		39

LEADERS IN TOTAL BASES

Year	Player and Club	T.B.	Year	Player and Club	T.B.
1900—(Not classed as major)			1903—John (Buck) Freeman, Boston		281
1901—Napoleon Lajoie, Philadelphia		345	1904—Napoleon Lajoie, Cleveland		304
1902—John (Buck) Freeman, Boston		287	1905—George Stone, St. Louis		260

LEADERS IN TOTAL BASES—Continued

Year	Player and Club	T.B.	Year	Player and Club	T.B.
1906—	George Stone, St. Louis	288	1946—	Theodore Williams, Boston	343
1907—	Tyrus Cobb, Detroit	286	1947—	Theodore Williams, Boston	335
1908—	Tyrus Cobb, Detroit	276	1948—	Joseph DiMaggio, New York	355
1909—	Tyrus Cobb, Detroit	296	1949—	Theodore Williams, Boston	368
1910—	Napoleon Lajoie, Cleveland	304	1950—	Walter Dropo, Boston	326
1911—	Tyrus Cobb, Detroit	367	1951—	Theodore Williams, Boston	295
1912—	Joseph Jackson, Cleveland	331	1952—	Albert Rosen, Cleveland	297
1913—	Samuel Crawford, Detroit	298	1953—	Albert Rosen, Cleveland	367
1914—	Tristram Speaker, Boston	287	1954—	Orestes (Minnie) Minoso, Chicago	304
1915—	Tyrus Cobb, Detroit	274	1955—	Albert Kaline, Detroit	321
1916—	Joseph Jackson, Chicago	293	1956—	Mickey Mantle, New York	376
1917—	Tyrus Cobb, Detroit	336	1957—	Roy Sievers, Washington	331
1918—	George Burns, Philadelphia	236	1958—	Mickey Mantle, New York	307
1919—	George (Babe) Ruth, Boston	284	1959—	Rocco Colavito, Cleveland	301
1920—	George Sisler, St. Louis	399	1960—	Mickey Mantle, New York	294
1921—	George (Babe) Ruth, New York	457	1961—	Roger Maris, New York	366
1922—	Kenneth Williams, St. Louis	367	1962—	Rocco Colavito, Detroit	309
1923—	George (Babe) Ruth, New York	399	1963—	Richard Stuart, Boston	319
1924—	George (Babe) Ruth, New York	391	1964—	Pedro (Tony) Oliva, Minnesota	374
1925—	Aloysius Simmons, Philadelphia	392	1965—	Zoilo Versalles, Minnesota	308
1926—	George (Babe) Ruth, New York	365	1966—	Frank Robinson, Baltimore	367
1927—	H. Louis Gehrig, New York	447	1967—	Carl Yastrzemski, Boston	360
1928—	George (Babe) Ruth, New York	380	1968—	Frank Howard, Washington	330
1929—	Aloysius Simmons, Philadelphia	373	1969—	Frank Howard, Washington	340
1930—	H. Louis Gehrig, New York	419	1970—	Carl Yastrzemski, Boston	335
1931—	H. Louis Gehrig, New York	410	1971—	C. Reginald Smith, Boston	302
1932—	James Foxx, Philadelphia	438	1972—	Bobby Murcer, New York	314
1933—	James Foxx, Philadelphia	403	1973—	David L. May, Milwaukee	295
1934—	H. Louis Gehrig, New York	409		George Scott, Milwaukee	295
1935—	Henry Greenberg, Detroit	389		Salvatore L. Bando, Oakland	295
1936—	Harold Trosky, Cleveland	405	1974—	Joseph Rudi, Oakland	287
1937—	Joseph DiMaggio, New York	418	1975—	George Scott, Milwaukee	318
1938—	James Foxx, Boston	398	1976—	George Brett, Kansas City	298
1939—	Theodore Williams, Boston	344	1977—	James Rice, Boston	382
1940—	Henry Greenberg, Detroit	384	1978—	James Rice, Boston	406
1941—	Joseph DiMaggio, New York	348	1979—	James Rice, Boston	369
1942—	Theodore Williams, Boston	338	1980—	Cecil Cooper, Milwaukee	335
1943—	Rudolph York, Detroit	301	1981—	Dwight Evans, Boston	215
1944—	John Lindell, New York	297	1982—	Robin Yount, Milwaukee	367
1945—	George Stirnweiss, New York	301	1983—	James Rice, Boston	344

RUNS BATTED IN LEADERS

Note—Runs batted in not compiled prior to 1907; officially adopted in 1920.

Year	Player and Club	RBI	Year	Player and Club	RBI
1907—	Tyrus Cobb, Detroit	116	1928—	George (Babe) Ruth, New York	142
1908—	Tyrus Cobb, Detroit	101		H. Louis Gehrig, New York	142
1909—	Tyrus Cobb, Detroit	115	1929—	Aloysius Simmons, Philadelphia	157
1910—	Samuel Crawford, Detroit	115	1930—	H. Louis Gehrig, New York	174
1911—	Tyrus Cobb, Detroit	144	1931—	H. Louis Gehrig, New York	184
1912—	J. Franklin Baker, Philadelphia	133	1932—	James Foxx, Philadelphia	169
1913—	J. Franklin Baker, Philadelphia	126	1933—	James Foxx, Philadelphia	163
1914—	Samuel Crawford, Detroit	112	1934—	H. Louis Gehrig, New York	165
1915—	Samuel Crawford, Detroit	116	1935—	Henry Greenberg, Detroit	170
1916—	Walter Pipp, New York	99	1936—	Harold Trosky, Cleveland	162
1917—	Robert Veach, Detroit	115	1937—	Henry Greenberg, Detroit	183
1918—	George Burns, Philadelphia	74	1938—	James Foxx, Boston	175
	Robert Veach, Detroit	74	1939—	Theodore Williams, Boston	145
1919—	George (Babe) Ruth, Boston	112	1940—	Henry Greenberg, Detroit	150
1920—	George (Babe) Ruth, New York	137	1941—	Joseph DiMaggio, New York	125
1921—	George (Babe) Ruth, New York	171	1942—	Theodore Williams, Boston	137
1922—	Kenneth Williams, St. Louis	155	1943—	Rudolph York, Detroit	118
1923—	George (Babe) Ruth, New York	131	1944—	Vernon Stephens, St. Louis	109
1924—	Leon (Goose) Goslin, Washington	129	1945—	Nicholas Etten, New York	111
1925—	Robert Meusel, New York	138	1946—	Henry Greenberg, Detroit	127
1926—	George (Babe) Ruth, New York	145	1947—	Theodore Williams, Boston	114
1927—	H. Louis Gehrig, New York	175	1948—	Joseph DiMaggio, New York	155

Year	Player and Club	RBI	Year	Player and Club	RBI
1949—	Theodore Williams, Boston	159	1966—	Frank Robinson, Baltimore	122
	Vernon Stephens, Boston	159	1967—	Carl Yastrzemski, Boston	121
1950—	Walter Dropo, Boston	144	1968—	Kenneth Harrelson, Boston	109
	Vernon Stephens, Boston	144	1969—	Harmon Killebrew, Minnesota	140
1951—	Gus Zernial, Chicago-Philadelphia	129	1970—	Frank Howard, Washington	126
1952—	Albert Rosen, Cleveland	105	1971—	Harmon Killebrew, Minnesota	119
1953—	Albert Rosen, Cleveland	145	1972—	Richard Allen, Chicago	113
1954—	Lawrence Doby, Cleveland	126	1973—	Reginald Jackson, Oakland	117
1955—	Raymond Boone, Detroit	116	1974—	Jeffrey Burroughs, Texas	118
	Jack Jensen, Boston	116	1975—	George Scott, Milwaukee	109
1956—	Mickey Mantle, New York	130	1976—	Lee May, Baltimore	109
1957—	Roy Sievers, Washington	114	1977—	Larry Hisle, Minnesota	119
1958—	Jack Jensen, Boston	122	1978—	James Rice, Boston	139
1959—	Jack Jensen, Boston	112	1979—	Donald Baylor, California	139
1960—	Roger Maris, New York	112	1980—	Cecil Cooper, Milwaukee	122
1961—	Roger Maris, New York	142	1981—	Eddie Murray, Baltimore	78
1962—	Harmon Killebrew, Minnesota	126	1982—	Harold McRae, Kansas City	133
1963—	Richard Stuart, Boston	118	1983—	Cecil Cooper, Milwaukee	126
1964—	Brooks Robinson, Baltimore	118		James Rice, Boston	126
1965—	Rocco Colavito, Cleveland	108			

BATTERS LEADING IN BASES ON BALLS

Note—Bases on balls not included in batting records in American League prior to 1913.

Year	Player and Club	BB.	Year	Player and Club	BB.
1913—	Burton Shotton, St. Louis	102	1948—	Theodore Williams, Boston	126
1914—	Owen (Donie) Bush, Detroit	112	1949—	Theodore Williams, Boston	162
1915—	Edward Collins, Chicago	119	1950—	Edward Yost, Washington	141
1916—	Burton Shotton, St. Louis	111	1951—	Theodore Williams, Boston	144
1917—	John Graney, Cleveland	94	1952—	Edward Yost, Washington	129
1918—	Raymond Chapman, Cleveland	84	1953—	Edward Yost, Washington	123
1919—	John Graney, Cleveland	105	1954—	Theodore Williams, Boston	136
1920—	George (Babe) Ruth, New York	148	1955—	Mickey Mantle, New York	113
1921—	George (Babe) Ruth, New York	144	1956—	Edward Yost, Washington	151
1922—	L. W. (Whitey) Witt, New York	89	1957—	Mickey Mantle, New York	146
1923—	George (Babe) Ruth, New York	170	1958—	Mickey Mantle, New York	129
1924—	George (Babe) Ruth, New York	142	1959—	Edward Yost, Detroit	135
1925—	William Kamm, Chicago	90	1960—	Edward Yost, Detroit	125
	John Mostil, Chicago	90	1961—	Mickey Mantle, New York	126
1926—	George (Babe) Ruth, New York	144	1962—	Mickey Mantle, New York	122
1927—	George (Babe) Ruth, New York	138	1963—	Carl Yastrzemski, Boston	95
1928—	George (Babe) Ruth, New York	135	1964—	Norman Siebern, Baltimore	106
1929—	Max Bishop, Philadelphia	128	1965—	Rocco Colavito, Cleveland	93
1930—	George (Babe) Ruth, New York	136	1966—	Harmon Killebrew, Minnesota	103
1931—	George (Babe) Ruth, New York	128	1967—	Harmon Killebrew, Minnesota	131
1932—	George (Babe) Ruth, New York	130	1968—	Carl Yastrzemski, Boston	119
1933—	George (Babe) Ruth, New York	114	1969—	Harmon Killebrew, Minnesota	145
1934—	James Foxx, Philadelphia	111	1970—	Frank Howard, Washington	132
1935—	H. Louis Gehrig, New York	132	1971—	Harmon Killebrew, Minnesota	114
1936—	H. Louis Gehrig, New York	130	1972—	Richard Allen, Chicago	99
1937—	H. Louis Gehrig, New York	127		Roy White, New York	99
1938—	James Foxx, Boston	119	1973—	John Mayberry, Kansas City	122
	Henry Greenberg, Detroit	119	1974—	F. Gene Tenace, Oakland	110
1939—	Harlond Clift, St. Louis	111	1975—	John Mayberry, Kansas City	119
1940—	Charles Keller, New York	106	1976—	D. Michael Hargrove, Texas	97
1941—	Theodore Williams, Boston	145	1977—	Colbert (Toby) Harrah, Texas	109
1942—	Theodore Williams, Boston	145	1978—	D. Michael Hargrove, Texas	107
1943—	Charles Keller, New York	106	1979—	Darrell Porter, Kansas City	121
1944—	Nicholas Etten, New York	97	1980—	Willie Randolph, New York	119
1945—	Roy Cullenbine, Cleveland-Detroit	112	1981—	Dwight Evans, Boston	85
1946—	Theodore Williams, Boston	156	1982—	Rickey Henderson, Oakland	116
1947—	Theodore Williams, Boston	162	1983—	Rickey Henderson, Oakland	103

BATTERS LEADING IN STRIKEOUTS

Note—Strikeouts not included in batting records in American League prior to 1913.

Year	Player and Club	SO.	Year	Player and Club	SO.
1913—	Daniel Moeller, Washington	106	1915—	John Lavan, St. Louis	83
1914—	August Williams, St. Louis	120	1916—	Walter Pipp, New York	82

BATTERS LEADING IN STRIKEOUTS —Continued

Year	Player and Club	SO.
1917—	Robert Roth, Cleveland	73
1918—	George (Babe) Ruth, Boston	58
1919—	Maurice Shannon, Phila.-Bos.	70
1920—	Aaron Ward, New York	84
1921—	Robert Meusel, New York	88
1922—	James Dykes, Philadelphia	98
1923—	George (Babe) Ruth, New York	93
1924—	George (Babe) Ruth, New York	81
1925—	Martin McManus, St. Louis	69
1926—	Anthony Lazzeri, New York	96
1927—	George (Babe) Ruth, New York	89
1928—	George (Babe) Ruth, New York	87
1929—	James Foxx, Philadelphia	70
1930—	James Foxx, Philadelphia	66
	Edward Morgan, Cleveland	66
1931—	James Foxx, Philadelphia	84
1932—	Bruce Campbell, Chicago-St. Louis	104
1933—	James Foxx, Philadelphia	93
1934—	Harlond Cliff, St. Louis	100
1935—	James Foxx, Philadelphia	99
1936—	James Foxx, Boston	119
1937—	Frank Crosetti, New York	105
1938—	Frank Crosetti, New York	97
1939—	Hank Greenberg, Detroit	95
1940—	Samuel Chapman, Philadelphia	96
1941—	James Foxx, Boston	103
1942—	Joseph Gordon, New York	95
1943—	Chester Laabs, St. Louis	105
1944—	J. Patrick Seerey, Cleveland	99
1945—	J. Patrick Seerey, Cleveland	97
1946—	Charles Keller, New York	101
	J. Patrick Seerey, Cleveland	101
1947—	Edwin Joost, Philadelphia	110
1948—	J. Patrick Seerey, Cleve.-Chicago	102
1949—	Richard Kokos, St. Louis	91
1950—	Gus Zernial, Chicago	110

Year	Player and Club	SO.
1951—	Gus Zernial, Chicago-Philadelphia	101
1952—	Lawrence Doby, Cleveland	111
	Mickey Mantle, New York	111
1953—	Lawrence Doby, Cleveland	121
1954—	Mickey Mantle, New York	107
1955—	Norbert Zauchin, Boston	105
1956—	James Lemon, Washington	138
1957—	James Lemon, Washington	94
1958—	James Lemon, Washington	120
	Mickey Mantle, New York	120
1959—	Mickey Mantle, New York	126
1960—	Mickey Mantle, New York	125
1961—	Jacob Wood, Detroit	141
1962—	Harmon Killebrew, Minnesota	142
1963—	David Nicholson, Chicago	175
1964—	Nelson Mathews, Kansas City	143
1965—	Zoilo Versalles, Minnesota	122
1966—	George Scott, Boston	152
1967—	Frank Howard, Washington	155
1968—	Reginald Jackson, Oakland	171
1969—	Reginald Jackson, Oakland	142
1970—	Reginald Jackson, Oakland	135
1971—	Reginald Jackson, Oakland	161
1972—	A. Bobby Darwin, Minnesota	145
1973—	A. Bobby Darwin, Minnesota	137
1974—	A. Bobby Darwin, Minnesota	127
1975—	Jeffrey Burroughs, Texas	155
1976—	James Rice, Boston	123
1977—	Clell (Butch) Hobson, Boston	162
1978—	Gary Alexander, Oakland-Cleveland	166
1979—	J. Gorman Thomas, Milwaukee	175
1980—	J. Gorman Thomas, Milwaukee	170
1981—	Antonio Armas, Oakland	115
1982—	Reginald Jackson, California	156
1983—	Ronald Kittle, Chicago	150

LEADING BASE STEALERS

Year	Player and Club	SB.
1900—	(Not classed as major)	
1901—	Frank Isbell Chicago	48
1902—	Fred (Topsy) Hartsel, Philadelphia	54
1903—	Harry Bay, Cleveland	46
1904—	Elmer Flick, Clev-Harry Bay, Clev	42
1905—	Daniel Hoffman, Philadelphia	46
1906—	Flick, Clev-Anderson, Wash.	39
1907—	Tyrus Cobb, Detroit	49
1908—	Patrick Dougherty, Chicago	47
1909—	Tyrus Cobb, Detroit	76
1910—	Edward Collins, Philadelphia	81
1911—	Tyrus Cobb, Detroit	83
1912—	J. Clyde Milan, Washington	88
1913—	J. Clyde Milan, Washington	75
1914—	Frederick Maisel, New York	74
1915—	Tyrus Cobb, Detroit	96
1916—	Tyrus Cobb, Detroit	68
1917—	Tyrus Cobb, Detroit	55
1918—	George Sisler, St. Louis	45
1919—	Edward Collins, Chicago	33
1920—	Edgar (Sam) Rice, Washington	63
1921—	George Sisler, St. Louis	35
1922—	George Sisler, St. Louis	51
1923—	Edward Collins, Chicago	49
1924—	Edward Collins, Chicago	42
1925—	John Mostil, Chicago	43
1926—	John Mostil, Chicago	35
1927—	George Sisler, St. Louis	27
1928—	Charles (Buddy) Myer, Boston	30

Year	Player and Club	SB.
1929—	Charles Gehringer, Detroit	27
1930—	Martin McManus, Detroit	23
1931—	W. Benjamin Chapman, New York	61
1932—	W. Benjamin Chapman, New York	38
1933—	W. Benjamin Chapman, New York	27
1934—	William Werber, Boston	40
1935—	William Werber, Boston	29
1936—	Lynford Lary, St. Louis	37
1937—	Werber, Phila-Chapman, Wash-Bos	35
1938—	Frank Crosetti, New York	27
1939—	George Case, Washington	51
1940—	George Case, Washington	35
1941—	George Case, Washington	33
1942—	George Case, Washington	44
1943—	George Case, Washington	61
1944—	George Stirnweiss, New York	55
1945—	George Stirnweiss, New York	33
1946—	George Case, Cleveland	28
1947—	Robert Dillinger, St. Louis	34
1948—	Robert Dillinger, St. Louis	28
1949—	Robert Dillinger, St. Louis	20
1950—	Dominic DiMaggio, Boston	15
1951—	Orestes (Minnie) Minoso, Clev-Chi	31
1952—	Orestes (Minnie) Minoso, Chicago	22
1953—	Orestes (Minnie) Minoso, Chicago	25
1954—	Jack Jensen, Boston	22
1955—	Manuel (Jim) Rivera, Chicago	25
1956—	Luis Aparicio, Chicago	21
1957—	Luis Aparicio, Chicago	28

Year	Player and Club	SB.	Year	Player and Club	SB.
1958	Luis Aparicio, Chicago	29	1971	Amos Otis, Kansas City	52
1959	Luis Aparicio, Chicago	56	1972	Dagoberto Campaneris, Oakland	52
1960	Luis Aparicio, Chicago	51	1973	Tommy Harper, Boston	54
1961	Luis Aparicio, Chicago	53	1974	William North, Oakland	54
1962	Luis Aparicio, Chicago	31	1975	John (Mickey) Rivers, California	70
1963	Luis Aparicio, Baltimore	40	1976	William North, Oakland	75
1964	Luis Aparicio, Baltimore	57	1977	Freddie Patek, Kansas City	53
1965	Dagoberto Campaneris, Kansas City	51	1978	Ronald LeFlore, Detroit	68
1966	Dagoberto Campaneris, Kansas City	52	1979	Willie Wilson, Kansas City	83
1967	Dagoberto Campaneris, Kansas City	55	1980	Rickey Henderson, Oakland	100
1968	Dagoberto Campaneris, Oakland	62	1981	Rickey Henderson, Oakland	56
1969	Tommy Harper, Seattle	73	1982	Rickey Henderson, Oakland	130
1970	Dagoberto Campaneris, Oakland	42	1983	Rickey Henderson, Oakland	108

SLUGGING LEADERS

Year	Player and Club	Slug. Avg.	Year	Player and Club	Slug. Avg.
1900	(Not classed as major)		1942	Theodore Williams, Boston	.648
1901	Napoleon Lajoie, Philadelphia	.635	1943	Rudolph York, Detroit	.527
1902	Edward Delahanty, Washington	.589	1944	Robert Doerr, Boston	5278
1903	Napoleon Lajoie, Cleveland	.533	1945	George Stirnweiss, New York	.476
1904	Napoleon Lajoie, Cleveland	.549	1946	Theodore Williams, Boston	.667
1905	Elmer Flick, Cleveland	.466	1947	Theodore Williams, Boston	.634
1906	George Stone, St. Louis	.496	1948	Theodore Williams, Boston	.615
1907	Tyrus Cobb, Detroit	.473	1949	Theodore Williams, Boston	.650
1908	Tyrus Cobb, Detroit	.475	1950	Joseph DiMaggio, New York	.585
1909	Tyrus Cobb, Detroit	.517	1951	Theodore Williams, Boston	.556
1910	Tyrus Cobb, Detroit	.554	1952	Lawrence Doby, Cleveland	.541
1911	Tyrus Cobb, Detroit	.621	1953	Albert Rosen, Cleveland	.613
1912	Tyrus Cobb, Detroit	.586	1954	Theodore Williams, Boston	.635
1913	Joseph Jackson, Cleveland	.551	1955	Mickey Mantle, New York	.611
1914	Tyrus Cobb, Detroit	.513	1956	Mickey Mantle, New York	.705
1915	Jacques F. Fournier, Chicago	.491	1957	Theodore Williams, Boston	.731
1916	Tristram Speaker, Cleveland	.502	1958	Rocco Colavito, Cleveland	.620
1917	Tyrus Cobb, Detroit	.571	1959	Albert Kaline, Detroit	.530
1918	George (Babe) Ruth, Boston	.555	1960	Roger Maris, New York	.581
1919	George (Babe) Ruth, Boston	.657	1961	Mickey Mantle, New York	.687
1920	George (Babe) Ruth, New York	.847	1962	Mickey Mantle, New York	.605
1921	George (Babe) Ruth, New York	.846	1963	Harmon Killebrew, Minnesota	.555
1922	George (Babe) Ruth, New York	.672	1964	John (Boog) Powell, Baltimore	.606
1923	George (Babe) Ruth, New York	.764	1965	Carl Yastrzemski, Boston	.536
1924	George (Babe) Ruth, New York	.739	1966	Frank Robinson, Baltimore	.637
1925	Kenneth Williams, St. Louis	.613	1967	Carl Yastrzemski, Boston	.622
1926	George (Babe) Ruth, New York	.737	1968	Frank Howard, Washington	.552
1927	George (Babe) Ruth, New York	.772	1969	Reginald Jackson, Oakland	.608
1928	George (Babe) Ruth, New York	.709	1970	Carl Yastrzemski, Boston	.592
1929	George (Babe) Ruth, New York	.697	1971	Pedro (Tony) Oliva, Minnesota	.546
1930	George (Babe) Ruth, New York	.732	1972	Richard Allen, Chicago	.603
1931	George (Babe) Ruth, New York	.700	1973	Reginald Jackson, Oakland	.531
1932	James Foxx, Philadelphia	.749	1974	Richard Allen, Chicago	.563
1933	James Foxx, Philadelphia	.703	1975	Fredric Lynn, Boston	.566
1934	H. Louis Gehrig, New York	.706	1976	Reginald Jackson, Baltimore	.502
1935	James Foxx, Philadelphia	.636	1977	James Rice, Boston	.593
1936	H. Louis Gehrig, New York	.696	1978	James Rice, Boston	.600
1937	Joseph DiMaggio, New York	.673	1979	Fredric Lynn, Boston	.637
1938	James Foxx, Boston	.704	1980	George Brett, Kansas City	.664
1939	James Foxx, Boston	.694	1981	Robert Grich, California	.543
1940	Henry Greenberg, Detroit	.670	1982	Robin Yount, Milwaukee	.578
1941	Theodore Williams, Boston	.735	1983	George Brett, Kansas City	.563

LEADING PITCHERS IN WINNING PERCENTAGE

(15 OR MORE VICTORIES)

Year	Pitcher	Club	Won	Lost	Pct.
1901—	Clark Griffith	Chicago	24	7	.774
1902—	William Bernhard	Philadelphia-Cleveland	18	5	.783
1903—	Earl Moore	Cleveland	22	7	.759
1904—	John Chesbro	New York	41	13	.759
1905—	Jess Tannehill	Boston	22	9	.710
1906—	Edward Plank	Philadelphia	19	6	.760
1907—	William Donovan	Detroit	25	4	.862
1908—	Edward Walsh	Chicago	40	15	.727
1909—	George Mullin	Detroit	29	8	.784
1910—	Albert (Chief) Bender	Philadelphia	23	5	.821
1911—	Albert (Chief) Bender	Philadelphia	17	5	.773
1912—	Joseph Wood	Boston	34	5	.872
1913—	Walter Johnson	Washington	36	7	.837
1914—	Albert (Chief) Bender	Philadelphia	17	3	.850
1915—	Joseph Wood	Boston	15	5	.750
1916—	Edward V. Cicotte	Chicago	15	7	.682
1917—	Ewell (Reb) Russell	Chicago	15	5	.750
1918—	Samuel Jones	Boston	16	5	.762
1919—	Edward V. Cicotte	Chicago	29	7	.806
1920—	James Bagby	Cleveland	31	12	.721
1921—	Carl Mays	New York	27	9	.750
1922—	Leslie (Joe) Bush	New York	26	7	.788
1923—	Herbert Pennock	New York	19	6	.760
1924—	Walter Johnson	Washington	23	7	.767
1925—	Stanley Coveleski	Washington	20	5	.800
1926—	George Uhle	Cleveland	27	11	.711
1927—	Waite Hoyt	New York	22	7	.759
1928—	Alvin Crowder	St. Louis	21	5	.808
1929—	Robert Grove	Philadelphia	20	6	.769
1930—	Robert Grove	Philadelphia	28	5	.848
1931—	Robert Grove	Philadelphia	31	4	.886
1932—	John Allen	New York	17	4	.810
1933—	Robert Grove	Philadelphia	24	8	.750
1934—	Vernon Gomez	New York	26	5	.839
1935—	Elden Auker	Detroit	18	7	.720
1936—	Monte Pearson	New York	19	7	.731
1937—	John Allen	Cleveland	15	1	.938
1938—	Charles (Red) Ruffing	New York	21	7	.750
1939—	Robert Grove	Boston	15	4	.789
1940—	Lynwood (Schoolboy) Rowe	Detroit	16	3	.842
1941—	Vernon Gomez	New York	15	5	.750
1942—	Ernest Bonham	New York	21	5	.808
1943—	Spurgeon (Spud) Chandler	New York	20	4	.833
1944—	Cecil (Tex) Hughson	Boston	18	5	.783
1945—	Harold Newhouser	Detroit	25	9	.735
1946—	David (Boo) Ferriss	Boston	25	6	.806
1947—	Allie Reynolds	New York	19	8	.704
1948—	John Kramer	Boston	18	5	.783
1949—	Ellis Kinder	Boston	23	6	.793
1950—	Victor Raschi	New York	21	8	.724
1951—	Robert Feller	Cleveland	22	8	.733
1952—	Robert Shantz	Philadelphia	24	7	.774
1953—	Edmund Lopat	New York	16	4	.800
1954—	Sandalio Consuegra	Chicago	16	3	.842
1955—	Thomas Byrne	New York	16	5	.762
1956—	Edward (Whitey) Ford	New York	19	6	.760
1957—	Richard Donovan	Chicago	16	6	.727
	Thomas Sturdivant	New York	16	6	.727
1958—	Robert Turley	New York	21	7	.750
1959—	Robert Shaw	Chicago	18	6	.750
1960—	James Perry	Cleveland	18	10	.643
1961—	Edward (Whitey) Ford	New York	25	4	.862
1962—	Raymond Herbert	Chicago	20	9	.690
1963—	Edward (Whitey) Ford	New York	24	7	.774
1964—	Wallace Bunker	Baltimore	19	5	.792
1965—	James (Mudcat) Grant	Minnesota	21	7	.750
1966—	Wilfred (Sonny) Siebert	Cleveland	16	8	.667
1967—	Joel Horlen	Chicago	19	7	.731

Year	Pitcher	Club	Won	Lost	Pct.
1968—	Dennis McLain	Detroit	31	6	.838
1969—	James Palmer	Baltimore	16	4	.800
1970—	Miguel (Mike) Cuellar	Baltimore	24	8	.750
1971—	David McNally	Baltimore	21	5	.808
1972—	James A. Hunter	Oakland	21	7	.750
1973—	James A. Hunter	Oakland	21	5	.808
1974—	Miguel (Mike) Cuellar	Baltimore	22	10	.688
1975—	Michael A. Torrez	Baltimore	20	9	.690
1976—	William Campbell	Minnesota	17	5	.773
1977—	Paul Splittorff	Kansas City	16	6	.727
1978—	Ronald Guidry	New York	25	3	.893
1979—	R. Michael Caldwell	Milwaukee	16	6	.727
1980—	Steven Stone	Baltimore	25	7	.781
1981—	Peter Vuckovich	Milwaukee	14	4	.778
1982—	Peter Vuckovich	Milwaukee	18	6	.750
1983—	Richard Dotson	Chicago	22	7	.759

Note—1981 percentages based on 10 or more victories.

LEADING PITCHERS—EARNED-RUN AVERAGE

(Based on Ten Complete Games Through 1950, Then 154 Innings Until A. L. Expanded in 1961, When It Became 162 Innings)

Year	Pitcher and Club	G.	IP.	ERA.
1913—	Johnson, Washington	48	346	1.14
1914—	Leonard, Boston	35	225	1.00
1915—	Wood, Boston	25	157	1.49
1916—	Ruth, Boston	44	324	1.75
1917—	Cicotte, Chicago	49	346	1.53
1918—	Johnson, Washington	39	325	1.27
1919—	Johnson, Washington	39	290	1.49
1920—	Shawkey, New York	38	267	2.45
1921—	Faber, Chicago	43	331	2.47
1922—	Faber, Chicago	43	353	2.80
1923—	S. Coveleski, Cleveland	33	228	2.76
1924—	Johnson, Washington	38	278	2.72
1925—	S. Coveleski, Wash.	32	241	2.84
1926—	Grove, Philadelphia	45	258	2.51
1927—	Moore, New York	50	213	2.28
1928—	Braxton, Washington	38	218	2.52
1929—	Grove, Philadelphia	42	275	2.81
1930—	Grove, Philadelphia	50	291	2.54
1931—	Grove, Philadelphia	41	289	2.06
1932—	Grove, Philadelphia	44	292	2.84
1933—	Pearson, Cleveland	19	135	2.33
1934—	Gomez, New York	38	282	2.33
1935—	Grove, Boston	35	273	2.70
1936—	Grove, Boston	35	253	2.81
1937—	Gomez, New York	34	278	2.33
1938—	Grove, Boston	24	164	3.07
1939—	Grove, Boston	23	191	2.54
1940—	Feller, Cleveland	43	320	2.62
1941—	T. Lee, Chicago	35	300	2.37
1942—	Lyons, Chicago	20	180	2.10
1943—	Chandler, New York	30	253	1.64
1944—	Trout, Detroit	49	352	2.12
1945—	Newhouser, Detroit	40	313	1.81
1946—	Newhouser, Detroit	37	293	1.94
1947—	Chandler, New York	17	128	2.46
1948—	Bearden, Cleveland	37	230	2.43
1949—	Parnell, Boston	39	295	2.78
1950—	Wynn, Cleveland	32	214	3.20
1951—	Rogovin, Det.-Chi.	27	217	2.78
1952—	Reynolds, New York	35	244	2.07
1953—	Lopat, New York	25	178	2.43
1954—	Garcia, Cleveland	45	259	2.64
1955—	Pierce, Chicago	33	206	1.97
1956—	Ford, New York	31	226	2.47
1957—	Shantz, New York	30	173	2.45
1958—	Ford, New York	30	219	2.01
1959—	Wilhelm, Baltimore	32	226	2.19
1960—	Baumann, Chicago	47	185	2.68
1961—	Donovan, Washington	23	169	2.40
1962—	Aguirre, Detroit	42	216	2.21
1963—	Peters, Chicago	41	243	2.33
1964—	Chance, Los Angeles	46	278	1.65
1965—	McDowell, Cleveland	42	273	2.18
1966—	Peters, Chicago	30	205	1.98
1967—	Horlen, Chicago	35	258	2.06
1968—	Tiant, Cleveland	34	258	1.60
1969—	Bosman, Washington	31	193	2.19
1970—	Segui, Oakland	47	162	2.56
1971—	Blue, Oakland	39	312	1.82
1972—	Tiant, Boston	43	179	1.91
1973—	Palmer, Baltimore	38	296	2.40
1974—	Hunter, Oakland	41	318	2.49
1975—	Palmer, Baltimore	39	323	2.09
1976—	Fidrych, Detroit	31	250	2.34
1977—	Tanana, California	31	241	2.54
1978—	Guidry, New York	35	274	1.74
1979—	Guidry, New York	33	236	2.78
1980—	May, New York	41	175	2.47
1981—	McCatty, Oakland	22	186	2.32
1982—	Sutcliffe, Cleveland	34	216	2.96
1983—	Honeycutt, Texas	25	174.2	2.42

Note—Wilcy Moore pitched only six complete games—he started 12—in 1927, but was recognized as leader because of 213 innings pitched; Ernie Bonham, New York, had 1.91 ERA and ten complete games in 1940, but appeared in only 12 games and 99 innings, and Bob Feller was recognized as leader.

Note—Earned-runs not tabulated in American League prior to 1913.

Note—1981 earned-run champion determined by taking team's leader who pitched as many innings as his total number of games played.

STRIKEOUT LEADERS—PITCHING

Year	Player and Club	SO.
1900—	(Not classed as major)	
1901—	Denton (Cy) Young, Boston	159
1902—	George (Rube) Waddell, Philadelphia	210
1903—	George (Rube) Waddell, Philadelphia	301
1904—	George (Rube) Waddell, Philadelphia	349
1905—	George (Rube) Waddell, Philadelphia	286
1906—	George (Rube) Waddell, Philadelphia	203
1907—	George (Rube) Waddell, Philadelphia	226
1908—	Edward Walsh, Chicago	269
1909—	Frank Smith, Chicago	177
1910—	Walter Johnson, Washington	313
1911—	Edward Walsh, Chicago	255
1912—	Walter Johnson, Washington	303
1913—	Walter Johnson, Washington	243
1914—	Walter Johnson, Washington	225
1915—	Walter Johnson, Washington	203
1916—	Walter Johnson, Washington	228
1917—	Walter Johnson, Washington	188
1918—	Walter Johnson, Washington	162
1919—	Walter Johnson, Washington	147
1920—	Stanley Coveleski, Cleveland	133
1921—	Walter Johnson, Washington	143
1922—	Urban Shocker, St. Louis	149
1923—	Walter Johnson, Washington	130
1924—	Walter Johnson, Washington	158
1925—	Robert Grove, Philadelphia	116
1926—	Robert Grove, Philadelphia	194
1927—	Robert Grove, Philadelphia	174
1928—	Robert Grove, Philadelphia	183
1929—	Robert Grove, Philadelphia	170
1930—	Robert Grove, Philadelphia	209
1931—	Robert Grove, Philadelphia	175
1932—	Charles (Red) Ruffing, New York	190
1933—	Vernon Gomez, New York	163
1934—	Vernon Gomez, New York	158
1935—	Thomas Bridges, Detroit	163
1936—	Thomas Bridges, Detroit	175
1937—	Vernon Gomez, New York	194
1938—	Robert Feller, Cleveland	240
1939—	Robert Feller, Cleveland	246
1940—	Robert Feller, Cleveland	261
1941—	Robert Feller, Cleveland	260
1942—	Louis (Bobo) Newsom, Washington	113
	Cecil (Tex) Hughson, Boston	113
1943—	Allie Reynolds, Cleveland	151
1944—	Harold Newhouser, Detroit	187
1945—	Harold Newhouser, Detroit	212
1946—	Robert Feller, Cleveland	348
1947—	Robert Feller, Cleveland	196
1948—	Robert Feller, Cleveland	164
1949—	Virgil Trucks, Detroit	153
1950—	Robert Lemon, Cleveland	170
1951—	Victor Raschi, New York	164
1952—	Allie Reynolds, New York	160
1953—	W. William Pierce, Chicago	186
1954—	Robert Turley, Baltimore	185
1955—	Herbert Score, Cleveland	245
1956—	Herbert Score, Cleveland	263
1957—	Early Wynn, Cleveland	184
1958—	Early Wynn, Chicago	179
1959—	James Bunning, Detroit	201
1960—	James Bunning, Detroit	201
1961—	Camilo Pascual, Minnesota	221
1962—	Camilo Pascual, Minnesota	206
1963—	Camilo Pascual, Minnesota	202
1964—	Alphonso Downing, New York	217
1965—	Samuel McDowell, Cleveland	325
1966—	Samuel McDowell, Cleveland	225
1967—	James Lonborg, Boston	246
1968—	Samuel McDowell, Cleveland	283
1969—	Samuel McDowell, Cleveland	279
1970—	Samuel McDowell, Cleveland	304
1971—	Michael Lolich, Detroit	308
1972—	L. Nolan Ryan, California	329
1973—	L. Nolan Ryan, California	383
1974—	L. Nolan Ryan, California	367
1975—	Frank Tanana, California	269
1976—	L. Nolan Ryan, California	327
1977—	L. Nolan Ryan, California	341
1978—	L. Nolan Ryan, California	260
1979—	L. Nolan Ryan, California	223
1980—	Leonard Barker, Cleveland	187
1981—	Leonard Barker, Cleveland	127
1982—	Floyd Bannister, Seattle	209
1983—	John Morris, Detroit	232

SHUTOUT LEADERS

Year	Player and Club	ShO.
1900—	(Not classed as major)	
1901—	Clark C. Griffith, Chicago	5
	Denton T. Young, Boston	5
1902—	Adrian Joss, Cleveland	5
1903—	Denton T. Young, Boston	7
1904—	Denton T. Young, Boston	10
1905—	Edward H. Killian, Detroit	8
1906—	Edward A. Walsh, Chicago	10
1907—	Edward S. Plank, Philadelphia	8
1908—	Edward A. Walsh, Chicago	12
1909—	Edward A. Walsh, Chicago	8
1910—	John W. Coombs, Philadelphia	13
1911—	Walter P. Johnson, Washington	6
	Edward S. Plank, Philadelphia	6
1912—	Joseph Wood, Boston	10
1913—	Walter P. Johnson, Washington	11
1914—	Walter P. Johnson, Washington	9
1915—	Walter P. Johnson, Washington	7
1916—	George H. Ruth, Boston	9
1917—	Stanley Coveleski, Cleveland	9
1918—	Walter P. Johnson, Washington	8
	Carl W. Mays, Boston	8
1919—	Walter P. Johnson, Washington	7
1920—	Carl W. Mays, New York	6
1921—	Samuel P. Jones, Boston	5
1922—	George E. Uhle, Cleveland	5
1923—	Stanley Coveleski, Cleveland	5
1924—	Walter P. Johnson, Washington	6
1925—	Theodore A. Lyons, Chicago	5
1926—	Edwin L. Wells, Detroit	4
1927—	Horace M. Lisenbee, Washington	4
1928—	Herbert J. Pennock, New York	5
1929—	George F. Blaeholder, St. Louis	4
	Alvin F. Crowder, St. Louis	4
	Samuel D. Gray, St. Louis	4
	Daniel K. MacFayden, Boston	4

Year	Player and Club	ShO.	Year	Player and Club	ShO.
1930—	Clinton H. Brown, Cleveland	3	1960—	Edward C. Ford, New York	4
	George L. Earnshaw, Philadelphia	3		James E. Perry, Cleveland	4
	George W. Pipgras, New York	3		Early Wynn, Chicago	4
1931—	Robert M. Grove, Philadelphia	4	1961—	Stephen D. Barber, Baltimore	8
	Victor G. Sorrell, Detroit	4		Camilo A. Pascual, Minnesota	8
1932—	Thomas D. Bridges, Detroit	4	1962—	Richard E. Donovan, Cleveland	5
	Robert M. Grove, Philadelphia	4		James L. Kaat, Minnesota	5
1933—	Oral C. Hildebrand, Cleveland	6		Camilo A. Pascual, Minnesota	5
1934—	Vernon L. Gomez, New York	6	1963—	Raymond E. Herbert, Chicago	7
	Melvin L. Harder, Cleveland	6	1964—	W. Dean Chance, Los Angeles	11
1935—	Lynwood T. Rowe, Detroit	6	1965—	James T. Grant, Minnesota	6
1936—	Robert M. Grove, Boston	6	1966—	Thomas E. John, Chicago	5
1937—	Vernon L. Gomez, New York	6		Samuel E. McDowell, Cleveland	5
1938—	Vernon L. Gomez, New York	4		Luis C. Tiant, Cleveland	5
1939—	Charles H. Ruffing, New York	5	1967—	Steven L. Hargan, Cleveland	6
1940—	Robert W. Feller, Cleveland	4		Joel E. Horlen, Chicago	6
	Theodore A. Lyons, Chicago	4		Thomas E. John, Chicago	6
	Albert J. Milnar, Cleveland	4		Michael S. Lolich, Detroit	6
1941—	Robert W. Feller, Cleveland	6		James E. McGlothlin, California	6
1942—	Ernest E. Bonham, New York	6	1968—	Luis C. Tiant, Cleveland	9
1943—	Spurgeon F. Chandler, New York	5	1969—	Dennis D. McLain, Detroit	9
	Paul H. Trout, Detroit	5	1970—	Charles T. Dobson, Oakland	5
1944—	Paul H. Trout, Detroit	7		James A. Palmer, Baltimore	5
1945—	Harold Newhouser, Detroit	8	1971—	Vida Blue, Oakland	8
1946—	Robert W. Feller, Cleveland	10	1972—	L. Nolan Ryan, California	9
1947—	Robert W. Feller, Cleveland	5	1973—	Rikalbert Blyleven, Minnesota	9
1948—	Robert G. Lemon, Cleveland	10	1974—	Luis C. Tiant, Boston	7
1949—	Edward M. Garcia, Cleveland	6	1975—	James A. Palmer, Baltimore	10
	Ellis R. Kinder, Boston	6	1976—	L. Nolan Ryan, California	7
	Virgil O. Trucks, Detroit	6	1977—	Frank Tanana, California	7
1950—	Arthur J. Houtteman, Detroit	4	1978—	Ronald Guidry, New York	9
1951—	Allie P. Reynolds, New York	7	1979—	L. Nolan Ryan, California	5
1952—	Edward M. Garcia, Cleveland	6		Michael Flanagan, Baltimore	5
	Allie P. Reynolds, New York	6		Dennis Leonard, Kansas City	5
1953—	Erwin C. Porterfield, Washington	9	1980—	Thomas John, New York	6
1954—	Edward M. Garcia, Cleveland	5	1981—	Richard Dotson, Chicago	4
	Virgil O. Trucks, Chicago	5		Kenneth Forsch, California	4
1955—	William F. Hoeft, Detroit	7		Steven McCatty, Oakland	4
1956—	Herbert J. Score, Cleveland	5		George Medich, Texas	4
1957—	James A. Wilson, Chicago	5	1982—	David Stieb, Toronto	5
1958—	Edward C. Ford, New York	7	1983—	Michael Boddicker, Baltimore	5
1959—	Camilo A. Pascual, Washington	6			

NATIONAL LEAGUE

PENNANT WINNERS

Year	Club	Manager	W.	L.	Pct.	*G.A.
1900—Brooklyn		Edward (Ned) Hanlon	82	54	.603	4½
1901—Pittsburgh		Frederick Clarke	90	49	.647	7½
1902—Pittsburgh		Frederick Clarke	103	36	.741	27½
1903—Pittsburgh		Frederick Clarke	91	49	.650	6½
1904—New York		John McGraw	106	47	.693	13
1905—New York		John McGraw	105	48	.686	9
1906—Chicago		Frank Chance	116	36	.763	20
1907—Chicago		Frank Chance	107	45	.704	17
1908—Chicago		Frank Chance	99	55	.643	1
1909—Pittsburgh		Frederick Clarke	110	42	.724	6½
1910—Chicago		Frank Chance	104	50	.675	13
1911—New York		John McGraw	99	54	.647	7½
1912—New York		John McGraw	103	48	.682	10
1913—New York		John McGraw	101	51	.664	12½
1914—Boston		George Stallings	94	59	.614	10½
1915—Philadelphia		Patrick Moran	90	62	.592	7
1916—Brooklyn		Wilbert Robinson	94	60	.610	2½
1917—New York		John McGraw	98	56	.636	10
1918—Chicago		Fred Mitchell	84	45	.651	10½
1919—Cincinnati		Patrick Moran	96	44	.686	9
1920—Brooklyn		Wilbert Robinson	93	61	.604	7
1921—New York		John McGraw	94	59	.614	4
1922—New York		John McGraw	93	61	.604	7
1923—New York		John McGraw	95	58	.621	4½
1924—New York		John McGraw	93	60	.608	1½
1925—Pittsburgh		William McKechnie	95	58	.621	8½
1926—St. Louis		Rogers Hornsby	89	65	.578	2
1927—Pittsburgh		Owen (Donie) Bush	94	60	.610	1½
1928—St. Louis		William McKechnie	95	59	.617	2
1929—Chicago		Joseph McCarthy	98	54	.645	10½
1930—St. Louis		Charles (Gabby) Street	92	62	.597	2
1931—St. Louis		Charles (Gabby) Street	101	53	.656	13
1932—Chicago		Rogers Hornsby, Charles Grimm	90	64	.584	4
1933—New York		William Terry	91	61	.599	5
1934—St. Louis		Frank Frisch	95	58	.621	2
1935—Chicago		Charles Grimm	100	54	.649	4
1936—New York		William Terry	92	62	.597	5
1937—New York		William Terry	95	57	.625	3
1938—Chicago		Charles Grimm, Gabby Hartnett	89	63	.586	2
1939—Cincinnati		William McKechnie	97	57	.630	4½
1940—Cincinnati		William McKechnie	100	53	.654	12
1941—Brooklyn		Leo Durocher	100	54	.649	2½
1942—St. Louis		William Southworth	106	48	.688	2
1943—St. Louis		William Southworth	105	49	.682	18
1944—St. Louis		William Southworth	105	49	.682	14½
1945—Chicago		Charles Grimm	98	56	.636	3
1946—St. Louis†		Edwin Dyer	98	58	.628	2
1947—Brooklyn		Burton Shotton	94	60	.610	5
1948—Boston		William Southworth	91	62	.595	6½
1949—Brooklyn		Burton Shotton	97	57	.630	1
1950—Philadelphia		Edwin Sawyer	91	63	.591	2
1951—New York‡		Leo Durocher	98	59	.624	1
1952—Brooklyn		Charles Dressen	96	57	.627	4½
1953—Brooklyn		Charles Dressen	105	49	.682	13
1954—New York		Leo Durocher	97	57	.630	5
1955—Brooklyn		Walter Alston	98	55	.641	13½
1956—Brooklyn		Walter Alston	93	61	.604	1
1957—Milwaukee		Fred Haney	95	59	.617	8
1958—Milwaukee		Fred Haney	92	62	.597	8
1959—Los Angeles§		Walter Alston	88	68	.564	2
1960—Pittsburgh		Daniel Murtaugh	95	59	.617	7
1961—Cincinnati		Frederick Hutchinson	93	61	.604	4
1962—San Francisco x		Alvin Dark	103	62	.624	1
1963—Los Angeles		Walter Alston	99	63	.611	6
1964—St. Louis		John Keane	93	69	.574	1
1965—Los Angeles		Walter Alston	97	65	.599	2

Year	Club	Manager	W.	L.	Pct.	✩G.A.
1966—Los Angeles	Walter Alston		95	67	.586	1½
1967—St. Louis	Albert (Red) Schoendienst		101	60	.627	10½
1968—St. Louis	Albert (Red) Schoendienst		97	65	.599	9
1969—New York (E)✩✩	Gilbert Hodges		100	62	.617	8
1970—Cincinnati (W)✩✩	George (Sparky) Anderson		102	60	.630	14½
1971—Pittsburgh (E)✩✩	Daniel Murtaugh		97	65	.599	7
1972—Cincinnati (W)✩✩	George (Sparky) Anderson		95	59	.617	10½
1973—New York (E)✩✩	Lawrence (Yogi) Berra		82	79	.509	1½
1974—Los Angeles (W)✩✩	Walter Alston		102	60	.630	4
1975—Cincinnati (W)✩✩	George (Sparky) Anderson		108	54	.667	20
1976—Cincinnati (W)✩✩	George (Sparky) Anderson		102	60	.630	10
1977—Los Angeles (W)✩✩	Thomas Lasorda		98	64	.605	10
1978—Los Angeles (W)✩✩	Thomas Lasorda		95	67	.586	2½
1979—Pittsburgh (E) ✩✩	Charles (Chuck) Tanner		98	64	.605	2
1980—Philadelphia (E)✩✩	G. Dallas Green		91	71	.562	1
1981—Los Angeles (W)✩✩	Thomas Lasorda		63	47	.573	y
1982—St. Louis (E)✩✩	Dorrel (Whitey) Herzog		92	70	.568	3
1983—Philadelphia (E)✩✩	Patrick Corrales, Paul Owens		90	72	.556	6

✩Games ahead of second-place club. †Defeated Brooklyn, two games to none, in playoff for pennant. ‡Defeated Brooklyn, two games to one, in playoff for pennant. §Defeated Milwaukee, two games to none, in playoff for pennant. xDefeated Los Angeles, two games to one, in playoff for pennant. yFirst half 36-21; second half 27-26. ✩✩Won Championship Series.

YEARLY FINISHES

Year	Atl.	Chi.	Cin.	Hou.	L.A.	N.Y.	Phil.	Pitt.	St.L.	S.F.
1900	†4	✩5	7	....	‡1	....	3	2	✩5	§8
1901	†5	6	8	....	‡3	....	2	1	4	§7
1902	†3	5	4	....	‡2	....	7	1	6	§8
1903	†6	3	4	....	‡5	....	7	1	8	§2
1904	†7	2	3	....	‡6	....	8	4	5	§1
1905	†7	3	5	....	‡8	....	4	2	6	§1
1906	†8	1	6	....	‡5	....	4	3	7	§2
1907	†7	1	6	....	‡5	....	3	2	8	§4
1908	†6	1	5	....	‡7	....	4	✩2	8	✩§2
1909	†8	2	4	....	‡6	....	5	1	7	§3
1910	†8	1	5	....	‡6	....	4	3	7	§2
1911	†8	2	6	....	‡7	....	4	3	5	§1
1912	†8	3	4	....	‡7	....	5	2	6	§1
1913	†5	3	7	....	‡6	....	2	4	8	§1
1914	†1	4	8	....	‡5	....	6	7	3	§2
1915	†2	4	7	....	‡3	....	1	5	6	§8
1916	†3	5	✩7	....	‡1	....	2	6	✩7	§4
1917	†6	5	4	....	‡7	....	2	8	3	§1
1918	†7	1	3	....	‡5	....	6	4	8	§2
1919	†6	3	1	....	‡5	....	8	4	7	§2
1920	†7	✩5	3	....	‡1	....	8	4	✩5	§2
1921	†4	7	6	....	‡5	....	8	2	3	§1
1922	†8	5	2	....	‡6	....	7	✩3	✩3	§1
1923	†7	4	2	....	‡6	....	8	3	5	§1
1924	†8	5	4	....	‡2	....	7	3	6	§1
1925	†5	8	3	....	✩‡6	....	✩6	1	4	§2
1926	†7	4	2	....	‡6	....	8	3	1	§5
1927	†7	4	5	....	‡6	....	8	1	2	§3
1928	†7	3	5	....	‡6	....	8	4	1	§2
1929	†8	1	7	....	‡6	....	5	2	4	§3
1930	†6	2	7	....	‡4	....	8	5	1	§3
1931	†7	3	8	....	‡4	....	6	5	1	§2
1932	†5	1	8	....	‡3	....	4	2	✩6	✩§6
1933	†4	3	8	....	‡6	....	7	2	5	§1
1934	†4	3	8	....	‡6	....	7	5	1	§2
1935	†8	1	6	....	‡5	....	7	4	2	§3
1936	†6	✩2	5	....	‡7	....	8	4	✩2	§1
1937	†5	2	8	....	‡6	....	7	3	4	§1
1938	†5	1	4	....	‡7	....	8	2	6	§3
1939	†7	4	1	....	‡3	....	8	6	2	§5

YEARLY FINISHES—Continued

Year	Atl.	Chi.	Cin.	Hous.	L.A.	N.Y.	Phil.	Pitt.	St.L.	S.F.
1940	†7	5	1	....	‡2	....	8	4	3	§6
1941	†7	6	3	....	‡1	....	8	4	2	§5
1942	†7	6	4	....	‡2	....	8	5	1	§3
1943	†6	5	2	....	‡3	....	7	4	1	§8
1944	†6	4	3	....	‡7	....	8	2	1	§5
1945	†6	1	7	....	‡3	....	8	4	2	§5
1946	†4	3	6	....	‡2	....	5	7	1	§8
1947	†3	6	5	....	‡1	....	*7	*7	2	§4
1948	†1	8	7	....	‡3	....	6	4	2	§5
1949	†4	8	7	....	‡1	....	3	6	2	§5
1950	†4	7	6	....	‡2	....	1	8	5	§3
1951	†4	8	6	....	‡2	....	5	7	3	§1
1952	†7	5	6	....	‡1	....	4	8	3	§2
1953	†2	7	6	....	‡1	....	*3	8	*3	§5
1954	†3	7	5	....	‡2	....	4	8	6	§1
1955	†2	6	5	....	‡1	....	4	8	7	§3
1956	†2	8	3	....	‡1	....	5	7	4	§6
1957	†1	*7	4	....	‡3	....	5	*7	2	§6
1958	†1	*5	4	....	7	....	8	2	*5	3
1959	†2	*5	*5	....	1	....	8	4	7	3
1960	†2	7	6	....	4	....	8	1	3	5
1961	†4	7	1	....	2	....	8	6	5	3
1962	†5	9	3	8	2	10	7	4	6	1
1963	†6	7	5	9	1	10	4	8	2	3
1964	†5	8	*2	9	*6	10	*2	*6	1	4
1965	†5	8	4	9	1	10	6	3	7	2
1966	5	10	7	8	1	9	4	3	6	2
1967	7	3	4	9	8	10	5	6	1	2
1968	5	3	4	10	*7	9	*7	6	1	2

	EAST DIVISION						WEST DIVISION					
Year	Chi.	Mon.	N.Y.	Phila.	Pitt.	St.L.	Atl.	Cin.	Hous.	L.A.	S.D.	S.F.
1969	2	6	1	5	3	4	1	3	5	4	6	2
1970	2	6	3	5	1	4	5	1	4	2	6	3
1971	*3	5	*3	6	1	2	3	*4	*4	2	6	1
1972	2	5	3	6	1	4	4	1	2	3	6	5
1973	5	4	1	6	3	2	5	1	4	2	6	3
1974	6	4	5	3	1	2	3	2	4	1	6	5
1975	*5	*5	*3	2	1	*3	5	1	6	2	4	3
1976	4	6	3	1	2	5	6	1	3	2	5	4
1977	4	5	6	1	2	3	6	2	3	1	5	4
1978	3	4	6	1	2	5	6	2	5	1	4	3
1979	5	2	6	4	1	3	6	1	2	3	5	4
1980	6	2	5	1	3	4	4	3	1	2	6	5
1981x	6	3	5	1	4	2	4	2	3	1	6	5
y	5	1	4	3	6	2	5	2	1	4	6	3
1982	5	3	6	2	4	1	1	6	5	2	4	3
1983	5	3	6	1	2	4	2	6	3	1	4	5

*Tied for position. †Record of predecessor Boston (1900-1952) and Milwaukee (1953-1965) clubs; ‡Brooklyn club; §New York Giants. xStandings for first half of split season. yStandings for second half of split season.

LEADING BATSMEN

Year	Player and Club	G.	AB.	R.	H.	TB.	2B.	3B.	HR.	RBI.	B.A.
1900—John (Honus) Wagner, Pittsburgh	134	528	107	201	302	45	22	4	....	.381
1901—Jesse Burkett, St. Louis	142	597	139	228	313	21	17	10	....	.382
1902—Clarence Beaumont, Pittsburgh	131	544	101	194	227	21	6	0	....	.357
1903—John (Honus) Wagner, Pittsburgh	129	512	97	182	265	30	19	5	....	.355
1904—John (Honus) Wagner, Pittsburgh	132	490	97	171	255	44	14	4	....	.349
1905—J. Bentley Seymour, Cincinnati	149	581	95	219	325	40	21	8	....	.377
1906—John (Honus) Wagner, Pittsburgh	140	516	103	175	237	38	9	2	....	.339
1907—John (Honus) Wagner, Pittsburgh	142	515	98	180	264	38	14	6	91	.350
1908—John (Honus) Wagner, Pittsburgh	151	568	100	201	308	39	19	10	106	.354
1909—John (Honus) Wagner, Pittsburgh	137	495	92	168	242	39	10	5	102	.339
1910—Sherwood Magee, Philadelphia	154	519	110	172	263	39	17	6	116	.331
1911—John (Honus) Wagner, Pittsburgh	130	473	87	158	240	23	16	9	108	.334
1912—Henry Zimmerman, Chicago	145	557	95	207	318	41	14	14	98	.372
1913—Jacob Daubert, Brooklyn	139	508	76	178	215	17	7	2	46	.350

Year	Player and Club	G.	AB.	R.	H.	TB.	2B.	3B.	HR.	RBI.	B.A.
1914—	Jacob Daubert, Brooklyn	126	474	89	156	205	17	7	6	44	.329
1915—	Lawrence Doyle, New York	150	591	86	189	261	40	10	4	68	.320
1916—	Harold Chase, Cincinnati	142	542	66	184	249	29	12	4	84	.339
1917—	Edd Roush, Cincinnati	136	522	82	178	237	19	14	4	62	.341
1918—	Zachariah Wheat, Brooklyn	105	409	39	137	158	15	3	0	48	.335
1919—	Edd Roush, Cincinnati	133	504	73	162	216	19	13	3	69	.321
1920—	Rogers Hornsby, St. Louis	149	589	96	218	329	44	20	9	94	.370
1921—	Rogers Hornsby, St. Louis	154	592	131	235	378	44	18	21	126	.397
1922—	Rogers Hornsby, St. Louis	154	623	141	250	450	46	14	42	152	.401
1923—	Rogers Hornsby, St. Louis	107	424	89	163	266	32	10	17	83	.384
1924—	Rogers Hornsby, St. Louis	143	536	121	227	373	43	14	25	94	.424
1925—	Rogers Hornsby, St. Louis	138	504	133	203	381	41	10	39	143	.403
1926—	Eugene Hargrave, Cincinnati	105	326	42	115	171	22	8	6	62	.353
1927—	Paul Waner, Pittsburgh	155	623	114	237	338	42	18	9	131	.380
1928—	Rogers Hornsby, Boston	140	486	99	188	307	42	7	21	94	.387
1929—	Frank O'Doul, Philadelphia	154	638	152	254	397	35	6	32	122	.398
1930—	William Terry, New York	154	633	139	254	392	39	15	23	129	.401
1931—	Chas. (Chick) Hafey, St. Louis	122	450	94	157	256	35	8	16	95	.349
1932—	Frank O'Doul, Brooklyn	148	595	120	219	330	32	8	21	90	.368
1933—	Charles Klein, Philadelphia	152	606	101	223	365	44	7	28	120	.368
1934—	Paul Waner, Pittsburgh	146	599	122	217	323	32	16	14	90	.362
1935—	J. Floyd (Arky) Vaughan, Pitts.	137	499	108	192	303	34	10	19	99	.385
1936—	Paul Waner, Pittsburgh	148	585	107	218	304	53	9	5	94	.373
1937—	Joseph Medwick, St. Louis	156	633	111	237	406	56	10	31	154	.374
1938—	Ernest Lombardi, Cincinnati	129	489	60	167	256	30	1	19	95	.342
1939—	John Mize, St. Louis	153	564	104	197	353	44	14	28	108	.349
1940—	Debs Garms, Pittsburgh	103	358	76	127	179	23	7	5	57	.355
1941—	Harold (Pete) Reiser, Brooklyn	137	536	117	184	299	39	17	14	76	.343
1942—	Ernest Lombardi, Boston	105	309	32	102	149	14	0	11	46	.330
1943—	Stanley Musial, St. Louis	157	617	108	220	347	48	20	13	81	.357
1944—	Fred (Dixie) Walker, Brooklyn	147	535	77	191	283	37	8	13	91	.357
1945—	Philip Cavarretta, Chicago	132	498	94	177	249	34	10	6	97	.355
1946—	Stanley Musial, St. Louis	156	624	124	228	366	50	20	16	103	.365
1947—	Harry Walker, St. Louis-Phila.	140	513	81	186	250	29	16	1	41	.363
1948—	Stanley Musial, St. Louis	155	611	135	230	429	46	18	39	131	.376
1949—	Jack Robinson, Brooklyn	156	593	122	203	313	38	12	16	124	.342
1950—	Stanley Musial, St. Louis	146	555	105	192	331	41	7	28	109	.346
1951—	Stanley Musial, St. Louis	152	578	124	205	355	30	12	32	108	.355
1952—	Stanley Musial, St. Louis	154	578	105	194	311	42	6	21	91	.336
1953—	Carl Furillo, Brooklyn	132	479	82	165	278	38	6	21	92	.344
1954—	Willie Mays, New York	151	565	119	195	377	33	13	41	110	.345
1955—	Richie Ashburn, Philadelphia	140	533	91	180	239	32	9	3	42	.338
1956—	Henry Aaron, Milwaukee	153	609	106	200	340	34	14	26	92	.328
1957—	Stanley Musial, St. Louis	134	502	82	176	307	38	3	29	102	.351
1958—	Richie Ashburn, Philadelphia	152	615	98	215	271	24	13	2	33	.350
1959—	Henry Aaron, Milwaukee	154	629	116	223	400	46	7	39	123	.355
1960—	Richard Groat, Pittsburgh	138	573	85	186	226	26	4	2	50	.325
1961—	Roberto Clemente, Pittsburgh	146	572	100	201	320	30	10	23	89	.351
1962—	H. Thomas Davis, Los Angeles	163	665	120	230	356	27	9	27	153	.346
1963—	H. Thomas Davis, Los Angeles	146	556	69	181	254	19	3	16	88	.326
1964—	Roberto Clemente, Pittsburgh	155	622	95	211	301	40	7	12	87	.339
1965—	Roberto Clemente, Pittsburgh	152	589	91	194	273	21	14	10	65	.329
1966—	Mateo Alou, Pittsburgh	141	535	86	183	225	18	9	2	27	.342
1967—	Roberto Clemente, Pittsburgh	147	585	103	209	324	26	10	23	110	.357
1968—	Peter Rose, Cincinnati	149	626	94	210	294	42	6	10	49	.335
1969—	Peter Rose, Cincinnati	156	627	120	218	321	33	11	16	82	.348
1970—	Ricardo Carty, Atlanta	136	478	84	175	279	23	3	25	101	.366
1971—	Joseph Torre, St. Louis	161	634	97	230	352	34	8	24	137	.363
1972—	Billy L. Williams, Chicago	150	574	95	191	348	34	6	37	122	.333
1973—	Peter Rose, Cincinnati	160	680	115	230	297	36	8	5	64	.338
1974—	Ralph Garr, Atlanta	143	606	87	214	305	24	17	11	54	.353
1975—	Bill Madlock, Chicago	130	514	77	182	246	29	7	7	64	.354
1976—	Bill Madlock, Chicago	142	514	68	174	257	36	1	15	84	.339
1977—	David Parker, Pittsburgh	159	637	107	215	338	44	8	21	88	.338
1978—	David Parker, Pittsburgh	148	581	102	194	340	32	12	30	117	.334
1979—	Keith Hernandez, St. Louis	161	610	116	210	313	48	11	11	105	.344
1980—	William Buckner, Chicago	145	578	69	187	264	41	3	10	68	.324
1981—	Bill Madlock, Pittsburgh	82	279	35	95	138	23	1	6	45	.341
1982—	Albert Oliver, Montreal	160	617	90	204	317	43	2	22	109	.331
1983—	Bill Madlock, Pittsburgh	130	473	68	153	210	21	0	12	68	.323

LEADERS IN RUNS SCORED

Year	Player and Club	Runs	Year	Player and Club	Runs
1900	Roy Thomas, Philadelphia	131	1941	Harold (Pete) Reiser, Brooklyn	117
1901	Jesse Burkett, St. Louis	139	1942	Melvin Ott, New York	118
1902	John (Honus) Wagner, Pittsburgh	105	1943	J. Floyd (Arky) Vaughan, Brooklyn	112
1903	Clarence Beaumont, Pittsburgh	137	1944	William Nicholson, Chicago	116
1904	George Browne, New York	99	1945	Edward Stanky, Brooklyn	128
1905	Michael Donlin, New York	124	1946	Stanley Musial, St. Louis	124
1906	John (Honus) Wagner, Pittsburgh	103	1947	John Mize, New York	137
	Frank Chance, Chicago	103	1948	Stanley Musial, St. Louis	135
1907	W. Porter Shannon, New York	104	1949	Harold (Pee Wee) Reese, Brooklyn	132
1908	Frederick Tenney, New York	101	1950	C. Earl Torgeson, Boston	120
1909	Thomas Leach, Pittsburgh	126	1951	Musial, St. Louis-Kiner, Pittsburgh	124
1910	Sherwood Magee, Philadelphia	110	1952	Musial, St. Louis-Hemus, St. Louis	105
1911	James Sheckard, Chicago	121	1953	Edwin (Duke) Snider, Brooklyn	132
1912	Robert Bescher, Cincinnati	120	1954	Musial, St. Louis-Snider, Brooklyn	120
1913	Thomas Leach, Chicago	99	1955	Edwin (Duke) Snider, Brooklyn	126
	Max Carey, Pittsburgh	99	1956	Frank Robinson, Cincinnati	122
1914	George Burns, New York	100	1957	Henry Aaron, Milwaukee	118
1915	Cliff. (Gavvy) Cravath, Philadelphia	89	1958	Willie Mays, San Francisco	121
1916	George Burns, New York	105	1959	Vada Pinson, Cincinnati	131
1917	George Burns, New York	103	1960	William Bruton, Milwaukee	112
1918	Henry Groh, Cincinnati	88	1961	Willie Mays, San Francisco	129
1919	George Burns, New York	86	1962	Frank Robinson, Cincinnati	134
1920	George Burns, New York	115	1963	Henry Aaron, Milwaukee	121
1921	Rogers Hornsby, St. Louis	131	1964	Richard Allen, Philadelphia	125
1922	Rogers Hornsby, St. Louis	141	1965	Tommy Harper, Cincinnati	126
1923	Ross Youngs, New York	121	1966	Felipe Alou, Atlanta	122
1924	Frank Frisch, New York	121	1967	Henry Aaron, Atlanta	113
	Rogers Hornsby, St. Louis	121		Louis Brock, St. Louis	113
1925	Hazen (Kiki) Cuyler, Pittsburgh	144	1968	Glenn Beckert, Chicago	98
1926	Hazen (Kiki) Cuyler, Pittsburgh	113	1969	Bobby Bonds, San Francisco	120
1927	Lloyd Waner, Pittsburgh	133		Peter Rose, Cincinnati	120
	Rogers Hornsby, New York	133	1970	Billy Williams, Chicago	137
1928	Paul Waner, Pittsburgh	142	1971	Louis Brock, St. Louis	126
1929	Rogers Hornsby, Chicago	156	1972	Joe Morgan, Cincinnati	122
1930	Charles (Chuck) Klein, Philadelphia	158	1973	Bobby Bonds, San Francisco	131
1931	Terry, New York-Klein, Philadelphia	121	1974	Peter Rose, Cincinnati	110
1932	Charles (Chuck) Klein, Philadelphia	152	1975	Peter Rose, Cincinnati	112
1933	John (Pepper) Martin, St. Louis	122	1976	Peter Rose, Cincinnati	130
1934	Paul Waner, Pittsburgh	122	1977	George Foster, Cincinnati	124
1935	August Galan, Chicago	133	1978	Ivan DeJesus, Chicago	104
1936	J. Floyd (Arky) Vaughan, Pittsburgh	122	1979	Keith Hernandez, St. Louis	116
1937	Joseph Medwick, St. Louis	111	1980	Keith Hernandez, St. Louis	111
1938	Melvin Ott, New York	116	1981	Michael Schmidt, Philadelphia	78
1939	William Werber, Cincinnati	115	1982	Lonnie Smith, St. Louis	120
1940	J. Floyd (Arky) Vaughan, Pittsburgh	113	1983	Timothy Raines, Montreal	133

LEADERS IN HITS

Year	Player and Club	Hits	Year	Player and Club	Hits
1900	William Keeler, Brooklyn	208	1919	Ivy Olson, Brooklyn	164
1901	Jesse Burkett, St. Louis	228	1920	Rogers Hornsby, St. Louis	218
1902	Clarence Beaumont, Pittsburgh	194	1921	Rogers Hornsby, St. Louis	235
1903	Clarence Beaumont, Pittsburgh	209	1922	Rogers Hornsby, St. Louis	250
1904	Clarence Beaumont, Pittsburgh	185	1923	Frank Frisch, New York	223
1905	J. Bentley Seymour, Cincinnati	219	1924	Rogers Hornsby, St. Louis	227
1906	Harry Steinfeldt, Chicago	176	1925	James Bottomley, St. Louis	227
1907	Clarence Beaumont, Boston	187	1926	Edward Brown, Boston	201
1908	John (Honus) Wagner, Pittsburgh	201	1927	Paul Waner, Pittsburgh	237
1909	Lawrence Doyle, New York	172	1928	Fred Lindstrom, New York	231
1910	John (Honus) Wagner, Pittsburgh	178	1929	Frank O'Doul, Philadelphia	254
	Robert Byrne, Pittsburgh	178	1930	William Terry, New York	254
1911	Roy Miller, Boston	192	1931	Lloyd Waner, Pittsburgh	214
1912	Henry Zimmerman, Chicago	207	1932	Charles Klein, Philadelphia	226
1913	Cliff. (Gavvy) Cravath, Philadelphia	179	1933	Charles Klein, Philadelphia	223
1914	Sherwood Magee, Philadelphia	171	1934	Paul Waner, Pittsburgh	217
1915	Lawrence Doyle, New York	189	1935	William Herman, Chicago	227
1916	Harold Chase, Cincinnati	184	1936	Joseph Medwick, St. Louis	223
1917	Henry Groh, Cincinnati	182	1937	Joseph Medwick, St. Louis	237
1918	Charles Hollocher, Chicago	161	1938	Frank McCormick, Cincinnati	209

Year	Player and Club	Hits
1939—	Frank McCormick, Cincinnati	209
1940—	Stanley Hack, Chicago	191
	Frank McCormick, Cincinnati	191
1941—	Stanley Hack, Chicago	186
1942—	Enos Slaughter, St. Louis	188
1943—	Stanley Musial, St. Louis	220
1944—	Musial, St. Louis-Cavarretta, Chi.	197
1945—	Thomas Holmes, Boston	224
1946—	Stanley Musial, St. Louis	228
1947—	Thomas Holmes, Boston	191
1948—	Stanley Musial, St. Louis	230
1949—	Stanley Musial, St. Louis	207
1950—	Edwin (Duke) Snider, Brooklyn	199
1951—	Richie Ashburn, Philadelphia	221
1952—	Stanley Musial, St. Louis	194
1953—	Richie Ashburn, Philadelphia	205
1954—	Donald Mueller, New York	212
1955—	Theodore Kluszewski, Cincinnati	192
1956—	Henry Aaron, Milwaukee	200
1957—	Al (Red) Schoendienst, N.Y.-Mil.	200
1958—	Richie Ashburn, Philadelphia	215
1959—	Henry Aaron, Milwaukee	223
1960—	Willie Mays, San Francisco	190
1961—	Vada Pinson, Cincinnati	208
1962—	H. Thomas Davis, Los Angeles	230
1963—	Vada Pinson, Cincinnati	204
1964—	Clemente, Pitts.-Flood, St. Louis	211
1965—	Peter Rose, Cincinnati	209
1966—	Felipe Alou, Atlanta	218
1967—	Roberto Clemente, Pittsburgh	209
1968—	Felipe Alou, Atlanta	210
	Peter Rose, Cincinnati	210
1969—	Mateo Alou, Pittsburgh	231
1970—	Peter Rose, Cincinnati	205
	Billy Williams, Chicago	205
1971—	Joseph Torre, St. Louis	230
1972—	Peter Rose, Cincinnati	198
1973—	Peter Rose, Cincinnati	230
1974—	Ralph Garr, Atlanta	214
1975—	David Cash, Philadelphia	213
1976—	Peter Rose, Cincinnati	215
1977—	David Parker, Pittsburgh	215
1978—	Steven Garvey, Los Angeles	202
1979—	Garry Templeton, St. Louis	211
1980—	Steven Garvey, Los Angeles	200
1981—	Peter Rose, Philadelphia	140
1982—	Albert Oliver, Montreal	204
1983—	Jose Cruz, Houston	189
	Andre Dawson, Montreal	189

ONE-BASE HIT LEADERS

Year	Player and Club	1B.
1900—	William H. Keeler, Brooklyn	179
1901—	Jesse C. Burkett, St. Louis	180
1902—	Clarence H. Beaumont, Pittsburgh	167
1903—	Clarence H. Beaumont, Pittsburgh	166
1904—	Clarence H. Beaumont, Pittsburgh	158
1905—	Michael J. Donlin, New York	162
1906—	Miller J. Huggins, Cincinnati	141
	William P. Shannon, St. Louis-NY	141
1907—	Clarence H. Beaumont, Pittsburgh	150
1908—	Michael J. Donlin, New York	153
1909—	Edward L. Grant, Philadelphia	147
1910—	Edward L. Grant, Philadelphia	134
1911—	Jacob E. Daubert, Brooklyn	146
	Roy O. Miller, Boston	146
1912—	William J. Sweeney, Boston	159
1913—	Jacob E. Daubert, Brooklyn	152
1914—	Beals Becker, Philadelphia	128
1915—	Lawrence J. Doyle, New York	135
1916—	David A. Robertson, New York	142
1917—	Benjamin M. Kauff, New York	141
	Edd J. Roush, Cincinnati	141
1918—	Charles J. Hollocher, Chicago	130
1919—	Ivan M. Olson, Brooklyn	140
1920—	Milton J. Stock, St. Louis	170
1921—	Carson L. Bigbee, Pittsburgh	161
1922—	Carson L. Bigbee, Pittsburgh	166
1923—	Frank F. Frisch, New York	169
1924—	Zachariah Wheat, Brooklyn	149
1925—	Milton J. Stock, Brooklyn	164
1926—	Edward W. Brown, Boston	160
1927—	Lloyd J. Waner, Pittsburgh	198
1928—	Lloyd J. Waner, Pittsburgh	180
1929—	Frank J. O'Doul, Philadelphia	181
	Lloyd J. Waner, Pittsburgh	181
1930—	William H. Terry, New York	177
1931—	Lloyd J. Waner, Pittsburgh	172
1932—	Frank J. O'Doul, Brooklyn	158
1933—	Charles P. Fullis, Philadelphia	162
1934—	William H. Terry, New York	169
1935—	Forrest D. Jensen, Pittsburgh	160
1936—	Joseph G. Moore, New York	160
1937—	Paul G. Waner, Pittsburgh	178
1938—	Frank A. McCormick, Cincinnati	160
1939—	John A. Hassett, Boston	162
1940—	Burgess U. Whitehead, New York	141
1941—	Stanley C. Hack, Chicago	141
1942—	Enos B. Slaughter, St. Louis	127
1943—	Nicholas J. Witek, New York	172
1944—	Philip J. Cavarretta, Chicago	142
1945—	Stanley C. Hack, Chicago	155
1946—	Stanley F. Musial, St. Louis	142
1947—	Thomas F. Holmes, Boston	146
1948—	Stanley A. Rojek, Pittsburgh	150
1949—	Albert F. Schoendienst, St. Louis	160
1950—	Edward S. Waitkus, Philadelphia	143
1951—	Richie Ashburn, Philadelphia	181
1952—	Robert H. Adams, Cincinnati	145
1953—	Richie Ashburn, Philadelphia	169
1954—	Donald F. Mueller, New York	165
1955—	Donald F. Mueller, New York	152
1956—	John E. Temple, Cincinnati	157
1957—	Richie Ashburn, Philadelphia	152
1958—	Richie Ashburn, Philadelphia	176
1959—	Don L. Blasingame, St. Louis	144
1960—	Richard M. Groat, Pittsburgh	154
1961—	Vada E. Pinson, Cincinnati	150
	Maurice M. Wills, Los Angeles	150
1962—	Maurice M. Wills, Los Angeles	179
1963—	Curtis C. Flood, St. Louis	152
1964—	Curtis C. Flood, St. Louis	178
1965—	Maurice M. Wills, Los Angeles	165
1966—	Roland T. Jackson, Houston	160
1967—	Maurice M. Wills, Pittsburgh	162
1968—	Curtis C. Flood, St. Louis	160
1969—	Mateo R. Alou, Pittsburgh	183
1970—	Mateo R. Alou, Pittsburgh	171
1971—	Ralph A. Garr, Atlanta	180
1972—	Louis C. Brock, St. Louis	156
1973—	Peter E. Rose, Cincinnati	181
1974—	David Cash, Philadelphia	167
1975—	David Cash, Philadelphia	166
1976—	Guillermo Montanez, San Fran.-Atl.	164
1977—	Garry Templeton, St. Louis	155
1978—	Lawrence Bowa, Philadelphia	153

ONE-BASE HIT LEADERS—Continued

Year	Player and Club	1B.	Year	Player and Club	1B.
1979—	Peter Rose, Philadelphia	159	1982—	William Buckner, Chicago	147
1980—	Eugene Richards, San Diego	155	1983—	Rafael Ramirez, Atlanta	160
1981—	Peter Rose, Philadelphia	117			

TWO-BASE HIT LEADERS

Year	Player and Club	2B.	Year	Player and Club	2B.
1900—	John (Honus) Wagner, Pittsburgh	45	1943—	Stanley Musial, St. Louis	48
1901—	Wagner, Pitts-Beckley, Cinn	39	1944—	Stanley Musial, St. Louis	51
1902—	John (Honus) Wagner, Pittsburgh	33	1945—	Thomas Holmes, Boston	47
1903—	Clarke, Pitts.-Mertes, N.Y.- Steinfeldt, Cincinnati	32	1946—	Stanley Musial, St. Louis	50
1904—	John (Honus) Wagner, Pittsburgh	44	1947—	Edward Miller, Cincinnati	38
1905—	J. Bentley Seymour, Cincinnati	40	1948—	Stanley Musial, St. Louis	46
1906—	John (Honus) Wagner, Pittsburgh	38	1949—	Stanley Musial, St. Louis	41
1907—	John (Honus) Wagner, Pittsburgh	38	1950—	Al (Red) Schoendienst, St. Louis	43
1908—	John (Honus) Wagner, Pittsburgh	39	1951—	Alvin Dark, New York	41
1909—	John (Honus) Wagner, Pittsburgh	39	1952—	Stanley Musial, St. Louis	42
1910—	Robert Byrne, Pittsburgh	43	1953—	Stanley Musial, St. Louis	53
1911—	Edward Konetchy, St. Louis	38	1954—	Stanley Musial, St. Louis	41
1912—	Henry Zimmerman, Chicago	41	1955—	Logan, Milwaukee-Aaron, Milwaukee	37
1913—	J. Carlisle Smith, Brooklyn	40	1956—	Henry Aaron, Milwaukee	34
1914—	Sherwood Magee, Philadelphia	39	1957—	Donald Hoak, Cincinnati	39
1915—	Lawrence Doyle, New York	40	1958—	Orlando Cepeda, San Francisco	38
1916—	O. Albert Niehoff, Philadelphia	42	1959—	Vada Pinson, Cincinnati	47
1917—	Henry Groh, Cincinnati	39	1960—	Vada Pinson, Cincinnati	37
1918—	Henry Groh, Cincinnati	28	1961—	Henry Aaron, Milwaukee	39
1919—	Ross Youngs, New York	31	1962—	Frank Robinson, Cincinnati	51
1920—	Rogers Hornsby, St. Louis	44	1963—	Richard Groat, St. Louis	43
1921—	Rogers Hornsby, St. Louis	44	1964—	A. Lee Maye, Milwaukee	44
1922—	Rogers Hornsby, St. Louis	46	1965—	Henry Aaron, Milwaukee	40
1923—	Edd Roush, Cincinnati	41	1966—	John Callison, Philadelphia	40
1924—	Rogers Hornsby, St. Louis	43	1967—	Daniel Staub, Houston	44
1925—	James Bottomley, St. Louis	44	1968—	Louis Brock, St. Louis	46
1926—	James Bottomley, St. Louis	40	1969—	Mateo Alou, Pittsburgh	41
1927—	J. Riggs Stephenson, Chicago	46	1970—	M. Wesley Parker, Los Angeles	47
1928—	Paul Waner, Pittsburgh	50	1971—	Cesar Cedeno, Houston	40
1929—	John Frederick, Brooklyn	52	1972—	Cesar Cedeno, Houston	39
1930—	Charles Klein, Philadelphia	59		Guillermo Montanez, Philadelphia	39
1931—	Earl (Sparky) Adams, St. Louis	46	1973—	Wilver Stargell, Pittsburgh	43
1932—	Paul Waner, Pittsburgh	62	1974—	Peter Rose, Cincinnati	45
1933—	Charles Klein, Philadelphia	44	1975—	Peter Rose, Cincinnati	47
1934—	Cuyler, Chicago-Allen, Philadelphia	42	1976—	Peter Rose, Cincinnati	42
1935—	William Herman, Chicago	57	1977—	David Parker, Pittsburgh	44
1936—	Joseph Medwick, St. Louis	64	1978—	Peter Rose, Cincinnati	51
1937—	Joseph Medwick, St. Louis	56	1979—	Keith Hernandez, St. Louis	48
1938—	Joseph Medwick, St. Louis	47	1980—	Peter Rose, Philadelphia	42
1939—	Enos Slaughter, St. Louis	52	1981—	William Buckner, Chicago	35
1940—	Frank McCormick, Cincinnati	44	1982—	Albert Oliver, Montreal	43
1941—	Reiser, Brooklyn-Mize, St. Louis	39	1983—	William Buckner, Chicago	38
1942—	Martin Marion, St. Louis	38		Albert Oliver, Montreal	38
				Johnny Ray, Pittsburgh	38

THREE-BASE HIT LEADERS

Year	Player and Club	3B.	Year	Player and Club	3B.
1900—	John (Honus) Wagner, Pittsburgh	22	1912—	John (Chief) Wilson, Pittsburgh	36
1901—	James Sheckard, Brooklyn	21	1913—	Victor Saier, Chicago	21
1902—	Samuel Crawford, Cincinnati	23	1914—	Max Carey, Pittsburgh	17
1903—	John (Honus) Wagner, Pittsburgh	19	1915—	Thomas Long, St. Louis	25
1904—	Harry Lumley, Brooklyn	18	1916—	William Hinchman, Pittsburgh	16
1905—	J. Bentley Seymour, Cincinnati	21	1917—	Rogers Hornsby, St. Louis	17
1906—	Clarke, Pittsburgh-Schulte, Chicago	13	1918—	Jacob Daubert, Brooklyn	15
1907—	Ganzel, Cin.-Alperman, Brklyn	16	1919—	Hi Myers, Brklyn-Southworth, Pitts.	14
1908—	John (Honus) Wagner, Pittsburgh	19	1920—	Henry (Hi) Myers, Brooklyn	22
1909—	Michael Mitchell, Cincinnati	17	1921—	Hornsby, St. Louis-Powell, Boston	18
1910—	Michael Mitchell, Cincinnati	18	1922—	Jacob Daubert, Cincinnati	22
1911—	Lawrence Doyle, New York	25	1923—	Carey, Pitts.-Traynor, Pitts.	19

Year	Player and Club	3B.
1924—	Edd Roush, Cincinnati	21
1925—	Hazen (Kiki) Cuyler, Pittsburgh	26
1926—	Paul Waner, Pittsburgh	22
1927—	Paul Waner, Pittsburgh	18
1928—	James Bottomley, St. Louis	20
1929—	Lloyd Waner, Pittsburgh	20
1930—	Adam Comorosky, Pittsburgh	23
1931—	William Terry, New York	20
1932—	Floyd (Babe) Herman, Cincinnati	19
1933—	J. Floyd (Arky) Vaughan, Pittsburgh.	19
1934—	Joseph Medwick, St. Louis	18
1935—	Ival Goodman, Cincinnati	18
1936—	Ival Goodman, Cincinnati	14
1937—	J. Floyd (Arky) Vaughan, Pittsburgh.	17
1938—	John Mize, St. Louis	16
1939—	William Herman, Chicago	18
1940—	J. Floyd (Arky) Vaughan, Pittsburgh.	15
1941—	Harold (Pete) Reiser, Brooklyn	17
1942—	Enos Slaughter, St. Louis	17
1943—	Stanley Musial, St. Louis	20
1944—	John Barrett, Pittsburgh	19
1945—	Luis Olmo, Brooklyn	13
1946—	Stanley Musial, St. Louis	20
1947—	Harry Walker, St. Louis-Philadelphia	16
1948—	Stanley Musial, St. Louis	18
1949—	Musial, St. L.-Slaughter, St. L.	13
1950—	Richie Ashburn, Philadelphia	14
1951—	Musial, St. Louis-Bell, Pittsburgh	12
1952—	Robert Thomson, New York	14
1953—	James Gilliam, Brooklyn	17
1954—	Willie Mays, New York	13
1955—	Mays, New York-Long, Pittsburgh	13
1956—	William Bruton, Milwaukee	15
1957—	Willie Mays, New York	20
1958—	Richie Ashburn, Philadelphia	13
1959—	Moon, L. A.-Neal, L. A.	11
1960—	William Bruton, Milwaukee	13
1961—	George Altman, Chicago	12
1962—	Callison, Philadelphia-Virdon, Pitt.	10
	W. Davis, Wills, Los Angeles	10
1963—	Vada Pinson, Cincinnati	14
1964—	Allen, Philadelphia-Santo, Chicago	13
1965—	John Callison, Philadelphia	16
1966—	J. Timothy McCarver, St. Louis	13
1967—	Vada Pinson, Cincinnati	13
1968—	Louis Brock, St. Louis	14
1969—	Roberto Clemente, Pittsburgh	12
1970—	William Davis, Los Angeles	16
1971—	Joe Morgan, Houston	11
	Roger Metzger, Houston	11
1972—	Lawrence Bowa, Philadelphia	13
1973—	Roger Metzger, Houston	14
1974—	Ralph Garr, Atlanta	17
1975—	Ralph Garr, Atlanta	11
1976—	David Cash, Philadelphia	12
1977—	Garry Templeton, St. Louis	18
1978—	Garry Templeton, St. Louis	13
1979—	Garry Templeton, St. Louis	19
1980—	Omar Moreno, Pittsburgh	13
	Rodney Scott, Montreal	13
1981—	G. Craig Reynolds, Houston	12
	Eugene Richards, San Diego	12
1982—	Richard Thon, Houston	10
1983—	Brett Butler, Atlanta	13

HOME RUN LEADERS

Year	Player and Club	HR.
1900—	Herman Long, Boston	12
1901—	Samuel Crawford, Cincinnati	16
1902—	Thomas Leach, Pittsburgh	6
1903—	James Sheckard, Brooklyn	9
1904—	Harry Lumley, Brooklyn	9
1905—	Fred Odwell, Cincinnati	9
1906—	Timothy Jordan, Brooklyn	12
1907—	David Brain, Boston	10
1908—	Timothy Jordan, Brooklyn	12
1909—	John (Red) Murray, New York	7
1910—	Fred Beck, Bos.-F. Schulte, Chi.	10
1911—	Frank Schulte, Chicago	21
1912—	Henry Zimmerman, Chicago	14
1913—	Cliff. (Gavvy) Cravath, Philadelphia	19
1914—	Cliff. (Gavvy) Cravath, Philadelphia	19
1915—	Cliff. (Gavvy) Cravath, Philadelphia	24
1916—	Robertson, New York-Williams, Chi.	12
1917—	Dave Robertson, New York	12
	Cliff. (Gavvy) Cravath, Philadelphia	12
1918—	Cliff. (Gavvy) Cravath, Philadelphia	8
1919—	Cliff. (Gavvy) Cravath, Philadelphia	12
1920—	Fred (Cy) Williams, Philadelphia	15
1921—	George Kelly, New York	23
1922—	Rogers Hornsby, St. Louis	42
1923—	Fred (Cy) Williams, Philadelphia	41
1924—	Jacques Fournier, Brooklyn	27
1925—	Rogers Hornsby, St. Louis	39
1926—	Lewis (Hack) Wilson, Chicago	21
1927—	Wilson, Chi.-Williams, Phila.	30
1928—	Lewis (Hack) Wilson, Chicago	31
	James Bottomley, St. Louis	31
1929—	Charles Klein, Philadelphia	43
1930—	Lewis (Hack) Wilson, Chicago	56
1931—	Charles Klein, Philadelphia	31
1932—	Klein, Philadelphia-Ott, New York	38
1933—	Charles Klein, Philadelphia	28
1934—	Collins, St. Louis-Ott, New York	35
1935—	Walter Berger, Boston	34
1936—	Melvin Ott, New York	33
1937—	Ott, New York-Medwick, St. Louis	31
1938—	Melvin Ott, New York	36
1939—	John Mize, St. Louis	28
1940—	John Mize, St. Louis	43
1941—	Adolph Camilli, Brooklyn	34
1942—	Melvin Ott, New York	30
1943—	William Nicholson, Chicago	29
1944—	William Nicholson, Chicago	33
1945—	Thomas Holmes, Boston	28
1946—	Ralph Kiner, Pittsburgh	23
1947—	Kiner, Pittsburgh-Mize, New York	51
1948—	Kiner, Pittsburgh-Mize, New York	40
1949—	Ralph Kiner, Pittsburgh	54
1950—	Ralph Kiner, Pittsburgh	47
1951—	Ralph Kiner, Pittsburgh	42
1952—	Kiner, Pittsburgh-Sauer, Chicago	37
1953—	Edwin Mathews, Milwaukee	47
1954—	Theodore Kluszewski, Cincinnati	49
1955—	Willie Mays, New York	51
1956—	Edwin (Duke) Snider, Brooklyn	43
1957—	Henry Aaron, Milwaukee	44
1958—	Ernest Banks, Chicago	47
1959—	Edwin Mathews, Milwaukee	46
1960—	Ernest Banks, Chicago	41
1961—	Orlando Cepeda, San Francisco	46
1962—	Willie Mays, San Francisco	49
1963—	H. Aaron, Milw.-McCovey, San Fran.	44
1964—	Willie Mays, San Francisco	47
1965—	Willie Mays, San Francisco	52
1966—	Henry Aaron, Atlanta	44
1967—	Henry Aaron, Atlanta	39

HOME RUN LEADERS—Continued

Year	Player and Club	HR.	Year	Player and Club	HR.
1968—	Willie McCovey, San Francisco	36	1976—	Michael Schmidt, Philadelphia	38
1969—	Willie McCovey, San Francisco	45	1977—	George Foster, Cincinnati	52
1970—	Johnny Bench, Cincinnati	45	1978—	George Foster, Cincinnati	40
1971—	Wilver Stargell, Pittsburgh	48	1979—	David Kingman, Chicago	48
1972—	Johnny Bench, Cincinnati	40	1980—	Michael Schmidt, Philadelphia	48
1973—	Wilver Stargell, Pittsburgh	44	1981—	Michael Schmidt, Philadelphia	31
1974—	Michael Schmidt, Philadelphia	36	1982—	David Kingman, New York	37
1975—	Michael Schmidt, Philadelphia	38	1983—	Michael Schmidt, Philadelphia	40

LEADERS IN TOTAL BASES

Year	Player and Club	T.B.	Year	Player and Club	T.B.
1900—	Elmer Flick, Philadelphia	305	1942—	Enos Slaughter, St. Louis	292
1901—	Jesse Burkett, St. Louis	313	1943—	Stanley Musial, St. Louis	347
1902—	Samuel Crawford, Cincinnati	256	1944—	William Nicholson, Chicago	317
1903—	Clarence Beaumont, Pittsburgh	272	1945—	Thomas Holmes, Boston	367
1904—	John (Honus) Wagner, Pittsburgh	255	1946—	Stanley Musial, St. Louis	366
1905—	J. Bentley Seymour, Cincinnati	325	1947—	Ralph Kiner, Pittsburgh	361
1906—	John (Honus) Wagner, Pittsburgh	237	1948—	Stanley Musial, St. Louis	429
1907—	John (Honus) Wagner, Pittsburgh	264	1949—	Stanley Musial, St. Louis	382
1908—	John (Honus) Wagner, Pittsburgh	308	1950—	Edwin (Duke) Snider, Brooklyn	343
1909—	John (Honus) Wagner, Pittsburgh	242	1951—	Stanley Musial, St. Louis	355
1910—	Sherwood Magee, Philadelphia	263	1952—	Stanley Musial, St. Louis	311
1911—	Frank Schulte, Chicago	308	1953—	Edwin (Duke) Snider, Brooklyn	370
1912—	Henry Zimmerman, Chicago	318	1954—	Edwin (Duke) Snider, Brooklyn	378
1913—	Cliff (Gavvy) Cravath, Philadelphia	298	1955—	Willie Mays, New York	382
1914—	Sherwood Magee, Philadelphia	277	1956—	Henry Aaron, Milwaukee	340
1915—	Cliff (Gavvy) Cravath, Philadelphia	266	1957—	Henry Aaron, Milwaukee	369
1916—	Zachariah Wheat, Brooklyn	262	1958—	Ernest Banks, Chicago	379
1917—	Rogers Hornsby, St. Louis	253	1959—	Henry Aaron, Milwaukee	400
1918—	Charles Hollocher, Chicago	202	1960—	Henry Aaron, Milwaukee	334
1919—	Henry (Hi) Myers, Brooklyn	223	1961—	Henry Aaron, Milwaukee	358
1920—	Rogers Hornsby, St. Louis	329	1962—	Willie Mays, San Francisco	382
1921—	Rogers Hornsby, St. Louis	378	1963—	Henry Aaron, Milwaukee	370
1922—	Rogers Hornsby, St. Louis	450	1964—	Richard Allen, Philadelphia	352
1923—	Frank Frisch, New York	311	1965—	Willie Mays, San Francisco	360
1924—	Rogers Hornsby, St. Louis	373	1966—	Felipe Alou, Atlanta	355
1925—	Rogers Hornsby, St. Louis	381	1967—	Henry Aaron, Atlanta	344
1926—	James Bottomley, St. Louis	305	1968—	Billy Williams, Chicago	321
1927—	Paul Waner, Pittsburgh	338	1969—	Henry Aaron, Atlanta	332
1928—	James Bottomley, St. Louis	362	1970—	Billy Williams, Chicago	373
1929—	Rogers Hornsby, Chicago	409	1971—	Joseph Torre, St. Louis	352
1930—	Charles Klein, Philadelphia	445	1972—	Billy Williams, Chicago	348
1931—	Charles Klein, Philadelphia	347	1973—	Bobby Bonds, San Francisco	341
1932—	Charles Klein, Philadelphia	420	1974—	Johnny Bench, Cincinnati	315
1933—	Charles Klein, Philadelphia	365	1975—	Gregory Luzinski, Philadelphia	322
1934—	James (Rip) Collins, St. Louis	369	1976—	Michael Schmidt, Philadelphia	306
1935—	Joseph Medwick, St. Louis	365	1977—	George Foster, Cincinnati	388
1936—	Joseph Medwick, St. Louis	367	1978—	David Parker, Pittsburgh	340
1937—	Joseph Medwick, St. Louis	406	1979—	David Winfield, San Diego	333
1938—	John Mize, St. Louis	326	1980—	Michael Schmidt, Philadelphia	342
1939—	John Mize, St. Louis	353	1981—	Michael Schmidt, Philadelphia	228
1940—	John Mize, St. Louis	368	1982—	Albert Oliver, Montreal	317
1941—	Harold (Pete) Reiser, Brooklyn	299	1983—	Andre Dawson, Montreal	341

RUNS BATTED IN LEADERS

Year	Player and Club	RBI	Year	Player and Club	RBI
1907—	John (Honus) Wagner, Pittsburgh	91	1917—	Henry Zimmerman, New York	100
1908—	John (Honus) Wagner, Pittsburgh	106	1918—	Frederick Merkle, Chicago	71
1909—	John (Honus) Wagner, Pittsburgh	102	1919—	Henry (Hi) Myers, Brooklyn	72
1910—	Sherwood Magee, Philadelphia	116	1920—	George Kelly, New York	94
1911—	Frank Schulte, Chicago	121		Rogers Hornsby, St. Louis	94
1912—	Henry Zimmerman, Chicago	98	1921—	Rogers Hornsby, St. Louis	126
1913—	Cliff (Gavvy) Cravath, Philadelphia	118	1922—	Rogers Hornsby, St. Louis	152
1914—	Sherwood Magee, Philadelphia	101	1923—	Emil Meusel, New York	125
1915—	Cliff (Gavvy) Cravath, Philadelphia	118	1924—	George Kelly, New York	136
1916—	Harold Chase, Cincinnati	84	1925—	Rogers Hornsby, St. Louis	143

Year	Player and Club	RBI	Year	Player and Club	RBI
1926—	James Bottomley, St. Louis	120	1956—	Stanley Musial, St. Louis	109
1927—	Paul Waner, Pittsburgh	131	1957—	Henry Aaron, Milwaukee	132
1928—	James Bottomley, St. Louis	136	1958—	Ernest Banks, Chicago	129
1929—	Lewis (Hack) Wilson, Chicago	159	1959—	Ernest Banks, Chicago	143
1930—	Lewis (Hack) Wilson, Chicago	190	1960—	Henry Aaron, Milwaukee	126
1931—	Charles Klein, Philadelphia	121	1961—	Orlando Cepeda, San Francisco	142
1932—	Frank (Don) Hurst, Philadelphia	143	1962—	H. Thomas Davis, Los Angeles	153
1933—	Charles Klein, Philadelphia	120	1963—	Henry Aaron, Milwaukee	130
1934—	Melvin Ott, New York	135	1964—	Kenton Boyer, St. Louis	119
1935—	Walter Berger, Boston	130	1965—	Deron Johnson, Cincinnati	130
1936—	Joseph Medwick, St. Louis	138	1966—	Henry Aaron, Atlanta	127
1937—	Joseph Medwick, St. Louis	154	1967—	Orlando Cepeda, St. Louis	111
1938—	Joseph Medwick, St. Louis	122	1968—	Willie McCovey, San Francisco	105
1939—	Frank McCormick, Cincinnati	128	1969—	Willie McCovey, San Francisco	126
1940—	John Mize, St. Louis	137	1970—	Johnny Bench, Cincinnati	148
1941—	Adolph Camilli, Brooklyn	120	1971—	Joseph Torre, St. Louis	137
1942—	John Mize, New York	110	1972—	Johnny Bench, Cincinnati	125
1943—	William Nicholson, Chicago	128	1973—	Wilver Stargell, Pittsburgh	119
1944—	William Nicholson, Chicago	122	1974—	Johnny Bench, Cincinnati	129
1945—	Fred (Dixie) Walker, Brooklyn	124	1975—	Gregory Luzinski, Philadelphia	120
1946—	Enos Slaughter, St. Louis	130	1976—	George Foster, Cincinnati	121
1947—	John Mize, New York	138	1977—	George Foster, Cincinnati	149
1948—	Stanley Musial, St. Louis	131	1978—	George Foster, Cincinnati	120
1949—	Ralph Kiner, Pittsburgh	127	1979—	David Winfield, San Diego	118
1950—	Delmer Ennis, Philadelphia	126	1980—	Michael Schmidt, Philadelphia	121
1951—	Monford Irvin, New York	121	1981—	Michael Schmidt, Philadelphia	91
1952—	Henry Sauer, Chicago	121	1982—	Dale Murphy, Atlanta	109
1953—	Roy Campanella, Brooklyn	142		Albert Oliver, Montreal	109
1954—	Theodore Kluszewski, Cincinnati	141	1983—	Dale Murphy, Atlanta	121
1955—	Edwin (Duke) Snider, Brooklyn	136			

BATTERS LEADING IN BASES ON BALLS

Year	Player and Club	BB.	Year	Player and Club	BB.
1910—	Miller Huggins, St. Louis	116	1948—	Robert Elliott, Boston	131
1911—	James Sheckard, Chicago	147	1949—	Ralph Kiner, Pittsburgh	117
1912—	James Sheckard, Chicago	122	1950—	Edward Stanky, New York	144
1913—	Robert Bescher, Cincinnati	94	1951—	Ralph Kiner, Pittsburgh	137
1914—	Miller Huggins, St. Louis	105	1952—	Ralph Kiner, Pittsburgh	110
1915—	Cliff. (Gavvy) Cravath, Philadelphia	86	1953—	Stanley Musial, St. Louis	105
1916—	Henry Groh, Cincinnati	84	1954—	Richie Ashburn, Philadelphia	125
1917—	George Burns, New York	75	1955—	Edwin Mathews, Milwaukee	109
1918—	Max Carey, Pittsburgh	62	1956—	Edwin (Duke) Snider, Brooklyn	99
1919—	George Burns, New York	82	1957—	Richie Ashburn, Philadelphia	94
1920—	George Burns, New York	76		John Temple, Cincinnati	94
1921—	George Burns, New York	80	1958—	Richie Ashburn, Philadelphia	97
1922—	Max Carey, Pittsburgh	80	1959—	James Gilliam, Los Angeles	96
1923—	George Burns, New York	101	1960—	Richie Ashburn, Chicago	116
1924—	Rogers Hornsby, St. Louis	89	1961—	Edwin Mathews, Milwaukee	93
1925—	Jacques Fournier, Brooklyn	86	1962—	Edwin Mathews, Milwaukee	101
1926—	Lewis (Hack) Wilson, Chicago	69	1963—	Edwin Mathews, Milwaukee	124
1927—	Rogers Hornsby, New York	86	1964—	Ronald Santo, Chicago	86
1928—	Rogers Hornsby, Boston	107	1965—	Joe Morgan, Houston	97
1929—	Melvin Ott, New York	113	1966—	Ronald Santo, Chicago	95
1930—	Lewis (Hack) Wilson, Chicago	105	1967—	Ronald Santo, Chicago	96
1931—	Melvin Ott, New York	80	1968—	Ronald Santo, Chicago	96
1932—	Melvin Ott, New York	100	1969—	James Wynn, Houston	148
1933—	Melvin Ott, New York	75	1970—	Willie McCovey, San Francisco	137
1934—	J. Floyd (Arky) Vaughan, Pittsburgh.	94	1971—	Willie Mays, San Francisco	112
1935—	J. Floyd (Arky) Vaughan, Pittsburgh.	97	1972—	Joe Morgan, Cincinnati	115
1936—	J. Floyd (Arky) Vaughan, Pittsburgh.	118	1973—	Darrell Evans, Atlanta	124
1937—	Melvin Ott, New York	102	1974—	Darrell Evans, Atlanta	126
1938—	Adolph Camilli, Brooklyn	119	1975—	Joe Morgan, Cincinnati	132
1939—	Adolph Camilli, Brooklyn	110	1976—	James Wynn, Atlanta	127
1940—	Elburt Fletcher, Pittsburgh	119	1977—	F. Gene Tenace, San Diego	125
1941—	Elburt Fletcher, Pittsburgh	118	1978—	Jeffrey Burroughs, Atlanta	117
1942—	Melvin Ott, New York	109	1979—	Michael Schmidt, Philadelphia	120
1943—	August Galan, Brooklyn	103	1980—	Daniel Driessen, Cincinnati	93
1944—	August Galan, Brooklyn	101		Joe Morgan, Houston	93
1945—	Edward Stanky, Brooklyn	148	1981—	Michael Schmidt, Philadelphia	73
1946—	Edward Stanky, Brooklyn	137	1982—	Michael Schmidt, Philadelphia	107
1947—	Henry Greenberg, Pittsburgh	104	1983—	Michael Schmidt, Philadelphia	128
	Harold (Pee Wee) Reese, Brooklyn...	104			

Note—Bases on balls not included in batting records in National League prior to 1910.

BATTERS LEADING IN STRIKEOUTS

Year	Player and Club	SO.	Year	Player and Club	SO.
1910—	John Hummell, Brooklyn	81	1946—	Ralph Kiner, Pittsburgh	109
1911—	Robert Coulson, Brooklyn	78	1947—	William Nicholson, Chicago	83
	Robert Bescher, Cincinnati	78	1948—	Henry Sauer, Cincinnati	85
1912—	Edward McDonald, Boston	91	1949—	Edwin (Duke) Snider, Brooklyn	92
1913—	George Burns, New York	74	1950—	Roy Smalley, Chicago	114
1914—	Frederick Merkle, New York	80	1951—	Gilbert Hodges, Brooklyn	99
1915—	H. Douglas Baird, Pittsburgh	88	1952—	Edwin Mathews, Boston	115
1916—	Cliff. (Gavvy) Cravath, Philadelphia	89	1953—	Stephen Bilko, St. Louis	125
1917—	Fred Williams, Chicago	78	1954—	Edwin (Duke) Snider, Brooklyn	96
1918—	Ross Youngs, New York	49	1955—	Walter Post, Cincinnati	102
	George Paskert, Chicago	49	1956—	Walter Post, Cincinnati	124
1919—	Raymond Powell, Boston	79	1957—	Edwin (Duke) Snider, Brooklyn	104
1920—	George Kelly, New York	92	1958—	Harry Anderson, Philadelphia	95
1921—	Raymond Powell, Boston	85	1959—	Walter Post, Philadelphia	101
1922—	Frank Parkinson, Philadelphia	93	1960—	J. Francisco Herrera, Philadelphia	136
1923—	George Grantham, Chicago	92	1961—	Richard Stuart, Pittsburgh	121
1924—	George Grantham, Chicago	63	1962—	Kenneth Hubbs, Chicago	129
1925—	Chas. (Gabby) Hartnett, Chicago	77	1963—	Donn Clendenon, Pittsburgh	136
1926—	Bernard Friberg, Philadelphia	77	1964—	Richard Allen, Philadelphia	138
1927—	Lewis (Hack) Wilson, Chicago	70	1965—	Richard Allen, Philadelphia	150
1928—	Lewis (Hack) Wilson, Chicago	94	1966—	Byron Browne, Chicago	143
1929—	Lewis (Hack) Wilson, Chicago	83	1967—	James Wynn, Houston	137
1930—	Lewis (Hack) Wilson, Chicago	84	1968—	Donn Clendenon, Pittsburgh	163
1931—	H. Nicholas Cullop, Cincinnati	86	1969—	Bobby Bonds, San Francisco	187
1932—	Lewis (Hack) Wilson, Brooklyn	85	1970—	Bobby Bonds, San Francisco	189
1933—	Walter Berger, Boston	77	1971—	Wilver Stargell, Pittsburgh	154
1934—	Adolph Camilli, Chicago-Philadelphia	94	1972—	Lee May, Houston	145
1935—	Adolph Camilli, Philadelphia	113	1973—	Bobby Bonds, San Francisco	148
1936—	Wilbur Brubaker, Pittsburgh	96	1974—	Michael Schmidt, Philadelphia	138
1937—	Vincent DiMaggio, Boston	111	1975—	Michael Schmidt, Philadelphia	180
1938—	Vincent DiMaggio, Boston	134	1976—	Michael Schmidt, Philadelphia	149
1939—	Adolph Camilli, Brooklyn	107	1977—	Gregory Luzinski, Philadelphia	140
1940—	Chester Ross, Boston	128	1978—	Dale Murphy, Atlanta	145
1941—	Adolph Camilli, Brooklyn	115	1979—	David Kingman, Chicago	131
1942—	Vincent DiMaggio, Pittsburgh	87	1980—	Dale Murphy, Atlanta	133
1943—	Vincent DiMaggio, Pittsburgh	126	1981—	David Kingman, New York	105
1944—	Vincent DiMaggio, Pittsburgh	83	1982—	David Kingman, New York	156
1945—	Vincent DiMaggio, Philadelphia	91	1983—	Michael Schmidt, Philadelphia	148

Note—Strikeouts not included in batting records in National League prior to 1910.

LEADING BASE STEALERS

Year	Player and Club	SB.	Year	Player and Club	SB.
1900—	James Barrett, Cincinnati	46	1925—	Max Carey, Pittsburgh	46
1901—	John (Honus) Wagner, Pittsburgh	48	1926—	Hazen (Kiki) Cuyler, Pittsburgh	35
1902—	John (Honus) Wagner, Pittsburgh	43	1927—	Frank Frisch, St. Louis	48
1903—	Sheckard, Brooklyn-Chance, Chicago	67	1928—	Hazen (Kiki) Cuyler, Chicago	37
1904—	John (Honus) Wagner, Pittsburgh	53	1929—	Hazen (Kiki) Cuyler, Chicago	43
1905—	Maloney, Chicago-Devlin, New York	59	1930—	Hazen (Kiki) Cuyler, Chicago	37
1906—	Frank Chance, Chicago	57	1931—	Frank Frisch, St. Louis	28
1907—	John (Honus) Wagner, Pittsburgh	61	1932—	Charles Klein, Philadelphia	20
1908—	John (Honus) Wagner, Pittsburgh	53	1933—	John (Pepper) Martin, St. Louis	26
1909—	Robert Bescher, Cincinnati	54	1934—	John (Pepper) Martin, St. Louis	23
1910—	Robert Bescher, Cincinnati	70	1935—	August Galan, Chicago	22
1911—	Robert Bescher, Cincinnati	81	1936—	John (Pepper) Martin, St. Louis	23
1912—	Robert Bescher, Cincinnati	67	1937—	August Galan, Chicago	23
1913—	Max Carey, Pittsburgh	61	1938—	Stanley Hack, Chicago	16
1914—	George Burns, New York	62	1939—	Hack, Chicago-Handley, Pittsburgh	17
1915—	Max Carey, Pittsburgh	36	1940—	Linus Frey, Cincinnati	22
1916—	Max Carey, Pittsburgh	63	1941—	Daniel Murtaugh, Philadelphia	18
1917—	Max Carey, Pittsburgh	46	1942—	Harold (Pete) Reiser, Brooklyn	20
1918—	Max Carey, Pittsburgh	58	1943—	J. Floyd (Arky) Vaughan, Brooklyn	20
1919—	George Burns, New York	40	1944—	John Barrett, Pittsburgh	28
1920—	Max Carey, Pittsburgh	52	1945—	Al. (Red) Schoendienst, St. Louis	26
1921—	Frank Frisch, New York	49	1946—	Harold (Pete) Reiser, Brooklyn	34
1922—	Max Carey, Pittsburgh	51	1947—	Jack Robinson, Brooklyn	29
1923—	Max Carey, Pittsburgh	51	1948—	Richie Ashburn, Philadelphia	32
1924—	Max Carey, Pittsburgh	49	1949—	Jack Robinson, Brooklyn	37

Year	Player and Club	SB.	Year	Player and Club	SB.
1950	Samuel Jethroe, Boston	35	1967	Louis Brock, St. Louis	52
1951	Samuel Jethroe, Boston	35	1968	Louis Brock, St. Louis	62
1952	Harold (Pee Wee) Reese, Brooklyn	30	1969	Louis Brock, St. Louis	53
1953	William Bruton, Milwaukee	26	1970	Robert Tolan, Cincinnati	57
1954	William Bruton, Milwaukee	34	1971	Louis Brock, St. Louis	64
1955	William Bruton, Milwaukee	35	1972	Louis Brock, St. Louis	63
1956	Willie Mays, New York	40	1973	Louis Brock, St. Louis	70
1957	Willie Mays, New York	38	1974	Louis Brock, St. Louis	118
1958	Willie Mays, San Francisco	31	1975	David Lopes, Los Angeles	77
1959	Willie Mays, San Francisco	27	1976	David Lopes, Los Angeles	63
1960	Maurice Wills, Los Angeles	50	1977	Franklin Taveras, Pittsburgh	70
1961	Maurice Wills, Los Angeles	35	1978	Omar Moreno, Pittsburgh	71
1962	Maurice Wills, Los Angeles	104	1979	Omar Moreno, Pittsburgh	77
1963	Maurice Wills, Los Angeles	40	1980	Ronald LeFlore, Montreal	97
1964	Maurice Wills, Los Angeles	53	1981	Timothy Raines, Montreal	71
1965	Maurice Wills, Los Angeles	94	1982	Timothy Raines, Montreal	78
1966	Louis Brock, St. Louis	74	1983	Timothy Raines, Montreal	90

SLUGGING LEADERS

Year	Player and Club	Slug. Avg.	Year	Player and Club	Slug. Avg.
1900	John (Honus) Wagner, Pittsburgh	.572	1942	John Mize, New York	.521
1901	James Sheckard, Brooklyn	.541	1943	Stanley Musial, St. Louis	.562
1902	John (Honus) Wagner, Pittsburgh	.467	1944	Stanley Musial, St. Louis	.549
1903	Fred Clarke, Pittsburgh	.532	1945	Tommy Holmes, Boston	.577
1904	John (Honus) Wagner, Pittsburgh	.520	1946	Stanley Musial, St. Louis	.587
1905	J. Bentley Seymour, Cincinnati	.559	1947	Ralph Kiner, Pittsburgh	.639
1906	Harry Lumley, Brooklyn	477	1948	Stanley Musial, St. Louis	.702
1907	John (Honus) Wagner, Pittsburgh	.513	1949	Ralph Kiner, Pittsburgh	.658
1908	John (Honus) Wagner, Pittsburgh	.542	1950	Stanley Musial, St. Louis	.596
1909	John (Honus) Wagner, Pittsburgh	.489	1951	Ralph Kiner, Pittsburgh	.627
1910	Sherwood Magee, Philadelphia	.507	1952	Stanley Musial, St. Louis	.538
1911	Frank Schulte, Chicago	.534	1953	Edwin (Duke) Snider, Brooklyn	.6271
1912	Henry Zimmerman, Chicago	.571	1954	Willie Mays, New York	.667
1913	Cliff. (Gavvy) Cravath, Philadelphia	.568	1955	Willie Mays, New York	.659
1914	Sherwood Magee, Philadelphia	.509	1956	Edwin (Duke) Snider, Brooklyn	.598
1915	Cliff. (Gavvy) Cravath, Philadelphia	.510	1957	Willie Mays, New York	.626
1916	Zachariah Wheat, Brooklyn	.461	1958	Ernest Banks, Chicago	.614
1917	Rogers Hornsby, St. Louis	.484	1959	Henry Aaron, Milwaukee	.636
1918	Edd Roush, Cincinnati	.455	1960	Frank Robinson, Cincinnati	.595
1919	Henry (Hi) Myers, Brooklyn	.436	1961	Frank Robinson, Cincinnati	.611
1920	Rogers Hornsby, St. Louis	.559	1962	Frank Robinson, Cincinnati	.624
1921	Rogers Hornsby, St. Louis	.659	1963	Henry Aaron, Milwaukee	.586
1922	Rogers Hornsby, St. Louis	.722	1964	Willie Mays, San Francisco	.607
1923	Rogers Hornsby, St. Louis	.627	1965	Willie Mays, San Francisco	.645
1924	Rogers Hornsby, St. Louis	.696	1966	Richard Allen, Philadelphia	.632
1925	Rogers Hornsby, St. Louis	.756	1967	Henry Aaron, Atlanta	.573
1926	Fred Williams, Philadelphia	.569	1968	Willie McCovey, San Francisco	.545
1927	Charles Hafey, St. Louis	.590	1969	Willie McCovey, San Francisco	.656
1928	Rogers Hornsby, Boston	.632	1970	Willie McCovey, San Francisco	.612
1929	Rogers Hornsby, Chicago	.679	1971	Henry Aaron, Atlanta	.669
1930	Lewis (Hack) Wilson, Chicago	.723	1972	Billy Williams, Chicago	.606
1931	Charles Klein, Philadelphia	.584	1973	Wilver Stargell, Pittsburgh	.646
1932	Charles Klein, Philadelphia	.646	1974	Michael Schmidt, Philadelphia	.546
1933	Charles Klein, Philadelphia	.602	1975	David Parker, Pittsburgh	.541
1934	James (Rip) Collins, St. Louis	.615	1976	Joe Morgan, Cincinnati	.576
1935	J. Floyd (Arky) Vaughan, Pittsburgh.	.607	1977	George Foster, Cincinnati	.631
1936	Melvin Ott, New York	.588	1978	David Parker, Pittsburgh	.585
1937	Joseph Medwick, St. Louis	.641	1979	David Kingman, Chicago	.613
1938	John Mize, St. Louis	.614	1980	Michael Schmidt, Philadelphia	.624
1939	John Mize, St. Louis	.626	1981	Michael Schmidt, Philadelphia	.644
1940	John Mize, St. Louis	.636	1982	Michael Schmidt, Philadelphia	.547
1941	Harold (Pete) Reiser, Brooklyn	.558	1983	Dale Murphy, Atlanta	.540

LEADING PITCHERS IN WINNING PERCENTAGE
(15 OR MORE VICTORIES)

Year	Pitcher	Club	Won	Lost	Pct.
1900—	Joseph McGinnity	Brooklyn	29	9	.763
1901—	John Chesbro	Pittsburgh	21	9	.700
1902—	John Chesbro	Pittsburgh	28	6	.824
1903—	Samuel Leever	Pittsburgh	25	7	.781
1904—	Joseph McGinnity	New York	35	8	.814
1905—	Samuel Leever	Pittsburgh	20	5	.800
1906—	Edward Reulbach	Chicago	19	4	.826
1907—	Edward Reulbach	Chicago	17	4	.810
1908—	Edward Reulbach	Chicago	24	7	.774
1909—	Christy Mathewson	New York	25	6	.806
	Howard Camnitz	Pittsburgh	25	6	.806
1910—	Leonard Cole	Chicago	20	4	.833
1911—	Richard (Rube) Marquard	New York	24	7	.774
1912—	Claude Hendrix	Pittsburgh	24	9	.727
1913—	Albert Humphries	Chicago	16	4	.800
1914—	Williams James	Boston	26	7	.788
1915—	Grover Alexander	Philadelphia	31	10	.756
1916—	Thomas Hughes	Boston	16	3	.842
1917—	Ferdinand Schupp	New York	21	7	.750
1918—	Claude Hendrix	Chicago	20	7	.741
1919—	Walter Ruether	Cincinnati	19	6	.760
1920—	Burleigh Grimes	Brooklyn	23	11	.676
1921—	William L. Doak	St. Louis	15	6	.714
1922—	Peter Donohue	Cincinnati	18	9	.667
1923—	Adolfo Luque	Cincinnati	27	8	.771
1924—	Emil Yde	Pittsburgh	16	3	.842
1925—	William Sherdel	St. Louis	15	6	.714
1926—	Ray Kremer	Pittsburgh	20	6	.769
1927—	Lawrence Benton	Boston-New York	17	7	.708
1928—	Lawrence Benton	New York	25	9	.735
1929—	Charles Root	Chicago	19	6	.760
1930—	Fred Fitzsimmons	New York	19	7	.731
1931—	Paul Derringer	St. Louis	18	8	.692
1932—	Lonnie Warneke	Chicago	22	6	.786
1933—	Benjamin Cantwell	Boston	20	10	.667
1934—	Jerome (Dizzy) Dean	St. Louis	30	7	.811
1935—	William Lee	Chicago	20	6	.769
1936—	Carl Hubbell	New York	26	6	.813
1937—	Carl Hubbell	New York	22	8	.733
1938—	William Lee	Chicago	22	9	.710
1939—	Paul Derringer	Cincinnati	25	7	.781
1940—	Fred Fitzsimmons	Brooklyn	16	2	.889
1941—	Elmer Riddle	Cincinnati	19	4	.826
1942—	Lawrence French	Brooklyn	15	4	.789
1943—	Morton Cooper	St. Louis	21	8	.724
1944—	Theodore Wilks	St. Louis	17	4	.810
1945—	Harry Breecheen	St. Louis	15	4	.789
1946—	Murry Dickson	St. Louis	15	6	.714
1947—	Lawrence Jansen	New York	21	5	.808
1948—	Harry Brecheen	St. Louis	20	7	.741
1949—	Elwin (Preacher) Roe	Brooklyn	15	6	.714
1950—	Salvatore Maglie	New York	18	4	.818
1951—	Elwin (Preacher) Roe	Brooklyn	22	3	.880
1952—	J. Hoyt Wilhelm	New York	15	3	.833
1953—	Carl Erskine	Brooklyn	20	6	.769
1954—	John Antonelli	New York	21	7	.750
1955—	Donald Newcombe	Brooklyn	20	5	.800
1956—	Donald Newcombe	Brooklyn	27	7	.794
1957—	Robert Buhl	Milwaukee	18	7	.720
1958—	Warren E. Spahn	Milwaukee	22	11	.667
	S. Lewis Burdette	Milwaukee	20	10	.667
1959—	ElRoy Face	Pittsburgh	18	1	.947
1960—	Ernest Broglio	St. Louis	21	9	.700
1961—	John Podres	Los Angeles	18	5	.783
1962—	Robert Purkey	Cincinnati	23	5	.821
1963—	Ronald Perranoski	Los Angeles	16	3	.842
1964—	Sanford Koufax	Los Angeles	19	5	.792
1965—	Sanford Koufax	Los Angeles	26	8	.765

Year	Pitcher	Club	Won	Lost	Pct.
1966—Juan Marichal	San Francisco		25	6	.806
1967—Richard Hughes	St. Louis		16	6	.727
1968—Stephen R. Blass	Pittsburgh		18	6	.750
1969—G. Thomas Seaver	New York		25	7	.781
1970—Robert Gibson	St. Louis		23	7	.767
1971—Donald E. Gullett	Cincinnati		16	6	.727
1972—Gary L. Nolan	Cincinnati		15	5	.750
1973—Thomas E. John	Los Angeles		16	7	.696
1974—John (Andy) Messersmith	Los Angeles		20	6	.769
1975—Donald E. Gullett	Cincinnati		15	4	.789
1976—Steven N. Carlton	Philadelphia		20	7	.741
1977—John R. Candelaria	Pittsburgh		20	5	.800
1978—Gaylord J. Perry	San Diego		21	6	.778
1979—G. Thomas Seaver	Cincinnati		16	6	.727
1980—James Bibby	Pittsburgh		19	6	.760
1981—G. Thomas Seaver	Cincinnati		14	2	.875
1982—Philip Niekro	Atlanta		17	4	.810
1983—John Denny	Philadelphia		19	6	.760

Note—1981 percentages based on 10 or more victories.

LEADING PITCHERS—EARNED-RUN AVERAGE

(Based on Ten Complete Games Through 1950, Then 154 Innings Until N. L. Expanded in 1962, When It Became 162 Innings)

Year	Pitcher and Club	G.	IP.	ERA.	Year	Pitcher and Club	G.	IP.	ERA.
1912—Tesreau, New York	36	243	1.96	1948—Brecheen, St. Louis	33	233	2.24
1913—Mathewson, New York	40	306	2.06	1949—Koslo, New York	38	212	2.50
1914—Doak, St. Louis	36	256	1.72	1950—Hearn, St.L.-N.Y.	22	134	2.49
1915—Alexander, Philadelphia	49	376	1.22	1951—Nichols, Boston	33	156	2.88
1916—Alexander, Philadelphia	48	390	1.55	1952—Wilhelm, New York	71	159	2.43
1917—Alexander, Philadelphia	45	388	1.83	1953—Spahn, Milwaukee	35	266	2.10
1918—Vaughn, Chicago	35	290	1.74	1954—Antonelli, New York	39	259	2.29
1919—Alexander, Chicago	30	235	1.72	1955—Friend, Pittsburgh	44	200	2.84
1920—Alexander, Chicago	46	363	1.91	1956—Burdette, Milwaukee	39	256	2.71
1921—Doak, St. Louis	32	209	2.58	1957—Podres, Brooklyn	31	196	2.66
1922—Ryan, New York	46	192	3.00	1958—Miller, San Francisco	41	182	2.47
1923—Luque, Cincinnati	41	322	1.93	1959—S. Jones, San Francisco	50	271	2.82
1924—Vance, Brooklyn	35	309	2.16	1960—McCormick, San Fran.	40	253	2.70
1925—Luque, Cincinnati	36	291	2.63	1961—Spahn, Milwaukee	38	263	3.01
1926—Kremer, Pittsburgh	37	231	2.61	1962—Koufax, Los Angeles	28	184	2.54
1927—Kremer, Pittsburgh	35	226	2.47	1963—Koufax, Los Angeles	40	311	1.88
1928—Vance, Brooklyn	38	280	2.09	1964—Koufax, Los Angeles	29	223	1.74
1929—Walker, New York	29	178	3.08	1965—Koufax, Los Angeles	43	336	2.04
1930—Vance, Brooklyn	35	259	2.61	1966—Koufax, Los Angeles	41	323	1.73
1931—Walker, New York	37	239	2.26	1967—P. Niekro, Atlanta	46	207	1.87
1932—Warneke, Chicago	35	277	2.37	1968—Gibson, St. Louis	34	305	1.12
1933—Hubbell, New York	45	309	1.66	1969—Marichal, San Francisco	37	300	2.10
1934—Hubbell, New York	49	313	2.30	1970—Seaver, New York	37	291	2.81
1935—Blanton, Pittsburgh	35	254	2.59	1971—Seaver, New York	36	286	1.76
1936—Hubbell, New York	42	304	2.31	1972—Carlton, Philadelphia	41	346	1.98
1937—Turner, Boston	33	257	2.38	1973—Seaver, New York	36	290	2.08
1938—W. Lee, Chicago	44	291	2.66	1974—Capra, Atlanta	39	217	2.28
1939—Walters, Cincinnati	39	319	2.29	1975—Jones, San Diego	37	285	2.24
1940—Walters, Cincinnati	36	305	2.48	1976—Denny, St. Louis	30	207	2.52
1941—E. Riddle, Cincinnati	33	217	2.24	1977—Candelaria, Pittsburgh	33	231	2.34
1942—M. Cooper, St. Louis	37	279	1.77	1978—Swan, New York	29	207	2.43
1943—Pollet, St. Louis	16	118	1.75	1979—Richard, Houston	38	292	2.71
1944—Heusser, Cincinnati	30	193	2.38	1980—Sutton, Los Angeles	32	212	2.21
1945—Borowy, Chicago	15	122	2.14	1981—Ryan, Houston	21	149	1.69
1946—Pollet, St. Louis	40	266	2.10	1982—Rogers, Montreal	35	277	2.40
1947—Spahn, Boston	40	290	2.33	1983—Hammaker, San Fran.	23	172.1	2.25

Note—Earned-run records not tabulated in National League prior to 1912.
Note—1981 earned-run champion determined by taking leader who pitched as many innings as his team's total number of games played.

STRIKEOUT LEADERS—PITCHING

Year	Player and Club	SO.
1900—	George (Rube) Waddell, Pittsburgh...	133
1901—	Frank (Noodles) Hahn, Cincinnati	233
1902—	Victor Willis, Boston	226
1903—	Christopher Mathewson, New York	267
1904—	Christopher Mathewson, New York	212
1905—	Christopher Mathewson, New York	206
1906—	Frederick Beebe, Chicago-St. Louis	171
1907—	Christopher Mathewson, New York	178
1908—	Christopher Mathewson, New York	259
1909—	Orval Overall, Chicago	205
1910—	Christopher Mathewson, New York	190
1911—	Richard (Rube) Marquard, N.Y.	237
1912—	Grover Alexander, Philadelphia	195
1913—	Thomas Seaton, Philadelphia	168
1914—	Grover Alexander, Philadelphia	214
1915—	Grover Alexander, Philadelphia	241
1916—	Grover Alexander, Philadelphia	167
1917—	Grover Alexander, Philadelphia	200
1918—	James (Hippo) Vaughn, Chicago	148
1919—	James (Hippo) Vaughn, Chicago	141
1920—	Grover Alexander, Chicago	173
1921—	Burleigh Grimes, Brooklyn	136
1922—	Arthur (Dazzy) Vance, Brooklyn	134
1923—	Arthur (Dazzy) Vance, Brooklyn	197
1924—	Arthur (Dazzy) Vance, Brooklyn	262
1925—	Arthur (Dazzy) Vance, Brooklyn	221
1926—	Arthur (Dazzy) Vance, Brooklyn	140
1927—	Arthur (Dazzy) Vance, Brooklyn	184
1928—	Arthur (Dazzy) Vance, Brooklyn	200
1929—	Perce (Pat) Malone, Chicago	166
1930—	William Hallahan, St. Louis	177
1931—	William Hallahan, St. Louis	159
1932—	Jerome (Dizzy) Dean, St. Louis	191
1933—	Jerome (Dizzy) Dean, St. Louis	199
1934—	Jerome (Dizzy) Dean, St. Louis	195
1935—	Jerome (Dizzy) Dean, St. Louis	182
1936—	Van Lingle Mungo, Brooklyn	238
1937—	Carl Hubbell, New York	159
1938—	Claiborne Bryant, Chicago	135
1939—	Claude Passeau, Phila.-Chi.	137
	William (Bucky) Walters, Cincinnati	137
1940—	W. Kirby Higbe, Philadelphia	137
1941—	John Vander Meer, Cincinnati	202
1942—	John Vander Meer, Cincinnati	186
1943—	John Vander Meer, Cincinnati	174
1944—	William Voiselle, New York	161
1945—	Elwin (Preacher) Roe, Pittsburgh	148
1946—	John Schmitz, Chicago	135
1947—	Ewell Blackwell, Cincinnati	193
1948—	Harry Brecheen, St. Louis	149
1949—	Warren Spahn, Boston	151
1950—	Warren Spahn, Boston	191
1951—	Warren Spahn, Boston	164
	Donald Newcombe, Brooklyn	164
1952—	Warren Spahn, Boston	183
1953—	Robin Roberts, Philadelphia	198
1954—	Robin Roberts, Philadelphia	185
1955—	Samuel Jones, Chicago	198
1956—	Samuel Jones, Chicago	176
1957—	John Sanford, Philadelphia	188
1958—	Samuel Jones, St. Louis	225
1959—	Donald Drysdale, Los Angeles	242
1960—	Donald Drysdale, Los Angeles	246
1961—	Sanford Koufax, Los Angeles	269
1962—	Donald Drysdale, Los Angeles	232
1963—	Sanford Koufax, Los Angeles	306
1964—	Robert Veale, Pittsburgh	250
1965—	Sanford Koufax, Los Angeles	382
1966—	Sanford Koufax, Los Angeles	317
1967—	James Bunning, Philadelphia	253
1968—	Robert Gibson, St. Louis	268
1969—	Ferguson Jenkins, Chicago	273
1970—	G. Thomas Seaver, New York	283
1971—	G. Thomas Seaver, New York	289
1972—	Steven Carlton, Philadelphia	310
1973—	G. Thomas Seaver, New York	251
1974—	Steven Carlton, Philadelphia	240
1975—	G. Thomas Seaver, New York	243
1976—	G. Thomas Seaver, New York	235
1977—	Philip Niekro, Atlanta	262
1978—	James R. Richard, Houston	303
1979—	James R. Richard, Houston	313
1980—	Steven Carlton, Philadelphia	286
1981—	Fernando Valenzuela, Los Angeles	180
1982—	Steven Carlton, Philadelphia	286
1983—	Steven Carlton, Philadelphia	275

SHUTOUT LEADERS

Year	Player and Club	ShO.
1900—	Clark C. Griffith, Chicago	4
	Frank G. Hahn, Cincinnati	4
	Charles A. Nichols, Boston	4
	Denton T. Young, St. Louis	4
1901—	John D. Chesbro, Pittsburgh	6
	Albert L. Orth, Philadelphia	6
	Victor G. Willis, Boston	6
1902—	John D. Chesbro, Pittsburgh	8
	Christopher Mathewson, New York	8
1903—	Samuel W. Leever, Pittsburgh	7
1904—	Joseph J. McGinnity, New York	9
1905—	Christopher Mathewson, New York	9
1906—	Mordecai P. Brown, Chicago	9
1907—	Orval Overall, Chicago	9
	Christopher Mathewson, New York	9
1908—	Christopher Mathewson, New York	12
1909—	Orval Overall, Chicago	9
1910—	Earl L. Moore, Philadelphia	7
1911—	Charles B. Adams, Pittsburgh	7
	Grover C. Alexander, Philadelphia	7
1912—	George N. Rucker, Brooklyn	6
1913—	Grover C. Alexander, Philadelphia	9
1914—	Charles M. Tesreau, New York	8
1915—	Grover C. Alexander, Philadelphia	12
1916—	Grover C. Alexander, Philadelphia	16
1917—	Grover C. Alexander, Philadelphia	8
1918—	George A. Tyler, Chicago	8
	James L. Vaughn, Chicago	8
1919—	Grover C. Alexander, Chicago	9
1920—	Charles B. Adams, Pittsburgh	8
1921—	Grover C. Alexander, Chicago	3
	Philip B. Douglas, New York	3
	Dana Filligim, Boston	3
	Adolph Luque, Cincinnati	3
	Clarence E. Mitchell, Brooklyn	3
	John D. Morrison, Pittsburgh	3
	Joseph C. Oeschger, Boston	3
	Jesse J. Haines, St. Louis	3
1922—	Arthur C. Vance, Brooklyn	6
1923—	Adolfo Luque, Cincinnati	6
1924—	Jesse L. Barnes, Boston	4
	A. Wilbur Cooper, Pittsburgh	4
	Remy P. Kremer, Pittsburgh	4
	Eppa Rixey, Cincinnati	4

Year	Player and Club	ShO.
	Allen S. Sothoron, St. Louis	4
	Emil O. Yde, Pittsburgh	4
1925	Harold G. Carlson, Philadelphia	4
	Adolfo Luque, Cincinnati	4
	Arthur C. Vance, Brooklyn	4
1926	Peter J. Donohue, Cincinnati	5
1927	Jesse J. Haines, St. Louis	6
1928	John F. Blake, Chicago	4
	Burleigh A. Grimes, Pittsburgh	4
	Charles F. Lucas, Cincinnati	4
	Douglas L. McWeeney, Brooklyn	4
	Arthur C. Vance, Brooklyn	4
1929	Perce L. Malone, Chicago	5
1930	Charles H. Root, Chicago	4
	Arthur C. Vance, Brooklyn	4
1931	William H. Walker, New York	6
1932	Lonnie Warneke, Chicago	4
	Jerome H. Dean, St. Louis	4
	Stephen A. Swetonic, Pittsburgh	4
1933	Carl O. Hubbell, New York	10
1934	Jerome H. Dean, St. Louis	7
1935	Darrell E. Blanton, Pittsburgh	4
	Freddie L. Fitzsimmons, New York	4
	Lawrence H. French, Chicago	4
	Van L. Mungo, Brooklyn	4
	James D. Weaver, Pittsburgh	4
1936	Darrell E. Blanton, Pittsburgh	4
	James O. Carleton, Chicago	4
	Lawrence H. French, Chicago	4
	William C. Lee, Chicago	4
	Alfred J. Smith, New York	4
	Williams H. Walters, Philadelphia	4
	Lonnie Warneke, Chicago	4
1937	Louis H. Fette, Boston	5
	Lee T. Grissom, Cincinnati	5
	James R. Turner, Boston	5
1938	William C. Lee, Chicago	9
1939	Louis H. Fette, Boston	6
1940	William L. Lohrman, New York	5
	Manuel L. Salvo, Boston	5
	J. Whitlow Wyatt, Brooklyn	5
1941	J. Whitlow Wyatt, Brooklyn	7
1942	Morton C. Cooper, St. Louis	10
1943	Hiram G. Bithorn, Chicago	7
1944	Morton C. Cooper, St. Louis	7
1945	Claude W. Passeau, Chicago	5
1946	Ewell Blackwell, Cincinnati	6
1947	Warren E. Spahn, Boston	7
1948	Harry D. Brecheen, St. Louis	7
1949	Kenneth A. Heintzelman, Phila.	5
	Donald Newcombe, Brooklyn	5
	Howard J. Pollet, St. Louis	5
	Kenneth D. Raffensberger, Cin.	5
1950	James T. Hearn, New York	5
	Lawrence J. Jansen, New York	5
	Salvatore A. Maglie, New York	5
	Robin E. Roberts, Philadelphia	5
1951	Warren E. Spahn, Boston	7
1952	Salvatore A. Maglie, New York	7
	Ken D. Raffensberger, Cincinnati	7
	Curtis T. Simmons, Philadelphia	7
1953	Harvey Haddix, St. Louis	6
1954	John A. Antonelli, New York	6
1955	Joseph H. Nuxhall, Cincinnati	5
1956	John A. Antonelli, New York	6
	S. Lewis Burdette, Milwaukee	6
1957	John L. Podres, Brooklyn	6
1958	Carlton F. Willey, Milwaukee	4
1959	John A. Antonelli, San Francisco	4
	Robert R. Buhl, Milwaukee	4
	S. Lewis Burdette, Milwaukee	4
	Roger L. Craig, Los Angeles	4
	Donald S. Drysdale, Los Angeles	4
	Sam Jones, San Francisco	4
	Warren E. Spahn, Milwaukee	4
1960	John S. Sanford, San Francisco	6
1961	Joseph R. Jay, Cincinnati	4
	Warren E. Spahn, Milwaukee	4
1962	Robert B. Friend, Pittsburgh	5
	Robert Gibson, St. Louis	5
1963	Sanford Koufax, Los Angeles	11
1964	Sanford Koufax, Los Angeles	7
1965	Juan A. Marichal, San Francisco	10
1966	James P. Bunning, Philadelphia	5
	Robert Gibson, St. Louis	5
	Lawrence C. Jackson, Philadelphia	5
	Larry E. Jaster, St. Louis	5
	Sanford Koufax, Los Angeles	5
	James W. Maloney, Cincinnati	5
1967	James P. Bunning, Philadelphia	6
1968	Robert Gibson, St. Louis	13
1969	Juan A. Marichal, San Francisco	8
1970	Gaylord J. Perry, San Francisco	5
1971	Stephen R. Blass, Pittsburgh	5
	Alphonso E. Downing, Los Angeles	5
	Robert Gibson, St. Louis	5
	Milton S. Pappas, Chicago	5
1972	Donald H. Sutton, Los Angeles	9
1973	John E. Billingham, Cincinnati	7
1974	Jonathan T. Matlack, New York	7
1975	John A. Messersmith, Los Angeles	7
1976	Jonathan T. Matlack, New York	6
	John J. Montefusco, San Francisco	6
1977	G. Thomas Seaver, N.Y.-Cin.	7
1978	Robert W. Knepper, San Francisco	6
1979	G. Thomas Seaver, Cincinnati	5
	Joseph F. Niekro, Houston	5
	Stephen D. Rogers, Montreal	5
1980	Jerry Reuss, Los Angeles	6
1981	Fernando Valenzuela, Los Angeles	8
1982	Steven N. Carlton, Philadelphia	6
1983	Stephen D. Rogers, Montreal	5

PRE-1900 PENNANT WINNERS

Year	Club	Manager	W.	L.	Pct.	Year	Club	Manager	W.	L.	Pct.
1876—Chicago		Albert Spalding	52	14	.788	1888—New York		James Mutrie	84	47	.641
1877—Boston		Harry Wright	31	17	.646	1889—New York		James Mutrie	83	43	.659
1878—Boston		Harry Wright	41	19	.683	1890—Brooklyn		Wm. McGunnigle	86	43	.667
1879—Providence		George Wright	55	23	.705	1891—Boston		Frank Selee	87	51	.630
1880—Chicago		Adrian Anson	67	17	.798	1892—Boston		Frank Selee	102	48	.680
1881—Chicago		Adrian Anson	56	28	.667	1893—Boston		Frank Selee	86	44	.662
1882—Chicago		Adrian Anson	55	29	.655	1894—Baltimore		Edward Hanlon	89	39	.695
1883—Boston		John Morrill	63	35	.643	1895—Baltimore		Edward Hanlon	87	43	.669
1884—Providence		Frank Bancroft	84	28	.750	1896—Baltimore		Edward Hanlon	90	39	.698
1885—Chicago		Adrian Anson	87	25	.777	1897—Boston		Frank Selee	93	39	.705
1886—Chicago		Adrian Anson	90	34	.726	1898—Boston		Frank Selee	102	47	.685
1887—Detroit		Wm. Watkins	79	45	.637	1899—Brooklyn		Edward Hanlon	88	42	.677

PRE-1900 YEARLY FINISHES

Year	Bos.	Bkn.	Chi.	Cin.	N.Y.	Phil.	Pitt.	St.L.	Balt.	Buf.	Clev.
1876	4	....	1	8	6	7	....	3	....	....	....
1877	1	....	5	6	....	....	....	4	....	....	....
1878	1	....	4	2	....	....	....	....	....	....	....
1879	2	....	*3	5	....	....	....	....	....	*3	6
1880	6	....	1	8	....	....	....	....	....	7	3
1881	6	....	1	....	....	....	....	....	....	3	7
1882	*3	....	1	....	....	....	....	....	....	*3	5
1883	1	....	2	....	6	8	....	....	....	5	4
1884	2	....	*4	....	*4	6	....	....	....	3	7
1885	5	....	1	....	2	3	....	8	....	7	....
1886	5	....	1	....	3	4	....	6	....	....	....
1887	5	....	3	....	4	2	6	....	....	....	....
1888	4	....	2	....	1	3	6	....	....	....	....
1889	2	....	3	....	1	4	5	....	....	....	6
1890	5	1	2	4	6	3	8	....	....	....	7
1891	1	6	2	7	3	4	8	....	....	....	5
1892	1	3	7	5	8	4	6	11	12	....	2
1893	1	*6	9	*6	5	4	2	10	8	....	3
1894	3	5	8	10	2	4	7	9	1	....	6
1895	*5	*5	4	8	9	3	7	11	1	....	2
1896	4	*9	5	3	7	8	6	11	1	....	2
1897	1	*6	9	4	3	10	8	12	2	....	5
1898	1	10	4	3	7	6	8	12	2	....	5
1899	2	1	8	6	10	3	7	5	4	....	12

Year	Det.	Hart.	Ind.	K.C.	Lou.	Mil.	Prov.	Syr.	Troy	Wash.	Wor.
1876	....	2	....	....	5	....	....	....	....	....	....
1877	....	3	....	....	2	....	....	....	....	....	....
1878	....	....	5	....	....	6	3	....	....	....	....
1879	....	....	....	....	....	....	1	8	7	....	....
1880	....	....	....	....	....	....	2	....	4	....	5
1881	4	....	....	....	....	....	2	....	5	....	8
1882	6	....	....	....	....	....	2	....	7	....	8
1883	7	....	....	....	....	....	3	....	....	....	....
1884	8	....	....	....	....	....	1	....	....	....	....
1885	6	....	....	....	....	....	4	....	....	....	....
1886	2	....	....	7	....	....	....	....	....	8	....
1887	1	....	8	....	....	....	....	....	....	7	....
1888	5	....	7	....	....	....	....	....	....	8	....
1889	....	....	7	....	....	....	....	....	....	8	....
1890	....	....	....	....	....	....	....	....	....	....	....
1891	....	....	....	....	....	....	....	....	....	....	....
1892	....	....	....	....	9	....	....	....	....	10	....
1893	....	....	....	....	11	....	....	....	....	12	....
1894	....	....	....	....	12	....	....	....	....	11	....
1895	....	....	....	....	12	....	....	....	....	10	....
1896	....	....	....	....	12	....	....	....	....	*9	....
1897	....	....	....	....	11	....	....	....	....	*6	....
1898	....	....	....	....	9	....	....	....	....	11	....
1899	....	....	....	....	9	....	....	....	....	11	....

*Tied for position

PRE-1900 LEADERS

LEADING BATSMEN

Year	Player and Club	G.	H.	Pct.
1876—	Barnes, Chicago	66	138	.404
1877—	White, Boston	48	82	.385
1878—	Dalrymple, Milwaukee	60	95	.356
1879—	Anson, Chicago	49	90	.407
1880—	Gore, Chicago	75	114	.365
1881—	Anson, Chicago	84	137	.399
1882—	Brouthers, Buffalo	84	129	.367
1883—	Brouthers, Buffalo	97	156	.371
1884—	O'Rourke, Buffalo	104	157	.350
1885—	Connor, New York	110	169	.371
1886—	Kelly, Chicago	118	175	.388
1887—	Anson, Chicago	122	*224	.421
1888—	Anson, Chicago	134	177	.343

Year	Player and Club	G.	H.	Pct.
1889—	Brouthers, Boston	126	181	.373
1890—	Glasscock, New York	124	172	.336
1891—	Hamilton, Philadelphia	133	179	.338
1892—	Brouthers, Brooklyn	152	197	.335
	Childs, Cleveland	144	185	.335
1893—	Duffy, Boston	131	203	.378
1894—	Duffy, Boston	124	236	.438
1895—	Burkett, Cleveland	132	235	.423
1896—	Burkett, Cleveland	133	240	.410
1897—	Keeler, Baltimore	128	243	.432
1898—	Keeler, Baltimore	128	214	.379
1899—	Delahanty, Philadelphia	145	234	.408

*Bases on balls counted as hits.

TWO-BASE HIT LEADERS

Year	Player and Club	2B.
1876—	Roscoe Barnes, Chicago	23
1877—	Adrian (Cap) Anson, Chicago	20
1878—	Lewis Brown, Providence	18
1879—	Charles Eden, Cleveland	31
1880—	Fred Dunlap, Cleveland	27
1881—	Michael (King) Kelly, Chicago	28
1882—	Michael (King) Kelly, Chicago	36
1883—	Edward Williamson, Chicago	50
1884—	Paul Hines, Providence	34
1885—	Adrian (Cap) Anson, Chicago	35
1886—	Dennis (Dan) Brouthers, Detroit	41
1887—	Dennis (Dan) Brouthers, Detroit	35

Year	Player and Club	2B.
1888—	James Ryan, Chicago	37
1889—	John Glasscock, Indianapolis	39
1890—	Samuel Thompson, Philadelphia	38
1891—	Michael Griffin, Brooklyn	36
1892—	Brouthers, Bkn.-Delahanty, Phil.	33
1893—	Oliver (Pat) Tebeau, Cleveland	35
1894—	Hugh Duffy, Boston	50
1895—	Edward Delahanty, Philadelphia	47
1896—	Edward Delahanty, Philadelphia	42
1897—	Jacob Stenzel, Baltimore	40
1898—	Napoleon Lajoie, Philadelphia	40
1899—	Edward Delahanty, Philadelphia	56

THREE-BASE HIT LEADERS

Year	Player and Club	3B.
1876—	George Hall, Athletics	12
1877—	Brown, Bos.-McVey, Chi.-White, Bos.	9
1878—	Thomas York, Providence	9
1879—	L. Dickerson, Cin.-M. Kelly, Cin	14
1880—	Harry Stovey, Worcester	14
1881—	John Rowe, Buffalo	11
1882—	Roger Connor, Troy	17
1883—	Dennis (Dan) Brouthers, Buffalo	17
1884—	William (Buck) Ewing, New York	18
1885—	R. Connor, N.Y.-J. O'Rourke, N.Y.	15
1886—	Roger Connor, New York	19
1887—	Samuel Thompson, Detroit	23

Year	Player and Club	3B.
1888—	R. Connor, N.Y.-R. Johnson, Bos	17
1889—	Connor, NY-Fogarty, Phil. Wilmot, Wash.	17
1890—	John McPhee, Cincinnati	25
1891—	Jacob Beckley, Pittsburgh	20
1892—	Dennis (Dan) Brouthers, Brooklyn	20
1893—	Perry Werden, St. Louis	33
1894—	Henry Reitz, Baltimore	29
1895—	A. Selbach, Wash.-S. Thompson, Phil.	22
1896—	McCreery, Lou.-G. Van Haltren, N.Y.	21
1897—	Harry Davis, Pittsburgh	28
1898—	John Anderson, Bkn.-Wash.	19
1899—	James Williams, Pittsburgh	27

HOME RUN LEADERS

Year	Player and Club	HR.
1876—	George Hall, Athletics	5
1877—	George Shaffer, Louisville	3
1878—	Paul Hines, Providence	4
1879—	Charles Jones, Boston	9
1880—	J. O'Rourke, Bos.-H. Stovey, Wor.	6
1881—	Dennis (Dan) Brouthers, Buffalo	8
1882—	George Wood, Detroit	7
1883—	William (Buck) Ewing, New York	10
1884—	Edward Williamson, Chicago	27
1885—	Abner Dalrymple, Chicago	11
1886—	Harding Richardson, Detroit	11
1887—	R. Connor, N.Y.-T. O'Brien, Wash.	17

Year	Player and Club	HR.
1888—	Roger Connor, New York	14
1889—	Samuel Thompson, Philadelphia	20
1890—	T. Burns, Bkn.-M. Tiernan, N.Y.	13
1891—	H. Stovey, Bos.-M. Tiernan, N.Y.	16
1892—	James Holliday, Cincinnati	13
1893—	Edward Delahanty, Philadelphia	19
1894—	H. Duffy, Boston-R. Lowe, Boston	18
1895—	William Joyce, Washington	17
1896—	Delahanty, Phil.-S. Thompson, Phil	13
1897—	Napoleon Lajoie, Philadelphia	10
1898—	James Collins, Boston	14
1899—	John (Buck) Freeman, Washington	25

Cap Anson, who won four pre-1900 batting titles, was the first batter to record 3,000 hits.

PRE-1900 LEADERS—Continued

STOLEN BASE LEADERS

Year	Player and Club	SB.	Year	Player and Club	SB.
1886	George Andrews, Philadelphia	56	1893	John M. Ward, New York	72
1887	John M. Ward, New York	111	1894	William Hamilton, Philadelphia	99
1888	William (Dummy) Hoy, Washington	82	1895	William Hamilton, Philadelphia	95
1889	James Fogarty, Philadelphia	99	1896	William Lange, Chicago	100
1890	William Hamilton, Philadelphia	102	1897	William Lange, Chicago	83
1891	William Hamilton, Philadelphia	115	1898	Frederick Clarke, Louisville	66
1892	John M. Ward, Brooklyn	94	1899	James Sheckard, Baltimore	78

LEADING PITCHERS IN WINNING PERCENTAGE
(15 OR MORE VICTORIES)

Year	Pitcher and Club	W.	L.	Pct.	Year	Pitcher and Club	W.	L.	Pct.
1876	Albert Spalding, Chicago	47	13	.783	1888	Timothy Keefe, New York	35	12	.745
1877	Thomas Bond, Boston	31	17	.646	1889	John Clarkson, Boston	49	19	.721
1878	Thomas Bond, Boston	40	19	.678	1890	Thomas Lovett, Brooklyn	32	11	.744
1879	Jom M. Ward, Providence	44	18	.710	1891	John Ewing, New York	22	8	.733
1880	Fred Goldsmith, Chicago	22	3	.880	1892	Denton (Cy) Young, Cleve	36	11	.766
1881	Chas. Radbourn, Prov.	25	11	.694	1893	Frank Killen, Pittsburgh	34	10	.773
1882	Lawrence Corcoran, Chi.	27	13	.675	1894	Jouett Meekin, New York	34	9	.791
1883	James McCormick, Cleve.	27	13	.675	1895	William Hoffer, Baltimore	30	7	.811
1884	Chas. Radbourn, Prov.	60	12	.833	1896	William Hoffer, Baltimore	26	7	.788
1885	Michael Welch, New York	44	11	.800	1897	Amos Rusie, New York	29	8	.784
1886	John Flynn, Chicago	24	6	.800	1898	Edward Lewis, Boston	25	8	.758
1887	Charles Getzein, Detroit	29	13	.690	1899	James Hughes, Brooklyn	28	6	.824

Lifetime Batting Leaders

Players With Career Batting Average of .300 or Better, Playing Ten or More Seasons or Collecting 1,000 or More Hits (178)

Player	Years	G.	AB.	R.	H.	B.A.
Tyrus R. Cobb	24	3033	*11429	2245	*4191	*.367
Rogers Hornsby	23	2259	8173	1579	2930	.358
Joseph J. Jackson	13	1330	4980	873	1772	.356
L. Rogers Browning	13	1180	4850	950	1719	.354
David L. Orr	8	788	3303	539	1163	.352
Dennis L. Brouthers	19	1658	6725	1507	2349	.349
Frank J. O'Doul	11	970	3264	624	1140	.349
Edward J. Delahanty	16	1825	7493	1596	2593	.346
Tristram Speaker	22	2790	10196	1881	3515	.345
William H. Keeler	19	2124	8564	1720	2955	.345
Theodore S. Williams	19	2292	7706	1798	2654	.344
William R. Hamilton	14	1578	6262	1690	2157	.344
Jacob C. Stenzel	9	753	2992	662	1028	.344
George H. Ruth	22	2503	8397	2174	2873	.342
Jesse C. Burkett	16	2063	8389	1708	2872	.342
Harry E. Heilmann	17	2145	7787	1291	2660	.342
William H. Terry	14	1721	6428	1120	2193	.341
George H. Sisler	15	2055	8267	1284	2812	.340
H. Louis Gehrig	17	2164	8001	1888	2721	.340
James E. O'Neill	10	1038	4197	865	1428	.340
Napoleon Lajoie	21	2475	*9589	1506	3252	.339
Adrian C. Anson	22	2253	9084	1712	3081	.339
Samuel L. Thompson	15	1405	6004	1259	2016	.336
J. Riggs Stephenson	14	1310	4508	714	1515	.336
William A. Lange	7	808	3194	692	1072	.336
Aloysius H. Simmons	20	2215	8761	1507	2927	.334
John J. McGraw	16	1082	3919	1019	1307	.334
Michael J. Donlin	12	1025	3859	670	1287	.334
Edward T. Collins	25	2826	9946	1816	3309	.333
Paul G. Waner	20	2549	9459	1627	3152	.333
Stanley F. Musial	22	3026	10972	1949	3630	.331
Dennis P. Lyons	13	1110	4248	920	1404	.331
Rodney C. Carew	17	2249	8543	1313	2832	.331
Henry E. Manush	17	2008	7654	1287	2524	.330
Hugh Duffy	17	1722	6999	1545	2307	.330
John P. Wagner	21	2785	10427	1740	3430	.329
Robert R. Fothergill	12	1106	3269	453	1064	.325
James E. Foxx	20	2317	8134	1751	2646	.325
Roger Connor	18	1987	7807	1607	2535	.325
Joseph P. DiMaggio	13	1736	6821	1390	2214	.325
Edd J. Roush	16	1748	6646	1000	2158	.325
Earle B. Combs	12	1455	5746	1186	1866	.325
Joseph M. Medwick	17	1984	7635	1198	2471	.324
Floyd C. Herman	13	1552	5603	882	1818	.324
Edgar C. Rice	20	2404	9269	1514	2987	.322
Ross Youngs	10	1211	4627	812	1491	.322
George E. VanHaltren	17	1978	8022	1650	2573	.321
Hazen S. Cuyler	18	1879	7161	1305	2299	.321
Joseph J. Kelley	17	1829	6989	1425	2245	.321
Harry D. Stovey	14	1482	5994	1467	1925	.321
Charles L. Gehringer	19	2323	8860	1774	2839	.320
Harold J. Traynor	17	1941	7559	1183	2416	.320
Charles H. Klein	17	1753	6486	1168	2076	.320
Gordon S. Cochrane	13	1482	5169	1041	1652	.320
James W. Holliday	10	901	3604	733	1152	.320
Kenneth R. Williams	14	1397	4860	860	1552	.319
J. Floyd Vaughan	14	1817	6622	1173	2103	.318
H. Earl Averill	13	1669	6352	1224	2019	.318
Roberto W. Clemente	18	2433	9454	1416	3000	.317
Zachariah D. Wheat	19	2406	9106	1289	2884	.317
Michael J. Tiernan	13	1474	5910	1312	1875	.317
Charles J. Hafey	13	1283	4625	777	1466	.317
Joseph Harris	10	970	3035	461	963	.317
Bill Madlock	11	1340	4912	714	1557	.317
Lloyd J. Waner	18	1993	7772	1201	2459	.316
Frank F. Frisch	19	2311	9112	1532	2880	.316

Lifetime Batting Leaders —Continued

Player	Years	G.	AB.	R.	H.	B.A.
Leon A. Goslin	18	2287	8656	1483	2735	.316
Henry E. Larkin	10	1178	4729	933	1493	.316
Lewis A. Fonseca	12	937	3404	518	1075	.316
George H. Brett	11	1358	5307	852	1676	.316
Frederick C. Clarke	21	2204	8584	1620	2703	.315
Elmer H. Flick	13	1480	5601	951	1767	.315
John T. Tobin	11	1322	5020	763	1579	.315
James E. Ryan	18	2008	8218	1640	2577	.314
James H. O'Rourke	19	1750	7365	1425	2314	.314
Cecil H. Travis	12	1328	4914	665	1544	.314
Hugh A. Jennings	18	1264	4840	989	1520	.314
Elmer E. Smith	14	1231	4686	931	1473	.314
Bibb A. Falk	12	1354	4656	656	1463	.314
William M. Dickey	17	1789	6300	930	1969	.313
Michael J. Kelly	16	1434	5922	1359	1853	.313
Jacques F. Fournier	15	1530	5207	821	1631	.313
Henry B. Greenberg	13	1394	5193	1051	1628	.313
Joseph W. Sewell	14	1903	7132	1141	2226	.312
John R. Mize	15	1884	6443	1118	2011	.312
Edmund J. Miller	16	1820	6212	946	1937	.312
Clarence A. Childs	13	1463	5624	1218	1757	.312
W. Barney McCosky	11	1170	4172	664	1301	.312
L. Dale Mitchell	11	1127	3984	555	1244	.312
Clarence H. Beaumont	12	1411	5647	953	1754	.311
Fred C. Lindstrom	13	1438	5611	895	1747	.311
William C. Jacobson	11	1472	5507	787	1714	.311
William Ewing	18	1281	5348	1118	1663	.311
Jack R. Robinson	10	1382	4877	947	1518	.311
Raymond A. Radcliff	10	1081	4074	598	1267	.311
Taft S. Wright	9	1029	3583	465	1115	.311
Lucius B. Appling	20	2422	8856	1319	2749	.310
James L. Bottomley	16	1991	7471	1177	2313	.310
Edwin J. McKean	13	1655	6902	1213	2139	.310
Robert H. Veach	14	1822	6659	954	2064	.310
Emil F. Meusel	11	1289	4900	701	1521	.310
Thomas P. Burns	11	1178	4678	876	1451	.310
Jonathan T. Stone	11	1199	4490	738	1391	.310
Eugene F. Hargrave	12	852	2533	314	786	.310
E. Gordon Phelps	11	726	2117	239	657	.310
Samuel Crawford	19	2505	9579	1392	2964	.309
Jacob P. Beckley	20	2373	9476	1601	2930	.309
Robert W. Meusel	11	1407	5475	826	1693	.309
Richie Ashburn	15	2189	8365	1322	2574	.308
John P. McInnis	19	2128	7822	872	2406	.308
Walter S. Brodie	12	1439	5686	873	1749	.308
George F. Gore	14	1301	5366	1324	1653	.308
Virgil L. Davis	16	1458	4255	388	1312	.308
Harvey L. Hendrick	11	922	2910	434	896	.308
Eugene N. DeMontreville	11	911	3589	535	1106	.308
Cecil C. Cooper	13	1397	5323	796	1639	.308
George H. Burns	16	1866	6573	901	2018	.307
J. Franklin Baker	13	1575	5983	887	1838	.307
Michael J. Griffin	12	1508	5963	1401	1830	.307
Joseph F. Vosmik	13	1414	5472	818	1682	.307
Charles S. Stahl	10	1299	5062	856	1552	.307
Lewis R. Wilson	12	1348	4760	884	1461	.307
John M. Pesky	10	1270	4745	867	1455	.307
Frederick M. Leach	10	991	3733	543	1147	.307
John F. Moore	10	846	3013	439	926	.307
Henry J. Bonura	8	917	3582	600	1099	.307
Mateo R. Alou	15	1667	5789	780	1777	.307
Fred R. Walker	18	1905	6740	1037	2064	.306
George C. Kell	15	1795	6702	881	2054	.306
Ernest N. Lombardi	17	1853	5855	601	1792	.306
James L. White	15	1278	5274	828	1612	.306
Charles W. Jones	11	825	3471	668	1062	.306
Ralph A. Garr	13	1317	5108	717	1562	.306
Peter E. Rose	21	3250	13037	2047	3990	.306
Henry L. Aaron	23	3298	12364	2174	3771	.305
James E. Rice	10	1334	5306	823	1620	.305

Player	Years	G.	AB.	R.	H.	B.A.
Albert Oliver	16	2153	8351	1132	2546	.305
David G. Parker	11	1301	4848	728	1479	.305
Melvin T. Ott	22	2730	9456	1859	2876	.304
William J. Herman	15	1922	7707	1163	2345	.304
Patrick J. Donovan	17	1809	7416	1321	2254	.304
Paul A. Hines	16	1456	6190	1054	1884	.304
J. Bentley Seymour	16	1500	5657	737	1720	.304
A. Harding Richardson	14	1313	5615	1112	1705	.304
W. Curtis Walker	12	1359	4858	718	1475	.304
Samuel A. Leslie	10	822	2460	311	749	.304
Pedro (Tony) Oliva	15	1676	6301	870	1917	.304
Manuel R. Mota	20	1536	3779	496	1149	.304
G. Kenneth Griffey	11	1292	4799	802	1460	.304
Jacob E. Daubert	15	2014	7673	1117	2326	.303
Charles S. Myer	17	1923	7038	1174	2131	.303
Harvey E. Kuenn	15	1833	6913	951	2092	.303
Charles D. Jamieson	18	1777	6560	1062	1990	.303
George W. Harper	11	1073	3398	505	1030	.303
Earl S. Smith	12	860	2264	225	686	.303
John E. Stivetts	11	523	1955	345	592	.303
Wm. Benjamin Chapman	15	1717	6478	1144	1958	.302
Harold A. Trosky	11	1347	5161	835	1561	.302
George F. Grantham	13	1444	4989	912	1508	.302
Thomas F. Holmes	11	1320	4992	698	1507	.302
Carl N. Reynolds	13	1222	4495	672	1357	.302
Charles T. Hickman	12	1062	3973	480	1199	.302
Homer W. Summa	10	840	3001	413	905	.302
Samuel D. Hale	10	883	2915	422	880	.302
Robert L. Caruthers	10	692	2508	503	758	.302
John J. Doyle	17	1535	6013	997	1814	.302
Willie H. Mays	22	2992	10881	2062	3283	.302
Joseph E. Cronin	20	2124	7579	1233	2285	.301
Stanley C. Hack	16	1938	7278	1239	2193	.301
Raymond B. Bressler	19	1302	3881	544	1170	.301
John A. Mostil	10	972	3507	618	1054	.301
Raymond F. Blades	10	767	2415	467	726	.301
Steven P. Garvey	15	1827	6931	928	2082	.300
Enos B. Slaughter	19	2380	7946	1247	2383	.300
William D. Goodman	16	1623	5644	807	1691	.300
Walter A. Berger	11	1350	5163	809	1550	.300
Ethan N. Allen	13	1281	4418	623	1325	.300
Earl H. Sheely	9	1234	4471	572	1340	.300

*Total in dispute. See explanation on Page 3.

.400 HITTERS IN MAJORS

(Bases on balls counted as hits in 1887)

American League

Napoleon Lajoie, Philadelphia—1901, .422*.
Tyrus R. Cobb, Detroit—1911, .420*; 1912, .410*; 1922, .401*.
Joseph J. Jackson, Cleveland—1911, .408*.
George Sisler, St. Louis—1920, .407*; 1922, .420*.
Harry E. Heilmann, Detroit—1923, .403.*
Theodore S. Williams, Boston—1941, .406*.

National League

Roscoe C. Barnes, Chicago—1876, .404* (66 games).
Adrian C. Anson, Chicago—1879, .407 (49 games); 1887, .421.
Dennis Brouthers, Detroit—1887, .419.
Sam Thompson, Detroit, Philadelphia—1887, .406; 1894, .404*.
Jacob Stenzel, Pittsburgh—1893, .409 (51 games).
Hugh Duffy, Boston—1894, .438*.
Edward J. Delahanty, Philadelphia—1894, .400*; 1899, .408*.
George Turner, Philadelphia—1894, .423 (77 games).
Jesse Burkett, Cleveland, St. Louis—1895, .423*; 1896, .410*; 1899, .402*.
Fred C. Clarke, Louisville—1897, .406*.
William H. Keeler, Baltimore—1897, .432*.
Rogers Hornsby, St. Louis—1922, .401*; 1924, .424*; 1925, .403*.
William H. Terry, New York—1930, .401*.

American Association

Harry D. Stovey, Philadelphia—1884, .404*; 1887, .402.
Thomas J. Esterbrook, N. Y. Mets—1884, .408*.
James (Tip) O'Neill, St. Louis—1887, .492*.
L. Rogers Browning, Louisville—1887, .471*.
Dennis P. Lyons, Athletics—1887, .469.
William Robinson, St. Louis—1887, .426.
Joseph Mack, Louisville—1887, 410.
Paul Radford, N. Y. Mets—1887, .404.
Tom Burns, Baltimore—1887, .401.
Robert L. Caruthers, St. Louis—1887, .459 (98 games).
Dave Orr, N. Y. Mets—1887, .403 (85 games).

Union Association

Fred Dunlap, St. Louis—1884, .420 (81 games)*.
*Qualify as .400 hitters under present rule 10.23 of Official Baseball Rules.

PLAYERS WITH 20 OR MORE PLAYING YEARS (55)

(See Page 52 for Pitchers)

Player	Yrs.	G.	Player	Yrs.	G.
James T. McGuire	26	1781	Napoleon Lajoie	21	2475
Edward T. Collins	25	2826	Ronald R. Fairly	21	2442
Roderick J. Wallace	25	2369	Wilver D. Stargell	21	2360
Tyrus R. Cobb	24	3033	Lafayette N. Cross	21	2259
Carl M. Yastrzemski	23	3308	Frederick C. Clarke	21	2204
Walter J. V. Maranville	23	2670	Robert A. O'Farrell	21	1492
Rogers Hornsby	23	2259	J. Timothy McCarver	21	1909
Henry L. Aaron	23	3298	John J. O'Connor	21	1404
Brooks C. Robinson	23	2896	Atanasio R. Perez	20	2557
Stanley F. Musial	22	3026	Paul G. Waner	20	2549
Willie H. Mays	22	2992	Max G. Carey	20	2469
Albert W. Kaline	22	2834	Lucius B. Appling	20	2422
Tristram Speaker	22	2789	Edgar C. Rice	20	2404
Melvin T. Ott	22	2730	Jacob P. Beckley	20	2373
Willie L. McCovey	22	2588	George S. Davis	20	2370
George H. Ruth	22	2503	James E. Foxx	20	2317
Harmon C. Killebrew	22	2435	Roger M. Cramer	20	2239
William F. Dahlen	22	2431	Aloysius H. Simmons	20	2215
James J. Dykes	22	2282	Joseph I. Judge	20	2170
Adrian C. Anson	22	2253	Charles J. Grimm	20	2166
Philip J. Cavarretta	22	2030	Joseph E. Cronin	20	2124
Harry H. Davis	22	1746	James B. Vernon	20	2409
William J. Gleason	22	1942	Charles L. Hartnett	20	1990
Peter E. Rose	21	3250	Elmer W. Valo	20	1806
Daniel J. Staub	21	2819	J. Luther Sewell	20	1630
Frank Robinson	21	2808	Manuel R. Mota	20	1536
John P. Wagner	21	2785	John W. Cooney	20	1172
Joe L. Morgan	21	2533			

PLAYERS BATTING .300 OR OVER TEN OR MORE YEARS (65)

50 OR MORE GAMES, SEASON

Player	Yrs.	Cns.	Player	Yrs.	Cns.
Henry L. Aaron	14	5	Joseph P. DiMaggio	11	7
Adrian C. Anson	20	*15	Patrick J. Donovan	10	6
Lucius B. Appling	14	9	Hugh Duffy	11	10
Jacob P. Beckley	13	6	William B. Ewing	10	8
Dennis L. Brouthers	15	14	James E. Foxx	12	5
L. Rogers Browning	10	7	Frank F. Frisch	13	11
Jesse C. Burkett	11	10	H. Louis Gehrig	12	12
Rodney C. Carew	15	15	Charles L. Gehringer	13	8
Frederick C. Clarke	11	5	Leon A. Goslin	11	7
Roberto W. Clemente	13	8	William R. Hamilton	12	12
Tyrus R. Cobb	23	23	Harry E. Heilmann	12	12
Edward T. Collins	17	9	Rogers Hornsby	14	12
Roger Connor	12	6	William H. Keeler	13	13
Samuel Crawford	10	4	Joseph J. Kelley	11	11
Hazen S. Cuyler	10	4	Napoleon Lajoie	15	10
Jacob E. Daubert	10	6	Ernest N. Lombardi	10	5
Virgil L. Davis	10	7	Mickey C. Mantle	10	5
Edward J. Delahanty	12	12	Henry E. Manush	11	7
William M. Dickey	11	6	Willie H. Mays	10	7

Player	Yrs.	Cns.	Player	Yrs.	Cns.
John P. McInnis	11	5	Tristram Speaker	18	10
Joseph M. Medwick	12	*10	J. Riggs Stephenson	12	8
Stanley F. Musial	17	*16	William H. Terry	11	10
Albert Oliver	10	8	Harold J. Traynor	10	6
James H. O'Rourke	13	5	George E. Van Haltren	13	9
Melvin T. Ott	10	3	J. Floyd Vaughan	12	*10
Edgar C. Rice	13	5	John P. Wagner	17	*17
Peter E. Rose	15	9	Fred R. Walker	10	6
Edd J. Roush	12	11	Lloyd J. Waner	10	6
George H. Ruth	17	8	Paul G. Waner	14	*12
James E. Ryan	13	7	Zachariah D. Wheat	13	6
Aloysius H. Simmons	13	*11	Kenneth R. Williams	10	7
George H. Sisler	13	9	Theodore S. Williams	16	*15
Enos B. Slaughter	10	5			

*From start of career.

PLAYERS WITH 2,300 OR MORE GAMES (49)

Player	G.	B.A.	Player	G.	B.A.
Carl M. Yastrzemski	3308	.285	Napoleon Lajoie	2475	.339
Henry L. Aaron	3298	.305	Max G. Carey	2469	.285
Peter E. Rose	3250	.306	Vada E. Pinson	2469	.286
Tyrus R. Cobb	3033	*.367	Ronald R. Fairly	2442	.266
Stanley F. Musial	3026	.331	Harmon C. Killebrew	2435	.256
Willie H. Mays	2992	.302	Roberto W. Clemente	2433	.317
Brooks C. Robinson	2896	.267	William F. Dahlen	2431	.275
Albert W. Kaline	2834	.297	William H. Davis	2429	.279
Edward T. Collins	2826	.333	Lucius B. Appling	2422	.310
Daniel J. Staub	2819	.280	James B. Vernon	2409	.286
Frank Robinson	2808	.294	Zachariah D. Wheat	2406	.317
Tristram Speaker	2790	.345	Edgar C. Rice	2404	.322
John P. Wagner	2785	.329	Mickey C. Mantle	2401	.298
Melvin T. Ott	2730	.304	Edwin L. Mathews	2391	.271
Walter J. V. Maranville	2670	.258	Enos B. Slaughter	2380	.300
Louis C. Brock	2616	.293	Jacob P. Beckley	2373	.309
Luis E. Aparicio	2599	.262	George S. Davis	2370	.297
Willie L. McCovey	2588	.270	Roderick J. Wallace	2369	.267
Atanasio R. Perez	2557	.280	J. Nelson Fox	2367	.288
Paul G. Waner	2549	.333	Wilver D. Stargell	2360	.282
Joe L. Morgan	2533	.272	Charles L. Gehringer	2323	.320
Ernest Banks	2528	.274	James E. Foxx	2317	.325
Samuel Crawford	2505	.309	Frank F. Frisch	2311	.316
George H. Ruth	2503	.342	Harry B. Hooper	2308	.281
Billy L. Williams	2488	.290			

*Average in dispute. See explanation on Page 3.

PLAYERS WITH 500 OR MORE CONSECUTIVE GAMES (29)

Player	Games	Player	Games
H. Louis Gehrig	2130	Santos C. Alomar	648
L. Everett Scott	1307	Edward W. Brown	618
Steven P. Garvey	1207	Roy D. McMillan	585
Billy L. Williams	1117	George B. Pinckney	577
Joseph W. Sewell	1103	Walter S. Brodie	574
Stanley F. Musial	895	Aaron L. Ward	565
Edward F. Yost	829	George J. LaChance	540
Augustus R. Suhr	822	John F. Freeman	535
J. Nelson Fox	798	Fred W. Luderus	533
*Peter E. Rose	745	J. Clyde Milan	511
Richie Ashburn	730	*Charles L. Gehringer	511
Ernest Banks	717	Vada E. Pinson	508
*Peter E. Rose	678	*Charles L. Gehringer	504
H. Earl Averill	673	Omar R. Moreno	503
Frank A. McCormick	652		

*Only players with two streaks.

PLAYERS WITH 9,000 OR MORE AT-BATS (37)

Player	AB.	Player	AB.
Peter E. Rose	13037	Jacob P. Beckley	9476
Henry L. Aaron	12364	Paul G. Waner	9459
Carl M. Yastrzemski	11988	Melvin T. Ott	9456
Tyrus R. Cobb	*11429	Roberto W. Clemente	9454
Stanley F. Musial	10972	Ernest Banks	9421
Willie H. Mays	10881	Max G. Carey	9363
Brooks C. Robinson	10654	Billy L. Williams	9350
John P. Wagner	10427	Edgar C. Rice	9269
Louis C. Brock	10332	Atanasio R. Perez	9258
Luis E. Aparicio	10230	J. Nelson Fox	9232
Tristram Speaker	10196	William H. Davis	9174
Albert W. Kaline	10116	Roger M. Cramer	9140
Walter J. Maranville	10078	Frank F. Frisch	9112
Frank Robinson	10006	Zachariah D. Wheat	9106
Edward T. Collins	9946	Adrian C. Anson	9084
Vada E. Pinson	9645	Lafayette N. Cross	9065
Daniel J. Staub	9603	George S. Davis	9027
Napoleon Lajoie	*9589	William F. Dahlen	9019
Samuel Crawford	9579		

*Total in dispute. See explanation on Page 3.

PLAYERS WITH 1,500 OR MORE RUNS (44)

Player	Runs	Player	Runs
Tyrus R. Cobb	2245	George E. VanHaltren	1650
George H. Ruth	2174	James E. Ryan	1640
Henry L. Aaron	2174	Paul G. Waner	1627
Willie H. Mays	2062	Albert W. Kaline	1622
Peter E. Rose	2047	Frederick C. Clarke	1620
Stanley F. Musial	1949	Louis C. Brock	1610
H. Louis Gehrig	1888	Roger Connor	1607
Tristram Speaker	1881	Jacob P. Beckley	1601
Melvin T. Ott	1859	Joe L. Morgan	1600
Frank Robinson	1829	Edward J. Delahanty	1596
Edward T. Collins	1816	William F. Dahlen	1594
Carl M. Yastrzemski	1816	Rogers Hornsby	1579
Theodore S. Williams	1798	George S. Davis	1546
Charles L. Gehringer	1774	Max G. Carey	1545
James E. Foxx	1751	Hugh Duffy	1545
John P. Wagner	1740	Frank F. Frisch	1532
William H. Keeler	1720	Edgar C. Rice	1514
Adrian C. Anson	1712	Edwin L. Mathews	1509
Jesse C. Burkett	1708	Thomas T. Brown	1507
William R. Hamilton	1690	Dennis L. Brouthers	1507
Mickey C. Mantle	1677	Aloysius H. Simmons	1507
John A. McPhee	1674	Napoleon Lajoie	1506

PLAYERS WITH 2,500 OR MORE HITS (58)

Player	Hits	Player	Hits
Tyrus R. Cobb	*4191	Frank Robinson	2943
Peter E. Rose	3990	Jacob P. Beckley	2930
Henry L. Aaron	3771	Rogers Hornsby	2930
Stanley F. Musial	3630	Aloysius H. Simmons	2927
Tristram Speaker	3515	Zachariah D. Wheat	2884
John P. Wagner	3430	Frank F. Frisch	2880
Carl M. Yastrzemski	3419	Melvin T. Ott	2876
Edward T. Collins	3309	George H. Ruth	2873
Willie H. Mays	3283	Jesse C. Burkett	2872
Napoleon Lajoie	3252	Brooks C. Robinson	2848
Paul G. Waner	3152	Charles L. Gehringer	2839
Adrian C. Anson	3081	Rodney C. Carew	2832
Louis C. Brock	3023	George H. Sisler	2812
Albert W. Kaline	3007	Vada E. Pinson	2757
Roberto W. Clemente	3000	Lucius B. Appling	2749
Edgar C. Rice	2987	Leon A. Goslin	2735
Samuel Crawford	2964	H. Louis Gehrig	2721
William H. Keeler	2955	Billy L. Williams	2711

Player	Hits	Player	Hits
Roger M. Cramer	2705	Walter J. Maranville	2605
Fred C. Clarke	2703	Edward J. Delahanty	2593
Daniel J. Staub	2685	Atanasio R. Perez	2588
George S. Davis	2683	Ernest Banks	2583
Luis E. Aparicio	2677	James Ryan	2577
Max Carey	2665	Richie Ashburn	2574
J. Nelson Fox	2663	George E. VanHaltren	2573
Harry E. Heilmann	2660	William H. Davis	2561
Lafayette N. Cross	2654	Albert Oliver	2546
Theodore S. Williams	2654	Roger Connor	2535
James E. Foxx	2646	Henry E. Manush	2524

*Total in dispute. See explanation on Page 3.

PLAYERS HITTING SAFELY IN 30 OR MORE CONSECUTIVE GAMES, SEASON (28)

Player	Club	Games	Year
Joseph P. DiMaggio	New York AL	56	1941
*William H. Keeler	Baltimore NL	44	1897
Peter E. Rose	Cincinnati NL	44	1978
William F. Dahlen	Chicago NL	42	1894
George H. Sisler	St. Louis AL	41	1922
Tyrus R. Cobb	Detroit AL	40	1911
Thomas F. Holmes	Boston NL	37	1945
William R. Hamilton	Philadelphia NL	36	1894
Fred C. Clarke	Louisville NL	35	1895
Tyrus R. Cobb	Detroit AL	35	1917
*George H. Sisler	St. Louis AL	34	1925
Jonathan T. Stone	Detroit AL	34	1930
George H. McQuinn	St. Louis AL	34	1938
Dominic P. DiMaggio	Boston AL	34	1949
George S. Davis	New York NL	33	1893
Rogers Hornsby	St. Louis NL	33	1922
Henry E. Manush	Washington AL	33	1933
Edward J. Delahanty	Philadelphia NL	31	1899
Edgar C. Rice	Washington AL	31	1924
Willie H. Davis	Los Angeles NL	31	1969
Ricardo A. J. Carty	Atlanta NL	31	1970
Kenneth F. Landreaux	Minnesota AL	31	1980
Elmer E. Smith	Cincinnati NL	30	1898
Tristram E. Speaker	Boston AL	30	1912
Leon A. Goslin	Detroit AL	30	1934
Stanley F. Musial	St. Louis NL	30	1950
*Ronald LeFlore	Detroit AL	30	1976
George H. Brett	Kansas City AL	30	1980

*From start of season.

PLAYERS WITH 200 HITS, FOUR OR MORE YEARS (27)

Player	Yrs.	Player	Yrs.
Peter E. Rose	10	Charles H. Klein	5
Tyrus R. Cobb	9	Napoleon Lajoie	5
H. Louis Gehrig	8	Vada E. Pinson	4
William H. Keeler	8	Harry E. Heilmann	4
Paul G. Waner	8	Joseph J. Jackson	4
Charles L. Gehringer	7	Henry E. Manush	4
Rogers Hornsby	7	Joseph M. Medwick	4
Jesse C. Burkett	6	Tristram Speaker	4
Stanley F. Musial	6	John T. Tobin	4
Edgar C. Rice	6	Lloyd J. Waner	4
Aloysius H. Simmons	6	Roberto W. Clemente	4
George H. Sisler	6	Louis C. Brock	4
William H. Terry	6	Rodney C. Carew	4
Steven P. Garvey	6		

PLAYERS WITH 2,000 OR MORE ONE-BASE HITS (36)

Player	1B.	Player	1B.
Tyrus R. Cobb	3052	Lucius B. Appling	2162
Peter E. Rose	2992	J. Nelson Fox	2161
Edward T. Collins	2641	Roberto W. Clemente	2154
William H. Keeler	2534	Jacob P. Beckley	2142
John P. Wagner	2426	George H. Sisler	2122
Tristram Speaker	2383	Richie Ashburn	2119
Napoleon Lajoie	2354	Luis E. Aparicio	2108
Adrian C. Anson	2330	Zachariah D. Wheat	2104
Jesse C. Burkett	2303	Samuel Crawford	2102
Henry L. Aaron	2294	Lafayette N. Cross	2077
Edgar C. Rice	2272	Fred C. Clarke	2061
Carl M. Yastrzemski	2262	Albert W. Kaline	2035
Stanley F. Musial	2253	Lloyd J. Waner	2032
Louis C. Brock	2247	Brooks C. Robinson	2030
Paul G. Waner	2244	Walter J. Maranville	2020
Rodney C. Carew	2217	Max Carey	2018
Frank F. Frisch	2171	George E. Van Haltren	2008
Roger M. Cramer	2163	George S. Davis	2007

PLAYERS WITH 400 OR MORE TWO-BASE HITS (73)

Player	2B.	Player	2B.
Tristram Speaker	793	James L. Bottomley	465
Stanley F. Musial	725	James E. Foxx	458
Tyrus R. Cobb	*724	Samuel Crawford	455
Peter E. Rose	711	Jacob P. Beckley	455
Napoleon Lajoie	652	James J. Dykes	453
John P. Wagner	651	Dennis J. Brouthers	446
Carl M. Yastrzemski	646	George H. Burns	444
Henry L. Aaron	624	Richard Bartell	442
Paul G. Waner	605	George S. Davis	442
Charles L. Gehringer	574	Lucius B. Appling	440
Harry E. Heilmann	542	Roberto W. Clemente	440
Rogers Hornsby	541	James E. Ryan	439
Joseph M. Medwick	540	Edward T. Collins	437
Aloysius H. Simmons	539	Joseph W. Sewell	436
H. Louis Gehrig	535	Harold A. McRae	435
Adrian C. Anson	530	Wallace Moses	435
Frank Robinson	528	Billy L. Williams	434
Theodore S. Williams	525	Joseph I. Judge	433
Willie H. Mays	523	Roger Connor	429
Joseph E. Cronin	516	Joe L. Morgan	428
Edward J. Delahanty	508	Albert F. Schoendienst	427
George H. Ruth	506	Sherwood R. Magee	425
Leon A. Goslin	500	George H. Sisler	425
Edgar C. Rice	498	Wilver D. Stargell	423
Albert W. Kaline	498	Rodney C. Carew	420
Daniel J. Staub	492	Max G. Carey	419
Albert Oliver	492	Orlando M. Cepeda	417
Henry E. Manush	491	Enos B. Slaughter	413
James B. Vernon	490	Ted L. Simmons	413
Melvin T. Ott	488	Joseph A. Kuhel	412
William J. Herman	486	W. Benjamin Chapman	407
Louis C. Brock	486	Ernest Banks	407
Vada F. Pinson	485	William F. Dahlen	403
Brooks C. Robinson	482	H. Earl Averill	401
Atanasio R. Perez	479	Martin J. McManus	401
Zachariah D. Wheat	476	Lafayette N. Cross	401
Frank F. Frisch	466		

*Total in dispute. See explanation on Page 3.

PLAYERS WITH 150 OR MORE THREE-BASE HITS (50)

Player	3B.	Player	3B.
Samuel Crawford	312	Jacob P. Beckley	246
Tyrus R. Cobb	298	Roger Connor	227
John P. Wagner	252	Tristram Speaker	222

Player	3B.	Player	3B.
Frederick C. Clarke	219	Sherwood R. Magee	166
Dennis L. Brouthers	212	Roberto W. Clemente	166
Paul G. Waner	191	Jacob E. Daubert	165
Joseph J. Kelley	189	Napoleon Lajoie	164
Edward T. Collins	186	George H. Sisler	164
Jesse C. Burkett	185	Harold J. Traynor	164
Harry D. Stovey	185	Edward J. Konetchy	163
Edgar C. Rice	184	H. Louis Gehrig	162
Edward J. Delahanty	182	Harry B. Hooper	160
John A. McPhee	180	Henry E. Manush	160
William B. Ewing	179	Max Carey	159
Walter J. Maranville	177	Joseph I. Judge	159
Stanley F. Musial	177	Michael J. Tiernan	159
Leon A. Goslin	173	George E. VanHaltren	159
Zachariah D. Wheat	172	Hazen S. Cuyler	157
Elmer H. Flick	170	William H. Keeler	155
Thomas W. Leach	170	Earle B. Combs	154
Rogers Hornsby	169	James E. Ryan	153
Joseph J. Jackson	168	Edwin J. McKean	152
Edd J. Roush	168	James L. Bottomley	151
George S. Davis	167	Thomas W. Corcoran	151
William F. Dahlen	166	Harry E. Heilmann	151

PLAYERS WITH 250 OR MORE HOME RUNS (75)

Player	HR.	Player	HR.
Henry L. Aaron	755	Graig Nettles	333
George H. Ruth	714	Bobby L. Bonds	332
Willie H. Mays	660	Henry B. Greenberg	331
Frank Robinson	586	Willie W. Horton	325
Harmon C. Killebrew	573	Roy E. Sievers	318
Mickey C. Mantle	536	C. Reginald Smith	314
James E. Foxx	534	Aloysius H. Simmons	307
Theodore S. Williams	521	Rogers Hornsby	301
Willie L. McCovey	521	Charles H. Klein	300
Edwin L. Mathews	512	Gregory M. Luzinski	294
Ernest Banks	512	James S. Wynn	291
Melvin T. Ott	511	Daniel J. Staub	290
H. Louis Gehrig	493	George A. Foster	289
Reginald M. Jackson	478	Robert L. Johnson	288
Stanley F. Musial	475	Henry J. Sauer	288
Wilver D. Stargell	475	Delmer Ennis	288
Carl M. Yastrzemski	452	Frank J. Thomas	286
Billy L. Williams	426	Kenton L. Boyer	282
Edwin D. Snider	407	Theodore B. Kluszewski	279
Albert W. Kaline	399	Rudolph P. York	277
Johnny L. Bench	389	James E. Rice	276
Michael J. Schmidt	389	Roger E. Maris	275
Frank O. Howard	382	George C. Scott	271
Orlando M. Cepeda	379	Brooks C. Robinson	268
Norman D. Cash	377	Victor W. Wertz	266
Rocco D. Colavito	374	Robert B. Thomson	264
Gilbert R. Hodges	370	Darrell W. Evans	262
Ralph M. Kiner	369	Joe L. Morgan	262
Atanasio R. Perez	369	W. Robert Allison	256
Joseph P. DiMaggio	361	Vada E. Pinson	256
John R. Mize	359	John C. Mayberry	255
Lawrence P. Berra	358	Joseph L. Gordon	253
Lee A. May	354	Lawrence E. Doby	253
Richard A. Allen	351	Joseph P. Torre	252
Ronald E. Santo	342	Ronald C. Cey	252
David A. Kingman	342	Bobby R. Murcer	252
John W. Powell	339	Fred Williams	251
Joseph W. Adcock	336		

PLAYERS WITH EIGHT OR MORE HOME RUNS WITH BASES FILLED (61)

Player	Total	Player	Total
H. Louis Gehrig	23	James E. Foxx	17
Willie L. McCovey	18	Theodore S. Williams	17

PLAYERS WITH EIGHT OR MORE HOME RUNS WITH BASES FILLED (61)—Continued

Player	Total	Player	Total
George H. Ruth	16	Richard L. Stuart	9
Henry L. Aaron	16	Gus E. Zernial	9
Gilbert R. Hodges	14	Orlando M. Cepeda	9
Joseph P. DiMaggio	13	Americo P. Petrocelli	9
Ralph M. Kiner	13	Willie W. Horton	9
Rudolph P. York	12	Daniel J. Staub	9
Rogers Hornsby	12	Reginald M. Jackson	9
Ernest Banks	12	Raymond A. Boone	8
Joseph O. Rudi	12	William M. Dickey	8
Henry B. Greenberg	11	Robert P. Doerr	8
Harmon C. Killebrew	11	Carl A. Furillo	8
Wilver D. Stargell	11	Robert L. Johnson	8
Lee A. May	11	George L. Kelly	8
Johnny L. Bench	11	Jack E. Jensen	8
David A. Kingman	11	Anthony M. Lazzeri	8
George A. Foster	11	Edwin L. Mathews	8
Aloysius H. Simmons	10	William B. Nicholson	8
Vernon D. Stephens	10	Ronald J. Northey	8
Victor W. Wertz	10	James T. Northrup	8
Joseph W. Adcock	10	Robert B. Thomson	8
Roy E. Sievers	10	Andrew W. Seminick	8
John D. Milner	10	Norman D. Cash	8
Jeffrey A. Burroughs	10	Willie H. Mays	8
Lawrence P. Berra	9	Richard J. McAuliffe	8
W. Walker Cooper	9	Vada E. Pinson	8
Samuel B. Chapman	9	Billy L. Williams	8
Mickey C. Mantle	9	Richard A. Allen	8
Stanley F. Musial	9	Donald E. Baylor	8
Albert L. Rosen	9		

PLAYERS WITH TEN OR MORE PINCH-HIT HOME RUNS (13)

Player	Total	Player	Total
Clifford Johnson	18	Joseph W. Adcock	12
Gerald T. Lynch	18	Fred C. Williams	11
Forrest H. Burgess	16	Fred D. Whitfield	11
William J. Brown	16	Gus E. Zernial	10
Willie L. McCovey	16	Walter C. Post	10
George D. Crowe	14	Donald R. Mincher	10
Robert H. Cerv	12		

PLAYERS WITH TWO OR MORE HOME RUNS IN ONE GAME, TWENTY-FIVE OR MORE TIMES (42)

Player	Total	Player	Total
George H. Ruth	72	Edwin D. Snider	34
Willie H. Mays	63	Michael J. Schmidt	34
Henry L. Aaron	62	Rocco D. Colavito	32
James E. Foxx	55	Gus E. Zernial	32
Frank Robinson	54	Richard A. Allen	32
Edwin L. Mathews	49	Henry J. Sauer	31
Melvin T. Ott	49	Billy L. Williams	31
Mickey C. Mantle	46	James E. Rice	31
Harmon C. Killebrew	46	Gilbert R. Hodges	30
Willie L. McCovey	44	John R. Mize	30
H. Louis Gehrig	43	Willie W. Horton	30
Ernest Banks	42	Joseph W. Adcock	28
Ralph M. Kiner	40	Charles H. Klein	28
Stanley F. Musial	37	Roy E. Sievers	27
Theodore S. Williams	37	Lewis R. Wilson	27
Wilver D. Stargell	36	Carl M. Yastrzemski	27
David A. Kingman	36	Frank O. Howard	26
Joseph P. DiMaggio	35	Ronald E. Santo	26
Henry B. Greenberg	35	Roger E. Maris	25
Lee A. May	35	Harold A. Trosky	25
Reginald M. Jackson	35	Norman D. Cash	25

PLAYERS WITH 4,000 OR MORE TOTAL BASES (41)

Player	TB.	Player	TB.
Henry L. Aaron	6856	Napoleon Lajoie	4478
Stanley F. Musial	6134	Paul G. Waner	4478
Willie H. Mays	6066	Edwin L. Mathews	4349
Tyrus R. Cobb	*5862	Samuel E. Crawford	4328
George H. Ruth	5793	Atanasio R. Perez	4328
Carl M. Yastrzemski	5539	Leon A. Goslin	4325
Peter E. Rose	5433	Brooks C. Robinson	4270
Frank Robinson	5373	Vada E. Pinson	4264
Tristram Speaker	5103	Edward T. Collins	4259
H. Louis Gehrig	5059	Charles L. Gehringer	4257
Melvin T. Ott	5041	Louis C. Brock	4238
James E. Foxx	4956	Willie L. McCovey	4219
John P. Wagner	4888	Wilver D. Stargell	4190
Theodore S. Williams	4884	Adrian C. Anson	4145
Albert W. Kaline	4852	Harmon C. Killebrew	4143
Rogers Hornsby	4712	Daniel J. Staub	4141
Ernest Banks	4706	Jacob P. Beckley	4138
Aloysius H. Simmons	4685	Zachariah D. Wheat	4100
Billy L. Williams	4599	Reginald M. Jackson	4091
Mickey C. Mantle	4511	Harry E. Heilmann	4053
Roberto W. Clemente	4492		

*Total in dispute. See explanation on Page 3.

SLUGGING AVERAGE, PLAYERS WITH 4,000 OR MORE TOTAL BASES (41)

Player	T.B.	S.A.	Player	T.B.	S.A.
George H. Ruth	5793	.690	Ernest Banks	4706	.500
Theodore S. Williams	4884	.634	Billy L. Williams	4599	.492
H. Louis Gehrig	5059	.632	Charles L. Gehringer	4257	.481
James E. Foxx	4956	.609	Albert W. Kaline	4852	.480
Rogers Hornsby	4712	.577	Roberto W. Clemente	4492	.475
Stanley F. Musial	6134	.559	Paul G. Waner	4478	.473
Mickey C. Mantle	4511	.557	John P. Wagner	4888	.469
Willie H. Mays	6066	.557	Napoleon Lajoie	4478	.467
Henry L. Aaron	6856	.555	Atanasio R. Perez	4328	.467
Frank Robinson	5373	.537	Carl M. Yastrzemski	5539	.462
Aloysius H. Simmons	4685	.535	Adrian C. Anson	4145	.456
Melvin T. Ott	5041	.533	Samuel E. Crawford	4328	.452
Wilver D. Stargell	4190	.529	Zachariah D. Wheat	4100	.450
Harry E. Heilmann	4053	.520	Vada E. Pinson	4264	.442
Willie L. McCovey	4219	.515	Jacob P. Beckley	4138	.437
Tyrus R. Cobb	*5862	*.513	Daniel J. Staub	4141	.431
Edwin L. Mathews	4349	.509	Edward T. Collins	4259	.428
Harmon C. Killebrew	4143	.509	Peter E. Rose	5433	.417
Reginald M. Jackson	4091	.504	Louis C. Brock	4238	.410
Leon A. Goslin	4325	.500	Brooks C. Robinson	4270	.401
Tristram Speaker	5103	.500			

*Total in dispute. See explanation on Page 3.

PLAYERS WITH 800 OR MORE LONG HITS (DOUBLES, TRIPLES, HOMERS) (43)

Player	Long Hits	Player	Long Hits
Henry L. Aaron	1477	Ernest Banks	1009
Stanley F. Musial	1377	John P. Wagner	1004
George H. Ruth	1356	Peter E. Rose	998
Willie H. Mays	1323	Aloysius H. Simmons	995
H. Louis Gehrig	1190	Albert W. Kaline	972
Frank Robinson	1186	Wilver D. Stargell	953
Carl M. Yastrzemski	1157	Mickey C. Mantle	952
Tyrus R. Cobb	*1139	Billy L. Williams	948
Tristram Speaker	1132	Edwin L. Mathews	938
James E. Foxx	1117	Atanasio R. Perez	925
Theodore S. Williams	1117	Leon A. Goslin	921
Melvin T. Ott	1071	Willie L. McCovey	920
Rogers Hornsby	1011	Reginald M. Jackson	915

PLAYERS WITH 800 OR MORE LONG HITS (DOUBLES, TRIPLES, HOMERS (43)—Continued

Player	Long Hits	Player	Long Hits
Paul G. Waner	909	Edwin D. Snider	850
Charles L. Gehringer	904	Roberto W. Clemente	846
Napoleon Lajoie	898	James L. Bottomley	835
Harmon C. Killebrew	887	Daniel J. Staub	829
Joseph P. DiMaggio	881	Orlando M. Cepeda	823
Harry E. Heilmann	876	Brooks C. Robinson	818
Vada E. Pinson	868	John R. Mize	809
Samuel E. Crawford	862	Joseph E. Cronin	803
Joseph M. Medwick	858		

*Total in dispute. See explanation on Page 3.

PLAYERS WITH 1,400 OR MORE EXTRA BASES ON LONG HITS (54)

Player	Extra Bases	Player	Extra Bases
Henry L. Aaron	3085	Johnny L. Bench	1596
George H. Ruth	2920	Leon A. Goslin	1590
Willie H. Mays	2783	Tristram Speaker	1588
Stanley F. Musial	2504	Michael J. Schmidt	1532
Frank Robinson	2430	Richard A. Allen	1531
H. Louis Gehrig	2338	Ronald E. Santo	1525
James E. Foxx	2310	Henry B. Greenberg	1514
Theodore S. Williams	2230	Vada E. Pinson	1507
Melvin T. Ott	2165	Gilbert R. Hodges	1501
Ernest Banks	2123	Lawrence P. Berra	1493
Carl M. Yastrzemski	2120	Roberto W. Clemente	1492
Mickey C. Mantle	2096	Lee A. May	1464
Harmon C. Killebrew	2057	Frank O. Howard	1461
Edwin L. Mathews	2034	John P. Wagner	1458
Willie L. McCovey	2008	Daniel J. Staub	1456
Wilver D. Stargell	1958	Norman D. Cash	1454
Reginald M. Jackson	1915	Robert L. Johnson	1450
Billy L. Williams	1888	Rocco D. Colavito	1447
Albert W. Kaline	1845	Charles L. Klein	1446
Rogers Hornsby	1782	Peter E. Rose	1443
Aloysius H. Simmons	1758	Bobby L. Bonds	1430
Edwin D. Snider	1749	James L. Bottomley	1424
Atanasio R. Perez	1740	Brooks C. Robinson	1422
Joseph P. DiMaggio	1734	C. Reginald Smith	1419
Tyrus R. Cobb	*1672	Charles L. Gehringer	1418
John R. Mize	1610	Joe L. Morgan	1406
Orlando M. Cepeda	1608	Ralph M. Kiner	1401

*Total in dispute. See explanation on Page 3.

PLAYERS WITH 1,200 OR MORE RUNS BATTED IN (57)

Player	R.B.I.	Player	R.B.I.
Henry L. Aaron	2297	Leon A. Goslin	1609
George H. Ruth	2204	Harmon C. Killebrew	1584
H. Louis Gehrig	1990	Albert W. Kaline	1583
Tyrus R. Cobb	1960	Rogers Hornsby	1579
Stanley F. Musial	1951	Atanasio R. Perez	1575
James E. Foxx	1921	Tristram Speaker	1562
Willie H. Mays	1903	Willie L. McCovey	1555
Melvin T. Ott	1860	Harry E. Heilmann	1551
Carl M. Yastrzemski	1844	Wilver D. Stargell	1540
Theodore S. Williams	1839	Joseph P. DiMaggio	1537
Aloysius H. Simmons	1827	Mickey C. Mantle	1509
Frank Robinson	1812	Billy L. Williams	1476
Ernest Banks	1636	Edwin L. Mathews	1453

Player	RBI.	Player	RBI.
Daniel J. Staub	1440	Roberto W. Clemente	1305
Reginald M. Jackson	1435	Enos B. Slaughter	1304
Lawrence P. Berra	1430	Delmer Ennis	1284
Charles L. Gehringer	1427	Robert L. Johnson	1283
Joseph E. Cronin	1423	Henry B. Greenberg	1276
James L. Bottomley	1422	Gilbert R. Hodges	1274
Joseph M. Medwick	1383	Harold J. Traynor	1273
Johnny L. Bench	1376	Zachariah D. Wheat	1265
Orlando M. Cepeda	1365	Robert P. Doerr	1247
Brooks C. Robinson	1357	Albert Oliver	1247
John R. Mize	1337	Lee A. May	1244
Edwin D. Snider	1333	Frank F. Frisch	1242
Ronald E. Santo	1331	William M. Dickey	1209
James B. Vernon	1311	Peter E. Rose	1209
Paul G. Waner	1309	Charles H. Klein	1201
Edward T. Collins	1307		

PLAYERS WITH 400 OR MORE STOLEN BASES (52)

Player	SB.	Player	SB.
Louis C. Brock	938	Cesar Cedeno	516
William R. Hamilton	937	Thomas F. M. McCarthy	506
Tyrus R. Cobb	892	Luis E. Aparicio	506
Walter A. Latham	791	J. Clyde Milan	495
Harry D. Stovey	744	Edward J. Delahanty	478
Edward T. Collins	743	James T. Sheckard	475
Max G. Carey	738	David E. Lopes	468
John P. Wagner	720	Bobby L. Bonds	461
Thomas T. Brown	697	Joseph J. Kelley	458
Joe L. Morgan	681	Ronald LeFlore	455
Dagoberto B. Campaneris	649	William A. Lange	453
George S. Davis	632	Michael J. Tiernan	449
William E. Hoy	605	Omar R. Moreno	449
John M. Ward	605	John J. McGraw	444
John A. McPhee	602	Sherwood R. Magee	441
Hugh A. Duffy	597	Charles A. Comiskey	440
William F. Dahlen	587	James E. Ryan	434
Maurice M. Wills	586	Tristram Speaker	433
John J. Doyle	560	Robert H. Bescher	428
Herman C. Long	554	Rickey H. Henderson	427
Michael J. Griffin	549	Thomas W. Corcoran	420
George E. Van Haltren	537	Frank F. Frisch	419
Patrick J. Donovan	531	Tommy Harper	408
Frederick C. Clarke	527	Thomas P. Daly	407
Curtis B. Welch	526	Owen J. Bush	405
William H. Keeler	519	Frank L. Chance	405

PLAYERS WITH TEN OR MORE STEALS OF HOME (31)

Player	Steals of home	Player	Steals of home
Tyrus R. Cobb	35	Max G. Carey	14
George J. Burns	27	W. Benjamin Chapman	14
Frank Schulte	22	Frederick C. Maisel	14
John J. Evers	21	Henry Zimmerman	13
Jack R. Robinson	19	Harry B. Hooper	11
Frank F. Frisch	19	George J. Moriarty	11
George H. Sisler	19	Robert F. Roth	11
James T. Sheckard	18	Fred C. Merkle	11
Edward T. Collins	17	John F. Collins	10
Joseph B. Tinker	17	Charles L. Herzog	10
Lawrence J. Doyle	17	Edgar C. Rice	10
Rodney C. Carew	17	George H. Ruth	10
Tristram Speaker	15	Ross M. Youngs	10
H. Louis Gehrig	15	James H. Johnston	10
Victor S. Saier	14	William M. Werber	10
John P. Wagner	14		

PLAYERS WITH 1,000 OR MORE BASES ON BALLS (49)

(Does not include any seasons in National League before 1910 and in American League prior to 1913)

Player	BB.	Player	BB.
George H. Ruth	2056	Charles L. Gehringer	1185
Theodore S. Williams	2019	Max F. Bishop	1153
Carl M. Yastrzemski	1845	Tristram Speaker	1146
Joe L. Morgan	1799	Darrell W. Evans	1127
Mickey C. Mantle	1734	Reginald M. Jackson	1118
Melvin T. Ott	1708	Ronald E. Santo	1108
Edward F. Yost	1614	Luzerne A. Blue	1092
Stanley F. Musial	1599	Stanley C. Hack	1092
Harmon C. Killebrew	1559	Paul G. Waner	1091
H. Louis Gehrig	1508	Michael J. Schmidt	1086
Willie H. Mays	1464	Robert L. Johnson	1073
James E. Foxx	1452	Harlond B. Clift	1070
Edwin L. Mathews	1444	Joseph E. Cronin	1059
Frank Robinson	1420	Ronald R. Fairly	1052
Peter E. Rose	1410	Billy L. Williams	1045
Henry L. Aaron	1402	Norman D. Cash	1043
Willie D. McCovey	1345	Edwin D. Joost	1041
Lucius B. Appling	1302	Max Carey	1040
Albert W. Kaline	1277	Rogers Hornsby	1038
Daniel J. Staub	1241	James Gilliam	1036
Kenneth W. Singleton	1225	Salvatore L. Bando	1031
James S. Wynn	1224	Enos B. Slaughter	1018
Edward T. Collins	1213	Ralph M. Kiner	1011
Harold H. Reese	1210	John W. Powell	1001
Richie Ashburn	1198		

PLAYERS WITH 1,000 OR MORE STRIKEOUTS (57)

Player	SO.	Player	SO.
Reginald M. Jackson	2106	Ernest Banks	1236
Wilver D. Stargell	1936	Roberto W. Clemente	1230
Atanasio R. Perez	1799	John W. Powell	1226
Bobby L. Bonds	1757	Vada E. Pinson	1196
Louis C. Brock	1730	Kenneth W. Singleton	1186
Mickey C. Mantle	1710	Orlando M. Cepeda	1169
Harmon C. Killebrew	1699	George A. Foster	1149
Lee A. May	1570	Dagoberto B. Campaneris	1142
Richard A. Allen	1556	Donn A. Clendenon	1140
Willie D. McCovey	1550	Gilbert R. Hodges	1137
Frank Robinson	1532	Leonardo A. Cardenas	1135
Willie H. Mays	1526	Robert S. Bailey	1126
Robert J. Monday	1497	C. Reginald Smith	1103
Edwin L. Mathews	1487	James L. Fregosi	1097
Frank O. Howard	1460	Joseph P. Torre	1094
David A. Kingman	1457	Norman D. Cash	1091
James S. Wynn	1427	Antonio Taylor	1083
Michael J. Schmidt	1427	Tommy Harper	1080
George C. Scott	1418	Robert A. Grich	1077
Gregory M. Luzinski	1415	John W. Callison	1064
Carl M. Yastrzemski	1393	Joseph W. Adcock	1059
Henry L. Aaron	1383	Douglas L. Rader	1057
Ronald E. Santo	1343	Peter E. Rose	1050
George H. Ruth	1330	Billy L. Williams	1046
Deron R. Johnson	1318	W. Robert Allison	1033
Willie W. Horton	1313	Albert W. Kaline	1020
James E. Foxx	1311	Kenton L. Boyer	1017
Johnny L. Bench	1278	Lawrence E. Doby	1011
Edwin D. Snider	1237		

PITCHERS WITH 600 OR MORE GAMES PITCHED (64)
OR 20 YEARS OF SERVICE (25)

Pitcher	Yrs.	G.	Pitcher	Yrs.	G.
J. Hoyt Wilhelm	21	1070	Albert W. Lyle	16	899
Lyndall D. McDaniel	21	987	James L. Kaat	25	898
Denton T. Young	22	906	Donald J. McMahon	18	874

Pitcher	Yrs.	G.
Roland G. Fingers	15	864
El Roy Face	16	848
Walter P. Johnson	21	802
Frank E. McGraw	18	799
Gaylord J. Perry	22	777
Darold D. Knowles	16	765
Warren E. Spahn	21	750
Philip H. Niekro	20	739
Ronald P. Perranoski	13	737
Ronald L. Kline	17	736
Clay P. Carroll	15	731
Thomas H. Burgmeier	16	728
Michael G. Marshall	14	723
John C. Klippstein	18	711
Stuart L. Miller	16	704
Ronald L. Reed	18	700
James F. Galvin	14	697
Grover C. Alexander	20	696
Robert L. Miller	17	694
Eppa Rixey	21	692
Grant D. Jackson	18	692
Early Wynn	23	691
Eddie G. Fisher	15	690
Theodore W. Abernathy	14	681
Robin E. Roberts	19	676
Waite C. Hoyt	21	675
Urban C. Faber	20	669
David J. Giusti	15	668
John P. Quinn	21	665
Ferguson A. Jenkins	19	664
H. Eugene Garber	14	661
Paul A. Lindblad	14	655
Wilbur F. Wood	18	651
Samuel P. Jones	22	647
David E. LaRoche	14	647
Kenton C. Tekulve	10	647
Emil J. Leonard	20	640
Gerald L. Staley	15	640
Diego P. Segui	15	639
Christopher Mathewson	17	635
Charles H. Root	17	632
James E. Perry	17	630
S. Lewis Burdette	18	626
Murry M. Dickson	18	625
Woodrow T. Fryman	18	625
Charles H. Ruffing	22	624
Steven N. Carlton	19	624
Donald H. Sutton	18	622
Charles A. Nichols	15	620
Herbert J. Pennock	22	617
Robert M. Grove	17	616
Burleigh A. Grimes	19	615
Thomas E. John	21	614
Richard W. Tidrow	12	609
Robert B. Friend	16	602
Allan F. Worthington	14	602
Elias Sosa	12	601
Louis N. Newsom	20	600
Theodore A. Lyons	21	594
Melvin L. Harder	20	582
Curtis T. Simmons	20	569
Adolfo Luque	20	550
Clark C. Griffith	20	416

PITCHERS WITH 500 OR MORE GAMES STARTED (28)

Pitcher	Games Started
Denton T. Young	818
Gaylord J. Perry	690
James F. Galvin	682
Walter P. Johnson	666
Warren E. Spahn	665
James L. Kaat	625
Early Wynn	612
Robin E. Roberts	609
Steven N. Carlton	606
Donald H. Sutton	605
Grover C. Alexander	598
Ferguson A. Jenkins	594
Philip H. Niekro	594
Timothy J. Keefe	593
Thomas E. John	569
Charles A. Nichols	561
G. Thomas Seaver	553
Eppa Rixey	552
Christopher Mathewson	551
Michael F. Welch	549
Charles H. Ruffing	536
James P. Bunning	519
John G. Clarkson	518
James A. Palmer	518
John J. Powell	517
Anthony J. Mullane	505
August Weyhing	503
Charles Radbourn	503

PITCHERS WITH 250 OR MORE COMPLETE GAMES PITCHED (76)

Pitcher	Complete Games
Denton T. Young	751
James F. Galvin	641
Timothy J. Keefe	554
Walter P. Johnson	531
Charles A. Nichols	531
Michael F. Welch	526
John G. Clarkson	485
Charles G. Radbourn	479
Anthony J. Mullane	464
James McCormick	462
August J. Weyhing	448
Grover C. Alexander	436
Christopher Mathewson	434
John J. Powell	422
William H. White	394
Amos W. Rusie	391
Victor G. Willis	387
Edward S. Plank	387
Warren E. Spahn	382
James E. Whitney	373
William J. Terry	368
Theodore A. Lyons	356
Charles G. Buffinton	350
Charles C. Fraser	342
George E. Mullin	339
Clark C. Griffith	337
Charles H. Ruffing	335
Charles F. King	327
Albert L. Orth	323
William F. Hutchinson	321
Burleigh A. Grimes	314
Joseph J. McGinnity	314

PITCHERS WITH 250 OR MORE COMPLETE GAMES —Continued

Pitcher	Complete Games	Pitcher	Complete Games
Frank L. Donahue	312	John J. McMahon	277
Guy J. Hecker	310	Charles H. Getzein	277
William H. Dinneen	305	Urban C. Faber	275
Robin E. Roberts	305	John F. Dwyer	270
Gaylord J. Perry	303	Jouett Meekin	270
Theodore P. Breitenstein	300	Ferguson A. Jenkins	267
Robert M. Grove	300	Jesse N. Tannehill	266
Robert L. Caruthers	299	Elton P. Chamberlain	264
Emerson P. Hawley	297	Matthew A. Kilroy	264
William V. Kennedy	297	Guy H. White	262
Edward Morris.	297	John D. Chesbro	261
Marcus E. Baldwin	296	George E. Waddell	261
Thomas H. Bond	294	Philip H. Ehret	260
William E. Donovan	290	Carl O. Hubbell	258
Eppa Rixey	290	Lawrence J. Corcoran	256
Early Wynn	290	Robert Gibson	255
Robert T. Mathews	289	Frank B. Killen	253
Ellsworth E. Cunningham	286	George B. Mercer	252
John C. Stivetts	281	Paul M. Derringer	251
A. Wilbur Cooper	279	Samuel P. Jones	250
Robert W. Feller	279	Edward A. Walsh	250
John W. Taylor	278	Steven N. Carlton	250

PITCHERS WITH 3500 OR MORE INNINGS PITCHED (52)

Pitcher	Innings	Pitcher	Innings
Denton T. Young	7377	Burleigh A. Grimes	4178
James F. Galvin	5959	Theodore A. Lyons	4162
Walter P. Johnson	5924	G. Thomas Seaver	4130⅓
Gaylord J. Perry	5352	Urban C. Faber	4087
Warren E. Spahn	5246	Victor G. Willis	3994
Grover C. Alexander	5188	Thomas E. John	3941⅓
Charles A. Nichols	5067	Robert M. Grove	3940
Timothy J. Keefe	5043	James A. Palmer	3929⅔
Michael F. Welch	4794	Robert Gibson	3885
Christopher Mathewson	4781	Samuel P. Jones	3884
Robin E. Roberts	4689	Robert W. Feller	3828
Philip H. Niekro	4619	Waite C. Hoyt	3762
Early Wynn	4566	James P. Bunning	3759
Steven N. Carlton	4557⅓	Louis N. Newsom	3758
Charles G. Radbourn	4543	Amos W. Rusie	3750
John G. Clarkson	4534	Paul M. Derringer	3646
James L. Kaat	4527⅔	Michael S. Lolich	3640
Anthony J. Mullane	4506	Robert B. Friend	3612
Ferguson A. Jenkins	4498⅔	Carl O. Hubbell	3591
Eppa Rixey	4494	Herbert J. Pennock	3572
John J. Powell	4390	Earl O. Whitehill	3563
Donald H. Sutton	4357	William H. White	3543
Charles H. Ruffing	4342	William J. Terry	3523
August P. Weyhing	4335	L. Nolan Ryan	3521⅔
James McCormick	4264	Jerry M. Koosman	3516
Edward S. Plank	4234	Juan A. Marichal	3506

PITCHERS WITH 1500 OR MORE RUNS ALLOWED (55)

Pitcher	Runs	Pitcher	Runs
James F. Galvin	3303	Early Wynn	2037
Denton T. Young	3168	Earl O. Whitehill	2018
August P. Weyhing	2770	Warren E. Spahn	2016
Michael F. Welch	2555	Samuel P. Jones	2008
Charles A. Nichols	2477	Eppa Rixey	1986
Timothy J. Keefe	2461	Charles C. Fraser	1984
John G. Clarkson	2396	John Powell	1976
Charles G. Radbourn	2300	Robin E. Roberts	1962
Gaylord J. Perry	2128	Philip H. Niekro	1917
Charles H. Ruffing	2117	Amos W. Rusie	1908
Theodore A. Lyons	2056	Louis N. Newsom	1908
Burleigh A. Grimes	2048	Walter P. Johnson	1902
James L. Kaat	2038	Ferguson A. Jenkins	1853

Pitcher	Runs	Pitcher	Runs
Grover C. Alexander	1851	Christopher Mathewson	1613
Charles F. King	1834	Irving D. Hadley	1609
Urban C. Faber	1813	George A. Dauss	1599
John E. Stivetts	1809	Thomas E. John	1598
Waite C. Hoyt	1780	Robert M. Grove	1594
Steven N. Carlton	1733	John P. Quinn	1569
Melvin L. Harder	1714	Robert W. Feller	1557
Albert L. Orth	1711	Jesse J. Haines	1556
Herbert J. Pennock	1699	Jonathan T. Zachary	1552
Donald H. Sutton	1662	Curtis T. Simmons	1551
Paul M. Derringer	1652	Michael S. Lolich	1537
Robert B. Friend	1652	James P. Bunning	1527
Victor G. Willis	1644	George E. Mullin	1507
Francis R. Donahue	1640	Fred L. Fitzsimmons	1505
George E. Uhle	1635		

PITCHERS WITH 4000 OR MORE HITS ALLOWED (28)

Pitcher	Hits	Pitcher	Hits
Denton T. Young	7078	Theodore A. Lyons	4489
James F. Galvin	*6334	Burleigh A. Grimes	4406
Gaylord J. Perry	4938	John G. Clarkson	*4376
Walter P. Johnson	4920	John J. Powell	4323
Grover C. Alexander	4868	Charles H. Ruffing	4294
Charles A. Nichols	4854	Early Wynn	4291
Warren E. Spahn	4830	Anthony J. Mullane	*4238
August P. Weyhing	*4669	Philip H. Niekro	4218
Michael F. Welch	*4646	Christopher Mathewson	4203
Eppa Rixey	4633	James McCormick	*4166
James L. Kaat	4620	Ferguson A. Jenkins	4142
Robin E. Roberts	4582	Urban C. Faber	4104
Timothy J. Keefe	*4524	Samuel P. Jones	4084
Charles Radbourn	*4500	Waite C. Hoyt	4037

*Includes 1887 bases on balls, scored as hits under rules in effect for that year.

PITCHERS WITH 200 OR MORE VICTORIES (82)

Pitcher	W.	L.	Pct.	Pitcher	W.	L.	Pct.
Denton T. Young	511	313	.620	Robert Gibson	251	174	.591
Walter P. Johnson	416	279	.599	Thomas E. John	248	184	.574
Christopher Mathewson	373	188	.665	Joseph J. McGinnity	247	145	.630
Grover C. Alexander	373	208	.642	John Powell	247	254	.493
Warren E. Spahn	363	245	.597	Victor G. Willis	244	204	.545
Charles A. Nichols	361	208	.634	Juan A. Marichal	243	142	.631
James F. Galvin	361	309	.539	Amos W. Rusie	241	158	.604
Timothy J. Keefe	342	224	.604	Clark C. Griffith	240	140	.632
John G. Clarkson	327	176	.650	Herbert J. Pennock	240	162	.597
Gaylord J. Perry	314	265	.542	Waite C. Hoyt	237	182	.566
Charles G. Radbourn	308	191	.617	Edward C. Ford	236	106	.690
Michael F. Welch	307	209	.595	Charles G. Buffinton	230	151	.604
Edward S. Plank	305	181	.628	Luis C. Tiant	229	172	.571
Robert M. Grove	300	141	.680	Samuel P. Jones	229	217	.513
Steven N. Carlton	300	200	.600	William H. White	227	167	.576
Early Wynn	300	244	.551	James A. Hunter	224	166	.574
Robin E. Roberts	286	245	.539	James P. Bunning	224	184	.549
Anthony J. Mullane	285	213	.572	Melvin L. Harder	223	186	.545
Ferguson A. Jenkins	284	226	.557	Paul Derringer	223	212	.513
James L. Kaat	283	237	.544	George Dauss	222	182	.550
G. Thomas Seaver	273	170	.616	L. Nolan Ryan	219	195	.529
Charles H. Ruffing	273	225	.548	Earl O. Whitehill	218	186	.540
Burleigh A. Grimes	270	212	.560	Robert L. Caruthers	217	101	.682
James A. Palmer	268	149	.643	Fred L. Fitzsimmons	217	146	.598
Philip H. Niekro	268	230	.538	Michael S. Lolich	217	191	.532
Robert W. Feller	266	162	.621	A. Wilbur Cooper	216	178	.548
Donald H. Sutton	266	206	.564	Stanley Coveleski	215	141	.604
Eppa Rixey	266	251	.515	James E. Perry	215	174	.553
James McCormick	265	215	.552	John P. Quinn	212	181	.539
August P. Weyhing	262	224	.539	George Mullin	212	181	.539
Theodore A. Lyons	260	230	.531	W. William Pierce	211	169	.555
Urban C. Faber	254	212	.545	Louis N. Newsom	211	222	.487
Carl O. Hubbell	253	154	.622	Edward V. Cicotte	210	149	.585

PITCHERS WITH 200 OR MORE VICTORIES—Continued

Pitcher	W.	L.	Pct.	Pitcher	W.	L.	Pct.
Jesse J. Haines	210	158	.571	Charles F. King	206	152	.575
Milton S. Pappas	209	164	.560	John E. Stivetts	205	128	.616
Donald S. Drysdale	209	166	.557	William J. Terry	205	197	.510
Mordecai P. Brown	208	111	.652	S. Lewis Burdette	203	144	.585
Charles A. Bender	208	112	.650	Jerry M. Koosman	202	190	.515
Carl W. Mays	208	126	.623	Charles H. Root	201	160	.557
Robert G. Lemon	207	128	.618	Richard W. Marquard	201	177	.532
Harold Newhouser	207	150	.580	George E. Uhle	200	166	.546

PITCHERS WITH 75 OR MORE SAVES (SINCE 1969) (32)

Pitcher	Saves	Pitcher	Saves
Roland G. Fingers	301	James T. Brewer	112
Albert W. Lyle	222	Darold D. Knowles	112
H. Bruce Sutter	215	Wayne A. Granger	104
Richard M. Gossage	206	Alan T. Hrabosky	97
Frank E. McGraw	179	Gregory B. Minton	96
Michael G. Marshall	178	Randall J. Moffitt	96
H. Eugene Garber	158	Thomas H. Burgmeier	95
Kenton C. Tekulve	145	Felix A. Martinez	93
J. David Giusti	140	Ronald L. Reed	91
Daniel R. Quisenberry	136	James L. Kern	88
David E. LaRoche	126	Elias Sosa	83
John F. Hiller	119	Kenneth G. Sanders	82
William R. Campbell	118	Thomas H. Hume	82
Terry J. Forster	116	Pedro R. Borbon	80
Gary R. Lavelle	115	Grant D. Jackson	77
Clay P. Carroll	113	Edward J. Farmer	75

ALL-TIME LEADERS IN 1-0 COMPLETE GAME VICTORIES (24) (10 OR MORE)

Pitcher	Games	Pitcher	Games
Walter P. Johnson	38	George N. Rucker	11
Grover C. Alexander	17	Charles A. Nichols	11
Christopher Mathewson	14	Ferguson A. Jenkins	11
Edward S. Plank	13	Leslie A. Bush	10
Edward A. Walsh	13	Paul Derringer	10
Guy Harris White	13	William L. Doak	10
Denton T. Young	13	Adrian C. Joss	10
W. Dean Chance	13	Richard Rudolph	10
Rikalbert Blyleven	13	James L. Vaughn	10
Stanley Coveleski	12	George A. Tyler	10
Gaylord J. Perry	12	Warren E. Spahn	10
Steven N. Carlton	12	Sanford Koufax	10

ALL-TIME LEADERS IN SHUTOUTS WON OR TIED (48) (40 OR MORE)

Pitcher	Games	Pitcher	Games
Walter P. Johnson	110	Early Wynn	49
Grover C. Alexander	90	Donald S. Drysdale	49
Christopher Mathewson	83	Luis C. Tiant	49
Denton T. Young	77	Ferguson A. Jenkins	49
Edward S. Plank	64	Charles A. Nichols	48
Warren E. Spahn	63	Charles B. Adams	46
Edward A. Walsh	58	John J. Powell	46
James F. Galvin	57	Guy Harris White	46
Robert Gibson	56	Charles H. Ruffing	46
Donald H. Sutton	56	Robert W. Feller	46
G. Thomas Seaver	56	Adrian C. Joss	45
Steven N. Carlton	55	Robin E. Roberts	45
James A. Palmer	53	Edward C. Ford	45
Gaylord J. Perry	53	Thomas E. John	44
Juan A. Marichal	52	Milton S. Pappas	43
L. Nolan Ryan	52	Philip H. Niekro	43
Mordecai P. Brown	50	William H. Walters	42
George E. Waddell	50	James A. Hunter	42
Victor G. Willis	50	Rikalbert Blyleven	42

Pitcher	Games	Pitcher	Games
Charles A. Bender	41	Sanford Koufax	40
Michael S. Lolich	41	James P. Bunning	40
James L. Vaughn	41	Melvin L. Stottlemyre	40
Michael Welch	41	Claude W. Osteen	40
Lawrence H. French	40	Timothy J. Keefe	40

PITCHERS WITH 1,200 OR MORE BASES ON BALLS (34)

Pitcher	BB.	Pitcher	BB.
L. Nolan Ryan	2022	Robert Gibson	1336
Early Wynn	1775	Charles C. Fraser	1332
Robert W. Feller	1764	Samuel E. McDowell	1312
Louis N. Newsom	1732	Michael F. Welch	1306
Amos W. Rusie	1637	Burleigh A. Grimes	1295
August P. Weyhing	1569	James A. Palmer	1294
Charles H. Ruffing	1541	Mark E. Baldwin	1285
Steven N. Carlton	1524	Allie P. Reynolds	1261
Philip H. Niekro	1452	Leslie A. Bush	1260
Irving G. Hadley	1442	Robert G. Lemon	1251
Warren E. Spahn	1434	Harold Newhouser	1249
Earl O. Whitehill	1431	Charles A. Nichols	1245
Samuel P. Jones	1396	William J. Terry	1244
Anthony J. Mullane	1379	Timothy J. Keefe	1225
Gaylord J. Perry	1379	Urban C. Faber	1213
Walter P. Johnson	1353	Denton T. Young	1209
Michael A. Torrez	1350	G. Thomas Seaver	1204

PITCHERS WITH 2,000 OR MORE STRIKEOUTS (35)

Pitchers	SO.	Pitcher	SO.
Steven N. Carlton	3709	James L. Kaat	2461
L. Nolan Ryan	3677	Samuel E. McDowell	2453
Gaylord J. Perry	3534	Luis C. Tiant	2416
Walter P. Johnson	3508	Sanford Koufax	2396
G. Thomas Seaver	3272	Jerry M. Koosman	2359
Ferguson A. Jenkins	3192	Robin E. Roberts	2357
Robert Gibson	3117	Early Wynn	2334
Donald H. Sutton	3065	George E. Waddell	2310
Philip H. Niekro	2912	Juan A. Marichal	2303
James P. Bunning	2855	Robert M. Grove	2266
Michael S. Lolich	2832	James A. Palmer	2208
Denton T. Young	2819	Grover C. Alexander	2198
Warren E. Spahn	2583	Camilo A. Pascual	2167
Robert W. Feller	2581	Edward S. Plank	2112
Timothy J. Keefe	2538	Louis N. Newsom	2082
Christopher Mathewson	2505	Arthur C. Vance	2045
Rikalbert Blyleven	2499	James A. Hunter	2012
Donald S. Drysdale	2486		

PITCHERS WITH 20 OR MORE VICTORIES, FIVE OR MORE YEARS (52)

Pitcher	Years	Pitcher	Years
Denton T. Young	16	Charles G. Buffinton	7
Christopher Mathewson	13	Clark C. Griffith	7
Warren E. Spahn	13	Timothy J. Keefe	7
Walter P. Johnson	12	Robert G. Lemon	7
Charles A. Nichols	11	Edward S. Plank	7
James F. Galvin	10	August Weyhing	7
Grover C. Alexander	9	Victor G. Willis	7
Charles Radbourn	9	Ferguson A. Jenkins	7
Michael F. Welch	9	Mordecai P. Brown	6
John G. Clarkson	8	Robert L. Caruthers	6
Robert M. Grove	8	Robert W. Feller	6
James McCormick	8	Wesley C. Ferrell	6
Joseph J. McGinnity	8	Juan A. Marichal	6
Anthony J. Mullane	8	Robin E. Roberts	6
Amos W. Rusie	8	Jesse N. Tannehill	6
James A. Palmer	8	Steven N. Carlton	6

PITCHERS WITH 20 OR MORE VICTORIES, FIVE OR MORE YEARS (52)—Continued

Pitcher	Years	Pitcher	Years
Thomas H. Bond	5	George E. Mullin	5
John D. Chesbro	5	Charles L. Phillippe	5
Lawrence J. Corcoran	5	John C. Stivetts	5
Stanley Coveleski	5	James L. Vaughn	5
Robert Gibson	5	William H. White	5
Burleigh A. Grimes	5	James E. Whitney	5
Carl O. Hubbell	5	Early Wynn	5
Charles F. King	5	James A. Hunter	5
John J. McMahon	5	G. Thomas Seaver	5
Carl W. Mays	5	Gaylord J. Perry	5

PITCHERS WITH 30 OR MORE VICTORIES, TWO OR MORE YEARS (32)

Pitcher	Years	Pitcher	Years
Charles A. Nichols	7	Grover C. Alexander	3
John G. Clarkson	6	Edward Morris	3
Timothy J. Keefe	6	Charles Radbourn	3
Anthony J. Mullane	5	Amos W. Rusie	3
Denton T. Young	5	George S. Haddock	2
Thomas H. Bond	4	Walter P. Johnson	2
Lawrence J. Corcoran	4	Guy J. Hecker	2
James McCormick	4	David L. Foutz	2
Christopher Mathewson	4	Frank B. Killen	2
Charles F. King	4	Joseph J. McGinnity	2
William H. White	4	John J. McMahon	2
Michael F. Welch	4	John M. Ward	2
James F. Galvin	3	John C. Stivetts	2
William F. Hutchison	3	Thomas A. Ramsey	2
Robert L. Caruthers	3	August Weyhing	2
Robert T. Mathews	3	James E. Whitney	2

PITCHERS ALLOWING SEVEN OR MORE HOME RUNS WITH BASES FILLED (18)

Pitcher	Total	Pitcher	Years
Ned F. Garver	9	James T. Brewer	8
Milton S. Pappas	9	Frank E. McGraw	8
Lyndall D. McDaniel	9	Lawrence H. French	7
Jerry Reuss	9	James T. Hearn	7
James L. Kaat	9	John S. Sanford	7
El Roy L. Face	8	Lonnie Warneke	7
Robert W. Feller	8	Raymond M. Sadecki	7
Early Wynn	8	Gaylord J. Perry	7
John C. Klippstein	8	Michael A. Torrez	7

LIFETIME EARNED-RUN AVERAGES BELOW 3.50

Pitchers with 3,000 or More Innings Pitched (46)

National League 1912 to date
American League 1913 to date

	IP.	ER.	ERA.
(a) Walter P. Johnson	4195	1103	2.37
(b) Grover C. Alexander	4822	1372	2.56
G. Thomas Seaver	4130⅓	1254	2.73
Edward C. Ford	3171	967	2.74
James A. Palmer	3929⅔	1235	2.83
Stanley Coveleski	3071	982	2.88
Juan A. Marichal	3506	1126	2.89
A. Wilbur Cooper	3482	1119	2.89
Robert Gibson	3885	1258	2.91
Carl W. Mays	3022	979	2.92
Donald S. Drysdale	3432	1124	2.95
Carl O. Hubbell	3591	1188	2.98
Rikalbert Blyleven	3177⅔	1063	3.01

	IP.	ER.	ERA.
Steven N. Carlton	4557⅓	1524	3.01
Robert M. Grove	3940	1339	3.06
Warren E. Spahn	5246	1798	3.08
Gaylord J. Perry	5352	1846	3.10
L. Nolan Ryan	3521⅔	1214	3.11
Donald H. Sutton	4357	1504	3.11
Thomas E. John	3941⅓	1369	3.13
Eppa Rixey	4494	1572	3.15
Urban C. Faber	4087	1430	3.15
Philip H. Niekro	4619	1640	3.20
Vida R. Blue	3056⅓	1091	3.21
Adolfo Luque	3221	1161	3.24
Robert W. Feller	3828	1384	3.25
Emil J. Leonard	3220	1162	3.25
James A. Hunter	3449	1248	3.26
James P. Bunning	3759	1366	3.27
W. William Pierce	3305	1201	3.27
Luis C. Tiant	3485⅔	1280	3.30
William H. Walters	3104	1139	3.30
Claude W. Osteen	3459	1268	3.30
George Dauss	3374	1244	3.32
Jerry M. Koosman	3516	1301	3.33
Ferguson A. Jenkins	4498⅔	1669	3.34
H. Lee Meadows	3151	1185	3.38
Robin E. Roberts	4689	1774	3.40
Lawrence C. Jackson	3262	1233	3.40
Milton S. Pappas	3186	1203	3.40
Michael S. Lolich	3640	1390	3.44
Lawrence H. French	3152	1206	3.44
James E. Perry	3287	1258	3.44
James L. Kaat	4527⅔	1738	3.46
Paul M. Derringer	3646	1401	3.46
Leslie A. Bush	3088	1193	3.49

(a) Does not include 1729 innings pitched 1907 through 1912; allowed 520 total runs in that period; earned-run total not available and if all the 520 runs were included in Johnson's earned-run total, his career earned-run average would be 2.47.

(b) Does not include 367 innings pitched in 1911; allowed 133 total runs in that year; earned-run total not available.

Roll Call of Majors' No-Hitters

National League, 112; American League, 87

(H)—Home.   (A)—Away.

PERFECT GAMES—NINE OR MORE INNINGS

Twelve perfect games have been pitched in major championship play including one in the 1956 World Series by Don Larsen of the New York Yankees and Harvey Haddix' 12-inning effort for Pittsburgh in 1959. The perfect games follow, with the letter in parentheses after the date indicating home or away:

Year	Score
1880—John Richmond, Worcester vs. Cleveland, N. L., June 12 (H)	1—0
John Ward, Providence vs. Buffalo, N. L., June 17 (H)	5—0
1904—Denton (Cy) Young, Boston vs. Philadelphia, A. L., May 5 (H)	3—0
1908—Adrian Joss, Cleveland vs. Chicago, A. L., October 2 (H)	1—0
1917—Ernest Shore, Boston vs. Washington, A. L., June 23, first game (H)	*4—0
1922—Charles Robertson, Chicago vs. Detroit, A. L., April 30 (A)	2—0
1956—Don Larsen, New York A. L., vs. Brooklyn N. L. (World Series), October 8 (H)	2—0
1959—Harvey Haddix, Pittsburgh vs. Milwaukee, N. L., May 26, night (A). (Pitched 12 perfect innings before Felix Mantilla, leading off in thirteenth, reached base on third baseman Don Hoak's throwing error. After Ed Mathews sacrificed and Hank Aaron was walked intentionally, Joe Adcock doubled to score Mantilla, ending the game)	0—1
1964—James Bunning, Philadelphia vs. New York, N. L., June 21, first game (A)	6—0
1965—Sanford Koufax, Los Angeles vs. Chicago, N. L., Sept. 9 (H)	1—0
1968—James A. Hunter, Oakland vs. Minnesota, A. L., May 8 (H)	4—0
1981—Leonard H. Barker, Cleveland vs. Toronto, A.L., May 15 (H)	3—0

*Shore's performance is classified as a perfect game even though he did not start the game. George (Babe) Ruth, Boston's starting pitcher was removed by Umpire Clarence (Brick) Owens after giving a base on balls to Ray Morgan, the first batter. Shore, without warming up, took Ruth's place. Morgan was retired trying to steal second. From then on, Shore faced 26 batters, with none reaching base.

NO-HIT GAMES—TEN OR MORE INNINGS

	Score
1884—Samuel Kimber, Brooklyn vs. Toledo, A. A., October 4 (H). (Game called in the eleventh on account of darkness.)	0—0
1906—Harry McIntire, Brooklyn vs. Pittsburgh, N. L., August 1 (H). (Pitched ten and two-thirds hitless innings before Claude Ritchey singled; lost on four hits in 13 innings.)	0—1
1908—George Wiltse, New York vs. Philadelphia, N. L., July 4, a.m. game, (H) (10 innings)	1—0
1917—Frederick Toney, Cincinnati vs. Chicago, N. L., May 2 (A). (James Vaughn, Chicago, pitched nine and one-third no-hit innings in the same game.)	1—0
1965—James Maloney, Cincinnati vs. New York, N. L., June 14 (H) (Pitched ten hitless innings before Johnny Lewis homered to lead off in eleventh; lost on two hits in 11 innings.)	0—1
James Maloney, Cincinnati vs. Chicago, N. L., August 19, first game (A) (10 innings)	1—0

NO HIT GAMES—NINE INNINGS

Year	Score
1876—George Bradley, St. Louis vs. Hartford, N. L., July 15 (H)	2—0
1880—Lawrence Corcoran, Chicago vs. Boston, N. L., August 19 (H)	6—0
James Galvin, Buffalo vs. Worcester, N. L., August 20 (A)	1—0
1882—Anthony Mullane, Louisville vs. Cincinnati, A. A., September 11 (A) (first at 50-foot distance)	2—0
Guy Hecker, Louisville vs. Pittsburgh, A. A., September 19 (A)	3—1
Lawrence Corcoran, Chicago vs. Worcester, N. L., Sept. 20 (H)	5—0
1883—Charles Radbourn, Providence vs. Cleveland, N. L., July 25 (A)	8—0
Hugh Daly, Cleveland vs. Philadelphia, N. L., September 13 (A)	1—0
1884—Albert Atkisson, Philadelphia vs. Pittsburgh, A. A., May 24 (H)	10—1
Edward Morris, Columbus vs. Pittsburgh, A. A., May 29 (A)	5—0
Frank Mountain, Columbus vs. Washington, A. A., June 5 (A)	12—0

Lawrence Corcoran, Chicago vs. Providence, N. L., June 27 (H) .... 6—0
James Galvin, Buffalo vs. Detroit, N. L., August 4 (A) .... 18—0
Richard Burns, Cincinnati vs. Kansas City, U. A., August 26 (A) .... 3—1
Edward Cushman, Milwaukee vs. Washington, U. A., Sept. 28 (H) .... 5—0
1885—John Clarkson, Chicago vs. Providence, N. L., July 27 (A) .... 4—0
    Charles Ferguson, Philadelphia vs. Providence, N. L., August 29 (H) .... 1—0
1886—Albert Atkisson, Philadelphia vs. New York, A. A., May 1 (H) .... 3—2
    William Terry, Brooklyn vs. St. Louis, A. A., July 24 (H) .... 1—0
    Matthew Kilroy, Baltimore vs. Pittsburgh, A. A., October 6 (A) .... 6—0
1888—William Terry, Brooklyn vs. Louisville, A. A., May 27 (H) .... 4—0
    Henry Porter, Kansas City vs. Baltimore, A. A., June 6 (A) .... 4—0
    Edward Seward, Philadelphia vs. Cincinnati, A. A., July 26 (H) .... 12—2
    August Weyhing, Philadelphia vs. Kansas City, A. A., July 31 (H) .... 4—0
1890—Ledell Titcomb, Rochester vs. Syracuse, A. A., September 15 (H) .... 7—0
1891—Thomas Lovett, Brooklyn vs. New York, N. L., June 22 (H) .... 4—0
    Amos Rusie, New York vs. Brooklyn, N. L., July 31 (H) .... 6—0
    Theodore Breitenstein, St. Louis vs. Louisville, A. A., October 4,
      first game (H) (first game he started in majors) .... 8—0
1892—John Stivetts, Boston vs. Brooklyn, N. L., August 6 (H) .... 11—0
    Alex Sanders, Louisville vs. Baltimore, N. L., August 22 (H) .... 6—2
    Charles Jones, Cincinnati vs. Pittsburgh, N. L., October 15 (H)
      (his first game in National League) .... 7—1
1893—William Hawke, Baltimore vs. Washington, N. L., August 16 (H)
      (first at 60-foot-six-inch distance.) .... 5—0
1897—Denton (Cy) Young, Cleveland vs. Cincinnati, N. L., September 18,
      first game (H) .... 6—0
1898—Theodore Breitenstein, Cincinnati vs. Pittsburgh, N. L., April 22 (H) .... 11—0
    James Hughes, Baltimore vs. Boston, N. L., April 22 (H) .... 8—0
    Frank Donohue, Philadelphia vs. Boston, N. L., July 8 (H) .... 5—0
    Walter Thornton, Chicago vs. Brooklyn, N. L., August 21, second
      game (H) .... 2—0
1899—Charles (Deacon) Phillippe, Louisville vs. New York, N. L., May 25 (H) .... 7—0
    Victor Willis, Boston vs. Washington, N. L., August 7 (H) .... 7—1
1900—Frank Hahn, Cincinnati vs. Philadelphia, N. L., July 12 (H) .... 4—0
1901—Christopher Mathewson, New York vs. St. Louis, N. L., July 15 (A) .... 5—0
    Earl Moore, Cleveland vs. Chicago, A. L., May 9 (H) (Pitched nine hitless
      innings before Samuel B. Mertes singled; lost on two hits in ten innings.) ... 2—4
1902—James Callahan, Chicago vs. Detroit, A. L., September 20, first game (H) ..... 3—0
1903—Charles (Chic) Fraser, Philadelphia vs. Chicago, N. L., September 18,
      second game (A) .... 10—0
1904—Robert Wicker, Chicago vs. New York, N. L., June 11 (A) (Pitched nine and
      one-third hitless innings before Samuel B. Mertes singled; won on one hit
      in 12 innings.) .... 1—0
    Jesse Tannehill, Boston vs. Chicago, A. L., August 17 (A) .... 6—0
1905—Christopher Mathewson, New York vs. Chicago, N. L., June 13 (A) .... 1—0
    Weldon Henley, Philadelphia vs. St. Louis, A. L., July 22, first game (A) .... 6—0
    Frank Smith, Chicago vs. Detroit, A. L., Sept. 6, second game (A) .... 15—0
    William Dinneen, Boston vs. Chicago, A. L., September 27, first game (H) .... 2—0
1906—John Lush, Philadelphia vs. Brooklyn, N. L., May 1 (A) .... 6—0
    Malcolm Eason, Brooklyn vs. St. Louis, N. L., July 20 (A) .... 2—0
1907—Frank Pfeffer, Boston vs. Cincinnati, N. L., May 8 (H) .... 6—0
    Nicholas Maddox, Pittsburgh vs. Brooklyn, N. L., Sept. 20 (H) .... 2—1
1908—Denton (Cy) Young, Boston vs. New York, A. L., June 30 (A) .... 8—0
    George (Nap) Rucker, Brooklyn vs. Boston, N. L., September 5,
      second game (H) .... 6—0
    Robert (Dusty) Rhoades, Cleveland vs. Boston, A. L., Septem-
      ber 18 (H) .... 2—1
    Frank Smith, Chicago vs. Philadelphia, A. L., September 20 (H) .... 1—0
1909—Leon Ames, New York vs. Brooklyn, N. L., April 15 (H) (Giants' opening
      game.) Ames pitched nine and one-third hitless innings before Charles Al-
      perman singled; lost on seven hits in 13 innings .... 0—3
1910—Adrian Joss, Cleveland vs. Chicago, A. L., April 20 (A) .... 1—0
    C. A. (Chief) Bender, Philadelphia vs. Cleveland A. L., May 12 (H) .... 4—0
    Thomas Hughes, New York vs. Cleveland, A. L., August 30, second
      game (H) (Pitched nine and one-third hitless innings before Harry
      Niles singled; lost on seven hits in 11 innings.) .... 0—5

1911—Joseph Wood, Boston vs. St. Louis, A. L., July 29, first game (H) .... 5—0
    Edward Walsh, Chicago vs. Boston, A. L., August 27 (H) .... 5—0
1912—George Mullin, Detroit vs. St. Louis, A. L., July 4 p.m. (H) .... 7—0
    Earl Hamilton, St. Louis vs. Detroit, A. L., August 30 (A) .... 5—1
    Charles (Jeff) Tesreau, New York vs. Philadelphia, N. L. September 6, first game (A) .... 3—0
1914—James Scott, Chicago vs. Washington, A. L., May 14 (A) (Pitched nine hitless innings before Chick Gandil singled; lost on two hits in ten innings) ..... 0—1
    Joseph Benz, Chicago vs. Cleveland, A. L., May 31 (H) .... 6—1
    George Davis, Boston vs. Philadelphia, N. L., September 9, second game (H) .... 7—0
1915—Richard Marquard, New York vs. Brooklyn, N. L., April 15 (H) .... 2—0
    James Lavender, Chicago vs. New York, N. L., August 31, first game (A) .... 2—0
1916—Thomas Hughes, Boston vs. Pittsburgh, N. L., June 16 (H) .... 2—0
    George Foster, Boston vs. New York, A. L., June 21 (H) .... 2—0
    Leslie (Joe) Bush, Philadelphia vs. Cleveland, A. L., August 26 (H) .... 5—0
    Hubert (Dutch) Leonard, Boston vs. St. Louis, A. L., Aug. 30 (H) .... 4—0
1917—Edward Cicotte, Chicago vs. St. Louis, A. L., April 14 (A) .... 11—0
    George Mogridge, New York vs. Boston, A. L., April 24 (A) .... 2—1
    James Vaughn, Chicago vs. Cincinnati, N. L., May 2 (H) (Pitched nine and one-third hitless innings before Larry Kopf singled; lost on two hits in ten innings. Fred Toney, Cincinnati, pitched ten no-hit innings in the same game.) .... 0—1
    Ernest Koob, St. Louis vs. Chicago, A. L., May 5 (H) .... 1—0
    Robert Groom, St. Louis vs. Chicago, A. L., May 6, second game (H) .... 3—0
1918—Hubert (Dutch) Leonard, Boston vs. Detroit, A. L., June 3 (A) .... 5—0
1919—Horace (Hod) Eller, Cincinnati vs. St. Louis, N. L., May 11 (H) .... 6—0
    Raymond Caldwell, Cleveland vs. New York, A. L., September 10, first game (A) .... 3—0
1920—Walter Johnson, Washington vs. Boston, A. L., July 1 (A) .... 1—0
1922—Jesse Barnes, New York vs. Philadelphia, N. L., May 7 (H) .... 6—0
1923—Samuel Jones, New York vs. Philadelphia, A. L., September 4 (A) .... 2—0
    Howard Ehmke, Boston vs. Philadelphia, A. L., September 7 (A) .... 4—0
1924—Jesse Haines, St. Louis vs. Boston, N. L., July 17 (H) .... 5—0
1925—Arthur (Dazzy) Vance, Brooklyn vs. Philadelphia, N. L., September 13, first game (H) .... 10—1
1926—Theodore Lyons, Chicago vs. Boston, A. L., August 21 (A) .... 6—0
1929—Carl Hubbell, New York vs. Pittsburgh, N. L., May 8 (H) .... 11—0
1931—Wesley Ferrell, Cleveland vs. St. Louis, A. L., April 29 (H) .... 9—0
    Robert Burke, Washington vs. Boston, A. L., August 8 (H) .... 5—0
1934—Louis (Buck) Newsom, St. Louis vs. Boston, A. L., September 18 (H) (Pitched nine and two-thirds hitless innings before Roy Johnson singled; lost on one hit in ten innings.) .... 1—2
    Paul Dean, St. Louis vs. Brooklyn N. L., September 21, second game (A) ...... 3—0
1935—Vernon Kennedy, Chicago vs. Cleveland, A. L., August 31 (H) .... 5—0
1937—William Dietrich, Chicago vs. St. Louis, A. L., June 1 (H) .... 8—0
1938—John Vander Meer, Cincinnati vs. Boston, N. L., June 11 (H) .... 3—0
    John Vander Meer, Cincinnati vs. Brooklyn, N. L., June 15 (A) (Vander Meer's two no-hitters were successive.) .... 6—0
    Monte Pearson, New York vs. Cleveland, A. L., August 27, second game (H) 13—0
1940—Robert Feller, Cleveland vs. Chicago, A. L., April 16 (A—opening day.) .... 1—0
    James (Tex) Carleton, Brooklyn vs. Cincinnati, N. L., April 30 (A) .... 3—0
1941—Lonnie Warneke, St. Louis vs. Cincinnati, N. L., August 30 (A) .... 2—0
1944—James Tobin, Boston vs. Brooklyn, N. L., April 27 (H) .... 2—0
    Clyde Shoun, Cincinnati vs. Boston, N. L. May 15 (H) .... 1—0
1945—Richard Fowler, Philadelphia vs. St. Louis, A. L., September 9, second game (H) .... 1—0
1946—Edward Head, Brooklyn vs. Boston, N. L., April 23 (H) .... 5—0
    Robert Feller, Cleveland vs. New York, A. L., April 30 (A) .... 1—0
1947—Ewell Blackwell, Cincinnati vs. Boston, N. L., June 18, (H) .... 6—0
    Donald Black, Cleveland vs. Philadelphia, A. L., July 10, first game (H) ...... 3—0
    William McCahan, Philadelphia vs. Washington, A. L., Sept. 3 (H) .... 3—0
1948—Robert Lemon, Cleveland vs. Detroit, A. L., June 30, (A) .... 2—0
    Rex Barney, Brooklyn vs. New York, N. L., Sept. 9, (A) .... 2—0
1950—Vernon Bickford, Boston vs. Brooklyn, N. L., August 11, (H) .... 7—0

1951—Clifford Chambers, Pittsburgh vs. Boston, N. L., May 6, second game (A) ..... 3—0
Robert Feller, Cleveland vs. Detroit, A. L., July 1, first game (H) .... 2—1
Allie Reynolds, New York vs. Cleveland, A. L., July 12, (A) .... 1—0
Allie Reynolds, New York vs. Boston, A. L., September 28, first game (H) .... 8—0
1952—Virgil Trucks, Detroit vs. Washington, A. L., May 15 (H) .... 1—0
Carl Erskine, Brooklyn vs. Chicago, N. L., June 19 (H) .... 5—0
Virgil Trucks, Detroit vs. New York, A. L., August 25 (A) .... 1—0
1953—Alva (Bobo) Holloman, St. Louis vs. Philadelphia, A. L., May 6 (H) (first
start in major leagues) .... 6—0
1954—James Wilson, Milwaukee vs. Philadelphia, N. L., June 12 (H) .... 2—0
1955—Samuel Jones, Chicago vs. Pittsburgh, N. L., May 12 (H) .... 4—0
1956—Carl Erskine, Brooklyn vs. New York, N. L., May 12 (H) .... 3—0
John Klippstein, Hershell Freeman and Joseph Black, Cincinnati vs. Milwaukee, N. L., May 26 (A) (Klippstein pitched seven innings, Freeman
the eighth and Black the remainder of the way; Jack Dittmer doubled for
first hit with two out in tenth inning, and Black lost on three hits in 11
innings.) .... 1—2
Melvin Parnell, Boston vs. Chicago, A. L., July 14 (H) .... 4—0
Salvatore Maglie, Brooklyn vs. Philadelphia, N. L., September 25 (H) .... 5—0
1957—Robert Keegan, Chicago vs. Washington, A. L., August 20, second game,
(H) .... 6—0
1958—James Bunning, Detroit vs. Boston, A. L., July 20, first game (A) .... 3—0
J. Hoyt Wilhelm, Baltimore vs. New York, A. L., Sept. 20 (H) .... 1—0
1960—Donald Cardwell, Chicago vs. St. Louis, N. L., May 15, second game (H) .... 4—0
S. Lewis Burdette, Milwaukee vs. Philadelphia, N. L., August 18 (H) .... 1—0
Warren Spahn, Milwaukee vs. Philadelphia, N. L., September 16 (H) .... 4—0
1961—Warren Spahn, Milwaukee vs. San Francisco, N. L., April 28 (H) .... 1—0
1962—Robert (Bo) Belinsky, Los Angeles vs. Baltimore, A. L., May 5 (H) .... 2—0
Earl Wilson, Boston vs. Los Angeles, A. L., June 26 (H) .... 2—0
Sanford Koufax, Los Angeles vs. New York, N. L., June 30 (H) .... 5—0
William Monbouquette, Boston vs. Chicago, A. L., August 1 (A) .... 1—0
John Kralick, Minnesota vs. Kansas City, A. L., August 26 (H) .... 1—0
1963—Sanford Koufax, Los Angeles vs. San Francisco, N. L., May 11 (H) .... 8—0
Donald Nottebart, Houston vs. Philadelphia, N. L., May 17 (H) .... 4—1
Juan Marichal, San Francisco vs. Houston, N. L., June 15 (H) .... 1—0
1964—Kenneth Johnson, Houston vs. Cincinnati, N. L., April 23 (H) .... 0—1
Sanford Koufax, Los Angeles vs. Philadelphia, N. L., June 4 (A) .... 3—0
1965—David Morehead, Boston vs. Cleveland, A. L., September 16 (H) .... 2—0
1966—Wilfred (Sonny) Siebert, Cleveland vs. Washington, A. L., June 10 (H) .... 2—0
1967—Stephen D. Barber and Stuart L. Miller, Baltimore vs. Detroit A. L., April 30,
first game (H) Barber pitched eight and two-thirds innings and Miller
one-third of an inning... 1—2
Donald E. Wilson, Houston vs. Atlanta, N. L., June 18 (H) .... 2—0
W. Dean Chance, Minnesota vs. Cleveland, A. L., August 25, second game
(A) .... 2—1
Joel E. Horlen, Chicago vs. Detroit, A. L., September 10, first game (H) .... 6—0
1968—Thomas H. Phoebus, Baltimore vs. Boston, A. L., April 27, (H) .... 6—0
George R. Culver, Cincinnati vs. Philadelphia, N. L., July 29, second game,
(A) .... 6—1
Gaylord J. Perry, San Francisco vs. St. Louis, N. L., September 17 (H) .... 1—0
Ray C. Washburn, St. Louis vs. San Francisco, N. L., September 18 (A) .... 2—0
1969—William H. Stoneman, Montreal vs. Philadelphia, N. L., April 17 (A) .... 7—0
James W. Maloney, Cincinnati vs. Houston, N. L., April 30 (H) .... 10—0
Donald E. Wilson, Houston vs. Cincinnati, N. L., May 1 (A) .... 4—0
James A. Palmer, Baltimore vs. Oakland, A. L., August 13 (H) .... 8—0
Kenneth D. Holtzman, Chicago vs. Atlanta, N. L., August 19 (H) .... 3—0
Robert R. Moose, Pittsburgh vs. New York, N. L., Sept. 20 (A) .... 4—0
1970—Dock P. Ellis, Pittsburgh vs. San Diego, N. L., June 12, first game, (A) .... 2—0
Clyde Wright, California vs. Oakland, A. L., July 3 (H) .... 4—0
William R. Singer, Los Angeles vs. Philadelphia, N. L., July 20, (H) .... 5—0
Vida Blue, Oakland vs. Minnesota, A. L., September 21 (H) .... 6—0
1971—Kenneth D. Holtzman, Chicago vs. Cincinnati, N. L., June 3 (A) .... 1—0
Richard C. Wise, Philadelphia vs. Cincinnati, N. L., June 23 (A) .... 4—0
Robert Gibson, St. Louis vs. Pittsburgh, N. L., August 14 (A) .... 11—0
1972—Burt C. Hooton, Chicago vs. Philadelphia, N. L., April 16 (H) .... 4—0
Milton S. Pappas, Chicago vs. San Diego, N. L., September 2 (H) .... 8—0
William H. Stoneman, Montreal vs. New York, N. L., October 2, first game
(H) .... 7—0

1973—Steven L. Busby, Kansas City vs. Detroit, A. L., April 27 (A) .... 3—0
　　　L. Nolan Ryan, California vs. Kansas City, A. L., May 15 (A) .... 3—0
　　　L. Nolan Ryan, California vs. Detroit, A. L., July 15 (A) .... 6—0
　　　James B. Bibby, Texas vs. Oakland, A. L., July 30 (A) .... 6—0
　　　Philip H. Niekro, Atlanta vs. San Diego, N. L., August 5 (H) .... 9—0
1974—Steven L. Busby, Kansas City vs. Milwaukee, A. L., June 19 (A) .... 2—0
　　　Richard A. Bosman, Cleveland vs. Oakland, A. L., July 19 (H) .... 4—0
　　　L. Nolan Ryan, California vs. Minnesota, A. L., September 28, (H) .... 4—0
1975—L. Nolan Ryan, California vs. Baltimore, A. L., June 1 (H) .... 1—0
　　　Edward L. Halicki, San Francisco vs. New York, N. L., August 24, second
　　　　game (H) .... 6—0
　　　Vida Blue, W. Glenn Abbott, Paul A. Lindblad and Roland G. Fingers, Oak-
　　　land vs. California, A. L., September 28, 1975, (H) Blue pitched five in-
　　　nings, Abbott, the sixth, Lindblad the seventh and Fingers the remainder
　　　of the way .... 5—0
1976—Lawrence E. Dierker, Houston vs. Montreal, N. L., July 9 (H) .... 6—0
　　　Johnny L. Odom and Francisco J. Barrios, Chicago vs. Oakland, A. L., July
　　　28 (A). Odom pitched five innings and Barrios four innings .... 2—1
　　　John R. Candelaria, Pittsburgh vs. Los Angeles, N. L., August 9 (H) .... 2—0
　　　John J. Montefusco, San Francisco vs. Atlanta, N. L., September 29 (A) .... 9—0
1977—James W. Colborn, Kansas City vs. Texas, A. L., May 14 (H) .... 6—0
　　　Dennis L. Eckersley, Cleveland vs. California, A. L., May 30 (H) .... 1—0
　　　Rikalbert Blyleven, Texas vs. California, A. L., September 22 (A) .... 6—0
1978—Robert H. Forsch, St. Louis vs. Philadelphia, N. L., April 16 (H) .... 5—0
　　　G. Thomas Seaver, Cincinnati vs. St. Louis, N. L., June 16 (H) .... 4—0
1979—Kenneth R. Forsch, Houston vs. Atlanta, N. L., April 7 (H) .... 6—0
1980—Jerry Reuss, Los Angeles vs. San Francisco, N. L., June 27 (A) .... 8—0
1981—Charles W. Lea, Montreal vs. San Francisco, N. L., May 10, second game
　　　(H) .... 4—0
　　　L. Nolan Ryan, Houston vs. Los Angeles, N. L., September 26 (H) .... 5—0
1983—David A. Righetti, New York vs. Boston, A. L., July 4 (H) .... 4—0
　　　Robert H. Forsch, St. Louis vs. Montreal, N. L., September 26 (H) .... 3—0
　　　Michael B. Warren, Oakland vs. Chicago, A. L., September 29 (H) .... 3—0

LESS THAN NINE INNINGS

1884—Lawrence J. McKeon, six innings, Indianapolis vs. Cincinnati, A. A., May 6
　　　(A) .... 0—0
　　　Charles Gagus, eight innings, Washington vs. Wilmington, U. A., August 21
　　　(H) .... 12—1
　　　Charles H. Getzein, six innings, Detroit vs. Philadelphia, N. L. October 1
　　　(H) .... 1—0
　　　Charles J. Sweeney and Henry J. Boyle, five innings, St. Louis vs. St. Paul,
　　　U. A., October 5 (H). Sweeney pitched three innings and Boyle two in-
　　　nings .... 0—1
1885—Fred L. Shaw, five innings, Providence vs. Buffalo, N. L., October 7, first
　　　game (A) .... 4—0
1888—George E. Van Haltren, six innings, Chicago vs. Pittsburgh, N. L., June 21
　　　(H) .... 1—0
　　　Edward N. Crane, seven innings, New York vs. Washington, N. L., Septem-
　　　ber 27 (H) .... 3—0
1889—Matthew A. Kilroy, seven innings, Baltimore vs. St. Louis, A. A., July 29,
　　　second game (H) .... 0—0
1890—Charles K. King, eight innings, Chicago vs. Brooklyn, P. L., June 21 (H) .... 0—1
　　　George E. Nicol, seven innings, St. Louis vs. Philadelphia, A. A., September
　　　23 (H) .... 21—2
　　　Henry C. Gastright, eight innings, Columbus vs. Toledo, A. A., October 12
　　　(H) .... 6—0
1892—John E. Stivetts, five innings, Boston vs. Washington, N. L., October 15 sec-
　　　ond game (A) .... 6—0
1893—Elton P. Chamberlain, seven innings, Cincinnati vs. Boston, N. L., Septem-
　　　ber 23, second game (H) .... 6—0
1894—Edward F. Stein, six innings, Brooklyn vs. Chicago, N. L., June 2 (H) .... 1—0
1903—Leon K. Ames, five innings, New York vs. St. Louis, N. L., September 14,
　　　second game (A) .... 5—0
1905—George E. Waddell, five innings, Philadelphia vs. St. Louis, A. L., August 15
　　　(H) .... 2—0

1906—John W. Weimer, seven innings, Cincinnati vs. Brooklyn, N. L., August 24,
    second game (H) .... 1—0
    James H. Dygert and George E. Waddell, five innings, Philadelphia vs. Chi-
    cago, A. L., August 29 (H). Dygert pitched three innings and Waddell two
    innings.. 4—3
    Grant McGlynn, seven innings, St. Louis vs. Brooklyn, N. L., September 24,
    second game (A) .... 1—1
    Albert P. Leifield, six innings, Pittsburgh vs. Philadelphia, N. L., September
    26, second game (A) .... 8—0
1907—Edward A. Walsh, five innings, Chicago vs. New York, A. L., May 26 (H) ..... 8—1
    Edwin Karger, seven perfect innings, St. Louis vs. Boston, N. L., August 11,
    second game (H) .... 4—0
    S. Howard Camnitz, five innings, Pittsburgh vs. New York, N. L., August 23,
    second game (A) .... 1—0
    Harry P. Vickers, five perfect innings, Philadelphia vs. Washington, A. L.,
    October 5, second game (A) .... 4—0
1908—John C. Lush, six innings, St. Louis vs. Brooklyn, N. L., August 6 (A) .... 2—0
1910—Leonard L. Cole, seven innings, Chicago vs. St. Louis, N. L., July 31, second
    game (A) .... 4—0
    J. Carl Cashion, six innings, Washington vs. Cleveland, A. L., August 20,
    second game (H) .... 2—0
1924—Walter P. Johnson, seven innings, Washington vs. St. Louis, A. L., August 25
    (H) .... 2—0
1937—Fred M. Frankhouse, seven and two-thirds innings, Brooklyn vs. Cincinnati,
    N. L., August 27 (H) .... 5—0
1940—John H. Whitehead, six innings, St. Louis vs. Detroit, A. L., August 5, second
    game (H) .... 4—0
1944—James A. Tobin, five innings, Boston vs. Philadelphia, N. L., June 22, second
    game (H) .... 7—0
1959—Michael F. McCormick, five innings, San Francisco vs. Philadelphia, N. L.,
    June 12 (A) .... 3—0
    Samuel Jones, seven innings, San Francisco vs. St. Louis, N. L., September
    26 (A) .... 4—0
1967—W. Dean Chance, five perfect innings, Minnesota vs. Boston, A. L., August 6
    (H) .... 2—0

Babe Ruth's 60 Home Runs—1927

HR No.	Team game No.	Date	Opposing Pitcher and Club	City	Inn.	O.B.
1	4	April 15	Howard J. Ehmke (R), Phila.	New York	1	0
2	11	April 23	George E. Walberg (L), Phila.	Philadelphia	1	0
3	12	April 24	Hollis Thurston (R), Wash.	Washington	6	0
4	14	April 29	Bryan W. Harriss (R), Boston	Boston	5	0
5	16	May 1	John P. Quinn (R), Phila.	New York	1	1
6	16	May 1	George E. Walberg (L), Phila.	New York	8	0
7	24	May 10	Milton Gaston (R), St. Louis	St. Louis	1	2
8	25	May 11	Ernest Nevers (R), St. Louis	St. Louis	1	1
9	29	May 17	H. Warren Collins (R), Detroit	Detroit	8	0
10	33	May 22	Benj. J. Karr (R), Cleveland	Cleveland	6	1
11	34	May 23	Hollis Thurston (R), Wash.	Washington	1	0
12	37	May 28*	Hollis Thurston (R), Wash.	New York	7	2
13	39	May 29	Daniel K. MacFayden (R), Boston	New York	8	0
14	41	May 30‡	George E. Walberg (L), Phila.	Philadelphia	11	0
15	42	May 31*	John P. Quinn (R), Phila.	Philadelphia	1	1
16	43	May 31†	Howard J. Ehmke (R), Phila.	Philadelphia	5	1
17	47	June 5	Earl O. Whitehill (L), Detroit	New York	6	0
18	48	June 7	Alphonse T. Thomas (R), Chi.	New York	4	0
19	52	June 11	Garland M. Buckeye (L), Cleve.	New York	3	1
20	52	June 11	Garland M. Buckeye (L), Cleve.	New York	5	0
21	53	June 12	George E. Uhle (R), Cleveland	New York	7	0
22	55	June 16	Jonathan T. Zachary (R), St. L.	New York	1	1
23	60	June 22*	Harold J. Wiltse (L), Boston	Boston	5	0
24	60	June 22*	Harold J. Wiltse (L), Boston	Boston	7	1
25	70	June 30	Bryan W. Harriss (R), Boston	New York	4	1
26	73	July 3	Horace O. Lisenbee (R), Wash.	Washington	1	0
27	78	July 8†	Donald W. Hankins (R), Detroit	Detroit	2	2
28	79	July 9*	Kenneth E. Holloway (R), Detroit	Detroit	1	1
29	79	July 9*	Kenneth E. Holloway (R), Detroit	Detroit	4	2
30	83	July 12	Joseph B. Shaute (L), Cleve.	Cleveland	9	1
31	94	July 24	Alphonse T. Thomas (R), Chi.	Chicago	3	0
32	95	July 26*	Milton Gaston (R), St. Louis	New York	1	1
33	95	July 26*	Milton Gaston (R), St. Louis	New York	6	0
34	98	July 28	Walter C. Stewart (L), St. L.	New York	8	1
35	106	Aug. 5	George S. Smith (R), Detroit	New York	8	0
36	110	Aug. 10	Jonathan T. Zachary (L), Wash.	Washington	3	2
37	114	Aug. 16	Alphonse T. Thomas (R), Chi.	Chicago	5	0
38	115	Aug. 17	George W. Connally (R), Chi.	Chicago	11	0
39	118	Aug. 20	J. Walter Miller (L), Cleveland	Cleveland	1	1
40	120	Aug. 22	Joseph B. Shaute (L), Cleve.	Cleveland	6	0
41	124	Aug. 27	Ernest Nevers (R), St. Louis	St. Louis	8	1
42	125	Aug. 28	J. Ernest Wingard (L), St. Louis	St. Louis	1	1
43	127	Aug. 31	Tony Welzer (R), Boston	New York	8	0
44	128	Sept. 2	George E. Walberg (L), Phila.	Philadelphia	1	0
45	132	Sept. 6*	Tony Welzer (R), Boston	Boston	6	2
46	132	Sept. 6*	Tony Welzer (R), Boston	Boston	7	1
47	133	Sept. 6†	Jack Russell (R), Boston	Boston	9	0
48	134	Sept. 7	Daniel K. MacFayden (R), Boston	Boston	1	0
49	134	Sept. 7	Bryan W. Harriss (R), Boston	Boston	8	1
50	138	Sept. 11	Milton Gaston (R), St. Louis	New York	4	0
51	139	Sept. 13*	G. Willis Hudlin (R), Cleveland	New York	7	1
52	140	Sept. 13†	Joseph B. Shaute (L), Cleveland	New York	4	0
53	143	Sept. 16	Ted Blankenship (R), Chicago	New York	3	0
54	147	Sept. 18†	Theodore A. Lyons (R), Chicago	New York	5	1
55	148	Sept. 21	Samuel B. Gibson (R), Detroit	New York	9	0
56	149	Sept. 22	Kenneth E. Holloway (R), Detroit	New York	9	1
57	152	Sept. 27	Robert M Grove (L), Phila.	New York	6	3
58	153	Sept. 29	Horace O. Lisenbee (R), Wash.	New York	1	0
59	153	Sept. 29	Paul Hopkins (R), Washington	New York	5	3
60	154	Sept. 30	Jonathan T. Zachary (L), Wash.	New York	8	1

*First game of doubleheader.　†Second game of doubleheader.
‡Afternoon game of split doubleheader.

New York A. L. played 155 games in 1927 (one tie on April 14), with Ruth participating in 151 games. (No home run for Ruth in game No. 155 on October 1).

Roger Maris' 61 Home Runs—1961

HR No.	Team game No.	Date	Opposing Pitcher and Club	City	Inn.	O.B.
1	11	April 26	Paul Foytack (R), Detroit	Detroit	5	0
2	17	May 3	Pedro Ramos (R), Minnesota	Minneapolis	7	2
3	20	May 6	Eli Grba (R), Los Angeles	Los Angeles	5	0
4	29	May 17	Peter Burnside (L), Washington	New York	8	1
5	30	May 19	James Perry (R), Cleveland	Cleveland	1	1
6	31	May 20	Gary Bell (R), Cleveland	Cleveland	3	0
7	32	May 21	Charles Estrada (R), Baltimore	New York	1	0
8	35	May 24	D. Eugene Conley (R), Boston	New York	4	1
9	38	May 28	Calvin McLish (R), Chicago	New York	2	1
10	40	May 30	D. Eugene Conley (R), Boston	Boston	6	2
11	40	May 30	Miguel Fornieles (R), Boston	Boston	8	2
12	41	May 31	Billy Muffett (R), Boston	Boston	3	0
13	43	June 2	Calvin McLish (R), Chicago	Chicago	3	2
14	44	June 3	Robert Shaw (R), Chicago	Chicago	8	2
15	45	June 4	Russell Kemmerer (R), Chicago	Chicago	3	0
16	48	June 6	Edwin Palmquist (R), Minnesota	New York	6	2
17	49	June 7	Pedro Ramos (R), Minnesota	New York	3	2
18	52	June 9	Raymond Herbert (R), Kan. City	New York	7	1
19	55	June 11†	Eli Grba (R), Los Angeles	New York	3	0
20	55	June 11†	John James (R), Los Angeles	New York	7	0
21	57	June 13	James Perry (R), Cleveland	Cleveland	6	0
22	58	June 14	Gary Bell (R), Cleveland	Cleveland	4	1
23	61	June 17	Donald Mossi (L), Detroit	Detroit	4	0
24	62	June 18	Jerry Casale (R), Detroit	Detroit	8	1
25	63	June 19	James Archer (L), Kansas City	Kansas City	9	0
26	64	June 20	Joseph Nuxhall (L), Kansas City	Kansas City	1	0
27	66	June 22	Norman Bass (R), Kansas City	Kansas City	2	1
28	74	July 1	David Sisler (R), Washington	New York	9	1
29	75	July 2	Peter Burnside (L), Washington	New York	3	2
30	75	July 2	John Klippstein (R), Washington	New York	7	1
31	77	July 4†	Frank Lary (R), Detroit	New York	8	1
32	78	July 5	Frank Funk (R), Cleveland	New York	7	0
33	82	July 9*	William Monbouquette (R), Bos.	New York	7	0
34	84	July 13	Early Wynn (R), Chicago	Chicago	1	1
35	86	July 15	Raymond Herbert (R), Chicago	Chicago	3	0
36	92	July 21	William Monbouquette (R), Bos.	Boston	1	0
37	95	July 25*	Frank Baumann (L), Chicago	New York	4	1
38	95	July 25*	Don Larsen (R), Chicago	New York	8	0
39	96	July 25†	Russell Kemmerer (R), Chicago	New York	4	0
40	96	July 25†	Warren Hacker (R), Chicago	New York	6	2
41	106	Aug. 4	Camilo Pascual (R), Minnesota	New York	1	2
42	114	Aug. 11	Peter Burnside (L), Washington	Washington	5	0
43	115	Aug. 12	Richard Donovan (R), Wash.	Washington	4	0
44	116	Aug. 13*	Bennie Daniels (R), Washington	Washington	4	0
45	117	Aug. 13†	Marion Kutyna (R), Washington	Washington	1	1
46	118	Aug. 15	Juan Pizarro (L), Chicago	New York	4	0
47	119	Aug. 16	W. William Pierce (L), Chicago	New York	1	1
48	119	Aug. 16	W. William Pierce (L), Chicago	New York	3	1
49	124	Aug. 20	James Perry (R), Cleveland	Cleveland	3	1
50	125	Aug. 22	Kenneth McBride (R), L. Angeles	Los Angeles	6	1
51	129	Aug. 26	Jerry Walker (R), Kansas City	Kansas City	6	0
52	135	Sept. 2	Frank Lary (R), Detroit	New York	6	0
53	135	Sept. 2	Henry Aguirre (L), Detroit	New York	8	1
54	140	Sept. 6	Thomas Cheney (R), Washington	New York	4	0
55	141	Sept. 7	Richard Stigman (L), Cleveland	New York	3	0
56	143	Sept. 9	James Grant (R), Cleveland	New York	7	0
57	151	Sept. 16	Frank Lary (R), Detroit	Detroit	3	1
58	152	Sept. 17	Terrence Fox (R), Detroit	Detroit	12	1
59	155	Sept. 20	Milton Pappas (R), Baltimore	Baltimore	3	0
60	159	Sept. 26	John Fisher (R), Baltimore	New York	3	0
61	163	Oct. 1	E. Tracy Stallard (R), Boston	New York	4	0

*First game of doubleheader. †Second game of doubleheader.

New York played 163 games in 1961 (one tie on April 22). Maris did not hit homer in this game. Maris played in 161 games.

Joe DiMaggio's 56-Game Hitting Streak

Date—1941 Opp. Pitcher and Club	AB.	R.	H.	2B.	3B.	HR.	RBI.
May 15—Smith, Chicago	4	0	1	0	0	0	1
16—Lee, Chicago	4	2	2	0	1	1	1
17—Rigney, Chicago	3	1	1	0	0	0	0
18—Harris (2), Niggeling (1), St. Louis	3	3	3	1	0	0	1
19—Galehouse, St. Louis	3	0	1	1	0	0	0
20—Auker, St. Louis	5	1	1	0	0	0	1
21—Rowe (1), Benton (1), Detroit	5	0	2	0	0	0	1
22—McKain, Detroit	4	0	1	0	0	0	1
23—Newsome, Boston	5	0	1	0	0	0	2
24—Johnson, Boston	4	2	1	0	0	0	2
25—Grove, Boston	4	0	1	0	0	0	0
27—Chase (1), Anderson (2), Carrasquel (1), Washington	5	3	4	0	0	1	3
28—Hudson, Washington (Night)	4	1	1	0	1	0	0
29—Sundra, Washington	3	1	1	0	0	0	0
30—Johnson, Boston	2	1	1	0	0	0	0
30—Harris, Boston	3	0	1	1	0	0	0
June 1—Milnar, Cleveland	4	1	1	0	0	0	0
1—Harder, Cleveland	4	0	1	0	0	0	0
2—Feller, Cleveland	4	2	2	1	0	0	0
3—Trout, Detroit	4	1	1	0	0	1	1
5—Newhouser, Detroit	5	1	1	0	1	0	1
7—Muncrief (1), Allen (1), Caster (1), St. Louis	5	2	3	0	0	0	1
8—Auker, St. Louis	4	3	2	0	0	2	4
8—Caster (1), Kramer (1), St. Louis	4	1	2	1	0	1	3
10—Rigney, Chicago	5	1	1	0	0	0	0
12—Lee, Chicago (Night)	4	1	2	0	0	1	1
14—Feller, Cleveland	2	0	1	1	0	0	1
15—Bagby, Cleveland	3	1	1	0	0	1	1
16—Milnar, Cleveland	5	0	1	1	0	0	0
17—Rigney, Chicago	4	1	1	0	0	0	0
18—Lee, Chicago	3	0	1	0	0	0	0
19—Smith (1), Ross (2), Chicago	3	2	3	0	0	1	2
20—Newsom (2), McKain (2), Detroit	5	3	4	1	0	0	1
21—Trout, Detroit	4	0	1	0	0	0	1
22—Newhouser (1), Newsom (1), Detroit	5	1	2	1	0	1	2
24—Muncrief, St. Louis	4	1	1	0	0	0	0
25—Galehouse, St. Louis	4	1	1	0	0	1	3
26—Auker, St. Louis	4	0	1	1	0	0	1
27—Dean, Philadelphia	3	1	2	0	0	1	2
28—Babich (1), Harris (1), Philadelphia	5	1	2	1	0	0	0
29—Leonard, Washington	4	1	1	1	0	0	0
29—Anderson, Washington	5	1	1	0	0	0	1
July 1—Harris (1), Ryba (1), Boston	4	0	2	0	0	0	1
1—Wilson, Boston	3	1	1	0	0	0	1
2—Newsome, Boston	5	1	1	0	0	1	3
5—Marchildon, Philadelphia	4	2	1	0	0	1	2
6—Babich (1), Hadley (3), Philadelphia	5	2	4	1	0	0	2
6—Knott, Philadelphia	4	0	2	0	1	0	2
10—Niggeling, St. Louis (Night)	2	0	1	0	0	0	0
11—Harris (3), Kramer (1), St. Louis	5	1	4	0	0	1	2
12—Auker (1), Muncrief (1), St. Louis	5	1	2	1	0	0	1
13—Lyons (2), Hallett (1), Chicago	4	2	3	0	0	0	0
13—Lee, Chicago	4	0	1	0	0	0	0
14—Rigney, Chicago	3	0	1	0	0	0	0
15—Smith, Chicago	4	1	2	1	0	0	2
16—Milnar (2), Krakauskas (1), Cleve.	4	3	3	1	0	0	0
Totals for 56 games	223	56	91	16	4	15	55

Stopped July 17 at Cleveland, New York won, 4 to 3. First inning, Alfred J. Smith pitching, thrown out by Keltner; fourth inning, Smith pitching, received base on balls; seventh inning, Smith pitching, thrown out by Keltner; eighth inning, James C. Bagby, Jr., pitching, grounded into double play.

All-Time Major League Records

Records for National League, 1876 to date. American Association, 1882 to 1891; Union Association, 1884; Players' League, 1890; American League, 1901 to date. (Does not include Federal League of 1914 and 1915.)

Major league championship games only, if included in official season averages.

Fewest for leader records are for season when 154 games or 162 games were scheduled, except for pitchers.

Two games in one day (a.m. and p.m.) are included with doubleheader records.

American League and National League records based on 154-game schedule, but if item was surpassed since adoption of 162-game schedule by American League in 1961 and National League in 1962, records for both length schedules are listed. Fewest 1972 and 1981 club and league records omitted due to cancellations of games on account of players' strike.

INDIVIDUAL SERVICE

Most Years Played in Major Leagues

26—James T. McGuire, Toledo, Cleveland, Rochester, Washington A. A.; Detroit, Philadelphia, Washington, Brooklyn N. L.; Detroit, New York, Boston, Cleveland A. L.; 1884 to 1912, except 1889, 1909, 1911 (4 in A. A.; 13 in N. L.; 9 in A. L.). 1781 games.

Most Years Played, League

A. L.—25—Edward T. Collins, Philadelphia, Chicago, 1906 through 1930, 2826 games.

N. L.—23—Walter J. Maranville, Boston, Pittsburgh, Chicago, Brooklyn, St. Louis, 1912 through 1935, except 1934, 2670 games.

Most Consecutive Years Played, League

A. L.—25—Edward T. Collins, Philadelphia, Chicago, 1906 through 1930, 2826 games.

N. L.—22—Adrian C. Anson, Chicago, 1876 through 1897, 2253 games.
Walter J. Maranville, Boston, Pittsburgh, Chicago, Brooklyn, St. Louis, 1912 through 1933, 2670 games.
Melvin T. Ott, New York, 1926 through 1947, 2730 games.
Stanley F. Musial, St. Louis, 1941 through 1963 (except 1945 in military service), 3026 games.
Willie H. Mays, original New York club, San Francisco, present New York club, 1951 through 1973 (except 1953 in military service), 2992 games.
Willie L. McCovey, San Francisco, San Diego, 1959 through 1980 (played in A.L. for part of 1976), 2577 games.

Most Leagues, Played, Season

3—William N. Murphy, 1884, N. L., A. A., U. A.
Walter F. Prince, 1884, N. L., A. A., U. A.
George A. Strief, 1884, A. A., U. A., N. L.

Most Leagues, Played, Lifetime

4—Held by 20 players. Last Time—Lafayette N. Cross, A. A., P. L., N. L., A. L., 21 years, 2259 games, 1887 through 1907.

Most Years, One Club

A. L.—23—Brooks C. Robinson, Baltimore, 1955 through 1977, 2896 games.
Carl M. Yastrzemski, Boston, 1961 through 1983, 3308 games.

N. L.—22—Adrian C. Anson, Chicago, 1876 through 1897, 2253 games.
Melvin T. Ott, New York, 1926 through 1947, 2730 games.
Stanley F. Musial, St. Louis, 1941 through 1963 (except 1945 in military service), 3026 games.

Most Consecutive Years, One Club

A. L.—23—Brooks C. Robinson, Baltimore, 1955 through 1977, 2896 games.
Carl M. Yastrzemski, Boston, 1961 through 1983, 3308 games.

N. L.—22—Adrian C. Anson, Chicago, 1876 through 1897, 2253 games.
Melvin T. Ott, New York, 1926 through 1947, 2730 games.
Stanley F. Musial, St. Louis, 1941 through 1963 (except 1945 in military service), 3026 games.

Most Clubs Played in Major Leagues

12—Charles M. Smith, Cincinnati, Cleveland, Worcester, Buffalo, Pittsburgh, Boston N. L.; Philadelphia, Baltimore, Louisville, Columbus, Pittsburgh, Washington, A. A., 1880 through 1891, 12 years, 1110 games.
James T. McGuire, Toledo, Cleveland, Rochester, Washington, A. A.; Detroit, Philadelphia, Washington, Brooklyn N. L.; Detroit, New York, Boston, Cleveland A. L.: 1884 to 1912, except 1889, 1909, 1911, 1781 games.

Most Clubs Played in Major Leagues, Since 1900

10—Robert Lane Miller, St. Louis N. L., New York N. L., Los Angeles N. L., Minnesota A. L., Cleveland A. L., Chicago A. L., Chicago N. L., San Diego N. L., Pittsburgh, N. L., Detroit A. L., 1957, 1959 through 1974 (17 years), 807 games.

H. Thomas Davis, Los Angeles N. L., New York N. L., Chicago A. L., Seattle A. L., Houston N. L., Chicago N. L., Oakland A. L., Baltimore A. L., California A. L., Kansas City A. L., 1959 through 1976 (18 years), 1999 games.

Kenneth A. Brett, Boston A.L., Milwaukee A.L., Philadelphia N.L., Pittsburgh N.L., New York A.L., Chicago A.L., California A.L., Minnesota A.L., Los Angeles N.L., Kansas City A.L., 1967, 1969 through 1981 (14 years), 349 games.

Most Clubs Played, League

N. L.—9—Dennis L. Brouthers, Troy, Buffalo, Detroit, Boston, Brooklyn, Baltimore, Louisville, Philadelphia, New York, 1879 through 1889, 1892 through 1896, 1904 (17 years).

A. L.—7—W. Edward Robinson, Cleveland, Washington, Chicago, Philadelphia, New York, Kansas City, Detroit, Baltimore, 1942 through 1957 (except 1943, 1944, 1945, in military service), (13 years), (Note: Kansas City considered part of Philadelphia franchise and is not considered a separate club).

Woodson G. Held, New York, Kansas City, Cleveland, Washington, Baltimore, California, Chicago, 1954, 1957 through 1969 (14 years).

Kenneth G. Sanders, Kansas City (first club), Boston, Oakland, Milwaukee, Minnesota, Cleveland, California, Kansas City (second club), 1964, 1966, 1968, 1970 through 1976 (10 years), (Note: Oakland considered part of first Kansas City franchise and is not considered a separate club).

Kenneth A. Brett, Boston, Milwaukee, New York, Chicago, California, Minnesota, Kansas City, 1967, 1969 through 1972, 1976 through 1981 (11 years).

N. L. since 1899—7—John C. Barry, Washington, Boston, Philadelphia, Chicago, Cincinnati, St. Louis, New York, 1899 through 1908 (10 years).

Joseph C. Schultz, Sr., Boston, Brooklyn, Chicago, Pittsburgh, St. Louis, Philadelphia, Cincinnati, 1912 through 1925, except 1914, 1917 and 1918 (11 years).

Frank J. Thomas, Pittsburgh, Cincinnati, Chicago, Milwaukee, New York, Philadelphia, Houston, 1951 through 1966 (16 years).

Most Clubs Played, League, One Season

N. L.—4—Thomas J. Dowse, Louisville, Cincinnati, Philadelphia, Washington, 63 games, 1892.

A. L.—4—Frank E. Huelsman, Chicago, Detroit, St. Louis, Washington, 112 games, 1904.

Paul E. Lehner, Philadelphia, Chicago, St. Louis, Cleveland, 65 games, 1951.

Theodore G. Gray, Chicago, Cleveland, New York, Baltimore, 14 games, 1955.

Most Clubs Played in Majors, One Season

4—Harry E. Wheeler, St. Louis A. A., Kansas City U. A., Chicago U. A., Pittsburgh U. A., Baltimore U. A., 72 games, 1884 (Note: Pittsburgh considered part of Chicago franchise and is not considered a separate club).

Since 1900—4—Held by many players—Last player—David A. Kingman, New York N. L., San Diego N. L., California A. L., New York A. L., 132 games, 1977.

Most Clubs Played, One Day

N. L.—2—Max O. Flack, Chicago, St. Louis, May 30 a.m., p.m., 1922.

Clifton E. Heathcote, St. Louis, Chicago, May 30 a.m., p.m., 1922.

Joel R. Youngblood, New York, Montreal, August 4, 1982.

Most Positions Played, One Season

N. L.—9—Lewis W. McAllister, Cleveland, 110 games, 1899.

Michael T. Walsh, Philadelphia, 84 games, 1911.

E. Eugene Paulette, St. Louis, 125 games, 1918.

A. L.—9—Samuel B. Mertes, Chicago, 129 games, 1902.

John H. Rothrock, Boston, 117 games, 1928.

Dagoberto B. Campaneris, Kansas City, 144 games, 1965.

Cesar L. Tovar, Minnesota, 157 games, 1968.

Most Positions Played, One Game

A. L.—9—Dagoberto B. Campaneris, Kansas City, September 8, 1965; played 8⅔ innings of 13-inning game.

Cesar L. Tovar, Minnesota, September 22, 1968.

Most Games, League

A. L.— 3308— Carl M. Yastrzemski, Boston, 23 years, 1961 through 1983.

N. L.— 3250— Peter E. Rose, Cincinnati, Philadelphia, 21 years, 1963 through 1983.

Most Consecutive Games, League

A. L.— 2130— H. Louis Gehrig, New York, June 1, 1925, through April 30, 1939.
N. L.— 1207— Steven P. Garvey, Los Angeles, San Diego, September 3, 1975, through July 29, 1983, first game.

Most Consecutive Games, League, From Start of Career

N. L.— 424— Ernest Banks, Chicago, September 17, 1953, through August 10, 1957.
A. L.— 394— Aloysius H. Simmons, Philadelphia, April 15, 1924, through July 20, 1926.

Most Games Played, Season

N. L. (162-game season) —165—Maurice M. Wills, Los Angeles, 1962.
N. L. (154-game season) —160—Henry K. Groh, Cincinnati, 1915.
                                   Thomas H. Griffith, Cincinnati, 1915.
A. L. (162-game season) —164—Cesar L. Tovar, Minnesota, 1967.
A. L. (154-game season) —162—James E. Barrett, Detroit, 1904.

Most Games Played, Season, With Two Clubs

N. L. (162-game season) —164—Franklin Taveras, Pittsburgh, New York, 1979.
N. L. (154-game season) —158—Ralph M. Kiner, Pittsburgh, Chicago, 1953.
A. L. (162-game season) —160—Julio L. Cruz, Seattle, Chicago, 1983.
A. L. (154-game season) —155—Patrick H. Dougherty, Boston, New York, 1904.
                                   W. Edward Robinson, Washington, Chicago, 1950.

Most Games, Season, as Pinch-Hitter

N. L. (162-game season) —94—Daniel J. Staub, New York, 1983.
N. L. (154-game season) —76—Gerald T. Lynch, Cincinnati, 1960.
A. L. —81—Elmer W. Valo, New York, Washington, 1960.

Most Years Leading League in Most Games

A. L.—7—H. Louis Gehrig, New York, 1927, 1930 (tied), 1932, 1934 (tied), 1936 (tied), 1937, 1938 (tied).
N. L.—6—Ernest Banks, Chicago, 1954 (tied), 1955 (tied), 1957 (tied), 1958, 1959 (tied), 1960.

Most Years Played All Clubs' Games

A. L.—13—H. Louis Gehrig, New York, 1926 through 1938 (consecutive).
N. L.—10—Peter E. Rose, Cincinnati, 1965, 1972, 1974, 1975, 1976, 1977, Philadelphia, 1979, 1980, 1981, 1982.

Most Consecutive Years Played All Clubs' Games

A. L.—13—H. Louis Gehrig, New York, 1926 through 1938.
N. L.— 7—Steven P. Garvey, Los Angeles, 1976 through 1982.

Fewest Games, Season, for Leader in Most Games (154 or 162 Game Schedule)

N. L.— 152— Stanley C. Hack, Chicago, 1938.
                William J. Herman, Chicago, 1938.
A. L.— 154— Held by many players.

Most Years, 100 or More Games in Major Leagues

22—Henry L. Aaron, 21 in National League, Milwaukee, Atlanta, 1954 through 1974; one in American League, Milwaukee, 1975.
     Carl M. Yastrzemski, 22 in American League, Boston, 1961 through 1983, except 1981.

Most Years, 100 or More Games, League

A. L.—22—Carl M. Yastrzemski, Boston, 1961 through 1982, except 1981.
N. L.—21—Stanley F. Musial, St. Louis, 1942 through 1963 (except 1945 in military service).
           Henry L. Aaron, Milwaukee, Atlanta, 1954 through 1974.
           Peter E. Rose, Cincinnati, Philadelphia, 1963 through 1983.

Most Consecutive Years, 100 or More Games, League

N. L.—21—Stanley F. Musial, St. Louis, 1942 through 1963 (except 1945 in military service).
           Henry L. Aaron, Milwaukee, Atlanta, 1954 through 1974.
           Peter E. Rose, Cincinnati, Philadelphia, 1963 through 1983.
A. L.—20—Carl M. Yastrzemski, Boston, 1961 through 1980.

Most Years, 150 or More Games, League

N. L.—17—Peter E. Rose, Cincinnati, Philadelphia, 1963 through 1983, except 1964, 1967, 1968, 1981.
A. L.—14—Brooks C. Robinson, Baltimore, 1960 through 1974, except 1965.

Most Consecutive Years, 150 or More Games, League

N. L.—13—Willie H. Mays, New York, San Francisco, 1954 through 1966.
A. L.—11—J. Nelson Fox, Chicago, 1952 through 1962.

INDIVIDUAL BATTING

Highest Batting Average, Season, 100 or More Games

N. L.—.438—Hugh Duffy, Boston, 124 games, 1894.
N. L. since 1900—.424—Rogers Hornsby, St. Louis, 143 games, 1924.
A. L.—.422—Napoleon Lajoie, Philadelphia, 131 games, 1901.

Highest Batting Average, Season, 100 or More Games, Second Best Batsman

A. L.—.408—Joseph J. Jackson, Cleveland, 147 games, 1911.
N. L.—.406—Fred C. Clarke, Louisville, 129 games, 1897.
N. L. since 1900—.393—Floyd C. Herman, Brooklyn, 163 games, 1930.

Lowest Batting Average, Season, 150 or More Games

A. L.—.182—Montford M. Cross, Philadelphia, 153 games, 1904.
N. L.—.201—C. Dallan Maxvill, St. Louis, 152 games, 1970.

Lowest Batting Average, Season, Batting Leader, 100 or More Games

A. L.—.301—Carl M. Yastrzemski, Boston, 157 games, 1968.
N. L.—.320—Lawrence J. Doyle, New York, 150 games, 1915.

Lowest Batting Average, Season, with Most At-Bats

N. L.—.000—Robert R. Buhl, Milwaukee, Chicago, 35 games, 1962, 70 at-bats.
A. L.—.000—William R. Wight, Chicago, 30 games, 1950, 61 at-bats.

Highest Batting Average, League, Fifteen or More Seasons

A. L.—.367—Tyrus R. Cobb, Detroit, Philadelphia, 24 years, 1905 through 1928, 11,429
          at-bats, 4,191 hits. (Cobb's totals are in dispute. See explanation on Page
          3)
N. L.—.359—Rogers Hornsby, St. Louis, New York, Boston, Chicago, 19 years, 1915
          through 1933, 8,058 at-bats, 2,895 hits.

Highest Batting Average, Five Consecutive Seasons, 100 or More Games

N. L.—.4024—Rogers Hornsby, St. Louis, 1921 through 1925.
A. L.—.3965—Tyrus R. Cobb, Detroit, 1909 through 1913.

Highest Batting Average, Four Consecutive Seasons, 100 or More Games

N. L.—.4039—Rogers Hornsby, St. Louis, 1922 through 1925.
A. L.—.4019—Tyrus R. Cobb, Detroit, 1910 through 1913.

Highest Batting Average, Three Consecutive Seasons, 100 or More Games

A. L.—.408—Tyrus R. Cobb, Detroit, 1911, 1912, 1913.
N. L.—.40647—William H. Keeler, Baltimore, 1895, 1896, 1897.
        .40627—Jesse C. Burkett, Cleveland, 1895, 1896, 1897.
N. L. since 1900—.405—Rogers Hornsby, St. Louis, 1923, 1924, 1925.

Highest Batting Average, Two Consecutive Seasons, 100 or More Games

N. L.—.417—Jesse C. Burkett, Cleveland, 1895, 1896.
A. L.—.415—Tyrus R. Cobb, Detroit, 1911, 1912.
N. L. since 1900—.413—Rogers Hornsby, St. Louis, 1924, 1925.

Highest Batting Average, Season, 100 or More Games, First Baseman

A. L.—.420—George H. Sisler, St. Louis, 142 games, 1922; 141 games at first base.
N. L.—.401—William H. Terry, New York, 154 games, 1930; 154 games at first base.

Highest Batting Average, Season, 100 or More Games, Second Baseman

N. L.—.424—Rogers Hornsby, St. Louis, 143 games, 1924; 143 games at second base.
A. L.—.422—Napoleon Lajoie, Philadelphia, 131 games, 1901; 130 games at second base.

Highest Batting Average, Season, 100 or More Games, Third Baseman

A. L.—.390—George H. Brett, Kansas City, 117 games, 1980; 112 games at third base.
N. L.—.390—John J. McGraw, Baltimore, 118 games, 1899; 118 games at third base.
N. L. since 1900—.379—Fred C. Lindstrom, New York, 148 games, 1930; 148 games at
          third base.

Highest Batting Average, Season, 100 or More Games, Shortstop

N. L.—.397—Hugh A. Jennings, Baltimore, 129 games, 1896; 129 games at shortstop.
A. L.—.388—Lucius B. Appling, Chicago, 138 games, 1936; 137 games at shortstop.
N. L. since 1900—.385—J. Floyd Vaughan, Pittsburgh, 137 games, 1935; 137 games at
          shortstop.

Highest Batting Average, Season, 100 or More Games, Catcher

A. L.—.362—William M. Dickey, New York, 112 games, 1936; caught in 107 games.
N. L.—.358—John T. Meyers, New York, 126 games, 1912; caught in 122 games.

Highest Batting Average, Season, 100 or More Games, Outfielder

N. L.—.438—Hugh Duffy, Boston, 124 games. 1894; 123 games in outfield.
A. L.—.420—Tyrus R. Cobb, Detroit, 146 games, 1911; 146 games in outfield.
N. L. since 1900—.398—Frank J. O'Doul, Philadelphia, 154 games, 1929; 154 games in outfield.

Highest Batting Average, Season, Pitcher (Only for Games as Pitcher)

A. L.—.440—Walter P. Johnson, Washington, 36 games, 1925; pitched 30 games.
N. L.—.406—John N. Bentley, New York, 52 games, 1923; pitched 31 games.

Most Years Leading League in Batting Average

A. L.—12—Tyrus R. Cobb, Detroit, 1907, 1908, 1909, 1910, 1911, 1912, 1913, 1914, 1915, 1917, 1918, 1919. (This record is in dispute. See explanation on Page 3.)
N. L.— 8—John P. Wagner, Pittsburgh, 1900, 1903, 1904, 1906, 1907, 1908, 1909, 1911.

Most Consecutive Years Leading League in Batting Average

A. L.—9—Tyrus R. Cobb, Detroit, 1907 through 1915. (This record is in dispute. See explanation on Page 3.)
N. L.—6—Rogers Hornsby, St. Louis, 1920 through 1925.

Most Years .400 or Over, 50 or More Games

N. L.—3—Jesse C. Burkett, Cleveland, St. Louis, 1895, 1896, 1899.
Rogers Hornsby, St. Louis, 1922, 1924, 1925.
A. L.—3—Tyrus R. Cobb, Detroit, 1911, 1912, 1922.

Most Consecutive Years .400 or Over, 50 or More Games

N. L.—2—Jesse C. Burkett, Cleveland, 1895, 1896.
Rogers Hornsby, St. Louis, 1924, 1925.
A. L.—2—Tyrus R. Cobb, Detroit, 1911, 1912.

Most Years .300 or Over, 50 or More Games

A. L.—23—Tyrus R. Cobb, Detroit, Philadelphia, 1906 through 1928.
N. L.—18—Adrian C. Anson, Chicago, 1876 to 1897, except 1877, 1879, 1891 and 1892.
N. L. since 1900—17—Stanley F. Musial, St. Louis, 1942 through 1958, and 1962 (except 1945, in military service).

Most Years .300 or Over, Pitcher

A. L.—8—Charles H. Ruffing, Boston, New York, 1928, 1929, 1930, 1931, 1932, 1935, 1939, 1941.
N. L.—5—John E. Stivetts, Boston, 1892, 1893, 1894, 1896, 1897.

Most Consecutive Years, .300 or Over, 50 or More Games

A. L.—23—Tyrus R. Cobb, Detroit, Philadelphia, 1906 through 1928.
N. L.—17—John P. Wagner, Louisville, Pittsburgh, 1897 through 1913.
N. L. since 1900—16—Stanley F. Musial, St. Louis, 1942 through 1958 (except 1945, in military service).

Most Consecutive Years, .300 or Over, 50 or More Games, Start of Career

N. L.—17—John P. Wagner, Louisville, Pittsburgh, 1897 through 1913.
N. L. since 1900—16—Stanley F. Musial, St. Louis, 1942 through 1958 (except 1945, in military service).
A. L.—15—Theodore S. Williams, Boston, 1939 through 1958 (except 1943-44-45 and 1952-53, in military service).

Highest Slugging Average, Season, 100 or More Games

A. L.—.847—George H. Ruth, New York, 142 games, 1920.
N. L.—.756—Rogers Hornsby, St. Louis, 138 games, 1925.

Highest Slugging Average, League, Thirteen or More Seasons

A. L.—.692—George H. Ruth, Boston, New York, 21 years, 1914 through 1934.
N. L.—.578—Rogers Hornsby, St. Louis, New York, Boston, Chicago, 19 years, 1915 through 1933.

Most Years Leading League in Slugging Average, 100 or More Games

A. L.— 13— George H. Ruth, Boston, New York, 1918 through 1931, except 1925.
(Played only 95 games in 1918, short season due to war.)
N. L.— 9— Rogers Hornsby, St. Louis, Boston, Chicago, 1917, 1920, 1921, 1922, 1923, 1924, 1925, 1928, 1929.

Lowest Slugging Average, Season, 150 or More Games

N. L.—.223—C. Dallan Maxvill, St. Louis, 152 games, 1970.
A. L.—.243—George F. McBride, Washington, 156 games, 1914.

Lowest Slugging Average, Season, Slugging Leader, 100 or More Games

N. L.—.436—Henry H. Myers, Brooklyn, 133 games, 1919.
A. L.—.466—Elmer H. Flick, Cleveland, 131 games, 1905.

Most At-Bats, League

N. L.—13,037—Peter E. Rose, Cincinnati, Philadelphia, 21 years, 1963 through 1983.
A. L.—11,988—Carl M. Yastrzemski, Boston, 23 years, 1961 through 1983.

Most Plate Appearances, League

N. L.—14,696—Peter E. Rose, Cincinnati, Philadelphia, 21 years, 1963 through 1983.
A. L.—13,990—Carl M. Yastrzemski, Boston, 23 years, 1961 through 1983.

Most At-Bats, Season

A. L. (162-game season)—705—Willie J. Wilson, Kansas City, 161 games, 1980.
A. L. (154-game season)—679—Harvey Kuenn, Detroit, 155 games, 1953.
N. L. (162-game season)—699—David Cash, Philadelphia, 162 games, 1975.
N. L. (154-game season)—696—Forrest D. Jensen, Pittsburgh, 153 games, 1936.

Most Plate Appearances, Season

N. L. (162-game season)—771—Peter E. Rose, Cincinnati, 163 games, 1974.
N. L. (154-game season)—755—Elwood G. English, Chicago, 156 games, 1930.
A. L. (162-game season)—754—Robert C. Richardson, New York, 161 games, 1962.
A. L. (154-game season)—757—Frank P. J. Crosetti, New York, 157 games, 1938.

Fewest At-Bats, Season, 150 or More Games

A. L.— 389— Tommy L. McCraw, Chicago, 151 games, 1966.
N. L.— 399— C. Dallan Maxvill, St. Louis, 152 games, 1970.

Most Years Leading League in At-Bats

A. L.—7—Roger M. Cramer, Philadelphia, Boston, Washington, Detroit, 1933, 1934, 1935, 1938, 1940, 1941, 1942.
N. L.—4—Abner F. Dalrymple, Chicago, 1880, 1882, 1884, 1885.
N. L. since 1900—4—Peter E. Rose, Cincinnati, 1965, 1972, 1973, 1977.

Most Consecutive Years Leading League in At-Bats

N. L.—3—Earl J. Adams, Chicago, 1925, 1926, 1927.
       David Cash, Philadelphia, 1974, 1975, 1976.
A. L.—3—Roger M. Cramer, Philadelphia, 1933, 1934, 1935.
       Roger M. Cramer, Boston, Washington, Detroit, 1940, 1941, 1942.
       Robert C. Richardson, New York, 1962, 1963, 1964.

Most Years 600 or More At-Bats, League

N. L.—17—Peter E. Rose, Cincinnati, 1963, 1965, 1966, 1968, 1969, 1970, 1971, 1972, 1973, 1974, 1975, 1976, 1977, 1978, Philadelphia, 1979, 1980, 1982.
A. L.—12—J. Nelson Fox, Chicago, 1951, 1952, 1953, 1954, 1955, 1956, 1957, 1958, 1959, 1960, 1961, 1962 (consecutive).

Most Consecutive Years, 600 or More At-Bats, League

N. L.—13—Peter E. Rose, Cincinnati, Philadelphia, 1968 through 1980.
A. L.—12—J. Nelson Fox, Chicago, 1951 through 1962.

Fewest At-Bats, Season, for Leader in At-Bats (154 or 162-Game Schedule)

N. L.— 585— Porter B. Shannon, New York, 155 games, 1907.
A. L.— 588— Tyrus R. Cobb, Detroit, 152 games, 1917.

Most At-Bats, Season, Pinch-Hitter

N. L. (162-game season)—81—Daniel J. Staub, New York, 94 games, 1983.
N. L. (154-game season)—72—Samuel A. Leslie, New York, 75 games, 1932.
A. L. (162-game season)—72—David E. Philley, Baltimore, 79 games, 1961.
A. L. (154-game season)—66—Julio Becquer, Washington, 70 games, 1957.

Most Times Faced Pitcher as Batsman, Inning

A. A.—3—Lawrence P. Murphy, Washington, June 17, 1891, first inning.
N. L. before 1900—3—Held by ten players.
N. L. since 1900—3—Martin Callaghan, Chicago, August 25, 1922, fourth inning.
       William R. Cox, Harold H. Reese and Edwin D. Snider, Brooklyn, all on May 21, 1952, first inning.
       Gilbert R. Hodges, Brooklyn, August 8, 1954, eighth inning.
       Johnnie B. Baker, Atlanta, September 20, 1972, second inning.
A. L.—3—Theodore S. Williams, Boston, July 4, 1948, seventh inning; Samuel C. White, G. Eugene Stephens, Thomas M. Umphlett, John J. Lipon and George C. Kell, Boston, all on June 18, 1953, seventh inning.

Most At-Bats, Game, Nine Innings

N. L.—8—Held by 18 players. Last player—William J. McCormick, Chicago, June 29, 1897.

N. L. since 1900—7—Held by many players. Last two players—Renaldo A. Stennett, Pittsburgh, September 16, 1975. Richard J. Hebner, Pittsburgh, September 16, 1975.

A. L.—7—Held by many players. Last player—Donald E. Baylor, California, August 25, 1979.

Most Times Faced Pitcher as Batsman, Game, Nine Innings

N. L. before 1900—8—Held by many players.

N. L. since 1900—8—Russell G. Wrightstone, Philadelphia, August 25, 1922.
Frank J. Parkinson, Philadelphia, August 25, 1922.
Taylor L. Douthit, St. Louis, July 6, 1929, second game.
Andrew A. High, St. Louis, July 6, 1929, second game.

A. L.—8—Clyde F. Vollmer, Boston, June 8, 1950.

Most At-Bats, Extra-Inning Game

N. L.—11—Carson L. Bigbee, Pittsburgh, August 22, 1917, 22 innings.
Charles Pick, Boston, May 1, 1920, 26 innings.
Norman D. Boeckel, Boston, May 1, 1920, 26 innings.
Ralph A. Garr, Atlanta, May 4, 1973, 20 innings.
David L. Schneck, New York, September 11, 1974, 25 innings.
David Cash, Montreal, May 21, 1977, 21 innings.

A. L.—11—John H. Burnett, Cleveland, July 10, 1932, 18 innings.
Edward Moran, Cleveland, July 10, 1932, 18 innings.
Irvin Hall, Philadelphia, July 21, 1945, 24 innings.
Robert C. Richardson, New York, June 24, 1962, 22 innings.

Most Times Faced Pitcher as Batsman, Extra-Inning Game

N. L.—12—Felix B. Millan, New York, September 11, 1974, 25 innings.
John D. Milner, New York, September 11, 1974, 25 innings.

A. L.—11—Held by many players.
Last Player—Robert C. Richardson, New York, June 24, 1962, 22 innings.

Most At-Bats, Doubleheader, 18 Innings.

N. L.—13—Walter J. Maranville, Pittsburgh, August 8, 1922.
William J. Herman, Chicago, August 21, 1935.

A. L.—13—David E. Philley, Chicago, May 30, 1950.

Most At-Bats, Doubleheader, More Than 18 Innings

N. L.—14—Joseph O. Christopher, New York, May 31, 1964, 32 innings.
James L. Hickman, New York, May 31, 1964, 32 innings.
Edward E. Kranepool, New York, May 31, 1964, 32 innings.
Roy D. McMillan, New York, May 31, 1964, 32 innings.
Frank J. Thomas, New York, May 31, 1964, 32 innings.

A. L.—14—Robert J. Monday, Kansas City, June 17, 1967, 28 innings.
Ramon A. Webster, Kansas City, June 17, 1967, 28 innings.

Most Times Faced Pitcher, Game, No Official At-Bats

N. L.—6—Charles M. Smith, Boston, April 17, 1890; 5 bases on balls, 1 hit by pitcher.
Walter Wilmot, Chicago, August 22, 1891. 6 bases on balls.
Miller J. Huggins, St. Louis, June 1, 1910; 4 bases on balls, 1 sacrifice hit, 1 sacrifice fly.
William M. Urbanski, Boston, June 13, 1934; 4 bases on balls, 2 sacrifice hits.

A. L.—6—James E. Foxx, Boston, June 16, 1938; 6 bases on balls.

Most Runs, League

A. L.—2,245—Tyrus R. Cobb, Detroit, Philadelphia, 24 years, 1905 through 1928.

N. L.—2,107—Henry L. Aaron, Milwaukee, Atlanta, 21 years, 1954 through 1974.

Most Runs, Season

N. L.— 196— William R. Hamilton, Philadelphia, 131 games, 1894.

A. L.— 177— George H. Ruth, New York, 152 games, 1921.

N. L. since 1900—158—Charles H. Klein, Philadelphia, 156 games, 1930.

Fewest Runs, Season, 150 or More Games

A. L.—25—Leonard A. Cardenas, California, 150 games, 1972.

N. L.—32—Michael J. Doolan, Philadelphia, 151 games, 1913.

Most Years Leading League in Runs

A. L.—8—George H. Ruth, Boston, New York, 1919, 1920, 1921, 1923, 1924, 1926, 1927, 1928.

N. L.—5—George J. Burns, New York, 1914, 1916, 1917, 1919, 1920.
Rogers Hornsby, St. Louis, New York, Chicago, 1921, 1922, 1924 (tied), 1927 (tied), 1929.
Stanley F. Musial, St. Louis, 1946, 1948, 1951 (tied), 1952 (tied), 1954 (tied).

Most Consecutive Years Leading League in Runs

  A. L.—5—Theodore S. Williams, Boston, 1940, 1941, 1942 (in military service 1943-44-45), 1946, 1947.
  N. L.—3—Michael J. Kelly, Chicago, 1884, 1885, 1886.
        Charles H. Klein, Philadelphia, 1930, 1931 (tied), 1932.
        Edwin D. Snider, Brooklyn, 1953, 1954 (tied), 1955.
        Peter E. Rose, Cincinnati, 1974, 1975, 1976.

Most Years 100 or More Runs, League

  N. L.—15—Henry L. Aaron, Milwaukee, Atlanta, 1955 through 1970, except 1968.
  A. L.—13—H. Louis Gehrig, New York, 1926 through 1938.

Most Consecutive Years 100 or More Runs, League

  A. L.—13—H. Louis Gehrig, New York, 1926 through 1938.
  N. L.—13—Henry L. Aaron, Milwaukee, Atlanta, 1955 through 1967.

Most Years 150 or More Runs, League

  A. L.—6—George H. Ruth, New York, 1920, 1921, 1923, 1927, 1928, 1930.
  N. L.—4—William R. Hamilton, Philadelphia, Boston, 1894, 1895, 1896, 1897.
  N. L. since 1900—2—Charles H. Klein, Philadelphia, 1930, 1932.

Fewest Runs, Season, for Leader in Runs (154-Game Schedule)

  N. L.—89—Clifford C. Cravath, Philadelphia, 150 games, 1915.
  A. L.—92—Harry H. Davis, Philadelphia, 149 games, 1905.

Most Runs, Inning

  N. L.—3—Thomas E. Burns, Chicago, September 6, 1883, seventh inning.
        Edward N. Williamson, Chicago, September 6, 1883, seventh inning.
  A. L.—3—Samuel C. White, Boston, June 18, 1953, seventh inning.
  N. L. since 1900—2—Held by many players.

Most Runs, Game

  A. A.—7—Guy J. Hecker, Louisville, August 15, 1886, second game.
  N. L.—6—James E. Whitney, Boston, June 9, 1883.
        Adrian C. Anson, Chicago, August 24, 1886.
        Michael J. Tiernan, New York, June 15, 1887.
        Michael J. Kelly, Boston, August 27, 1887.
        Ezra B. Sutton, Boston, August 27, 1887.
        James Ryan, Chicago, July 25, 1894.
        Robert L. Lowe, Boston, May 3, 1895.
        Clarence H. Beaumont, Pittsburgh, July 22, 1899.
        Melvin T. Ott, New York, August 4, 1934, second game; April 30, 1944, first game.
        Frank J. Torre, Milwaukee, September 2, 1957, first game.
  A. L.—6—John Pesky, Boston, May 8, 1946.

Most Runs, Game, by Pitcher

  A. A.—7—Guy J. Hecker, Louisville, August 15, 1886, second game.
  N. L.—5—George B. Cuppy, Cleveland, August 9, 1895.
  N. L. since 1900 and A. L.—4—Held by many pitchers.
  N. L.—Last Pitcher—James A. Tobin, Boston, September 12, 1940, first game.
  A. L.—Last Pitcher—William F. Hoeft, Detroit, May 5, 1956.

Most Runs, Doubleheader, 18 Innings

  N. L.—9—Herman A. Long, Boston, May 30, 1894.
  A. L.—9—Melo Almada, Washington, July 25, 1937.
  N. L. since 1900—8—Charles H. Klein, Chicago, August 21, 1935.

Most Runs, Two Consecutive Games, 18 Innings

  A. A.—11—Guy J. Hecker, Louisville, August 12, August 15, second game, 1886.
  N. L.— 9—Herman A. Long, Boston, May 30, 30, 1894.
        James Ryan, Chicago, July 24, 25, 1894.
        William F. Dahlen, Chicago, September 20, 21, 1894.
  A. L.— 9—Melo Almada, Washington, July 25, 25, 1937.
  N. L. since 1900—8—Hazen S. Cuyler, Pittsburgh, June 20, 22, 1925.
        John H. Frederick, Brooklyn, May 17, 18, 1929.
        Melvin T. Ott, New York, August 4, second game, August 5, 1934.
        Charles H. Klein, Chicago, August 21, 21, 1935.
        Stanley F. Musial, St. Louis, May 19, 20, 1948.

Most Consecutive Games Scoring One or More Runs, Season

  N. L.—24—William R. Hamilton, Philadelphia, July 6 through August 2, 1894, 35 runs.
  A. L.—18—Robert A. Rolfe, New York, August 9 through August 25, second game, 1939, 30 runs.

N. L. since 1900—17—Theodore B. Kluszewski, Cincinnati, August 27 through September 13, 1954, 24 runs.

Most Times Five or More Runs in One Game, Season

N. L.—1876 through 1899—2—Held by many players.
N. L. since 1900—2—Hazen S. Cuyler, Pittsburgh, May 12, second game, June 20, 1925.
          Melvin T. Ott, New York, April 30, first game, June 12, 1944.
          Philip Weintraub, New York, April 30, first game, June 12, 1944.
          Willie H. Mays, San Francisco, April 24, September 19, 1964.
A. L.—2—H. Louis Gehrig, New York, May 3, July 28, 1936.

Most Times Five or More Runs in One Game, League

N. L.—6—James E. Ryan, Chicago, 1887, 1889, 1891, 1894 (2), 1897.
          William H. Keeler, Baltimore, Brooklyn, 1895 (2), 1897 (2), 1901, 1902.
A. L.—3—H. Louis Gehrig, New York, 1928, 1936 (2).
          James E. Foxx, Philadelphia, Boston, 1932, 1935, 1939.
N. L. since 1900—3—Melvin T. Ott, New York, 1934, 1944 (2).
          Willie H. Mays, New York, San Francisco, 1954 (1), 1964 (2).

Most Times, Five or More Runs in One Game, in Major Leagues

6—George F. Gore, Chicago N. L., 1880, 1881, 1882 (2), 1883, New York P. L. 1890.
   James E. Ryan, Chicago N. L., 1887, 1889, 1891, 1894 (2), 1897.
   William H. Keeler, Baltimore N. L., 1895 (2), 1897 (2), Brooklyn N. L., 1901, 1902.

Most Hits, League

A. L.—4,191—Tyrus R. Cobb, Detroit, Philadelphia, 24 years, 1905 through 1928. (This record is in dispute. See explanation on Page 3.)
N. L.—3,990—Peter E. Rose, Cincinnati, Philadelphia, 21 years, 1963 through 1983.

Most Hits, Season

(Except 1887 when bases on balls counted as hits.)
A. L.— 257— George H. Sisler, St. Louis, 154 games, 1920.
N. L.— 254—Frank J. O'Doul, Philadelphia, 154 games, 1929.
          William H. Terry, New York, 154 games, 1930.

Most Games, One or More Hits, Season

N. L.— 135— Charles H. Klein, Philadelphia, 156 games, 1930.
A. L.— 133— Aloysius H. Simmons, Philadelphia, 153 games, 1925.

Fewest Hits, Season, 150 or More Games

N. L.—80—C. Dallan Maxvill, St. Louis, 152 games, 1970.
A. L.—82—Edwin A. Brinkman, Washington, 154 games, 1965.

Most Years Leading League in Hits

A. L.—8—Tyrus R. Cobb, Detroit, 1907, 1908, 1909, 1911, 1912, 1915, 1917, 1919 (tied).
N. L.—7—Peter E. Rose, Cincinnati, 1965, 1968 (tied), 1970 (tied), 1972, 1973, 1976, Philadelphia 1981.

Most Consecutive Years Leading League in Hits

N. L.—3—Clarence H. Beaumont, Pittsburgh, 1902, 1903, 1904.
          Rogers Hornsby, St. Louis, 1920, 1921, 1922.
          Frank A. McCormick, Cincinnati, 1938, 1939, 1940 (tied).
          Stanley F. Musial, St. Louis, 1943, 1944 (in military service 1945), 1946.
A. L.—3—Tyrus R. Cobb, Detroit, 1907, 1908, 1909.
          John M. Pesky, Boston, 1942, 1946, 1947 (in military service 1943, 1944, 1945).
          Pedro (Tony) Oliva, Minnesota, 1964, 1965, 1966.

Most Years 200 or More Hits, League

N. L.—10—Peter E. Rose, Cincinnati, 1965, 1966, 1968, 1969, 1970, 1973, 1975, 1976, 1977, Philadelphia, 1979.
A. L.— 9— Tyrus R. Cobb, Detroit, 1907, 1909, 1911, 1912, 1915, 1916, 1917, 1922, 1924.

Most Consecutive Years 200 or More Hits, League

N. L.—8—William H. Keeler, Baltimore, Brooklyn, 1894 through 1901.
A. L.—5—Aloysius H. Simmons, Philadelphia, Chicago, 1929 through 1933.
          Charles L. Gehringer, Detroit, 1933 through 1937.
N. L. since 1900—5—Charles H. Klein, Philadelphia, 1929 through 1933.

Most Hits, Two Consecutive Seasons, League

N. L.— 485— Rogers Hornsby, St. Louis, 235 in 1921, 250 in 1922.
A. L.— 475— Tyrus R. Cobb, Detroit, 248 in 1911, 227 in 1912.

Fewest Hits, Season, for Leader in Hits (154 or 162-Game Schedule)

N. L.— 171— Sherwood R. Magee, Philadelphia, 146 games, 1914.
A. L.— 177— Dagoberto B. Campaneris, Oakland, 159 games, 1968.

Most Times Six Hits in Six Times at Bat, Game, League

N. L.—2—James L. Bottomley, St. Louis, September 16, 1924; August 5, 1931, second game.

A. L.—2—Roger M. Cramer, Philadelphia, June 20, 1932; July 13, 1935.

Most Times Six Hits in Six Times at Bat, Game, Major Leagues

2—Edward J. Delahanty, Cleveland, P. L., June 2, 1890; Philadelphia, N. L., June 16, 1894.

Six or More Hits in One Game
National League (68 times)

H—At Home. A—On Road.

Player Club Date	Place	AB	R	H	2B	3B	HR
David Force, Philadelphia, June 27, 1876	H	6	3	6	1	0	0
Calvin A. McVey, Chicago, July 22, 1876	H	7	4	6	1	0	0
Calvin A. McVey, Chicago, July 25, 1876	H	7	4	6	1	0	0
Roscoe C. Barnes, Chicago, July 27, 1876	H	6	3	6	1	1	0
Paul A. Hines, Providence, Aug. 26, 1879 (10 inn.)	H	6	1	6	0	0	0
George Gore, Chicago, May 7, 1880	H	6	5	6	0	0	0
Lew P. Dickerson, Worcester, June 16, 1881	H	6	3	6	0	1	0
Samuel W. Wise, Boston, June 20, 1883	H	7	5	6	1	1	0
Dennis L. Brouthers, Buffalo, July 19, 1883	H	6	3	6	2	0	0
Daniel Richardson, New York, June 11, 1887	H	7	2	6	0	0	0
Michael J. Kelly, Boston, August 27, 1887	H	7	6	6	1	0	1
Jeremiah Denny, Indianapolis, May 4, 1889	H	6	3	6	1	0	1
Lawrence Twitchell, Cleveland, August 15, 1889	H	6	5	6	1	3	1
John W. Glasscock, New York, September 27, 1890	A	6	2	6	0	0	0
Robert L. Lowe, Boston, June 11, 1891	H	6	4	6	1	0	1
Henry Larkin, Washington, June 7, 1892	H	7	3	6	0	1	0
Wilbert Robinson, Balt., June 10, 1892 (1st game)	H	7	1	7	1	0	0
John J. Boyle, Philadelphia, July 6, 1893 (11 inn.)	A	6	1	6	1	0	0
Richard Cooley, St. Louis, Sept. 30, 1893 (2nd game)	A	6	1	6	1	1	0
Edward J. Delahanty, Philadelphia, June 16, 1894	H	6	4	6	1	0	0
Walter S. Brodie, Baltimore, July 9, 1894	H	6	2	6	2	1	0
Charles L. Zimmer, Cleveland, July 11, 1894 (10 inn.)	H	6	3	6	2	0	0
Samuel L. Thompson, Philadelphia, August 17, 1894	H	7	4	6	1	1	1
Roger Connor, St. Louis, June 1, 1895	A	6	4	6	2	1	0
George S. Davis, New York, August 15, 1895	A	6	3	6	2	1	0
Jacob C. Stenzel, Pittsburgh, May 14, 1896	H	6	3	6	0	0	0
Fred C. Tenney, Boston, May 31, 1897	H	8	3	6	1	0	0
Richard Harley, St. Louis, June 24, 1897 (12 inn.)	A	6	2	6	1	0	0
William J. McCormick, Chicago, June 29, 1897	H	8	5	6	0	1	1
Thomas J. Tucker, Washington, July 15, 1897	A	6	1	6	1	0	0
William H. Keeler, Baltimore, September 3, 1897	H	6	5	6	0	1	0
John J. Doyle, Baltimore, September 3, 1897	H	6	2	6	2	0	0
Charles S. Stahl, Boston, May 31, 1899	H	6	4	6	0	0	0
Clarence H. Beaumont, Pittsburgh, July 22, 1899	H	6	6	6	0	0	0
Albert K. Selbach, New York, June 9, 1901	A	7	4	6	2	0	0
George W. Cutshaw, Brooklyn, August 9, 1915	A	6	2	6	0	0	0
Carson L. Bigbee, Pittsburgh, Aug. 22, 1917 (22 inn.)	A	11	0	6	0	0	0
David J. Bancroft, New York, June 28, 1920	A	6	2	6	0	0	0
John B. Gooch, Pittsburgh, July 7, 1922 (18 inn.)	H	8	1	6	1	0	0
Max Carey, Pittsburgh, July 7, 1922 (18 inn.)	H	6	3	6	1	0	0
Jacques F. Fournier, Brooklyn, June 29, 1923	A	6	1	6	2	0	1
Hazen S. Cuyler, Pittsburgh, Aug. 9, 1924 (1st game)	A	6	3	6	3	1	0
Frank F. Frisch, New York, Sept. 10, 1924 (1st game)	H	7	3	6	0	0	1
James L. Bottomley, St. Louis, September 16, 1924	A	6	3	6	1	0	2
Paul G. Waner, Pittsburgh, August 26, 1926	H	6	1	6	2	1	0
Lloyd J. Waner, Pittsburgh, June 15, 1929 (14 inn.)	H	8	2	6	1	1	0
John H. DeBerry, Brooklyn, June 23, 1929 (14 inn.)	H	7	0	6	0	0	0
Walter J. Gilbert, Brooklyn, May 30, 1931 (2nd game)	A	7	3	6	1	0	0
James L. Bottomley, St. L., Aug. 5, 1931 (2nd game)	A	6	2	6	1	0	0
Anthony F. Cuccinello, Cin., Aug. 13, 1931 (1st game)	A	6	4	6	2	1	0
Terry B. Moore, St. Louis, September 5, 1935	H	6	2	6	1	0	0
Ernest N. Lombardi, Cincinnati, May 9, 1937	A	6	3	6	1	0	0
Frank Demaree, Chi., July 5, 1937 (1st game, 14 inn.)	H	7	2	6	3	0	0
Harry A. Lavagetto, Brkn., Sept. 23, 1939 (1st game)	A	6	4	6	1	1	0
W. Walker Cooper, Cincinnati, July 6, 1949	H	7	5	6	0	0	3
John L. Hopp, Pittsburgh, May 14, 1950 (2nd game)	A	6	3	6	0	0	2
Cornelius J. Ryan, Philadelphia, April 16, 1953	A	6	3	6	2	0	0
Richard M. Groat, Pitts., May 13, 1960	A	6	2	6	3	0	0
Jesus M. Alou, San Francisco, July 10, 1964	A	6	1	6	0	0	1

Player Club Date	Place	AB	R	H	2B	3B	HR
Joe L. Morgan, Houston, July 8, 1965 (12 inn.)	A	6	4	6	0	1	2
Felix B. Millan, Atlanta, July 6, 1970	H	6	2	6	1	1	0
Donald E. Kessinger, Chicago, July 17, 1971 (10 inn.)	H	6	3	6	1	0	0
Willie H. Davis, Los Angeles, May 24, 1973 (19 inn.)	H	9	1	6	0	0	0
Bill Madlock, Chicago, July 26, 1975 (10 inn.)	H	6	1	6	0	1	0
Renaldo A. Stennett, Pittsburgh, September 16, 1975	A	7	5	7	2	1	0
Jose D. Cardenal, Chicago, May 2, 1976, (1st game, 14 inn.)	A	7	2	6	1	0	1
Eugene Richards, San Diego, July 26, 1977, (2nd game, 15 inns.)	H	7	1	6	1	0	0
Joseph H. Lefebvre, San Diego, September 13, 1982 (16 inn.)	A	8	1	6	1	0	1

Six or More Hits in One Game
American League (36 times)

Player Club Date	Place	AB	R	H	2B	3B	HR
Michael J. Donlin, Baltimore, June 24, 1901	H	6	5	6	2	2	0
William G. Nance, Detroit, July 13, 1901	H	6	3	6	1	0	0
Erwin K. Harvey, Cleveland, April 25, 1902	A	6	3	6	0	0	0
Daniel F. Murphy, Philadelphia, July 8, 1902	A	6	3	6	0	0	1
James T. Williams, Baltimore, August 25, 1902	H	6	1	6	1	1	0
Robert H. Veach, Detroit, Sept. 17, 1920 (12 inn.)	H	6	2	6	1	1	1
George H. Sisler, St. Louis, Aug. 9, 1921 (19 inn.)	A	9	2	6	0	1	0
Frank W. Brower, Cleveland, August 7, 1923	A	6	3	6	1	0	0
George H. Burns, Cleve., June 19, 1924 (1st game)	A	6	2	6	3	1	0
Tyrus R. Cobb, Detroit, May 5, 1925	A	6	4	6	1	0	3
James E. Foxx, Phila., May 30, 1930 (a.m. game, 13 inn.)	H	7	0	6	2	1	0
Roger M. Cramer, Philadelphia, June 20, 1932	A	6	3	6	0	0	0
James E. Foxx, Phil., July 10, 1932, (18 inn.)	A	9	4	6	1	0	3
John H. Burnett, Cleve., July 10, 1932, (18 inn.)	H	11	4	9	2	0	0
Samuel West, St. Louis, April 13, 1933, (11 inn.)	H	6	2	6	1	0	0
Myril O. Hoag, New York, June 6, 1934 (first game)	A	6	3	6	0	0	0
Rob. Johnson, Phil., June 16, 1934, (2nd game, 11 inn.)	H	6	3	6	1	0	2
Roger M. Cramer, Phila., July 13, 1935, (1st game)	H	6	3	6	1	0	0
Bruce D. Campbell, Cleve., July 2, 1936, (1st game)	A	6	1	6	1	0	0
Raymond A. Radcliff, Chi., July 18, 1936, (2nd game)	A	7	4	6	2	0	0
Henry Steinbacher, Chicago, June 22, 1938	H	6	3	6	1	0	0
George Myatt, Washington, May 1, 1944	A	6	3	6	1	0	0
Stanley O. Spence, Washington, June 1, 1944	A	6	2	6	0	0	1
George C. Kell, Detroit, September 20, 1946	A	7	4	6	1	0	0
James R. Fridley, Cleve., April 29, 1952	A	6	4	6	0	0	0
James A. Piersall, Bos., June 10, 1953, (1st game)	A	6	2	6	1	0	0
Joseph P. DeMaestri, K.C., July 8, 1955 (11 inn.)	A	6	2	6	0	0	0
James E. Runnels, Bos., Aug. 30, 1960, (1st game, 15 inn.)	H	7	1	6	1	0	0
Rocco D. Colavito, Detroit, June 24, 1962, (22 inn.)	H	10	1	7	0	1	0
Floyd A. Robinson, Chicago, July 22, 1962	A	6	1	6	0	0	0
Robert L. Oliver, Kansas City, May 4, 1969	A	6	2	6	1	0	1
James T. Northrup, Detroit, August 28, 1969, (13 inn.)	H	6	2	6	0	0	2
Cesar D. Gutierrez, Detroit, June 21, 1970, (2nd game, 12 inn.)	A	7	3	7	1	0	0
John E. Briggs, Milwaukee, Aug. 4, 1973	A	6	2	6	2	0	0
Jorge Orta, Cleveland, June 15, 1980	H	6	4	6	1	0	0
Gerald P. Remy, Boston, September 3, 1981, (20 inn.)	H	10	2	6	0	0	0

American Association (15 times)

Player Club Date	Place	AB	R	H	2B	3B	HR
William W. Carpenter, Cincinnati, Sept. 12, 1883	H	7	5	6	0	0	0
John G. Reilly, Cincinnati, September 12, 1883	H	7	6	6	1	1	1
Oscar Walker, Brooklyn, May 31, 1884	H	6	2	6	1	1	0
Alonzo Knight, Philadelphia, July 30, 1884	H	6	5	6	0	1	0
David L. Orr, New York, June 12, 1885	H	6	4	6	2	1	1
Henry Larkin, Philadelphia, June 16, 1885	H	6	4	6	2	1	1
George B. Pinckney, Brooklyn, June 25, 1885	H	6	5	6	0	0	0
Walter A. Latham, St. Louis, April 24, 1886	H	6	5	6	0	1	0
Guy J. Hecker, Louisville, Aug. 15, 1886, (2nd game)	H	7	7	6	0	0	3
H. Dennis Lyons, Philadelphia, April 26, 1887	H	6	4	6	2	1	0
Peter J. Hotaling, Cleveland, June 6, 1888	H	7	5	6	0	1	0
James J. McTamany, Kansas City, June 15, 1888	H	6	3	6	0	0	1
William D. O'Brien, Brooklyn, August 8, 1889	A	6	1	6	3	0	0
William B. Weaver, Louisville, August 12, 1890	H	6	3	6	1	2	1
Frank Sheibeck, Toledo, September 27, 1890	H	6	4	6	1	1	0

Players League (twice)

Player Club Date	Place	AB	R	H	2B	3B	HR
Edward J. Delahanty, Cleveland, June 2, 1890	H	6	4	6	1	1	0
William Shindle, Philadelphia, August 26, 1890	H	6	3	6	2	1	0

Most Times Five or More Hits in One Game, Season

N. L.—4—William H. Keeler, Baltimore, July 17, August 14, September 3, September 6, first game, 1897.
Stanley F. Musial, St. Louis, April 30, May 19, June 22, September 22, 1948.
A. L.—4—Tyrus R. Cobb, Detroit, May 7, July 7, second game, July 12, July 17, 1922.

Most Times Five or More Hits in One Game, League

A. L.—14—Tyrus R. Cobb, Detroit, Philadelphia, 1908 to 1927.
N. L.— 9—Max G. Carey, Pittsburgh, Brooklyn, 1914 to 1927.
Peter E. Rose, Cincinnati, Philadelphia, 1963 to 1982.

Most Times Five Hits in One Game, by Pitcher, Major Leagues

3—James J. Callahan, Chicago N. L., 1897, Chicago A. L., 1902, 1903.

Most Clubs, One or More Hits, One Day

N. L.—2—Joel R. Youngblood, New York, Montreal, August 4, 1982.

Most Hits, League, by Pinch-Hitter

N. L.— 150— Manuel Mota, San Francisco, Pittsburgh, Montreal, Los Angeles, 20 years, 1962 through 1982, 599 games.
A. L.— 107— William J. Brown, Detroit, 13 years, 1963 through 1975, 525 games.

Most Hits, Season, by Pinch-Hitter

N. L. (162-game season)—25—Jose M. Morales, Montreal, 82 games, 1976.
N. L. (154-game season)—22—Samuel A. Leslie, New York, 75 games, 1932.
A. L. (162-game season)—24—David E. Philley, Baltimore, 79 games, 1961.
A. L. (154-game season)—20—Parke E. Coleman, St. Louis, 74 games, 1936.

Most Hits, Inning

N. L.—3—Thomas E. Burns, Chicago, September 6, 1883, seventh inning; 2 doubles, 1 home run.
Fred N. Pfeffer, Chicago, September 6, 1883, seventh inning; 2 singles, 1 double.
Edward N. Williamson, Chicago, September 6, 1883, seventh inning; 2 singles, 1 double.
A. L.—3—G. Eugene Stephens, Boston, June 18, 1953, seventh inning; 2 singles, 1 double.

Most Hits, Inning, First Game in Majors

A. L.—2—Alfred M. Martin, New York, April 18, 1950, eighth inning.

Most Times Two Hits in One Inning, One Game

N. L.—2—Max Carey, Pittsburgh, June 22, 1925, first and eighth innings; 2 singles, each inning.
Renaldo A. Stennett, Pittsburgh, September 16, 1975, first inning, single and double; fifth inning, double and single.
A. L.—2—John Hodapp, Cleveland, July 29, 1928, second and sixth innings, 2 singles, each inning.
J. Sherman Lollar, Chicago, April 23, 1955, second inning, single and home run; sixth inning, 2 singles.

Most Hits, Game, Nine Innings

N. L.—7—Wilbert Robinson, Baltimore, June 10, 1892, first game; 6 singles, 1 double (consecutive).
Renaldo A. Stennett, Pittsburgh, September 16, 1975, 4 singles, 2 doubles, 1 triple (consecutive).
N. L. since 1900—6—22 times. Held by 21 players.
A. L.—6—23 times. Held by 22 players.

Most Hits, Extra-Inning Game

A. L.—9—John H. Burnett, Cleveland, July 10, 1932, 18 innings, 7 singles. 2 doubles.
N. L.—6—Held by 13 players. Last Player—Eugene Richards, San Diego, July 26, 1977, second game, 15 innings, 5 singles, 1 double.

Most At-Bats, Extra-Inning Game, No Hits

N. L.—11—Charles Pick, Boston, May 1, 1920, 26 innings.
A. L.—10—George C. Kell, Philadelphia, July 21, 1945, 24 innings.

Most At-Bats, Doubleheader (9-Inning Games), No Hits

A. L.—11—Albert G. Pearson, Los Angeles, July 1, 1962.
N. L.—10—Held by many players.

Most At-Bats, Doubleheader (More than 18 innings), No Hits

N. L.—12—Albert F. Schoendienst, St. Louis, June 9, 1947, 24 innings.
A. L.—12—Robert P. Saverine, Washington, June 8, 1966, 23 innings.

Making All Club's Hits, Game (Most)

A. L.—4—Norman Elberfeld, New York, August 1, 1903, 4 singles.
N. L.—4—Billy L. Williams, Chicago, September 5, 1969, 2 doubles, 2 homers.

Most Hits, First Game in Majors

N. L.—5—Fred C. Clarke, Louisville, June 30, 1894; 4 singles, 1 triple.
A. L.—5—Cecil H. Travis, Washington, May 16, 1933, 12 innings; 5 singles.
A. L.—Nine innings— 4—Raymond W. Jansen, St. Louis, September 30, 1910; 4 singles
    (only game in major league career).
    Charles A. Shires, Chicago, August 20, 1928; 3 singles, 1 triple.
    Russell P. Van Atta, New York, April 25, 1933; 4 singles.
    Forrest V. Jacobs, Philadelphia, April 13, 1954; 4 singles.
    W. Ted Cox, Boston, September 18, 1977; 3 singles, 1 double (consecutive).
N. L. since 1900—4—Charles D. Stengel, Brooklyn, September 17, 1912; 4 singles, 1 base
    on balls.
    Willie L. McCovey, San Francisco, July 30, 1959; 2 singles, 2 triples (consecu-
    tive).
    Mack Jones, Milwaukee, July 13, 1961; 3 singles, 1 double.

Most Times Reached First Base Safely, Inning

N. L.—3—Edward N. Williamson, Chicago, September 6, 1883, seventh inning.
    Thomas E. Burns, Chicago, September 6, 1883, seventh inning.
    Fred N. Pfeffer, Chicago, September 6, 1883, seventh inning.
    Herman A. Long, Boston, June 18, 1894, a.m. game, first inning.
    Robert L. Lowe, Boston, June 18, 1894, a.m. game, first inning.
    Hugh Duffy, Boston, June 18, 1894, a.m. game, first inning.
    Harold H. Reese, Brooklyn, May 21, 1952, first inning.
A. L.—3—Samuel C. White, Boston, June 18, 1953, seventh inning.
    G. Eugene Stephens, Boston, June 18, 1953, seventh inning.
    Thomas M. Umphlett, Boston, June 18, 1953, seventh inning.

Most Times Reached First Base Safely, Nine-Inning Game (Batting 1.000)

N. L.—8—Frank G. Ward, Cincinnati, June 18, 1893, 2 singles, 5 bases on balls, 1 hit by
    pitcher.
A. L.—7—W. Benjamin Chapman, New York, May 24, 1936, 2 doubles, 5 bases on balls.
N. L. since 1900—7—Clifton E. Heathcote, Chicago, August 25, 1922, 3 singles, 2 doubles,
    2 bases on balls.
    Harry A. Lavagetto, Brooklyn, September 23, 1939, first game, 4 singles, 1
    double, 1 triple, 1 base on balls.
    Melvin T. Ott, New York, April 30, 1944, first game, 2 singles, 5 bases on balls.
    Renaldo A. Stennett, Pittsburgh, September 16, 1975, 4 singles, 2 doubles, 1
    triple.

Most Times Reached First Base Safely, Extra-Inning Game (Batting 1.000)

N. L.—9—Max Carey, Pittsburgh, July 7, 1922, 18 innings; 5 singles, 1 double, 3 bases on
    balls.
A. L.—7—Cesar D. Gutierrez, Detroit, June 21, 1970, second game, 12 innings; 6 singles,
    1 double.

Most Consecutive Times Reached Base Safely, Season

A. L.—16—Theodore S. Williams, Boston, September 17 (1), 18 (1), 20 (1), 21 (4), 22
    (4), 23 (5), 1957; 2 singles, 4 home runs, 9 bases on balls, 1 hit by pitcher.

Most Hits, First Doubleheader in Majors

N. L.-A.L.—6—Held by many players.

Most Hits, Game, by Pitcher

A. A.—6—Guy J. Hecker, Louisville, August 15, 1886, second game.
N. L.-A. L.—5—Held by many pitchers.
N. L.—Last pitcher, Peter J. Donohue, Cincinnati, May 22, 1925, 4 singles, 1 home run.
A. L.—Last pitcher, Melvin L. Stottlemyre, New York, September 26, 1964, 4 singles, 1
    double.

Most Hits, Opening Day of Season

N. L.-A. L.—5—Held by many players.
N. L.—Last Player—William J. Herman, Chicago, April 14, 1936, 1 single, 3 doubles, 1
    home run.
A. L.—Last Player—J. Nelson Fox, Chicago, April 10, 1959, 14 innings, 3 singles, 1 dou-
    ble, 1 home run.

Most Hits, Two Consecutive Games

N. L.—12—Calvin A. McVey, Chicago, July 22 (6), July 25 (6), 1876.
N. L. since 1900—10—Roberto W. Clemente, Pittsburgh, August 22 (5), August 23 (5),
          1970, 25 innings.
          Renaldo A. Stennett, Pittsburgh, September 16 (7), September 17 (3), 1975.
A. L.—11—John H. Burnett, Cleveland, July 9, second game, (2), July 10, (9), 1932, 27
          innings.
A. L.—Nine-inning games—Last Player—9—Don E. Baylor, Baltimore, August 13 (4),
          14 (5), 1973.

Most Hits, Doubleheader

A. A.—9—Fred H. Carroll, Pittsburgh, July 5, 1886.
N. L.—9—Wilbert Robinson, Baltimore, June 10, 1892.
          Joseph J. Kelley, Baltimore, September 3, 1894 (consecutive).
          Fred C. Lindstrom, New York, June 25, 1928.
          William H. Terry, New York, June 18, 1929.
A. L.—9—Ray Morehart, Chicago, August 31, 1926.
          George W. Case, Washington, July 4, 1940.
          James E. Runnels, Boston, August 30, 1960, 25 innings.
          J. Leroy Thomas, Los Angeles, September 5, 1961.

Most Hits, Doubleheader, Pinch-Hitter

N. L.-A. L.—2—Held by many pinch-hitters.

Most Hits, Two Consecutive Games, by Pitcher

A. A.—10—Guy J. Hecker, Louisville, August 12, 15, second game, 1886.
A. L.— 8—George L. Earnshaw, Philadelphia, June 9, 12, second game, 1931.
N. L. since 1900—8—W. Kirby Higbe, Brooklyn, August 11, 17, first game, 1941.

Most Hits, Three Consecutive Games

N. L.—15—Calvin A. McVey, Chicago, July 20 (3), 22 (6), 25 (6), 1876.
N. L.—14—William H. Keeler, Baltimore, September 3, 4, 6, first game, 1897.
A. L.—13—Joseph E. Cronin, Washington, June 19, 21, 22, 1933.
          Walter O. Dropo, Detroit, July 14, 15, 15, 1952.
N. L. since 1900—12—William H. Keeler, Brooklyn, June 19, 20, 21, 1901.
          Milton J. Stock, Brooklyn, June 30, July 1, 2, 1925.
          Stanley F. Musial, St. Louis, August 11, 11, 12, 1946.
          Renaldo A. Stennett, Pittsburgh, September 16 (7), 17 (3), 18 (2), 1975.

Most Hits, Four Consecutive Games

N. L.—17—Calvin A. McVey, Chicago, July 20 (3), July 22 (6), July 25 (6), July 27 (2),
          1876.
          William H. Keeler, Baltimore, September 2, 3, 4, 6, first game, 1897.
N. L. since 1900—16—Milton J. Stock, Brooklyn, June 30, July 1, 2, 3, 1925.
A. A.—17—Guy J. Hecker, Louisville, August 8, 10, 12, 15, second game, 1886.
A. L.—15—John K. Lewis, Jr., Washington, July 25, 25, 27, 28, 1937.
          Walter O. Dropo, Detroit, July 14, 15, 15, 16, 1952.

Most Hits, Two Consecutive Doubleheaders

A. L.—14—Tyrus R. Cobb, Detroit, July 17 (7), 19 (7), 1912.
N. L.—14—William D. White, St. Louis, July 17 (8), 18 (6), 1961.

Most Consecutive Hits, Start of Career

A. L.—6—W. Ted Cox, Boston, September 18, 19, 1977.

Most Consecutive Hits During Season (Bases on Balls, Shown in Streak)

A. L.—12—Michael F. Higgins, Boston, June 19, 19, 21, 21, 1938. (2 B.B.)
          Walter O. Dropo, Detroit, July 14, 15, 15, 1952. (0 B.B.)
N. L.—10—Edward J. Delahanty, Philadelphia, July 13, 13, 14, 1897. (1 B.B.)
          Jacob Gettman, Washington, September 10, 11, 11, 1897. (0 B.B.)
          Edward J. Konetchy, Brooklyn, June 28, second game, June 29, July 1, 1919.
          (0 B.B.)
          Hazen S. Cuyler, Pittsburgh, September 18, 19, 21, 1925. (1 B.B.)
          Charles J. Hafey, St. Louis, July 6, second game, July 8, 9, 1929. (2 B.B.)
          Joseph M. Medwick, St. Louis, July 19, 19, 21, 1936. (1 B.B.)
          John A. Hassett, Boston, June 9, second game, June 10, 14, 1940. (1 B.B.)
          Woodrow W. Williams, Cincinnati, September 5, second game, September 6,
          6, 1943. (1 B.B.)

Most Consecutive Hits During Season by Pinch-Hitter

N. L.—8—David E. Philley, Philadelphia, September 9 through September 28, 1958.
          Daniel J. Staub, New York, June 11 through June 26, first game, 1983.
A. L.—7—William R. Stein, Texas, April 14 through May 25, 1981.

Most Consecutive Hits, League, by Pinch-Hitter

   N. L.—9—David E. Philley, Philadelphia, September 9 through September 28, 1958; April 16, 1959.

Most Consecutive Games Batted Safely During Season

   A. L.—56—Joseph P. DiMaggio, New York, May 15 through July 16, 1941.
   N. L.—44—William H. Keeler, Baltimore, April 22 through June 18, 1897.
        Peter E. Rose, Cincinnati, June 14 through July 31, 1978.

Most Consecutive Games Batted Safely, Start of Season

   N. L.—44—William H. Keeler, Baltimore, April 22 through June 18, 1897.
   A. L.—34—George H. Sisler, St. Louis, April 14 through May 19, 1925.
   N. L. since 1900—25—Charles J. Grimm, Pittsburgh, April 17 through May 16, 1923.

Most Consecutive-Game Batting Streaks (20 or More Games) Season

   A. L.—3—Tristram E. Speaker, Boston, 1912.
   N. L.—2—Held by many players. Last player—Steven P. Garvey, Los Angeles, 1978.

Most Consecutive-Game Batting Streaks (20 or More Games) Season, League

   A. L.—7—Tyrus R. Cobb, Detroit, Philadelphia, 1906, 1911, 1912, 1917, 1918, 1926, 1927.
   N. L.—7—Peter E. Rose, Cincinnati, Philadelphia, 1967, 1968, 1977 (2), 1978, 1979, 1982.

Most Consecutive Games, Three or More Hits, Season

   A. L.—6—George H. Brett, Kansas City, May 8, 9, 10, 11, 12, 13, 1976.

Most One-Base Hits, League

   A. L.—3,052—Tyrus R. Cobb, Detroit, Philadelphia, 24 years, 1905 through 1928.
   N.L.—2,992—Peter E. Rose, Cincinnati, Philadelphia, 21 years, 1963 through 1983.

Most One-Base Hits, Season

   N. L.— 202— William H. Keeler, Baltimore, 128 games, 1898.
   N. L. since 1900—198—Lloyd J. Waner, Pittsburgh, 150 games, 1927.
   A. L.— 184— Willie J. Wilson, Kansas City, 161 games, 1980.

Fewest One-Base Hits, Season, 150 or More Games

   A. L.—58—F. Gene Tenace, Oakland, 158 games, 1974.
   N.L.—63—Michael J. Schmidt, Philadelphia, 160 games, 1979.

Most Years Leading League in One-Base Hits

   A. L.—8—J. Nelson Fox, Chicago, 1952, 1954, 1955, 1956, 1957, 1958, 1959, 1960.
   N. L.—4—Clarence H. Beaumont, Pittsburgh, Boston, 1902, 1903, 1904, 1907.
        Lloyd J. Waner, Pittsburgh, 1927, 1928, 1929 (tied), 1931.
        Richie Ashburn, Philadelphia, 1951, 1953, 1957, 1958.
        Maurice M. Wills, Los Angeles, Pittsburgh, 1961 (tied), 1962, 1965, 1967.

Most Consecutive Years Leading League in One-Base Hits

   A. L.—7—J. Nelson Fox, Chicago, 1954, 1955, 1956, 1957, 1958, 1959, 1960.
   N. L.—3—Clarence H. Beaumont, Pittsburgh, 1902, 1903, 1904.
        Lloyd J. Waner, Pittsburgh, 1927, 1928, 1929 (tied).

Fewest One-Base Hits, Season, Leader in One-Base Hits (154 or 162-Game Schedule)

   A. L.— 129— Donald A. Buford, Chicago, 155 games, 1965.
   N. L.— 127— Enos B. Slaughter, St. Louis, 152 games, 1942.

Most One-Base Hits, Game, Nine Innings

   N. L.-A. A.-A. L.—6—Held by many players.
   N. L.—Last time—David J. Bancroft, New York, June 28, 1920.
   A. L.—Last time—Floyd A. Robinson, Chicago, July 22, 1962.

Most One-Base Hits, Extra-Inning Game

   A. L.—7—John H. Burnett, Cleveland, July 10, 1932, 18 innings.
   N. L.—6—Held by many players. Last player—Willie H. Davis, Los Angeles, May 24, 1973, 19 innings.

Most One-Base Hits, Inning

   N. L.-A. L.—2—Held by many players.

Most One-Base Hits, Doubleheader

   N. L.-A. L.—8—Held by many players.
   A. L.—Last player—H. Earl Averill, Cleveland, May 7, 1933.
   N. L.—Last player—Kenneth D. Hubbs, Chicago, May 20, 1962.

Most One-Base Hits, Game, Each Batting in Three Runs

N. L.-A. L.—1—Held by many players.
N. L.—Last player—Guillermo N. Montanez, Philadelphia, September 8, 1974, eighth inning.
A. L.—Last player—H. Thomas Davis, Baltimore, August 29, 1974, fourth inning.

Most Two-Base Hits, League

A. L.— 793— Tristram Speaker, Boston, Cleveland, Washington, Philadelphia, 22 years, 1907 through 1928.
N. L.— 725— Stanley F. Musial, St. Louis, 22 years, 1941 through 1963 (except 1945, in military service).

Most Two-Base Hits, Season

A. L.—67—Earl W. Webb, Boston, 151 games, 1931.
N. L.—64—Joseph M. Medwick, St. Louis, 155 games, 1936.

Most Two-Base Hits, Season, Catcher

A. L.—42—Gordon S. Cochrane, Philadelphia, 130 games, 1930; caught 130 games.
N. L.—40—Johnny L. Bench, Cincinnati, 154 games, 1968; caught 154 games.
    Terrence E. Kennedy, San Diego, 153 games, 1982; caught 139 games (also had 2 doubles as first baseman).

Fewest Two-Base Hits, Season, 150 or More Games

N. L.—5—C. Dallan Maxvill, St. Louis, 152 games, 1970.
A. L.—6—William P. Purtell, Chicago, Boston, 151 games, 1910.

Most Years Leading League in Two-Base Hits

N. L.—8—John P. Wagner, Pittsburgh, 1900, 1901 (tied), 1902, 1904, 1906, 1907, 1908, 1909.
    Stanley F. Musial, St. Louis, 1943, 1944, 1946, 1948, 1949, 1952, 1953, 1954.
A. L.—8—Tristram Speaker, Boston, Cleveland, 1912, 1914, 1916 (tied), 1918, 1920, 1921, 1922, 1923.

Most Consecutive Years Leading League in Two-Base Hits

N. L.—4—John P. Wagner, Pittsburgh, 1906, 1907, 1908, 1909.
A. L.—4—Tristram Speaker, Cleveland, 1920, 1921, 1922, 1923.

Most Years 50 or More Two-Base Hits, League

A. L.—5—Tristram Speaker, Boston, Cleveland, 1912, 1920, 1921, 1923, 1926.
N. L.—3—Paul G. Waner, Pittsburgh, 1928, 1932, 1936.
    Stanley F. Musial, St. Louis, 1944, 1946, 1953.

Fewest Two-Base Hits, Season, Leader in Two-Base Hits (154 or 162-Game Schedule)

A. L.—32—Salvatore L. Bando, Oakland, 162 games, 1973.
    Pedro Garcia, Milwaukee, 160 games, 1973.
N. L.—34—Henry L. Aaron, Milwaukee, 153 games, 1956.

Most Two-Base Hits, Inning

N. L.-A. L.—2—Held by many players.
N. L.—Last Player—Michael W. Ivie, San Diego, May 30, 1977, first game, seventh inning.
A. L.—Last Player—Robert O. Jones, Texas, July 3, 1983, fifteenth inning.

Most Two-Base Hits, Inning, by Pitcher

N. L.—2—Fred Goldsmith, Chicago, September 6, 1883, seventh inning.
    Henry L. Borowy, Chicago, May 5, 1946, first game, seventh inning.
A. L.—2—Joseph Wood, Boston, July 4, 1913, a.m. game, fourth inning.
    Theodore A. Lyons, Chicago, July 28, 1935, first game, second inning.

Most Two-Base Hits, Game

N. L.—4—17 times (Held by 17 players). Last player—Billy L. Williams, Chicago, April 9, 1969, consecutive.
A. L.—4—15 times (Held by 15 players). Last Player—Richard A. Miller, Boston, May 11, 1981.
A. A.—4—2 times (held by 2 players).

Most Consecutive Two-Base Hits, Game, Nine Innings

N. L.—4—Richard Bartell, Philadelphia, April 25, 1933.
    Ernest N. Lombardi, Cincinnati, May 8, 1935, first game.
    Willie E. Jones, Philadelphia, April 20, 1949.
    Billy L. Williams, Chicago, April 9, 1969.

A. L.—4—William M. Werber, Boston, July 17, 1935, first game.
Michael A. Kreevich, Chicago, September 4, 1937.
John H. Lindell, New York, August 17, 1944.
Victor W. Wertz, Cleveland, September 26, 1956.
William H. Bruton, Detroit, May 19, 1963.
David E. Duncan, Baltimore, June 30, 1975, second game.

Most Two-Base Hits, Opening Game of Season

A. L.—4—Frank Dillon, Detroit, April 25, 1901.
N. L.—4—James R. Greengrass, Cincinnati, April 13, 1954.

Most Two-Base Hits, Game, by Pitcher

N. L.—3—George E. Hemming, Baltimore, August 1, 1895.
John A. Messersmith, Los Angeles, April 25, 1975.
A. L.—3—George Mullin, Detroit, April 27, 1903.
Walter P. Johnson, Washington, July 29, 1917.
George H. Ruth, Boston, May 9, 1918, 10 innings.
George E. Uhle, Cleveland, June 1, 1923.

Most Two-Base Hits, Doubleheader

A. L.—6—Henry Majeski, Philadelphia, August 27, 1948.
N. L.—5—Charles J. Hafey, Cincinnati, July 23, 1933.
Joseph M. Medwick, St. Louis, May 30, 1935.
Albert F. Schoendienst, St. Louis, June 6, 1948.
Michael W. Ivie, San Diego, May 30, 1977.

Most Two-Base Hits, Two Consecutive Games

N. L.—6—Adrian C. Anson, Chicago, July 3, July 4, morning game, 1883.
Samuel L. Thompson, Philadelphia, June 29 (3) July 1 (3), 1895, 22 innings.
Albert F. Schoendienst, St. Louis, June 5, 6, first game, 1948.
A. L.—6—Joseph A. Dugan, Philadelphia, September 24, 25, 1920.
Earl H. Sheely, Chicago, May 20, 21, 1926.
Henry Majeski, Philadelphia, August 27, 28, 1948.

Most Two-Base Hits, Three Consecutive Games

N. L.—8—Albert F. Schoendienst, St. Louis, June 5, 6, 6, 1948.
A. L.—7—Joseph A. Dugan, Philadelphia, September 23, 24, 25, 1920.
Earl H. Sheely, Chicago, May 20, 21, 22, 1926.

Most Two-Base Hits, Three Consecutive Games, Pinch-Hitter

N. L.—3—Berthold Haas, Brooklyn, September 18, 19, 20, 1937.
Douglas H. Clemens, Philadelphia, June 6, 6, 7, 1967.
A. L.—Never accomplished.

Most Two-Base Hits, Game, Each Batting in Three Runs

N. L.—2—Robert J. Gilks, Cleveland, August 5, 1890, 1 in second, 1 in eighth.
Harry H. Davis, New York, June 27, 1896, 1 in fifth, 1 in ninth.
William B. Douglas, Philadelphia, July 11, 1898, 1 in second, 1 in sixth.
Clifford C. Cravath, Philadelphia, August 8, 1915, 1 in fourth, 1 in eighth.
A. L.—1—Held by many players.

Most Three-Base Hits in Major Leagues

312—Samuel Crawford, Cincinnati N. L., Detroit A. L., 19 years, 1899 through 1917; 62 in N. L. and 250 in A. L.

Most Three-Base Hits, League

A. L.— 298— Tyrus R. Cobb, Detroit, Philadephia, 24 years, 1905 through 1928.
N. L.— 252— John P. Wagner, Louisville, Pittsburgh, 21 years, 1897 through 1917.
N. L. since 1900—231—John P. Wagner, Pittsburgh, 18 years, 1900 through 1917.

Most Three-Base Hits, Season

N. L.—36—J. Owen Wilson, Pittsburgh, 152 games, 1912.
A. L.—26—Joseph J. Jackson, Cleveland, 152 games, 1912.
Samuel Crawford, Detroit, 157 games, 1914.

Fewest Three-Base Hits, Season, Most At-Bats

N. L.—0—Octavio R. Rojas, Philadelphia, 152 games, 1968, 621 at-bats.
A. L.—0—James F. Morrison, Chicago, 162 games, 1980, 604 at-bats.

Most Years Leading Major Leagues in Three-Base Hits, Since 1900

6—Samuel Crawford, Cincinnati N. L., 1902; Detroit A. L., 1903, 1910, 1913, 1914, 1915.

Most Years Leading League in Three-Base Hits, Since 1900

A. L.—5—Samuel Crawford, Detroit, 1903, 1910, 1913, 1914, 1915.
N. L.—5—Stanley F. Musial, St. Louis, 1943, 1946, 1948, 1949 (tied), 1951 (tied).

Most Consecutive Years Leading League in Three-Base Hits, Since 1900

N. L.—3—Garry L. Templeton, St. Louis, 1977, 1978, 1979.
A. L.—3—Elmer H. Flick, Cleveland, 1905, 1906, 1907.
    Samuel Crawford, Detroit, 1913, 1914, 1915.
    Zoilo Versalles, Minnesota, 1963, 1964 (tied), 1965 (tied).

Most Years, 20 or More Three-Base Hits in Major Leagues

5—Samuel Crawford, Cincinnati N. L., 1902; Detroit A. L., 1903, 1912, 1913, 1914.

Most Years, 20 or More Three-Base Hits, League

A. L.—4—Samuel Crawford, Detroit, 1903, 1912, 1913, 1914.
    Tyrus R. Cobb, Detroit, 1908, 1911, 1912, 1917.
N. L.—2—Held by many players.

**Fewest Three-Base Hits, Season, for Leader in Three-Base Hits
    (154 or 162-Game Schedule)**

A. L.— 8—Delbert B. Unser, Washington, 153 games, 1969.
N. L.—10—John W. Callison, Philadelphia, 157 games, 1962.
    William H. Davis, Los Angeles, 157 games, 1962.
    William C. Virdon, Pittsburgh, 156 games, 1962.
    Maurice M. Wills, Los Angeles, 165 games, 1962.
    Richard W. Thon, Houston, 136 games, 1982.

Most Three-Base Hits, Inning

N. L.—2—Joseph Hornung, Boston, May 6, 1882, eighth inning.
    Henry Peitz, St. Louis, July 2, 1895, first inning.
    William F. Shugart, Louisville, July 30, 1895, fifth inning.
    John B. Freeman, Boston, July 25, 1900, first inning.
    William F. Dahlen, Brooklyn, August 30, 1900, eighth inning.
    W. Curtis Walker, Cincinnati, July 22, 1926, second inning.
A. A.—2—Harry Wheeler, Cincinnati, June 28, 1882, eleventh inning.
    Harry D. Stovey, Philadelphia, August 18, 1884, eighth inning.
A. L.—2—Allen L. Zarilla, St. Louis, July 13, 1946, fourth inning.
    Gilbert F. Coan, Washington, April 21, 1951, sixth inning.

Most Three-Base Hits, Game

A. A.—4—George A. Strief, Philadelphia, June 25, 1885.
N. L.—4—William Joyce, New York, May 18, 1897.
N. L. since 1900—3—Held by many players.
N. L.—Last player—G. Craig Reynolds, Houston, May 16, 1981.
A. L.—3—Held by many players.
A. L.—Last player—Kenneth F. Landreaux, Minnesota, July 3, 1980.

Most Three-Base Hits, Game, by Pitcher

N. L.—3—Jouett Meekin, New York, July 4, 1894, first game.

Most Consecutive Three-Base Hits, Game, Nine Innings

N. L.-A. L.—3—Held by many players.
N. L.—Last player—Roberto W. Clemente, Pittsburgh, September 8, 1958.
A. L.—Last player—Joseph P. DiMaggio, New York, August 27, 1938, first game.

Most Times 3 Three-Base Hits, Game, Nine or More Innings, Season

N. L.—2—David L. Brain, St. Louis, May 29, 1905; Pittsburgh, August 8, 1905.
A. L.—1—Held by many players.

Most Times, 3 Three-Base Hits, Game, Nine or More Innings, League

N. L.—2—John G. Reilly, Cincinnati, 1890, 1891.
    George S. Davis, Cleveland, New York, 1891, 1894.
    William F. Dahlen, Chicago, 1896, 1898.
    David L. Brain, St. Louis, Pittsburgh, 1905 (2).
A. L.—1—Held by many players.

Most Three-Base Hits With Bases Filled, League

A. L.—8—John F. Collins, Chicago, Boston, 1910, 1915, 1916, 1918 (3), 1920 (2).
N. L.—7—Stanley F. Musial, St. Louis, 1946, 1947 (2), 1948, 1949, 1951, 1954.

Most Three-Base Hits, With Bases Filled, Season

A. L.—3—John F. Collins, Chicago, 103 games, 1918.
    Elmer W. Valo, Philadelphia, 150 games, 1949.
    Jack E. Jensen, Boston, 151 games, 1956.
N. L.—3—George J. Burns, New York, 154 games, 1914.
    Ted C. Sizemore, Los Angeles, 159 games, 1969.
    Manuel de J. Sanguillen, Pittsburgh, 138 games, 1971.

Most Three-Base Hits, With Bases Filled, Game

N. L.—2—Samuel L. Thompson, Detroit, May 7, 1887.
    Henry P. Reitz, Baltimore, June 4, 1894, 1 in third inning, 1 in seventh inning.
    William Clark, Pittsburgh, September 17, 1898, second game, 1 in first inning, 1 in seventh inning.
    William H. Bruton, Milwaukee, August 2, 1959, second game, 1 in first inning, 1 in sixth inning.
A. L.—2—Elmer W. Valo, Philadelphia, May 1, 1949, first game, 1 in third inning, 1 in seventh inning.
    Duane E. Kuiper, Cleveland, July 27, 1978, second game, 1 in first inning, 1 in fifth inning.

Most Three-Base Hits, First Major League Game

A. L.—2—Edward Irwin, Detroit, May 18, 1912. (Only major league game.)
    Roy Weatherly, Cleveland, June 27, 1936.
N. L.—2—Willie L. McCovey, San Francisco, July 30, 1959.
    John W. Sipin, San Diego, May 24, 1969.

Three-Base Hit and Home Run, First Major League Game

A. L.—Henry I. Arft, St. Louis, July 27, 1948.
N. L.—Lloyd A. Merriman, Cincinnati, April 24, 1949, first game.
    Frank Ernaga, Chicago, May 24, 1957.

Most Three-Base Hits, Doubleheader

A. A.—4—William R. Hamilton, Kansas City, June 28, 1889.
N. L.—4—Michael J. Donlin, Cincinnati, September 22, 1903.
A. L.—3—Held by many players.

Most Three-Base Hits, 5 Consecutive Games

N. L.—6—J. Owen Wilson, Pittsburgh, June 17, 18, 19, 20, 20 (2), 1912.

Most Home Runs in Major Leagues

755—Henry L. Aaron, 733 in National League, Milwaukee, Atlanta, 21 years, 1954 through 1975 (375 at home, 358 on road), 22 in American League, Milwaukee, 2 years, 1975, 1976. (10 at home, 12 on road).

Most Home Runs, League

N. L.— 733— Henry L. Aaron, Milwaukee, Atlanta, 21 years, 1954 through 1974, (375 at home, 358 on road).
A. L.— 708— George H. Ruth, Boston (49), New York (659), 21 years, 1914 through 1934, (345 at home, 363 on road).

Most Home Runs, One Club, League

N. L.— 733— Henry L. Aaron, Milwaukee, Atlanta, 21 years, 1954 through 1974 (375 at home, 358 on road).
A. L.— 659— George H. Ruth, New York, 15 years, 1920 through 1934 (333 at home, 326 on road).

Most Home Runs, Season

A. L. (162-game season)—61—Roger E. Maris, New York, 161 games, 1961.
A. L. (154-game season)—60—George H. Ruth, New York, 151 games, 1927.
N. L. (154-game season)—56—Lewis R. Wilson, Chicago, 155 games, 1930.
N. L. (162-game season)—52—Willie H. Mays, San Francisco, 157 games, 1965.
    George A. Foster, Cincinnati, 158 games, 1977.

Most Home Runs, Season, for Runner-Up in Home Runs

A. L. (162-game season)—54—Mickey C. Mantle, New York, 153 games, 1961.
A. L. (154-game season)—50—James E. Foxx, Boston, 149 games, 1938.
N. L. (154-game season)—47—Theodore B. Kluszewski, Cincinnati, 153 games, 1955.
N. L. (162-game season)—47—Henry L. Aaron, Atlanta, 139 games, 1971.

Most Home Runs, Two Consecutive Seasons

A. L.— 114— George H. Ruth, New York, 60 in 1927; 54 in 1928.
N. L.— 101— Ralph M. Kiner, Pittsburgh, 54 in 1949; 47 in 1950.

Fewest Home Runs, Season, Most At-Bats

N. L.—0—Walter J. Maranville, Pittsburgh, 155 games, 1922; 672 at-bats.
A. L.—0—Roger M. Cramer, Boston, 148 games, 1938; 658 at-bats.

Most Years Leading League in Home Runs

A. L.—12—George H. Ruth, Boston, New York, 1918 (tied), 1919, 1920, 1921, 1923, 1924, 1926, 1927, 1928, 1929, 1930, 1931 (tied).
N. L.— 7—Ralph M. Kiner, Pittsburgh, 1946, 1947 (tied), 1948 (tied), 1949, 1950, 1951, 1952 (tied).

Most Consecutive Years Leading League in Home Runs
N. L.—7—Ralph M. Kiner, Pittsburgh, 1946, 1947 (tied), 1948 (tied), 1949, 1950, 1951, 1952 (tied).
A. L.—6—George H. Ruth, New York, 1926 through 1931 (tied in 1931).

Players With 40 or More Home Runs in One Season

National League (69 Times)

HR.	Player and Club	Year	HR.	Player and Club	Year
56	Lewis R. Wilson, Chicago	1930	43	Ernest Banks, Chicago	1957
54	Ralph M. Kiner, Pittsburgh	1949	43	David A. Johnson, Atlanta	1973
52	Willie H. Mays, San Francisco	1965	42	Rogers Hornsby, St. Louis	1922
52	George A. Foster, Cincinnati	1977	42	Melvin T. Ott, New York	1929
51	Ralph M. Kiner, Pittsburgh	1947	42	Ralph M. Kiner, Pittsburgh	1951
51	John R. Mize, New York	1947	42	Edwin D. Snider, Brooklyn	1953
51	Willie H. Mays, New York	1955	42	Gilbert R. Hodges, Brooklyn	1954
49	Theodore B. Kluszewski, Cin	1954	42	Edwin D. Snider, Brooklyn	1955
49	Willie H. Mays, San Francisco	1962	42	Billy L. Williams, Chicago	1970
48	Wilver D. Stargell, Pittsburgh	1971	41	Fred Williams, Philadelphia	1923
48	David A. Kingman, Chicago	1979	41	Roy Campanella, Brooklyn	1953
48	Michael J. Schmidt, Phila.	1980	41	Henry J. Sauer, Chicago	1954
47	Ralph M. Kiner, Pittsburgh	1950	41	Willie H. Mays, New York	1954
47	Edwin L. Mathews, Milwaukee	1953	41	Edwin L. Mathews, Milwaukee	1955
47	Theodore B. Kluszewski, Cin	1955	41	Ernest Banks, Chicago	1960
47	Ernest Banks, Chicago	1958	41	Darrell W. Evans, Atlanta	1973
47	Willie H. Mays, San Francisco	1964	41	Jeffrey A. Burroughs, Atlanta	1977
47	Henry L. Aaron, Atlanta	1971	40	Charles H. Klein, Philadelphia	1930
46	Edwin L. Mathews, Milwaukee	1959	40	Ralph M. Kiner, Pittsburgh	1948
46	Orlando M. Cepeda, S. Fran	1961	40	John R. Mize, New York	1948
45	Ernest Banks, Chicago	1959	40	Gilbert R. Hodges, Brooklyn	1951
45	Henry L. Aaron, Milwaukee	1962	40	Theodore B. Kluszewski, Cin	1953
45	Willie L. McCovey, S. Fran	1969	40	Edwin D. Snider, Brooklyn	1954
45	Johnny L. Bench, Cincinnati	1970	40	Edwin L. Mathews, Milwaukee	1954
45	Michael J. Schmidt, Phila.	1979	40	Walter C. Post, Cincinnati	1955
44	Ernest Banks, Chicago	1955	40	Edwin D. Snider, Brooklyn	1957
44	Henry L. Aaron, Milwaukee	1957	40	Henry L. Aaron, Milwaukee	1960
44	Henry L. Aaron, Milwaukee	1963	40	Willie H. Mays, San Francisco	1961
44	Willie L. McCovey, S. Fran	1963	40	Richard A. Allen, Philadelphia	1966
44	Henry L. Aaron, Atlanta	1966	40	Atanasio R. Perez, Cincinnati	1970
44	Henry L. Aaron, Atlanta	1969	40	Johnny L. Bench, Cincinnati	1972
44	Wilver D. Stargell, Pittsburgh	1973	40	Henry L. Aaron, Atlanta	1973
43	Charles H. Klein, Philadelphia	1929	40	George A. Foster, Cincinnati	1978
43	John R. Mize, St. Louis	1940	40	Michael J. Schmidt, Phila.	1983
43	Edwin D. Snider, Brooklyn	1956			

American League (63 Times)

HR.	Player and Club	Year	HR.	Player and Club	Year
61	Roger E. Maris, New York	1961	46	James E. Gentile, Baltimore	1961
60	George H. Ruth, New York	1927	46	Harmon C. Killebrew, Minn.	1961
59	George H. Ruth, New York	1921	46	James E. Rice, Boston	1978
58	James E. Foxx, Philadelphia	1932	45	Rocco D. Colavito, Detroit	1961
58	Henry B. Greenberg, Detroit	1938	45	Harmon C. Killebrew, Minn.	1963
54	George H. Ruth, New York	1920	45	J. Gorman Thomas, Milwaukee	1979
54	George H. Ruth, New York	1928	44	James E. Foxx, Philadelphia	1934
54	Mickey C. Mantle, New York	1961	44	Henry B. Greenberg, Detroit	1946
52	Mickey C. Mantle, New York	1956	44	Harmon C. Killebrew, Minn.	1967
50	James E. Foxx, Boston	1938	44	Carl M. Yastrzemski, Boston	1967
49	George H. Ruth, New York	1930	44	Frank O. Howard, Washington	1968
49	H. Louis Gehrig, New York	1934	44	Frank O. Howard, Washington	1970
49	H. Louis Gehrig, New York	1936	43	Theodore S. Williams, Boston	1949
49	Harmon C. Killebrew, Minn.	1964	43	Albert L. Rosen, Cleveland	1953
49	Frank Robinson, Baltimore	1966	42	Harold A. Trosky, Cleveland	1936
49	Harmon C. Killebrew, Minn.	1969	42	Gus E. Zernial, Philadelphia	1953
48	James E. Foxx, Philadelphia	1933	42	Roy E. Sievers, Washington	1957
48	Harmon C. Killebrew, Minn.	1962	42	Mickey C. Mantle, New York	1958
48	Frank O. Howard, Washington	1969	42	Rocco D. Colavito, Cleveland	1959
47	George H. Ruth, New York	1926	42	Harmon C. Killebrew, Wash.	1959
47	H. Louis Gehrig, New York	1927	42	Richard L. Stuart, Boston	1963
47	Reginald M. Jackson, Oakland	1969	41	George H. Ruth, New York	1923
46	George H. Ruth, New York	1924	41	Henry L. Gehrig, New York	1930
46	George H. Ruth, New York	1929	41	George H. Ruth, New York	1932
46	H. Louis Gehrig, New York	1931	41	James E. Foxx, Boston	1936
46	George H. Ruth, New York	1931	41	Henry B. Greenberg, Detroit	1940
46	Joseph P. DiMaggio, New York	1937	41	Rocco D. Colavito, Cleveland	1958

HR.	Player and Club	Year
41	Norman D. Cash, Detroit	1961
41	Harmon C. Killebrew, Minn	1970
41	Reginald M. Jackson, New York	1980
41	Benjamin A. Oglivie, Milwaukee	1980
40	Henry B. Greenberg, Detroit	1937

HR.	Player and Club	Year
40	Mickey C. Mantle, New York	1960
40	Americo Petrocelli, Boston	1969
40	Carl M. Yastrzemski, Boston	1969
40	Carl M. Yastrzemski, Boston	1970

Most Home Runs, Season, for all Clubs

American League

Baltimore—Frank Robinson, 1966 49
St. Louis—Kenneth R. Williams,
1922 39
Boston—James E. Foxx, 1938 50
California—Reginald M. Jackson, 1982 .. 39
Los Angeles—Leon L. Wagner, 1962 37
Chicago—Richard A. Allen, 1972 37
Cleveland—Albert L. Rosen, 1953 43
Detroit—Henry B. Greenberg, 1938 58
*Kansas City—John C. Mayberry, 1975 .. 34
Milwaukee—J. Gorman Thomas, 1979 ... 45
Seattle—Donald R. Mincher, 1969 25
Minnesota—Harmon C. Killebrew,
1964, 1969 49

Wash.—Roy E. Sievers, 1957 42
Harmon Killebrew, 1959 42
New York—Roger E. Maris, 1961 61
Oakland—Reginald M. Jackson, 1969 47
Kansas City—Robert H. Cerv, 1958 38
Philadelphia—James E. Foxx, 1932 58
§Seattle—Willie W. Horton, 1979 29
Texas—Jeffrey A. Burroughs, 1973 30
Toronto—John C. Mayberry, 1980 30
†Washington—Frank O. Howard, 1969... 48
†Second Washington club. *Present Kansas City club. §Present Seattle club.

National League

Atlanta—Henry L. Aaron, 1971 47
Milwaukee—Edwin L. Mathews,
1953 47
Boston—Walter A. Berger, 1930 38
Chicago—Lewis R. Wilson, 1930 56
Cincinnati—George A. Foster, 1977 52
Houston—James S. Wynn, 1967 37
Los Angeles—Steven P. Garvey, 1977 ... 33
Brooklyn—Edwin D. Snider, 1956 43
Montreal—Andre F. Dawson, 1983 32
*New York—David A. Kingman, 1976... 37
David A. Kingman, 1982.....37

Philadelphia—Michael J. Schmidt,
1980 48
Pittsburgh—Ralph M. Kiner, 1949 54
St. Louis—John R. Mize, 1940 43
San Diego—Nathan Colbert, 1970 38
Nathan Colbert, 1972 38
S. Francisco—Willie H. Mays, 1965 52
New York—John R. Mize, 1947 51
Willie H. Mays, 1955......... 51
*Present New York club.

Most Home Runs by Rookie, Season, for All Clubs

American League

Baltimore—Calvin E. Ripken, 1982 28
St. Louis—Walter Judnich, 1940 24
Boston—Walter O. Dropo, 1950 34
Chicago—Ronald D. Kittle, 1983 35
Cleveland—Albert L. Rosen, 1950 37
Detroit—Rudolph P. York, 1937 35
*Kansas City—Robert L. Oliver, 1969 13
LA—California—Kenneth L. Hunt,
1961 25
Milwaukee—Darrell R. Porter, 1973 16
Seattle—Steven E. Hovley, 1969 3
Daniel J. Walton, 1969.... 3
Minnesota—Jimmie R. Hall, 1963 33
Washington—W. Robert Allison,
1959 30

New York—Joe P. DiMaggio, 1936 29
Oakland—Wayne D. Gross, 1977 22
Kansas City—Woodson G. Held,
1957 20
Philadelphia—Robert L. Johnson,
1933 21
§Seattle—Ruppert S. Jones, 1977 24
Texas—David A. Hostetler, 1982 22
†Washington—Don W. Lock, 1962 12
Toronto—Jesse L. Barfield, 1982 18
*Present Kansas City club.
†Second Washington club. ‡Present Seattle club.

National League

Atlanta—Earl C. Williams, 1971 33
Milwaukee—Ricardo Carty, 1964 22
Boston—Walter A. Berger, 1930 38
Chicago—Billy L. Williams, 1961 25
Cincinnati—Frank Robinson, 1956 38
Houston—Joe L. Morgan, 1965 14
Los Angeles—Frank Howard, 1960 23
Brooklyn—Adel. Bissonette, 1928 25
Montreal—Andre F. Dawson, 1977 19
*New York—Darryl E. Strawberry,
1983 26

Philadelphia—Guillermo N.
Montanez, 1971 30
Pittsburgh—John C. Rizzo, 1938 23
Ralph M. Kiner, 1946 23
St. Louis—Ray L. Jablonski, 1953 21
San Diego—John M. Grubb, 1973 8
Michael W. Ivie, 1975 8
San Francisco—Jas. R. Hart, 1964 31
New York—Robert B. Thomson,
1947 29
*Present New York club.

Most Home Runs, Season, First Baseman

    A. L.—58—Henry B. Greenberg, Detroit, 155 games, 1938; 154 games at first base.

    N. L.—51—John R. Mize, New York, 154 games, 1947; 154 games at first base.

Most Home Runs, Season, Second Baseman

    N. L. (154-game season)—42—Rogers Hornsby, St. Louis, 154 games, 1922; 154 games at second base.

    N. L. (162-game season)—42—David A. Johnson, Atlanta, 157 games, 1973; 156 games at second base (also had 1 home run as pinch-hitter).

    A. L.—32—Joseph L. Gordon, Cleveland, 144 games, 1948; 144 games at second base.

Most Home Runs, Season, Third Baseman

    N. L.—48—Michael J. Schmidt, Philadelphia, 150 games, 1980; 149 games at third base.

    A. L.—43—Albert L. Rosen, Cleveland, 155 games, 1953; 154 games at third base.

Most Home Runs, Season, Shortstop

    N. L.—47—Ernest Banks, Chicago, 154 games, 1958; 154 games at shortstop.

    A. L.—40—Americo Petrocelli, Boston, 154 games, 1969; 153 games at shortstop.

Most Home Runs, Season, Outfielder

    A. L. (162-game season)—61—Roger E. Maris, New York, 161 games, 1961; 160 games in outfield.

    A. L. (154-game season)—60—George H. Ruth, New York, 151 games, 1927; 151 games in outfield.

    N. L.—56—Lewis R. Wilson, Chicago, 155 games, 1930; 155 games in outfield.

Most Home Runs, Season, Catcher

    N. L.—41—Roy Campanella, Brooklyn, 144 games, 1953; caught 140 games.
        (Johnny L. Bench, Cincinnati, 1970, had 38 home runs in 140 games as catcher; 6 home runs in 23 games as outfielder; 1 home run in 12 games as first baseman.)

    A. L.—32—Lance M. Parrish, Detroit, 133 games, 1982; caught 132 games.

Most Home Runs, Season, Pitcher (Only those hit in games as pitcher)

    A. L.—9—Wesley C. Ferrell, Cleveland, 48 games, 1931; pitched 40 games.

    N. L.—7—Donald Newcombe, Brooklyn, 57 games, 1955; pitched 34 games.
        Donald S. Drysdale, Los Angeles, 47 games, 1958; pitched 44 games.
        Donald S. Drysdale, Los Angeles, 58 games, 1965; pitched 44 games.

Most Home Runs, Season, at Home Grounds

    A. L.—39—Henry B. Greenberg, Detroit, 1938.

    N. L.—34—Theodore B. Kluszewski, Cincinnati, 1954.

Most Home Runs, Season, on Road

    A. L.—32—George H. Ruth, New York, 1927.

    N. L.—31—George A. Foster, Cincinnati, 1977.

Most Home Runs, Season, at Home Grounds Against One Club

    A. L.—10—Gus E. Zernial, Philadelphia vs. St. Louis, at Philadelphia, 1951.

    N. L.— 9—Stanley F. Musial, St. Louis vs. New York at St. Louis, 1954.

Most Home Runs, Season, Against One Club

    A. L.—14—(8-club league)—H. Louis Gehrig, New York vs. Cleveland, 1936; 6 at New York, 8 at Cleveland.

        13—(10-club league)—Roger E. Maris, New York vs. Chicago, 1961; 8 at New York, 5 at Chicago.

        11—(12-club league)—Harmon C. Killebrew, Minnesota vs. Oakland, 1969; 6 at Minnesota, 5 at Oakland.

    N. L.—13—(8-club league)—Henry J. Sauer, Chicago vs. Pittsburgh, 1954; 8 at Chicago, 5 at Pittsburgh.
        Joseph W. Adcock, Milwaukee vs. Brooklyn, 1956; 5 at Milwaukee, 7 at Brooklyn, 1 at Jersey City.

        11—(10-club league)—Frank Robinson, Cincinnati vs. Milwaukee, 1962; 8 at Cincinnati, 3 at Milwaukee.
        (12-club league)—Wilver D. Stargell, Pittsburgh vs. Atlanta, 1971; 6 at Pittsburgh, 5 at Atlanta. (12 scheduled games).

Most Home Runs, League, First Baseman

    A. L.—493—H. Louis Gehrig, New York, 17 years, 1923 through 1939.

    N. L.—439—Willie L. McCovey, San Francisco, San Diego, 22 years, 1959 through 1980.

Most Home Runs, Major Leagues, Second Baseman

    264—Rogers Hornsby, 263 in National League, St. Louis, New York, Boston, Chicago, 15 years, 1916, 1919 through 1931, 1933; 1 in American League, 1 year, 1937.

Most Home Runs, League, Second Baseman

N. L.— 263— Rogers Hornsby, St. Louis, New York, Boston, Chicago, 15 years, 1916, 1919 through 1931, 1933.

A. L.— 246— Joseph L. Gordon, New York, Cleveland, 11 years, 1938 through 1950, (except 1944, 1945 in military service).

Most Home Runs, Major Leagues, Third Baseman

486—Edwin L. Mathews, 482 in National League, Boston, Milwaukee, Atlanta, Houston, 16 years, 1952 through 1967; 4 in American League, 1 year, 1967.

Most Home Runs, League, Third Baseman

N. L.— 482— Edwin L. Mathews, Boston, Milwaukee, Atlanta, Houston, 16 years, 1952 through 1967.

A. L.— 319— Graig Nettles, Minnesota, Cleveland, New York, 16 years, 1968 through 1983.

Most Home Runs, League, Shortstop

N. L.— 293— Ernest Banks, Chicago, 9 years, 1953 through 1961.

A. L.— 213— Vernon D. Stephens, St. Louis, Boston, Chicago, 13 years, 1942 through 1952, except 1951.

Most Home Runs, Major Leagues, Outfielder

692—George H. Ruth, 686 in American League, Boston, New York, 17 years, 1918 through 1934; 6 in National League, 1 year, Boston, 1935.

Most Home Runs, League, Outfielder

A. L.— 686— George H. Ruth, Boston, New York, 17 years, 1918 through 1934.

N. L.— 661— Henry L. Aaron, Milwaukee, Atlanta, 21 years, 1954 through 1974.

Most Home Runs, League, Catcher

N. L.— 325— Johnny L. Bench, Cincinnati, 17 years, 1967 through 1983.

A. L.— 313— Lawrence P. Berra, New York, 18 years, 1946 through 1963.

Most Home Runs, League, Pitcher

A. L.—36—Wesley C. Ferrell, Cleveland, Boston, Washington, New York, 13 years, 1927 through 1939. (Also 1 home run as pinch-hitter, 1935; 1 home run as pitcher, Boston N. L., 1941).

N. L.—35—Warren E. Spahn, Boston, Milwaukee, New York, San Francisco, 21 years, 1942 through 1965, (except 1943, 1944, 1945 in military service).

Most Home Runs, Season, on Road, Against One Club

A. L.—10—Harry E. Heilmann, Detroit at Philadelphia, 12 games, 1922.

N. L.— 9—Joseph W. Adcock, Milwaukee at Brooklyn, 11 games, 1954.
Willie H. Mays, New York at Brooklyn, 11 games, 1955.

Most Years, 50 or More Home Runs, League

A. L.—4—George H. Ruth, New York, 1920, 1921, 1927, 1928.

N. L.—2—Ralph Kiner, Pittsburgh, 1947, 1949.
Willie H. Mays, New York, 1955; San Francisco, 1965.

Most Consecutive Years, 50 or More Home Runs, Season, League

A. L.—2—George H. Ruth, New York, 1920, 1921 and 1927, 1928.

N. L.—No player with two consecutive years.

Most Years, 40 or More Home Runs, League

A. L.—11—George H. Ruth, New York, 1920, 1921, 1923, 1924, 1926, 1927, 1928, 1929, 1930, 1931, 1932.

N. L.— 8—Henry L. Aaron, Milwaukee, Atlanta, 1957, 1960, 1962, 1963, 1966, 1969, 1971, 1973.

Most Consecutive Years, 40 or More Home Runs, League

A. L.—7—George H. Ruth, New York, 1926 through 1932.

N. L.—5—Ralph M. Kiner, Pittsburgh, 1947 through 1951.
Edwin D. Snider, Brooklyn, 1953 through 1957.

Most Years, 30 or More Home Runs, League

N. L.—15—Henry L. Aaron, Milwaukee, Atlanta, 1957 through 1973, except 1964, 1968.

A. L.—13—George H. Ruth, New York, 1920 through 1933, except 1925.

Most Consecutive Years, 30 or More Home Runs, League

A. L.—12—James E. Foxx, Philadelphia, Boston, 1929 through 1940.

N. L.— 9—Edwin L. Mathews, Milwaukee, 1953 through 1961.

Most Years, 20 or More Home Runs, League

N. L.—20—Henry L. Aaron, Milwaukee, Atlanta, 1955 through 1974.
A. L.—16—George H. Ruth, Boston, New York, 1919 through 1934.
           Theodore S. Williams, Boston, 1939, 1940, 1941, 1942, 1946, 1947, 1948, 1949,
           1950, 1951, 1954, 1955, 1956, 1957, 1958, 1960.

Most Consecutive Years, 20 or More Home Runs, League

N. L.—20—Henry L. Aaron, Milwaukee, Atlanta, 1955 through 1974.
A. L.—16—George H. Ruth, Boston, New York, 1919 through 1934.

Most Times, Three or More Home Runs, Game, Season

N. L.—2—John R. Mize, St. Louis, twice, July 13, July 20, second game, 1938; May 13,
        September 8, first game, 1940.
        Ralph M. Kiner, Pittsburgh, August 16, September 11, second game, 1947.
        Willie H. Mays, San Francisco, April 30, 4 home runs, June 29, first game,
        1961.
        Wilver D. Stargell, Pittsburgh, April 10, April 21, 1971.
        David A. Kingman, Chicago, May 17, July 28, 1979.
A. L.—2—Theodore S. Williams, Boston, May 8, June 13, 1957.
        Douglas V. DeCinces, California, August 3, August 8, 1982.

Most Times, Three or More Home Runs, Game, in Major Leagues

6—John R. Mize, St. Louis N. L., 1938 (2), 1940 (2), New York N. L., 1947 (1), New York
    A. L., 1950 (1).

Most Times, Three or More Home Runs, Game, League

N. L.—5—John R. Mize, St. Louis, 1938 (2), 1940 (2), New York, 1947.
A. L.—4—H. Louis Gehrig, New York, 1927, 1929, 1930, 1932.

Most Times, Three Home Runs in a Doubleheader (Connecting in Both Games), League

A. L.—7—George H. Ruth, New York, 1920, 1922, 1926, 1927, 1930, 1933 (2).
N. L.—5—Melvin T. Ott, New York, 1929, 1931, 1932, 1933, 1944.

Most Times, Three Consecutive Home Runs, Game, in Major Leagues

4—John R. Mize, St. Louis, N. L., 1938, 1940, New York, N. L., 1947, New York
    A. L., 1950.

Most Times, Three or More Consecutive Home Runs, Game, League

N. L.—3—John R. Mize, St. Louis, 1938, 1940, New York, 1947.
A. L.—2—Joseph P. DiMaggio, New York, 1937, 1948.
        Rocco D. Colavito, Cleveland, 1959; Detroit, 1962.

Most Times, Two or More Home Runs, Game, in Major Leagues

72—George H. Ruth, Boston A. L., New York A. L., Boston N. L., 22 years, 1914-1935; 71
    in American League, 1 in National League.

Most Times, Two or More Home Runs, Game, League

A. L.—71—George H. Ruth, Boston, New York, 21 years, 1914 through 1934.
N. L.—63—Willie H. Mays, original New York club, San Francisco present New York
           club, 22 years, 1951 through 1973 (except 1953 in military service), 2 home
           runs, game, 60 times; 3 home runs, game, 2 times; 4 home runs, game, 1
           time.

Most Times, Two Home Runs Game, League, by Pitcher

A. L.—5—Wesley C. Ferrell, Cleveland, Boston, 1931, 1934 (2), 1935, 1936.
N. L.—3—Donald Newcombe, Brooklyn, 1955 (2), 1956.

Most Times, Two Home Runs, Game, Season, by Pitcher

A. L.—2—Wesley C. Ferrell, Boston, 1934.
        Jack E. Harshman, Baltimore, 1958.
        Richard E. Donovan, Cleveland, 1962.
N. L.—2—Donald Newcombe, Brooklyn, 1955.
        Tony L. Cloninger, Atlanta, 1966.
        Richard C. Wise, Philadelphia, 1971.

Most Times, Two or More Home Runs, Game, Season

A. L.—11—Henry B. Greenberg, Detroit, 1938.
N. L.—10—Ralph M. Kiner, Pittsburgh, 1947.

Most Home Runs, With Bases Filled, League

A. L.—23—H. Louis Gehrig, New York, 17 years, 1923 through 1939.
N. L.—18—Willie L. McCovey, San Francisco, San Diego, 22 years, 1959 through 1980.

Most Home Runs With Bases Filled, Season

N. L. (154-game season)—5—Ernest Banks, Chicago, 154 games, 1955.
N. L. (162-game season)—3—Held by many players. Last player—C. Ray Knight, Cin-
                  cinnati, 162 games, 1980.
A. L. (162-game season)—5—James E. Gentile, Baltimore, 148 games, 1961.
A. L. (154-game season)—4—George H. Ruth, Boston, 130 games, 1919.
                  H. Louis Gehrig, New York, 154 games, 1934.
                  Rudolph P. York, Detroit, 135 games, 1938.
                  Thomas D. Henrich, New York, 146 games, 1948.
                  Albert L. Rosen, Cleveland, 154 games, 1951.
                  Raymond O. Boone, Cleveland-Detroit, 135 games, 1953.

Most Home Runs With Bases Filled, by Pinch-Hitter, Season

N. L.—2—David A. Johnson, Philadelphia, April 30, June 3, 1978.
        Michael W. Ivie, San Francisco, May 28, June 30, first game, 1978.
A. L.—1—Held by many pinch-hitters.

Most Home Runs With Bases Filled, One Month

A. L.—3—Rudolph P. York, Detroit, May 16, 22, 30, first game, 1938.
        James T. Northrup, Detroit, June 24 (2), 29, 1968.
        Larry A. Parrish, Texas, July 4, 7, 10, first game, 1982
N. L.—2—Held by many players. Last player—George A. Foster, New York, August 14,
        20, 1983.

Most Home Runs With Bases Filled, One Week (Sunday Through Saturday)

A. L.—3—James T. Northrup, Detroit, June 24 (2), 29, 1968.
        (H. Louis Gehrig, New York, hit homers with bases filled on Saturday, Au-
        gust 29, Monday, August 31, Tuesday, September 1, 1931, second game. On
        Sunday, August 30, home run 1 on; September 1, first game, home run, 1
        on).
        Larry A. Parrish, Texas, July 4, 7, 10, first game, 1982.
N. L.—2—Held by many players. Last player—George A. Foster, New York, August 14,
        20, 1983.

Most Home Runs With Bases Filled, Game

A. L.—2—Anthony M. Lazzeri, New York, May 24, 1936, second and fifth innings.
        James R. Tabor, Boston, July 4, 1939, second game, third and sixth innings.
        Rudolph P. York, Boston, July 27, 1946, second and fifth innings.
        James E. Gentile, Baltimore, May 9, 1961, first and second innings.
        James T. Northrup, Detroit, June 24, 1968, fifth and sixth innings.
        Frank Robinson, Baltimore, June 26, 1970, fifth and sixth innings.
N. L.—2—Tony L. Cloninger, Atlanta, July 3, 1966, first and fourth innings.

Most Home Runs With Bases Filled, First Major League Game

N. L.—1—William Duggleby, Philadelphia, April 21, 1898, second inning, on first at bat.
        Bobby L. Bonds, San Francisco, June 25, 1968, sixth inning on third at bat.
A. L.—Never accomplished.

Most HRs, Bases Filled, Two Consecutive Games (Connecting in Each Game)

N. L.—2—James H. Bannon, Boston, August 6, 7, 1894.
        James T. Sheckard, Brooklyn, September 23, 24, 1901.
        Philip M. Garner, Pittsburgh, September 14, 15, 1978.
A. L.—2—George H. Ruth, New York, September 27, 29, 1927; also August 6, second
        game, August 7, first game, 1929.
        William M. Dickey, New York, August 3, second game, August 4, 1937.
        James E. Foxx, Boston, May 20, 21, 1940.
        James F. Busby, Cleveland, July 5, July 6, 1956.
        Brooks C. Robinson, Baltimore, May 6, May 9, 1962.
        Willie M. Aikens, California, June 13, second game, June 14, 1979.

Most Home Runs, Game, by Pitcher

A. A.—3—Guy J. Hecker, Louisville, August 15, 1886, second game.
N. L.—3—James A. Tobin, Boston, May 13, 1942.
A. L.—2—Held by many pitchers. Last pitcher—Wilfred C. Siebert, Boston, September 2,
        1971.

Fewest Home Runs, Season, for Leader in Home Runs (154-Game Schedule)

A. L.—7—Samuel Crawford, Detroit, 152 games, 1908.
        Robert F. Roth, Chicago, Cleveland, 109 games, 1915.
N. L.—7—John J. Murray, New York, 149 games, 1909.

Most Home Runs, Inning

N. L.—2—Charles Jones, Boston, June 10, 1880, eighth inning.
Robert L. Lowe, Boston, May 30, 1894, p.m. game, third inning.
Jacob C. Stenzel, Pittsburgh, June 6, 1894, third inning.
Lewis R. Wilson, New York, July 1, 1925, second game, third inning.
Henry Leiber, New York, August 24, 1935, second inning.
Andrew W. Seminick, Philadelphia, June 2, 1949, eighth inning.
Sidney Gordon, New York, July 31, 1949, second game, second inning.
Willie L. McCovey, San Francisco, April 12, 1973, fourth inning and San Francisco, June 27, 1977, sixth inning.
John D. Boccabella, Montreal, July 6, 1973, first game, sixth inning.
Lee A. May, Houston, April 29, 1974, sixth inning.
Andre F. Dawson, Montreal, July 30, 1978, third inning.
C. Ray Knight, Cincinnati, May 13, 1980, fifth inning.

P. L.—2—Louis Bierbauer, Brooklyn, July 12, 1890, third inning.

A. A.—2—Edward Cartwright, St. Louis, September 23, 1890, third inning.

A. L.—2—Kenneth R. Williams, St. Louis, August 7, 1922, sixth inning.
William Regan, Boston, June 16, 1928, fourth inning.
Joseph P. DiMaggio, New York, June 24, 1936, fifth inning.
Albert W. Kaline, Detroit, April 17, 1955, sixth inning.
James R. Lemon, Washington, September 5, 1959, third inning.
Joseph A. Pepitone, New York, May 23, 1962, eighth inning.
Frederic C. Reichardt, California, April 30, 1966, eighth inning.
Clifford Johnson, New York, June 30, 1977, eighth inning.

Most Home Runs, Game

N. L.—4—Robert L. Lowe, Boston, May 30, 1894, p.m. game, consecutive.
Edward J. Delahanty, Philadelphia, July 13, 1896.
Charles H. Klein, Philadelphia, July 10, 1936, 10 innings.
Gilbert R. Hodges, Brooklyn, August 31, 1950.
Joseph W. Adcock, Milwaukee, July 31, 1954.
Willie H. Mays, San Francisco, April 30, 1961.
Michael J. Schmidt, Philadelphia, April 17, 1976, 10 innings, consecutive.

A. L.—4—H. Louis Gehrig, New York, June 3, 1932, consecutive.
J. Patrick Seerey, Chicago, July 18, 1948, first game, 11 innings.
Rocco D. Colavito, Cleveland, June 10, 1959, consecutive.

Most Consecutive Home Runs, Game

N. L.—4—Robert L. Lowe, Boston, May 30, 1894, p.m. game.
Michael J. Schmidt, Philadelphia, April 17, 1976, 10 innings.

A. L.—4—H. Louis Gehrig, New York, June 3, 1932.
Rocco D. Colavito, Cleveland, June 10, 1959.

Most Consecutive Home Runs, Two Games (*also base on balls)

A. L.—4—James E. Foxx, Philadelphia, June 7 (1), June 8 (3), 1933.
Henry B. Greenberg, Detroit, July 26 (2), July 27 (2), 1938.
Charles R. Maxwell, Detroit, May 3, first game (1) May 3, second game (3), 1959.
Willie C. Kirkland, Cleveland, July 9, second game (3), July 13 (1), 1961; also 2 bases on balls and 1 sacrifice hit.
Mickey C. Mantle, New York, July 4, second game (2), July 6 (2), 1962.
*Bobby R. Murcer, New York, June 24, first game (1), June 24, second game (3), 1970.
Michael P. Epstein, Oakland, June 15 (2), June 16 (2), 1971.
*Don E. Baylor, Baltimore, July 1 (1), July 2 (3), 1975.
Larry D. Herndon, Detroit, May 16 (1), May 18 (3), 1982.

N. L.—4—*William B. Nicholson, Chicago, July 22 (1), July 23, first game (3), 1944.
*Ralph M. Kiner, Pittsburgh, August 15 (1), August 16 (3), 1947.
Ralph M. Kiner, Pittsburgh, September 11 (2), September 13 (2), 1949.
*Stanley F. Musial, St. Louis, July 7, second game (1), July 8 (3), 1962.
Arthur L. Shamsky, Cincinnati, August 12 (3), August 14 (1), 1966.
Deron R. Johnson, Philadelphia, July 10, second game (1), July 11 (3), 1971.
Michael J. Schmidt, Philadelphia, July 6 (1), July 7 (3), 1979.

Most Consecutive Home Runs, Three Games

A. L.—4—John E. Blanchard, New York, July 21 (1), 22 (1), 26 (2), 1961.
N. L.—Never accomplished.

Most Consecutive Home Runs, Four Games

A. L.—4—Theodore S. Williams, Boston, September 17, 20, 21, 22, 1957 (4 bases on balls in streak).
N. L.—Never accomplished.

NATIONAL LEAGUE

Capitalized name denotes consecutive home runs (bases on balls excluded) in following two categories; H—at home; A—on road.

Four Home Runs in One Game (7 times)

ROBERT L. LOWE, Boston, May 30, 1894, p.m. game, (H).
Edward J. Delahanty, Philadelphia, July 13, 1896, (A), (3 consecutive).
Charles H. Klein, Philadelphia, July 10, 1936, 10 innings, (A), (3 consecutive).
Gilbert R. Hodges, Brooklyn, August 31, 1950, (H).
Joseph W. Adcock, Milwaukee, July 31, 1954, (A), (3 consecutive).
Willie H. Mays, San Francisco, April 30, 1961, (A).
MICHAEL J. SCHMIDT, Philadelphia, April 17, 1976, 10 innings, (A).

Three Home Runs in One Game (133 times)

Edward N. Williamson, Chicago, May 30, 1884, p.m. game, (H).
ADRIAN C. ANSON, Chicago, August 6, 1884, (H).
JOHN E. MANNING, Philadelphia, October 9, 1884, (A).
Dennis L. Brouthers, Detroit, September 10, 1886, (A).
Roger Connor, New York, May 9, 1888, (A).
W. Frank Shugart, St. Louis, May 10, 1894, (A).
WILLIAM JOYCE, Washington, August 20, 1894, (H).
Thomas L. McCreery, Louisville, July 12, 1897, (A).
Jacob P. Beckley, Cincinnati, September 26, 1897, first game, (A).
Walter J. Henline, Philadelphia, September 15, 1922, (H).
Fred C. Williams, Philadelphia, May 11, 1923, (H).
GEORGE L. KELLY, New York, September 17, 1923, (A).
George L. Kelly, New York, June 14, 1924, (H).
Jacques F. Fournier, Brooklyn, July 13, 1926, (A).
Lester R. Bell, Boston, June 2, 1928, (H).
GEORGE W. HARPER, St. Louis, September 20, 1928, first game, (A).
Lewis R. Wilson, Chicago, July 26, 1930, (A).
MELVIN T. OTT, New York, August 31, 1930, second game, (H).
ROGERS HORNSBY, Chicago, April 24, 1931, (A).
GEORGE A. WATKINS, St. Louis, June 24, 1931, second game, (A).
William H. Terry, New York, August 13, 1932, first game, (H).
Floyd C. Herman, Chicago, July 20, 1933, (H).
Harold B. Lee, Boston, July 6, 1934, (A).
George H. Ruth, Boston, May 25, 1935, (A).
JOHN F. MOORE, Philadelphia, July 22, 1936, (H).
Alexander Kampouris, Cincinnati, May 9, 1937, (A).
JOHN R. MIZE, St. Louis, July 13, 1938, (H).
John R. Mize, St. Louis, July 20, 1938, second game, (H).
HENRY C. LEIBER, Chicago, July 4, 1939, first game, (H).
John R. Mize, St. Louis, May 13, 1940, 14 innings, (A).
JOHN R. MIZE, St. Louis, September 8, 1940, first game, (H).
JAMES A. TOBIN, Boston, May 13, 1942, (H).
CLYDE E. McCULLOUGH, Chicago, July 26, 1942, first game, (A).
WILLIAM B. NICHOLSON, Chicago, July 23, 1944, first game, (A).
JOHN R. MIZE, New York, April 24, 1947, (A).
WILLARD MARSHALL, New York, July 18, 1947, (H).
RALPH M. KINER, Pittsburgh, August 16, 1947, (H).
RALPH M. KINER, Pittsburgh, September 11, 1947, second game, (H).
Ralph M. Kiner, Pittsburgh, July 5, 1948, first game, (H).
EUGENE V. HERMANSKI, Brooklyn, August 5, 1948, (H).
Andrew W. Seminick, Philadelphia, June 2, 1949, (H).
W. Walker Cooper, Cincinnati, July 6, 1949, (H).
ROBERT I. ELLIOTT, Boston, September 24, 1949, (A).
EDWIN D. SNIDER, Brooklyn, May 30, 1950, p.m. game, (H).
Wesley N. Westrum, New York, June 24, 1950, (H).
ANDREW W. PAFKO, Chicago, August 2, 1950, second game, (A).
ROY CAMPANELLA, Brooklyn, August 26, 1950, (A).
HENRY J. SAUER, Chicago, August 28, 1950, first game, (H).
THOMAS M. BROWN, Brooklyn, September 18, 1950, (H).
Ralph M. Kiner, Pittsburgh, July 18, 1951, (A).
DELBERT Q. WILBER, Philadelphia, August 27, 1951, second game, (H).
Donald F. Mueller, New York, September 1, 1951, (H).
Henry J. Sauer, Chicago, June 11, 1952, (H).
EDWIN L. MATHEWS, Boston, September 27, 1952, (A).
JAMES L. RHODES, New York, August 26, 1953, (H).
James T. Pendleton, Milwaukee, August 30, 1953, first game, (A).
Stanley F. Musial, St. Louis, May 2, 1954, first game, (H).

Three Home Runs in One Game (133 times) —Continued

HENRY C. THOMPSON, New York, June 3, 1954, (A).
JAMES L. RHODES, New York, July 28, 1954, (H).
Edwin D. Snider, Brooklyn, June 1, 1955, (H).
DAVID R. BELL, Cincinnati, July 21, 1955, (A).
Delmer Ennis, Philadelphia, July 23, 1955, (H).
Forrest H. Burgess, Cincinnati, July 29, 1955, (H).
Ernest Banks, Chicago, August 4, 1955, (H).
DAVID R. BELL, Cincinnati, May 29, 1956, (A).
L. Edgar Bailey, Cincinnati, June 24, 1956, first game, (A).
Theodore B. Kluszewski, Cincinnati, July 1, 1956, first game, 10 innings, (A).
ROBERT B. THURMAN, Cincinnati, August 18, 1956, (H).
ERNEST BANKS, Chicago, September 14, 1957, second game, (H).
R. Lee Walls, Chicago, April 24, 1958, (A).
Roman G. Mejias, Pittsburgh, May 4, 1958, first game, (A).
Walter J. Moryn, Chicago, May 30, 1958, second game, (H).
FRANK J. THOMAS, Pittsburgh, August 16, 1958, (A).
Donald L. Demeter, Los Angeles, April 21, 1959, 11 innings, (H).
Henry L. Aaron, Milwaukee, June 21, 1959, (A).
FRANK ROBINSON, Cincinnati, August 22, 1959, (H).
RICHARD L. STUART, Pittsburgh, June 30, 1960, second game, (H).
Willie H. Mays, San Francisco, June 29, 1961, 10 innings, (A).
WILLIAM D. WHITE, St. Louis, July 5, 1961, (A).
Donald L. Demeter, Philadelphia, September 12, 1961, (A).
ERNEST BANKS, Chicago, May 29, 1962, (H).
STANLEY F. MUSIAL, St. Louis, July 8, 1962, (A).
Willie H. Mays, San Francisco, June 2, 1963, (A).
Ernest Banks, Chicago, June 9, 1963, (H).
WILLIE L. McCOVEY, San Francisco, September 22, 1963, (H).
WILLIE L. McCOVEY, San Francisco, April 22, 1964, (A).
JOHN W. CALLISON, Philadelphia, September 27, 1964, (H).
John W. Callison, Philadelphia, June 6, 1965, second game (A).
Wilver D. Stargell, Pittsburgh, June 24, 1965, (A).
JAMES L. HICKMAN, New York, September 3, 1965, (A).
Eugene G. Oliver, Atlanta, July 30, 1966, second game, (H).
ARTHUR L. SHAMSKY, Cincinnati, August 12, 1966, 13 innings (H).
Willie L. McCovey, San Francisco, September 17, 1966, 10 innings (H).
Roberto W. Clemente, Pittsburgh, May 15, 1967, 10 innings (A).
ADOLFO E. PHILLIPS, Chicago, June 11, 1967, second game (H).
JAMES S. WYNN, Houston, June 15, 1967, (H).
Wilver D. Stargell, Pittsburgh, May 22, 1968, (A).
Billy L. Williams, Chicago, September 10, 1968, (H).
RICHARD A. ALLEN, Philadelphia, September 29, 1968, (A).
J. ROBERT TILLMAN, Atlanta, July 30, 1969, first game, (A).
ROBERTO W. CLEMENTE, Pittsburgh, August 13, 1969, (A).
Ricardo A. Carty, Atlanta, May 31, 1970, (H).
Michael K. Lum, Atlanta, July 3, 1970, first game, (H).
JOHNNY L. BENCH, Cincinnati, July 26, 1970, (H).
ORLANDO M. CEPEDA, Atlanta, July 26, 1970, first game, (A).
Wilver D. Stargell, Pittsburgh, April 10, 1971, 12 innings, (A).
WILVER D. STARGELL, Pittsburgh, April 21, 1971, (H).
DERON R. JOHNSON, Philadelphia, July 11, 1971, (H).
ROBERT J. MONDAY, Chicago, May 16, 1972, (A).
Nathan Colbert, San Diego, August 1, 1972, second game, (A).
Johnny L. Bench, Cincinnati, May 9, 1973, (A).
Lee A. May, Houston, June 21, 1973, (A).
George E. Mitterwald, Chicago, April 17, 1974, (H).
James S. Wynn, Los Angeles, May 11, 1974, (A).
David E. Lopes, Los Angeles, August 20, 1974, (A).
C. Reginald Smith, St. Louis, May 22, 1976, (A).
David A. Kingman, New York, June 4, 1976, (A).
William H. Robinson, Pittsburgh, June 5, 1976, 15 innings, (H).
Gary N. Matthews, San Francisco, September 25, 1976, (H).
GARY E. CARTER, Montreal, April 20, 1977, (H).
LARRY A. PARRISH, Montreal, May 29, 1977, (H).
GEORGE A. FOSTER, Cincinnati, July 14, 1977, (H).
Peter E. Rose, Cincinnati, April 29, 1978, (A).
David A. Kingman, Chicago, May 14, 1978, (A).
LARRY A. PARRISH, Montreal, July 30, 1978, (A).
David A. Kingman, Chicago, May 17, 1979 (H).
Dale B. Murphy, Atlanta, May 18, 1979, (H).
MICHAEL J. SCHMIDT, Philadelphia, July 7, 1979, (H).
DAVID A. KINGMAN, Chicago, July 28, 1979 (A).

Larry A. Parrish, Montreal, April 25, 1980, (A).
Johnny L. Bench, Cincinnati, May 29, 1980, (A).
Claudell Washington, New York, June 22, 1980, (A).
Darrell W. Evans, San Francisco, June 15, 1983, (H).

AMERICAN LEAGUE

Capitalized name denotes consecutive home runs (Bases on Balls, excluded) in following two categories; H—at home; A—on road.

Four Home Runs in One Game (3 times)

H. LOUIS GEHRIG, New York, June 3, 1932, (A).
J. Patrick Seerey, Chicago, July 18, 1948, first game, (A), (11 innings—3 consecutive).
ROCCO D. COLAVITO, Cleveland, June 10, 1959, (A).

Three Home Runs In One Game (118 times)

Kenneth R. Williams, St. Louis, April 22, 1922, (H).
Joseph H. Hauser, Philadelphia, August 2, 1924, (A).
Leon A. Goslin, Washington, June 19, 1925, 12 innings, (A).
Tyrus R. Cobb, Detroit, May 5, 1925 (A).
Gordon S. Cochrane, Philadelphia, May 21, 1925, (A).
Anthony M. Lazzeri, New York, June 8, 1927, (H).
H. Louis Gehrig, New York, June 23, 1927 (A).
H. Louis Gehrig, New York, May 4, 1929, (A).
George H. Ruth, New York, May 21, 1930, first game, (A).
H. Louis Gehrig, New York, May 22, 1930, second game, (A).
CARL N. REYNOLDS, Chicago, July 2, 1930, second game, (A).
LEON A. GOSLIN, St. Louis, August 19, 1930, (A).
H. EARL AVERILL, Cleveland, September 17, 1930, first game, (H).
Leon A. Goslin, St. Louis, June 23, 1932, (H).
W. Benjamin Chapman, New York, July 9, 1932, second game, (H).
James E. Foxx, Philadelphia, July 10, 1932, 18 innings, (A).
Aloysius H. Simmons, Philadelphia, July 15, 1932, (H).
JAMES E. FOXX, Philadelphia, June 8, 1933 (H).
HAROLD A. TROSKY, Cleveland, May 30, 1934, second game, (H).
PARKE E. COLEMAN, Philadelphia, August 17, 1934, first game, (H).
M. FRANK HIGGINS, Philadelphia, June 27, 1935 (H).
JULIUS J. SOLTERS, St. Louis, July 7, 1935 (A).
Anthony M. Lazzeri, New York, May 24, 1936, (A).
JOSEPH P. DiMAGGIO, New York, June 13, 1937, second game, 11 innings, (A).
Harold A. Trosky, Cleveland, July 5, 1937, first game, (A).
MERVYN J. CONNORS, Chicago, September 17, 1938, second game, (H).
KENNETH F. KELTNER, Cleveland, May 25, 1939 (A).
James R. Tabor, Boston, July 4, 1939, second game, (A).
WILLIAM M. DICKEY, New York, July 26, 1939, (H).
M. FRANK HIGGINS, Detroit, May 20, 1940, (H):
Charles E. Keller, New York, July 28, 1940, first game, (A).
Rudolph P. York, Detroit, September 1, 1941, first game, (H).
J. Patrick Seerey, Cleveland, July 13, 1945, (A).
Theodore S. Williams, Boston, July 14, 1946, first game, (H).
Samuel B. Chapman, Philadelphia, August 15, 1946, (A).
JOSEPH P. DiMAGGIO, New York, May 23, 1948, first game, (A).
Patrick J. Mullin, Detroit, June 26, 1949, second game, (A).
Robert P. Doerr, Boston, June 8, 1950, (H).
LAWRENCE E. DOBY, Cleveland, August 2, 1950, (H).
Joseph P. DiMaggio, New York, September 10, 1950, (A).
JOHN R. MIZE, New York, September 15, 1950, (A).
Gus E. Zernial, Chicago, October 1, 1950, second game, (H).
Robert F. Avila, Cleveland, June 20, 1951, (A).
Clyde F. Vollmer, Boston, July 26, 1951, (H).
Albert L. Rosen, Cleveland, April 29, 1952, (A).
WILLIAM V. GLYNN, Cleveland, July 5, 1954, first game, (A).
Albert W. Kaline, Detroit, April 17, 1955, (A).
Mickey C. Mantle, New York, May 13, 1955, (H).
Norbert H. Zauchin, Boston, May 27, 1955, (H).
JAMES R. LEMON, Washington, August 31, 1956, (H).
Theodore S. Williams, Boston, May 8, 1957, (A).
Theodore S. Williams, Boston, June 13, 1957, (A).
Hector H. Lopez, Kansas City, June 26, 1958, (A).
PRESTON M. WARD, Kansas City, September 9, 1958, (H).
CHARLES R. MAXWELL, Detroit, May 3, 1959, second game, (H).
Robert H. Cerv, Kansas City, August 20, 1959, (H).
WILLIE C. KIRKLAND, Cleveland, July 9, 1961, second game, (H).
Rocco D. Colavito, Detroit, August 27, 1961, second game, (A).

Three Home Runs in One Game (118 times) —Continued

J. Leroy Thomas, Los Angeles, Sept. 5, 1961, second game, (A).
ROCCO D. COLAVITO, Detroit, July 5, 1962, (A).
Stephen Boros, Detroit, August 6, 1962, (A).
DONALD G. LEPPERT, Washington, April 11, 1963, (H).
W. ROBERT ALLISON, Minnesota, May 17, 1963, (A).
JOHN W. POWELL, Baltimore, August 10, 1963, (A).
Harmon C. Killebrew, Minnesota, September 21, 1963, first game (A).
James H. King, Washington, June 8, 1964, (H).
John W. Powell, Baltimore, June 27, 1964 (A).
MANUEL E. JIMENEZ, Kansas City, July 4, 1964, (A).
THOMAS M. TRESH, New York, June 6, 1965, second game (H).
John W. Powell, Baltimore, August 15, 1966, (A).
Tommy L. McCraw, Chicago, May 24, 1967 (A).
Curtis L. Blefary, Baltimore, June 6, 1967, first game, (A).
KENNETH S. HARRELSON, Boston, June 14, 1968, (A).
Michael P. Epstein, Washington, May 16, 1969, (A).
Joseph M. Lahoud, Boston, June 11, 1969, (A).
WILLIAM E. MELTON, Chicago, June 24, 1969, second game, (A).
Reginald M. Jackson, Oakland, July 2, 1969, (H).
Paul L. Blair, Baltimore, April 29, 1970, (A).
Anthony Horton, Cleveland, May 24, 1970, second game, (H).
Willie Horton, Detroit, June 9, 1970, (H).
BOBBY R. MURCER, New York, June 24, 1970, second game, (H).
William A. Freehan, Detroit, August 9, 1971 (A).
GEORGE A. HENDRICK, Cleveland, June 19, 1973, (H).
Antonio L. (Pedro) Oliva, Minnesota, July 3, 1973, (A).
Leroy B. Stanton, California, July 10, 1973, 10 innings, (A).
Bobby R. Murcer, New York, July 13, 1973, (H).
ROBERT GRICH, Baltimore, June 18, 1974, (H).
Fredric M. Lynn, Boston, June 18, 1975, (A).
John C. Mayberry, Kansas City, July 1, 1975, (A).
DONALD E. BAYLOR, Baltimore, July 2, 1975, (A).
TOLIA SOLAITA, Kansas City, September 7, 1975, 11 innings, (A).
Carl M. Yastrzemski, Boston, May 19, 1976, (A).
Willie W. Horton, Texas, May 15, 1977, (A).
JOHN C. MAYBERRY, Kansas City, June 1, 1977, (A).
CLIFFORD JOHNSON, New York, June 30, 1977, (A).
JAMES E. RICE, Boston, August 29, 1977, (H).
Albert Oliver, Texas, May 23, 1979, (H).
Benjamin A. Oglivie, Milwaukee, July 8, 1979, first game, (H).
Claudell Washington, Chicago, July 14, 1979, (H).
George H. Brett, Kansas City, July 22, 1979, (A).
Cecil C. Cooper, Milwaukee, July 27, 1979, (H).
EDDIE C. MURRAY, Baltimore, August 29, 1979, second game, (A).
CARNEY R. LANSFORD, California, September 1, 1979, (A).
Otoniel Velez, Toronto, May 4, 1980, 10 innings, first game, (H).
Freddie J. Patek, California, June 20, 1980, (A).
ALBERT OLIVER, Texas, August 17, 1980, second game, (A).
Eddie C. Murray, Baltimore, September 14, 1980, 13 innings, (A).
Jeffrey A. Burroughs, Seattle, August 14, 1981, second game, (A).
Paul L. Molitor, Milwaukee, May 12, 1982, (A).
LARRY D. HERNDON, Detroit, May 18, 1982, (A).
BENJAMIN A. OGLIVIE, Milwaukee, June 20, 1982, (A).
HAROLD D. BAINES, Chicago, July 7, 1982, (H).
DOUGLAS V. DeCINCES, California, August 3, 1982, (H).
Douglas V. DeCinces, California, August 8, 1982, (A).
George H. Brett, Kansas City, April 20, 1983, (A).
Benjamin A. Oglivie, Milwaukee, May 14, 1983, (H).
Darnell G. Ford, Baltimore, July 20, 1983, (A).
James E. Rice, Boston, August 29, 1983, second game, (A).

AMERICAN ASSOCIATION

Three Home Runs in One Game

Guy J. Hecker, Louisville, August 15, 1886, second game, (H).

Most Inside-the-Park Home Runs, Game

N. L.—2—Walter J. Maranville, Boston, July 1, 1919.
                Maurice C. Rath, Cincinnati at New York, September 20, 1920, second game.
                Terry B. Moore, St. Louis at Pittsburgh, August 16, 1939, first game.
                Henry C. Thompson, New York at New York, August 16, 1950.

A. L.—2—Benjamin Paschal, New York at New York, September 22, 1925, first game.
W. Benjamin Chapman, New York at New York, July 9, 1932, second game.
Richard A. Allen, Chicago at Minnesota, July 31, 1972.

Most Home Runs Game, In Extra Innings

A. L.—2—Vernon D. Stephens, St. Louis, September 29, 1943, first game, consecutive, eleventh and thirteenth innings.
Willie C. Kirkland, Cleveland, June 14, 1963, second game, eleventh and nineteenth innings.
N. L.—2—Arthur L. Shamsky, Cincinnati, August 12, 1966, consecutive, tenth and eleventh innings.
Ralph A. Garr, Atlanta, May 17, 1971, consecutive, tenth and twelfth innings.

Most Home Runs in Extra Innings, League

N. L.—22—Willie H. Mays, original New York club, San Francisco, present New York club, 22 years, 1951 through 1973 (except 1953 in military service).
A. L.—16—George H. Ruth, Boston, New York, 21 years, 1914 through 1934.

Home Run, First Plate Appearance in Major Leagues (N.L. 25 Times; A.L. 23 Times; A.A. 1 Time)
*On First Pitch

A. A.—Michael J. Griffin, Baltimore, April 16, 1887.
N. L.—William J. Duggleby, Philadelphia, April 21, 1898.
John W. Bates, Boston, April 12, 1906.
E. Clise Dudley, Brooklyn, April 27, 1929.*
Gordon L. Slade, Brooklyn, May 24, 1930.
Edwin Morgan, St. Louis, April 14, 1936.*
Ernest Koy, Brooklyn, April 19, 1938.
Emmett J. Mueller, Philadelphia, April 19, 1938.
Clyde F. Vollmer, Cincinnati, May 31, 1942, second game*.
John J. Kerr, New York, September 8, 1943.
Carroll W. Lockman, New York, July 5, 1945.
Daniel P. Bankhead, Brooklyn, August 26, 1947.
Lester L. Layton, New York, May 21, 1948.
Edward R. Sanicki, Philadelphia, September 14, 1949.
Theodore N. Tappe, Cincinnati, September 14, 1950, first game.
J. Hoyt Wilhelm, New York, April 23, 1952.
Wallace W. Moon, St. Louis, April 13, 1954.
Charles W. Tanner, Milwaukee, April 12, 1955.*
William D. White, New York, May 7, 1956.
Frank Ernaga, Chicago, May 24, 1957.
Donald G. Leppert, Pittsburgh, June 18, 1961, first game.
Facundo A. Barragan, Chicago, September 1, 1961.
Benigno F. Ayala, New York, August 27, 1974.
Jose Y. Sosa, Houston, July 30, 1975.
Johnnie L. LeMaster, San Francisco, September 2, 1975.
Michael R. Fitzgerald, New York, September 13, 1983.
A. L.—H. Earl Averill, Cleveland, April 16, 1929.
Clarence M. Parker, Philadelphia, April 30, 1937.
Wilfred H. Lefebvre, Boston, June 10, 1938.*
James E. Miller, Detroit, April 23, 1944, second game.
Edward C. Pellagrini, Boston, April 22, 1946.
George S. Vico, Detroit, April 20, 1948.*
Robert C. Nieman, St. Louis, September 14, 1951.
John E. Kennedy, Washington, September 5, 1962, first game.
Leslie F. Narum, Baltimore, May 3, 1963.
W. Gates Brown, Detroit, June 19, 1963.
Dagoberto B. Campaneris, Kansas City, July 23, 1964.*
William A. Roman, Detroit, September 30, 1964, second game.
Garrabrant R. Alyea, Washington, September 12, 1965.*
John Miller, New York, September 11, 1966.
W. Richard Renick, Minnesota, July 11, 1968.
Joseph W. Keough, Oakland, August 7, 1968, second game.
Gene W. Lamont, Detroit, September 2, 1970, second game.
Donald G. Rose, California, May 24, 1972.*
Reginald J. Sanders, Detroit, September 1, 1974.
David L. McKay, Minnesota, August 22, 1975.
Alvis Woods, Toronto, April 7, 1977.
David R. Machemer, California, June 21, 1978.
Gary J. Gaetti, Minnesota, September 20, 1981.*

Most Home Runs, First Game in Major Leagues

A. A.—2—Charles T. Reilly, Columbus, October 9, 1889 (on third and fifth times at bat).
A. L.—2—Robert C. Nieman, St. Louis, September 14, 1951 (on first 2 times at bat).
  Dagoberto B. Campaneris, Kansas City, July 23, 1964 (on first and fourth times at bat).
N. L.—1—Held by many players.

Most Home Runs, First Two Major League Games

N. L.—3—Joseph R. Cunningham, St. Louis, June 30 (1), July 1 (2), 1954.
A. L.—2—H. Earl Averill, Cleveland, April 16 (1), April 17 (1), 1929.
  Robert C. Nieman, St. Louis, September 14 (2), September 15 (0), 1951.
  Dagoberto B. Campaneris, Kansas City, July 23 (2), July 24 (0), 1964.
  Curtis L. Blefary, Baltimore, April 14 (0), April 17 (2), 1965.
  Joseph H. Lefebvre, New York, May 22 (1), May 23 (1), 1980.
  David L. Stapleton, Boston, May 30 (0), May 31 (2), 1980.
  Timothy J. Laudner, Minnesota, August 28 (1), August 29 (1), 1981.

Most Home Runs as Leadoff Batter, Season

N. L.—11—Bobby L. Bonds, San Francisco, 160 games, 1973, 39 home runs for season.
A. L.— 6—Edwin D. Joost, Philadelphia, 135 games, 1948, 16 home runs for season.
  Edward F. Yost, Detroit, 148 games, 1959, 21 home runs for season.
  Tommy Harper, Milwaukee, 154 games, 1970, 31 home runs for season.
  Dagoberto B. Campaneris, Oakland, 147 games, 1970, 22 home runs for season.
  Brian J. Downing, California, 158 games, 1982, 28 home runs for season.

Most Home Runs as Leadoff Batter in Major Leagues

35—Bobby L. Bonds, 30 in National League, San Francisco, 9 years, 1968 through 1974, St. Louis, 1980, Chicago, 1981; 5 in American League, 5 years, New York, 1975, California, 1976 and 1977, Chicago and Texas, 1978, Cleveland, 1979.

Most Home Runs as Leadoff Batter, League

N. L.—30—Bobby L. Bonds, San Francisco, St. Louis, Chicago, 9 years, 1968 through 1974, 1980 through 1981.
A. L.—28—Edward F. Yost, Washington, Detroit, Los Angeles, 17 years, 1944 through 1962 (except 1945, 1946 in military service).

Home Run, First Time at Bat in Major Leagues, by Pinch-Hitter

N. L.—Edwin Morgan, St. Louis, April 14, 1936, seventh inning.
  Lester L. Layton, New York, May 21, 1948, ninth inning.
  Theodore N. Tappe, Cincinnati, September 14, 1950, first game, eighth inning.
  Charles W. Tanner, Milwaukee, April 12, 1955, eighth inning.
A. L.—Clarence M. Parker, Philadelphia, April 30, 1937, ninth inning.
  John E. Kennedy, Washington, September 5, 1962, first game, sixth inning.
  W. Gates Brown, Detroit, June 19, 1963, fifth inning.
  William A. Roman, Detroit, September 30, 1964, second game, seventh inning.
  Garrabrant R. Alyea, Washington, September 12, 1965, sixth inning.
  Joseph W. Keough, Oakland, August 7, 1968, second game, eighth inning.
  Alvis Woods, Toronto, April 7, 1977, fifth inning.

Most Home Runs by Pinch-Hitter, Season

N. L.—6—John H. Frederick, Brooklyn, 1932.
A. L.—5—Joseph E. Cronin, Boston, 1943.

Most Home Runs With Bases Filled, by Pinch-Hitter, Game

A. L.—N. L.—1—Held by many players.

Most Home Runs, Consecutive At-Bats, Pinch-Hitter

N. L.—3—Leondaus Lacy, Los Angeles, May 2, 6, 17, 1978 (includes 1 base on balls during streak).
  Delbert B. Unser, Philadelphia, June 30, July 5, 10, 1979.
A. L.—2—Raymond B. Caldwell, New York, June 10, 11, 1915.
  Joseph E. Cronin, Boston, June 17, first game, 17, second game, 1943.
  Charles E. Keller, New York, September 12, 14, 1948.
  Delbert Q. Wilber, Boston, May 6, 10, 1953.
  Theodore S. Williams, Boston, September 17, 20, 1957 (includes 1 base on balls during streak).
  John E. Blanchard, New York, July 21, 22, 1961.
  Charles T. Schilling, Boston, April 30, May 1, 1965.
  Raymond H. Barker, New York, June 20, June 22, first game, 1965.
  Curtell H. Motton, Baltimore, May 15, 17, 1968.
  W. Gates Brown, Detroit, August 9, 11, first game, 1968.
  Gary W. Alexander, Cleveland, July 5, 6, 1980.
  Daryl A. Sconiers, California, April 30, May 7, 1983.

Most Home Runs, Doubleheader, Pinch-Hitter

A. L.—2—Joseph E. Cronin, Boston, June 17, 1943.
N. L.—2—Harold N. Breeden, Montreal, July 13, 1973.

Most Home Runs With Bases Filled, by Pinch-Hitter, League

N. L.—3—Ronald J. Northey, St. Louis, September 3, 1947; May 30, 1948, second game; Chicago, September 18, 1950.
Willie L. McCovey, San Francisco, June 12, 1960; September 10, 1965; San Diego, May 30, 1975.
A. L.—3—Richard B. Reese, Minnesota, August 3, 1969, June 7, 1970, July 9, 1972.

Most Home Runs by Pinch-Hitter

Both Leagues—18—Clifford Johnson, Houston N. L., New York A. L., Cleveland A. L., Chicago N. L., Oakland A. L., Toronto A. L., 1974 (5), 1975 (1), 1976 (1), 1977 (3), 1978 (2), 1979 (1), 1980 (3), 1981 (1), 1983 (1).
N. L.—18—Gerald T. Lynch, Cincinnati, Pittsburgh, 1957 (3), 1958 (1), 1959 (1), 1961 (5), 1962 (1), 1963 (4), 1964 (1), 1965 (1), 1966 (1).
A. L.—16—William J. Brown, Detroit, 1963 (1), 1964 (1), 1965 (1), 1966 (2), 1968 (3), 1970 (1), 1971 (2), 1972 (1), 1974 (3), 1975 (1).

Two Home Runs, Game, One Home Run Righthanded, One Lefthanded— (N.L. 18 times; A.L. 36 times)

N. L.—August J. Galan, Chicago, June 25, 1937.
James W. Russell, Boston, June 7, 1948.
James W. Russell, Brooklyn, July 26, 1950.
Albert F. Schoendienst, St. Louis, July 8, 1951, second game.
Maurice M. Wills, Los Angeles, May 30, 1962, first game.
Ellis N. Burton, Chicago, August 1, 1963.
Ellis N. Burton, Chicago, September 7, 1964, first game.
James K. Lefebvre, Los Angeles, May 7, 1966.
M. Wesley Parker, Los Angeles, June 5, 1966, first game.
Peter E. Rose, Cincinnati, August 30, 1966.
Peter E. Rose, Cincinnati, August 2, 1967.
Ted L. Simmons, St. Louis, April 17, 1975.
C. Reginald Smith, St. Louis, May 4, 1975.
C. Reginald Smith, St. Louis, May 22, 1976 (2 righthanded, 1 lefthanded).
Lee L. Mazzilli, New York, September 3, 1978.
Ted L. Simmons, St. Louis, June 11, 1979.
Alan D. Ashby, Houston, September 27, 1982.
Charles T. Davis, San Francisco, June 5, 1983.
A. L.—Walter H. Schang, Philadelphia, September 8, 1916.
John Lucadello, St. Louis, September 16, 1940.
Mickey C. Mantle, New York, May 13, 1955 (1 righthanded, 2 lefthanded).
Mickey C. Mantle, New York, August 15, 1955, second game.
Mickey C. Mantle, New York, May 18, 1956.
Mickey C. Mantle, New York, July 1, 1956, second game.
Mickey C. Mantle, New York, June 12, 1957.
Mickey C. Mantle, New York, July 28, 1958.
Mickey C. Mantle, New York, September 15, 1959.
Mickey C. Mantle, New York, April 26, 1961.
Mickey C. Mantle, New York, May 6, 1962, second game.
Thomas M. Tresh, New York, September 1, 1963.
Thomas M. Tresh, New York, July 13, 1964.
Mickey C. Mantle, New York, August 12, 1964.
Thomas M. Tresh, New York, June 6, 1965, second game (1 righthanded, 2 left-handed).
C. Reginald Smith, Boston, August 20, 1967, first game.
C. Reginald Smith, Boston, August 11, 1968, second game.
Donald A. Buford, Baltimore, April 9, 1970.
Roy H. White, New York, May 7, 1970.
C. Reginald Smith, Boston, July 2, 1972, first game.
C. Reginald Smith, Boston, April 16, 1973.
Roy H. White, New York, August 13, 1973.
Roy H. White, New York, April 23, 1975.
Kenneth J. Henderson, Chicago, August 29, 1975.
Roy H. White, New York, August 18, 1976.
Eddie C. Murray, Baltimore, August 3, 1977.
Roy H. White, New York, June 13, 1978.
Lawrence W. Milbourne, Seattle, July 15, 1978.
Willie J. Wilson, Kansas City, June 15, 1979.
Eddie C. Murray, Baltimore, August 29, 1979, second game (2 righthanded, 1 lefthanded).

Two Home Runs, Game, One Home Run Righthanded, One Lefthanded—N.L. 18 Times; A.L. 36 Times) —Continued

  U. L. Washington, Kansas City, September 21, 1979.
  Eddie C. Murray, Baltimore, August 16, 1981.
  Eddie C. Murray, Baltimore, April 24, 1982.
  Ted L. Simmons, Milwaukee, May 2, 1982.
  Eddie C. Murray, Baltimore, August 26, 1982.
  Roy F. Smalley, New York, September 5, 1982.

Most Consecutive Games Hitting Homer Each Game

  N. L.—8—R. Dale Long, Pittsburgh, May 19, 20, first game, 20, second game, 22, 23, 25, 26, 28, 1956, 8 home runs.
  A. L.—6—Kenneth R. Williams, St. Louis, July 28, 29, 30, 31, August 1, 2, 1922, 6 home runs.
      H. Louis Gehrig, New York, August 28, 29, 30, 31, September 1, first game, 1, second game, 1931, 6 home runs.
      Roy E. Sievers, Washington, July 29, second game, 30, 31, August 1, 2, 3, 1957, 6 home runs.
      Roger E. Maris, New York, August 11, 12, 13, 13, 15, 16 (2), 1961, 7 home runs.
      Frank O. Howard, Washington, May 12 (2), 14 (2), 15 (1), 16 (2), 17 (1), 18 (2), 1968, 10 home runs.
      Reginald M. Jackson, Baltimore, July 18, 19, 20, 21, 22, 23, 1976, 6 home runs.

Most Home Runs, Doubleheader, Hitting Homers Each Game

  N. L.—5—Stanley F. Musial, St. Louis, May 2, 1954.
      Nathan Colbert, San Diego, August 1, 1972.
  A. L.—4—H. Earl Averill, Cleveland, September 17, 1930.
      James E. Foxx, Philadelphia, July 2, 1933, 19 innings.
      James R. Tabor, Boston, July 4, 1939.
      Gus E. Zernial, Chicago, October 1, 1950.
      Charles R. Maxwell, Detroit, May 3, 1959, consecutive.
      Roger E. Maris, New York, July 25, 1961.
      Rocco D. Colavito, Detroit, August 27, 1961.
      Harmon C. Killebrew, Minnesota, September 21, 1963.
      Bobby R. Murcer, New York, June 24, 1970, consecutive.
      Graig Nettles, New York, April 14, 1974.
      Otoniel Velez, Toronto, May 4, 1980, 19 innings.
      Albert Oliver, Texas, August 17, 1980.

Most Home Runs, Two Consecutive Games, Hitting Homer Each Game

  N. L.—5—Adrian C. Anson, Chicago, August 5 (2), August 6 (3), 1884.
      Ralph M. Kiner, Pittsburgh, August 15 (2), 16 (3), 1947, also September 11 (3), September 12 (2), 1947.
      Donald F. Mueller, New York, September 1 (3), September 2 (2), 1951.
      Stanley F. Musial, St. Louis, May 2, first game (3), May 2, second game (2), 1954.
      Joseph W. Adcock, Milwaukee, July 30 (1), 31 (4), 1954.
      Billy L. Williams, Chicago, September 8 (2), 10 (3), 1968.
      Nathan Colbert, San Diego, August 1, first game (2), second game (3), 1972.
      Michael J. Schmidt, Philadelphia, April 17 (4), April 18 (1), 1976.
      David A. Kingman, Chicago, July 27 (2), July 28 (3), 1979.
  A. L.—5—Tyrus R. Cobb, Detroit, May 5 (3), 6 (2), 1925.
      Anthony M. Lazzeri, New York, May 23, second game (2), 24 (3), 1936.
      Carl M. Yastrzemski, Boston, May 19 (3), May 20 (2), 1976.

Most Home Runs, Three Consecutive Games, Hitting Homer in Each Game

  A. L.—6—Anthony M. Lazzeri, New York, May 23 (1), 23 (2), 24 (3), 1936.
      Gus E. Zernial, Philadelphia, May 13, second game (2), 15 (2), 16 (2), 1951.
  N. L.—6—Ralph M. Kiner, Pittsburgh, August 14 (1), 15 (2), 16 (3), 1947, also September 10 (2), 11 (1), 11 (3), 1947.
      Frank J. Thomas, New York, August 1 (2), 2 (2), 3 (2), 1962.
      Lee A. May, Cincinnati, May 24 (2), May 25 (2), May 28 (2), 1969.
      Michael J. Schmidt, Philadelphia, April 17 (4), April 18 (1), April 20 (1), 1976.

Most Home Runs, Four Consecutive Games, Hitting Homer in Each Game

  N. L.—8—Ralph M. Kiner, Pittsburgh, September 10 (2), 11 (1), 11 (3), 12 (2), 1947.
  A. L.—7—Anthony M. Lazzeri, New York, May 21 (1), 23 (1), 23 (2), 24 (3), 1936.
      Gus E. Zernial, Philadelphia, May 13, second game (2), 15 (2), 16 (2), 17 (1), 1951.
      Frank O. Howard, Washington, May 12 (2), 14 (2), 15 (1), 16 (2), 1968.

Most Home Runs, First Four Consecutive Games of Season, Hitting Homer in Each Game

  N. L.—4—Willie H. Mays, San Francisco, April 6 (1), April 7 (1), April 8 (1), April 10 (1), 1971.

Most Home Runs, Five Consecutive Games, Hitting Homer in Each Game

A. L.—8—Frank O. Howard, Washington, May 12 (2), 14 (2), 15 (1), 16 (2), 17 (1), 1968.
Frank O. Howard, Washington, May 14 (2), 15 (1), 16 (2), 17 (1), 18 (2), 1968.
7—George H. Ruth, New York, June 10 (1), 11 (1), 12 (1), 13 (2), 14 (2), 1921.
Victor W. Wertz, Detroit, July 27 (1), 28 (2), 29 (1), 30 (1), August 1 (2), 1950.
N. L.—7—James L. Bottomley, St. Louis, July 5 (1), 6 (2), 6 (1), 8 (1), 9 (2), 1929.
Johnny L. Bench, Cincinnati, May 30 (2), 31 (1), June 1 (1), 2 (2), 3 (1), 1972.
Michael J. Schmidt, Philadelphia, July 6 (1), 7 (3), 8 (1), 9 (1), 10 (1), 1979.

Most Home Runs, Six Consecutive Games, Hitting Homer in Each Game

A. L.—10—Frank O. Howard, Washington, May 12 (2), 14 (2), 15 (1), 16 (2), 17 (1), 18 (2), 1968.
N. L.— 7—George L. Kelly, New York, July 11, 12 (2), 13, 14, 15, 16, 1924.
W. Walker Cooper, New York, June 22 (2), 23, 24, 25, 27, 28, 1947.
Willie H. Mays, New York, September 14 (2), 16, 17, 18, 20, 20, 1955.

Most Home Runs, Seven Consecutive Games, Hitting Homer in Each Game

N. L.—7—R. Dale Long, Pittsburgh, May 19, 20, 20, 22, 23, 25, 26, 1956.
A. L.—Never accomplished.

Most Home Runs, Eight Consecutive Games, Hitting Homer in Each Game

N. L.—8—R. Dale Long, Pittsburgh, May 19, 20, 20, 22, 23, 25, 26, 28, 1956.
A. L.—Never accomplished.

Most Consecutive Games, Hitting Homer, Pitcher

N. L.—4—Kenneth A. Brett, Philadelphia, June 9, 13, 18, 23, 1973. (Starting pitcher).
A. L.—2—0100Held by many pitchers.

Most Home Runs, Two Consecutive Days

A. L.—6—George H. Ruth, New York, May 21 (3), 21 (0), 22 (2), 22 (1), 1930, 4 games.
Anthony M. Lazzeri, New York May 23 (1), 23 (2), 24 (3), 1936, 3 games.
N. L.—6—Ralph M. Kiner, Pittsburgh, September 11 (1), 11 (3), 12 (2), 1947, 3 games.

Most Hits, All Home Runs, Consecutive Games

N. L.—6—Frank O. Hurst, Philadelphia, July 28 through August 2, 1929, 6 games.
A. L.—5—Kenneth R. Williams, St. Louis, July 28 through August 1, 1922, 5 games.

Most Home Runs, One Week (Sunday through Saturday)

A. L.—10—Frank O. Howard, Washington, May 12 through May 18, 1968, 6 games.
N. L.— 8—Ralph M. Kiner, Pittsburgh, September 7 through 13, 1947, 7 games.
Theodore B. Kluszewski, Cincinnati, July 1, first game, through 7, 1956, 7 games.
Nathan Colbert, San Diego, July 30, first game, through August 5, 1972, 9 games.

Most Home Runs, One Month (From first through last day of month)

A. L.—18—Rudolph P. York, Detroit, August, 1937.
N. L.—17—Willie H. Mays, San Francisco, August, 1965.

Most Home Runs Month of April

N¢ L.—11—Wilver D. Stargell, Pittsburgh, April 1971.
Michael J. Schmidt, Philadelphia, April 1976.
A. L.—11—Graig Nettles, New York, April 1174.

Most Home Runs Month of May

A. L.—16—Mickey C. Mantle, New York, May 1956.
N. L.—15—Fred Williams, Philadelphia, May 1923.

Most Home Runs Month of June

A. L.—15—George H. Ruth, New York, June 1930.
Robert L. Johnson, Philadelphia, June 1934.
Roger E. Maris, New York, June 1961.
N. L.—14—Ralph M. Kiner, Pittsburgh, June 1947.
Michael J. Schmidt, Philadelphia, June, 1977.

Most Home Runs Month of July

A. L.—15—Joseph P. DiMaggio, New York, July 1937.
Henry B. Greenberg, Detroit, July 1938.
N. L.—15—Joseph W. Adcock, Milwaukee, July 1956.

Most Home Runs Month of August

A. L.—18—Rudolph P. York, Detroit, August 1937.
N. L.—17—Willie H. Mays, San Francisco, August 1965.

Most Home Runs Month of September

A. L.—17—George H. Ruth, New York, September 1927.
N. L.—16—Ralph M. Kiner, Pittsburgh, September 1949.

Most Home Runs Month of October

N. L.—4—Edward N. Williamson, Chicago, October 1884.
        Michael J. Schmidt, Philadelphia, October 1980.
A. L.—4—Gus E. Zernial, Chicago, October 1950.

Home Run Winning Longest Extra-Inning Game

A. L.—John B. Reed, New York, 22 innings, 1 on base, New York won vs. Detroit, 9-7,
        June 24, 1962.
N. L.—Lawrence J. Doyle, New York, 21 innings, 1 on base, New York won vs. Pitts-
        burgh, 3-1, July 17, 1914.
        Mervin W. Rettenmund, San Diego, 21 innings, 2 on base, San Diego won vs.
        Montreal, 11-8, May 21, 1977.

Home Run Winning Longest 1 to 0 Game

N. L.—Charles G. Radbourn, Providence, August 17, 1882, 18 innings.
N. L. since 1900—Willie H. Mays, San Francisco, July 2, 1963, 16 innings.
A. L.—William J. Skowron, New York, April 22, 1959, 14 innings.

Home Run by Pitcher Winning 1-0 Extra-Inning Game and Pitching Complete Game

A. L.—Thomas J. Hughes, Washingtof, August 3, 1906, 10 innings.
        Charles H. Ruffing, New York, August 13, 1932, 10 innings.
N. L.—Never accomplished—(John C. Klippstein, Cincinnati, August 6, 1962, hit home
        run in thirteenth inning, after relieving Robert T. Purkey, who had pitched
        first 10 innings).

Most National League Parks, One or More Home Runs, During Career

22—Henry L. Aaron, Milwaukee, Atlanta, 21 years, 1954 through 1974.
     Willie H. Mays, New York, San Francisco, 22 years, 1951 through 1973 except 1953.
     Willie L. McCovey, San Francisco, San Diego, 22 years, 1959 through 1980.

Hitting Home Runs All Major League Parks (15) in Use During Career

Harry E. Heilmann, Detroit A. L., 1914, 1916 through 1929, Cincinnati N. L., 1930, 1932.
J. Geoffrey Heath, Cleveland A. L., 1936 through 1945, Washington A. L., 1946, St. Louis
     A. L., 1946, 1947, Boston N. L., 1948, 1949 (League Park and Municipal Stadium,
     Cleveland).
John R. Mize, St. Louis N. L., 1936 through 1941, New York N. L., 1942, 1946 through
     1949, New York A. L., 1949 through 1953.

Most Major League Parks, One or More Home Runs During Career

32—Frank Robinson, Cincinnati N. L., Baltimore A. L., Los Angeles N. L., California
     A. L., Cleveland A. L., 21 years, 1956 through 1976.
     Daniel J. Staub, Houston N. L., Montreal N. L., New York N. L., Detroit A. L.,
     Texas A. L., 21 years, 1963 through 1983.
31—Henry L. Aaron, Milwaukee N. L., Atlanta N. L., Milwaukee A. L., 23 years, 1954
     through 1976.

Hitting Home Runs all Twelve Parks, Season, League

N. L.—Willie L. McCovey, San Francisco, 1970.
        Joseph A. Pepitone, Houston, Chicago, 1970.
        Wilver D. Stargell, Pittsburgh, 1970, (13 including both Pittsburgh parks).
        Johnny L. Bench, Cincinnati, 1972.
        George A. Foster, Cincinnati, 1977.
        Michael J. Schmidt, Philadelphia, 1979.
A. L.—Reginald M. Jackson, Oakland, 1975.

Most Years Hitting Home Runs All Parks, League

A. L.—11—George H. Ruth, Boston, New York, 1919, 1920, 1921, 1923, 1924, 1926, 1927,
        1928, 1929, 1930, 1931.
N. L.— 9—Henry L. Aaron, Milwaukee, Atlanta, 1954, 1955, 1956, 1957, 1958, 1959, 1960,
        1963, 1966.

Most Home Runs Through April 30

N. L.—11—Wilver D. Stargell, Pittsburgh, 1971.
        Michael J. Schmidt, Philadelphia, 1976.
A. L.—11—Graig Nettles, New York, 1974.

Most Home Runs Through May 31

A. L.—20—Mickey C. Mantle, New York, 1956.
N. L.—18—Fred Williams, Philadelphia, 1923.
        Willie H. Mays, San Francisco, 1964.
        Atanasio R. Perez, Cincinnati, 1970.

Most Home Runs Through June 30

A. L.—30—George H. Ruth, New York, 1928; also 1930.
N. L.—28—Wilver D. Stargell, Pittsburgh, 1971.

Most Home Runs Through July 31

A. L.—41—George H. Ruth, New York, 1928.
    James E. Foxx, Philadelphia, 1932.
N. L.—36—Willie H. Mays, New York, 1954.
    Johnny L. Bench, Cincinnati, 1970.
    Wilver D. Stargell, Pittsburgh, 1971.
    Michael J. Schmidt, Philadelphia, 1979.

Most Home Runs Through August 31

A. L. (162-game season)—51—Roger E. Maris, New York, 1961.
A. L. (154-game season)—48—George H. Ruth, New York, 1921.
    James E. Foxx, Philadelphia, 1932.
N. L.—46—Lewis R. Wilson, Chicago, 1930.

Most Home Runs Through September 30

A. L.—60—George H. Ruth, New York, 1927.
    Roger E. Maris, New York, 1961.
N. L.—56—Lewis R. Wilson, Chicago, 1930.

Most Home Runs, Opening Game of Season

N. L.—2—23 times—Held by 21 players—Last player, Albert Oliver, Montreal, April 6,
    1983.
A. L.—2—23 times—Held by 23 players—Last players, Gary J. Gaetti, Minnesota, April
    6, 1982; David G. Bell, Texas, April 8, 1982.

Most Consecutive At-Bats, Without Hitting Home Run, League

N. L.—3,347—Thomas J. Thevenow, St. Louis, Philadelphia, Pittsburgh, Cincinnati,
    Boston, September 24, 1926 through October 2, 1938 (end of career).
A. L.—3,278—Edward C. Foster, Washington, Boston, St. Louis, April 20, 1916 through
    August 5, 1923 (end of career).

Most Total Bases in Major Leagues

6856—Henry L. Aaron, National League, 6591, Milwaukee, Atlanta, 21 years, 1954
    through 1974; American League, 265, 2 years, Milwaukee, 1975, 1976.

Most Total Bases, League

N. L.—6591—Henry L. Aaron, Milwaukee, Atlanta, 21 years, 1954 through 1974.
A. L.—5860—Tyrus R. Cobb, Detroit, Philadelphia, 24 years, 1905 through 1928.

Most Total Bases, Season

A. L.—457—George H. Ruth, New York, 152 games, 1921.
N. L.—450—Rogers Hornsby, St. Louis, 154 games, 1922.

Players With 400 or More Total Bases in One Season

AMERICAN LEAGUE (12 times)			NATIONAL LEAGUE (10 times)		
T.B.	Player and Club	Year	T.B.	Player and Club	Year
457	George H. Ruth, New York	1921	450	Rogers Hornsby, St. Louis	1922
447	H. Louis Gehrig, N. Y.	1927	445	Charles H. Klein, Phil'phia	1930
438	James E. Foxx, Phil'phia	1932	429	Stanley F. Musial, St. L.	1948
419	H. Louis Gehrig, N. Y.	1930	423	Lewis R. Wilson, Chicago	1930
418	Joseph P. DiMaggio, N. Y.	1937	420	Charles H. Klein, Phil'phia	1932
417	George H. Ruth, New York	1927	416	Floyd C. Herman, Brook.	1930
410	H. Louis Gehrig, N. Y.	1931	409	Rogers Hornsby, Chicago	1929
409	H. Louis Gehrig, N. Y.	1934	406	Joseph M. Medwick, St. L.	1937
406	James E. Rice, Boston	1978	405	Charles H. Klein, Phil'phia	1929
405	Harold A. Trosky, Cleve.	1936	400	Henry L. Aaron, Milw.	1959
403	H. Louis Gehrig, N. Y.	1936			
403	James E. Foxx, Phila.	1933			

Fewest Total Bases, Season, 150 or More Games

N. L.—89—C. Dallan Maxvill, St. Louis, 152 games, 1970.
A. L.—114—Edwin A. Brinkman, Washington, 154 games, 1965.

Most Years Leading League in Total Bases

N. L.—8—Henry L. Aaron, Milwaukee, Atlanta, 1956, 1957, 1959, 1960, 1961, 1963, 1967,
    1969.
A. L.—6—Tyrus R. Cobb, Detroit, 1907, 1908, 1909, 1911, 1915, 1917.
    George H. Ruth, Boston, New York, 1919, 1921, 1923, 1924, 1926, 1928.
    Theodore S. Williams, Boston, 1939, 1942, 1946, 1947, 1949, 1951.

Most Consecutive Years Leading League in Total Bases

N. L.—4—John P. Wagner, Pittsburgh, 1906, 1907, 1908, 1909.
   Charles H. Klein, Philadelphia, 1930, 1931, 1932, 1933.
A. L.—3—Tyrus R. Cobb, Detroit, 1907, 1908, 1909.
   Theodore S. Williams, Boston, 1942, 1946, 1947 (in military service 1943-44-
      45).
   James E. Rice, Boston, 1977, 1978, 1979.

Most Years, 400 or More Total Bases, League

A. L.—5—H. Louis Gehrig, New York, 1927, 1930, 1931, 1934, 1936.
N. L.—3—Charles H. Klein, Philadelphia, 1929, 1930, 1932.

Most Consecutive Years, 400 or More Total Bases, League

A. L.—2—H. Louis Gehrig, New York, 1930, 1931.
   James E. Foxx, Philadelphia, 1932, 1933.
N. L.—2—Charles H. Klein, Philadelphia, 1929, 1930.

Most Years, 300 or More Total Bases, League

N. L.—15—Henry L. Aaron, Milwaukee, Atlanta, 1955 through 1971, except 1964, 1970.
A. L.—13—H. Louis Gehrig, New York, 1926 through 1938.

Most Consecutive Years, 300 or More Total Bases, League

A. L.—13—H. Louis Gehrig, New York, 1926 through 1938.
N. L.—13—Willie H. Mays, New York, San Francisco, 1954 through 1966.

Fewest Total Bases, Season, for Leader in Total Bases (154-game Schedule)

N. L.— 237— John P. Wagner, Pittsburgh, 140 games, 1906.
A. L.— 260— George H. Stone, St. Louis, 154 games, 1905.

Most Total Bases, Inning

N. L.-A. L.—8—Held by many players.
A. L.—Last player—Clifford Johnson, New York, June 30, 1977, eighth inning, 2 home
      runs.
N. L.—Last player—C. Ray Knight, Cincinnati, May 13, 1980, fifth inning, 2 home runs.

Most Total Bases, Game, Nine Innings

N. L.—18—Joseph W. Adcock, Milwaukee, July 31, 1954; 4 home runs, 1 double.
A. L.—16—Tyrus R. Cobb, Detroit, May 5, 1925; 3 home runs, 1 double, 2 singles.
   H. Louis Gehrig, New York, June 3, 1932; 4 home runs.
   Rocco D. Colavito, Cleveland, June 10, 1959; 4 home runs.
   Fredric M. Lynn, Boston, June 18, 1975; 3 home runs, 1 triple, 1 single.

Most Total Bases, Extra-Inning Game, Since 1900

N. L.—17—Michael J. Schmidt, Philadelphia, April 17, 1976, 10 innings; 4 home runs, 1
      single.
A. L.—16—James E. Foxx, Philadelphia, July 10, 1932, 18 innings; 3 home runs, 1 dou-
      ble, 2 singles.
   James P. Seerey, Chicago, July 18, 1948, first game, 11 innings; 4 home runs.

Most Total Bases, Doubleheader, Nine-Inning Games

N. L.—22—Nathan Colbert, San Diego, August 1, 1972.
A. L.—21—Albert Oliver, Texas, August 17, 1980.

Most Total Bases, Doubleheader (More Than 18 Innings)

A. L.—21—James E. Foxx, Philadelphia, July 2, 1933, 19 innings.
N. L.—19—Ralph M. Kiner, Pittsburgh, September 11, 1947, 22 innings.

Most Total Bases, Two Consecutive Games

A. L.—25—Tyrus R. Cobb, Detroit, May 5, 6, 1925.
N. L.—25—Joseph W. Adcock, Milwaukee, July 30, 31, 1954.

Most Total Bases, Nine-Inning Game by Pitcher

A. A.—15—Guy J. Hecker, Louisville, August 15, 1886, second game, 3 home runs, 3
      singles.
N. L.—12—James Tobin, Boston, May 13, 1942; 3 home runs.
A. L.—10—Lewis D. Wiltse, Philadelphia, August 10, 1901, second game, 2 triples, 2 dou-
      bles.
   Charles H. Ruffing, New York, June 17, 1936, first game, 2 singles and 2
      home runs.
   Jack E. Harshman, Baltimore, September 23, 1958, 2 home runs, 1 double.

Most Total Bases, Extra-Inning Game by Pitcher

A. L.—10—George H. Ruth, Boston, May 9, 1918, 10 innings, 1 single, 3 doubles, 1 triple.

Most Long Hits in Major Leagues

1477—Henry L. Aaron, 1429 in National League, Milwaukee, Atlanta, 21 years, 1954
    through 1974; 48 in American League, 2 years, Milwaukee, 1975, 1976, 624 dou-
    bles, 98 triples, 755 home runs.

Most Long Hits, League

N. L.— 1429— Henry L. Aaron, Milwaukee, Atlanta, 21 years, 1954 through 1974, 600
    doubles, 96 triples, 733 home runs.
A. L.— 1350— George H. Ruth, Boston, New York, 21 years, 1914 through 1934, 506 dou-
    bles, 136 triples, 708 home runs.

Most Long Hits, Season

A. L.— 119— George H. Ruth, New York, 152 games, 1921; 44 doubles, 16 triples, 59 home
    runs.
N. L.— 107— Charles H. Klein, Philadelphia, 156 games, 1930; 59 doubles, 8 triples, 40
    home runs.

Most Years Leading League in Doubles, Triples, Home Runs (Same Season)

A. A.—1—James E. O'Neill, St. Louis, 123 games, 1887, 46 doubles, 24 triples, 13 home
    runs. Also led in batting, .492.
N. L.-A. L.—Never accomplished.

Twenty or More Doubles, Triples and Homers, Season

N. L.—John F. Freeman, Washington, 155 games, 1899 (20 doubles, 26 triples, 25 home
    runs).
    Frank M. Schulte, Chicago, 154 games, 1911 (30 doubles, 21 triples, 21 homers).
    James L. Bottomley, St. Louis, 149 games, 1928 (42 doubles, 20 triples, 31
    homers).
    Willie H. Mays, New York, 152 games, 1957 (26 doubles, 20 triples, 35 homers).
A. L.—J. Geoffrey Heath, Cleveland, 151 games, 1941 (32 doubles, 20 triples, 24 homers).
    George H. Brett, Kansas City, 154 games, 1979 (42 doubles, 20 triples, 23
    homers).

Fewest Long Hits, Season, 150 or More Games

N. L.— 7—C. Dallan Maxvill, St. Louis, 152 games, 1970, 5 doubles, 2 triples.
A. L.—12—Michael Tresh, Chicago, 150 games, 1945, 12 doubles.

Most Years Leading League in Long Hits

N. L.—7—John P. Wagner, Pittsburgh, 1900, 1902, 1903, 1904, 1907, 1908, 1909.
    Stanley F. Musial, St. Louis, 1943, 1944, 1946, 1948, 1949, 1950, 1953.
A. L.—7—George H. Ruth, Boston, New York, 1918, 1919, 1920, 1921, 1923, 1924, 1928.

Most Consecutive Years Leading League in Long Hits

A. L.—4—George H. Ruth, Boston, New York, 1918, 1919, 1920, 1921.
N. L.—3—Held by many players. Last player—Edwin D. Snider, Brooklyn, 1954, 1955
    (tied), 1956.

Fewest Long Hits, Season, for Leader in Long Hits (154-game Schedule)

N. L.—50—Sherwood R. Magee, Philadelphia, 154 games, 1906; 36 doubles, 8 triples, 6
    home runs.
A. L.—54—Samuel Crawford, Detroit, 156 games, 1915; 31 doubles, 19 triples, 4 home
    runs.

Most Times, Four or More Long Hits, Game, League

A. L.—5—H. Louis Gehrig, New York, 1926, 1928, 1930, 1932, 1934.
    Joseph P. DiMaggio, New York, 1936, 1937, 1941, 1948, 1950.
N. L.—4—Wilver D. Stargell, Pittsburgh, 1965, 1968, 1970, 1973.

Most Times, Four Long Hits, Game, Season

A. L.—2—George H. Burns, Cleveland, June 19, first game, July 23, 1924.
    James E. Foxx, Philadelphia, April 24, July 2, second game, 1933.
N. L.—2—Joseph M. Medwick, St. Louis, May 12, August 4, 1937.
    Billy L. Williams, Chicago, April 9, September 5, 1969.

Most Long Hits, Inning

N. L.—3—Thomas E. Burns, Chicago, September 6, 1883, seventh inning, 2 doubles, 1
    home run.
A. L.-N. L. since 1900—2—Held by many players.
A. L.—Last player—Robert O. Jones, Texas, July 3, 1983, fifteenth inning, 2 doubles.
N. L.—Last player—Darrell W. Evans, San Francisco, May 13, 1983, fourth inning, 1
    double, 1 home run.

Most Long Hits, Game

A. A.—5—George A. Strief, Philadelphia, June 25, 1885; 4 triples, 1 double, consecutive.
N. L.—5—George F. Gore, Chicago, July 9, 1885; 2 triples, 3 doubles, consecutive.
Lawrence Twitchell, Cleveland, August 15, 1889; 1 double, 3 triples, 1 home run.
Joseph W. Adcock, Milwaukee, July 31, 1954; 4 home runs, 1 double, consecutive.
Wilver D. Stargell, Pittsburgh, August 1, 1970; 3 doubles, 2 home runs.
Steven P. Garvey, Los Angeles, August 28, 1977; 3 doubles, 2 home runs, consecutive.
A. L.—5—Louis Boudreau, Cleveland, July 14, 1946; first game; 4 doubles, 1 home run.

Most Long Hits, Opening Game of Season

N. L.—4—George D. Myers, Indianapolis, April 20, 1888; 3 doubles, 1 home run.
William J. Herman, Chicago, April 14, 1936; 3 doubles, 1 home run.
James R. Greengrass, Cincinnati, April 13, 1954; 4 doubles.
A. L.—4—Frank Dillon, Detroit, April 25, 1901; 4 doubles.
Don E. Baylor, Baltimore, April 6, 1973; 2 doubles, 1 triple, 1 home run.

Most Long Hits, Inning, Pitcher

N. L.—2—Fred Goldsmith, Chicago, September 6, 1883, seventh inning, 2 doubles.
William J. Terry, Chicago, May 19, 1895, third inning, 1 home run, 1 double.
Henry L. Borowy, Chicago, May 5, 1946; first game, seventh inning, 2 doubles.
A. L.—2—Joseph Wood, Boston, July 4, 1913, a.m. game, fourth inning, 2 doubles.
J. Robert Shawkey, New York, July 12, 1923, third inning, 1 triple, 1 double.
Theodore A. Lyons, Chicago, July 28, 1935, first game, second inning, 2 doubles.

Most Long Hits, Game, Pitcher, Nine Innings

A. A.—4—Robert L. Caruthers, St. Louis, August 16, 1886, 2 home runs, 1 triple, 1 double.
A. L.—4—Lewis D. Wiltse, Philadelphia, August 10, 1901, second game, 2 triples, 2 doubles.
N. L.—3—Held by many pitchers—Last pitcher—John A. Messersmith, Los Angeles, April 25, 1975, 3 doubles.

Most Long Hits, Extra-Inning Game, Pitcher

A. L.—4—George H. Ruth, Boston, May 9, 1918, 10 innings, 3 doubles, 1 triple.

Most Long Hits, Doubleheader, Nine-Inning Games

N. L.—6—Joseph M. Medwick, St. Louis, May 30, 1935, 5 doubles, 1 triple.
Albert F. Schoendienst, St. Louis, June 6, 1948, 5 doubles, 1 home run.
A. L.—6—John T. Stone, Detroit, April 30, 1933, 4 doubles, 2 home runs.
Henry Majeski, Philadelphia, August 27, 1948, 6 doubles.
Harold A. McRae, Kansas City, August 27, 1974, 5 doubles, 1 home run.
Albert Oliver, Texas, August 17, 1980, 1 double, 1 triple, 4 home runs.

Most Long Hits, Doubleheader (More Than 18 Innings)

N. L.—6—Charles J. Hafey, St. Louis, July 28, 1928, 21 innings, 4 doubles, 2 home runs.
Melvin T. Ott, New York, June 19, 1929, 20 innings, 4 doubles, 2 home runs.
James L. Rhodes, New York, 20 innings, August 29, 1954, 2 doubles, 2 triples, 2 home runs (played 12 innings, 7 at-bats).
A. L.—6—James E. Foxx, Philadelphia, July 2, 1933, 19 innings, 1 double, 1 triple, 4 home runs.

Most Long Hits, Two Consecutive Games

N. L.—7—Edward J. Delahanty, Philadelphia, July 13, 14, 1896, 2 doubles, 1 triple, 4 home runs.
Albert F. Schoendienst, St. Louis, June 5, 6, first game, 1948, 6 doubles, 1 home run.
Joseph W. Adcock, Milwaukee, July 30, 31, 1954, 2 doubles, 5 home runs.
A. L.—7—Earl H. Sheely, Chicago, May 20, 21, 1926, 6 doubles, 1 home run.

Most Long Hits, Three Consecutive Games

N. L.—9—Albert Schoendienst, St. Louis, June 5, 6, 6, 1948, 8 doubles, 1 home run.
A. L.—8—Earl H. Sheely, Chicago, May 20, 21, 22, 1926, 7 doubles, 1 home run.

Most Consecutive Long Hits, Season

A. L.—7—Elmer J. Smith, Cleveland, September 4, 5, 5, 1921, 3 doubles, 4 home runs. (2 bases on balls in streak).
Earl H. Sheely, Chicago, May 20, 21, 1926, 6 doubles, 1 home run (1 sacrifice hit in streak).
N. L.—5—Held by many players.

Most Consecutive Games, One or More Long Hits, Season

N. L.—14—Paul G. Waner, Pittsburgh, June 3 through June 19, 1927; 12 doubles, 4 triples, 4 home runs.

A. L.— 9—George H. Ruth, New York, August 28 through September 5, 1921, second game; 7 doubles, 1 triple, 3 home runs.

Most Extra Bases on Long Hits, in Major Leagues

3085—Henry L. Aaron, 2991 in National League, Milwaukee, Atlanta, 21 years, 1954 through 1974; 94 in American League, Milwaukee, 2 years, 1975, 1976.

Most Extra Bases on Long Hits, League

N. L.— 2991— Henry L. Aaron, Milwaukee, Atlanta, 21 years, 1954 through 1974.

A. L.— 2902— George H. Ruth, Boston, New York, 21 years, 1914 through 1934.

Most Extra Bases on Long Hits, Season

A. L.— 253— George H. Ruth, New York, 152 games, 1921.

N. L.— 215— Lewis R. Wilson, Chicago, 155 games, 1930.

Fewest Extra Bases on Long Hits, Season, 150 or More Games

N. L.— 9—C. Dallan Maxvill, St. Louis, 152 games, 1970.

A. L.—11—Michael Tresh, Chicago, 150 games, 1945.

Most Years Leading League in Extra Bases on Long Hits

A. L.—9—George H. Ruth, Boston, New York, 1918, 1919, 1920, 1921, 1923, 1924, 1926, 1928, 1929.

N. L.—6—John P. Wagner, Pittsburgh, 1900, 1902, 1903, 1907, 1908, 1909.
　　　　Michael J. Schmidt, Philadelphia, 1974, 1975, 1976, 1980, 1981, 1982.

Most Consecutive Years Leading League in Extra Bases on Long Hits

A. L.—4—George H. Ruth, Boston, New York, 1918, 1919, 1920, 1921.

N. L.—3—Held by many players.
　　　　Last player—Michael J. Schmidt, Philadelphia, 1980, 1981, 1982.

Most Years 200 or More Extra Bases on Long Hits

A. L.—4—George H. Ruth, New York, 1920, 1921, 1927, 1928.

N. L.—1—Rogers Hornsby, St. Louis, 1922.
　　　　Lewis R. Wilson, Chicago, 1930.

Most Consecutive Years 200 or More Extra Bases on Long Hits

A. L.—2—George H. Ruth, New York, 1920, 1921, also 1927, 1928.

N. L.—No player with 2 consecutive years.

Most Years 100 or More Extra Bases on Long Hits

N. L.—19—Henry L. Aaron, Milwaukee, Atlanta, 1955 through 1973.

A. L.—16—Theodore S. Williams, Boston, 1939, 1940, 1941, 1942, 1946, 1947, 1948, 1949, 1950, 1951, 1954, 1955, 1956, 1957, 1958, 1960.

Most Consecutive Years 100 or More Extra Bases on Long Hits

N. L.—19—Henry L. Aaron, Milwaukee, Atlanta, 1955 through 1973.

A. L.—15—Theodore S. Williams, Boston, 1939, 1940, 1941, 1942 (in military service, 1943, 1944, 1945), 1946, 1947, 1948, 1949, 1950, 1951 (in military service, most of seasons, 1952, 1953), 1954, 1955, 1956, 1957, 1958.
　　　　14—H. Louis Gehrig, New York, 1925 through 1938.

Fewest Extra Bases on Long Hits, Season, for Leader in Extra Bases (154 or 162-game Schedule)

N. L.—74—Harry G. Lumley, Brooklyn, 131 games, 1906.
　　　　John P. Wagner, Pittsburgh, 137 games, 1909.

A. L.—80—Samuel Crawford, Detroit, 144 games, 1907.

Most Extra Bases on Long Hits, Inning

N. L.-A. L.—6—Held by many players.

Most Extra Bases on Long Hits, Nine-Inning Game

N. L.—13—Joseph W. Adcock, Milwaukee, July 31, 1954; 4 home runs, 1 double.

A. L.—12—H. Louis Gehrig, New York, June 3, 1932; 4 home runs.
　　　　Rocco D. Colavito, Cleveland, June 10, 1959; 4 home runs.

Most Extra Bases on Long Hits, Extra-Inning Game

N. L.—12—Charles H. Klein, Philadelphia, July 10, 1936, 10 innings; 4 home runs.
　　　　Michael J. Schmidt, Philadelphia, April 17, 1976, 10 innings; 4 home runs.

A. L.—12—J. Patrick Seerey, Chicago, July 18, 1948, first game, 11 innings; 4 home runs.

Most Extra Bases on Long Hits, Doubleheader, Nine-Inning Games

N. L.—15—Stanley F. Musial, St. Louis, May 2, 1954.
      Nathan Colbert, San Diego, August 1, 1972.
A. L.—15—Albert Oliver, Texas, August 17, 1980.

Most Extra Bases on Long Hits, Doubleheader, More Than 18 Innings

A. L.—15—James E. Foxx, Philadelphia, July 2, 1933, 19 innings.
N. L.—13—Ralph M. Kiner, Pittsburgh, September 11, 1947, 22 innings.

Most Extra Bases on Long Hits, Two Consecutive Games

A. L.—17—Anthony M. Lazzeri, New York, May 23, second game, May 24, 1936; 5 home
      runs, 1 triple
N. L.—17—Joseph W. Adcock, Milwaukee, July 30, July 31, 1954; 5 home runs, 2 doubles.

Most Times Hitting for Cycle
(single, double, triple, home run, game)

A. L.—3—Robert W. Meusel, New York, 1921, 1922, 1928.
N. L.—3—Floyd C. Herman, Brooklyn, 1931 (2), Chicago, 1933.
Two Leagues—3—John G. Reilly, Cincinnati A. A., 1883 (2), Cincinnati N. L., 1890.

Hitting for Cycle, Game
(single, double, triple, home run)

N. L.—98 times—Last Players—Ivan DeJesus, Chicago, April 22, 1980; Michael A.
      Easler, Pittsburgh, June 12, 1980.
A. L.—80 times—Last Player—Frank White, Kansas City, August 3, 1982.

Hitting for Cycle, Both Leagues
(single, double, triple, home run, game)

Robert J. Watson, Houston N. L., June 24, 1977; Boston A. L., September 15, 1979.

Most Runs Batted In, Major Leagues

2297—Henry L. Aaron, 2202 in National League, Milwaukee, Atlanta, 21 years, 1954
      through 1974; 95 in American League, Milwaukee, 2 years, 1975, 1976.

Most Runs Batted In, League

N. L.— 2202— Henry L. Aaron, Milwaukee, Atlanta, 21 years, 1954 through 1974.
A. L.— 2192— George H. Ruth, Boston, New York, 21 years, 1914 through 1934.

Most Runs Batted In, Season

N. L.— 190— Lewis R. Wilson, Chicago, 155 games, 1930.
A. L.— 184— H. Louis Gehrig, New York, 155 games, 1931.

Most Runs Batted In, Season, Catcher

N. L.— 142— Roy Campanella, Brooklyn, 144 games, 1953; caught 140 games.
A. L.— 133— William M. Dickey, New York, 140 games, 1937; caught 137 games.

Fewest Runs Batted In, Season, 150 or More Games

N. L.—20—Richie Ashburn, Philadelphia, 153 games, 1959.
A. L.—23—Owen Bush, Detroit, 157 games, 1914.

Most Years Leading League, Runs Batted In

A. L.—6—George H. Ruth, Boston, New York, 1919, 1920, 1921, 1923, 1926, 1928 (tied).
N. L.—4—Rogers Hornsby, St. Louis, 1920 (tied), 1921, 1922, 1925.
      Henry L. Aaron, Milwaukee, Atlanta, 1957, 1960, 1963, 1966.

Most Consecutive Years Leading League, Runs Batted In

A. L.—3—Tyrus R. Cobb, Detroit, 1907, 1908, 1909.
      George H. Ruth, Boston, New York, 1919, 1920, 1921.
N. L.—3—John P. Wagner, Pittsburgh, 1907, 1908, 1909.
      Rogers Hornsby, St. Louis, 1920 (tied), 1921, 1922
      Joseph M. Medwick, St. Louis, 1936, 1937, 1938.
      George A. Foster, Cincinnati, 1976, 1977, 1978.

Most Years, 100 or More Runs Batted In

A. L.—13—George H. Ruth, Boston, New York, 1919 through 1933, except 1922 and 1925.
      H. Louis Gehrig, New York, 1926 through 1938.
      James E. Foxx, Philadelphia, Boston, 1929 through 1941.
N. L.—11—Henry L. Aaron, Milwaukee, Atlanta, 1955, 1957, 1959, 1960, 1961, 1962, 1963,
      1966, 1967, 1970, 1971.

Most Consecutive Years, 100 or More Runs Batted In, League

A. L.—13—H. Louis Gehrig, New York, 1926 through 1938.
      James E. Foxx, Philadelphia, Boston, 1929 through 1941.
N. L.— 8—Melvin T. Ott, New York, 1929 through 1936.
      Willie H. Mays, San Francisco, 1959 through 1966.

Most Years, 150 or More Runs Batted In, League

A. L.—7—H. Louis Gehrig, New York, 1927, 1930, 1931, 1932, 1934, 1936, 1937.
N. L.—2—Lewis R. Wilson, Chicago, 1929, 1930.

Most Consecutive Years, 150 or More Runs Batted In

A. L.—3—George H. Ruth, New York, 1929, 1930, 1931.
     H. Louis Gehrig, New York, 1930, 1931, 1932.
N. L.—2—Lewis R. Wilson, Chicago, 1929, 1930.

Fewest Runs Batted In, Season, for Leader In Runs Batted In, Since 1920 (154 or 162-Game Schedule)

N. L.— 94— George L. Kelly, New York, 155 games, 1920.
     Rogers Hornsby, St. Louis, 149 games, 1920.
A. L.— 105— Albert L. Rosen, Cleveland, 148 games, 1952.

Most Runs Batted In, Inning

N. L.—6—Fred C. Merkle, New York, May 13, 1911, first inning.
     James R. Hart, San Francisco, July 8, 1970 fifth inning.
A. L.—6—Robert L. Johnson, Philadelphia, August 29, 1937, first game, first inning.
     Thomas R. McBride, Boston, August 4, 1945, second game, fourth inning.
     Joseph H. Astroth, Philadelphia, September 23, 1950, sixth inning.
     Gilbert J. McDougald, New York, May 3, 1951, ninth inning.
     Sabath A. Mele, Chicago, June 10, 1952, fourth inning.
     James R. Lemon, Washington, September 5, 1959, third inning.

Most Runs Batted In, Game

N. L.—12—James L. Bottomley, St. Louis, September 16, 1924.
A. L.—11—Anthony M. Lazzeri, New York, May 24, 1936.

Most Runs Batted In, Game, Pitcher

N. L.—9—Tony L. Cloninger, Atlanta, July 3, 1966.
A. L.—7—Victor J. Raschi, New York, August 4, 1953.

Most Runs Batted In, Doubleheader

N. L.—13—Nathan Colbert, San Diego, August 1, 1972.
A. L.—11—H. Earl Averill, Cleveland, September 17, 1930, 17 innings.
     James R. Tabor, Boston, July 4, 1939, 18 innings.
     John W. Powell, Baltimore, July 6, 1966, 20 innings.

Batting In All Club's Runs, Game (Most)

N. L.—8—George L. Kelly, New York vs. Cincinnati, June 14, 1924; New York won, 8 to 6.
A. L.—8—Robert L. Johnson, Philadelphia vs. St. Louis, June 12, 1938; Philadelphia won, 8-3.

Most Runs Batted In, Two Consecutive Games

A. L.—15—Anthony M. Lazzeri, New York, May 23, second game (4), May 24, (11) 1936.
N. L.—13—Nathan Colbert, San Diego, August 1, first game (5), August 1, second game (8), 1972.

Most Consecutive Games, Season, One or More Runs Batted In

N. L.—17—Oscar R. Grimes, Chicago, June 27 through July 23, 1922; 27 runs batted in.
A. L.—13—Taft S. Wright, Chicago, May 4 through May 20, 1941; 22 runs batted in.

Most Runs Batted In, Two Consecutive Innings

A. L.—8—James E. Gentile, Baltimore, May 9, 1961, first and second innings.
     James T. Northrup, Detroit, June 24, 1968, fifth and sixth innings .
     Frank Robinson, Baltimore, June 26, 1970, fifth and sixth innings.
N. L.—7—Charles A. Nichols, Boston, September 19, 1892, fifth and sixth innings.
     Anthony Piet, Pittsburgh, July 28, 1932, second game, second and third innings.
     John J. Rucker, New York, September 29, 1940, second and third innings.
     Delmer Ennis, Philadelphia, July 27, 1950, seventh and eighth innings.
     C. Earl Torgeson, Boston, June 30, 1951, seventh and eighth innings.
     Ralph M. Kiner, Pittsburgh, July 4, 1951, second game, third and fourth innings.
     Joe L. Morgan, Cincinnati, August 19, 1974, second and third innings.

Most Game-Winning RBIs, Season (Since 1980)

A. L.—22—Harold D. Baines, Chicago, 156 games, 1983.
N. L.—21—Jack A. Clark, San Francisco, 157 games, 1982.
     Keith Hernandez, St. Louis, 160 games, 1982.

Most Game-Winning RBIs, Season, by Pitcher (Since 1980)

N. L.—2—Held by many pitchers.

Fewest Game-Winning RBIs, Season, 150 or More Games (Since 1980)

N. L.—1—Stephen L. Sax, Los Angeles, 150 games, 1982.
A. L.—2—Alfredo C. Griffin, Toronto, 155 games, 1980.
       Julio L. Cruz, Seattle, 154 games, 1982.
       Gary J. Gaetti, Minnesota, 157 games, 1983.
       Alfredo C. Griffin, Toronto, 162 games, 1983.

Most Game-Winning RBIs, Doubleheader (Since 1980)

N. L.-A. L.—2—Held by many players.

Most Consecutive Games With Game-Winning RBI, Season (Since 1980)

A. L.—4—George H. Brett, Kansas City, August 13 through 17, 1980.
N. L.—3—Held by many players.

Most Consecutive Winning Games With Game-Winning RBI, Season (Since 1980)

N. L.—5—J. Robert Horner, Atlanta, May 1 through May 8, 1983, 2 losses in streak.
A. L.—4—Jeffrey L. Newman, Oakland, June 22 through July 3, 1980, 7 losses in streak.
       George H. Brett, Kansas City, August 13 through 17, 1980, 0 losses in streak.
       Roy F. Smalley, Minnesota, April 26, second game, through May 1, 1981, 1 loss in streak.
       Donald E. Baylor, California, May 1 through May 9, 1982, 4 losses in streak.
       Antonio R. Armas, Oakland, June 9 through June 14, 1982, 1 loss in streak.
       Wade A. Boggs, Boston, July 22 through July 26, 1983, 2 losses in streak.

Home Run and Triple With Bases Filled, Game

N. L.—Dennis L. Brouthers, Detroit, May 17, 1887.
      Charles A. Nichols, Boston, September 19, 1892.
      Jacob C. Stenzel, Pittsburgh, July 15, 1893.
      Adelphia L. Bissonette, Brooklyn, April 21, 1930.
      Edward D. Phillips, Pittsburgh, May 28, 1931.
      Luis R. Olmo, Brooklyn, May 18, 1945.
A. L.—George H. Sisler, St. Louis, July 11, 1925.
      Harry E. Heilmann, Detroit, July 26, 1928, second game.

Most Bases on Balls in Major Leagues

2056—George H. Ruth, Boston A. L., New York A. L., Boston N. L., 22 years, 1914 through 1935 (2036 in A. L., 20 in N. L.).

Most Bases on Balls, League

A. L.— 2036— George H. Ruth, Boston, New York, 21 years, 1914 through 1934.
N. L.— 1799— Joe L. Morgan, Houston, Cincinnati, San Francisco, Philadelphia, 21 years, 1963 through 1983.

Most Bases on Balls, Season

A. L.— 170— George H. Ruth, New York, 152 games, 1923.
N. L.— 148— Edward R. Stanky, Brooklyn, 153 games, 1945.
       James S. Wynn, Houston, 149 games, 1969.

Most Bases on Balls, Season, Pinch-Hitter

A. L.—18—Elmer W. Valo, New York, Washington, 81 games, 1960.
N. L.—16—Harry H. McCurdy, Philadelphia, 71 games, 1933.
       Mervin W. Rettenmund, San Diego, 86 games, 1977.

Fewest Bases on Balls, Season, 150 or More Games

N. L.—12—Harold C. Lanier, San Francisco, 151 games, 1968.
A. L.—14—Timothy J. Foli, California, 150 games, 1982.

Most Years Leading League in Bases on Balls

A. L.—11—George H. Ruth, New York, 1920, 1921, 1923, 1924, 1926, 1927, 1928, 1930, 1931, 1932, 1933.
N. L.— 6—Melvin T. Ott, New York, 1929, 1931, 1932, 1933, 1937, 1942.

Most Consecutive Years Leading in Bases on Balls

A. L.—6—Theodore S. Williams, Boston, 1941, 1942, 1946, 1947, 1948, 1949 (except 1943, 1944, 1945, in military service).
N. L.—3—George J. Burns, New York, 1919, 1920, 1921.
      Melvin T. Ott, New York, 1931, 1932, 1933.
      J. Floyd Vaughan, Pittsburgh, 1934, 1935, 1936.
      Edwin L. Mathews, Milwaukee, 1961, 1962, 1963.
      Ronald E. Santo, Chicago, 1966, 1967, 1968.
      Michael J. Schmidt, Philadelphia, 1981, 1982, 1983.

Most Years, 100 or More Bases on Balls, League

A. L.—13—George H. Ruth, Boston, New York, 1919, 1920, 1921, 1923, 1924, 1926, 1927, 1928, 1930, 1931, 1932, 1933, 1934.

N. L.—10—Melvin T. Ott, New York, 1929, 1930, 1932, 1936, 1937, 1938, 1939, 1940, 1941, 1942.

Most Consecutive Years 100 or More Bases on Balls, League

N. L.—7—Melvin T. Ott, New York, 1936 through 1942.

A. L.—6—Theodore S. Williams, Boston, 1941 through 1949 (except 1943-44-45 in military service).

Edwin D. Joost, Philadelphia, 1947 through 1952.

Fewest Bases on Balls, Season, Leader in Bases on Balls (154 or 162-Game Schedule)

N. L.—69—Lewis R. Wilson, Chicago, 142 games, 1926.

A. L.—89—Lawton W. Witt, New York, 140 games, 1922.

Most Bases on Balls, Inning

N. L.-A. L.—2—Held by many players.

N. L.—Last Player—Franklin Taveras, Pittsburgh, June 29, 1976, first inning.

A. L.—Last Player—Dagoberto B. Campaneris, Oakland, June 18, 1975, seventh inning.

Most Bases on Balls, Nine-Inning Game

N. L.—6—Walter Wilmot, Chicago, August 22, 1891 (consecutive).

A. L.—6—James E. Foxx, Boston, June 16, 1938 (consecutive).

N. L. since 1900—5—Held by many players.

N. L.—Last Player—Dale B. Murphy, Atlanta, April 22, 1983.

Most Bases on Balls, Doubleheader

A. L.—8—Max Bishop, Philadelphia, May 21, 1930; Boston, July 8, 1934.

N. L.—6—Melvin T. Ott, New York, October 5, 1929.

John R. Mize, St. Louis, August 26, 1939.

Melvin T. Ott, New York, April 30, 1944.

Clayton E. Dalrymple, Philadelphia, July 4, 1967, 19 innings.

Cleon J. Jones, New York, June 25, 1971.

Most Bases on Balls, First Major League Game

A. L.—4—Otto H. Saltzgaver, New York, April 12, 1932.

Milton Galatzer, Cleveland, June 25, 1933, first game.

N. L.—3—Held by many players.

Most Bases on Balls, Game, Pitcher

A. A.—4—Joseph Miller, Philadelphia, September 13, 1886.

A. L.—4—Urban C. Faber, Chicago, June 18, 1915, consecutive.

Charles K. Stobbs, Boston, June 8, 1950, consecutive.

N. L.—3—Held by many pitchers.

Most Intentional Bases on Balls in Major Leagues, Since 1955

293—Henry L. Aaron, 289 in National League, Milwaukee, Atlanta, 20 years, 1955 through 1974; 4 in American League, Milwaukee, 2 years, 1975, 1976.

Most Intentional Bases on Balls, League, Since 1955

N. L.—289—Henry L. Aaron, Milwaukee, Atlanta, 20 years, 1955 through 1974.

A. L.—190—Carl M. Yastrzemski, Boston, 23 years, 1961 through 1983.

Most Intentional Bases on Balls, Season, Since 1955

N. L.—45—Willie L. McCovey, San Francisco, 149 games, 1969.

A. L.—33—Theodore S. Williams, Boston, 132 games, 1957.

Fewest Intentional Bases on Balls, Season, Most At-Bats

N. L.—0—Lawrence R. Bowa, Philadelphia, 162 games, 1974; 669 at-bats.

A. L.—0—Calvin E. Ripken, Baltimore, 162 games, 1983; 663 at-bats.

Most Years Leading League in Intentional Bases on Balls, Since 1955

N. L.—4—Frank Robinson, Cincinnati, 1961, 1962 (tied), 1963, 1964.

Willie L. McCovey, San Francisco, 1969, 1970, 1971 (tied), 1973.

A. L.—3—Theodore S. Williams, Boston, 1955, 1956, 1957.

Harmon C. Killebrew, Minnesota, 1966, 1967 (tied), 1969 (tied).

Rodney C. Carew, Minnesota, 1975, 1977, 1978.

Most Consecutive Years Leading League in Intentional Bases on Balls, Since 1955

N. L.—4—Frank Robinson, Cincinnati, 1961, 1962 (tied), 1963, 1964.

A. L.—3—Theodore S. Williams, Boston, 1955, 1956, 1957.

Most Years, 10 or More Intentional Bases on Balls

N. L.—16—Henry L. Aaron, Milwaukee, Atlanta, 1957 through 1973, except 1964.
A. L.— 9—Pedro Oliva, Minnesota, 1965 through 1975 except 1971, 1972.

Most Intentional Bases on Balls, Game

N. L.—5—Melvin T. Ott, New York, October 5, 1929, second game.
A. L.—4—Roger E. Maris, New York, May 22, 1962, 12 innings.

Most Consecutive Bases on Balls, During Season

A. L.—7—William G. Rogell, Detroit, August 17, second game, August 18, August 19,
         first game, 1938.
N. L.—7—Melvin T. Ott, New York, June 16, 17, 18, 1943.
         Edward R. Stanky, New York, August 29, 30, 1950.

Most Consecutive Games, Season, One or More Bases on Balls

A. L.—22—Roy J. Cullenbine, Detroit, July 2 through July 22, 1947, 34 bases on balls.
A. A.—16—William H. Robinson, St. Louis, September 15, through October 2, 1888, 23
         bases on balls.
N. L.—15—Darrell W. Evans, Atlanta, April 9 through April 27, 1976, 19 bases on balls.

Most Times Five Bases on Balls, Game, League

N. L.—4—Melvin T. Ott, New York, 1929, 1933, 1943, 1944.
A. L.—2—Max F. Bishop, Philadelphia, 1929, 1930.

Most Times Two Bases on Balls, Inning, League

A. L.—4—George A. Selkirk, New York, 1936 (2), 1938, 1940.
N. L.—2—Edward R. Stanky, New York, 1950 (2).

Most Times Two Bases on Balls, Inning, Season

A. L.—2—George A. Selkirk, New York, June 24, August 28, second game, 1936.
         James L. Webb, Chicago, July 30, September 3, 1940.
N. L.—2—Edward R. Stanky, New York, June 27, August 22, 1950.

Most Strikeouts, League

A. L.— 2106— Reginald M. Jackson, Kansas City, Oakland, Baltimore, New York, Cali-
         fornia, 17 years, 1967 through 1983.
N. L.— 1936— Wilver D. Stargell, Pittsburgh, 21 years, 1962 through 1982.

Fewest Strikeouts, League, 14 or More Seasons, Except Pitchers

A. L.— 113— Joseph W. Sewell, Cleveland, New York, 14 years, 1903 games, 1920
         through 1933.
N. L.— 173— Lloyd J. Waner, Pittsburgh, Boston, Cincinnati, Philadelphia, Brooklyn, 18
         years, 1993 games, 1927 through 1945, except 1943.

Most Strikeouts, Season

N. L. (162-game season)—189—Bobby L. Bonds, San Francisco, 157 games, 1970.
A. L. (162-game season)—175—David L. Nicholson, Chicago, 126 games, 1963.
         J. Gorman Thomas, Milwaukee, 156 games, 1979.
A. L. (154-game season)—138—James R. Lemon, Washington, 146 games, 1956.
N. L. (154-game season)—136—J. Francisco Herrera, Philadelphia, 145 games, 1960.

Fewest Strikeouts, Season, 150 or More Games

A. L.—4—Joseph W. Sewell, Cleveland, 155 games, 1925; 152 games, 1929.
N. L.—5—Charles J. Hollocher, Chicago, 152 games, 1922.

Most Strikeouts, Season, by Pitcher Since 1900

A. L.—65—Wilbur F. Wood, Chicago, 49 games, 1972.
N. L.—62—Jerry M. Koosman, New York, 35 games, 1968.

Fewest Strikeouts, Season, for Leader in Most Strikeouts (154-Game Schedule)

N. L.—63—George F. Grantham, Chicago, 127 games, 1924.
A. L.—66—James E. Foxx, Philadelphia, 153 games, 1930.
         Edward Morgan, Cleveland, 150 games, 1930.

Most Years Leading League in Strikeouts

A. L.—7—James E. Foxx, Philadelphia, Boston, 1929, 1930 (tied), 1931, 1933, 1935, 1936,
         1941.
N. L.—6—Vincent P. DiMaggio, Boston, Pittsburgh, Philadelphia, 1937, 1938, 1942, 1943,
         1944, 1945.

Most Consecutive Years Leading League in Strikeouts

N. L.—4—Lewis R. Wilson, Chicago, 1927 through 1930.
         Vincent P. DiMaggio, Pittsburgh, Philadelphia, 1942 through 1945.
A. L.—4—Reginald M. Jackson, Oakland, 1968 through 1971.

Most Years, 100 or More Strikeouts, League

A. L.—15—Reginald M. Jackson, Oakland, Baltimore, New York, California, 1968 through 1980, 1982 through 1983.
N. L.—13—Wilver D. Stargell, Pittsburgh, 1965 through 1976, 1979.

Most Consecutive Years, 100 or More Strikeouts, League

A. L.—13—Reginald M. Jackson, Oakland, Baltimore, New York, 1968 through 1980.
N. L.—12—Wilver D. Stargell, Pittsburgh, 1965 through 1976.

Most Years Leading League in Fewest Strikeouts, 150 or More Games

A. L.—11—J. Nelson Fox, Chicago, 1952 through 1962.
N. L.— 4—Stanley F. Musial, St. Louis, 1943, 1948, 1952, 1956 (tied).
       Richard M. Groat, Pittsburgh, St. Louis, 1955, 1958, 1964, 1965 (tied).

Most Consecutive Games, Season, No Strikeouts

A. L.— 115— Joseph W. Sewell, Cleveland, May 17 through September 19, 1929, 437 at-bats.
N. L.— 77— Lloyd J. Waner, Pittsburgh, Boston, Cincinnati, April 24 through September 16, 1941.

Most Strikeouts, Inning

N. L.—2—18 times (held by 18 players). Last player—Larry D. McWilliams, Atlanta, April 22, 1979, fourth inning.
A. L.—2—15 times (held by 15 players). Last player—Deron R. Johnson, Oakland, September 23, 1973, fifth inning.

Most Strikeouts, Game, Nine Innings

N. L.—5—Oscar Walker, Buffalo, June 20, 1879 (consecutive).
      Henry Dowling, Louisville, August 15, 1899 (consecutive).
      L. Floyd Young, Pittsburgh, September 29, 1935, second game (consecutive).
      Robert Sadowski, Milwaukee, April 20, 1964, (consecutive).
      Richard A. Allen, Philadelphia, June 28, 1964, first game (consecutive).
      Ronald A. Swoboda, New York, June 22, 1969, first game (consecutive).
      Steve E. Whitaker, San Francisco, April 14, 1970 (consecutive).
      Richard A. Allen, St. Louis, May 24, 1970 (consecutive).
      William E. Russell, Los Angeles, June 9, 1971, (consecutive).
      Jose M. Mangual, Montreal, August 11, 1975, (consecutive).
      Franklin Taveras, New York, May 1, 1979 (consecutive).
A. L.—5—Robert M. Grove, Philadelphia, June 10, 1933, first game (consecutive).
      John J. Broaca, New York, June 25, 1934 (consecutive).
      Chester P. Laabs, Detroit, October 2, 1938, first game (consecutive).
      Lawrence E. Doby, Cleveland, April 25, 1948 (consecutive).
      James H. Landis, Chicago, July 28, 1957 (consecutive).
      W. Robert Allison, Minnesota, September 2, 1965, (consecutive).
      Reginald M. Jackson, Oakland, September 27, 1968, (consecutive).
      Raymond A. Jarvis, Boston, April 20, 1969 (consecutive).
      Robert J. Monday, Oakland, April 29, 1970, (consecutive).
      Frank O. Howard, Washington, September 19, 1970, first game (consecutive).
      Donald A. Buford, Baltimore, August 26, 1971, (consecutive).
      Richard E. Manning, Cleveland, May 15, 1977 (consecutive).

Most Strikeouts, Extra-Inning Game

A. L.—6—Carl Weilman, St. Louis, July 25, 1913, 15 innings (consecutive).
      Frederic C. Reichardt, California, May 31, 1966, 17 innings.
      Billy R. Cowan, California, July 9, 1971, 20 innings.
      Cecil C. Cooper, Boston, June 14, 1974, 15 innings.
N. L.—6—Donald A. Hoak, Chicago, May 2, 1956, 17 innings.

Most Times, Four or More Strikeouts, Game, Major Leagues

15—Richard A. Allen, Philadelphia N. L., 1964 (2), 1966 (1), 1968 (7), 1969 (2), St. Louis N.L., 1970 (1), Chicago A.L., 1974 (2).

Most Times, Four or More Strikeouts, Game, League

N. L.—13—Richard A. Allen, Philadelphia, 1964 (2), 1966, 1968 (7), 1969 (2), St. Louis, 1970.
A. L.—10—Mickey C. Mantle, New York, 1952, 1954, 1959, 1964, 1965, 1966, 1967, 1968 (3).

Most Times, Four or More Strikeouts, Game, Season

N. L.—7—Richard A. Allen, Philadelphia, April 13, May 1, 9, June 29, July 16, 21, August 19, 1968.
A. L.—5—Reginald M. Jackson, Oakland, April 7, second game, April 21, May 18, June 4, September 21, first game, 1971.
      A. Bobby Darwin, Minnesota, May 12-13, June 23, July 14, August 6, first game, August 10, 1972.

Most Strikeouts, First Major League Game

N. L.—4—William A. Sunday, Chicago, May 22, 1883.
          Wesley O. Bales, Atlanta, August 7, 1966.
A. A.—4—Hercules H. Burnett, Louisville, June 26, 1888.
A. L.—4—Roleine C. Naylor, Philadelphia, September 14, 1917.
          Samuel J. Ewing, Chicago, September 11, 1973.

Most Strikeouts, Doubleheader

A. L.—7—J. Patrick Seerey, Chicago, July 24, 1948 (19 innings).
          David L. Nicholson, Chicago, June 12, 1963 (17 innings).
          Frank O. Howard, Washington, July 9, 1965 (18 innings).
          William E. Melton, Chicago, July 24, 1970 (18 innings).
N. L.—7—Michael L. Vail, New York, September 26, 1975 (24 innings).

Most Strikeouts, Two Consecutive Games (More Than 18 Innings)

A. L.—8—Pedro Ramos, Cleveland, August 19, 23, 1963 (22 innings).
          Roy F. Smalley, Minnesota, August 28, 29, 1976 (26 innings).
N. L.—8—Adolfo E. Phillips, Chicago, June 10, 11, 1966 (19 innings).
          Byron E. Browne, Chicago, July 19, 20, first game, 1966 (27 innings).
          Richard A. Allen, St. Louis, May 24 (5), May 26 (3), 1970 (19 innings).

Most Strikeouts, Two Consecutive Games (18 Innings)

A. L.—8—Robert J. Monday, Oakland, April 28 (3), April 29 (5), 1970.
          J. Gorman Thomas, Milwaukee, July 27, second game (4), July 28 (4), 1975.
N. L.—8—Wayne L. Twitchell, Philadelphia, May 16 (4), May 22 (4), 1973.
          Ruppert S. Jones, San Diego, July 16 (4), July 17 (4), 1982.

Most Strikeouts, Three Consecutive Games

N. L.—10—Adolfo E. Phillips, Chicago, June 8 (2), June 10 (5), June 11 (3), 1966.
           Wayne L. Twitchell, Philadelphia, May 16 (4), May 22 (4), May 27 (2), 1973.
A. L.—10—William E. Melton, Chicago, July 24 (4), July 24 (3), July 28, (3), 1970.
           Richard A. Drago, Kansas City, September 5 (3), September 10, second
           game (4), September 17 (3), 1970.
           James H. Fuller, Baltimore, September 25 (3), September 27 (4), September
           28, first game (3), 1973.
           J. Gorman Thomas, Milwaukee, July 27, second game (4), July 28 (4), July
           29, (2), 1975.

Most Strikeouts, Four Consecutive Games

N. L.—12—Adolfo E. Phillips, Chicago, June 7 (2), June 8 (2), June 10 (5), June 11 (3),
           1966.
A. L.—12—James J. Hannan, Washington, July 24 (4), July 29 (2), August 3 (3), Au-
           gust 8 (3), 1968.
           William E. Melton, Chicago, July 23 (2), July 24 (4), July 24 (3), July 28
           (3), 1970.

Ten or More Consecutive Strikeouts, Season (Consecutive Plate Appearances)

N. L.—12—Sanford Koufax, Brooklyn, June 24 to September 24, second game, 1955. (12
           at-bats for season, 12 strikeouts.)
       10—Tommie W. Sisk, Pittsburgh, July 27 (2), August 1 (3), August 6 (4), August
           12, (1), 1966.
A. L.—11—W. Dean Chance, Los Angeles, July 24 (1), July 30 (2), August 4, first game
           (3), August 9 (4), August 13 (1), 1966.
       10—Joseph C. Grzenda, Washington, April 7 (2), April 22 (1), May 26 (4), June
           13 (1), June 16 (1), August 3 (1), 1970.

Most Consecutive Strikeouts, Season (Not Consecutive Plate Appearances)

N. L.—14—William A. Hands, Chicago, June 9, second game through July 11, 1968, sec-
           ond game; also 1 base on balls and 2 sacrifice hits.
           Juan T. Eichelberger, San Diego, June 30 through August 15, 1980; also 1
           sacrifice hit.
A. L.—13—James J. Hannan, Washington, July 24, through August 13, 1968; also 2 bases
           on balls.

Most Sacrifices, League

A. L.—511—Edward T. Collins, Philadelphia, Chicago, 25 years, 1906 through 1930.
N. L.—392—Jacob E. Daubert, Brooklyn, Cincinnati, 15 years, 1910 through 1924.

Most Sacrifices, Season (Including Sacrifice Scoring Flies)

A. L.—67—Raymond J. Chapman, Cleveland, 156 games, 1917.
N. L.—46—James T. Sheckard, Chicago, 148 games, 1909.

Most Sacrifices, Season (No Sacrifice Flies)

A. L.—46—William J. Bradley, Cleveland, 139 games, 1907.
N. L.—43—William Gleason, Philadelphia, 155 games, 1905.

Fewest Sacrifice Hits, Season, Most At-Bats

N. L.—0—David Cash, Philadelphia, 162 games, 1975; 699 at-bats.
A. L.—0—Aloysius H. Simmons, Philadelphia, 154 games, 1932; 670 at-bats.

Fewest Sacrifices, Season, for Leader in Sacrifices (No Sacrifice Flies) (154 or 162-Game Schedule)

A. L.—13—Alfred M. Martin, Detroit, 131 games, 1958.
    Anthony C. Kubek, New York, 132 games, 1959.
    James H. Landis, Chicago, 149 games, 1959.
    Alfred J. Pilarcik, Baltimore, 130 games, 1959.
    Victor P. Power, Minnesota, 138 games, 1963.
    Paul L. Blair, Baltimore, 150 games, 1969.
    Dennis D. McLain, Detroit, 42 games, 1969.
N. L.—13—Maurice M. Wills, Los Angeles, 148 games, 1961.

Most Years Leading League in Sacrifices

A. L.—6—George W. Haas, Philadelphia, Chicago, 1930, 1931, 1932, 1933, 1934, 1936.
N. L.—4—Franz O. Knabe, Philadelphia, 1907, 1908, 1910, 1913.

Most Consecutive Years Leading League in Sacrifices

A. L.—5—George W. Haas, Philadelphia, Chicago, 1930 through 1934.
N. L.—2—Held by many players. N. L.—Last Player—John E. Temple, Cincinnati, 1957, 1958 (tied).

Most Sacrifice Hits, Game

A. L.—4—Wade H. Killefer, Washington, August 27, 1910, first game.
    John J. Barry, Boston, August 21, 1916.
    Raymond J. Chapman, Cleveland, August 31, 1919.
N. L.—4—Jacob E. Daubert, Brooklyn, August 15, 1914, second game.

Most Sacrifice Hits, Inning

A. L.—2—J. Alton Benton, Detroit, August 6, 1941, third inning.
N. L.—1—Held by many players.

Most Sacrifice Hits, Doubleheader

N. L.—6—Jacob E. Daubert, Brooklyn, August 15, 1914.
A. L.—5—Wade H. Killefer, Washington, August 27, 1910.

Most Years Leading League in Sacrifice Flies

A. L.—4—Brooks C. Robinson, Baltimore, 1962 (tied), 1964, 1967 (tied), 1968 (tied).
N. L.—3—Ronald E. Santo, Chicago, 1963, 1967, 1969.
    Johnny L. Bench, Cincinnati, 1970, 1972, 1973 (tied).

Most Sacrifice Flies in Major Leagues

121—Henry L. Aaron, 113 in N. L., Milwaukee, Atlanta, 21 years, 1954 through 1974; 8 in A. L., Milwaukee, 2 years, 1975, 1976.

Most Sacrifice Flies, League

A. L.— 114— Brooks C. Robinson, Baltimore, 23 years, 1955 through 1977.
N. L.— 113— Henry L. Aaron, Milwaukee, Altanta, 21 years, 1954 through 1974.

Most Sacrifice Flies, Game (Batting in Run)

N. L.—3—Harry M. Steinfeldt, Chicago, May 5, 1909.
    Ernest Banks, Chicago, June 2, 1961.
A. L.—3—Robert W. Meusel, New York, September 15, 1926.
    Russell E. Nixon, Boston, August 31, 1965, second game.

Most Sacrifice Flies, Season (Batting in Run)

N. L.—19—Gilbert R. Hodges, Brooklyn, 154 games, 1954.
A. L.—17—Roy H. White, New York, 147 games, 1971.
    (Harold J. Traynor, Pittsburgh, N. L., 144 games, 1928, had 31 sacrifice flies, advancing runners to second base, third base and home.)

Fewest Sacrifice Flies, Season, Most At-Bats

N. L.—0—Peter E. Rose, Cincinnati, 160 games, 1973; 680 at-bats.
    Franklin Taveras, Pittsburgh, New York, 164 games, 1979; 680 at-bats.
A. L.—0—Zoilo Versalles, Minnesota, 159 games, 1963; 621 at-bats.

Most Hit by Pitch, League

N. L.— 243— Ronald K. Hunt, New York, Los Angeles, San Francisco, Montreal, St. Louis, 12 years, 1963 through 1974.
A. L.— 189— Orestes A. Minoso, Cleveland, Chicago, Washington, 16 years, 1949 through 1964 (except 1950, 1962), 1976, 1980.

Most Hit by Pitch, Season

N. L.—50—Ronald K. Hunt, Montreal, 152 games, 1971.
A. L.—24—Norman A. Elberfeld, Washington, 127 games, 1911.
            William A. Freehan, Detroit, 155 games, 1968.

Fewest Hit by Pitch, Season, Most At-Bats

A. L.—0—Santos C. Alomar, California, 162 games, 1971, 689 at-bats.
N. L.—0—Hugh M. Critz, Cincinnati, New York, 152 games, 1930, 662 at-bats.
            Granville W. Hamner, Philadelphia, 154 games, 1949, 662 at-bats.

Most Years Leading League, Hit by Pitch

A. L.—10—Orestes A. Minoso, Cleveland, Chicago, 1951, 1952, 1953, 1954, 1956, 1957,
            1958, 1959, 1960, 1961.
N. L.— 7—Ronald K. Hunt, San Francisco, Montreal, St. Louis, 1968, 1969, 1970, 1971,
            1972, 1973, 1974.

Most Consecutive Years, Leading League, Hit by Pitch

N. L.—7—Ronald K. Hunt, San Francisco, Montreal, St. Louis, 1968 through 1974.
A. L.—6—Orestes A. Minoso, Chicago, Cleveland, 1956 through 1961.

Fewest Hit by Pitch, Season, for Leader in Hit by Pitch (154 or 162-Game Schedule)

A. L.—5—Frank P. J. Crosetti, New York, 138 games, 1934.
            Frank A. Pytlak, Cleveland, 91 games, 1934.
N. L.—6—Robert G. Blattner, New York, 126 games, 1946.
            Andre F. Dawson, Montreal, 151 games, 1980.
            Daniel Driessen, Cincinnati, 154 games, 1980.
            Timothy J. Foli, Pittsburgh, 127 games, 1980.
            Gregory M. Luzinski, Philadelphia, 106 games, 1980.
            Elliott Maddox, New York, 130 games, 1980.
            Peter E. Rose, Philadelphia, 162 games, 1980.

Most Hit by Pitch, Inning

N. L.—2—Willard R. Schmidt, Cincinnati, April 26, 1959, third inning.
            Frank J. Thomas, New York, April 29, 1962, first game, fourth inning.
A. L.—1—Held by many players.

Most Hit by Pitch, Game, Nine Innings

N. L.—3—13 times (held by 10 players). Last Player—Rigoberto P. Fuentes, San Fran-
            cisco, September 13, 1973.
A. A.—3—5 times (held by 5 players).
A. L.—3—4 times (held by 4 players). Last Player—William A. Freehan, Detroit, Au-
            gust 16, 1968 (consecutive).

Most Hit by Pitch, Extra-Inning Game

N. L.—3—Ronald K. Hunt, San Francisco, April 29, 1969, 13 innings.
A. L.—3—J. Garland Stahl, Washington, April 15, 1904, 10 innings.
            Craig R. Kusick, Minnesota, August 27, 1975, 11 innings.

Most Hit by Pitch, Doubleheader

N. L.—5—Frank L. Chance, Chicago, May 30, 1904.
A. L.—3—Bertram C. Daniels, New York, June 20, 1913.
            Alphonse E. Smith, Chicago, June 21, 1961.

Most Times Three Hit by Pitch, Game, League

N. L.—3—Hugh A. Jennings, Baltimore, 1894, 1896, 1898.
N. L. since 1900—2—Frank Chance, Chicago, 1902, 1904.
A. L.—1—Held by 5 players.

Most Grounding Into Double Plays, in Major Leagues

328—Henry L. Aaron, 305 in National League, Milwaukee, Atlanta, 21 years, 1954
        through 1974; 23 in American League, Milwaukee, 2 years, 1975, 1976.

Most Grounding Into Double Plays, League

A. L.— 311— Carl M. Yastrzemski, Boston, 23 years, 1961 through 1983.
N. L.— 305— Henry L. Aaron, Milwaukee, Atlanta, 21 years, 1954 through 1974.

Most Grounding Into Double Plays, Game, Nine Innings

A. L.—4—Leon A. Goslin, Detroit, April 28, 1934 (consecutive).
            Michael A. Kreevich, Chicago, August 4, 1939 (consecutive).
N. L.—4—Joseph P. Torre, New York, July 21, 1975 (consecutive).

Most Grounding Into Double Plays, Two Consecutive Games

N. L.—5—Henry J. Bonura, New York, July 8 (3), second game, July 9 (2), 1939.
A. L.—4—Held by many players.

Most Grounding Into Double Plays, Season

    A. L.—32—Jack E. Jensen, Boston, 152 games, 1954.

    N. L.—30—Ernest N. Lombardi, Cincinnati, 129 games, 1938.

Fewest Grounding Into Double Plays, Season, 150 or More Games

    N. L.—0—August J. Galan, Chicago, 154 games, 1935.

    A. L.—0—Richard J. McAuliffe, Detroit, 151 games, 1968.

Fewest Grounding Into Double Plays for Leader in Most Grounding Into Double Plays, Season (154 or 162-Game Schedule)

    N. L.—19—Andrew W. Seminick, Philadelphia, 124 games 1946.

            George J. Kurowski, St. Louis, 146 games, 1947.

            Andrew Pafko, Chicago, 129 games, 1947.

    A. L.—21—Brooks C. Robinson, Baltimore, 158 games, 1967.

Most Years Leading League, Grounding Into Double Plays, Season

    N. L.—4—Ernest N. Lombardi, Cincinnati, New York, 1933, 1934, 1938, 1944.

    A. L.—3—Jack E. Jensen, Boston, 1954, 1956, 1957.

            George Scott, Boston, Milwaukee, 1966 (tied), 1974, 1975 (tied).

Most Years Leading in Fewest Grounded Into Double Plays, 150 Games

    N. L.—6—Richie Ashburn, Philadelphia, Chicago, 1951, 1952, 1953, 1954, 1958, 1960 (tied).

    A. L.—2—Held by ten players. Last player—Willie J. Wilson, Kansas City, 1979, 1980.

Most First on Error, Inning, Fair-Hit Balls

    A. L.—2—Emory E. Rigney, Detroit, August 21, 1922, sixth inning.

            Fred Spurgeon, Cleveland, April 14, 1925, eighth inning.

            John C. Bassler, Detroit, June 17, 1925, sixth inning.

            Edgar C. Rice, Washington, July 10, 1926, eighth inning.

    N. L.—2—Stuart Martin, St. Louis, June 22, 1940, sixth inning.

Most First on Error, Game, Fair-Hit Balls

    P. L.—4—Michael J. Griffin, Philadelphia, June 23, 1890.

    N. L.—3—George Gore, New York, August 15, 1887.

            Alphonso R. Lopez, Boston, July 16, 1936.

            Gerald W. Grote, New York, September 5, 1975.

    A. L.—2—Held by many players.

Most Times Awarded First Base, Season, on Catcher's Interference

    N. L.—7—Dale A. Berra, Pittsburgh, 161 games, 1983.

    A. L.—6—G. Robert Stinson, Seattle, 124 games, 1978.

Most Times Awarded First Base, Game, on Catcher's Interference

    N. L.—2—Benjamin Geraghty, Brooklyn, April 26, 1936.

            Patrick Corrales, Philadelphia, September 29, 1965.

    A. L.—2—Daniel T. Meyer, Seattle, May 3, 1977.

            G. Robert Stinson, Seattle, July 24, 1979.

Most Times Out, Hit by Batted Ball, Game

    N. L.—2—Walter Wilmot, Chicago, September 30, 1890.

    A. L.—2—Ernest G. Shore, Boston, July 28, 1917, second game.

Most Runners Left on Base, Game

    N. L.—12—Glenn A. Beckert, Chicago, September 16, 1972.

    A. L.—11—W. Frank Isbell, Chicago, August 10, 1901.

            John A. Donahue, Chicago, June 23, 1907, 12 innings.

Most Times Grounding Into Infield Triple Play, Game or Season

    N. L.-A. L.—1—Held by many players.

Most Batting Departments Leading League or Tied, Season

    A. L.—12—Tyrus R. Cobb, Detroit, 146 games, 1911—runs, hits, one-base hits, two-base hits, three-base hits, total bases, long hits, extra bases on long hits, stolen bases, runs batted in, batting average, slugging average.

    N. L.—12—Joseph M. Medwick, St. Louis, 156 games, 1937—games, at-bats, runs, hits, two-base hits, home runs (tied), total bases, long hits, extra bases on long hits, runs batted in, batting average, slugging average.

            Stanley F. Musial, St. Louis, 156 games, 1946—games (tied), at-bats, runs, hits, one-base hits, two-base hits, three-base hits, total bases, long hits, extra bases on long hits, batting average, slugging average. (Also tied in fewest grounding into double plays.)

Pinch-Runner and Pinch-Hitter in Same Game (Different Innings)

    A. L.—Tharon P. Collins, St. Louis, June 8, 1923; pinch-runner in third inning, pinch-hitter in ninth inning.

TRIPLE CROWN BATTING CHAMPIONS

Leading in Batting Average, Home Runs and Runs Batted In, Same Season

N. L.—Rogers Hornsby, St. Louis, 1922, 1925.
　　　　Henry Zimmerman, Chicago, 1912.
　　　　Charles H. Klein, Philadelphia, 1933.
　　　　Joseph M. Medwick, St. Louis, 1937.
A. L.—Theodore S. Williams, Boston, 1942, 1947.
　　　　Tyrus R. Cobb, Detroit, 1909.
　　　　James E. Foxx, Philadelphia, 1933.
　　　　H. Louis Gehrig, New York, 1934.
　　　　Mickey C. Mantle, New York, 1956.
　　　　Frank Robinson, Baltimore, 1966.
　　　　Carl M. Yastrzemski, Boston, 1967.

30 or More Stolen Bases, 30 or More Home Runs, Same Season

	Year	Games	Stolen Bases	Home Runs
A. L.—Kenneth R. Williams, St. Louis	1922	153	37	39
Tommy Harper, Milwaukee	1970	154	38	31
Bobby L. Bonds, New York	1975	145	30	32
Bobby L. Bonds, California	1977	158	41	37
Bobby L. Bonds, Chicago, Texas	1978	156	43	31
N. L.—Willie H. Mays, New York	1956	152	40	36
Willie H. Mays, New York	1957	152	38	35
Henry L. Aaron, Milwaukee	1963	161	31	44
Bobby L. Bonds, San Francisco	1969	158	45	32
Bobby L. Bonds, San Francisco	1973	160	43	39
Dale B. Murphy, Atlanta	1983	162	30	36

50 or More Stolen Bases, 20 or More Home Runs, Same Season

	Year	Games	Stolen Bases	Home Runs
N. L.—Louis C. Brock, St. Louis	1967	159	52	21
Cesar Cedeno, Houston	1972	139	55	22
Cesar Cedeno, Houston	1973	139	56	25
Joe L. Morgan, Cincinnati	1973	157	67	26
Cesar Cedeno, Houston	1974	160	57	26
Joe Morgan, Cincinnati	1974	149	58	22
Joe Morgan, Cincinnati	1976	141	60	27
A. L.—Never accomplished.				

Most Times Reached First Base Safely, Season (On hits, bases on balls, hit by pitch)
AMERICAN LEAGUE

		Year	Games	Hits	B.B.	H.P.	Tot.
Baltimore	Kenneth W. Singleton	1975	155	176	118	1	295
Boston	Theodore S. Williams	1949	155	194	162	2	358
California	Albert G. Pearson	1963	154	176	92	3	271
Chicago	Luzerne A. Blue	1931	155	179	127	3	309
Cleveland	Tristram Speaker	1920	150	214	97	5	316
Detroit	Tyrus R. Cobb	1915	156	208	118	10	336
Kansas City*	Norman L. Siebern	1962	162	185	110	1	296
Kansas City‡	John C. Mayberry	1975	156	161	119	4	284
	Darrell R. Porter	1979	157	155	121	8	284
Milwaukee	Paul L. Molitor	1982	160	201	69	1	271
Minnesota	Rodney C. Carew	1977	155	239	69	3	311
New York	George H. Ruth	1923	152	205	170	4	xx379
Oakland	Rickey H. Henderson	1980	158	179	117	5	301
Philadelphia	James E. Foxx	1932	154	213	116	0	329
St. Louis	George H. Sisler	1920	154	257	46	2	305
Seattle††	Tommy Harper	1969	148	126	95	1	222
Seattle†	Ruppert S. Jones	1979	162	166	85	3	254
Texas	D. Michael Hargrove	1977	153	160	103	6	269
Toronto	Willie C. Upshaw	1983	160	177	61	5	243
Washington**	Edward F. Yost	1950	155	169	141	8	318
Washington‡‡	Frank O. Howard	1970	161	160	132	2	294

xxAmerican League record. *Original Kansas City club (now Oakland). ‡Present Kansas City club. **Original Washington club (now Minnesota). ‡‡Second Washington club (now Texas). ††Original Seattle club. †Present Seattle club.

Most Times Reached First Base Safely, Season (On hits, bases on balls, hit by pitch) — Continued

NATIONAL LEAGUE

		Year	Games	Hits	B.B.	H.P.	Tot.
Atlanta	Darrell W. Evans	1973	161	167	124	3	294
Boston	Thomas F. Holmes	1945	154	224	70	4	298
Brooklyn	Floyd C. Herman	1930	153	241	66	4	311
Chicago	Elwood G. English	1930	156	214	100	6	320
Cincinnati	Peter E. Rose	1969	156	218	88	5	311
Houston	James S. Wynn	1969	149	133	148	3	284
Los Angeles	M. Wesley Parker	1970	161	196	79	0	275
Milwaukee	Henry L. Aaron	1963	161	201	78	0	279
Montreal	Kenneth W. Singleton	1973	162	169	123	2	294
New York*	Edward R. Stanky	1950	152	158	144	12	314
New York‡	Lee L. Mazzilli	1979	158	181	93	0	274
Philadelphia	Frank J. O'Doul	1929	154	254	76	4	xx334
Pittsburgh	J. Floyd Vaughan	1936	156	190	118	5	313
St. Louis	Rogers Hornsby	1924	143	227	89	2	318
San Diego	David M. Winfield	1979	159	184	85	2	271
San Francisco	Willie H. Mays	1958	152	208	78	1	287

xxNational League record. *Original New York club (now San Francisco). ‡Present New York club.

INDIVIDUAL BATTING—ROOKIE SEASON

Most Games, Rookie Season

A. L. (162-game season) —162—Jacob Wood, Detroit, 1961.
        Robert F. Knoop, Los Angeles, 1964.
        George Scott, Boston, 1966.
A. L. (154-game season) —155—Emory E. Rigney, Detroit, 1922.
        Anthony M. Lazzeri, New York, 1926.
        Dale Alexander, Detroit, 1929.
        William R. Johnson, New York, 1943.
        Richard C. Wakefield, Detroit, 1943.
        Albert L. Rosen, Cleveland, 1950.
        Harvey E. Kuenn, Detroit, 1953.
N. L. (162-game season) —162—Richard A. Allen, Philadelphia, 1964.
        Johnny C. Ray, Pittsburgh, 1982.
N. L. (154-game season) —157—Raymond L. Jablonski, St. Louis, 1953.

Highest Batting Average, Rookie Season, 100 or More Games

N. L.—.373—George A. Watkins, St. Louis, 119 games, 1930.
A. L.—.349—Wade A. Boggs, Boston, 104 games, 1982.

Leading Batsmen, Rookie Season

N. L.—.356—Abner L. Dalrymple, Milwaukee, 60 games, 1878.
A. L.—.323—Pedro Oliva, Minnesota, 161 games, 1964.

Highest Slugging Average, Rookie Season, 100 or More Games

N. L.—.621—George A. Watkins, St. Louis, 119 games, 1930.
A. L.—.609—Theodore S. Williams, Boston, 149 games, 1939.

Most At-Bats, Rookie Season

A. L. (162-game season) —672—Pedro Oliva, Minnesota, 161 games, 1964.
A. L. (154-game season) —679—Harvey E. Kuenn, Detroit, 155 games, 1953.
N. L. (154-game season) —643—Frank C. Baumholtz, Cincinnati, 151 games, 1947.
N. L. (162-game season) —661—Kenneth D. Hubbs, Chicago, 160 games, 1962.

Most Hits, Rookie Season

N. L.— 223— Lloyd J. Waner, Pittsburgh, 150 games, 1927.
A. L. (162-game season) —217—Pedro Oliva, Minnesota, 161 games, 1964.
A. L. (154-game season) —215—Dale Alexander, Detroit, 155 games, 1929.

Most Runs, Rookie Season

A. A.— 152— Michael J. Griffin, Baltimore, 136 games, 1887.
N. L.— 135— Roy Thomas, Philadelphia, 148 games, 1899.
N. L. since 1900—133—Lloyd J. Waner, Pittsburgh, 150 games, 1927.
A. L.— 132— Joseph P. DiMaggio, New York, 138 games, 1936.

200 or More Hits, Rookie Season

N. L.— 223— Lloyd J. Waner, Pittsburgh, 150 games, 1927.
     219— James T. Williams, Pittsburgh, 153 games, 1899.
     206— John H. Frederick, Brooklyn, 148 games, 1929.
     201— Richard A. Allen, Philadelphia, 162 games, 1964.
A. L.— 217— Pedro Oliva, Minnesota, 161 games, 1964.
     215— Dale Alexander, Detroit, 155 games, 1929.
     209— Harvey E. Kuenn, Detroit, 155 games, 1953.
     206— Joseph P. DiMaggio, New York, 138 games, 1936.
     206— Harold A. Trosky, Cleveland, 154 games, 1934.
     205— John M. Pesky, Boston, 147 games, 1942.
     201— Roy C. Johnson, Detroit, 148 games, 1929.
     200— Richard C. Wakefield, Detroit, 155 games, 1943.

Most Consecutive Games, Batted Safely, Rookie Season

N. L.—27—James T. Williams, Pittsburgh, August 8 through September 7, 1899.
A. L.—26—Guy P. Curtright, Chicago, June 6, first game, through July 1, 1943.
N. L. since 1900—23—Joseph A. Rapp, Philadelphia, July 7, through July 30, second
        game, 1921.
        Richie Ashburn, Philadelphia, May 9, first game, through June 5, second
        game, 1948.
        Alvin R. Dark, Boston, June 20, first game, through July 11, 1948.
        Michael L. Vail, New York, August 22 through September 15, 1975.

Most One-Base Hits, Rookie Season

N. L.— 198— Lloyd J. Waner, Pittsburgh, 150 games, 1927.
A. L.— 167— Harvey E. Kuenn, Detroit, 155 games, 1953.

Most Two-Base Hits, Rookie Season

N. L.—52—John H. Frederick, Brooklyn, 148 games, 1929.
A. L. (162-game season)—47—Frederic M. Lynn, Boston, 145 games, 1975.
A. L. (154-game season)—45—Roy C. Johnson, Detroit, 148 games, 1929.
                           Harold A. Trosky, Cleveland, 154 games, 1934.

Most Three-Base Hits, Rookie Season

N. L.—27—James T. Williams, Pittsburgh, 153 games, 1899.
N. L. since 1900—22—Paul G. Waner, Pittsburgh, 144 games, 1926.
A. L.—15—Dale Alexander, Detroit, 155 games, 1929.
        Joseph P. DiMaggio, New York, 138 games, 1936.

Most Home Runs, Rookie Season

N. L.—38—Walter A. Berger, Boston, 151 games, 1930.
        Frank Robinson, Cincinnati, 152 games, 1956.
A. L. —37—Albert L. Rosen, Cleveland, 155 games, 1950.

Most Total Bases, Rookie Season

A. L. (154-game season)—374—Harold A. Trosky, Cleveland, 154 games, 1934.
A. L. (162-game season)—374—Pedro Oliva, Minnesota, 161 games, 1964.
N. L. (162-game season)—352—Richard A. Allen, Philadelphia, 162 games, 1964.
N. L. (154-game season)—342—John H. Frederick, Brooklyn, 148 games, 1929.

Most Long Hits, Rookie Season

A. L.—89—Harold A. Trosky, Cleveland, 154 games, 1934; 45 doubles, 9 triples, 35 home
        runs.
N. L.—82—John H. Frederick, Brooklyn, 148 games, 1929; 52 doubles, 6 triples, 24 home
        runs.

Most Extra Bases on Long Hits, Rookie Season

N. L.— 169— Walter A. Berger, Boston, 151 games, 1930.
A. L.— 168— Harold A. Trosky, Cleveland, 154 games, 1934.

Most Runs Batted In, Rookie Season

A. L.— 145— Theodore S. Williams, Boston, 149 games, 1939.
N. L.— 119— Walter A. Berger, Boston, 151 games, 1930.

Most Game-Winning RBIs, Rookie Season (Since 1980)

A. L.—11—Von F. Hayes, Cleveland, 150 games, 1982.
        Calvin E. Ripken, Baltimore, 160 games, 1982.
N. L.—11—Gary E. Redus, Cincinnati, 125 games, 1983.
        Darryl E. Strawberry, New York, 122 games, 1983.

Most Bases on Balls, Rookie Season

A. L.— 107— Theodore S. Williams, Boston, 149 games, 1939.
N. L.— 100— James Gilliam, Brooklyn, 151 games, 1953.

Most Intentional Bases on Balls, Rookie Season, Since 1955

   N. L.—14—Guillermo N. Montanez, Philadelphia, 158 games, 1971.
   A. L.—13—George C. Scott, Boston, 162 games, 1966.

Most Strikeouts, Rookie Season

   A. L. (162-game season)—152—George C. Scott, Boston, 162 games, 1966.
   A. L. (154-game season)—101—Robert J. Hoover, Detroit, 144 games, 1943.
   N. L. (162-game season)—152—Larry E. Hisle, Philadelphia, 145 games, 1969.
   N. L. (154-game season)—115—Edwin L. Matthews, Boston, 145 games, 1952.

Fewest Strikeouts, Rookie Season, 150 or More Games

   N. L.—17—John A. Hassett, Brooklyn, 156 games, 1936.
   A. L.—25—Thomas Oliver, Boston, 154 games, 1930.

Most Sacrifices, Rookie Season (Includes Sacrifice Scoring Flies)

   A. L.—39—Emory E. Rigney, Detroit, 155 games, 1922.
   N. L.—29—John B. Miller, Pittsburgh, 150 games, 1909.

Most Sacrifices, Rookie Season, Since 1931 (Excludes Sacrifice Flies)

   A. L.—28—Robert J. Hoover, Detroit, 144 games, 1943.
   N. L.—28—Jack R. Robinson, Brooklyn, 151 games, 1947.
           Osborne E. Smith, San Diego, 159 games, 1978.

Most Sacrifice Flies, Rookie Season

   N. L.—13—Guillermo N. Montanez, Philadelphia, 158 games, 1971.
   A. L.—13—Gary J. Gaetti, Minnesota, 145 games, 1982.

Most Stolen Bases, Rookie Season

   A. A.—98—Michael J. Griffin, Baltimore, 136 games, 1887.
   N. L.—82—William E. Hoy, Washington, 136 games, 1888.
   A. L.—49—Rolla H. Zeider, Chicago, 136 games, 1910.
   N. L. since 1900—71—Timothy Raines, Montreal, 88 games, 1981.

Most Caught Stealing, Rookie Season

   A. L. (162-game season)—21—Michael L. Edwards, Oakland, 142 games, 1978.
   A. L. (154-game season)—17—Luzerne A. Blue, Detroit, 153 games, 1921.
   N. L. (162-game season)—20—Gregory E. Gross, Houston, 156 games, 1974.
   N. L. (154-game season)—18—Joseph A. Rapp, New York-Philadelphia, 110 games, 1921.

Most Hit by Pitch, Rookie Season

   A. A.—29—Thomas J. Tucker, Baltimore, 136 games, 1887.
   N. L.—20—Frank Robinson, Cincinnati, 152 games, 1956.
   A. L.—17—Henry E. Manush, Detroit, 109 games, 1923.

Most Grounded Into Double Plays, Rookie Season

   A. L.—27—William R. Johnson, New York, 155 games, 1943.
           Albert L. Rosen, Cleveland, 155 games, 1950.
   N. L. (162-game season)—20—Kenneth D. Hubbs, Chicago, 160 games, 1962.
                         George A. Foster, San Francisco, Cincinnati, 140 games, 1971.
   N. L. (154-game season)—19—Robert B. Schmidt, San Francisco, 127 games, 1958.

Fewest Grounded Into Double Plays, Rookie Season, 150 or More Games

   A. L.—4—Manuel J. Rivera, St. Louis-Chicago, 150 games, 1952.
   N. L.—4—Joe L. Morgan, Houston, 157 games, 1965.

INDIVIDUAL BATTING—RIGHTHANDERS

Data Showing Season Record for Players Who Batted Righthanded

Most Games, Righthander, Season

   N. L. (162-game season)—164—Jose A. Pagan, San Francisco, 1962.
                         Ronald E. Santo, Chicago, 1965.
                         Franklin Taveras, Pittsburgh, New York, 1979.
   N. L. (154-game season)—160—Henry K. Groh, Cincinnati, 1915.
   A. L. (162-game season)—164—Cesar L. Tovar, Minnesota, 1967.
   A. L. (154-game season)—159—Napoleon Lajoie, Cleveland, 1910.
                         Derrill B. Pratt, St. Louis, 1915.

Highest Batting Average, Righthander, Season, 100 or More Games

   N. L.—.438—Hugh Duffy, Boston, 124 games, 1894.
   N. L. since 1900—.424—Rogers Hornsby, St. Louis, 143 games, 1924.
   A. L.—.422—Napoleon Lajoie, Philadelphia, 131 games, 1910.

Highest Slugging Average, Righthander, Season, 100 or More Games

N. L.—.756—Rogers Hornsby, St. Louis, 138 games, 1925.
A. L.—.749—James E. Foxx, Philadelphia, 154 games, 1932.

Most At-Bats, Righthander, Season

A. L. (162-game season)—692—Robert C. Richardson, New York, 161 games, 1962.
A. L. (154-game season)—679—Harvey Kuenn, Detroit, 155 games, 1953.
N. L. (162-game season)—699—David Cash, Philadelphia, 162 games, 1975.
N. L. (154-game season)—672—Walter J. Maranville, Pittsburgh, 155 games, 1922.

Most Runs, Righthander, Season

N. L.— 167— Joseph J. Kelley, Baltimore, 129 games, 1894.
N. L. since 1900—156—Rogers Hornsby, Chicago, 156 games, 1929.
A. L.— 152— Aloysius H. Simmons, Philadelphia, 138 games, 1930.

Most Hits, Righthander, Season

A. L.— 253— Aloysius H. Simmons, Philadelphia, 153 games, 1925.
N. L.— 250— Rogers Hornsby, St. Louis, 154 games, 1922.

Most Consecutive Games Batted Safely, Righthander, During Season

A. L.—56—Joseph P. DiMaggio, New York, May 15 through July 16, 1941.
N. L.—42—William F. Dahlen, Chicago, June 20 through August 6, 1894.
N. L. since 1900—33—Rogers Hornsby, St. Louis, August 13 through September 19, 1922.

Most One-Base Hits, Righthander, Season

A. L.— 174— Aloysius H. Simmons, Philadelphia, 153 games, 1925.
N. L. (162-game season)—178—Curtis C. Flood, St. Louis, 162 games, 1964.
N. L. (154-game season)—172—Nicholas J. Witek, New York, 153 games, 1943.

Most Two-Base Hits, Righthander, Season

A. L.—64—George H. Burns, Cleveland, 151 games, 1926.
N. L.—64—Joseph M. Medwick, St. Louis, 155 games, 1936.

Most Three-Base Hits, Righthander, Season

N. L.—33—Perry W. Werden, St. Louis, 124 games, 1893.
N. L. since 1900—26—Hazen S. Cuyler, Pittsburgh, 153 games, 1925.
A. L.—23—James T. Williams, Baltimore, 125 games, 1902.

Most Home Runs, Righthander, Season

A. L.—58—James E. Foxx, Philadelphia, 154 games, 1932.
            Henry B. Greenberg, Detroit, 155 games, 1938.
N. L.—56—Lewis R. Wilson, Chicago, 155 games, 1930.

Most Home Runs, Righthander, Two Consecutive Seasons

A. L.— 106— James E. Foxx, Philadelphia, 58 in 1932; 48 in 1933.
N. L.— 101— Ralph Kiner, Pittsburgh, 54 in 1949; 47 in 1950.

Most Home Runs, Righthander in Major Leagues

755—Henry L. Aaron, 733 in National League, Milwaukee, Atlanta, 21 years, 1954 through 1974; 22 in American League, 2 years, Milwaukee, 1975, 1976.

Most Home Runs, Righthander, League

N. L.— 733— Henry L. Aaron, Milwaukee, Atlanta, 21 years, 1954 through 1974.
A. L.— 573— Harmon C. Killebrew, Washington, Minnesota, Kansas City, 22 years, 1954 through 1975.

Most Home Runs, Righthander, One Month

A. L.—18—Rudolph P. York, Detroit, August, 1937.
N. L.—17—Willie H. Mays, San Francisco, August, 1965.

Most Home Runs, Righthander, Season at Home Grounds

A. L.—39—Henry B. Greenberg, Detroit, 1938.
N. L.—33—Lewis R. Wilson, Chicago, 1930.

Most Home Runs, Righthander, Season on Road

N. L.—31—George A. Foster, Cincinnati, 1977.
A. L.—28—Harmon C. Killebrew, Minnesota, 1962.

Most Total Bases, Righthander, Season

N. L.— 450— Rogers Hornsby, St. Louis, 154 games, 1922.
A. L.— 438— James E. Foxx, Philadelphia, 154 games, 1932.

Most Long Hits, Righthander, Season

A. L.— 103— Henry B. Greenberg, Detroit, 154 games, 1937; 49 doubles, 14 triples, 40 home runs.

N. L.— 102— Rogers Hornsby, St. Louis, 154 games, 1922; 46 doubles, 14 triples, 42 home runs.

Most Extra Bases on Long Hits, Righthander, Season

A. L.— 225— James E. Foxx, Philadelphia, 154 games, 1932.
N. L.— 215— Lewis R. Wilson, Chicago, 155 games, 1930.

Most Bases on Balls, Righthander, Season

A. L.— 151— Edward F. Yost, Washington, 152 games, 1956.
N. L.— 148— Edward R. Stanky, Brooklyn, 153 games, 1945.
James S. Wynn, Houston, 149 games, 1969.

Most Intentional Bases on Balls, Season, Righthander, Since 1955

N. L.—29—Adolfo E. Phillips, Chicago, 144 games, 1967.
A. L.—29—Frank O. Howard, Washington, 161 games, 1970.

Most Strikeouts, Righthander, Season

N. L. (162-game season)—189—Bobby L. Bonds, San Francisco, 157 games, 1970.
A. L. (162-game season)—175—David L. Nicholson, Chicago, 126 games, 1963.
J. Gorman Thomas, Milwaukee, 156 games, 1979.
A. L. (154-game season)—138—James R. Lemon, Washington, 146 games, 1956.
N. L. (154-game season)—136—J. Francisco Herrera, Philadelphia, 145 games, 1960.

Fewest Strikeouts, Righthander, Season, 150 or More Games

N. L.—8—Emil M. Verban, Philadelphia, 155 games, 1947.
A. L.—9—John P. McInnis, Boston, 152 games, 1921.
Louis Boudreau, Cleveland, 152 games, 1948.

Most Sacrifices, Righthander, Season

A. L.—67—Raymond J. Chapman, Cleveland, 156 games, 1917 (includes a few sacrifice scoring flies).
N. L.—43—William Gleason, Philadelphia, 155 games, 1905 (does not include sacrifice flies).

Most Sacrifice Flies, Righthander, Season (Batting in Run)

N. L.—19—Gilbert R. Hodges, Brooklyn, 154 games, 1954.
A. L.—16—Charles A. Gandil, Washington, 145 games, 1914.

Most Runs Batted In, Righthander, Season

N. L.— 190— Lewis R. Wilson, Chicago, 155 games, 1930.
A. L.— 183— Henry B. Greenberg, Detroit, 154 games, 1937.

Most Hit by Pitch, Righthander, Season

N. L.—50—Ronald K. Hunt, Montreal, 152 games, 1971.
A. L.—24—William A. Freehan, Detroit, 155 games, 1968.

Most Grounded Into Double Plays, Righthander, Season

A. L.—32—Jack E. Jensen, Boston, 152 games, 1954.
N. L.—30—Ernest N. Lombardi, Cincinnati, 129 games, 1938.

Fewest Grounded Into Double Plays, Righthander, Season, 150 or More Games

N. L.—1—Ronald K. Hunt, Montreal, 152 games, 1971.
A. L.—2—Cesar L. Tovar, Minnesota, 157 games, 1968.
Mark Belanger, Baltimore, 152 games, 1975.

INDIVIDUAL BATTING—LEFTHANDERS
Data Showing Season Record for Players Who Batted Lefthanded
Most Games, Lefthander, Season

N. L. (162-game season)—164—Billy L. Williams, Chicago, 1965.
N. L. (154-game season)—160—Thomas H. Griffith, Cincinnati, 1915.
A. L. (162-game season)—163—Leon L. Wagner, Cleveland, 1964.
Albert Oliver, Texas, 1980.
A. L. (154-game season)—162—James E. Barrett, Detroit, 1904.

Highest Batting Average, Lefthander, Season, 100 or More Games

N. L.— .432— William H. Keeler, Baltimore, 128 games, 1897.
A. L.—.41979—George H. Sisler, St. Louis, 142 games, 1922.
.41962—Tyrus R. Cobb, Detroit, 146 games, 1911.
N. L. since 1900—.401—William H. Terry, New York, 154 games, 1930.

Highest Slugging Average, Lefthander, Season, 100 or More Games

    A. L.—.847—George H. Ruth, New York, 142 games, 1920.
    N. L.—.702—Stanley F. Musial, St. Louis, 155 games, 1948.

Most At-Bats, Lefthander, Season

    N. L.—(162-game season)—698—Mateo R. Alou, Pittsburgh, 162 games, 1969.
    N. L.—(154-game season)—696—Forrest D. Jensen, Pittsburgh, 153 games, 1936.
    A. L.—(162-game season)—672—Pedro Oliva, Minnesota, 162 games, 1964.
    A. L.—(154-game season)—671—John T. Tobin, St. Louis, 150 games, 1921.

Most Runs, Lefthander, Season

    N. L.— 196— William R. Hamilton, Philadelphia, 131 games, 1894.
    A. L.— 177— George H. Ruth, New York, 152 games, 1921.
    N. L. since 1900—158—Charles H. Klein, Philadelphia, 156 games, 1930.

Most Hits, Lefthander, Season

    A. L.— 257— George H. Sisler, St. Louis, 154 games, 1920.
    N. L.— 254— Frank J. O'Doul, Philadelphia, 154 games, 1929.
                 William H. Terry, New York, 154 games, 1930.

Most Consecutive Games Batted Safely, Lefthander, During Season

    N. L.—44—William H. Keeler, Baltimore, April 22 to June 18, 1897.
    A. L.—41—George H. Sisler, St. Louis, July 27 to September 17, 1922.
    N. L. since 1900—37—Thomas F. Holmes, Boston, June 6, first game, to July 8, second game, 1945.

Most One-Base Hits, Lefthander, Season

    N. L.— 202— William H. Keeler, Baltimore, 128 games, 1898.
    N. L. since 1900—198—Lloyd J. Waner, Pittsburgh, 150 games, 1927.
    A. L.— 182— Edgar C. Rice, Washington, 152 games, 1925.

Most Two-Base Hits, Lefthander, Season

    A. L.—67—Earl W. Webb, Boston, 151 games, 1931.
    N. L.—62—Paul G. Waner, Pittsburgh, 154 games, 1932.

Most Three-Base Hits, Lefthander, Season

    N. L.—36—J. Owen Wilson, Pittsburgh, 152 games, 1912.
    A. L.—26—Joseph J. Jackson, Cleveland, 152 games, 1912.
                 Samuel Crawford, Detroit, 157 games, 1914.

Most Home Runs, Lefthander, Season

    A. L.—(162-game season)—61—Roger E. Maris, New York, 161 games, 1961.
    A. L.—(154-game season)—60—George H. Ruth, New York, 151 games, 1927.
    N. L.—51—John R. Mize, New York, 154 games, 1947.

Most Home Runs, Lefthander, Two Consecutive Seasons

    A. L.— 114— George H. Ruth, New York, 60 in 1927; 54 in 1928.
    N. L.— 96— Theodore B. Kluszewski, Cincinnati, 49 in 1954; 47 in 1955.

Most Home Runs, Lefthander, Major Leagues

    714—George H. Ruth, Boston A. L., New York A. L., Boston N. L., 22 years, 1914 through 1935, 708 in A. L. and 6 in N. L.

Most Home Runs, Lefthander, League

    A. L.— 708— George H. Ruth, Boston, New York, 21 years, 1914 through 1934.
    N. L.— 521— Willie L. McCovey, San Francisco, 22 years, 1959 through 1980.

Most Home Runs, Lefthander, One Month

    A. L.—17—George H. Ruth, New York, September, 1927.
    N. L.—15—Fred Williams, Philadelphia, May, 1923.
                 Edwin D. Snider, Brooklyn, August, 1953.

Most Home Runs, Lefthander, Season at Home Grounds

    N. L.—34—Theodore B. Kluszewski, Cincinnati, 1954.
    A. L.—32—George H. Ruth, New York, 1921.
                 Kenneth R. Williams, St. Louis, 1922.

Most Home Runs, Lefthander, Season, on Road

    A. L.—32—George H. Ruth, New York, 1927.
    N. L.—30—Edwin L. Mathews, Milwaukee, 1953.

Most Total Bases, Lefthander, Season

    A. L.— 457— George H. Ruth, New York, 152 games, 1921.
    N. L.— 445— Charles H. Klein, Philadelphia, 156 games, 1930.

Most Long Hits, Lefthander, Season

    A. L.— 119— George H. Ruth, New York, 152 games, 1921; 44 doubles, 16 triples, 59 home runs.

    N. L.— 107— Charles H. Klein, Philadelphia, 156 games, 1930; 59 doubles, 8 triples, 40 home runs.

Most Extra Bases on Long Hits, Lefthander, Season

    A. L.— 253— George H. Ruth, New York, 152 games, 1921.

    N. L.— 199— Stanley F. Musial, St. Louis, 155 games, 1948.

Most Bases on Balls, Lefthander, Season

    A. L.— 170— George H. Ruth, New York, 152 games, 1923.

    N. L.— 147— James T. Sheckard, Chicago, 156 games, 1911.

Most Intentional Bases on Balls, Lefthander, Season, Since 1955

    N. L.— 45— Willie L. McCovey, San Francisco, 149 games, 1969.

    A. L.— 33— Theodore S. Williams, Boston, 132 games, 1957.

Most Strikeouts, Lefthander, Season

    A. L. (162-game season) —171—Reginald M. Jackson, Oakland, 154 games, 1968.

    A. L. (154-game season) —121—Lawrence E. Doby, Cleveland, 149 games, 1953.

    N. L. (162-game season) —154—Wilver D. Stargell, Pittsburgh, 141 games, 1971.

    N. L. (154-game season) —115—Edwin L. Mathews, Boston, 145 games, 1952.

Fewest Strikeouts, Lefthander, Season, 150 or More Games

    A. L.—4—Joseph W. Sewell, Cleveland, 155 games, 1925; 152 games, 1929.

    N. L.—5—Charles J. Hollocher, Chicago, 152 games, 1922.

Most Sacrifices, Lefthander, Season

    A. L.—52—Robert S. Ganley, Washington, 150 games, 1908 (includes a few sacrifice scoring flies).

    N. L.—46—James T. Sheckard, Chicago, 148 games, 1909 (includes a few sacrifice scoring flies).

Most Sacrifice Flies, Lefthander, Season (Batting in Run)

    A. L.—16—Samuel E. Crawford, Detroit, 157 games, 1914.

    N. L.—13—Guillermo N. Montanez, Philadelphia, 158 games, 1971.

Most Runs Batted in, Lefthander, Season

    A. L.— 184— H. Louis Gehrig, New York, 155 games, 1931.

    N. L.— 170— Charles H. Klein, Philadelphia, 156 games, 1930.

Most Hit by Pitcher, Lefthander, Season

    N. L.—31—Louis R. Evans, St. Louis, 151 games, 1910.

    A. L.—20—Harry H. Gessler, Washington, 128 games, 1911.

Most Grounded Into Double Plays, Lefthander, Season

    A. L.— (162-game season) —30—Carl M. Yastrzemski, Boston, 151 games, 1964.

    A. L.— (154-game season) —23—Richard J. Wakefield, Detroit, 155 games, 1943.

                               George S. Vico, Detroit, 144 games, 1948.

    N. L.— (162-game season) —26—Guillermo N. Montanez, Philadelphia, San Francisco, 156 games, 1975.

    N. L.— (154-game season) —23—Edwin D. Snider, Brooklyn, 150 games, 1951.

Fewest Grounded Into Double Plays, Lefthander, Season, 150 or More Games

    A. L.—0—Richard J. McAuliffe, Detroit, 151 games, 1968.

    N. L.—2—Louis C. Brock, St. Louis, 155 games, 1965.

            Louis C. Brock, St. Louis, 157 games, 1969.

INDIVIDUAL BATTING—SWITCH HITTERS

Data Showing Season Record for Players Who Were Switch Hitters

Most Games, Switch Hitter, Season

    N. L. (162-game season) —165—Maurice M. Wills, Los Angeles, 1962.

    A. L. (162-game season) —163—Donald A. Buford, Chicago, 1966.

Highest Batting Average, Switch Hitter, Season, 100 or More Games

    N. L.—.373—George S. Davis, New York, 133 games, 1893.

    A. L.—.365—Mickey C. Mantle, New York, 144 games, 1957.

    N. L. since 1900—.348—Frank F. Frisch, New York, 151 games, 1923.

                  .348—Peter E. Rose, Cincinnati, 156 games, 1969.

Highest Slugging Average, Switch Hitter, Season

   A. L.—.705—Mickey C. Mantle, New York, 150 games, 1956.
   N. L.—.615—James A. Collins, St. Louis, 154 games, 1934.

Most At-Bats, Switch Hitter, Season

   A. L.— 705— Willie J. Wilson, Kansas City, 161 games, 1980.
   N. L.— 695— Maurice M. Wills, Los Angeles, 165 games, 1962.

Most Runs, Switch Hitter, Season

   N. L.— 140— Max G. Carey, Pittsburgh, 155 games, 1922.
   A. L.— 133— Willie J. Wilson, Kansas City, 161 games, 1980.

Most Hits, Switch Hitter, Season

   N. L.— 230— Peter E. Rose, Cincinnati, 160 games, 1973.
   A. L.— 230— Willie J. Wilson, Kansas City, 161 games, 1980.

Switch Hitters With 100 or More Hits, Both Sides of Plate, Season

   N. L.—Garry L. Templeton, St. Louis, 154 games, 1979; 111 hits lefthanded, 100 hits
      righthanded.
   A. L.—Willie J. Wilson, Kansas City, 161 games, 1980; 130 hits lefthanded, 100 hits right-
      handed.

Most Consecutive Games, Batted Safely, Switch Hitter, Season

   N. L.—44—Peter E. Rose, Cincinnati, June 14 through July 31, 1978.
   A. L.—20—Walter H. Schang, Philadelphia, June 16 through July 7, 1916.
       David E. Philley, Philadelphia, June 12, through July 1, 1953.

Most One-Base Hits, Switch Hitter, Season

   A. L.— 184— Willie J. Wilson, Kansas City, 161 games, 1980.
   N. L.— 181— Peter E. Rose, Cincinnati, 160 games, 1973.

Most Two-Base Hits, Switch Hitter, Season

   N. L.—51—Peter E. Rose, Cincinnati, 159 games, 1978.
   A. L.—47—John J. Anderson, Milwaukee, 138 games, 1901.

Most Three-Base Hits, Switch Hitter, Season

   N. L.—26—George S. Davis, New York, 133 games, 1893.
   N. L. since 1900—19—Max G. Carey, 153 games, 1923.
       Garry L. Templeton, St. Louis, 154 games, 1979.
   A. L.—15—Luzerne A. Blue, Chicago, 155 games, 1931.
       Alfredo C. Griffin, Toronto, 155 games, 1980.
       Willie J. Wilson, Kansas City, 161 games, 1980.
       Willie J. Wilson, Kansas City, 136 games, 1982.

Most Home Runs, Switch Hitter, Season

   A. L.—54—Mickey C. Mantle, New York, 153 games, 1961.
   N. L.—35—James A. Collins, St. Louis, 154 games, 1934.

Most Home Runs, Switch Hitter, Two Consecutive Seasons

   A. L.—94—Mickey C. Mantle, New York, 40 in 1960, 54 in 1961.
   N. L.—61—C. Reginald Smith, Los Angeles, 32 in 1977, 29 in 1978.

Most Home Runs, Switch Hitter, League

   A. L.— 536— Mickey C. Mantle, New York, 18 years, 1951 through 1968.
   N. L.— 172— Ted L. Simmons, St. Louis, 13 years, 1968 through 1980.

Most Home Runs, Switch Hitter, One Month

   A. L.—16—Mickey C. Mantle, New York, May, 1956.
   N. L.—11—James A. Collins, St. Louis, June, 1935.

Most Home Runs, Switch Hitter, Season at Home Grounds

   A. L.—27—Mickey C. Mantle, New York, 1956.
   N. L.—22—James A. Collins, St. Louis, 1934.

Most Home Runs, Switch Hitter, Season on Road

   A. L.—30—Mickey C. Mantle, New York, 1961.
   N. L.—17—C. Reginald Smith, Los Angeles, 1977.

Most Games, Switch Hitting Home Runs, Season

   A. L.—2—Mickey C. Mantle, New York, 1955, 1956.
       Eddie C. Murray, Baltimore, 1982.
   N. L.—1—Held by many players.

Most Games, Switch Hitting Home Runs, League

    A. L.—10—Mickey C. Mantle, New York, 1955 (2), 1956 (2), 1957, 1958, 1959, 1961, 1962, 1964.
    N. L.— 2—James W. Russell, Boston, 1948, Brooklyn, 1950.
             Ellis N. Burton, Chicago, 1963, 1964.
             Peter E. Rose, Cincinnati, 1966, 1967.
             C. Reginald Smith, St. Louis, 1975, 1976.
             Ted L. Simmons, St. Louis, 1975, 1979.

Most Total Bases, Switch Hitter, Season

    A. L.— 376— Mickey C. Mantle, New York, 150 games, 1956.
    N. L.— 369— James A. Collins, St. Louis, 154 games, 1934.

Most Long Hits, Switch Hitter, Season

    N. L.—87—James A. Collins, St. Louis, 154 games, 1934.
    A. L.—79—Mickey C. Mantle, New York, 150 games, 1956.

Most Extra Bases on Long Hits, Switch Hitter, Season

    A. L.— 190— Mickey C. Mantle, New York, 153 games, 1961.
    A. L.— 169— James A. Collins, St. Louis, 154 games, 1934.

Most Bases on Balls, Switch Hitter, Season

    A. L.— 146— Mickey C. Mantle, New York, 144 games, 1957.
    N. L.— 116— Miller J. Huggins, St. Louis, 151 games, 1910.

Most Intentional Bases on Balls, Switch Hitter, Season, Since 1955

    N. L.—25—Ted L. Simmons, St. Louis, 150 games, 1977.
    A. L.—23—Mickey C. Mantle, New York, 144 games, 1957.

Most Strikeouts, Switch Hitter, Season

    A. L.— 126— Mickey C. Mantle, New York, 144 games, 1959.
    N. L.— 112— Samuel Jethroe, Boston, 151 games, 1952.

Fewest Strikeouts, Switch Hitter, Season

    N. L.—10—Frank F. Frisch, St. Louis, 153 games, 1927.
    A. L.—23—George D. Weaver, Chicago, 151 games, 1920.

Most Sacrifices, Switch Hitter, Season

    A. L.—52—Owen J. Bush, Detroit, 157 games, 1909 (includes a few sacrifice scoring flies).
    N. L.—35—Leo G. Magee, St. Louis, 142 games, 1914 (includes sacrifice flies).

Most Sacrifice Flies, Switch Hitter, Season

    A. L.—17—Roy H. White, New York, 147 games, 1971.
    N. L.—13—C. Reginald Smith, Los Angeles, 128 games, 1978.

Most Runs Batted In, Switch Hitter, Season

    A. L.— 130— Mickey C. Mantle, New York, 150 games, 1956.
    N. L.— 128— James A. Collins, St. Louis, 154 games, 1934.

Most Hit by Pitch, Switch Hitter, Season

    N. L.—11—Samuel Jethroe, Boston, 148 games, 1951.
             Peter E. Rose, Cincinnati, 162 games, 1975.
    A. L.—10—Fred L. Valentine, Washington, 146 games, 1966.
             Fred L. Valentine, Washington, 151 games, 1967.

Most Grounded Into Double Play, Switch Hitter, Season

    A. L.—29—David E. Philley, Philadelphia, 151 games, 1952.
    N. L.—29—Ted L. Simmons, St. Louis, 161 games, 1973.

Fewest Grounded Into Double Play, Switch Hitter, Season

    N. L.—0—August J. Galan, Chicago, 154 games, 1935.
    A. L.—1—Willie J. Wilson, Kansas City, 154 games, 1979.

CLUB BATTING—SEASON RECORDS

Highest Batting Average, Season

    N. L.—.343—Philadelphia, 132 games, 1894.
    N. L. since 1900—.319—New York, 154 games, 1930.
    A. L.—.316—Detroit, 154 games, 1921.

Lowest Batting Average, Season

    N. L.—.207—Washington, 136 games, 1888.
    A. L.—.212—Chicago, 156 games, 1910.
    N. L. since 1900—.213—Brooklyn, 154 games, 1908.

Most Years Leading League in Batting Average, Since 1900

N. L.—21—Pittsburgh, 1902, 1907, 1909, 1922, 1923 (tied), 1925, 1927, 1928, 1933, 1936
(tied), 1938 (tied), 1942, 1960, 1961, 1966, 1967, 1969 (tied), 1970 (tied),
1972, 1974, 1982.
A. L.—16—Detroit, 1907, 1908, 1909, 1915, 1916, 1917, 1921, 1924, 1929, 1934, 1935, 1937,
1940 (tied), 1943, 1956, 1961 (tied).

Most Consecutive Years, Leading League in Batting Average

A. L.—5—Philadelphia, 1910, 1911, 1912, 1913, 1914.
Boston, 1938, 1939, 1940 (tied), 1941, 1942.
N. L.—4—Philadelphia, 1892 (tied), 1893, 1894, 1895.
New York, 1910, 1911, 1912, 1913.
St. Louis, 1941 (tied), 1942, 1943, 1944.

Highest Batting Average, Pennant Winner, Season

N. L.—.328—Baltimore, 129 games, 1894.
N. L. since 1900—.314—St. Louis, 154 games, 1930.
A. L.—.307—New York, 155 games, 1927.

Lowest Batting Average, Pennant Winner, Season

A. L.—.228—Chicago, 154 games, 1906; last in batting.
N. L.—.242—New York, 162 games, 1969; tied for seventh in batting.

Lowest Batting Average, Season, Club Leader in Batting

A. L.—.240—Oakland, 163 games, 1968.
N. L.—.254—Pittsburgh, 157 games, 1907; St. Louis, 157 games, 1915.

Most Players Batting .300 or Over, Season, 50 or More Games, One Club

A. L.—10—Philadelphia, 1927.
N. L.—10—St. Louis, 1930.

Most Players Batting .400 or Over, Season, 50 or More Games, One Club

N. L.—3—Philadelphia, 1894.
N. L. since 1900—1—St. Louis, 1922, 1924, 1925; New York, 1930.
A. L.—1—Philadelphia, 1901; Detroit, 1911, 1912, 1922, 1923; Cleveland, 1911; St. Louis,
1920, 1922; Boston, 1941.

Highest Batting Average, Outfield, Season

N. L.—.405—Philadelphia, 132 games, 1894.
A. L.—.367—Detroit, 156 games, 1925.
N. L. since 1900—.350—Chicago, 156 games, 1929.

Highest Slugging Average, Season

A. L.—.489—New York, 155 games, 1927.
N. L.—.481—Chicago, 156 games, 1930.

Most Years Leading League in Slugging Average, Since 1900

A. L.—28—New York, 1920, 1921, 1923, 1924, 1926, 1927, 1928, 1930, 1931, 1936, 1937,
1938, 1939, 1943, 1944, 1945, 1947, 1948, 1951, 1953, 1954, 1955, 1956, 1957,
1958, 1960, 1961, 1962.
N. L.—18—New York-San Francisco, 1904, 1905, 1908, 1910, 1911, 1919, 1923, 1924, 1927,
1928, 1935, 1945, 1947, 1948, 1952 (tied), 1961, 1962, 1963.

Most Consecutive Years Leading League in Slugging Average, Since 1900

N. L.—7—Brooklyn, 1949, 1950, 1951, 1952 (tied), 1953, 1954, 1955.
A. L.—6—New York, 1953, 1954, 1955, 1956, 1957, 1958.

Lowest Slugging Average, Season (150 or More Games)

A. L.—.261—Chicago, 156 games, 1910.
N. L.—.274—Boston, 155 games, 1909.

Most At-Bats, Season

N. L.— 5767— Cincinnati, 163 games, 1968.
A. L.— 5733— Milwaukee, 163 games, 1982.

Fewest At-Bats, Season

N. L.— 4725— Philadelphia, 149 games, 1907.
A. L.— 4827— Chicago, 153 games, 1913.

Most Runs, Season

N. L.— 1221— Boston, 133 games, 1894.
A. L.— 1067— New York, 155 games, 1931.
N. L. since 1900—1004—St. Louis, 154 games, 1930.

Most Runs, Season, at Home, Since 1900

A. L.— 625— Boston, 77 games, 1950.
N. L.— 543— Philadelphia, 77 games, 1930.

Most Runs, Season, on Road, Since 1900

A. L.— 591— New York, 78 games, 1930.
N. L.— 492— Chicago, 78 games, 1929.

Most Runs, Season, Against One Club, Since 1900

N. L.— 218— Chicago vs. Philadelphia 24 games, 1930 (117 at home, 101 at Philadelphia).
190— St. Louis vs. Philadelphia, 22 games, 1930 (103 at home, 87 at Philadelphia).
A. L.— 216— Boston vs. St. Louis, 22 games, 1950 (118 at home, 98 at St. Louis).

Most Runs, One Month, Since 1900

A. L.— 275— New York, August 1938, 36 games.
N. L.— 260— New York, June 1929, 33 games.

Fewest Runs, Season

N. L.— 372— St. Louis, 154 games, 1908.
A. L.— 380— Washington, 156 games, 1909.

Most Runs, Season, Pennant Winner

N. L.— 1170— Baltimore, 129 games, 1894.
A. L.— 1065— New York, 155 games, 1936.
N. L. since 1900—1004—St. Louis, 154 games, 1930.

Fewest Runs, Season, Pennant Winner

A. L.— 550— Boston, 156 games, 1916.
N. L.— 571— Chicago, 155 games, 1907.

Fewest Runs, Season, for Leader in Most Runs

N. L.— 590— St. Louis, 157 games, 1915.
A. L.— 622— Philadelphia, 152 games, 1905.

Most Players Scoring 100 or More Runs, One Club, Season

N. L.—7—Boston, 1894.
A. L.—6—New York, 1931.
N. L. since 1900—6—Brooklyn, 1953.

Most Games, Season, Scoring 20 or More Runs

N. L.—8—Boston, 1894.
N. L. since 1900—3—Philadelphia, 1900.
A. L.—3—New York, 1939.
        Boston, 1950.

Most Games, League, Scoring 20 or More Runs

N. L.—38—Chicago, 1876 to date.
A. L.—19—New York, 1903 to date.
N. L. since 1900—15—Brooklyn, 1900 through 1957.

Most Innings, Season, Scoring 10 or More Runs

N. L.—5—Boston, 1894.
A. L.—3—Washington, 1930.
N. L. since 1900—3—Brooklyn, 1943.

Most Innings, League, Scoring 10 or More Runs

N. L.—30—Chicago, 1876 to date.
A. L.—21—Boston, 1901 to date.
N. L. since 1900—19—Brooklyn-Los Angeles, 1900 through 1957 in Brooklyn, 1958 to date in Los Angeles.

Most Opponents' Runs, Season

N. L.— 1199— Philadelphia, 156 games, 1930.
A. L.— 1064— St. Louis, 155 games, 1936.

Fewest Opponents' Runs, Season

N. L.— 379— Chicago, 154 games, 1906.
A. L.— 435— Philadelphia, 155 games, 1910.

Most Hits, Season

N. L.— 1783— Philadelphia, 156 games, 1930.
A. L.— 1724— Detroit, 154 games, 1921.

Fewest Hits, Season

N. L.— 1044— Brooklyn, 154 games, 1908.
A. L.— 1061— Chicago, 156 games, 1910.

Most Players, 200 or More Hits, Season

N. L.—4—Philadelphia, 1929.
A. L.—4—Detroit, 1937.

Most Players, 100 or More Hits, Season

N. L.—9—Pittsburgh, 1921, 1972, 1976; Philadelphia, 1923; New York, 1928; St. Louis, 1979.
A. L.—9—Philadelphia, 1925; Detroit, 1934; Baltimore, 1973; Kansas City, 1974, 1977; Oakland, 1975; Texas, 1976, 1978; Chicago, 1977; New York, 1977; California, 1978; Milwaukee, 1978; Detroit, 1980; Kansas City, 1980; California, 1982; Kansas City, 1982; Toronto, 1983.

Fewest Players, 100 or More Hits, Season

N. L.—0—New York, 1972.
A. L.—2—Washington, 1965.

Most One-Base Hits, Season

N. L.— 1338— Philadelphia, 132 games, 1894.
A. L.— 1298— Detroit, 154 games, 1921.
N. L. since 1900—1297—Pittsburgh, 155 games, 1922.

Fewest One-Base Hits, Season

A. L.— 811— Baltimore, 162 games, 1968.
N. L.— 843— New York, 156 games, 1972.

Most Two-Base Hits, Season

N. L.— 373— St. Louis, 154 games, 1930.
A. L.— 358— Cleveland, 154 games, 1930.

Fewest Two-Base Hits, Season

N. L.— 110— Brooklyn, 154 games, 1908.
A. L.— 116— Chicago, 156 games, 1910.

Most Consecutive Years Leading League in Two-Base Hits

A. L.—8—Cleveland, 1916 through 1923.
N. L.—5—St. Louis, 1920 through 1924.

Most Three-Base Hits, Season

N. L.— 153— Baltimore, 129 games, 1894.
N. L. since 1900—129—Pittsburgh, 152 games, 1912.
A. L.— 112— Baltimore, 134 games, 1901.
              Boston, 141 games, 1903.

Fewest Three-Base Hits, Season

A. L.—17—New York, 163 games, 1967.
            Boston, 162 games, 1968.
            Texas, 154 games, 1972.
            New York, 162 games, 1973.
            Texas, 162 games, 1975.
N. L.—17—Atlanta, 155 games, 1972.

Most Consecutive Years Leading League in Three-Base Hits

A. L.—7—Washington, 1931 through 1937, (tied 1934).
N. L.—6—Pittsburgh, 1932 through 1937.

Most Home Runs, Season

A. L. (162-game season)—240—New York, 163 games, 1961 (112 at home, 128 on road).
A. L. (154-game season)—193—New York, 155 games, 1960 (92 at home, 101 on road).
N. L. (154-game season)—221—New York, 155 games, 1947 (131 at home, 90 on road).
                               Cincinnati, 155 games, 1956 (128 at home, 93 on road).
N. L. (162-game season)—207—Atlanta, 163 games, 1966 (119 at home, 88 on road).

Most Home Runs, Season, at Home by Home Club

A. L.— 133— Cleveland, 1970, 81 games.
N. L.— 131— New York, 1947, 76 games.

Most Home Runs, Season at Home by Opponents

A. L.— 132— at Kansas City, 1964, 81 games.
N. L.— 120— at New York, 1962, 80 games.

Most Home Runs, Season, on Road

    A. L.— 128— New York, 1961, 82 games.
    N. L.— 124— Milwaukee, 1957, 77 games.

Most Home Runs, One Month

    N. L.—55—New York, July, 1947.
    A. L.—55—Minnesota, May, 1964.

Most Times Hitting Two or More Consecutive Home Runs, Season

    A. L.—16—Boston, 161 games, 1977.
                Milwaukee, 163 games, 1982.
    N. L.—12—Cincinnati, 155 games, 1956.

Most Home Runs, Season, Each Club

American League			National League		
Club	Year	Tot.	Club	Year	Tot.
Baltimore	1979	181	Atlanta	1966	207
St. Louis	1940	118	Milwaukee	1957	199
Boston	1977	213	Boston	1950	148
California	1961	189	Chicago	1958	182
Chicago	1977	192	Cincinnati	1956	221
Cleveland	1970	183	Houston	1972, 1973	134
Detroit	1962	209	Los Angeles	1977	191
*Kansas City	1977	146	Brooklyn	1953	208
Milwaukee	1982	216	Montreal	1979	143
Seattle	1969	125	*New York	1962	139
Minnesota	1963	225	Philadelphia	1977	186
Washington	1959	163	Pittsburgh	1966	158
Oakland	1970	171	St. Louis	1955	143
Kansas City	1957, 1964	166	San Diego	1970	172
Philadelphia	1932	173	San Francisco	1962	204
New York	1961	240	New York	1947	221
†Seattle	1977	133	*Present New York club.		
Texas	1979	140			
Toronto	1983	167			
‡Washington	1969	148			

    ‡Second Washington club.
    *Present Kansas City club.
    †Present Seattle club.

Fewest Home Runs, Season (154 or 162-Game Schedule)

    N. L.—9—Pittsburgh, 157 games, 1917.
    A. L.—3—Chicago, 156 games, 1908.

Fewest Home Runs, Season, Each Club (154 or 162-Game Schedule)

American League			National League		
Club	Year	Tot.	Club	Year	Tot.
Baltimore	1954	52	Atlanta	1968	80
St. Louis	1906	9	Milwaukee	1954	139
Boston	1906	12	Boston	1909	15
California	1975	55	Chicago	1905	12
Chicago	1908	3	Cincinnati	1908, 1916	14
Cleveland	1910	8	Houston	1979	49
Detroit	1906	9	Los Angeles	1968	67
*Kansas City	1976	65	Brooklyn	1915	14
Milwaukee	1972, 1976	88	Montreal	1974	86
Seattle	1969	125	*New York	1980	61
Minnesota	1976	81	Philadelphia	1908	11
Washington	1917	4	Pittsburgh	1917	9
Oakland	1968	94	St. Louis	1906	10
Kansas City	1967	69	San Diego	1976	64
Philadelphia	1915, 1917	16	San Francisco	1980	80
New York	1913	8	New York	1906	15
‡Seattle	1978	97	*Present New York club.		
Texas	1972	56			
Toronto	1979	95			
†Washington	1971	86			

    †Second Washington club.
    *Present Kansas City club.
    ‡Present Seattle club.

Most Home Runs at Parks, Season

American League

Club	Year	Tot.	Club	Year	Tot.
Baltimore	1982	174	Milwaukee	1979	172
Boston	1977	219	Minnesota	1963	211
California			New York	1961	171
Anaheim	1982	168	Oakland	1971	158
Wrigley Field	1961	248	Philadelphia	1932	189
Chavez Ravine	1964	102	St. Louis	1940	135
Chicago	1970	175	Seattle	1969	167
Cleveland	1970	236	†Seattle	1979, 1982	182
Detroit	1962, 1982	208	Texas	1977	140
Kansas City	1964	239	Toronto	1983	185
*Kansas City	1979	134	Washington		
			Griffith Stadium	1956	158

*Present Kansas City club.
†Present Seattle club.

National League

Club	Year	Tot.	Club	Year	Tot.
Atlanta	1970	211	New York		
Boston	1945	131	Polo Grounds	1962	213
Brooklyn	1950	207	Shea Stadium	1966	145
Chicago	1970	201	Philadelphia		
Cincinnati			Baker Field	1929	160
Crosley Field	1957	219	Shibe Park	1955	154
Riverfront Stadium	1977	166	Veterans Stadium	1977	164
Houston	1970	115	Pittsburgh		
Los Angeles			Forbes Field	1947	182
Coliseum	1958	193	Three Rivers Stadium	1979	151
Dodger Stadium	1977, 1979	161	St. Louis		
Milwaukee	1965	173	Busch Stadium	1955	176
Montreal			Busch Mem. Stadium	1979	113
Jarry Park	1970	168	San Diego	1983	135
Olympic Stadium	1977	131	San Francisco	1962	183

Most Years Leading League in Home Runs, Since 1900

A. L.—34—New York, 1915, 1916, 1917, 1919, 1920, 1921, 1923, 1924, 1925, (tied), 1926, 1927, 1928, 1929, 1930, 1931, 1933, 1936, 1937, 1938, 1939, 1940, 1941, 1942, 1943, 1944, 1945, 1946, 1947, 1951 (tied), 1955, 1956, 1958, 1960, 1961.

N. L.—27—New York-San Francisco, 1904, 1905, 1907, 1909, 1912, 1917, 1924, 1925, 1927, 1928, 1931, 1933, 1934, 1935, 1937, 1938, 1939, 1942, 1943, 1945, 1946, 1947, 1948 (tied), 1954 (tied), 1963, 1964, 1972.

Most Consecutive Years Leading League or Tied, in Home Runs

A. L.—12—New York, 1936 through 1947.
N. L.— 7—Brooklyn, 1949 through 1955, (1954 tied).

Most Consecutive Years, 100 or More Home Runs, Season

A. L.—35—Boston, 1946 through 1980.
N. L.—29—New York-San Francisco, 1945 through 1957 in New York, through 1973 in San Francisco.
        Cincinnati, 1952 through 1980.

Most Years 200 or More Home Runs, Season

N. L.—2—Brooklyn, 208 in 1953; 201 in 1955.
       New York-San Francisco, 221 in 1947; 204 in 1962.
       Atlanta, 207 in 1966; 206 in 1973
A. L.—2—Minnesota, 225 in 1963; 221 in 1964.
       Boston, 203 in 1970; 213 in 1977.
       Milwaukee, 203 in 1980; 216 in 1982.

Most Years 100 or More Home Runs, Season, Since 1900

A. L.—58—New York, 1920, 1921, 1923, 1925, 1926, 1927, 1928, 1929, 1930, 1931, 1932, 1933, 1934, 1935, 1936, 1937, 1938, 1939, 1940, 1941, 1942, 1943, 1946, 1947, 1948, 1949, 1950, 1951, 1952, 1953, 1954, 1955, 1956, 1957, 1958, 1959, 1960, 1961, 1962, 1963, 1964, 1965, 1966, 1967, 1968, 1970, 1972, 1973, 1974, 1975, 1976, 1977, 1978, 1979, 1980, 1981, 1982, 1983.

N. L.—47—New York-San Francisco, 1925, 1927, 1928, 1929, 1930, 1931, 1932, 1934, 1935, 1937, 1938, 1939, 1942, 1945, 1946, 1947, 1948, 1949, 1950, 1951, 1952, 1953, 1954, 1955, 1956, 1957, in New York, 1958, 1959, 1960, 1961, 1962, 1963, 1964, 1965, 1966, 1967, 1968, 1969, 1970, 1971, 1972, 1973, 1977, 1978, 1979, 1982, 1983 in San Francisco.

Most Times, Two or More Home Runs by One Player, Game, Season, One Club

A. L.—24—New York, 1961.
N. L.—24—Atlanta, 1966.

Most Players, Three or More Home Runs, Game, Season, One Club

N. L.—4—Brooklyn, 1950 (Snider, Campanella, Hodges, Brown).
      Cincinnati, 1956 (Bell, Bailey, Kluszewski, Thurman).
A. L.—2—New York, 1927, 1930, 1932, 1950.
      Philadelphia, 1932 (Foxx, Simmons).
      Boston, 1957 (Williams twice).
      Kansas City, 1958 (Lopez, Ward).
      Detroit, 1962 (Colavito, Boros).
      Minnesota, 1963 (Allison, Killebrew).
      Kansas City, 1975 (Mayberry, Solaita).
      Milwaukee, 1979 (Oglivie, Cooper).
      Milwaukee, 1982 (Molitor, Oglivie).
      California, 1982 (DeCinces twice).

Most Times, Three or More Home Runs, Inning, Season, One Club

N. L.—5—New York, 1954.
      Chicago, 1955.
A. L.—4—Minnesota, 1964.

Most Times, Three or More Home Runs, Inning, One Club, League

N. L.—40—New York-San Francisco, 1883 to date.
A. L.—37—New York, 1903 to date.

Most Times, Three or More Consecutive Home Runs, Inning, One Club, League

N. L.—11—New York-San Francisco, 1932, 1939 (2), 1948, 1949, 1953, 1954, 1956 in New York, 1963, 1969, 1982 in San Francisco.
A. L.— 7—Cleveland, 1902, 1939, 1950, 1951, 1962, 1963, 1970.

Most Times, Five or More Home Runs, Game, Season, One Club

A. L.—8—Boston, 1977.
N. L.—6—New York, 1947.

Most Home Runs With Bases Filled, Season, One Club

A. L.—10—Detroit, 1938.
N. L.— 9—Chicago, 1929.

Most Home Runs, With Bases Filled, Pinch-Hitter, Season, One Club

N. L.—3—San Francisco, 1973 (Arnold, Bonds, Goodson), 1978 (Ivie 2, Clark).
      Chicago, 1975 (Summers, LaCock, Hosley).
      Philadelphia, 1978 (Johnson 2, McBride).
A. L.—3—Baltimore, 1982 (Ayala, Ford, Crowley).

Most Home Runs, Pinch-Hitter, Season, One Club

N. L.—12—Cincinnati, 1957.
      New York, 1983.
A. L.—11—Baltimore, 1982.

Most Players, 50 or More Home Runs, Season, One Club

A. L.—2—New York, 1961 (Maris 61, Mantle, 54).
N. L.—1—Chicago, 1930; Pittsburgh, 1947, 1949; New York, 1947, 1955; San Francisco, 1965; Cincinnati, 1977.

Most Players, 40 or More Home Runs, Season, One Club

A. L.—2—New York, 1927 (Ruth 60, Gehrig 47), 1930 (Ruth 49, Gehrig 41) 1931 (Ruth 46, Gehrig 46), 1961 (Maris 61, Mantle 54).
      Detroit, 1961 (Colavito 45, Cash 41).
      Boston, 1969 (Petrocelli 40, Yastrzemski 40).
N. L.—3—Atlanta, 1973 (Johnson 43, Evans 41, Aaron 40).
      2—Brooklyn, 1953 (Snider 42, Campanella 41).
      Brooklyn, 1954 (Hodges 42, Snider 40).
      Cincinnati, 1955 (Kluszewski 47, Post 40).
      San Francisco, 1961 (Cepeda 46, Mays 40).
      Cincinnati, 1970 (Bench 45, Perez 40).

Most Players, 30 or More Home Runs, Season, One Club

N. L.—4—Los Angeles, 1977.
      3—Philadelphia, 1929; New York, 1947; Brooklyn, 1950, 1953; Cincinnati, 1956; Milwaukee, 1961; San Francisco, 1963, 1964, 1966; Milwaukee, 1965; Atlanta, 1966, 1973; Cincinnati, 1970.
A. L.—3—New York, 1941; Washington, 1959; Minnesota, 1963, 1964; Boston, 1977; Milwaukee, 1982.

HOME RUNS BY CLUBS, 1901 THROUGH 1983

AMERICAN LEAGUE

*Denotes leader or tie.

Year	Balt.	Bos.	Calif.	Chi.	Cleve.	K.C.	Det.	Minn.	N.Y.	Oak.	Mil.	Tex.	Lg.
1901	..	*36	..	31	11	..	29	34	..	34	..	..	226
1902	29	43	..	14	32	..	21	*47	..	38	..	..	256
1903	11	*48	..	14	30	..	12	17	18	32	..	..	182
1904	10	26	..	14	22	..	14	9	27	*31	..	..	153
1905	16	*29	..	11	22	..	10	25	17	23	..	..	153
1906	20	12	..	7	12	..	9	26	17	*31	..	..	134
1907	19	14	..	7	11	..	11	11	15	*22	..	..	101
1908	*21	13	..	3	18	..	19	8	12	20	..	..	114
1909	10	*21	..	4	10	..	20	8	16	20	..	..	109
1910	12	*44	..	7	8	..	28	8	19	18	..	..	144
1911	16	*35	..	20	19	..	28	15	25	*35	..	..	193
1912	19	*28	..	17	10	..	18	17	18	22	..	..	149
1913	18	17	..	23	16	..	24	19	8	*33	..	..	158
1914	17	18	..	19	11	..	25	18	12	*28	..	..	148
1915	19	13	..	25	20	..	23	12	*31	16	..	..	159
1916	14	14	..	17	16	..	17	12	*35	19	..	..	144
1917	15	14	..	19	13	..	25	4	*27	16	..	..	133
1918	5	16	..	8	9	..	13	4	20	*22	..	..	97
1919	32	33	..	25	24	..	23	24	*45	35	..	..	241
1920	50	22	..	36	35	..	30	36	*115	46	..	..	370
1921	66	17	..	35	42	..	58	42	*134	83	..	..	477
1922	97	45	..	45	32	..	54	45	95	*111	..	..	524
1923	82	34	..	42	59	..	41	26	*105	52	..	..	441
1924	67	30	..	41	40	..	35	22	*98	63	..	..	396
1925	*110	41	..	38	52	..	50	56	*110	76	..	..	533
1926	72	32	..	32	27	..	36	43	*121	61	..	..	424
1927	55	28	..	36	26	..	51	29	*158	56	..	..	439
1928	63	38	..	24	34	..	62	40	*133	89	..	..	483
1929	47	28	..	37	62	..	110	48	*142	122	..	..	596
1930	75	47	..	63	72	..	82	57	*152	125	..	..	673
1931	76	37	..	27	71	..	43	49	*155	118	..	..	576
1932	67	53	..	36	78	..	80	61	160	*173	..	..	708
1933	64	50	..	43	50	..	57	60	*144	140	..	..	608
1934	62	51	..	71	100	..	74	51	135	*144	..	..	688
1935	73	69	..	74	93	..	106	32	104	*112	..	..	663
1936	79	86	..	60	123	..	94	62	*182	72	..	..	758
1937	71	100	..	67	103	..	150	47	*174	94	..	..	806
1938	92	98	..	67	113	..	137	85	*174	98	..	..	864
1939	91	124	..	64	85	..	124	44	*166	98	..	..	796
1940	118	145	..	73	101	..	134	52	*155	105	..	..	883
1941	91	124	..	47	103	..	81	52	*151	85	..	..	734
1942	98	103	..	25	50	..	76	40	*108	33	..	..	533
1943	78	57	..	33	55	..	77	47	*100	26	..	..	473
1944	72	69	..	23	70	..	60	33	*96	36	..	..	459
1945	63	50	..	22	65	..	77	27	*93	33	..	..	430
1946	84	109	..	37	79	..	108	60	*136	40	..	..	653
1947	90	103	..	53	112	..	103	42	*115	61	..	..	679
1948	63	121	..	55	*155	..	78	31	139	68	..	..	710
1949	117	*131	..	43	112	..	88	81	115	82	..	..	769
1950	106	161	..	93	*164	..	114	76	159	100	..	..	973
1951	86	127	..	86	*140	..	104	54	*140	102	..	..	839
1952	82	113	..	80	*148	..	103	50	129	89	..	..	794
1953	112	101	..	74	*160	..	108	69	139	116	..	..	879
1954	52	132	..	94	*156	..	90	81	133	94	..	..	823
1955	54	137	..	116	148	..	130	80	*175	121	..	..	961
1956	91	139	..	128	153	..	150	112	*190	112	..	..	1075
1957	87	153	..	106	140	..	116	111	145	*166	..	..	1024
1958	108	155	..	101	161	..	109	121	*164	138	..	..	1057
1959	109	125	..	97	*167	..	160	163	153	117	..	..	1091
1960	123	124	..	112	127	..	150	147	*193	110	..	..	1086
1961	149	112	189	138	150	..	180	167	*240	90	..	119	1534
1962	156	146	137	92	180	..	*209	185	199	116	..	132	1552
1963	146	171	95	114	169	..	148	*225	188	95	..	138	1489
1964	162	186	102	106	164	..	157	*221	162	166	..	125	1551
1965	125	*165	92	125	156	..	162	150	149	110	..	136	1370
1966	175	145	122	87	155	..	*179	144	162	70	..	126	1365
1967	138	*158	114	89	131	..	152	131	100	69	..	115	1197
1968	133	125	83	71	75	..	*185	105	109	94	..	124	1104

HOME RUNS BY CLUBS, 1901 THROUGH 1983—Continued

AMERICAN LEAGUE

*Denotes leader or tie.

Year	Balt.	Bos.	Calif.	Chi.	Cleve.	K.C.	Det.	Minn.	N.Y.	Oak.	Mil.	Tex.	Lg.
1969	175	*197	88	112	119	98	182	163	94	148	y125	148	1649
1970	179	*203	114	123	183	97	148	153	111	171	126	138	*1746
1971	158	161	96	138	109	80	*179	116	97	160	104	86	1484
1972	100	124	78	108	91	78	122	93	103	*134	88	56	1175
1973	119	147	93	111	*158	114	157	120	131	147	145	110	1552
1974	116	109	95	*135	131	89	131	111	101/	132	120	99	1369
1975	124	134	55	94	*153	118	125	121	110	151	146	134	1465
1976	119	*134	63	73	85	65	101	81	120	113	88	80	1122
Totals	5910	6392	1616	4437	6386	739	6576	5068	8223	6228	942	1866	54,466

Year	Balt.	Bos.	Calif.	Chi.	Clev.	K.C.	Det.	Minn.	N.Y.	Oak.	Mil.	Tex.	Sea.	Tor.	Lg.
1977	148	*213	131	192	100	146	166	123	184	117	125	135	133	100	2013
1978	154	172	108	106	106	98	129	82	125	100	*173	132	97	98	1680
1979	181	*194	164	127	138	116	164	112	150	108	185	140	132	95	2006
1980	156	162	106	91	89	115	143	99	189	137	*203	124	104	126	1844
1981	88	90	97	76	39	61	65	47	100	*104	96	49	89	61	1062
1982	179	136	186	136	109	132	177	148	161	149	*216	115	130	106	2080
1983	*168	142	154	157	86	109	156	141	153	121	132	106	111	167	1903
Tot.	6984	7501	2562	5322	7053	1516	7576	5820	9285	7064	2072	2667	796	753	67,054

Note: Figures in Baltimore column 1902-1953 are for St. Louis (3012); in Oakland column 1901-54 are for Philadelphia (3498), Kansas City 1955-67 (1480); Minnesota column 1901-1960 are for old Washington club (2782). Texas column represents second Washington club, 1961 through 1971. Figures in Totals column are all inclusive. (Baltimore had 24 in 1901 and 32 in 1902 and Milwaukee had 27 in 1901); these are included in League Totals but not in Club Totals. yPredecessor Seattle club. California column represents the Los Angeles Angels for 1961 through September 1, 1965.

HOME RUNS BY CLUBS, 1900 THROUGH 1983

NATIONAL LEAGUE

*Denotes leaders or tie.

Year	Atl.	Chi.	Cinn.	Hous.	L.A.	Mont.	N.Y.	Phila.	Pitts.	St.L.	S.D.	S.F.	Lg.
1900	*47	33	30	..	27	..	..	28	26	37	..	23	251
1901	28	18	38	..	32	..	..	23	28	*39	..	19	225
1902	13	7	18	..	*19	..	..	5	18	10	..	6	96
1903	25	10	28	..	14	..	..	12	*33	5	..	20	147
1904	24	22	21	..	15	..	..	23	15	24	..	*31	175
1905	17	12	27	..	29	..	..	16	22	20	..	*39	182
1906	16	20	16	..	*25	..	..	12	12	10	..	15	126
1907	22	13	15	..	18	..	..	12	19	10	..	*23	141
1908	17	19	14	..	*28	..	..	11	25	17	..	20	151
1909	15	20	22	..	16	..	..	12	25	15	..	*26	151
1910	31	*34	23	..	25	..	..	22	33	15	..	31	214
1911	37	54	21	..	28	..	..	*60	48	27	..	39	314
1912	35	42	19	..	32	..	..	42	39	27	..	*48	284
1913	32	59	27	..	39	..	..	*73	35	15	..	31	311
1914	35	41	16	..	31	..	..	*62	18	33	..	30	266
1915	17	53	15	..	14	..	..	*58	24	20	..	24	225
1916	22	*46	14	..	28	..	..	42	20	25	..	42	239
1917	22	17	26	..	25	..	..	38	9	26	..	*39	202
1918	13	20	15	..	10	..	..	25	15	*27	..	13	138
1919	24	21	19	..	25	..	..	*42	17	18	..	40	206
1920	23	34	18	..	28	..	..	*64	16	32	..	46	261
1921	61	37	20	..	59	..	..	*88	37	83	..	75	460
1922	32	42	45	..	56	..	..	*116	52	107	..	80	530
1923	32	90	45	..	62	..	..	*112	49	63	..	85	538
1924	25	66	36	..	72	..	..	94	43	67	..	*95	498
1925	41	85	44	..	64	..	..	100	77	109	..	*114	634
1926	16	66	35	..	40	..	..	75	44	*90	..	73	439
1927	37	74	29	..	39	..	..	57	54	84	..	*109	483
1928	52	92	32	..	66	..	..	85	52	113	..	*118	610
1929	32	139	34	..	99	..	..	*153	60	100	..	136	753
1930	66	*171	74	..	122	..	..	126	86	104	..	143	892
1931	34	83	21	..	71	..	..	81	41	60	..	*101	492
1932	63	69	47	..	109	..	..	*122	47	76	..	116	549
1933	54	72	34	..	62	..	..	60	39	57	..	*82	460
1934	83	101	55	..	79	..	..	56	52	104	..	*126	656
1935	75	88	73	..	59	..	..	92	66	86	..	*123	662
1936	68	76	82	..	33	..	..	*103	60	88	..	97	607

HOME RUNS BY CLUBS, 1900 THROUGH 1983—Continued

NATIONAL LEAGUE

*Denotes leaders or tie.

Year	Atl.	Chi.	Cinn.	Hous.	L.A.	Mont.	N.Y.	Phila.	Pitts.	St.L.	S.D.	S.F.	Lg.
1937	63	96	73	..	37	..	..	103	47	94	..	*111	624
1938	54	65	110	..	61	..	..	40	65	91	..	*125	611
1939	56	91	98	..	78	..	..	49	63	98	..	*116	649
1940	59	86	89	..	93	..	..	75	76	*119	..	91	688
1941	48	99	64	..	*101	..	..	64	56	70	..	95	597
1942	68	75	66	..	62	..	..	44	54	60	..	*109	538
1943	39	52	43	..	39	..	..	66	42	70	..	*81	432
1944	79	71	51	..	56	..	..	55	70	*100	..	93	575
1945	101	57	56	..	57	..	..	56	72	64	..	*114	577
1946	44	56	65	..	55	..	..	80	60	81	..	*121	562
1947	85	71	95	..	83	..	..	60	156	115	..	*221	886
1948	95	87	104	..	91	..	..	91	108	105	..	*164	845
1949	103	97	86	..	*152	..	..	122	126	102	..	147	935
1950	148	161	99	..	*194	..	..	125	138	102	..	133	1100
1951	130	103	88	..	*184	..	..	108	137	95	..	179	1024
1952	110	107	104	..	*153	..	..	93	92	97	..	151	907
1953	156	137	166	..	*208	..	..	115	99	140	..	176	1197
1954	139	159	147	..	*186	..	..	102	76	119	..	*186	1114
1955	182	164	181	..	*201	..	..	132	91	143	..	169	1263
1956	177	142	*221	..	179	..	..	121	110	124	..	145	1219
1957	*199	147	187	..	147	..	..	117	92	132	..	157	1178
1958	167	*182	123	..	172	..	..	124	134	111	..	170	1183
1959	*177	163	161	..	148	..	..	113	112	118	..	167	1159
1960	*170	119	140	..	126	..	..	99	120	138	..	130	1042
1961	*188	176	158	..	157	..	..	103	128	103	..	183	1196
1962	181	126	167	105	140	..	139	142	108	137	..	*204	1449
1963	139	127	122	62	110	..	96	126	108	128	..	*197	1215
1964	159	145	130	70	79	..	103	130	121	109	..	*165	1211
1965	*196	134	183	97	78	..	107	144	111	109	..	159	1318
1966	*207	140	149	112	108	..	98	117	158	108	..	181	1378
1967	*158	128	109	93	82	..	83	103	91	115	..	140	1102
1968	80	*130	106	66	67	..	81	100	80	73	..	108	891
1969	141	142	*171	104	97	125	109	137	119	90	99	136	1470
1970	160	179	*191	129	87	136	120	101	130	113	172	165	*1683
1971	153	128	138	71	95	88	98	123	*154	95	96	140	1379
1972	144	133	124	134	98	91	105	98	110	70	102	*150	1359
1973	*206	117	137	134	110	125	85	134	154	75	112	161	1550
1974	120	110	135	110	*139	86	96	95	114	83	99	93	1280
1975	107	95	124	84	118	98	101	125	*138	81	78	84	1233
1976	82	105	*141	66	91	94	102	110	110	63	64	85	1113
1977	139	111	181	114	*191	138	88	186	133	96	120	134	1631
1978	123	72	136	70	*149	121	86	133	115	79	75	117	1276
1979	126	135	132	49	*183	143	74	119	148	100	93	125	1427
1980	144	107	113	75	*148	114	61	117	116	101	67	80	1243
1981	64	57	64	45	*82	81	57	69	55	50	32	63	719
1982	*146	102	82	74	138	133	97	112	134	67	81	133	1299
1983	130	140	107	97	*146	102	112	125	121	83	93	142	1398
Totals	7228	7372	6865	1961	7156	1675	2098	7105	6308	6468	1383	8774	64,393

Note: Figures in Atlanta column 1900-1952 are for Boston (2588) and 1953-65 for Milwaukee (2230); in Los Angeles column 1900-1957 are for Brooklyn (4017); San Francisco column 1900-1957 are for New York Giants (5162); New York column represents the present Met franchise. Figures in Totals columns are all inclusive.

Most Players, 20 or More Home Runs, Season, One Club

A. L.—6—New York, 1961; Minnesota, 1964.
N. L.—6—Milwaukee, 1965.

Most Home Runs By Two Players, Season on One Club

A. L. (162-game season)—115—New York, 1961, Roger E. Maris 61. Mickey Mantle 54.
A. L. (154-game season)—107—New York, 1927, George H. Ruth, 60, H. Louis Gehrig, 47.
N. L. (154-game season)— 93—Chicago, 1930, Lewis R. Wilson, 56, Charles L. Hartnett, 37.
N. L. (162-game season)— 91—San Francisco, 1965, Willie H. Mays, 52, Willie L. McCovey, 39.

Most Home Runs By Three Players, Season, One Club

A. L. (162-game season)—143—New York, 1961, Maris 61, Mantle, 54, Skowron, 28.
A. L. (154-game season)—125—New York, 1927, Ruth 60, Gehrig 47, Lazzeri 18.
N. L. (162-game season)—124—Atlanta, 1973, Johnson 43, Evans 41, Aaron 40.
N. L. (154-game season)—122—New York, 1947, Mize 51, Marshall 36, Cooper 35.

Most Home Runs, Season, Against One Club

A. L.—48—New York vs. Kansas City, 1956.
N. L.—44—Cincinnati vs. Brooklyn, 1956.

Most Total Bases, Season

A. L.— 2703— New York, 155 games, 1936.
N. L.— 2684— Chicago, 156 games, 1930.

Fewest Total Bases, Season

A. L.— 1310— Chicago, 156 games, 1910.
N. L.— 1358— Brooklyn, 154 games, 1908.

Most Long Hits, Season

A. L.— 580— New York, 155 games, 1936; 315 doubles, 83 triples, 182 home runs.
N. L.— 566— St. Louis, 154 games, 1930; 373 doubles, 89 triples, 104 home runs.

Fewest Long Hits, Season

A. L.— 179— Chicago, 156 games, 1910; 116 doubles, 56 triples, 7 home runs.
N. L.— 182— Boston, 155 games, 1909; 124 doubles, 43 triples, 15 home runs.

Most Extra Bases on Long Hits, Season

A. L.— 1027— New York, 155 games, 1936.
N. L.— 1016— Brooklyn, 155 games, 1953.

Fewest Extra Bases on Long Hits, Season

A. L.— 249— Chicago, 156 games, 1910.
N. L.— 255— Boston, 155 games, 1909.

Most Runs Batted In, Season

A. L.— 995— New York, 155 games, 1936.
N. L.— 942— St. Louis, 154 games, 1930.

Fewest Runs Batted In, Season, Since 1920

N. L.— 354— Philadelphia, 151 games, 1942.
A. L.— 424— Texas, 154 games, 1972.

Most Players, 100 or More Runs Batted In, Season, One Club

A. L.—5—New York 1936.
N. L.—4—Pittsburgh, 1925; Chicago, 1929; Philadelphia, 1929.

Most Game-Winning RBIs, Season, Club (Since 1980)

A. L.—96—New York, 1980, 103 games won.
N. L.—87—Philadelphia, 1980, 91 games won.
        St. Louis, 1982, 92 games won.

Fewest Game-Winning RBIs, Season, Club (Since 1980)

N. L.—53—Cincinnati, 1982, 61 games won.
A. L.—55—Seattle, 1980, 59 games won.

Most Games Won With No Game-Winning RBI, Season (Since 1980)

A. L.—12—Detroit, 1980, 84 games won.
N. L.—12—Houston, 1980, 93 games won.

Fewest Games Won With No Game-Winning RBI, Season (Since 1980)

A. L.—0—New York, 1982, 79 games won.
N. L.—2—Los Angeles, 1982, 88 games won.
        Montreal, 1983, 80 games won.

Most Bases on Balls, Season

A. L.— 835— Boston, 155 games, 1949.
N. L.— 732— Brooklyn, 155 games, 1947.

Fewest Bases on Balls, Season

N. L.— 283— Philadelphia, 153 games, 1920.
A. L.— 356— Philadelphia, 156 games, 1920.

Most Intentional Bases on Balls, Season, Since 1955

N. L. (162-game season)—102—Pittsburgh, 163 games, 1979.
N. L. (154-game season)— 91—Brooklyn, 154 games, 1956.

Most Intentional Bases on Balls, Season, Since 1955—Continued

    A. L. (162-game season)— 79—Minnesota, 162 games, 1965.
    A. L. (154-game season)— 66—New York, 154 games, 1957.

Fewest Intentional Bases on Balls, Season, Since 1955

    A. L. (162-game season)—10—Kansas City, 162 games, 1961.
    A. L. (154-game season)—20—Washington, 154 games, 1959.
    N. L. (154-game season)—22—Los Angeles, 154 games, 1958.
    N. L. (162-game season)—34—New York, 163 games, 1964.

Most Strikeouts, Season

    N. L.— 1203— New York, 163 games, 1968.
    A. L.— 1125— Washington, 162 games, 1965.

Fewest Strikeouts, Season

    N. L.— 308— Cincinnati, 153 games, 1921.
    A. L.— 326— Philadelphia, 155 games, 1927.

Most Sacrifice Hits, Season, Includes Sacrifice Scoring Flies

    A. L.— 310— Boston, 157 games, 1917.
    N. L.— 270— Chicago, 158 games, 1908.

Most Sacrifice Hits, Season, No Sacrifice Flies

    N. L.— 231— Chicago, 154 games, 1906.
    A. L.— 207— Chicago, 154 games, 1906.

Fewest Sacrifice Hits, Season, No Sacrifice Flies

    A. L.—22—Minnesota, 162 games, 1982.
    N. L.—32—New York, 154 games, 1957.

Most Sacrifice Flies, Season (Run Scoring)

    A. L. (162-game season)—76—Kansas City, 162 games, 1979.
    A. L. (154-game season)—63—Boston, 155 games, 1915.
    N. L. (162-game season)—74—Philadelphia, 162 games, 1977.
    N. L. (154-game season)—66—New York, 154 games, 1912.
                               St. Louis, 153 games, 1954.

Fewest Sacrifice Flies, Season (Run Scoring)

    N. L.—19—San Diego, 161 games, 1971.
    A. L.—23—California, 161 games, 1967.

Most Hit by Pitch, Season

    N. L.— 148— Baltimore, 154 games, 1898.
    A. L.— 80— Washington, 154 games, 1911.
    N. L. since 1900—78—St. Louis, 153 games, 1910.
                          Montreal, 162 games, 1971.

Fewest Hit by Pitch, Season

    A. L.—5—Philadelphia, 154 games, 1937.
    N. L.—9—Philadelphia, 152 games, 1939.

Most Grounded Into Double Play, Season

    A. L.— 171— Boston, 162 games, 1982, 1983.
    N. L.— 166— St. Louis, 154 games, 1958.

Fewest Grounded Into Double Play, Season

    N. L.—75—St. Louis, 155 games, 1945.
    A. L.—79—Kansas City, 161 games, 1967.

INNING, GAME, DOUBLEHEADER

Most Men Facing Pitcher, as Batsmen, Inning

    A. L.—23—Boston vs. Detroit, June 18, 1953, seventh inning.
    N. L.—23—Chicago vs. Detroit, September 6, 1883, seventh inning.
    N. L. since 1900—21—Brooklyn vs. Cincinnati, May 21, 1952, first inning.

Most Batters Facing Pitcher, Three Times, Inning, One Club

    N. L.—5—Chicago vs. Detroit, September 6, 1883, seventh inning.
    A. L.—5—Boston vs. Detroit, June 18, 1953, seventh inning.
    N. L. since 1900—3—Brooklyn vs. Cincinnati, May 21, 1952, first inning.

Most Official At-Bats, Game, Nine Innings, One Club

    N. L.—66—Chicago vs. Buffalo, July 3, 1883.
    N. L. since 1900—58—New York vs. Philadelphia, September 2, 1925, second game.
                    New York vs. Philadelphia, July 11, 1931, first game.
    A. L.—56—New York vs. Philadelphia, June 28, 1939, first game.

Most Men Facing Pitcher, as Batsmen, Game, Nine Innings, One Club

N. L.—71—Chicago vs. Louisville, June 29, 1897.
N. L. since 1900—66—Philadelphia vs. Chicago, August 25, 1922. St. Louis vs. Philadelphia, July 6, 1929, second game.
A. L.—64—Boston vs. St. Louis, June 8, 1950.

Most Men Facing Pitcher, as Batsmen, Extra-Inning Game, One Club

N. L.— 103— New York vs. St. Louis, September 11, 1974, 25 innings.
A. L.— 96— New York vs. Detroit, June 24, 1962, 22 innings.

Most Men Facing Pitcher, as Batsmen, Game, Nine Innings, Both Clubs

N. L.— 125— Philadelphia 66, Chicago 59, August 25, 1922.
A. L.— 108— Cleveland 58, Philadelphia 50, April 29, 1952.

Most Official At-Bats, Extra-Inning Game, One Club

N. L.—89—New York vs. St. Louis, September 11, 1974, 25 innings.
A. L.—85—New York vs. Detroit, June 24, 1962, 22 innings.

Most Official At-Bats, Game, Nine Innings, Both Clubs

N. L.— 106— Chicago 64, Louisville 42, July 22, 1876.
N. L. since 1900—99—New York 56, Cincinnati 43, June 9, 1901.
                   New York 58, Philadelphia 41, July 11, 1931, first game.
A. L.—96—Cleveland 51, Philadelphia 45, April 29, 1952.

Most Men Facing Pitcher as Batsmen, Extra-Inning Game, Both Clubs

N. L.— 202— New York 103, St. Louis 99, September 11, 1974, 25 innings.
A. L.— 191— New York 96, Detroit 95, June 24, 1962, 22 innings.

Most Official At-Bats, Extra-Inning Game, Both Clubs

N. L.— 175— New York 89, St. Louis 86, September 11, 1974, 25 innings.
A. L.— 167— New York 85, Detroit 82, June 24, 1962, 22 innings.

Most Official At-Bats, Doubleheader, One Club, 18 Innings

A. L.—99—New York vs. Philadelphia, June 28, 1939.
N. L.—98—Pittsburgh vs. Philadelphia, August 8, 1922.

Most Official At-Bats, Doubleheader, Both Clubs, 18 Innings

N. L.— 176— Pittsburgh 98, Philadelphia 78, August 8, 1922.
A. L.— 172— Boston 89, Philadelphia 83, July 4, 1939.

Most Official At-Bats, Doubleheader, Both Clubs, More Than 18 Innings

N. L.— 234— New York 119, San Francisco 115, May 31, 1964, 32 innings.
A. L.— 215— Kansas City 112, Detroit 103, June 17, 1967, 28 innings.

Fewest Official At-Bats, Game, One Club, Nine Innings

A. L.—23—Chicago vs. St. Louis, May 6, 1917.
          Cleveland vs. Chicago, May 9, 1961.
          Detroit vs. Baltimore, May 6, 1968.
N. L.—24—Cincinnati vs. Brooklyn, July 22, 1911.
          Boston vs. Cincinnati, May 15, 1951.
          Pittsburgh vs. Chicago, May 12, 1955.

Fewest Official At-Bats, Game, One Club, Eight Innings

A. L.—19—Baltimore vs. Kansas City, September 12, 1964.
N. L.—21—Pittsburgh vs. St. Louis, September 8, 1908.

Fewest Official At-Bats, Game, Both Clubs, Nine Innings

N. L.—48—Boston 25, Philadelphia 23, April 22, 1910.
          Brooklyn 24, Cincinnati 24, July 22, 1911.
A. L.—46—Kansas City 27, Baltimore 19, September 12, 1964.

Fewest Official At-Bats, Doubleheader, One Club

A. L.—50—Boston vs. Chicago, August 28, 1912.
N. L.—52—Brooklyn vs. St. Louis, July 24, 1909.

Fewest Official At-Bats, Doubleheader, Both Clubs

N. L.— 109— St. Louis 57, Brooklyn 52, July 24, 1909.
A. L.— 111— Cleveland 56, Chicago 55, May 28, 1916.

Most Runs, Inning, One Club

N. L.—18—Chicago vs. Detroit, September 6, 1883, seventh inning.
A. L.—17—Boston vs. Detroit, June 18, 1953, seventh inning.
N. L. since 1900—15—Brooklyn vs. Cincinnati, May 21, 1952, first inning.

Most Runs, Inning, Both Clubs

A. L.—19—Cleveland 13, Boston 6, April 10, 1977, eighth inning.
A. A.—19—Washington 14, Baltimore 5, June 17, 1891, first inning.
N. L.—18—Chicago 18, Detroit 0, September 6, 1883, seventh inning.
N. L. since 1900—17—Boston 10, New York 7, June 20, 1912, ninth inning.

Most Runs, Two Consecutive Innings, One Club

N. L.—21—Pittsburgh vs. Boston, June 6, 1894; 12 in third inning; 9 in fourth inning.
A. L.—19—Boston vs. Philadelphia, May 2, 1901; 9 in second inning, 10 in third inning.
    Boston vs. Detroit, June 18, 1953; 2 in sixth inning, 17 in seventh inning.
N. L. since 1900—17—New York vs. Boston, September 3, 1926; 5 in fourth inning, 12 in
    fifth inning.

Most Times Ten or More Runs, Inning, Game, One Club

N. L.—2—Chicago vs. Philadelphia, August 25, 1922; 10 in second, 14 in fourth inning.
    St. Louis vs. Philadelphia, July 6, 1929, second game; 10 in first, 10 in fifth
    inning.
    Brooklyn vs. Pittsburgh, July 10, 1943; 10 in first, 10 in fourth inning.
A. L.—1—Made in many games.

Most Runs, First Inning, One Club

N. L.—16—Boston vs. Baltimore, June 18, 1894, a.m. game.
N. L. since 1900—15—Brooklyn vs. Cincinnati, May 21, 1952.
A. L.—14—Cleveland vs. Philadelphia, June 18, 1950, second game.

Most Runs, First Inning, Both Clubs

A. A.—19—Washington 14, Baltimore 5, June 17, 1891.
N. L.—16—Boston 16, Baltimore 0, June 18, 1894, a.m. game.
N. L. since 1900—15—Brooklyn 15, Cincinnati 0, May 21, 1952.
A. L.—14—Cleveland 14, Philadelphia 0, June 18, 1950, second game.
    Chicago 11, Baltimore 3, August 3, 1956.

Most Runs, Second Inning, One Club

N. L.—13—New York vs. Cleveland, July 19, 1890, first game.
    Atlanta vs. Houston, September 20, 1972.
A. L.—13—Kansas City vs. Chicago, April 21, 1956.

Most Runs, Second Inning, Both Clubs

A. L.—14—Philadelphia 10, Detroit 4, September 23, 1913.
    New York 11, Detroit 3, August 28, 1936, second game.
N. L.—13—New York 13, Cleveland 0, July 19, 1890, first game.
    Chicago 10, Philadelphia 3, August 25, 1922.
    Brooklyn 11, New York 2, April 29, 1930.
    Atlanta 13, Houston 0, September 20, 1972.

Most Runs, Third Inning, One Club

N. L.—14—Cleveland vs. Washington, August 7, 1889.
N. L. since 1900—13—San Francisco vs. St. Louis, May 7, 1966.
A. L.—12—New York vs. Washington, September 11, 1949, first game.

Most Runs, Third Inning, Both Clubs

N. L.—14—Cleveland 14, Washington 0, August 7, 1889.
N. L. since 1900—13—San Francisco 13, St. Louis 0, May 7, 1966.
    St. Louis 7, Atlanta 6, August 21, 1973.
A. L.—12—Boston 8, Washington 4, August 12, 1949, second game.
    New York 12, Washington 0, September 11, 1949, first game.

Most Runs, Fourth Inning, One Club

N. L.—15—Hartford vs. New York, May 13, 1876.
N. L. since 1900—14—Chicago vs. Philadelphia, August 25, 1922.
A. L.—13—Chicago vs. Washington, September 26, 1943, first game.

Most Runs, Fourth Inning, Both Clubs

N. L.—15—Hartford 15, New York 0, May 13, 1876.
    Chicago 14, Philadelphia 1, August 25, 1922.
A. L.—13—Chicago 13, Washington 0, September 26, 1943, first game.

Most Runs, Fifth Inning, One Club

A. L.—14—New York vs. Washington, July 6, 1920.
N. L.—13—Chicago vs. Pittsburgh, August 16, 1890.
N. L. since 1900—12—New York vs. Boston, September 3, 1926.
    Cincinnati vs. Atlanta, April 25, 1977.

Most Runs, Fifth Inning, Both Clubs

N. L.—16—Brooklyn 11, New York 5, June 3, 1890.
N. L. since 1900—15—Brooklyn 10, Cincinnati 5, June 12, 1949.
          Philadelphia 9, Pittsburgh 6, April 16, 1953.
A. L.—14—New York 14, Washington 0, July 6, 1920.

Most Runs, Sixth Inning, One Club

P. L.—14—Philadelphia vs. Buffalo, June 26, 1890.
A. L.—13—Cleveland vs. Boston, July 7, 1923, first game.
          Detroit vs. New York, June 17, 1925.
N. L.—12—Chicago vs. Cincinnati, May 8, 1890.
          Philadelphia vs. Chicago, July 21, 1923, first game.
          Chicago vs. Philadelphia, August 21, 1935, second game.

Most Runs, Sixth Inning, Both Clubs

A. L.—15—Philadelphia 10, New York 5, September 5, 1912, first game.
          Detroit 10, Minnesota 5, June 13, 1967.
N. L.—15—New York 10, Cincinnati 5, June 12, 1979.

Most Runs, Seventh Inning, One Club

N. L.—18—Chicago vs. Detroit, September 6, 1883.
A. L.—17—Boston vs. Detroit, June 18, 1953.
N. L. since 1900—12—Chicago vs. Cincinnati, May 28, 1925.
          Brooklyn vs. St. Louis, August 30, 1953.

Most Runs, Seventh Inning, Both Clubs

N. L.—18—Chicago 18, Detroit 0, September 6, 1883.
A. L.—17—Boston 17, Detroit 0, June 18, 1953.

Most Runs, Eighth Inning, One Club

A. L.—13—Philadelphia vs. Cleveland, June 15, 1925.
          Cleveland vs. Boston, April 10, 1977.
N. L.—13—Brooklyn vs. Cincinnati, August 8, 1954.

Most Runs, Eighth Inning, Both Clubs

A. L.—19—Cleveland 13, Boston 6, April 10, 1977.
N. L.—14—New York 11, Pittsburgh 3, May 25, 1954.
          Brooklyn 13, Cincinnati 1, August 8, 1954.

Most Runs, Ninth Inning, One Club

N. L.—14—Baltimore vs. Boston, April 24, 1894.
N. L. since 1900—12—San Francisco vs. Cincinnati, August 23, 1961.
A. L.—13—California vs. Texas, September 14, 1978.

Most Runs, Ninth Inning, Both Clubs

N. L.—17—Boston 10, New York 7, June 20, 1912.
A. L.—14—Cleveland 9, Philadelphia 5, July 25, 1939.

Most Runs, Ninth Inning, With Two Out

A. L.—9—Cleveland vs. Washington, May 23, 1901; won 14 to 13.
          Boston vs. Milwaukee, June 2, 1901; won 13 to 2.
          Cleveland vs. New York, August 4, 1929, second game; won 14 to 6.
N. L.—7—Chicago vs. Cincinnati, June 29, 1952, first game; won 9 to 8.
          San Francisco vs. Pittsburgh, May 1, 1973; won 8 to 7.

Most Runs, Ninth Inning, With Two Out, None on Base

A. L.—9—Cleveland vs. Washington, May 23, 1901; won 14 to 13.
          Boston vs. Milwaukee, June 2, 1901; won 13 to 2.
N. L.—7—Chicago vs. Cincinnati, June 29, 1952, first game; won 9 to 8.

Most Runs, Tenth Inning, One Club

A. L.—11—Minnesota vs. Oakland, June 21, 1969.
N. L.—10—Boston vs. New York, June 17, 1887, a.m. game.
N. L. since 1900—9—Cincinnati vs. Philadelphia, August 24, 1947, first game.

Most Runs, Tenth Inning, Both Clubs

A. L.—12—Minnesota 11, Oakland 1, June 21, 1969.
N. L.—11—New York 6, Brooklyn 5, April 24, 1955.

Most Runs, Eleventh Inning, One Club

N. L.—10—Kansas City vs. Detroit, July 21, 1886.
A. L.— 8—Philadelphia vs. Detroit, May 1, 1951.
N. L. since 1900—8—Brooklyn vs. Milwaukee, August 29, 1954, first game.

Most Runs, Eleventh Inning, Both Clubs

A. L.—11—Seattle 6, Boston 5, May 16, 1969.
N. L.—11—New York 6, Chicago 5, June 30, 1979.

Most Runs, Twelfth Inning, One Club

A. L.—11—New York vs. Detroit, July 26, 1928, first game.
N. L.— 9—Chicago vs. Pittsburgh, July 23, 1923.

Most Runs, Twelfth Inning, Both Clubs

A. L.—11—New York 11, Detroit 0, July 26, 1928, first game.
N. L.— 9—Chicago 9, Pittsburgh 0, July 23, 1923.
                New York 8, Brooklyn 1, May 30, 1940, second game.
                Houston 8, Cincinnati 1, June 2, 1966.
                San Diego 5, Houston 4, July 5, 1969.

Most Runs, Thirteenth Inning, One Club

N. L.—10—Cincinnati vs. Brooklyn, May 15, 1919.
A. L.— 9—Cleveland vs. Detroit, August 5, 1933, first game.

Most Runs, Fourteenth Inning, One Club

N. L.—8—New York vs. Pittsburgh, June 15, 1929.
A. L.—7—Cleveland vs. St. Louis, June 3, 1935.

Most Runs, Fifteenth Inning, One Club

A. L.—12—Texas vs. Oakland, July 3, 1983.
N. L.— 7—St. Louis vs. Boston, September 28, 1928.

Most Runs, Sixteenth Inning, One Club

A. L.—8—Chicago vs. Washington, May 20, 1920.
N. L.—5—Cincinnati vs. New York, August 20, 1973.

Most Runs, Seventeenth Inning, One Club

N. L.—7—New York vs. Pittsburgh, July 16, 1920.
A. L.—6—New York vs. Detroit, July 20, 1941.

Most Runs, Eighteenth Inning, One Club

N. L.—5—Chicago vs. Boston, May 14, 1927.
A. L.—4—Minnesota vs. Seattle, July 19, 1969.

Most Runs, Nineteenth Inning, One Club

N. L.—4—New York vs. Los Angeles, May 24, 1973.
A. L.—3—Chicago vs. Boston, July 13, 1951.

Most Runs, Nineteenth Inning, Both Clubs

N. L.—6—Brooklyn 3, Philadelphia 3, April 30, 1919.
A. L.—5—Chicago 3, Boston 2, July 13, 1951.

Most Runs, Twentieth Inning, One Club

N. L.—4—Brooklyn vs. Boston, July 5, 1940.
A. L.—3—Boston vs. Seattle, July 27, 1969.
                Washington vs. Cleveland, September 14, second game, finished September
                20, 1971.

Most Runs, Twentieth Inning, Both Clubs

N. L.—4—Brooklyn 4, Boston 0, July 5, 1940.
A. L.—4—Boston 3, Seattle 1, July 27, 1969.
                Washington 3, Cleveland 1, September 14, second game, finished September
                20, 1971.

Most Runs, Twenty-First Inning, One Club

A. L.—4—Chicago vs. Cleveland, May 26, finished May 28, 1973.
N. L.—3—San Diego vs. Montreal, May 21, 1977.

Most Runs, Twenty-Second Inning, One Club

A. L.—2—New York vs. Detroit, June 24, 1962.
N. L.—1—Brooklyn vs. Pittsburgh, August 22, 1917.
                Chicago vs. Boston, May 17, 1927.

Most Runs, Twenty-Third Inning, One Club

N. L.—2—San Francisco vs. New York, May 31, 1964, second game.
A. L.—0—Boston vs. Philadelphia, September 1, 1906.
                Philadelphia vs. Boston, September 1, 1906.
                Detroit vs. Philadelphia, July 21, 1945.
                Philadelphia vs. Detroit, July 21, 1945.

Most Runs, Twenty-Fourth Inning, One Club

A. L.—3—Philadelphia vs. Boston, September 1, 1906.
N. L.—1—Houston vs. New York, April 15, 1968.

Most Runs, Twenty-Fifth Inning, One Club

N. L.—1—St. Louis vs. New York, September 11, 1974.
A. L.—No twenty-five inning game.

Most Runs, Twenty-Sixth Inning, One Club

N. L.—0—Boston vs. Brooklyn, May 1, 1920.
　　　　　Brooklyn vs. Boston, May 1, 1920.
A. L.—No twenty-six inning game.

Most Runs, Extra Inning, One Club

A. L.—12—Texas vs. Oakland, July 3, 1983, fifteenth inning.
N. L.—10—Kansas City vs. Detroit, July 21, 1886, eleventh inning.
　　　　　Boston vs. New York, June 17, 1887, a.m. game, tenth inning.
　　　　　Cincinnati vs. Brooklyn, May 15, 1919, thirteenth inning.

Most Runs, Extra Inning, Both Clubs

A. L.—12—Minnesota 11, Oakland 1, June 21, 1969, tenth inning.
　　　　　Texas 12, Oakland 0, July 3, 1983, fifteenth inning.
N. L.—11—New York 8, Pittsburgh 3, June 15, 1929, fourteenth inning.
　　　　　New York 6, Brooklyn 5, April 24, 1955, tenth inning.
　　　　　New York 6, Chicago 5, June 30, 1979, eleventh inning.

Most Runs, Start of Game, With None Out

N. L.—10—New York vs. St. Louis, May 13, 1911, first inning.
A. L.— 8—Cleveland vs. Baltimore, July 6, 1954, first inning.
　　　　　New York vs. Baltimore, April 24, 1960, first inning.

Most Runs, Start of Inning, With None Out

N. L.—13—Chicago vs. Detroit, September 6, 1883, seventh inning.
A. L.—11—Detroit vs. New York, June 17, 1925, sixth inning.
N. L. since 1900—12—Brooklyn vs. Philadelphia, May 24, 1953, eighth inning.

Most Runs, Inning, With Two Out

A. L.—13—Cleveland vs. Boston, July 7, 1923, first game, sixth inning.
　　　　　Kansas City vs. Chicago, April 21, 1956, second inning.
N. L.—12—Brooklyn vs. Cincinnati, May 21, 1952, first inning.
　　　　　Brooklyn vs. Cincinnati, August 8, 1954, eighth inning.

Most Runs, Inning, With Two Out, None on Base

N. L.—12—Brooklyn vs. Cincinnati, August 8, 1954, eighth inning.
A. L.—10—Chicago vs. Detroit, September 2, 1959, second game, fifth inning.

Most Runs, Game, One Club

N. L.—36—Chicago vs. Louisville (7), June 29, 1897.
A. L.—29—Boston vs. St. Louis (4), June 8, 1950.
　　　　　Chicago vs. Kansas City (6), April 23, 1955.
N. L. since 1900—28—St. Louis vs. Philadelphia (7), July 6, 1929, second game.

Most Runs, Opening Game of Season, One Club

P. L.—23—Buffalo vs. Cleveland, April 19, 1890 (23-2).
A. L.—21—Cleveland vs. St. Louis, April 14, 1925 (21-14).
N. L.—19—Philadelphia vs. Boston, April 19, 1900, 10 innings (19-17).

Most Runs, Game, Both Clubs

N. L.—49—Chicago 26, Philadelphia 23, August 25, 1922.
A. L.—36—Boston 22, Philadelphia 14, June 29, 1950.

Most Runs, Opening Game of Season, Both Clubs

N. L.—36—Philadelphia 19, Boston 17, April 19, 1900, 10 innings.
A. L.—35—Cleveland 21, St. Louis 14, April 14, 1925.

Most Runs, Doubleheader, One Club

N. L.—43—Boston vs. Cincinnati, August 21, 1894.
A. L.—36—Detroit vs. St. Louis, August 14, 1937.
N. L. since 1900—34—St. Louis vs. Philadelphia, July 6, 1929.

Most Runs, Doubleheader, Both Clubs

N. L.—54—Boston 43, Cincinnati 11, August 21, 1894.
A. L.—54—Boston 35, Philadelphia 19, July 4, 1939.
N. L. since 1900—50—Brooklyn 26, Philadelphia 24, May 18, 1929.
　　　　　St. Louis 34, Philadelphia 16, July 6, 1929.

Longest Extra-Inning Game, Without a Run, One Club

N. L.—24 innings— New York vs. Houston, April 15, 1968.
A. L.—18 innings— Washington vs. Detroit, July 16, 1909.
                   Detroit vs. Washington, July 16, 1909.
                   Chicago vs. Washington, May 15, 1918.
                   Chicago vs. Washington, June 8, 1947, first game.

Fewest Runs, Longest Doubleheader, One Club

N. L.—0—St. Louis vs. New York, July 2, 1933, 27 innings.
         New York vs. Philadelphia, October 2, 1965, 27 innings.
A. L.—0—Held by many clubs, 18 innings. Last doubleheader—Cleveland vs. Boston, September 26, 1975.

Fewest Runs, Doubleheader, Both Clubs

N. L.—1—Boston 1, Pittsburgh 0, September 4, 1902.
         Philadelphia 1, Boston 0, September 5, 1913.
A. L.—2—Washington 1, St. Louis 1, September 25, 1904.
         Philadelphia 1, Boston 1, June 1, 1909.
         Philadelphia 1, Boston 1, September 11, 1909.
         Los Angeles 1, Detroit 1, August 18, 1964.
         Washington 1, Kansas City 1, May 2, 1967.
         Baltimore 2, Boston 0, September 2, 1974.

Most Runs, Two Consecutive Games, One Club

N. L.—53—Chicago, July 22, 25, 1876.
A. L.—49—Boston vs. St. Louis, June 7, 8, 1950.
N. L. since 1900—45—Pittsburgh, June 20, 22, 1925.

Most Runs, Three Consecutive Games, One Club

N. L.—71—Chicago, July 20, 22, 25, 1876.
A. L.—56—Boston vs. St. Louis, June 7, 8, 9, 1950.

Most Runs, Four Consecutive Games, One Club

N. L.—88—Chicago, July 20, 22, 25, 27, 1876.
A. L.—65—Boston, June 5, 6, 7, 8, 1950.

Most Players, Six Runs in One Game, One Club

N. L.—2—Boston vs. Pittsburgh, August 27, 1887, (M. J. Kelly, Ezra B. Sutton).
N. L. since 1900—1—New York vs. Philadelphia, August 4, 1934, second game, (Melvin T. Ott).
         New York vs. Brooklyn, April 30, 1944, first game, (Melvin T. Ott).
         Milwaukee vs. Chicago, September 2, 1957, first game, (Frank J. Torre).
A. L.—1—Boston vs. Chicago, May 8, 1946, (John Pesky).

Most Players, Five or More Runs in One Game, One Club

N. L.—3—Chicago vs. Cleveland, July 24, 1882.
         Boston vs. Philadelphia, June 20, 1883.
         Boston vs. Pittsburgh, August 27, 1887.
         New York vs. Brooklyn, April 30, 1944, first game.
         Chicago vs. Boston, July 3, 1945.
A. L.—2—Cleveland vs. Baltimore, September 2, 1902.
         Chicago vs. Kansas City, April 23, 1955.

Most Players, Four or More Runs in One Game, One Club

N. L.—6—Chicago vs. Cleveland, July 24, 1882.
         Chicago vs. Louisville, June 29, 1897.
N. L. since 1900—4—St. Louis vs. Philadelphia, July 6, 1929, second game.
A. L.—4—Boston vs. St. Louis, June 8, 1950.

Most Players, Three or More Runs in One Game, One Club

N. L.—9—Chicago vs. Buffalo, July 3, 1883.
A. L.—7—Boston vs. St. Louis, June 8, 1950.
N. L. since 1900—6—New York vs. Philadelphia, September 2, 1925, second game.

Most Players, Six or More Runs in One Game, Both Clubs

N. L.—2—Boston 2 (M. J. Kelly, Ezra B. Sutton), Pittsburgh 0, August 27, 1887.
A. L.—1—Boston 1 (John Pesky) Chicago 0, May 8, 1946.

Most Players Five or More Runs in One Game, Both Clubs

N. L.—3—Chicago 3, Cleveland 0, July 24, 1882.
         Boston 3, Philadelphia 0, June 20, 1883.
         Boston 3, Pittsburgh 0, August 27, 1887.
         New York 3, Brooklyn 0, April 30, 1944, first game.
         Chicago 3, Boston 0, July 3. 1945

A. L.—2—Cleveland, 2, Baltimore 0, September 2, 1902.
Chicago 2, Kansas City 0, April 23, 1955.

Most Players, Four or More Runs in One Game, Both Clubs

N. L.—6—Chicago 6, Cleveland 0, July 24, 1882.
Chicago 6, Louisville 0, June 29, 1897.
N. L. since 1900—4—St. Louis 4, Philadelphia 0, July 6, 1929, second game.
A. L.—4—Boston 4, St. Louis 0, June 8, 1950.

Most Players, Three or More Runs in One Game, Both Clubs

N. L.—9—Chicago 9, Buffalo 0, July 3, 1883.
A. L.—7—Boston 7, St. Louis 0, June 8, 1950.
N. L. since 1900—6—New York 6, Philadelphia 0, September 2, 1925, second game.

Most Players, Two or More Runs in One Game, Both Clubs

N. L.—16—Chicago 9, Philadelphia 7, August 25, 1922.
A. L.—13—Boston 9, Philadelphia 4, June 29, 1950.

Most Players, One or More Runs in One Game, Both Clubs

N. L.—22—Philadelphia 13, Chicago 9, August 25, 1922.
A. L.—18—Boston 10, Philadelphia 8, June 29, 1950.

Most Players, Two or More Runs in One Inning, One Club

N. L.—7—Chicago vs. Detroit, September 6, 1883, seventh inning.
N. L. since 1900—6—Brooklyn vs. Cincinnati, May 21, 1952, first inning.
A. L.—5—New York vs. Washington, July 6, 1920, fifth inning.
New York vs. Boston, June 21, 1945, fifth inning.
Boston vs. Philadelphia, July 4, 1948, seventh inning.
Cleveland vs. Philadelphia, June 18, 1950, second game, first inning.
Boston vs. Detroit, June 18, 1953, seventh inning.

Most Players, Two or More Runs in One Game, One Club

N. L.—10—Chicago vs. Louisville, June 29, 1897.
A. L.— 9—New York vs. Cleveland, July 14, 1904.
Cleveland vs. Boston, July 7, 1923, first game.
New York vs. Chicago, July 26, 1931, second game.
New York vs. Philadelphia, May 24, 1936.
Boston vs. Philadelphia, June 29, 1950.
N. L. since 1900—9—St. Louis vs. Chicago, April 16, 1912.
Chicago vs. Philadelphia, August 25, 1922.
St. Louis vs. Philadelphia, July 6, 1929, second game.

Most Players, One or More Runs in One Game, One Club

N. L.—13—Cincinnati vs. Boston, June 4, 1911.
New York vs. Boston, June 20, 1912.
Philadelphia vs. Chicago, August 25, 1922.
A. L.—13—Washington vs. St. Louis, July 10, 1926.
New York vs. St. Louis, August 7, 1949, first game.
Oakland vs. Kansas City, September 20, 1975.

Most Runs by Two Players, One Game, One Club

N. L.—12—Boston vs. Pittsburgh, August 27, 1887; Michael J. Kelly 6, Ezra B. Sutton 6.
N. L. since 1900—11—New York vs. Brooklyn, April 30, 1944, first game; Melvin T. Ott 6, Joseph M. Medwick 5.
A. L.—10—Cleveland vs. Baltimore, September 2, 1902; Harry E. Bay 5, William J. Bradley 5.
Chicago vs. Kansas City, April 23, 1955; Alfonso Carrasquel 5, Orestes A. Minoso 5.

Most Runs, Inning, One Club, Pinch-Hitters

N. L.—3—Boston vs. Philadelphia, April 19, 1900, ninth inning.
Brooklyn vs. Philadelphia, September 9, 1926, ninth inning.
San Francisco vs. Pittsburgh, May 5, 1958, ninth inning.
A. L.—3—Chicago vs. Philadelphia, September 19, 1916, ninth inning.
Philadelphia vs. Detroit, September 18, 1940, second game, ninth inning.
Cleveland vs. Detroit, August 7, 1941, ninth inning.

Most Runs, Inning, One Club, Pinch-Runners

A. L.—3—Chicago vs. Minnesota, September 16, 1967, ninth inning.
Chicago vs. Oakland, May 19, 1968, second game, fifth inning.
Oakland vs. California, May 7, 1975, seventh inning.
N. L.—2—Made in many innings. Last time—Philadelphia vs. Pittsburgh, May 19, 1974, first game, eighth inning.

Most Runs by Infield, Game, One Club

N. L.—16—Chicago vs. Philadelphia, June 29, 1897.
Chicago vs. Boston, July 3, 1945.
A. L.—16—Boston vs. St. Louis, June 8, 1950.

Most Runs by Outfield, Game, One Club

A. A.—14—Kansas City vs. Philadelphia, September 30, 1888.
N. L.—14—New York vs. Cincinnati, June 9, 1901.
New York vs. Brooklyn, April 30, 1944, first game.
A. L.—11—Chicago vs. Philadelphia, September 11, 1936.
New York vs. Washington, August 12, 1953.

Most Innings Scored, Nine-Inning Game, One Club (Scoring in Every Inning)

A. A.—9—Columbus vs. Pittsburgh, June 14, 1883.
Kansas City vs. Brooklyn, May 20, 1889.
N. L.—9—Cleveland vs. Boston, August 15, 1889.
Washington vs. Boston, June 22, 1894.
Cleveland vs. Philadelphia, July 12, 1894.
Chicago vs. Louisville, June 29, 1897.
New York vs. Philadelphia, June 1, 1923.
St. Louis vs. Chicago, September 13, 1964.
A. L.—8—Boston vs. Cleveland, September 16, 1903, did not bat in ninth.
Cleveland vs. Boston, July 7, 1923, first game, did not bat in ninth.
New York vs. St. Louis, July 26, 1939, did not bat in ninth.
Chicago vs. Boston, May 11, 1949, did not bat in ninth.

Most Innings Scored, Game, Nine Innings, Both Clubs

N. L.—15—Philadelphia 8, Detroit 7, July 1, 1887.
Washington 9, Boston 6, June 22, 1894.
A. A.—15—Kansas City 9, Brooklyn 6, May 20, 1889.
P. L.—15—New York 8, Chicago 7, May 23, 1890.
A. L.—14—Baltimore 8, Philadelphia 6, May 7, 1901.
St. Louis 7, Detroit 7, April 23, 1927.
Detroit 7, Chicago 7, July 2, 1940.
N. L. since 1900—14—New York 9, Philadelphia 5, June 1, 1923.
Pittsburgh 8, Chicago 6, July 6, 1975.
Los Angeles 8, Chicago 6, May 25, 1976.

Most Consecutive Innings Scored During Season, One Club

A. L.—17—Boston, September 15 (last 3 innings), September 16 (8 innings), September 17 (first 6 innings), 1903 (3 games).
N. L.—14—Pittsburgh, July 31 (last 5 innings), August 1 (8 innings), August 2 (first inning), 1894 (3 games).
New York, July 18 (last 3 innings) July 19 (8 innings), July 20 (first 3 innings), 1949 (3 games).

Most Runs, Game, to Overcome and Win

A. L.—12—Detroit vs. Chicago, June 18, 1911, at Detroit.

Chicago	7	0	0		3	3	0		2	0	0—15
Detroit	0	1	0		0	4	3		0	5	3—16

Philadelphia vs. Cleveland, June 15, 1925, at Philadelphia.

Cleveland	0	4	2		2	4	2		1	0	0—15
Philadelphia	0	1	1		0	0	1		1	13	x—17

N. L.—11—St. Louis vs. New York, June 15, 1952, first game, at New York.

St. Louis	0	0	0		0	7	0		3	2	2—14
New York	0	5	6		0	0	0		0	0	1—12

Philadelphia vs. Chicago, April 17, 1976, at Chicago, 10 innings.

Philadelphia	0	1	0		1	2	0		3	5	3—18
Chicago	0	7	5		1	0	0		0	0	2	1—16

Most Hits, Inning, One Club

N. L.—18—Chicago vs. Detroit, September 6, 1883, seventh inning.
A. L.—14—Boston vs. Detroit, June 18, 1953, seventh inning.
N. L. since 1900—12—St. Louis vs. Cincinnati, April 22, 1925, first inning.

Most Hits, Game, Nine Innings, One Club

N. L.—36—Philadelphia vs. Louisville, August 17, 1894.
N. L. since 1900—31—New York vs. Cincinnati, June 9, 1901.
A. L.—30—New York vs. Boston, September 28, 1923.

Most Hits, Game, Nine Innings, Both Clubs

N. L.—51—Philadelphia 26, Chicago 25, August 25, 1922.
A. L.—45—Philadelphia 27, Boston 18, July 8, 1902.
Detroit 28, New York 17, September 29, 1928.

Most Hits, Extra-Inning Game, One Club

N. L.—Less than nine-inning game.
N. L.—since 1900—Less than nine-inning game.
A. L.—33—Cleveland vs. Philadelphia, July 10, 1932, 18 innings.

Most Hits, Extra-Inning Game, Both Clubs

A. L.—58—Cleveland 33, Philadelphia 25, July 10, 1932, 18 innings.
N. L.—52—New York 28, Pittsburgh 24, June 15, 1929, 14 innings.

Most Hits, Doubleheader, One Club

N. L.—46—Pittsburgh vs. Philadelphia, August 8, 1922
A. L.—43—New York vs. Philadelphia, June 28, 1939.

Most Hits, Doubleheader, Both Clubs

N. L.—73—Washington 41, Philadelphia 32, July 4, 1896.
       St. Louis 43, Philadelphia 30, July 6, 1929.
A. L.—65—Boston 35, Philadelphia 30, July 4, 1939.

Fewest Hits, Game, One Club

N. L., U. A., A. A., A. L.—0—Made in many games.

Fewest Hits, Extra-Inning Game, One Club

A. A.—0—Toledo vs. Brooklyn, October 4, 1884, 10 innings.
N. L.—0—Philadelphia vs. New York, July 4 1908, a.m. game, 10 innings.
       Chicago vs. Cincinnati, May 2, 1917, 10 innings.
       Chicago vs. Cincinnati, August 19, 1965, first game, 10 innings.
N. L.—1—Milwaukee vs. Pittsburgh, May 26, 1959, 13 innings.
A. L.—1—Cleveland vs. Chicago, September 6, 1903, 10 innings.
       Boston vs. St. Louis, September 18, 1934, 10 innings.
       Los Angeles vs. New York, May 22, 1962, 12 innings.

Fewest Hits, Nine-Inning Game, Both Clubs

N. L.—1—Los Angeles 1, Chicago 0, September 9, 1965.
A. A.—2—Philadelphia 1, Baltimore 1, August 20, 1886.
A. L.—2—Cleveland 1, St. Louis 1, April 23, 1952.
       Chicago 1, Baltimore 1, June 21, 1956.
       Baltimore 1, Kansas City 1, September 12, 1964.
       Baltimore 2, Detroit 0, April 30, 1967, first game.

Fewest Hits, Doubleheader, One Club

N. L.—3—Brooklyn vs. St. Louis, September 21, 1934.
       New York vs. Philadelphia, June 21, 1964.
A. L.—3—Chicago vs. Boston, May 27, 1945.
       California vs. Cleveland, June 8, 1969.

Fewest Hits, Doubleheader, Both Clubs

A. L.—11—Detroit 7, St. Louis 4, May 30, 1914.
N. L.—12—Chicago 6, Pittsburgh 6, September 3, 1905.
       St. Louis 6, Brooklyn 6, July 24, 1909.

Fewest Hits, Two Consecutive Nine-Inning Games, One Club

N. L.—2—New York vs. Providence, June 17 (1), 18 (1), 1884.
       Cincinnati vs. Brooklyn, July 5 (1), 6 (1), 1900.
       Boston vs. New York, September 28, second game (1); September 30, first
         game (1), 1916.
       New York vs. Milwaukee, September 10, (1), September 11 (1), 1965.
       Los Angeles vs. Houston, September 26 (0), 27 (2), 1981.
A. A.—2—Baltimore vs. St. Louis-Louisville, July 28 (1), 29 (1), 1886.
A. L.—2—New York vs. Cleveland, September 25 (1), 26 (1), 1907.
       St. Louis vs. Washington, Philadelphia, September 25, second game (1), Sep-
         tember 27, 1910 (1), first game.
       Chicago vs. Washington, August 10 (1), 11 (1), 1917.
       Milwaukee vs. Kansas City, June 18 (2), June 19 (0), 1974.

Most Hits, Two Consecutive Games, One Club

N. L.—55—Philadelphia vs. Louisville, August 16, 17, 1894.
A. L.—51—Boston vs. St. Louis, June 7, 8, 1950.
N. L. since 1900—49—Pittsburgh vs. Philadelphia, August 7, August 8, first game, 1922.

Most Consecutive Hits, Game, One Club

N. L.—12—St. Louis vs. Boston, September 17, 1920, fourth and fifth innings.
       Brooklyn vs. Pittsburgh, June 23, 1930, sixth and seventh innings.
A. L.—10—Boston vs. Milwaukee, June 2, 1901, ninth inning.
       Detroit vs. Baltimore, September 20, 1983, first inning (1 walk during
         streak).

Most Consecutive Hits, Inning, One Club

N. L.—10—St. Louis vs. Boston, September 17, 1920, fourth inning.
　　　　　St. Louis vs. Philadelphia, June 12, 1922, sixth inning.
　　　　　Chicago vs. Boston, September 7, 1929, first game, fourth inning.
　　　　　Brooklyn vs. Pittsburgh, June 23, 1930, sixth inning.
A. L.—10—Boston vs. Milwaukee, June 2, 1901, ninth inning.
　　　　　Detroit vs. Baltimore, September 20, 1983, first inning (1 walk during
　　　　　　streak).

Most Consecutive Hits, Start of Game, One Club, With None Out

N. L.—8—Philadelphia vs. Chicago, August 5, 1975, 4 singles, 2 doubles, 2 home runs.
　　　　　Pittsburgh vs. Atlanta, August 26, 1975, 7 singles, 1 triple.
A. L.—8—Oakland vs. Chicago, September 27, 1981, first game, 8 singles.

Most Batters Reaching First Base Safely, Inning, One Club

A. L.—20—Boston vs. Detroit, June 18, 1953, seventh inning.
N. L.—19—Boston vs. Baltimore, June 18, 1894, a.m. game, first inning.
　　　　　Brooklyn vs. Cincinnati, May 21, 1952, first inning.

Most Consecutive Batters Reaching First Base Safely, Inning, One Club

N. L.—19—Brooklyn vs. Cincinnati, May 21, 1952, first inning.
A. L.—13—Kansas City vs. Chicago, April 21, 1956, second inning.

Most Batters Reaching First Base Safely Three Times, Inning, One Club

N. L.—3—Chicago vs. Detroit, September 6, 1883, seventh inning.
　　　　　Boston vs. Baltimore, June 18, 1894, a.m. game, first inning.
N. L. since 1900—1—Brooklyn vs. Cincinnati, May 21, 1952, first inning.
A. L.—3—Boston vs. Detroit, June 18, 1953, seventh inning.

Most Players, Six Hits One Game, Nine Innings, One Club

A. A.—2—Cincinnati vs. Pittsburgh, September 12, 1883.
N. L.—2—Baltimore vs. St. Louis, September 3, 1897.
A. L.—1—Made in many games.

Most Players Making Two or More Hits, Inning, One Club

N. L.—6—Chicago vs. Detroit, September 6, 1883, seventh inning.
A. L.—5—Philadelphia vs. Boston, July 8, 1902, sixth inning.
　　　　　New York vs. Philadelphia, September 10, 1921, ninth inning.

Most Players, Five or More Hits in Game, One Club

N. L.—4—Philadelphia vs. Louisville, August 17, 1894.
N. L. since 1900—3—New York vs. Cincinnati, June 9, 1901.
　　　　　New York vs. Philadelphia, June 1, 1923.
A. L.—3—Detroit vs. Washington, July 30, 1917.
　　　　　Cleveland vs. Philadelphia, July 10, 1932, 18 innings.
　　　　　Washington vs. Cleveland, May 16, 1933, 12 innings.
　　　　　Chicago vs. Philadelphia, September 11, 1936.

Most Players, Four or More Hits, Game, Nine Innings, One Club

N. L.—7—Chicago vs. Cleveland, July 24, 1882.
N. L. since 1900—5—San Francisco vs. Los Angeles, May 13, 1958.
A. L.—4—Detroit vs. New York, September 29, 1928.
　　　　　Chicago vs. Philadelphia, September 11, 1936.
　　　　　Boston vs. St. Louis, June 8, 1950.

Most Players, Three or More Hits, Game, Nine Innings, One Club

N. L.—8—Chicago vs. Detroit, September 6, 1883.
N. L. since 1900—7—Pittsburgh vs. Philadelphia, June 12, 1928.
A. L.—7—New York vs. Philadelphia, June 28, 1939, first game.
　　　　　Chicago vs. Kansas City, April 23, 1955.

Most Players, Two or More Hits, Game, Nine Innings, One Club

A. A.—10—Brooklyn vs. Philadelphia, June 25, 1885.
N. L.—10—Pittsburgh vs. Philadelphia, August 7, 1922.
　　　　　New York vs. Philadelphia, September 2, 1925, second game.
A. L.— 9—Held by many clubs.

Most Players, One or More Hits, Game, Nine Innings, One Club

A. L.—14—Cleveland vs. St. Louis, August 12, 1948, second game.
N. L.—13—St. Louis vs. Philadelphia, May 11, 1923.
　　　　　St. Louis vs. Philadelphia, September 16, 1926, first game.
　　　　　Montreal vs. Cincinnati, May 7, 1978, first game.
　　　　　Montreal vs. Atlanta, July 30, 1978.
　　　　　Montreal vs. Houston, June 17, 1979.

Most Players, Five or More Hits, Game, Extra Innings, Both Clubs

A. L.—5—Cleveland 3, Philadelphia 2, July 10, 1932, 18 innings.

Most Players, Five or More Hits, Game, Nine Innings, Both Clubs

N. L.—4—Philadelphia 4, Louisville 0, August 17, 1894.
N. L. since 1900—3—New York 3, Cincinnati 0, June 9, 1901.
        New York 3, Philadelphia 0, June 1, 1923.
A. L.—3—Detroit 3, Washington 0, July 30, 1917.
        Washington 3, Cleveland 0, May 16, 1933, 12 innings.
        Chicago 3, Philadelphia 0, September 11, 1936.

Most Players, Four or More Hits, Game, Nine Innings, Both Clubs

N. L.—7—Chicago 7, Cleveland 0, July 24, 1882.
N. L. since 1900—5—St. Louis 4, Philadelphia 1, July 6, 1929, second game.
        San Francisco 5, Los Angeles 0, May 13, 1958.
A. L.—4—Detroit 4, New York 0, September 29, 1928.
        Chicago 4, Philadelphia 0, September 11, 1936.
        Boston 4, St. Louis 0, June 8, 1950.

Most Players, One or More Hits, Game, Nine Innings, Both Clubs

N. L.—23—St. Louis 13, Philadelphia 10, May 11, 1923.
A. L.—22—New York 12, Cleveland 10, July 18, 1934.

Each Player, One or More Hits, Consecutive Games, One Club

N. L.—5—Pittsburgh, August 5, 7, 8, 9, 10, 1922.

Most Hits, Inning, One Club, Pinch-Hitters

N. L.—4—Chicago vs. Brooklyn, May 21, 1927, second game, ninth inning.
        Philadelphia vs. Pittsburgh, September 12, 1974, eighth inning.
A. L.—4—Philadelphia vs. Detroit, September 18, 1940, second game, ninth inning.

Most Hits, Game, Nine Innings, One Club, Pinch-Hitters

N. L.—6—Brooklyn vs. Philadelphia, September 9, 1926.
A. L.—4—Cleveland vs. Chicago, April 22, 1930.
        Philadelphia vs. Detroit, September 18, 1940, second game.
        Detroit vs. Chicago, April 22, 1953.
        Kansas City vs. Detroit, September 1, 1958, a.m. game.
        Cleveland vs. Boston, September 21, 1967.
        Oakland vs. Detroit, August 30, 1970.
        Chicago vs. Oakland, September 7, 1970, second game.

Most Consecutive Hits, Inning, One Club, Pinch-Hitters

N. L.-A. L.—3—Made in many innings.
N. L.—Last time, Pittsburgh vs. San Francisco, July 2, 1961, first game, eighth inning.
A. L.—Last time, Boston vs. Chicago, June 4, 1975, ninth inning.

Most Hits by Infield, Game, One Club

N. L.—18—Boston vs. St. Louis, May 31, 1897.
A. L.—16—Boston vs. St. Louis, June 8, 1950.
N. L. since 1900—16—Pittsburgh vs. Chicago, September 16, 1975.

Most Hits by Outfield, Game, One Club

N. L.—16—New York vs. Cincinnati, June 9, 1901.
A. L.—12—Baltimore vs. Detroit, June 24, 1901.
        Detroit vs. Washington, July 30, 1917.
        Cleveland vs. Philadelphia, April 29, 1952.
        Boston vs. Baltimore, July 11, 1969, second game.

Most Hits by Pitchers, Doubleheader, One Club

A. L.—8—New York vs. Cleveland, June 17, 1936.

Most Hits by Pitchers, Two Consecutive Games, One Club

N. L.—9—Chicago, May 19, 20, 1895.

Most Hits, Game, No Runs, One Club

N. L.—14—New York vs. Chicago, September 14, 1913; lost 7 to 0, 15 total bases.
A. L.—14—Cleveland vs. Washington, July 10, 1928, second game; lost 9 to 0, 16 total
        bases.

Most Hits, Extra-Inning Game, No Runs, One Club

N. L.—15—Boston vs. Pittsburgh, July 10, 1901, 12 innings, 16 total bases; lost 1 to 0.
        Boston vs. Pittsburgh, August 1, 1918, 21 innings, 15 total bases; lost 2 to 0.
A. L.—15—Boston vs. Washington, July 3, 1913, 15 innings, 19 total bases; lost 1 to 0.

Most One-Base Hits, Inning, One Club

N. L.—11—St. Louis vs. Cincinnati, April 22, 1925, first inning.
A. L.—11—Boston vs. Detroit, June 18, 1953, seventh inning.

Most Consecutive One-Base Hits, Inning, One Club

N. L.—10—St. Louis vs. Boston, September 17, 1920, fourth inning.
A. L.— 8—Washington vs. Cleveland, May 7, 1951, fourth inning.
        Oakland vs. Chicago, September 27, 1981, first game, first inning.

Most One-Base Hits, Game, One Club

N. L.—28—Philadelphia vs. Louisville, August 17, 1894.
        Boston vs. Baltimore, April 20, 1896.
A. L.—24—Cleveland vs. New York, July 29, 1928.
        Boston vs. Detroit, June 18, 1953.
N. L. since 1900—23—New York vs. Chicago, September 21, 1931.

Most One-Base Hits, Game, Both Clubs

N. L.—37—Baltimore 21, Washington 16, August 8, 1896.
N. L. since 1900—36—New York 22, Cincinnati 14, June 9, 1901.
A. L.—36—Chicago 21, Boston 15, August 15, 1922.

Most Two-Base Hits, Inning, One Club

N. L.—7—Boston vs. St. Louis, August 25, 1936, first game, first inning.
A. L.—6—Washington vs. Boston, June 9, 1934, eighth inning.

Most Players, Two Two-Base Hits, Inning, Game, One Club

N. L.—3—Boston vs. St. Louis, August 25, 1936, first game, first inning.
A. L.—2—New York vs. Boston, July 3, 1932, sixth inning.
       Toronto vs. Baltimore, June 26, 1978, second inning.

Most Consecutive Two-Base Hits, Inning, Game, One Club

A. L.—5—Washington vs. Boston, June 9, 1934, eighth inning.
N. L.—4—Held by many clubs.
Last time—St. Louis vs. Pittsburgh, August 30, 1952, third inning.

Most Two-Base Hits, Game, One Club

N. L.—14—Chicago vs. Buffalo, July 3, 1883.
N. L. since 1900—13—St. Louis vs. Chicago, July 12, 1931, second game.
A. L.—11—Detroit vs. New York, July 14, 1934.

Most Two-Base Hits, Game, by Pinch-Hitters

A. L.—3—Cleveland vs. Washington, June 27, 1948, first game.
       Chicago vs. New York, May 7, 1971.
N. L.—3—San Francisco vs. Pittsburgh, May 5, 1958.

Most Two-Base Hits, Game, Both Clubs

N. L.—23—St. Louis 13, Chicago 10, July 12, 1931, second game.
A. L.—16—Cleveland 9, New York 7, July 21, 1921.

Most Two-Base Hits, Doubleheader, One Club

N. L.—17—St. Louis vs. Chicago, July 12, 1931.
A. L.—14—Philadelphia vs. Boston, July 8, 1905.

Most Two-Base Hits, Doubleheader, Both Clubs

N. L.—32—St. Louis 17, Chicago 15, July 12, 1931.
A. L.—26—Philadelphia 14, Boston 12, July 8, 1905.

Most Two-Base Hits, With Bases Filled, Game, One Club

N. L.-A. L.—2—Made in many games.

Most Two-Base Hits, With Bases Filled, Game, Both Clubs

N. L.-A. L.—2—Made in many games.

Most Three-Base Hits, Inning, One Club

A. L.—5—Chicago vs. Milwaukee, September 15, 1901, second game, eighth inning.
N. L.—4—Boston vs. Troy, May 6, 1882, eighth inning.
       Baltimore vs. St. Louis, July 27, 1892, seventh inning.
       St. Louis vs. Chicago, July 2, 1895, first inning.
       Chicago vs. St. Louis, April 17, 1899, fourth inning.
       Brooklyn vs. Pittsburgh, August 23, 1902, third inning.
       Cincinnati vs. Boston, July 22, 1926, second inning.
       New York vs. Pittsburgh, July 17, 1936, first inning.

Most Consecutive Three-Base Hits, Inning, One Club

A. L.—4—Boston vs. Detroit, May 6, 1934, fourth inning.
N. L.—3—Made in many innings. Last times—Chicago vs. Philadelphia, April 25, 1981,
fourth inning; Montreal vs. San Diego, May 6, 1981, ninth inning.

Most Three-Base Hits, Game, One Club

N. L.—9—Baltimore vs. Cleveland, September 3, 1894, first game.
N. L. since 1900—8—Pittsburgh vs. St. Louis, May 30, 1925, second game.
A. L.—6—Chicago vs. Milwaukee, September 15, 1901; second game.
    Chicago vs. New York, September 17, 1920.
    Detroit vs. New York, June 17, 1922.

Most Three-Base Hits, Game, Both Clubs

N. L.—11—Baltimore 9, Cleveland 2, September 3, 1894, first game.
N. L. since 1900—9—Pittsburgh 6, Chicago 3, July 4, 1904, p.m. game.
    Pittsburgh 8, St. Louis 1, May 30, 1925, second game.
A. L.— 9—Detroit 6, New York 3, June 17, 1922.

Longest Extra-Inning Game, Without a Three-Base Hit, One Club

N. L.—26 innings— Brooklyn vs. Boston, May 1, 1920.
A. L.—24 innings— Detroit vs. Philadelphia, July 21, 1945.
    Philadelphia vs. Detroit, July 21, 1945.

Longest Extra-Inning Game, Without a Three-Base Hit, Both Clubs

N. L.—25 innings— New York 0, St. Louis 0, September 11, 1974.
A. L.—24 innings— Detroit 0, Philadelphia 0, July 21, 1945.

Most Three-Base Hits, Doubleheader, One Club

N. L.—9—Baltimore vs. Cleveland, September 3, 1894.
    Cincinnati vs. Chicago, May 27, 1922.
A. L.—9—Chicago vs. Milwaukee, September 15, 1901.

Most Three-Base Hits, Doubleheader, Both Clubs

N. L.—11—Baltimore 9, Cleveland 2, September 3, 1894.
N. L. since 1900—10—Cincinnati 9, Chicago 1, May 27, 1922.
    New York 7, Pittsburgh 3, July 30, 1923.
A. L.—10—Chicago 9, Milwaukee 1, September 15, 1901.

Most Three-Base Hits With Bases Filled, Game, One Club

N. L.—2—Detroit vs. Indianapolis, May 7, 1887.
    Pittsburgh vs. Brooklyn, September 17, 1898.
    Chicago vs. Philadelphia, May 14, 1904.
    Brooklyn vs. St. Louis, August 25, 1917, first game.
    Cincinnati vs. Brooklyn, September 25, 1925.
    Pittsburgh vs. St. Louis, September 10, 1938.
    Chicago vs. Boston, June 12, 1936.
    Brooklyn vs. Philadelphia, May 24, 1953, both in eighth inning.
    Milwaukee vs. St. Louis, August 2, 1959, second game.
    Montreal vs. Cincinnati, September 1, 1979.
A. A.—2—Kansas City vs. Philadelphia, August 22, 1889.
A. L.—2—Boston vs. St. Louis, August 16, 1926, second game.
    Philadelphia vs. Washington, April 26, 1928.
    Philadelphia vs. Washington, May 1, 1949, first game.
    Detroit vs. New York, June 9, 1950.
    Cleveland vs. New York, July 27, 1978, second game.

Most Three-Base Hits With Bases Filled, Game, Both Clubs, Each Club Connecting

N. L.—2—Made in many games. Last time—Chicago 1, St. Louis 1, April 22, 1938.
A. L.—2—Made in many games. Last time—Washington 1, New York 1, July 4, 1950,
    first game.

NATIONAL LEAGUE

Capitalized names denote three or more home runs were consecutive.

Five Home Runs in One Inning, One Club (3 times)

Date	Inning	Club and Players
June 6, 1939	Fourth	New York (Danning, Demaree, WHITEHEAD, SALVO, MOORE).
June 2, 1949	Eighth	Philadelphia (Ennis, Seminick, Jones, Rowe, Seminick).
Aug. 23, 1961	Ninth	San Francisco (Cepeda, F. Alou, Davenport, Mays, Orsino).

Four Home Runs in One Inning, One Club (11 times)

Date		Inning	Club and Players
June 6, 1894		Third	Pittsburgh (Stenzel, Lyons, Bierbauer, Stenzel).
May 12, 1930		Seventh	Chicago (Heathcote, Wilson, Grimm, Beck).
Aug. 13, 1939	(first)	Fourth	New York (Bonura, KAMPOURIS, LOHR-MAN, MOORE).
June 6, 1948	(first)	Sixth	St. Louis (Dusak, Schoendienst, Slaughter, Jones).
May 28, 1954		Eighth	New York (Williams, Dark, Irvin, Gardner).
July 8, 1956	(first)	Fourth	New York (Mays, THOMPSON, SPENCER, WESTRUM).
June 8, 1961		Seventh	Milwaukee (MATHEWS, AARON, ADCOCK, THOMAS).
June 8, 1965		Tenth	Milwaukee (Torre, Mathews, Aaron, Oliver).
July 10, 1970		Ninth	San Diego (Murrell, Spiezio, Campbell, Gaston).
June 21, 1971	(first)	Eighth	Atlanta (Lum, King, H. Aaron, Evans).
July 30, 1978		Third	Montreal (Dawson, Parrish, Cash, Dawson).

Three Consecutive Home Runs in One Inning, One Club (43 times including four and five homer innings)

Date		Inning	Club and Players
May 10, 1894		Seventh	St. Louis (SHUGART, MILLER, PEITZ).
Aug. 13, 1932	(first)	Fourth	New York (TERRY, OTT, LINDSTROM).
June 10, 1935		Eighth	Pittsburgh (P. WANER, VAUGHAN, YOUNG).
July 9, 1938		Third	Boston (CUCCINELLO, WEST, FLETCHER).
Aug. 11, 1941		Fifth	Chicago (CAVARRETTA, HACK, NICH-OLSON).
June 11, 1944	(second)	Eighth	St. Louis (W. COOPER, KUROWSKI, LIT-WHILER).
Aug. 11, 1946	(first)	Eighth	Cincinnati (HATTON, WEST, MUELLER).
June 20, 1948	(second)	Eighth	New York (MIZE, MARSHALL, GORDON).
June 4, 1949		Sixth	New York (LOCKMAN, GORDON, MAR-SHALL).
April 19, 1952		Seventh	Brooklyn, (CAMPANELLA, PAFKO, SNIDER).
Sept. 27, 1952		Seventh	Pittsburgh (KINER, GARAGIOLA, BELL).
Sept. 4, 1953		Fourth	New York (WESTRUM, CORWIN, LOCK-MAN).
June 20, 1954		Sixth	New York (HOFMAN, WESTRUM, RHODES).
Aug. 15, 1954		Ninth	Cincinnati (BELL, KLUSZEWSKI, GREEN-GRASS).
April 16, 1955		Second	Chicago (JACKSON, BANKS, FONDY).
July 6, 1955	(first)	Sixth	Pittsburgh (LYNCH, THOMAS, LONG).
May 30, 1956	(first)	First	Milwaukee (MATHEWS, AARON, THOM-SON).
May 31, 1956		Ninth	Cincinnati (BELL, KLUSZEWSKI, ROB-INSON).
June 29, 1956		Ninth	Brooklyn (SNIDER, JACKSON, HODGES).
April 21, 1957	(first)	Third	Pittsburgh (THOMAS, SMITH, GROAT).
June 26, 1957		Fifth	Milwaukee (AARON, MATHEWS, COVING-TON).
May 7, 1958		Fifth	Pittsburgh (SKINNER, KLUSZEWSKI, THOMAS).
May 31, 1958		First	Milwaukee (AARON, MATHEWS, COVING-TON).
June 18, 1961		Third	Milwaukee (AARON, ADCOCK, THOMAS).
April 28, 1962		Sixth	New York (THOMAS, NEAL, HODGES).
Aug. 27, 1963		Third	San Francisco (MAYS, CEPEDA, F. ALOU).
July 18, 1964		Eighth	St. Louis (BOYER, WHITE, McCARVER).
Aug. 5, 1969	(first)	Fifth	San Francisco (MARSHALL, HUNT, BONDS).
May 18, 1970		Eighth	New York (MARSHALL, FOY, GROTE).
Aug. 1, 1970		Seventh	Pittsburgh (ROBERTSON, STARGELL, PAGAN).
July 16, 1974		Ninth	San Diego (COLBERT, McCOVEY, WIN-FIELD).
July 20, 1974		Fifth	New York (THEODORE, STAUB, JONES).
May 17, 1977		Fifth	Chicago (BIITTNER, MURCER, MORALES).
Sept. 30, 1977		Second	Philadelphia (LUZINSKI, HEBNER, MAD-DOX).
Aug. 14, 1978		Third	Atlanta (MATTHEWS, BURROUGHS, HORNER).

June 17, 1979	Fourth	Montreal (PEREZ, CARTER, VALENTINE).
July 11, 1979	First	San Diego (TURNER, WINFIELD, TENACE).
May 27, 1980	Third	Cincinnati (GRIFFEY, FOSTER, DRIESSEN).
July 11, 1982	Second	San Francisco (SMITH, MAY, SUMMERS).

AMERICAN LEAGUE

Capitalized names denote three or more home runs were consecutive.

Five Home Runs in One Inning, One Club

Date	Inning	Club and Players
June 9, 1966	Seventh	Minnesota (Rollins, Versalles, OLIVA, MINCHER, KILLEBREW).

Four Home Runs in One Inning, One Club (11 times)

Date	Inning	Club and Players
Sept. 24, 1940 (first)	Sixth	Boston (WILLIAMS, FOXX, CRONIN, Tabor).
June 23, 1950	Fourth	Detroit (Trout, Priddy, Wertz, Evers).
May 22, 1957	Sixth	Boston (Mauch, Williams, Gernert, Malzone).
Aug. 26, 1957	Seventh	Boston (Zauchin, Lepcio, Piersall, Malzone).
July 31, 1963 (second)	Sixth	Cleveland (HELD, RAMOS, FRANCONA, BROWN).
May 2, 1964	Eleventh	Minnesota (OLIVA, ALLISON, HALL, KILLEBREW).
May 17, 1967	Seventh	Baltimore (Etchebarren, Bowens, Powell, D. Johnson).
July 29, 1974	First	Detroit (KALINE, FREEHAN, STANLEY, Brinkman).
June 17, 1977	First	Boston (Burleson, Lynn, Fisk, Scott).
July 4, 1977	Eighth	Boston (LYNN, RICE, YASTRZEMSKI, Scott).
May 31, 1980	Fourth	Boston (Stapleton, PEREZ, FISK, HOBSON).
May 16, 1983	Ninth	Minnesota (Engle, Mitchell, Gaetti, Hatcher).

Three Consecutive Home Runs in One Inning, One Club (51 times including four and five homer innings)

Date	Inning	Club and Players
June 30, 1902 (first)	Sixth	Cleveland (LAJOIE, HICKMAN, BRADLEY).
May 2, 1922	Fourth	Philadelphia (WALKER, PERKINS, MILLER).
Sept. 10, 1925 (first)	Fourth	New York (MEUSEL, RUTH, GEHRIG).
May 4, 1929	Seventh	New York (RUTH, GEHRIG, MEUSEL).
June 18, 1930	Fifth	Philadelphia (SIMMONS, FOXX, MILLER).
July 17, 1934	Fourth	Philadelphia (JOHNSON, FOXX, HIGGINS).
June 25, 1939 (first)	Seventh	Cleveland (CHAPMAN, TROSKY, HEATH).
May 23, 1946	Fifth	New York (DiMAGGIO, ETTEN, GORDON).
April 23, 1947	Eighth	Detroit (CULLENBINE, WAKEFIELD, EVERS).
May 13, 1947	Sixth	New York (KELLER, DiMAGGIO, LINDELL).
April 19, 1948 (a.m.)	Second	Boston (SPENCE, STEPHENS, DOERR).
June 6, 1948 (second)	Sixth	Boston (WILLIAMS, SPENCE, STEPHENS).
July 28, 1950	Third	Cleveland (DOBY, ROSEN, EASTER).
Sept. 2, 1951	First	Cleveland (SIMPSON, ROSEN, EASTER).
July 16, 1953 (first)	Fifth	St. Louis (COURTNEY, KRYHOSKI, DYCK).
July 7, 1956	Seventh	Detroit (KUENN, TORGESON, MAXWELL).
Sept. 7, 1959	Second	Boston (BUDDIN, CASALE, GREEN).
April 30, 1961 (second)	Seventh	Baltimore (GENTILE, TRIANDOS, HANSEN).
May 23, 1961	Ninth	Detroit (CASH, BOROS, BROWN).
June 27, 1961	First	Washington (GREEN, TASBY, LONG).
June 17, 1962 (first)	Second	Cleveland (KINDALL, PHILLIPS, MAHONEY).
Aug. 19, 1962	Seventh	Kansas City (CIMOLI, CAUSEY, BRYAN).
Aug. 28, 1962	Fourth	Los Angeles (J. L. THOMAS, WAGNER, RODGERS).
Sept. 10, 1965	Eighth	Baltimore (ROBINSON, BLEFARY, ADAIR).
June 29, 1966	Third	New York (RICHARDSON, MANTLE, PEPITONE).
July 2, 1966	Sixth	Washington (HOWARD, LOCK, McMULLEN).
June 22, 1969 (first)	Third	Oakland (KUBIAK, JACKSON, BANDO).
Aug. 10, 1969	Sixth	New York (MURCER, MUNSON, MICHAEL).

Sept. 4, 1969	Ninth	Baltimore (F. ROBINSON, POWELL, B. C. ROBINSON).
Aug. 22, 1970	Sixth	Cleveland (SIMS, NETTLES, LEON).
April 17, 1971	Seventh	Detroit (NORTHRUP, CASH, HORTON).
June 27, 1972	First	Detroit (RODRIGUEZ, KALINE, HORTON).
July 15, 1973	Eighth	Minnesota (MITTERWALD, LIS, HOLT).
May 11, 1977	Second	California (BONDS, BAYLOR, JACKSON).
July 4, 1977	Eighth	Boston (LYNN, RICE, YASTRZEMSKI).
Aug. 13, 1977	Sixth	Boston (SCOTT, HOBSON, EVANS).
May 8, 1979	Sixth	Baltimore (MURRAY, MAY, ROENICKE).
June 3, 1980	Third	Oakland (REVERING, PAGE, ARMAS).
May 28, 1982	Sixth	Milwaukee (COOPER, MONEY, THOMAS).
June 5, 1982	Seventh	Milwaukee (YOUNT, COOPER, OGLIVIE).
June 7, 1982	Eighth	Minnesota (WASHINGTON, BRUNANSKY, HRBEK).
Sept. 12, 1982	Third	Milwaukee (COOPER, SIMMONS, OGLIVIE).
Aug. 2, 1983	Third	Seattle (S. HENDERSON, D. HENDERSON, RAMOS).
Sept. 9, 1983	First	Chicago (FISK, PACIOREK, LUZINSKI).

PLAYERS LEAGUE

Three Consecutive Home Runs in One Inning, One Club

| Date | Inning | Club and Players |
| May 31, 1890 | Eighth | New York (GORE, EWING, CONNOR). |

Most Home Runs, Inning, One Club

N. L.—5—New York vs. Cincinnati, June 6, 1939, fourth inning.
   Philadelphia vs. Cincinnati, June 2, 1949, eighth inning.
   San Francisco vs. Cincinnati, August 23, 1961, ninth inning.
A. L.—5—Minnesota vs. Kansas City, June 9, 1966, seventh inning.

Most Home Runs, Inning, Both Clubs

A. L.—5—St. Louis 3, Philadelphia 2, June 8, 1928, ninth inning.
   Detroit 4, New York 1, June 23, 1950, fourth inning.
   Minnesota 5, Kansas City 0, June 9, 1966, seventh inning.
   Baltimore 4, Boston 1, May 17, 1967, seventh inning.
   Minnesota 4, Oakland 1, May 16, 1983, ninth inning.
N. L.—5—New York 5, Cincinnati 0, June 6, 1939, fourth inning.
   Philadelphia 5, Cincinnati 0, June 2, 1949, eighth inning.
   New York 3, Boston 2, July 6, 1951, third inning.
   Cincinnati 3, Brooklyn 2, June 11, 1954, seventh inning.
   San Francisco 5, Cincinnati 0, August 23, 1961, ninth inning.
   Philadelphia 3, Chicago 2, April 17, 1964, fifth inning.
   Chicago 3, Atlanta 2, July 3, 1967, first inning.
   Pittsburgh 3, Atlanta 2, August 1, 1970, seventh inning.
   Cincinnati 3, Chicago 2, July 28, 1977, first inning.
   San Francisco 3, Atlanta 2, May 25, 1979, fourth inning.

Most Consecutive Home Runs, Inning, One Club

N. L.—4—Milwaukee vs. Cincinnati, June 8, 1961, seventh inning.
A. L.—4—Cleveland vs. Los Angeles, July 31, 1963, second game, sixth inning.
   Minnesota vs. Kansas City, May 2, 1964, eleventh inning.

Most Home Runs, Inning, One Club, None on Base

N. L.—4—New York vs. Philadelphia, August 13, 1939, first game, fourth inning.
A. L.—4—Cleveland vs. Los Angeles, July 31, 1963, second game, sixth inning (consecutive).
   Minnesota vs. Kansas City, May 2, 1964, eleventh inning (consecutive).
   Minnesota vs. Kansas City, June 9, 1966, seventh inning (also 1 home run with 1 on base).
   Boston vs. New York, June 17, 1977, first inning.
   Boston vs. Toronto, July 4, 1977, eighth inning.
   Boston vs. Milwaukee, May 31, 1980, fourth inning.

Most Home Runs, Game, One Club

A. L.—8—New York vs. Philadelphia, June 28, 1939, first game.
   Minnesota vs. Washington, August 29, 1963, first game.
   Boston vs. Toronto, July 4, 1977.
N. L.—8—Milwaukee vs. Pittsburgh, August 30, 1953, first game.
   Cincinnati vs. Milwaukee, August 18, 1956.
   San Francisco vs. Milwaukee, April 30, 1961.
   Montreal vs. Atlanta, July 30, 1978.

Most Home Runs, One Club, Opening Game of Season
A. L.—5—New York vs. Philadelphia, April 12, 1932.
      Boston vs. Washington, April 12, 1965.
N. L.—5—Chicago vs. St. Louis, April 14, 1936.
      San Francisco vs. Milwaukee, April 14, 1964.

Most Home Runs, Night Game, One Club
N. L.—8—Cincinnati vs. Milwaukee, August 18, 1956.
A. L.—7—Baltimore vs. Boston, May 17, 1967.
      Milwaukee vs. Cleveland, April 29, 1980.

Most Home Runs, Game, One Club, No Other Runs
N. L.—5—New York vs. Chicago, June 16, 1930.
      St. Louis vs. Brooklyn, September 1, 1953.
      Cincinnati vs. Milwaukee, April 16, 1955.
      Chicago vs. Pittsburgh, April 21, 1964.
      Pittsburgh vs. Los Angeles, May 7, 1973.
A. L.—5—Oakland vs. Washington, June 16, 1971.

Most Home Runs, Game, Both Clubs, No Other Runs
N. L.—5—San Francisco 3, Milwaukee 2, August 30, 1962.
A. L.—4—Cleveland 4, New York 0, August 2, 1956.
      New York 4, Baltimore 0, May 13, 1973, first game.

Most Home Runs, Inning, One Club, With Two Out
N. L.—5—New York vs. Cincinnati, June 6, 1939, fourth inning.
A. L.—3—Cleveland vs. Philadelphia, June 25, 1939, first game, seventh inning.
      New York vs. Philadelphia, June 28, 1939, first game, third inning.
      Minnesota vs. Kansas City, June 9, 1966, seventh inning.
      Washington vs. New York, July 2, 1966, sixth inning.
      Oakland vs. Minnesota, June 22, 1969, first game, third inning.

Most Home Runs, Shutout Game, One Club, No Other Runs
A. L.—4—Cleveland vs. New York, August 2, 1956.
      New York vs. Baltimore, May 13, 1973, first game.
N. L.—3—St. Louis vs. New York, July 19, 1923.
      Philadelphia vs. Cincinnati, August 27, 1951, second game.
      San Francisco vs. Milwaukee, August 14, 1964.
      Cincinnati vs. Pittsburgh, September 25, 1968.
      New York vs. Philadelphia, June 29, 1971.
      New York vs. Pittsburgh, September 17, 1971.
      New York vs. Cincinnati, August 29, 1972.

Most Home Runs, Nine-Inning Game, One Club, None on Bases
A. L.—7—Boston vs. Toronto, July 4, 1977 (8 home runs in game by Boston).
N. L.—6—New York vs. Philadelphia, August 13, 1939, first game (7 home runs in game
        by New York).
      New York vs. Cincinnati, June 24, 1950 (7 home runs in game by New York).
      Atlanta vs. Chicago, August 3, 1967 (7 home runs in game by Atlanta).
      Chicago vs. San Diego, August 19, 1970 (7 home runs in game by Chicago).

Most Home Runs, Game, Both Clubs, None on Bases, Nine-Inning Game
A. L.—7—Minnesota 6, Cleveland 1, April 29, 1962, second game.
      Chicago 5, Cleveland 2, June 18, 1974.
N. L.—7—Chicago 6, San Diego 1, August 19, 1970.
      Pittsburgh 4, Cincinnati 3, June 7, 1976.

Most Home Runs, Game, Both Clubs, Nine Innings
A. L.—11—New York 6, Detroit 5, June 23, 1950.
       Boston 6, Milwaukee 5, May 22, 1977, first game.
N. L.—11—Chicago 7, New York 4, June 11, 1967, second game.

Most Home Runs, Both Clubs, Opening Game of Season
A. L.—7—New York 5, Philadelphia 2, April 12, 1932.
      Boston 5, Washington 2, April 12, 1965.
N. L.—6—Chicago 5, St. Louis 1, April 14, 1936.

Most Home Runs, Night Game, Both Clubs, Nine Innings
A. L.—11—New York 6, Detroit 5, June 23, 1950.
N. L.—10—Cincinnati 8, Milwaukee 2, August 18, 1956.
       Cincinnati 7, Atlanta 3, April 21, 1970.

Most Home Runs, Extra-Inning Game, Both Clubs
N. L.—11—Pittsburgh 6, Cincinnati 5, August 12, 1966, 13 innings.
       Chicago 6, Cincinnati 5, July 28, 1977, 13 innings.
       Chicago 6, Philadelphia 5, May 17, 1979, 10 innings.
A. L.— 9—Washington 7, Chicago 2, May 3, 1949, 10 innings.
       Cleveland 6, New York 3, May 24, 1970, second game, 11 innings.

Most Home Runs, Game Both Clubs, First-Game Players
N. L.—2—Brooklyn 1 (Ernest Koy), Philadelphia 1 (Emmett J. Mueller), April 19, 1938 (each in first inning).

Most Players Two or More Home Runs, Nine-Inning Game, One Club
N. L.—3—Pittsburgh vs. St. Louis, August 16, 1947.
New York vs. Pittsburgh, July 8, 1956, first game.
Cincinnati vs. Milwaukee, August 18, 1956.
A. L.—3—Boston vs. St. Louis, June 8, 1950.
New York vs. Boston, May 30, 1961.

Most Players Two or More Home Runs, Extra-Inning Game, One Club
N. L.—3—Chicago vs. St. Louis, April 16, 1955, 14 innings.

Most Players Two or More Home Runs, Nine-Inning Game, Both Clubs
N. L.—4—Pittsburgh 3, St. Louis 1, August 16, 1947.
A. L.—3—Boston 3, St. Louis 0, June 8, 1950.
New York 2, Kansas City 1, July 28, 1958.
New York 3, Boston 0, May 30, 1961.
Detroit 2, California 1, July 4, 1968.
Chicago 2, Cleveland 1, June 18, 1974.

Most Players One or More Home Runs, Nine-Inning Game, One Club
A. L.—7—Baltimore vs. Boston, May 17, 1967 (7 home runs in game by Baltimore).
N. L.—7—Los Angeles vs. Cincinnati, May 25, 1979 (7 home runs in game by Los Angeles).

Most Players One or More Home Runs, Ten-Inning Game, One Club
A. L.—6—Washington vs. Chicago, May 3, 1949.
N. L.—5—New York vs. Pittsburgh, July 10, 1923.

Most Players One or More Home Runs, Game, Both Clubs
N. L.—9—New York 5, Brooklyn 4, September 2, 1939, first game.
New York 6, Pittsburgh 3, July 11, 1954, first game.
Chicago 5, Pittsburgh 4, April 21, 1964.
Cincinnati 6, Atlanta 3, April 21, 1970.
Cincinnati 5, Chicago 4, July 28, 1977, 13 innings.
A. L.—9—New York 5, Detroit 4, June 23, 1950.
Minnesota 5, Boston 4, May 25, 1965.
Baltimore 7, Boston 2, May 17, 1967.
California 5, Cleveland 4, August 30, 1970.
Boston 5, Milwaukee 4, May 22, 1977, first game.

Most Players One or More Home Runs, Ten-Inning Game, Both Clubs
A. L.—8—Washington 6, Chicago 2, May 3, 1949.
N. L.—7—Brooklyn 4, Chicago 3, April 30, 1957.

Most Home Runs, Doubleheader, One Club
A. L.—13—New York vs. Philadelphia, June 28, 1939.
N. L.—12—Milwaukee vs. Pittsburgh, August 30, 1953.

Most Home Runs, Doubleheader, Both Clubs
N. L.—15—Milwaukee 9, Chicago 6, May 30, 1956.
A. L.—14—New York 9, Philadelphia 5, May 22, 1930.

Longest Extra-Inning Game Without a Home Run, Both Clubs
N. L. 26 innings—0—Boston 0, Brooklyn 0, May 1, 1920.
A. L. 24 innings—0—Boston 0, Philadelphia 0, September 1, 1906.
Detroit 0, Philadelphia 0, July 21, 1945.

Most Home Runs, Infield, Game, One Club
N. L.—6—Milwaukee vs. Brooklyn, July 31, 1954.
Montreal vs. Atlanta, July 30, 1978.
A. L.—5—New York vs. Philadelphia, June 3, 1932.
New York vs. Philadelphia, May 24, 1936.
Cleveland vs. Philadelphia, June 18, 1941.
Boston vs. St. Louis, June 8, 1950.

Most Home Runs, Outfield, Game, One Club
N. L.—6—Cincinnati vs. Milwaukee, August 18, 1956.
San Francisco vs. Milwaukee, April 30, 1961.
A. L.—5—New York vs. Chicago, July 22, 1940, first game.
Cleveland vs. New York, July 13, 1945.
New York vs. Boston, May 30, 1961.

Most Home Runs, Start of Game, One Club
A. A.—2—Boston vs. Baltimore, June 25, 1891 (Brown, Joyce).
Philadelphia vs. Boston, August 21, 1891 (McTamany, Larkin).

A. L.—2—Chicago vs. Boston, September 2, 1937, first game (Berger, Kreevich).
        Detroit vs. Philadelphia, June 22, 1939 (McCosky, Averill).
        New York vs. Chicago, April 27, 1955 (Bauer, Carey).
        Kansas City vs. Boston, September 18, 1958 (Tuttle, Maris).
        Minnesota vs. Cleveland, May 10, 1962 (Green, Power).
        Boston vs. Minnesota, May 1, 1971 (Aparicio, Smith).
        Cleveland vs. Detroit, June 19, 1971 (Nettles, Pinson).
        Boston vs. Milwaukee, June 20, 1973, (Miller, Smith).
        Milwaukee vs. Boston, July 29, 1975, (Money, Porter).
        Boston vs. New York, June 17, 1977, (Burleson, Lynn).
        Oakland vs. Toronto, September 9, 1983 (Henderson, Davis).
N. L.—2—Boston vs. Chicago, August 6, 1937, first game (Johnson, Warstler).
        Pittsburgh vs. Boston, July 6, 1945, second game (Coscarart, Russell).
        Cincinnati vs. Pittsburgh, April 19, 1952 (Hatton, Adams).
        San Francisco vs. St. Louis, July 6, 1958 (Lockman, Kirkland).
        St. Louis vs. Los Angeles, August 17, 1958, first game (Flood, Freese).
        San Francisco vs. St. Louis, May 27, 1964, (Hiller, Snider).
        Cincinnati vs. Los Angeles, April 7, 1969 (Rose, Tolan).
        Cincinnati vs. Pittsburgh, August 17, 1969 (Rose, Tolan).
        Cincinnati vs. Houston, June 28, 1970 (Rose, Tolan).
        Pittsburgh vs. Houston, July 5, 1982 (Moreno, Ray).

Most Consecutive Games, One or More Home Runs, One Club

A. L.—25—New York, June 1, second game, through June 29, second game, 1941 (40 home runs).
N. L.—24—Brooklyn, June 18 through July 10, 1953 (39 home runs).

Most Home Runs, Two Consecutive Games, One Club

N. L.—13—San Francisco, April 29, 30, 1961.
A. L.—13—New York, June 28, 28, 1939.

Most Home Runs, 3 Consecutive Games, One Club (Connecting in Each Game)

A. L.—16—Boston, June 17 through June 19, 1977.
N. L.—14—Milwaukee, August 30, 30, September 2, 1953.
        Milwaukee, May 30, 30, 31, 1956.
        San Francisco, April 29, 30, May 2, 1961.
        Milwaukee, June 8, 9, 10, 1961.

Most Home Runs, 4 Consecutive Games, One Club (Connecting in Each Game)

A. L.—18—Boston, June 16 through June 19, 1977.
N. L.—16—Milwaukee, August 30, 30, September 2, 3, 1953.
        Milwaukee, May 28, 30, 30, 31, 1956.
        Milwaukee, June 8, 9, 10, 11, first game, 1961.

Most Home Runs, 5 Consecutive Games, One Club (Connecting in Each Game)

A. L.—21—Boston, June 14 through June 19, 1977.
N. L.—19—New York, July 7 through July 11, first game, 1954.

Most Home Runs, 6 Consecutive Games, One Club (Connecting in Each Game)

A. L.—24—Boston, June 17 through June 22, 1977.
N. L.—22—New York, July 6 through July 11, first game, 1954.

Most Home Runs, 7 Consecutive Games, One Club (Connecting in Each Game)

A. L.—26—Boston, June 16 through June 22, 1977.
N. L.—24—New York, July 5, second game through July 11, first game, 1954.

Most Home Runs, 8 Consecutive Games, One Club (Connecting in Each Game)

A. L.—29—Boston, June 14 through June 22, 1977.
N. L.—26—New York, July 5, first game through July 11, first game, 1954.

Most Home Runs, 9 Consecutive Games, One Club (Connecting in Each Game)

A. L.—30—Boston, June 14 through June 23, 1977.
        Boston, June 16 through June 24, 1977.
N. L.—27—New York, July 4, second game through July 11, first game, 1954.

Most Home Runs, 10 Consecutive Games, One Club (Connecting in Each Game)

A. L.—33—Boston, June 14 through June 24, 1977.
N. L.—28—New York, July 4, first game through July 11, first game, 1954.

Most Home Runs, 11 Consecutive Games, One Club (Connecting in Each Game)

N. L.—30—New York, June 22 through July 3, 1947.
A. L.—27—Boston, April 15 through April 27, 1969.

Most Home Runs, 12 Consecutive Games, One Club (Connecting in Each Game)

N. L.—31—New York, June 21 through July 3, 1947.
A. L.—26—New York, May 24 through June 5, first game, 1961.
          Boston, June 11 through June 22, 1963.
          Milwaukee, June 19 through July 1, 1982.
          Milwaukee, June 20 through July 2, 1982.
          Milwaukee, June 21 through July 3, 1982.

Most Home Runs, 13 Consecutive Games, One Club (Connecting in Each Game)

N. L.—33—New York, June 20 through July 3, 1947.
A. L.—30—Milwaukee, June 19 through July 2, 1982.
          Milwaukee, June 20 through July 3, 1982.

Most Home Runs, 14 Consecutive Games, One Club (Connecting in Each Game)

N. L.—34—New York, June 20 through July 4, a.m. game, 1947.
A. L.—34—Milwaukee, June 19 through July 3, 1982.

Most Home Runs, 15 Consecutive Games, One Club (Connecting in Each Game)

N. L.—35—New York, June 20 through July 4, p.m. game, 1947.
A. L.—35—Milwaukee, June 18 through July 3, 1982.

Most Home Runs, 16 Consecutive Games, One Club (Connecting in Each Game)

N. L.—37—New York, June 20 through July 5, 1947.
A. L.—31—New York, May 22 through June 7, 1961.

Most Home Runs, 17 Consecutive Games, One Club (Connecting in Each Game)

N. L.—34—Cincinnati, August 9 through August 24, 1956.
A. L.—32—New York, May 22 through June 8, first game, 1961.

Most Home Runs, 18 Consecutive Games, One Club (Connecting in Each Game)

N. L.—36—Cincinnati, August 8 through August 24, 1956.
A. L.—31—New York, June 2 through June 24, 1941.

Most Home Runs, 19 Consecutive Games, One Club (Connecting in Each Game)

N. L.—38—Cincinnati, August 7 through August 24, 1956.
A. L.—33—New York, June 1, second game, through June 24, 1941.

Most Home Runs, 20 Consecutive Games, One Club (Connecting in Each Game)

N. L.—39—Cincinnati, August 4 through August 23 (also August 6 through August 24), 1956.
A. L.—34—New York, June 1, second game, through June 25, 1941

Most Home Runs, 21 Consecutive Games, One Club (Connecting in Each Game)

N. L.—41—Cincinnati, August 4 through August 24, 1956.
A. L.—35—New York, June 1, second game, through June 26, 1941.

Most Home Runs, 22 Consecutive Games, One Club (Connecting in Each Game)

N. L.—39—Milwaukee, July 8 through July 31, 1956.
A. L.—36—New York, June 1, second game, through June 27, 1941.

Most Home Runs, 23 Consecutive Games, One Club (Connecting in Each Game)

N. L.—38—Brooklyn, June 18 through July 9, 1953.
A. L.—37—New York, June 1, second game, through June 28, 1941.

Most Home Runs, 24 Consecutive Games, One Club (Connecting in Each Game)

N. L.—39—Brooklyn, June 18 through July 10, 1953.
A. L.—38—New York, June 1, second game, through June 29, first game, 1941.

Most Home Runs, 25 Consecutive Games, One Club (Connecting in Each Game)

A. L.—40—New York, June 1, second game, through June 29, second game, 1941.
N. L.—Never accomplished.

Most Consecutive Games, Start of Season, One or More Home Runs, One Club

N. L.—13—Chicago, April 13 through May 2, second game, 1954, (28 home runs).
A. L.— 8—New York, April 12 through April 23, 1932, (20 home runs).

Most Consecutive Games, Season, Two or More Home Runs, One Club

A. L.—9—Cleveland, May 13, first game through May 21, 1962 (28 home runs).
N. L.—8—Milwaukee, July 19 through July 26, 1956, (20 home runs).

Most Home Runs With Bases Filled, Game, One Club

A. L.—2—Chicago vs. Detroit, May 1, 1901 (Hoy, MacFarland).
         Philadelphia vs. Boston, July 8, 1902 (Murphy, Davis).
         Boston vs. Chicago, May 13, 1934 (Walters, Morgan).
         New York vs. Philadelphia, May 24, 1936 (Lazzeri 2).

Boston vs. Philadelphia, July 4, 1939, second game (Tabor 2).
Boston vs. St. Louis, July 27, 1946 (York 2).
Detroit vs. Philadelphia, June 11, 1954, first game (Boone, Kaline).
Baltimore vs. New York, April 24, 1960 (Pearson, Klaus).
Boston vs. Chicago, May 10, 1960 (Wertz, Repulski).
Baltimore vs. Minnesota, May 9, 1961 (Gentile 2).
Minnesota vs. Cleveland, July 18, 1962, first inning (Allison, Killebrew).
Detroit vs. Cleveland, June 24, 1968 (Northrup 2).
Baltimore vs. Washington, June 26, 1970 (Frank Robinson 2).
Milwaukee vs. Chicago, June 17, 1973 (Porter, Lahoud).
Milwaukee vs. Boston, April 12, 1980 (Cooper, Money).
California vs. Detroit, April 27, 1983 (Lynn, Sconiers).

N. L.—2—Chicago vs. Pittsburgh, August 16, 1890, (Burns, Kittredge).
Brooklyn vs. Cincinnati, September 23, 1901 (Kelley, Sheckard).
Boston vs. Chicago, August 12, 1903, second game (Stanley, Moran).
Philadelphia vs. Boston, April 28, 1921 (Miller, Meadows).
New York vs. Philadelphia, September 5, 1924, second game (Kelly, Jackson).
Pittsburgh vs. St. Louis, June 22, 1925 (Grantham, Traynor).
St. Louis vs. Philadelphia, July 6, 1929, second game (Bottomley, Hafey).
Pittsburgh vs. Philadelphia, May 1, 1933 (Vaughan, Grace).
Boston vs. Philadelphia, April 30, 1938 (Moore, Maggert).
New York vs. Brooklyn, July 4, 1938, second game (Bartell, Mancuso).
New York vs. St. Louis, July 13, 1951 (Westrum, Williams).
Cincinnati vs. Pittsburgh, July 29, 1955 (Thurman, Burgess).
Atlanta vs. San Francisco, July 3, 1966 (Cloninger 2).
Houston vs. New York, July 30, 1969, first game (Menke, Wynn).
San Francisco vs. Montreal, April 26, 1970, first game (McCovey, Dietz).
Pittsburgh vs. Chicago, September 14, 1982 (Hebner, Madlock).

Most Home Runs With Bases Filled, Inning, One Club

A. L.—2—Minnesota vs. Cleveland, July 18, 1962, first inning (Allison, Killebrew).
Milwaukee vs. Boston, April 12, 1980, second inning (Cooper, Money).
N. L.—2—Chicago vs. Pittsburgh, August 16, 1890, fifth inning (Burns, Kittredge).
Houston vs. New York, July 30, 1969, first game, ninth inning (Menke, Wynn).

Most Home Runs With Bases Filled, Inning, Both Clubs

N. L.—2—Chicago 2, (Burns, Kittredge), Pittsburgh 0, August 16, 1890, fifth inning.
New York 1, (Irvin), Chicago 1 (Walker), May 18, 1950, sixth inning.
Houston 2 (Menke, Wynn), New York 0, July 30, 1969, first game, ninth inning.
Atlanta 1, (Evans), Cincinnati 1, (Geronimo), September 12, 1974, first game, second inning.
A. L.—2—Washington 1 (Tasby), Boston 1 (Pagliaroni), June 18, 1961, first game, ninth inning.
Minnesota 2 (Allison, Killebrew), Cleveland 0, July 18, 1962, first inning.
Milwaukee 2 (Cooper, Money), Boston 0, April 12, 1980, second inning.
Cleveland 1 (Orta), Texas 1 (Sundberg), April 14, 1980, first inning.

Most Home Runs With Bases Filled, Game, Both Clubs (Each Club Connecting)

N. L. - A. L.—2—Made in many games.
A. L.—Last time—Cleveland 1 (Orta), Texas 1 (Sundberg), April 14, 1980.
N. L.—Last time—San Francisco 1 (Martin), Cincinnati 1 (Oester), June 2, 1981.

Most Home Runs With Bases Filled, Two Consecutive Games, One Club

N. L.—3—Brooklyn, September 23 (2), September 24 (1), 1901.
Pittsburgh, June 20 (1), June 22 (2), 1925.
A. L.—3—Milwaukee, April 10 (1), April 12 (2), 1980.

Most Consecutive Games, One or More Home Runs With Bases Filled, One Club

A. L.—3—Milwaukee, April 6, 7, 8, 1978. (First three games of season.)
N. L.—2—Held by many clubs.

Most Home Runs With Bases Filled, Game, Both Clubs, by Pinch-Hitters

N. L.—2—New York, 1 (Crawford), Boston 1 (Bell), May 26, 1929.
A. L.—1—Held by many clubs.

Most Home Runs With Bases Filled, Doubleheader, One Club

N. L.-A. L.—2—Made in many doubleheaders.
N. L.—Last time—Cincinnati vs. Atlanta, September 12, 1974.
A. L.—Last time—Baltimore vs. Chicago, August 14, 1976.

Most Home Runs With Bases Filled, Doubleheader, Both Clubs

N. L.—3—Cincinnati 2, Atlanta 1, September 12, 1974.
A. L.—2—Last time—Baltimore 2, Chicago 0, August 14, 1976.

Most Home Runs, Inning, One Club, by Pinch-Hitters

N. L.—2—New York vs. St. Louis, June 20, 1954, sixth inning (Hofman, Rhodes).
San Francisco vs. Milwaukee, June 4, 1958, tenth inning (Sauer, Schmidt, consecutive).
Los Angeles vs. Chicago, August 8, 1963, fifth inning (Howard, Skowron, consecutive).
Los Angeles vs. St. Louis, July 23, 1975, ninth inning (Crawford, Lacy, consecutive).
A. L.—2—New York vs. Kansas City, July 23, 1955, ninth inning (Cerv, Howard).
Baltimore vs. Boston, August 26, 1966, ninth inning (Roznovsky, Powell, consecutive).
Seattle vs. New York, April 27, 1979, eighth inning (Stinson, Meyer).
Minnesota vs. Oakland, May 16, 1983, ninth inning (Engle, Hatcher).

Most Home Runs, Game, One Club, by Pinch-Hitters

N. L.—2—Philadelphia vs. New York, May 30, 1925, second game.
Philadelphia vs. St. Louis, June 2, 1928.
St. Louis vs. Brooklyn, July 21, 1930, first game.
St. Louis vs. Cincinnati, May 12, 1951, second game.
Chicago vs. Philadelphia, June 9, 1954, second game.
New York vs. St. Louis, June 20, 1954.
San Francisco vs. Milwaukee, June 4, 1958.
Philadelphia vs. Pittsburgh, August 13, 1958.
New York vs. Philadelphia, August 15, 1962, second game, 13 innings.
Los Angeles vs. Chicago, August 8, 1963, 10 innings.
New York vs. Philadelphia, September 17, 1963.
New York vs. San Francisco, August 4, 1966.
Montreal vs. Atlanta, July 13, 1973, first game.
Chicago vs. Pittsburgh, September 10, 1974.
Los Angeles vs. St. Louis, July 23, 1975.
Chicago vs. Houston August 23, 1975.
Los Angeles vs. Chicago, August 27, 1982.
A. L.—2—Cleveland vs. Philadelphia, May 26, 1937.
New York vs. Kansas City, July 23, 1955.
Cleveland vs. Minnesota, August 15, 1965, second game, 11 innings.
Baltimore vs. Boston, August 26, 1966, 12 innings.
Detroit vs. Boston, August 11, 1968, first game, 14 innings.
Seattle vs. New York August 2, 1969.
Minnesota vs. Detroit, July 31, 1970.
Minnesota vs. California, July 28, 1974, second game.
Seattle vs. New York, April 27, 1979.
Chicago vs. Oakland, July 6, 1980, second game.
Minnesota vs. Oakland, May 16, 1983.

Most Home Runs, Game, Both Clubs, by Pinch-Hitters

N. L.—3—Philadelphia 2, St. Louis 1, June 2, 1928.
St. Louis 2, Brooklyn 1, July 21, 1930, first game.
A. L.—2—Made in many games. Last time—Baltimore 1, Cleveland 1, September 15, 1981.

Most Home Runs, Doubleheader, One Club, by Pinch-Hitters

N. L.—3—Montreal vs. Atlanta, July 13, 1973.
A. L.—2—Made in many doubleheaders.

Most Home Runs, Doubleheader, Both Clubs, by Pinch-Hitters

N. L.—4—St. Louis 2, Brooklyn 2, July 21, 1930.
A. L.—2—Made in many doubleheaders.

Most Total Bases, Inning, One Club

N. L.—29—Chicago vs. Detroit, September 6, 1883, seventh inning.
N. L. since 1900—27—San Francisco vs. Cincinnati, August 23, 1961, ninth inning.
A. L.—25—Boston vs. Philadelphia, September 24, 1940, first game, sixth inning.

Most Total Bases, Game, One Club

A. L.—60—Boston vs. St. Louis, June 8, 1950.
N. L.—58—Montreal vs. Atlanta, July 30, 1978.

Most Total Bases, Nine-Inning Game, Both Clubs

N. L.—79—St. Louis 41, Philadelphia 38, May 11, 1923.
A. L.—77—New York 50, Philadelphia 27, June 3, 1932.

Most Total Bases, Extra-Inning Game, Both Clubs

N. L.—97—Chicago 49, Philadelphia 48, May 17, 1979, 10 innings.
A. L.—85—Cleveland 45, Philadelphia 40, July 10, 1932, 18 innings.

Most Total Bases, Doubleheader, One Club

A. L.—87—New York vs. Philadelphia, June 28, 1939.
N. L.—73—Milwaukee vs. Pittsburgh, August 30, 1953.

Most Total Bases, Doubleheader, Both Clubs

A. L.— 114— New York 73, Philadelphia 41, May 22, 1930.
N. L.— 108— St. Louis 62, Philadelphia 46, July 6, 1929.

Most Total Bases, Two Consecutive Games, One Club

A. L.— 102— Boston vs. St. Louis, June 7 (42), June 8 (60), 1950.
N. L.— 89— Pittsburgh, June 20 (46), June 22 (43), 1925.

Most Long Hits, Inning, One Club

N. L.—8—Chicago vs. Detroit, September 6, 1883, seventh inning.
N. L. since 1900—7—Boston vs. St. Louis, August 25, 1936, first game, first inning.
    Philadelphia vs. Cincinnati, June 2, 1949, eighth inning.
A. L.—7—St. Louis vs. Washington, August 7, 1922, sixth inning.
    Boston vs. Philadelphia, September 24, 1940, first game, sixth inning.
    New York vs. St. Louis, May 3, 1951, ninth inning.

Most Long Hits, Game, One Club

A. L.—17—Boston vs. St. Louis, June 8, 1950.
N. L.—16—Chicago vs. Buffalo, July 3, 1883.
N. L. since 1900—14—Pittsburgh vs. Atlanta, August 1, 1970.
    Montreal vs. Atlanta, July 30, 1978.

Most Long Hits, Game, Both Clubs

N. L.—24—St. Louis 13, Chicago 11, July 12, 1931, second game.
A. L.—19—Minnesota 12, Toronto 7, May 8, 1979.

Most Long Hits, Doubleheader, One Club

N. L.—21—Baltimore vs. Cleveland, September 3, 1894.
N. L. since 1900—18—Chicago vs. St. Louis, July 12, 1931.
A. L.—18—New York vs. Washington, July 4, 1927.
    New York vs. Philadelphia, June 28, 1939.

Most Long Hits, Doubleheader, Both Clubs

N. L.—35—Chicago 18, St. Louis 17, July 12, 1931.
A. L.—28—Boston 16, Detroit 12, May 14, 1967.

Longest Game Without a Long Hit, One Club

N. L.—26 Innings—Brooklyn vs. Boston, May 1, 1920.
A. L.—19 Innings—Detroit vs. New York, August 23, 1968, second game.

Longest Game Without a Long Hit, Both Clubs

A. L.—18 Innings—Chicago 0, New York 0, August 21, 1933.
N. L.—17 Innings—Boston 0, Chicago 0, September 21, 1901.

Longest Doubleheader Without a Long Hit, One Club

A. L.—26 Innings—Cleveland vs. Detroit, August 6, 1968.

Most Extra Bases on Long Hits, Inning, One Club

N. L.—18—Philadelphia vs. Cincinnati, June 2, 1949, eighth inning.
A. L.—17—Boston vs. Philadelphia, September 24, 1940, first game, sixth inning.

Most Extra Bases on Long Hits, Game, One Club

A. L.—32—Boston vs. St. Louis, June 8, 1950.
N. L.—30—Montreal vs. Atlanta, July 30, 1978.

Most Extra Bases on Long Hits, Game, Both Clubs

N. L.—47—Philadelphia 24, Chicago 23, May 17, 1979, 10 innings.
N. L.—40—Milwaukee 27, Brooklyn 13, July 31, 1954, nine innings.
    Chicago 26, New York 14, June 11, 1967, second game, nine innings.
A. L.—41—New York 27, Philadelphia 14, June 3, 1932.

Most Extra Bases on Long Hits, Doubleheader, One Club

A. L.—44—New York vs. Philadelphia, June 28, 1939.
N. L.—41—Milwaukee vs. Pittsburgh, August 30, 1953.

Most Extra Bases on Long Hits, Two Consecutive Games, One Club

A. L.—51—Boston vs. St. Louis, June 7 (19), 8 (32), 1950.
N. L.—44—Milwaukee vs. Brooklyn, July 31 (27), August 1 (17), 1954.

Most Runs Batted In, Inning, One Club
A. L.—17—Boston vs. Detroit, June 18, 1953, seventh inning.
N. L.—15—Chicago vs. Detroit, September 6, 1883, seventh inning.
    Brooklyn vs. Cincinnati, May 21, 1952, first inning.

Most Runs Batted In, Game, One Club
A. L.—29—Boston vs. St. Louis, June 8, 1950.
N. L.—26—New York vs. Brooklyn, April 30, 1944, first game.

Most Runs Batted In, Game, Both Clubs
N. L.—45—Philadelphia 23, Chicago 22, May 17, 1979, 10 innings.
N. L.—43—Chicago 24, Philadelphia 19, August 25, 1922, 9 innings.
A. L.—35—Boston 21, Philadelphia 14, June 29, 1950.

Most Runs Batted In, Doubleheader, One Club
A. L.—34—Boston vs. Philadelphia, July 4, 1939.
N. L.—31—St. Louis vs. Philadelphia, July 6, 1929.

Most Runs Batted In, Doubleheader, Both Clubs
A. L.—49—Boston 34, Philadelphia 15, July 4, 1939.
N. L.—45—St. Louis 31, Philadelphia 14, July 6, 1929.

Most Runs Batted In, Two Consecutive Games, One Club
A. L.—49—Boston vs. St. Louis, June 7 (20), 8 (29), 1950.
N. L.—39—Pittsburgh, June 20 (19), June 22 (20), 1925.

Longest Game, Without a Run Batted In, Both Clubs
N. L.—19 innings—0—Cincinnati 0, Brooklyn 0, September 11, 1946.
A. L.—18 innings—0—Washington 0, Detroit 0, July 16, 1909.
    Washington 0, Chicago 0, May 15, 1918.

Most Bases on Balls, Inning, One Club
A. L.—11—New York vs. Washington, September 11, 1949, first game, third inning.
N. L.— 9— Cincinnati vs. Chicago, April 24, 1957, fifth inning.

Most Consecutive Bases on Balls, Inning, One Club
A. L.—7—Chicago vs. Washington, August 28, 1909, first game, second inning.
N. L.—7—Atlanta vs. Pittsburgh, May 25, 1983, third inning.

Most Players, Two Bases on Balls, Inning, Game, One Club
A. L.—4—New York vs. Washington, September 11, 1949, first game, third inning.
N. L.—2—Made in many innings.

Most Consecutive Bases on Balls, Start of Game
N. L.—5—New York vs. Cincinnati, June 16, 1941.
A. L.—3—Made in many games.

Most Bases on Balls, Inning, One Club, Pinch-Hitters
N. L.—3—Pittsburgh vs. Philadelphia, June 3, 1911, ninth inning.
    Brooklyn vs. New York, April 22, 1922, seventh inning.
    Boston vs. Brooklyn, June 2, 1932, first game, ninth inning.
    Chicago vs. Philadelphia, July 29, 1947, seventh inning.
A. L.—3—Baltimore vs. Washington, April 22, 1955, seventh inning.
    Washington vs. Boston, May 14, 1961, second game, ninth inning, consecutive.

Most Consecutive Bases on Balls, Inning, One Club, by Pinch-Hitters
N. L.—3—Brooklyn vs. New York, April 22, 1922, seventh inning.
    Boston vs. Brooklyn, June 2, 1932, first game, ninth inning.
A. L.—3—Washington vs. Boston, May 14, 1961, second game, ninth inning.

Most Bases on Balls, Game, Nine Innings, One Club
A. A.—19—Louisville vs. Cleveland, September 21, 1887.
A. L.—18—Detroit vs. Philadelphia, May 9, 1916.
    Cleveland vs. Boston, May 20, 1948.
N. L.—17—Chicago vs. New York, May 30, 1887, a.m. game.
    Brooklyn vs. Philadelphia, August 27, 1903.
    New York vs. Brooklyn, April 30, 1944, first game.

Most Bases on Balls, Game, Nine Innings, Both Clubs
A. L.—30—Detroit 18, Philadelphia 12, May 9, 1916.
N. L.—26—Houston 13, San Francisco 13, May 4, 1975, second game.

Most Bases on Balls, Extra-Inning Game, One Club
A. L.—20—Boston vs. Detroit, September 17, 1920, 12 innings.
N. L.—16—Cincinnati vs. Atlanta, October 1, 1978, 14 innings.

Most Bases on Balls, Extra-Inning Game, Both Clubs
A. L.—28—Boston 20, Detroit 8, September 17, 1920, 12 innings.
N. L.—25—Chicago 15, Cincinnati 10, August 9, 1942, first game, 18 innings.
    San Diego 13, Chicago 12, June 17, 1974, 13 innings.

Most Bases on Balls, Doubleheader, One Club
N. L.—25—New York vs. Brooklyn, April 30, 1944.
A. L.—23—Cleveland vs. Philadelphia, June 18, 1950.

Most Bases on Balls, Doubleheader, Both Clubs
N. L.—42—Houston 21, San Francisco 21, May 4, 1975.
A. L.—32—Baltimore 18, Chicago 14, May 28, 1954.
Detroit 20, Kansas City 12, August 1, 1962.

Longest Game Without a Base on Balls, One Club
N. L.—21 innings—New York vs. Pittsburgh, July 17, 1914.
A. L.—20 innings—Philadelphia vs. Boston, July 4, 1905, p.m. game.

Longest Game Without a Base on Balls, Both Clubs
A. L.—13 innings—Washington 0, Detroit 0, July 22, 1904.
Boston 0, Philadelphia 0, September 9, 1907.
N. L.—12 innings—Chicago 0, Los Angeles 0, July 27, 1980.

Longest Doubleheader Without a Base on Balls, One Club
N. L.—27 innings—St. Louis vs. New York, July 2, 1933.
A. L.—20 innings—Detroit vs. Philadelphia, August 28, 1908.

Most Bases on Balls, Two Consecutive Games, One Club
A. L.—29—Detroit vs. Philadelphia, May 9, 10, 1916.
N. L.—25—New York vs. Brooklyn, April 30, 30, 1944.

Most Bases on Balls, Two Consecutive Games, Both Clubs
A. L.—48—Detroit 29, Philadelphia 19, May 9, 10, 1916.

Fewest Bases on Balls, Doubleheader, Both Clubs
N. L.—1—Cincinnati 1, Brooklyn 0, August 6, 1905.
Cincinnati 1, Pittsburgh 0, September 7, 1924.
Brooklyn 1, St. Louis 0, September 22, 1929.
A. L.—2—Philadelphia 2, Detroit 0, August 28, 1908, 20 innings.
Philadelphia 1, Chicago 1, July 12, 1912.
Cleveland 2, Chicago 0, September 6, 1930.

Most Bases on Balls, Game, Nine Innings, No Runs, One Club
A. L.—11—St. Louis vs. New York, August 1, 1941.
N. L.— 9—Cincinnati vs. St. Louis, September 1, 1958, first game.

Most Bases on Balls, Extra-Inning Game, No Runs, One Club
N. L.—10—Chicago vs. Cincinnati, August 19, 1965, first game, 10 innings.
A. L.—Less than nine-inning game.

Most Intentional Bases on Balls, Inning, One Club
N. L.-A. L.—3—Made in many innings.

Most Intentional Bases on Balls, Game, Nine Innings, One Club
N. L.—6—San Francisco vs. St. Louis, July 19, 1975.
A. L.—5—California vs. New York, May 10, 1967.
Washington vs. Cleveland, September 2, 1970.

Most Intentional Bases on Balls, Extra-Inning Game, One Club
N. L.—6—Houston vs. San Francisco, July 11, 1970, 14 innings.
New York vs. San Diego, August 26, 1980, 18 innings.
A. L.—5—Chicago vs. Washington, June 29, 1958, second game, 11 innings.
Minnesota vs. Milwaukee, May 12, 1972, 22-inning suspended game; completed May 13.
New York vs. California, August 29, 1978.

Most Intentional Bases on Balls, Game, Nine Innings, Both Clubs
A. L.—6—California 5, New York 1, May 10, 1967.
N. L.—6—San Francisco 6, St. Louis 0, July 19, 1975.

Most Intentional Bases on Balls, Extra-Inning Game, Both Clubs
N. L.—10—New York 6, San Diego 4, August 26, 1980, 18 innings.
A. L.— 7—Minnesota 5, Milwaukee 2, May 12, 1972, 22 innings.

Most Consecutive Strikeouts, Game, One Club
N. L.—10—San Diego vs. New York, April 22, 1970; 1 in sixth inning, 3 in seventh inning, 3 in eighth inning, 3 in ninth inning.
A. L.— 8—Boston vs. California, July 9, 1972; 2 in first inning, 3 in second inning, 3 in third inning.
Milwaukee vs. California, August 7, 1973; 1 in first inning, 3 in second inning, 3 in third inning, 1 in fourth inning.

Most Strikeouts, Start of Game, One Club (Consecutive)

N. L.—9—Cleveland vs. New York, August 28, 1884.
A. L.—6—Cleveland vs. Detroit, August 6, 1968, first game.
    California vs. Boston, May 11, 1970.
    California vs. Minnesota, September 16, 1970.
N. L. since 1900—6—Philadelphia vs. Los Angeles, May 28, 1973.
    Philadelphia vs. New York, May 1, 1980.

Most Strikeouts, Inning, One Club

A. A.—4—Pittsburgh vs. Philadelphia, September 30, 1885, seventh inning.
N. L.—4—Chicago vs. New York, October 4, 1888, fifth inning, consecutive.
    Cincinnati vs. New York, May 15, 1906, fifth inning, consecutive.
    St. Louis vs. Chicago, May 27, 1956, first game, sixth inning, consecutive.
    Milwaukee vs. Cincinnati, August 11, 1959, first game, sixth inning.
    Cincinnati vs. Los Angeles, April 12, 1962, third inning, consecutive.
    Philadelphia vs. Los Angeles, April 17, 1965, second inning, consecutive.
    Pittsburgh vs. St. Louis, June 7, 1966, fourth inning.
    Montreal vs. Chicago, July 31, 1974, first game, second inning, consecutive.
    Pittsburgh vs. Atlanta, July 29, 1977, sixth inning.
A. L.—4—Boston vs. Washington, April 15, 1911, fifth inning.
    Philadelphia vs. Cleveland, June 11, 1916, sixth inning, consecutive.
    Chicago vs. Los Angeles, May 18, 1961, seventh inning.
    Washington vs. Cleveland, September 2, 1964, seventh inning.
    California vs. Baltimore, May 29, 1970, fourth inning, consecutive.
    Seattle vs. Cleveland, July 21, 1978, fifth inning, consecutive.

Most Strikeouts, Inning, One Club, by Pinch-Hitters

A. L.—3—Philadelphia vs. Washington, September 3, 1910, eighth inning, consecutive.
    Chicago vs. Boston, June 5, 1911, ninth inning, consecutive.
    Detroit vs. Cleveland, September 19, 1945, eighth inning, consecutive.
    Philadelphia vs. Cleveland, September 9, 1952, ninth inning.
    Cleveland vs. New York, May 12, 1953, eighth inning, consecutive.
    New York vs. Philadelphia, September 24, 1954, ninth inning, consecutive.
    Detroit vs. Cleveland, August 4, 1967, eighth inning.
    California vs. Minnesota, May 17, 1971, ninth inning, consecutive.
N. L.—3—Pittsburgh vs. Cincinnati, June 5, 1953, ninth inning, consecutive.
    Cincinnati vs. Brooklyn, August 8, 1953, ninth inning.
    St. Louis vs. Cincinnati, May 10, 1961, ninth inning.
    Cincinnati vs. Houston, June 2, 1966, eighth inning, consecutive.
    Atlanta vs. Houston, June 18, 1967, eighth inning, consecutive.
    Cincinnati vs. Houston, September 27, 1969, eighth inning.
    St. Louis vs. Montreal, July 4, 1970, eighth inning.
    Philadelphia vs. Pittsburgh, July 6, 1970, ninth inning.

Most Strikeouts, Game, Nine Innings, One Club, by Pinch-Hitters

A. L.—5—Detroit vs. New York, September 8, 1979.
N. L.—4—Brooklyn vs. Philadelphia, April 27, 1950.
    Philadelphia vs. Milwaukee, September 16, 1960.
    Chicago vs. New York, September 21, 1962.
    Chicago vs. New York, May 3, 1969.
    Cincinnati vs. Houston, September 27, 1969.
    Montreal vs. Philadelphia, June 24, 1972.

Most Strikeouts, Game, Nine Innings, Both Clubs, by Pinch-Hitters

A. L.—5—New York 4, Boston 1, July 4, 1955, first game.
    Washington 4, Cleveland 1, May 1, 1957.
    Detroit 4, Cleveland 1, August 4, 1967.
N. L.—4—Made in many games. Last time—Montreal 4, Philadelphia 0, June 24, 1972.

Most Strikeouts, Game, One Club, Nine Innings

N. L.—19—Boston vs. Providence, June 7, 1884.
    New York vs. St. Louis, September 15, 1969.
    San Diego vs. New York, April 22, 1970.
U. A.—19—Boston vs. Chicago, July 7, 1884.
A. L.—19—Detroit vs. Cleveland, September 18, 1966, first nine innings of ten-inning game.
    Boston vs. California, August 12, 1974.

Most Strikeouts, Game, Both Clubs, Nine Innings

N. L.—29—Boston 19, Providence 10, June 7, 1884.
U. A.—29—Boston 19, Chicago 10, July 7, 1884.
    St. Louis 18, Boston 11, July 19, 1884.
N. L. since 1900—28—Cincinnati 15, San Diego 13, September 15, 1972.

BASEBALL RECORD BOOK

A. L.—27—Detroit 19, Cleveland 8, September 18, 1966, first nine innings of ten-inning game.
Baltimore 14, Cleveland 13, April 7, 1970.

Most Strikeouts, Doubleheader, One Club (18 Innings)

N. L.—26—Philadelphia vs. New York, September 9, 1970.
San Diego vs. New York, May 29, 1971.
San Francisco vs. Houston, September 5, 1971.
A. L.—25—Los Angeles vs. Cleveland, July 31, 1963.

Most Strikeouts, Doubleheader, One Club (More Than 18 Innings)

N. L.—31—Pittsburgh vs. Philadelphia, September 22, 1958, 23 innings.
New York vs. Philadelphia, October 2, 1965, 27 innings.
A. L.—27—Cleveland vs. Boston, August 25, 1963, 24 innings.

Most Strikeouts, Doubleheader, Both Clubs, 18 Innings

N. L.—41—Philadelphia 26, New York 15, September 9, 1970.
San Diego 26, New York 15, May 29, 1971.
Chicago 21, New York 20, September 15, 1971.
A. L.—40—Cleveland 23, Los Angeles 17, September 29, 1962.

Most Strikeouts, Doubleheader, Both Clubs (More Than 18 Innings)

N. L.—51—New York 30, Philadelphia 21, September 26, 1975, 24 innings.
A. L.—44—Cleveland 27, Boston 17, August 25, 1963, 24 innings.

Most Strikeouts, Extra-Inning Game, One Club

A. L.—26—California vs. Oakland July 9, 1971, 20 innings.
N. L.—22—New York vs. San Francisco, May 31, 1964, second game, 23 innings.
Cincinnati vs. Los Angeles, August 8, 1972, 19 innings.
A. L.—21—Baltimore vs. Washington, September 12, 1962, 16 innings.
Detroit vs. Cleveland, September 18, 1966, 10 innings.
Washington vs. Baltimore, June 4, 1967, 19 innings.

Most Strikeouts, Extra-Inning Game, Both Clubs

A. L.—43—California 26, Oakland 17, July 9, 1971, 20 innings.
N. L.—36—New York 22, San Francisco 14, May 31, 1964, second game, 23 innings.
Pittsburgh 19, Cincinnati 17, September 30, 1964, 16 innings.

Most Strikeouts, Two Consecutive Nine-Inning Games, One Club

N. L.—29—San Diego vs. New York, April 21 (10), April 22 (19), 1970.
A. L.—29—Boston vs. California, July 9, (16), vs. Oakland, July 10, (13), 1972.

Most Strikeouts, Two Consecutive (More Than 18 Innings) Games, One Club

A. L.—35—California vs. Oakland, July 9, (26) 20 innings, July 10 (9) 9 innings, 1971, (29 innings).
33—Boston vs. Cleveland, April 15 (17), 12 innings; April 16 (16), 10 innings, 1966, (22 innings).
N. L.—31—Pittsburgh vs. Philadelphia, September 22, first game, 14 innings (21), September 22, second game, 9 innings (10), 1958, 23 innings.
New York vs. Philadelphia, October 2, first game, 9 innings (10), October 2, second game, 18 innings (21), 1965, 27 innings.

Longest Extra-Inning Game Without a Strikeout, One Club

N. L.—17 innings— New York vs. Cincinnati, June 26, 1893.
Cincinnati vs. New York, August 27, 1920, first game.
A. L.—16 innings— Cleveland vs. New York, June 7, 1936.

Longest Extra-Inning Game Without a Strikeout, Both Clubs

A. L.—12 innings— Chicago 0, St. Louis 0, July 7, 1931.
N. L.—10 innings— Boston 0, New York 0, April 19, 1928.

Longest Doubleheader Without a Strikeout, One Club

N. L.—21 innings— Pittsburgh vs. Philadelphia, July 12, 1924.
A. L.—20 innings— Boston vs. St. Louis, July 28, 1917.

Fewest Strikeouts, Doubleheader, Both Clubs

A. L.—1—Cleveland 1, Boston 0, August 28, 1926.
N. L.—2—Brooklyn 2, New York 0, August 13, 1932.
Pittsburgh 2, St. Louis 0, September 6, 1948.

Most Sacrifice Hits, Inning, One Club; No Sacrifice Flies

A. L.—3—Cleveland vs. St. Louis, July 10, 1949, fifth inning.
Detroit vs. Baltimore, July 12, 1970, first game, second inning (consecutive).
Cleveland vs. Chicago, June 8, 1980, sixth inning (consecutive).

Most Sacrifice Hits, Inning, One Club; No Sacrifice Flies—Continued

N. L.—3—Chicago vs. Milwaukee, August 26, 1962, sixth inning, (consecutive).
  Philadelphia vs. Los Angeles, September 23, 1967, seventh inning, (consecutive).
  Los Angeles vs. San Francisco, May 23, 1972, sixth inning.
  Houston vs. San Diego, April 29, 1975, seventh inning.
  Houston vs. Atlanta, July 6, 1975, ninth inning.

Most Sacrifices, Game, One Club; Includes Sacrifice Flies

A. L.—8—New York vs. Boston, May 4, 1918, 2 sacrifice scoring flies.
  Chicago vs. Detroit, July 11, 1927.
  St. Louis vs. Cleveland, July 23, 1928.
  Texas vs. Chicago, August 1, 1977.
N. L.—8—Cincinnati vs. Philadelphia, May 6, 1926.

Most Sacrifices, Game, Both Clubs; Includes Sacrifice Flies

A. L.—11—Washington 7, Boston 4, September 1, 1926.
N. L.— 9—New York 5, Chicago 4, August 29, 1921.
  Cincinnati 8, Philadelphia 1, May 6, 1926.
  San Francisco 6, San Diego 3, May 23, 1970, 15 innings, (no sacrifice flies in game).

Most Sacrifices, Doubleheader, One Club; Includes Sacrifice Flies

A. L.—10—Detroit vs. Chicago, July 7, 1921.
N. L.— 9—Held by many clubs.

Most Sacrifices, Doubleheader, Both Clubs; Includes Sacrifice Flies

A. L.—13—Boston 9, Chicago 4, July 17, 1926.

Longest Extra-Inning Game Without a Sacrifice

A. L.—24 innings— Detroit vs. Philadelphia, July 21, 1945.
N. L.—23 innings— Brooklyn vs. Boston, June 27, 1939.

Longest Extra-Inning Game Without a Sacrifice, Both Clubs

N. L.—19 innings— Philadelphia 0, Cincinnati 0, September 15, 1950, second game.
A. L.—18 innings— Washington 0, St. Louis 0, June 20, 1952.

Fewest Sacrifices, Doubleheader, One Club

N. L.-A. L.—0—Made in many doubleheaders.

Longest Doubleheader Without a Sacrifice, Both Clubs

N. L.—28 innings— 0—Cincinnati 0, Philadelphia 0, September 15, 1950.
A. L.—18 innings— 0—Made in many doubleheaders.

Most Sacrifice Flies, Inning, One Club (Run Batted In)

A. L.—3—Chicago vs. Cleveland, July 1, 1962, second game, fifth inning.
N. L.—2—Made in many innings.

Most Sacrifice Flies, Game, One Club (Run Batted In)

A. L.—4—Boston vs. Detroit, May 13, 1913.
  Cleveland vs. Seattle, June 1, 1980.
  Cleveland vs. Texas, August 13, 1980.
N. L.—4—New York vs. San Francisco, July 26, 1967.
  New York vs. Philadelphia, September 23, 1972.
  St. Louis vs. Cincinnati, September 2, 1980.
  Cincinnati vs. Houston, May 5, 1982.

Most Sacrifice Flies, Game, Both Clubs (Run Batted In)

A. L.—5—Boston 3, Washington 2, August 31, 1965, second game.
  Cleveland 4, Seattle 1, June 1, 1980.
  Cleveland 4, Texas 1, August 13, 1980.
N. L.—5—St. Louis 4, Cincinnati 1, September 2, 1980.

Most Hit by Pitch, Inning, One Club

N. L.—4— Boston vs. Pittsburgh, August 19, 1893, first game, second inning.
N. L. since 1900—3—New York vs. Pittsburgh, September 25, 1905, first inning.
  Chicago vs. Boston, September 17, 1928, ninth inning.
  Philadelphia vs. Cincinnati, May 15, 1960, first game, eighth inning.
  Atlanta vs. Cincinnati, July 2, 1969, second inning.
  Cincinnati vs. Pittsburgh, May 1, 1974, first inning, consecutive.
A. L.—3—New York vs. Washington, June 20, 1913, second game, first inning.
  Cleveland vs. New York, August 25, 1921, eighth inning.
  Boston vs. New York, June 30, 1954, third inning.
  Baltimore vs. California, August 9, 1968, seventh inning.
  California vs. Chicago, September 10, 1977, first inning, consecutive.

Most Hit by Pitch, Game, One Club, Nine Innings

A. A.—6—Brooklyn vs. Baltimore, April 25, 1887.
A. L.—6—New York vs. Washington, June 20, 1913, second game.
N. L.—5—Pittsburgh vs. Cleveland, April 23, 1890.
          Washington vs. Chicago, June 13, 1893.
          Philadelphia vs. New York, April 23, 1896.
          Washington vs. Pittsburgh, May 9, 1896.
          Atlanta vs. Cincinnati, July 2, 1969.

Most Hit by Pitch, Extra-Inning Game, One Club

N. L.—6—New York vs. Chicago, June 16, 1893, 11 innings.

Most Hit by Pitch, Game, Both Clubs, Nine Innings

N. L.—8— Washington 5, Pittsburgh 3, May 9, 1896.
N. L. since 1900—7—Brooklyn 4, New York 3, July 17, 1900.
          New York 4, Boston 3, August 1, 1903, second game.
A. L.—7—Detroit 4, Washington 3, August 24, 1914, second game.
          Minnesota 4, Kansas City 3, April 13, 1971.

Most Hit by Pitch, Doubleheader, One Club

N. L.—8—New York vs. Boston, August 1, 1903.
A. L.—6—New York vs. Washington, June 20, 1913.

Most Hit by Pitch, Doubleheader, Both Clubs

N. L.—11—New York 8, Boston 3, August 1, 1903.
A. L.— 8—Detroit 5, Washington 3, August 24, 1914.

Most Grounded Into Double Play, Game, Nine Innings, One Club

A. L.—6—Washington vs. Cleveland, August 5, 1948.
          Boston vs. California, May 1, 1966, first game.
          Baltimore vs. Kansas City, May 6, 1972.
          Cleveland vs. New York, April 29, 1975.
N. L.—6—Cincinnati vs. New York, May 2, 1957.

Most Grounded Into Double Play, Game, Nine Innings, Both Clubs

A. L.—9—Boston 6, California 3, May 1, 1966, first game.
N. L.—8—Boston 5, Chicago 3, September 18, 1928.

Most Grounded Into Double Play, Extra-Inning Game, One Club

A. L.—6—Toronto vs. Minnesota, August 29, 1977, first game, 10 innings.

Most Grounded Into Double Play, Extra-Inning Game, Both Clubs

N. L.—9—Los Angeles 5, New York 4, May 24, 1973, 19 innings.

Most Times Reaching First Base on Error, Inning, One Club

N. L.—4—St. Louis vs. Pittsburgh, August 5, 1901, eighth inning.
A. L.—4—St. Louis vs. Boston, June 8, 1911, fourth inning.

Most Times Reaching First Base on Error, Game, One Club

N. L.—10—Chicago vs. Cleveland, July 24, 1882.
A. L.— 8—Detroit vs. Chicago, May 6, 1903.

Most Times Reaching First Base on Error, Game, Both Clubs

N. L.—16—Chicago 10, Cleveland 6, July 24, 1882.
A. L.—12—Detroit 8, Chicago 4, May 6, 1903.

LEAGUE BATTING

Most Games, Season, Since 1900

A. L.— (14-club league) —1135 in 1982, 1983.
A. L.— (12-club league) —973 in 1969, 1970, 1974.
A. L.— (10-club league) —814 in 1964.
A. L.— (8-club league) —631 in 1914.
N. L.— (12-club league) —974 in 1983.
N. L.— (10-club league) —813 in 1965, 1968.
N. L.— (8-club league) —625 in 1914, 1917.

Fewest Games, Season, Since 1900 (Except 1918, short season due to war)

A.L.—608 in 1933.   N. L.—608 in 1934.

Most Unplayed Games, Season, Since 1900 (Except 1918)

A.L.—19 in 1901.   N. L.—14 in 1938.

Fewest Unplayed Scheduled Games, Season, Since 1900 (Except 1918)

N. L.-A. L.—0—Made in many years.

Fewest Unplayed Games, Season, Both Leagues

0 in 1930, 1947, 1949, 1951, 1954, 1956, 1959, 1960, 1964, 1972, 1982, 1983 (12 years).

Most Postponed Games, Season

A. L.—(8-club league)—97 in 1935.
A. L.—(12-club league)—53 in 1975.
N. L.—(8-club league)—49 in 1956.
N. L.—(10-club league)—49 in 1967.
N. L.—(12-club league)—41 in 1974.

Fewest Postponed Games, Season

A.L.—23 in 1957. N. L.—26 in 1963.

Most Postponed Doubleheaders, Season

A. L.—14 in 1945.   N. L.—5 in 1959.

Fewest Postponed Doubleheaders, Season

A. L.—0 in 1914, 1957.   N. L.—0 in 1961, 1966, 1970.

Most Times Two Games in One Day, Season

A. L.—153 in 1943.   N. L.—146 in 1943.

Most Night Games, Season (Includes Twilight Games)

N. L.—(12-club league)—799 in 1983.
N. L.—(10-club league)—487 in 1968.
A. L.—(14-club league)—822 in 1982.
A. L.—(12-club league)—661 in 1976.
A. L.—(10-club league)—472 in 1965.

Most Night Games, Season, Both Leagues (Includes Twilight Games)

1432 in 1983 (14-club, A. L.; 12-club, N. L.)—633 in A. L., 799 in N. L.
1274 in 1975 (12-club leagues)—651 in A. L., 623 in N. L.
 960 in 1968 (10-club leagues)—487 in N. L., 473 in A. L.

Most At-Bats, Season, Since 1900

N. L.—(12-club league)—66,700 in 1977.
N. L.—(10-club league)—55,449 in 1962.
N. L.—(8-club league)—43,891 in 1936.
A. L.—(14-club league)—77,888 in 1980.
A. L.—(12-club league)—66,276 in 1973.
A. L.—(10-club league)—55,239 in 1962.
A. L.—(8-club league)—43,747 in 1930.

Most Players 600 or More At-Bats, Season, Since 1900

N. L.—19 in 1962.   A. L.—17 in 1962.

Most Runs, Season, Since 1900

N. L.—(12-club league)—8771 in 1970.
N. L.—(10-club league)—7278 in 1962.
N. L.—(8-club league)—7025 in 1930.
A. L.—(14-club league)—10527 in 1979.
A. L.—(12-club league)—8314 in 1973.
A. L.—(10-club league)—7342 in 1961.
A. L.—(8-club league)—7009 in 1936.

Fewest Runs, Season, Since 1900

N. L.—4136 in 1908.   A. L.—4272 in 1909.

Most Games, Season, 20 or More Runs

N. L.—32 in 1894.
N. L. since 1900—5 in 1900, 1925.
A. L.—5 in 1923.

Most Games, League, 20 or More Runs

N. L.—1876 to date—247.
N. L. since 1900 to date—83.
A. L.—1901 to date—81.

Most Innings, Season, 10 or More Runs

N. L.—12 in 1894.
N. L. since 1900—6 in 1922.
A. L.—6 in 1936, 1950, 1979.

Most Innings, League, 10 or More Runs

N. L.—1876 to date—216.

N. L. since 1900 to date—122.
A. L.—1901 to date—148.

Most Runs, League, One Day, 3 Games
A. L.—62, May 3, 1949.
N. L.—59, August 13, 1959.

Most Runs, League, One Day, 4 Games
N. L.—101, May 17, 1887
N. L. since 1900—88, April 29, 1901.
A. L.—77, July 9, 1937.

Most Runs, League, One Day, 5 Games
N. L.—105, May 20, 1897.   A. L.—97, September 9, 1937.

Most Runs, League, One Day, 6 Games
A. L.—112, July 10, 1932.   N. L.—Less than for 5 games.

Most Runs, League, One Day, 7 Games
N. L.—159—August 7, 1894.
N. L. since 1900—118, July 21, 1923.   A. L.—91, July 7, 1923.

Most Runs, League, One Day, 8 Games
N. L.—Less than for 7 games.   A. L.—99, July 5, 1937.

Most Runs, Both Leagues, One Day, 15 Games
188 on July 16, 1950; 99 in N. L. (7 games); 89 in A. L. (8 games).

Most Runs, Both Leagues, One Day, 16 Games
191 on May 30, 1950; 104 in N. L. (8 games); 87 in A. L. (8 games).

Most Runs, League, Opening Day of Season, 4 Games
N. L.—67, April 19, 1900.   A. L.—65, April 14, 1925.

Fewest Runs, League, Opening Day of Season, 4 Games
A. L.—11, April 16, 1940.   N. L.—13, April 18, 1944.

Most Players Scoring 5 or More Runs, Game, Season, Since 1900
N. L.—7 in 1930.   A. L.—5 in 1939.

Fewest Players Scoring 5 or More Runs, Game, Season, Since 1900
N. L.-A. L.—None in many seasons.

Most Players 100 or More Runs, Season, Since 1900
A. L.—24 in 1936.   N. L.—19 in 1929.

Most Hits, Season, Since 1900
N. L.—(12-club league)—17,465 in 1977.
N. L.—(10-club league)—14,453 in 1962.
N. L.—(8-club league)—13,260 in 1930.
A. L.—(14-club league)—20,958 in 1980.
A. L.—(12-club league)—17,193 in 1973.
A. L.—(10-club league)—14,068 in 1962.
A. L.—(8-club league)—12,657 in 1962.

Most Hits, League, One Day, 4 Games
A. L.—119, June 2, 1925.
N. L.—115, July 6, 1934.

Most Hits, League, One Day, 6 Games
A. L.—190, July 10, 1932.

Most Hits, League, One Day, 7 Games
N. L.—175, July 16, 1950.
A. L.—Less than for 6 games.

Most Hits, League, One Day, 8 Games
N. L.—183, July 21, 1963.
A. L.—165, May 30, 1950.

Most Hits, Both Leagues, One Day, 15 Games
337 on July 16, 1950; 175 in N. L. (7 games); 162 in A. L. (8 games).

Most Hits, Both Leagues, One Day, 16 Games
Less than for 15 games.

Fewest Hits, Season, Since 1900

N. L.—9566 in 1907.   A. L.—9719 in 1908.

Most Players 200 or More Hits, Season

N. L.—12 in 1929 and 1930.   A. L.—9 in 1936 and 1937.

Fewest Players 200 or More Hits, Season, Since 1900

N. L.—0— (26 years) 1902, 1904, 1906, 1907, 1909, 1910, 1911, 1913, 1914, 1915, 1916, 1917, 1918, 1919, 1940, 1941, 1942, 1944, 1947, 1950, 1952, 1955, 1960, 1972, 1981, 1983.

A. L.—0— (26 years) 1902, 1903, 1905, 1908, 1913, 1914, 1918, 1919, 1945, 1951, 1952, 1956, 1957, 1958, 1959, 1960, 1961, 1963, 1965, 1966, 1967, 1968, 1969, 1972, 1975, 1981.

Most Players 5 or More Hits, Game, Season, Since 1900

N. L.—27 in 1930.   A. L.—22 in 1936.

Fewest Players 5 or More Hits, Game, Season, Since 1900

N. L.—1 in 1914.   A. L.—2 in 1913, 1914, 1963.

Most One-Base Hits, Season, Since 1900

A. L.— (14-club league)—15,072 in 1980.
A. L.— (12-club league)—12,729 in 1974.
A. L.— (10-club league)— 9,878 in 1962.
A. L.— (8-club league)— 9,214 in 1921.
N. L.— (12-club league)—12,564 in 1980.
N. L.— (10-club league)—10,476 in 1922.
N. L.— (8-club league)— 9,476 in 1962.

Fewest One-Base Hits, Since 1900

N. L.—7466 in 1956.   A. L.—7573 in 1959.

Most Two-Base Hits, Season, Since 1900

A. L.— (14-club league)—3710 in 1983.
A. L.— (12-club league)—2624 in 1973.
A. L.— (8-club league)—2400 in 1936.
N. L.— (12-club league)—3033 in 1977.
N. L.— (8-club league)—2386 in 1930.

Fewest Two-Base Hits, Season, Since 1900

N. L.—1148 in 1907.   A. L.—1348 in 1910.

Most Players With 40 or More Two-Base Hits, Season, Since 1900

N. L.—12 in 1920.   A. L.—12 in 1937.

Most Three-Base Hits, Season, Since 1900

A. L.— (14-club league)—644 in 1977.
A. L.— (12-club league)—467 in 1976.
A. L.— (8-club league)—694 in 1921.
N. L.— (12-club league)—554 in 1970.
N. L.— (8-club league)—685 in 1912.

Fewest Three-Base Hits, Season, Since 1900

A. L.—267 in 1959.   N. L.—323 in 1942.

Most Players With 20 or More Three-Base Hits, Since 1900

A. L.—4 in 1912.   N. L.—3 in 1911, 1912.

Most Home Runs, Season

A. L.— (14-club league)—2080 in 1982.
A. L.— (12-club league)—1746 in 1970.
A. L.— (10-club league)—1552 in 1962.
A. L.— (8-club league)—1091 in 1959.
N. L.— (12-club league)—1683 in 1970.
N. L.— (10-club league)—1449 in 1962.
N. L.— (8-club league)—1263 in 1965.

Most Home Runs, Season, Both Leagues

(14-club A. L., 12-club N. L.)—3644 in 1977 (2013 in A. L., 1631 in N. L.)
(12-club league)—3429 in 1970 (1746 in A. L., 1683 in N. L.)
(10-club league)—3001 in 1962 (1552 in A. L., 1449 in N. L.)

Fewest Home Runs, Season, Since 1900 (154-Game Schedule)

A. L.—101 in 1907.   N. L.—126 in 1906.

Most Players Two or More Home Runs, Game, Season

N. L.— (12-club league) —98 in 1970.
N. L.— (10-club league) —82 in 1966.
N. L.— (8-club league) —84 in 1955.
A. L.— (14-club league) —117 in 1977.
A. L.— (12-club league) —93 in 1969.
A. L.— (10-club league) —98 in 1964.
A. L.— (8-club league) —62 in 1960.

Fewest Players Two or More Home Runs, Game, Season

N. L.—0 in 1907, 1918.   A. L.—0 in 1908, 1915.

Most Players Two or More Home Runs, Game, One Day

N. L.— (12-club league) —5—May 8, 1970.
N. L.— (10-club league) —5—June 5, 1966.
N. L.— (8-club league) —5—August 16, 1947; April 16, 1955.
A. L.— (14-club league) —6—August 2, 1983.
A. L.— (10-club league) —5—June 11, 1961; May 20, 1962.
A. L.— (8-club league) —4—April 30, 1933; May 30, 1956.

Most Players Two or More Home Runs, Game, One Day, Both Leagues

6 on May 30, 1956; 4 in A. L., 2 in N. L.
    May 23, 1970; 4 in N. L., 2 in A. L.
    August 2, 1983; 6 in A. L., 0 in N. L.

Most Players Three or More Home Runs, Game, Season

N. L.—7 in 1950.   A. L.—7 in 1979.

Most Players, Three or More Home Runs, Game, Season, Both Leagues

12 in 1950; 7 in N. L.; 5 in A. L.

Most Players 20 or More Home Runs, Season

A. L.— (14-club league) —35 in 1982.
A. L.— (12-club league) —25 in 1970.
A. L.— (10-club league) —25 in 1964.
A. L.— (8-club league) —18 in 1959.
N. L.— (12-club league) —29 in 1970.
N. L.— (10-club league) —25 in 1962.
N. L.— (8-club league) —23 in 1956.

Most Players 30 or More Home Runs, Season

A. L.— (14-club league) —10 in 1982.
A. L.— (12-club league) —10 in 1969.
A. L.— (10-club league) — 9 in 1964.
N. L.— (12-club league) —12 in 1970.
N. L.— (10-club league) —10 in 1965.

Most Players 40 or More Home Runs, Season

N. L.— (12-club league) —4 in 1973.
N. L.— (8-club league) —6 in 1954, 1955.
A. L.— (12-club league) —5 in 1969.
A. L.— (10-club league) —6 in 1961.
A. L.— (8-club league) —3 in 1936.

Most Players, 50 or More Home Runs, Season

A. L.—2 in 1938, 1961.   N. L.—2 in 1947.

Most Home Runs, One Day, One Game, One League

N. L.—7, August 3, 1967.

Most Home Runs, One Day, Two Games, One League

A. L.—13, June 28, 1939.   N. L.—9, September 1, 1953, May 29, 1962.

Most Home Runs, One Day, Three Games, One League

A. L.—14, May 3, 1949.   N. L.—14, August 26, 1953; May 2, 1956; August 13, 1959.

Most Home Runs, One Day, Four Games, One League

N. L.—20, April 14, 1955; April 16, 1955.   A. L.—18, June 23, 1950; July 16, 1973.

Most Home Runs, Opening Day of Season, Four Games, One League

A. L.—13, April 14, 1925.   N. L.—12, April 19, 1938.

Most Home Runs, One Day, Five Games, One League

A. L.—25, July 13, 1964.   N. L.—21, May 2, 1954.

Most Home Runs, One Day, Six Games, One League
N. L.—20, April 29, 1956; July 3, 1966.   A. L.—19, July 25, 1937; June 18, 1975.

Most Home Runs, One Day, Seven Games, One League
N. L.—30, May 8, 1970.   A. L.—27, May 28, 1961.

Most Home Runs, One Day, Eight Games, One League
N. L.—28, July 8, 1962.   A. L.—27, April 29, 1962.

Most Home Runs, One Day, One League, Nine Games
N. L.—Less than for 8 games.   A. L.—28, July 19, 1964.

Most Home Runs, One Day, One League, 10 Games
A. L.—30, June 10, 1962; June 14, 1964.   N. L.—24, June 10, 1962.

Most Home Runs, One Day, One League, 11 Games
A. L.—28, July 25, 1971.

Most Home Runs, One Day, Both Leagues, Eight Games
30, June 23, 1950; 18 in A. L. (4 games); 12 in N. L. (4 games).
June 2, 1960; 18 in A. L. (5 games); 12 in N. L. (3 games).

Most Home Runs, One Day, Both Leagues, Nine Games
31, May 6, 1950; 16 in A. L. (5 games); 15 in N. L. (4 games).

Most Home Runs, One Day, Both Leagues, 10 Games
35, July 13, 1964; 25 in A. L. (5 games); 10 in N. L. (5 games).

Most Home Runs, One Day, Both Leagues, 11 Games
39, May 28, 1961; 27 in A. L. (7 games); 12 in N. L. (4 games).

Most Home Runs, One Day, Both Leagues, 12 Games
42, May 8, 1972; 30 in N. L. (7 games); 12 in A. L. (5 games).

Most Home Runs, One Day, Both Leagues, 13 Games
Less than for 12 games.

Most Home Runs, One Day, Both Leagues, 14 Games
46, May 10, 1970; 25 in A. L. (7 games); 21 in N. L. (7 games).

Most Home Runs, One Day, Both Leagues, 15 Games
45, July 8, 1962; 28 in N. L. (8 games); 17 in A. L. (7 games).

Most Home Runs, One Day, Both Leagues, 16 Games
50, May 30, 1956; 26 in N. L. (8 games); 24 in A. L. (8 games).

Most Home Runs, One Day, Both Leagues, 17 Games
Less than for 16 games.

Most Home Runs, One Day, Both Leagues, 18 Games
Less than for 16 games.

Most Home Runs, One Day, Both Leagues, 19 Games
Less than for 16 games.

Most Home Runs, One Day, Both Leagues, 20 Games
54 on June 10, 1962; 30 in A. L. (10 games); 24 in N. L. (10 games).

Most Home Runs, One Day, by Pitchers
A. L.—4—July 31, 1935
N. L.—3—June 3, 1892; May 13, 1942; July 2, 1961; June 23, 1971.

Most Home Runs, One Day, by Pinch-Hitters
N. L.—4—June 2, 1928; July 21, 1930.
A. L.—3—May 26, 1937; August 13, 1947; August 2, 1961; July 6, 1962; May 6, 1964; August 26, 1966; August 11, 1968; August 3, 1969, June 7, 1970; September 25, 1970, July 6, 1980.

Most Home Runs, Season, by Pinch-Hitters
N. L.—(12-club league)—55 in 1983.
N. L.—(10-club league)—45 in 1962.
N. L.—(8-club league)—42 in 1958.
A. L.—(14-club league)—53 in 1980.
A. L.—(12-club league)—49 in 1970.
A. L.—(10-club league)—50 in 1961.
A. L.—(8-club league)—29 in 1953.

Most Home Runs, Season, by Pinch-Hitters, Both Leagues

96 in 1977 (14-club A. L., 12-club N. L.) —49 in N. L., 47 in A. L.
95 in 1970 (12-club leagues) —49 in A. L., 46 in N. L.
84 in 1962 (10-club leagues) —45 in N. L., 39 in A. L.

Most Home Runs With Bases Filled, Season

A. L.— (14-club league) —50 in 1979.
A. L.— (12-club league) —39 in 1970.
A. L.— (10-club league) —48 in 1961.
A. L.— (8-club league) —37 in 1938.
N. L.— (12-club league) —49 in 1970, 1977.
N. L.— (10-club league) —37 in 1962.
N. L.— (8-club league) —35 in 1950.

Most Home Runs With Bases Filled, Season, Both Leagues

88 in 1970— (12-club league) —49 in N. L.; 39 in A. L.
77 in 1961— (10-club league in A. L., 8-club league in N. L.) —48 in A. L.;
    29 in N. L.

Fewest Home Runs With Bases Filled, Season

A. L.—0 in 1918 (Short season due to war).
N. L.—1 in 1920.
A. L.—1 in 1907, 1909, 1915.

Fewest Home Runs With Bases Filled, Season, Both Leagues

3—1907 (2 in N. L., 1 in A. L.).

Most Home Runs With Bases Filled, Season, by Pinch-Hitters

A. L.— (14-club league) —5 in 1982.
A. L.— (12-club league) —3 in 1970, 1971, 1973.
A. L.— (10-club league) —7 in 1961.
A. L.— (8-club league) —5 in 1953.
N. L.— (12-club league) —9 in 1978.
N. L.— (8-club league) —4 in 1959.

Most Home Runs With Bases Filled, Season, by Pinch-Hitters, Both Leagues

(14-club A. L.—12-club N. L.) —13 in 1978 (9 in N. L.; 4 in A. L.).
(12-club leagues) —9 in 1973 (6 in N. L.; 3 in A. L.).
(8-club leagues) —8 in 1953 (5 in A. L.; 3 in N. L.).

Most Home Runs With Bases Filled, One Day

N. L.—3—May 20, 1927; May 26, 1929; September 18, 1949; June 1, 1950; August 13, 1959;
    July 3, 1966; April 26, 1970; June 20, 1971; September 12, 1974.
A. L.—3—May 13, 1934; July 31, 1941; July 5, 1954; July 27, 1959; April 24, 1960; May 10,
    1960; August 19, 1962; August 3, 1969; June 15, 1970; June 24, 1974; September 19, 1982.

Most Home Runs With Bases Filled, One Day, Both Leagues

4—September 18, 1949 (3 in N. L.; 1 in A. L.).
    April 24, 1960 (3 in A. L.; 1 in N. L.).
    August 22, 1963 (2 in A. L.; 2 in N. L.).
    May 10, 1969 (2 in N. L.; 2 in A. L.).
    August 3, 1969 (3 in A. L.; 1 in N. L.).
    June 20, 1971 (3 in N. L.; 1 in A. L.).
    June 24, 1974 (3 in A. L.; 1 in N. L.).
    September 8, 1974 (2 in A. L.; 2 in N. L.).

Most Times 3 or More Home Runs, Inning, Club, Season

N. L.— (12-club league) —10 in 1970.
N. L.— (8-club league) —13 in 1954, 1955.
A. L.— (14-club league) —11 in 1982.
A. L.— (12-club league) — 7 in 1966, 1973, 1974.
A. L.— (10-club league) —10 in 1961, 1962.
A. L.— (8-club league) — 5 in 1936, 1947, 1953, 1954, 1956, 1957, 1959.

Most Clubs 100 or More Home Runs, Season

A. L.— (14-club league) —14 in 1977, 1982.
A. L.— (12-club league) —11 in 1970, 1973.
A. L.— (10-club league) —10 in 1964.
A. L.— (8-club league) — 8 in 1958, 1960.
N. L.— (12-club league) —11 in 1970.
N. L.— (10-club league) —10 in 1962.
N. L.— (8-club league) — 8 in 1956, 1958, 1959, 1961.

Most Players Hitting Home Runs, All Parks, 8-Club League, Season

N. L.—11 in 1956 (8 parks, excluding Jersey City; 5 of 11 connected there).
A. L.— 7 in 1953 (8 parks).

Most Players Hitting Home Runs, All Parks, 10-Club League, Season
> A. L.—4 in 1962.
> N. L.—3 in 1963.

Most Players Hitting Home Runs, All Parks, 12-Club League, Season
> N. L.—3 in 1970.
> A. L.—1 in 1975.

Most Times 5 or More Home Runs, Game, Club, Season
> N. L.— (8-club league) —15 in 1954.
> N. L.— (12-club league) —10 in 1970.
> N. L.— (10-club league) — 8 in 1966.
> A. L.— (14-club league) — 9 in 1982.
> A. L.— (8-club league) — 8 in 1950.
> A. L.— (10-club league) — 7 in 1966.
> A. L.— (12-club league) — 8 in 1969.

Most Total Bases, Season, Since 1900
> A. L.— (14-club league) —31,337 in 1982.
> A. L.— (12-club league) —25,281 in 1973.
> A. L.— (10-club league) —21,762 in 1962.
> A. L.— (8-club league) —18,427 in 1936.
> N. L.— (12-club league) —26,443 in 1977.
> N. L.— (10-club league) —21,781 in 1962.
> N. L.— (8-club league) —19,572 in 1930.

Most Players 300 or More Total Bases, Season, Since 1900
> N. L.—14 in 1930.   A. L.—12 in 1930, 1937.

Most Players 400 or More Total Bases, Season
> N. L.—3 in 1930.   A. L.—2 in 1927, 1936.

Most Long Hits, Season, Since 1900
> A. L.— (14-club league) —6163 in 1983.
> A. L.— (12-club league) —4611 in 1970.
> A. L.— (10-club league) —4190 in 1962.
> A. L.— (8-club league) —3706 in 1936.
> N. L.— (12-club league) —5190 in 1977.
> N. L.— (10-club league) —3977 in 1962.
> N. L.— (8-club league) —3903 in 1930.

Most Extra Bases on Long Hits, Season, Since 1900
> A. L.— (14-club league) —10,771 in 1982.
> A. L.— (12-club league) —8476 in 1970.
> A. L.— (10-club league) —7694 in 1962.
> A. L.— (8-club league) —5842 in 1940.
> N. L.— (12-club league) —8978 in 1977.
> N. L.— (10-club league) —7328 in 1962.
> N. L.— (8-club league) —6312 in 1930.

Most Runs Batted In, Season
> A. L.— (14-club league) —9908 in 1979.
> A. L.— (12-club league) —7769 in 1973.
> A. L.— (10-club league) —6842 in 1961.
> A. L.— (8-club league) —6520 in 1936.
> N. L.— (12-club league) —8173 in 1970.
> N. L.— (10-club league) —6760 in 1962.
> N. L.— (8-club league) —6582 in 1930.

Most Players 100 or More Runs Batted In, Season
> A. L.—18 in 1936.   N. L.—17 in 1930.

Most Sacrifices, Season, Including Scoring Flies, Since 1900
> A. L.—1731 in 1917.   N. L.—1655 in 1908.

Most Sacrifices, Season, No Sacrifice Flies
> A. L.—1349 in 1906.   N. L.—1349 in 1907.

Fewest Sacrifices, Season, No Sacrifice Flies
> N. L.—510 in 1957.   A. L.—531 in 1958.

Most Sacrifice Flies, Season
> A. L.— (14-club league) —765 in 1979.
> A. L.— (12-club league) —624 in 1976.
> A. L.— (10-club league) —448 in 1961.
> A. L.— (8-club league) —370 in 1954.

N. L.—(12-club league)—580 in 1982.
N. L.—(10-club league)—410 in 1962.
N. L.—(8-club league)—425 in 1954.

Fewest Sacrifice Flies, Season

N. L.—(12-club league)—430 in 1969.
N. L.—(10-club league)—363 in 1966.
N. L.—(8-club league)—304 in 1959.
A. L.—(12-club league)—484 in 1969.
A. L.—(10-club league)—348 in 1967.
A. L.—(8-club league)—312 in 1959.

Most Stolen Bases, Season, Since 1900

N. L.—(12-club league)—1839 in 1980.
N. L.—(8-club league)—1691 in 1911.
A. L.—(14-club league)—1533 in 1983.
A. L.—(12-club league)—1690 in 1976.
A. L.—(8-club league)—1810 in 1912.

Fewest Stolen Bases, Season, Since 1900

A. L.—(8-club league)—278 in 1950.
A. L.—(12-club league)—863 in 1970.
N. L.—(8-club league)—337 in 1954.
N. L.—(12-club league)—817 in 1969.

Most Caught Stealing, Season

A. L.—(14-club league)—936 in 1977.
A. L.—(12-club league)—867 in 1976.
A. L.—(10-club league)—471 in 1968.
A. L.—(8-club league)—707 in 1920.
N. L.—(12-club league)—870 in 1983.
N. L.—(10-club league)—494 in 1966.
N. L.—(8-club league)—517 in 1925.

Fewest Caught Stealing, Season

N. L.—(12-club league)—492 in 1971.
N. L.—(10-club league)—409 in 1962.
N. L.—(8-club league)—218 in 1953.
A. L.—(12-club league)—539 in 1972.
A. L.—(10-club league)—270 in 1963.
A. L.—(8-club league)—231 in 1950.

Most Bases on Balls, Since 1900

A. L.—(14-club league)—7413 in 1979.
A. L.—(12-club league)—7032 in 1969.
A. L.—(10-club league)—5902 in 1961.
A. L.—(8-club league)—5627 in 1949.
N. L.—(12-club league)—6919 in 1970.
N. L.—(10-club league)—5265 in 1962.
N. L.—(8-club league)—4537 in 1950.

Fewest Bases on Balls, Season, Since 1900

A. L.—(12-club league)—6128 in 1976.
A. L.—(8-club league)—3797 in 1922.
N. L.—(12-club league)—5964 in 1982.
N. L.—(8-club league)—2906 in 1921.

Most Intentional Bases on Balls, Season

N. L.—(12-club league)—862 in 1973.
A. L.—(12-club league)—668 in 1969.

Fewest Intentional Bases on Balls, Season

A. L.—(12-club league)—471 in 1976.
N. L.—(12-club league)—685 in 1976.

Most Players 100 or More Bases on Balls, Season

A. L.—(12-club league)—7 in 1970.
N. L.—(12-club league)—5 in 1970.
A. L.—8 in 1949.   N. L.—4 in 1949, 1951.

Most Strikeouts, Season, Since 1900

N. L.—(12-club league)—11,628 in 1969.
N. L.—(10-club league)—9649 in 1965.
N. L.—(8-club league)—6824 in 1960.
A. L.—(14-club league)—11,234 in 1977.

Most Strikeouts, Season, Since 1900—Continued

A. L.—(12-club league)—10,957 in 1970.
A. L.—(10-club league)—9956 in 1964.
A. L.—(8-club league)—6081 in 1959.

Fewest Strikeouts, Season, Since 1900

A. L.—(8-club league)—3245 in 1924.
N. L.—(8-club league)—3359 in 1926.
A. L.—(12-club league)—9143 in 1976.
N. L.—(12-club league)—9602 in 1976.

Most Players 100 or More Strikeouts, Season

N. L.—(12-club league)—16 in 1970.
N. L.—(10-club league)—17 in 1965.
N. L.—(8-club league)— 4 in 1960.
A. L.—(14-club league)—15 in 1977.
A. L.—(12-club league)—11 in 1970.
A. L.—(10-club league)—15 in 1967.
A. L.—(8-club league)— 3 in 1958, 1959, 1960.

Most Hit by Pitch, Season

A. L.—(14-club league)—461 in 1977.
A. L.—(12-club league)—439 in 1969.
A. L.—(8-club league)—464 in 1911.
N. L.—(12-club league)—443 in 1969.
N. L.—(8-club league)—415 in 1903.

Fewest Hit by Pitch, Season

A. L.—(14-club league)—372 in 1982.
N. L.—(12-club league)—292 in 1983.
A. L.—(12-club league)—374 in 1976.
A. L.—(8-club league)—132 in 1947.
N. L.—(8-club league)—157 in 1943.

Most Grounded Into Double Play, Season

A. L.—(14-club league)—1968 in 1980.
A. L.—(12-club league)—1608 in 1973.
A. L.—(10-club league)—1256 in 1961.
A. L.—(8-club league)—1181 in 1950.
N. L.—(12-club league)—1547 in 1971.
N. L.—(10-club league)—1251 in 1962.
N. L.—(8-club league)—1047 in 1958.

Fewest Grounded Into Double Play, Season

N. L.—(8-club league)— 820 in 1945.
N. L.—(12-club league)—1350 in 1982.
A. L.—(12-club league)—1440 in 1976.
A. L.—(8-club league)— 890 in 1945.

Highest Batting Average, Season, Since 1900

N. L.—.303 in 1930.   A. L.—.29244 in 1921.

Lowest Batting Average, Season, Since 1900

A. L.—.23011 in 1968.   N. L.—.23895 in 1908.

Most .300 Batsmen, Season, Qualifiers For the Batting Championship

N. L.—33 in 1930.   A. L.—26 in 1924.

Fewest .300 Batsmen, Season, Qualifiers For the Batting Championship

A. L.—1 in 1968.   N. L.—4 in 1907.

Most .400 Batsmen, Season, Qualifiers For the Batting Championship

N. L.—3 in 1894.   A. L.—2 in 1911, 1922.
N. L. Since 1900—1 in 1922, 1924, 1925, 1930.

Most Clubs Batting .300 or Over, Season, Since 1900

N. L.—6 in 1930.   A. L.—4 in 1921.

Highest Slugging Average, Season, Since 1900

N. L.—.448 in 1930.   A. L.—.421 in 1930, 1936.

Lowest Slugging Average, Season, Since 1900

N. L.—.306 in 1908.   A. L.—.312 in 1910.

Most Left on Bases, Season, Since 1900
    A. L.—(14-club league) —15,954 in 1980.
    A. L.—(12-club league) —13,925 in 1973.
    A. L.—(10-club league) —11,680 in 1961.
    A. L.—(8-club league) — 9,628 in 1936.
    N. L.—(12-club league) —14,468 in 1975.
    N. L.—(10-club league) —11,416 in 1962.
    N. L.—(8-club league) — 9,424 in 1945.

Fewest Left on Bases, Season, Since 1900
    A. L.—(12-club league) —13,494 in 1976.
    A. L.—(10-club league) —10,668 in 1966.
    A. L.—(8-club league) — 8,619 in 1958.
    N. L.—(12-club league) —13,525 in 1982.
    N. L.—(10-club league) —10,994 in 1966.
    N. L.—(8-club league) — 8,254 in 1920.

Most Players, Season, Since 1900
    A. L.—(14-club league) —515 in 1982.
    A. L.—(12-club league) —440 in 1969.
    A. L.—(10-club league) —369 in 1962.
    A. L.—(8-club league) —323 in 1955.
    N. L.—(12-club league) —461 in 1983.
    N. L.—(10-club league) —373 in 1967.
    N. L.—(8-club league) —333 in 1946.

Fewest Players, Season, Since 1900
    A. L.—(12-club league) —412 in 1976.
    A. L.—(8-club league) —166 in 1904.
    N. L.—(12-club league) —420 in 1979.
    N. L.—(8-club league) —188 in 1905.

Most Players in 150 or More Games, Season, Since 1900
    N. L.—(12-club league) —40 in 1978, 1979.
    N. L.—(10-club league) —34 in 1965.
    N. L.—(8-club league) —23 in 1953.
    A. L.—(14-club league) —42 in 1977.
    A. L.—(12-club league) —32 in 1976.
    A. L.—(10-club league) —30 in 1962.
    A. L.—(8-club league) —19 in 1921, 1936.

Most Players Playing All Games, Season, Since 1900
    N. L.—10 in 1932.   A. L.—10 in 1933.

Fewest Players Playing All Games, Season
    A. L.—0—1910, 1963.
    N. L.—0—1914.

Most Players With Two or More Clubs, Season, Since 1900
    A. L.—47 in 1952.   N. L.—31 in 1919.

Fewest Players With Two or More Clubs, Since 1900
    A. L.—2 in 1940.   N. L.—5 in 1935.

Most Players With Three or More Clubs, Season, Since 1900
    A. L.—4 in 1952.   N. L.—3 in 1919.

Most Times Players Used as Pinch-Hitters, Season
    A. L.— (12-club league) —2993 in 1970.
    A. L.— (10-club league) —2403 in 1967.
    A. L.—(8-club league) —1950 in 1960.
    N. L.—(12-club league) —3071 in 1975.
    N. L.—(10-club league) —2448 in 1965.
    N. L.—(8-club league) —1911 in 1960.

Most Times Players Used as Pinch-Hitters, Season, Both Leagues
    5804 in 1970— (12-club leagues) —2993 in A. L., 2811 in N. L.
    4723 in 1967— (10-club leagues) —2403 in A. L., 2320 in N. L.
    3861 in 1960—(8-club leagues) —1950 in A. L., 1911 in N. L.

Most Managers, Season, Since 1900
    A. L.— (14-club league) —19 in 1977, 1981.
    A. L.— (12-club league) —16 in 1969, 1975.
    A. L.— (10-club league) —15 in 1966.
    A. L.—(8-club league) —12 in 1933, 1946.

Most Managers, Season, Since 1900—Continued

N. L.— (12-club league) —16 in 1972 (Leo E. Durocher, Chicago, Houston, counted as one).
N. L.— (10-club league) —12 in 1965, 1966, 1967, 1968.
N. L.— (8-club league) —12 in 1902, 1948 (Leo E. Durocher, Brooklyn, New York, counted as one in 1948).

Most Playing Managers, Season, Both Leagues

10 in 1934 (8-club leagues) —6 in N. L., 4 in A. L.

Most Managerial Changes, Start of Season

A. L.— (8-club league) —6 in 1955.   N. L.— (8-club league) —4 in 1909, 1913.

Most Tie Games, Season

A. L.—19 in 1910.   N. L.—16 in 1913.

Most Tie Games, One Day

N. L.—3, April 26, 1897.   A. L.—2, made on many days.

Fewest Tie Games, Season

N. L.—0 in 1925, 1954, 1958, 1970, 1976, 1977, 1978, 1982.
A. L.—0 in 1930, 1963, 1965, 1971, 1972, 1973, 1975, 1976, 1977, 1978, 1979.

Most 0-0 Games, Season

A. L.—6 in 1904.   N. L.—3 in 1917.

Most No-Hit Games, Season, Major Leagues

8 in 1884, 4 in A. A., 2 in N. L., 2 in U. A.
Since 1900—7 in 1917, 5 in A. L., 2 in N. L.

Most No-Hit Games, Season

A. A.—4 in 1884, 1888.   A. L.—5 in 1917.   N. L.—5 in 1969.

Fewest No-Hit Games, Season

N. L.—0—Made in many seasons—Last season—1982.
A. L.—0—Made in many seasons—Last season—1982.

Most No-Hit Games, One Day

N. L.—2, April 22, 1898.   A. L.—1, made on many days.

Most One-Hit Games, Season, Nine or More Innings

N. L.— (12-club league) —12 in 1971.
N. L.— (10-club league) —13 in 1965.
N. L.— (8-club league) —12 in 1906, 1910.
A. L.— (14-club league) —13 in 1979.
A. L.— (12-club league) —11 in 1973.
A. L.— (10-club league) —11 in 1968.
A. L.— (8-club league) —12 in 1910, 1915.

Fewest One-Hit Games, Season, Nine or More Innings

A. L.—0 in 1922, 1927, 1930.   N. L.—0 in 1924, 1929, 1932, 1952.

Most Shutouts, Season

A. L.— (14-club league) —161 in 1978.
A. L.— (12-club league) —193 in 1972.
A. L.— (10-club league) —154 in 1968.
A. L.— (8-club league) —146 in 1909.
N. L.— (12-club league) —166 in 1969.
N. L.— (10-club league) —185 in 1968.
N. L.— (8-club league) —164 in 1908.

Most Extra-Inning Shutouts, Season

A. L.— (12-club league) —12 in 1976.
A. L.— (10-club league) —10 in 1968.
A. L.— (8-club league) —12 in 1918.
N. L.— (12-club league) —12 in 1976.
N. L.— (10-club league) —11 in 1965.
N. L.— (8-club league) — 8 in 1908, 1909, 1910.

Fewest Shutouts, Season

A. L.— (14-club league) —116 in 1979.
A. L.— (12-club league) —110 in 1970.
A. L.— (8-club league) — 41 in 1930.
N. L.— (12-club league) —115 in 1983.
N. L.— (8-club league) — 48 in 1925.

Most Shutouts, One Day

N. L.—5—July 13, 1888 (6 games); June 24, 1892 (8 games); July 21, 1896 (7 games);
July 8, 1907 (5 games); September 7, 1908 (8 games); September 9,1916 (7
games); May 31, 1943 (8 games); June 17, 1969 (9 games).
A. L.—5—September 7, 1903 (8 games); August 5, 1909 (6 games); May 6, 1945 (8
games); June 4, 1972 (9 games).

Most Shutouts, One Day, Both Leagues

8—June 4, 1972, 5 in A. L. (9 games), 3 in N. L. (7 games).
7—September 7, 1908, 5 in N. L. (8 games); 2 in A. L. (8 games). August 23, 1942, 4 in
A. L. (8 games); 3 in N. L. (8 games). May 14, 1944, 4 in N. L. (8 games); 3 in A.L. (8
games). May 24, 1964, 4 in N. L. (8 games); 3 in A. L. (9 games). August 26, 1968, 4
in N. L. (8 games); 3 in A. L. (5 games).

Most 1-0 Games, Season

N. L.— (12-club league)—38 in 1976.
N. L.— (10-club league)—44 in 1968.
N. L.—(8-club league)—43 in 1907.
A. L.—(14-club league)—26 in 1980.
A. L.—(12-club league)—42 in 1971.
A. L.—(10-club league)—38 in 1968.
A. L.—(8-club league)—41 in 1908.

Fewest 1-0 Games, Season

A. L.—(14-club league)—12 in 1982.
A. L.—(12-club league)—15 in 1970.
A. L.—(8-club league)— 4 in 1930, 1936.
N. L.—(12-club league)—13 in 1983.
N. L.—(8-club league)— 5 in 1932, 1956.

Most 1-0 Games, One Day

A. L.—3, May 14, 1914. N. L.—3, July 4, 1918; July 17, 1962; September 12, 1969; September 1, 1976.

Most Extra-Inning Games, Season

A. L.— (14-club league)—107 in 1977, 1980.
A. L.— (12-club league)—116 in 1976.
A. L.— (10-club league)— 91 in 1965.
A. L.—(8-club league)— 91 in 1943.
N. L.— (12-club league)—109 in 1982.
N. L.— (10-club league)— 93 in 1967.
N. L.—(8-club league)— 86 in 1916.

Most Extra-Inning Games, One Day

N. L.—5—May 30, 1892.
N. L. since 1900—4—May 12, 1963; May 29, 1966.
A. L.—4—June 11, 1969; June 4, 1976.

Most Extra-Inning Games, One Day, Both Leagues

6 on August 22, 1951; 3 in N. L. (5 games), 3 in A. L. (5 games).
6 on May 12, 1963; 4 in N. L. (8 games), 2 in A. L. (7 games).

Most Games Won by One Run, Season

A. L.— (14-club league)—368 in 1978.
A. L.— (12-club league)—332 in 1969.
A. L.— (10-club league)—281 in 1967, 1968.
A. L.—(8-club league)—217 in 1943.
N. L.— (12-club league)—344 in 1980.
N. L.— (10-club league)—294 in 1968.
N. L.—(8-club league)—223 in 1946.

Fewest Games Won by One Run, Season

A. L.— (14-club league)—318 in 1983.
A. L.— (12-club league)—279 in 1973.
A. L.—(8-club league)—157 in 1938.
N. L.— (12-club league)—294 in 1970.
N. L.—(8-club league)—170 in 1949.

Most Games Won by One Run, One Day

A. L.—6—May 30, 1967, (10 games); August 22, 1967, (9 games).
N. L.—6—June 6, 1967 (7 games), June 8, 1969 (6 games).

Most Games Won by One Run, One Day Both Leagues

10 on May 30, 1967. A. L. 6 (10 games), N. L. 4 (7 games).

Most Games Won by Home Clubs, One Day, League
N. L.-A. L.— (8-club leagues)—8—on many days.

Most Games Won by Home Clubs, One Day, Both Leagues
14 on May 30, 1903 (A. L. won 8, lost 0; N. L. won 6, lost 2).

Most Games Won by Home Clubs, Season
A. L.— (14-club league)—649 in 1978 (lost 482).
A. L.— (12-club league)—540 in 1969 (lost 431).
A. L.— (10-club league)—454 in 1961 (lost 353).
A. L.— (8-club league)—360 in 1945 (lost 244) and 1949 (lost 256).
N. L.— (12-club league)—556 in 1978 (lost 415) and 1980 (lost 416).
N. L.— (10-club league)—464 in 1967 (lost 345).
N. L.— (8-club league)—358 in 1931 (lost 256) and 1955 (lost 257).

Most Games Won by Visiting Clubs, One Day, League
N. L.-A. L.— (8-club leagues)—8—on many days.

Most Games Won by Visiting Clubs, One Day, Both Leagues
(8-club leagues)
12 on July 4, 1935 (N. L. won 7, lost 1; A. L. won 5, lost 3).
12 on August 5, 1951 (N. L. won 7, lost 0; A. L. won 5, lost 2).
12 on June 15, 1958 (A. L. won 8, lost 0; N. L. won 4, lost 1).

Most Games Won by Visiting Clubs, Season
N. L.— (12-club league)—473 in 1982 (lost 499).
                        462 in 1973 (lost 508).
N. L.— (10-club league)—400 in 1968 (lost 410).
N. L.— (8-club league)—307 in 1948 (lost 308).
A. L.— (14-club league)—547 in 1980 (lost 582).
A. L.— (12-club league)—469 in 1971 (lost 497).
A. L.— (10-club league)—391 in 1968 (lost 418).
A. L.— (8-club league)—312 in 1953 (lost 301).

Most Clubs Winning 100 or More Games, Season
A. L.— (14-club league)—2 in 1977, 1980.
A. L.— (12-club league)—2 in 1971.
A. L.— (10-club league)—2 in 1961.
A. L.— (8-club league)—2 in 1915, 1954.
N. L.— (12-club league)—2 in 1976.
N. L.— (10-club league)—2 in 1962.
N. L.— (8-club league)—2 in 1909, 1942.

Most Clubs Winning 90 or More Games, Season
N. L.— (12-club league)—4 in 1969, 1976, 1980.
N. L.— (10-club league)—4 in 1962, 1964.
N. L.— (8-club league)—3 in many seasons.
A. L.— (14-club league)—6 in 1977.
A. L.— (12-club league)—4 in 1975.
A. L.— (10-club league)—3 in 1961, 1963, 1964, 1965, 1967.
A. L.— (8-club league)—4 in 1950.

Most Clubs Losing 100 or More Games, Season
N. L.— (12-club league)—2 in 1969.
N. L.— (10-club league)—2 in 1962.
N. L.— (8-club league)—2 in 1898, 1905, 1908, 1923, 1938.
A. L.— (14-club league)—2 in 1978, 1979.
A. L.— (12-club league)—1 in 1970, 1971 1972, 1973, 1975.
A. L.— (10-club league)—2 in 1961, 1964, 1965.
A. L.— (8-club league)—2 in 1912, 1932, 1949, 1954.

MAJOR LEAGUE FIELDING RECORDS

FIRST BASEMEN

Most Years, League
N. L.—22—Willie L. McCovey, San Francisco, San Diego, 1959 through 1980, 2,045 games.
A. L.—20—Joseph I. Judge, Washington, Boston, 1915 through 1934, (consecutive), 2,084 games.

Most Games in Majors

2,368—Jacob P. Beckley, Pittsburgh, N. L., Pittsburgh, P. L., New York, N. L., Cincinnati, N. L., St. Louis, N. L., 1888 through 1907, 20 years.

Since 1900—2,237—James B. Vernon, Washington, A. L., Cleveland, A. L., Boston, A. L., Milwaukee, N. L., 1939 through 1959, except 1944, 1945 (in military service), 19 years.

Most Games, League

N. L.—2,247—Jacob P. Beckley, Pittsburgh, New York, Cincinnati, St. Louis, 1888 through 1907, except 1890; 19 years.

A. L.—2,227—James B. Vernon, Washington, Cleveland, Boston, 1939 through 1958, except 1944, 1945 (in military service); 18 consecutive years. (Also 10 games with Milwaukee, N. L., 1959).

N. L. since 1900—2,132—Charles J. Grimm, St. Louis, Pittsburgh, Chicago, 1918 through 1936; 19 consecutive years.

Most Consecutive Games, League

A. L.— 885— H. Louis Gehrig, New York, June 2, 1925, through September 27, 1930.

N. L.— 652— Frank A. McCormick, Cincinnati, April 19, 1938, through May 24, 1942, second game.

Most Games, Season

A. L. (162-game season)—162—Norman L. Siebern, Kansas City, 1962.

A. L. (154-game season)—157—George LaChance, Boston, 1904.
John A. Donahue, Chicago, 1907.
H. Louis Gehrig, New York, 1937, 1938.*

N. L. (162-game season)—162—William D. White, St. Louis, 1963.
Ernest Banks, Chicago, 1965.
Steven P. Garvey, Los Angeles, 1976, 1979, 1980.
Peter E. Rose, Philadelphia, 1980, 1982.

N. L. (154-game season)—158—Edward J. Konetchy, St. Louis, 1911; Boston, 1916.
Richard C. Hoblitzel, Cincinnati, 1911.
Ellsworth T. Dahlgren, Pittsburgh, 1944.
Gilbert R. Hodges, Brooklyn, 1951.

Most Years Leading League in Most Games

A. L.—7—H. Louis Gehrig, New York, 1926, 1927, 1928 (tied), 1932, 1936, 1937, 1938.

N. L.—7—Steven P. Garvey, Los Angeles, 1975, 1976, 1977, 1978, 1979, 1980 (tied), 1981.

Fewest Games for Leader in Most Games

A. L.— 121— Victor P. Power, Cleveland, 1959.

N. L.— 134— Edward F. Bouchee, Philadelphia, 1959.

Highest Fielding Average, Season, 150 or More Games

A. L.—.999—John P. McInnis, Boston, 152 games, 1921.

N. L.—.998—Steven P. Garvey, Los Angeles, 162 games, 1976.

Highest Fielding Average, Season, 100 or More Games

A. L.—.999—John P. McInnis, Boston, 152, games, 1921.
James L. Spencer, California, Texas, 125 games, 1973.

N. L.—.999—Frank A. McCormick, Philadelphia, 134 games, 1946.
M. Wesley Parker, Los Angeles, 114 games, 1968.
Steven P. Garvey, Los Angeles, 110 games, 1981.

Highest Fielding Average, League, 1000 or More Games

N. L.—.9957—M. Wesley Parker, Los Angeles, 1964 through 1972, 9 years, 1,108 games.

A. L.— .995—James L. Spencer, California, Texas, Chicago, New York, Oakland, 1968 through 1982, 15 years, 1221 games.

Lowest Fielding Average, Season, 100 or More Games

N. L.—.954—Alex McKinnon, New York, 112 games, 1884.

N. L. since 1900—.970—John J. Doyle, New York, 130 games, 1900.

A. L.—.972—Harry H. Davis, Philadelphia, 100 games, 1903.
Patrick H. Newnam, St. Louis, 103 games, 1910.

Most Years Leading League in Fielding Average, 100 or More Games

N. L.—9—Charles J. Grimm, Pittsburgh, Chicago, 1920, 1922 (tied), 1923, 1924, 1928 (tied), 1930, 1931, 1932 (tied), 1933.

A. L.—6—Joseph I. Judge, Washington, 1923, 1924 (tied), 1925, 1927, 1929, 1930.

Most Consecutive Years Leading League in Fielding, 100 or More Games

N. L.—5—Theodore B. Kluszewski, Cincinnati, 1951, 1952, 1953, 1954, 1955.

A. L.—4—Charles A. Gandil, Cleveland, Chicago, 1916, 1917, 1918, 1919.

Lowest Fielding Average, Season, for Leader, 100 or More Games

N. L.—.978—Alex McKinnon, St. Louis, 100 games, 1885.
A. L.—.981—John J. Anderson, Milwaukee, 125 games, 1901.
N. L. since 1900—.986—Dennis L. McGann, St. Louis, 113 games, 1901.
                          William E. Bransfield, Pittsburgh, 100 games, 1902.

Most Putouts in Majors

23,696—Jacob P. Beckley, Pittsburgh, N. L., Pittsburgh, P. L., New York, N. L., Cincinnati, N. L., St. Louis, N. L., 1888 through 1907, 20 years.

Most Putouts, League

N. L.—22,438—Jacob P. Beckley, New York, Pittsburgh, Cincinnati, St. Louis, 1888 through 1907, except 1890; 19 years.
N. L. since 1900—20,700—Charles J. Grimm, St. Louis, Pittsburgh, Chicago, 1918 through 1936; 19 consecutive years.
A. L.—19,754—James B. Vernon, Washington, Cleveland, Boston, 1939 through 1958, except 1944, 1945 (in military service); 18 consecutive years.

Most Putouts, Season

A. L.— 1846— John A. Donahue, Chicago, 157 games, 1907.
N. L.— 1759— George L. Kelly, New York, 155 games, 1920.

Most Years Leading League in Putouts

N. L.—6—Jacob P. Beckley, Pittsburgh, Cincinnati, St. Louis, 1892, 1894, 1895, 1900, 1902, 1904.
      Frank A. McCormick, Cincinnati, 1939, 1940, 1941, 1942, 1944, 1945.
A. L.—4—Walter C. Pipp, New York, 1915, 1919, 1920, 1922.

Fewest Putouts, Season, 150 or More Games

A. L.— 1159— Richard L. Stuart, Boston, 155 games, 1964.
N. L.— 1162— Gordon C. Coleman, Cincinnati, 150 games, 1961.

Fewest Putouts, Game, Nine Innings

A. A.—0—Allen B. McCauley, Washington, August 6, 1891.
A. L.—0—John W. Clancy, Chicago, April 27, 1930.
      Rudolph P. York, Detroit, June 18, 1943.
      Frank Robinson, Baltimore, July 1, 1971.
      F. Gene Tenace, Oakland, September 1, 1974.
N. L.—0—James A. Collins, St. Louis, August 21, 1935; also Chicago, June 29, 1937.
      Adolph Camilli, Philadelphia, July 30, 1937.
      C. Earl Torgeson, Boston, May 30, 1947, first game.
      Gary L. Thomasson, San Francisco, July 31, 1977.

Fewest Putouts, Season, for Leader in Most Putouts

A. L.— 971— Victor W. Wertz, Cleveland, 133 games, 1956.
N. L.— 1127— Edward F. Bouchee, Philadelphia, 134 games, 1959.

Most Putouts, Game, Nine Innings

A. L.—22—Thomas Jones, St. Louis, May 11, 1906.
      Harold H. Chase, New York, September 21, 1906, first game.
N. L.—22—Ernest Banks, Chicago, May 9, 1963.

Most Putouts, Extra-Inning Game

N. L.—42—Walter L. Holke, Boston, May 1, 1920, 26 innings.
A. L.—32—Michael P. Epstein, Washington, June 12, 1967, 22 innings.
      Rodney C. Carew, California, April 13, 1982, 20 innings (completed April 14).

Most Assists in Majors

1535—George H. Sisler, St. Louis, A. L., Washington, A. L., Boston, N. L., 1915 through 1930, except 1923; 15 years.

Most Assists, League

A. L.— 1444— James B. Vernon, Washington, Cleveland, Washington, Boston, 1939 through 1958, except 1944, 1945, (in military service), 18 consecutive years.
N. L.— 1365— Fred C. Tenney, Boston, New York, 1897 through 1911, except 1910; 14 years.

Most Assists, Season

N. L.— 161— William J. Buckner, Chicago, 144 games, 1983.
A. L.— 155— James B. Vernon, Cleveland, 153 games, 1949.

Most Years Leading League in Assists

N. L.—8—Fred C. Tenney, Boston, 1899, 1901, 1902, 1903, 1904, 1905, 1906, 1907.
A. L.—6—George H. Sisler, St. Louis, 1919, 1920, 1922, 1924, 1925, 1927.
      Victor P. Power, Kansas City, Cleveland, Minnesota, 1955, 1957, 1959, 1960, 1961, 1962.

Fewest Assists, Season, 150 or More Games
N. L.—54—James L. Bottomley, St. Louis, 154 games, 1926.
A. L.—58—H. Louis Gehrig, New York, 154 games, 1931.

Fewest Assists, Season, for Leader in Most Assists
N. L.—83—Herman Reich, Chicago, 85 games, 1949.
A. L.—85—Walter C. Pipp, New York, 134 games, 1915.

Most Assists, Game, Nine Innings
N. L.—8—Robert E. Robertson, Pittsburgh, June 21, 1971.
A. L.—7—George T. Stovall, St. Louis, August 7, 1912.

Most Assists, Extra-Inning Game
N. L.—8—Robert R. Skinner, Pittsburgh, July 22, 1954, 14 innings.
A. L.—7—Ferris R. Fain, Philadelphia, June 9, 1949, 12 innings.

Most Assists, Inning
A. L.—3—Richard L. Stuart, Boston, June 28, 1963, first inning.
        James M. Maler, Seattle, April 29, 1982, third inning.
N. L.—3—Andre Thornton, Chicago, August 22, 1975, fifth inning.

Most Assists, Doubleheader
A. L.—8—Charles C. Carr, Detroit, June 26, 1904.
        George H. Sisler, St. Louis, September 12, 1926.
        Rudolph P. York, Chicago, September 27, 1947.
        James L. Spencer, California, August 25, 1970, 21 innings.
N. L.—8—Gilbert R. Hodges, Brooklyn, July 24, 1952, 20 innings.
        R. Dale Long, Pittsburgh, May 1, 1955.

Most Consecutive Games With One or More Assists, Season
A. L.—16—Victor P. Power, Cleveland, June 9 through June 25, 1960, 29 assists.
N. L.—14—William H. Terry, New York, May 13 through May 27, 1930; 16 assists.

Most Chances Accepted (Excludes Errors) in Majors
25,000—Jacob P. Beckley, Pittsburgh, N. L., Pittsburgh, P. L., New York N. L., Cincin-
        nati, N. L., St. Louis, N. L., 1888-1907, 20 years.

Most Chances Accepted (Excludes Errors) League
N. L.—23,687—Jacob P. Beckley, Pittsburgh, New York, Cincinnati, St. Louis, 1888
        through 1907, except 1890; 19 years.
N. L. since 1900—21,914—Charles J. Grimm, St. Louis, Pittsburgh, Chicago, 1918-1936;
        19 consecutive years.
A. L.—21,198—James B. Vernon, Washington, Cleveland, Boston, 1939 through 1958,
        except 1944, 1945 (in military service) 18 consecutive years.

Most Chances Accepted (Excludes Errors), Season
A. L.—1986— John A. Donahue, Chicago, 157 games, 1907.
N. L.—1862— George L. Kelly, New York, 155 games, 1920.

Most Years Leading League in Chances Accepted (Excludes Errors)
N. L.—6—Jacob P. Beckley, Pittsburgh, Cincinnati, St. Louis, 1892, 1894, 1895, 1900,
        1902, 1904.
        William H. Terry, New York, 1927 (tied), 1928, 1929, 1930, 1932, 1934.
A. L.—4—Walter C. Pipp, New York, 1915, 1919, 1920, 1922.

Fewest Chances Accepted (Excludes Errors), Season, 150 or More Games
N. L.— 1251— Deron R. Johnson, Philadelphia, 154 games, 1970.
A. L.— 1263— Richard L. Stuart, Boston, 155 games, 1964.

Fewest Chances Accepted (Excl. Errors), Season, by Leader in Chances Accepted
A. L.— 1048— William J. Skowron, New York, 120 games, 1956.
        Victor W. Wertz, Cleveland, 133 games, 1956.
N. L.— 1222— Edward F. Bouchee, Philadelphia, 134 games, 1959.

Most Chances Accepted (Excludes Errors) Game, 9 Innings
22—Held by many first basemen in both leagues.
A. L.—Last first baseman—John P. McInnis, Boston, July 19, 1918, 21 putouts, 1 assist.
N. L.—Last first baseman—Ernest Banks, Chicago, May 9, 1963, 22 putouts.

Most Chances Accepted (Excludes Errors) Extra-Inning Game
N. L.—43—Walter L. Holke, Boston, May 1, 1920, 26 innings.
A. L.—34—Rudolph P. York, Detroit, July 21, 1945, 24 innings.
        Michael P. Epstein, Washington, June 12, 1967, 22 innings.
        Rodney C. Carew, California, April 13, 1982, 20 innings (completed April 14).

Most Chances Accepted (Excludes Errors), Doubleheader, 18 Innings
A. L.—38—Harold H. Chase, New York, August 5, 1905.
N. L.—35—Harold H. Chase, New York, August 26, 1919.

Most Chances Accepted (Excludes Errors), Two Consecutive Games
   N. L.—39—Harvey L. Cotter, Chicago, July 10, 1924, second game; July 11, 1924.
   A. L.—38—Harold H. Chase, New York, August 5, 5, 1905.

Fewest Chances Offered, Game, 9 Innings in Field
   A. A.—0—Allen B. McCauley, Washington, August 6, 1891.
   A. L.—0—John W. Clancy, Chicago, April 27, 1930.
               F. Gene Tenace, Oakland, September 1, 1974.
   N. L.—0—James A. Collins, Chicago, June 29, 1937.

Fewest Chances Offered, Game, 8 Innings in Field
   A. A.—0—Guy J. Hecker, Louisville, October 9, 1887.
   A. L.—0—Norman D. Cash, Detroit, June 27, 1963.
   N. L.—1—Held by many first basemen.

Fewest Chances Offered, Doubleheader, 18 Innings
   N. L.—7—Adrian C. Anson, Chicago, July 19, 1896.
               Frank E. Bowerman, Pittsburgh, August 19, 1899.
   N. L. since 1900—8—Edward S. Waitkus, Chicago, May 31, 1948.
               George D. Crowe, Cincinnati, June 2, 1957.
   A. L.—9—Henry B. Greenberg, Detroit, August 26, 1935.

Fewest Chances Offered, Two Consecutive Games, 18 Innings
   A. L.—6—Richard D. Kryhoski, New York, April 29 (3), 30 (3), 1949.
   N. L.—7—Adrian C. Anson, Chicago, July 19 (5), 19 (2), 1896.
               Frank E. Bowerman, Pittsburgh, August 19 (5), 19 (2), 1899.
               Philip J. Cavarretta, Chicago, April 25 (6), 26 (1), 1935.

Fewest Chances Offered, Two Consecutive Games, 17 Innings
   A. L.—5—F. Gene Tenace, Oakland, August 31 (5), September 1 (0), 1974.

Most Errors, Season
   U. A.—62—Joseph J. Quinn, St. Louis, 100 games, 1884.
   N. L.—58—Adrian C. Anson, Chicago, 108 games, 1884.
   N. L. since 1900—43—John J. Doyle, New York, 130 games, 1900.
   A. L.—41—Jeremiah Freeman, Washington, 154 games, 1908.

Most Errors, League
   N. L.—568—Adrian C. Anson, Chicago, 1879 through 1897, 19 years.
   A. L.—285—Harold H. Chase, New York, Chicago, 1905 through 1914, 10 years, 1175 games.
   N. L. since 1900—252—Fred C. Tenney, Boston, New York, 1900 through 1911, except 1910, 11 years.

Most Years Leading Major Leagues in Errors
   7—Richard L. Stuart, Pittsburgh N. L. 1958 (tied) 1959, 1960 (tied), 1961, 1962 (tied); Boston, A. L., 1963, 1964.

Most Years Leading League in Errors
   N. L.—5—Adrian C. Anson, Chicago, 1882, 1884, 1885, 1886, 1892.
               Richard L. Stuart, Pittsburgh, 1958 (tied), 1959, 1960 (tied), 1961, 1962 (tied).
               Willie L. McCovey, San Francisco, 1967 (tied), 1968, 1970, 1971, 1977.
   A. L.—5—Harold H. Chase, New York, Chicago, 1905, 1909, 1911, 1912 (tied), 1913.
               George H. Sisler, St. Louis, 1916, 1917, 1924, 1925, 1927.
               Ferris R. Fain, Philadelphia, 1947 (tied), 1948, 1949, 1950, 1952.

Fewest Errors, Season, 150 or More Games
   A. L.—1—John P. McInnis, Boston, 152 games, 1921.
   N. L.—3—Steven P. Garvey, Los Angeles, 162 games, 1976.

Fewest Errors, Season, for Leader in Most Errors
   A. L.—10—Victor P. Power, Kansas City, 144 games, 1955.
               Augustus Triandos, Baltimore, 103 games, 1955.
   N. L.—13—Stanley F. Musial, St. Louis, 114 games, 1946.
               Dee V. Fondy, Chicago, 147 games, 1955.
               R. Dale Long, Pittsburgh, 119 games, 1955.
               Atanasio R. Perez, Cincinnati, 151 games, 1973.
               David A. Kingman, San Francisco, 91 games, 1974.
               Willie L. McCovey, San Francisco, 136 games, 1977.
               William J. Buckner, Chicago, 144 games, 1983.
               Keith Hernandez, St. Louis, New York, 144 games, 1983.
               Albert Oliver, Montreal, 153 games, 1983.

Most Errors, Inning

N. L.—3—Adolph Camilli, Philadelphia, August 2, 1935, first inning.
Albert Oliver, Pittsburgh, May 23, 1969, fourth inning.
A. L.—3—George M. Metkovich, Boston, April 17, 1945, seventh inning.
Tommy L. McCraw, Chicago, May 3, 1968, third inning.

Most Errors, Game, 9 Innings

N. L.—5—John C. Carbine, Louisville, April 29, 1876.
George Zettlein, Philadelphia, June 22, 1876.
Everett Mills, Hartford, October 7, 1876.
Thomas J. Esterbrook, Buffalo, July 27, 1880.
Roger Connor, Troy City, May 27, 1882.
A. A.—5—Lewis J. Brown, Louisville, September 10, 1883.
U. A.—5—John F. Gorman, Kansas City, June 28, 1884.
Joseph J. Quinn, St. Louis, July 4, 1884.
N. L. since 1900—4—John Menefee, Chicago, October 6, 1901.
John C. Lush, Philadelphia, June 11, 1904, and September 15, 1904, second game.
Fred C. Tenney, Boston, July 12, 1905, first game.
A. L.—4—Harold H. Chase, Chicago, July 23, 1913.
George H. Sisler, St. Louis, April 14, 1925.
James C. Wasdell, Washington, May 3, 1939.

Most Errors, Two Consecutive Games

A. A.—8—Lewis J. Brown, Louisville, September 9, 10, 1883.

Longest Errorless Game

N. L.—26 innings—Walter L. Holke, Boston, May 1, 1920.
Edward J. Konetchy, Brooklyn, May 1, 1920.
A. L.—24 innings—Myron Grimshaw, Boston, September 1, 1906.
Richard W. Siebert, Philadelphia, July 21, 1945.

Most Consecutive Errorless Games, Season

N. L.— 131— Frank A. McCormick, Philadelphia, April 16 through September 23, 1946
(1256 chances accepted).
A. L.— 119— John P. McInnis, Boston, May 21, first game, through October 2, 1921 (1300 chances accepted).

Most Consecutive Errorless Games, League

A. L.— 178— J. Michael Hegan, Milwaukee, Oakland, September 24, 1970, through May 20, 1973; 8 in 1970; 92 in 1971; 64 in 1972; 14 in 1973 (758 chances accepted).
A. L.— 163— John P. McInnis, Boston, Cleveland, May 31, 1921, first game, through June 2, 1922; 119 in 1921, 44 in 1922 (1700 chances accepted).
N. L.— 138— Frank A. McCormick, Cincinnati, Philadelphia, September 26, first game, 1945 through September 23, 1946; 7 in 1945, 131 in 1946 (1325 chances accepted).

Most Chances Accepted, Season, No Errors

A. L.— 1300— John P. McInnis, Boston, May 31, first game, through October 2, 1921, 119 games.
N. L.— 1256— Frank A. McCormick, Philadelphia, April 16 through September 23, 1946, 131 games.

Most Chances Accepted, League, No Errors

A. L.— 1700— John P. McInnis, Boston, Cleveland, May 31, 1921, first game, through June 2, 1922, 163 games (1300 in 1921, 400 in 1922).
N. L.— 1325— Frank A. McCormick, Cincinnati, Philadelphia, September 26, first game, 1945 through September 23, 1946 (69 in 1945, 1256 in 1946).

Most Double Plays, Season

A. L.— 194— Ferris R. Fain, Philadelphia, 150 games, 1949.
N. L.— 182— Donn A. Clendenon, Pittsburgh, 152 games, 1966.

Most Double Plays in Major Leagues

2044—James B. Vernon, Washington, A. L., Cleveland, A. L., Boston, A. L., Milwaukee, N. L., 1939 through 1959, except 1944, 1945 (in military service) 19 consecutive years, 2237 games; 2041 in A. L., 3 in N. L.

Most Double Plays, League

A. L.— 2041— James B. Vernon, Washington, Cleveland, Boston, 1939 through 1958, except 1944, 1945 (in military service) 18 consecutive years, 2227 games.
N. L.— 1708— Charles J. Grimm, St. Louis, Pittsburgh, Chicago, 1918 through 1936, 19 consecutive years, 2132 games.

Most Years Leading League in Double Plays

N. L.—5—Adrian C. Anson, Chicago, 1884, 1886, 1888, 1891, 1895.
Donn Clendenon, Pittsburgh, 1963, 1965, 1966, 1967, 1968.
A. L.—4—John P. McInnis, Philadelphia, Boston, 1912, 1914, 1919, 1920 (tied).
Walter C. Pipp, New York, 1915, 1916, 1917 (tied), 1920 (tied).
Cecil C. Cooper, Milwaukee, 1980, 1981, 1982, 1983.

Fewest Double Plays, Season, 150 or More Games

A. L.—87—H. Louis Gehrig, New York, 155 games, 1926.
N. L.—89—William J. Buckner, Chicago, 161 games, 1982.

Fewest Double Plays, Season, for Leader in Most Double Plays

A. L.— 98— Victor P. Power, Cleveland, 121 games, 1959.
N. L.— 109— William D. White, St. Louis, 123 games, 1960.

Most Double Plays, Game, 9 Innings

N. L.—7—Curtis L. Blefary, Houston, May 4, 1969.
A. L.—6—Ferris R. Fain, Philadelphia, September 1, 1947, second game.
George S. Vico, Detroit, May 19, 1948.
W. Edward Robinson, Cleveland, August 5, 1948.
J. Leroy Thomas, Los Angeles, August 23, 1963.
Robert L. Oliver, Kansas City, May 14, 1971.
John C. Mayberry, Kansas City, May 6, 1972.
Robert L. Oliver, New York, April 29, 1975.

Most Double Plays, Extra-Inning Game

A. L.—6—James E. Foxx, Philadelphia, August 24, 1935, 15 innings.
Rodney C. Carew, Minnesota, August 29, 1977, first game, 10 innings.
N. L.—6—Theodore B. Kluszewski, Cincinnati, May 1, 1955, 16 innings.

Most Double Plays, Doubleheader, 18 Innings

N. L.—8—Raymond E. Sanders, St. Louis, June 11, 1944.
A. L.—8—Walter F. Judnich, St. Louis, September 16, 1947.
Walter O. Dropo, Boston, June 25, 1950.

Most Double Plays, Doubleheader, More than 18 Innings

A. L.—10—James B. Vernon, Washington, August 18, 1943, 23 innings.

Most Double Plays Started, Game, 9 Innings

A. L.—3—Luzerne A. Blue, Detroit, September 8, 1922.
Walter F. Judnich, St. Louis, September 6, 1947.
Victor P. Power, Philadelphia, September 26, 1954.
N. L.—3—Frank O. Hurst, Philadelphia, September 17, 1930.
Tommie L. Aaron, Milwaukee, May 27, 1962.

Most Unassisted Double Plays, Season

A. L.—8—James L. Bottomley, St. Louis, 140 games, 1936.
N. L.—8—William D. White, St. Louis, 151 games, 1961.

Most Unassisted Double Plays, Game

N. L.—2—Held by 14 first basemen. Last first baseman—Steven P. Garvey, Los Angeles,
August 31, 1976.
A. L.—2—Held by 12 first basemen. Last first baseman—Daniel L. Briggs, California,
April 16, 1977.

Most Innings Played, Game

N. L.—26—Walter L. Holke, Boston, May 1, 1920.
Edward J. Konetchy, Brooklyn, May 1, 1920.
A. L.—24—Myron Grimshaw, Boston, September 1, 1906.
Rudolph P. York, Detroit, July 21, 1945.
Richard W. Siebert, Philadelphia, July 21, 1945.

SECOND BASEMEN'S FIELDING RECORDS

Most Years, League

A. L.—21—Edward T. Collins, Philadelphia, Chicago, 1908 through 1928, consecutive
(2,651 games).
N. L.—21—Joe L. Morgan, Houston, Cincinnati, San Francisco, Philadelphia, 1963
through 1983 (2,427 games).

Most Games, League

A. L.— 2651— Edward T. Collins, Philadelphia, Chicago, 21 years, 1908 through 1928.
N. L.— 2427— Joe L. Morgan, Houston, Cincinnati, San Francisco, Philadelphia, 1963
through 1983, 21 years.

Most Consecutive Games Played, League

A. L.— 798— J. Nelson Fox, Chicago, August 7, 1955, through September 3, 1960.
N. L.— 443— David Cash, Pittsburgh, Philadelphia, September 20, 1973 through August 5, 1976.

Most Games, Season

A. L. (162-game season) —162—Jacob Wood, Detroit, 1961.
                       Robert Grich, Baltimore, 1973.
A. L. (154-game season) —158—Derrill B. Pratt, St. Louis, 1915; also in 1916.
N. L. (162-game season) —163—William S. Mazeroski, Pittsburgh, 1967.
N. L. (154-game season) —156—Claude C. Ritchey, Pittsburgh, 1904.
                       Miller J. Huggins, Cincinnati, 1907.
                       Rogers Hornsby, Chicago, 1929.
                       William J. Herman, Chicago, 1939.
                       Jack R. Robinson, Brooklyn, 1949.

Most Years Leading League in Games

A. L.—8—J. Nelson Fox, Chicago, 1952, 1953, 1954, 1955, 1956, 1957, 1958, 1959.
N. L.—7—William J. Herman, Chicago, Brooklyn, 1932 (tied), 1933, 1935, 1936 (tied), 1938, 1939, 1942.

Fewest Games, Season, for Leader in Most Games

A. L.— 133— Frank LaPorte, St. Louis, 1911.
N. L.— 134— George W. Cutshaw, Pittsburgh, 1917.

Highest Fielding Average, Season, 150 or More Games

A. L.—.99471—Robert Grich, Baltimore, 162 games, 1973.
N. L.—.99310—Rigoberto P. Fuentes, San Francisco, 160 games, 1973.
     .99307—Joe L. Morgan, Cincinnati, 151 games, 1977.

Highest Fielding Average, Season, 100 or More Games

N. L.—.9956 —Kenneth G. Boswell, New York, 101 games, 1970.
A. L.—.99481—Robert D. Wilfong, Minnesota, 120 games, 1980.
     .99471—Robert A. Grich, Baltimore, 162 games, 1973.

Highest Fielding Average, League, 1000 or More Games

A. L.—.984—J. Nelson Fox, Philadelphia, Chicago, 1947 through 1963, 17 consecutive years, 2179 games.
N. L.—.984—David Cash, Pittsburgh, Philadelphia, Montreal, San Diego, 1969 through 1980, 12 years, 1,330 games.

Lowest Fielding Average, Season, 100 or More Games

N. L.—.893—Fred N. Pfeffer, Chicago, 109 games, 1885.
A. L.—.914—Frank H. Truesdale, St. Louis, 122 games, 1910.
N. L. since 1900—.927—John S. Farrell, St. Louis, 118 games, 1903.

Most Years Leading League in Fielding Average, 100 or More Games

A. L.—9—Edward T. Collins, Philadelphia, Chicago, 1909, 1910, 1914, 1915, 1916, 1920, 1921, 1922, 1924.
N. L.—7—Albert F. Schoendienst, St. Louis, New York, Milwaukee, 1946, 1949, 1953, 1955, 1956, 1957 (tied), 1958.

Most Consecutive Years Leading League in Fielding, 100 or More Games

N. L.—6—Claude C. Ritchey, Pittsburgh, 1902, 1903, 1904 (tied), 1905, 1906, 1907.
A. L.—4—Charles L. Gehringer, Detroit, 1934 (tied), 1935, 1936, 1937.

Lowest Fielding Average for Leader, Season, 100 or More Games

N. L.—.928—Charles E. Bassett, Indianapolis, 119 games, 1887.
N. L. since 1900—.953—John B. Miller, Pittsburgh, 150 games, 1909.
A. L.—.960—James T. Williams, New York, 132 games, 1903.

Most Putouts, League

A. L.— 6526— Edward T. Collins, Philadelphia, Chicago, 1908 through 1928, 21 years.
N. L.— 5541— Joe L. Morgan, Houston, Cincinnati, San Francisco, Philadelphia, 1963 through 1983, 21 years.

Most Putouts, Season

A. A.— 525— John A. McPhee, Cincinnati, 140 games, 1886.
A. L. (162-game season) —484—Robert Grich, Baltimore 160 games, 1974.
A. L. (154-game season) —479—Stanley R. Harris, Washington, 154 games, 1922.
N. L. (154-game season) —466—William J. Herman, Chicago, 153 games, 1933.

Most Years Leading League in Putouts

A. L.—10—J. Nelson Fox, Chicago, 1952, 1953, 1954, 1955, 1956, 1957, 1958, 1959, 1960, 1961.

N. L.— 7—Fred N. Pfeffer, Chicago, 1884, 1885, 1886, 1887, 1888, 1889, 1891.
William J. Herman, Chicago, Brooklyn, 1933, 1935, 1936, 1938, 1939, 1940 (tied), 1942.

Fewest Putouts, Season, 150 or More Games

N. L.— 260— John B. Miller, Pittsburgh, 150 games, 1909.

A. L.— 287— Daniel F. Murphy, Philadelphia, 150 games, 1905.

Fewest Putouts, Season, for Leader in Most Putouts

N. L.— 292— Lawrence J. Doyle, New York, 144 games, 1909.

A. L.— 304— Charles L. Gehringer, Detroit, 121 games, 1927.

Most Putouts, Game, Nine Innings

A. A.—12—Louis Bierbauer, Philadelphia, June 22, 1888.

A. L.—12—Robert F. Knoop, California, August 30, 1966.

N. L.—11—Samuel W. Wise, Washington, May 9, 1893.
John A. McPhee, Cincinnati, April 21, 1894.
Napoleon Lajoie, Philadelphia, April 25, 1899.
William J. Herman, Chicago, June 28, 1933, first game.
Eugene W. Baker, Chicago, May 27, 1955.
Charles L. Neal, Los Angeles, July 2, 1959.
M. Julian Javier, St. Louis, June 27, 1964.

Most Putouts, Two Consecutive Nine-Inning Games

A. A.—19—William F. Greenwood, Rochester, July 15, 16, 1890.

Most Putouts, Extra-Inning Game

N. L.—15—Jacob Pitler, Pittsburgh, August 22, 1917, 22 innings.

A. L.—12—William F. Gardner, Baltimore, May 21, 1957, 16 innings.
Vern G. Fuller, Cleveland, April 11, 1969, 16 innings.

Most Putouts, Doubleheader, 18 Innings

N. L.—16—Fred N. Pfeffer, Chicago, May 31, 1897.
William J. Herman, Chicago, June 28, 1933.

A. L.—15—Casimer E. Michaels, Washington, July 30, 1950.

Fewest Putouts, Longest Doubleheader

A. L.— 0—Edward C. Foster, Washington, July 5, 1917, 21⅓ innings.

N. L.— 0—Claude C. Ritchey, Pittsburgh, September 2, 1901, 18 innings.
Eugene N. DeMontreville, Boston, September 20, 1901, 18 innings.
John J. Evers, Boston, August 3, 1916, 18 innings.
John W. Rawlings, Boston, September 10, 1917, 18 innings.
Lee C. Magee, Cincinnati, August 18, 1918, 18 innings.
Charles L. Herzog, Boston, June 2, 1919, 18 innings.
Milton J. Stock, Brooklyn, August 10, 1925, 18 innings.
Rogers Hornsby, Boston, September 10, 1928, 18 innings.
Carvel W. Rowell, Boston, July 4, 1941, 18 innings.
William J. Rigney, New York, September 1, 1947, 18 innings.
Cornelius J. Ryan, Philadelphia, June 14, 1953, 18 innings.
Antonio Taylor, Philadelphia, August 9, 1960, 18 innings.
Gerald P. Buchek, New York, May 28, 1967, 18 innings.

Longest Game, No Putouts

A. L.—15 innings—Stephen D. Yerkes, Boston, June 11, 1913.
Robert D. Doyle, California, June 14, 1974.

N. L.—12 innings—Kenneth G. Boswell, New York, August 7, 1972 (none out in 13th inning).

Most Assists, League

A. L.— 7630— Edward T. Collins, Philadelphia, Chicago, 21 years, 1908 through 1928.

N. L.— 6738— Joe L. Morgan, Houston, Cincinnati, San Francisco, Philadelphia, 1963 through 1983, 21 years.

Most Assists, Season

N. L.— 641— Frank F. Frisch, St. Louis, 153 games, 1927.

A. L.— 572— Oscar D. Melillo, St. Louis, 148 games, 1930.

Most Years Leading League in Assists

N. L.—9—William S. Mazeroski, Pittsburgh, 1958, 1960, 1961, 1962, 1963, 1964, 1966, 1967, 1968.

A. L.—7—Charles L. Gehringer, Detroit, 1927, 1928, 1933, 1934, 1935, 1936, 1938.

Most Consecutive Years, Leading League in Assists
A. L.—6—Horace M. Clarke, New York, 1967 through 1972.
N. L.—5—William S. Mazeroski, Pittsburgh, 1960 through 1964.

Fewest Assists, Season, 150 or More Games
A. L.— 350— William F. Gardner, Baltimore, 151 games, 1958.
N. L.— 358— Antonio Taylor, Philadelphia, 150 games, 1964.

Fewest Assists, Season, for Leader in Most Assists
N. L.— 381— Emil M. Verban, Philadelphia, 138 games, 1946.
A. L.— 396— J. Nelson Fox, Chicago, 154 games, 1956.

Most Years With 500 or More Assists
A. L.—6—Charles L. Gehringer, Detroit, 1928, 1929, 1930, 1933, 1934, 1936.
N. L.—5—Hugh M. Critz, Cincinnati, New York, 1925, 1926, 1930, 1933, 1934.
    William S. Mazeroski, Pittsburgh, 1961, 1962, 1963, 1964, 1966.

Most Assists, Game, Nine Innings
N. L.—12—John M. Ward, Brooklyn, June 10, 1892, first game.
    James Gilliam, Jr., Brooklyn, July 21, 1956.
A. L.—12—Donald W. Money, Milwaukee, June 24, 1977.

Most Assists, Extra-Inning Game
N. L.—15—Lafayette N. Cross, Philadelphia, August 5, 1897, 12 innings.
N. L. since 1900—13—Maurice C. Rath, Cincinnati, August 26, 1919, 15 innings.
A. L.—13—Roberto Avila, Cleveland, July 1, 1952, 19 innings.
    William L. Randolph, New York, August 25, 1976, 19 innings.

Most Chances Accepted (Excludes Errors), League
A. L.—14,156—Edward T. Collins, Philadelphia, Chicago, 1908 through 1928, 21 years.
N. L.—12,279—Joe L. Morgan, Houston, Cincinnati, San Francisco, Philadelphia, 1963
    through 1983, 21 years.

Most Chances Accepted (Excludes Errors), Season
N. L.— 1037— Frank F. Frisch, St. Louis, 153 games, 1927.
A. L.— 988— Napoleon Lajoie, Cleveland, 156 games, 1908.

Most Years Leading League in Chances, Accepted (Excludes Errors)
A. L.—9—J. Nelson Fox, Chicago, 1952, 1953, 1954, 1955, 1956, 1957, 1958, 1959, 1960.
N. L.—8—William S. Mazeroski, Pittsburgh, 1958, 1960, 1961, 1962, 1963, 1964, 1966,
    1967.

Fewest Chances Accepted, Season, 150 or More Games
A. L.— 674— Daniel F. Murphy, Philadelphia, 150 games, 1905.
N. L.— 683— Antonio Taylor, Philadelphia, 150 games, 1964.

Fewest Chances Accepted (Excl. Errors), Season, by Leader in Chances Accepted
N. L.— 686— John B. Miller, Pittsburgh, 150 games, 1909.
A. L.— 697— Edward T. Collins, Philadelphia, 132 games, 1911.

Most Years With 900 or More Chances Accepted (Excludes Errors)
N. L.—5—William J. Herman, Chicago, 1932, 1933, 1935, 1936, 1938.
A. L.—4—Charles L. Gehringer, Detroit, 1929, 1930, 1933, 1936.

Most Chances Accepted (Excludes Errors), Game, Nine Innings
A. A.—18—Clarence L. Childs, Syracuse, June 1, 1890.
N. L.—18—Terry W. Harmon, Philadelphia, June 12, 1971.
A. L.—18—Julio L. Cruz, Seattle, June 7, 1981 (first nine innings of 11-inning game; 19
    total chances accepted in game).
    17—James J. Dykes, Philadelphia, August 28, 1921.
    J. Nelson Fox, Chicago, June 12, 1952.

Most Chances Accepted (Excludes Errors), Doubleheader
N. L.—26—Frank J. Parkinson, Philadelphia, September 5, 1922.
A. L.—24—Casimer E. Michaels, Washington, July 30, 1950.
    Alfred M. Martin, New York, September 24, 1952, 19 innings.

Most Chances Accepted (Excludes Errors), Extra-Inning Game
N. L.—21—Eddie Moore, Boston vs. Chicago, May 17, 1927, 22 innings.
A. L.—20—William L. Randolph, New York, August 25, 1976, 19 innings.

Most Chances Accepted (Excludes Errors), Two Consecutive Games
A. A.—31—William F. Greenwood, Rochester, July 15, 16, 1890.
N. L.—28—Fred N. Pfeffer, Chicago, August 13, 14, 1884.
    John N. Ward, New York, July 18, July 19, first game, 1893.
A. L.—28—Robert P. Doerr, Boston, May 30, second game, June 3, first game, 1946.
N. L. since 1900—26—Frank J. Parkinson, Philadelphia, September 5, 5, 1922.
    Emil Verban, Philadelphia, August 1, 2, 1947.

Fewest Chances Offered, Doubleheader
N. L.—1—Charles L. Herzog, Boston, June 2, 1919.
A. L.—1—Edward C. Foster, Washington, July 5, 1917, 21⅓ innings.

Most Chances Accepted (Excludes Errors), Two Consecutive Games, More Than 18 Innings
A. L.—34—Minter C. Hayes, Chicago, July 14, 15, 1932, 22 innings.
N. L.—Less than two nine-inning games.

Longest Game, No Chances Offered
A. L.— (15 -club league)—Stephen D. Yerkes, Boston, June 11, 1919.
N. L.— (12 -club league)—Kenneth G. Boswell, New York, August 7, 1972, (none out in 13th inning).

Fewest Chances Offered, Two Consecutive Games
N. L.—1—Charles L. Herzog, Boston, April 28, 30, 1919, 19 innings, also June 2, 2, 1919, 18 innings.
   Gerald P. Buchek, New York, May 28, second game, (1), May 29, 1967, (0), 17 innings.
A. L.—1—Robert G. Young, St. Louis, April 19, 20, 1951, 17 innings.
   Roberto Avila, Cleveland, April 19, 20, first game, 1952, 18 innings.
   Edward C. Foster, Washington, July 5, 5, 1917, 21⅓ innings.

Fewest Chances Offered, Three Consecutive Games
N. L.—3—Edward R. Stanky, Boston, April 25, 26, 27, 1949, 26 innings.
A. L.—4—Held by many second basemen.

Fewest Chances Offered, Four Consecutive Games
N. L.—5—Charles L. Herzog, Boston, June 2, 2, 3, 3, 1919, 37 innings.
A. L.—6—Held by many second basemen.

Most Errors, Season
N. L.—88—Charles M. Smith, Cincinnati, 80 games, 1880.
   Robert Ferguson, Philadelphia, 85 games, 1883.
A. A.—87—William Robinson, St. Louis, 129 games, 1886.
   William H. McClellan, Brooklyn, 136 games, 1887.
A. L.—61—William Gleason, Detroit, 136 games, 1901.
   Hobart Ferris, Boston, 138 games, 1901.
N. L. since 1900—55—George F. Grantham, Chicago, 150 games, 1923.

Most Errors in Major Leagues
828—Fred N. Pfeffer, Troy, N. L., Chicago, N. L., Chicago, P. L., Louisville, N. L., New York, N. L., 16 years, 1882 through 1897; 654 in N. L., 74 in P. L.

Most Errors, League
N. L.— 754— Fred N. Pfeffer, Troy, Chicago, Louisville, New York, 1882 through 1897, except 1890, 15 years.
A. L.— 435— Edward T. Collins, Philadelphia, Chicago, 1908 through 1928, 21 consecutive years.
N. L. since 1900—443—Lawrence J. Doyle, New York, Chicago, 1907 through 1920, 14 consecutive years.

Most Years Leading League in Errors
N. L.—5—Fred N. Pfeffer, Chicago, 1884, 1885, 1886, 1887, 1888, consecutive.
A. L.—4—William A. Wambsganss, Cleveland, Boston, 1917, 1919, 1920, 1924.
   Joseph L. Gordon, New York, 1938, 1941, 1942, 1943 (tied).
N. L. since 1900—4—William J. Herman, Chicago, 1932, 1933, 1937, 1939.
   Glenn A. Beckert, Chicago, 1966, 1967, 1969, 1970 (tied).
Both Leagues —4—Rigoberto Fuentes, San Francisco, N. L., 1971, 1972; San Diego, N. L., 1976; Detroit, A. L., 1977.

Fewest Errors, Season, 150 or More Games
A. L.—5—K. Jerry Adair, Baltimore, 153 games, 1964.
   Robert Grich, Baltimore, 162 games, 1973.
N. L.—5—Joe L. Morgan, Cincinnati, 151 games, 1977.

Fewest Errors, Season, for Leader in Most Errors
A. L.—14—Hector H. Lopez, Kansas City, 96 games, 1958.
N. L.—15—Ted C. Sizemore, Chicago, 96 games, 1979.
   Glenn D. Hubbard, Atlanta, 91 games, 1979.

Most Consecutive Errorless Games, League
N. L.—91—Joe L. Morgan, Cincinnati, July 6, 1977 through April 22, 1978, 410 chances accepted.
A. L.—89—K. Jerry Adair, Baltimore, July 22, 1964 through May 6, 1965, 458 chances accepted.

Most Consecutive Errorless Games, Season

N. L.—89—J. Manuel Trillo, Philadelphia, April 9 through July 30, 1982, 473 chances accepted.

A. L.—86—Richard F. Dauer, Baltimore, April 10 through September 29, 1978, 418 chances accepted.

Most Consecutive Chances Accepted, Season, No Errors

N. L.— 479— J. Manuel Trillo, Philadelphia, April 8 (part) through July 31 (part), 1982, 91 games.

A. L.— 425— Richard F. Dauer, Baltimore, April 10 through September 30 (part), 1978, 87 games.

Most Errors, Inning

N. L.—3—John A. McPhee, Cincinnati, September 23, 1894; first game, second inning.
Claude S. Ritchey, Pittsburgh, September 22, 1900, sixth inning.
Carvel W. Rowell, Boston, September 25, 1941, third inning.
Edward R. Stanky, Chicago, June 20, 1943, first game, eighth inning.
George J. Hausmann, New York, August 13, 1944, second game, fourth inning.
Kermit E. Wahl, Cincinnati, September 18, 1945, first game, eleventh inning.
David E. Lopes, Los Angeles, June 2, 1973, first inning.
Ted C. Sizemore, St. Louis, April 17, 1975, sixth inning.

A. L.—3—Derrill B. Pratt, St. Louis, September 1, 1914, second game, fourth inning.
William A. Wambsganss, Cleveland, May 15, 1923, fourth inning.
Timothy L. Cullen, Washington, August 30, 1969, eighth inning, consecutive.

Most Errors, Game, Nine Innings

N. L.—9—Andrew J. Leonard, Boston, June 14, 1876.

A. L.—5—Charles Hickman, Washington, September 29, 1905.
Napoleon Lajoie, Philadelphia, April 22, 1915.

N. L. since 1900—4—Held by six second basemen. Last second baseman—Kendall C. Wise, Chicago, May 3, 1957.

Most Errors, Two Consecutive Games

N. L.—11—Andrew J. Leonard, Boston, June 10, 14, 1876.

Most Errors, Three Consecutive Games

N. L.—13—Andrew J. Leonard, Boston, June 10, 14, 15, 1876.

Longest Errorless Game

N. L.—25 innings— Felix B. Millan, New York, September 11, 1974.
Ted C. Sizemore, St. Louis, September 11, 1974.

A. L.—24 innings— Hobart Ferris, Boston, September 1, 1906.
Irvin Hall, Philadelphia, July 21, 1945.

Most Double Plays, Season

N. L.— 161— William S. Mazeroski, Pittsburgh, 162 games, 1966.

A. L.— 150— Gerald E. Priddy, Detroit, 157 games, 1950.

Most Double Plays, League

N. L.— 1706— William S. Mazeroski, Pittsburgh, 17 years, 1956 through 1972.

A. L.— 1568— J. Nelson Fox, Philadelphia, Chicago, 17 years, 1947 through 1963.

Most Years Leading League in Double Plays

N. L.—8—William S. Mazeroski, Pittsburgh, 1960, 1961, 1962, 1963, 1964, 1965, 1966, 1967.

A. L.—5—Napoleon Lajoie, Cleveland, 1903, 1906, 1907, 1908, 1909 (tied).
Edward T. Collins, Philadelphia, Chicago, 1909 (tied), 1910, 1912, 1916, 1919.
Stanley R. Harris, Washington, 1921, 1922, 1923, 1924 (tied), 1925.
Robert P. Doerr, Boston, 1938, 1940, 1943, 1946, 1947.
J. Nelson Fox, Chicago, 1954, 1956, 1957, 1958, 1960.

Fewest Double Plays, Season, 150 or More Games

N. L.—65—George J. Hausmann, New York, 154 games, 1945.

A. L. (154-game season)—83—Edward T. Collins, Chicago, 152 games, 1924.

A. L. (162-game season)—83—Jacob Wood, Detroit, 162 games, 1961.

Fewest Double Plays, Season, for Leader in Most Double Plays

N. L.—81—Rogers Hornsby, St. Louis, 154 games, 1922.

A. L.—84—Charles L. Gehringer, Detroit, 121 games, 1927.

Most Double Plays, Game, Nine Innings

A. L.—6—Robert F. Knoop, California, May 1, 1966, first game.

N. L.—5—Held by many second basemen.
Last player—Teodoro N. Martinez, Los Angeles, August 21, 1977.

Most Double Plays, Doubleheader

    A. L.—8—Robert P. Doerr, Boston, June 25, 1950.
           Robert F. Knoop, California, May 1, 1966.
    N. L.—6—Held by many second basemen.

Most Double Plays, Extra-Inning Game

    A. L.—6—Joseph L. Gordon, Cleveland, August 31, 1949, first game, 14 innings.
    N. L.—6—Felix B. Millan, Atlanta, August 5, 1971, 17 innings.

Most Unassisted Double Plays, Game

    N. L.—2—David W. Force, Buffalo, September 15, 1881.
           Claude C. Ritchey, Louisville, July 9, 1899, first game.
    A. L.—2—Michael L. Edwards, Oakland, August 10, 1978.

Most Double Plays Started, Game

    A. L.—5—Gerald E. Priddy, Detroit, May 20, 1950.
    N. L.—4—Fred C. Dunlap, Detroit, June 11, 1887.
           Frank W. Gustine, Pittsburgh, August 22, 1940, second game.
           Emil Verban, Philadelphia, July 18, 1947.
           Albert F. Schoendienst, St. Louis, August 20, 1954.
           Felix B. Millan, Atlanta, August 5, 1971, 17 innings.

Most Innings Played, Game

    N. L.—26—Charles Pick, Boston, May 1, 1920.
           Ivan M. Olson, Brooklyn, May 1, 1920.
    A. L.—24—Daniel L. Murphy, Philadelphia, September 1, 1906.
           Hobart Ferris, Boston, September 1, 1906.
           Irvin Hall, Philadelphia, July 21, 1945.
           Edward J. Mayo, Detroit, July 21, 1945.

THIRD BASEMEN'S FIELDING RECORDS

Most Years, League

    A. L.—23—Brooks C. Robinson, Baltimore, 1955 through 1977, 2870 games.
    N. L.—16—Harold J. Traynor, Pittsburgh, 1921 through 1937 except 1936, 1,864 games.
           Stanley C. Hack, Chicago, 1932 through 1947, 1,836 games.
           Edwin L. Mathews, Boston, Milwaukee, Atlanta, Houston, 1952 through 1967, 2,154 games.

Most Games, League

    A. L.— 2870— Brooks C. Robinson, Baltimore, 23 years, 1955 through 1977.
    N. L.— 2154— Edwin L. Mathews, Boston, Milwaukee, Atlanta, Houston, 16 years, 1952 through 1967.

Most Consecutive Games, League

    A. L.— 576— Edward F. Yost, Washington, July 3, 1951, to May 11, 1955.
    N. L.— 364— Ronald E. Santo, Chicago, April 19, 1964 through May 31, 1966.

Most Games, Season

    A. L. (162-game season) —163—Brooks C. Robinson, Baltimore, 1961, also 1964.
    A. L. (154-game season) —157—George C. Kell, Detroit, 1950.
           Edward F. Yost, Washington, 1952.
    N. L. (162-game season) —164—Ronald E. Santo, Chicago, 1965.
    N. L. (154-game season) —157—Arthur Devlin, New York, 1908.
           J. Carlisle Smith, Boston, 1915.
           Willie E. Jones, Philadelphia, 1950.
           Edwin L. Mathews, Milwaukee, 1953.
           Raymond L. Jablonski, St. Louis, 1953.

Most Years Leading League in Most Games

    A. L.—8—Brooks C. Robinson, Baltimore, 1960, 1961, 1962, 1963, 1964, 1966, (tied), 1968 (tied), 1970.
    N. L.—7—Ronald E. Santo, Chicago, 1961 (tied), 1963, 1965, 1966, 1967, 1968, 1969 (tied).

Fewest Games, Season, for Leader in Most Games

    N. L.— 111— Arthur C. Whitney, Boston, 1934.
    A. L.— 131— George C. Kell, Philadelphia, Detroit, 1946.

Highest Fielding Average, Season, 100 or More Games

    A. L.—.989—Donald W. Money, Milwaukee, 157 games, 1974.
    N. L.—.983—Henry K. Groh, New York, 145 games, 1924.

Highest Fielding Average, Season, 150 or More Games

A. L.—.989—Donald W. Money, Milwaukee, 157 games, 1974.
N. L.—.980—Kenneth J. Reitz, St. Louis, 157 games, 1977.

Highest Fielding Average, League, 1,000 or More Games

A. L.—.971—Brooks C. Robinson, Baltimore, 23 years, 1955 through 1977, 2870 games.
N. L.—.970—Kenneth J. Reitz, St. Louis, San Francisco, Chicago, Pittsburgh, 11 years, 1972 through 1982, 1,321 games.

Lowest Fielding Average, Season, 100 or More Games

N. L.—.836—Charles Hickman, New York, 118 games, 1900.
A. L.—.860—Hunter B. Hill, Washington, 135 games, 1904.

Most Years Leading League in Fielding Average, 100 or More Games

A. L.—11—Brooks C. Robinson, Baltimore, 1960, 1961, 1962, 1963, 1964, 1966, 1967, 1968, 1969 (tied), 1972, 1975.
N. L.— 6—Henry K. Groh, Cincinnati, New York, 1915 (tied), 1917, 1918, 1922, 1923, 1924.
            Kenneth J. Reitz, St. Louis, Chicago, 1973, 1974, 1977, 1978, 1980, 1981.

Most Consecutive Years Leading in Fielding Average, 100 or More Games

A. L.—6—William E. Kamm, Chicago, 1924 through 1929.
N. L.—4—Willie E. Jones, Philadelphia, 1953 through 1956.

Lowest Fielding Average for Leader, Season, 100 or More Games

N. L.—.891—Edward N. Williamson, Chicago, 111 games, 1885.
            N. L. since 1900—.917—Robert L. Lowe, Boston, 111 games, 1901.
            Charles Irwin, Cincinnati, Brooklyn, 131 games, 1901.
A. L.—.936—William J. Bradley, Cleveland, 133 games, 1901.

Most Putouts, League

A. L.— 2697— Brooks C. Robinson, Baltimore, 23 years, 1955 through 1977.
N. L.— 2288— Harold J. Traynor, Pittsburgh, 16 years, 1921 through 1937, except 1936.

Most Putouts, Season

A. A.— 252— Dennis P. Lyons, Philadelphia, 137 games, 1887.
N. L.— 252— James J. Collins, Boston, 142 games, 1900.
A. L.— 243— William E. Kamm, Chicago, 155 games, 1928.

Most Years Leading League in Putouts

A. L.—8—Edward F. Yost, Washington, Detroit, 1948, 1950, 1951, 1952, 1953, 1954 (tied), 1956, 1959.
N. L.—7—Harold J. Traynor, Pittsburgh, 1923, 1925, 1926, 1927, 1931, 1933, 1934.
            Willie E. Jones, Philadelphia, 1949, 1950, 1952, 1953, 1954, 1955, 1956.
            Ronald E. Santo, Chicago, 1962, 1963, 1964, 1965, 1966, 1967, 1969.

Fewest Putouts, Season, 150 or More Games

N. L.— 86— Kenneth J. Reitz, St. Louis, 150 games, 1980.
A. L.— 101— Paul Schaal, Los Angeles, 153 games, 1965.

Most Putouts, Game, Nine Innings

N. L.—10—William J. Kuehne, Pittsburgh, May 24, 1889.
N. L. since 1900—9—Robert L. Dillard, St. Louis, June 18, 1900.
A. L.— 7—William J. Bradley, Cleveland, September 21, 1901, first game; also May 13, 1909.
            Harry P. Riconda, Philadelphia, July 5, 1924, second game.
            Oswald L. Bluege, Washington, June 18, 1927.
            Raymond O. Boone, Detroit, April 24, 1954.

Longest Game With No Putouts

N. L.—20 innings—Lewis A. Malone, Brooklyn, April 30, 1919.
A. L.—18⅓ innings—Vernon D. Stephens, Boston, July 13, 1951.

Most Consecutive Games, No Putouts

A. L.—10—Felix Torres, Los Angeles, June 14 through June 23, 1963.
N. L.— 8—Kenton L. Boyer, St. Louis, August 4, first game through August 11, 1963.

Fewest Putouts, Season, for Leader in Most Putouts

N. L.— 116— Harold J. Traynor, Pittsburgh, 110 games, 1934.
A. L.— 131— David G. Bell, Texas, 145 games, 1982.
            Gary J. Gaetti, Minnesota, 154 games, 1983.

Most Assists, League

A. L.— 6205— Brooks C. Robinson, Baltimore, 23 years, 1955 through 1977.
N. L.— 4532— Ronald E. Santo, Chicago, 14 years, 1960 through 1973.

Most Assists, Season

A. L. (154-game season) —405—Harlond B. Clift, St. Louis, 155 games, 1937.
A. L. (162-game season) —412—Graig Nettles, Cleveland, 158 games, 1971.
N. L. (154-game season) —384—William Shindle, Baltimore, 134 games, 1892.
N. L. (162-game season) —404—Michael J. Schmidt, Philadelphia, 162 games, 1974.
N. L. since 1900 (154-game season) —371—Thomas W. Leach, Pittsburgh, 146 games, 1904.

Most Years Leading League in Assists

A. L.—8—Brooks C. Robinson, Baltimore, 1960, 1963, 1964, 1966, 1967, 1968, 1969, 1974.
N. L.—7—Ronald E. Santo, Chicago, 1962, 1963, 1964, 1965, 1966, 1967, 1968.
        Michael J. Schmidt, Philadelphia, 1974, 1976, 1977, 1980, 1981, 1982, 1983.

Fewest Assists, Season, 150 or More Games

A. L.— 221— Harry Lord, Chicago, 150 games, 1913.
N. L.— 247— Stanley C. Hack, Chicago, 150 games, 1937.

Fewest Assists, Season, for Leader in Most Assists

N. L.— 227— Arthur C. Whitney, Boston, 111 games, 1934.
A. L.— 258— Oswald L. Bluege, Washington, 134 games, 1930.

Most Assists, Game, Nine Innings

N. L.—11—James L. White, Buffalo, May 16, 1884.
        Jeremiah Denny, New York, May 29, 1890.
        Damon R. Phillips, Boston, August 29, 1944.
A. L.—11—Kenneth L. McMullen, Washington, September 26, 1966, first game.
        Michael D. Ferraro, New York, September 14, 1968.

Most Assists, Extra-Inning Game

N. L.—12—Robert M. Byrne, Pittsburgh, June 8, 1910, second game, 11 innings.
A. L.—11—J. Franklin Baker, New York, May 24, 1918, 19 innings.
        Douglas V. DeCinces, California, May 7, 1983, 12 innings.

Most Innings, No Assists, Extra-Inning Game

A. L.—17—Colbert D. Harrah, Texas, September 17, 1977.

Most Chances Accepted (Excludes Errors), League

A. L.— 8902— Brooks C. Robinson, Baltimore, 23 years, 1955 through 1977.
N. L.— 6462— Ronald E. Santo, Chicago, 14 years, 1960 through 1973.

Most Chances Accepted (Excludes Errors), Season

A. L.— 603— Harlond B. Clift, St. Louis, 155 games, 1937.
N. L.— 601— James J. Collins, Boston, 151 games, 1899.
N. L. since 1900—583—Thomas W. Leach, Pittsburgh, 146 games, 1904.

Most Years Leading League in Chances Accepted (Excludes Errors)

N. L.—9—Ronald E. Santo, Chicago, 1961, 1962, 1963, 1964, 1965, 1966, 1967, 1968, 1969
        (tied).
A. L.—8—J. Franklin Baker, Philadelphia, New York, 1909, 1910, 1912, 1913, 1914, 1917,
        1918, 1919.
        Brooks C. Robinson, Baltimore, 1960, 1963, 1964, 1966, 1967, 1968, 1969, 1974.

Fewest Chances Accepted (Excludes Errors), Season, 150 or More Games

A. L.— 364— Harry Lord, Chicago, 150 games, 1913.
N. L.— 366— Peter E. Rose, Cincinnati, 161 games, 1977.

Fewest Chances Accepted (Excludes Errors), Season, Leader in Chances Accepted

N. L.— 332— Arthur C. Whitney, Boston, 111 games, 1934.
A. L.— 396— Oswald L. Bluege, Washington, 134 games, 1930.

Most Chances Accepted (Excludes Errors), Game, Nine Innings

N. L.—13—William J. Kuehne, Pittsburgh, May 24, 1889.
        Jeremiah Denny, New York, May 19, 1890.
        William Shindle, Baltimore, September 28, 1893.
        William M. Joyce, Washington, May 26, 1894.
        Arthur Devlin, New York, May 23, 1908, first game.
        Anthony F. Cuccinello, Brooklyn, July 12, 1934, first game.
        Roy J. Hughes, Chicago, August 29, 1944, second game.
A. L.—13—William Conroy, Washington, September 25, 1911.

Most Chances Accepted (Excludes Errors), Extra-Inning Game

N. L.—16—Jeremiah Denny, Providence, August 17, 1882, 18 innings.
A. L.—14—James J. Collins, Boston, June 21, 1902, 15 innings.
        Benjamin F. Dyer, Detroit, July 16, 1919, 14 innings.
N. L. since 1900—14—Donald A. Hoak, Cincinnati, May 4, 1958, second game, 14 innings.

Most Chances Accepted (Excludes Errors), Two Consecutive Games

N. L.—23—Joseph F. Farrell, Detroit, June 30, July 1, 1884.
N. L. since 1900—18—Harry M. Steinfeldt, Cincinnati, June 14, 16, 1902.
      Robert M. Byrne, Pittsburgh, June 15, 17, 1910.
      Edward D. Zimmerman, Brooklyn, July 4, 4, 1911.
      Ralph A. Pinelli, Cincinnati, July 11, second game, July 13, 1925.
      Lee Handley, Pittsburgh, June 15, 16, first game, 1946.
A. L.—18—Hobart Ferris, St. Louis, July 12, 13, 1909, first game.
      Terrence L. Turner, Cleveland, May 21, June 1, 1916, first game.
      Aaron L. Ward, New York, April 20, 21, 1921.

Most Chances Accepted (Excludes Errors), Doubleheader

N. L.—18—Edward D. Zimmerman, Brooklyn, July 4, 1911.
A. L.—16—William P. Purtell, Chicago, July 14, 1909.

Longest Game With No Chances Offered

N. L.—15 innings—Harry M. Steinfeldt, Chicago, August 22, 1908.
       Henry K. Groh, Cincinnati, August 26, 1919, second game.
       Norman D. Boeckel, Boston, June 16, 1921; also September 12, 1921, first game.
A. L.—12⅔ innings—James R. Tabor, Boston, July 7, 1943.

Longest Doubleheader With No Chances Offered

A. L.—21⅔ innings—William L. Gardner, Cleveland, August 23, 1920.
N. L.—19 innings—Norman D. Boeckel, Boston, July 26, 1922.

Most Errors, Season

N. L.—91—Charles Hickman, New York, 118 games, 1900.
A. L.—64—Samuel N. Strang, Chicago, 137 games, 1902.

Most Errors in Major Leagues

780—Walter A. Latham, St. Louis A. A., Chicago P. L., Cincinnati N. L., St. Louis N. L., 14 years, 1883 through 1896.

Most Errors, League

N. L.—553—Jeremiah Denny, Providence, St. Louis, Indianapolis, New York, Cleveland, Philadelphia, Louisville, 1881 through 1894, except 1892, 13 years.
A. L.—359—James P. Austin, New York, St. Louis, 1909 through 1922; 1925, 1926, 1929, 17 years, 1,433 games.
N. L. since 1900—324—Harold J. Traynor, Pittsburgh, 1921 through 1935; 1937, 16 years, 1,864 games.

Most Years Leading League in Errors

N. L.—5—Harold J. Traynor, Pittsburgh, 1926, 1928 (tied), 1931, 1932, 1933.
A. L.—5—James R. Tabor, Boston, 1939, 1940 (tied), 1941, 1942, 1943 (tied).

Fewest Errors, Season, 150 or More Games

A. L.—5—Donald W. Money, Milwaukee, 157 games, 1974.
N. L.—8—Kenneth J. Reitz, St. Louis, 150 games, 1980.

Fewest Errors, Season, for Leader in Most Errors

N. L.—16—Edwin L. Mathews, Milwaukee, 147 games, 1957.
      Gene L. Freese, Pittsburgh, 74 games, 1957.
A. L.—17—Cecil T. Travis, Washington, 56 games, 1946.

Most Consecutive Errorless Games, League

N. L.—97—James H. Davenport, San Francisco, July 29, 1966 through April 28, 1968, 209 chances accepted. (Played other positions during streak.)
A. L.—88—Donald W. Money, Milwaukee, September 28, 1973, second game, through July 16, 1974, 261 chances accepted.

Most Consecutive Errorless Games, Season

A. L.—86—Donald W. Money, Milwaukee, April 5 through July 16, 1974, 257 chances accepted.
N. L.—64—James H. Davenport, San Francisco, May 22 through September 30, 1967, first game, 137 chances accepted. (Played other positions during streak.)
    57—Robert T. Aspromonte, Houston, July 14 through September 18, 1962, second game, 145 chances accepted.

Most Consecutive Chances Accepted, League, No Errors

A. L.—261—Donald W. Money, Milwaukee, September 28, 1973, first game (part) through July 16, 1974, 88 games.

Most Consecutive Chances Accepted, Season, No Errors

   A. L.— 257— Donald W. Money, Milwaukee, April 5 through July 16, 1974, 88 games.

   N. L.— 163— Donald W. Money, Philadelphia, July 27, first game through September 11, 1972, 48 games.

Most Errors, Game, Nine Innings

   U. A.—6—James B. Donnelly, Kansas City, July 16, 1884.

   A. A.—6—James H. Moffett, Toledo, August 2, 1884.

        Joseph Werrick, Louisville, July 28, 1888.

        William C. Alvord, Toledo, May 22, 1890.

   N. L.—6—Joseph H. Mulvey, Philadelphia, July 30, 1884.

   N. L. since 1900—5—David L. Brain, Boston, June 11, 1906.

   A. L.—4—Held by 19 third basemen. Last third baseman—Thomas D. Brookens, Detroit, September 6, 1980.

Most Errors, Inning

   N. L.—4—Lewis Whistler, New York, June 19, 1891, fourth inning.

   A. L.—4—James T. Burke, Milwaukee, May 27, 1901, fourth inning.

   N. L. since 1900—3—Phil Geier, Boston, June 6, 1904, tenth inning.

        Harry H. Mowrey, Cincinnati, April 30, 1907, second inning.

        Lewis S. Riggs, Brooklyn, September 13, 1942, second game, fifth inning.

        William R. Cox, Brooklyn, August 6, 1949, eighth inning.

        Thomas Glaviano, St. Louis, May 18, 1950, ninth inning.

        Ronald E. Santo, Chicago, September 3, 1963, second inning.

        Jose A. Pagan, Pittsburgh, August 18, 1966, fourth inning.

        James K. Lefebvre, Los Angeles, April 25, 1967, fourth inning.

        Darrell W. Evans, San Francisco, April 11, 1980, seventh inning.

        Hubert Brooks, New York, May 10, 1981, fourth inning.

Most Errors, Doubleheader, Since 1900

   N. L.—5—William J. Bradley, Chicago, May 30, 1900.

        Thomas W. Leach, Pittsburgh, August 20, 1903.

   A. L.—4—Held by many third basemen. Last third baseman—Herbert E. Plews, Washington, June 3, 1958.

Most Errors, Two Consecutive Games

   A. A.—9—Thomas J. Esterbrook, New York, July 15, 26, 1883.

Longest Errorless Game

   N. L.—26 innings—Norman D. Boeckel, Boston, May 1, 1920

               James H. Johnston, Brooklyn, May 1, 1920.

   A. L.—24 innings—John W. Knight, Philadelphia, September 1, 1906.

               James E. Morgan, Boston, September 1, 1906.

               George C. Kell, Philadelphia, July 21, 1945.

               Robert P. Maier, Detroit, July 21, 1945.

Most Double Plays, Season

   A. L. (162-game season)—54—Graig Nettles, Cleveland, 158 games, 1971.

   A. L. (154-game season)—50—Harlond B. Clift, St. Louis, 155 games, 1937.

   N. L. (162-game season)—45—Darrell W. Evans, Atlanta, 160 games, 1974.

   N. L. (154-game season)—43—Henry Thompson, New York, 138 games, 1950.

Most Double Plays, League

   A. L.— 618— Brooks C. Robinson, Baltimore, 23 years, 1955 through 1977.

   N. L.— 389— Ronald E. Santo, Chicago, 14 years, 1960 through 1973.

Most Years Leading League in Double Plays

   N. L.—6—Henry K. Groh, Cincinnati, New York, 1915, 1916, 1918, 1919, 1920 (tied), 1922.

        Ronald E. Santo, Chicago, 1961, 1964, 1966, 1967, 1968 (tied), 1971.

   A. L.—5—James P. Austin, New York, St. Louis, 1909, 1911, 1913, 1915, 1917.

        Kenneth F. Keltner, Cleveland, 1939, 1941, 1942, 1944, 1947.

        Frank J. Malzone, Boston, 1957, 1958, 1959, 1960, 1961.

Fewest Double Plays, Season, 150 or More Games

   N. L.—10—Robert T. Aspromonte, Houston, 155 games, 1964.

   A. L.—17—R. Maxwell Alvis, Cleveland, 156 games, 1965.

Fewest Double Plays, Season, for Leader in Most Double Plays

   N. L.—17—Joseph V. Stripp, Brooklyn, 140 games, 1933.

        John L. Vergez, New York, 123 games, 1933.

        George J. Kurowski, St. Louis, 138 games, 1946.

        James R. Tabor, Philadelphia, 124 games, 1946.

   A. L.—23—Martin J. McManus, Detroit, 130 games, 1930.

Most Unassisted Double Plays, Season

A. L.—4—Joseph A. Dugan, New York, 148 games, 1924.
N. L.—2—Held by many third basemen. Last third baseman—T. Michael Shannon, St.
        Louis, 156 games, 1968.

Most Unassisted Double Plays, Game

N. L.-A. L.—1—Held by many third basemen.

Most Unassisted Double Plays, Two Consecutive Games

A. L.—2—James Delahanty, Detroit, August 28, 29, 1911.
         Marvin J. Owen, Detroit, April 28, 29, 1934.
N. L.—Never accomplished.

Most Double Plays Started, Game, Nine Innings

N. L.—4—Harold J. Traynor, Pittsburgh, July 9, 1925, first game.
         John L. Vergez, Philadelphia, August 15, 1935.
A. L.—4—Felix Torres, Los Angeles, August 23, 1963.
         Kenneth L. McMullen, Washington, August 13, 1965.

Most Double Plays, Game

N. L.—4—Harold J. Traynor, Pittsburgh, July 9, 1925, first game.
         John L. Vergez, Philadelphia, August 15, 1935.
A. L.—4—Andrew A. Carey, New York, July 31, 1955, second game.
         Felix Torres, Los Angeles, August 23, 1963.
         Kenneth L. McMullen, Washington, August 13, 1965.

Most Innings Played, Game

N. L.—26—Norman D. Boeckel, Boston, May 1, 1920.
          James H. Johnston, Brooklyn, May 1, 1920.
A. L.—24—John W. Knight, Philadelphia, September 1, 1906.
          James E. Morgan, Boston, September 1, 1906.
          George C. Kell, Philadelphia, July 21, 1945.
          Robert P. Maier, Detroit, July 21, 1945.

SHORTSTOPS' FIELDING RECORDS

Most Years in Majors

20—William F. Dahlen, Chicago N. L., Brooklyn N. L., New York N. L., Boston N. L.,
    1891 through 1911, except 1910, 2,139 games.
    Roderick J. Wallace, St. Louis N. L., St. Louis A. L., 1899 through 1918, 1,828 games.
    Lucius B. Appling, Chicago A. L., 1930 through 1950 (except 1944, in military ser-
    vice), 2,218 games.

Most Years, League

N. L.—20—William F. Dahlen, Chicago, Brooklyn, New York, Boston, 1891 through
          1911, except 1910, 2,139 games.
A. L.—20—Lucius B. Appling, Chicago, 1930 through 1950, except 1944 (in military ser-
          vice), 2,219 games.
N. L. since 1900—19—Walter J. Maranville, Boston, Pittsburgh, Chicago, Brooklyn, St.
          Louis, 1912 through 1931, except 1924, 2,153 games.

Most Games, League

A. L.— 2581— Luis E. Aparicio, Chicago, Baltimore, Boston, 18 years, 1956 through 1973.
N. L.— 2153— Walter J. Maranville, Boston, Pittsburgh, Chicago, Brooklyn, St. Louis,
             19 years, 1912-31, except 1924.

Most Consecutive Games, League

A. L.— 1307— L. Everett Scott, Boston, New York, June 20, 1916, through May 5, 1925.
N. L.— 584— Roy D. McMillan, Cincinnati, September 16, 1951, first game through Au-
             gust 6, 1955.

Most Games, Season

N. L. (162-game season)—165—Maurice M. Wills, Los Angeles, 1962.
N. L. (154-game season)—157—Joseph B. Tinker, Chicago, 1908.
                              Granville W. Hamner, Philadelphia, 1950.
A. L. (162-game season)—162—Richard D. Howser, Cleveland, 1964.
                              James L. Fregosi, California, 1966.
                              Edwin A. Brinkman, Detroit, 1973.
                              Alfredo C. Griffin, Toronto, 1982.
                              Calvin E. Ripken, Baltimore, 1983.
A. L. (154-game season)—158—Edward E. Lake, Detroit, 1947.

Most Years Leading League in Games

N. L.—6—Michael J. Doolan, Philadelphia, 1906, 1909, 1910, 1911, 1912, 1913.
J. Floyd Vaughan, Pittsburgh, 1933 (tied), 1934, 1936, 1938, 1939, 1940.
Roy D. McMillan, Cincinnati, Milwaukee, 1952, 1953, 1954 (tied), 1956, 1957, 1961.
A. L.—5—Luis E. Aparicio, Chicago, 1956, 1957, 1958, 1959, 1960 (tied).

Fewest Games, Season, for Leader in Most Games

N. L.— 141— Walter J. Maranville, Pittsburgh, 1923.
A. L.— 142— Luis Aparicio, Chicago, 1957.

Most Games, Season, Lefthanded Shortstop

N. L.—73—William B. Hulen, Philadelphia, 1896.

Highest Fielding Average, Season, 100 or More Games

N. L.—.991—Lawrence R. Bowa, Philadelphia, 146 games, 1979.
A. L.—.990—Edwin A. Brinkman, Detroit, 156 games, 1972.

Highest Fielding Average, Season, 150 or More Games

A. L.— .990— Edwin A. Brinkman, Detroit, 156 games, 1972.
N. L.— .987— Lawrence R. Bowa, Philadelphia, 157 games, 1971.
Lawrence R. Bowa, Philadelphia, 150 games, 1972.

Highest Fielding Average, League, 1000 or More Games

N. L.—.981—Lawrence R. Bowa, Philadelphia, Chicago, 14 years, 1970 through 1983, 2,015 games.
A. L.—.977—Mark H. Belanger, Baltimore, 17 years, 1965 through 1981, 1,898 games.

Lowest Fielding Average, Season, 100 or More Games

A. L.—.861—William H. Keister, Baltimore, 114 games, 1901.
N. L.—.884—Thomas E. Burns, Chicago, 111 games, 1885.
N. L. since 1900—.891—Otto A. Krueger, St. Louis, 107 games, 1902.

Most Years Leading League in Fielding Average, 100 or More Games

A. L.—8—L. Everett Scott, Boston, New York, 1916, 1917, 1918, 1919, 1920, 1921, 1922, 1923, consecutive.
Louis Boudreau, Cleveland, 1940, 1941, 1942, 1943, 1944, 1946, 1947, 1948.
Luis E. Aparicio, Chicago, Baltimore, 1959, 1960, 1961, 1962, 1963, 1964, 1965, 1966, consecutive.
N. L.—6—Lawrence R. Bowa, Philadelphia, Chicago, 1971, 1972, 1974, 1978, 1979, 1983.

Most Consecutive Years Leading League in Fielding Average

A. L.—8—L. Everett Scott, Boston, New York, 1916 through 1923.
Luis E. Aparicio, Chicago, Baltimore, 1959 through 1966.
N. L.—5—Hugh A. Jennings, Baltimore, 1894 through 1898.
N. L. since 1900—4—Edward R. Miller, Boston, Cincinnati, 1940 through 1943.

Lowest Fielding Average, Season, for Leader, 100 or More Games

N. L.—.900—John W. Glasscock, Indianapolis, 109 games, 1888.
Arthur A. Irwin, Philadelphia, 121 games, 1888.
A. L.—.934—Fred N. Parent, Boston, 139 games, 1903; Montford M. Cross, Philadelphia, 138 games, 1903.
N. L. since 1900—.936—Thomas W. Corcoran, Cincinnati, 150 games, 1904.

Most Putouts, League

N. L.— 5133— Walter J. Maranville, Boston, Pittsburgh, Chicago, Brooklyn, St. Louis, 1912 through 1931 except 1924; 19 years.
A. L.— 4548— Luis E. Aparicio, Chicago, Baltimore, Boston, 18 years, 1956 through 1973.

Most Putouts, Season

N. L.— 425— Hugh A. Jennings, Baltimore, 131 games, 1895.
A. L.— 425— Owen Bush, Detroit, 157 games, 1914.
N. L. since 1900—407—Walter J. Maranville, Boston, 156 games, 1914.

Most Years Leading League in Putouts

N. L.—6—Walter J. Maranville, Boston, Pittsburgh, 1914, 1915 (tied), 1916, 1917, 1919, 1923.
A. L.—4—Joseph W. Sewell, Cleveland, 1924, 1925, 1926, 1927.
Louis Boudreau, Cleveland, 1941, 1943, 1944, 1946.
Edwin D. Joost, Philadelphia, 1947, 1948, 1949, 1951.
Luis E. Aparicio, Chicago, Baltimore, 1956, 1958, 1959, 1966.

Fewest Putouts, Season, 150 or More Games

N. L.— 180— Lawrence R. Bowa, Philadelphia, 156 games, 1976.
A. L.— 229— Zoilo Versalles, Minnesota, 159 games, 1967.

Fewest Putouts, Season, for Leader in Most Putouts

A. L.— 248— Joseph P. DeMaestri, Kansas City, 134 games, 1957.
N. L.— 257— Roy D. McMillan, Milwaukee, 154 games, 1961.
    L. Eugene Alley, Pittsburgh, 146 games, 1967.

Most Putouts, Game, Nine Innings

N. L.—11—William Fuller, New York, August 20, 1895.
    Horace H. Ford, Cincinnati, September 18, 1929.
A. L.—11—Joseph P. Cassidy, Washington, August 30, 1904, first game.

Most Putouts, Opening Game of Season, Nine Innings

N. L.—9—William F. Dahlen, Brooklyn, April 19, 1900.

Most Putouts, Extra-Inning Game

N. L.—14—Montford M. Cross, Philadelphia, July 7, 1899, 11 innings.
A. L.—Less than nine-inning game.

Most Putouts, Game, No Assists

N. L.—9—Charles L. Herzog, Cincinnati, May 26, 1916.

Most Assists, League

A. L.— 8016— Luis E. Aparicio, Chicago, Baltimore, Boston, 18 years, 1956 through 1973.
N. L.— 7414— William F. Dahlen, Chicago, Brooklyn, New York, Boston 1891 through
    1911, except 1910; 20 years.
N. L.—since 1900—7338—Walter J. Maranville, Boston, Pittsburgh, Chicago, Brooklyn,
    St. Louis, 1912 through 1931, except 1924; 19 years.

Most Assists, Season

N. L. (162-game season)—621—Osborne E. Smith, San Diego, 158 games, 1980.
N. L. (154-game season)—601—F. Glenn Wright, Pittsburgh, 153 games, 1924.
A. L. (162-game season)—572—Roy F. Smalley, Minnesota, 161 games, 1979.
A. L. (154-game season)—570—Terrence L. Turner, Cleveland, 147 games, 1906.

Most Years Leading League in Assists

A. L.—7—Lucius B. Appling, Chicago, 1933, 1935, 1937, 1939, 1941, 1943, 1946.
    Luis E. Aparicio, Chicago, 1956, 1957, 1958, 1959, 1960, 1961, 1968.
N. L.—5—Michael J. Doolan, Philadelphia, 1906, 1909, 1910, 1912, 1913.

Most Consecutive Years Leading League in Assists

A. L.—6—Luis E. Aparicio, Chicago, 1956 through 1961.
N. L.—4—George J. Smith, Cincinnati, 1891 through 1894.
    Osborne E. Smith, San Diego, St. Louis, 1979 through 1982.

Fewest Assists, Season, 150 or More Games

A. L.— 369— Edwin A. Brinkman, Washington, 150 games, 1965.
N. L.— 401— Derrel M. Harrelson, New York, 156 games, 1970.

Most Years With 500 or More Assists

A. L.—6—Owen Bush, Detroit, 1909, 1911, 1912, 1913, 1914, 1915.
N. L.—6—Donald E. Kessinger, Chicago, 1968 through 1973.

Fewest Assists, Season, for Leader in Most Assists

A. L.— 438— Joseph W. Sewell, Cleveland, 137 games, 1928.
N. L.— 440— John Logan, Milwaukee, 129 games, 1957.

Most Assists, Game, Nine Innings

N. L.—14—Thomas W. Corcoran, Cincinnati, August 7, 1903.
A. L.—13—Robert E. Reeves, Washington, August 7, 1927.

Most Assists, Extra-Inning Game

A. L.—15—Richard P. Burleson, California, April 13, 1982, 20 innings (completed April
    14).
N. L.—14—Herman C. Long, Boston, May 6, 1892, 14 innings.
    Derrel M. Harrelson, New York, May 24, 1973, 19 innings.

Fewest Assists, Longest Extra-Inning Game

N. L.—0—John F. Coffey, Boston, July 26, 1909, 17 innings.
A. L.—0—John P. Gochnauer, Cleveland, July 14, 1903, 12 innings.

Most Chances Accepted (Excluding Errors), League

A. L.—12,564—Luis E. Aparicio, Chicago, Baltimore, Boston, 18 years, 1956 through
    1973.
N. L.—12,471—Walter J. Maranville, Boston, Pittsburgh, Chicago, Brooklyn, St. Louis,
    1912 through 1931 except 1924, 19 years.

Most Chances Accepted (Excluding Errors), Season

   N. L.— 984— David J. Bancroft, New York, 156 games, 1922.
   A. L.— 969— Owen Bush, Detroit, 157 games, 1914.

Most Years Leading League in Chances Accepted (Excluding Errors)

   A. L.—7—Luis E. Aparicio, Chicago, 1956, 1957, 1958, 1959, 1960, 1961, 1968.
   N. L.—5—John W. Glasscock, Cleveland, St. Louis, Indianapolis, 1881, 1885, 1886, 1887,
        1889.
        Roy D. McMillan, Cincinnati, Milwaukee, 1952, 1953, 1955, 1956, 1961.

Most Chances Accepted (Excluding Errors), Game, Nine Innings

   N. L.—19—Daniel Richardson, Washington, June 20, 1892, first game.
        Edwin D. Joost, Cincinnati, May 7, 1941.
   A. L.—17—Roderick J. Wallace, St. Louis, June 10, 1902.

Most Chances Accepted (Excluding Errors), Extra-Inning Game

   N. L.—21—Edward R. Miller, Boston, June 27, 1939, 23 innings.
   A. L.—18—Fred A. Parent, Boston, July 9, 1902, 17 innings.
        Alfonso Carrasquel, Chicago, July 13, 1951, 19 innings.
        James L. Webb, Detroit, July 21, 1945, 24 innings.
        James E. Runnels, Washington, June 3, 1952, 17 innings.
        Ronald L. Hansen, Chicago, August 29, 1965, first game, 14 innings.

Most Chances Accepted (Excluding Errors), Doubleheader

   N. L.—25—Daniel Richardson, Washington, June 20, 1892.
   N. L. since 1900—24—John H. Sand, Philadelphia, July 4, 1924.
        David J. Bancroft, Boston, July 31, 1926.
   A. L.—24—George F. McBride, Washington, August 19, 1908.
        Roger T. Peckinpaugh, New York, September 8, 1919.
        Emory E. Rigney, Boston, July 15, 1926.

Most Chances Accepted, Doubleheader, More Than 18 Innings

   A. L.—28—Ronald L. Hansen, Chicago, August 29, 1965, 23 innings.
   N. L.—26—J. Floyd Vaughan, Pittsburgh, August 22, 1940, 21 innings.

Longest Game With No Chances Offered

   N. L.—12 innings— Irving B. Ray, Boston, August 15, 1888.
   A. L.—12 innings— John P. Gochnauer, Cleveland, July 14, 1903.
        11⅔ innings —William G. Rogell, Detroit, June 16, 1937.
   N. L. since 1900—11⅔ innings—Edward Feinberg, Philadelphia, May 19, 1939.
        11 innings— William F. Jurges, New York, September 22, 1942 (None out in
        12th).

Fewest Chances Offered, Opening Game of Season

   A. L.—0—Frank P. J. Crosetti, New York, April 16, 1940, 9⅔ innings.
   N. L.—0—John P. Wagner, Pittsburgh, April 14, 1910, 9 innings.

Fewest Chances Offered, Doubleheader

   A. L.—0—Colbert D. Harrah, Texas, June 25, 1976, 18 innings.
   N. L.—1—Travis C. Jackson, New York, May 30, 1934, 18 innings.

Fewest Chances Offered, Two Consecutive Games

   A. L.—0—Thomas M. Tresh, New York, July 31, August 1, 1968, 18 innings.
        Colbert D. Harrah, Texas, June 25, 25, 1976, 18 innings.
   N. L.—1—Travis C. Jackson, New York, May 30, 1934, 18 innings.
        Humberto P. Fernandez, Philadelphia, May 7, 8, 1957, 18 innings.
        Michael T. Fischlin, Houston, June 18, 20, 1978, 18 innings.

Fewest Chances Offered, Three Consecutive Games

   A. L.—0—Thomas M. Tresh, New York, July 30, 31, August 1, 1968, 26 innings.
   N. L.—3—Humberto P. Fernandez, Philadelphia, May 5, second game, 7, 8, 1957, 27
        innings.

Most Chances, Three Consecutive Games

   A. L.—37—Walter Gerber, St. Louis, May 27, 29, 30, first game, 1923.
   N. L.—35—George S. Davis, New York, May 23, 24, 25, 1899.
        George S. Davis, New York, July 19, 20, 21, 1900.

Most Chances Accepted (Excludes Errors), Four Consecutive Games

   A. L.—48—Walter Gerber, St. Louis, May 27, 29, 30, 30, 1923.
   N. L.—45—George S. Davis, New York, May 23, 24, 25, 26, 1899.
   N. L. since 1900—44—George S. Davis, New York, July 18, 19, 20, 21, 1900.

Fewest Chances Accepted (Excludes Errors), Season, 150 or More Games

A. L.— 623— Edward E. Lake, Detroit, 155 games, 1946.
N. L.— 670— William E. Russell, Los Angeles, 150 games, 1979.

Fewest Chances Accepted (Excludes Errors), Season, for Leader in Most Chances Accepted

A. L.— 695— Luis E. Aparicio, Chicago, 142 games, 1957.
N. L.— 703— John Logan, Milwaukee, 129 games, 1957.

Most Errors, Season

P. L.— 115— William Shindle, Philadelphia, 132 games, 1890.
N. L.— 106— Joseph D. Sullivan, Washington, 127 games, 1893.
A. L.— 95— John P. Gochnauer, Cleveland, 128 games, 1903.
N. L. since 1900—81—Rudolph E. Hulswitt, Philadelphia, 138 games, 1903.

Most Errors in Major Leagues

1037—Herman C. Long, Kansas City, A. A., Boston N. L., New York A. L., Detroit A. L.,
15 years, 1889 through 1903.

Most Errors, League

N. L.— 972— William F. Dahlen, Chicago, Brooklyn, New York, Boston, 1891 through
1911, except 1910, 20 years, 2,139 games.
A. L.— 689— Owen J. Bush, Detroit, Washington, 1908 through 1921, 14 years, 1,866
games.
N. L. since 1900—676—John P. Wagner, Pittsburgh, 1901 through 1917, 17 years, 1,887
games.

Fewest Errors, Season, 150 or More Games

A. L.—7—Edwin A. Brinkman, Detroit, 156 games, 1972.
N. L.—9—Lawrence R. Bowa, Philadelphia, 150 games, 1972.

Most Years Leading League in Errors

N. L.—6—Richard M. Groat, Pittsburgh, St. Louis, 1955, 1956, 1959, 1961, 1962, 1964.
A. L.—5—Lucius B. Appling, Chicago, 1933, 1935, 1937, 1939, 1946.

Fewest Errors, Season, for Leader in Most Errors

A. L.—24—Vernon D. Stephens, Boston, 155 games, 1948.
N. L.—27—Solomon J. Hemus, St. Louis, 150 games, 1953.

Most Errors, Inning

N. L.—4—William Fuller, Washington, August 17, 1888, second inning.
Leonard R. Merullo, Chicago, September 13, 1942, second game, second inning.
A. L.—4—Raymond J. Chapman, Cleveland, June 20, 1914, fifth inning.

Most Errors, Game, Nine Innings

N. L.—7—James H. Hallinan, New York, July 29, 1876.
A. A.—7—George Smith, Brooklyn, June 17, 1885.
N. L. since 1900—5—Charles Babb, New York, August 24, 1903, first game; also with
Brooklyn, June 20, 1904.
Phil Lewis, Brooklyn, July 20, 1905.
A. L.—5—Owen Bush, Detroit, August 25, 1911, first game.

Most Errors, Extra-Inning Game

A. L.—6—William J. O'Neill, Boston, May 21, 1904, 13 innings.
N. L.—5—Held by many shortstops.

Most Errors, Opening Game of Season, Nine Innings

N. L.—5—John J. Troy, New York, May 1, 1883.
N. L. since 1900—4—Louis B. Stringer, Chicago, April 15, 1941.
A. L.—3—Held by many shortstops.

Most Errors, First Major League Game

N. L.—4—Louis B. Stringer, Chicago, April 15, 1941.
A. L.—3—Held by many shortstops.

Most Errors, Doubleheader, 18 Innings

P. L.—9—Edward J. Delahanty, Cleveland, July 4, 1890.
N. L.—7—William Shindle, Baltimore, April 23, 1892.
N. L. since 1900—6—Samuel N. Strang, Chicago, Ocotber 8, 1900.
A. L.—5—John P. Gochnauer, Cleveland, September 10, 1902.
Albert Brancato, Philadelphia, September 13, 1940.
Zoilo Versalles, Minnesota, July 5, 1963.

Most Errors, Two Consecutive Nine-Inning Games

A. A.—10—George Smith, Brooklyn, June 16, 17, 1885.
N. L.— 9—Fred N. Pfeffer, Troy, September 7, 9, 1882.
A. L.— 6— Juan J. Beniquez, Boston, July 13 (3), July 14 (3), 1972.

Longest Errorless Game

N.L.—26 innings— Walter J. Maranville, Boston, May 1, 1920.
A. L.—24 innings— Fred N. Parent, Boston, September 1, 1906.

Most Consecutive Errorless Games, Season

A. L.—72—Edwin A. Brinkman, Detroit, May 21 through August 4, 1972, 331 chances
            accepted.
N. L.—59—Roger H. Metzger, Houston, June 8 through August 14, 1976, 269 chances
            accepted.

Most Consecutive Errorless Games, League

A. L.—72—Edwin A. Brinkman, Detroit, May 21 through August 4, 1972, 331 chances
            accepted.
N. L.—68—John J. Kerr, New York, July 28, second game, 1946 through May 24, 1947,
            52 in 1946; 16 in 1947, 375 chances accepted.

Most Consecutive Chances Accepted, Season, No Errors

A. L.— 331— Edwin A. Brinkman, Detroit, May 21 through August 4, 1972, 72 games.
N. L.— 286— John J. Kerr, New York, July 28, first game (part), through September 29,
            1946, 53 games.

Most Consecutive Chances Accepted, League, No Errors

N. L.—383— John J. Kerr, New York, July 28, first game (part), 1946 through May 25,
            1947 (part); 286 in 1946; 97 in 1947; 70 games.
A. L.— 331— Edwin A. Brinkman, Detroit, May 21 through August 4, 1972, 72 games.

Most Double Plays, Season

A. L.— 147— Richard P. Burleson, Boston, 155 games, 1980.
N. L.—137— Robert P. Wine, Montreal, 159 games, 1970.

Most Double Plays, League

A. L.— 1553— Luis E. Aparicio, Chicago, Baltimore, Boston, 18 years, 1956 through 1973.
N. L.— 1304— Roy D. McMillan, Cincinnati, Milwaukee, New York, 16 years, 1951
            through 1966.

Most Years Leading League in Double Plays

A. L.—6—George F. McBride, Washington, 1908, 1909, 1910, 1911, 1912 (tied), 1914.
N. L.—5—Michael J. Doolan, Philadelphia, 1907, 1909 (tied), 1910, 1911, 1913.
            Richard M. Groat, Pittsburgh, St. Louis, 1958, 1959, 1961, 1962, 1964.

Fewest Double Plays, Season, 150 or More Games

N. L.—64—William E. Russell, Los Angeles, 150 games, 1982.
            Ivan DeJesus, Philadelphia, 158 games, 1983.
A. L.—65—L. Everett Scott, New York, 152 games, 1923.

Fewest Double Plays, Season, for Leader in Most Double Plays

A. L.—81—Roger Peckinpaugh, Washington, 155 games, 1924.
N. L.—81—John J. Kerr, New York, 148 games, 1945.

Most Double Plays, Nine-Inning Game

A. L.—5—29 times. Held by 25 shortstops. Last shortstop—Nelson A. Norman, Texas,
            April 23, 1979.
N. L.—5—18 times. Held by 18 shortstops. Last shortstop—David E. Concepcion, Cincin-
            nati, June 25, 1975.

Most Double Plays, Extra-Inning Game

A. L.—6—Dagoberto B. Campaneris, Oakland, September 13, 1970 first game, 11 in-
            nings.
N. L.—5—John C. Ryan, Philadelphia, April 21, 1935.

Most Double Plays Started, Game

A. L.—5—Charles T. O'Leary, Detroit, July 23, 1905.
            John P. Sullivan, Washington, August 13, 1944, second game.
            James L. Fregosi, California, May 1, 1966, first game.
N. L.—4—William L. Kopf, Boston, April 28, 1922.
            James E. Cooney, Chicago, June 13, 1926.
            William H. Myers, Cincinnati, June 4, 1939.
            Alvin R. Dark, New York, July 21, 1955.
            Donald E. Kessinger, July 21, 1971.

Most Unassisted Double Plays, Game

    A. L.—2—Lee Ford Tannehill, Chicago, August 4, 1911, first game.
    N. L.—1—Held by many shortstops.

Most Innings Played, Game

    N. L.—26—Charles W. Ward, Brooklyn, May 1, 1920.
               Walter J. Maranville, Boston, May 1, 1920.
    A. L.—24—Fred N. Parent, Boston, September 1, 1906.
               Montford M. Cross, Philadelphia, September 1, 1906.
               Edgar J. Busch, Philadelphia, July 21, 1945.
               James L. Webb, Detroit, July 21, 1945.

OUTFIELDERS' FIELDING RECORDS

Most Years, League

    A. L.—24—Tyrus R. Cobb, Detroit, Philadelphia, 1905 through 1928, 2938 games.
    N. L.—22—Willie H. Mays, original New York club, San Francisco, present New York club, 1951 through 1973 (except 1953 in military service), 2843 games.

Most Games, League

    A. L.— 2938— Tyrus R. Cobb, Detroit, Philadelphia, 1905 through 1928, 24 years.
    N. L.— 2843— Willie H. Mays, original New York club, San Francisco, present New York club, 1951 through 1973, 22 years, (except 1953 in military service).

Most Games, Season

    A. L. (162-game season)—163—Leon L. Wagner, Cleveland, 1964.
    A. L. (154-game season)—162—James E. Barrett, Detroit, 1904.
    N. L. (162-game season)—164—Billy L. Williams, Chicago, 1965.
    N. L. (154-game season)—160—Thomas H. Griffith, Cincinnati, 1915.

Most Consecutive Games Played, League

    N. L.— 897— Billy L. Williams, Chicago, September 22, 1963 through June 13, 1969.
    A. L.— 511— J. Clyde Milan, Washington, August 12, 1910, through October 3, 1913, second game.

Most Years Leading League in Most Games

    N. L.—6—George J. Burns, New York, Cincinnati, 1914 (tied), 1916 (tied), 1919, 1920 (tied), 1922, 1923 (tied).
           Billy L. Williams, Chicago, 1964 (tied), 1965, 1966, 1967, 1968, 1970 (tied).
    A. L.—5—Rocco D. Colavito, Cleveland, Detroit, 1959, 1961, 1962, 1963, 1965.

Fewest Games, Season, for Leader in Most Games

    A. L.— 147— Theodore S. Williams, Boston, 1951.
    N. L.— 149— Max Carey, Pittsburgh, 1924.
            Chester J. Ross, Boston, 1940.

Highest Fielding Average, Season, 100 or More Games

    N. L.—1.000—Daniel W. Litwhiler, Philadelphia, 151 games, 1942.
                Willard W. Marshall, Boston, 136 games, 1951.
                A. Antonio Gonzalez, Philadelphia, 114 games, 1962.
                Donald L. Demeter, Philadelphia, 119 games, 1963.
                Curtis C. Flood, St. Louis, 159 games, 1966.
                John W. Callison, Philadelphia, 109 games, 1968.
                Terry S. Puhl, Houston, 152 games, 1979.
                Gary L. Woods, Chicago, 103 games, 1982.
    A. L.—1.000—Rocco D. Colavito, Cleveland, 162 games, 1965.
                Russell H. Snyder, Baltimore, 106 games, 1965.
                Kenneth S. Harrelson, Boston, 132 games, 1968.
                Mitchell J. Stanley, Detroit, 130 games, 1968.
                A. Kent Berry, Chicago, 120 games, 1969.
                Mitchell J. Stanley, Detroit, 132 games, 1970.
                Roy H. White, New York, 145 games, 1971.
                Albert W. Kaline, Detroit, 129 games, 1971.
                A. Kent Berry, California, 116 games, 1972.
                Carl M. Yastrzemski, Boston, 140 games, 1977.
                William A. Sample, Texas, 103 games, 1979.
                Gary S. Roenicke, Baltimore, 113 games, 1980.
                Robert C. Clark, California, 102 games, 1982.
                Brian J. Downing, California, 158 games, 1982.
                John L. Lowenstein, Baltimore, 112 games, 1982.

Highest Fielding Average, Season, 150 or More Games

N. L.—1.000—Daniel W. Litwhiler, Philadelphia, 151 games, 1942.
Curtis C. Flood, St. Louis, 159 games, 1966.
Terry S. Puhl, Houston, 152 games, 1979.
A. L.—1.000—Rocco D. Colavito, Cleveland, 162 games, 1965.
Brian J. Downing, California, 158 games, 1982.

Highest Fielding Average, League, 1000 or More Games

N. L.—.9917—Peter E. Rose, Cincinnati, Philadelphia, 13 years, 1963, 1967 through 1976, 1978, 1983, 1,299 games.
A. L.—.9907—Joseph O. Rudi, Kansas City, Oakland, California, Boston, 16 years, 1967 through 1982, 1,195 games.
.9907—Mitchell J. Stanley, Detroit, 15 years, 1964 through 1978, 1,989 games.

Lowest Fielding Average, Season, 100 or More Games

N. L.—.843—John Manning, Philadelphia, 103 games, 1884.
A. L.—.872—William J. O'Neill, Washington, 112 games, 1904.
N. L.—since 1900—.900—Michael J. Donlin, Cincinnati, 118 games, 1903.

Lowest Fielding Average, Season, for Leader, 100 or More Games

N. L.—.941—Patrick Gillespie, New York, 102 games, 1885.
A. L.—.959—Charles S. Stahl, Boston, 130 games, 1901.
N. L. since 1900—.968—John J. Murray, New York, 143 games, 1912.
Max Carey, Pittsburgh, 150 games, 1912.
Zachariah D. Wheat, Brooklyn, 120 games, 1912.

Most Years Leading in Fielding Average, 100 or More Games (162-Game Season, 108 or More Games)

A. L.—5—Amos E. Strunk, Philadelphia, Boston, Chicago, 1912, 1914, 1917, (tied), 1918, 1920.
N. L.—4—Joseph Hornung, Boston, 1881, 1882, 1883, 1887.
Walter S. Brodie, Boston, Pittsburgh, Baltimore, 1890, 1891, 1897, 1899.
N. L. since 1900—3—Stanley F. Musial, St. Louis, 1949, 1954, 1961.
A. Antonio Gonzalez, Philadelphia, 1962, 1964, 1967.
Peter E. Rose, Cincinnati, 1970, 1971 (tied), 1974.

Most Consecutive Years Leading League in Fielding Average, 100 or More Games

N. L.—3—Joseph Hornung, Boston, 1881, 1882, 1883.
A. L.—3—Eugene R. Woodling, New York, 1951 (tied), 1952, 1953 (tied).
N. L. since 1900—2—Held by many outfielders. Last outfielder—Peter E. Rose, Cincinnati, 1970, 1971 (tied).

Most Putouts, League

N. L.—7095—Willie H. Mays, original New York club, San Francisco, present New York club, 22 years, 1951 through 1973 (except 1953 in military service).
A. L.—6794—Tristram Speaker, Boston, Cleveland, Washington, Philadelphia, 1907-1928, 22 years.

Most Years Leading League in Putouts

N. L.—9—Max Carey, Pittsburgh, 1912, 1913, 1916, 1917, 1918, 1921, 1922, 1923, 1924.
Richie Ashburn, Philadelphia, 1949, 1950, 1951, 1952, 1953, 1954, 1956, 1957, 1958.
A. L.—7—Tristram Speaker, Boston, Cleveland, 1909, 1910, 1913, 1914, 1915, 1918, 1919.

Most Putouts, Season

N. L.— 547— Taylor L. Douthit, St. Louis, 154 games, 1928.
A. L.— 512— Chester E. Lemon, Chicago, 149 games, 1977.

Fewest Putouts, Season, 150 or More Games

A. L.— 182— Edgar Hahn, Chicago, 156 games, 1907.
N. L.— 210— Samuel L. Thompson, Philadelphia, 151 games, 1892.
N. L. since 1900—221—Frank M. Schulte, Chicago, 150 games, 1910.

Fewest Putouts, Season, for Leader in Most Putouts

A. L.— 319— Tristram Speaker, Boston, 142 games, 1909.
N. L.— 321— Roy Thomas, Philadelphia, 139 games, 1904.

Most Years With 500 or More Putouts

N. L.—4—Richie Ashburn, Philadelphia, 1949, 1951, 1956, 1957.
A. L.—1—Dominic P. DiMaggio, Boston, 1948.
Chester E. Lemon, Chicago, 1977.
Dwayne K. Murphy, Oakland, 1980.

Most Years With 400 or More Putouts

N. L.—9—Richie Ashburn, Philadelphia, 1949, 1950, 1951, 1952, 1953, 1954, 1956, 1957, 1958.
A. L.—4—Samuel F. West, Washington, St. Louis, 1931, 1932, 1935, 1936.
     Dominic P. DiMaggio, Boston, 1942, 1947, 1948, 1949.
     Samuel B. Chapman, Philadelphia, 1941, 1947, 1949, 1950.
     J. Gorman Thomas, Milwaukee, Cleveland, 1979, 1980, 1982, 1983.

Most Putouts, Game, Nine Innings, Center Field

N. L.—12—Earl B. Clark, Boston, May 10, 1929.
A. L.—12—Lyman W. Bostock, Minnesota, May 25, 1977, second game.

Most Putouts, Extra-Inning Game, Center Field

A. L.—12—Harry D. Bay, Cleveland, July 19, 1904, 12 innings.
     Ruppert S. Jones, Seattle, May 16, 1978, 16 innings.
     Richard E. Manning, Milwaukee, July 11, 1983, 15 innings.
N. L.—12—Carden E. Gillenwater, Boston, September 11, 1946, 17 innings.
     Lloyd Merriman, Cincinnati, September 7, 1951, 18 innings.

Most Putouts, Game, Nine Innings, Left Field

N. L.—11—Richard J. Harley, St. Louis, June 30, 1898.
     T. Frederick Hartsel, Chicago, September 10, 1901.
A. L.—11—Paul E. Lehner, Philadelphia, June 25, 1950, second game.
     Willie Horton, Detroit, July 18, 1969.

Most Putouts, Extra-Inning Game, Left Field

A. L.—12—Thomas McBride, Washington, July 2, 1948, 12 innings.
N. L.—Less than nine-inning game.

Most Putouts, Game, Right Field

A. L.—11—Antonio R. Armas, Oakland, June 12, 1982.
N. L.—10—William B. Nicholson, Chicago, September 17, 1945.

Most Putouts, Doubleheader, Center Field, 18 Innings

N. L.—18—Lloyd J. Waner, Pittsburgh, June 26, 1935.
A. L.—17—Lyman W. Bostock, Minnesota, May 25, 1977.

Most Consecutive Putouts, Game

A. L.—7—W. Benjamin Chapman, Boston, June 25, 1937, right field.
N. L.—6—Edd J. Roush, Cincinnati, July 4, 1919, a.m. game, center field.

Most Assists, League

A. L.— 450— Tristram Speaker, Boston, Cleveland, Washington, Philadelphia, 1907 through 1928, 22 years.
N. L.— 356— James E. Ryan, Chicago, 1885 through 1900 except 1890; 15 years.
N. L. since 1900—339—Max Carey, Pittsburgh, Brooklyn, 1910 through 1929; 20 years.

Most Assists, Season

N. L.—45—A. Harding Richardson, Buffalo, 78 games, 1881.
N. L. since 1900—44—Charles H. Klein, Philadelphia, 156 games, 1930.
A. L.—35—Samuel Mertes, Chicago, 123 games, 1902.
     Tristram Speaker, Boston, 142 games, 1909, also 153 games, 1912.

Most Years Leading League in Assists

A. L.—7—Carl M. Yastrzemski, Boston, 1962, 1963, 1964 (tied), 1966, 1969, 1971, 1977.
N. L.—5—Roberto W. Clemente, Pittsburgh, 1958, 1960, 1961, 1966, 1967.

Fewest Assists, Season, 150 or More Games

A. L.—1—Harmon C. Killebrew, Minnesota, 157 games, 1964.
N. L.—3—Billy L. Williams, Chicago, 162 games, 1967.
     Louis C. Brock, St. Louis, 159 games, 1973.

Fewest Assists, Season, for Leader in Most Assists

A. L.—13—A. Kent Berry, California, 116 games, 1972.
     Carlos May, Chicago, 145 games, 1972.
N. L.—14—William H. Bruton, Milwaukee, 141 games, 1954.
     Donald F. Mueller, New York, 153 games, 1954.
     Frank J. Thomas, Pittsburgh, 153 games, 1954.

Most Assists, Game, Nine Innings

N. L.—4—Harry C. Schafer, Boston, September 26, 1877.
     William W. Crowley, Buffalo, May 24, 1880.
     William W. Crowley, Buffalo, August 27, 1880.
     Frederick C. Clarke, Pittsburgh, August 23, 1910.
     Walter A. Berger, Boston, April 27, 1931.

Most Assists, Game, Nine Innings—Continued

A. L.—4—William J. Holmes, Chicago, August 21, 1903.
Lee C. Magee, New York, June 28, 1916.
Oscar C. Felsch, Chicago, August 14, 1919.
Robert W. Meusel, New York, September 5, 1921, second game.
Elton Langford, Cleveland, May 1, 1928.

Most Assists, Extra-Inning Game

N. L.—4—Charles B. Miller, May 30, 1895, second game, 11 innings.
A. L.—3—Held by many outfielders.

Most Assists, Game, Outfielder to Catcher

N. L.—3—William E. Hoy, Washington, June 19, 1899.
James T. Jones, New York, June 30, 1902.
John McCarthy, Chicago, April 26, 1905.
A. L.—2—Held by many outfielders.

Most Assists, Inning

N. L.—2—Held by many outfielders.
A. L.—2—Held by many outfielders.

Most Chances Accepted (Excludes Errors), Season

N. L.— 557— Taylor L. Douthit, St. Louis, 154 games, 1928.
A. L.— 524— Chester E. Lemon, Chicago, 149 games, 1977.

Most Years Leading League in Chances Accepted (Excludes Errors)

N. L.—9—Max Carey, Pittsburgh, 1912, 1913, 1916, 1917, 1918, 1921, 1922, 1923, 1924.
Richie Ashburn, Philadelphia, 1949, 1950, 1951, 1952, 1953, 1954, 1956, 1957, 1958.
A. L.—8—Tristram Speaker, Boston, Cleveland, 1909, 1910, 1912, 1913, 1914, 1915, 1918, 1919.

Fewest Chances Accepted (Excludes Errors), Season, 150 or More Games

A. L.— 206— Edgar Hahn, Chicago, 156 games, 1907.
N. L.— 235— Johnnie B. Baker, Los Angeles, 152 games, 1977.

Fewest Chances Accepted (Excludes Errors), Season, for Leaders in Chances Accepted

A. L.— 333— Samuel Crawford, Detroit, 144 games, 1907.
N. L.— 342— Roy Thomas, Philadelphia, 139 games, 1904.

Most Chances Accepted (Excludes Errors), League

N. L.— 7290— Willie H. Mays, original New York club, San Francisco, present New York club, 22 years, 1951 through 1973 (except 1953 in military service).
A. L.— 7244— Tristram Speaker, Boston, Cleveland, Washington, Philadelphia, 22 years, 1907 through 1928.

Most Chances Accepted (Excludes Errors), Game, Nine Innings, Center Field

N. L.—13—Earl B. Clark, Boston, May 10, 1929.
A. L.—12—Oscar C. Felsch, Chicago, June 23, 1919.
John A. Mostil, Chicago, May 22, 1928.
Lyman W. Bostock, Minnesota, May 25, 1977, second game.

Most Chances Accepted (Excludes Errors), Extra-Inning Game, Center Field

A. L.—12—Harry D. Bay, Cleveland, July 19, 1904, 12 innings.
Ruppert S. Jones, Seattle, May 16, 1978, 16 innings.
Richard E. Manning, Milwaukee, July 11, 1983, 15 innings.
N. L.—12—Carden E. Gillenwater, Boston, September 11, 1946, 17 innings.
Lloyd Merriman, Cincinnati, September 7, 1951, 18 innings.

Most Chances Accepted (Excludes Errors), Game, Nine Innings, Left Field

N. L.—11—Joseph Hornung, Boston, September 23, 1881.
Richard J. Harley, St. Louis, June 30, 1898.
T. Frederick Hartsel, Chicago, September 10, 1901.
A. L.—11—Paul E. Lehner, Philadelphia, June 25, 1950, second game.
Willie Horton, Detroit July 18, 1969.

Most Chances Accepted (Excludes Errors), Extra-Inning Game, Left Field

A. L.—12—Thomas McBride, Washington, July 2, 1948, 12 innings.
N. L.—Less than nine-inning game.

Most Chances Accepted (Excludes Errors), Game, Nine Innings, Right Field

A. L.—12—Antonio R. Armas, Oakland, June 12, 1982.
N. L.—11—Harry C. Schafer, Boston, September 26, 1877.

N. L. since 1900—10—Alfred E. Neale, Cincinnati, July 13, 1920.
    Charles D. Stengel, Philadelphia, July 30, 1920.
    William B. Nicholson, Chicago, September 17, 1945.
    Arnold R. McBride, Philadelphia, September 8, 1978, second game.

Most Chances Accepted (Excludes Errors), Doubleheader, Center Field, 18 Innings

N. L.—18—Lloyd J. Waner, Pittsburgh, June 26, 1935.
A. L.—17—Lyman W. Bostock, Minnesota, May 25, 1977.

Most Chances Accepted (Excludes Errors), Doubleheader, Center Field (One Extra-Inning Game Included)

A. L.—Less than 18-inning doubleheader.
N. L.—Less than 18-inning doubleheader.

Most Chances Accepted (Excl. Errors), Two Consecutive Games, Center Field

A. L.—21—Oscar C. Felsch, Chicago, June 23, 24, 1919.
N. L.—20—Earl B. Clark, Boston, May 10, 11, 1929.

Longest Game With No Chances Offered

A. L.—22 innings— William H. Bruton, Detroit, June 24, 1962.
    Charles A. Peterson, Washington, June 12, 1967.
N. L.—18 innings— Lance Richbourg, Boston, May 14, 1927.
    Arthur L. Shamsky, Cincinnati, July 19, 1966.

Longest Game With No Chances Offered, Center Field

A. L.—22 innings— William H. Bruton, Detroit, June 24, 1962.
N. L.—17⅓ innings—Earnest R. Orsatti, St. Louis, July 2, 1933, first game.

Longest Game With No Chances Offered, Left Field

N. L.—16 innings— Joseph Delahanty, St. Louis, July 19, 1908.
A. L.—16 innings— Robert L. Johnson, Philadelphia, June 5, 1942.
    Patrick J. Mullin, Detroit, May 9, 1952.

Longest Game With No Chances Offered, Right Field

A. L.—22 innings— Charles A. Peterson, Washington, June 12, 1967.
N. L.—18 innings— Lance Richbourg, Boston, May 14, 1927.
    Arthur L. Shamsky, Cincinnati, July 19, 1966.

Longest Season Opening Game With No Chances Offered

A. L.—14 innings— Charles J. Hemphill, New York, April 14, 1910.
    Arthur C. Engle, New York, April 14, 1910.
N. L.—13 innings— Charles L. Herzog, New York, April 15, 1909.
    William O'Hara, New York, April 15, 1909.

Longest Doubleheader With No Chances Offered

A. L.—24 innings— Roger E. Maris, New York, August 6, 1961.
N. L.—21 innings— Dain E. Clay, Cincinnati, September 21, 1944.

Most Consecutive Games With No Chances Offered

A. L.—7—William C. Jacobson, Boston, June 18, 19, 20, 21, 24, 25, 25, 1926, 64⅓ innings, right field.
N. L.—6—Frank M. Schulte, Chicago, June 25, 25, 26, 27, 28, 29, 1912, right field.

Most Errors, Season

P. L.—52—Edward Beecher, Buffalo, 125 games, 1890.
N. L.—47—George H. Van Haltren, Baltimore, Pittsburgh, 143 games, 1892.
N. L. since 1900—36—J. Bentley Seymour, Cincinnati, 135 games, 1903.
A. L.—31—Roy C. Johnson, Detroit, 146 games, 1929.

Most Errors, Major Leagues

384—William E. Hoy, Washington N. L., Buffalo P. L., St. Louis, A. A., Cincinnati N. L., Louisville N. L., Chicago A. L., 14 years, 1888 through 1902, except 1900.

Most Errors, League

N. L.— 347— George F. Gore, Chicago, New York, St. Louis, 13 years, 1879 through 1892, except 1890.
A. L.— 271— Tyrus R. Cobb, Detroit, Philadelphia, 24 years, 1905 through 1928.
N. L. since 1900—235—Max Carey, Pittsburgh, Brooklyn, 20 years, 1910 through 1929.

Most Years Leading League in Errors

N. L.—7—Louis C. Brock, Chicago, St. Louis, 1964, 1965, 1966, 1967, 1968 (tied), 1972, 1973 (tied).
A. L.—5—Burton E. Shotton, St. Louis, Washington, 1912 (tied), 1914, 1915 (tied), 1916, 1918.
    Reginald M. Jackson, Oakland, Baltimore, 1968, 1970, 1972, 1975, 1976 (tied).

Fewest Errors, Season, 150 or More Games

N. L.—0—Daniel W. Litwhiler, Philadelphia, 151 games, 1942.
Curtis C. Flood, St. Louis, 159 games, 1966.
Terry S. Puhl, Houston, 152 games, 1979.
A. L.—0—Rocco D. Colavito, Cleveland, 162 games, 1965.
Brian J. Downing, California, 158 games, 1982.

Fewest Errors, Season, for Leader in Most Errors

A. L.— 9—Roger E. Maris, Cleveland-Kansas City, 146 games, 1958.
Reginald M. Jackson, Oakland, 135 games, 1972.
N. L.—10—Samuel Jethroe, Boston, 140 games, 1951.
Walter C. Post, Philadelphia, 91 games, 1958.
Joseph R. Cunningham, St. Louis, 116 games, 1960.

Most Errors, Inning

N. L.—3—George Gore, Chicago, August 8, 1883, first inning.
Larry D. Herndon, San Francisco, Septembr 6, 1980, fourth inning.
A. A.—3—James A. Donahue, Kansas City, July 4, 1889, p.m. game. first inning.
A. L.—3—Albert C. Selbach, Washington, June 23, 1904, eighth inning.
Harry D. Bay, Cleveland, June 29, 1905, second game, ninth inning.
Harry E. Heilmann, Detroit, May 22, 1914, first inning.
Herschel E. Bennett, St. Louis, April 14, 1925, eighth inning.

Most Errors, Game, Nine Innings

N. L.—5—John E. Manning, Boston, May 1, 1876.
Charles N. Snyder, Louisville, July 29, 1876.
James H. O'Rourke, Boston, June 21, 1877.
Charles W. Bennett, Milwaukee, June 15, 1878.
Michael J. Dorgan, New York, May 24, 1884.
Michael J. Tiernan, New York, May 16, 1887.
Martin C. Sullivan, Chicago, May 18, 1887.
A. A.—5—James S. Clinton, Baltimore, May 3, 1884.
U. A.—5—Frederick C. Tenney, Washington, May 29, 1884.
A. L.—5—Albert C. Selbach, Baltimore, August 19, 1902.
N. L. since 1900—4—Fred Nicholson, Boston, June 16, 1922.

Longest Errorless Game

N. L.—26 innings— Walton E. Cruise, Boston, May 1, 1920.
Leslie Mann, Boston, May 1, 1920.
Bernard E. Neis, Brooklyn, May 1, 1920.
Raymond R. Powell, Boston, May 1, 1920.
Zachariah D. Wheat, Brooklyn, May 1, 1920.
A. L.—24 innings— T. Frederick Hartsel, Philadelphia, September 1, 1906.
John F. Hayden, Boston, September 1, 1906.
John Hoey, Boston, September 1, 1906.
Briscoe Lord, Philadelphia, September 1, 1906.
Ralph Q. Seybold, Philadelphia, September 1, 1906.
Charles S. Stahl, Boston, September 1, 1906.
Roger M. Cramer, Detroit, July 21, 1945.
Roy J. Cullenbine, Detroit, July 21, 1945.
Roberto Estalella, Philadelphia, July 21, 1945.
William M. McGhee, Philadelphia, July 21, 1945.
Harold A. Peck, Philadelphia, July 21, 1945.

Most Consecutive Errorless Games, Season

A. L.— 162— Rocco D. Colavito, Cleveland, April 13 through October 3, 1965 (274 chances accepted).
N. L.— 159— Curtis C. Flood, St. Louis, April 13 through October 2, 1966 (396 chances accepted).

Most Consecutive Errorless Games, Major Leagues

266—Donald L. Demeter, Philadelphia, N. L., Detroit A. L., September 3, 1962, first game, through July 6, 1965 (449 chances accepted).

Most Consecutive Errorless Games, League

A. L.— 244— Brian J. Downing, California, May 25, 1981 through July 21, second game 1983 (471 chances accepted).
N. L.— 226— Curtis C. Flood, St. Louis, September 3, 1965 through June 2, 1967 (566 chances accepted) also first two chances on June 4, for total of 568.

Most Consecutive Chances Accepted, League, No Errors

N. L.— 568— Curtis C. Flood, St. Louis, September 3, 1965 through June 4 (part) 1967, 227 games.
A. L.— 510— A. Kent Berry, California, September 16, 1971 through July 27, 1973, 211 games.

Most Double Plays, Season

    A. L.—15—Oscar C. Felsch, Chicago, 125 games, 1919.
    N. L.—12—Melvin T. Ott, New York, 149 games, 1929.

Most Double Plays, League

    A. L.— 135— Tristram Speaker, Boston, Cleveland, Washington, Philadelphia, 22 years, 1907 through 1928.
    N. L.— 86— Max Carey, Pittsburgh, Brooklyn, 20 years, 1910 through 1929.

Most Years Leading League in Double Plays

    A. L.—5—Tristram Speaker, Boston, Cleveland, 1909, 1912, 1914, 1915, 1916.
    N. L.—4—Willie H. Mays, New York, San Francisco, 1954, 1955, 1956, 1965.

Fewest Double Plays, Season, 150 or More Games

    N. L.-A. L.—0—Held by many outfielders.
    N. L.—Last outfielder—Dale B. Murphy, Atlanta, 160 games, 1983.
    A. L.—Last outfielder—Richard E. Manning, Cleveland, Milwaukee, 158 games, 1983.

Fewest Double Plays, Season, for Leader in Most Double Plays

    N. L.—4—Held by 5 players. Last outfielder—Brett M. Butler, Atlanta, 143 games, 1983.
    A. L.—4—Held by 19 players. Last 2 outfielders—Antonio R. Armas, Oakland 112 games, 1977; Roy H. White, New York, 135 games, 1977.

Most Double Plays Started, Game

    A. A.—3—John Nelson, New York, June 9, 1887.
    N. L.—3—John McCarthy, Chicago, April 26, 1905.
    A. L.—3—Ira Flagstead, Boston, April 19, 1926, p.m. game.

Most Triple Plays Started, Season

    A. L.—2—Charles D. Jamieson, Cleveland, May 23, June 9, 1928.
    N. L.—1—Held by many outfielders.

Most Unassisted Double Plays, Season

    A. L.—2—Ralph O. Seybold, Philadelphia, August 15, September 10, first game, 1907.
          Tristram Speaker, Cleveland, April 18, April 29, 1918.
          Jose D. Cardenal, Cleveland, June 8, July 16, 1968.
    N. L.—2—Adam Comorosky, Pittsburgh, May 31, June 13, 1931.

Most Unassisted Double Plays, Major Leagues

    4—Tristram Speaker, Boston A. L., Cleveland A. L., 1909 (1), 1914 (1), 1918 (2).
       Elmer J. Smith, Cleveland A. L., New York A. L., Cincinnati N. L., 1915 (1), 1920 (1), 1923 (1), 1925 (1); (3 in A. L., 1 in N. L.)

Most Unassisted Double Plays, League

    A. L.—4—Tristram Speaker, Boston, Cleveland, 1 in 1909, 1 in 1914, 2 in 1918.
    N. L.—2—Held by many outfielders.

Most Unassisted Double Plays, Game

    N. L.-A. L.—1—Held by many outfielders.
    N. L.—Last outfielder—Bobby L. Bonds, San Francisco, May 31, 1972, fourth inning.
    A. L.—Last outfielder—William A. North, Oakland, July 28, 1974, second game, fifth inning.

Most Innings Played, Game

    N. L.—26—Walton E. Cruise, Boston, May 1, 1920.
          Leslie Mann, Boston, May 1, 1920.
          Bernard E. Neis, Brooklyn, May 1, 1920.
          Raymond R. Powell, Boston, May 1, 1920.
          Zachariah D. Wheat, Brooklyn, May 1, 1920.
    A. L.—24—T. Frederick Hartsel, Philadelphia, September 1, 1906.
          John F. Hayden, Boston, September 1, 1906.
          John Hoey, Boston, September 1, 1906.
          Briscoe Lord, Philadelphia, September 1, 1906.
          Ralph O. Seybold, Philadelphia, September 1, 1906.
          Charles S. Stahl, Boston, September 1, 1906.
          Roger Cramer, Detroit, July 21, 1945.
          Roy J. Cullenbine, Detroit, July 21, 1945.
          Roberto Estalella, Philadelphia, July 21, 1945.
          William M. McGhee, Philadelphia, July 21, 1945.
          Harold A. Peck, Philadelphia, July 21, 1945.

CATCHERS' FIELDING RECORDS

Most Years in Majors

25—James T. McGuire, Toledo, Cleveland, Rochester, Washington A. A.; Detroit, Phila-delphia, Washington, Brooklyn N. L.; Detroit, New York, Boston, Cleveland A. L., 1884 through 1912, except 1889, 1908, 1909, 1911 4 (part) in A. A.; 14 (part) in N. L.; (9 in A. L.) 1,608 games.

Most Years, League

N. L.—21—Robert A. O'Farrell, Chicago, St. Louis, New York, Cincinnati, 1915 through 1935, 1,338 games.

A. L.—20—J. Luther Sewell, Cleveland, Washington, Chicago, St. Louis, 1921 through 1942 except 1940, 1941.

Most Games in Majors

1,918—Alfonso R. Lopez, Brooklyn, N. L., Boston, N. L., Pittsburgh, N. L., Cleveland, A. L., 1928 through 1947, except 1929, 19 years; 1,861 in N. L., 57 in A. L.

Most Games, League

N. L.—1,861—Alfonso R. Lopez, Brooklyn, Boston, Pittsburgh, 1928 through 1946, ex-cept 1929, 18 years.

A. L.—1,806—Richard B. Ferrell, St. Louis, Boston, Washington, 1929 through 1947, ex-cept 1946, 18 years.

Most Consecutive Games, League

A. L.— 312— Frank W. Hayes, St. Louis, Philadelphia, Cleveland, October 2, second game, 1943 through April 21, 1946.

N. L.— 233— Ray C. Mueller, Cincinnati, July 31, 1943, through May 5, 1946 (spent en-tire 1945 season in military service).

Most Years With 100 or More Games, League

A. L.—13—William M. Dickey, New York, 1929 through 1941.

N. L.—13—Johnny L. Bench, Cincinnati, 1968 through 1980.

Most Consecutive Years With 100 or More Games, League

A. L.—13—William M. Dickey, New York, 1929 through 1941.

N. L.—13—Johnny L. Bench, Cincinnati, 1968 through 1980.

Most Games, Season

N. L. (162-game season)—160—C. Randolph Hundley, Chicago, 1968 (147 complete).

A. L. (162-game season)—155—James H. Sundberg, Texas, 1975.

A. L. (154-game season)—155—Frank W. Hayes, Philadelphia, 1944 (135 complete).

N. L. (154-game season)—155—Ray C. Mueller, Cincinnati, 1944 (135 complete).

Catching All Club's Games, Season (Not Complete)

N. L.— 155— Ray C. Mueller, Cincinnati, 1944 (135 complete).

A. L.— 155— Frank W. Hayes, Philadelphia, 1944 (135 complete), (Hayes also caught the full schedule in 1945, when he played for two clubs—151 games, 32 with Philadelphia, 119 with Cleveland).

150— Michael Tresh, Chicago, 1945 (125 complete).

Most Consecutive Games, Season

A. L.— 155— Frank W. Hayes, Philadelphia, April 18 through October 1, second game, 1944 (135 complete).

N. L.— 155— Ray C. Mueller, Cincinnati, April 18 through October 1, 1944 (135 com-plete).

Most Games, Rookie Season

N. L.— 154— Johnny L. Bench, Cincinnati, 1968.

A. L.— 150— Robert L. Rodgers, Los Angeles, 1962.

Most Years Leading League in Games

A. L.—8—Lawrence P. Berra, New York, 1950, 1951, 1952, 1953, 1954, 1955, 1956, 1957.

N. L.—6— Gary E. Carter, Montreal, 1977, 1978, 1979, 1980, 1981, 1982.

Fewest Games, Season, for Leader in Most Games

N. L.—96—Ernest N. Lombardi, New York, 1945.

A. L.—98—Jacob W. Early, Washington, 1942.

Most Games, Season, Lefthanded Catcher

N. L.— 105— John T. Clements, Philadelphia, 1891.

A. L.— 23— John A. Donahue, St. Louis, 1902.

Highest Fielding Average, Season, 100 or More Games

A. L.—1.000—Warren V. Rosar, Philadelphia, 117 games, 1946.

N. L.— .999—Wesley N. Westrum, New York, 139 games, 1950.

Highest Fielding Average, Season, 150 or More Games

N. L.—.996—C. Randolph Hundley, Chicago, 152 games, 1967.
A. L.—.995—James H. Sundberg, Texas, 150 games, 1979.

Highest Fielding Average, League, 1,000 or More Games

A. L.—.9933—William A. Freehan, Detroit, 15 years, 1961, 1963 through 1976, 1,483 games.
N. L.— .992—John A. Edwards, Cincinnati, St. Louis, Houston, 14 years, 1961 through 1974, 1,392 games.

Lowest Fielding Average, Season, 100 or More Games

A. L.—.934—Samuel Agnew, St. Louis, 102 games, 1915.
N. L. since 1900—.947—Charles S. Dooin, Philadelphia, 140 games, 1909.

Most Years Leading League in Fielding Average, 100 or More Games

A. L.—8—Raymond W. Schalk, Chicago, 1913, 1914, 1915, 1916, 1917, 1920, 1921, 1922.
N. L.—7—Charles L. Hartnett, Chicago, 1925, 1928, 1930, 1934, 1935, 1936, 1937.

Most Consecutive Years Leading in Fielding Average, 100 or More Games

A. L.—6—William A. Freehan, Detroit, 1965, 1966, 1967 (tied), 1968, 1969 (tied), 1970.
N. L.—4—John G. Kling, Chicago, 1902 through 1905.
Charles L. Hartnett, Chicago, 1934 through 1937.

Lowest Fielding Average, Season, for Leader, 100 or More Games, Since 1900

A. L.—.954—Maurice R. Powers, Philadelphia, 111 games, 1901.
N. L.—.958—Charles L. Hartnett, Chicago, 110 games, 1925.

Most Putouts, League

A. L.— 9941— William A. Freehan, Detroit, 15 years, 1961, 1963 through 1976.
N. L.— 9260— Johnny L. Bench, Cincinnati, 17 years, 1967 through 1983.

Most Putouts, Season

N. L. (162-game season)—1135—John A. Edwards, Houston, 151 games, 1969.
N. L. (154-game season)— 877—John Roseboro, Los Angeles, 125 games, 1961.
A. L. (162-game season)— 971—William A. Freehan, Detroit, 138 games, 1968.
A. L. (154-game season)— 785—Ossee F. Schreckengost, Philadelphia, 114 games, 1905.

Fewest Putouts, Season, 150 or More Games

N. L.— 471— Ray C. Mueller, Cincinnati, 155 games, 1944.
A. L.— 575— Michael Tresh, Chicago, 150 games, 1945.

Most Years Leading League in Putouts

A. L.—9—Raymond W. Schalk, Chicago, 1913, 1914, 1915, 1916, 1917, 1918, 1919, 1920, 1922.
N. L.—6—John G. Kling, Chicago, 1902, 1903, 1904, 1905, 1906, 1907 (tied).
Roy Campanella, Brooklyn, 1949, 1950, 1951, 1953, 1955, 1956.
Gary E. Carter, Montreal, 1977, 1978, 1979, 1980, 1981, 1982.

Fewest Putouts, Season, for Leader in Most Putouts

N. L.— 409— Charles L. Hartnett, Chicago, 110 games, 1925.
A. L.— 446— George R. Tebbetts, Detroit, 97 games, 1942.

Most Putouts, Game, Nine Innings

N. L.—20—Gerald W. Grote, New York April 22, 1970, 19 strikeouts.
A. L.—19—William A. Freehan, Detroit, June 15, 1965, 18 strikeouts.
Eliseo C. Rodriguez, California, August 12, 1974, 19 strikeouts.

Most Putouts, Extra-Inning Game

N. L.—22—Robert B. Schmidt, San Francisco, June 22, 1958, first game, 14 innings, 19 strikeouts.
Thomas F. Haller, San Francisco, May 31, 1964, second game, 23 innings, 22 strikeouts.
Stephen W. Yeager, Los Angeles, August 8, 1972, 19 innings, 22 strikeouts.
A. L.—21—Eliseo C. Rodriguez, California, June 14, 1974, 15 innings, 20 strikeouts.
20—Kenneth L. Retzer, Washington, September 12, 1962, 16 innings, 21 strikeouts.
19—Jose J. Azcue, Cleveland, July 3, 1968, 10 innings, 19 strikeouts.

Longest Game, No Putouts

A. L.—14 innings— Walter H. Schang, Boston, September 13, 1920.
Eugene A. Desautels, Cleveland, August 11, 1942, first game.
N. L.—13 innings— James Wilson, Philadelphia, August 31, 1927, first game.
Harold Finney, Pittsburgh, September 22, 1931.

Most Consecutive Putouts, Start of Game

N. L.—9—Arthur E. Wilson, New York, May 30, 1911, a.m. game 4 strikeouts, 3 fouled
   out, 1 tagged out, 1 forced out.
   John A. Bateman, Houston, July 14, 1968, second game, 9 strikeouts,
A. L.—8—Tony Mike Brumley, Washington, September 4, 1965, 8 strikeouts.

Most Consecutive Putouts, Game

N. L.—10—Gerald W. Grote, New York, April 22, 1970, 1 in sixth inning; 3 in seventh
   inning; 3 in eighth inning; 3 in ninth inning; 10 strikeouts.
A. L.— 8—Tony Mike Brumley, Washington, September 4, 1965, 3 in first inning; 3 in
   second inning; 2 in third inning; 8 strikeouts.
   John H. Stephenson, California, July 9, 1972, 2 in first inning; 3 in second
   inning; 3 in third inning; 8 strikeouts.
   Arthur W. Kusnyer, California, July 15, 1973, 1 in first inning; 3 in second
   inning; 3 in third inning; 1 in fourth inning.

Most Putouts, Two Consecutive Games

N. L.—31—Gerald W. Grote, New York, April 21 (11), April 22 (20), 1970; 29 strikeouts.
A. L.—29—Arndt Jorgens, New York, June 2 (14), June 3 (15) 1933; 28 strikeouts.

Most Putouts, Doubleheader, 18 Innings

N. L.—25—John A. Bateman, Houston, September 10, 1968, 22 strikeouts.
A. L.—25—Henry Severeid, St. Louis, July 13, 1920, 21 strikeouts.

Most Fouls Caught, Inning

N. L.—3—Arnold M. Owen, Brooklyn, August 4, 1941, third inning.
   Wesley N. Westrum, New York, August 24, 1949, ninth inning.
   Wesley N. Westrum, New York, September 23, 1956, fifth inning.
A. L.—3—Matthew D. Batts, Detroit, August 2, 1953, second game, fourth inning.

Most Fouls Caught, Game

N. L.—6—Wesley N. Westrum, New York, August 24, 1949.
A. L.—6—J. Sherman Lollar, Chicago, April 10, 1962.

Most Assists in Majors

1,835—James T. McGuire, Toledo, Cleveland, Rochester, Washington, A. A., Detroit,
   Philadelphia, Washington, Brooklyn, N. L., Detroit, New York, Boston, Cleveland, A. L., 1884 through 1912, except 1889, 1908, 1909, 1911; 25 years.

Most Assists, League

A. L.—1,810—Raymond W. Schalk, Chicago, 1912 through 1928; 17 consecutive years.
N. L.—1,593—Charles S. Dooin, Philadelphia, Cincinnati, New York, 1902 through 1916;
   15 consecutive years.

Most Assists, Season

N. L.— 214— Patrick J. Moran, Boston, 107 games, 1903
A. L.— 212— Oscar H. Stanage, Detroit, 141 games, 1911.

Fewest Assists, Season, 150 or More Games

N. L.—59—C. Randolph Hundley, Chicago, 152 games, 1967.
A. L.—73—James E. Hegan, Cleveland, 152 games, 1949.
   Robert L. Rodgers, Los Angeles, 150 games, 1962.

Most Years Leading League in Assists

N. L.—6—Charles L. Hartnett, Chicago, 1925, 1927, 1928 (tied), 1930, 1934, 1935.
   Delmar W. Crandall, Milwaukee, 1953, 1954, 1957, 1958, 1959, 1960.
A. L.—6—James H. Sundberg, Texas, 1975, 1976, 1977, 1978, 1980, 1981.

Fewest Assists, Season, for Leader in Most Assists

N. L.—52—Philip S. Masi, Boston, 95 games, 1945.
A. L.—60—Samuel C. White, Boston, 114 games, 1956.
   Earl J. Battey, Minnesota, 131 games, 1961.

Most Assists, Game, Nine Innings

N. L.—9—Michael P. Hines, Boston, May 1, 1883.
A. L.—8— Walter H. Schang, Boston, May 12, 1920.
N. L. since 1900—7—Edward McFarland, Philadelphia, May 7, 1901.
   William Bergen, Brooklyn, August 23, 1909, second game.
   James P. Archer, Pittsburgh, May 24, 1918.
   John B. Adams, Philadelphia, August 21, 1919.

Most Assists, Inning

A. A.—3—John A. Milligan, Philadelphia, July 26, 1887, third inning.

A. L.—3—Leslie G. Nunamaker, New York, August 3, 1914, second inning.
Raymond W. Schalk, Chicago, September 30, 1921, eighth inning.
William M. Dickey, New York, May 13, 1929, sixth inning.
James H. Sundberg, Texas, September 3, 1976, fifth inning.
N. L.—3—C. Bruce Edwards, Brooklyn, August 15, 1946, fourth inning.
James R. Campbell, Houston, June 16, 1963, second game, third inning.

Most Chances Accepted (Excludes Errors) League

A. L.—10,662—William A. Freehan, Detroit, 15 years, 1931, 1963 through 1976.
N. L.—10,110—Johnny L. Bench, Cincinnati, 17 years, 1967 through 1983.

Most Chances Accepted (Excludes Errors) Season

N. L. (162-game season)—1214—John A. Edwards, Houston, 151 games, 1969.
N. L. (154-game season)— 933—John Roseboro, Los Angeles, 125 games, 1961.
A. L. (162-game season)—1044—William A. Freehan, Detroit, 138 games, 1968.
A. L. (154-game season)— 924—Charles E. Street, Washington, 137 games, 1909.

Fewest Chances Accepted (Excludes Errors), Season, 150 or More Games

N. L.— 536— Ray C. Mueller, Cincinnati, 155 games, 1944.
A. L.— 677— Michael Tresh, Chicago, 150 games, 1945.

Most Years Leading League in Chances Accepted (Excludes Errors)

A. L.—8—Raymond W. Schalk, Chicago, 1913, 1914, 1915, 1916, 1917, 1919, 1920, 1922.
Lawrence P. Berra, New York, 1950, 1951, 1952, 1954, 1955, 1956, 1957, 1959.
N. L.—6—Roy Campanella, Brooklyn, 1949, 1950, 1951, 1953, 1955, 1956.
Gary E. Carter, Montreal, 1977, 1978, 1979, 1980, 1981, 1982.

Fewest Chances Accepted (Excludes Errors), Season for Leader in Chances Accepted

N. L.— 474— Ernest N. Lombardi, New York, 96 games, 1945.
A. L.— 515— George R. Tebbetts, Detroit, 97 games, 1942.

Most Chances Accepted (Excludes Errors), Inning

N. L.—5—Joseph H. Garagiola, St. Louis, June 17, 1949, eighth inning, 3 putouts, 2 assists.
A. L.—4—Held by many catchers. Last catcher—F. Gene Tenace, Oakland, May 24, 1975, fifth inning, 3 putouts, 1 assist.

Most Chances Accepted (Excludes Errors), Game, Nine Innings

U. A.—23—George Bignall, Milwaukee, October 3, 1884, 18 strikeouts.
N. L.—22—Vincent Nava, Providence, June 7, 1884, 19 strikeouts.
N. L. since 1900—20—Gerald W. Grote, New York, April 22, 1970, 19 strikeouts.
A. L.—20—Eliseo C. Rodriguez, California, August 12, 1974, 19 strikeouts.

Most Chances Accepted (Excludes Errors), Ten Innings, Since 1900

N. L.—20—John H. DeBerry, Brooklyn, July 20, 1925, 17 strikeouts.
A. L.—19—Jose J. Azcue, Cleveland, July 3, 1968, 10 innings, 19 strikeouts.

Most Chances Accepted (Excludes Errors), Extra-Inning Game

A. L.—26—Maurice R. Powers, Philadelphia, September 1, 1906, 24 innings, 18 strikeouts.
N. L.—24—Stephen W. Yeager, Los Angeles, August 8, 1972, 19 innings, 22 strikeouts.

Most Chances Accepted (Excludes Errors), Doubleheader, 18 Innings

A. L.—27—Henry Severeid, St. Louis, July 13, 1920, 21 strikeouts.
N. L.—26—John A. Bateman, Houston, September 10, 1968, 22 strikeouts.

Most Chances Accepted (Excludes Errors), Two Consecutive, 9-Inning Games

N. L.—31—Gerald W. Grote, New York, April 21 (11) April 22 (20), 1970; 29 strikeouts.
A. L.—30—Arndt Jorgens, New York, June 2, 3, 1933, 28 strikeouts.

Longest Game With No Chances Offered

A. L.—14 innings— Eugene A. Desautels, Cleveland, August 11, 1942, first game.
N. L.—13 innings— James Wilson, Philadelphia, August 31, 1927, first game.

Longest Night Game With No Chances Offered

A. L.—11 innings— Alfred H. Evans, Washington, September 6, 1946.
N. L.—10 innings— Ernest N. Lombardi, New York, August 4, 1944.

Fewest Chances Offered, Doubleheader

N. L.—0—Harry H. McCurdy, St. Louis, July 10, 1923.
A. L.—2—Everett Yaryan, Chicago, May 26, 1921.
Henry Severeid, St. Louis, September 5, 1921.
J. Luther Sewell, Cleveland, August 28, 1926.

Fewest Chances Offered, Two Consecutive Games

A. L.—0—Ralph Perkins, Philadelphia, September 16, 17, 1922.
N. L.—0—Harry H. McCurdy, St. Louis, July 10, 1923.
      Andrew W. Seminick, Cincinnati, September 15, 16, 1953.

Most Errors, Season

N. L.—94—Nathan W. Hicks, New York, 45 games, 1876.
N. L. since 1900—40—Charles S. Dooin, Philadelphia, 140 games, 1909.
A. A.—85—Edward Whiting, Baltimore, 72 games, 1882.
A. L.—41—Oscar H. Stanage, Detroit, 141 games, 1911.

Most Errors, League, Since 1900

N. L.— 234— Ivy B. Wingo, St. Louis, Cincinnati 17 years, 1911 through 1929, except 1927, 1928.
A. L.— 218— Walter H. Schang, Philadelphia, Boston, New York, St. Louis, Detroit, 19 years, 1913 through 1931.

Most Years Leading League in Errors

N. L.—7—Ivy B. Wingo, St. Louis, Cincinnati, 1912 (tied), 1913, 1916, 1917, 1918, 1920, 1921.
A. L.—6—George R. Tebbetts, Detroit, Boston, 1939, 1940 (tied), 1942 (tied), 1947, 1948, 1949.

Fewest Errors, Season, 150 or More Games

N. L.—4—C. Randolph Hundley, Chicago, 152 games, 1967.
A. L.—4—James H. Sundberg, Texas, 150 games, 1979.

Fewest Errors, Season, 100 or More Games

A. L.—0—Warren V. Rosar, Philadelphia, 117 games, 1946.
N. L.—1—R. Earl Grace, Pittsburgh, 114 games, 1932.
      Wesley N. Westrum, New York, 139 games, 1950.

Fewest Errors, Season, for Leaders in Most Errors

A. L.—7—Richard B. Ferrell, St. Louis, 137 games, 1933.
N. L.—9—Henry L. Foiles, Pittsburgh, 109 games, 1957.

Most Errors, Inning

N. L.—4—George F. Miller, St. Louis, May 24, 1895, second inning.
    3—Edward Rowan, Boston, June 10, 1882, fifth inning.
A. L.—3—Edward Sweeney, New York, July 10, 1912, first inning.
    John Peters, Cleveland, May 16, 1918, first inning.
N. L. since 1900—2—Held by many catchers.

Most Errors, Game, Nine Innings (All Fielding Errors)

N. L.—7—John C. Rowe, Buffalo, May 16, 1883.
    Lowe, Detroit, June 26, 1884.
A. A.—7—William H. Taylor, Baltimore, May 29, 1886, a.m. game.
N. L. since 1900—4—Charles E. Street, Boston, June 7, 1905.
A. L.—4—John Peters, Cleveland, May 16, 1918.
    William G. Styles, Philadelphia, July 29, 1921.
    William H. Moore, Boston, September 26, 1927, second game.

Longest Errorless Game

A. L.—24 innings— Maurice R. Powers, Philadelphia, September 1, 1906.
             Warren V. Rosar, Philadelphia, July 21, 1945.
             Robert V. Swift, Detroit, July 21, 1945.
N. L.—24 innings— Harold King, Houston, April 15, 1968.
             Gerald W. Grote, New York, April 15, 1968 (caught 23⅓ innings).

Most Errors, Doubleheader

A. A.—8—James A. Donahue, Kansas City, August 31, 1889.
N. L.—8—Lewis Graulich, Philadelphia, September 19, 1891.
N. L. since 1900—4—Held by many catchers.
A. L.—4—Held by many catchers.

Most Consecutive Errorless Games, League

A. L.— 148— Lawrence P. Berra, New York, July 28, 1957, second game, through May 10, 1959, second game, 950 chances accepted.
N. L.— 138— John A. Edwards, Houston, July 11, 1970, through August 20, 1971, 805 chances accepted.

Most Consecutive Errorless Games, Season

A. L.— 117— Warren V. Rosar, Philadelphia, April 16 through September 29, 1946, first game, 605 chances accepted.
N. L.— 110— R. Earl Grace, Pittsburgh, April 12 through September 7, 1932, 400 chances accepted.

Most Consecutive Errorless Games, Start of Career

A. L.—93—Frank A. Pytlak, Cleveland, April 22, 1932, through May 5, 1934.

Most Consecutive Chances Accepted, League, No Errors

A. L.— 950— Lawrence P. Berra, New York, 148 games, July 28, 1957, second game through May 10, 1959, second game.

N. L.— 805— John A. Edwards, Houston, July 11, 1970 through August 20, 1971, 805 chances accepted.

Most Consecutive Chances Accepted, Season, No Errors

A. L.— 605— Warren V. Rosar, Philadelphia, 117 games, April 16 through September 29, 1946, first game.

N. L.— 476— Arnold M. Owen Brooklyn, 100 games, April 15 through August 29, 1941.

Most Passed Balls, Season

N. L.—99—Charles N. Snyder, Boston, 58 games, 1881.
Michael P. Hines, Boston, 56 games, 1883.

N. L. since 1900—29—Frank Bowerman, New York 73, games, 1900.

A. L.—33—Joseph C. Martin, Chicago, 112 games, 1965.

Most Years Leading League in Passed Balls

N. L.—10—Ernest N. Lombardi, Cincinnati, Boston, New York, 1932, 1935, 1936 (tied), 1937, 1938, 1939, 1940 (tied), 1941, 1942, 1945.

A. L.— 5—Richard B. Ferrell, St. Louis, Washington, 1931 (tied), 1939, 1940, 1944, 1945.

Fewest Passed Balls, Season, 100 or More Games

N. L.—0—Alfred C. Todd, Pittsburgh, 128 games, 1937.
Alfonso R. Lopez, Pittsburgh, 114 games, 1941.
Johnny L. Bench, Cincinnati, 121 games, 1975.

A. L.—0—William M. Dickey, New York, 125 games, 1931.

Fewest Passed Balls, Season, 150 or More Games

N. L.—1—Gary E. Carter, Montreal, 152 games, 1978.

A. L.—4—James E. Hegan, Cleveland, 152 games, 1949.
Carlton E. Fisk, Boston, 151 games, 1977.

Fewest Passed Balls, Season, for Leader in Most Passed Balls

A. L.—6—Gordon S. Cochrane, Philadelphia, 117 games, 1931.
Charles F. Berry, Boston, 102 games, 1931.
Richard B. Ferrell, St. Louis, 108 games, 1931.

N. L.—7—Held by five catchers.

Most Passed Balls, Game

A. L.—12—Frank Gardner, Washington, May 10, 1884.

N. L.—10—Patrick E. Dealey, Boston, May 1886.

N. L. since 1900—6—Harry Vickers, Cincinnati, October 4, 1902.

A. L.—5—Thomas P. Egan, California, July 28, 1970.

Most Passed Balls, Two Consecutive Games

N. L.—13— Peter J. Hotaling, Worcester, September 20, 21, 1881.

Longest Game With No Passed Balls

A. L.—24 innings— Maurice R. Powers, Philadelphia, September 1, 1906.
Warren V. Rosar, Philadelphia, July 21, 1945.
Robert V. Swift, Detroit, July 21, 1945.

N. L.—24 innings— Harold King, Houston, April 15, 1968.
Gerald W. Grote, New York, April 15, 1968 (caught 23⅓ innings).

Most Passed Balls, Inning

A. A.—5—Daniel C. Sullivan, St. Louis, August 9, 1885, third inning.

N. L.—4—Raymond F. Katt, New York, September 10, 1954, eighth inning.

A. L.—3—Augustus R. Triandos, Baltimore, May 4, 1960, sixth inning.
Myron N. Ginsberg, Baltimore, May 10, 1960, second inning.
Charles R. Lau, Baltimore, June 14, 1962, eighth inning.
Joseph J. Azcue, California, August 30, 1969, seventh inning, consecutive.

Most Double Plays, Season

A. L.—29—Frank W. Hayes, Philadelphia, Cleveland, 151 games, 1945.

N. L.—23—Thomas F. Haller, Los Angeles, 139 games, 1968.

Most Double Plays, League

A. L.— 217— Raymond W. Schalk, Chicago, 17 years, 1912 through 1928.

N. L.— 163— Charles L. Hartnett, Chicago, New York, 20 years, 1922 through 1941.

Most Years Leading League in Double Plays

   N. L.—6—Charles L. Hartnett, Chicago, 1925 (tied), 1927, 1930 (tied), 1931, 1934, 1935.
   A. L.—6—Lawrence P. Berra, New York, 1949, 1950, 1951, 1952, 1954, 1956.

Fewest Double Plays, Season, for Leader in Most Double Plays

   N. L.—8—Philip S. Masi, Boston-Pittsburgh, 81 games, 1949.
          Clyde E. McCullough, Pittsburgh, 90 games, 1949.
   A. L.—9—Earl J. Battey, Minnesota, 131 games, 1961.
          Augustus R. Triandos, Baltimore, 114 games, 1961.

Most Double Plays, Nine-Inning Game

   N. L.—3—John J. O'Neill, Chicago, April 26, 1905.
          J. Frank Hogan, New York, August 19, 1931.
          Edward St. Claire, Boston, August 9, 1951.
   A. L.—3—Charles F. Berry, Chicago, May 17, 1932.
          Joseph C. Martin, Chicago, June 23, 1963, first game.
          Earl J. Battey, Minnesota, August 11, 1966.
          Edward M. Herrmann, Chicago, July 4, 1972.
          J. Rikard Dempsey, Baltimore, June 1, 1977.

Most Double Plays, Extra-Inning Game

   N. L.—3—Robert A. O'Farrell, Chicago, July 9, 1919, second game, 10⅓ innings.
          Ronald W. Hodges, New York, April 23, 1978, 11⅔ innings.
   A. L.—3—William J. Sullivan, Chicago, July 25, 1912, 10 innings.

Most Double Plays Started, Game

   N. L.—3—J. Frank Hogan, New York, August 19, 1931.
   A. L.—2—Held by many catchers.

Most Unassisted Double Plays, Game

   N. L.—1—Held by many players.
   A. L.—1—Held by many players.

Most Unassisted Double Plays, Season

   A. L.—2—Frank P. Crossin, St. Louis, 1914.
   N. L.—1—Held by many catchers.

Most Unassisted Double Plays, League

   A. L.—2—Charles Schmidt, Detroit, 1906, 1907.
          Frank P. Crossin, St. Louis, 1914 (2).
          Clinton D. Courtney, Baltimore, 1954, 1960.
          Lawrence P. Berra, New York, 1947, 1962.
          Robert L. Rodgers, Los Angeles, 1965; California, 1969.
   N. L.—2—Miguel A. Gonzalez, St. Louis, 1915, 1918.
          Christopher J. Cannizzaro, New York, 1964, 1965.
          L. Edgar Bailey, San Francisco, 1963; Chicago, 1965.
          Robert D. Taylor, New York, 1964, 1967.

Most Innings Caught, Game

   A. L.—24—Maurice R. Powers, Philadelphia, September 1, 1906.
           Warren V. Rosar, Philadelphia, July 21, 1945.
           Robert V. Swift, Detroit, July 21, 1945.
   N. L.—24—Harold King, Houston, April 15, 1968.
           Gerald W. Grote, New York, April 15, 1968, (caught 23⅓ innings).

Most Innings Caught, Doubleheader

   A. L.—29—Ossee F. Schreckengost, Philadelphia, July 4, 1905.
   N. L.—27—William C. Fischer, Chicago, June 28, 1916.
           August R. Mancuso, New York, July 2, 1933.

Most Stolen Bases Off Catcher, Game

   A. A.—19—Grant Briggs, Syracuse, April 22, 1890.
   N. L.—17—George F. Miller, Pittsburgh, May 23, 1890.
   N. L. since 1900—11—William C. Fischer, St. Louis, August 13, 1916, second game, five
          innings.
   A. L.—13—W. Branch Rickey, New York, June 28, 1907.

Most Stolen Bases Off Catcher, Inning

   A. L.—8—Stephen F. O'Neill, Cleveland, July 19, 1915, first inning.
   N. L.—8—Miguel A. Gonzalez, New York, July 7, 1919, first game, ninth inning.

Most Runners Caught Stealing, Game, Nine Innings

   N. L.—8—Charles A. Farrell, Washington, May 11, 1897.
   N. L. since 1900—7—William Bergen, Brooklyn, August 23, 1909, second game.
   A. L.—6—Walter H. Schang, Philadelphia, May 12, 1915.

Most Runners Caught Stealing, Inning

A. A.—3—John Milligan, Philadelphia, July 26, 1887, third inning.
A. L.—3—Leslie G. Nunamaker, New York, August 3, 1914, second inning.
N. L.—2—Held by many catchers.

Most No-Hit Games Caught, League (Entire Game)

A. L.—4—Raymond W. Schalk, Chicago, 1914 (2), 1917, 1922.
N. L.—3—Roy Campanella, Brooklyn, 1952, 1956 (2).
      Delmar W. Crandall, Milwaukee, 1954, 1960 (2).
Both Leagues—3—Jeffrey A. Torborg, Los Angeles N. L., 1965, 1970; California A.L.,
      1973.

Most No-Hit, Winning Games Caught, League (Entire Game)

A. L.—3—Raymond W. Schalk, Chicago, 1914, 1917, 1922.
      William F. Carrigan, Boston, 1911, 1916 (2).
      J. Luther Sewell, Cleveland, 1931, Chicago, 1935, 1937.
      James E. Hegan, Cleveland, 1947, 1948, 1951.
N. L.—3—Roy Campanella, Brooklyn, 1952, 1956 (2).
      Delmar W. Crandall, Milwaukee, 1954, 1960 (2).
Both Leagues—3—Jeffrey A. Torborg, Los Angeles N. L., 1965, 1970; California A. L.
      1973.

PITCHERS' FIELDING RECORDS

Most Games Pitched in Major Leagues

1070—J. Hoyt Wilhelm, New York N. L., St. Louis N. L., Cleveland A. L., Baltimore
      A. L., Chicago A. L., California A. L., Atlanta N. L., Chicago N. L., Los Angeles
      N. L., 21 years, 1952 through 1972, 448 in N. L., 622 in A. L.

Most Games, Pitched League

N. L.— 846— El Roy L. Face, Pittsburgh, Montreal, 16 years, 1953 through 1969, except
      1954.
A. L.— 807— Albert W. Lyle, Boston, New York, Texas, Chicago, 15 years, 1967 through
      1982, except 1981.

Most Games, Pitched Season

N. L.— 106— Michael G. Marshall, Los Angeles, 208 innings, 1974.
A. L.— 90— Michael G. Marshall, Minnesota, 143 innings, 1979.

Most Years Leading League in Games Pitched in Major Leagues

7—Joseph J. McGinnity, Brooklyn N. L., Baltimore A. L., New York N. L., 1900, 1901,
      1903, 1904, 1905, 1906, 1907.

Most Years Leading League in Games Pitched

N. L.—6—Joseph J. McGinnity, Brooklyn, New York, 1900, 1903, 1904, 1905, 1906, 1907.
A. L.—6—Fred Marberry, Washington, 1924, 1925, 1926, 1928, 1929, 1932.

Fewest Games, Season, for Leader in Most Games Pitched

A. L.—40—Joseph W. Haynes, Chicago, 1942 (103 innings).
N. L.—41—Remy Kremer, Pittsburgh, 1924 (259 innings).
      John D. Morrison, Pittsburgh, 1924 (238 innings).

Highest Fielding Average, Most Chances Accepted, Season

N. L.—1.000—Randall L. Jones, San Diego, 1976, 40 games, 31 putouts, 81 assists, 112
      chances accepted.
A. L.—1.000—Walter P. Johnson, Washington, 1913, 48 games, 21 putouts, 82 assists, 103
      chances accepted.

Most Years, Highest Fielding Average, With Most Chances Accepted, Season

N. L.—4—Claude W. Passeau, Phiadelphia, Chicago, 1939, 1942, 1943, 1945.
      Lawrence C. Jackson, St. Louis, Chicago, Philadelphia, 1957, 1964, 1965, 1968.
A. L.—3—Walter P. Johnson, Washington, 1913, 1917, 1922 (tied).

Most Putouts, Season

N. L.—52—Albert G. Spalding, Chicago, 60 games, 1876.
A. L.—49—Nicholas Altrock, Chicago, 38 games, 1904.
N. L. since 1900—39—Victor G. Willis, Boston, 43 games, 1904.

Most Putouts, Major Leagues, Since 1900

363—Ferguson A. Jenkins, Philadelphia N.L., Chicago N.L., Texas A.L., Boston A.L., 19
      years, 1965 through 1983.

Most Putouts, League, Since 1900

N. L.— 340— Philip H. Niekro, Milwaukee, Atlanta, 20 years, 1964 through 1983.
A. L.— 291— James A. Palmer, Baltimore, 18 years, 1965 through 1983, except 1968.

Most Years Leading League in Putouts

A. L.—5—Robert G. Lemon, Cleveland, 1948, 1949, 1952, 1953, 1954.
N. L.—4—Grover C. Alexander, Philadelphia, 1914, 1915, 1916, 1917.
          Fred L. Fitzsimmons, New York, 1926, 1928, 1930, 1934.

Fewest Putouts, Season, for Leader in Most Putouts

N. L.—14—S. Howard Camnitz, Pittsburgh, 38 games, 1910.
          Arthur N. Nehf, New York, 37 games, 1922.
          Anthony C. Kaufmann, Chicago, 37 games, 1922.
A. L.—16—Roxie Lawson, Detroit, 27 games, 1937.

Most Putouts, Game, Nine Innings

N. L.-A. L.—5—Held by many pitchers.
N. L.—Last pitchers—Richard D. Ruthven, Atlanta, April 19, 1978; Mark Lemongello, Houston, August 9, 1978.
A. L.—Last pitcher—James L. Beattie, New York, September 13, 1978.

Most Putouts, Extra-Inning Game

A. L.—7—Richard J. Fowler, Philadelphia, June 9, 1949, 12 innings.
N. L.—6—Robert T. Purkey, Pittsburgh, July 22, 1954, pitched 11 innings of 14-inning game.

Most Putouts, Inning

A. L.—3—James C. Bagby, Jr., Boston, September 26, 1940, fourth inning.
          Robert F. Heffner, Boston, June 28, 1963, first inning.
          James L. Beattie, New York, September 13, 1978, second inning.
N. L.—3—Ricky E. Reuschel, Chicago, April 25, 1975, third inning.

Most Assists, Season

A. L.— 227— Edward A. Walsh, Chicago, 56 games, 1907.
N. L.— 168— John G. Clarkson, Boston, 72 games, 1889.
N. L. since 1900—141—Christopher Mathewson, New York, 56 games, 1908.

Most Assists, League, Since 1900

N. L.— 1489— Christopher Mathewson, New York, Cincinnati, 17 years, 1900 through 1916.
A. L.— 1337— Walter P. Johnson, Washington, 21 years, 1907 through 1927.

Most Years Leading League in Assists

A. L.—6—Robert G. Lemon, Cleveland, 1948, 1949, 1951, 1952, 1953, 1956.
N. L.—5—Christopher Mathewson, New York, 1901, 1905, 1908, 1910, 1911.

Fewest Assists, Season, for Leader in Most Assists

N. L.—48—Donald S. Drysdale, Los Angeles, 44 games, 1959.
A. L.—49—William R. Wight, Cleveland, Baltimore, 36 games, 1955.

Most Assists, Game, Nine Innings

N. L.—11—Truett B. Sewell, Pittsburgh, June 6, 1941, second game.
A. L.—11—Albert C. Orth, New York, August 12, 1906.
          Edward A. Walsh, Chicago, April 19, 1907.
          Edward A. Walsh, Chicago, August 12, 1907.
          George N. McConnell, New York, September 2, 1912, second game.
          Meldon J. Wolfgang, Chicago, August 29, 1914.

Most Assists, Extra-Inning Game

N. L.—12—Leon J. Cadore, Brooklyn, May 1, 1920, 26 innings.
A. L.—12—Nicholas Altrock, Chicago, June 7, 1908, 10 innings.
          Edward A. Walsh, Chicago, July 16, 1907, 13 innings.

Most Assists, Inning

N. L.-A. L.—3—Held by many pitchers.

Most Chances Accepted (Excludes Errors), Season

A. L.— 262— Edward A. Walsh, Chicago, 56 games, 1907.
N. L.— 206— John G. Clarkson, Boston, 72 games, 1889.
N. L. since 1900—168—Christopher Mathewson, New York, 56 games, 1908.

Most Chances Accepted, League, Since 1900

N. L.— 1761— Christopher Mathewson, New York, Cincinnati, 17 years, 1900 through 1916.
A. L.— 1606— Walter P. Johnson, Washington, 21 years, 1907 through 1927.

Most Years Leading League in Chances Accepted (Excludes Errors)

A. L.—8—Robert G. Lemon, Cleveland, 1948, 1949, 1950, 1951, 1952, 1953, 1954, 1956.
N. L.—7—Burleigh A. Grimes, Brooklyn, New York, Pittsburgh, 1921, 1922, 1923, 1924, 1925, 1927, 1928.

Fewest Chances Accepted (Excl. Errors) Season, for Leader in Chances Accepted

A. L.—63—Franklin L. Sullivan, Boston, 35 games, 1955.
     Raymond E. Herbert, Kansas City, 37 games, 1960.
     James E. Perry, Cleveland, 41 games, 1960.
N. L.—67—Paul E. Minner, Chicago, 31 games, 1953.
     Robin E. Roberts, Philadelphia, 44 games, 1953.
     James T. Hearn, New York, 39 games, 1955.

Most Chances Accepted, Inning

N. L.—4—Philip R. Regan, Chicago, June 6, 1969, sixth inning, 1 putout, 3 assists.
A. L.—3—Held by many pitchers.

Most Chances Accepted (Excludes Errors) Game, Nine Innings

A. L.—13—Nicholas Altrock, Chicago, August 6, 1904, 3 putouts, 10 assists.
     Edward A. Walsh, Chicago, April 19, 1907, 2 putouts, 11 assists.
N. L.—12—Truett B. Sewell, Pittsburgh, June 6, 1941, second game, 1 putout, 11 assists.

Most Chances Accepted (Excludes Errors) Extra-Inning Game

A. L.—15—Edward A. Walsh, Chicago, July 16, 1907, 13 innings.
N. L.—13—Leon J. Cadore, Brooklyn, May 1, 1920, 26 innings.

Most Chances Accepted (Excludes Errors), Two Consecutive Games

A. L.—20—Edward A. Walsh, Chicago, April 13, 19, 1907, 2 putouts, 18 assists.

Longest Game, No Chances Offered

N. L.—20 innings— Milton Watson, Philadelphia, July 17, 1918.
A. L.—15 innings— Charles H. Ruffing, New York, July 23, 1932, first game.

Fewest Chances Offered, Two Consecutive Games More Than 18 Innings

A. A.—0—John Neagle, Pittsburgh, July 13, 17, 1884, 12 innings each.
N. L.-A. L.—1—Held by many pitchers.

Fewest Chances Offered, Doubleheader

A. A.—1—Thomas Ramsey, Louisville, July 5, 1886, 1 putout.
N. L.—3—Joseph J. McGinnity, New York, August 1, 1903, 1 putout, 1 assist, 1 error.
     Grover C. Alexander, Philadelphia, September 3, 1917, 1 putout, 2 assists.
     Herman S. Bell, St. Louis, July 19, 1924, 1 putout, 2 assists.
A. L.—3—Edward A. Walsh, Chicago, September 29, 1908, 0 putouts, 3 assists.

Most Errors, League, Since 1900

N. L.—64—James L. Vaughn, Chicago, 9 years, 1913 through 1921.
A. L.—55—Edward A. Walsh, Chicago, 13 years, 1904 through 1916.

Most Errors, Season

A. A.—63—Timothy J. Keefe, New York, 68 games, 1883.
N. L.—28—James E. Whitney, Boston, 63 games, 1881.
N. L. since 1900—17—Eustace J. Newton, Cincinnati, Brooklyn, 33 games, 1901.
A. L.—15—John D. Chesbro, New York, 55 games, 1904.
     George E. Waddell, Philadelphia, 46 games, 1905.
     Edward A. Walsh, Chicago, 62 games, 1912.

Most Years Leading League in Errors

N. L.—5—James L. Vaughn, Chicago, 1914, 1915 (tied), 1917 (tied), 1919, 1920.
     Warren E. Spahn, Boston, Milwaukee, 1949 (tied), 1950, 1952 (tied), 1954
     (tied), 1964 (tied).
A. L.—4—Allan S. Sothoron, St. Louis, 1917, 1918 (tied), 1919, 1920.
     L. Nolan Ryan, California, 1975, 1976, 1977 (tied), 1978.

Fewest Errors, Season, for Leader in Most Errors

N. L.-A. L.—4—Held by many pitchers.

Most Errors, Inning

N. L.—3—J. Bentley Seymour, New York, May 21, 1898, sixth inning.
A. L.—2—Held by many pitchers.

Most Errors, Game

N. L.—5—Edward R. Doheny, New York, August 15, 1899.
N. L. since 1900—4—Eustace J. Newton, Cincinnati, September 13, 1900, first game.
     Lafayette S. Winham, Pittsburgh, September 21, 1903, first game.
A. L.—4—Chester Ross, Boston, May 17, 1925.

Longest Errorless Game

N. L.—26 innings— Leon J. Cadore, Brooklyn, May 1, 1920.
     Joseph Oeschger, Boston, May 1, 1920.
A. L.—24 innings— John W. Coombs, Philadelphia, September 1, 1906.
     Joseph Harris, Boston, September 1, 1906.

Most Consecutive Errorless Games, Season

A. L.—88—Wilbur F. Wood, Chicago, April 10 through September 29, 1968 (32 chances accepted).

N. L.—84—Theodore W. Abernathy, Chicago, April 12, through October 3, 1965 (52 chances accepted).

Most Consecutive Errorless Games, League

A. L.— 385— Paul A. Lindblad, Kansas City, Oakland, Texas, August 27, 1966, first game, through April 30, 1974, 126 chances accepted.

N. L.— 274— Rawlins J. Eastwick, Cincinnati, St. Louis, Philadelphia, September 12, 1974, first game through September 29, 1979.

Most Consecutive Chances Accepted, League, No Errors

N. L.— 273— Claude W. Passeau, Chicago, September 21, first game, 1941 through May 20, 1946, 145 games.

A. L.— 230— J. Rick Langford, Oakland, April 13, 1977 to October 2, 1980, 142 games.

Most Double Plays, Season

A. L.—15—Robert G. Lemon, Cleveland, 41 games, 1953.

N. L.—12—Arthur N. Nehf, New York, 40 games, 1920.
      Curtis B. Davis, Philadelphia, 51 games, 1934.
      Randall L. Jones, San Diego, 40 games, 1976.

Most Double Plays, League

N. L.—82—Warren E. Spahn, Boston, Milwaukee, New York, San Francisco, 21 years, 1942 through 1965 (except 1943, 1944, 1945, in military service).

A. L.—78—Robert G. Lemon, Cleveland, 13 years, 1946 through 1958.

Most Years Leading League in Double Plays

N. L.—5—William H. Walters, Philadelphia, Cincinnati, 1937, 1939, 1941 (tied), 1943 (tied), 1944 (tied).
      Warren E. Spahn, Milwaukee, 1953 (tied), 1956, 1960 (tied), 1961 (tied), 1963.

A. L.—4—G. Willis Hudlin, Cleveland, 1929, 1930, 1931, 1934.

Fewest Double Plays, Season, For Leader in Most Double Plays

N. L.-A. L.—5—Held by many pitchers.

Most Double Plays Started, Game

A. L.—4—Milton Gaston, Chicago, May 17, 1932.
      Harold Newhouser, Detroit, May 19, 1948.

N. L.—3—Held by 5 pitchers.
      Last pitcher—D. Eugene Conley, Milwaukee, July 19, 1957.

Most Unassisted Double Plays, Game

N. L.—1—18 times. Held by many pitchers.
      Last pitcher—James C. McAndrew, New York, August 17, 1968.

A. L.—1—14 times. Held by many pitchers.
      Last pitcher—James H. Umbarger, Texas, August 19, 1975.

Most Unassisted Double Plays, League

N. L.—2—James O. Carleton, Chicago, Brooklyn, 1935, 1940.
      Claude W. Passeau, Philadelphia, Chicago, 1938, 1945.

A. L.—1—Held by many pitchers.

Most Triple Plays Started, Season

N. L.—2—A. Wilbur Cooper, Pittsburgh, July 7, August 21, 1920.

A. L.—1—Held by many pitchers.

Most Innings, Pitched, Game

N. L.—26 innings— Leon J. Cadore, Brooklyn, May 1, 1920.
      Joseph Oeschger, Boston, May 1, 1920.

A. L.—24 innings— John W. Coombs, Philadelphia, September 1, 1906.
      Joseph Harris, Boston, September 1, 1906.

CLUB FIELDING LEADERS—ALL-TIME

(Leaders for Each City Included for Clubs Which Moved)

FIRST BASEMEN
American League

Highest Fielding Average, Season, 100 or More Games, Each Club

Club	Player	Year	G.	P.O.	Assts.	E.	F.A.
Boston	John P. McInnis	1921	152	1549	102	1	.999
*Washington	Joseph I. Judge	1930	117	1050	67	2	.998
§Kansas City	Victor P. Power	1957	113	968	99	2	.998
Chicago	James L. Spencer	1976	143	1206	112	2	.998
New York	Joseph A. Pepitone	1965	115	1036	71	3	.997
	C. Christopher Chambliss	1978	155	1366	111	4	.997
Philadelphia	James E. Foxx	1935	121	1109	77	3	.997
Detroit	Norman D. Cash	1964	137	1105	92	4	.997
	Enos M. Cabell	1983	106	830	79	3	.997
Cleveland	John W. Powell	1975	121	997	69	3	.997
Baltimore	Eddie C. Murray	1978	157	1504	106	5	.997
	Eddie C. Murray	1982	149	1269	97	4	.997
‡Kansas City	R. Pierre LaCock	1979	108	829	68	3	.997
Milwaukee	Cecil C. Cooper	1980	142	1336	106	5	.997
	Cecil C. Cooper	1982	154	1428	98	5	.997
California	J. Leroy Thomas	1963	104	961	84	4	.996
	James L. Spencer	1971	145	1296	93	5	.996
	Victor P. Power	1965	107	419	41	2	.996
ySeattle	Bruce A. Boch	1980	133	1273	98	6	.996
St. Louis	George H. McQuinn	1941	125	1138	109	6	.995
	Charles A. Stevens	1946	120	1020	86	6	.995
Oakland	Danny A. Cater	1968	121	985	68	5	.995
	F. Gene Tenace	1974	106	816	41	4	.995
xSeattle	Donald R. Mincher	1969	122	1033	93	6	.995
Toronto	John C. Mayberry	1979	135	1192	74	6	.995
Minnesota	Victor P. Power	1962	142	1193	134	10	.994
	Rodney C. Carew	1977	151	1459	121	10	.994
	Ronnie D. Jackson	1979	157	1447	137	9	.994
Texas	D. Michael Hargrove	1977	152	1393	100	11	.993
	Peter M. O'Brien	1983	133	1144	120	9	.993
†Washington	Michael P. Epstein	1970	122	1100	70	10	.992

*Original Washington club (now Minnesota). †Washington second club (now Texas).
‡Present Kansas City club. §Original Kansas City club (now Oakland).
xOriginal Seattle club (now Milwaukee). yPresent Seattle club.

National League

Highest Fielding Average, Season, 100 or More Games, Each Club

Club	Player	Year	G.	P.O.	Assts.	E.	F.A.
Philadelphia	Frank A. McCormick	1946	134	1185	98	1	.999
Los Angeles	M. Wesley Parker	1968	114	939	69	1	.999
	Steven P. Garvey	1981	110	1019	55	1	.999
†New York	Edward E. Kranepool	1971	108	786	61	2	.998
Cincinnati	Daniel Driessen	1982	144	1239	78	3	.998
Boston	Walter L. Holke	1921	150	1471	86	4	.997
Milwaukee	Joseph W. Adcock	1962	112	907	57	3	.997
Chicago	Ernest Banks	1969	153	1419	87	4	.997
Houston	Denis J. Menke	1971	101	845	59	3	.997
Pittsburgh	Wilver D. Stargell	1979	113	949	47	3	.997
Atlanta	C. Christopher Chambliss	1981	107	1046	94	4	.997
*New York	William H. Terry	1935	143	1379	99	6	.996
	John R. Mize	1947	154	1381	118	6	.996
St. Louis	William D. White	1964	160	1513	101	6	.996
	Joseph P. Torre	1969	144	1270	83	6	.996
San Diego	Nathan Colbert	1972	150	1290	103	6	.996

FIRST BASEMEN—Continued

Club	Player	Year	G.	P.O.	Assts.	E.	F.A.
Brooklyn	Adolph L. Camilli	1938	145	1356	95	8	.995
	Gilbert R. Hodges	1949	156	1336	80	7	.995
	Gilbert R. Hodges	1954	154	1381	132	7	.995
Montreal	Ronald R. Fairly	1970	118	944	90	5	.995
	Michael Jorgensen	1973	123	990	80	5	.995
San Francisco	Guillermo N. Montanez	1975	134	1150	81	8	.993
	Darrell W. Evans	1983	113	979	88	7	.993

*Original New York club (now San Francisco Giants). †Present New York club.

SECOND BASEMEN
American League

Highest Fielding Average, Season, 100 or More Games, Each Club

Club	Player	Year	G.	P.O.	Assts.	E.	F.A.
Baltimore	Robert Grich	1973	162	431	509	5	.995
Minnesota	Robert D. Wilfong	1980	120	238	337	3	.995
†Washington	Timothy L. Cullen	1970	112	211	262	3	.994
New York	George H. Stirnweiss	1948	141	346	364	5	.993
Boston	Robert P. Doerr	1948	138	366	430	6	.993
St. Louis	Oscar D. Melillo	1933	130	362	451	7	.991
‡Kansas City	Octavio R. Rojas	1971	111	252	293	5	.991
Chicago	J. Nelson Fox	1962	154	376	428	8	.990
§Kansas City	Richard L. Green	1964	120	262	361	6	.990
California	Santos C. Alomar	1971	137	350	432	9	.989
	Robert A. Grich	1980	146	326	463	9	.989
Philadelphia	Max F. Bishop	1932	106	232	340	7	.988
	Peter Suder	1948	148	342	461	10	.988
Milwaukee	Ron M. Theobald	1972	113	193	299	6	.988
Oakland	Richard L. Green	1973	133	264	297	7	.988
Cleveland	Duane E. Kuiper	1979	140	345	380	9	.988
Detroit	Louis R. Whitaker	1982	149	331	470	10	.988
ySeattle	Julio L. Cruz	1978	141	286	472	10	.987
	Julio L. Cruz	1982	151	320	434	10	.987
*Washington	Charles S. Myer	1931	137	333	398	12	.984
Texas	David E. Nelson	1973	140	327	364	11	.984
	Elliott T. Wills	1980	144	340	473	13	.984
Toronto	David L. McKay	1978	140	310	408	12	.984
xSeattle	No second basemen in 100 games.						

*Original Washington club (now Minnesota). †Washington second club (now Texas). ‡Present Kansas City club. §Former Kansas City club (now Oakland). xOriginal Seattle club (now Milwaukee). yPresent Seattle club.

National League

Highest Fielding Average, Season, 100 or More Games, Each Club

Club	Player	Year	G.	P.O.	Assts.	E.	F.A.
†New York	Kenneth G. Boswell	1970	101	204	244	2	.996
Philadelphia	J. Manuel Trillo	1982	149	343	441	5	.994
Cincinnati	Joe L. Morgan	1977	151	351	359	5	.993
San Francisco	Rigoberto P. Fuentes	1973	160	386	478	6	.993
Pittsburgh	William S. Mazeroski	1966	162	411	538	8	.992
Brooklyn	Jack R. Robinson	1951	150	390	435	7	.992
St. Louis	Thomas M. Herr	1981	103	211	374	5	.992
Los Angeles	Charles L. Neal	1959	151	386	413	9	.989
Milwaukee	Frank E. Bolling	1962	119	252	298	6	.989
Houston	Tommy V. Helms	1973	145	325	438	9	.988
	Joe L. Morgan	1980	130	244	348	7	.988
Atlanta	Felix B. Millan	1972	120	273	339	8	.987
San Diego	David Cash	1980	123	290	326	8	.987

Club	Player	Year	G.	P.O.	Assts.	E.	F.A.
Chicago	Glenn A. Beckert	1971	129	275	382	9	.986
	Ryne D. Sandberg	1983	157	330	571	13	.986
Montreal	David Cash	1977	153	343	443	11	.986
	David Cash	1978	159	362	400	11	.986
	R. Douglas Flynn	1983	107	205	290	7	.986
*New York	Hugh M. Critz	1933	133	316	541	16	.982
	David C. Williams	1954	142	353	396	14	.982
Boston	Edward R. Stanky	1949	135	357	354	15	.979

*Original New York club (now San Francisco Giants). †Present New York club.

THIRD BASEMEN
American League

Highest Fielding Average, Season, 100 or More Games, Each Club

Club	Player	Year	G.	P.O.	Assts.	E.	F.A.
Milwaukee	Donald W. Money	1974	157	131	336	5	.989
Philadelphia	Henry Majeski	1947	134	160	263	5	.988
Detroit	Aurelio Rodriguez	1978	131	79	228	4	.987
Cleveland	William E. Kamm	1933	131	153	221	6	.984
California	Carney R. Lansford	1979	157	135	263	7	.983
Texas	David G. Bell	1980	120	125	282	8	.981
Chicago	Floyd W. Baker	1947	101	84	253	7	.980
Baltimore	Brooks C. Robinson	1967	158	147	405	11	.980
Boston	Grady E. Hatton	1955	111	97	225	8	.976
	Americo Petrocelli	1971	156	118	334	11	.976
†Washington	Kenneth L. McMullen	1969	154	185	347	13	.976
New York	Graig Nettles	1978	159	109	326	11	.975
St. Louis	Mark J. Christman	1944	145	172	316	14	.972
§Kansas City	Edwin D. Charles	1965	128	150	251	12	.971
Oakland	Salvatore L. Bando	1971	153	141	267	12	.971
Minnesota	Michael L. Cubbage	1978	115	65	233	9	.971
Toronto	S. Rance Mulliniks	1983	116	70	161	7	.971
*Washington	Oswald L. Bluege	1932	149	158	295	14	.970
‡Kansas City	Joseph A. Foy	1969	113	117	209	12	.964
ySeattle	William A. Stein	1977	147	146	255	15	.964
xSeattle					No third basemen in 100 games.		

*Original Washington club (now Minnesota). †Washington second club (now Texas).
‡Present Kansas City club. §Former Kansas City club (now Oakland). xOriginal Seattle club (now Milwaukee). yPresent Seattle club.

National League

Highest Fielding Average, Season, 100 or More Games, Each Club

Club	Player	Year	G.	P.O.	Assts.	E.	F.A.
*New York	Henry K. Groh	1924	145	121	286	7	.983
Philadelphia	Arthur C. Whitney	1937	130	136	238	7	.982
St. Louis	Kenneth J. Reitz	1977	157	121	320	9	.980
San Francisco	James H. Davenport	1959	121	91	221	7	.978
Los Angeles	Ronald C. Cey	1979	150	123	265	9	.977
Chicago	Stanley C. Hack	1945	146	195	312	13	.975
Cincinnati	Grady E. Hatton	1949	136	143	290	11	.975
Houston	Robert T. Aspromonte	1964	155	133	261	11	.973
Pittsburgh	Philip M. Garner	1977	107	98	240	10	.971
Brooklyn	William R. Cox	1952	100	100	157	8	.970
Atlanta	Cletis L. Boyer	1967	150	166	291	14	.970
	J. Robert Horner	1982	137	102	217	10	.970
Boston	Arthur C. Whitney	1934	111	105	227	11	.968
Milwaukee	Edwin L. Mathews	1963	121	113	276	13	.968
†New York	Leonard S. Randle	1978	124	108	215	11	.967
Montreal	Robert S. Bailey	1971	120	69	194	11	.960

THIRD BASEMEN—Continued

Club	Player	Year	G.	P.O.	Assts.	E.	F.A.
San Diego	David W. Roberts	1974	103	83	170	12	.955
	Douglas L. Rader	1976	137	109	318	20	.955

*Original New York club (now San Francisco Giants). †Present New York club.

SHORTSTOPS
American League

Highest Fielding Average, Season, 100 or More Games, Each Club

Club	Player	Year	G.	P.O.	Assts.	E.	F.A.
Detroit	Edwin A. Brinkman	1972	156	233	495	7	.990
Cleveland	Frank T. Duffy	1973	115	198	377	8	.986
Minnesota	Leonardo A. Cardenas	1971	153	266	445	11	.985
Baltimore	Mark H. Belanger	1977	142	244	417	10	.985
	Mark H. Belanger	1978	134	184	409	9	.985
California	Timothy J. Foli	1982	139	235	432	10	.985
New York	Frederick B. Stanley	1976	110	145	251	7	.983
Chicago	Ronald L. Hansen	1963	144	247	483	13	.983
Boston	Vernon D. Stephens	1950	146	258	431	13	.981
	Americo Petrocelli	1969	153	269	466	14	.981
	Richard P. Burleson	1978	144	285	482	15	.981
§Kansas City	Joseph P. DeMaestri	1957	134	248	387	13	.980
	Joseph P. DeMaestri	1958	137	226	417	13	.980
†Washington	Edwin A. Brinkman	1967	109	160	309	10	.979
Texas	Russell E. Dent	1983	129	150	369	11	.979
*Washington	Mark J. Christman	1947	106	203	291	11	.978
Oakland	Dagoberto Campaneris	1972	148	283	494	18	.977
Toronto	Luis Gomez	1978	153	247	400	16	.976
Philadelphia	Edwin D. Joost	1951	140	325	422	20	.974
Milwaukee	Robin R. Yount	1983	139	256	420	19	.973
‡Kansas City	Freddie J. Patek	1972	136	230	510	22	.971
St. Louis	Vernon D. Stephens	1947	149	283	494	24	.970
	G. William Hunter	1953	152	284	512	25	.970
ySeattle	Mario Mendoza	1979	148	177	422	19	.969
xSeattle	Raymond F. Oyler	1969	106	143	266	15	.965

*Original Washington club (now Minnesota Twins). †Washington second club (now Texas). ‡Present Kansas City club. §Former Kansas City club (now Oakland). xOriginal Seattle club (now Milwaukee). yPresent Seattle club.

National League

Highest Fielding Average, Season, 100 or More Games, Each Club

Club	Player	Year	G.	P.O.	Assts.	E.	F.A.
Philadelphia	Lawrence R. Bowa	1979	146	229	448	6	.991
Houston	Roger H. Metzger	1976	150	253	462	10	.986
Cincinnati	David I. Concepcion	1977	156	280	490	11	.986
Chicago	Ernest Banks	1959	154	271	519	12	.985
St. Louis	Osborne E. Smith	1982	139	279	535	13	.984
Boston	Edward R. Miller	1942	142	285	450	13	.983
*New York	John J. Kerr	1946	126	240	400	12	.982
Montreal	Robert P. Wine	1971	119	221	321	10	.982
	Chris E. Speier	1982	155	291	405	13	.982
San Francisco	Chris E. Speier	1975	136	247	420	12	.982
Pittsburgh	Timothy J. Foli	1980	125	212	402	12	.981
†New York	Derrel M. Harrelson	1973	103	153	315	10	.979
Los Angeles	Maurice M. Wills	1971	144	220	484	16	.978
Brooklyn	Harold H. Reese	1949	155	316	454	18	.977
Milwaukee	William F. Woodward	1965	107	146	243	9	.977
San Diego	Osborne E. Smith	1979	155	256	555	20	.976
	Osborne E. Smith	1981	110	220	422	16	.976
Atlanta	Luis Gomez	1980	119	135	319	15	.968

*Original New York club (now San Francisco Giants). †Present New York club.

OUTFIELDERS
American League

Highest Fielding Average, Season, 100 or More Games, Each Club

Club	Player	Year	G.	P.O.	Assts.	E.	F.A.
Cleveland	Rocco D. Colavito	1965	162	265	9	0	1.000
Baltimore	Russell H. Snyder	1965	106	188	4	0	1.000
	Gary S. Roenicke	1980	113	197	8	0	1.000
	John L. Lowenstein	1982	112	202	2	0	1.000
Detroit	Mitchell J. Stanley	1968	130	297	7	0	1.000
	Mitchell J. Stanley	1970	132	317	3	0	1.000
	Albert W. Kaline	1971	129	207	6	0	1.000
New York	Roy H. White	1971	145	306	8	0	1.000
Boston	Kenneth S. Harrelson	1968	132	241	8	0	1.000
	Carl M. Yastrzemski	1977	140	287	16	0	1.000
Chicago	A. Kent Berry	1969	120	215	7	0	1.000
California	A. Kent Berry	1972	116	272	13	0	1.000
	Brian J. Downing	1982	158	321	9	0	1.000
	Robert C. Clark	1982	102	88	2	0	1.000
Texas	William A. Sample	1979	103	173	7	0	1.000
†Washington	James A. Piersall	1962	132	308	5	1	.997
St. Louis	Milton J. Byrnes	1943	114	289	13	1	.997
Minnesota	Ted O. Uhlaender	1969	150	278	8	1	.997
	Stephen R. Brye	1974	129	301	10	1	.997
	Robert V. Mitchell	1982	121	350	8	1	.997
‡Kansas City	Amos J. Otis	1982	125	308	5	1	.997
*Washington	Samuel F. West	1928	116	210	13	1	.996
Oakland	Joseph O. Rudi	1971	121	249	5	1	.996
Milwaukee	William H. Sharp	1975	124	294	12	2	.994
Toronto	Lloyd A. Moseby	1982	145	361	4	3	.992
Philadelphia	David E. Philley	1952	149	442	13	4	.991
ySeattle	Ruppert S. Jones	1979	161	453	13	5	.989
§Kansas City	William R. Tuttle	1958	145	311	12	4	.988
	William R. Tuttle	1960	148	381	16	5	.988
	N. Michael Hershberger	1965	144	238	14	3	.988
xSeattle	H. Wayne Comer	1969	139	287	14	6	.980

*Original Washington club (now Minnesota Twins). †Washington second club (now Texas). ‡Present Kansas City club. §Former Kansas City club (now Oakland). xOriginal Seattle club (now Milwaukee). yPresent Seattle club.

National League

Highest Fielding Average, Season, 100 or More Games, Each Club

Club	Player	Year	G.	P.O.	Assts.	E.	F.A.
Philadelphia	Daniel W. Litwhiler	1942	151	308	9	0	1.000
	A. Antonio Gonzalez	1962	114	268	8	0	1.000
	Donald L. Demeter	1963	119	166	6	0	1.000
	John W. Callison	1968	109	187	10	0	1.000
Boston	Willard W. Marshall	1951	136	220	11	0	1.000
St. Louis	Curtis C. Flood	1966	159	391	5	0	1.000
Houston	Terry S. Puhl	1979	152	352	7	0	1.000
Chicago	Gary L. Woods	1982	103	161	6	0	1.000
Cincinnati	Harry F. Craft	1940	109	284	7	1	.997
	Lloyd Merriman	1951	102	309	5	1	.997
	Peter E. Rose	1970	159	309	8	1	.997
	Peter E. Rose	1974	163	346	11	1	.997
	George A. Foster	1980	141	295	6	1	.997
Pittsburgh	Omar R. Moreno	1981	103	302	6	1	.997
*New York	Monford Irvin	1951	112	237	10	1	.996
Los Angeles	Johnnie B. Baker	1976	106	254	3	1	.996
	Derrel O. Thomas	1979	119	269	10	1	.996
Brooklyn	Leonard Koenecke	1934	121	310	6	2	.994
	John W. Cooney	1936	130	336	11	2	.994
San Francisco	Bobby L. Bonds	1971	154	329	10	2	.994

OUTFIELDERS—Continued

Club	Player	Year	G.	P.O.	Assts.	E.	F.A.
Atlanta	Rowland J. Office	1974	119	171	0	1	.994
San Diego	Ruppert S. Jones	1981	104	295	9	2	.993
†New York	Lee L. Mazzilli	1977	156	386	9	3	.992
Montreal	Timothy Raines	1982	120	232	7	2	.992
Milwaukee	William H. Bruton	1959	133	309	6	3	.991

*Original New York club (now San Francisco). †Present New York club.

CATCHERS
American League

Highest Fielding Average, Season, 100 or More Games, Each Club

Club	Player	Year	G.	P.O.	Assts.	E.	F.A.
Philadelphia	Warren V. Rosar	1946	117	532	73	0	1.000
Chicago	J. Sherman Lollar	1961	107	464	48	1	.998
New York	Elston G. Howard	1964	146	939	67	2	.998
	Thurman L. Munson	1971	117	547	67	1	.998
Cleveland	James E. Hegan	1955	111	593	34	2	.997
Detroit	William A. Freehan	1970	114	742	42	2	.997
Minnesota	Glenn D. Borgmann	1974	128	652	52	2	.997
Texas	James H. Sundberg	1978	148	769	91	3	.997
Baltimore	J. Rikard Dempsey	1983	127	591	65	2	.997
St. Louis	Clinton D. Courtney	1952	113	487	60	2	.996
Milwaukee	Ted L. Simmons	1982	121	570	62	3	.995
Oakland	David E. Duncan	1972	113	661	43	5	.993
California	Brian J. Downing	1978	128	681	82	5	.993
ySeattle	Larry E. Cox	1980	104	412	45	3	.993
*Washington	Alfred H. Evans	1949	107	322	47	3	.992
Boston	Michael J. Ryan	1966	114	685	50	6	.992
†Washington	Paulino O. Casanova	1969	122	583	59	5	.992
Toronto	L. Ernest Whitt	1983	119	554	50	5	.992
§Kansas City	Philip A. Roof	1967	113	677	55	7	.991
‡Kansas City	Edgar L. Kirkpatrick	1972	108	590	49	6	.991
xSeattle	Gerald E. McNertney	1969	122	697	67	9	.988

*Original Washington club (now Minnesota). †Washington second club (now Texas). ‡Present Kansas City club. §Former Kansas City club (now Oakland). xOriginal Seattle club (now Milwaukee). yPresent Seattle club.

National League

Highest Fielding Average, Season, 100 or More Games, Each Club

Club	Player	Year	G.	P.O.	Assts.	E.	F.A.
*New York	Wesley N. Westrum	1950	139	608	71	1	.999
Pittsburgh	R. Earl Grace	1932	114	364	48	1	.998
St. Louis	J. Timothy McCarver	1967	130	819	67	3	.997
San Francisco	Thomas F. Haller	1967	136	797	64	3	.997
Cincinnati	Johnny L. Bench	1976	128	651	60	2	.997
Chicago	Charles L. Hartnett	1934	129	605	86	3	.996
	Charles L. Hartnett	1937	103	436	65	2	.996
	C. Randolph Hundley	1967	152	865	59	4	.996
Milwaukee	Delmar W. Crandall	1956	109	448	44	2	.996
Los Angeles	Joe V. Ferguson	1973	122	757	57	3	.996
Boston	Raymond P. Berres	1941	120	356	64	2	.995
Brooklyn	Arnold M. Owen	1941	128	530	64	3	.995
Houston	John A. Edwards	1970	139	854	74	5	.995
	John A. Edwards	1971	104	555	44	3	.995
†New York	Gerald W. Grote	1975	111	706	55	4	.995
Philadelphia	Virgil L. Davis	1931	114	420	78	3	.994
Atlanta	Robert D. Didier	1969	114	633	52	4	.994
San Diego	Fred L. Kendall	1976	146	582	54	4	.994
Montreal	Gary E. Carter	1980	149	822	108	7	.993
	Gary E. Carter	1981	100	509	58	4	.993

*Original New York club (now San Francisco). †Present New York club.

PITCHERS
American League

Highest Fielding Average, Season, with Most Chances Accepted

Club	Player	Year	G.	P.O.	A.	E.	C.A.	F.A.
*Washington	Walter P. Johnson	1913	48	21	82	0	103	1.000
Boston	Jack E. Russell	1929	35	15	69	0	84	1.000
zPhiladelphia	John W. Coombs	1912	54	16	66	0	82	1.000
Chicago	Joel E. Horlen	1967	35	29	53	0	82	1.000
	Thomas E. John	1969	33	16	66	0	82	1.000
Detroit	Harold Newhouser	1945	40	16	66	0	82	1.000
New York	George A. Mogridge	1917	29	16	61	0	77	1.000
	Leslie A. Bush	1922	39	16	61	0	77	1.000
Cleveland	Clinton H. Brown	1931	39	9	67	0	76	1.000
Milwaukee	James W. Colborn	1973	43	19	55	0	74	1.000
aSt. Louis	Leslie A. Bush	1925	33	17	54	0	71	1.000
ySeattle	Michael E. Parrott	1979	38	27	39	0	66	1.000
Oakland	J. Rick Langford	1979	34	26	36	0	62	1.000
Minnesota	James E. Perry	1971	41	17	44	0	61	1.000
†Washington	Claude W. Osteen	1964	37	9	51	0	60	1.000
‡Kansas City	Alan J. Fitzmorris	1974	34	20	39	0	59	1.000
	Lawrence C. Gura	1980	36	9	50	0	59	1.000
Baltimore	Milton S. Pappas	1964	37	25	30	0	55	1.000
California	Thomas E. John	1983	34	16	39	0	55	1.000
Toronto	Luis E. Leal	1982	38	17	31	0	48	1.000
§Kansas City	Jerry A. Walker	1962	31	15	27	0	42	1.000
Texas	Wilfred C. Siebert	1973	25	13	25	0	38	1.000
xSeattle	Diego P. Segui	1969	66	8	23	0	31	1.000

*Original Washington club (now Minnesota). †Washington second club (now Texas). ‡Present Kansas City club. §Former Kansas City club (now Oakland). xOriginal Seattle club (now Milwaukee). yPresent Seattle club. zOriginal Philadelphia club (now Oakland). aOriginal St. Louis club (now Baltimore).

National League

Highest Fielding Average, Season With Most Chances Accepted

Club	Player	Year	G.	P.O.	A.	E.	C.A.	F.A.
San Diego	Randall L. Jones	1976	40	31	81	0	112	1.000
Chicago	Lawrence C. Jackson	1964	40	24	85	0	109	1.000
Philadelphia	Eppa Rixey	1917	39	15	93	0	108	1.000
aNew York	Hal H. Schumacher	1935	33	14	89	0	103	1.000
bBoston	James R. Turner	1938	35	17	72	0	89	1.000
San Francisco	Gaylord J. Perry	1969	40	18	67	0	85	1.000
Pittsburgh	Charles B. Adams	1914	40	13	62	0	75	1.000
St. Louis	Grover C. Alexander	1927	37	8	66	0	74	1.000
Cincinnati	John D. Couch	1922	43	9	65	0	74	1.000
cBrooklyn	Arthur C. Vance	1928	38	17	55	0	72	1.000
Atlanta	Philip H. Niekro	1977	44	20	51	0	71	1.000
Houston	J. Rodney Richard	1977	36	26	44	0	70	1.000
dMilwaukee	Warren E. Spahn	1957	39	18	47	0	65	1.000
Los Angeles	Thomas E. John	1972	29	11	45	0	56	1.000
Montreal	Stephen D. Rogers	1983	36	28	28	0	56	1.000
eNew York	Gary E. Gentry	1969	35	13	41	0	54	1.000

aOriginal New York club, now San Francisco. bNow Atlanta. cNow Los Angeles. dBoston club transferred to Milwaukee, then to Atlanta. eSecond New York club.

CLUB FIELDING

Season Records

Highest Fielding Average, Season

A. L. (162-game season) —.9849—Baltimore, 162 games, 1980.
A. L. (154-game season) — .983—Cleveland, 157 games, 1947, Cleveland, 154 games, 1949.
N. L. (162-game season) —.9846—Cincinnati, 162 games, 1977.
N. L. (154-game season) —.9831—Cincinnati, 154 games, 1958.

Lowest Fielding Average, Season, Since 1900

N. L. (162-game season) —.967—New York, 161 games, 1962, New York, 162 games, 1963.
N. L. (154-game season) —.936—Philadelphia, 155 games, 1904.
A. L. (162-game season) —.970—Oakland, 161 games, 1977.
A. L. (154-game season) —.928—Detroit, 136 games, 1901.

Most Consecutive Years Leading League in Fielding

A. L.—6—Boston, 1916 through 1921.
N. L.—4—Chicago, 1905 through 1908.

Most Putouts, Season

A. L. (162-game season) —4520—New York, 164 games, 1964.
A. L. (154-game season) —4396—Cleveland, 161 games, 1910.
N. L. (162-game season) —4480—Pittsburgh, 163 games, 1979.
N. L. (154-game season) —4359—Philadelphia, 159 games, 1913.

Fewest Putouts, Season

N. L. (162-game season) —4223—Atlanta, 160 games, 1979.
N. L. (154-game season) —3887—Philadelphia, 149 games, 1907.
A. L. (162-game season) —4188—Detroit, 159 games, 1975.
A. L. (154-game season) —3907—Cleveland, 147 games, 1945.

Most Assists, Season

N. L. (162-game season) —2104—Chicago, 162 games, 1977.
N. L. (154-game season) —2293—St. Louis, 154 games, 1917.
A. L. (162-game season) —2077—California, 162 games, 1983.
A. L. (154-game season) —2446—Chicago, 157 games, 1907.

Fewest Assists, Season

N. L. (154-game season) —1437—Philadelphia, 156 games, 1957.
A. L. (162-game season) —1443—Detroit, 161 games, 1962.

Most Consecutive Years Leading League in Assists

A. L.—6—Chicago, 1905 through 1910.
N. L.—6—New York, 1933 through 1938.

Most Chances Accepted (Excludes Errors), Season

A. L. (162-game season) —6499—California, 162 games, 1983.
A. L. (154-game season) —6655—Chicago, 157 games, 1907.
N. L. (162-game season) —6508—Chicago, 162 games, 1977.
N. L. (154-game season) —6472—New York, 155 games, 1920.

Fewest Chances Accepted (Excludes Errors), Season

A. L. (154-game season) —5470—Cleveland, 147 games, 1945.
N. L. (154-game season) —5545—Philadelphia, 154 games 1955.

Most Errors, Season

N. L.— 867— Washington, 122 games, 1886.
A. L.— 425— Detroit, 136 games, 1901.
N. L. since 1900—408—Brooklyn, 155 games, 1905.

Fewest Errors, Season

A. L. (162-game season) —95—Baltimore, 163 games, 1964.
                                  Baltimore, 162 games, 1980.
N. L. (162-game season) —95—Cincinnati, 162 games, 1977.

Most Errorless Games, Season

N. L. (162-game season) —94—Cincinnati, 162 games, 1977 (95 errors).
N. L. (154-game season) —82—Cincinnati, 154 games, 1958 (100 errors).
A. L. (162-game season) —92—Baltimore, 162 games, 1980 (95 errors).
A. L. (154-game season) —84—Detroit, 156 games, 1972 (96 errors).

Most Consecutive Years Leading League in Errors

    N. L.—7—Philadelphia, 1930 through 1936.
    A. L.—6—Philadelphia, 1936 through 1941
           St. Louis, 1948 through 1953.

Most Years Leading League, Fewest Errors

    N. L. since 1900—19—Cincinnati.

Most Double Plays, Season

    A. L. (154-game season)—217—Philadelphia, 154 games, 1949.
    A. L. (162-game season)—206—Boston, 160 games, 1980.
                        Toronto, 162 games, 1980.
    N. L. (162-game season)—215—Pittsburgh, 162 games, 1966.
    N. L. (154-game season)—198—Los Angeles, 154 games, 1958.

Most Years, 200 or More Double Plays

    A. L.—3—Philadelphia, 1949 (217), 1950 (208), 1951 (204).
    N. L.—1—Pittsburgh, 1966 (215).

Fewest Double Plays, Season (A. L.—Since 1912; N. L.—Since 1919)

    A. L. (154-game season)—74—Boston, 151 games, 1913.
    N. L. (154-game season)—94—Pittsburgh, 153 games, 1935.

Most Times Five or More Double Plays, Game, Season

    N. L.—3—New York, 1950.
    A. L.—3—Cleveland, 1970.
           Kansas City, 1971.

Most Triple Plays, Season

    A. A.—3—Cincinnati, 1882.
           Rochester, 1890.
    A. L.—3—Detroit, 1911; Boston, 1924, 1979; Oakland, 1979.
    N. L.—3—Philadelphia, 1964; Chicago 1965.

Most Passed Balls, Season

    N. L.— 167— Boston, 98 games, 1883.
    A. L. (154-game season)—49—Baltimore, 155 games, 1959.
    N. L. (154-game season)—since 1900—42—Boston, 156 games, 1905.
    N. L. (162-game season)—42—Atlanta, 162 games, 1967.

Fewest Passed Balls, Season

    A. L. (162-game season)—3—Boston, 160 games, 1975.
    A. L. (154-game season)—0—New York, 155 games, 1931.
    N. L. (162-game season)—2—New York, 162 games, 1980.
    N. L. (154-game season)—2—Boston, 153 games, 1943.

CLUB FIELDING
Inning, Game, Doubleheader

Most Assists, Inning, One Club

    A. L.—10—Cleveland vs. Philadelphia, August 17, 1921, first inning.
              Boston vs. New York, May 10, 1952, fifth inning.
    N. L.— 8—Boston vs. Philadelphia, May 1, 1911, fourth inning.

Most Assists, Game, Nine Innings, One Club

    N. L.—28—Pittsburgh vs. New York, June 7, 1911.
    A. L.—27—St. Louis vs. Philadelphia, August 16, 1919.

Most Assists, Game, Nine Innings, Both Clubs

    A. L.—45—New York 23, Chicago 22, August 21, 1905.
    N. L.—44—Brooklyn 23, New York 21, April 21, 1903.
           New York 25, Cincinnati 19, May 15, 1909.

Most Assists, Extra-Inning Game, One Club

    N. L.—41—Boston vs. Brooklyn, May 1, 1920, 26 innings.
    A. L.—38—Detroit vs. Philadelphia, July 21, 1945, 24 innings.
           Washington vs. Chicago, June 12, 1967, 22 innings.

Most Assists, Extra-Inning Game, Both Clubs

    N. L.—72—Boston 41, Brooklyn 31, May 1, 1920, 26 innings.
    A. L.—72—Detroit 38, Philadelphia 34, July 21, 1945, 24 innings.

Most Assists, Two Consecutive Games, One Club

N. L.—48—Boston vs. New York, June 24, 25, 1918.
A. L.—43—Washington vs. St. Louis, August 19, 20, 1923.

Fewest Assists, Game, Eight Innings, One Club

A. L.—0—St. Louis vs. Cleveland, August 8, 1943, second game.
N. L.—1—Held by many clubs.

Fewest Assists, Game, Nine Innings, One Club

A. L.—0—Cleveland vs. New York, July 4, 1945, first game.
N. L.—1—Chicago vs. Philadelphia, August 23, 1932.
        Cincinnati vs. Brooklyn, August 6, 1938.
        Pittsburgh vs. Chicago, August 13, 1950, first game.
        New York vs. Chicago, May 6, 1953.
        Philadelphia vs. Chicago, July 17, 1955, second game.
        Philadelphia vs. Chicago, May 2, 1957.
        Philadelphia vs. Milwaukee, June 16, 1965.
        Philadelphia vs. Cincinnati, June 7, 1966.
        Philadelphia vs. Cincinnati, May 18, 1967.
        Houston vs. Cincinnati, May 1, 1969.
        St. Louis vs. Los Angeles, May 25, 1969.
        New York vs. San Diego, April 22, 1970.
        Atlanta vs. Cincinnati, June 25, 1971, first game.
        Philadelphia vs. Chicago, August 6, 1974.
        Pittsburgh vs. Montreal, September 17, 1977.
        New York vs. Atlanta, September 4, 1981.

Fewest Assists, Game, Nine Innings, Both Clubs

A. L.—5—Baltimore 3, Cleveland 2, August 31, 1955.
N. L.—6—Chicago 5, Philadelphia 1, May 2, 1957.
        San Francisco 3, Philadelphia 3, May 13, 1959.

Fewest Assists, Two Consecutive Nine-Inning Games, One Club

N. L.—5—Chicago vs. Philadelphia, Brooklyn, August 23 (1), 24 (4), 1932.
A. L.—7—Chicago vs. Boston, June 11 (2), 11 (5), 1960, 17 innings.
        Kansas City vs. Milwaukee, California, April 16 (3), April 17 (4), 1970, 18
        innings.

Most Assists, Doubleheader, Nine-Inning Games, One Club

N. L.—42—New York vs. Boston, September 30, 1914.
A. L.—41—Boston vs. Detroit, September 20, 1927.
        Boston vs. Washington, September 26, 1927.

Most Assists, Doubleheader, Nine-Inning Games, Both Clubs

N. L.—70—Brooklyn 36, Philadelphia 34, September 5, 1922.
A. L.—68—Detroit 34, Philadelphia 34, September 5, 1901.
        Cleveland 35, Boston 33, September 7, 1935.
        St. Louis 39, Boston 29, July 23, 1939.

Fewest Assists, Doubleheader, Nine-Inning Games, One Club

A. L.—8—Philadelphia vs. New York July 7, 1946.
        Minnesota vs. Los Angeles, July 19, 1961, 17⅔ innings.
      7—Chicago vs. Boston, June 11, 1960, 17 innings.
N. L.—7—New York vs. San Diego, May 29, 1971.

Fewest Assists, Doubleheader, Both Clubs

N. L.—22—Milwaukee 14, Philadelphia 8, September 12, 1954.
A. L.—25—Washington 13, New York 12, July 4, 1931.

Most Chances Accepted (Excludes Errors), Nine-Inning Game, One Club

N. L.—55—Pittsburgh vs. New York, June 7, 1911.
A. L.—54—St. Louis vs. Philadelphia, August 16, 1919.

Most Chances Accepted (Excludes Errors), Extra-Inning Game, One Club

N. L.—119—Boston vs. Brooklyn, May 1, 1920, 26 innings.
A. L.—110—Detroit vs. Philadelphia, July 21, 1945, 24 innings.

Most Chances Accepted (Excludes Errors), Nine-Inning Game, Both Clubs

N. L.—98—Brooklyn 50, New York 48, April 21, 1903.
        New York 52, Cincinnati 46, May 15, 1909.
A. L.—98—Cleveland 49, St. Louis 49, May 7, 1909.

Most Errors, Game, One Club

N. L.—24—Boston vs. St. Louis, June 14, 1876.

A. L.—12—Detroit vs. Chicago, May 1, 1901.
Chicago vs. Detroit, May 6, 1903.
N. L. since 1900—11—St. Louis vs. Pittsburgh, April 19, 1902.
Boston vs. St. Louis, June 11, 1906.
St. Louis vs. Cincinnati, July 3, 1909, second game.

Most Errors, Game, Both Clubs

N. L.—40—Boston 24, St. Louis 16, June 14, 1876.
A. L.—18—Chicago 12, Detroit 6, May 6, 1903.
N. L. since 1900—15—St. Louis 11, Pittsburgh 4, April 19, 1902.
Boston 10, Chicago 5, October 3, 1904.

Longest Game With No Errors, One Club

A. L.—22 innings— Chicago vs. Washington, June 12, 1967.
Washington vs. Chicago, June 12, 1967.
N. L.—21 innings— Boston vs. Pittsburgh, August 1, 1918.
Chicago vs. Philadelphia, July 17, 1918.
San Francisco vs. Cincinnati, September 1, 1967.
San Diego vs. Montreal, May 21, 1977.

Longest Game With No Errors, Both Clubs

A. L.—22 innings— Chicago 0, Washington 0, June 12, 1967.
N. L.—21 innings— Chicago 0, Philadelphia 0, July 17, 1918, none out for Philadelphia in
21st inning.

Most Errors, Inning, One Club, Since 1900

A. L.—7—Cleveland vs. Chicago, September 20, 1905, eighth inning.
N. L.—6—Pittsburgh vs. New York, August 20, 1903, first game, first inning.

Most Consecutive Errorless Games, Season, One Club

A. L.—12—Detroit, July 29 through August 7, 1963, 105⅔ innings.
N. L.—15—Cincinnati, June 15, second game, through June 30, 1975, 144 innings.

Most Errors, Doubleheader, One Club, Since 1900

N. L.—17—Cincinnati vs. Brooklyn, September 13, 1900.
Chicago vs. Cincinnati, October 8, 1900.
St. Louis vs. Cincinnati, July 3, 1909.
A. L.—16—Cleveland vs. Washington, September 21, 1901.

Most Errors, Doubleheader, Both Clubs, Since 1900

N. L.—25—Chicago 17, Cincinnati 8, October 8, 1900.
A. L.—22—Cleveland 16, Washington 6, September 21, 1901.

Longest Doubleheader Without an Error, One Club

A. L.—27 innings— Detroit vs. New York, August 23, 1968, (first game, Detroit fielded 8
innings; second game 19 innings).
N. L.—25 innings— Philadelphia vs. Cincinnati, July 8, 1924.

Longest Doubleheader Without an Error, Both Clubs

A. L.—24 innings— New York 0, Philadelphia 0, July 4, 1925.
Washington 0, New York 0, August 14, 1960.
N. L.—20 innings— Boston 0, Chicago 0, September 18, 1924.
New York 0, Chicago 0, August 27, 1951.

Most Double Plays, Game, One Club

A. L.—7—New York vs. Philadelphia, August 14, 1942.
N. L.—7—Houston vs. San Francisco, May 4, 1969.
Atlanta vs. Cincinnati, June 27, 1982, 14 innings.

Most Double Plays, Game, Nine Innings, Both Clubs

A. L.—9—Detroit 5, Washington 4, May 21, 1925.
Cleveland 6, Detroit 3, September 27, 1952.
New York 6, Kansas City 3, July 31, 1955, second game.
Cleveland 5, Boston 4, May 9, 1965, second game.
California 6, Boston 3, May 1, 1966, first game.
Cleveland 5, Chicago 4, May 5, 1970.
Kansas City 6, Oakland 3, May 14, 1971.
N. L.—9—Chicago 5, Cincinnati 4, July 3, 1929.
Los Angeles 5, Pittsburgh 4, April 15, 1961.

Most Double Plays, Extra-Inning Game, Both Clubs

N. L.—10—Boston 5, Cincinnati 5, June 7, 1925, 12 innings.
Cincinnati 6, New York 4, May 1, 1955, 16 innings.

Most Double Plays, Two Consecutive Nine-Inning Games, One Club

   N. L.—10—New York vs. Brooklyn, August 12, August 13, first game, 1932.
   A. L.—10—Detroit vs. Boston, May 18 (4), 19 (6), 1948.
              Cleveland vs. Kansas City, May 3 (5); vs. Chicago, May 5 (5); 1970.
              Kansas City vs. Baltimore, May 5 (4), May 6 (6), 1972.

Most Double Plays, Doubleheader, One Club

   A. L.—10—Washington vs. Chicago, August 18, 1943, 22⅓ innings.
   N. L.— 9—St. Louis vs. Cincinnati, June 11, 1944, 18 innings.

Most Double Plays, Doubleheader, Both Clubs

   N. L.—13—New York 7, Philadelphia 6, September 28, 1939.
              Pittsburgh 8, St. Louis 5, September 6, 1948.
   A. L.—12—Philadelphia 9, Cleveland 3, September 14, 1931.
              Boston 7, Chicago 5, September 15, 1947.
              New York 7, Kansas City 5, July 31, 1955.
              California 8, Boston 4, May 1, 1966.

Most Consecutive Games Making One or More Double Plays

   A. L.—25—Boston, May 7 through June 4, second game, 1951.
              Cleveland, August 21, second game through September 12, 1953.
   N. L.—23—Brooklyn, August 7, second game through August 27, 1952.

Most Double Plays, Three Consecutive Games, Club (Making One Each Game)

   N. L.—12—New York, August 9 through August 13 first game, 1932.
   A. L.—12—Boston, June 25 through June 27, 1950.
              New York, April 19 through April 21, 1952.
              Chicago, September 2 (6), September 3, first game (2), September 3, second
              game (4), 1973.

Most Double Plays, Four Consecutive Games, Club (Making One Each Game)

   A. L.—14—Chicago, July 12 through July 14, 1951.
              New York, April 18 through April 21, 1952.
   N. L.—14—Cincinnati, April 30 through May 4, 1955.

Most Double Plays, Five Consecutive Games, Club (Making One Each Game)

   A. L.—16—New York, April 19 through April 23, 1952.
   N. L.—15—Cincinnati, April 30 through May 6, 1955.

Most Double Plays, Six Consecutive Games, Club (Making One Each Game)

   A. L.—18—New York, April 18 through April 23, 1952.
   N. L.—16—New York, September 4, first game through September 8, 1950.

Most Double Plays, Seven Consecutive Games, Club (Making One Each Game)

   A. L.—19—New York, April 17 through April 23, 1952.
   N. L.—18—New York, September 2 through September 8, 1950.

Most Double Plays, Eight Consecutive Games, Club (Making One Each Game)

   A. L.—20—New York, April 16 through April 23, 1952.
              Los Angeles, August 16 through August 24, 1963.
   N. L.—19—New York, September 2 through September 9, 1950.
              Los Angeles, June 24, first game through July 1, 1958.

Most Double Plays, Nine Consecutive Games, Club (Making One Each Game)

   A. L.—22—Philadelphia, May 8 through May 18, 1951.
              Los Angeles, August 16 through August 25, 1963.
   N. L.—21—Los Angeles, June 24, first game, through July 3, first game, 1958.

Most Double Plays, 10 Consecutive Games, Club (Making One Each Game)

   A. L.—24—Philadelphia, May 8 through May 20, first game, 1951.
   N. L.—22—Los Angeles, June 23 through July 3, first game, 1958.

Most Double Plays, 11 Consecutive Games, Club (Making One Each Game)

   A. L.—26—Philadelphia, May 8 through May 20, second game, 1951.
   N. L.—23—New York, September 2 through September 13, 1950.
              Milwaukee, August 19 through August 28, 1956.
              Los Angeles, June 22, second game, through July 3, first game, 1958.

Most Double Plays, 12 Consecutive Games, Club (Making One Each Game)

   A. L.—26—Washington, September 1 through September 9, first game, 1937.
              Los Angeles, August 16 through August 29, 1963.
              Chicago, September 4, second game, through September 17, 1963.
   N. L.—25—New York, September 4, first game through September 14, second game,
              1950.

Most Double Plays, 13 Consecutive Games, Club (Making One Each Game)

A. L.—29—Los Angeles, August 16 through August 30, 1963.
N. L.—27—New York, September 2 through September 14, second game 1950.

Most Double Plays, 14 Consecutive Games, Club (Making One Each Game)

A. L.—31—Los Angeles, August 16 through August 31, 1963.
N. L.—28—New York, September 2 through September 15, 1950.

Most Double Plays, 15 Consecutive Games, Club (Making One Each Game)

A. L.—34—Los Angeles, August 16 through September 1, 1963.
N. L.—29—Philadelphia, July 11 through July 26, 1953.

Most Double Plays, 16 Consecutive Games, Club (Making One Each Game)

A. L.—35—Los Angeles, August 15 through September 1, 1963.
N. L.—29—Cincinnati, May 11 through May 29, 1954.
Philadelphia, July 15 through July 30, 1961.

Most Double Plays, 17 Consecutive Games, Club (Making One Each Game)

A. L.—36—Los Angeles, August 14 through September 1, 1963.
N. L.—27—Brooklyn, August 7, second game through August 22, second game, 1952.

Most Double Plays, 18 Consecutive Games, Club (Making One Each Game)

A. L.—38—Los Angeles, August 13 through September 1, 1963.
N. L.—29—Brooklyn, August 7, second game, through August 23, 1952.
Montreal, July 19, second game, through August 5, first game, 1970.

Most Double Plays, 19 Consecutive Games, Club (Making One Each Game)

A. L.—31—Cleveland, August 22 through September 7, first game, 1953.
N. L.—30—Brooklyn, August 7, second game, through August 24, 1952.

Most Double Plays, 20 Consecutive Games, Club (Making One Each Game)

N. L.—33—Brooklyn, August 7, second game, through August 25, first game, 1952.
A. L.—32—Boston, May 7 through June 1, 1951.
Cleveland, August 21, second game, through September 7, first game, 1953.

Most Double Plays, 21 Consecutive Games, Club (Making One Each Game)

N. L.—34—Brooklyn, August 7, second game, through August 25, second game, 1952.
A. L.—34—Cleveland, August 23, second game, through September 11, 1953.

Most Double Plays, 22 Consecutive Games, Club (Making One Each Game)

N. L.—35—Brooklyn, August 7, second game, through August 26, 1952.
A. L.—35—Cleveland, August 23, first game, through September 11, 1953.

Most Double Plays, 23 Consecutive Games, Club (Making One Each Game)

N. L.—36—Brooklyn, August 7, second game, through August 27, 1952.
A. L.—36—Cleveland, August 22 through September 11, 1953.

Most Double Plays, 24 Consecutive Games, Club (Making One Each Game)

A. L.—37—Boston, May 7 through June 4, first game, 1951.
Cleveland, August 21, second game, through September 11, 1953.
N. L.—No performance.

Most Double Plays, 25 Consecutive Games, Club (Making One Each Game)

A. L.—38—Boston, May 7 through June 4, second game, 1951.
Cleveland, August 21, second game, through September 12, 1953.
N. L.—No performance.

Most Unassisted Double Plays, Game, One Club

N. L.-A. L.—2—Made in many games.

Most Unassisted Double Plays, Game, Both Clubs

N. L.-A. L.—2—Made in many games.

Most Consecutive Games, One or More Double or Triple Plays, One Club

N. L.—26—New York, August 21 through September 16, second game, 1951 (44 double plays, 1 triple play)
A. L.—25—Boston, May 7 through June 4, second game, 1951 (38 double plays).
Cleveland, August 21, second game, through September 12, 1953 (38 double plays).

Most Triple Plays, Game, One Club

N. L.—1—Made in many games.   A. L.—1—Made in many games.

Most Triple Plays, Game, Both Clubs

N. L.—1—Made in many games.   A. L.—1—Made in many games.

Most Triple Plays, Two Consecutive Games, One Club

    A. L.—2—Detroit vs. Boston, June 6, 7, 1908.
    N. L.—1—Held by many clubs.

Most Passed Balls, Game, One Club

    A. A.—12—Washington vs. New York, May 10, 1884.
    N. L.—10—Boston vs. Washington, May 3, 1886.
    N. L. since 1900—6—Cincinnati vs. Pittsburgh, October 4, 1902.
    A. L.— 5—California vs. New York, July 28, 1970.

Most Passed Balls, Game, Both Clubs

    A. A.—14—Washington 12, New York 2, May 10, 1884.
    N. L.—11—Troy 7, Cleveland 4, June 16, 1880.
    N. L. since 1900—6—Cincinnati 6, Pittsburgh 0, October 4, 1902.
    A. L.— 5—California 5, New York 0, July 28, 1970.

Longest Game With No Passed Balls, One Club

    N. L.—26 innings— Boston vs. Brooklyn, May 1, 1920.
                         Brooklyn vs. Boston, May 1, 1920.
    A. L.—24 innings— Boston vs. Philadelphia, September 1, 1906.
                         Philadelphia vs. Boston, September 1, 1906.
                         Detroit vs. Philadelphia, July 21, 1945.
                         Philadelphia vs. Detroit, July 21, 1945.

Longest Game With No Passed Balls, Both Clubs

    N. L.—26 innings— Boston 0, Brooklyn 0, May 1, 1920.
    A. L.—24 innings— Boston 0, Philadelphia 0, September 1, 1906.
                         Detroit 0, Philadelphia 0, July 21, 1945.

Most Players One or More Putouts, Game, Nine Innings, One Club

    A. L.—14—New York vs. Cleveland, July 17, 1952, first game.
    N. L.—13—St. Louis vs. Los Angeles, April 13, 1960.
            Chicago vs. New York, August 8, 1965, second game.

Most Players One or More Putouts, Game, Nine Innings, Both Clubs

    A. L.—22—New York 14, Cleveland 8, July 17, 1952, first game.
    N. L.—22—Chicago 13, New York 9, August 8, 1965, second game.

Most Players One or More Assists, Game, Nine Innings, One Club

    A. L.—11—Washington vs. Philadelphia, October 3, 1920.
            Boston vs. Philadelphia, May 1, 1929.
            Washington vs. Baltimore, April 29, 1956, first game.
            Chicago vs. Kansas City, September 22, 1970, second game.
    N. L.—11—Brooklyn vs. Philadelphia, April 22, 1953.

CLUB FIELDING

RECORDS FOR INFIELD
FIRST BASE, SECOND BASE, THIRD BASE AND SHORTSTOP

Most Putouts, Infield, Game, Nine Innings, One Club

    A. L.—25—New York vs. Washington, June 23, 1911.
            Cleveland vs. Boston, August 9, 1922.
            Detroit vs. Chicago, September 26, 1924.
            Boston vs. Cleveland, June 24, 1931.
            Detroit vs. Philadelphia, June 20, 1937, first game.
            Detroit vs. New York, May 6, 1941.
    N. L.—25—Chicago vs. Philadelphia, September 24, 1927.
            Pittsburgh vs. New York, June 6, 1941, second game.
            St. Louis vs. Boston, July 17, 1947.
            Chicago vs. Pittsburgh, May 9, 1963.

Most Putouts, Infield, Game, Nine Innings, Both Clubs

    N. L.—46—Cincinnati 24, New York 22, May 7, 1941.
            St. Louis 25, Boston 21, July 17, 1947.
    A. L.—45—Detroit 24, Washington 21, September 15, 1945, second game.
            Boston, 24, Cleveland 21, July 11, 1977.

Fewest Putouts, Infield, Game, Nine Innings, One Club

    A. L.—3—St. Louis vs. New York, July 20, 1945, second game.
    N. L.—3—New York vs. San Diego, April 22, 1970.

Most Assists, Infield, Game, Nine Innings, One Club

A. L.—21—Detroit vs. Washington, September 2, 1901, second game.
N. L.—21—New York vs. Pittsburgh, July 13, 1919.
    Philadelphia vs. Boston, May 30, 1931, p.m. game.
    Brooklyn vs. Pittsburgh, August 18, 1935, second game.

Most Assists, Infield, Game, Nine Innings, Both Clubs

N. L.—38—Brooklyn 20, Cincinnati 18, June 10, 1917.
A. L.—35—Detroit 19, Cleveland 16, April 18, 1924.
    Chicago 18, Boston 17, September 17, 1945, second game.

Fewest Assists, Infield, Game, Nine Innings, One Club

N. L.—0—Pittsburgh vs. Chicago, July 19, 1902.
    New York vs. Philadelphia, July 29, 1934, first game.
    Chicago vs. Cincinnati, April 26, 1935.
    Cincinnati vs. Brooklyn, August 6, 1938.
    Boston vs. Pittsburgh, June 17, 1940, first game.
    New York vs. Chicago, May 6, 1953.
    Philadelphia vs. Chicago, May 2, 1957.
    Houston vs. Cincinnati, September 10, 1968, first game.
    Pittsburgh vs. Montreal, September 17, 1977.
A. L.—0—Boston, vs. Chicago, August 13, 1924, first game.
    Cleveland vs. New York, July 4, 1945, first game.
    St. Louis vs. New York, July 20, 1945, second game.
    Washington vs. St. Louis, May 20, 1952.

Fewest Assists, Infield, Game, Nine Innings, Both Clubs

A. L.—2—Philadelphia 2, Washington 0, May 5, 1910, Washington fielded only 8 innings.
N. L.—2—Chicago 2, Philadelphia 0, May 2, 1957.

Most Chances Accepted, Infield, Game, Nine Innings, One Club

N. L.—45—New York vs. Pittsburgh, July 13, 1919.
    Chicago vs. Philadelphia, September 24, 1927.
    Chicago vs. Pittsburgh, May 9, 1963.
A. L.—44—Detroit vs. Washington, September 2, 1901, second game.

Most Chances Accepted, Infield, Game, Nine Innings, Both Clubs

N. L.—78—Cincinnati 41, New York 37, May 7, 1941.
A. L.—76—Boston 43, Cleveland 33, June 24, 1931.

Fewest Chances Offered, Infield, Game, Nine Innings, One Club

A. L.—3—St. Louis vs. New York, July 20, 1945, second game.
N. L.—4—New York vs. San Diego, April 22, 1970.

Fewest Chances Offered, Infield, Game, Nine Innings, Both Clubs

A. L.—18—Cleveland 9, Baltimore 9, August 31, 1955.
N. L.—19—Chicago 10, Philadelphia 9, May 2, 1957.

Most Errors, Infield, Game, Nine Innings, One Club

N. L.—17—Boston vs. St. Louis, June 14, 1876.
A. L.—10—Detroit vs. Chicago, May 1, 1901

Most Errors, Infield, Game, Nine Innings, Both Clubs

N. L.—22—Boston 17, St. Louis 5, June 14, 1876.
A. L.—13—Chicago 8, Detroit 5, May 6, 1903.

Longest Game, Without An Error, Infield, One Club

A. L.—24 innings— Boston vs. Philadelphia, September 1, 1906.
N. L.—24 innings— Houston vs. New York, April 15, 1968.

RECORDS FOR OUTFIELD

Most Putouts, Outfield, Game, Nine Innings, One Club

N. L.—19—Pittsburgh vs. Cincinnati, July 5, 1948, second game.
A. L.—18—Cleveland vs. St. Louis, September 28, 1929.
    New York vs. Boston, October 1, 1933.

Most Putouts, Outfield, Game, Nine Innings, Both Clubs

N. L.—30—Chicago 16, Philadelphia 14, August 7, 1953.
A. L.—29—Washington 17, St. Louis 12, May 3, 1939.

Most Putouts, Outfield, Extra-Inning Game, One Club

N. L.—23—Brooklyn vs. Boston, May 1, 1920, 26 innings.
    Chicago vs. Boston, May 17, 1927, 22 innings
A. L.—22—Chicago vs. Washington, May 15, 1918, 18 innings.

Most Putouts, Outfield, Extra-Inning Game, Both Clubs

N. L.—42—New York 21, Pittsburgh 21, July 17, 1914, 21 innings.
A. L.—38—Washington 20, St. Louis 18, July 19, 1924, 16 innings.

Longest Game, Outfield, With No Putouts, One Club

N. L.—13 innings— New York vs. Brooklyn, April 15, 1909.
A. L.—11 innings— St. Louis vs. Cleveland, April 23, 1905.

Fewest Putouts, Outfield, Game, Nine Innings, Both Clubs

A. A.—1—St. Louis 1, New York 0, June 30, 1886.
N. L.—1—Pittsburgh 1, Brooklyn 0, August 26, 1910.
A. L.—2—New York 2, Detroit 0, May 9, 1930.

Most Putouts, Outfield, Doubleheader, One Club, More Than 18 Innings

N. L.—29—Boston vs. New York, September 3, 1933, 23 innings.
A. L.—Less than for 18 innings.

Most Putouts, Outfield, Doubleheader, One Club

N. L.—27—Pittsburgh vs. Cincinnati, July 5, 1948.
A. L.—24—Detroit vs. Philadelphia, June 28, 1931.

Most Putouts, Outfield, Doubleheader, Both Clubs

N. L.—47—Pittsburgh 26, Boston 21, June 26, 1935.
A. L.—43—Detroit 24, Philadelphia 19, June 28, 1931.

Most Assists, Outfield, Game, One Club

N. L.—5—Pittsburgh vs. Philadelphia, August 23, 1910.
A. L.—5—New York vs. Boston, September 5, 1921, second game.
    Cleveland vs. St. Louis, May 1, 1928.

Most Assists, Game, Outfield to Catcher With Base Runner Thrown Out

N. L.—3—Washington vs. Indianapolis, June 19, 1889.
    New York vs. Boston, June 30, 1902.
    Chicago vs. Pittsburgh, April 26, 1905.
A. L.—2—Made in many games.

Longest Game, Outfield, With No Assists, One Club

N. L.—26 innings— Boston vs. Brooklyn, May 1, 1920.
A. L.—24 innings— Boston vs. Philadelphia, September 1, 1906.
    Philadelphia vs. Detroit, July 21, 1945.

Longest Game, Outfield, With No Assists, Both Clubs

N. L.—24 innings— Houston 0, New York 0, April 15, 1968.
A. L.—22 innings— Chicago 0, Washington 0, June 12, 1967.

Most Chances Accepted (Excludes Errors), Outfield, Game, One Club

N. L.—20—Pittsburgh vs. Cincinnati, July 5, 1948, second game.
A. L.—18—Cleveland vs. St. Louis, September 28, 1929.
    New York vs. Boston, October 1, 1933.
    Philadelphia vs. Boston, May 27, 1941, second game.
    New York vs. Cleveland, June 26, 1955, second game.

Most Chances Accepted (Excludes Errors), Outfield, Game, Both Clubs

A. L.—30—Washington 17, St. Louis 13, May 3, 1939.
N. L.—30—Chicago 16, Philadelphia 14, August 7, 1953.

Most Chances Accepted (Excl. Errors), Outfield, Overtime Game, One Club

N. L.—24—Brooklyn vs. Boston, May 1, 1920, 26 innings.
    Chicago vs. Boston, May 17, 1927, 22 innings.
A. L.—22—Chicago vs. Washington, May 15, 1918, 18 innings.

Most Chances Accepted (Excl. Errors), Outfield, Overtime Game, Both Clubs

N. L.—43—New York 22, Pittsburgh 21, July 17, 1914, 21 innings.
A. L.—40—Washington 21, St. Louis 19, July 19, 1924, 16 innings.

Fewest Chances Offered, Outfield, Game, Nine Innings, One Club

N. L.—0—Made in many games.
A. L.—0—Made in many games.

Longest Game, Outfield, With No Chances Offered, One Club

A. L.—11 innings— St. Louis vs. Cleveland, April 23, 1905.
N. L.—10 innings— New York vs. Louisville, August 8, 1899.
N. L. since 1900—1—Made in many extra-inning games (0 in many nine-inning games).

Fewest Chances Offered, Outfield, Game, Nine Innings, Both Clubs

    A. A.—2—St. Louis 2, New York 0, June 30, 1886.
    N. L.—2—Pittsburgh 1, Brooklyn 1, August 26, 1910.
             Cincinnati 1, New York 1, May 7, 1941.
    A. L.—3—St. Louis 2, Chicago 1, April 24, 1908.
             New York 2, Boston 1, May 4, 1911.
             New York 2, Detroit 1, May 9, 1930.

Fewest Chances Offered, Outfield, Two Consecutive Games, One Club

    U. A.—0—Milwaukee vs. Boston, October 4, 5, 1884.
    A. L.—1—St. Louis, April 16, 10 innings, April 17, 1908.
    N. L.—2—Held by many clubs.

Most Chances Accepted, Outfield, Doubleheader, One Club

    N. L.—28—Pittsburgh vs. Cincinnati, July 5, 1948.
    A. L.—24—Detroit vs. Philadelphia, June 28, 1931.
             Philadelphia vs. Boston, May 27, 1941.

Most Chances Accepted, Outfield, Doubleheader, Both Clubs

    N. L.—48—Pittsburgh 26, Boston 22, June 26, 1935.
    A. L.—44—Detroit 24, Philadelphia 20, June 28, 1931.

Most Errors, Outfield, Game, Nine Innings, One Club

    N. L.—11—Boston vs. Hartford, May 1, 1876.
    A. L.— 5—Baltimore vs. St. Louis, August 19, 1902.
    N. L. since 1900—4—Made in many games. Last time—San Francisco vs. Los Angeles,
        July 4, 1971.

LEAGUE FIELDING RECORDS

Highest Fielding Percentage, Season

    A. L.—(14-club league)—.97985 in 1982.
    A. L.—(12-club league)—.97975 in 1964.
    A. L.—(8-club league)—.97881 in 1957, 1958.
    N. L.—(12-club league)—.97967 in 1971.
    N. L.—(8-club league)—.97728 in 1956.

Lowest Fielding Percentage, Season, Since 1900

    A. L.—(14-club league)—.97736 in 1977.
    A. L.—(12-club league)—.9754 in 1975.
    A. L.—(8-club league)—.937 in 1901.
    N. L.—(12-club league)—.9765 in 1969.
    N. L.—(8-club league)—.949 in 1903.

Most Putouts, Season, Since 1900

    A. L.—(14-club league)—61,005 in 1982.
    A. L.—(12-club league)—52,510 in 1969.
    A. L.—(10-club league)—43,847 in 1964.
    A. L.—(8-club league)—33,830 in 1916.
    N. L.—(12-club league)—52,630 in 1982.
    N. L.—(10-club league)—44,042 in 1968.
    N. L.—(8-club league)—33,724 in 1917.

Fewest Putouts, Season, Since 1900

    A. L.—(14-club league)—60,155 in 1979.
    A. L.—(12-club league)—51,821 in 1975.
    A. L.—(8-club league)—32,235 in 1938.
    N. L.—(12-club league)—52,000 in 1978.
    N. L.—(8-club league)—32,296 in 1906.

Most Assists, Season, Since 1900

    A. L.—(14-club league)—25,626 in 1980.
    A. L.—(12-club league)—21,786 in 1976.
    A. L.—(10-club league)—17,269 in 1961.
    A. L.—(8-club league)—17,167 in 1910.
    N. L.—(12-club league)—22,341 in 1980.
    N. L.—(10-club league)—18,205 in 1968.
    N. L.—(8-club league)—16,759 in 1920.

Fewest Assists, Season, Since 1900

    A. L.—(14-club league)—24,938 in 1983.
    A. L.—(12-club league)—21,001 in 1971.
    A. L.—(8-club league)—13,219 in 1958.
    N. L.—(12-club league)—21,038 in 1970.
    N. L.—(8-club league)—13,345 in 1956.

Most Errors, Season, Since 1900

A. L.— (14-club league) —1,989 in 1977.
A. L.— (12-club league) —1,747 in 1974.
A. L.— (8-club league) —2,889 in 1901.
N. L.— (12-club league) —1,859 in 1975.
N. L.— (10-club league) —2,590 in 1904.

Fewest Errors, Season, Since 1900

A. L.— (8-club league) —1,002 in 1958.
A. L.— (12-club league) —1,261 in 1964.
A. L.— (14-club league) —1,768 in 1982.
N. L.— (8-club league) —1,082 in 1956.
N. L.— (12-club league) —1,389 in 1968.

Most Chances Accepted, Season, Since 1900

A. L.— (14-club league) —86,621 in 1980.
A. L.— (12-club league) —74,191 in 1976.
A. L.— (10-club league) —60,997 in 1964.
A. L.— (8-club league) —50,870 in 1910.
N. L.— (12-club league) —74,930 in 1980.
N. L.— (10-club league) —62,247 in 1968.
N. L.— (8-club league) —50,419 in 1920.

Fewest Chances Accepted, Season, Since 1900

A. L.— (14-club league) —85,616 in 1979.
A. L.— (12-club league) —72,875 in 1971.
A. L.— (8-club league) —40,086 in 1938.
N. L.— (12-club league) —73,273 in 1970.
N. L.— (8-club league) —46,404 in 1955.

Most Passed Balls, Season, Since 1900

A. L.— (14-club league) —181 in 1979.
A. L.— (12-club league) —247 in 1969.
A. L.— (10-club league) —211 in 1965.
A. L.— (8-club league) —178 in 1914.
N. L.— (12-club league) —217 in 1969.
N. L.— (10-club league) —216 in 1962.
N. L.— (8-club league) —202 in 1905.

Fewest Passed Balls, Season

A. L.— (8-club league) — 53 in 1949.
A. L.— (10-club league) —147 in 1963, 1966.
A. L.— (12-club league) —127 in 1976.
A. L.— (14-club league) —128 in 1977.
N. L.— (8-club league) — 65 in 1936.
N. L.— (10-club league) —148 in 1968.
N. L.— (12-club league) —122 in 1980.

Most Double Plays, Season

A. L.— (14-club league) —2,368 in 1980.
A. L.— (12-club league) —1,994 in 1973.
A. L.— (10-club league) —1,585 in 1961.
A. L.— (8-club league) —1,487 in 1949.
N. L.— (12-club league) —1,888 in 1971.
N. L.— (10-club league) —1,596 in 1962.
N. L.— (8-club league) —1,337 in 1951.

Fewest Double Plays, Season (A. L.—Since 1912; N. L.—Since 1920)

A. L.— (8-club league) — 818 in 1912.
A. L.— (12-club league) —1,388 in 1967, 1968.
A. L.— (14-club league) —2,143 in 1977.
N. L.— (8-club league) —1,007 in 1920.
N. L.— (12-club league) —1,431 in 1963.

Most Double Plays, One Day, Four Games, One League

N. L.—19—May 7, 1941.
A. L.—21—May 20, 1941.

Most Double Plays, One Day, Five Games, One League

N. L.—23—September 28, 1939.
A. L.—21—May 13, 1970.

Most Double Plays, One Day, Six Games, One League

A. L.—23—June 4, 1970.
N. L.—22—April 26, 1972.

Most Double Plays, One Day, Seven Games, One League

    A. L.—25—August 7, 1974.
    N. L.—23—August 15, 1937.

Most Double Plays, One Day, Eight Games, One League

    A. L.—29—July 23, 1972.
    N. L.—25—June 24, 1975.

Most Double Plays, One Day, Nine Games, One League

    N. L.—28—July 24, 1976.
    A. L.—25—July 8, 1973; August 7, 1973.

Most Double Plays, One Day, Ten Games, One League

    A. L.—27—July 4, 1969; July 26, 1973.
    N. L.—25—July 1, 1973.

Most Times, Five or More Double Plays, One Club, Season

    A. L.—9 in 1970.
    N. L.—7 in 1950, 1962.

Most Unassisted Double Plays, Season, by First Basemen

    A. L.—38 in 1949.
    N. L.—32 in 1953.

Most Unassisted Double Plays, Season, by Catchers

    N. L.—5 in 1965.
    A. L.—3 in 1914, 1969.

Most Unassisted Double Plays, Season, by Pitchers

    N. L.—3 in 1935, 1940.
    A. L.—2 in 1908, 1932.

Most Triple Plays, Season

    N. L.—(12-club league) —4 in 1969, 1971, 1978.
    N. L.—(8-club league) —7 in 1891, 1905, 1910, 1929.
    A. L.—(14-club league) —10 in 1979.
    A. L.—(12-club league) —3 in 1972.
    A. L.—(8-club league) —7 in 1922, 1936.

Fewest Triple Plays, Season

    N. L.—0 in 1928, 1938, 1941, 1943, 1945, 1946, 1959, 1961, 1974.
    A. L.—0 in 1904, 1933, 1942, 1956, 1961, 1962, 1974, 1975.

Fewest Triple Plays, Season, Both Leagues

    0 in 1974 (0 in A. L., 0 in N. L.)

Most Triple Plays, One Day

    N. L.—2—May 29, 1897; August 30, 1921.
    A. L.—1—Made on many days.

Most First Basemen With 100 or More Assists, Season

    A. L.—6 in 1962, 1976, 1977, 1978.
    N. L.—6 in 1982.

Most Second Basemen With 500 or More Assists, Season

    N. L.—4 in 1924.
    A. L.—3 in 1930.

Most Shortstops With 500 or More Assists, Season

    N. L.—5 in 1978.
    A. L.—5 in 1979.

Most Outfielders With 400 or More Putouts, Season

    A. L.—5 in 1979, 1980.
    N. L.—4 in 1954, 1982.

Most Catchers Catching 100 or More Games, Season

    N. L.—(12-club league) —10 in 1969, 1977, 1980, 1982.
    N. L.—(10-club league) — 9 in 1965, 1966.
    N. L.—(8-club league) — 8 in 1931, 1941.
    A. L.—(14-club league) —11 in 1977.
    A. L.—(12-club league) — 8 in 1972, 1974.
    A. L.—(10-club league) — 9 in 1966.
    A. L.—(8-club league) — 8 in 1921, 1952.

Fewest Catchers Catching 100 or More Games, Season, Since 1890

A. L.—0 in 1902, 1903, 1942.

N. L.—0 in 1893, 1896, 1900, 1945.

UNASSISTED TRIPLE PLAYS (8)

Neal Ball, shortstop, Cleveland A. L., vs. Boston at Cleveland, July 19, 1909, first game, second inning. Ball caught McConnell's liner, touched second, retiring Wagner, who was on his way to third base, and then tagged Stahl as he came up to second.

William A. Wambsganss, second baseman, Cleveland A. L. vs. Brooklyn N. L., in World Series game at Cleveland, October 10, 1920, fifth inning. Wambsganss caught Mitchell's line drive, stepped on second to retire Kilduff, then tagged Miller coming from first.

George H. Burns, first baseman, Boston A. L., vs. Cleveland at Boston, September 14, 1923, second inning. Burns caught Brower's liner, tagged Lutzke off first and then ran to second and reached that bag before Stephenson could return from third base.

Ernest K. Padgett, shortstop, Boston N. L., vs. Philadelphia at Boston, October 6, 1923, second game, fourth inning. Padgett caught Holke's liner, ran to second to retire Tierney, then tagged Lee before he could return to first.

F. Glenn Wright, shortstop, Pittsburgh N. L., vs. St. Louis at Pittsburgh, May 7, 1925, ninth inning. Wright caught Bottomley's liner, ran to second to retire Cooney and then tagged Hornsby, who was en route to second.

James E. Cooney, shortstop, Chicago N. L., vs. Pittsburgh at Pittsburgh, May 30, 1927, a.m. game, fourth inning. Cooney caught Paul Waner's liner, stepped on second to retire Lloyd Waner, then tagged Barnhart off first.

John H. Neun, first baseman, Detroit A. L., vs. Cleveland at Detroit, May 31, 1927, ninth inning. Neun caught Summa's liner, ran over and tagged Jamieson between first and second and then touched second base before Myatt could return.

Ronald L. Hansen, shortstop, Washington A. L., vs. Cleveland at Cleveland, July 30, 1968, first inning. With the count 3 and 2 on Azcue, Nelson broke for third base. Hansen caught Azcue's liner, stepped on second to double Nelson and then tagged Snyder going into second base.

(All above unassisted triple plays made with runners on first and second bases only.)

MAJOR LEAGUE PITCHING RECORDS

Most Years Pitched in Major Leagues

25—James L. Kaat, Washington A.L., Minnesota A.L., Chicago A.L., Philadelphia N.L., New York A.L., St. Louis N.L., 1959 through 1983.

Most Years Pitched, League

A. L.—23—Early Wynn, Washington, Cleveland, Chicago, 1939, 1941 through 1963 (except 1945, in military service), 691 games.

N. L.—21—Eppa Rixey, Philadelphia, Cincinnati, 1912 through 1933 (except 1918, in military service), 692 games.

           Warren E. Spahn, Boston, Milwaukee, New York, San Francisco, 1942 through 1965 (except 1943, 1944, 1945, in military service), 750 games.

Most Consecutive Years Pitched in Major Leagues

25—James L. Kaat, Washington A. L., Minnesota A. L., Chicago A. L., Philadelphia N. L., New York A. L., St. Louis N. L., 1959 through 1983.

Most Consecutive Years Pitched, League

A. L.—22—Herbert J. Pennock, Philadelphia, Boston, New York, 1912 through 1934 (except 1918, in military service).

           Samuel P. Jones, Cleveland, Boston, New York, St. Louis, Washington, Chicago, 1914 through 1935.

           Early Wynn, Washington, Cleveland, Chicago, 1941 through 1963 (except 1945, in military service).

           Charles H. Ruffing, Boston, New York, Chicago, 1924 through 1947 (except 1943, 1944 in military service).

N. L.—21—Eppa Rixey, Philadelphia, Cincinnati, 1912 through 1933 (except 1918, in military service).

           Warren E. Spahn, Boston, Milwaukee, New York, San Francisco, 1942 through 1965 (except 1943, 1944, 1945, in military service).

Most Years Pitched, One Club

A. L.—21—Walter P. Johnson, Washington, 1907 through 1927, 802 games.

           Theodore A. Lyons, Chicago, 1923 through 1946 (except 1943, 1944, 1945, in military service), 594 games.

N. L.—20—Warren E. Spahn, Boston, Milwaukee, 1942 through 1964 (except 1943, 1944, 1945, in military service), 714 games.

Most Consecutive Years Pitched, One Club

A. L.—21—Walter P. Johnson, Washington, 1907 through 1927, 802 games.

Theodore A. Lyons, Chicago, 1923 through 1946 (except 1943, 1944, 1945, in military service), 594 games.

N. L.—20—Warren E. Spahn, Boston, Milwaukee, 1942 through 1964 (except 1943, 1944, 1945, in military service), 714 games.

Most Clubs Pitched On, Major Leagues

10—Robert Lane Miller, St. Louis N. L., New York N. L., Los Angeles N. L., Minnesota A. L., Cleveland A. L., Chicago A. L., Chicago N. L., San Diego N. L., Pittsburgh N. L., Detroit A. L., 1957, 1959 through 1974, 17 years, 694 games.

Kenneth A. Brett, Boston A. L., Milwaukee A. L., Philadelphia N. L., Pittsburgh N. L., New York A. L., Chicago A. L., California A. L., Minnesota A. L., Los Angeles N. L., Kansas City A. L., 1967, 1969 through 1981, 14 years, 349 games.

Most Clubs Pitched On, League

N. L.—6—Burleigh A. Grimes, Pittsburgh, Brooklyn, New York, Boston, St. Louis, Chicago, 1916 through 1934, 19 years, 605 games.

Robert Lane Miller, St. Louis, New York, Los Angeles, Chicago, San Diego, Pittsburgh, 1957 through 1974 except 1958, 1968, 1969, 15 years, 549 games.

A. L.—(12-club league)—7—Kenneth G. Sanders, Kansas City No. 1, 1964, Boston, Kansas City No. 1, 1966, Oakland, 1968, Milwaukee, 1970, 1971, 1972, Minnesota, 1973, Cleveland, 1973, 1974, California, 1974, Kansas City No. 2, 1976, 9 years, 348 games. (Note: Oakland considered part of Kansas City No. 1 franchise and is not considered as separate club).

Kenneth A. Brett, Boston, Milwaukee, New York, Chicago, California, Minnesota, Kansas City, 1967, 1969 through 1972, 1976 through 1981, 11 years, 238 games.

A. L.—(8-club league)—6—Samuel P. Jones, Cleveland, Boston, New York, St. Louis, Washington, Chicago, 1914 through 1935, 22 years, 647 games.

Peter W. Appleton, Cleveland, Boston, New York, Washington, Chicago, St. Louis, 1930 through 1945 except 1934, 1935, 1943, 1944, 12 years, 304 games.

Louis N. Newsom, St. Louis, Washington, Boston, Detroit, Philadelphia, New York, 1934 through 1947, also Washington, 1952, Philadelphia, 1952, 1953, 16 years, 555 games.

William R. Wight, New York, Chicago, Boston, Detroit, Cleveland, Baltimore, 1946 through 1957, except 1954, 11 years, 312 games.

Most Leagues Pitched In

4—Edward Bakely, A. A., U. A., N. L., P. L.

Edward N. Crane, U. A., N. L., P. L., A. A.

Francis I. Foreman, U. A., A. A., N. L., A. L.

Cornelius B. Murphy, U. A., N. L., P. L., A. A.

Most Clubs Pitched On, One Season, in Major Leagues

4—G. Willis Hudlin, Cleveland A. L., Washington A. L., St. Louis A. L., New York N. L., 19 games, 1940.

Theodore G. Gray, Chicago A. L., Cleveland A. L., New York A. L., Baltimore A. L., 14 games, 1955.

Michael D. Kilkenny, Detroit A. L., Oakland A. L., San Diego N. L., Cleveland A. L., 29 games, 1972.

Most Clubs Pitched On, One Season, League

A. L.—4—Theodore G. Gray, Chicago, Cleveland, New York, Baltimore, 14 games, 1955.

N. L.—3—Held by many pitchers. Last pitcher—Robert L. Miller, Chicago, San Diego, Pittsburgh, 56 games, 1971.

Most Games Pitched, Major Leagues

1070—J. Hoyt Wilhelm, New York N. L., St. Louis N. L., Cleveland A. L., Baltimore A. L., Chicago A. L., California A. L., Atlanta N. L., Chicago N. L., Los Angeles N. L., 21 years, 1952 through 1972, 448 games in N. L., 622 in A. L.

Most Games Pitched, League

N. L.— 846— El Roy L. Face, Pittsburgh, Montreal, 16 years, 1953 through 1969, except 1954, started 27, relieved 819.

A. L.— 807— Albert W. Lyle, Boston, New York, Texas, Chicago, 15 years, 1967 through 1982, except 1981, started 0, relieved 807.

Most Games Pitched, One Club

A. L.— 802— Walter P. Johnson, Washington, 21 years, 1907 through 1927, started 666, relieved 136.

N. L.— 802— El Roy L. Face, Pittsburgh, 15 years, 1953 through 1968 except 1954, started 27, relieved 775.

Most Games Pitched, Season

N. L.— 106— Michael G. Marshall, Los Angeles, 1974 (208 innings).
A. L.— 90— Michael G. Marshall, Minnesota, 1979 (143 innings).

Most Games Pitched, Rookie Season

A. L.—78—Edward J. Vande Berg, Seattle, 1982 (0 complete, 76 innings).
N. L.—77—Clarence E. Metzger, San Diego, 1976 (0 complete, 123 innings).

Most Years Leading Major Leagues in Most Games

7—Joseph J. McGinnity, Brooklyn N. L., Baltimore A. L., New York N. L., 1900, 1901, 1903, 1904, 1905, 1906, 1907.

Most Years Leading League in Most Games

N. L.—6—Joseph J. McGinnity, Brooklyn, New York, 1900, 1903, 1904, 1905, 1906, 1907.
A. L.—6—Fred Marberry, Washington, 1924, 1925, 1926, 1928, 1929, 1932.

Fewest Games Pitched, Season, for Leader in Most Games

A. L.—40—Joseph W. Haynes, Chicago, 1942 (103 innings).
N. L.—41—Remy Kremer, Pittsburgh, 1924 (259 innings).
    John D. Morrison, Pittsburgh, 1924 (238 innings).

Most Times Pitched Opening Game of Season

A. L.—14—Walter P. Johnson, Washington, 1910 to 1926. Won 9, lost 5.
N. L.—14—G. Thomas Seaver, New York, 1968 to 1977, 1983; Cincinnati, 1978 to 1979, 1981. Won 6, lost 1.

Most Games Started in Major Leagues

818—Denton T. Young, Cleveland N. L., St. Louis N. L., Boston A. L., Cleveland A. L., Boston N. L., 22 years, 1890 through 1911; 460 in N. L., 358 in A. L.

Most Games, Started, League

A. L.— 666— Walter P. Johnson, Washington, 21 years, 1907 through 1927.
N. L.— 665— Warren E. Spahn, Boston, Milwaukee, New York, San Francisco, 21 years, 1942 through 1965 (except 1943, 1944, 1945, in military service).

Most Consecutive Starting Assignments, League, Since 1900

N. L.— 463— Steven N. Carlton, St. Louis, Philadelphia, May 15, 1971 through 1983.
A. L.— 272— Melvin L. Stottlemyre, New York, April 10, 1967 through June 11, 1974.

Most Games Started, Season

N. L.—74—William H. White, Cincinnati, 1879 (pitched 75 games).
A. L.—51—John D. Chesbro, New York, 1904 (pitched 55 games).
N. L. since 1900—48—Joseph J. McGinnity, New York, 1903 (pitched 55 games).

Most Years Leading League in Games Started

N. L.—6—Robin E. Roberts, Philadelphia, 1950 (tied), 1951, 1952, 1953, 1954, 1955.
A. L.—5—Robert W. Feller, Cleveland, 1940, 1941, 1946, 1947, 1948.
    Early Wynn, Washington, Cleveland, Chicago, 1943 (tied), 1951 (tied), 1954, 1957, 1959 (tied).

All Games Started, Season, None as Relief Pitcher (Most), Since 1900

A. L.—49—Wilbur F. Wood, Chicago, 1972 (20 complete).
N. L.—44—Philip H. Niekro, Atlanta, 1979 (23 complete).

Most Consecutive Appearances as Relief Pitcher, Major Leagues

899—Albert W. Lyle, Boston A.L., New York A.L., Texas A.L., Philadelphia N.L., Chicago A.L., 1967 through 1982, 807 in A.L., 92 in N.L.

Most Consecutive Appearances as Relief Pitcher, League

A. L.— 807— Albert W. Lyle, Boston, New York, Texas, Chicago, July 4, 1967 through September 9, 1980; April 9, 1982 through August 12, 1982.
N. L.— 657— El Roy Face, Pittsburgh, August 4, 1957, first game, through August 31, 1968; Montreal, N. L., April 29 through August 15, 1969.

All Games Pitched, Season, None Started (Most)

N. L.— 106— Michael G. Marshall, Los Angeles, 1974 (finished 83), 208 innings.
A. L.— 83— Kenneth G. Sanders, Milwaukee, 1971 (finished 77), 136 innings.

Most Games Pitched Major Leagues, All in Relief (None Started)

899—Albert W. Lyle, Boston A.L., New York A.L., Texas A.L., Philadelphia N.L., Chicago A.L., 1967 through 1982, 807 in A.L., 92 in N.L.

Most Games Pitched League, All in Relief (None Started)

A. L.— 807— Albert W. Lyle, Boston, New York, Texas, Chicago, July 4, 1967 through September 9, 1980; April 9, 1982 through August 12, 1982.
N. L.— 647— Kenton C. Tekulve, Pittsburgh, May 20, 1974 through 1983.

Most Consecutive Complete Games Pitched, Season, Since 1900

N. L.—39—John W. Taylor, St. Louis, April 15 through October 6, first game, 1904 (352 innings, including two games finished in relief).

A. L.—37—William H. Dinneen, Boston, April 16 through October 10, first game, 1904 (337 innings).

Most Complete Games Pitched in Major Leagues

751—Denton T. Young, Cleveland N. L., St. Louis N. L., Boston A. L., Cleveland A. L., Boston N. L., 22 years, 1890 through 1911; 428 in N. L., 323 in A. L.

Most Complete Games, League, Righthander

N. L.— 557— James F. Galvin, Buffalo, Pittsburgh, St. Louis, 12 years, 1879 through 1892, except 1886, 1890.

A. L.— 531— Walter P. Johnson, Washington, 21 years, 1907 through 1927.

N. L. since 1900—437—Grover C. Alexander, Philadelphia, Chicago, St. Louis, 20 years, 1911 through 1930.

Most Complete Games, League, Lefthander

A. L.— 387— Edward S. Plank, Philadelphia, St. Louis, 16 years, 1901 through 1917, except 1915.

N. L.— 382— Warren E. Spahn, Boston, Milwaukee, New York, San Francisco, 21 years, 1942 through 1965, except 1943, 1944, 1945 in military service.

Most Complete Games, Season

N. L.—74—William H. White, Cincinnati, 1879; pitched in 75 games.

A. L.—48—John D. Chesbro, New York, 1904; pitched in 55 games.

N. L. since 1900—45—Victor G. Willis, Boston, 1902; pitched in 51 games.

Most Years Leading League in Complete Games

N. L.—9—Warren E. Spahn, Boston, Milwaukee, 1949, 1951, 1957, 1958, 1959, 1960 (tied), 1961, 1962, 1963.

A. L.—6—Walter P. Johnson, Washington, 1910, 1911, 1913, 1914, 1915, 1916.

Most Complete Games, Rookie Season

N. L.—67—James A. Devlin, Louisville, 1876 (67 games).

N. L. since 1900—41—Irving M. Young, Boston, 1905 (43 games).

A. L.—36—Roscoe C. Miller, Detroit, 1901 (38 games).

Fewest Complete Games, Season, for Leader in Most Complete Games

N. L.—14—Stephen D. Rogers, Montreal, 1980.

A. L.—15—Frank S. Lary, Detroit, 1960.
    W. Dean Chance, Los Angeles, 1964.

All Games Pitched, Season, None Complete (Most)

N. L.— 106— Michael G. Marshall, Los Angeles, 1974, started none (208 innings).

A. L.— 90— Michael G. Marshall, Minnesota, 1979, started one (143 innings).

Games Started, Season, None Complete (Most)

N. L.—31—Fredie H. Norman, Cincinnati, 1978.

A. L.—28—Paul W. Splittorff, Kansas City, 1982.

Most Games Finished, Major Leagues

651—J. Hoyt Wilhelm, New York N. L., St. Louis N. L., Cleveland A. L., Baltimore A. L., Chicago A. L., California A. L., Atlanta N. L., Chicago N. L., Los Angeles N. L., 21 years, 1952 through 1972, 245 in N. L., 406 in A. L.

Most Games Finished, League

A. L.— 599— Albert W. Lyle, Boston, New York, Texas, Chicago, 15 years, 1967 through 1982, except 1981.

N. L.— 574— El Roy L. Face, Pittsburgh, Montreal, 16 years, 1953 through 1969, except 1954.

Most Games Finished, Season

A. L.—84—Michael G. Marshall, Minnesota, 1979 (90 games).

N. L.—83—Michael G. Marshall, Los Angeles, 1974 (106 games).

Most Games in Major Leagues as Relief Pitcher

1018—J. Hoyt Wilhelm, New York N. L., St. Louis N. L., Cleveland A. L., Baltimore A. L., Chicago A. L., California A. L., Atlanta N. L., Chicago N. L., Los Angeles N. L., 21 years, 1952 through 1972; 448 in N. L., 570 in A. L.

Most Games, League, as Relief Pitcher

N. L.— 819— El Roy L. Face, Pittsburgh, Montreal, 16 years, 1953 through 1969, except 1954.

A. L.— 807— Albert W. Lyle, Boston, New York, Texas, Chicago, 15 years, 1967 through 1982, except 1981.

Most Games, Season, as Relief Pitcher

N. L.— 106— Michael G. Marshall, Los Angeles, 1974, started none, 208 innings.
A. L.— 89— Michael G. Marshall, Minnesota, 1979, 141 innings (also started 1 game— 2 innings).

Most Years Leading League in Games Finished

Both Leagues—5—Michael G. Marshall, Montreal, Los Angeles, NL, 1971, 1972, 1973, 1974, Minnesota, AL, 1979.
A. L.—5—Fred Marberry, Washington, 1924, 1925, 1926, 1928, 1929.
N. L.—4—Ace T. Adams, New York, 1942, 1943, 1944, 1945.
        El Roy L. Face, Pittsburgh, 1958, 1960, 1961, 1962.
        Michael G. Marshall, Montreal, Los Angeles, 1971, 1972, 1973, 1974.

Most Consecutive Games Pitched as Relief Pitcher

N. L.—13—Michael G. Marshall, Los Angeles, June 18 through July 3, first game, 1974, 24⅔ innings.
A. L.— 8—Bennett Flowers, Boston, July 25 through August 1, 1953, 12⅔ innings.

Most Games Taken Out as Starting Pitcher, Season

A. L.—36—Stanley R. Bahnsen, Chicago, 1972 (started 41).
N. L.—35—Dennis P. Lamp, Chicago, 1980 (started 37).

Most Innings Pitched in Major Leagues

7377—Denton T. Young, Cleveland N. L., St. Louis N. L., Boston A. L., Cleveland A.L., Boston N.L., 22 years, 1890 through 1911, 4143 in N.L., 3234 in A.L.

Most Innings Pitched, League

A. L.— 5924— Walter P. Johnson, Washington, 21 years, 1907 through 1927.
N. L.— 5246— Warren E. Spahn, Boston, Milwaukee, New York, San Francisco, 21 years, 1942 through 1965 (except 1943, 1944, 1945, in military service).

Most Innings Pitched, Season

N. L.— 683— William H. White, Cincinnati, 75 games, 1879.
A. L.— 464— Edward A. Walsh, Chicago, 66 games, 1908.
N. L. since 1900—434—Joseph J. McGinnity, New York, 55 games, 1903.

Most Innings Pitched, Rookie Season, Since 1900

N. L.— 378— Irving M. Young, Boston, 43 games, 1905.
A. L.— 316— Ewell A. Russell, Chicago, 43 games, 1913.

Most Innings, Season, as Relief Pitcher

N. L.— 208— Michael G. Marshall, Los Angeles, 1974, pitched 106 games as relief pitcher.
A. L.—168⅓—Robert W. Stanley, Boston, 1982, pitched 48 games as relief pitcher. (William R. Campbell, Minnesota, hurled 167⅔ innings, rounded to 168, as a relief pitcher in 1976.)

Most Innings, Major Leagues as Relief Pitcher

1870—J. Hoyt Wilhelm, New York N. L., St. Louis N. L., Cleveland A. L., Baltimore A. L., Chicago A. L., California A. L., Atlanta N. L., Chicago N. L., Los Angeles N. L., 21 years, 1952 through 1972; 916 in N. L., 954 in A. L.

Most Innings, League, as Relief Pitcher

A. L.— 1265— Albert W. Lyle, Boston, New York, Texas, Chicago, 15 years, 1967 through 1982, except 1981.
N. L.—1264⅔—Frank E. McGraw, New York, Philadelphia, 18 years, 1965 through 1983, except 1968.

Most Years Leading League in Innings Pitched

N. L.—7—Grover C. Alexander, Philadelphia, Chicago, 1911, 1912 (tied), 1914, 1915, 1916, 1917, 1920
A. L.—5—Walter P. Johnson, Washington, 1910, 1913, 1914, 1915, 1916.
        Robert W. Feller, Cleveland, 1939, 1940, 1941, 1946, 1947.

Fewest Innings Pitched, Season, for Leader in Most Innings

A. L.— 256— Early Wynn, Chicago, 37 games, 1959.
N. L.— 266— Howard J. Pollet, St. Louis, 40 games, 1946.

Most Years, 200 or More Innings, Pitched, Major Leagues

19—Denton T. Young, Cleveland N. L., St. Louis N. L., Boston A. L., Cleveland A.L., 1891 through 1909, consecutive; 10 in N. L., 9 in A. L.

Most Years, 200 or More Innings, Pitched League

A. L.—18—Walter P. Johnson, Washington, 1908 through 1926, except 1920.
N. L.—17—Warren E. Spahn, Boston, Milwaukee, 1947 through 1963, consecutive.

Most Years, 300 or More Innings, Pitched, Major Leagues

16—Denton T. Young, Cleveland N. L., St. Louis N. L., Boston A. L., 1891 through 1907, except 1906. 10 in N. L., 6 in A. L.

Most Years, 300 or More Innings Pitched League

N. L.—12—Charles A. Nichols, Boston, 1890 through 1899, 1901, 1904.

N. L. since 1900—11—Christopher Mathewson, New York, 1901, 1903, 1904, 1905, 1907, 1908, 1910, 1911, 1912, 1913, 1914.

A. L.—9—Walter P. Johnson, Washington, 1910 through 1918, consecutive.

Most Consecutive Years, 300 or More Innings Pitched, League, Since 1900

A. L.—9—Walter P. Johnson, Washington, 1910 through 1918.

N. L.—7—Grover C. Alexander, Philadelphia, 1911 through 1917.

Most Years, 400 or More Innings Pitched, League, Since 1900

N. L.—2—Joseph J. McGinnity, New York, 1903, (434), 1904 (408).

A. L.—2—Edward A. Walsh, Chicago, 1907 (419), 1908 (464).

Most Innings Pitched, Game

N. L.—26—Leon J. Cadore, Brooklyn, May 1, 1920, tie 1-1.
  Joseph Oeschger, Boston, May 1, 1920, tie 1-1.

A. L.—24—John W. Coombs, Philadelphia, September 1, 1906, won 4-1.
  Joseph Harris, Boston, September 1, 1906, lost 4-1.

Most Innings Pitched, Game, as Relief Pitcher Finishing Game

N. L.—18⅓—George W. Zabel, Chicago, June 17, 1915 (Chicago 4, Brooklyn 3, 19 innings).

A. L.—17 —Edwin A. Rommel, Philadelphia, July 10, 1932 (Philadelphia 18, Cleveland 17, 18 innings).

Most Consecutive Innings Pitched, Season, Without Relief, Since 1900

N. L.— 352— John Taylor, St. Louis, April 15 through October 6, first game, 1904; complete season, 39 complete games and 2 games finished.

A. L.— 337— William H. Dinneen, Boston, April 16 through October 10, first game, 1904; complete season, 37 complete games.

Most Consecutive Innings Pitched, League, Without Relief, Since 1900

N. L.— 1727— John W. Taylor, Chicago, St. Louis, June 20, 1901, second game, through August 9, 1906, 203 games, 188 complete games, 15 finished.

Most Doubleheaders Pitched in Major Leagues

5—Joseph J. McGinnity, Baltimore A. L., 1901 (2); New York N. L., 1903 (3); 2 in A.L., 3 in N. L., Won 3 in N. L., Lost 2 in A. L.

Most Doubleheaders Pitched, League

N. L.—3—Joseph J. McGinnity, New York, 1903.

A. L.—2—Held by many pitchers.

Most Doubleheaders Pitched, Season

N. L.—3—Joseph J. McGinnity, New York, August 1, 8, 31, 1903. Won 3, Lost 0.

A. L.—2—Joseph J. McGinnity, Baltimore, 1901. Won 0, Lost 2.
  John R. Watson, Philadelphia, 1918. Won 0, Lost 2.

Most Doubleheaders Won, League

N. L.—3—Joseph J. McGinnity, New York, 1903, Lost 0.

A. L.—2—Edward A. Walsh, Chicago, 1905, 1908, Lost 0.

Most Doubleheaders Won, Season (Complete Games)

N. L.—3—Joseph J. McGinnity, New York, 1903.

A. L.—1—Held by many pitchers. Last pitcher, Emil H. Levsen, Cleveland vs. Boston, at Boston, August 28, 1926. Won 6-1, 5-1.

Most Games Won in Major Leagues

511—Denton T. Young, Cleveland N. L., St. Louis N. L., Boston A. L., Cleveland A. L., Boston N. L., 22 years, 1890 through 1911, (won 289 in N. L., won 222 in A. L.).

Most Games Won, League, Righthanded Pitcher

A. L.— 416— Walter P. Johnson, Washington, 21 years, 1907 through 1927, (won 416, lost 279—.599).

N. L.— 373— Christopher Mathewson, New York, Cincinnati, 17 years, 1900 through 1916, (won 373, lost 188—.665).
  Grover C. Alexander, Philadelphia, Chicago, St. Louis, 20 years, 1911 through 1930, (won 373, lost 208—.642).

Most Games Won, League, Lefthanded Pitcher

N. L.— 363— Warren E. Spahn, Boston, Milwaukee, New York, San Francisco, 21 years, 1942 through 1965 except 1943, 1944, 1945, in military service. (Won 363, lost 245—.597)

A. L.— 305— Edward S. Plank, Philadelphia, St. Louis 16 years, 1901 through 1917, except 1915 (won 305, lost 181—.628).

Most Games Won, Season, Righthanded Pitcher

N. L.—60—Charles G. Radbourn, Providence, 1884 (won 60, lost 12—.833).

A. L.—41—John D. Chesbro, New York, 1904 (won 41, lost 13—.759).

N. L. since 1900—37—Christopher Mathewson, New York, 1908 (won 37, lost 11— .771).

Most Games Won, Season, Lefthanded Pitcher

N. L.—42—Charles B. Baldwin, Detroit, 1886 (won 42, lost 14—.750).

A. L.—31—Robert M. Grove, Philadelphia, 1931 (won 31, lost 4—.886).

N. L. since 1900—27—Sanford Koufax, Los Angeles, 1966 (won 27, lost 9—.750).
    Steven N. Carlton, Philadelphia, 1972 (won 27, lost 10— .730).

Most Games Won in Major Leagues as Relief Pitcher

124—J. Hoyt Wilhelm, New York N. L., St. Louis N. L., Cleveland A. L., California A. L., Atlanta N. L., Baltimore A. L., Chicago A. L., Chicago N. L., Los Angeles N. L., 21 years, 1952 through 1972, won 73 in A. L., won 51 in N. L.; lost 102, lost 67 in A. L.; lost 35 in N. L.

Most Games Won, League, as Relief Pitcher

N. L.—96—El Roy L. Face, Pittsburgh, Montreal, 16 years, 1953 through 1969, except 1954 (lost 82).

A. L.—87—Albert W. Lyle, Boston, New York, Texas, Chicago, 15 years, 1967 through 1982, except 1981 (lost 67).

Most Games Won, Season, All as Relief Pitcher

N. L.—18—El Roy L. Face, Pittsburgh, 1959 (won 18, lost 1—.947).

A. L.—17—John F. Hiller, Detroit, 1974 (won 17, lost 14—.548).
    William R. Campbell, Minnesota, 1976 (won 17, lost 5—.773).

Fewest Games Won, Season, for Leader in Most Games Won

A. L.—18—Edward C. Ford, New York, 1955 (won 18, lost 7).
    Robert G. Lemon, Cleveland, 1955 (won 18, lost 10).
    Franklin L. Sullivan, Boston, 1955 (won 18, lost 13).
    Charles L. Estrada, Baltimore, 1960 (won 18, lost 11).
    James E. Perry, Cleveland, 1960, (won 18, lost 10).

N. L.—19—James T. Elliott, Philadelphia, 1931 (won 19, lost 14).
    William A. Hallahan, St. Louis, 1931 (won 19, lost 9).
    Henry W. Meine, Pittsburgh, 1931 (won 19, lost 13).
    John A. Denny, Philadelphia, 1983 (won 19, lost 6).

Most Years Leading League in Games Won

N. L.—8—Warren E. Spahn, Boston, Milwaukee, 1949, 1950, 1953 (tied), 1957, 1958 (tied), 1959 (tied), 1960 (tied), 1961 (tied).

A. L.—6—Walter P. Johnson, Washington, 1913, 1914, 1915, 1916, 1918, 1924.
    Robert W. Feller, Cleveland, 1939, 1940, 1941, 1946 (tied), 1947, 1951.

Most Games Won, Rookie Season

N. L.—47—Albert G. Spalding, Chicago, 1876 (won 47, lost 13—.783).

N. L. since 1900—28—Grover C. Alexander, Philadelphia, 1911 (won 28, lost 13— .683).

A. L.—24—O. Edgar Summers, Detroit, 1908 (won 24, lost 12—.667).

Most Games Won, League, From One Club

N. L.—70—Grover C. Alexander, Philadelphia, Chicago, St. Louis, vs. Cincinnati, 20 years, 1911 through 1930.

A. L.—66—Walter P. Johnson, Washington, vs. Detroit, 21 years, 1907 through 1927.

Most Consecutive Games Won, League, From One Club

N. L.—24—Christopher Mathewson, New York, vs. St. Louis, June 16, 1904 through September 15, 1908.

A. L.—23—Carl W. Mays, Boston, New York, vs. Philadelphia, August 30, 1918, to July 24, 1923.

Most Games Won, Season, From One Club

N. L.—12—Charles G. Radbourn, Providence vs. Cleveland, 1884.

N. L. since 1900—9—Edward M. Reulbach, Chicago vs. Brooklyn, 1908 (won 9, lost 0).

A. L.— 9—Edward A. Walsh, Chicago vs. New York 1908 (won 9, lost 1), and vs. Boston, 1908 (won 9, lost 0).

Most Years Winning 30 or More Games, League

N. L.— 7— Charles A. Nichols, Boston, 1891, 1892, 1893, 1894, 1896, 1897, 1898.
N. L. since 1900—4—Christopher Mathewson, New York, 1903, 1904, 1905, 1908.
A. L.—2—Denton T. Young, Boston, 1901, 1902.
    Walter P. Johnson, Washington, 1912, 1913.

Most Years Winning 20 or More Games in Major Leagues

16—Denton T. Young, Cleveland N. L., 1891, 1892, 1893, 1894, 1895, 1896, 1897, 1898; St. Louis, N. L., 1899, 1900; Boston, A. L., 1901, 1902, 1903, 1904, 1907, 1908. Ten in N. L. Six in A. L. (14 consecutive).

Most Years Winning 20 or More Games, League, Righthanded Pitcher

N. L.—13—Christopher Mathewson, New York, 1901, 1903, 1904, 1905, 1906, 1907, 1908, 1909, 1910, 1911, 1912, 1913, 1914 (12 consecutive).
A. L.—12—Walter P. Johnson, Washington, 1910, 1911, 1912, 1913, 1914, 1915, 1916, 1917, 1918, 1919, 1924, 1925 (10 consecutive).

Most Years Winning 20 or More Games, League, Lefthanded Pitcher

N. L.—13—Warren E. Spahn, Boston, Milwaukee, 1947, 1949, 1950, 1951, 1953, 1954, 1956, 1957, 1958, 1959, 1960, 1961, 1963.
A. L.— 8—Robert M. Grove, Philadelphia, Boston, 1927, 1928, 1929, 1930, 1931, 1932, 1933, 1935.

Most Consecutive Years, Winning 20 or More Games, Major Leagues

14—Denton T. Young, Cleveland N. L., St. Louis N. L., 1891 through 1900; Boston A. L., 1901 through 1904; 10 in N. L.; 4 in A. L.

Most Consecutive Years, Winning 20 or More Games, League

N. L.—12—Christopher Mathewson, New York, 1903 through 1914.
A. L.—10—Walter P. Johnson, Washington, 1910 through 1919.

Most Consecutive Years Winning 20 or More Games, League, Start of Career

N. L.—10—Charles A. Nichols, Boston, 1890 through 1899. (Also won 21 with St. Louis, 1904.)
A. L.— 3—Sylveanus A. Gregg, Cleveland, 1911, 1912, 1913.

Most Consecutive Games Won, League

N. L.—24—Carl O. Hubbell, New York, July 17, 1936, through May 27, 1937; 16 in 1936, 8 in 1937.
A. L.—17—John T. Allen, Cleveland, September 10, 1936, through September 30, 1937, first game; 2 in 1936, 15 in 1937.
    David A. McNally, Baltimore, September 22, 1968 through July 30, 1969; 2 in 1968, 15 in 1969.

Most Consecutive Games Won, Season

N. L.—19—Timothy J. Keefe, New York, June 23 through August 10, 1888.
    Richard W. Marquard, New York, April 11 through July 3, 1912, first game.
A. L.—16—Walter P. Johnson, Washington, July 3, second game, through August 23, 1912, first game.
    Joseph Wood, Boston, July 8 through September 15, 1912, second game.
    Robert M. Grove, Philadelphia, June 8 through August 19, 1931.
    Lynwood T. Rowe, Detroit, June 15 through August 25, 1934.

Most Consecutive Games Won, Season, Relief Pitcher

N. L.—17—El Roy L. Face, Pittsburgh, April 22, through August 30, second game, 1959.
A. L.—12—Luis E. Arroyo, New York, July 1 through September 9, 1961.

Most Consecutive Games Won, Start of Season

N. L.—19—Richard W. Marquard, New York, April 11 through July 3, 1912, first game.
A. L.—15—John T. Allen, Cleveland, April 23, 1937, through September 30, 1937, first game.
    David A. McNally, Baltimore, April 12 through July 30, 1969.

Most Season Opening Games Won, League

A. L.—9—Walter P. Johnson, Washington, all complete, 1910, 1913, 1914, 1915, 1916, 1917, 1919, 1924, 1926; seven shutouts. Lost (5), 1912, 1918, 1920, 1921, 1923, no shutouts.
N. L.—6—Juan A. Marichal, San Francisco, five complete, 1962, 1964, 1966, 1971, 1972, 1973. Lost 1965, 1967, 2 shutouts, 2 no decisions, 1968, 1969.
    G. Thomas Seaver, New York, Cincinnati, 2 complete, 1971, 1972, 1973, 1975, 1976, 1977. One game lost, 1979, 7 no decisions, 1968, 1969, 1970, 1974, 1978, 1981, 1983.

Most Consecutive Games Won, Rookie Season

N. L.—17—John P. Luby, Chicago, August 6, second game, through October 3, 1890.
N. L. since 1900—12—George L. Wiltse, New York, May 29, through September 15, 1904.
A. L.—12—R. Atley Donald, New York, May 9 through July 25, 1939.
        Russell W. Ford, New York, August 9 through October 6, 1910.

Most Consecutive Games Won as Starting Pitcher, Rookie Season

N. L.—17—John P. Luby, Chicago, August 6, second game, through October 3, 1890.
N. L. since 1900—12—George L. Wiltse, New York, May 29 through September 15, 1904.
A. L.—12—R. Atley Donald, New York, May 9 through July 25, 1939.

Most Consecutive Games Won as Relief Pitcher, Rookie Season

N. L.—10—John E. Yuhas, St. Louis, June 5, through September 25, 1952; end of season.
        Clarence E. Metzger, San Diego, April 20, through August 8, 1976.
A. L.— 9—Joseph W. Pate, Philadelphia, April 15 through August 10, 1926.

Most Consecutive Games Won, Start of Career, League, As Starting Pitcher

N. L.—12—George L. Wiltse, New York, May 29 through September 15, 1904.
A. L.— 9—Edward C. Ford, New York, July 17 through September 24, second game,
        1950.

Most Consecutive Games Won, Start of Career, League, As Relief Pitcher

N. L.—12—Clarence E. Metzger, San Francisco, 1974 (1), San Diego, 1975 (1), 1976
        (10), September 21, 1974 through August 8, 1976.
A. L.— 9—Joseph W. Pate, Philadelphia, April 15 through August 10, 1926.

Most Consecutive Games Won, Relief Pitcher, 3 Consecutive Games

A. L.—3—Harold G. White, Detroit, September 26, second game, 27, 28, 1950, 5⅓ innings.
        Grant D. Jackson, Baltimore, September 29, 30, October 1, 1974, 5⅓ innings.
        Albert W. Lyle, New York, August 29, 30, 31, 1977, 7⅔ innings.
N. L.—3—Michael G. Marshall, Los Angeles, June 21, 22, 23, 1974, 7 innings.
        H. Eugene Garber, Philadelphia, May 15 (second game), 16, 17, 1975, 5⅔ innings.
        Alan T. Hrabosky, St. Louis, July 12, 13, 17, 1975, 5 innings.
        Kenton C. Tekulve, Pittsburgh, May 6, 7, 9, 1980, 5⅓ innings.

Most Consecutive Games Won, End of Season

N. L.—17—John P. Luby, Chicago, August 6, second game, through October 3, 1890.
N. L. since 1900—16—Carl O. Hubbell, New York, July 17 through September 23, 1936.
A. L.—15—Alvin F. Crowder, Washington, August 2 through September 25, 1932.

Most Games Won by Two Pitchers, Season, One Club

N. L.—77—Providence 1884; Charles G. Radbourn, 60, Charles J. Sweeney, 17.
        76—New York, 1885; Michael F. Welch, 44, Timothy J. Keefe, 32.
N. L. since 1900—68—New York, 1904; Joseph J. McGinnity, 35, Christopher Mathew-
        son, 33.
A. L.—64—New York, 1904; John D. Chesbro, 41, John Powell, 23.

Most Games Won, One Month

N. L.—15—John G. Clarkson, Chicago, June 1885, won 15, lost 1.
N. L. since 1900—9—Christopher Mathewson, New York, August, 1903; won 9, lost 1.
        Christopher Mathewson, New York, August, 1904; won 9, lost 1.
        Grover C. Alexander, Chicago, May 1920, won 9, lost 0.
A. L.—10—George E. Waddell, Philadelphia, July 1902; won 10, lost 1, tied 1.

PITCHERS WINNING 20 OR MORE GAMES IN A SEASON

NATIONAL LEAGUE

(Number in parentheses after club denotes position of team at close of season)

1876 (5)	W.	L.
Albert Spalding, Chicago (1)	47	13
George Bradley, St. Louis (2)	45	19
Thomas H. Bond, Hartford (3)	32	13
James Devlin, Louisville (5)	30	34
Robert Mathews, New York (6)	21	34

1877 (3)	W.	L.
Thomas H. Bond, Boston (1)	31	17
James Devlin, Louisville (2)	28	20
Frank Larkin, Hartford (3)	22	21

1878 (4)	W.	L.
Thomas Bond, Boston (1)	40	19
William White, Cincinnati (2)	29	21
Frank Larkin, Chicago (4)	29	26
John Ward, Providence (3)	22	13

1879 (6)	W.	L.
John Ward, Providence (1)	44	18
William White, Cincinnati (5)	43	31
Thomas Bond, Boston (2)	42	19
James Galvin, Buffalo (3T)	37	27
Frank Larkin, Chicago (3T)	30	23
James McCormick, Cleve. (6)	20	40

1880 (8)	W.	L.
James McCormick, Cleve. (3)	45	28
Lawrence Corcoran, Chi. (1)	43	14
John Ward, Providence (2)	40	23
Michael Welch, Troy (4)	34	30
John Richmond, Worc. (5)	31	33
Thomas Bond, Boston (6)	26	29
Frederick Goldsmith, Chi. (1)	22	3
James Galvin, Buffalo (7)	20	37

1881 (9)	W.	L.
Lawrence Corcoran, Chi. (1)	31	14
James Whitney, Boston (6)	31	33
James Galvin, Buffalo (3)	29	24
George Derby, Detroit (4)	29	26
James McCormick, Cleve. (7)	26	30
Charles Radbourn, Prov. (2)	25	11
Frederick Goldsmith, Chi. (1)	25	13
John Richmond, Worcester (8)	25	27
Michael Welch, Troy (5)	21	18

1882 (7)	W.	L.
James McCormick, Cleve. (5)	36	29
Charles Radbourn, Prov. (2)	31	19
James Galvin, Buffalo (3T)	28	22
Frederick Goldsmith, Chi. (1)	28	16
Lawrence Corcoran, Chi. (1)	27	13
George Weidman, Detroit (6)	26	20
James Whitney, Boston (3T)	24	22

1883 (9)	W.	L.
Charles Radbourn, Prov. (3)	49	25
James Galvin, Buffalo (5)	46	29
James Whitney, Boston (1)	38	22
Lawrence Corcoran, Chi. (2)	31	21
Frederick Goldsmith, Chi. (2)	28	18
James McCormick, Cleve. (4)	27	13
Michael Welch, New York (6)	25	23
Charles Buffinton, Boston (1)	24	13
Hugh Daly, Cleveland (4)	24	18

1884 (7)	W.	L.
Charles Radbourn, Prov. (1)	60	12
Charles Buffinton, Boston (2)	47	16
James Galvin, Buffalo (3)	46	22
Michael Welch, New York (4T)	39	21
Lawrence Corcoran, Chi. (4T)	35	23
James Whitney, Boston (2)	24	17
Charles Ferguson, Phila. (6)	21	24

1885 (9)	W.	L.
John Clarkson, Chicago (1)	53	16
Michael Welch, New York (2)	44	11
Timothy Keefe, New York (2)	32	13
Charles Ferguson, Phila. (3)	26	19
Charles Radbourn, Prov. (4)	26	20
Edward Dailey, Phila. (3)	26	22
Frederick Shaw, Prov. (4)	23	26
Charles Buffinton, Boston (5)	22	27
James McCormick, 1-3 Providence (4) 20-4 Chicago (1)	21	7

1886 (11)	W.	L.
Charles Baldwin, Detroit (2)	42	13
Timothy Keefe, New York (3)	42	20
John Clarkson, Chicago (1)	35	17
Michael Welch, New York (3)	33	22
Charles Ferguson, Phila. (4)	32	9
Charles Getzein, Detroit (2)	31	11
James McCormick, Chicago (1)	31	11
Charles Radbourn, Boston (5)	27	30
Daniel Casey, Philadelphia (4)	25	19
John Flynn, Chicago (1)	24	6
William Stemmeyer, Boston (5)	22	18

1887 (11)	W.	L.
John Clarkson, Chicago (3)	38	21
Timothy Keefe, New York (4)	35	19
Charles Getzein, Detroit (1)	29	13
Daniel Casey, Philadelphia (2)	28	13
James Galvin, Pittsburgh (6)	28	21
James Whitney, Wash. (7)	24	21
Charles Radbourn, Boston (5)	24	23
Michael Welch, New York (4)	22	15
Michael Madden, Boston (5)	22	14
Charles Ferguson, Phila. (2)	21	10
Charles Buffinton, Phila. (2)	21	17

1888 (8)	W.	L.
Timothy Keefe, New York (1)	35	12
John Clarkson, Boston (4)	33	20
Peter Conway, Detroit (5)	30	14
Edward Morris, Pittsburgh (6)	29	23
Charles Buffinton, Phila. (3)	28	17
Michael Welch, New York (1)	26	19
August Krock, Chicago (2)	25	14
James Galvin, Pittsburgh (6)	23	25

1889 (10)	W.	L.
John Clarkson, Boston (2)	49	19
Timothy Keefe, New York (1)	28	13
Michael Welch, New York (1)	27	12
Charles Buffinton, Phila. (4)	26	17
James Galvin, Pittsburgh (5)	23	16
John O'Brien, Cleveland (6)	22	17
Henry Staley, Pittsburgh (5)	21	26
Charles Radbourn, Boston (2)	20	11
Edward Beatin, Cleveland (6)	20	14
Henry Boyle, Indianapolis (7)	20	23

1890 (13)	W.	L.
William Hutchinson, Chi. (2)	42	25
William Gleason, Phila. (3)	38	16
Thomas Lovett, Brooklyn (1)	32	11
Amos Rusie, New York (6)	29	30
William Rhines, Cincinnati (4)	28	17
Charles Nichols, Boston (5)	27	19
John Clarkson, Boston (5)	26	18
William Terry, Brooklyn (1)	25	16
Charles Getzein, Boston (5)	24	18
Robert Caruthers, Brooklyn (1)	23	11
Thomas Vickery, Phila. (3)	22	23
Edward Beatin, Cleveland (7)	22	31
John Luby, Chicago (2)	21	9

1891 (12)	W.	L.
William Hutchinson, Chi. (2)	43	19
John Clarkson, Boston (1)	34	18
Amos Rusie, New York (3)	32	19
Charles Nichols, Boston (1)	30	17
Denton Young, Cleveland (5)	27	20
William Gleason, Phila. (4)	24	19
Anthony Mullane, Cin. (7)	24	25
John Ewing, New York (3)	22	8
Henry Staley, 4-3 Pittsburgh (8) 17-10 Boston (1)	21	13
Thomas Lovett, Brooklyn (6)	21	20
Marcus Baldwin, Pitts. (8)	21	27
Charles Esper, Philadelphia (4)	20	14

1892 (22)	W.	L.
William Hutchinson, Chi. (7)	37	34
Denton Young, Cleveland (2)	36	11
Charles Nichols, Boston (1)	35	16
John Stivetts, Boston (1)	33	14
George Haddock, Brooklyn (3)	31	13
Amos Rusie, New York (8)	31	28
Frank Killen, Washington (10)	30	23

1892 (22) —Cont.

	W.	L.
George Cuppy, Cleveland (2)	28	12
August Weyhing, Phila. (4)	28	18
Marcus Baldwin, Pitts. (6)	27	20
Edward Stein, Brooklyn (3)	26	16
Henry Staley, Boston (1)	24	11
John Clarkson, 8-6 Boston (1)		
16-10 Cleveland (2)	24	16
Addison Gumbert, Chicago (7)	23	21
Charles King, New York (8)	22	24
Anthony Mullane, Cin. (5)	21	10
William Terry 2-4, Balt. (12)		
19-6 Pittsburgh (6)	21	10
John Dwyer 3-11, St. Louis (11)		
18-8 Cincinnati (5)	21	19
Scott Stratton, Louisville (9)	21	19
Elton Chamberlain, Cin. (5)	20	22
William Gleason, St. Louis (11)	20	24
John McMahon, Baltimore (12)	20	25

1893 (7)

	W.	L.
Frank Killen, Pittsburgh (2)	34	10
Charles Nichols, Boston (1)	34	14
Denton Young, Cleveland (3)	32	16
Amos Rusie, New York (5)	29	18
William Kennedy, Brkn. (6T)	26	19
John McMahon, Baltimore (8)	24	16
August Weyhing, Phila. (4)	24	16

1894 (13)

	W.	L.
Amos Rusie, New York (2)	36	13
Jouett Meekin, New York (2)	34	9
Charles Nichols, Boston (3)	32	13
John Stivetts, Boston (3)	28	13
Theo. Breitenstein, St. L. (9)	27	22
John McMahon, Baltimore (1)	25	8
Edward Stein, Brooklyn (5)	25	15
Denton Young, Cleveland (6)	25	22
George Cuppy, Cleveland (6)	23	17
John Taylor, Philadelphia (4)	22	11
William Kennedy, Brkn. (5)	22	20
Clark Griffith, Chicago (8)	21	11
John Dwyer, Cincinnati (10)	20	18

1895 (9)

	W.	L.
Denton Young, Cleveland (2)	35	10
Emerson Hawley, Pitts. (7)	32	21
William Hoffer, Baltimore (1)	30	7
John Taylor, Philadelphia (3)	26	13
Wilfred Carsey, Phila. (3)	26	15
Charles Nichols, Boston (5T)	26	16
Clark Griffith, Chicago (4)	25	13
George Cuppy, Cleveland (2)	25	15
William Terry, Chicago (4)	23	13
Amos Rusie, New York (9)	22	21
George Hemming, Balti. (1)	20	10
William Rhines, Cincinnati (8)	20	10
Theo. Breitenstein, St. L. (11)	20	29

1896 (12)

	W.	L.
Charles Nichols, Boston (4)	30	14
Frank Killen, Pittsburgh (6)	29	15
Denton Young, Cleveland (2)	29	16
William Hoffer, Baltimore (1)	26	7
Jouett Meekin, New York (7)	26	13
John Dwyer, Cincinnati (3)	25	10
George Cuppy, Cleveland (2)	25	15
George Mercer, Wash. (9T)	25	19
Clark Griffith, Chicago (5)	22	13
John Stivetts, Boston (4)	22	13
John Taylor, Philadelphia (8)	21	20
Emerson Hawley, Pitts. (6)	21	21

1897 (13)

	W.	L.
Charles Nichols, Boston (1)	31	11

1897 (13) —Cont.

	W.	L.
Amos Rusie, New York (3)	29	8
Frederick Klobedanz, Bos. (1)	25	8
Joseph Corbett, Baltimore (2)	24	8
George Mercer, Wash. (6T)	24	21
Theo. Breitenstein, Cin. (4)	23	12
William Hoffer, Baltimore (2)	22	10
Denton Young, Cleveland (5)	21	18
Clark Griffith, Chicago (9)	21	19
Jeremiah Nops, Baltimore (2)	20	7
Jouett Meekin, New York (3)	20	11
Edward Lewis, Boston (1)	20	12
J. Bentley Seymour, N.Y. (3)	20	14

1898 (17)

	W.	L.
Charles Nichols, Boston (1)	31	12
Ellsw'th Cunningham, Lou. (9)	28	15
James McJames, Baltimore (2)	27	14
Emerson Hawley, Cin. (3)	26	12
Clark Griffith, Chicago (4)	26	10
Edward Lewis, Boston (1)	25	8
Denton Young, Cleveland (5)	25	14
J. Bentley Seymour, N. Y. (7)	25	17
Wiley Piatt, Philadelphia (6)	24	14
Jesse Tannehill, Pitts. (8)	24	14
John Powell, Cleveland (5)	24	15
Victor Willis, Boston (1)	23	12
James Hughes, Baltimore (2)	21	11
Theo. Breitenstein, Cin. (3)	21	14
Albert Maul, Baltimore (2)	20	7
Amos Rusie, New York (7)	20	10
James Callahan, Chicago (4)	20	11

1899 (17)

	W.	L.
James Hughes, Brooklyn (1)	28	6
Joseph McGinnity, Balti. (4)	28	17
Victor Willis, Boston (2)	27	10
Denton Young, St. Louis (5)	26	15
Frank Hahn, Cincinnati (6)	23	7
James Callahan, Chicago (8)	23	12
Jesse Tannehill, Pitts. (7)	23	14
Wiley Piatt, Philadelphia (3)	23	15
John Powell, St. Louis (5)	23	21
Frank Donahue, Phila. (3)	22	7
Clark Griffith, Chicago (8)	22	13
John Dunn, Brooklyn (1)	21	12
Charles Fraser, Phila. (3)	21	13
Charles Nichols, Boston (2)	21	19
Frank Kitson, Baltimore (4)	20	16
Charles Phillippe, Louis. (9)	20	17
Samuel Leever, Pittsburgh (7)	20	23

1900 (5)

	W.	L.
Joseph McGinnity, Brkn. (1)	29	9
William Kennedy, Brkn. (1)	22	13
William Dinneen, Boston (4)	21	15
Jesse Tannehill, Pitts (2)	20	7
Denton Young, St. Louis (5T)	20	18

1901 (8)

	W.	L.
William Donovan, Brkn. (3)	25	15
Charles Phillippe, Pitts. (1)	22	12
Frank Hahn, Cincinnati (8)	22	19
John Chesbro, Pittsburgh (1)	21	9
Albert Orth, Philadelphia (2)	20	12
Charles Harper, St. Louis (4)	20	12
Frank Donahue, Phila. (2)	20	13
Christ. Mathewson, N. Y. (7)	20	17

1902 (7)

	W.	L.
John Chesbro, Pittsburgh (1)	28	6
Charles Pittinger, Boston (3)	27	14
Victor Willis, Boston (3)	27	19
John Taylor, Chicago (5)	22	10
Frank Hahn, Cincinnati (4)	22	12
Jesse Tannehill, Pitts. (1)	20	6
Charles Phillippe, Pitts. (1)	20	9

1903 (9)	W.	L.
Joseph McGinnity, N. Y. (2)	31	20
Christ. Mathewson, N. Y. (2)	30	13
Samuel Leever, Pitts. (1)	25	7
Charles Phillippe, Pitts. (1)	25	9
Frank Hahn, Cincinnati (4)	22	12
Harry Schmidt, Brooklyn (5)	22	13
John Taylor, Chicago (3)	21	14
Jacob Weimer, Chicago (3)	20	8
Robert Wicker, 0-0, St. Louis (8)		
20-9 Chicago (3)	20	9

1904 (7)	W.	L.
Joseph McGinnity, N. Y. (1)	35	8
Christ. Mathewson, N. Y. (1)	33	12
Charles Harper, Cincinnati (3)	23	9
Charles Nichols, St. Louis (5)	21	13
Luther Taylor, New York (1)	21	15
Jacob Weimer, Chicago (2)	20	14
John Taylor, St. Louis (5)	20	19

1905 (8)	W.	L.
Christ. Mathewson, N. Y. (1)	31	9
Charles Pittinger, Phila. (4)	23	14
Leon Ames, New York (1)	22	8
Joseph McGinnity, N. Y. (1)	21	15
Samuel Leever, Pittsburgh (2)	20	5
Robert Ewing, Cincinnati (5)	20	11
Charles Phillippe, Pitts. (2)	20	13
Irving Young, Boston (7)	20	21

1906 (8)	W.	L.
Joseph McGinnity, N. Y. (2)	27	12
Mordecai Brown, Chicago (1)	26	6
Victor Willis, Pittsburgh (3)	23	13
Samuel Leever, Pittsburgh (3)	22	7
Christ. Mathewson, N. Y. (2)	22	12
John Pfiester, Chicago (1)	20	8
John Taylor, 8-3 St. Louis (7)		
12-3 Chicago (1)	20	12
Jacob Weimer, Cincinnati (6)	20	14

1907 (6)	W.	L.
Christ. Mathewson, N. Y. (4)	24	12
Orval Overall, Chicago (1)	23	8
Frank Sparks, Philadelphia (3)	22	8
Victor Willis, Pittsburgh (2)	21	11
Mordecai Brown, Chicago (1)	20	6
Albert Leifield, Pittsburgh (2)	20	16

1908 (7)	W.	L.
Christ. Mathewson, N. Y. (2T)	37	11
Mordecai Brown, Chicago (1)	29	9
Edward Reulbach, Chicago (1)	24	7
Nicholas Maddox, Pitts. (2T)	23	8
Victor Willis, Pittsburgh (2T)	23	11
George Wiltse, New York (2T)	23	14
George McQuillan, Phila. (4)	23	17

1909 (6)	W.	L.
Mordecai Brown, Chicago (2)	27	9
S. Howard Camnitz, Pitts. (1)	25	6
Christ. Mathewson, N. Y. (3)	25	6
Victor Willis, Pittsburgh (1)	22	11
George Wiltse, New York (3)	20	11
Orval Overall, Chicago (2)	20	11

1910 (5)	W.	L.
Christ. Mathewson, N. Y. (2)	27	9
Mordecai Brown, Chicago (1)	25	14
Earl Moore, Philadelphia (4)	22	15
Leonard Cole, Chicago (1)	20	4
George Suggs, Cincinnati (5)	20	12

1911 (8)	W.	L.
Grover Alexander, Phila. (4)	28	13
Christ. Mathewson, N. Y. (1)	26	13
Richard Marquard, N. Y. (1)	24	7
Robert Harmon, St. Louis (5)	23	16

1911 (8)—Cont.	W.	L.
Charles Adams, Pittsburgh (3)	22	12
George Rucker, Brooklyn (7)	22	18
Mordecai Brown, Chicago (2)	21	11
S. Howard Camnitz, Pitts. (3)	20	15

1912 (5)	W.	L.
Lawrence Cheney, Chicago (3)	26	10
Richard Marquard, N. Y. (1)	26	11
Claude Hendrix, Pitts. (2)	24	9
Christ. Mathewson, N. Y. (1)	23	12
S. Howard Camnitz, Pitts. (2)	22	12

1913 (7)	W.	L.
Thomas Seaton, Phila. (2)	27	12
Christ. Mathewson, N. Y. (1)	25	11
Richard Marquard, N. Y. (1)	23	10
Grover Alexander, Phila. (2)	22	8
Charles Tesreau, New York (1)	22	13
Charles Adams, Pittsburgh (4)	21	10
Lawrence Cheney, Chicago (3)	21	14

1914 (9)	W.	L.
Richard Rudolph, Boston (1)	27	10
Grover Alexander, Phila. (6)	27	15
William James, Boston (1)	26	7
Charles Tesreau, New York (2)	26	10
Christ. Mathewson, N. Y. (2)	24	13
Edward Pfeffer, Brooklyn (5)	23	12
James Vaughn, Chicago (4)	21	13
J. Erskine Mayer, Phila. (6)	21	19
Lawrence Cheney, Chicago (4)	20	18

1915 (5)	W.	L.
Grover Alexander, Phila. (1)	31	10
Richard Rudolph, Boston (2)	22	19
Albert Mamaux, Pittsburgh (5)	21	8
J. Erskine Mayer, Phila. (1)	21	15
James Vaughn, Chicago (4)	20	12

1916 (4)	W.	L.
Grover Alexander, Phila. (2)	33	12
Edward Pfeffer, Brooklyn (1)	25	11
Eppa Rixey, Philadelphia (2)	22	10
Albert Mamaux, Pittsburgh (6)	21	15

1917 (5)	W.	L.
Grover Alexander, Phila. (2)	30	13
Fred Toney, Cincinnati (4)	24	16
James Vaughn, Chicago (5)	23	13
Ferdinand Schupp, N. Y. (1)	21	7
Peter Schneider, Cin. (4)	20	19

1918 (2)	W.	L.
James Vaughn, Chicago (1)	22	10
Claude Hendrix, Chicago (1)	20	7

1919 (3)	W.	L.
Jesse Barnes, New York (2)	25	9
Harry Sallee, Cincinnati (1)	21	7
James Vaughn, Chicago (3)	21	14

1920 (7)	W.	L.
Grover Alexander, Chi. (5T)	27	14
A. Wilbur Cooper, Pitts. (4)	24	15
Burleigh Grimes, Brooklyn (1)	23	11
Fred Toney, New York (2)	21	11
Arthur Nehf, New York (2)	21	12
William Doak, St. Louis (5T)	20	12
Jesse Barnes, New York (2)	20	15

1921 (4)	W.	L.
Burleigh Grimes, Brooklyn (5)	22	13
A. Wilbur Cooper, Pitts. (2)	22	14
Arthur Nehf, New York (1)	20	10
Joseph Oeschger, Boston (4)	20	14

1922 (3)	W.	L.
Eppa Rixey, Cincinnati (2)	25	13
A. Wilbur Cooper, Pitts. (3T)	23	14
Walter Ruether, Brooklyn (6)	21	12

1923 (7) — W. L.
Adolfo Luque, Cincinnati (2) 27   8
John Morrison, Pittsburgh (3) 25   13
Grover Alexander, Chicago (4) 22   12
Peter Donohue, Cincinnati (2) 21   15
Burleigh Grimes, Brooklyn (6) 21   18
Jesse Haines, St. Louis (5) 20   13
Eppa Rixey, Cincinnati (2) 20   15

1924 (4) — W. L.
Arthur Vance, Brooklyn (2) 28   6
Burleigh Grimes, Brooklyn (2) 22   13
Carl Mays, Cincinnati (4) 20   9
A. Wilbur Cooper, Pitts. (3) 20   14

1925 (3) — W. L.
Arthur Vance, Brooklyn (6T) 22   9
Eppa Rixey, Cincinnati (3) 21   11
Peter Donohue, Cincinnati (3) 21   14

1926 (4) — W. L.
Remy Kremer, Pittsburgh (3) 20   6
Charles Rhem, St. Louis (1) 20   7
H. Lee Meadows, Pitts. (3) 20   9
Peter Donohue, Cincinnati (2) 20   14

1927 (4) — W. L.
Charles Root, Chicago (4) 26   15
Jesse Haines, St. Louis (2) 24   10
Carmen Hill, Pittsburgh (1) 22   11
Grover Alexander, St. L. (2) 21   10

1928 (6) — W. L.
Lawrence Benton, N. Y. (2) 25   9
Burleigh Grimes, Pitts. (4) 25   14
Arthur Vance, Brooklyn (6) 22   10
William Sherdel, St. Louis (1) 21   10
Jesse Haines, St. Louis (1) 20   8
Fred Fitzsimmons, N. Y. (2) 20   9

1929 (1) — W. L.
Perce Malone, Chicago (1) 22   10

1930 (2) — W. L.
Perce Malone, Chicago (2) 20   9
Remy Kremer, Pittsburgh (5) 20   12

1931 (0)

1932 (2) — W. L.
Lonnie Warneke, Chicago (1) 22   6
W. William Clark, Brkn. (3) 20   12

1933 (4) — W. L.
Carl Hubbell, New York (1) 23   12
Benjamin Cantwell, Boston (4) 20   10
Guy Bush, Chicago (3) 20   12
Jerome Dean, St. Louis (5) 20   18

1934 (4) — W. L.
Jerome Dean, St. Louis (1) 30   7
Harold Schumacher, N. Y. (2) 23   10
Lonnie Warneke, Chicago (3) 22   10
Carl Hubbell, New York (2) 21   12

1935 (5) — W. L.
Jerome Dean, St. Louis (2) 28   12
Carl Hubbell, New York (3) 23   12
Paul Derringer, Cin. (6) 22   13
William C. Lee, Chicago (1) 20   6
Lonnie Warneke, Chicago (1) 20   13

1936 (2) — W. L.
Carl Hubbell, New York (1) 26   6
Jerome Dean, St. Louis (2T) 24   13

1937 (4) — W. L.
Carl Hubbell, New York (1) 22   8
Clifford Melton, New York (1) 20   9
Louis Fette, Boston (5) 20   10
James Turner, Boston (5) 20   11

1938 (2) — W. L.
William C. Lee Chicago (1) 22   9
Paul Derringer, Cincinnati (4) 21   14

1939 (4) — W. L.
William Walters, Cin. (1) 27   11
Paul Derringer, Cincinnati (1) 25   7
Curtis Davis, St. Louis (2) 22   16
Luke Hamlin, Brooklyn (3) 20   13

1940 (3) — W. L.
William Walters, Cin. (1) 22   10
Paul Derringer, Cincinnati (1) 20   12
Claude Passeau, Chicago (5) 20   13

1941 (2) — W. L.
W. Kirby Higbe, Brooklyn (1) 22   9
J. Whitlow Wyatt, Brkn. (1) 22   10

1942 (2) — W. L.
Morton Cooper, St. Louis (1) 22   7
John Beazley, St. Louis (1) 21   6

1943 (3) — W. L.
Morton Cooper, St. Louis (1) 21   8
Truett Sewell, Pittsburgh (4) 21   9
Elmer Riddle, Cincinnati (2) 21   11

1944 (4) — W. L.
William Walters, Cin. (3) 23   8
Morton Cooper, St. Louis (1) 22   7
Truett Sewell, Pittsburgh (2) 21   12
William Voiselle, New York (5) 21   16

1945 (2) — W. L.
Charles Barrett, 2-3 Boston (6)
   21-9 St. Louis (2) 23   12
Henry Wyse, Chicago (1) 22   10

1946 (2) — W. L.
Howard Pollet, St. Louis (1) 21   10
John Sain, Boston (4) 20   14

1947 (5) — W. L.
Ewell Blackwell, Cin. (5) 22   8
Lawrence Jansen, N. Y. (4) 21   5
Warren Spahn, Boston (3) 21   10
Ralph Branca, Brooklyn (1) 21   12
John Sain, Boston (3) 21   12

1948 (2) — W. L.
John Sain, Boston (1) 24   15
Harry Brecheen, St. Louis (2) 20   7

1949 (2) — W. L.
Warren Spahn, Boston (4) 21   14
Howard Pollet, St. Louis (2) 20   9

1950 (3) — W. L.
Warren Spahn, Boston (4) 21   17
Robin Roberts, Phila. (1) 20   11
John Sain, Boston (4) 20   13

1951 (7) — W. L.
Salvatore Maglie, N. Y. (1) 23   6
Lawrence Jansen, N. Y. (1) 23   11
Elwin Roe, Brooklyn (2) 22   3
Warren Spahn, Boston (4) 22   14
Robin Roberts, Phila. (5) 21   15
Donald Newcombe, Brkn. (2) 20   9
Murry Dickson, Pitts. (7) 20   16

1952 (1) — W. L.
Robin Roberts, Phila. (4) 28   7

1953 (4) — W. L.
Warren Spahn, Milwaukee (2) 23   7
Robin Roberts, Phila. (3T) 23   16
Carl Erskine, Brooklyn (1) 20   6
Harvey Haddix, St. Louis (3T) 20   9

1954 (3) — W. L.
Robin Roberts, Phila. (4) 23   15
John Antonelli, New York (1) 21   7
Warren Spahn, Milwaukee (3) 21   12

1955 (2)	W.	L.
Robin Roberts, Phila. (4)	23	14
Donald Newcombe, Brook. (1)	20	5

1956 (3)	W.	L.
Donald Newcombe, Brook. (1)	27	7
Warren Spahn, Milwaukee (2)	20	11
John Antonelli, New York (6)	20	13

1957 (1)	W.	L.
Warren Spahn, Milwaukee (1)	21	11

1958 (3)	W.	L.
Warren Spahn, Milwaukee (1)	22	11
Robert Friend, Pittsburgh (2)	22	14
S. Lewis Burdette, Milw. (1)	20	10

1959 (3)	W.	L.
S. Lewis Burdette, Milw. (2)	21	15
Warren Spahn, Milwaukee (2)	21	15
Samuel Jones, San Fran. (3)	21	15

1960 (3)	W.	L.
Ernest Broglio, St. Louis (3)	21	9
Warren Spahn, Milwaukee (2)	21	10
Vernon Law, Pittsburgh (1)	20	9

1961 (2)	W.	L.
Joseph Jay, Cincinnati (1)	21	10
Warren Spahn, Milwaukee (4)	21	13

1962 (4)	W.	L.
Donald Drysdale, L. A. (2)	25	9
John Sanford, S. F. (1)	24	7
Robert Purkey, Cincinnati (3)	23	5
Joseph Jay, Cincinnati (3)	21	14

1963 (5)	W.	L.
Sanford Koufax, L. A. (1)	25	5
Juan A. Marichal, S. F. (3)	25	8
James W. Maloney, Cinn. (5)	23	7
Warren E. Spahn, Milw. (6)	23	7
Richard C. Ellsworth, Chi. (7)	22	10

1964 (3)	W.	L.
Lawrence C. Jackson, Chi. (8)	24	11
Juan A. Marichal, San F. (4)	21	8
Raymond M. Sadecki, St.L. (1)	20	11

1965 (7)	W.	L.
Sanford Koufax, L. A. (1)	26	8
Tony Cloninger, Milw. (5)	24	11
Donald Drysdale, L. A. (1)	23	12
Samuel J. Ellis, Cincinnati (4)	22	10
Juan A. Marichal, S. F. (2)	22	13
James W. Maloney, Cin. (4)	20	9
Robert Gibson, St. Louis (7)	20	12

1966 (5)	W.	L.
Sanford Koufax, L. A. (1)	27	9
Juan A. Marichal, S. F. (2)	25	6
Gaylord J. Perry, S. F. (2)	21	8
Robert Gibson, St. Louis (6)	21	12
Christopher J. Short, Phila. (4)	20	10

1967 (2)	W.	L.
Michael F. McCormick, S.F. (2)	22	10
Ferguson A. Jenkins, Chi. (3)	20	13

1968 (3)	W.	L.
Juan A. Marichal, S. F. (2)	26	9
Robert Gibson, St. Louis (1)	22	9
Ferguson A. Jenkins, Chi. (3)	20	15

1969 (9)	W.	L.
G. Thomas Seaver, N. Y. (1E)	25	7
Philip H. Niekro, Atl. (1W)	23	13
Juan A. Marichal, S. F. (2W)	21	11

1969 (9) —Cont.	W.	L.
Ferguson A. Jenkins, Chi. (2E)	21	15
William R. Singer, L. A. (4W)	20	12
Lawrence E. Dierker, Hou. (5W)	20	13
Robert Gibson, St. Louis (4E)	20	13
William A. Hands, Chi. (2E)	20	14
Claude W. Osteen, L. A. (4W)	20	15

1970 (4)	W.	L.
Robert Gibson, St. Louis (4E)	23	7
Gaylord J. Perry, S. F. (3W)	23	13
Ferguson A. Jenkins, Chi. (2E)	22	16
James J. Merritt, Cin. (1W)	20	12

1971 (4)	W.	L.
Ferguson A. Jenkins, Chi. (3ET)	24	13
Alphonso E. Downing, L. A. (2W)	20	9
Steven N. Carlton, St. L. (2E)	20	9
G. Thomas Seaver, N. Y. (3ET)	20	10

1972 (4)	W.	L.
Steven N. Carlton, Phila. (6E)	27	10
G. Thomas Seaver, N. Y. (3E)	21	12
Claude W. Osteen, L. A. (3W)	20	11
Ferguson A. Jenkins, Chi. (2E)	20	12

1973 (1)	W.	L.
Ronald R. Bryant, San Fran. (3W)	24	12

1974 (2)	W.	L.
John A. Messersmith, Los Ang. (1W)	20	6
Philip H. Niekro, Atlanta (3W)	20	13

1975 (2)	W.	L.
G. Thomas Seaver, N. Y. (3ET)	22	9
Randall L. Jones, San Diego (4W)	20	12

1976 (5)	W.	L.
Randall L. Jones, S. D. (5W)	22	14
Jerry M. Koosman, N. Y. (3E)	21	10
Donald H. Sutton, L. A. (2W)	21	10
Steven N. Carlton, Phila. (1E)	20	7
James R. Richard, Hou. (3W)	20	15

1977 (6)	W.	L.
Steven N. Carlton, Phila. (1E)	23	10
G. Thomas Seaver, N.Y.-Cin. (2W)	21	6
John R. Candelaria, Pitts. (2E)	20	5
Robert H. Forsch, St. L. (3E)	20	7
Thomas E. John, L. A. (1W)	20	7
Ricky E. Reuschel, Chi. (4E)	20	10

1978 (2)	W.	L.
Gaylord J. Perry, S. D. (3W)	21	6
Ross A. Grimsley, Mon. (4E)	20	11

1979 (2)	W.	L.
Joseph F. Niekro, Hou. (2W)	21	11
Philip H. Niekro, Atl. (6W)	21	20

1980 (2)	W.	L.
Steven N. Carlton, Phila. (1E)	24	9
Joseph F. Niekro, Hou. (1W)	20	12

1981 (0)	W.	L.

1982 (1)	W.	L.
Steven N. Carlton, Phila. (2E)	23	11

1983 (0)	W.	L.

AMERICAN LEAGUE

1901 (5)	W.	L.
Denton Young, Boston (2)	33	10
Joseph McGinnity, Balt. (5)	26	21
Clark Griffith, Chicago (1)	24	7
C. Roscoe Miller, Detroit (3)	23	13
Charles Fraser, Phila. (4)	20	15

1902 (7)	W.	L.
Denton Young, Boston (3)	32	10
George Waddell, Phila. (1)	23	7
Frank Donahue, St. Louis (2)	22	11
John Powell, St. Louis (2)	22	17
William Dinneen, Boston (3)	21	21
Roy Patterson, Chicago (4)	20	12
Edward Plank, Phila. (1)	20	15

1903 (7)	W.	L.
Denton Young, Boston (1)	28	10
Edward Plank, Phila. (2)	23	16
Thomas Hughes, Boston (1)	21	7
William Dinneen, Boston (1)	21	11
William Sudhoff, St. Louis (6)	21	15
John Chesbro, New York (4)	21	15
George Waddell, Phila. (2)	21	16

1904 (9)	W.	L.
John Chesbro, New York (2)	41	13
Denton Young, Boston (1)	26	16
Edward Plank, Phila. (5)	26	17
George Waddell, Phila. (5)	25	19
William Bernhard, Cleve. (4)	23	13
William Dinneen, Boston (1)	23	14
John Powell, New York (2)	23	19
Jesse Tannehill, Boston (1)	21	11
Frank Owen, Chicago (3)	21	15

1905 (9)	W.	L.
George Waddell, Phila. (1)	26	11
Edward Plank, Phila. (1)	25	12
Nicholas Altrock, Chicago (2)	24	12
Edward Killian, Detroit (3)	23	13
Jesse Tannehill, Boston (4)	22	9
Frank Owen, Chicago (2)	21	13
George Mullin, Detroit (3)	21	20
Adrian Joss, Cleveland (5)	20	11
Frank Smith, Chicago (2)	20	14

1906 (8)	W.	L.
Albert Orth, New York (2)	27	17
John Chesbro, New York (2)	24	16
Robert Rhoades, Cleveland (3)	22	10
Frank Owen, Chicago (1)	22	13
Adrian Joss, Cleveland (3)	21	9
George Mullin, Detroit (6)	21	18
Nicholas Altrock, Chicago (1)	20	13
Otto Hess, Cleveland (3)	20	17

1907 (10)	W.	L.
Adrian Joss, Cleveland (4)	27	10
G. Harris White, Chicago (3)	27	13
William Donovan, Detroit (1)	25	4
Edward Killian, Detroit (1)	25	13
Edward Plank, Phila. (2)	24	16
Edward Walsh, Chicago (3)	24	18
Frank Smith, Chicago (3)	22	11
Denton Young, Boston (7)	22	15
James Dygert, Phila. (2)	20	9
George Mullin, Detroit (1)	20	20

1908 (4)	W.	L.
Edward Walsh, Chicago (3)	40	15
Adrian Joss, Cleveland (2)	24	11
Oren Summers, Detroit (1)	24	12
Denton Young, Boston (5)	21	11

1909 (3)	W.	L.
George Mullin, Detroit (1)	29	8
Frank Smith, Chicago (4)	25	17
R. Edgar Willett, Detroit (1)	22	9

1910 (5)	W.	L.
John Coombs, Phila. (1)	31	9
Russell Ford, New York (2)	26	6
Walter Johnson, Wash. (7)	25	17
Charles Bender, Phila. (1)	23	5
George Mullin, Detroit (3)	21	12

1911 (7)	W.	L.
John Coombs, Phila. (1)	28	12
Edward Walsh, Chicago (4)	27	18
Walter Johnson, Wash. (7)	25	13
Sylveanus Gregg, Cleve. (3)	23	7
Joseph Wood, Boston (5)	23	17
Edward Plank, Phila. (1)	22	8
Russell Ford, New York (6)	22	11

1912 (8)	W.	L.
Joseph Wood, Boston (1)	34	5
Walter Johnson, Wash. (2)	32	12
Edward Walsh, Chicago (4)	27	17
Edward Plank, Phila. (3)	26	6
Robert Groom, Wash. (2)	24	13
John Coombs, Phila. (3)	21	10
Hugh Bedient, Boston (1)	20	10
Sylveanus Gregg, Cleve. (5)	20	13

1913 (6)	W.	L.
Walter Johnson, Wash. (2)	36	7
Fred Falkenberg, Cleve. (3)	23	10
Ewell Russell, Chicago (5)	22	16
Charles Bender, Phila. (1)	21	10
Sylveanus Gregg, Cleve. (3)	20	13
James Scott, Chicago (5)	20	20

1914 (3)	W.	L.
Walter Johnson, Wash. (3)	28	18
Harry Coveleski, Detroit (4)	22	12
Ray Collins, Boston (2)	20	13

1915 (5)	W.	L.
Walter Johnson, Wash. (4)	27	13
James Scott, Chicago (3)	24	11
George Dauss, Detroit (2)	24	13
Urban Faber, Chicago (3)	24	14
Harry Coveleski, Detroit (2)	22	13

1916 (4)	W.	L.
Walter Johnson, Wash. (7)	25	20
Robert Shawkey, New York (4)	24	14
George Ruth, Boston (1)	23	12
Harry Coveleski, Detroit (3)	21	11

1917 (5)	W.	L.
Edward Cicotte, Chicago (1)	28	12
George Ruth, Boston (2)	24	13
James Bagby, Cleveland (3)	23	13
Walter Johnson, Wash. (5)	23	16
Carl Mays, Boston (2)	22	9

1918 (4)	W.	L.
Walter Johnson, Wash. (3)	23	13
Stanley Coveleski, Cleve. (2)	22	13
Carl Mays, Boston (1)	21	13
Scott Perry, Philadelphia (8)	20	19

1919 (7)	W.	L.
Edward Cicotte, Chicago (1)	29	7
Claude Williams, Chicago (1)	23	11
Stanley Coveleski, Cleve. (2)	23	12
George Dauss, Detroit (4)	21	9
Allan Sothoron, St. Louis (5)	21	11

1919 (7)—Cont.

	W.	L.
Robert Shawkey, New York (3) ...	20	13
Walter Johnson, Wash. (7)	20	14

1920 (10)

	W.	L.
James Bagby, Cleveland (1)	31	12
Carl Mays, New York (3)	26	11
Stanley Coveleski, Cleve. (1)	24	14
Urban Faber, Chicago (2)	23	13
Claude Williams, Chicago (2)	22	14
Richard Kerr, Chicago (2)	21	9
Edward Cicotte, Chicago (2)	21	10
Raymond Caldwell, Cleve. (1)	20	10
Urban Shocker, St. Louis (4)	20	10
Robert Shawkey, New York (3) ...	20	13

1921 (5)

	W.	L.
Carl Mays, New York (1)	27	9
Urban Shocker, St. Louis (3)	27	12
Urban Faber, Chicago (7)	25	15
Stanley Coveleski, Cleve. (2)	23	13
Samuel Jones, Boston (5)	23	16

1922 (6)

	W.	L.
Edwin Rommel, Phila. (7)	27	13
Leslie Bush, New York (1)	26	7
Urban Shocker, St. Louis (2)	24	17
George Uhle, Cleveland (4)	22	16
Urban Faber, Chicago (5)	21	17
Robert Shawkey, New York (1) ...	20	12

1923 (5)

	W.	L.
George Uhle, Cleveland (3)	26	16
Samuel Jones, New York (1)	21	8
George Dauss, Detroit (2)	21	13
Urban Shocker, St. Louis (5)	20	12
Howard Ehmke, Boston (8)	20	17

1924 (4)

	W.	L.
Walter Johnson, Wash. (1)	23	7
Herbert Pennock, N. Y. (2)	21	9
Hollis Thurston, Chicago (8)	20	14
Joseph Shaute, Cleveland (6)	20	17

1925 (4)

	W.	L.
Edwin Rommel, Phila. (2)	21	10
Theodore Lyons, Chicago (5)	21	11
Stanley Coveleski, Wash. (1)	20	5
Walter Johnson, Wash. (1)	20	7

1926 (2)

	W.	L.
George Uhle, Cleveland (2)	27	11
Herbert Pennock, N. Y. (1)	23	11

1927 (3)

	W.	L.
Waite Hoyt, New York (1)	22	7
Theodore Lyons, Chicago (5)	22	14
Robert Grove, Phila. (2)	20	13

1928 (5)

	W.	L.
Robert Grove, Phila. (2)	24	8
George Pipgras, New York (1)	24	13
Waite Hoyt, New York (1)	23	7
Alvin Crowder, St. Louis (3)	21	5
Samuel Gray, St. Louis (3)	20	12

1929 (3)

	W.	L.
George Earnshaw, Phila. (1)	24	8
Wesley Ferrell, Cleveland (3)	21	10
Robert Grove, Phila. (1)	20	6

1930 (5)

	W.	L.
Robert Grove, Phila. (1)	28	5
Wesley Ferrell, Cleveland (4)	25	13
George Earnshaw, Phila. (1)	22	13
Theodore Lyons, Chicago (7)	22	15
Walter Stewart, St. Louis (6)	20	12

1931 (5)

	W.	L.
Robert Grove, Phila. (1)	31	4
Wesley Ferrell, Cleveland (4)	22	12
George Earnshaw, Phila. (1)	21	7
Vernon Gomez, New York (2)	21	9
George Walberg, Phila. (1)	20	12

1932 (5)

	W.	L.
Alvin Crowder, Washington (3)	26	13
Robert Grove, Phila. (2)	25	10
Vernon Gomez, New York (1)	24	7
Wesley Ferrell, Cleveland (4)	23	13
Monte Weaver, Washington (3)	22	10

1933 (3)

	W.	L.
Robert Grove, Phila. (3)	24	8
Alvin Crowder, Washington (1)	24	15
Earl Whitehill, Washington (1)	22	8

1934 (4)

	W.	L.
Vernon Gomez, New York (2)	26	5
Lynwood Rowe, Detroit (1)	24	8
Thomas Bridges, Detroit (1)	22	11
Melvin Harder, Cleveland (3)	20	12

1935 (4)

	W.	L.
Wesley Ferrell, Boston (4)	25	14
Melvin Harder, Cleveland (3)	22	11
Thomas Bridges, Detroit (1)	21	10
Robert Grove, Boston (4)	20	12

1936 (5)

	W.	L.
Thomas Bridges, Detroit (2)	23	11
L. Vernon Kennedy, Chi. (3)	21	9
John Allen, Cleveland (5)	20	10
Charles Ruffing, New York (1)	20	12
Wesley Ferrell, Boston (6)	20	15

1937 (2)

	W.	L.
Vernon Gomez, New York (1)	21	11
Charles Ruffing, New York (1)	20	7

1938 (2)

	W.	L.
Charles Ruffing, New York (1)	21	7
Louis Newsom, St. Louis (7)	20	16

1939 (4)

	W.	L.
Robert Feller, Cleveland (3)	24	9
Charles Ruffing, New York (1)	21	7
Emil Leonard, Wash. (6)	20	8
Louis Newsom, (3-1) St. L. (8) (17-10) Detroit (5)	20	11

1940 (2)

	W.	L.
Robert Feller, Cleveland (2)	27	11
Louis Newsom, Detroit (1)	21	5

1941 (2)

	W.	L.
Robert Feller, Cleveland (4T)	25	13
Thornton Lee, Chicago (3)	22	11

1942 (2)

	W.	L.
Cecil Hughson, Boston (2)	22	6
Ernest Bonham, New York (1)	21	5

1943 (2)

	W.	L.
Spurgeon Chandler, N. Y. (1)	20	4
Paul Trout, Detroit (5)	20	12

1944 (2)

	W.	L.
Harold Newhouser, Detroit (2)	29	9
Paul Trout, Detroit, (2)	27	14

1945 (3)

	W.	L.
Harold Newhouser, Detroit (1)	25	9
David Ferriss, Boston (7)	21	10
Roger Wolff, Washington (2)	20	10

1946 (5)	W.	L.
Harold Newhouser, Detroit (2)	26	9
Robert Feller, Cleveland (6)	26	15
David Ferriss, Boston (1)	25	6
Spurgeon Chandler, N. Y. (3)	20	8
Cecil Hughson, Boston (1)	20	11

1947 (1)	W.	L.
Robert Feller, Cleveland (4)	20	11

1948 (3)	W.	L.
Harold Newhouser, Detroit (5)	21	12
H. Eugene Bearden, Cleve. (1)	20	7
Robert Lemon, Cleveland (1)	20	14

1949 (5)	W.	L.
Melvin Parnell, Boston (2)	25	7
Ellis Kinder, Boston (2)	23	6
Robert Lemon, Cleveland (3)	22	10
Victor Raschi, New York (1)	21	10
Alexander Kellner, Phila. (5)	20	12

1950 (2)	W.	L.
Robert Lemon, Cleveland (4)	23	11
Victor Raschi, New York (1)	21	8

1951 (6)	W.	L.
Robert Feller, Cleveland (2)	22	8
Edmund Lopat, New York (1)	21	9
Victor Raschi, New York (1)	21	10
Ned Garver, St. Louis (8)	20	12
Edward Garcia, Cleveland (2)	20	13
Early Wynn, Cleveland (2)	20	13

1952 (5)	W.	L.
Robert Shantz, Phila. (4)	24	7
Early Wynn, Cleveland (2)	23	12
Edward Garcia, Cleveland (2)	22	11
Robert Lemon, Cleveland (2)	22	11
Allie Reynolds, New York (1)	20	8

1953 (4)	W.	L.
Ervin Porterfield, Wash. (5)	22	10
Melvin Parnell, Boston (4)	21	8
Robert Lemon, Cleveland (2)	21	15
Virgil Trucks,		
5-4 St. Louis (8)		
15-6 Chicago (3)	20	10

1954 (3)	W.	L.
Robert Lemon, Cleveland (1)	23	7
Early Wynn, Cleveland (1)	23	11
Robert Grim, New York (2)	20	6

1955 (0)

1956 (6)	W.	L.
Frank Lary, Detroit (5)	21	13
Herbert Score, Cleveland (2)	20	9
Early Wynn, Cleveland (2)	20	9
W. William Pierce, Chicago (3)	20	9
Robert Lemon, Cleveland (2)	20	14
William Hoeft, Detroit (5)	20	14

1957 (2)	W.	L.
James Bunning, Detroit (4)	20	8
W. William Pierce, Chicago (2)	20	12

1958 (1)	W.	L.
Robert Turley, New York (1)	21	7

1959 (1)	W.	L.
Early Wynn, Chicago (1)	22	10

1960 (0)

1961 (2)	W.	L.
Edward Ford, New York (1)	25	4
Frank Lary, Detroit (2)	23	9

1962 (4)	W.	L.
Ralph Terry, New York (1)	23	12
Raymond Herbert, Chicago (5)	20	9

1962 (4) —Cont.	W.	L.
Richard Donovan, Cleve. (6)	20	10
Camilo Pascual, Minnesota (2)	20	11

1963 (5)	W.	L.
Edward C. Ford, New York (1)	24	7
James A. Bouton, N. Y. (1)	21	7
Camilo Pascual, Minnesota (3)	21	9
Wm. C. Monbouquette, Bos. (7)....	20	10
Stephen D. Barber, Balt. (4)	20	13

1964 (2)	W.	L.
W. Dean Chance, L. A. (5)	20	9
Gary C. Peters, Chicago (2)	20	8

1965 (2)	W.	L.
James T. Grant, Minn. (1)	21	7
M. L. Stottlemyre, N. Y. (6)	20	9

1966 (2)	W.	L.
James L. Kaat, Minnesota (2)	25	13
Dennis D. McLain, Detroit (3)	20	14

1967 (3)	W.	L.
James R. Lonborg, Boston (1)	22	9
R. Earl Wilson, Detroit (2T)	22	11
W. Dean Chance, Minn. (2T)	20	14

1968 (4)	W.	L.
Dennis D. McLain, Detroit (1)	31	6
David A. McNally, Balt. (2)	22	10
Luis C. Tiant, Cleveland (3)	21	9
M. L. Stottlemyre, N. Y. (5)	21	12

1969 (6)	W.	L.
Dennis D. McLain, Det. (2E)	24	9
Miguel Cuellar, Balt. (1E)	23	11
James E. Perry, Minn. (1W)	20	6
David A. McNally, Balt. (1E)	20	7
David W. Boswell, Minn. (1W)	20	12
M. L. Stottlemyre, N. Y. (5E)	20	14

1970 (7)	W.	L.
Miguel Cuellar, Baltimore (1E)	24	8
David A. McNally, Balt. (1E)	24	9
James E. Perry, Minn. (1W)	24	12
Clyde Wright, Calif. (3W)	22	12
James A. Palmer, Balt. (1E)	20	10
Fred I. Peterson, N. Y. (2E)	20	11
Samuel E. McDowell,		
Clev. (5E)	20	12

1971 (10)	W.	L.
Michael S. Lolich, Detroit (2E)	25	14
Vida Blue, Oakland (1W)	24	8
Wilbur F. Wood, Chicago (3W)	22	13
David A. McNally, Balt. (1E)	21	5
James A. Hunter, Oak. (1W)	21	11
Patrick E. Dobson, Balt. (1E)	20	8
James A. Palmer, Balt. (1E)	20	9
Miguel Cuellar, Balt. (1E)	20	9
Joseph H. Coleman, Det. (2E)	20	9
John A. Messersmith, Calif.		
(4W)	20	13

1972 (6)	W.	L.
Gaylord J. Perry, Clev. (5W)	24	16
Wilbur F. Wood, Chicago (2W)	24	17
Michael S. Lolich, Det. (1E)	22	14
James A. Hunter, Oak. (1W)	21	7
James A. Palmer, Balt. (3E)	21	10
Stanley R. Bahnsen, Chi. (2W)	21	16

1973 (12)	W.	L.
Wilbur F. Wood, Chicago (5W)	24	20
Joseph H. Coleman, Det. (3E)	23	15
James A. Palmer, Balt. (1E)	22	9
James A. Hunter, Oak. (1W)	21	5
Kenneth D. Holtzman, Oakland		
(1W)	21	13
L. Nolan Ryan, Calif. (4W)	21	16

1973 (12) —Cont.

	W.	L.
Vida Blue, Oakland (1W)	20	9
Paul W. Splittorff, K. C. (2W)	20	11
James W. Colborn, Mil. (5E)	20	12
Luis C. Tiant, Boston (2E)	20	13
William R. Singer, Calif. (4W)	20	14
Bert R. Blyleven, Minn. (3W)	20	17

1974 (9)

	W.	L.
James A. Hunter, Oak. (1W)	25	12
Ferguson, A. Jenkins, Tex. (2W)	25	12
Miguel Cuellar, Balt. (1E)	22	10
Luis C. Tiant, Boston (3E)	22	13
Steven L. Busby, K. C. (5W)	22	14
L. Nolan Ryan, Calif. (6W)	22	16
James L. Kaat, Chicago (4W)	21	13
Gaylord J. Perry, Cleve. (4E)	21	13
Wilbur F. Wood, Chi. (4W)	20	19

1975 (5)

	W.	L.
James A. Palmer, Balt. (2E)	23	11
James A. Hunter, N. Y. (3E)	23	14
Vida Blue, Oakland (W1)	22	11
Michael A. Torrez, Balt. (2E)	20	9
James L. Kaat, Chicago (W5)	20	14

1976 (3)

	W.	L.
James A. Palmer, Balt. (2E)	22	13
Luis C. Tiant, Boston (3E)	21	12
Marcus W. Garland, Balt. (2E)	20	7

1977 (3)

	W.	L.
James A. Palmer, Balt. (2TE)	20	11
David A. Goltz, Minn. (4W)	20	11
Dennis P. Leonard, K. C. (1W)	20	12

1978 (6)

	W.	L.
Ronald A. Guidry, N. Y. (1E)	25	3
R. Michael Caldwell, Milw. (3E)	22	9
James A. Palmer, Balt. (4E)	21	12
Dennis P. Leonard, K. C. (1W)	21	17
Dennis L. Eckersley, Bos. (2E)	20	8
Eduardo Figueroa, N. Y. (1E)	20	9

1979 (3)

	W.	L.
Michael K. Flanagan, Balt. (1E)	23	9
Thomas E. John, N. Y. (4E)	21	9
Jerry M. Koosman, Minn. (4W)	20	13

1980 (5)

	W.	L.
Steven M. Stone, Balt. (2E)	25	7
Thomas E. John, N. Y. (1E)	22	9
Michael K. Norris, Oak. (2W)	22	9
Scott H. McGregor, Balt. (2E)	20	8
Dennis P. Leonard, K. C. (1W)	20	11

1981 (0)

1982 (0)

1983 (4)

	W.	L.
D. LaMarr Hoyt, Chi. (1W)	24	10
Richard E. Dotson, Chi. (1W)	22	7
Ronald A. Guidry, N.Y. (3E)	21	9
John S. Morris, Det. (2E)	20	13

20-Game Winners, Two Leagues, One Season, Since 1900

	W.	L.
1902—Joseph J. McGinnity	21	18
13-10 Baltimore A. L. (8)		
8-8 New York N. L. (8)		
1904—Patrick J. Flaherty	21	11
2-2 Chicago A. L. (3)		
19-9 Pittsburgh N. L. (4)		
1945—Henry L. Borowy	21	7
10-5 New York A. L. (4)		
11-2 Chicago N. L. (1)		

AMERICAN ASSOCIATION

1882 (5)

	W.	L.
William White, Cincinnati (1)	40	12
Anthony Mullane, L'isville (2)	30	24
Samuel H. Weaver, Phila. (3)	26	15
George W. McGinnis, St. L. (5)	25	21
Henry H. Salisbury, Pitts. (5)	20	19

1883 (8)

	W.	L.
William H. White, Cin. (3)	43	22
Timothy J. Keefe, N. Y. (4)	41	27
Anthony Mullane, St. L. (2)	35	15
Robert T. Mathews, Phila. (1)	30	14
George W. McGinnis, St. L. (2)	29	15
Guy Hecker, Louisville (5)	28	25
Frank Mountain, Columbus (6)	26	33
Samuel H. Weaver, L'isville (5)	24	20

1884 (12)

	W.	L.
Guy Hecker, Louisville (3)	52	20
John H. Lynch, New York (1)	37	15
Edward Morris, Columbus (2)	35	13
Timothy J. Keefe, N. Y. (1)	37	17
Anthony Mullane, Toledo (8)	35	25
William H. White, Cin. (5)	34	18
Robert D. Emslie, Balt. (6)	32	18
Robert T. Mathews, Phila. (7)	30	18
J. Harding Henderson, Balt. (6)	27	22
George McGinnis, St. Louis (4)	24	16
Frank Mountain, Columbus (2)	24	17
William R. Mountjoy, Cin. (5)	20	12

1885 (9)

	W.	L.
Robert L. Caruthers, St. L. (1)	40	13
Edward Morris, Pittsburgh (3)	39	24
David Foutz, St. Louis (1)	33	14
Henry Porter, Brooklyn (5T)	33	21
Robert T. Mathews, Phila. (4)	30	17
Guy Hecker, Louisville (5T)	30	24
J. Harding Henderson, Balt. (8)	26	35
John H. Lynch, New York (7)	23	21
Lawrence J. McKeon, Cin. (2)	20	13

1886 (11)

	W.	L.
David Foutz, St. Louis (1)	41	16
Edward Morris, Pittsburgh (2)	41	20
Thomas Ramsey, Louisville (4)	37	27
Anthony Mullane, Cin. (5)	31	27
Robert Caruthers, St. Louis (1)	30	14
James Galvin, Pittsburgh (2)	29	21
Matthew Kilroy, Baltimore (8)	29	34
Henry Porter, Brooklyn (3)	28	20
Guy Hecker, Louisville (4)	27	23
Albert Atkisson, Phila. (6)	25	17
John H. Lynch, New York (7)	20	20

1887 (10)

	W.	L.
Matthew Kilroy, Baltimore (3)	46	20
Thomas Ramsey, Louisville (4)	39	27
Charles F. King, St. Louis (1)	34	11
Elmer E. Smith, Cincinnati (2)	33	18
Anthony Mullane, Cin. (2)	31	17

1887 (10)—Cont.	W.	L.
Robert Caruthers, St. L. (1)	29	9
John F. Smith, Baltimore (3)	29	29
August Weyhing, Phila. (5)	26	25
Edward Seward, Phila. (5)	25	24
David Foutz, St. Louis (1)	24	12

1888 (12)	W.	L.
Charles F. King, St. L. (1)	45	21
Edward Seward, Phila (3)	34	19
Robert Caruthers, Brooklyn (2)	29	15
August Weyhing, Phila. (3)	29	19
Elton Chamberlain	25	12
9-8 Louisville (7)		
16-4 St. Louis (1)		
Leon Viau, Cincinnati (4)	27	14
Anthony Mullane, Cin. (4)	26	16
Nathaniel Hudson, St. L. (1)	25	11
Michael Hughes, Brooklyn (2)	25	13
Edward Bakely, Cleveland (6)	25	33
Elmer E. Smith, Cin. (4)	22	17
Ellsworth Cunningham, Ba. (5)	22	29

1889 (11)	W.	L.
Robert Caruthers, Brooklyn (1)	40	12
Elton Chamberlain, St. L. (2)	35	15
Charles F. King, St. L. (2)	33	17
James W. Duryea, Cin. (4)	32	21
August Weyhing, Phila. (3)	28	19
Matthew Kilroy, Baltimore (5)	28	25
Mark Baldwin, Columbus (6)	26	24

1889 (11)—Cont.	W.	L.
Francis Foreman, Balt. (5)	25	21
William Terry, Brooklyn (1)	21	16
Edward Seward, Phila. (3)	21	16
Leon Viau, Cincinnati (4)	21	19

1890 (8)	W.	L.
John McMahon	36	21
29-19 Philadelphia (8)		
7- 2 Baltimore (6)		
Scott Stratton, Louisville (1)	34	13
Henry Gastright, Col. (2)	29	13
John Stivetts, St. Louis (3)	29	20
Robert M. Barr, Rochester (5)	28	25
Thomas Ramsey, St. Louis (3)	26	16
Philip Ehret, Louisville (1)	25	14
John J. Healy, Toledo (4)	22	23

1891 (8)	W.	L.
George S. Haddock, Boston (1)	34	12
John McMahon, Baltimore (3)	34	25
John Stivetts, St. Louis (2)	33	22
August Weyhing, Phila. (4)	31	20
Charles Buffinton, Boston (1)	28	9
Philip H. Knell, Columbus (5)	27	26
Elton Chamberlain, Phila. (4)	23	23
William McGill	22	13
8-8 Cincinnati (5)		
14-5 St. Louis (2)		

UNION ASSOCIATION

1884 (9)	W.	L.
William J. Sweeney, Balt. (3)	40	21
Hugh I. Daly, Chi. 22-25 (6)		
1-1 Washington (5)		
5-4 Pittsburgh (8)	28	30
William H. Taylor, St. L. (1)	25	4
Richard S. Burns, Cin. (2)	25	15
Charles Sweeney, St. L. (1)	24	8
William E. Wise, Wash. (5)	23	20
James McCormick, Cin. (2)	22	4
Fred L. Shaw, Boston (4)	22	15
George Bradley, Cincinnati (2)	21	13

PLAYERS' LEAGUE

1890 (10)	W.	L.
Charles F. King, Chicago (4)	32	22
Mark Baldwin, Chicago (4)	32	24
August Weyhing, Brooklyn (2)	30	14
Charles Radbourn, Boston (1)	27	12
Addison Gumbert, Boston (1)	24	11
Henry O'Day, New York (3)	22	13
Henry Gruber, Cleve. (7)	22	23
Philip H. Knell, Phila. (5)	21	10
Henry Staley, Pittsburgh (6)	21	23
William Daley, Boston (1)	20	8

20-Game Winners, Two Leagues, One Season

	W.	L.
1884—William H. Taylor	43	16
25- 4 St. Louis U. A. (1)		
18-12 Phila. A. A. (7)		
1884—Charles Sweeney	41	15
17-7 Providence N. L. (1)		
24-8 St. Louis U. A. (1)		

	W.	L.
1884—James McCormick	41	26
19-22 Cleveland N. L. (7)		
22- 4 Cincinnati U. A. (2)		
1884—Fred L. Shaw	30	33
8-18 Detroit N. L. (8)		
22-15 Boston U. A. (4)		

Winning Two Complete Games in One Day
NATIONAL LEAGUE

		Innings	Scores	
September 9, 1876	William A. Cummings, Hartford	9—9	14-4	8-4
August 9, 1878	John M. Ward, Providence	9—9	12-6	8-5
July 12, 1879	James F. Galvin, Buffalo	9—12	4-3	5-4
July 4, 1881	Michael F. Welch, Troy	9—9	8-0	12-3
July 4, 1882	James F. Galvin, Buffalo	9—9	9-5	18-8
May 30, 1884	Charles M. Radbourn, Providence	9—9	12-9	9-2
October 7, 1885	Fred L. Shaw, Providence	5—5	4-0	6-1
October 10, 1885	Fred L. Shaw, Providence	6—5	3-0	7-3
October 9, 1886	Charles J. Ferguson, Philadelphia	9—6	5-1	6-1
August 20, 1887	James E. Whitney, Washington	9—9	3-1	4-3
September 12, 1889	John G. Clarkson, Boston	9—9	3-2	5-0
May 30, 1890	William F. Hutchinson, Chicago	9—9	6-4	11-7
October 4, 1890	Denton T. Young, Cleveland	9—9	5-1	7-3
September 12, 1891	Mark E. Baldwin, Pittsburgh	9—9	13-3	8-4

		Innings	Scores	
September 28, 1891	Amos W. Rusie, New York	9—6	10-4	13-5
May 30, 1892	Mark E. Baldwin, Pittsburgh	9—9	11-1	4-3
October 4, 1892	Amos W. Rusie, New York	9—9	6-4	9-5
June 3, 1897	J. Bentley Seymour, New York	9—7	6-1	10-6
August 1, 1903	Joseph J. McGinnity, New York	9—9	4-1	5-2
August 8, 1903	Joseph J. McGinnity, New York	9—9	6-1	4-3
August 31, 1903	Joseph J. McGinnity, New York	9—9	4-1	9-2
October 3, 1905	William D. Scanlon, Brooklyn	9—9	4-0	3-2
September 26, 1908	Edward M. Reulbach, Chicago	9—9	5-0	3-0
September 9, 1916	William D. Perritt, New York	9—9	3-1	3-0
September 20, 1916	Albert W. Demaree, Philadelphia	9—9	7-0	3-2
September 23, 1916	Grover C. Alexander, Philadelphia	9—9	7-3	4-0
July 1, 1917	Fred A. Toney, Cincinnati	9—9	4-1	5-1
September 3, 1917	Grover C. Alexander, Philadelphia	9—9	5-0	9-3
September 18, 1917	William H. Doak, St. Louis	9—9	2-0	12-4
August 13, 1921	John R. Watson, Boston	9—9	4-3	8-0
July 10, 1923	John D. Stuart, St. Louis	9—9	11-1	6-3
July 19, 1924	Herman S. Bell, St. Louis	9—9	6-1	2-1

AMERICAN LEAGUE

		Innings	Scores	
July 1, 1905	Frank M. Owen, Chicago	9—9	3-2	2-0
September 26, 1905	Edward A. Walsh, Chicago	9—8	10-5	3-1
September 22, 1906	George E. Mullin, Detroit	9—9	5-3	4-3
September 25, 1908	Oren E. Summers, Detroit	9—10	7-2	1-0
September 29, 1908	Edward A. Walsh, Chicago	9—9	5-1	2-0
September 22, 1914	Ray W. Collins, Boston	9—8	5-3	5-0
July 29, 1916	Arthur D. Davenport, St. Louis	9—9	3-1	3-2
August 30, 1918	Carl W. Mays, Boston	9—9	12-0	4-1
September 6, 1924	Urban J. Shocker, St. Louis	9—9	6-2	6-2
August 28, 1926	Emil H. Levsen, Cleveland	9—9	6-1	5-1

AMERICAN ASSOCIATION

		Innings	Scores	
July 4, 1883	Timothy J. Keefe, New York	9—9	9-1	3-0
July 4, 1884	Guy J. Hecker, Louisville	9—9	5-4	8-2
July 26, 1887	Matthew A. Kilroy, Baltimore	7—9	8-0	9-1
October 1, 1887	Matthew A. Kilroy, Baltimore	9—7	5-2	8-1
September 20, 1888	Anthony J. Mullane, Cincinnati	9—9	1-0	2-1

PLAYERS' LEAGUE

		Innings	Scores	
July 26, 1890	Henry Gruber, Cleveland	9—9	6-1	8-7
August 20, 1890	Ellsworth E. Cunningham, Buffalo	9—9	6-2	7-0
September 27, 1890	Edward N. Crane, New York	9—9	9-8	8-3

Consecutive Games Won, Season (12 or more)
National League

Year—Pitcher	Won	Year—Pitcher	Won
1888—Timothy Keefe, New York	19	1880—Lawrence Corcoran, Chi.	13
1912—Richard Marquard, N. Y.	19	1884—Charles Buffinton, Boston	13
1884—Charles Radbourn, Provi.	18	1892—Denton Young, Cleveland	13
1885—Michael Welch, New York	17	1896—Frank Dwyer, Cincinnati	13
1890—John Luby, Chicago	17	1909—Chris. Mathewson, N. Y.	13
1959—El Roy Face, Pittsburgh	17	1910—Charles Phillippe, Pitts.	13
1886—James McCormick, Chi.	16	1927—Burleigh Grimes, New York	13
1936—Carl Hubbell, New York	16	1956—Brooks Lawrence, Cinn.	13
1947—Ewell Blackwell, Cinn.	16	1966—Philip Regan, Los Angeles	13
1962—John S. Sanford, San Fran.	16	1971—Dock P. Ellis, Pittsburgh	13
1924—Arthur Vance, Brooklyn	15	1885—John Clarkson, Chicago.	13
1968—Robert Gibson, St. Louis	15	1886—Charles Ferguson, Phila.	12
1972—Steven N. Carlton, Phila.	15	1902—John Chesbro, Pittsburgh	12
1885—James McCormick, Chicago	14	1904—George Wiltse, New York	12
1886—John Flynn, Chicago	14	1906—Edward Reulbach, Chicago	12
1904—Joseph McGinnity, N. Y.	14	1914—Richard Rudolph, Boston	12
1909—Edward Reulbach, Chicago	14	1975—Burt C. Hooton, Los Angeles	12

Consecutive Games Won, Season (12 or More)—Continued
American League

Year—Pitcher	Won	Year—Pitcher	Won
1912—Walter Johnson, Wash.	16	1949—Ellis Kinder, Bos.	13
1912—Joseph Wood, Bos.	16	1971—David A. McNally, Baltimore	13
1931—Robert Grove, Phila.	16	1973—James A. Hunter, Oakland	13
1934—Lynwood Rowe, Det.	16	1978—Ronald A. Guidry, N.Y.	13
1932—Alvin Crowder, Wash.	15	1983—D. LaMarr Hoyt, Chicago	13
1937—John Allen, Cleve.	15	1901—Denton Young, Bos.	12
1969—David A. McNally, Balt.	15	1910—Russell Ford, N. Y.	12
1974—Gaylord J. Perry, Cleveland	15	1914—Hubert Leonard, Boston	12
1904—John Chesbro, N. Y.	14	1929—Jonathan Zachary, N. Y.	12
1913—Walter Johnson, Wash.	14	1931—George L. Earnshaw, Phila.	12
1914—Charles Bender, Phila.	14	1938—John Allen, Cleve.	12
1928—Robert Grove, Phila.	14	1939—Atley Donald, N. Y.	12
1961—Edward C. Ford, N. Y.	14	1946—David Ferriss, Bos.	12
1980—Steven M. Stone, Balt.	14	1961—Luis Arroyo, New York	12
1924—Walter Johnson, Wash.	13	1963—Edward C. Ford, N. Y.	12
1925—Stanley Coveleski, Wash.	13	1968—David A. McNally, Baltimore	12
1930—Wesley Ferrell, Cleve.	13	1971—Patrick E. Dobson, Baltimore	12
1940—Louis Newsom, Det.	13		

American Association

Year—Pitcher	Won
1890—Scott Stratton, St. Louis.	15
1884—John H. Lynch, New York	14
1882—William White, Cinn.	12

Union Association

Year—Pitcher	Won
1884—James McCormick, Cinn.	14

Consecutive Games Lost, Season (12 or more)
National League

Year—Pitcher	Lost	Year—Pitcher	Lost
1910—Clifton Curtis, Bos	18	1948—Robert McCall, Chi.	13
1963—Roger L. Craig, N. Y.	18	1880—William Purcell, Cinn.	12
1876—Henry Dean, Cinn.	16	1883—John Coleman, Phila.	12
1899—James Hughey, Cleve.	16	1902—Henry Thielman, Cinn.	12
1962—N. Craig Anderson, N. Y.	16	1905—Malcolm Eason, Brook.	12
1887—Frank Gilmore, Wash.	14	1914—Richard Marquard, N. Y.	12
1899—Fred Bates, Cleve.	14	1914—Peter Schneider, Cinn.	12
1908—James Pastorius, Brook	14	1928—Russell Miller, Phila.	12
1911—Charles Brown, Bos.	14	1933—Silas Johnson, Cinn.	12
1884—L. R. Moffatt, Cleve.	13	1939—A. Butcher, Phila.-Pitts.	12
1917—Burleigh Grimes, Pitts.	13	1940—Hugh Mulcahy, Phila.	12
1922—Joseph Oeschger, Bos	13	1962—Robert L. Miller, N. Y.	12
1935—Benjamin Cantwell, Bos	13	1972—Kenneth L. Reynolds, Phila.	12

American League

Year—Pitcher	Lost	Year—Pitcher	Lost
1909—Robert Groom, Washington	19	1930—Frank Henry, Chi.	13
1916—John Nabors, Phila.	19	1943—Luman Harris, Phila.	13
1980—Michael E. A. Parrott, Seattle	16	1982—Terry L. Felton, Minn.	13
1906—Joseph W. Harris, Boston	14	1929—Charles Ruffing, Bos.	12
1949—Howard Judson, Chi.	14	1940—Walter Masterson, Wash.	12
1949—L. Paul Calvert, Wash.	14	1945—Louis Newsom, Phila.	12
1979—Matthew L. Keough, Oakland	14	1945—Stephen Gerkin, Phila.	12
1914—Guy Morton, Cleve.	13	1953—Charles T. Bishop, Phila.	12
1920—Roy D. Moore, Phila.	13		

American Association

Year—Pitcher	Lost	Year—Pitcher	Lost
1882—Frederick Nichols, Balt.	12	1889—William Crowell, Cleve.	12

Highest Percentage Games Won, League, 200 or More Decisions

A. L.—.690—Edward C. Ford, New York, 16 years, 1950 through 1967, (except 1951, 1952, in military service). Won 236, lost 106.

N. L.—.665—Christopher Mathewson, New York, Cincinnati, 17 years, 1900 through 1916. Won 373, lost 188.

Highest Percentage Games Won, Season, 70 or More Decisions

N. L.—.833—Charles Radbourn, Providence, 1884; won 60, lost 12.

Highest Percentage Games Won, Season, 34 or More Decisions

A. L.—.886—Robert M. Grove, Philadelphia, 1931; won 31, lost 4.
N. L.—.824—John D. Chesbro, Pittsburgh, 1902; won 28, lost 6.
          Arthur C. Vance, Brooklyn, 1924; won 28, lost 6.

Highest Percentage Games Won, Season, 16 or More Decisions

N. L.—.947—El Roy Face, Pittsburgh, 1959; won 18, lost 1.
A. L.—.938—John T. Allen, Cleveland, 1937; won 15, lost 1.

Highest Percentage Games Won, Season, 20 or More Victories

A. L.—.893—Ronald A. Guidry, New York, 1978; won 25, lost 3.
N. L.— 880— Fred E. Goldsmith, Chicago, 1880; won 22, lost 3.
          Elwin C. Roe, Brooklyn, 1951; won 22, lost 3.

Most Years Leading in Highest Percentage Games Won, 15 or More Victories

A. L.—5—Robert M. Grove, Philadelphia, Boston, 1929, 1930, 1931, 1933, 1939.
N. L.—3—Edward M. Reulbach, Chicago, 1906, 1907, 1908.

Most Saves, Major Leagues (Since 1969)

301—Roland G. Fingers, Oakland A. L., San Diego N. L., Milwaukee A.L.; 15 years, 1968
    through 1982; saved 193 in A. L., saved 108 in N. L.

Most Saves, League (Since 1969)

A. L.— 216— Albert W. Lyle, Boston, New York, Texas, Chicago, 13 years, 1969 through
          1982, except 1981.
N. L.— 215— H. Bruce Sutter, Chicago, St. Louis, 8 years, 1976 through 1983.

Most Saves, Season (Since 1969)

A. L.—45—Daniel R. Quisenberry, Kansas City; 69 games in relief, finished 62.
N. L.—37—Clay P. Carroll, Cincinnati, 1972; 65 games in relief, finished 54.
        Roland G. Fingers, San Diego, 1978; 67 games in relief, finished 62.
        H. Bruce Sutter, Chicago, 1979; 62 games in relief, finished 56.

Most Games Lost in Major Leagues

313—Denton T. Young, Cleveland, N. L., St. Louis, N. L., Boston, A. L., Cleveland, A. L.,
    Boston, N. L.; 22 years, 1890-1911; lost 172 in N. L., lost 141 in A. L.

Most Games Lost, League, Righthander

A. L.— 279— Walter P. Johnson, Washington, 21 years, 1907 through 1927.
N. L.— 268— James F. Galvin, Buffalo, Pittsburgh, St. Louis, 12 years, 1879 through
          1892, except 1886 and 1890.
N. L. since 1900—226—Robert B. Friend, Pittsburgh, New York, 16 years, 1951 through
    1966.

Most Games Lost, League, Lefthander

N. L.— 251— Eppa Rixey, Philadelphia, Cincinnati, 21 years, 1912 through 1933, (except
          1918, in military service).
A. L.— 191— James L. Kaat, Washington, Minnesota, Chicago, New York, 19 years,
          1959 through 1975, 1979 through 1980.

Most Games Lost, Season

N. L.—48—John H. Coleman, Philadelphia, 1883 (won 11, lost 48, .186).
N. L. since 1900—29—Victor G. Willis, Boston, 1905 (won 12, lost 29, .293).
A. L.—26—John Townsend, Washington, 1904 (won 5, lost 26, .161).
        Robert B. Groom, Washington, 1909 (won 6, lost 26, .188).

Fewest Games Lost, Season, for Leader in Most Games Lost

A. L.—14—Theodore G. Gray, Detroit, 1951; won 7, lost 14.
        Alexander R. Kellner, Philadelphia, 1951; won 11, lost 14.
        Robert G. Lemon, Cleveland 1951; won 17 lost 14.
        W. William Pierce, Chicago, 1951; won 15, lost 14.
        Duane X. Pillette, St. Louis, 1951; won 6, lost 14.
        Paul H. Trout, Detroit, 1951; won 9, lost 14.
N. L.—16—Ronald L. Kline, Pittsburgh, 1958; won 13, lost 16.

Most Games Lost, Season, All as Relief Pitcher

N. L.—16—H. Eugene Garber, Atlanta, 1979 (won 6, lost 16—.273).
A. L.—14—Darold D. Knowles, Washington, 1970 (won 2, lost 14—.125).
        John F. Hiller, Detroit, 1974 (won 17, lost 14—.548).
        Michael G. Marshall, Minnesota, 1979 (won 10, lost 14—.417, also lost 1 game
        as starter).

Most Games Lost, Rookie Season

N. L.—34—James A. Devlin, Louisville, 1876 (won 30, lost 34, .469).
         Robert T. Mathews, New York, 1876 (won 21, lost 34, .382).
A. L.—26—Robert B. Groom, Washington, 1909 (won 6, lost 26, .188).
N. L. since 1900—25—Harry McIntire, Brooklyn, 1906 (won 8, lost 25, .242).

Most Years Leading League in Games Lost

A. L.—4—Louis N. Newsom, St. Louis, Washington, Detroit, Philadelphia 1934, 1935,
         1941, 1945.
         Pedro Ramos, Washington, Minnesota, 1958, 1959, 1960, 1961.
N. L.—4—Philip H. Niekro, Atlanta, 1977 (tied), 1978, 1979, 1980.

Most Consecutive Games Lost, League

N. L.—23—Clifton G. Curtis, Boston, June 13, 1910, first game, through May 22, 1911; 18
         in 1910, 5 in 1911.
A. L.—19—Robert Groom, Washington, June 19, first game through September 25, 1909.
         John H. Nabors, Philadelphia, April 28 through September 28, 1916.

Most Consecutive Games Lost, Season

A. L.—19—Robert Groom, Washington, June 19, first game, through September 25,
         1909.
         John H. Nabors, Philadelphia, April 28 through September 28, 1916.
N. L.—18—Clifton G. Curtis, Boston, June 13, first game, through September 20, first
         game, 1910.
         Roger L. Craig, New York, May 4 through August 4, 1963.

Most Consecutive Games Lost, Rookie Season

A. L.—19—Robert Groom, Washington, June 19, first game, through September 25,
         1909.
N. L.—16—Henry Dean, Cincinnati, July 11 through September 12, 1876.
N. L. since 1900—12—Henry Thielman, Cincinnati, June 29 through September 1, morn-
         ing game, 1902.
         Peter J. Schneider, Cincinnati, July 20 through September 26, first game,
         1914.

Most Consecutive Games Lost, Start of Career

A. L.—16—Terry L. Felton, Minnesota, April 18, 1980, second game, through September
         12, 1982.
A. A.—10—Charles Stecher, Philadelphia, September 6, through October 9, 1890.

Most Consecutive Games Lost, Start of Season

A. L.—14—Joseph W. Harris, Boston, May 10 through July 25, 1906.
         Matthew L. Keough, Oakland, April 15 through August 8, 1979.
N. L.—12—Russell L. Miller, Philadelphia, May 12 through August 12, 1928.
         Robert Lane Miller, New York, April 21 through September 10, 1962.
         Kenneth L. Reynolds, Philadelphia, May 29, second game, through August
         25, 1972.

Most Consecutive Games Lost, End of Season

A. L.—19—John Nabors, Philadelphia, April 28 through September 28, 1916.
N. L.—18—Clifton G. Curtis, Boston, June 13, first game, through September 20, 1910,
         first game.

Most Games Lost, Season to One Club, Since 1900

N. L.—7—Held by 7 pitchers.
         Last Time—Calvin C. McLish, Cincinnati vs. Pittsburgh, 1960 (won 0, lost 7).
A. L.—7—Held by 4 pitchers.
         Last Time—Camilo A. Pascual, Washington vs. New York, 1956 (won 0, lost
         7).

Most Consecutive Games Lost, League to One Club

N. L.—13—Donald H. Sutton, Los Angeles vs. Chicago, April 23, 1966 through July 24,
         1969 (start of career).
A. L.—10—David M. Morehead, Boston vs. Los Angeles, July 28, 1963 through Septem-
         ber 28, 1965 (start of career).

Most At-Bats, Game

N. L.—66—George H. Derby, Buffalo, July 3, 1883.
A. L.—53—Roy Patterson, Chicago, May 5, 1901.
N. L. since 1900—49—Harley Parker, Cincinnati, June 21, 1901.
         William C. Phillips, Cincinnati, June 24, 1901, second game.

Most Men Facing Pitcher, Nine-Inning Game

N. L.—67—George H. Derby, Buffalo, July 3, 1883.

A. L.—57—Roy Patterson, Chicago, May 5, 1901.
N. L. since 1900—53—William C. Phillips, Cincinnati, June 24, 1901, second game.

Most Men Facing Pitcher, Inning

N. L.—22—Anthony J. Mullane, Baltimore, June 18, 1894, a.m. game, first inning.
N. L. since 1900—16—Harold Kelleher, Philadelphia, May 5, 1938, eighth inning.
A. L.—16—Merle T. Adkins, Boston, July 8, 1902, sixth inning.
      Frank J. O'Doul, Boston, July 7, 1923, first game, sixth inning.
      Howard J. Ehmke, Boston, September 28, 1923, sixth inning

Most At-Bats, Season

N. L.—2808— William H. White, Cincinnati, 75 games, 1879; 683 innings.
A. L.—1690— Edward A. Walsh, Chicago, 66 games, 1908; 464 innings.
N. L. since 1900—1658—Joseph J. McGinnity, New York, 55 games, 1903; 434 innings.

Most At-Bats, League

A. L.—21,663—Walter P. Johnson, Washington, 21 years, 1907 through 1927.
N. L.—19,778—Warren E. Spahn, Boston, Milwaukee, New York, San Francisco, 21 years, 1942 through 1965, (except 1943, 1944, 1945 in military service).

Most Years Leading League in Most At-Bats

N. L.—6—Grover C. Alexander, Philadelphia, Chicago, 1911, 1914, 1915, 1916, 1917, 1920.
A. L.—4—Edward A. Walsh, Chicago, 1908, 1910, 1911, 1912.
      Walter P. Johnson, Washington, 1913, 1914, 1915, 1916.
      Robert G. Lemon, Cleveland, 1948, 1950, 1952, 1953.

Most Consecutive Years Leading League in Most At-Bats

A. L.—4—Walter P. Johnson, Washington, 1913, 1914, 1915, 1916.
N. L.—4—Grover C. Alexander, Philadelphia, 1914, 1915, 1916, 1917.
      Robin E. Roberts, Philadelphia, 1952, 1953, 1954, 1955.

Fewest Official At-Bats, Season, for Leader in Most At-Bats

A. L.— 942— James P. Bunning, Detroit, 250 innings, 1959.
N. L.— 1009— George B. Koslo, New York, 265 innings, 1946.

Most Runs Allowed, Season

N. L.— 544— John Coleman, Philadelphia, 63 games, 538 innings, 1883.
A. L.— 219— Joseph J. McGinnity, Baltimore, 48 games, 378 innings, 1901.
N. L. since 1900—224—William M. Carrick, New York, 45 games, 342 innings, 1900.

Most Runs Allowed, League

A. L.— 2117— Charles H. Ruffing, Boston, New York, Chicago, 1924 through 1947, except 1943, 1944, 22 years.
N. L.— 2037— Burleigh A. Grimes, Pittsburgh, Brooklyn, New York, Boston, St. Louis, Chicago, 1916 through 1934, 19 years.

Fewest Runs, Season, for Leader in Most Runs Allowed

N. L.— 102— George A. Smith, New York, Philadelphia, 196 innings, 1919.
A. L.— 108— James C. Bagby, Cleveland, 280 innings, 1918.

Most Runs Allowed, Inning

N. L.—16—Anthony J. Mullane, Baltimore, June 18, 1894, a.m. game, first inning.
A. L.—13—Frank J. O'Doul, Boston, July 7, 1923, first game, sixth inning.
N. L. since 1900—12—Harold Kelleher, Philadelphia, May 5, 1938, eighth inning.

Most Runs Allowed, Game

N. L.—35—David E. Rowe, Cleveland, July 24, 1882.
A. L.—24—Aloysius J. Travers, Detroit, May 18, 1912.
N. L. since 1900—21—Harley Parker, Cincinnati, June 21, 1901.

Fewest Runs Allowed, Doubleheader

N. L.—0—Edward M. Reulbach, Chicago, September 26, 1908.
A. L.—1—Edward A. Walsh, Chicago, September 29, 1908.
      Carl W. Mays, Boston, August 30, 1918.

Most Years Leading League in Most Runs Allowed

N. L.—3—Burleigh A. Grimes, Brooklyn, Pittsburgh, 1923, 1924, 1928.
      Robin E. Roberts, Philadelphia, 1955, 1956, 1957.
      Philip H. Niekro, Atlanta, 1977, 1978, 1979.
A. L.—3—Wilbur F. Wood, Chicago, 1972, 1973, 1975.

Most Earned Runs, Allowed Season, Since 1900

A. L.— 186— Louis N. Newsom, St. Louis, 330 innings, 1938.
N. L.— 155— Guy T. Bush, Chicago, 225 innings, 1930.

Fewest Earned Runs, Season, for Leader in Most Earned Runs Allowed

A. L.—83—William Adams, Philadelphia, 169 innings, 1918
George Dauss, Detroit, 250 innings, 1918.
N. L.—85—Peter J. Schneider, Cincinnati, 217 innings, 1918.
Arthur N. Nehf, Boston, 284 innings, 1918.
A. Wilbur Cooper, Pittsburgh, 287 innings, 1919.

Most Years Leading League in Most Earned Runs Allowed

N. L.—3—Burleigh A. Grimes, Brooklyn, 1922, 1924, 1925.
Murry M. Dickson, St. Louis, Pittsburgh, 1948, 1951, 1952 (tied).
Robin E. Roberts, Philadelphia, 1955, 1956, 1957.
John H. Fisher, New York, 1964 (tied), 1965 (tied), 1967
A. L.—3—Louis N. Newsom, St. Louis, Washington, Philadelphia, 1938, 1942, 1945.
Wilbur F. Wood, Chicago, 1972, 1973, 1975.

Lowest Earned-Run Average, League, 300 or More Games Won

A. L.—2.47—Walter P. Johnson, Washington, 802 games, 21 years, 1907 through 1927
(See notation on Page 58), righthander.
3.06—Robert M. Grove, Philadelphia, Boston, 616 games, 17 years, 1925 through
1941, lefthander.
N. L.—2.56—Grover C. Alexander, Philadelphia, Chicago, St. Louis, 696 games, 20
years, 1911 through 1930. (See notation on Page 58) righthander.

Lowest Earned-Run Average, League, 200 or More Games Won

A. L.—2.47—Walter P. Johnson, Washington, 802 games, 21 years, 1907 through 1927
(See notation on Page 58), righthander.
2.74—Edwin C. Ford, New York, 498 games, 16 years, 1950 through 1967 (except
1951, 1952 in military service), lefthander.
N. L.—2.56—Grover C. Alexander, Philadelphia, Chicago, St. Louis, 696 games, 20
years, 1911 through 1930 (See notation on Page 58), righthander.
2.73—G. Thomas Seaver, New York, Cincinnati, 559 games, 17 years, 1967
through 1983, righthander.

Lowest Earned-Run Average, League, 2000 or More Innings

N. L.—2.33—James L. Vaughn, Chicago, 2,217 innings, 305 games, 9 years, 1913 through
1921, lefthander.
A. L.—2.47—Walter P. Johnson, Washington, 5,924 innings, 802 games, 21 years, 1907
through 1927 (See notation on Page 58), righthander.
2.74—Edwin C. Ford, New York, 3,171 innings, 498 games, 16 years, 1950
through 1967 (except 1951, 1952 in military service), lefthander.

Lowest Earned-Run Average, 200 or More Innings, Season

A. L.—1.00—Hubert B. Leonard, Boston, 225 innings, 1914.
N. L.—1.12—Robert Gibson, St. Louis, 305 innings, 1968.

Lowest Earned-Run Average, 300 or More Innings, Season

N. L.—1.12—Robert Gibson, St. Louis, 305 innings, 1968.
A. L.—1.14—Walter P. Johnson, Washington, 346 innings, 1913.

Lowest Earned-Run Average, Season, 300 or More Innings, Righthanded Pitcher

N. L.—1.12—Robert Gibson, St. Louis, 305 innings, 1968.
A. L.—1.14—Walter P. Johnson, Washington, 346 innings, 1913.

Lowest Earned-Run Average, Season, 300 or More Innings, Lefthanded Pitcher

N. L.—1.66—Carl O. Hubbell, New York, 309 innings, 1933.
A. L.—1.75—George H. Ruth, Boston, 324 innings, 1916.

Most Years Leading League in Lowest Earned-Run Average

A. L.—9—Robert M. Grove, Philadelphia, Boston, 1926, 1929, 1930, 1931, 1932, 1935,
1936, 1938, 1939.
N. L.—5—Grover C. Alexander, Philadelphia, Chicago, 1915, 1916, 1917, 1919, 1920.
Sanford Koufax, Los Angeles, 1962, 1963, 1964, 1965, 1966.

Most Consecutive Years Leading League in Lowest Earned-Run Average

N. L.—5—Sanford Koufax, Los Angeles, 1962, 1963, 1964, 1965, 1966.
A. L.—4—Robert M. Grove, Philadelphia, 1929, 1930, 1931, 1932.

Highest Earned-Run Average, Season, for Leader in Earned-Run Average

A. L.—3.20—Early Wynn, Cleveland, 214 innings, 1950.
N. L.—3.08—William H. Walker, New York, 178 innings, 1929.

Most Consecutive Scoreless Innings, Game

N. L.—21—Joseph Oeschger, Boston, May 1, 1920; 6th through 26th inning.
A. L.—20—Joseph Harris, Boston, September 1, 1906; 4th through 23rd inning.

Most Consecutive Scoreless Innings, Season, Righthanded Pitcher

N. L.— 58 — Donald S. Drysdale, Los Angeles, from first inning, May 14 through fourth inning, June 8, 1968.
A. L.—55⅔—Walter P. Johnson, Washington, from second inning, April 10 through third inning, May 14, 1913 (includes 2 relief appearances).

Most Consecutive Scoreless Innings, Season, Lefthanded Pitcher

N. L.—45⅓—Carl O. Hubbell, New York, from seventh inning, July 13 through fifth inning, August 1, 1933 (includes 2 relief appearances).
A. L.— 45 — G. Harris White, Chicago, September 12 through September 30, 1904.

Most Consecutive Scoreless Innings, Start of Career

N. L.—25—George W. McQuillan, Philadelphia, from first inning, May 8, through ninth inning, September 29, first game, 1907.
A. L.—22—David M. Ferriss, Boston, from first inning, April 29, through fourth inning, May 13, 1945.

Pitching Longest Shutout Game

N. L.—18 innings— John M. Ward, Providence, August 17, 1882, won 1-0.
         Carl O. Hubbell, New York, July 2, 1933, first game, won 1-0.
A. L.—18 innings— O. Edgar Summers, Detroit, July 16, 1909, tie 0-0.
         Walter P. Johnson, Washington, May 15, 1918, won 1-0.

Pitching Longest No-Hit Complete Game

A. A.—10 innings— Samuel J. Kimber, Brooklyn, vs. Toledo, October 4, 1884.
N. L.—10 innings— George L. Wiltse, New York vs. Philadelphia, July 4, 1908, a.m. game.
         Frederick A. Toney, Cincinnati vs. Chicago, May 2, 1917.
         James W. Maloney, Cincinnati vs. Chicago, August 19, 1965, first game.
A. L.— 9 innings— Held by many pitchers

Pitching Longest One-Hit Complete Game

N. L.—12⅔ innings—Harvey Haddix, Pittsburgh vs. Milwaukee, May 26, 1959, one double.
A. L.—10   innings—G. Harris White, Chicago vs. Cleveland, September 6, 1903, one double.
         Louis N. Newsom, St. Louis vs. Boston, September 18, 1934, one single.
         Rikalbert Blyleven, Texas vs. Oakland, June 21, 1976, one single.

Most Shutout Games Won or Tied, Season, Righthanded Pitcher

N. L.—16—George W. Bradley, St. Louis, 1876.
         Grover C. Alexander, Philadelphia, 1916.
A. L.—13—John W. Coombs, Philadelphia, 1910.

Most Shutout Games Won or Tied, Season, Lefthanded Pitcher

A. A.—12—Edward Morris, Pittsburgh, 1886.
N. L.—11—Sanford Koufax, Los Angeles, 1963.
A. L.— 9—George H. Ruth, Boston, 1916.
         Ronald A. Guidry, New York, 1978.

Most Shutout Games Won or Tied, League, Righthanded Pitcher

A. L.—110— Walter P. Johnson, Washington, 21 years, 1907 through 1927.
N. L.— 90— Grover C. Alexander, Philadelphia, Chicago, St. Louis, 20 years, 1911 through 1930.

Most Shutout Games Won or Tied, League, Lefthanded Pitcher

A. L.—64—Edward S. Plank, Philadelphia, St. Louis, 16 years, 1901 through 1917, except 1915.
N. L.—63—Warren E. Spahn, Boston, Milwaukee, New York, San Francisco, 21 years, 1942 through 1965 (except 1943, 1944, 1945, in military service).

Most Shutout Games Participated in, Season

N. L.—20—Grover C. Alexander, Philadelphia, 1916 (won 16, lost 4).
A. L.—18—Edward A. Walsh, Chicago, 1908 (won 12, lost 6).

Most Shutout Games Won or Tied, One Month

A. L.—6—G. Harris White, Chicago, September, 1904.
         Edward A. Walsh, Chicago, August, 1906, September, 1908.
N. L.—5—George W. Bradley, St. Louis, May, 1876.
         Thomas H. Bond, Hartford, June, 1876.
         James F. Galvin, Buffalo, August, 1884.
         A. Ben Sanders, Philadelphia, September, 1888.

Most Shutout Games Won or Tied, One Month—Continued

> Donald S. Drysdale, Los Angeles, May, 1968.
> Robert Gibson, St. Louis, June, 1968.

Most Years Leading League in Shutout Games Won or Tied

> N. L.—7—Grover C. Alexander, Philadelphia, Chicago, 1911 (tied), 1913, 1915, 1916, 1917, 1919, 1921 (tied).
> A. L.—7—Walter P. Johnson, Washington, 1911 (tied), 1913, 1914, 1915, 1918 (tied), 1919, 1924.

Most Shutout Games Won or Tied, Rookie Season

> N. L.—16—George W. Bradley, St. Louis, 1876.
> N. L. since 1900—8—Fernando Valenzuela, Los Angeles, 1981.
> A. L.— 8—Russell W. Ford, New York, 1910.
> Ewell A. Russell, Chicago, 1913.

Most Shutout Games Won, League, From One Club

> A. L.—23—Walter P. Johnson, Washington, vs. Philadelphia, 21 years, 1907 through 1927.
> N. L.—20—Grover C. Alexander, Philadelphia, Chicago, St. Louis, vs. Cincinnati, 20 years, 1911 through 1930.

Most Shutout Games Won, Season, From One Club

> N. L.—(8-club league)—5—Charles B. Baldwin, Detroit vs. Philadelphia, 1886.
> Grover C. Alexander, Philadelphia vs. Cincinnati, 1916.
> A. A.—(8-club league)—5—Anthony J. Mullane, Cincinnati vs. New York, 1887.
> A. L.—(8-club league)—5—Thomas J. Hughes, Washington vs. Cleveland, 1905.
> A. L.—(10-club league)—4—William C. Monbouquette, Boston vs. Washington, 1964.
> N. L.—(10-club league)—5—Larry E. Jaster, St. Louis vs. Los Angeles, 1966, consecutive.
> A. L.—(12-club league)—4—Melvin L. Stottlemyre, New York vs. California, 1972, consecutive.

Most Shutouts Won or Tied, Opening Games of Season

> A. L.—7—Walter P. Johnson, 1910 to 1926.
> N. L.—3—Truett B. Sewell, Pittsburgh, 1943, 1947, 1949.
> Christopher J. Short, Philadelphia, 1965, 1968, 1970.

Most Years 10 or More Shutouts, Won or Tied

> A. L.—2—Edward A. Walsh, Chicago, 1906, 1908.
> Walter P. Johnson, Washington, 1913, 1914.
> N. L.—2—Grover C. Alexander, Philadelphia, 1915, 1916.

Most Clubs Shut Out (Won or Tied), One Season

> N. L.—(10-club league)—8—Robert Gibson, St. Louis, 1968 (all clubs except Los Angeles).
> N. L.—(8-club league)—7—James Galvin, Buffalo, 1884.
> Christopher Mathewson, New York, 1907.
> Grover C. Alexander, Philadelphia, 1913 and 1916; also with Chicago, 1919.
> A. L.—(12-club league)—8—L. Nolan Ryan, California, 1972 (all clubs, except Kansas City, New York, Oakland).
> A. L.—(8-club league)—7—Denton T. Young, Boston, 1904.
> John W. Coombs, Philadelphia, 1910.

Most 1-0 Games Won, League

> A. L.—38—Walter P. Johnson, Washington, 21 years, 1907 through 1927.
> N. L.—17—Grover C. Alexander, Philadelphia, Chicago, St. Louis, 20 years, 1911 through 1930.

Most 1-0 Complete Games Won, Season

> A. L.—5—Ewell A. Russell, Chicago, 1913.
> Walter P. Johnson, Washington, 1913, 1919.
> Leslie A. Bush, Boston, 1918.
> W. Dean Chance, Los Angeles, 1964 (also 1 incomplete).
> N. L.—5—Carl O. Hubbell, New York, 1933.

Most Years Leading League in 1-0 Games Won

> A. L.—8—Walter P. Johnson, Washington, 1913 (tied), 1914, 1915 (tied), 1919, 1920 (tied), 1922, 1923 (tied), 1926 (tied).
> N. L.—4—Grover C. Alexander, Philadelphia, Chicago, 1913 (tied), 1916 (tied), 1917 (tied), 1922 (tied).
> William C. Lee, Chicago, Philadelphia, Boston, 1934 (tied), 1936, 1944 (tied), 1945 (tied).

Most 1-0 Games Won, Season, From One Club

A. L.—3—Stanley Coveleski, Cleveland vs. Detroit, 1917.
Walter P. Johnson, Washington vs. Philadelphia, 1919.
James C. Bagby, Jr., Cleveland vs. Detroit, 1943.
N. L.—2—Held by many pitchers.

Fewest Shutout Games Pitched, Season, for Leader in Most Shutouts (Won or Tied)

N. L.—3—Held by eight pitchers in 1921.
A. L.—3—Held by three pitchers in 1930.

Shutout, First Major League Game, Nine Innings

N. L.—Held by 34 pitchers; Last pitcher—Harry R. Rasmussen, St. Louis, July 21, 1975.
A. L.—Held by 35 pitchers; Last pitcher—Michael K. Norris, Oakland, April 10, 1975.

Most Shutouts, First Two Major League Games

N. L.—2—Albert G. Spalding, Chicago, April 25, 27, 1876.
John M. Ward, Providence, July 18, 20, 1878.
James Hughes, Baltimore, April 18, 22, 1898.
Allan F. Worthington, New York, July 6, 11, 1953.
Karl B. Spooner, Brooklyn, September 22, 26, 1954.

A. L.—2—Joseph Doyle, New York, August 25, first game, August 30, first game, 1906.
John A. Marcum, Philadelphia, September 7, September 11, second game, 1933.
David M. Ferriss, Boston, April 29, first game, May 6, first game, 1945.
Thomas H. Phoebus, Baltimore, September 15, first game, September 20, 1966.

Most Shutouts Won or Tied, Four Consecutive Days

A. L.—3—James H. Dygert, Philadelphia, October 1, 3, 4, second game, 1907.
Walter P. Johnson, Washington, September 4, 5, 7, first game, 1908.
N. L.—2—Held by many pitchers.

Most Shutouts Won or Tied, Five Consecutive Days

N. L.—3—George W. Bradley, St. Louis, July 11, 13, 15, 1876.
John G. Clarkson, Chicago, May 21, 22, 25, 1885.

Most Consecutive Shutout Games Won or Tied, Season

N. L.—6—Donald S. Drysdale, Los Angeles, May 14, 18, 22, 26, 31, June 4, 1968.
A. L.—5—G. Harris White, Chicago, September 12, 16, 19, 25, 30, 1904.

Most Doubleheader Shutouts

N. L.—1—Edward M. Reulbach, Chicago vs. Brooklyn, September 26, 1908. (Won 5 to 0; 3 to 0).
A. L.—None.

Most Shutout Games Lost, League

A. L.—65—Walter P. Johnson, Washington, 21 years, 1907 through 1927. (Won 112, tied 1, lost 65).
N. L.—40—Christopher Mathewson, New York, Cincinnati, 17 years, 1900 through 1916. (Won 83, lost 40).

Most Shutout Games Lost, Season

N. L.—14—James A. Devlin, Louisville, 1876 (won 5, lost 14).
N. L. since 1900—11—Arthur L. Raymond, St. Louis, 1908 (won 5, lost 11).
A. L.—10—Walter P. Johnson, Washington, 1909 (won 4, lost 10).

Most Consecutive Shutout Games, Lost, Season

N. L.—4—James C. McAndrew, New York, July 21, first game, August 4, second game, August 10, second game, August 17, 1968, (allowed 6 runs).
A. L.—2—Held by many pitchers.

Most Shutout Games Lost, Season, to One Club

N. L.—5—James A. Devlin, Louisville vs. Hartford, 1876.
A. L.—5—Walter P. Johnson, Washington vs. Chicago, 1909.
N. L. since 1900—4—Irving M. Young, Boston vs. Pittsburgh, 1906.

Most Shutout Games Lost, One Month

A. L.—5—Walter P. Johnson, Washington, July, 1909.
N. L.—4—James A. Devlin, Louisville, June, 1876.
Fred L. Fitzsimmons, New York, September, 1934.
James C. McAndrew, New York, August, 1968.

Most 1-0 Games Lost, League

A. L.—26—Walter P. Johnson, Washington, 21 years, 1907 through 1927. (Won 38, lost 26).

N. L.—13—H. Lee Meadows, St. Louis, Philadelphia, Pittsburgh, 15 years, 1915 through 1929. (Won 7, lost 13).

Most 1-0 Games Lost, Season

A. L.—5—William E. Donovan, Detroit, 1903. (Won 1, lost 5).
 John M. Warhop, New York, 1914. (Won 0, lost 5).

N. L.—5—George W. McQuillan, Philadelphia, 1908. (Won 2, lost 5).
 Roger L. Craig, New York, 1963. (Won 0, lost 5).
 James P. Bunning, Philadelphia, 1967. (Won 1, lost 5).
 Ferguson A. Jenkins, Chicago, 1968. (Won 0, lost 5).

Most 1-0 Games Lost, Season, to One Club

A. L.—3—John M. Warhop, New York vs. Washington, 1914.

N. L.—2—Held by many pitchers.

Most No-Hit Games Pitched, Two Major Leagues, Nine or More Innings

5—L. Nolan Ryan, California, A. L., 1973 (2), 1974, 1975; Houston, N. L., 1981.
3—Denton T. Young, Cleveland, N. L., 1897; Boston, A. L., 1904, 1908.
2—James P. Bunning, Detroit, A. L., 1958; Philadelphia, N. L., 1964.

Most No-Hit Games, League

N. L.—4—Sanford Koufax, Los Angeles, 1962, 1963, 1964, 1965.
 3—Lawrence J. Corcoran, Chicago, 1880, 1882, 1884.
 James W. Maloney, Cincinnati, 1965 (2), 1969 (1).

A. L.—4—L. Nolan Ryan, California, 1973 (2), 1974 (1), 1975 (1).
 3—Robert W. Feller, Cleveland, 1940, 1946, 1951.

Most No-Hit Games, Season

N. L.—2—John S. Vander Meer, Cincinnati, June 11, 15, 1938, consecutive.
 James W. Maloney, Cincinnati, June 14, (first 10 innings of 11-inning game), August 19, 1965, first game, 10 innings.

A. L.—2—Allie P. Reynolds, New York, July 12, September 28, first game, 1951.
 Virgil O. Trucks, Detroit, May 15, August 25, 1952.
 L. Nolan Ryan, California, May 15, July 15, 1973.

Most Consecutive No-Hit Games

N. L.—2—John S. Vander Meer, Cincinnati, June 11, 15, 1938.

A. L.—Never accomplished.

Most Consecutive One-Hit Games

U. A.—2—Hugh Daily, Chicago, July 7, 10, 1884.

N. L.—2—Charles G. Buffinton, Philadelphia, August 6, 9, 1887.
 Lonnie Warneke, Chicago, April 17, 22, 1934 (His first two games of season).
 Morton C. Cooper, St. Louis, May 31, first game, June 4, 1943.

A. A.—2—Thomas Ramsey, Louisville, July 29, 31, 12 innings, 1886.

A. L.—2—Edward C. Ford, New York, September 2, 7, 1955.
 Samuel E. McDowell, Cleveland, April 25, May 1, 1966.

Most Low-Hit (No-Hit and One-Hit) Games, Season, Nine or More Innings

U. A.—4—Hugh Daily, Chicago, 1884.

N. L.—4—Grover C. Alexander, Philadelphia, 1915.

A. L.—3—Adrian C. Joss, Cleveland, 1907.
 Robert W. Feller, Cleveland, 1946.
 Virgil O. Trucks, Detroit, 1952.
 L. Nolan Ryan, California, 1973.
 Dennis L. Eckersley, Cleveland, 1977.

Most Low-Hit (No-Hit and One-Hit) Games, League, Nine or More Innings

A. L.—14—Robert W. Feller, Cleveland, 1938 through 1955, 3 no-hit; 11 one-hit. (Also lost one 8-inning one-hit game on April 23, 1952).

N. L.— 8—Charles G. Radbourn, Providence, Boston, 1881 to 1888, 1 no-hit; 7 one-hit.
 James W. Maloney, Cincinnati, 3 no-hit, 1965 (2), 1969 (1); 5 one-hit, 1963, 1964, 1965, 1968, 1969.

Fewest Hits Allowed, First Major League Game, Nine Innings

N. L.—0—Charles L. Jones, Cincinnati, October 15, 1892.

A. L.—1—Adrian C. Joss, Cleveland, April 26, 1902, single in seventh inning.
 Miguel Fornieles, Washington, September 2, 1952, second game, single in second inning.
 William J. Rohr, Boston, April 14, 1967, single, 2 out in ninth inning.

N. L. since 1900—1—Juan A. Marichal, San Francisco, July 19, 1960, single, 2 out in eighth inning.

Fewest Hits Allowed, Opening Game of Season, Nine Innings

A. L.—0—Robert W. Feller, Cleveland, April 16, 1940.
N. L.—1—Held by many pitchers. (Leon Ames, New York, allowed 0 hits in 9⅓ innings
    on April 15, 1909, but lost on 7 hits in 13 innings.)
    Last time—Lonnie Warneke, Chicago, April 17, 1934.

Most Years Leading League in Most Hits Allowed

N. L.—5—Robin E. Roberts, Philadelphia, 1952, 1953, 1954, 1955, 1956.
A. L.—4—James L. Kaat, Minnesota, Chicago, 1965, 1966, 1967, 1975.

Most Hits Allowed, League

N. L.—5490— James F. Galvin, Buffalo, Pittsburgh, St. Louis, 12 years, 1879 through
    1892, except 1886, 1890.
A. L.— 4920— Walter P. Johnson, Washington, 21 years, 1907 through 1927.
N. L. since 1900—4868—Grover C. Alexander, Philadelphia, Chicago, St. Louis, 20 years,
    1911 through 1930.

Most Hits Allowed, Major Leagues

7078—Denton T. Young, Cleveland N. L., St. Louis N. L., Boston A. L., Cleveland A. L.,
    Boston N. L., 22 years, 1890 through 1911. 4282 hits in N. L., 2796 hits in A. L.

Most Hits Allowed, Season

N. L.— 809— John H. Coleman, Philadelphia, 63 games, 548 innings, 1883.
A. L.— 401— Joseph J. McGinnity, Baltimore, 48 games, 378 innings, 1901.
N. L. since 1900—415—William M. Carrick, New York, 45 games, 342 innings, 1900.

Fewest Hits Allowed, Season, for Leader in Most Hits

A. L.— 243— Melvin L. Stottlemyre, New York, 279 innings, 1968.
N. L.— 251— George B. Koslo, New York, 265 innings, 1946.

Most Consecutive Hitless Innings, Season

A. L.—24—Denton T. Young, Boston, from seventh inning, April 25 through sixth in-
    ning, May 11, 1904.
N. L.—21—John S. Vander Meer, Cincinnati, from first inning, June 11 through third
    inning, June 19, first game, 1938.

Most Consecutive Batsmen Retired, Season

N. L.—41—James L. Barr, San Francisco, August 23 (last 21), August 29 (first 20),
    1972.
A. L.—33—Steven L. Busby, Kansas City, June 19 (last 24), June 24 (first 9), 1974.
    John E. Montague, Seattle, July 22 (last 13), July 24 (first 20), first game,
    1977.

Most Hits Allowed, Inning

N. L.—13—George E. Weidman, Detroit, September 6, 1883, seventh inning.
A. L.—12—Merle T. Adkins, Boston, July 8, 1902, sixth inning.
N. L. since 1900—11—Reginald Grabowski, Philadelphia, August 4, 1934, second game,
    ninth inning.

Most Consecutive Hits Allowed, Start of Game

N. L.—7—William G. Bonham, Chicago, August 5, 1975, 3 singles, 2 doubles, 2 homers.
A. L.—5—Frank D. Tanana, California, May 18, 1980, 1 single, 2 doubles, 2 triples.
    Luis E. Leal, Toronto, June 2, 1980, 2 singles, 3 doubles.
    Ross Baumgarten, Chicago, September 27, 1981, first game, 5 singles.

Most Consecutive Hits Allowed, Inning or Game

A. L.—10—William Reidy, Milwaukee, June 2, 1901, ninth inning.
N. L.— 9—J. Erskine Mayer, Philadelphia, August 18, 1913, ninth inning.

Most Hits Allowed, Game

N. L.—36—John Wadsworth, Louisville, August 17, 1894.
N. L. since 1900—26—Harley Parker, Cincinnati, June 21, 1901.
A. L.—26—Horace O. Lisenbee, Philadelphia, September 11, 1936.

Most Hits Allowed, Extra-Inning Game

A. L.—29—Edwin A. Rommel, Philadelphia, July 10, 1932, pitched last 17 innings of
    18-inning game.
N. L.—23—Edward J. Pfeffer, Brooklyn, June 1, 1919, 18 innings.

Most Hits Allowed, Two Consecutive Games

N. L.—48—James J. Callahan, Chicago, September 6 (25), September 11, first game
    (23), 1900.

Most Hits Allowed, Shutout Game, Nine Innings

N. L.—14—Lawrence D. Cheney, Chicago vs. New York, September 14, 1913 (Won 7-0).
A. L.—14—Milton Gaston, Washington vs. Cleveland, July 10, 1928, second game (Won 9-0).

Fewest Hits Allowed, Doubleheader, 18 Innings

A. A.—3—Timothy J. Keefe, New York, July 4, 1883.
N. L.—6—Fred Toney, Cincinnati, July 1, 1917.
       Herman S. Bell, St. Louis, July 19, 1924.
A. L.—7—Frank M. Owen, Chicago, July 1, 1905.
       Edward A. Walsh, Chicago, September 29, 1908.

Fewest Hits Allowed, Two Consecutive Games, 18 Innings

N. L.—0—John S. Vander Meer, Cincinnati, June 11, 15, 1938.
     1—James F. Galvin, Buffalo, August 2 (1), 4 (0), 1884.
        Alexander B. Sanders, Louisville, August 22 (0), 26 (1), 1892.
        Arthur C. Vance, Brooklyn, September 8, first game (1), September 12, first game (0), 1925.
        James A. Tobin, Boston, April 23, first game (1), April 27 (0), 1944.
     2—Charles G. Buffinton, Philadelphia, August 6 (1), 9 (1), 1887.
        James Hughes, Baltimore, April 18 (2), 22 (0), 1898. (First 2 major league games of career.)
        Lonnie Warneke, Chicago, April 17 (1), 22 (1), 1934. (His first 2 games of season.)
        Morton C. Cooper, St. Louis, May 31, first game (1), June 4, 1943 (1).
        Ewell Blackwell, Cincinnati, June 18 (0), 22 (2), first game, 1947.
        Warren E. Spahn, Milwaukee, April 28 (0), May 3 (2), 1961.
A. L.—1—Howard J. Ehmke, Boston, September 7 (0), 11 (1), 1923.
     2—Samuel P. Jones, New York, September 4 (0), 10 (2), 1923.
        Edward C. Ford, New York, September 2 (1), 7 (1), 1955.
        Samuel E. McDowell, Cleveland, April 25 (1), May 1, 1966 (1).
        L. Nolan Ryan, California, June 1, (0) June 6 (2), 1975.
U. A.—1—Edward L. Cushman, Milwaukee, September 28 (0), October 4, 1884 (1).
A. A.—2—Thomas Ramsey, Louisville, July 29 (1), 31 (1) (12 innings), 1886.

Fewest Hits Allowed, Three Consecutive Games

N. L.—3—John S. Vander Meer, Cincinnati, June 5 (3), 11 (0), 15 (0), 1938.
A. L.—5—Held by many pitchers.

Most Bases on Balls, Major Leagues

2022—L. Nolan Ryan, New York N.L., California A.L., Houston N.L., 17 years, 1966, 1968 through 1983.

Most Bases on Balls, League

A. L.—1775—Early Wynn, Washington, Cleveland, Chicago, 23 years, 1939, 1941 through 1963 (except 1945, in military service).
N. L.—1637—Amos W. Rusie, Indianapolis, New York, Cincinnati, 10 years, 1889 through 1901, except 1896, 1899, 1900.
N. L. since 1900—1524—Steven N. Carlton, St. Louis, Philadelphia, 19 years, 1965 through 1983.

Most Bases on Balls, Season

N. L.— 276— Amos W. Rusie, New York, 64 games, 1890.
A. L.— 208— Robert W. Feller, Cleveland, 278 innings, 1938.
N. L. since 1900—185—Samuel Jones, Chicago, 242 innings, 1955.

Most Years Leading League in Most Bases on Balls

A. L.—6—L. Nolan Ryan, California, 1972, 1973, 1974, 1976, 1977, 1978 (also led N. L. in 1980, 1982, for total of 8 seasons).
N. L.—5—Amos W. Rusie, New York, 1890, 1891, 1892, 1893, 1894.
N. L. since 1900—4—James J. Ring, Philadelphia, 1922, 1923, 1924, 1925.
         W. Kirby Higbe, Chicago, Philadelphia, Pittsburgh, Brooklyn, 1939, 1940, 1941, 1947.
         Samuel Jones, Chicago, St. Louis, San Francisco, 1955, 1956, 1958, 1959.
         Robert A. Veale, Pittsburgh, 1964, 1965 (tied), 1967, 1968.

Most Bases on Balls, Inning

A. L.—8—William D. Gray, Washington, August 28, 1909, first game, second inning.
N. L.—7—Anthony J. Mullane, Baltimore, June 18, 1894, a.m. game, first inning.
        Robert Ewing, Cincinnati, April 19, 1902, fourth inning. (His first major league game).

Most Consecutive Bases on Balls, Inning

    A. L.—7—William D. Gray, Washington, August 28, 1909, first game, second inning.
    N. L.—6—William H. Kennedy, Brooklyn, August 31, 1900, second inning.

Most Bases on Balls, Game, 9 Innings

    N. L.—16—William George, New York, May 30, 1887, first game.
            George H. Van Haltren, Chicago, June 27, 1887.
    P. L.—16—Henry Gruber, Cleveland, April 19, 1890.
    A. L.—16—Bruno P. Haas, Philadelphia, June 23, 1915. (His first major league game).
    N. L. since 1900—14—Henry Mathewson, New York, October 5, 1906.

Most Bases on Balls, Extra-Inning Game

    A. L.—16—Thomas J. Byrne, St. Louis, August 22, 1951, 13 innings.
    N. L.—13—J. Bentley Seymour, New York, May 24, 1899, 10 innings.

Longest Game Without Base on Balls

    N. L.—(21-club league)—Charles B. Adams, Pittsburgh, July 17, 1914.
    A. L.—(20-club league)—Denton T. Young, Boston, July 4, 1905, p.m. game.

Most Bases on Balls, Shutout Game

    A. L.—11—Vernon Gomez, New York, August 1, 1941.
            Melvin L. Stottlemyre, New York, May 21, 1970; pitched first 8⅓ innings.
    N. L.— 9—Wilmer D. Mizell, St. Louis, September 1, 1958, first game.

Most Bases on Balls, Shutout Game Over 9 Innings

    N. L.—10—James W. Maloney, Cincinnati, August 19, 1965, first game, (10 innings).
            James R. Richard, Houston, July 6, 1976, (10 innings).
    A. L.—Less than 9-inning game.

Fewest Bases on Balls, Doubleheader, Nine-Inning Games

    A. A.—0—Guy J. Hecker, Louisville, July 4, 1884.
    A. L.—1—Edward A. Walsh, Chicago, September 29, 1908.
    N. L.—1—Grover C. Alexander, Philadelphia, September 23, 1916; September 3, 1917.

Fewest Bases on Balls, Season, 250 or More Innings

    N. L.—18—Charles B. Adams, Pittsburgh, 263 innings, 1920.
    A. L.—28—Denton T. Young, Boston, 380 innings, 1904.

Most Consecutive Innings With No Bases on Balls, Season

    A. L.—84⅓—William C. Fischer, Kansas City, August 3 through September 30, 1962.
    N. L.—68 —Christopher Mathewson, New York, June 19 through July 18, 1913.
            Randall L. Jones, San Diego, May 17, eighth inning, through June 22, 1976,
            seventh inning.

Most Consecutive Innings With No Bases on Balls, Start of Season

    N. L.—52—Grover C. Alexander, Chicago, April 18 through May 17, 1923.

Most Intentional Bases on Balls, Season

    N. L.—23—Michael D. Garman, St. Louis, 66 games, 79 innings, 1975.
            Dale A. Murray, Cincinnati, New York, 68 games, 119 innings, 1978.
            Kenton C. Tekulve, Pittsburgh, 85 games, 128⅔ innings, 1982.
    A. L.—19—John F. Hiller, Detroit, 59 games, 150 innings, 1974.

Most Strikeouts, League

    N. L.—3709— Steven N. Carlton, St. Louis, Philadelphia, 19 years, 1965 through 1983.
    A. L.—3508— Walter P. Johnson, Washington, 21 years, 1907 through 1927.

Most Strikeouts, League, Righthanded Pitcher

    A. L.—3508— Walter P. Johnson, Washington, 21 years, 1907 through 1927.
    N. L.—3272— G. Thomas Seaver, New York, Cincinnati, 17 years, 1967 through 1983.

Most Strikeouts, League, Lefthanded Pitcher

    N. L.—3709— Steven N. Carlton, St. Louis, Philadelphia, 19 years, 1965 through 1983.
    A. L.—2679— Michael S. Lolich, Detroit, 13 years, 1963 through 1975 (also had 153 for
            New York, San Diego, NL, 1976, 1978, 1979, for major league total of
            2832).

Most Strikeouts, Season

    A. A.— 505— Matthew A. Kilroy, Baltimore, 65 games, 570 innings, 1886.
    N. L.— 411— Charles G. Radbourn, Providence, 72 games, 679 innings, 1884.
    A. L.— 383— L. Nolan Ryan, California, 41 games, 326 innings, 1973.
    N. L. since 1900—382—Sanford Koufax, Los Angeles, 43 games, 336 innings, 1965.

Most Strikeouts, Season, Righthanded Pitcher

U. A.— 483— Hugh I. Daily, Chicago, Pittsburgh, Washington, 58 games, 501 innings, 1884.
N. L.— 411— Charles G. Radbourn, Providence, 72 games, 679 innings, 1884.
A. L.— 383— L. Nolan Ryan, California, 41 games, 326 innings, 1973.
N. L. since 1900—313—James R. Richard, Houston, 38 games, 292 innings, 1979.

Most Strikeouts, Season, Lefthanded Pitcher

A. A.— 505— Matthew A. Kilroy, Baltimore, 65 games, 570 innings, 1886.
N. L.— 382— Sanford Koufax, Los Angeles, 43 games, 336 innings, 1965.
A. L.— 349— George E. Waddell, Philadelphia, 46 games, 384 innings, 1904.

Most Strikeouts, Season, Relief Pitcher

A. L.— 181— Richard R. Radatz, Boston, 1964, 79 games, 157 innings.
N. L.— 151— Richard M. Gossage, Pittsburgh, 1977, 72 games, 133 innings.

Fewest Strikeouts, Season, for Leader in Most Strikeouts

A. L.— 113— Cecil C. Hughson, Boston, 281 innings, 1942.
          Louis N. Newsom, Washington, 214 innings, 1942.
N. L.— 133— George E. Waddell, Pittsburgh, 213 innings, 1900.

Most Years Leading League in Most Strikeouts

A. L.—12—Walter P. Johnson, Washington, 1910, 1912, 1913, 1914, 1915, 1916, 1917, 1918, 1919, 1921, 1923, 1924.
N. L.— 7—Arthur C. Vance, Brooklyn, 1922 through 1928.

Most Consecutive Years Leading League in Strikeouts

A. L.—8—Walter P. Johnson, Washington, 1912 through 1919.
N. L.—7—Arthur C. Vance, Brooklyn, 1922 through 1928.

Most Years 100 or More Strikeouts in Major Leagues

18—Denton T. Young, Cleveland N. L., St. Louis N. L., Boston A. L., Cleveland A. L., 1891 through 1909, except 1897; 9 in National League; 9 in American League.
    Walter P. Johnson, Washington A. L., 1908 through 1926, except 1920.
    Gaylord J. Perry, San Francisco N. L., Cleveland A. L., Texas A. L., San Diego N. L., New York A. L., Atlanta N. L., Seattle A. L., 1964 through 1982, except 1981; 10 in National League; 8 in American League.
    Donald H. Sutton, Los Angeles N. L., Houston N. L., Milwaukee A. L., 1966 through 1983; 17 in National League; 1 in American League.

Most Consecutive Years 100 or More Strikeouts in Major Leagues

18—Donald H. Sutton, Los Angeles N. L., Houston N. L., Milwaukee A. L., 1966 through 1983; 17 in National League; 1 in American League.

Most Years 100 or More Strikeouts, League

A. L.—18—Walter P. Johnson, Washington, 1908 through 1926, except 1920.
N. L.—17—Warren E. Spahn, Boston, Milwaukee, 1947 through 1963.
          Steven N. Carlton, St. Louis, Philadelphia, 1967 through 1983.
          Donald H. Sutton, Los Angeles, Houston, 1966 through 1982.

Most Consecutive Years 100 or More Strikeouts, League

N. L.—17—Warren E. Spahn, Boston, Milwaukee, 1947 through 1963.
          Steven N. Carlton, St. Louis, Philadelphia, 1967 through 1983.
          Donald H. Sutton, Los Angeles, Houston, 1966 through 1982.
A. L.—13—Edward S. Plank, Philadelphia, 1902 through 1914.
          Michael S. Lolich, Detroit, 1963 through 1975.

Most Years 200 or More Strikeouts, League

N.L.—10—G. Thomas Seaver, New York, Cincinnati, 1968 through 1976, 1978.
A. L.— 7—George E. Waddell, Philadelphia, St. Louis, 1902 through 1908.
          Walter P. Johnson, Washington, 1910 through 1916.
          Michael S. Lolich, Detroit, 1965, 1969, 1970, 1971, 1972, 1973, 1974.
          L. Nolan Ryan, California, 1972, 1973, 1974, 1976, 1977, 1978, 1979.

Most Consecutive Years 200 or More Strikeouts, League

N. L.—9—G. Thomas Seaver, New York, 1968 through 1976.
A. L.—7—George E. Waddell, Philadelphia, St. Louis, 1902 through 1908.
          Walter P. Johnson, Washington, 1910 through 1916.

Most Years, 300 or More Strikeouts, Major Leagues

5—L. Nolan Ryan, California A. L., 1972, 1973, 1974, 1976, 1977.
3—Timothy J. Keefe, New York A. A., 1883, 1884, New York N. L., 1888.
  Amos W. Rusie, New York N. L., 1890, 1891, 1892.
  Sanford Koufax, Los Angeles N. L., 1963, 1965, 1966.

Most Years, 300 or More Strikeouts, League

A. L.—5—L. Nolan Ryan, California, 1972 (329), 1973 (383), 1974 (367), 1976 (327), 1977 (341).

N. L.—3—Amos W. Rusie, New York, 1890 (345), 1891 (321), 1892 (303).
Sanford Koufax, Los Angeles, 1963 (303), 1965 (382), 1966 (317).

Most Years, 400 or More Strikeouts, League

A. A.—1—505—Matthew A. Kilroy, Baltimore, 1886.
494—Thomas A. Ramsey, Louisville, 1886.

U. A.—1—484—Hugh I. Daily, Chicago, Pittsburgh, Washington, 1884.

U. A., N. L.—455—Fred L. Shaw, Detroit N. L., Boston U. A., 1884.

N. L.—1—411—Charles G. Radbourn, Providence, 1884.
402—Charles G. Buffinton, Boston, 1884.

Most Strikeouts, Rookie Season, Since 1900

A. L.— 245— Herbert J. Score, Cleveland, 227 innings, 1955.

N. L.— 227— Grover C. Alexander, Philadelphia, 367 innings, 1911.

Most Strikeouts, Inning

A. A.—4—Robert T. Mathews, Philadelphia, September 30, 1885, seventh inning.

N. L.—4—Edward N. Crane, New York, October 4, 1888, fifth inning, consecutive.
George L. Wiltse, New York, May 15, 1906, fifth inning, consecutive.
James B. Davis, Chicago, May 27, 1956, first game, sixth inning, consecutive.
Joseph H. Nuxhall, Cincinnati, August 11, 1959, first game, sixth inning.
Peter G. Richert, Los Angeles, April 12, 1962, third inning, consecutive.
Donald S. Drysdale, Los Angeles, April 17, 1965, second inning, consecutive.
Robert Gibson, St. Louis, June 7, 1966, fourth inning.
William G. Bonham, Chicago, July 31, 1974, first game, second inning, consecutive.
Philip H. Niekro, Atlanta, July 29, 1977, sixth inning.

A. L.—4—Walter P. Johnson, Washington, April 15, 1911, fifth inning.
Guy Morton, Cleveland, June 11, 1916, sixth inning, consecutive.
Rinold G. Duren, Los Angeles, May 18, 1961, seventh inning.
A. Lee Stange, Cleveland, September 2, 1964, seventh inning.
Miguel Cuellar, Baltimore, May 29, 1970, fourth inning, consecutive.
Michael D. Paxton, Cleveland, July 21, 1978, fifth inning, consecutive.

Three Strikeouts, Inning, on 9 Pitched Balls

A. L.—George E. Waddell, Philadelphia, July 1, 1902, third inning.
Hollis O. Thurston, Chicago, August 22, 1923, twelfth inning.
Robert M. Grove, Philadelphia, August 23, 1928, second inning; also September 27, 1928, seventh inning.
James P. Bunning, Detroit, August 2, 1959, ninth inning.
Alphonso E. Downing, New York, August 11, 1967, first game, second inning.
L. Nolan Ryan, California, July 9, 1972, second inning.

N. L.—D. Patrick Ragan, Brooklyn, October 5, 1914, second game, eighth inning.
Horace O. Eller, Cincinnati, August 21, 1917, ninth inning.
Joseph Oeschger, Boston, September 8, 1921, first game, fourth inning.
Arthur C. Vance, Brooklyn, September 14, 1924, third inning.
Sanford Koufax, Los Angeles, June 30, 1962, first inning.
Sanford Koufax, Los Angeles, April 18, 1964, third inning.
Robert J. Bruce, Houston, April 19, 1964, eighth inning.
L. Nolan Ryan, New York, April 19, 1968, third inning.
Robert Gibson, St. Louis, May 12, 1969, seventh inning.
Lynn E. McGlothen, St. Louis, August 19, 1975, second inning.
H. Bruce Sutter, Chicago, September 8, 1977, ninth inning.

Most Strikeouts, Game, 9 Innings

N. L.—19—Charles Sweeney, Providence, June 7, 1884.
Steven N. Carlton, St. Louis, September 15, 1969.
G. Thomas Seaver, New York, April 22, 1970.
18—Sanford Koufax, Los Angeles, August 31, 1959.
Sanford Koufax, Los Angeles, April 24, 1962.
Donald E. Wilson, Houston, July 14, 1968, second game.
William L. Gullickson, Montreal, September 10, 1980.

U. A.—19—Hugh Daly, Chicago, July 7, 1884.

A. L.—19—L. Nolan Ryan, California, August 12, 1974.
18—Robert W. Feller, Cleveland, October 2, 1938, first game.
L. Nolan Ryan, California, September 10, 1976.
Ronald A. Guidry, New York, June 17, 1978.

Most Strikeouts, Night Game, 9 Innings

N. L.—19—Steven N. Carlton, St. Louis, September 15, 1969.

A. L.—19—L. Nolan Ryan, California, August 12, 1974.

Most Strikeouts, Extra-Inning Game

A. L.—21—Thomas E. Cheney, Washington vs. Baltimore, September 12, 1962, 16 innings.

A. L.—19—Luis C. Tiant, Cleveland, July 3, 1968, 10 innings.

        L. Nolan Ryan, California, June 14, 1974, first 12 innings of 15-inning game.

        L. Nolan Ryan, California, August 20, 1974, 11 innings.

        L. Nolan Ryan, California, June 8, 1977, first 10 innings of 13-inning game.

N. L.—18—Warren E. Spahn, Boston vs. Chicago, June 14, 1952, 15 innings.

        James W. Maloney, Cincinnati vs. New York, June 14, 1965, 11 innings.

        Christopher J. Short, Philadelphia vs. New York, October 2, 1965, second game, first 15 innings of 18-inning game.

Most Strikeouts, Game, 9 Innings, Righthanded Pitcher

N. L.—19—Charles Sweeney, Providence, June 7, 1884.

        G. Thomas Seaver, New York, April 22, 1970.

A. L.—19—L. Nolan Ryan, California, August 12, 1974.

Most Strikeouts, Game, 9 Innings, Lefthanded Pitcher

N. L.—19—Steven N. Carlton, St. Louis, September 15, 1969.

A. L.—18—Ronald A. Guidry, New York, June 17, 1978.

Most Strikeouts, Extra-Inning Game, Righthanded Pitcher

A. L.—21—Thomas A. Cheney, Washington, September 12, 1962, 16 innings.

N. L.—18—James W. Maloney, Cincinnati, June 14, 1965, 11 innings.

Most Strikeouts, Extra-Inning Game, Lefthanded Pitcher

N. L.—18—Warren E. Spahn, Boston, June 14, 1952, 15 innings.

        Christopher J. Short, Philadelphia, October 2, 1965, second game, first 15 innings of 18-inning game.

A. L.—17—George E. Waddell, Philadelphia, September 5, 1905, 13 innings.

        George E. Waddell, St. Louis, September 20, 1908, 10 innings.

        Vida Blue, Oakland, July 9, 1971, pitched 11 innings of 20-inning game.

Most Consecutive Strikeouts, Game

N. L.—10—G. Thomas Seaver, New York, April 22, 1970, 1 in sixth inning, 3 in seventh inning, 3 in eighth inning, 3 in ninth inning.

A. L.— 8—L. Nolan Ryan, California, July 9, 1972, 2 in first inning, 3 in second inning, 3 in third inning.

        L. Nolan Ryan, California, July 15, 1973, 1 in first inning, 3 in second inning, 3 in third inning, 1 in fourth inning.

        Ronald G. Davis, New York, May 4, 1981, 2 in seventh inning, 3 in eighth inning, 3 in ninth inning.

Most Consecutive Strikeouts, First Major League Game

A. L.—7—Samuel L. Stewart, Baltimore, September 1, 1978, second game, 3 in second inning, 3 in third inning, 1 in fourth inning.

N. L.—6—Karl B. Spooner, Brooklyn, September 22, 1954, 3 in seventh inning, 3 in eighth inning.

        Peter G. Richert, Los Angeles, April 12, 1962, 1 in second inning, 4 in third inning, 1 in fourth inning (first six batters he faced in majors).

Most Strikeouts, Game, by Relief Pitcher

N. L.—14—Richard W. Marquard, New York, May 13, 1911 (last 8 innings of nine-inning game).

A. L.—14—Dennis D. McLain, Detroit, June 15, 1965, 6⅔ innings of nine-inning game.

Most Consecutive Strikeouts, Game, by Relief Pitcher

A. L.—8—Ronald G. Davis, New York, May 4, 1981, 2 in seventh inning, 3 in eighth inning, 3 in ninth inning.

N. L.—6—John R. Meyer, Philadelphia, September 22, 1958, first game, 3 in twelfth inning, 3 in thirteenth inning, (first 6 batters he faced).

        Peter G. Richert, Los Angeles, April 12, 1962, 1 in second inning, 4 in third inning, 1 in fourth inning (first 6 batters he faced in majors).

        Ronald P. Perranoski, Los Angeles, September 12, 1966, 3 in fifth inning, 3 in sixth inning, (first 6 batters he faced).

        Richard A. Kelley, Atlanta, September 8, 1967, 2 in sixth inning, 3 in seventh inning, 1 in eighth inning.

        Joseph W. Hoerner, St. Louis, June 1, 1968, 3 in ninth inning, 3 in tenth inning.

        Donald L. Gullett, Cincinnati, August 23, 1970, second game, 3 in sixth inning, 3 in seventh inning, (first 6 batters he faced).

        H. Bruce Sutter, Chicago, September 8, 1977, 3 in eighth inning, 3 in ninth inning, (first 6 batters he faced).

        Guillermo Hernandez, Philadelphia, July 3, 1983, 3 in eighth inning, 3 in ninth inning (all 6 batters he faced).

Most Consecutive Strikeouts, Start of Game

N. L.—9—Michael Welch, New York, August 28, 1884.
A. L.—6—John F. Hiller, Detroit, August 6, 1968, first game.
    Raymond L. Culp, Boston, May 11, 1970.
    Rikalbert Blyleven, Minnesota, September 16, 1970.
N. L. since 1900—6—John A. Messersmith, Los Angeles, May 28, 1973.
    Peter Falcone, New York, May 1, 1980.

Most Strikeouts, Losing Pitcher, Game, 9 Innings

N. L.—19—Steven N. Carlton, St. Louis, September 15, 1969, lost 4 to 3.
U. A.—18—Fred L. Shaw, Boston, July 19, 1884, lost 1 to 0.
    Henry Porter, Milwaukee, October 3, 1884, lost 5 to 4.
A. L.—18—Robert W. Feller, Cleveland, October 2, 1938, first game, lost 4 to 1.
A. A.—17—Guy J. Hecker, Louisville, August 26, 1884, lost 4 to 3.

Most Strikeouts, Losing Pitcher, Extra-Inning Game

A. L.—19—L. Nolan Ryan, California, August 20, 1974, 11 innings, lost 1-0.
N. L.—18—Warren E. Spahn, Boston, June 14, 1952, 15 innings, lost 3-1.
    James W. Maloney, Cincinnati, June 14, 1965, 11 innings. lost 1-0.

Most Strikeouts, First Major League Game, Since 1900

N. L.—15—Karl B. Spooner, Brooklyn, September 22, 1954.
    James R. Richard, Houston, September 5, 1971, second game.
A. L.—12—Elmer G. Myers, Philadelphia, October 6, 1915, second game.

Most Strikeouts, Two Consecutive Games

U. A.—34—Fred L. Shaw, Boston, July 19 (18), July 21 (16), 1884, 19 innings.
A. L.—32—Luis C. Tiant, Cleveland, June 29, first game (13), July 3 (19) 1968, 19 innings.
    L. Nolan Ryan, California, August 7 (13), August 12 (19), 1974, 17 innings.
    30—Samuel E. McDowell, Cleveland, May 1 (16), May 6 (14), 1968, 18 innings.
    L. Nolan Ryan, California, July 15 (17), July 19 (13), 1973, 19⅓ innings.
N. L.—31—Sanford Koufax, Los Angeles, August 24, August 31, 1959, 18 innings.

Most Strikeouts, Three Consecutive Games

U. A.—48—Fred L. Shaw, Boston, July 16, 19, 21, 1884, 28 innings.
A. L.—47—L. Nolan Ryan, California, August 12 (19), August 16 (9), August 20 (19), 1974, 27⅓ innings.
    41—Luis C. Tiant, Cleveland, June 23, first game (9), June 29, first game (13), July 3, (19), 1968, 28 innings.
    L. Nolan Ryan, California, July 11 (11), July 15 (17), July 19 (13), 1973, 25⅓ innings.
    L. Nolan Ryan, California, August 7 (13), August 12 (19), August 16 (9), 1974, 24⅓ innings.
N. L.—41—Sanford Koufax, Los Angeles, August 24, August 31, September 6, first game (ten innings), 1959, 28 innings.

Most Times, Ten or More Strikeouts, Game, Major Leagues

151—L. Nolan Ryan, 36 in National League, New York, Houston, 9 years, 1966, 1968 through 1971, 1980 through 1983; 114 in American League, California, 8 years, 1972 through 1979.

Most Times, Ten or More Strikeouts, Game, League

A. L.—114—L. Nolan Ryan, California, 8 years, 1972 through 1979.
N. L.— 97—Sanford Koufax, Brooklyn, Los Angeles, 12 years, 1955 through 1966.

Most Times, Ten or More Strikeouts, Game, Season

A. L.—23—L. Nolan Ryan, California, 1973.
N. L.—21—Sanford Koufax, Los Angeles, 1965.

Most Times, Fifteen or More Strikeouts, Game, League

A. L.—19—L. Nolan Ryan, California, 1972 (4), 1973 (2), 1974 (6), 1976 (3), 1977 (2), 1978 (1); 1979 (1); also 2 in National League with New York, 1970 (1), 1971 (1).
N. L.— 8—Sanford Koufax, Brooklyn, Los Angeles, 1959 (2), 1960 (2), 1961 (1), 1962 (2), 1966 (1).

Most Hit Batsmen, League

A. L.—206—Walter P. Johnson, Washington, 21 years, 1907 through 1927.
N. L.—195—Emerson P. Hawley, St. Louis, Pittsburgh, Cincinnati, New York, 9 years, 1892 through 1900.
N. L.—Since 1900—154—Donald S. Drysdale, Brooklyn, Los Angeles, 14 years, 1956 through 1969.

Most Hit Batsmen, Season

    A. A.—54—Phillip H. Knell, Columbus, 58 games, 1891.
    N. L.—41—Joseph J. McGinnity, Brooklyn, 45 games, 1900.
    A. L.—31—Charles C. Fraser, Philadelphia, 39 games, 1901.

Fewest Hit Batsmen, Season, for Leader in Most Hit Batsmen

    A. L.—6—Held by five pitchers. Last two pitchers—Spurgeon F. Chandler, New York,
        1940. Alfred J. Smith, Cleveland, 1940.
    N. L.—6—Held by five pitchers. Last three pitchers—Rex E. Barney, Brooklyn, 1948.
        Sheldon L. Jones, New York, 1948. Kent F. Peterson, Cincinnati, 1948.

Most Years Leading League in Most Hit Batsmen

    A. L.—6—Howard J. Ehmke, Detroit, Boston, Philadelphia, 1920, 1921, (tied), 1922,
        1923 (tied), 1925, 1927.
    N. L.—5—Donald S. Drysdale, Los Angeles, 1958, 1959, 1960, 1961, 1965 (tied).

Fewest Hit Batsmen, Season, Most Innings

    A. L.—0—Alvin F. Crowder, Washington, 50 games, 327 innings, 1932.
    N. L.—0—Sanford Koufax, Los Angeles, 41 games, 323 innings, 1966.

Fewest Hit Batsmen, Three Consecutive Seasons, Most Innings

    N. L.—0—Lawrence J. Benton, New York, Cincinnati, 1928, 1929, 1930 (755 innings).
        William A. Hallahan, St. Louis, 1932, 1933, 1934 (583 innings).
    A. L.—0—William R. Wight, Chicago, Boston, 1949, 1950, 1951 (569 innings).

Most Hit Batsmen, Inning

    N. L.—3—John P. Luby, Chicago, September 5, 1890, sixth inning.
        Emerson P. Hawley, St. Louis, July 4, 1894, first game, first inning, consecu-
          tive.
        Emerson P. Hawley, Pittsburgh, May 9, 1896, seventh inning.
        Walter M. Thornton, Chicago, May 18, 1898, fourth inning (consecutive).
        Charles L. Phillippe, Pittsburgh, September 25, 1905, first inning.
        Raymond J. Boggs, Boston, September 17, 1928, ninth inning.
        Raul R. Sanchez, Cincinnati, May 15, 1960, first game, eighth inning.
        Dock P. Ellis, Pittsburgh, May 1, 1974, first inning, (consecutive).
    A. L.—3—Melvin A. Gallia, Washington, June 20, 1913, second game, first inning.
        Harry C. Harper, New York, August 25, 1921, eighth inning.
        Thomas S. Morgan, New York, June 30, 1954, third inning.
        Wilbur F. Wood, Chicago, September 10, 1977, first inning, (consecutive).

Most Hit Batsmen, Game, 9 Innings

    A. A.—6—Edward Knouff, Baltimore, April 25, 1887.
    N. L.—5—Samuel E. Shaw, Chicago, June 13, 1893.
        Emerson P. Hawley, Pittsburgh, May 9, 1896.
        Fred C. Bates, Cleveland, July 17, 1899, second game.
    N. L. since 1900—4—Held by five pitchers. Last time—Myron W. Drabowsky, Chicago,
        June 2, 1957, first game.
    A. L.—4—Held by nine pitchers. Last time—Thomas E. John, Chicago, June 15, 1968.

Most Hit Batsmen, Two Consecutive Games

    N. L.—9—Samuel E. Shaw, Chicago, June 13 (5), June 16 (4), 1893.

Longest Game Without Hit Batsman

    N. L.—26 innings— Leon Cadore, Brooklyn, May 1, 1920.
                  Joseph Oeschger, Boston, May 1, 1920.
    A. L.—21 innings— Theodore A. Lyons, Chicago, May 24, 1929.

Most Wild Pitches, Season

    N. L.—64— William Stemmeyer, Boston, 41 games, 1886.
    N. L. since 1900—30—Leon K. Ames, New York, 263 innings, 1905.
    A. L.—21—Walter P. Johnson, Washington, 374 innings, 1910.
        R. Earl Wilson, Boston, 211 innings, 1963.
        L. Nolan Ryan, California, 299 innings, 1977.

Fewest Wild Pitches, Season, for Leader in Most Wild Pitches

    N. L.—6—W. Kirby Higbe, Brooklyn, 211 innings, 1946.
        Charles M. Schanz, Philadelphia, 116 innings, 1946.
    A. L.—7—Held by eight pitchers. Last two pitchers—George L. Earnshaw, Philadelphia,
        1928. Joseph B. Shaute, Cleveland, 1928.

Most Wild Pitches, League

    N. L.— 200— Philip H. Niekro, Milwaukee, Atlanta, 20 years, 1964 through 1983.
    A. L.— 156— Walter P. Johnson, Washington, 21 years, 1907 through 1927.

Most Years Leading League in Most Wild Pitches

    N. L.—6—Lawrence R. Cheney, Chicago, Brooklyn, 1912, 1913, 1914, 1916, 1917 (tied), 1918.
    A. L.—3—Walter P. Johnson, Washington, 1910, 1911, 1914 (tied).
          Leslie A. Bush, Philadelphia, New York, 1916, 1923, 1924 (tied).
          Samuel E. McDowell, Cleveland, 1965, 1967, 1970 (tied).
          L. Nolan Ryan, California, 1972, 1977, 1978.

Fewest Wild Pitches, Season, Most Innings

    N. L.—0—Joseph J. McGinnity, New York, 340 innings, 1906.
    A. L.—0—Alvin F. Crowder, Washington, 327 innings, 1932.

Fewest Wild Pitches and Hit Batsmen, Season, Most Innings

    A. L.—0—Alvin F. Crowder, Washington, 327 innings, 1932.
    N. L.—0—Jesse L. Barnes, Boston, 268 innings, 1924.

Most Wild Pitches, Inning

    P. L.—5—Ellsworth Cunningham, Buffalo, September 15, 1890, second game, first inning.
    A. L.—4—Walter P. Johnson, Washington, September 21, 1914, fourth inning.
    N. L.—4—Philip H. Niekro, Atlanta, August 4, 1979, second game, fifth inning.

Most Wild Pitches, Game

    N. L.—10—John J. Ryan, Louisville, July 22, 1876.
    N. L. since 1900—6—James R. Richard, Houston, April 10, 1979.
          Philip H. Niekro, Atlanta, August 14, 1979, second game.
          William L. Gullickson, Montreal, April 10, 1982.
    A. L.— 5—Charles Wheatley, Detroit, September 27, 1912.

Most Wild Pitches, First Major League Game

    A. A.—5—Thomas Seymour, Pittsburgh, September 23, 1882 (his only game in majors).
    N. L.—5—Michael Corcoran, Chicago, July 15, 1884 (his only game in majors).
          George E. Winkelman, Washington, August 2, 1886.

Most Wild Pitches, Opening Game of Season

    N. L.—4—Lawrence R. Cheney, Chicago, April 14, 1914.

Longest Game Without Wild Pitch

    N. L.—26 innings— Leon Cadore, Brooklyn, May 1, 1920.
    A. L.—24 innings— John W. Coombs, Philadelphia, September 1, 1906.
          Joseph Harris, Boston, September 1, 1906.

Most Sacrifices Allowed, Season (Sacrifice Hits and Sacrifice Flies)

    A. L.—54—Stanley Coveleski, Cleveland, 316 innings, 1921.
          Edwin A. Rommel, Philadelphia, 298 innings, 1923.
    N. L.—49—Eppa Rixey, Philadelphia, 284 innings, 1920.
          John W. Scott, Philadelphia, 233 innings, 1927.

Most Sacrifice Hits Allowed, Season, No Sacrifice Flies

    N. L.—35—Edward A. Brandt, Boston, 283 innings, 1933.
    A. L.—28—Earl O. Whitehill, Detroit, 272 innings, 1931.

Fewest Sacrifice Hits, Season, for Leader in Sacrifice Hits Allowed, No Sacrifice Flies

    N. L.—13—John A. Antonelli, San Francisco, 242 innings, 1958.
          Richard J. Farrell, Philadelphia, 94 innings, 1958.
          Ronald L. Kline, Pittsburgh, 237 innings, 1958.
    A. L.—11—Gaylord J. Perry, Seattle, Kansas City, 186⅓ innings, 1983.
          Robert W. Stanley, Boston, 145⅓ innings, 1983.

Fewest Sacrifice Hits Allowed, Season, Most Innings

    N. L.—0—Carlton F. Willey, New York, 30 games, 183 innings, 1963.

Most Years Leading League in Most Sacrifices Allowed

    N. L.—3—Eppa Rixey, Philadelphia, Cincinnati, 1920, 1921, 1928.
    A. L.—3—Earl O. Whitehill, Detroit, Washington, 1931, 1934, 1935.

Most Sacrifice Flies Allowed in Major Leagues

    141—James L. Kaat, Washington A. L., Minnesota A. L., Chicago A. L., Philadelphia N. L., New York A. L., St. Louis N. L., 25 years, 1959 through 1983, 108 in A. L., 33 in N. L.

Most Sacrifice Flies Allowed, League

    A. L.—108—James L. Kaat, Washington, Minnesota, Chicago, New York, 19 years, 1959 through 1975, 1979 through 1980.
    N. L.— 95— Robert Gibson, St. Louis, 17 years, 1959 through 1975.

Most Sacrifice Flies Allowed, Season

A. L.—17—Lawrence C. Gura, Kansas City, 200⅓ innings, 1983.
N. L.—15—Randy L. Lerch, Philadelphia, 214 innings, 1979.

Fewest Sacrifice Flies Allowed, Season, Most Innings

N. L.—0—Philip H. Niekro, Atlanta, 40 games, 284 innings, 1969.

Most Balks, Season

N. L.—11—Steven N. Carlton, Philadelphia, 251 innings, 1979.
A. L.— 8—Frank D. Tanana, California, 239 innings, 1978.

Most Balks, Inning

A. L.—3—Milburn J. Shoffner, Cleveland, May 12, 1930, third inning.
N. L.—3—James P. Owens, Cincinnati, April 24, 1963, second inning.
       Robert J. Shaw, Milwaukee, May 4, 1963, third inning.

Most Balks, Game

N. L.—5—Robert J. Shaw, Milwaukee, May 4, 1963.
A. L.—4—Victor J. Raschi, New York, May 3, 1950.

Most One-Base Hits Allowed, Game

N. L.—28—John Wadsworth, Louisville, August 17, 1894.
A. L.—23—Charles Baker, Cleveland, April 28, 1901.

Most One-Base Hits Allowed, Inning

N. L.—10—Reginald Grabowski, Philadelphia, August 4, 1934, second game, ninth inning.
A. L.—10—Eldon L. Auker, Detroit, September 29, 1935, second game, second inning.

Most Two-Base Hits Allowed, Game

N. L.—14—George H. Derby, Buffalo, July 3, 1883.
A. L.— 8—Edward F. LaFitte, Detroit, October 8, 1911, first game.

Most Two-Base Hits Allowed, Inning

A. L.—6—Robert M. Grove, Boston, June 9, 1934, eighth inning.
N. L.—5—Charles Esper, Washington, April 21, 1894, second inning.

Most Three-Base Hits Allowed, Game

N. L.—9—Michael J. Sullivan, Cleveland, September 3, 1894, first game.
A. L.—5—Barney Pelty, St. Louis, April 27, 1907.
       Aloysius J. Travers, Detroit, May 18, 1912.

Most Three-Base Hits Allowed, Inning

A. L.—4—Fred Marberry, Detroit, May 6, 1934, fourth inning.
       Aloysius J. Travers, Detroit, May 18, 1912.

Most Home Runs Allowed, Game

N. L.—7—Charles J. Sweeney, St. Louis, June 12, 1886.
N. L. Since 1900—6—Lawrence J. Benton, New York, May 12, 1930.
       Hollis J. Thurston, Brooklyn, August 13, 1932, first game.
       Wayman W. Kerksieck, Philadelphia, August 13, 1939, first game.
A. L.—6—Alphonse T. Thomas, St. Louis, June 27, 1936.
       George J. Caster, Philadelphia, September 24, 1940, first game.

Most Home Runs Allowed, Inning

N. L.—4—William Lampe, Boston, June 6, 1894, third inning.
       Lawrence J. Benton, New York, May 12, 1930, seventh inning.
       Wayman W. Kerksieck, Philadelphia, August 13, 1939, first game, fourth inning.
       Charles Bicknell, Philadelphia, June 6, 1948, first game, sixth inning.
       Benjamin S. Wade, Brooklyn, May 28, 1954, eighth inning.
A. L.—4—George J. Caster, Philadelphia, September 24, 1940, first game, sixth inning.
       Calvin C. McLish, Cleveland, May 22, 1957, sixth inning.
       Paul E. Foytack, Los Angeles, July 31, 1963, second game, sixth inning, consecutive.
       James A. Hunter, New York, June 17, 1977, first inning.
       R. Michael Caldwell, Milwaukee, May 31, 1980, fourth inning.

Most Consecutive Home Runs Allowed, Inning

A. L.—4—Paul E. Foytack, Los Angeles, July 31, 1963, second game, sixth inning.
N. L.—3—Held by many pitchers. Last pitcher—Donald H. Sutton, Los Angeles, May 27, 1980, third inning.

Most Home Runs Allowed, League

N. L.— 434— Warren E. Spahn, Boston, Milwaukee, New York, San Francisco, 21 years, 1942 through 1965 (except 1943, 1944, 1945, in military service).

A. L.— 374— James A. Hunter, Kansas City, Oakland, New York, 15 years, 1965 through 1979.

Most Home Runs Allowed in Major Leagues

502—Robin E. Roberts, Philadelphia N. L., Baltimore A. L., Houston N. L., Chicago N. L., 19 years, 1948 through 1966; 415 in N. L., 87 in A. L.

Most Years Allowing 30 or More Home Runs, League

N. L.—8—Robin E. Roberts, Philadelphia, 1953, 1954, 1955, 1956, 1957, 1958, 1959, 1960; (Also 1963 Baltimore A. L.)

A. L.—4—James T. Grant, Cleveland, Minnesota, 1961, 1963, 1964, 1965.
Dennis D. McLain, Detroit, Washington, 1966, 1967, 1968, 1971.

Fewest Home Runs Allowed, Season (Most Innings)

A. L.—0—Allan S. Sothoron, St. Louis, Boston, Cleveland, 29 games, 178 innings, 1921.

N. L.—1—Eppa Rixey, Cincinnati, 40 games, 301 innings, 1921.

Fewest Home Runs Allowed, Season, Since 1950, 250 or More Innings

N. L.—5—Robert A. Veale, Pittsburgh, 39 games, 266 innings, 1965.
Ronald L. Reed, Atlanta, St. Louis, 34 games, 250 innings, 1975.

A. L.—6—Edward M. Garcia, Cleveland, 45 games, 259 innings, 1954.

Most Years Leading League in Most Home Runs Allowed

N. L.—5—Robin E. Roberts, Philadelphia, 1954, 1955, 1956, 1957, 1960.
Ferguson A. Jenkins, Chicago, 1967, 1968 (tied), 1971, 1972, 1973 (also led A. L., 1975, 1979).

A. L.—3—Pedro Ramos, Washington, Minnesota, 1957, 1958, 1961.
Dennis D. McLain, Detroit, 1966, 1967, 1968.

Most Home Runs Allowed, Season

N. L.—46—Robin E. Roberts, Philadelphia, 43 games, 297 innings, 1956.

A. L.—43—Pedro Ramos, Washington, 43 games, 231 innings, 1957.

Most Home Runs Allowed, Season, vs. One Club

A. L.—15—James E. Perry, Cleveland vs. New York, 1960.

N. L.—13—Warren L. Hacker, Chicago vs. Brooklyn, 1956.
Warren E. Spahn, Milwaukee vs. Chicago, 1958.

Most Home Runs Allowed With Bases Filled, Season

A. L.—4—Raymond E. Narleski, Detroit, 1959.

N. L.—4—Frank E. McGraw, Philadelphia, 1979.

Most Home Runs Allowed With Bases Filled in Major Leagues

9—Milton S. Pappas, Baltimore A. L., Cincinnati N. L., Atlanta N. L., Chicago N. L., 1959, 1961 (3), 1962, 1965, 1966, 1970; 6 in A. L., 3 in N. L.

Ned F. Garver, St. Louis A. L., Detroit A. L., Kansas City A. L., 1949, 1950 (2), 1951, 1952, 1954, 1955 (2), 1959.

Lyndall D. McDaniel, St. Louis N. L., Chicago N. L., New York A. L., 1955, 1959, 1962, 1963 (3), 1970, 1972, 1973; 6 in N. L., 3 in A. L.

Jerry Reuss, St. Louis N. L., Houston N. L., Pittsburgh N. L., Los Angeles N. L., 1971 (2), 1972, 1973, 1974, 1976 (2), 1979, 1980.

James L. Kaat, Minnesota A. L., Chicago A. L., Philadelphia N. L., St. Louis N. L., 1962, 1963, 1973, 1974, 1975, 1978, 1980, 1982, 1983.

Most Home Runs Allowed With Bases Filled, League

A. L.—9—Ned F. Garver, St. Louis, Detroit, Kansas City, 1949, 1950 (2), 1951, 1952, 1954, 1955 (2), 1959.

N. L.—9—Jerry Reuss, St. Louis, Houston, Pittsburgh, Los Angeles, 1971 (2), 1972, 1973, 1974, 1976 (2), 1979, 1980.

Most Long Hits Allowed, Game

N. L.—16—George H. Derby, Buffalo, July 3, 1883.

A. L.—10—Dale D. Gear, Washington, August 10, 1901, second game.

Most Total Bases Allowed, Inning

N. L.—23—William C. Rhodes, Louisville, June 18, 1893, first inning.

A. L.—22—George J. Caster, Philadelphia, September 24, 1940, first game, sixth inning.

N. L. since 1900—18—Charles Bicknell, Philadelphia, June 6, 1948, first game, sixth inning.

Most Total Bases Allowed, Game

N. L.—55—William C. Rhodes, Louisville, June 18, 1893.
A. L.—41—Dale D. Gear, Washington, August 10, 1901, second game.
N. L. since 1900—39—Luther H. Taylor, New York, September 23, 1903.

CLUB PITCHING RECORDS

Most Players Used as Pitchers, Season

A. L. (162-game season)—25—Seattle, 1969.
A. L. (154-game season)—27—Philadelphia, 1915.
                               Kansas City, 1955.
N. L. (162-game season)—27—New York, 1967.
N. L. (154-game season)—24—Cincinnati, 1912.
                               Philadelphia, 1946.

Fewest Players Used As Pitchers, Season, One Club

A. L. (162-game season)—11—Baltimore, 1972, 1974; Oakland, 1974; Boston, 1976.
A. L. (154-game season)— 5—Boston, 1904.
N. L. (162-game season)—11—Philadelphia, 1976; Atlanta, 1980.
N. L. (154-game season)— 5—Boston, 1901.

Most Complete Games, Season

A. L. (154-game season)—148—Boston, 157 games, 1904.
A. L. (162-game season)— 94—Oakland, 162 games, 1980.
N. L. (154-game season)—146—St. Louis, 155 games, 1904.
N. L. (162-game season)— 77—San Francisco, 163 games, 1968.

Fewest Complete Games, Season

N. L.— 6—San Diego, 162 games, 1977.
A. L.—11—Texas, 154 games, 1972.
       16—Kansas City, 162 games, 1982.

Most Relief Appearances, Season

N. L.— 382— San Diego, 1977.

Most Consecutive Games, None Complete

N. L.—74—San Diego, May 5 through July 25, 1977.
A. L.—50—Milwaukee, June 9 through September 27, 1981.

Most Saves, Season

N. L.—60—Cincinnati, 162 games, 1970.
             Cincinnati, 154 games, 1972.
A. L.—58—Minnesota, 162 games, 1970.

Fewest Saves, Season

A. L.—11—Toronto, 162 games, 1979.
N. L.—13—Chicago, 162 games, 1971.
             St. Louis, 156 games, 1972.

Most Innings, Season

A. L. (162-game season)—1507—New York, 164 games, 1964.
A. L. (154-game season)—1465—Cleveland, 161 games, 1910.
N. L. (162-game season)—1493—Pittsburgh, 163 games, 1979.
N. L. (154-game season)—1453—Philadelphia, 159 games, 1913.

Most Pitchers, 300 or More Innings, Season

N. L. (154-game season)—3—Boston, 1905, 1906.
A. L. (154-game season)—3—Detroit, 1904.

Most Opponents' Official At-Bats, Season

N. L.— 5763— Philadelphia, 156 games, 1930.
A. L.— 5671— Boston, 163 games, 1978.

Fewest Opponents' Official At-Bats, Season

A. L.— 4933— Cleveland, 147 games, 1945.
N. L.— 5062— Philadelphia, 155 games, 1947.

Most Opponents' Men Facing Pitcher, Season

N. L.— 6549— Philadelphia, 156 games, 1930.
A. L.— 6436— Oakland, 162 games, 1979.

Fewest Opponents' Men Facing Pitcher, Season

A. L.— 5335— Cleveland, 159 games, 1976.
N. L.— 5684— Brooklyn, 154 games, 1956.

Most Opponents' Runs, Season

N. L. (154-game season) —1199—Philadelphia, 156 games, 1930.
N. L. (162-game season) — 948—New York, 161 games, 1962.
A. L. (154-game season) —1064—St. Louis, 155 games, 1936.
A. L. (162-game season) — 863—Kansas City, 162 games, 1961.

Fewest Opponents' Runs, Season

A. L. (154-game season) —408—Philadelphia, 153 games, 1909.
A. L. (162-game season) —491—Chicago, 162 games, 1967.
N. L. (154-game season) —379—Chicago, 154 games, 1906.
N. L. (162-game season) —472—St. Louis, 162 games, 1968.

Most Opponents' Earned Runs, Season

N. L.— 1024— Philadelphia, 156 games, 1930.
A. L.— 935— St. Louis, 155 games, 1936.

Fewest Opponents' Earned Runs, Season

N. L.— 332— Philadelphia, 153 games, 1915.
A. L.— 343— Chicago, 156 games, 1917.

Most Opponents' Hits, Season

N. L.— 1993— Philadelphia, 156 games, 1930.
A. L.— 1776— St. Louis, 155 games, 1936.

Fewest Opponents' Hits, Season

A. L.— 1087— Cleveland, 162 games, 1968.
N. L.— 1174— Pittsburgh, 153 games, 1909.

Most No-Hit Games, Season

A. A.—2—Louisville 1882; Columbus 1884; Philadelphia 1888.
A. L.—2—Boston 1904; Cleveland 1908; Chicago 1914; Boston 1916; St. Louis 1917; New
         York 1951; Detroit 1952; Boston 1962; California 1973.
N. L.—2—Brooklyn 1906; Cincinnati 1938; Brooklyn 1956; Milwaukee 1960; Cincinnati
         1965; Chicago 1972.

Most No-Hit Games by Opponents, Season

A. A.—2—Pittsburgh 1884.
N. L.—2—Providence 1885; Boston 1898; Philadelphia 1960; Chicago 1965; Cincinnati
         1971.
A. L.—2—Cleveland 1910; Chicago 1917; Philadelphia 1923; Detroit 1967, 1973; Califor-
         nia 1977.

Most Consecutive Years With No-Hit Games by Pitchers

N. L.—4—Los Angeles, 1962, 1963, 1964, 1965.
A. L.—3—Boston, 1916, 1917, 1918.
         Cleveland, 1946, 1947, 1948.
         Baltimore, 1967, 1968, 1969.
         California, 1973, 1974, 1975.

Most Consecutive Years Without No-Hit Games by Pitchers

N. L.—57—Philadelphia, 1907 through 1963.
A. L.—39—Detroit, 1913 through 1951.

Most Consecutive Years Without Losing No-Hit Games

N. L.—40—St. Louis, 1920 through 1959.
A. L.—29—Washington, 1918 through 1946.

Most One-Hit Games, Season

A. L. (162-game season) —5—Baltimore, 1964.
A. L. (154-game season) —4—Cleveland, 1907.
                            New York, 1934.
N. L. (162-game season) —4—Philadelphia, 1979
N. L. (154-game season) —4—Chicago, 1906, 1909.
                            Philadelphia, 1907, 1911, 1915.

Most Consecutive One-Hit Nine-Inning Games

N. L.—2—Providence vs. New York, June 17, 18, 1884.
         Brooklyn vs. Cincinnati, July 5, 6, 1900.
         New York vs. Boston, September 28, second game, 30, first game, 1916.
         Milwaukee vs. New York, September 10, 11, 1965.
         New York vs. Chicago, Philadelphia, May 13, 15, 1970.
         Houston vs. Philadelphia, New York, June 18, 19, 1972.
A. L.—2—Cleveland vs. New York, September 25, 26, 1907.
         Washington vs. Chicago, August 10, 11, 1917.

Most One-Hit Games by Opponents, Season

A. L.—5—St. Louis, 1910.
    Cleveland, 1915.
N. L.—4—New York, 1965.

Most Home Runs Allowed, Season

A. L. (162-game season)—220—Kansas City, 163 games, 1964.
A. L. (154-game season)—187—Kansas City, 154 games, 1956.
N. L. (162-game season)—192—New York, 161 games, 1962.
N. L. (154-game season)—185—St. Louis, 154 games, 1955.

Most Home Runs With Bases Filled, Allowed, Season

A. L.—9—Chicago, 153 games, 1934.
        St. Louis, 156 games, 1938.
        St. Louis, 154 games, 1950.
N. L.—8—Philadelphia, 152 games, 1933.
        Pittsburgh, 155 games, 1951.
        Chicago, 156 games, 1961.
        Los Angeles, 161 games, 1970.
        Philadelphia, 162 games, 1974.

Fewest Home Runs With Bases Filled, Allowed, Season

N. L.-A. L.—0—Held by many clubs.
N. L.—Last club, San Diego, 1980.
A. L.—Last clubs, California, Kansas City, Toronto, 1980.

Most Sacrifice Hits Allowed, Season

N. L. (162-game season)—112—San Diego, 162 games, 1975.
N. L. (154-game season)—106—New York, 154 games, 1956.
A. L. (162-game season)—106—Chicago, 163 games, 1961.
A. L. (154-game season)—110—Kansas City, 158 games, 1960.

Fewest Sacrifice Hits Allowed, Season

A. L.—32—Detroit, 162 games, 1983.
N. L.—44—Montreal, 156 games, 1972.

Most Sacrifice Flies Allowed, Season

N. L.—79—Pittsburgh, 154 games, 1954.
A. L.—70—Toronto, 161 games, 1977.
        Oakland, 162 games, 1979.

Fewest Sacrifice Flies Allowed, Season

N. L.—17—San Francisco, 162 games, 1963.
A. L.—17—Detroit, 164 games, 1968.

Most Bases on Balls, Season

A. L. (162-game season)—770—Cleveland, 162 games, 1971.
A. L. (154-game season)—812—New York, 155 games, 1949.
N. L. (162-game season)—716—Montreal, 162 games, 1970.
N. L. (154-game season)—671—Brooklyn, 157 games, 1946.

Fewest Bases on Balls, Season

N. L.— 295— New York, 153 games, 1921.
A. L.— 359— Detroit, 158 games, 1909.

Most Intentional Bases on Balls, Season

N. L.— 116— San Diego, 162 games, 1974.
A. L.— 94— Seattle, 163 games, 1980.

Fewest Intentional Bases on Balls, Season

N. L.— 9—Los Angeles, 162 games, 1974.
A. L.—16—Minnesota, 162 games, 1973.
        New York, 159 games, 1976.

Most Strikeouts, Season

N. L. (162-game season)—1221—Houston, 162 games, 1969.
N. L. (154-game season)—1122—Los Angeles, 154 games, 1960.
A. L. (162-game season)—1189—Cleveland, 162 games, 1967.
A. L. (154-game season)—1000—California, 155 games, 1972.

Fewest Strikeouts, Season

A. L.— 356— Boston, 154 games, 1930.
N. L.— 357— New York, 153 games, 1921.

Most Hit Batsmen, Season

N. L.—85—Pittsburgh, 134 games, 1895.
A. L.—81—Philadelphia, 152 games, 1911.
N. L. since 1900—68—Brooklyn, 139 games, 1903.

Fewest Hit Batsmen, Season

A. L. (154-game season)— 5—St. Louis, 154 games, 1945.
A. L. (162-game season)—10—Baltimore, 162 games, 1983.
N. L. (154-game season)—10—St. Louis, 155 games, 1948.
N. L. (162-game season)—12—San Diego, 162 games, 1978.
                                Los Angeles, 163 games, 1980.
                                San Diego, 163 games, 1980.

Most Wild Pitches, Season

N. L. (162-game season)—91—Houston, 162 games, 1970.
N. L. (154-game season)—70—Los Angeles, 154 games, 1958.
A. L. (162-game season)—87—Cleveland, 162 games, 1973.
A. L. (154-game season)—67—Philadelphia, 154 games, 1936.

Fewest Wild Pitches, Season

N. L.— 9—Cincinnati, 155 games, 1944.
A. L.—10—St. Louis, 154 games, 1930.
         Cleveland, 153 games, 1943.

Most Balks, Season

N. L.—25—San Diego, 162 games, 1977.
A. L.—16—Seattle, 162 games, 1983.

Fewest Balks, Season

A. L.-N. L.—0—Held by many clubs.

Most Balks, Game, One Club, Nine Innings

N. L.—6—Milwaukee vs. Chicago, May 4, 1963.
A. L.—4—New York vs. Chicago, May 3, 1950.

Most Balks, Game, Both Clubs, Nine Innings

N. L.—7—Pittsburgh 4, Cincinnati 3, April 13, 1963.
         Milwaukee 6, Chicago 1, May 4, 1963.
A. L.—5—Cleveland 3, Philadelphia 2, May 12, 1930.

Lowest Earned-Run Average, Season

A. L.—2.16—Chicago, 156 games, 1917.
N. L.—2.18—Philadelphia, 153 games, 1915.

Highest Earned-Run Average, Season

N. L.—6.70—Philadelphia, 156 games, 1930.
A. L.—6.24—St. Louis, 155 games, 1936.

Most Pitchers Winning 20 or More Games, Season, Since 1900

A. L.—4—Chicago, 1920.
         Baltimore, 1971.
N. L.—3—Pittsburgh, 1902.
         Chicago, 1903.
         New York, 1904, 1905, 1913, 1920.
         Cincinnati, 1923.

Most Consecutive Years With Pitchers Winning 20 or More Games

A. L.—13—Baltimore, 1968 through 1980.
N. L.—12—New York, 1903 through 1914.

Most Consecutive Years Without Pitchers Winning 20 or More Games

N. L.—32—Philadelphia, 1918 through 1949.
A. L.—15—Philadelphia, 1934 through 1948.
         St. Louis, 1904 through 1918.

Most Pitchers Losing 20 or More Games, Season, Since 1900

N. L.—4—Boston, 1905, 1906.
A. L.—3—Washington, 1904.
         St. Louis, 1905.
         Philadelphia, 1916.

Most Shutout Games Participated, Season

A. L. (154-game season)—47—Chicago, won 22, lost 24 (1 tie), 1910.
A. L. (162-game season)—44—California, won 28, lost 16, 1964.
N. L. (154-game season)—46—St. Louis, won 13, lost 33, 1908.
N. L. (162-game season)—47—New York, won 25, lost 22, 1968.

Fewest Shutout Games Participated, Season

A. L.—5—Chicago, won 3, lost 2, 1977.
N. L.—6—Philadelphia, won 3, lost 3, 1930.

Most Shutout Games Won or Tied, Season

N. L. (162-game season)—30—St. Louis, 1968.
N. L. (154-game season)—32—Chicago, 1907, 1909.
A. L. (162-game season)—28—California, 1964.
A. L. (154-game season)—32—Chicago, 1906 (including 2 ties).

Fewest Shutout Games Won or Tied, Season, 150 or More Games

N. L.—0—Brooklyn, 1898.
          Washington, 1898.
          St. Louis, 1898.
          Cleveland, 1899.
A. L.—1—Chicago, 1924.
          Washington, 1956.
          Seattle, 1977.
N. L. since 1900—1—Boston, 1928.

Most Shutout Games Lost, Season

N. L.—33—St. Louis, 1908.
A. L.—29—Washington, 1909 (also 1 tie).

Most Shutout Games Lost, Season, League Champion

N. L. (154-game season)—15—New York, 1913 (also 1 tie).
                              Philadelphia, 1915.
N. L. (162-game season)—17—Los Angeles, 1966.
A. L. (154-game season)—14—Chicago, 1906 (also 2 ties).
                              Philadelphia, 1913.
                              Detroit, 1945.
A. L. (162-game season)—15—Boston, 1967.

Fewest Shutout Games Lost, Season, 150 or More Games

A. L.—0—New York, 156 games, 1932 (no tie games).
N. L.—1—Brooklyn, 155 games, 1953 (no tie games).
          Cincinnati, 162 games, 1970, (no tie games).

Most Consecutive Games Without Being Shut Out, League

A. L.— 308— New York, August 3, 1931 through August 2, 1933.
N. L.— 182— Philadelphia, August 17, 1893 through May 10, 1895.

Most Consecutive Shutout Games Won, Season

N. L.—6—Pittsburgh, June 2 through June 6, 1903, (51 innings).
A. L.—5—Baltimore, September 2, 2, 4, 6, 6, 1974 (45 innings).

Most Consecutive Innings Shut Out Opponent, Season

N. L.—56—Pittsburgh, June 1 (last 2 innings) through June 9 (first 3 innings), 1903.
A. L.—54—Baltimore, September 1, (last inning) through September 7, 1974, (first 8 innings).

Most Consecutive Shutouts Lost, Season

N. L.—4—Boston, May 19 through 23, 1906.
          Cincinnati, July 30 through August 3, 1908.
          Cincinnati, July 31 through August 3, 1931.
          Houston, June 20, 21, 22, 23, first game, 1963.
          Houston, September 9, 10, 11, 11, 1966.
          Chicago, June 16, 16, 19, 20, 1968, 38 innings.
A. L.—4—Boston, August 2 through 6, 1906.
          Philadelphia, September 23 through September 25, 1906.
          St. Louis, August 25 through August 30, 1913.
          Washington, September 19, 20, 21, 22, 1958.
          Washington, September 1, 2, 4, 5, 1964.

Most Consecutive Innings Shut Out by Opponent, Season

A. L.—48—Philadelphia, September 22, last 7 innings, through September 26, first 5 innings, 1906.
N. L.—48—Chicago, June 15, last 8 innings, through June 21, first 2 innings, 1968.

Most Shutouts Won From One Club, Season

N. L. (162-game season)— 7—New York vs. Philadelphia, 1969, (lost 1).
N. L. (154-game season)—10—Pittsburgh vs. Boston, 1906, (lost 1).
A. L. (162-game season)— 6—Baltimore vs. Washington, 1969, (lost 1).

A. L. (154-game season)— 8—Chicago vs. Boston, 1906, (lost 1).
　　　　　　　　　　　　　　Cleveland vs. Washington, 1956, (lost 0).
　　　　　　　　　　　　　　Oakland vs. Cleveland, 1968, (lost 1).

Winning Two 1-0 Games, One Day

N. L.—12 times by clubs. Last time—Pittsburgh vs. St. Louis October 3, 1976.
A. L.— 1 time—Baltimore vs. Boston, September 2, 1974.

Most 1-0 Games Won, Season

A. L.—11—Washington, 1914, (lost 4).
N. L.—10—Pittsburgh, 1908, (lost 1).

Fewest 1-0 Games Won, Season

N. L.-A. L.—0—Held by many clubs.
N. L.—Last clubs—Atlanta, Chicago, Cincinnati, Montreal, St. Louis, San Diego, 1983.
A. L.—Last clubs—Boston, California, Detroit, Toronto, 1983.

Most 1-0 Games Lost, Season

N. L.—10—Pittsburgh, 1914; Chicago, 1916; Philadelphia, 1967.
A. L.— 9—New York, 1914; Chicago, 1968.

Fewest 1-0 Games Lost, Season

N. L.-A. L.—0—Held by many clubs.
N. L.—Last clubs—Atlanta, New York, 1983.
A. L.—Last clubs—Cleveland, Texas, Toronto, 1983.

Most 1-0 Games Won, Season, From One Club

N. L.—4—Held by four clubs. Last club—Cincinnati vs. Brooklyn, 1910.
A. L.—4—Held by four clubs. Last club—Detroit vs. Boston, 1917.

Most Consecutive 1-0 Games Won, Season

A. L.—3—Chicago, April 25, 26, 27, 1909.
N. L.—3—St. Louis, August 31, second game (5 innings), September 1, 1, 1917.

Most Consecutive 1-0 Games Lost, Season

A. L.—3—St. Louis, April 25, 26, 27, 1909.
　　　　　　Washington, May 7, 8, 10, (11 innings), 1909.
N. L.—3—Brooklyn, September 7, 7, 8 (11 innings), 1908.
　　　　　　Pittsburgh, August 31, second game (5 innings), September 1, 1, 1917.
　　　　　　Philadelphia, May 11, 12, 13, 1960.

Doubleheader Shutouts Since 1900; 100 in National League, 87 in American League

N. L.— Last— October 3, 1976, Pittsburgh vs. St. Louis, 1-0, 1-0, Pittsburgh winner.
A. L.— Last— September 25, 1977, New York vs. Toronto, 15-0, 2-0, New York winner.

LEAGUE PITCHING RECORDS

Most Complete Games, Season

A. L.—(8-club league)—1100 in 1904.
A. L.—(10-club league)— 426 in 1968.
A. L.—(12-club league)— 650 in 1975.
A. L.—(14-club league)— 645 in 1978.
N. L.—(8-club league)—1089 in 1904.
N. L.—(10-club league)— 471 in 1968.
N. L.—(12-club league)— 546 in 1971.

Fewest Complete Games, Season

A. L.—312 in 1960. N. L.—289 in 1982.

Most Runs, Season

A. L.—(14-club league)—10,527 in 1979.
A. L.—(12-club league)—8314 in 1973.
A. L.—(10-club league)—7342 in 1961.
A. L.—(8-club league)—7009 in 1936.
N. L.—(12-club league)—8771 in 1970.
N. L.—(10-club league)—7278 in 1962.
N. L.—(8-club league)—7025 in 1930.

Fewest Runs, Season

N. L.—4136 in 1908.   A. L.—4272 in 1909.

Most Earned Runs, Season

  A. L.— (14-club league) —9393 in 1979.
  A. L.— (12-club league) —7376 in 1973.
  A. L.— (10-club league) —6451 in 1961.
  A. L.— (8-club league) —6120 in 1936.
  N. L.— (12-club league) —7827 in 1970.
  N. L.— (10-club league) —6345 in 1962.
  N. L.— (8-club league) —6046 in 1930.

Fewest Earned Runs, Season

  N. L.—3258 in 1916.   A. L.—3414 in 1914.

Most Bases on Balls, Season

  A. L.— (14-club league) —7413 in 1979.
  A. L.— (12-club league) —7032 in 1969.
  A. L.— (10-club league) —5902 in 1961.
  A. L.— (8-club league) —5627 in 1949.
  N. L.— (12-club league) —6919 in 1970.
  N. L.— (10-club league) —5265 in 1962.
  N. L.— (8-club league) —4537 in 1950.

Most Intentional Bases on Balls, Season

  N. L.— (12-club league) —862 in 1973.
  N. L.— (10-club league) —804 in 1967.
  N. L.— (8-club league) —504 in 1956.
  A. L.— (14-club league) —646 in 1980.
  A. L.— (12-club league) —668 in 1969.
  A. L.— (10-club league) —534 in 1965.
  A. L.— (8-club league) —353 in 1957.

Fewest Bases on Balls, Season

  N. L.—2906 in 1921.   A. L.—3797 in 1922.

Most Strikeouts, Season

  N. L.— (12-club league) —11,628 in 1969.
  N. L.— (10-club league) —9649 in 1965.
  N. L.— (8-club league) —6824 in 1960.
  A. L.— (14-club league) —11,234 in 1977.
  A. L.— (12-club league) —10,957 in 1970.
  A. L.— (10-club league) —9956 in 1964.
  A. L.— (8-club league) —6081 in 1959.

Fewest Strikeouts, Season

  A. L.—3245 in 1924.   N. L.—3359 in 1926.

Most Pitchers, 100 or More Strikeouts, Season

  N. L.—45 in 1970.
  A. L.—39 in 1977.

Most Pitchers, 200 or More Strikeouts, Season

  N. L.—12 in 1969.
  A. L.— 7 in 1967, 1973.

Most Pitchers, 300 or More Strikeouts, Season

  A. A.— 6 in 1884.
  N. L.— 4 in 1884.
  U. A.— 3 in 1884.
  A. L.— 2 in 1971.
  N. L.—since 1900—1 in 1963, 1965, 1966, 1972, 1978, 1979.

Most Hit Batsmen, Season

  N. L.— (12-club league) —443 in 1969.
  N. L.— (8-club league) —415 in 1903.
  A. L.— (14-club league) —461 in 1977.
  A. L.— (12-club league) —439 in 1969.
  A. L.— (8-club league) —435 in 1909.

Fewest Hit Batsmen, Season

  A. L.—132 in 1947. N. L.—157 in 1943.

Most Wild Pitches, Season

  N. L.— (12-club league) —648 in 1969.
  N. L.— (10-club league) —550 in 1965.
  N. L.— (8-club league) —356 in 1961.

A. L.— (14-club league) —653 in 1979.
A. L.— (12-club league) —636 in 1969.
A. L.— (10-club league) —513 in 1966.
A. L.— (8-club league) —325 in 1936.

Fewest Wild Pitches, Season

A. L.—166 in 1931. N. L.—174 in 1943.

Most Balks, Season

N. L.— (12-club league) —184 in 1978.
N. L.— (10-club league) —147 in 1963.
A. L.— (14-club league) —111 in 1982.
A. L.— (12-club league) — 60 in 1976.
A. L.— (10-club league) — 51 in 1966.

Fewest Balks, Season

N. L.—13 in 1936, 1946, 1956. A. L.—18 in 1933, 1941.

Lowest Earned-Run Average, Season

N. L.—2.62 in 1916.   A. L.—2.73 in 1914.

Highest Earned-Run Average, Season

A. L.—5.04 in 1936.   N. L.—4.97 in 1930.

Most Pitchers Winning 20 or More Games, Season, Since 1900

A. L.— (12-club league) —12 in 1973.
A. L.— (8-club league) —10 in 1907, 1920.
N. L.— (12-club league) —9 in 1969.
N. L.— (8-club league) —9 in 1903.

Fewest Pitchers Winning 20 or More Games, Season, Since 1900

N. L.—0 in 1931, 1983.   A. L.—0 in 1955, 1960, 1982.

Most Pitchers Losing 20 or More Games, Season

N. L.—8 in 1905.   A. L.—7 in 1904.

Fewest Pitchers Losing 20 or More Games, Season

A. L.—0 in 1911, 1914, 1917, 1918, 1923, 1924, 1926, 1935, 1940, 1944, 1946, 1947, 1949, 1951,
    1955, 1958, 1959, 1960, 1962, 1964, 1965, 1967, 1968, 1970, 1972, 1976, 1977, 1978,
    1979, 1981, 1982, 1983 (32 years).
N. L.—0 in 1911, 1915, 1918, 1923, 1925, 1926, 1929, 1930, 1931, 1932, 1937, 1939, 1941, 1946,
    1947, 1948, 1949, 1951, 1953, 1956, 1958, 1959, 1961, 1967, 1968, 1970, 1971, 1975,
    1976, 1978, 1980, 1981, 1982, 1983 (34 years).

Most Shutouts, Season

A. L.— (12-club league) —193 in 1972.
A. L.— (10-club league) —154 in 1968.
A. L.— (8-club league) —146 in 1909.
N. L.— (12-club league) —166 in 1969.
N. L.— (10-club league) —185 in 1968.
N. L.— (8-club league) —164 in 1908.

Most Extra-Inning Shutouts, Season

A. L.— (12-club league) —12 in 1976.
A. L.— (10-club league) —10 in 1968.
A. L.— (8-club league) —12 in 1918.
N. L.— (12-club league) —12 in 1976.
N. L.— (10-club league) —11 in 1965.
N. L.— (8-club league) —8 in 1908, 1909, 1910.

Fewest Shutouts, Season

A. L.— (8-club league) —41 in 1930.
A. L.— (10-club league) —100 in 1961.
A. L.— (12-club league) —110 in 1970.
A. L.— (14-club league) —116 in 1979.
N. L.— (8-club league) —48 in 1925.
N. L.— (10-club league) —95 in 1962.
N. L.— (12-club league) —115 in 1983.

Most Shutouts, One Day

N. L.—5—July 13, 1888 (6 games).
        June 24, 1892 (8 games).
        July 21, 1896 (7 games).
        July 8, 1907 (5 games).
        September 7, 1908 (8 games).

Most Shutouts, One Day—Continued
September 9, 1916 (7 games).
May 31, 1943 (8 games).
June 17, 1969 (9 games).
A. L.—5—September 7, 1903 (8 games).
August 5, 1909 (6 games).
May 6, 1945 (8 games).
June 4, 1972 (9 games).

Most Shutouts, One Day, Both Leagues
8—June 4, 1972, 5 in A. L. (9 games), 3 in N. L. (7 games).
7—September 7, 1908, 5 in N. L. (8 games), 2 in A. L. (8 games).
August 23, 1942, 4 in A. L. (8 games), 3 in N. L. (8 games).
May 14, 1944, 4 in N. L. (8 games), 3 in A. L. (8 games).
May 24, 1964, 4 in N. L. (8 games, 3 in A. L. (9 games).
August 26, 1968, 4 in N. L. (8 games), 3 in A. L. (5 games).

Most 1-0 Games, Season
N. L.—(12-club league)—38 in 1976.
N. L.—(10-club league)—44 in 1968.
N. L.—(8-club league)—43 in 1907.
A. L.—(12-club league)—42 in 1971.
A. L.—(10-club league)—38 in 1968.
A. L.—(8-club league)—41 in 1908.

Fewest 1-0 Games, Season
A. L.—(8-club league)—4 in 1930, 1936.
A. L.—(10-club league)—16 in 1961.
A. L.—(12-club league)—15 in 1970.
A. L.—(14-club league)—12 in 1982.
N. L.—(8-club league)—5 in 1932, 1956.
N. L.—(10-club league)—13 in 1962.
N. L.—(12-club league)—13 in 1983.

Most 1-0 Games, One Day
A. L.—3—May 14, 1914; July 17, 1962.
N. L.—3—July 4, 1918; September 12, 1969; September 1, 1976.

Most No-Hit Games (Nine or More Innings), Season, Major Leagues
8 in 1884, 4 in A. A., 2 in N. L., 2 in U. A.
Since 1900—7 in 1917, 5 in A. L., 2 in N. L.

Most No-Hit Games (Nine or More Innings), Season
A. L.—(12-club league)—4 in 1973.
A. L.—(10-club league)—3 in 1967.
A. L.—(8-club league)—5 in 1917.
N. L.—(12-club league)—5 in 1969.
N. L.—(10-club league)—3 in 1965, 1968.
N. L.—(8-club league)—4 in 1880.

No-Hit Games (Nine or More Innings), League
N. L.—1876—to date—112—Cincinnati 15, Chicago 14, Houston 7, Los Angeles 6, (Brooklyn 11), Atlanta 1, (Milwaukee 4), (Boston 7), Montreal 3, New York (present club) 0, St. Louis 8, Pittsburgh 6, Philadelphia 6, San Diego 0, San Francisco 4 (original New York club 9), Baltimore 2, Buffalo 2, Cleveland 2, Louisville 2, Providence 2, Worcester 1.
N. L.—1901—to date— 86—Cincinnati 12, Chicago 9, Houston 7, Los Angeles 6, (Brooklyn 10), Atlanta 1, (Milwaukee 4), (Boston 5), Montreal 3, New York (present club) 0, Philadelphia 4, Pittsburgh 6, St. Louis 7, San Diego 0, San Francisco 4 (original New York club 8).
A. L.—1901—to date— 87—Baltimore 4 (St. Louis 5), Boston 14 California 6, Chicago 14, Cleveland 15, Detroit 4, Kansas City (present club) 3, Milwaukee 0 (Seattle 0), Minnesota 2, (original Washington club 2), New York 7, Oakland 4 (Kansas City 0), (Philadelphia 5), Texas 2 (Washington second club 0).

Fewest No-Hit Games, Season
N. L.—0—Made in many seasons—Last season—1982.
A. L.—0—Made in many seasons—Last season—1982.

Most No-Hit Games, One Day
N. L.—2 on April 22, 1898.   A. L.—1 made on many days.

Most One-Hit Games, Season, Nine or More Innings

    A. L.— (14-club league)—13 in 1979.
    A. L.— (12-club league)—11 in 1973.
    A. L.— (10-club league)—11 in 1968.
    A. L.— (8-club league)—12 in 1910, 1915.
    N. L.— (12-club league)—12 in 1971.
    N. L.— (10-club league)—13 in 1965.
    N. L.— (8-club league)—12 in 1906, 1910.

Fewest One-Hit Games, Season, Nine or More Innings

    A. L.— (12-club league)—4—in 1971.
    A. L.— (8-club league)—0—1922, 1926, 1927, 1930.
    N. L.— (12-club league)—4—in 1980.
    N. L.— (8-club league)—0—1924, 1929, 1932, 1952.

Most Pitchers, League, One Day, 1 Game

    N. L.—13—October 2, 1962.
    A. L.— 8—June 11, 1973.

Most Pitchers, League, One Day, 2 Games

    N. L.—19—May 4, 1954.   A. L.—18—August 10, 1959.

Most Pitchers, League, One Day, 3 Games

    N. L.—32—May 2, 1956.   A. L.—26—May 11, 1970.

Most Pitchers, League, One Day, 4 Games

    N. L.—39—May 6, 1950.   A. L.—33—September 10, 1955.

Most Pitchers, League, One Day, 5 Games

    A. L.—41—August 22, 1962.
            August 17, 1968.
            May 25, 1971.
    N. L.—39—May 13, 1969.

Most Pitchers, League, One Day, 6 Games

    A. L.—52—June 11, 1969.   N. L.—43—September 17, 1972.

Most Pitchers, League, One Day, 7 Games

    N. L.—51—September 23, 1973.   A. L.—49—September 7, 1959.

Most Pitchers, League, One Day, 8 Games

    N. L.—59—May 30, 1956.   A. L.—56—April 16, 1967.

Most Pitchers, League, One Day, 9 Games

    A. L.—66—May 30, 1969, July 20, 1969.   N. L.—50—July 29, 1973.

Most Pitchers, League, One Day, 10 Games

    N. L.—72—September 7, 1964.   A. L.—62—August 9, 1970.

Most Pitchers, Both Leagues, One Day, 8 Games

    60—April 22, 1960, 31 in N. L. (4 games), 29 in A. L. (4 games).

Most Pitchers, Both Leagues, One Day, 9 Games

    64—May 6, 1950, 39 in N. L. (4 games), 25 in A. L. (5 games).

Most Pitchers, Both Leagues, One Day, 10 Games

    71—August 22, 1962, 41 in A. L. (5 games), 30 in N. L. (5 games).

Most Pitchers, Both Leagues, One Day, 11 Games

    73—May 13, 1969, 39 in N. L. (5 games), 34 in A. L. (6 games).

Most Pitchers, Both Leagues, One Day, 12 Games

    87—June 11, 1969, 52 in A. L. (6 games), 35 in N. L. (6 games).

Most Pitchers, Both Leagues, One Day, 13 Games

    87—May 31, 1970, 45 in N. L. (7 games), 42 in A. L. (6 games).

Most Pitchers, Both Leagues, One Day, 14 Games

    88—April 16, 1967, 56 in A. L. (8 games), 32 in N. L. (6 games).

Most Pitchers, Both Leagues, One Day, 15 Games

    96—July 8, 1962, 54 in N. L. (8 games), 42 in A. L. (7 games).

Most Pitchers, Both Leagues, One Day, 16 Games

    108—May 30, 1969, 66 in A. L. (9 games), 42 in N. L. (7 games).

Most Pitchers, Both Leagues, One Day, 17 Games
Less than for 16 games.

Most Pitchers, Both Leagues, One Day, 18 Games
121—September 7, 1964, 72 in N. L. (10 games), 49 in A. L. (8 games).

Most Pitchers, Both Leagues, One Day, 19 Games
Less than for 18 games.

Most Pitchers, Both Leagues, One Day, 20 Games
104—June 10, 1962, 52 in N. L. (10 games), 52 in A. L. (10 games).

Most Pitchers, 300 or More Innings, Season
A. L.—(8-club league)—12 in 1904.
A. L.—(12-club league)—7 in 1973, 1974.
N. L.—(8-club league)—10 in 1905.
N. L.—(12-club league)—8 in 1969.

Most Pitchers Allowing 30 or More Home Runs, Season
A. L.—(10-club league)—10 in 1982.
N. L.—(12-club league)—5 in 1970.

Most Pitchers, League, Season
A. L.—(14-club league)—220 in 1979.
A. L.—(12-club league)—189 in 1970.
A. L.—(10-club league)—170 in 1962.
A. L.—(8-club league)—141 in 1946, 1955.
N. L.—(12-club league)—188 in 1970.
N. L.—(10-club league)—167 in 1967.
N. L.—(8-club league)—152 in 1946.

INDIVIDUAL BASE-RUNNING RECORDS

Most Stolen Bases, League
N. L.— 938—Louis C. Brock, Chicago, St. Louis, 19 years, 1961 through 1979.
A. L.— 892—Tyrus R. Cobb, Detroit, Philadelphia, 24 years, 1905 through 1928.

Highest Stolen Base Percentage, League (minimum 300 attempts)
A. L.—.842—Willie J. Wilson, Kansas City, 1976 through 1983.
N. L.—.831—David E. Lopes, Los Angeles, 1972 through 1981.

Most Stolen Bases, Season
A. A.— 156—Harry D. Stovey, Philadelphia, 130 games, 1888.
A. L.— 130—Rickey H. Henderson, Oakland, 149 games, 1982 (42 caught stealing).
N. L.— 118—Louis C. Brock, St. Louis, 153 games, 1974 (33 caught stealing).

Fewest Stolen Bases, Season, Most At-Bats
A. L.—0—Calvin E. Ripken, Baltimore, 162 games, 1983; 663 at-bats, 4 caught stealing.
N. L.—0—Peter E. Rose, Cincinnati, 162 games, 1975; 662 at-bats, 1 caught stealing.

Most Years, No Stolen Bases, League, 150 or More Games
Both Leagues—4—Deron R. Johnson, Cincinnati N. L., Philadelphia N. L., Chicago A. L.,
         Boston A. L., 1965, 1970, 1971, 1975; 3 in National League, 1 in
         American League.
A. L.—4—Kenneth W. Singleton, Baltimore, 1977, 1980, 1982, 1983.
N. L.—3—C. Dallan Maxvill, St. Louis, 1967, 1968, 1970.
         Deron R. Johnson, Cincinnati, Philadelphia, 1965, 1970, 1971 (also 1 year in
         American League, Chicago, Boston, 1975).

Most Times Stole Home, League
A. L.—35—Tyrus R. Cobb, Detroit, Philadelphia, 24 years, 1905 through 1928.
N. L.—27—George J. Burns, New York, Cincinnati, Philadelphia, 15 years, 1911 through
         1925.

Most Times Stole Home, Season
N. L.—7—Harold P. Reiser, Brooklyn, 122 games, 1946 (34 stolen bases).
A. L.—7—Rodney C. Carew, Minnesota, 123 games, 1969 (19 stolen bases).

Most Years Leading League in Most Stolen Bases
N. L.—10—Max Carey, Pittsburgh, 1913, 1915, 1916, 1917, 1918, 1920, 1922, 1923, 1924,
         1925.
A. L.— 9—Luis E. Aparicio, Chicago, Baltimore, 1956 through 1964.

Most Consecutive Years Leading League in Most Stolen Bases

A. L.—9—Luis E. Aparicio, Chicago, Baltimore, 1956 through 1964.
N. L.—6—Maurice M. Wills, Los Angeles, 1960 through 1965.

Most Years, 50 or More Stolen Bases, League

N. L.—12—Louis C. Brock, St. Louis, 1965, 1966, 1967, 1968, 1969, 1970, 1971, 1972, 1973, 1974, 1975, 1976.
A. L.— 8—Tyrus R. Cobb, Detroit, 1909, 1910, 1911, 1912, 1913, 1915, 1916, 1917.

Most Consecutive Years, 50 or More Stolen Bases, League

N. L.—12—Louis C. Brock, St. Louis, 1965 through 1976.
A. L.— 5—Tyrus R. Cobb, Detroit, 1909 through 1913.
Dagoberto B. Campaneris, Kansas City, Oakland, 1965 through 1969.

Fewest Stolen Bases, Season, for Leader in Most Stolen Bases

A. L.—15—Dominic P. DiMaggio, Boston, 141 games, 1950.
N. L.—16—Stanley C. Hack, Chicago, 152 games, 1938.

Most Caught Stealing, Season

A. L.—42—Rickey H. Henderson, Oakland, 149 games, 1982, 130 stolen bases.
N. L.—36—Miller J. Huggins, St. Louis, 148 games, 1914, 32 stolen bases.

Fewest Caught Stealing, Season, 50 or More Stolen Bases

N. L.—2—Max Carey, Pittsburgh, 155 games, 1922, 51 stolen bases.
A. L.—8—Luis E. Aparicio, Chicago, 153 games, 1960, 51 stolen bases.
Dagoberto B. Campaneris, Oakland, 135 games, 1969, 62 stolen bases.
Amos J. Otis, Kansas City, 147 games, 1971, 52 stolen bases.
Willie J. Wilson, Kansas City, 137 games, 1983, 59 stolen bases.

Fewest Caught Stealing, Season, 150 or More Games

N. L.-A. L.—0—Held by many players.

Fewest Caught Stealing, Season, for Leader in Caught Stealing

A. L.— 9—Walter A. Evers, Detroit, 143 games, 1950.
Manuel J. Rivera, Chicago, 139 games, 1956.
N. L.—10—Willie H. Mays, New York, 152 games, 1956.

Most Stolen Bases, With No Caught Stealing, Season

A. L.—16—Jimmy D. Sexton, Oakland, 69 games, 1982.
N. L.—12—Miguel A. Dilone, Pittsburgh, 29 games, 1977.

Most Stolen Bases, Consecutive, With No Caught Stealing, League

N. L.—38—David E. Lopes, Los Angeles, June 10, through August 24, 1975.
A. L.—32—Willie J. Wilson, Kansas City, July 23 through September 23, 1980.
Julio L. Cruz, Seattle, September 22, 1980 through June 11, 1981.

Most Consecutive Games With No Caught Stealing in Major Leagues

1206—Augustus Triandos, New York A. L., Baltimore A. L., Detroit A. L., Philadelphia N. L., Houston N. L., August 3, 1953 through August 15, 1965 (1 stolen base).

Most Consecutive Games With No Caught Stealing, League

A. L.—1079— August Triandos, New York, Baltimore, Detroit, August 3, 1953, through September 28,1963 (1 stolen base).
N. L.— 592— Frank J. Torre, Milwaukee, Philadelphia, April 20,1956 through August 10,1962 (4 stolen bases).

Most Stolen Bases, Game

N. L.—7—George F. Gore, Chicago, June 25, 1881.
William R. Hamilton, Philadelphia, August 31, 1894; second game.
A. L.—6—Edward T. Collins, Philadelphia, September 11, 1912; also September 22, 1912, first game.
N. L. since 1900—5—Dennis L. McGann, New York, May 27, 1904.
David E. Lopes, Los Angeles, August 24, 1974.
Lonnie Smith, St. Louis, September 4, 1982.

Most Stolen Bases, Two Consecutive Games

N. L.—8—Walter Wilmot, Chicago, August 6 (4), 7 (4), 1894.
A. L.—7—Edward T. Collins, Philadelphia, September 10 (1), 11 (6), 1912.
Amos J. Otis, Kansas City, April 30 (3), May 1 (4), 1975, 13 innings.
Rickey H. Henderson, Oakland, July 3 (4), 15 innings, July 4 (3), 1983.

Most Stolen Bases, Inning

N. L.—3—Held by many players. Last player—Peter E. Rose, Philadelphia, May 11, 1980, seventh inning.
A. L.—3—Held by many players. Last player—David E. Nelson, Texas, August, 30, 1974, first inning.

Most Stolen Bases, Inning, by Pinch-Runner

N. L.—2—William A. O'Hara, New York, September 1, 1909, sixth inning.
    William A. O'Hara, New York, September 2, 1909, ninth inning.
    Jacob A. Pitler, Pittsburgh, May 24, 1918, ninth inning.
    David I. Concepcion, Cincinnati, July 7, 1974, first game, seventh inning.
    Ronald LeFlore, Montreal, October 5, 1980, eighth inning.
A. L.—2—Raymond L. Dowd, Philadelphia, July 9, 1919, second game, ninth inning.
    Allan S. Lewis, Kansas City, July 15, 1967, seventh inning.
    Dagoberto B. Campaneris, Oakland, October 4, 1972, fourth inning.
    Donald Hopkins, Oakland, April 20, 1975, second game, seventh inning.

Most Times Stole Way First to Home, Inning, League

N. L.—3—John P. Wagner, Pittsburgh, 1902, 1907, 1909.
A. L.—3—Tyrus R. Cobb, Detroit, 1909, 1911, 1912.
N. L.—Last player—Peter E. Rose, Philadelphia, May 11, 1980, seventh inning.
A. L.—Last player—David E. Nelson, Texas, August 30, 1974, first inning.

Most Times Stole Home, Game

N. L.—2—Joseph B. Tinker, Chicago, June 28, 1910.
    Lawrence J. Doyle, New York, September 18, 1911.
    Walter P. Gautreau, Boston, September 3, 1927, first game.
A. L.—2—Joseph J. Jackson, Cleveland, August 11, 1912.
    Guy Zinn, New York, August 15, 1912.
    Edward T. Collins, Philadelphia, September 6, 1913.
    Tyrus R. Cobb, Detroit, June 18, 1915.
    William J. Barrett, Chcago, May 1, 1924.
    Victor P. Power, Cleveland, August 14, 1958, 9⅔ innings.

Most Caught Off Base, Game

A. A.—3—John Stricker, Philadelphia, August 29, 1883.
N. L.—3—Benjamin M. Kauff, New York, May 26, 1916.

Most Caught Stealing, League

N. L.— 307— Louis C. Brock, Chicago, St. Louis, 19 years, 1961 through 1979.
A. L.— 199— Dagoberto B. Campaneris, Kansas City, Oakland, Texas, California, New
     York, 19 years, 1964 through 1983.

Most Years Leading League in Caught Stealing

N. L. —7—Maurice M. Wills, Los Angeles, Pittsburgh, Montreal, 1961, 1962 (tied), 1963,
     1965, 1966, 1968, 1969.
    Louis C. Brock, Chicago, St. Louis, 1964, 1967, 1971, 1973, 1974, 1976, 1977
     (tied).
A. L.—6—Orestes A. Minoso, Chicago, Cleveland, 1952, 1953, 1954, 1957, 1958, 1960.

Most Caught Stealing, Inning

A. L.—2—Don E. Baylor, Baltimore, June 15, 1974, ninth inning.
N. L.—1—Held by many players.

Most Caught Stealing, Game

N. L.-A. L.—3—Held by many players.

CLUB BASE-RUNNING RECORDS

Most Stolen Bases, Season

A. A.— 638— Philadelphia, 137 games, 1887.
N. L.— 426— New York, 136 games, 1893.
N. L. since 1900—347—New York, 154 games, 1911.
A. L.— 341—Oakland, 161 games, 1976.

Most Players, 50 or More Stolen Bases, Season

A. L.—3—Oakland, 161 games, 1976. William A. North (75), Dagoberto B. Campaneris
    (54), Don E. Baylor (52).
N. L.—3—San Diego, 163 games, 1980. Eugene Richards (61), Osborne E. Smith (57),
    Jerry W. Mumphrey (52).

Most Years Leading League, Stolen Bases (Since 1900)

A. L.—30—Chicago.
N. L.—21—Brooklyn-Los Angeles (12-Brooklyn, 9-Los Angeles).
    15—Pittsburgh.

Most Times Stole Home, Season

A. L.—18—New York, 153 games, 1912 (245 stolen bases).
N. L.—17—Chicago, 157 games, 1911 (214 stolen bases).
    New York, 154 games, 1912 (319 stolen bases).

Fewest Stolen Bases, Season

A. L. (154-game season)—13—Washington, 154 games, 1957.
A. L. (162-game season)—18—Boston, 162 games, 1964.
N. L. (154-game season)—17—St. Louis, 157 games, 1949.
N. L. (162-game season)—22—San Francisco, 162 games, 1967.

Most Caught Stealing, Season, Since 1920

N. L.—149—Chicago, 154 games, 1924.
A. L.—123—Oakland, 161 games, 1976.

Fewest Caught Stealing, Season

N. L.— 8—Milwaukee, 154 games, 1958 (26 stolen bases).
A. L.—11—Kansas City, 155 games, 1960 (16 stolen bases).
       Cleveland, 161 games, 1961 (34 stolen bases).

Most Stolen Bases, Game, One Club

A. A.—19—Philadelphia vs. Syracuse, April 22, 1890.
N. L.—17—New York vs. Pittsburgh, May 23, 1890.
A. L.—15—New York vs. St. Louis, September 28, 1911
N. L. since 1900—11—New York vs. Boston, June 20, 1912.
       St. Louis vs. Pittsburgh, August 13, 1916, second game, 5 innings.

Most Stolen Bases, Game, Both Clubs

A. A.—21—Philadelphia 19, Syracuse 2, April 22, 1890.
N. L.—20—New York 17, Pittsburgh 3, May 23, 1890.
N. L. since 1900—16—New York 11, Boston 5, June 20, 1912.
A. L.—15—New York 15, St. Louis 0, September 28, 1911.
       St. Louis 8, Detroit 7, October 1, 1916.

Most Triple Steals, Game, One Club

A. L.—2—Philadelphia vs. Cleveland, July 25, 1930, first and fourth innings.
N. L.—1—Made in many games.

Most Triple Steals, Game, Both Clubs

A. L.—2—Philadelphia 2, Cleveland 0, July 25, 1930.
N. L.—1—Made in many games.

Longest Game Without Stolen Base, One Club

N. L.—26 innings— Boston vs. Brooklyn, May 1, 1920.
A. L.—24 innings— Detroit vs. Philadelphia, July 21, 1945.
       Philadelphia vs. Detroit, July 21, 1945.

Longest Game Without Stolen Base, Both Clubs

A. L.—24 innings— Detroit 0, Philadelphia 0, July 21, 1945.
N. L.—23 innings— San Francisco 0, New York 0, May 31, 1964, second game.

Most Stolen Bases, Inning, One Club

A. L.—8—Washington vs. Cleveland, July 19, 1915, first inning.
N. L.—8—Philadelphia vs. New York, July 7, 1919, first game, ninth inning.

Most Times Stole Home, Game, One Club

A. L.—3—Chicago vs. St. Louis, July 2, 1909.
       New York vs. Philadelphia, April 17, 1915.
N. L.—3—Chicago vs. Boston, August 23, 1909.
       New York vs. Pittsburgh, September 18, 1911.

Most Times Stole Home, Game, Both Clubs

A. L.—3—Chicago 3, St. Louis 0, July 2, 1909.
       New York 3, Philadelphia 0, April 17, 1915.
       Detroit 2, St. Louis 1, April 22, 1924.
N. L.—3—Chicago 3, Boston 0, August 23, 1909.
       New York 3, Pittsburgh 0, September 18, 1911.

Most Times Stole Home, Inning, One Club

N. L.—2—Made in many innings. Last time—St. Louis vs. Brooklyn, September 19, 1925,
       seventh inning.
A. L.—2—Made in many innings. Last time—Oakland vs. Kansas City, May 28, 1980,
       first inning.

Most Caught Stealing, Game, One Club

N. L.—8—Baltimore vs. Washington, May 11, 1897.
N. L. since 1900—7—St. Louis vs. Brooklyn, August 23, 1909, second game.
A. L.—6—St. Louis vs. Philadelphia, May 12, 1915.
       Chicago vs. Philadelphia, June 18, 1915.

Most Caught Stealing, Inning, One Club

A. A.—3—Cincinnati vs. Philadelphia, July 26, 1887, third inning.
A. L.—3—Detroit vs. New York, August 3, 1914, second inning.
N. L.—2—Made in many innings.

Most Left on Base, Season

A. L. (154-game season)—1334—St. Louis, 157 games, 1941.
A. L. (162-game season)—1263—Minnesota, 163 games, 1974.
N. L. (154-game season)—1278—Brooklyn, 155 games, 1947.
N. L. (162-game season)—1328—Cincinnati, 162 games, 1976.

Fewest Left on Base, Season

A. L. (154-game season)— 925—Kansas City, 154 games, 1957.
A. L. (162-game season)— 995—Kansas City, 160 games, 1966.
N. L. (154-game season)— 964—Chicago, 154 games, 1924.
N. L. (162-game season)—1019—San Francisco, 161 games, 1966.

Most Left on Base, Game, Nine Innings, One Club

A. L.—20—New York vs. Boston, September 21, 1956.
A. A.—18—Baltimore vs. Cincinnati, July 7, 1891.
N. L.—18—Boston vs. Baltimore, August 5, 1897.
              Pittsburgh vs. Cincinnati, September 8, 1905.
              Boston vs. St. Louis, July 11, 1923.
              St. Louis vs. Philadelphia, September 15, 1928, second game.
              New York vs. Philadelphia, August 7, 1943.
              St. Louis vs. Cincinnati, June 10, 1944.
              St. Louis vs. Philadelphia, September 14, 1950.
              Pittsburgh vs. Boston, June 5, 1951.

Most Left on Base, Game, Eight Innings, One Club

N. L.—17—Philadelphia vs. Chicago, June 15, 1926.
              New York vs. St. Louis, June 17, 1938.
              St. Louis vs. Chicago, September 23, 1951, first game.
A. L.—16—Made in many games.

Most Left on Base, 9-Inning Shutout Defeat, One Club

A. L.—15—New York vs. St. Louis, May 22, 1913.
              Washington vs. Cleveland, July 29, 1931.
              St. Louis vs. New York, August 1, 1941.
              Kansas City vs. Detroit, May 12, 1975.
N. L.—14—Pittsburgh vs. Philadelphia, May 10, 1913.
              St. Louis vs. Chicago, April 15, 1958.
              Los Angeles vs. Chicago, April 23, 1966.
              Philadelphia vs. Montreal, September 22, 1971.

Most Left on Base, 10-Inning Shutout Defeat, One Club

N. L.—14—Cincinnati vs. St. Louis, April 20, 1937.
A. L.—Less than 9-inning shutout game.

Most Left on Base, 10-Inning Game, One Club

N. L.—19—San Francisco vs. Los Angeles, September 21, 1969.
A. L.—19—Baltimore vs. Milwaukee, September 13, 1973.
              Texas vs. Detroit, August 26, 1975.

Most Left on Base, 11-Inning Game, One Club

A. L.—20—Philadelphia vs. Detroit, May 12, 1916.
              New York vs. Minnesota, April 24, 1971.
N. L.—20—New York vs. Philadelphia, April 23, 1929.

Most Left on Base, 12-Inning Game, One Club

N. L.-A. L.—Less than 11-inning game.

Most Left on Base, 13-Inning Game, One Club

A. L.—22—Boston vs. St. Louis, August 22, 1951.
N. L.—20—Pittsburgh vs. Philadelphia September 22, 1931.
              Brooklyn vs. Milwaukee, August 2, 1954.
              Cincinnati vs. San Diego, May 23, 1974.

Most Left on Base, 14-Inning Game, One Club

N. L.—25—Houston vs. San Francisco, July 11, 1970.
A. L.—22—Texas vs. Detroit, August 9, 1974.

Most Left on Base, 15-Inning Game, One Club

A. L.—23—Chicago vs. Cleveland, May 27, 1956, first game.
N. L.—22—St. Louis vs. Cincinnati, September 3, 1949.

Most Left on Base, 16-Inning Game, One Club

N. L.—20—Philadelphia vs. Brooklyn, September 4, 1922, second game.
A. L.—Less than for 15-inning game.

Most Left on Base, 17-Inning Game, One Club

N. L.—24—St. Louis vs. Pittsburgh, August 2, 1982.
A. L.—23—Cleveland vs. Philadelphia, August 14, 1929.

Most Left on Base, 18-Inning Game, One Club

A. L.—24—Cleveland vs. Philadelphia, July 10, 1932.
N. L.—23—Chicago vs. Cincinnati, August 9, 1942, first game.

Most Left on Base, 19-Inning Game, One Club

N. L.—26—San Diego vs. Pittsburgh, August 25, 1979.
A. L.—Less than for 18-inning game.

Most Left on Base, 20-Inning Game, One Club

N. L.—27—Atlanta vs. Philadelphia, May 4, 1973.
A. L.—Less than for 18-inning game.

Most Left on Base, Nine-Inning Game, Both Clubs

N. L.—30—Brooklyn 16, Pittsburgh 14, June 30, 1893.
New York 17, Philadelphia 13, July 18, 1943, first game.
A. L.—30—New York 15, Chicago 15, August 27, 1935, first game.
Los Angeles 15, Washington 15, July 21, 1961.

Most Left on Base, Ten-Inning Game, Both Clubs

N. L.—32—Philadelphia 18, Brooklyn 14, September 8, 1925, second game.
A. L.—Less than for 9-inning game.

Most Left on Base, 11-Inning Game, Both Clubs

A. L.—36—Philadelphia 20, Detroit 16, May 12, 1916.
N. L.—Less than for 10-inning game.

Most Left on Base, 12-Inning Game, Both Clubs

N. L.—33—Pittsburgh 18, New York 15, August 22, 1940, first game.
A. L.—Less than for 11-inning game.

Most Left on Base, 13-Inning Game, Both Clubs

A. L.—37—New York 19, Boston 18, September 29, 1956.
N. L.—37—Cincinnati 20, San Diego 17, May 23, 1974.

Most Left on Base, 14-Inning Game, Both Clubs

N. L.—37—Houston 20, Cincinnati 17, July 2, 1976, first game.
A. L.—Less than for 13-inning game.

Most Left on Base, 15-Inning Game, Both Clubs

A. L.—40—Chicago 23, Cleveland 17, May 27, 1956, first game.
N. L.—40—St. Louis 22, Cincinnati 18, September 3, 1949.

Most Left on Base, 16-Inning Game, Both Clubs

A. L.—37—Chicago 21, Detroit 16, May 9, 1952.
N. L.—Less than for 15-inning game.

Most Left on Base, 17-Inning Game, Both Clubs

A. L.—38—Boston 21, Baltimore 17, June 23, 1954.
N. L.—37—St. Louis 24, Pittsburgh 13, August 2, 1982.

Most Left on Base, 18-Inning Game, Both Clubs

N. L.—44—Chicago 23, Cincinnati 21, August 9, 1942, first game.
A. L.—44—Minnesota 23, Seattle 21, July 19, 1969.

Most Left on Base, 19-Inning Game, Both Clubs

A. L.—Less than for 18-inning game.
N. L.—Less than for 18-inning game.

Most Left on Base, 20-Inning Game, Both Clubs

N. L.—38—Atlanta 27, Philadelphia 11, May 4, 1973.
A. L.—Less than for 18-inning game.

Most Left on Base, 21-Inning Game, Both Clubs

N. L.—Less than for 18-inning game.
A. L.—Less than for 18-inning game

Most Left on Base, 22-Inning Game, Both Clubs

   A. L.—43—Detroit 23, New York 20, June 24, 1962.
   N. L.—42—Pittsburgh 24, Brooklyn 18, August 22, 1917.

Most Left on Base, 25-Inning Game, Both Clubs

   N. L.—45—New York 25, St. Louis 20, September 11, 1974.
   A. L.—No 25-inning game.

Most Left on Base, Extra-Inning Game, One Club

   N. L.—27—Atlanta vs. Philadelphia, May 4, 1973, 20 innings.
   A. L.—24—Cleveland vs. Philadelphia, July 10, 1932, 18 innings.

Most Left on Base, Extra-Inning Game, Both Clubs

   N. L.—45—New York 25, St. Louis 20, September 11, 1974, 23 innings.
   A. L.—44—Minnesota 23, Seattle 21, July 19, 1969, 18 innings.

Fewest Left on Base, 9-Inning Game, One Club

   A. L.-N. L.—0—Made in many games.

Fewest Left on Base, Extra-Inning Game, One Club

   A. L.—0—Philadelphia vs. New York, June 22, 1929, second game, 14 innings.
   N. L.—No game over nine-innings with none left on base.

Fewest Left on Base, Extra-Inning Game, Both Clubs

   N. L.—3—Chicago 2, Cincinnati 1, May 2, 1917, 10 innings.
   A. L.—4—Made in many games.

Fewest Left on Base, Game, Both Clubs

   N. L.—1—Los Angeles 1, Chicago 0, September 9, 1965.
   A. L.—2—Made in many games. Last time—Cleveland 1, Oakland 1, July 19, 1974.

Fewest Left on Base, Two Consecutive Games, One Club

   A. L.—2—Washington, May 27 (2), May 29 (0), 1952, (18 innings).
                Chicago vs. California, September 18 (1), September 19 (1), 1971, (17 innings).
   N. L.—2—San Francisco, May 6 (2), May 7 (0), 1960 (16 innings).
                San Francisco, June 13 (1), 10 innings, June 14 (1), 8 innings (18 innings), 1963.

Most Left on Base, Doubleheader, One Club, 18 Innings

   A. L.—30—Philadelphia vs. St. Louis, June 12, 1949, 18 innings.
   N. L.—29—St. Louis vs. Philadelphia, September 15, 1928, 18 innings.
                Philadelphia vs. Milwaukee, May 15, 1955, 18 innings.

Most Left on Base, Doubleheader, One Club, More Than 18 Innings

   A. L.—34—Cleveland vs. New York, August 18, 1943, 21⅓ innings.
   N. L.—30—Pittsburgh vs. Brooklyn, June 4, 1946, 20 innings.
                Philadelphia vs. Brooklyn, May 30, 1950 19 innings.

Most Left on Base, Doubleheader, Both Clubs, 18 Innings

   N. L.—49—Brooklyn 25, Pittsburgh 24, July 24, 1926.
   A. L.—49—New York 27, Chicago 22, August 27, 1935.

Fewest Left on Base, Doubleheader, One Club

   A. L.—3—Washington vs. New York, August 6, 1963, 17 innings.
   N. L.—3—San Francisco vs. Houston, September 24, 1978, 16 innings.

Fewest Left on Base, Doubleheader, Both Clubs

   N. L.—10—St. Louis 6, Boston 4, July 19, 1924.
   A. L.—13—Chicago 9, Philadelphia 4, July 18, 1918.

Most Men Caught Off Base, Game, One Club

   N. L.—5—Chicago vs. Brooklyn, June 24, 1901.
   A. A.—3—Philadelphia vs. Louisville, August 29, 1883.
   A. L.—3—New York vs. Washington, June 29, 1910.

CLUB RECORDS FOR SEASON

American League—1901 Through 1983

Present Franchise		Total Games	Won	Lost	Tied	Pct.
Baltimore	1954-83	4730	2610	2111	9	.553
Boston	1901-83	12828	6484	6261	83	.509
*California	1961-83	3664	1745	1916	3	.477
Chicago	1901-83	12837	6419	6318	100	.504
Cleveland	1901-83	12842	6552	6201	89	.514
Detroit	1901-83	12869	6613	6162	94	.518
Kansas City	1969-83	2364	1236	1126	2	.523
Milwaukee	1970-83	2208	1068	1138	2	.484
Minnesota	1961-83	3662	1849	1806	7	.506
New York	1903-83	12545	7119	5341	85	.571
Oakland	1968-83	2530	1297	1232	1	.513
Seattle	1977-83	1081	426	653	2	.395
Texas	1972-83	1880	888	988	4	.473
Toronto	1977-83	1076	437	639	0	.406
Present Totals		87116	44743	41892	481	.516

*Known as Los Angeles 1961-1965.

American League—1901 Through 1971

Extinct Franchises		Total Games	Won	Lost	Tied	Pct.
Baltimore	1901-02	276	118	153	5	.437
Kansas City	1955-67	2060	829	1224	7	.404
Milwaukee	1901	139	48	89	2	.353
Philadelphia	1901-54	8213	3886	4248	79	.478
St. Louis	1902-53	7974	3414	4465	95	.434
Seattle	1969	163	64	98	1	.396
aWashington	1901-60	9188	4223	4864	101	.465
bWashington	1961-71	1773	740	1032	1	.418
Extinct Totals		29786	13322	16173	291	.452
American League Totals		116902	58065	58065	772	.500

aOriginal Washington club.
bSecond Washington club.

National League—1876 Through 1983

Present Franchise		Total Games	Won	Lost	Tied	Pct.
Atlanta	1966-83	2853	1369	1478	6	.481
Chicago	1876-83	15781	8131	7499	151	.520
Cincinnati	1890-83	14404	7224	7058	122	.506
Houston	1962-83	3505	1664	1837	4	.475
Los Angeles	1958-83	4130	2281	1844	5	.553
Montreal	1969-83	2368	1118	1248	2	.473
New York	1962-83	3503	1498	1997	8	.429
Philadelphia	1883-83	15173	7002	8060	111	.465
Pittsburgh	1887-83	14787	7627	7034	126	.520
St. Louis	1892-83	14132	7047	6960	125	.503
San Diego	1969-83	2369	995	1372	2	.420
San Francisco	1958-83	4127	2156	1966	5	.523
Present Totals		97132	48112	48353	667	.499

National League—1876 Through 1965

Extinct Franchise		Total Games	Won	Lost	Tied	Pct.
Baltimore	1892-99	1117	644	447	26	.588
Boston	1876-52	10852	5118	5598	136	.478
Brooklyn	1890-57	10253	5214	4926	113	.514
Buffalo	1879-85	656	314	333	9	.486
Cincinnati	1876-80	348	125	217	6	.368
Cleveland	1879-84	549	242	299	8	.448
Cleveland	1889-99	1534	738	764	32	.492
Detroit	1881-88	879	426	437	16	.494
Hartford	1876-77	129	78	48	3	.619
Indianapolis	1878	63	24	36	3	.405
Indianapolis	1887-89	398	146	249	3	.371
Kansas City	1886	126	30	91	5	.258
Louisville	1876-77	130	65	61	4	.515

National League—1876 Through 1965—Continued

Extinct Franchise		Total Games	Won	Lost	Tied	Pct.
Louisville	1892-99	1121	419	683	19	.382
Milwaukee	1878	61	15	45	1	.254
Milwaukee	1953-65	2044	1146	890	8	.563
New York	1876	57	21	35	1	.377
New York	1883-57	11116	6067	4898	151	.553
Philadelphia	1876	60	14	45	1	.242
Providence	1878-85	725	438	278	9	.610
St. Louis	1876-77	124	73	51	0	.589
St. Louis	1885-86	236	79	151	6	.347
Syracuse	1879	71	22	48	1	.317
Troy	1879-82	330	134	191	5	.414
Washington	1886-89	514	163	337	14	.331
Washington	1892-99	1125	410	697	18	.372
Worcester	1880-82	252	90	159	3	.363
Extinct Totals		44870	22255	22014	601	.503
National League Totals		142002	70367	70367	1268	.500

American Association—1882 Through 1891

		Total Games	Won	Lost	Tied	Pct.
Baltimore	1882-89	944	403	519	22	.439
Baltimore	1890-91	174	87	81	6	.517
Boston	1891	139	93	42	4	.684
Brooklyn	1884-89	783	410	354	19	.536
Brooklyn	1890	101	26	74	1	.262
Cincinnati	1882-89	957	549	396	12	.580
Cincinnati	1891	102	43	57	2	.431
Cleveland	1887-88	268	89	174	5	.341
Columbus	1883-84	207	101	104	2	.493
Columbus	1889-91	418	200	209	9	.489
Indianapolis	1884	110	29	78	3	.277
Kansas City	1888-89	271	98	171	2	.365
Louisville	1882-91	1233	575	638	20	.475
Milwaukee	1891	36	21	15	0	.583
New York	1883-87	592	270	309	13	.467
Philadelphia	1882-91	1223	633	564	26	.528
Pittsburgh	1882-86	538	236	296	6	.444
Richmond	1884	46	12	30	4	.304
Rochester	1890	133	63	63	7	.500
St. Louis	1882-91	1235	782	433	20	.641
Syracuse	1890	128	55	72	1	.434
Toledo	1884	110	46	58	6	.446
Toledo	1890	134	68	64	2	.515
Washington	1884	63	12	51	0	.191
Washington	1891	139	43	92	4	.324
Association Totals		10084	4944	4944	196	.500

Most Games, League

N. L.—15,781—Chicago, 108 years, 1876 to date.
A. L.—12,869—Detroit, 83 years, 1901 to date.

Most Games Won, League

N. L.—8,131—Chicago, 108 years, 1876 to date.
A. L.—7,119—New York, 81 years, 1903 to date.

Most Games Lost, League

N. L.—8,060—Philadelphia, 101 years, 1883 to date.
A. L.—6,318—Chicago, 83 years, 1901 to date.

Most Games, Season

N. L. (162-game season)—165—Los Angeles, San Francisco, 1962 (3 playoffs).
N. L. (154-game season)—160—Cincinnati, 1915 (6 tied).
A. L. (162-game season)—164—Cleveland, 1964 (2 tied). New York, 1964 (2 tied).
Minnesota, 1967 (2 tied). Detroit, 1968 (2 tied).
New York, 1968 (2 tied).
A. L. (154-game season)—162—Detroit, 1904 (10 tied, 2 unplayed).

Most Times Two Games in One Day, Season

    A. L. (154-game season)—44—Chicago, 1943. (Won 11, lost 10, split 23).
    A. L. (162-game season)—29—Chicago, 1967. (Won 9, lost 5, split 15).
                               Kansas City, 1967. (Won 3, lost 9, split 17).
    N. L. (154-game season)—43—Philadelphia, 1943. (Won 11, lost 14, split 18).
    N. L. (162-game season)—28—New York, 1962. (Won 3, lost 15, split 10).

Fewest Times Two Games in One Day, Season

    N. L. (162-game season)—1—Los Angeles, 1979 (Won 0, lost 0, split 1).
    A. L. (162-game season)—0—Seattle, 1983 (Won 0, lost 0, split 0).

Most Games Won, One Month, by Clubs

American League, Since 1901

aMilwaukee ....11, May 1901, July 1901.
St. Louis.........................23, August 1945.
bBaltimore ....25, June 1966.
Boston ....24, July 1948, August 1949, August 1950.
cLos Angeles ....19, June 1963, June 1964, July 1964.
California ....20, June 1967.
Chicago..........................23, September 1905.
Cleveland........................26, August 1954.
Detroit............................23, July 1908, August 1915, August 1934, August 1935.
dKansas City ....25, September 1977.
kSeattle..........................14, June 1969, September 1969.
eMilwaukee ....21, June 1978.
fWashington...................24, August 1945.
Minnesota......................23, July 1969.
gBaltimore ....16, July 1901.
New York ....28, August 1938.
Philadelphia...................26, July 1931.
hKansas City ....19, July 1959.
Oakland ....23, August 1971.
iWashington...................19, July 1967.
Texas..............................21, September 1978.
jSeattle...........................16, June 1979.
Toronto ....18, May 1983.

    aOriginal Milwaukee club, 1901; bPresent Baltimore club; cName changed to California on September 2, 1965; dPresent Kansas City club; ePresent Milwaukee club; fOriginal Washington club; gBaltimore club 1901-1902; hOriginal Kansas City club; iWashington second club. jPresent Seattle club. kOriginal Seattle club.

National League, Since 1900

Boston ....26, September 1914.
Milwaukee ....23, August 1953, August 1958.
Atlanta...........................20, September 1966, September 1969.
Chicago..........................26, August 1906, July 1935, July 1945.
Cincinnati......................24, August 1918, July 1973.
Houston..........................20, May 1969, July 1976, June 1979.
Brooklyn........................25, July 1947, August 1953.
Los Angeles ....21, May 1962, July 1963, June 1973.
Montreal........................23, September 1979.
aNew York.....................23, September 1969.
Philadelphia...................22, September 1916, July 1950, July 1952, May 1976, September
                               1983.
Pittsburgh ....25, September 1901, September 1908, July 1932.
St. Louis.........................26, July 1944.
San Diego ....17, June 1974, July 1978, June 1982, June 1983.
bNew York.....................29, September 1916.
San Francisco................21, September 1965, August 1968.

    aPresent New York club; bOriginal New York club.

Most Games Lost, One Month, by Clubs

American League, Since 1901

Milwaukee ....18, June 1901, July 1901, September 1901.
St. Louis.........................24, September 1939, July 1952.
bBaltimore ....25, August 1954.
Boston ....24, July 1925, June 1927, July 1928.
cLos Angeles ....22, June 1961, May 1964.
California ....22, August 1968.
Chicago..........................24, June 1934, August 1968.
Cleveland........................24, July 1914.
Detroit............................24, June 1975.

Most Games Lost, One Month, by Clubs—Continued

dKansas City ....20, September 1974.
Seattle ....22, August 1969.
eMilwaukee ....23, August 1977.
fWashington...................29, July 1909.
Minnesota......................26, May 1981, May 1982.
gBaltimore ....23, September 1902.
New York ....24, July 1908.
Philadelphia...................28, July 1916.
hKansas City ....26, August 1961.
Oakland ....24, June 1979.
iWashington...................24, August 1961.
Texas...............................24, August 1973.
jSeattle............................22, August 1977.
Toronto...........................23, May 1979.

aMilwaukee club, 1901; bPresent Baltimore club; cName changed to California on September 2, 1965; dPresent Kansas City club; ePresent Milwaukee club; fOriginal Washington club; gBaltimore club, 1901-1902; hOriginal Kansas City club; iWashington second club; jPresent Seattle club.

National League, Since 1900

Boston ....25, September 1928, September 1935.
Milwaukee ....18, June 1954.
Atlanta.............................21, May 1976.
Chicago............................24, July 1957.
Cincinnati........................26, September 1914.
Houston............................24, July 1962.
Brooklyn..........................27, September 1908.
Los Angeles ....20, July 1968, June 1979.
Montreal..........................23, August 1969, September 1976.
aNew York.......................26, August 1962.
Philadelphia....................27, September 1939.
Pittsburgh.......................24, September 1916.
St. Louis..........................27, September 1908.
San Diego ....22, June 1969, August 1969, May 1974.
bNew York.......................25, August 1953.
San Francisco.................21, May 1972.

aPresent New York club; bOriginal New York club.

Fewest Games, Season

A. L. (154-game season)—147—Cleveland, 1945 (2 tied, 9 unplayed).
N. L. (154-game season)—149—Philadelphia, 1907 (2 tied, 7 unplayed), 1934 (5 unplayed).
A. L. (162-game season)—158—Baltimore, 1971 (4 unplayed).
N. L. (162-game season)—160—Cincinnati, 1966 (2 unplayed).
Atlanta, Montreal, 1979 (2 unplayed).

Most Night Games, Season (Includes Twilight Games)

A. L. (162-game season)—135—Texas, 1979 (won 68, lost 67).
N. L. (162-game season)—125—Houston, 1977 (won 67, lost 58).
Houston, 1983 (won 68, lost 57).

Most Night Games Won, Season

A. L. (154-game season)—47—Baltimore, 1960, lost 40.
A. L. (162-game season)—79—Baltimore, 1980, lost 44.
N. L. (154-game season)—61—Los Angeles, 1961, lost 44.
N. L. (162-game season)—72—Cincinnati, 1970, lost 41.
Los Angeles, 1977, lost 44.
Los Angeles, 1978, lost 44.

Most Night Games Lost, Season

N. L. (154-game season)—67—Philadelphia, 1961, won 23.
N. L. (162-game season)—82—Atlanta, 1977, won 43.
A. L. (154-game season)—48—Kansas City, 1956, won 20.
A. L. (162-game season)—83—Seattle, 1980, won 44.

Most Tie Games, Season

A. L.—10—Detroit, 1904.
N. L.— 9—St. Louis, 1911.

Fewest Tie Games, Season

N. L.-A. L.—0—By all clubs in many seasons.
N. L.—Last season, 1982.
A. L.—Last season, 1979.

Most Extra-Inning Games, Season

A. L.—31—Boston, 1943 (won 15, lost 14, 2 tied).
N. L.—27—Boston, 1943 (won 14, lost 13).
       Los Angeles, 1967 (won 10, lost 17).

Most Years, League

N. L.— 108— Chicago, 1876 to date (consecutive).
        Boston-Milwaukee-Atlanta, 1876 to date (consecutive).
A. L.— 83— Boston, Chicago, Cleveland, Detroit, Washington-Minnesota, 1901 to date (consecutive).

Highest Percentage Games Won, Season

U. A.—.850—St. Louis, won 91, lost 16, 1884.
N. L.—.798—Chicago, won 67, lost 17, 1880.
N. L. since 1900—.763—Chicago, won 116, lost 36, 1906.
A. L.—.721—Cleveland, won 111, lost 43, 1954.

Highest Percentage Games Won, Season, for League Champions Since 1969

A. L.—.673—Baltimore, won 109, lost 53, 1969.
N. L.—.667—Cincinnati, won 108, lost 54, 1975.

Highest Percentage Games Won, Season, for Second-Place Team

N. L.—.759—New York, won 85, lost 27, 1885.
N. L. since 1900—.680—Chicago, won 104, lost 49, 1909.
A. L.—.669—New York, won 103, lost 51, 1954.

Highest Percentage Games Won, Season, for Third-Place Team

N. L.—.691—Hartford, won 47, lost 21, 1876.
A. L.—.617—New York, won 95, lost 59, 1920.
N. L. since 1900—.608—Pittsburgh, won 93, lost 60, 1906.

Highest Percentage Games Won, Season, for Fourth-Place Team

N. L.—.623—Philadelphia, won 71, lost 43, 1886.
N. L. (10-club league)—.578—Pittsburgh, won 93, lost 68, 1962.
N. L. since 1900 (8-club League)—.569—Pittsburgh, won 87, lost 66, 1904.
A. L.—.597—Cleveland, won 92, lost 62, 1950.

Highest Percentage Games Won, Season, for Fifth-Place Team

A. L. (10-club league)—.537—Cleveland, won 87, lost 75, 1965.
A. L. (8-club league)—.536—Philadelphia, won 81, lost 70, 1904.
N. L.—.571—Boston, won 76, lost 57, 1882.
N. L. (10-club league)—.543—Milwaukee, won 88, lost 74, 1964.
N. L. since 1900 (8-club league)—.529—Chicago, won 81, lost 72, 1924.

Highest Percentage Games Won, Season, for Sixth-Place Team

N. L. (10-club league)—.528—Philadelphia, won 85, lost 76, 1965.
N. L.—.506—Detroit, won 42, lost 41, 1882.
N. L. since 1900 (8-club league)—.503—Brooklyn, won 77, lost 76, 1928.
A. L.—.513—Detroit, won 79, lost 75, 1962.

Highest Percentage Games Won, Season, for Seventh-Place Team

A. L.—.497—Washington, won 76, lost 77, 1916.
N. L. (10-club league)—.506—Chicago, won 82, lost 80, 1963.
N. L. (8-club league)—.464—Brooklyn, won 70, lost 81, 1917.

Highest Percentage Games Won, Season, for Eighth-Place Team

A. L.—(10-club league)—.475—Boston, won 76, lost 84, 1962.
N. L.—(10-club league)—.469—Chicago, won 76, lost 86, 1964.
       Los Angeles, won 76, lost 86, 1968 (tied for seventh).

Highest Percentage Games Won, Season, for Ninth-Place Team

N. L.—(10-club league)—.451—New York, won 73, lost 89, 1968.
A. L.—(10-club league)—.444—Kansas City, won 72, lost 90, 1962.
       Boston, won 72, lost 90, 1966.
       New York, won 72, lost 90, 1967.

Highest Percentage Games Won, Season, for Tailender

N. L.—(8-club league)—.454—New York, won 69, lost 83, 1915.
A. L.—(8-club league)—.431—Chicago, won 66, lost 87, 1924.
A. L.—(10-club league)—.440—New York, won 70, lost 89, 1966.

Most Games Won, Season

N. L. (162-game season)—108—Cincinnati, 1975 (won 108, lost 54).
N. L. (154-game season)—116—Chicago, 1906 (won 116, lost 36).

Most Games Won, Season—Continued

A. L. (162-game season)—109—New York, 1961 (won 109, lost 53).
Baltimore, 1969 (won 109, lost 53).
A. L. (154-game season)—111—Cleveland, 1954 (won 111, lost 43).

Fewest Games Won, Season

N. L. (154-game season)—20—Cleveland, 1899 (won 20, lost 134).
A. L. (154-game season)—36—Philadelphia, 1916 (won 36, lost 117).
N. L. since 1900 (154-game season)—38—Boston, 1935 (won 38, lost 115).
N. L. since 1900 (162-game season)—40—New York, 1962 (won 40, lost 120).
A. L. (162-game season)—53—Toronto, 1979 (won 53, lost 109).

Most Games Won From One Club, Season

N. L.—(8-club league)—21—Chicago vs. Boston, 1909 (won 21, lost 1).
Pittsburgh vs. Cincinnati, 1937 (won 21, lost 1).
Chicago vs. Cincinnati, 1945 (won 21, lost 1).
N. L.—(12-club league)—17—Atlanta vs. San Diego, 1974 (won 17, lost 1).
A. L.—(8-club league)—21—New York vs. St. Louis, 1927 (won 21, lost 1).
A. L.—(12-club league)—15—Baltimore vs. Milwaukee, 1973 (won 15, lost 3).

Most Games Won From League Champions, Season

N. L.—16—St. Louis vs. Chicago, 1945 (won 16, lost 6).
A. L.—14—Philadelphia vs. Detroit, 1909 (won 14, lost 8).
Minnesota vs. Oakland, 1973 (won 14, lost 4).

Most Consecutive Games Won From One Club, League

A. L.—(12-club league)—23—Baltimore vs. Kansas City, May 10, 1969 through August
2, 1970, last 11 in 1969, all 12 in 1970.
N. L.—(8-club league)—21—Boston vs. Philadelphia, all 14 in 1883, first 7 in 1884.
A. L.—(8-club league)—21—New York vs. St. Louis, first 21 in 1927.
N. L. since 1900—(8-club league)—20—Pittsburgh vs. Cincinnati, last 17 in 1937, first
3 in 1938.

Most Consecutive Games Lost to One Club, League

A. L.—(12-club league)—23—Kansas City vs. Baltimore, May 9, 1969 through August
2, 1970, last 11 in 1969, all 12 in 1970.
A. L.—(8-club league)—21—St. Louis vs. New York, first 21 in 1927.
N. L.—(8-club league)—21—Philadelphia vs. Boston, all 14 in 1883, first 7 in 1884.
N. L. since 1900—(8-club league)—20—Cincinnati vs. Pittsburgh, last 17 in 1937, first 3
in 1938.

Most Games Won From One Club, Two Consecutive Seasons

N. L.—(8-club league)—40—Pittsburgh vs. St. Louis, 1907, 1908.
A. L.—(8-club league)—37—Philadelphia vs. St. Louis, 1910, 1911.
Chicago vs. Philadelphia, 1915, 1916.
New York vs. Philadelphia, 1919, 1920.
New York vs. St. Louis, 1926, 1927.

Fewest Games Won From One Club, Season

A. A.—(8-club league)—1—Cleveland vs. St. Louis, won 1, lost 18, 1887.
Louisville vs. Brooklyn, won 1, lost 19, 1889.
N. L.—(8-club league)—1—Kansas City vs. Chicago, won 1, lost 17, 1886.
Washington vs. Chicago, won 1, lost 17, 1886.
Washington vs. Detroit, won 1, lost 17, 1886.
Indianapolis vs. Philadelphia, won 1, lost 17, 1887.
Boston vs. Chicago, won 1 lost 21, 1909.
Boston vs. Pittsburgh, won 1, lost 20, 1909.
Cincinnati vs. Pittsburgh, won 1, lost 21, 1937.
Cincinnati vs. Chicago, won 1, lost 21, 1945.
N. L.—(12-club league)—0—Baltimore vs. Boston, won 0, lost 13, 1892.
Cleveland vs. Brooklyn, won 0, lost 14, 1899.
Cleveland vs. Cincinnati, won 0, lost 14, 1899.
N. L. since 1900—(12-club league)—1—San Diego vs. Atlanta, won 1, lost 17, 1974.
Chicago vs. Cincinnati, won 1, lost 11, 1975.
Atlanta vs. St. Louis, won 1, lost 11, 1977.
Atlanta vs. Montreal, won 1, lost 9, 1979.
Chicago vs. Houston, won 1, lost 11, 1980.
New York vs. San Diego, won 1, lost 11, 1980.
Pittsburgh vs. Atlanta, won 1, lost 11, 1980.
Montreal vs. Los Angeles, won 1, lost 11, 1980.
Philadelphia vs. Los Angeles, won 1, lost 11,
1983.
N. L.—(10-club league)—1—Houston vs. Philadelphia, won 1, lost 17, 1962.
A. L.—(8-club league)—1—St. Louis vs. New York, won 1, lost 21, 1927.

A. L.—(10-club league)—1—Boston vs. Minnesota, won 1, lost 17, 1965.
A. L.—(12-club league)—0—Kansas City vs. Baltimore, won 0, lost 12, 1970.
A. L.—(14-club league)—0—Oakland vs. Baltimore, won 0, lost 11, 1978.

Most Consecutive Games Won From One Club, League, at Home

A. L.—22—Boston vs. Philadelphia, all 11 in 1949; all 11 in 1950; April 27, 1949 to September 10, 1950, inclusive.
N. L.—18—Milwaukee-Atlanta vs. New York, last 6 in 1964, all 9 in 1965, first 3 in 1966; June 27, 1964 through April 24, 1966, first game.

Most Games Won From One Club, Season, at Home

N. L.—16—Brooklyn vs. Pittsburgh, won 16, lost 2, 1890.
Philadelphia vs. Pittsburgh, won 16, lost 1, 1890.
N. L. since 1900—13—New York vs. Philadelphia, won 13, lost 2, 1904.
A. L.—12—Chicago vs. St. Louis, won 12, lost 0, 1915.

Most Consecutive Games Won From One Club, League, on Road

N. L.—18—Brooklyn vs. Philadelphia, all 11 in 1945; first 7 in 1946; May 5, first game, 1945 through August 10, 1946.
St. Louis vs. Pittsburgh, last 8 in 1964, all 9 in 1965, first 1 in 1966; May 7, 1964 through April 15, 1966.
A. L.—13—New York vs. St. Louis, all 11 in 1939, first 2 in 1940; May 10, 1939 through June 15, 1940.
Cleveland vs. California, last 1 in 1973; all 6 in 1974 and 1975, July 18, 1973 through July 13, 1975.

Most Games Won From One Club, Season, on Road

N. L.—(8-club league)—11—Pittsburgh vs. St. Louis, won 11, lost 0, 1908.
Chicago vs. Boston, won 11, lost 0, 1909.
Brooklyn vs. Philadelphia, won 11, lost 0, 1945.
A. L.—(8-club league)—11—Chicago vs. Philadelphia, won 11, lost 0, 1915.
New York vs. St. Louis, won 11, lost 0, 1927.
New York vs. St. Louis, won 11, lost 0, 1939.
Cleveland vs. Boston, won 11, lost 0, 1954.

Most One Run Decision Games, Season

A. L. (162-game season)—74—Chicago, won 30, lost 44, 1968.
A. L. (154-game season)—60—Philadelphia, won 22, lost 38, 1945.
N. L. (162-game season)—75—Houston, won 32, lost 43, 1971.
N. L. (154-game season)—69—Cincinnati, won 28, lost 41, 1946.

Fewest One Run Decision Games, Season

A. L. (154-game season)—27—Cleveland, won 9, lost 18, 1948.
A. L. (162-game season)—34—Milwaukee, won 12, lost 22, 1980.
N. L. (154-game season)—28—Brooklyn, won 16, lost 12, 1949.
N. L. (162-game season)—38—Chicago, won 17, lost 21, 1970.

Most Games Won, Season, by One Run

N. L. (162-game season)—42—San Francisco, won 42, lost 26, 1978.
N. L. (154-game season)—41—Cincinnati, won 41, lost 17, 1940.
A. L. (162-game season)—40—Baltimore, won 40, lost 15, 1970.
Baltimore, won 40, lost 21, 1974.
A. L. (154-game season)—38—New York, won 38, lost 23, 1943.

Most Games Lost, Season, by One Run

A. L. (162-game season)—44—Chicago, won 30, lost 44, 1968.
N. L. (162-game season)—43—Houston, won 32, lost 43, 1971.
N. L. (154-game season)—41—Cincinnati, won 28, lost 41, 1946.

Fewest Games Won, Season, by One Run

A. L. (154-game season)— 9—Cleveland, won 9, lost 18, 1948.
A. L. (162-game season)—12—Minnesota, won 12, lost 27, 1973.
Milwaukee, won 12, lost 22, 1980.
N. L. (154-game season)— 9—New York, won 9, lost 24, 1953.
N. L. (162-game season)—16—Montreal, won 16, lost 29, 1969.
Atlanta, won 16, lost 30, 1973.
St. Louis, won 16, lost 32, 1978.

Fewest Games Lost, Season, by One Run

A. L. (154-game season)—11—Boston, won 21, lost 11, 1950.
A. L. (162-game season)—12—Kansas City, won 29, lost 12, 1980.
Boston, won 23, lost 13, 1975.
Kansas City, won 31, lost 13, 1977.
N. L. (154-game season)—12—Brooklyn, won 16, lost 12, 1949.
N. L. (162-game season)—14—Philadelphia, won 26, lost 14, 1962.
St. Louis, won 29, lost 14, 1975.

Most Games Won at Home, Season

A. L. (162-game season)—65—New York, won 65, lost 16, 1961.
A. L. (154-game season)—62—New York, won 62, lost 15, 1932.
N. L. (154-game season)—61—Boston, won 61, lost 15, 1898.
N. L. (162-game season)—64—Cincinnati, won 64, lost 17, 1975.
N. L. (154-game season)—since 1900—60—St. Louis, won 60, lost 17, 1942.
                                    Brooklyn, won 60, lost 17, 1953.

Most Games Won on Road, Season

N. L. (162-game season)—53—Cincinnati, won 53, lost 25, 1972.
N. L. (154-game season)—60—Chicago, won 60, lost 15, 1906.
A. L. (162-game season)—55—Oakland, won 55, lost 25, 1971.
A. L. (154-game season)—54—New York, won 54, lost 20, 1939.

Best Gain in Games by Pennant Winner, One Season

A. A.—64 games—Louisville, won 88, lost 44, .667—1890. (In 1889 won 27, lost 111, .196; in
    eighth place, last.)
N. L.—41½ games—Brooklyn, won 88, lost 42, .677—1899. (In 1898 won 54, lost 91, .372;
    in tenth place.)
A. L.—(8-club league)—33 games—Boston, won 104, lost 50, .675—1946. (In 1945, won
    71, lost 83, .461; in seventh place.)
N. L. since 1900—(8-club league)—27 games—New York won 97, lost 57, .630— 1954. (In
    1953, won 70, lost 84, .455; in fifth place.)
N. L. (12-club league)—27 games—New York, won 100, lost 62, .617, 1969. (In 1968, won
    73, lost 89, .451; in ninth place.)

Best Gain in Position From Previous Season by Pennant Winner Through 1968

N. L.—Tenth to first—Brooklyn, 1899—won 88, lost 42, .677. (In 1898 finished tenth in
    12-club league, won 54, lost 91, .372.) (41½ games.)
A. A.—Eighth (last) to first—Louisville, 1890—won 88, lost 44, .667. (In 1889 finished
    eighth, won 27, lost 111, .196.) (64 games.)
A. L. (8-club league)—Seventh to first—New York, 1926—won 91, lost 63, .591. (In 1925
    finished seventh, won 69, lost 85, .448.) (22 games.)
    Seventh to first—Boston, 1946—won 104, lost 50, .675. (In 1945 finished seventh,
    won 71, lost 83, .461.) (33 games.)
A. L. (10-club league)—Ninth to first—Boston, 1967—won 92, lost 70, .568. (In 1966 fin-
    ished ninth in 10-club league, won 72, lost 90, .444.) (20 games.)
N. L. since 1900—(8-club league)—Seventh to first—Los Angeles, 1959—won 88, lost, 68,
    .564. (In 1958 finished seventh, won 71, lost 83, .461.) (16 games.)
N. L. (12-club league)—Ninth to first—New York, 1969—won 100, lost 62, .617. (In 1968,
    finished ninth in 10-club league, won 73, lost 89, .451.) (27 games.)

Best Gain in Games by Club From Previous Season

A. A.— 64— Louisville, won 88, lost 44, .667-1890, first place. (In 1889 won 27, lost 111,
    .196; in eighth place, last.)
N. L.—41½—Brooklyn, won 88, lost 42, .677-1899, first place. (In 1898 won 54, lost 91,
    .372; in tenth place.)
A. L.— 33— Boston, won 104, lost 50, .675-1946, first place. (In 1945, won 71, lost 83, .461;
    in seventh place.)
N. L.—(8-club league) since 1900—32½—Boston, won 71, lost 83, .461-1936, in sixth
    place. (In 1935, won 38, lost 115, .248; in eighth place.)
N. L.—(12-club league)—27 games—New York, won 100, lost 62, .617-1969, in first
    place. (In 1968, won 73, lost 89, .451, in ninth place.)

Most Games Leading League, Season

N. L.—(8-club league)—27½—Pittsburgh, 1902.
A. L.—(8-club league)—19½—New York, 1936.
A. L.—(14-club league)—20—Chicago, 1983.

Fewest Games Leading League, Season

N. L.—(8-club league)—0—St. Louis and Brooklyn, 1946 (before playoff); New York
    and Brooklyn, 1951 (before playoff); Los Angeles and Milwaukee, 1959 (be-
    fore playoff); San Francisco and Los Angeles, 1962 (before playoff); Houston
    and Los Angeles, 1980 (before playoff).
A. L.—(8-club league)—0—Cleveland and Boston, 1948 (before playoff).
    (14-club league)—New York and Boston, 1978 (before playoff).

Most Games Behind Pennant Winner, Season Through 1968

N. L.—(12-club league)—80—Cleveland, 1899.
N. L.—(8-club league) since 1900—66½—Boston, 1906.
A. L.—(8-club league)—64½—St. Louis, 1939.

Fewest Games Behind Pennant Winner, Season, for Last-Place Club Through 1968

N. L.—(8-club league)—21—New York, 1915.

A. L.—(8-club league)—25—Washington, 1944. (In shortened season of 1918, Philadelphia was 24 games behind.)

Fewest Games Behind Western Division Leader, Season, Last-Place Club, Since 1969

A. L.—22—California, 1974.
N. L.—19½—San Diego, 1980.

Fewest Games Behind Eastern Division Leader, Season, Last-Place Club, Since 1969

N. L.—11½—Philadelphia, 1973.
A. L.—17—Toronto, 1982.
Cleveland, 1982.

Most Games Behind Western Division Leader, Season, Last-Place Club, Since 1969

N. L.—43½—Houston, 1975.
A. L.—42—Chicago, 1970.

Most Games Behind Eastern Division Leader, Season, Last-Place Club, Since 1969

A. L.—50½—Toronto, 1979.
N. L.—48—Montreal, 1969.

Largest Lead for Pennant Winner on July 4, P. M. Through 1968

N. L.—14½ games—New York, 1912.
A. L.—12 games—New York, 1928.

Most Games Behind for Pennant Winner on July 4, P. M. Through 1968

N. L.—15 games—Boston, 1914 (8th place).
A. L.—6½ games—Detroit, 1907 (4th place).

Fewest Games Played for Pennant Clinching (154-Game Schedule)

A. L.— 136— New York, September 4, 1941 (won 91, lost 45, .669).
N. L.— 137— New York, September 22, 1904 (won 100, lost 37, .730).

Earliest Date for Pennant Clinching (154-Game Schedule) Through 1968

A. L.—September 4, 1941—New York (won 91, lost 45, .669, 136th game).
N. L.—September 8, 1955—Brooklyn (won 92, lost 46, .667, 138th game).

Earliest Date for Western Division Clinching, Since 1969

A. L.—September 15, 1971, first game. Oakland (won 94, lost 55, .631, 148th game).
N. L.—September 7, 1975, Cincinnati (won 95, lost 47, .669, 142nd game).

Earliest Date for Eastern Division Clinching, Since 1969

A. L.—September 13, 1969, Baltimore (won 101, lost 45, .690, 146th game).
N. L.—September 21, 1972, Pittsburgh (won 91, lost 53, .632, 144th game).

Most Days in First Place, Season

N. L. (162-game season)—182—Los Angeles, entire season, April 5 through October 2, 1974.
N. L. (154-game season)—174—New York, N. L., 1923, entire season, April 17 through October 7, 1923 (1 day tied, April 17, 173 days alone).
A. L. (154-game season)—174—New York, A. L., 1927, entire season, April 12 through October 2, 1927 (8 days tied, 166 days alone).

Fewest Days in First Place, Season for Pennant Winner Through 1968

N. L.— 3—New York, 1951. (Before playoff).
A. L.—20—Boston, 1967 (6 days alone).

Highest Percentage Games Won, One Month

U. A.—.947—St. Louis, May, 1884, won 18, lost 1.
N. L.—.944—Providence, August 1884, won 17, lost 1.
N. L. (since 1900)—.897—Chicago, August 1906, won 26, lost 3.
A. L.—.862—New York, July 1941, won 25, lost 4; .852, Philadelphia, May 1931, won 23, lost 4.

Most Games Won, One Month

N. L.—29—New York, September, 1916, won 29, lost 5.
A. L.—28—New York, August, 1938, won 28, lost 8.

Most Years Winning 100 or More Games

A. L.—14—New York, 1927, 1928, 1932, 1936, 1937, 1939, 1941, 1942, 1954, 1961, 1963, 1977, 1978, 1980.
N. L.— 5—Chicago, 1906, 1907, 1909, 1910, 1935.
New York-San Francisco, 1904, 1905, 1912, 1913 in New York, 1962 in San Francisco.
St. Louis, 1931, 1942, 1943, 1944, 1967.

Most Consecutive Years Winning 100 or More Games

A. L. (162-game season)—3—Baltimore, 1969, 1970, 1971.
A. L. (154-game season)—3—Philadelphia, 1929, 1930, 1931.
N. L. (154-game season)—3—St. Louis, 1942, 1943, 1944.
N. L. (162-game season)—2—Cincinnati, 1975, 1976.
                              Philadelphia, 1976, 1977.

Most Games Won, Two Consecutive Seasons

N. L. (154-game season)—223—Chicago, 1906, 1907 (lost 81).
N. L. (162-game season)—210—Cincinnati, 1975, 1976 (lost 114).
A. L. (162-game season)—217—Baltimore, 1969, 1970 (lost 107).
A. L. (154-game season)—211—New York, 1927, 1928 (lost 97).

Most Games Won, Three Consecutive Seasons

N. L. (154-game season)—322—Chicago, 1906, 1907, 1908 (lost 130).
N. L. (162-game season)—308—Cincinnati, 1974, 1975, 1976 (lost 178).
A. L. (162-game season)—318—Baltimore, 1969, 1970, 1971 (lost 164).
A. L. (154-game season)—313—Philadelphia, 1929, 1930, 1931 (lost 143).

Lowest Percentage Games Won, Season

N. L.—.130—Cleveland, won 20, lost 134, 1899.
A. L.—.235—Philadelphia, won 36, lost 117, 1916.
N. L. since 1900—.248—Boston, won 38, lost 115, 1935.

Lowest Percentage Games Won, Season, for Pennant Winner Through 1968

N. L.—.564—Los Angeles, won 88, lost 68, 1959.
A. L. (154-game season)—.575—Detroit won 88, lost 65, 1945.
A. L. (162-game season)—.568—Boston won 92, lost 70, 1967.

Lowest Percentage Games Won, Season, for League Champion Since 1969

N. L.—.509—New York, won 82, lost 79, 1973.
A. L.—.556—Oakland, won 90, lost 72, 1974.

Lowest Percentage Games Won, Season, for Second-Place Team Through 1968

A. L.—.532—Chicago, won 82, lost 72, 1958.
N. L.—(8-club league)—.543—Brooklyn, won 75, lost 63, 1902.
N. L.—(10-club league)—.543—San Francisco, won 88, lost 74, 1968.

Lowest Percentage Games Won, Season, for Third-Place Team Through 1968

A. L.—.500—Chicago, won 77, lost 77, 1941.
N. L.—(8-club league)—.508—Chicago, won 67, lost 65, 1889.
N. L.—(8-club league)—Since 1900—.519—New York, won 80, lost 74, 1955.
                                          San Francisco won 80, lost 74, 1958.
N. L.—(10-club league)—.519—Chicago, won 84, lost 78, 1968.

Lowest Percentage Games Won, Season, for Fourth-Place Team Through 1968

A. L.—.448—Boston, won 69, lost 85, 1954.
N. L.—.464—Philadelphia, won 71, lost 82, 1906.

Lowest Percentage Games Won, Season, for Fifth-Place Team Through 1968

A. L.—.409—St. Louis, won 63, lost 91, 1931.
N. L.—.411—Boston, won 46, lost 66, 1885.
N. L. since 1900—.434—Brooklyn, won 66, lost 86, 1906.

Lowest Percentage Games Won, Season, for Sixth-Place Team Through 1968

N. L.—.250—Milwaukee, won 15, lost 45, 1878 (six-club league).
N. L. since 1900—.359—Brooklyn, won 55, lost 98, 1909.
A. L.—.386—St. Louis, won 59, lost 94, 1948.

Lowest Percentage Games Won, Season, for Seventh-Place Team Through 1968

N. L.—.237—Philadelphia, won 14, lost 45, 1876.
N. L. since 1900—.327—Boston, won 50, lost 103, 1928.
A. L.—.325—Chicago, won 49, lost 102, 1932.

Lowest Percentage Games Won, Season, for Eighth-Place Team Through 1968

N. L.—.130—Cleveland, won 20, lost 134, 1899, last in 12-club league.
A. L.—(8-club league)—.235—Philadelphia, won 36, lost 117, 1916.
N. L.—(8-club league)—since 1900—.248—Boston, won 38, lost 115, 1935.
N. L.—(10-club league)—.400—Houston, won 64, lost 96, 1962.
A. L.—(10-club league)—.414—California, won 67, lost 95, 1968.
                                          Chicago, won 67, lost 95, 1968.

Lowest Percentage Games Won, Season, for Ninth-Place Team Through 1968

N. L.—(10-club league)—.364—Chicago, won 59, lost 103, 1962.
A. L.—(10-club league)—.379—Kansas City, won 61, lost 100, 1961.
                                          Washington, won 61, lost 100, 1961.

Most Games Lost, Season

N. L. (154-game season)—134—Cleveland, won 20, lost 134, 1899.
A. L. (154-game season)—117—Philadelphia, won 36, lost 117, 1916.
N. L. since 1900 (162-game season)—120—New York, won 40, lost 120, 1962.
N. L. since 1900 (154-game season)—115—Boston, won 38, lost 115, 1935.
A. L. (162-game season)—109—Toronto, won 53, lost 109, 1979.

Most Games Lost, One Month

A. L.—29—Washington, July, 1909, won 5, lost 29.
N. L.—27—Pittsburgh, August, 1890, won 1, lost 27.
        Cleveland, September, 1889, won 1, lost 27.
        St. Louis, September, 1908, won 7, lost 27.
        Brooklyn, September, 1908, won 6, lost 27.
        Philadelphia, September, 1939, won 6, lost 27.

Lowest Percentage Games Won, One Month

N. L.—.036—Pittsburgh, August, 1890, won 1, lost 27; Cleveland, September, 1899, won
        1, lost 27.
A. L.—.067—Philadelphia, July, 1916, won 2, lost 28.
N. L. since 1900—.120—Philadelphia, May, 1928, won 3, lost 22.

Most Games Lost on Road, Season

N. L. (162-game season)— 64—New York, won 17, lost 64, 1963.
N. L. (154-game season)—102—Cleveland, won 11, lost 102, 1899.
N. L. since 1900 (154-game season)—65—Boston, won 13, lost 65, 1935.
A. L. (154-game season)— 64—Philadelphia, won 13, lost 64, 1916.
A. L. (162-game season)— 60—Toronto, won 21, lost 60, 1979.

Most Games Lost at Home, Season

A. L. (154-game season)—59—St. Louis, won 18, lost 59, 1939.
A. L. (162-game season)—55—Kansas City, won 26, lost 55, 1964.
                            Toronto, won 25, lost 55, 1977.
N. L. (162-game season)—58—New York, won 22, lost 58, 1962.
N. L. (154-game season)—55—Philadelphia, won 20, lost 55, 1923.
                            Boston, won 22, lost 55, 1923.
                            Philadelphia, won 22, lost 55, 1945.

Most Years Losing 100 or More Games

A. L.—15—Philadelphia-Kansas City, 1915, 1916, 1919, 1920, 1921, 1936, 1940, 1943, 1946,
        1950, 1954 in Philadelphia, 1956, 1961, 1964, 1965 in Kansas City.
N. L.—14—Philadelphia, 1904, 1921, 1923, 1927, 1928, 1930, 1936, 1938, 1939, 1940, 1941,
        1942, 1945, 1961.

Most Consecutive Years Losing 100 or More Games

N. L.—5—Philadelphia, 1938 through 1942.
A. L.—4—Washington, 1961 through 1964.

Most Games Lost, Two Consecutive Seasons

N. L. (162-game season)—231—New York, 1962-63 (won 91).
A. L. (154-game season)—226—Philadelphia, 1915-16 (won 79).
A. L. (162-game season)—211—Toronto, 1978-79 (won 112).

Most Games Lost, Three Consecutive Seasons

N. L. (162-game season)—340—New York, 1962 through 1964 (won 144).
A. L. (154-game season)—324—Philadelphia, 1915 through 1917 (won 134).

Most Times Winning Two Games in One Day, Season

N. L. (162-game season)—11—New York, won 11, lost 3, 1969.
N. L. (154-game season)—20—Chicago, won 20, lost 3, 1945.
A. L. (162-game season)—15—Chicago, won 15, lost 7, 1961.
A. L. (154-game season)—14—New York, won 14, lost 7, 1943.
                            Cleveland, won 14, lost 8, 1943.
                            Washington, won 14, lost 8, 1945.
                            Boston, won 14, lost 9, 1946.

Most Times Winning Two Games in One Day, From One Club, Season

A. L. (154-game season)—7—Chicago vs. Philadelphia, 1943. (Won 7, lost 0).
N. L. (154-game season)—7—Chicago vs. Cincinnati, 1945. (Won 7, lost 0).

Fewest Times Winning Two Games in One Day, Season

A. L. (154-game season)—0—Detroit, 1952, lost 13, split 9.
                            Washington, 1957, lost 7, split 11.
A. L. (162-game season)—0—Held by many clubs. Last clubs—Boston, 1983, lost 2, split
                            6; Seattle, 1983, lost 0, split 0.

Fewest Times Winning Two Games in One Day, Season—Continued

   N. L. (154-game season)—1—Held by many clubs.
   N. L. (162-game season)—0—Held by many clubs. Last clubs—Chicago, 1983, lost 3,
           split 2; Cincinnati, 1983, lost 2, split 4.

Most Times Losing Two Games in One Day, Season

   A. L. (162-game season)—13—Chicago, 1970 (won 1).
   A. L. (154-game season)—18—Philadelphia, 1943 (won 4).
   N. L. (162-game season)—17—New York, 1962 (won 3).
   N. L. (154-game season)—19—Chicago, 1950 (won 4).

Fewest Times Losing Two Games in One Day, Season

   N. L.-A. L.—0—Held by many clubs.

Most Championships Won, Club

   A. L.—33—New York, 1921, 1922, 1923, 1926, 1927, 1928, 1932, 1936, 1937, 1938, 1939,
           1941, 1942, 1943, 1947, 1949, 1950, 1951, 1952, 1953, 1955, 1956, 1957, 1958,
           1960, 1961, 1962, 1963, 1964, 1976, 1977, 1978.
   N. L.—20—Brooklyn-Los Angeles, 1890, 1899, 1900, 1916, 1920, 1941, 1947, 1949, 1952,
           1953, 1955, 1956, in Brooklyn, 1959, 1963, 1965, 1966, 1974, 1977, 1978, 1981
           in Los Angeles.
   N. L. since 1900—18—Brooklyn-Los Angeles, 1900, 1916, 1920, 1941, 1947, 1949, 1952,
           1953, 1955, 1956, in Brooklyn, 1959, 1963, 1965, 1966, 1974, 1977,
           1978, 1981 in Los Angeles.

Most Consecutive Championships Won, Club

   A. L.—5—New York, 1949, 1950, 1951, 1952, 1953 (Charles D. Stengel, Manager).
       New York, 1960, 1961, 1962, 1963, 1964 (Charles D. Stengel, Ralph G. Houk,
       Lawrence P. Berra, Managers).
   A. A.—4—St. Louis, 1885, 1886, 1887, 1888 (Charles A. Comiskey, Manager).
   N. L.—4—New York, 1921, 1922, 1923, 1924 (John J. McGraw, Manager).

Fewest Championships Won, Present Clubs in Present Cities

   A. L.—0—California, Texas, Seattle, Toronto.
   N. L.—0—Atlanta, Houston, Montreal, San Diego.

Most Consecutive Years Without Winning Championship, League

   A. L.—42—St. Louis, 1902 through 1943.
   N. L.—38—Chicago, 1946 through 1983.

Most Times Finished in Last Place

   A. L.—24—Philadelphia-Kansas City-Oakland, 1915, 1916, 1917, 1918, 1919, 1920, 1921,
           1935, 1936, 1938, 1940, 1941, 1942, 1943, 1945, 1946, 1950, 1954 in Philadel-
           phia, 1956, 1960, 1961 (tied), 1964, 1965, 1967 in Kansas City.
   N. L.—24—Philadelphia, 1883, 1904, 1919, 1920, 1921, 1923, 1926, 1927, 1928, 1930, 1936,
           1938, 1939, 1940, 1941, 1942, 1944, 1945, 1947 (tied), 1958, 1959, 1960, 1961,
           1972 (E).

Most Times Lowest Percentage Games Won, League

   N. L.—24—Philadelphia, 1883, 1904, 1919, 1920, 1921, 1923, 1926, 1927, 1928, 1930, 1936,
           1938, 1939, 1940, 1941, 1942, 1944, 1945, 1946 (tied), 1958, 1959, 1960, 1961,
           1972.
   A. L.—24—Philadelphia-Kansas City, 1915, 1916, 1917, 1918, 1919, 1920, 1921, 1935, 1936,
           1938, 1940, 1941, 1942, 1943, 1945, 1946, 1950, 1954 in Philadelphia, 1956,
           1960, 1961 (tied), 1964, 1965, 1967 in Kansas City.

Fewest Times Lowest Percentage Games Won, Season, Present Clubs in Present Cities

   A. L.—0—Baltimore.
   N. L.—0—Los Angeles, San Francisco.

Most Consecutive Times Finished in Last Place

   A. L.—7—Philadelphia, 1915 through 1921.
   N. L.—5—Philadelphia, 1938 through 1942.

Most Consecutive Times Lowest Percentage Games Won, Season

   A. L.—7—Philadelphia, 1915 through 1921.
   N. L.—5—Philadelphia, 1938 through 1942.

Most Consecutive Years, First Division Finish

   A. L.—39—New York, 1926 through 1964.
   N. L.—14—Chicago, 1878 through 1891.
          Pittsburgh, 1900 through 1913.
          Chicago, 1926 through 1939.

Most Consecutive Years, Second Division Finish

N. L.—20—Chicago, 1947 through 1966.
A. L.—16—Philadelphia-Kansas City-Oakland, 1953 through 1968.

Most Consecutive Years Without Lowest Percentage Games Won

N. L.—77—Brooklyn-Los Angeles, 1906 through 1982.
A. L.—54—Cleveland, 1915 through 1968.

CONSECUTIVE GAMES WON IN SEASON
(13 or More)
NATIONAL LEAGUE

Year—Club	G.	Home	Rd.	Year—Club	G.	Home	Rd.
1916— New York (1 tie)	26	26	0	1899— Cincinnati	14	10	4
1880— Chicago	21	11	10	1903— Pittsburgh	14	7	7
1935— Chicago	21	18	3	1906— Chicago	14	14	0
1884— Providence	20	16	4	1909— Pittsburgh	14	12	2
1885— Chicago	18	14	4	1913— New York	14	6	8
1894— Baltimore	18	13	5	1932— Chicago	14	14	0
1904— New York	18	13	5	1935— St. Louis	14	12	2
1897— Boston	17	16	1	1965— San Francisco	14	6	8
1907— New York	17	14	3	1890— Cincinnati	13	13	0
1916— New York	17	0	17	1892— Chicago	13	11	2
1887— Philadelphia	16	5	11	1905— New York	13	8	5
1890— Philadelphia	16	14	2	1911— Pittsburgh	13	9	4
1892— Philadelphia	16	11	5	1922— Pittsburgh	13	2	11
1909— Pittsburgh	16	12	4	1928— Chicago	13	13	0
1912— New York	16	11	5	1938— Pittsburgh	13	5	8
1951— New York	16	13	3	1947— Brooklyn	13	2	11
1886— Detroit	15	12	3	1953— Brooklyn	13	7	6
1903— Pittsburgh	15	11	4	1962— Los Angeles	13	8	5
1924— Brooklyn	15	3	12	1965— Los Angeles	13	7	6
1936— Chicago	15	11	4	1977— Philadelphia	13	8	5
1936— New York	15	7	8	1982— Atlanta	13	5	8
1895— Baltimore	14	13	1				

AMERICAN LEAGUE

Year—Club	G.	Home	Rd.	Year—Club	G.	Home	Rd.
1906— Chicago (1 tie)	19	11	8	1941— New York	14	6	8
1947— New York	19	6	13	1951— Chicago	14	3	11
1953— New York	18	3	15	1973— Baltimore	14	10	4
1912— Washington	17	1	16	1908— Chicago	13	12	1
1931— Philadelphia	17	5	12	1910— Philadelphia	13	12	1
1926— New York	16	12	4	1927— Detroit (1 tie)	13	13	0
1977— Kansas City	16	9	7	1931— Philadelphia	13	13	0
1906— New York	15	12	3	1933— Washington	13	1	12
1913— Philadelphia	15	13	2	1942— Cleveland	13	4	9
1946— Boston	15	11	4	1948— Boston	13	12	1
1960— New York	15	9	6	1951— Cleveland	13	7	6
1909— Detroit	14	14	0	1954— New York	13	8	5
1916— St. Louis	14	13	1	1961— New York	13	12	1
1934— Detroit	14	9	5	1978— Baltimore	13	3	10

UNION ASSOCIATION

Year—Club	G.	Home	Rd.
1884— St. Louis	20	16	4

AMERICAN ASSOCIATION

Year—Club	G.	Home	Rd.
1887— St. Louis	15	15	0

CONSECUTIVE GAMES LOST IN SEASON
(13 or More)
AMERICAN LEAGUE

Year—Club	G.	Home	Rd.	Year—Club	G.	Home	Rd.
1906— Boston	20	19	1	1907— Boston (2 ties)	16	9	7
1916— Philadelphia	20	1	19	1927— Boston	15	10	5
1943— Philadelphia	20	3	17	1937— Philadelphia	15	10	5
1975— Detroit	19	9	10	1972— Texas	15	5	10
1920— Philadelphia	18	0	18	1911— St. Louis	14	6	8
1948— Washington	18	8	10	1930— Boston	14	3	11
1959— Washington	18	3	15	1940— St. Louis	14	0	14
1926— Boston	17	14	3	1945— Philadelphia	14	0	14

CONSECUTIVE GAMES LOST IN SEASON—Continued

Year—Club	G.	Home	Rd.	Year—Club	G.	Home	Rd.
1953— St. Louis	14	14	0	1924— Chicago	13	2	11
1954— Baltimore	14	7	7	1935— Philadelphia	13	10	3
1961— Washington	14	11	3	1936— St. Louis	13	2	11
1970— Washington	14	4	10	1953— Detroit (2 ties)	13	12	1
1977— Oakland	14	9	5	1958— Washington	13	4	9
1982— Minnesota	14	6	8	1959— Kansas City	13	4	9
1904— Wash. (1 tie)	13	7	6	1961— Minnesota	13	0	13
1913— New York	13	7	6	1962— Washington	13	7	6
1920— Detroit	13	5	8				

NATIONAL LEAGUE

Year—Club	G.	Home	Rd.	Year—Club	G.	Home	Rd.
1899— Cleveland	24	3	21	1883— Philadelphia	14	4	10
1961— Philadelphia	23	6	17	1896— St. Louis	14	5	9
1890— Pittsburgh	23	1	22	1899— Cleveland	14	0	14
1894— Louisville	20	0	20	1911— Boston	14	14	0
1969— Montreal	20	12	8	1916— St. Louis	14	0	14
1906— Boston	19	3	16	1935— Boston	14	4	10
1914— Cincinnati	19	6	13	1936— Philadelphia	14	10	4
1876— Cincinnati	18	9	9	1937— Brooklyn	14	0	14
1894— Louisville	18	0	18	1937— Cincinnati	14	10	4
1894— Washington	17	7	10	1885— Providence	13	2	11
1962— New York	17	7	10	1886— Washington	13	13	0
1977— Atlanta	17	8	9	1902— New York	13	5	8
1882— Troy	16	5	11	1909— Boston	13	13	0
1884— Detroit	16	5	11	1910— St. Louis	13	5	8
1899— Cleveland	16	0	16	1919— Philadelphia	13	0	13
1907— Boston	16	5	11	1919— Philadelphia	13	7	6
1911— Boston	16	8	8	1930— Cincinnati	13	1	12
1944— Brooklyn	16	0	16	1942— Philadelphia	13	4	9
1909— Boston	15	0	15	1944— Chicago	13	7	6
1909— St. Louis	15	11	4	1944— New York	13	0	13
1927— Boston	15	0	15	1945— Cincinnati	13	2	11
1935— Boston	15	0	15	1955— Philadelphia	13	9	4
1963— New York	15	8	7	1962— New York	13	9	4
1982— New York	15	6	9	1976— Atlanta	13	6	7
1878— Milwaukee	14	7	7	1980— New York	13	3	10
1882— Worcester	14	2	12	1982— Chicago	13	7	6

AMERICAN ASSOCIATION

Year—Club	G.	Home	Rd.	Year—Club	G.	Home	Rd.
1889— Louisville	26	5	21	1882— Baltimore	15	0	15
1890— Philadelphia	22	6	16	1884— Washington	15	0	15

Most Consecutive Games Won, Season

  N. L.—26—New York, September 7 through September 30, first game, 1916 (1 tie).
  A. L.—19—Chicago, August 2 through August 23, 1906 (1 tie).
         New York, June 29, second game, through July 17, second game, 1947.

Most Consecutive Games Won, Start of Season

  U. A.—20—St. Louis, April 20 through May 22, 1884.
  N. L.—13—Atlanta, April 6 through April 21, 1982.
  A. L.—11—Oakland, April 9 through April 19, first game, 1981.

Most Home Games Won Consecutively, Season

  N. L.—26—New York, September 7 through September 30, first game, 1916 (1 tie).
  A. L.—22—Philadelphia, July 15, first game, through August 31, 1931, not inclusive.

Most Road Games Won Consecutively, Season

  N. L.—17—New York, May 9 through May 29, 1916.
  A. L.—16—Washington, May 30, p.m. game, through June 15, 1912.

Most Consecutive Games Won, Season, No Tie Games

  N. L.—21—Chicago, June 2 through July 8, 1880.
         Chicago, September 4 through September 27, second game, 1935.
  A. L.—19—New York, June 29, second game through July 17, second game, 1947.

Most Consecutive Games Lost, Season

  A. A.—26—Louisville, May 22 through June 22, 1889, second game.

N. L.—24—Cleveland, August 26 through September 16, 1899.
A. L.—20—Boston, May 1 through May 24, 1906.
    Philadelphia, July 21 through August 8, 1916.
    Philadelphia, August 7 through August 24, first game, 1943.
N. L. since 1900—23—Philadelphia, July 29 through August 20, 1961, first game.

Most Consecutive Games Lost, Start of Season

A. L.—13—Washington, April 14 through May 4, 1904 (1 tie).
    Detroit, April 14 through May 2, 1920.
N. L.—11—Detroit, May 1 through May 15, 1884.
N. L. since 1900—9—Brooklyn, April 16 through April 26, 1918.
    Boston, April 19, morning game, through May 6, 1919.
    New York, April 11 through April 22, 1962.
    Houston, April 5 through April 13, 1983.

Most Home Games Lost Consecutively, Season

A. L.—20—St. Louis, June 3 through July 7, 1953, not inclusive.
A. L.—19—Boston, May 2 through May 24, 1906.
N. L.—14—Boston, May 8 through May 24, 1911.

Most Road Games Lost Consecutively, Season

N. L.—22—Pittsburgh, August 13 through September 2, 1890.
    New York, June 16, first game through July 28, 1963, not inclusive.
A. L.—19—Philadelphia, July 25 through August 8, 1916.

Most Consecutive Doubleheaders Played, Season, Club

N. L.—9—Boston, September 4 through September 15, 1928.
A. L.—8—Washington, July 27 through August 5, 1909.

Most Consecutive Doubleheaders Won, Season (No Other Games in Between)

A. L.—5—New York, August 30 through September 4, 1906.
N. L.—4—Brooklyn, September 1 through September 4, 1924.
    New York, September 10 through September 14, 1928.

Most Consecutive Doubleheaders Lost, Season (No Other Games in Between)

N. L.—5—Boston, September 8 through September 14, 1928.
A. L.—4—Boston, June 29 through July 5, 1921.

Most Games Postponed, Start of Season

A. L.—5—Chicago, April 6 through 10, 1982.
    New York, April 6 through 10, 1982.
N. L.—4—New York, April 12 through 15, 1933.

Most Consecutive Games Postponed, Season

N. L.—9—Philadelphia, August 10 through August 19, 1903.
A. L.—7—Detroit, May 14 through May 18, 1945.
    Philadelphia, May 14 through May 18, 1945.
    Washington, April 23 through April 29, 1952.

Most Consecutive Games Between Same Clubs, Season

A. L.—11—Detroit vs. St. Louis, September 8 through September 14, 1904.
N. L.—10—Chicago vs. Philadelphia, August 7 through August 16, 1907.

Most Consecutive Doubleheaders Between Same Clubs, Season

A. L.—5—Philadelphia vs. Washington, August 5, 7, 8, 9, 10, 1901.
N. L.—4—New York vs. Boston, September 10, 11, 13, 14, 1928.

Most Consecutive Extra-Inning Games, One Club

A. L.—5—Detroit, September 9 through September 13, 1908 (54 innings).
N. L.—4—Pittsburgh, August 18 through August 22, 1917 (59 innings).

Most Consecutive Extra-Inning Games, Same Clubs

A. L.—4—Chicago and Detroit, September 9 through September 12, 1908 (43 innings).
    Cleveland and St. Louis, May 1, 2, 4, 5, 1910 (46 innings).
    Boston and St. Louis, May 31, first game, to June 2, second game, 1943 (45 innings).
N. L.—4—New York and Pittsburgh, May 24, 25, June 23, 24, 1978 (44 innings; both clubs played other teams between these contests).
    3—Brooklyn and Pittsburgh, August 20, through August 22, 1917 (45 innings).
    Chicago and Pittsburgh, August 18, 19, 20, 1961 (33 innings).
    Cincinnati and New York, May 5, 6, 7, 1980 (36 innings).

Most Innings, Two Consecutive Extra-Inning Games, One Club

N. L.—45—Boston, May 1, 3, 1920.
A. L.—37—Minnesota vs. Milwaukee, May 12, (22), May 13 (15), 1972.
        Milwaukee vs. Minnesota, May 12, (22), May 13 (15), 1972.

Most Innings, Two Consecutive Extra-Inning Games, Same Clubs

N. L.—40—Boston and Chicago, May 14 (18), 17 (22), 1927.
A. L.—37—Minnesota and Milwaukee, May 12 (22), May 13 (15), 1972.

Most Innings, Three Consecutive Extra-Inning Games, One Club

N. L.—58—Brooklyn, May 1 to May 3, 1920.
A. L.—41—Cleveland, April 16 to April 21, 1935.
        Boston, April 8 (12), 10 (13), 11 (16), 1969.

Most Innings, Three Consecutive Extra-Inning Games, Same Clubs

N. L.—45—Brooklyn and Pittsburgh, August 20 through August 22, 1917.
A. L.—40—Chicago and Washington, August 24 through August 26, 1915.
        Detroit and Philadelphia, May 12 through May 14, 1943.

Most Innings, Four Consecutive Extra-Inning Games, One Club

N. L.—59—Pittsburgh, August 18 through August 22, 1917.
A. L.—51—Chicago, August 23 through August 26, 1915.
        Detroit, May 11, second game, through May 14, 1943.

Most Innings, Four Consecutive Extra-Inning Games, Same Clubs

A. L.—46—Cleveland and St. Louis, May 1, 2, 4, 5, 1910.
N. L.—No performance.

NUMBER OF PLAYERS, ALL POSITIONS

Most Players, Club, One Season

A. L. (162-game season)—53—Seattle, 1969.
    (154-game season)—56—Philadelphia, 1915.
N. L. (162-game season)—54—New York, 1967.
    (154-game season)—53—Brooklyn, 1944.

Fewest Players, One Club, One Season

A. L. (154-game season)—18—Boston, 1905.
A. L. (162-game season)—30—New York, 1963; Boston, 1965; Baltimore, 1969.
N. L. (162-game season)—29—Cincinnati, 1975.
N. L. (154-game season)—20—Chicago, 1905.

Most Players Used as Pitchers, Season, One Club

A. L. (162-game season)—25—Kansas City, 1965.
                 Seattle, 1969.
A. L. (154-game season)—27—Philadelphia, 1915.
                 Kansas City, 1955.
N. L. (162-game season)—27—New York, 1967.
N. L. (154-game season)—24—Cincinnati, 1912.
                 Philadelphia, 1946.

Fewest Players Used as Pitchers, Season, One Club

A. L. (162-game season)—11—Baltimore, 1972; Oakland, 1974; Baltimore, 1974.
A. L. (154-game season)— 5—Boston, 1904.
N. L. (162-game season)—11—Philadelphia, 1976; Atlanta, 1980.
N. L. (154-game season)— 5—Boston, 1901.

Most Players, Nine-Inning Game, One Club

A. L.—27—Kansas City vs. California, September 10, 1969.
N. L.—25—St. Louis vs. Los Angeles, April 16, 1959.
        Milwaukee vs. Philadelphia, September 26, 1964.

Most Players, Extra-Inning Game, One Club

A. L.—30—Oakland vs. Chicago, September 19, 1972, 15 innings.
N. L.—27—Philadelphia vs. St. Louis, September 13, 1974, 17 innings.
        Chicago vs. Pittsburgh, September 21, 1978, 14 innings.

Most Players, Nine-Inning Game, Both Clubs

N. L.—45—Chicago 24, Montreal 21, September 5, 1978.
A. L.—42—Oakland 24, Kansas City 18, September 20, 1975.

Most Players, Extra-Inning Game, Both Clubs

A. L.—51—Oakland 30, Chicago 21, September 19, 1972, 15 innings.
N. L.—51—Philadelphia 27, St. Louis 24, September 13, 1974, 17 innings.

Most Players Used, Doubleheader, One Club
A. L.—41—Chicago vs. Oakland, September 7, 1970.
N. L.—41—San Diego vs. San Francisco, May 30, 1977.

Most Players Used, Doubleheader, One Club, More Than 18 Innings
N. L.—42—St. Louis vs. Brooklyn, August 29, 1948, 19 innings.
       Montreal vs. Pittsburgh, September 5, 1975, 19 innings.

Most Players Used, Doubleheader, Both Clubs
N. L.—74—San Diego 41, San Francisco 33, May 30, 1977.
A. L.—70—Oakland 36, Texas 34, September 7, 1975.

Most Players Used, Doubleheader, Both Clubs, More Than 18 Innings
N. L.—74—Montreal 42, Pittsburgh 32, September 5, 1975, 19 innings.
A. L.—73—Washington 37, Cleveland 36, September 14, finished September 20, 1971, 29
       innings.

Most First Basemen, Nine-Inning Game, One Club
A. L.—5—Chicago vs. New York, June 25, 1953.
N. L.—3—Made in many games.

Most First Basemen, Extra-Inning Game, One Club
N. L.—4—Philadelphia vs. Milwaukee, July 23, 1964, 10 innings.
A. L.—4—Detroit vs. Philadelphia, September 30, 1907, 17 innings.

Most First Basemen, Nine-Inning Game, Both Clubs
A. L.—6—Chicago 5, New York 1, June 25, 1953.
N. L.—5—Los Angeles 3, New York 2, September 12, 1966.
       Cincinnati 3, New York 2, August 24, 1968.

Most First Basemen, Extra-Inning Game, Both Clubs
N. L.—5—Los Angeles 3, Houston 2, June 8, 1962, 13 innings.
       Philadelphia 3, Houston 2, July 17, 1963, 10 innings.
       Philadelphia 4, Milwaukee 1, July 23, 1964, 10 innings.
A. L.—5—Detroit 4, Philadelphia 1, September 30, 1907, 17 innings.

Most Second Basemen, Nine-Inning Game, One Club
N. L.—4—Brooklyn vs. New York, April 21, 1948.
       Chicago vs. New York, August 21, 1952, second game.
A. L.—4—Made in six games—Last time—Oakland vs. California, September 27, 1975.

Most Second Basemen, Extra-Inning Game, One Club
A. L.—6—Oakland vs. Chicago, September 19, 1972, 15 innings.
N. L.—5—New York vs. Cincinnati, July 20, 1954, 13 innings.

Most Second Basemen, Nine-Inning Game, Both Clubs
A. L.—6—Oakland 4, Cleveland 2, May 5, 1973.
       Oakland 4, Cleveland 2, May 6, 1973, first game.
       Oakland 4, Cleveland 2, May 6, 1973, second game.
N. L.—5—Brooklyn 4, New York 1, April 21, 1948.
       Chicago 4, New York 1, August 21, 1952, second game.

Most Second Basemen, Extra-Inning Game, Both Clubs
A. L.—8—Oakland 6, Chicago 2, September 19, 1972, 15 innings.
N. L.—7—New York 5, Cincinnati 2, July 20, 1954, 13 innings.

Most Third Basemen, Nine-Inning Game, One Club
N. L.—5—Atlanta vs. Philadelphia, April 21, 1966.
       Philadelphia vs. Pittsburgh, August 6, 1971.
A. L.—4—Kansas City vs. California, September 10, 1969.
       Minnesota vs. Seattle, September 28, 1969, first game.
       Cleveland vs. Minnesota, August 27, 1970.
       Milwaukee vs. Kansas City, September 6, 1971.
       Oakland vs. Cleveland, July 20, 1974.

Most Third Basemen, Extra-Inning Game, One Club
N. L.—4—Made in many games.
A. L.—4—Made in many games.

Most Third Basemen, Nine-Inning Game, Both Clubs
N. L.—7—Philadelphia 5, Pittsburgh 2, August 6, 1971.
A. L.—6—Minnesota 3, Cleveland 3, July 27, 1969.

Most Third Basemen, Extra-Inning Game, Both Clubs

A. L.—6—Detroit 3, Cleveland 3, July 10, 1969, 11 innings.
N. L.—5—Made in many games.

Most Shortstops, Nine-Inning Game, One Club

A. L.—4—New York vs. Washington, September 5, 1954.
       Minnesota vs. Oakland, September 22, 1968.
N. L.—3—Made in many games.

Most Shortstops, Nine-Inning Game, Both Clubs

A. L.—6—Detroit 3, Washington 3, September 21, 1968.
N. L.—5—Cincinnati 3, Houston 2, July 13, 1969.
       Montreal 3, Pittsburgh 2, October 1, 1969.

Most Shortstops, Extra-Inning Game, One Club

N. L.—5—Philadelphia vs. Cincinnati, May 8, 1949, 12 innings.
A. L.—4—Detroit vs. New York, July 28, 1957, second game, 15 innings.
       Baltimore vs. New York, September 26, 1958, 12 innings.

Most Right Fielders, Nine-Inning Game, One Club

N. L.—4—Philadelphia vs. St. Louis, June 2, 1928.
       Los Angeles vs. Houston, June 10, 1962, first game.
A. L.—4—Baltimore vs. Washington, September 25, 1955.

Most Right Fielders, Nine-Inning Game, Both Clubs

N. L.—6—Los Angeles 4, Houston 2, June 10, 1962, first game.
A. L.—5—Chicago 3, St. Louis 2, May 6, 1917, first game.
       Baltimore 4, Washington 1, September 25, 1955.
       Cleveland 3, Detroit 2, June 2, 1962.
       Cleveland 3, Kansas City 2, June 26, 1966, second game.
       Boston 3, California 2, August 20, 1967, second game.
       California 3, Chicago 2, July 20, 1968.
       California 3, Chicago 2, April 14, 1969.
       Oakland 3, Chicago 2, September 7, 1970, second game.
       Boston 3, Oakland 2, May 20, 1975.

Most Right Fielders, Extra-Inning Game, One Club

A. L.—6—Kansas City vs. California, September 8, 1965, 13 innings.
N. L.—4—St. Louis vs. Philadelphia, April 28, 1961, 11 innings.
       St. Louis vs. Chicago, April 13, 1962, 15 innings.
       Los Angeles vs. San Francisco, September 27, 1969, 11 innings.

Most Right Fielders, Extra-Inning Game, Both Clubs

A. L.—7—Kansas City 6, California 1, September 8, 1965, 13 innings.
N. L.—6—Los Angeles 3, San Francisco 3, June 25, 1964, 13 innings.

Most Center Fielders, Nine-Inning Game, One Club

A. L.—5—Minnesota vs. Oakland, September 22, 1968.
N. L.—4—Cincinnati vs. St. Louis, May 30, 1942, second game.

Most Center Fielders, Extra-Inning Game, One Club

N. L.—4—Boston vs. Brooklyn, April 25, 1917, 12 innings.
       Philadelphia vs. St. Louis, September 25, 1966, 13 innings.
A. L.—3—Made in many games.

Most Center Fielders, Nine-Inning Game, Both Clubs

A. L.—7—Minnesota 5, Oakland 2, September 22, 1968.
N. L.—6—Cincinnati 4, St. Louis 2, May 30, 1942, second game.

Most Center Fielders, Extra-Inning Game, Both Clubs

N. L.—5—Made in many games.
A. L.—5—Made in many games.

Most Left Fielders, Nine-Inning Game, One Club

A. L.—4—Baltimore vs. Detroit, September 14, 1960.
       Minnesota vs. California, July 9, 1970.
       Oakland vs. Cleveland, July 20, 1974.
N. L.—4—Brooklyn vs. Philadelphia, September 26, 1946.
       Los Angeles vs. New York, June 4, 1966.

Most Left Fielders, Nine-Inning Game, Both Clubs

N. L.—6—New York 3, San Francisco 3, September 22, 1963.
A. L.—6—Oakland 4, Cleveland 2, July 20, 1974.

Most Left Fielders, Extra-Inning Game, One Club

N. L.—5—Philadelphia vs. Milwaukee, July 23, 1964, 10 innings.
A. L.—4—Boston vs. Chicago, August 16, 1916, first game, 16 innings.
New York vs. Boston, September 26, 1953, 11 innings.

Most Left Fielders, Extra-Inning Game, Both Clubs

N. L.—7—Los Angeles 4, St. Louis 3, May 12, 1962, 15 innings.
A. L.—6—Minnesota 3, Baltimore 3, April 16, 1961, second game, 11 innings.
Minnesota 3, Oakland 3, September 6, 1969, 18 innings.

Most Catchers, Nine-Inning Game, One Club

N. L.—4—Boston vs. New York, October 6, 1929.
Brooklyn vs. St. Louis, May 5, 1940.
New York vs. St. Louis, September 2, 1962.
A. L.—4—Minnesota vs. California, September 27, 1967.

Most Catchers, Nine-Inning Game, Both Clubs

A. L.—6—Chicago 3, Philadelphia 3, July 10, 1926.
N. L.—6—Boston 4, New York 2, October 6, 1929.
Brooklyn 4, St. Louis 2, May 5, 1940.
New York 4, St. Louis 2, September 2, 1962.

Most Catchers, Extra-Inning Game, One Club

A. L.—4—Kansas City vs. Chicago, September 21, 1973, 12 innings.
N. L.—3—Made in many games.

Most Catchers, Extra-Inning Game, Both Clubs

A. L.—6—Chicago 3, New York 3, September 10, 1955, 10 innings.
California 3, Oakland 3, September 28, 1969, 11 innings.
Kansas City 4, Chicago 2, September 21, 1972, 12 innings.
N. L.—5—Made in many games.

Most Pitchers, Nine-Inning Game, One Club

A. L.—9—St. Louis vs. Chicago, October 2, 1949, first game.
N. L.—8—Held by many clubs.

Most Pitchers, Shutout Game, Winning Club

A. L.—7—Kansas City vs. Cleveland, September 15, 1966, 11 innings (won 1-0).
N. L.—6—Los Angeles vs. Milwaukee, October 3, 1965 (won 3-0).

Most Pitchers, No-Hit Game, Winning Club

A. L.—4—Oakland vs. California, September 28, 1975 (won 5-0).

Most Pitchers, Nine-Inning Game, Both Clubs

N. L.—14—Chicago 7, New York 7, July 23, 1944, second game.
Cincinnati 8, Milwaukee 6, April 26, 1959.
Houston 8, Chicago 6, September 11, 1967.
Houston 8, Los Angeles 6, September 17, 1972.
Montreal 8, Chicago 6, September 5, 1978.
A. L.—14—Kansas City 7, Cleveland 7, April 23, 1961.

Most Pitchers, Extra-Inning Game, One Club

N. L.—9—Cincinnati vs. Houston, July 8, 1962, second game, 13 innings.
A. L.—9—Los Angeles vs. Minnesota, April 16, 1963, 13 innings.
Minnesota vs. Chicago, July 25, 1964, 13 innings.
Washington vs. Cleveland, September 14, finished, September 20, 1971, 20 innings.
Cleveland vs. Washington, September 14, finished, September 20, 1971, 20 innings.

Most Pitchers, Extra-Inning Game, Both Clubs

A. L.—18—Washington 9, Cleveland 9, September 14, finished, September 20, 1971, night game, 20 innings.
N. L.—16—St. Louis 8, Chicago 8, October 3, 1982.

Most Pitchers, Inning, One Club

A. L.—6—Oakland vs. Cleveland, September 3, 1983, ninth inning.
N. L.—5—Made in many innings. Last time—St. Louis vs. Chicago, April 29, 1981, first game, eighth inning.

Most Pitchers, Inning, Both Clubs

N. L.—7—Cincinnati 5, Philadelphia 2, June 1, 1949, tenth inning.
Cincinnati 5, Brooklyn 2, June 12, 1949, fifth inning.
Atlanta 5, St. Louis 2, July 22, 1967, ninth inning.
St. Louis 4, Chicago 3, May 16, 1970, ninth inning.

Most Pitchers, Inning, Both Clubs—Continued

St. Louis 5, Cincinnati 2, June 15, 1980, ninth inning.
A. L.—7—Chicago 4, Baltimore 3, July 16, 1955, ninth inning.

Most Pitchers, Doubleheader (Nine-Inning Games), One Club

N. L.—13—San Diego vs. San Francisco, May 30, 1977.
A. L.—12—Cleveland vs. Detroit, September 7, 1959.
California vs. Detroit, September 30, 1967.

Most Pitchers, Doubleheader, One Club, More Than 18 Innings

N. L.—13—Milwaukee vs. Philadelphia, May 12, 1963, 23 innings.
12—St. Louis vs. Cincinnati, July 1, 1956, 19 innings.
Cincinnati vs. Houston, July 8, 1962, 22 innings.
Houston vs. St. Louis, July 11, 1968, 19 innings.
A. L.—12—Washington vs. Chicago, May 30, 1969, 19 innings.
New York vs. Baltimore, August 9, 1970, 20 innings.
Washington vs. Cleveland, September 14, finished September 20, 1971, 29 innings.

Most Pitchers, Doubleheader, 18 Innings, Both Clubs

N. L.—22—Milwaukee 11, New York 11, July 26, 1964.
A. L.—21—Detroit 11, Kansas City 10, July 23, 1961.

Most Pitchers, Doubleheader, Both Clubs, More Than 18 Innings

A. L.—22—Washington 12, Cleveland 10, September 14, finished September 20, 1971, 29 innings.
N. L.—20—St. Louis 12, Cincinnati 8, July 1, 1956, 19 innings.

Most Pinch-Hitters, Inning, One Club

N. L.—6—San Francisco vs. Pittsburgh, May 5, 1958, ninth inning.
A. L.—6—Detroit vs. New York, September 5, 1971, seventh inning.

Most Consecutive Pinch-Hitters, Inning, One Club

N. L.-A. L.—5—Made in many innings.
N. L.—Last time—New York vs. San Francisco, September 16, 1966, ninth inning.
A. L.—Last time—Texas vs. Chicago, July 9, 1979, eighth inning.

Most Pinch-Hitters, Inning, Both Clubs

A. L.—8—Chicago 5, Baltimore 3, May 18, 1957, seventh inning.
N. L.—8—Philadelphia 5, St. Louis 3, April 30, 1961, eighth inning.
New York 5, San Francisco 3, September 16, 1966, ninth inning.

Most Pinch-Hitters, Nine-Inning Game, One Club

N. L.—9—Los Angeles vs. St. Louis, September 22, 1959.
Montreal vs. Pittsburgh, September 5, 1975, second game.
A. L.—8—Baltimore vs. Chicago, May 28, 1954, first game.

Most Pinch-Hitters, Nine-Inning Game, Both Clubs

N. L.—11—Chicago 7, Los Angeles 4, October 1, 1961.
A. L.—10—Baltimore 6, New York 4, April 26, 1959, second game.

Most Pinch-Hitters, Extra-Inning Game, One Club

A. L.—10—Oakland vs. Chicago, September 17, 1972, 15 innings.
N. L.— 7—New York vs. Chicago, May 2, 1956, 17 innings.
Chicago vs. New York, May 2, 1956, 17 innings.

Most Pinch-Hitters, Extra-Inning Game, Both Clubs

N. L.—14—New York 7, Chicago 7, May 2, 1956, 17 innings.
A. L.—14—Oakland 10, Chicago 4, September 17, 1972, 15 innings.

Most Pinch-Hitters, Doubleheader, Nine-Inning Games, One Club

A. L.—10—New York vs. Boston, September, 6, 1954.
Baltimore vs. Washington, April 19, 1959.
N. L.—10—St. Louis vs. Chicago, May 11, 1958.
St. Louis vs. Pittsburgh, July 13, 1958.

Most Pinch-Hitters, Doubleheader, Nine-Inning Games, Both Clubs

N. L.—15—Milwaukee 8, San Francisco 7, August 30, 1964.
A. L.—14—New York 10, Boston 4, September 6, 1954.

Most Pinch-Hitters, Doubleheader, One Club, More Than 18 Innings

N. L.—15—Montreal vs. Pittsburgh, September 5, 1975, 19 innings.
A. L.— 9—New York vs. Washington, August 14, 1960, 24 innings.

Most Pinch-Hitters, Doubleheader, Both Clubs, More Than 18 Innings

N. L.—19—Montreal 15, Pittsburgh 4, September 5, 1975, 19 innings.
A. L.—17—New York 9, Washington 8, August 14, 1960, 24 innings.

Most Pinch-Runners, Inning, One Club

A. L.—4—Chicago vs. Minnesota, September 16, 1967, ninth inning.
N. L.—3—Made in many innings.

Most Pinch-Runners, Inning, Both Clubs

N. L.—4—Made in many innings.
A. L.—4—Made in many innings.

VARIOUS CLUB RECORDS FOR GAMES

Longest Game, by Innings

N. L.—26 innings— Brooklyn 1, Boston 1, May 1, 1920 at Boston.
A. L.—24 innings— Philadelphia 4, Boston 1, September 1, 1906 at Boston.
                  Detroit 1, Philadelphia 1, July 21, 1945 at Philadelphia.

Longest Opening Game, by Innings

A. L.—15 innings— Washington 1, Philadelphia 0, April 13, 1926 at Washington.
                  Detroit 4, Cleveland 2, April 19, 1960 at Cleveland.
N. L.—14 innings— Philadelphia 5, Brooklyn 5, April 17, 1923 at Brooklyn.
                  New York 1, Brooklyn 1, April 16, 1933 at Brooklyn (opener for New
                    York only).
                  Pittsburgh 4, Milwaukee 3, April 15, 1958 at Milwaukee.
                  Pittsburgh 6, St. Louis 2, April 8, 1969 at St. Louis.
                  Cincinnati 2, Los Angeles 1, April 7, 1975, at Cincinnati.

Longest Night Game, by Innings

N. L.—25 innings— St. Louis 4, New York 3, September 11, 1974 at New York.
A. L.—22 innings— Washington 6, Chicago 5, June 12, 1967 at Washington.
                  (Milwaukee at Minnesota played 21 innings May 12, 1972 with score
                    tied 3-3; called due to curfew, suspended game completed May 13,
                    1972 with Milwaukee winning 4-3.)

Longest 1-0 Day Game

N. L.—18 innings— Providence 1, Detroit 0, August 17, 1882 at Providence.
                  New York 1, St. Louis 0, July 2, 1933, first game at New York.
A. L.—18 innings— Washington 1, Chicago 0, May 15, 1918 at Washington.
                  Washington 1, Chicago 0, June 8, 1947, first game at Chicago.

Longest 1-0 Night Game

N. L.—24 innings— Houston 1, New York 0, April 15, 1968, at Houston.
A. L.—20 innings— Oakland 1, California 0, July 9, 1971, at Oakland.

Longest 0-0 Game

N. L.—19 innings— Brooklyn vs. Cincinnati, September 11, 1946 at Brooklyn.
A. L.—18 innings— Detroit vs. Washington, July 16, 1909 at Detroit.

Longest 0-0 Night Game

N. L.—18 innings— Philadelphia vs. New York, October 2, 1965, second game, at New
                  York.
A. L.—None.

Longest Shutout Game

N. L.—24 innings— Houston 1, New York 0, April 15, 1968 at Houston.
A. L.—20 innings— Oakland 1, California 0, July 9, 1971 at Oakland.

Longest Tie Game

N. L.—26 innings— Boston 1, Brooklyn 1, May 1, 1920 at Boston.
A. L.—24 innings— Detroit 1, Philadelphia 1, July 21, 1945 at Philadelphia.

Most Innings, One Day

N. L.—32—San Francisco and New York, May 31, 1964 at New York.
A. L.—29—Boston and Philadelphia, July 4, 1905 at Boston.
          Boston and New York, August 29, 1967, at New York.

Most Games, One Day

N. L.—3—Brooklyn and Pittsburgh, September 1, 1890 (Brooklyn won 3).
         Baltimore and Louisville, September 7, 1896 (Baltimore won 3).
         Pittsburgh and Cincinnati, October 2, 1920 (Cincinnati won 2).
A. L.—2—Made on many days.

Most Games Won, Two Consecutive Days

N. L.—5—Baltimore, September 7 (3), 8 (2), 1896.
A. L.—4—Made on many days.

Most Games Lost, Two Consecutive Days

N. L.—5—Pittsburgh, August 30 (2), September 1 (3), 1890.
      Louisville, September 7 (3), 8 (2), 1896.
A. L.—4—Made on many days.

Longest Game by Time, Nine Innings

N. L.—4 hours, 18 minutes—Los Angeles 8, San Francisco 7, October 2, 1962.
A. L.—4 hours, 11 minutes—Milwaukee 12, Chicago 9, July 10, 1983.

Longest Extra-Inning Game, by Time

N. L.—7 hours, 23 minutes—San Francisco 8, New York 6, May 31, 1964, second game
      (23 innings).
A. L.—7 hours, 0 minutes—New York 9, Detroit 7, June 24, 1962 (22 innings).

Longest 1-0 Game, by Time, Nine Innings

A. L.—3 hours, 2 minutes—Milwaukee 1, Minnesota 0, June 29, 1977.
N. L.—2 hours, 46 minutes—Philadelphia 1, New York 0, June 30, 1966.

Longest Extra-Inning 1-0 Game, by Time

N. L.—6 hours, 6 minutes—Houston 1, New York 0, April 15, 1968, 24 innings.
A. L.—5 hours, 5 minutes—Oakland 1, California 0, July 9, 1971, 20 innings.

Longest Extra-Inning 1-0 Night Game, by Time

N. L.—6 hours, 6 minutes—Houston 1, New York 0, April 15, 1968, 24 innings.
A. L.—5 hours, 5 minutes—Oakland 1, California 0, July 9, 1971, 20 innings.

Longest Night Game, by Time, Nine Innings

N. L.—4 hours, 2 minutes—Milwaukee 11, San Francisco 9, June 22, 1962.
A. L.—3 hours, 56 minutes—Texas 11, Chicago 6, August 1, 1977.

Longest Night Game, by Time, Ten Innings

A. L.—3 hours, 59 minutes—Boston 3, New York 3, July 5, 1958.
N. L.—3 hours, 56 minutes—New York 8, St. Louis 7, July 16, 1952.

Longest Extra-Inning Night Game, by Time

N. L.—7 hours, 4 minutes—St. Louis 4, New York 3, 25 innings at New York, September
      11, 1974.
A. L.—6 hours, 38 minutes—Washington 6, Chicago 5, 22 innings at Washington, June 12,
      1967.

Shortest Game, by Time, Nine Innings

N. L.—51 minutes—New York 6, Philadelphia 1, September 28, 1919, first game.
A. L.—55 minutes—St. Louis 6, New York 2, September 26, 1926, second game.

Shortest Night Game, by Time, Nine Innings

N. L.—1 hour, 15 minutes—Boston 2, Cincinnati 0, August 10, 1944.
A. L.—1 hour, 29 minutes—Chicago 1, Washington 0, May 21, 1943.

Shortest 1-0 Game, by Time

N. L.—57 minutes—New York 1, Brooklyn 0, August 30, 1918.
A. L.—1 hour, 13 minutes—Detroit 1, New York 0, August 8, 1920.

Shortest Doubleheader, by Time, 18 Innings

A. L.—2 hours, 7 minutes—New York at St. Louis, September 26, 1926.
N. L.—2 hours, 20 minutes—Chicago at Brooklyn, August 14, 1919.

Longest Doubleheader, by Time, 18 Innings

A. L.—6 hours, 50 minutes—Detroit at Kansas City, July 23, 1961.
N. L.—6 hours, 46 minutes—Brooklyn at New York, August 7, 1952.

Longest Doubleheader, by Time, More Than 18 Innings

N. L.—9 hours, 52 minutes—San Francisco at New York, May 31, 1964, 32 innings.
A. L.—9 hours, 5 minutes—Kansas City at Detroit, June 17, 1967, 28 innings.

Largest Score, Shutout Day Game

N. L.— 28-0— Providence vs. Philadelphia, August 21, 1883.
N. L. since 1900—22-0—Pittsburgh vs. Chicago, September 16, 1975.
A. L.— 21-0— Detroit vs. Cleveland, September 15, 1901, 8 innings.
              New York vs. Philadelphia, August 13, 1939, second game, 8 innings.

Largest Score, Shutout Night Game

N. L.— 19-0— Pittsburgh vs. St. Louis, August 3, 1961, at St. Louis.
Los Angeles vs. San Diego, June 28, 1969, at San Diego.
A. L.— 17-0— Los Angeles vs. Washington, August 23, 1963, at Washington.

Most Runs, Shutout Doubleheader, One Club

A. L.—26—Detroit vs. St. Louis, September 22, 1936, 12 to 0; 14 to 0.
N. L.—19—New York vs. Cincinnati, July 31, 1949, 10 to 0; 9 to 0.

AMERICAN LEAGUE EXTRA-INNING GAMES

24 Innings— (2)

Philadelphia 4, Boston 1, September 1, 1906 at Boston.
Detroit 1, Philadelphia 1 (tie), July 21, 1945 at Philadelphia.

22 Innings— (3)

New York 9, Detroit 7, June 24, 1962 at Detroit.
Washington 6, Chicago 5, June 12, 1967 at Washington.
Milwaukee 4, Minnesota 3, May 12, 1972 (21 innings), finished May 13, 1972 (1 inning) at Minnesota.

21 Innings— (3)

Detroit 6, Chicago 5, May 24, 1929 at Chicago.
Oakland 5, Washington 3, June 4, 1971 at Washington.
Chicago 6, Cleveland 3, May 26, 1973, finished May 28, 1973 at Chicago.

20 Innings— (8)

Philadelphia 4, Boston 2, July 4, 1905, p.m. game at Boston.
Washington 9, Minnesota 7, August 9, 1967 at Minnesota.
New York 4, Boston 3, August 29, 1967, second game, at New York.
Boston 5, Seattle 3, July 27, 1969, at Seattle.
Oakland 1, California 0, July 9, 1971, at Oakland.
Washington 8, Cleveland 6, September 14, 1971, second game (16 innings), finished September 20, 1971 (4 innings), started in Cleveland, finished at Washington.
Seattle 8, Boston 7, September 3, 1981 (19 innings), finished September 4, 1981 (2 innings) at Boston.
California 4, Seattle 3, April 13, 1982 (17 innings), finished April 14, 1982 (3 innings), at California.

19 Innings— (12)

Washington 5, Philadelphia 4, September 27, 1912 at Philadelphia.
Chicago 5, Cleveland 4, June 24, 1915 at Cleveland.
Cleveland 3, New York 2, May 24, 1918 at New York.
St. Louis 8, Washington 6, August 9, 1921 at Washington.
Chicago 5, Boston 4, July 13, 1951 at Chicago.
Cleveland 4, St. Louis 3, July 1, 1952 at Cleveland.
Cleveland 3, Washington 2, June 14, 1963, second game, at Cleveland.
Baltimore 7, Washington 5, June 4, 1967 at Baltimore.
Kansas City 6, Detroit 5, June 17, 1967, second game, at Detroit.
Detroit 3, New York 3, (tie), August 23, 1968, second game, at New York.
Oakland 5, Chicago 3, August 10, 1972 (17 innings), finished August 11, 1972 (2 innings) at Oakland.
New York 5, Minnesota 4, August 25, 1976 at New York.

18 Innings— (19)

Chicago 6, New York 6 (tie), June 25, 1903 at Chicago.
Washington 0, Detroit 0 (tie), July 16, 1909 at Detroit.
Washington 1, Chicago 0, May 15, 1918 at Washington.
Detroit 7, Washington 6, August 4, 1918 at Detroit.
Boston 12, New York 11, September 5, 1927, first game, at Boston.
Philadelphia 18, Cleveland 17, July 10, 1932 at Cleveland.
New York 3, Chicago 3 (tie), August 21, 1933 at Chicago.
Washington 1, Chicago 0, June 8, 1947, first game, at Chicago.
Washington 5, St. Louis 5 (tie), June 20, 1952 at St. Louis.
Chicago 1, Baltimore 1 (tie), August 6, 1959 at Baltimore.
New York 7, Boston 6, April 16, 1967 at New York.
Minnesota 3, New York 2, July 26, 1967, second game, at New York.
Baltimore 3, Boston 2, August 25, 1968 at Baltimore.
Minnesota 11, Seattle 7, July 19, 1969 (16 innings), finished July 20, 1969 (2 innings) at Seattle.
Oakland 9, Baltimore 8, August 24, 1969, second game at Oakland.
Minnesota 8, Oakland 6, September 6, 1969, at Oakland.
Washington 2, New York 1, April 22, 1970 at Washington.

18 Innings— (19) —Continued

Texas 4, Kansas City 3, May 17, 1972 at Kansas City.
Detroit 4, Cleveland 3, June 9, 1982 (14 innings), finished September 24, 1982 (4 innings), at Detroit.

NATIONAL LEAGUE EXTRA-INNING GAMES

26 Innings— (1)

Brooklyn 1, Boston 1 (tie), May 1, 1920 at Boston.

25 Innings— (1)

St. Louis 4, New York 3, September 11, 1974, at New York.

24 Innings— (1)

Houston 1, New York 0, April 15, 1968, at Houston.

23 Innings— (2)

Brooklyn 2, Boston 2 (tie), June 27, 1939 at Boston.
San Francisco 8, New York 6, May 31, 1964, second game, at New York.

22 Innings— (2)

Brooklyn 6, Pittsburgh 5, August 22, 1917 at Brooklyn.
Chicago 4, Boston 3, May 17, 1927 at Boston.

21 Innings— (7)

New York 3, Pittsburgh 1, July 17, 1914 at Pittsburgh.
Chicago 2, Philadelphia 1, July 17, 1918 at Chicago.
Pittsburgh 2, Boston 0, August 1, 1918 at Boston.
San Francisco 1, Cincinnati 0, September 1, 1967, at Cincinnati.
Houston 2, San Diego 1, September 24, 1971, first game, at San Diego.
San Diego 11, Montreal 8, May 21, 1977, at Montreal.
Los Angeles 2, Chicago 1, August 17, 1982 (17 innings), finished August 18, 1982 (4 innings), at Chicago.

20 Innings— (8)

Chicago 7, Cincinnati 7 (tie), June 30, 1892 at Cincinnati.
Chicago 2, Philadelphia 1, August 24, 1905 at Philadelphia.
Brooklyn 9, Philadelphia 9 (tie), April 30, 1919 at Philadelphia.
St. Louis 8, Chicago 7, August 28, 1930 at Chicago.
Brooklyn 6, Boston 2, July 5, 1940 at Boston.
Philadelphia 5, Atlanta 4, May 4, 1973, at Philadelphia.
Pittsburgh 5, Chicago 4, July 6, 1980, at Pittsburgh.
Houston 3, San Diego 1, August 15, 1980, at San Diego.

19 Innings— (13)

Chicago 3, Pittsburgh 2, June 22, 1902 at Chicago.
Pittsburgh 7, Boston 6, July 31, 1912 at Boston.
Chicago 4, Brooklyn 3, June 17, 1915 at Chicago.
St. Louis 8, Philadelphia 8 (tie), June 13, 1918 at Philadelphia.
Boston 2, Brooklyn 1, May 3, 1920 at Boston.
Chicago 3, Boston 2, August 17, 1932 at Chicago.
Brooklyn 9, Chicago 9 (tie), May 17, 1939 at Chicago.
Cincinnati 0, Brooklyn 0 (tie), September 11, 1946 at Brooklyn.
Philadelphia 8, Cincinnati 7, September 15, 1950, second game, at Philadelphia.
Pittsburgh 4, Milwaukee 3, July 19, 1955, at Pittsburgh.
Cincinnati 2, Los Angeles 1, August 8, 1972, at Cincinnati.
New York 7, Los Angeles 3, May 24, 1973, at Los Angeles.
Pittsburgh 4, San Diego 3, August 25, 1979, at San Diego.

18 Innings— (25)

Providence 1, Detroit 0, August 17, 1882 at Providence.
Brooklyn 7, St. Louis 7 (tie), August 17, 1902 at St. Louis.
Chicago 2, St. Louis 1, June 24, 1905 at St. Louis.
Pittsburgh 3, Chicago 2, June 28, 1916, second game, at Chicago.
Philadelphia 10, Brooklyn 9, June 1, 1919 at Brooklyn.
New York 9, Pittsburgh 8, July 7, 1922 at Pittsburgh.
Chicago 7, Boston 2, May 14, 1927 at Boston.
New York 1, St. Louis 0, July 2, 1933, first game, at New York.
St. Louis 8, Cincinnati 6, July 1, 1934, first game, at Cincinnati.
Chicago 10, Cincinnati 8, August 9, 1942, first game, at Cincinnati.
Philadelphia 4, Pittsburgh 3, June 9, 1949 at Philadelphia.
Cincinnati 7, Chicago 6, September 7, 1951, at Cincinnati.
Philadelphia 0, New York 0 (tie), October 2, 1965, second game, at New York.
Cincinnati 3, Chicago 2, July 19, 1966 at Chicago.

Philadelphia 2, Cincinnati 1, May 21, 1967 at Philadelphia.
Pittsburgh 1, San Diego 0, June 7, 1972, second game, at San Diego.
New York 3, Philadelphia 2, August 1, 1972, first game, at New York.
Montreal 5, Chicago 4, June 27, 1973, finished June 28, 1973 at Chicago.
Chicago 8, Montreal 7, June 28, 1974, first game, at Montreal.
New York 4, Montreal 3, September 16, 1975, at New York.
Pittsburgh 2, Chicago 1, August 10, 1977, at Pittsburgh.
Chicago 9, Cincinnati 8, May 10, 1979, finished July 23 at Chicago.
Houston 3, New York 2, June 18, 1979, at Houston.
San Diego 8, New York 6, August 26, 1980, at New York.
St. Louis 3, Houston 1, May 27, 1983, at Houston.

Managers' and Umpires' Records

Most Years as Manager, Major Leagues

53—Connie Mack, Pittsburgh N. L. (1894 through 1896), Philadelphia A. L. (1901 through 1950).

Most Years as Manager, League

A. L.—50—Connie Mack, Philadelphia, 1901 through 1950.
N. L.—32—John J. McGraw, Baltimore, 1899; New York, 1902 through 1932.

Most Clubs Managed, Major Leagues

7—Frank C. Bancroft, Worcester N. L., Detroit N. L., Cleveland N. L., Providence N. L., Philadelphia A. A., Indianapolis N. L., Cincinnati N. L.

Most Clubs Managed, Major Leagues Since 1899

6—James Dykes, Chicago A. L., Philadelphia A. L., Baltimore A. L., Cincinnati N. L., Detroit A. L., Cleveland A. L.
5—Patrick J. Donovan, Pittsburgh N. L., St. Louis N. L., Washington A. L., Brooklyn N. L., Boston A. L.
   Stanley R. Harris, Washington A. L., Detroit A. L., Boston A. L., Philadelphia N. L., New York A. L.
   Rogers Hornsby, St. Louis N. L., Chicago N. L., Boston N. L., St. Louis A. L., Cincinnati N. L.
   Charles W. Dressen, Cincinnati N. L., Brooklyn N. L., Washington A. L., Milwaukee N. L., Detroit A. L.
   Alfred M. Martin, Minnesota A. L., Detroit A. L., Texas A. L., New York A. L., Oakland A. L.

Most Clubs Managed, League, Season

U. A.—2—Theodore P. Sullivan, St. Louis, Kansas City, 1884.
A. A.—2—William S. Barnie, Baltimore, Philadelphia, 1891.
N. L.—2—Leo E. Durocher, Brooklyn, New York, 1948.
       Leo E. Durocher, Chicago, Houston, 1972.
A. L.—2—James J. Dykes, Detroit, Cleveland, 1960.
       Joseph L. Gordon, Cleveland, Detroit, 1960.
       Alfred M. Martin, Detroit, Texas, 1973.
       Alfred M. Martin, Texas, New York, 1975.
       Robert G. Lemon, Chicago, New York, 1978.

Most Clubs Managed, Different Major Leagues, Season

2—Joseph V. Battin, 1884 (Pittsburgh A. A. and Pittsburgh U. A.).
   William H. Watkins, 1888 (Detroit N. L., Kansas City A. A.).
   Gustavus H. Schmelz, 1890 (Cleveland N. L., Columbus A. A.).
   John J. McGraw, 1902 (Baltimore A. L., New York N. L.).
   Rogers Hornsby, 1952 (St. Louis A. L., Cincinnati N. L.).
   William C. Virdon, 1975 (New York A. L., Houston N. L.).

Most Different Times as Manager, One Major League Club

N. L.—4—Daniel E. Murtaugh, Pittsburgh, 1957 (part) through 1964; 1967 (part), 1970, 1971, 1973 (part), 1974 through 1976, 15 years.
     3—Arthur A. Irwin, Washington, 1889 (part), 1892 (part), 1898 (part), 1899 (complete).
       Christian F. Von Der Ahe, St. Louis, 1892 (complete), 1895 (part), 1897 (part).
       Charles J. Grimm, Chicago, 1932 (part) to 1938 (part), 1944 (part) to 1949 (part), 1960 (part).
A. L.—3—Stanley R. Harris, Washington, 1924 through 1928, 1935 through 1942, 1950 through 1954, 18 years.

Most Clubs as Manager, League

N. L.—6—Frank C. Bancroft, Worcester, Detroit, Cleveland, Providence, Indianapolis, Cincinnati.
N. L. since 1900—4—William B. McKechnie, Pittsburgh, St. Louis, Boston, Cincinnati.
    Rogers Hornsby, St. Louis, Chicago, Boston, Cincinnati.
    Leo E. Durocher, Brooklyn, New York, Chicago, Houston.
A. L.—5—James Dykes, Chicago, Philadelphia, Baltimore, Detroit, Cleveland.
    Alfred M. Martin, Minnesota, Detroit, Texas, New York, Oakland.

Most Years Championship Manager, League

N. L.—10—John J. McGraw, New York, 1904, 1905, 1911, 1912, 1913, 1917, 1921, 1922, 1923, 1924.
A. L.—10—Charles D. Stengel, New York, 1949, 1950, 1951, 1952, 1953, 1955, 1956, 1957, 1958, 1960.

Most Consecutive Years Championship Manager

A. L.—5—Charles D. Stengel, New York, 1949 through 1953 (first 5 years as New York manager).
    4—Joseph V. McCarthy, New York, 1936 through 1939.
    Charles D. Stengel, New York, 1955 through 1958.
A. A.—4—Charles A. Comiskey, St. Louis, 1885 through 1888.
N. L.—4—John J. McGraw, New York, 1921 through 1924.

Most Years Managed, Major Leagues, No Championships Won

23—Eugene W. Mauch, Philadelphia N. L., 1960 into 1968; Montreal N. L., 1969 through 1975; Minnesota A. L., 1976 into 1980; California A.L., 1981 through 1982.
21—James J. Dykes, Chicago A. L., 1934 through 1946, Philadelphia A. L., 1951 through 1953, Baltimore A. L., 1954, Cincinnati N. L., 1958, Detroit A. L., 1959, 1960, Cleveland A. L., 1960, 1961.

Most Years Managed, League, No Championships Won

A. L.—20—James J. Dykes, Chicago, 1934 through 1946, Philadelphia, 1951 through 1953, Baltimore, 1954, Detroit, 1959, 1960, Cleveland, 1960, 1961.
N. L.—16—Eugene W. Mauch, Philadelphia, 1960 into 1968; Montreal, 1969 through 1975.

Most Consecutive Years Managed, League, No Championships Won

Both Leagues—23—Eugene W. Mauch, Philadelphia N. L., 1960 into 1968; Montreal N. L., 1969 through 1975; Minnesota A. L., 1976 into 1980; California A.L., 1981 through 1982.
A. L.—19—Connie Mack, Philadelphia, 1932 through 1950.
N. L.—16—Eugene W. Mauch, Philadelphia, 1960 into 1968; Montreal, 1969 through 1975.

Most Managers, One Club, Season

A. A.—7—Louisville, 1889.
N. L.—4—Washington, 1892, 1898.
    St. Louis, 1895, 1896, 1897.
N. L.—since 1900—3—Cincinnati, 1902.
        New York, 1902.
        St. Louis, 1905, 1940, 1980.
        Pittsburgh, 1917.
        Chicago, 1925.
        Philadelphia, 1948.
A. L.—4—Texas, 1977.
    3—Boston, 1907.
    St. Louis, 1918, 1933.
    New York, 1946.
    Detroit, 1966.

Most Years Umpired

N. L.—37—William J. Klem, 1905 through 1941.
A. L.—31—Thomas H. Connolly, 1901 through 1931. (Connolly also umpired 3 years in the National League, 1898-1899-1900).

Longest Day Game, Plate Umpire by Time

N. L.—7 hours, 23 minutes—Edward L. Sudol, San Francisco at New York, May 31, 1964, second game, 23 innings. San Francisco won 8-6.

Longest Night Game, Plate Umpire by Time

N. L.—7 hours, 4 minutes—Edward L. Sudol, St. Louis at New York, September 11, 1974, 25 innings. St. Louis won 4-3.

AMERICAN LEAGUE MANAGERS, 1901 THROUGH 1983

BALTIMORE ORIOLES (ST. LOUIS BROWNS PRIOR TO 1954)

James R. McAleer, 1902 through 1909; John O'Connor, 1910; Roderick J. Wallace, 1911-12; George Stovall, 1912-13; James P. Austin, 1913; Branch Rickey, 1913 through 1915; Fielder Jones, 1916 through 1918; James P. Austin, 1918; James Burke, 1918 through 1920; Lee A. Fohl, 1921 through 1923; James Austin, 1923; George H. Sisler, 1924 through 1926; Daniel P. Howley, 1927 through 1929; William Killefer, 1930 through 1933; Allen S. Sothoron, 1933; Rogers Hornsby, 1933 through 1937; James Bottomley, 1937; Charles Street, 1938; Fred Haney, 1939 through 1941; J. Luther Sewell, 1941 through August 30, 1946; James W. Taylor, August 30, 1946 to end of season; Herold D. Ruel, 1947; James W. Taylor, 1948 through 1951; Rogers Hornsby, 1952; Martin W. Marion, 1952-53; James J. Dykes, 1954; Paul R. Richards, 1955 to September, 1961; C. Luman Harris, 1961; William C. Hitchcock, 1962-63; Henry A. Bauer, 1964 through July 10, 1968. Earl S. Weaver, July 11, 1968 through 1982; Joseph S. Altobelli, 1983. (John J. McGraw, 1901-02 and Wilbert Robinson, 1902, managed earlier Baltimore club.)

BOSTON RED SOX

James J. Collins, 1901 through 1906; Charles Stahl, 1906; George Huff, 1907; Robert Unglaub, 1907; James McGuire, 1907-08; Fred Lake, 1908-09; Patrick J. Donovan, 1910-11; J. Garland Stahl, 1912-13; William Carrigan, 1913 through 1916; John J. Barry, 1917; Edward G. Barrow, 1918 through 1920; Hugh Duffy, 1921-22; Frank Chance, 1923; Lee A. Fohl, 1924 through 1926; William Carrigan, 1927 through 1929; Charles Wagner, 1930; John F. Collins, 1931-32; Martin J. McManus, 1932-33; Stanley R. Harris, 1934; Joesph E. Cronin, 1935 through 1947; Joseph C. McCarthy, 1948 through 1950; Stephen F. O'Neill, 1950-51; Louis Boudreau, 1952 through 1954; Michael F. Higgins, 1955 through 1959; William F. Jurges, 1959-60; Michael F. Higgins, 1960 through 1962; John M. Pesky, 1963-64; William J. Herman, 1965 through September 7, 1966; James E. Runnels, September 8, 1966 to end of season; Richard H. Williams, 1967 through September 22, 1969; Edward J. Popowski, September 23, 1969 to end of season; Edward M. Kasko, 1970 through September 29, 1973; Edward J. Popowski, September 30, 1973; Darrell D. Johnson, 1974 through July 18, 1976; Donald W. Zimmer, July 19, 1976 through September 30, 1980; John M. Pesky, October 1 to end of season; Ralph G. Houk, 1981 through 1983.

CALIFORNIA ANGELS (LOS ANGELES ANGELS PRIOR TO 1966)

William J. Rigney, 1961 through May 25, 1969; Howard R. Phillips, May 27, 1969 through 1971; Delbert W. Rice, 1972; Bobby B. Winkles, 1973 through June 26, 1974; Richard H. Williams, July 1, 1974 through July 22, 1976; Norman B. Sherry, July 24, first game, 1976 through July 10, 1977; David Garcia, July 11, 1977 to June 1, 1978; James L. Fregosi, June 1, 1978 through May 27, 1981; Eugene W. Mauch, May 30, 1981 through 1982; John F. McNamara, 1983.

CHICAGO WHITE SOX

Clark C. Griffith, 1901-02; James J. Callahan, 1903-04; Fielder A. Jones, 1904 through 1908; William J. Sullivan, 1909; Hugh Duffy, 1910-11; James J. Callahan, 1912 through 1914; Clarence H. Rowland, 1915 through 1918; William Gleason, 1919 through 1923; Frank L. Chance, 1924; John J. Evers, 1924; Edward T. Collins, 1925-26; Ray W. Schalk, 1927-28; Russell Blackburne, 1928-29; Owen J. Bush, 1930-31; Lewis A. Fonseca, 1932 through 1934; James J. Dykes, 1934 through 1946; Theodore A. Lyons, 1946 through 1948; John J. Onslow, 1949-50; John M. Corriden, 1950; Paul R. Richards, 1951 through 1954; Martin W. Marion, 1954 through 1956; Alfonso R. Lopez, 1957 through 1965; Edward R. Stanky, 1966 through July 11, 1968; Alfonso R. Lopez, July 14, 1968 first game through May 1, 1969; Donald J. Gutteridge, May 3, 1969 through September 1, 1970; Charles W. Tanner, September 18, 1970 through 1975; Paul R. Richards, 1976; Robert G. Lemon, 1977 to June 30, 1978; Lawrence E. Doby, June 30, 1978 to end of season; Donald E. Kessinger, 1979 through August 2, 1979; Anthony LaRussa, August 3, 1979 through 1983.

CLEVELAND INDIANS

James R. McAleer, 1901; William R. Armour, 1902 through 1904; Napoleon Lajoie, 1905 through 1909; James McGuire, 1909 through 1911; George Stovall, 1911; Harry H. Davis, 1912; Joseph L. Birmingham, 1912 through 1915; Lee A. Fohl, 1915 through 1919; Tristram Speaker, 1919 through 1926; John (Jack) McCallister, 1927; Roger Peckinpaugh, 1928 through 1933; Walter P. Johnson, 1933 through 1935; Stephen F. O'Neill, 1935 through 1937; Oscar Vitt, 1938 through 1940; Roger Peckinpaugh, 1941; Louis Boudreau, 1942 through 1950; Alfonso R. Lopez, 1951 through 1956; M. Kerby Farrell, 1957; Robert R. Bragan, 1958; Joseph L. Gordon, 1958 through August 2, 1960; James J. Dykes, August 3, 1960 through 1961; F. Melvin McGaha, 1962; George R. Tebbetts, 1963 through August 19, 1966; George H. Strickland, August 20, 1966 to end of season; Joseph W. Adcock, 1967; Alvin R. Dark, 1968 through July 29, 1971; John J. Lipon, July 30, 1971 to end of season; Kenneth J. Aspromonte, 1972 through 1974; Frank Robinson, 1975 through June 18, 1977; Jeffrey A. Torborg, June 19, 1977 through July 22, 1979; David Garcia, July 23, 1979 through 1982; Michael D. Ferraro, 1983 to July 30, 1983; Patrick Corrales, July 31, 1983 through end of season.

DETROIT TIGERS

George Stallings, 1901; J. Frank Dwyer, 1902; Edward G. Barrow, 1903-04; Robert L. Lowe, 1904; William R. Armour, 1905-06; Hugh A. Jennings, 1907 through 1920; Tyrus R. Cobb 1921 through 1926; George Moriarty, 1927-28; Stanley R. Harris, 1929 through 1933; Delmer Baker, 1933; Gordon S. Cochrane, 1934 through 1938; Delmer Baker, 1938 through 1942; Stephen F. O'Neill, 1943 through 1948; Robert Rolfe, 1949 through 1952; Fredrick C. Hutchinson, 1952 through 1954; Stanley R. Harris, 1955 through 1956; John T. Tighe, 1957 to 1958; Willis P. Norman, 1958 through May 2, 1959; James J. Dykes, May 3, 1959 through August 2, 1960; Joseph L. Gordon, August 3, 1960 through end of season; Robert B. Scheffing, 1961 to June 18, 1963; Charles W. Dressen, June 18, 1963 through May 15, 1966; Robert V. Swift, May 16, 1966 through July 13, 1966; Francis M. Skaff, July 14, 1966 to end of season; E. Mayo Smith, 1967 through 1970; Alfred M. Martin, 1971 through August 30, 1973; Joseph C. Schultz, August 30, 1973 to end of season; Ralph G. Houk, 1974 through 1978; J. Lester Moss, 1979 to June 12, 1979; George L. Anderson, June 14, 1979 through 1983.

KANSAS CITY ROYALS

Joseph L. Gordon, 1969; Charles Metro, April 7, 1970 through June 7, 1970, second game; Robert G. Lemon, June 9, 1970 through 1972; John McKeon, 1973 through July 23, 1975; Dorrel N. E. Herzog, July 25, 1975 through 1979; James G. Frey, 1980 through August 29, 1981; Richard D. Howser, August 31, 1981 through 1983.

MILWAUKEE BREWERS

J. David Bristol, 1970 through May 27, 1972; Roy D. McMillan, May 28, 29, 1972; Delmar W. Crandall, May 30, 1972 through September 27, 1975; Harvey E. Kuenn, September 28, 1975; Alexander P. Grammas, 1976 through 1977; George I. Bamberger, 1978 through 1979; Robert L. Rodgers, 1980 through June 4, 1980; George I. Bamberger, June 6, 1980 through September 7, 1980; Robert L. Rodgers, September 9, 1980 through June 1, 1982; Harvey E. Kuenn, June 2, 1982 through 1983.

MINNESOTA TWINS (WASHINGTON SENATORS PRIOR TO 1961)

James H. Manning, 1901; Thomas J. Loftus, 1902-03; Malachi J. Kittredge, 1904; Patrick J. Donovan, 1904; J. Garland Stahl, 1905-06; Joseph Cantillon, 1907 through 1909; James R. McAleer, 1910-11; Clark C. Griffith, 1912 through 1920; George F. McBride, 1921; Clyde Milan, 1922; Owen J. Bush, 1923; Stanley R. Harris, 1924 through 1928; Walter P. Johnson, 1929 through 1932; Joseph E. Cronin, 1933-34; Stanley R. Harris, 1935 through 1942; Oswald L. Bluege, 1943 through 1947; Joseph Kuhel, 1948-49; Stanley R. Harris, 1950 through 1954; Charles W. Dressen, 1955 through May 6, 1957; Harry A. Lavagetto, May 7, 1957 through June 22, 1961; Sabath A. Mele, June 23, 1961 through June 8, 1967; Calvin C. Ermer, June 9, 1967 through 1968; Alfred M. Martin, 1969; William J. Rigney, 1970 through July 5, 1972; Frank R. Quilici, July 6, 1972 through 1975; Eugene W. Mauch, 1976 through August 24, 1980; John A. Goryl, August 25, 1980 through May 21, 1981; William F. Gardner, May 22, 1981 through 1983.

NEW YORK YANKEES

Clark C. Griffith, 1903 through 1908; Norman Elberfeld, 1908; George S. Stallings, 1909-10; Harold H. Chase, 1910-11; Harry Wolverton, 1912; Frank Chance, 1913-14; Roger Peckinpaugh, 1914; William E. Donovan, 1915 through 1917; Miller J. Huggins, 1918 through 1929; Arthur Fletcher, 1929; J. Robert Shawkey, 1930; Joseph V. McCarthy, 1931 through 1946; William M. Dickey, 1946; John Neun, 1946; Stanley R. Harris, 1947-48; Charles D. Stengel, 1949 through 1960; Ralph G. Houk, 1961 through 1963; Lawrence P. Berra, 1964; John J. Keane, 1965 to May 6, 1966; Ralph G. Houk, May 7, 1966 through 1973; William C. Virdon, 1974 through August 1, 1975; Alfred M. Martin, August 2, 1975 through July 23, 1978; Robert G. Lemon, July 25, 1978 through June 17, 1979; Alfred M. Martin, June 19, 1979 to end of season; Richard D. Howser, 1980; Eugene R. Michael, 1981 through September 5, 1981; Robert G. Lemon, September 6, 1981 through April 25, 1982; Eugene R. Michael, April 27, 1982 through August 3, 1982; Clyde E. King, August 4, 1982 through end of season; Alfred M. Martin, 1983.

OAKLAND ATHLETICS (KANSAS CITY ATHLETICS 1955 THROUGH 1967, PHILADELPHIA A'S PRIOR TO 1955)

Connie Mack, 1901 through 1950; James J. Dykes, 1951 through 1953; Edwin D. Joost, 1954; Louis Boudreau, 1955 through 1957; Harry F. Craft, 1957 through 1959; Robert I. Elliott, 1960; Joseph L. Gordon, 1961; Henry A. Bauer, 1961-62; Edmund W. Lopat, 1963 to June 11, 1964; F. Melvin McGaha, June 11, 1964 through May 15, 1965; Haywood C. Sullivan, May 16, 1965, to end of season; Alvin R. Dark, 1966 through August 19, 1967; Lucius B. Appling, August 21, 1967 to end of season; Robert D. Kennedy, 1968; Henry A. Bauer, 1969 through September 18, 1969; John F. McNamara, September 19, 1969 through 1970; Richard H. Williams, 1971 through 1973; Alvin R. Dark, 1974 through 1975; Charles W. Tanner, 1976; John A. McKeon, 1977 through June 9, 1977; Bobby B. Winkles, June 10, 1977 to May 23, 1978; John A. McKeon, May 23, 1978 to end of season; R. James Marshall, 1979 to end of season; Alfred M. Martin, 1980 through 1982; Stephen Boros, 1983.

SEATTLE PILOTS
Joseph C. Schultz, 1969.

SEATTLE MARINERS
Darrell D. Johnson, 1977 through August 3, 1980; Maurice M. Wills, August 4 through May 5, 1981; Rene G. Lachemann, May 6, 1981 through June 24, 1983; Delmar W. Crandall, June 25, 1983 through end of season.

TEXAS RANGERS (WASHINGTON SENATORS, 1961 THROUGH 1971)
James B. Vernon, 1961 to May 21, 1963; Edward F. Yost, May 22, 1963; Gilbert R. Hodges, May 23, 1963 through 1967; James R. Lemon, 1968; Theodore S. Williams, 1969 through 1972; Dorrel N. E. Herzog, start of 1973 season through September 4, 1973; Delbert Q. Wilber, September 7, 1973; Alfred M. Martin, September 8, 1973 through July 20, second game, 1975; Frank J. Lucchesi, July 21, 1975 through June 21, 1977; Edward R. Stanky, June 22, 1977; Cornelius J. Ryan, June 23 through 27, 1977; G. William Hunter, June 28, 1977 to September 30, 1978; Patrick Corrales, October 1, 1978 through 1980; Donald W. Zimmer, 1981 through July 28, 1982; Darrell D. Johnson, July 30, 1982 through end of season; Douglas L. Rader, 1983.

TORONTO BLUE JAYS
Roy T. Hartsfield, 1977 through 1979; Robert J. Mattick, 1980 through 1981; Robert J. Cox, 1982 through 1983.

NATIONAL LEAGUE MANAGERS, 1876 THROUGH 1983
(CURRENT CLUBS)
ATLANTA BRAVES (MILWAUKEE BRAVES 1953-1965; BOSTON BRAVES PRIOR TO 1953)
Harry Wright, 1876 through 1881; John F. Morrill, 1882 through 1888; James A. Hart, 1889; Frank Selee, 1890 through 1901; Albert C. Buckenberger, 1902 through 1904; Fred Tenney, 1905 through 1907; Joseph J. Kelley, 1908; Frank Bowerman, 1909; Harry Smith, 1909; Fred Lake, 1910; Fred Tenney, 1911; John Kling, 1912; George Stallings, 1913 through 1920; Fred Mitchell, 1921 through 1923; David Bancroft, 1924 through 1927; John Slattery, 1928; Rogers Hornsby, 1928; Emil Fuchs, 1929; Walter Maranville, 1929; William B. McKechnie, 1930 through 1937; Charles D. Stengel, 1938 through 1943; Robert Coleman, 1944-45; Adelphia Bissonette, 1945; William H. Southworth, 1946 through 1949; John Cooney, 1949; William H. Southworth, 1950-51; Thomas F. Holmes, 1951-52; Charles J. Grimm, 1952 to 1956; Fred G. Haney, 1956 through 1959; Charles W. Dressen, 1960-61; George R. Tebbetts, 1962; Robert R. Bragan, 1963 to August 8, 1966; William C. Hitchcock, August 9, 1966 through September 28, 1967; Kenneth J. Silvestri, September 29, 30, October 1, 1967; C. Luman Harris, 1968 through August 6, 1972; Edwin L. Mathews, August 7, 1972 through July 21, 1974; Clyde E. King, July 25, 1974 through August 29, 1975; Cornelius J. Ryan, August 31, 1975, first game to end of season; J. David Bristol, 1976 through May 10, 1977; Robert E. (Ted) Turner, May 11, 1977; J. David Bristol, May 12, 1977 to end of season; Robert J. Cox, 1978 through 1981. Joseph P. Torre, 1982 through 1983. (John J. Chapman managed 1878, Milwaukee N. L. club and Hugh Duffy managed 1901 Milwaukee A. L. club.)

CHICAGO CUBS
Albert Spalding, 1876-77; Robert Ferguson, 1878; Adrian C. Anson, 1879 through 1897; Thomas Burns, 1898-99; Thomas Loftus, 1900-01; Frank Selee, 1902 through 1905; Frank Chance, 1905 through 1912; John Evers, 1913; Henry F. O'Day, 1914; Roger Bresnahan, 1915; Joseph Tinker, 1916; Fred Mitchell, 1917 through 1920; John Evers, 1921; William Killefer, 1921 through 1925; Walter Maranville, 1925; George Gibson, 1925; Joseph V. McCarthy, 1926 through 1930; Rogers Hornsby, 1930 through 1932; Charles J. Grimm, 1932 through 1938; Charles Hartnett, 1938 through 1940; James Wilson, 1941 to 1944; Charles J. Grimm, 1944 through 1949; Frank F. Frisch, 1949 through 1951; Philip J. Cavarretta, 1951 through 1953; Stanley C. Hack, 1954 through 1956; Robert B. Scheffing, 1957 through 1959; Charles J. Grimm, 1960; Louis Boudreau, 1960; eight coaches handled managerial duties in 1961 through 1965; Leo E. Durocher, 1966 through July 23, 1972; Carroll W. Lockman, July 27, 1972 through July 21, 1974; R. James Marshall, July 25, 1974 through 1976; Herman L. Franks, 1977 through September 23, 1979; J. Joseph Amalfitano, September 24, 1979 to end of season; Pedro W. (Preston) Gomez, 1980 through July 23, 1980; J. Joseph Amalfitano, July 25, 1980 through 1981; Lee C. Elia, 1982 through August 21, 1983; Charles F. Fox, August 22, 1983 through end of season.

CINCINNATI REDS
Charles Gould, 1876; Lipman Pike, 1877; Calvin McVey, 1878-79; James White, 1879; John Clapp, 1880; Thomas Loftus, 1890-91; Charles A. Comiskey, 1892 through 1894; William Ewing, 1895 through 1899; Robert Allen, 1900; John McPhee, 1901-02; Frank C. Bancroft, 1902; Joseph Kelley, 1902 through 1905; Edward Hanlon, 1906-07; John Ganzel, 1908; Clark C. Griffith, 1909 through 1911; Henry F. O'Day, 1912; Joseph Tinker, 1913; Charles Herzog, 1914 through 1916; Christopher Mathewson, 1916 through 1918; Patrick

J. Moran, 1919 through 1923; John C. Hendricks, 1924 through 1929; Daniel P. Howley, 1930 through 1932; Owen J. Bush, 1933; Robert O'Farrell, 1934; Charles W. Dressen, 1934 through 1937; Roderick J. Wallace, 1937; Willaim B. McKechnie, 1938 through 1946; John Neun, 1947-48; William Walters, 1948-49; J. Luther Sewell, 1949 through 1952; Rogers Hornsby, 1952-53; C. Buster Mills, 1953; George R. Tebbetts, 1954 through 1958; James J. Dykes, 1958; E. Mayo Smith, 1959; Frederick C. Hutchinson, 1959 through 1964; Richard A. Sisler, 1965; Donald H. Heffner, 1966 to July 12 that year; J. David Bristol, July 13, 1966 through 1969; George L. Anderson, 1970 through 1978; John F. McNamara, 1979 through July 20, 1982; Russell E. Nixon, July 21, 1982 through 1983.

HOUSTON ASTROS

Harry F. Craft, 1962 through September 19, 1964; C. Luman Harris, September 19, 1964 through 1965; Grady E. Hatton, 1966 through June 17, 1968; Harry W. Walker, June 18, 1968, first game through August 25, 1972; Leo E. Durocher, August 27, 1972 through 1973; Pedro W. (Preston) Gomez, 1974 through August 18, 1975; William C. Virdon, August 19, 1975 through 1982; Robert P. Lillis, 1983.

LOS ANGELES DODGERS
(BROOKLYN DODGERS PRIOR TO 1958)

William McGunnigle, 1890; John Montgomery Ward, 1891-92; David Foutz, 1893 through 1896; William Barnie, 1897-98; Michael Griffin, 1898; Charles H. Ebbets, 1898; Edward Hanlon, 1899 through 1905; Patrick J. Donovan, 1906 through 1908; Harry Lumley, 1909; William Dahlen, 1910 through 1913; Wilbert Robinson, 1914 through 1931; Max Carey, 1932-33; Charles D. Stengel, 1934 through 1936; Burleigh Grimes, 1937-38; Leo Durocher, 1939 through 1946; Clyde L. Sukeforth, April 15, 1947; Burton E. Shotton, 1947; Leo Durocher, 1948; Burton E. Shotton, 1948 through 1950; Charles W. Dressen, 1951 through 1953; Walter E. Alston, 1954 through September 28, 1976; Thomas C. Lasorda, September 29, 1976 through 1983.

MONTREAL EXPOS

Eugene W. Mauch, 1969 through 1975; Karl O. Kuehl, 1976 through September 3, 1976; Charles F. Fox, September 4, 1976 to end of season; Richard H. Williams, 1977 through September 7, 1981; W. James Fanning, September 8, 1981 through 1982; William C. Virdon, 1983.

NEW YORK METS

Charles D. Stengel, 1962 through July 24, 1965; Wesley N. Westrum, July 25, 1965 through September 21 1967; Francis J. Parker, September 22, 1967 to end of season; Gilbert R. Hodges, 1968 through 1971; Lawrence P. Berra, 1972 through August 5, 1975, second game; Roy D. McMillan, August 6, 1975 to end of season; Joseph F. Frazier, 1976 through May 30, 1977; Joseph P. Torre, May 31, 1977 through 1981; George I. Bamberger, 1982 through June 2, 1983; Frank O. Howard, June 3, 1983 through end of season.

PHILADELPHIA PHILLIES

A. L. H. Wright, 1876; Horace Phillips, 1883; Robert Ferguson, 1883; Harry Wright, 1884 through 1893; Arthur Irwin, 1894-95; William Shettsline, 1896; George Stallings, 1897-98; William Shettsline, 1899 through 1902; Charles Zimmer, 1903; Hugh Duffy, 1904 through 1906; William Murray, 1907 through 1909; Charles Dooin, 1910 through 1914; Patrick J. Moran, 1915 through 1918; John Coombs, 1919; Clifford Cravath, 1919-20; William E. Donovan, 1921; Irving Wilhelm, 1921-22; Arthur Fletcher, 1923 through 1926; John P. McInnis, 1927; Burt Shotton, 1928 through 1933; James Wilson, 1934 through 1938; James T. Prothro, 1939 through 1941; John Lobert, 1942; Stanley R. Harris, 1943; Fred Fitzsimmons, 1943 through 1945; W. Benjamin Chapman, 1945 through 1948; Allen L. Cooke, 1948; Edwin M. Sawyer, 1948 through 1952; Stephen F. O'Neill, 1952 through 1954; Terry B. Moore, 1954; E. Mayo Smith, 1955 through 1958; Edwin M. Sawyer, 1958 through April 12, 1960; Eugene W. Mauch, April 16, 1960 through June 14, 1968, first game; Robert R. Skinner, June 16, 1968 through August 6, 1969; George E. Myatt, August 8, 1969 to end of season; Frank J. Lucchesi, 1970 through July 9, 1972; Paul F. Owens, July 10, 1972 to end of 1972; Daniel L. Ozark, 1973 through August 30, 1979; G. Dallas Green, August 31, 1979 through 1981; Patrick Corrales, 1982 through July 17, 1983; Paul F. Owens, July 18, 1983 through end of season.

PITTSBURGH PIRATES

Horace B. Phillips, 1887 through 1889; Fred Dunlap, 1889; Edward Hanlon, 1889; Guy Hecker, 1890; Edward Hanlon, 1891; William McGunnigle, 1891; Thomas E. Burns, 1892; Albert C. Buckenberger, 1892 through 1894; Connie Mack, 1894 through 1896; Patrick J. Donovan, 1897; William H. Watkins, 1898-99; Patrick J. Donovan, 1899; Fred Clarke, 1900 through 1915; James J. Callahan, 1916-17; John Wagner, 1917; Hugo Bezdek, 1917 through 1919; George Gibson, 1920 through 1922; William B. McKechnie, 1922 through 1926; Owen J. Bush, 1927 through 1929; Jewel Ens, 1929 through 1931; George Gibson, 1932 through 1934; Harold J. Traynor, 1934 through 1939; Frank F. Frisch, 1940 through 1946; Virgil L. Davis, 1946; William J. Herman, 1947; William E. Burwell, 1947; William A. Meyer, 1948 through 1952; Fred G. Haney, 1953 through 1955; Robert R. Bragan, 1956-57; Daniel E. Murtaugh, 1957 through 1964; Harry W. Walker, 1965 through July

17, 1967; Daniel E. Murtaugh, July 18, 1967 to end of season; Lawrence W. Shepard, 1968 through September 25, 1969; Alexander P. Grammas, September 26, 1969 to end of season; Daniel E. Murtaugh, 1970 through 1971; William C. Virdon, 1972 through September 5, 1973; Daniel E. Murtaugh, September 6, 1973 through 1976; Charles W. Tanner, 1977 through 1983.

ST. LOUIS CARDINALS

S. Mason Graffen, 1876; J. R. Lucas, 1877; George McManus, 1877; Fred Dunlop, 1886; Benjamin Fine, 1885; Henry V. Lucas, 1885; Gus Schmelz, 1886; Chris Von der Ahe, 1892; William H. Watkins, 1893; George Miller, 1894; H. B. Martin, 1894; Albert C. Buckenberger, 1895; Joseph Quinn, 1895; Lewis Phelan, 1895; Chris Von der Ahe, 1895; Henry Diddlebock, 1896; Walter A. Latham, 1896; Roger Connor, 1896; Thomas J. Dowd, 1896-97; Hugh Nicol, 1897; William Hallman, 1897; Chris Von der Ahe, 1897; Timothy Hurst, 1898; Oliver Tebeau, 1899-1900; Louis Heilbroner, 1900; Patrick J. Donovan, 1901 through 1903; Charles Nichols, 1904-05; James T. Burke, 1905; M. Stanley Robison, 1905; John L. McCloskey, 1906 through 1908; Roger Bresnahan, 1909 through 1912; Miller J. Huggins, 1913 through 1917; John C. Hendricks, 1918; Branch Rickey, 1919 through 1925; Rogers Hornsby, 1925-26; Robert O'Farrell, 1927; William B. McKechnie, 1928; William H. Southworth, 1929; William B. McKechnie, 1929; Charles Street, 1930 through 1933; Frank F. Frisch, 1933 through 1938; Miguel A. Gonzalez, 1938; Ray Blades, 1939-40; Miguel A. Gonzalez, 1940; William H. Southworth, 1940 through 1945; Edwin H. Dyer, 1946 through 1950; Martin W. Marion, 1951; Edward R. Stanky, 1952 through 1955 (part); Harry W. Walker, 1955; Frederick C. Hutchinson, 1956 through 1958 (part); Stanley C. Hack (part 1958); Solomon J. Hemus, 1959-60-61; John J. Keane, 1961 through 1964; Albert F. Schoendienst, 1965 through 1976; Vern Rapp, 1977 through April 25, 1978; Kenton L. Boyer, April 29, 1978 through June 8, 1980, first game; Dorrel N. E. Herzog, June 9 through August 28, 1980; Albert F. Schoendienst, August 29, 1980 to end of season; Dorrel N. E. Herzog, 1981 through 1983.

SAN DIEGO PADRES

Pedro W. (Preston) Gomez, 1969 through April 26, 1972; Donald W. Zimmer, April 27, 1972 through 1973; John F. McNamara, 1974 through May 28, 1977; Alvin R. Dark, May 30, 1977 to March 21, 1978; Roger L. Craig, March 21, 1978 through 1979; Gerald F. Coleman, 1980; Frank O. Howard, 1981; Richard H. Williams, 1982 through 1983.

SAN FRANCISCO GIANTS
(NEW YORK GIANTS PRIOR TO 1958)

William H. Cammeyer, 1876; John Clapp, 1883; James Price, 1884; James Mutrie, 1885 through 1891; Patrick Powers, 1892; John Montgomery Ward, 1893-94; George Davis, 1895; John J. Doyle, 1895; Harvey Watkins, 1895; Arthur Irwin, 1896; William Joyce, 1896 through 1898; Adrian C. Anson, 1898; John B. Day, 1899; Frederick C. Hoey, 1899; William Ewing, 1900; George Davis, 1900-01; Hor- ace Fogel, 1902; George Smith, 1902; John J. McGraw, 1902 through 1932; William H. Terry, 1932 through 1941; Melvin T. Ott, 1942 through 1948; Leo F. Durocher, 1948 through 1955; William J. Rigney, 1956 through 1960 (part); Thomas Sheehan, 1960; Alvin R. Dark, 1961 through 1964; Herman L. Franks, 1965 through 1968; Clyde E. King, 1969 through May 23, 1970; Charles F. Fox, May 24, 1970, first game through June 27, 1974; Wesley N. Westrum, June 28, 1974 through 1975; William J. Rigney, 1976; Joseph S. Altobelli, 1977 through September 5, 1979; J. David Bristol, September 6, 1979 through 1980; Frank Robinson, 1981 through 1983.

MAJOR LEAGUE MANAGERS, 1876 THROUGH 1983
LISTED ALPHABETICALLY

A

Adcock, Joseph W.—Cleveland AL 1967.

Allen, Robert G.—Cincinnati NL 1900.

Alston, Walter E.—Brooklyn NL 1954 through 1957; Los Angeles NL 1958 to 1976 (part).

Altobelli, Joseph S.—San Francisco NL 1977 through September 6, 1979; Baltimore AL 1983.

Amalfitano, J. Joseph—Chicago NL September 24, 1979 to end of season, July 25, 1980 through 1981.

Anderson, George L.—Cincinnati NL 1970 through 1978; Detroit AL June 14, 1979 through 1983.

Anson, Adrian C.—Chicago NL 1879 through 1897; New York NL 1898.

Appling, Lucius B.—Kansas City AL 1967.

Armour, William R.—Cleveland AL 1902 through 1904; Detroit AL 1905-06.

Aspromonte, Kenneth J.—Cleveland AL 1972 through 1974.

Austin, James P.—St. Louis AL 1913-18-23.

B

Baker, Delmer B.—Detroit AL 1933, 1938 through 1942.

Bamberger, George I.—Milwaukee AL 1978 through 1979; 1980 (part); New York NL 1982 to 1983 (part).

Bancroft, David J.—Boston NL 1924 through 1927.

Bancroft, Frank C.—Worcester NL 1880; Detroit NL 1881-82; Cleveland NL 1883; Providence NL 1884-85; Philadelphia AA 1887; Indianapolis NL 1889; Cincinnati NL 1902.

Barkley, Samuel W.—Kansas City AA 1888.

Barnie, William S.—Baltimore AA 1883 through 1891; Philadelphia AA 1891; Washington NL 1892; Louisville NL 1893-94; Brooklyn NL 1897-98.

Barrow, Edward G.—Detroit AL 1903-04; Boston AL 1918 through 1920.

Barry, John J.—Boston AL 1917.

Battin, Joseph V.—Pittsburgh AA 1884; Pittsburgh UA 1884.

Bauer, Henry A.—Kansas City AL 1961-62; Baltimore AL 1964 through 1968 (part); Oakland AL 1969 (part).

Berra, Lawrence P.—New York AL 1964; New York NL 1972 through August 5, 1975, second game.

Bezdek, Hugo F.—Pittsburgh NL 1917 through 1919.

Birmingham, Joseph L.—Cleveland AL 1912 through 1915.

Bissonette, Adelphia L.—Boston NL 1945.

Blackburne, Russell A.—Chicago AL 1928-29.

Blades, Raymond F.—St. Louis NL 1939-40.

Bluege, Oswald L.—Washington AL 1943 through 1947.

Bond, Thomas H.—Worcester NL 1882.

Boros, Stephen—Oakland AL 1983.

Bottomley, James L.—St. Louis AL 1937.

Boudreau, Louis—Cleveland AL 1942 through 1950; Boston AL 1952 through 1954; Kansas City AL 1955 through 1957; Chicago NL 1960.

Bowerman, Frank E.—Boston NL 1909.

Boyer, Kenton L.—St. Louis NL April 29, 1978 through June 8, 1980, first game.

Bragan, Robert R.—Pittsburgh NL 1956-57; Cleveland AL 1958; Milwaukee NL 1963 through 1965; Atlanta NL 1966.

Bresnahan, Roger P.—St. Louis NL 1909 through 1912; Chicago NL 1915.

Bristol, J. David—Cincinnati NL 1966 through 1969; Milwaukee AL 1970 through May 27, 1972; Atlanta NL 1976 through May 10, 1977; May 12, 1977 to end of season; San Francisco NL September 6, 1979 through 1980.

Brown, Freeman—Worcester NL 1880 through 1882.

Brown, Robert M.—Louisville AA 1889.

Brown, Thomas T.—Washington NL 1897-98.

Buckenberger, Albert C.—Columbus AA 1889-90; Pittsburgh NL 1892 through 1894; St. Louis NL 1895; Boston NL 1902 through 1904.

Buffinton, Charles G.—Philadelphia PL 1890.

Bullock, James L.—Providence NL 1880-81.

Burke, James T.—St. Louis NL 1905; St. Louis AL 1918 through 1920.

Burnham, George W.—Indianapolis NL 1887.

Burns, Thomas E.—Pittsburgh NL 1892; Chicago NL 1898-99.

Burwell, William E.—Pittsburgh NL 1947.

Bush, Owen J.—Washington AL 1923; Pittsburgh NL 1927 through 1929; Chicago AL 1930-31; Cincinnati NL 1933.

Butler, Ormond H.—Pittsburgh AA 1883.

Byrne, Charles H.—Brooklyn AA 1885 through 1887.

C

Callahan, James J.—Chicago AL 1903-04 and 1912 through 1914; Pittsburgh NL 1916-17.

Cammeyer, William H.—New York NL 1876.

Campau, Charles C.—St. Louis AA 1890.

Cantillon, Joseph D.—Washington AL 1907 through 1909.

Carey, Max G.—Brooklyn NL 1932-33.

Carrigan, William F.—Boston AL 1913 through 1916, 1927 through 1929.

Cavarretta, Philip J.—Chicago NL 1951 through 1953.

Caylor, Oliver P.—Cincinnati AA 1885-86; New York AA 1887.

Chance, Frank L.—Chicago NL 1905 through 1912; New York AL 1913-14; Boston AL 1923.

Chapman, W. Benjamin—Philadelphia NL 1945 through 1948.

Chapman, John C.—Louisville NL 1877; Milwaukee NL 1878; Worcester NL 1882; Detroit NL 1883-84; Buffalo NL 1885; Louisville AA 1889 through 1891; Louisville NL 1892.

Chase, Harold H.—New York AL 1910-11.

Clapp, John E.—Indianapolis NL 1878; Cincinnati NL 1880; New York NL 1883.

Clarke, Frederick C.—Louisville NL 1897 through 1899; Pittsburgh NL 1900 through 1915.

Cobb, Tyrus R.—Detroit AL 1921 through 1926.

Cochrane, Gordon S.—Detroit AL 1934 through 1938.

Coleman, Gerald F.—San Diego NL 1980.

Coleman, Robert—Boston NL 1944-45.

Collins, Edward T.—Chicago AL 1925-26.

Collins, James J.—Boston AL 1901 through 1906.

Collins, John F.—Boston AL 1931-32.

Comiskey, Charles A.—St. Louis AA 1883, 1885 through 1889; Chicago PL 1890; St. Louis AA 1891; Cincinnati NL 1892 through 1894.

Connor, Roger—St. Louis NL 1896.

Cooke, Allen L.—Philadelphia NL 1948.

Coombs, John W.—Philadelphia NL 1919.

Cooney, John W.—Boston NL 1949.

Corrales, Patrick—Texas AL 1978 (part) through 1980; Philadelphia NL 1982 to 1983 (part); Cleveland AL 1983 (part).

Corriden, John M.—Chicago AL 1950.

Cox, Robert J.—Atlanta NL 1978 through 1981; Toronto AL 1982 through 1983.

Craft, Harry F.—Kansas City AL 1957 through 1959; Houston NL 1962 through 1964.

Craig, Roger L.—San Diego NL March 21, 1978 through 1979.

Crandall, Delmar W.—Milwaukee AL May 30, 1972 to 1975 (part); Seattle AL 1983 (part).

Crane, Samuel N.—Buffalo NL 1880; Cincinnati UA 1884.

Cravath, Clifford C.—Philadelphia NL 1919-20.

Creamer, George W.—Pittsburgh AA 1884.

Cronin, Joseph E.—Washington AL 1933-34; Boston AL 1935 through 1947.

Cross, Lafayette N.—Cleveland NL 1899.

D

Dahlen, William F.—Brooklyn NL 1910 through 1913.

Dark, Alvin R.—San Francisco NL 1961 through 1964; Kansas City AL 1966-67; Cleveland AL 1968 through July 29, 1971; Oakland AL 1974-75; San Diego NL May 30, 1977 to March 21, 1978.

Davidson, M. H.—Louisville AA 1888-89.

Davis, George S.—New York NL 1895, 1900-01.

Davis, Harry H.—Cleveland AL 1912.

Davis, Virgil L.—Pittsburgh NL 1946.

Day, John B.—New York NL 1899.

Dennis, Walter L.—Washington NL 1887.

Dickey, William M.—New York AL 1946.

Diddlebock, Henry H.—St. Louis NL 1896.

Doby, Lawrence E.—Chicago AL June 30, 1978 to end of season.

Donovan, Patrick J.—Pittsburgh NL 1897 through 1899; St. Louis NL 1901 through 1903; Washington AL 1904; Brooklyn NL 1906 through 1908; Boston AL 1910-11.

Donovan, William E.—New York AL 1915 through 1917; Philadelphia NL 1921.

Dooin, Charles S.—Philadelphia NL 1910 through 1914.

Dowd, Thomas J.—St. Louis NL 1896-97.

Doyle, John J.—New York NL 1895; Washington NL 1898.

Doyle, Joseph J.—Brooklyn AA 1885.

Dressen, Charles W.—Cincinnati NL 1934 through 1937; Brooklyn NL 1951 through 1953; Washington AL 1955 through 1957; Milwaukee NL 1960-61; Detroit AL 1963 through 1966.

Duffy, Hugh—Milwaukee AL 1901; Philadelphia NL 1904 through 1906; Chicago AL 1910-11; Boston AL 1921-22.

Dunlap, Frederick C.—St. Louis UA 1884; St. Louis NL 1885; Pittsburgh NL 1889.

Durocher, Leo E.—Brooklyn NL 1939 through 1946 and 1948; New York NL 1948 through 1955; Chicago NL 1966 through July 23, 1972; Houston NL August 27, 1972 through 1973.

Dwyer, J. Francis—Detroit AL 1902.

Dyer, Edwin H.—St. Louis NL 1946 through 1950.

Dykes, James J.—Chicago AL 1934 through 1946; Philadelphia AL 1951 through 1953; Baltimore AL 1954; Cincinnati NL 1958; Detroit AL 1959-60; Cleveland AL 1960-61.

Dyler, John F.—Louisville AA 1882.

E

Ebbets, Charles H.—Brooklyn NL 1898.

Elberfeld, Norman A.—New York AL 1908.

Elia, Lee C.—Chicago NL 1982 to 1983 (part).

Ellick, Joseph J.—Chicago UA 1884.

Elliott, Robert I.—Kansas City AL 1960.

Ens, Jewel W.—Pittsburgh NL 1929 through 1931.

Ermer, Calvin C.—Minnesota AL 1967 through 1968.

Evans, J. Ford—Cleveland NL 1882.

Evers, John J.—Chicago NL 1913, 1921; Chicago AL 1924.

Ewing, William—New York PL 1890; Cincinnati NL 1895 through 1899; New York NL 1900.

F

Faatz, James S.—Cleveland PL 1890.

Fanning, W. James—Montreal NL 1981 (part) through 1982.

Farrell, M. Kerby—Cleveland AL 1957.

Ferguson, Robert V.—Hartford NL 1876-77; Chicago NL 1878; Troy NL 1879 through 1882; Philadelphia NL 1883; Pittsburgh AA 1884; New York AA 1886-87.

Ferraro, Michael D.—Cleveland AL 1983 (part).

Fessenden, Wallace C.—Syracuse AA 1890.

Fine, Benjamin—St. Louis NL 1885.

Fitzsimmons, Frederick L.—Philadelphia NL 1943 through 1945.

Fletcher, Arthur—Philadelphia NL 1923 through 1926; New York AL 1929.

Fogel, Horace S.—Indianapolis NL 1887; New York NL 1902.

Fohl, Lee A.—Cleveland AL 1915 through 1919; St. Louis AL 1921 through 1923; Boston AL 1924 through 1926.

Fonseca, Lewis A.—Chicago AL 1932 through 1934.

Foutz, David L.—Brooklyn NL 1893 through 1896.

Fox, Charles F.—San Francisco NL 1970 (part) to 1974 (part); Montreal NL 1976 (part); Chicago NL 1983 (part).

Franks, Herman L.—San Francisco NL 1965 through 1968; Chicago NL 1977 through September 23, 1979.

Frazer, George K.—Syracuse AA 1890.

Frazier, Joseph F.—New York NL 1976 through May 30, 1977.

Fregosi, James L.—California AL June 1, 1978 through May 27, 1981.

Frey, James G.—Kansas City AL 1980 through August 19, 1981.

Frisch, Frank F.—St. Louis NL 1933 through 1938; Pittsburgh NL 1940 through 1946; Chicago NL 1949 through 1951.

Fuchs, Emil B.—Boston NL 1929.

Fulmer, Charles J.—Louisville NL 1876; Cincinnati AA 1882.

Furniss, Thomas—Boston UA 1884.

G

Gaffney, John H.—Washington NL 1886-87.

Galvin, James F.—Buffalo NL 1885.

Ganzel, John H.—Cincinnati NL 1908.

Garcia, David—California AL July 11, 1977 to June 1, 1978; Cleveland AL July 23, 1979 through 1982.

Gardner, William F.—Minnesota AL 1981 (part) through 1983.

Gerhardt, Joseph J.—Louisville AA 1883-84.

Gibson, George—Pittsburgh NL 1920 through 1922; Chicago NL 1925; Pittsburgh NL 1932 through 1934.

Gifford, James H.—Indianapolis AA 1884; New York AA 1885-86.

Glasscock, John W.—Indianapolis NL 1889.

Gleason, William J.—Chicago AL 1919 through 1923.

Gomez, Pedro W. (Preston)—San Diego NL, 1969 through April 26, 1972; Houston NL, 1974 through August 18, 1975; Chicago NL 1980 to July 23, 1980.

Gonzalez, Miguel A.—St. Louis NL 1938,

1940.

Gordon, Joseph L.—Cleveland AL 1958 through 1960 (part); Detroit AL 1960; Kansas City AL 1961; 1969.

Goryl, John A.—Minnesota AL August 25, 1980 through May 21, 1981.

Gould, Charles H.—Cincinnati NL 1876.

Graffen, S. Mason—St. Louis NL 1876.

Grammas, Alexander P.—Pittsburgh, September 26, 1969 to end of season; Milwaukee AL 1976 through 1977.

Green, G. Dallas—Philadelphia NL August 31, 1979 through 1981.

Griffin, Michael J.—Brooklyn NL 1898.

Griffin, Tobias—Washington AA 1891.

Griffith, Clark C.—Chicago AL 1901-02; New York AL 1903 through 1908; Cincinnati NL 1909 through 1911; Washington AL 1912 through 1920.

Grimes, Burleigh A.—Brooklyn NL 1937-38.

Grimm, Charles J.—Chicago NL 1932 through 1938; 1944 through 1949; Boston NL 1952; Milwaukee NL 1953 through 1956; Chicago NL 1960.

Gutteridge, Donald J.—Chicago AL 1969, 1970 (part).

H

Hack, Stanley C.—Chicago NL 1954 through 1956; St. Louis NL 1958 (part).

Hackett, Charles M.—Cleveland NL 1884; Brooklyn AA 1885.

Hallman, William W.—St. Louis NL 1897.

Haney, Fred G.—St. Louis AL 1939 through 1941; Pittsburgh NL 1953 through 1955; Milwaukee NL 1956 through 1959.

Hanlon, Edward H.—Pittsburgh NL 1889; Pittsburgh PL 1890; Pittsburgh NL 1891; Baltimore NL 1892 through 1898; Brooklyn NL 1899 through 1905; Cincinnati NL 1906-07.

Harris, C. Luman—Baltimore AL 1961; Houston NL 1964-65; Atlanta NL 1968 through August 6, 1972.

Harris, Stanley R.—Washington AL 1924 through 1928; Detroit AL 1929 through 1933; Boston AL 1934; Washington AL 1935 through 1942; Philadelphia NL 1943; New York AL 1947-48; Washington AL 1950 through 1954; Detroit AL 1955-56.

Hart, James A.—Louisville AA 1885-86; Boston NL 1889.

Hartnett, Charles L.—Chicago NL 1938 through 1940.

Hartsfield, Roy T.—Toronto AL 1977 through 1979.

Hatton, Grady E.—Houston NL 1966 through 1968 (part).

Hecker, Guy J.—Pittsburgh NL 1890.

Heffner, Donald H.—Cincinnati NL 1966.

Heilbroner, Louis—St. Louis NL 1900.

Hemus, Solomon J.—St. Louis NL 1959-60-61.

Henderson, William C.—Baltimore UA 1884.

Hendricks, John C.—St. Louis NL 1918; Cincinnati NL 1924 through 1929.

Hengle, Edward S.—Chicago UA 1884.

Herman, William J.—Pittsburgh NL 1947; Boston AL 1964 (part); 1965, 1966 (part).

Herzog, Charles L.—Cincinnati NL 1914 through 1916.

Herzog, Dorrel N. E.—Texas AL 1973 (part); Kansas City AL 1975 (part) through 1979; St. Louis NL 1980 (part), 1981 through 1983.

Hewitt, Walter S.—Washington NL 1888.

Higgins, Michael F.—Boston AL 1955 through 1959 (part); 1960 through 1962.

Hilt, Benjamin F.—Philadelphia PL 1890.

Hitchcock, William C.—Baltimore AL 1962-63; Atlanta NL 1966-67.

Hodges, Gilbert R.—Washington AL 1963 through 1967; New York NL 1968 through 1971.

Hoey, Frederick C.—New York NL 1899.

Hollingshead, John S.—Washington AA 1884.

Holmes, Thomas F.—Boston NL 1951-52.

Hornsby, Rogers—St. Louis NL 1925-26; Boston NL 1928; Chicago NL 1930 through 1932; St. Louis AL 1933 through 1937, 1952; Cincinnati NL 1952-53.

Houk, Ralph G.—New York AL 1961 through 1963 and 1966 through 1973; Detroit AL 1974 through 1978; Boston AL 1981 through 1983.

Howard, Frank O.—San Diego NL 1981; New York NL 1983 (part).

Howley, Daniel P.—St. Louis AL 1927 through 1929; Cincinnati NL 1930 through 1932.

Howser, Richard D.—New York AL 1980; Kansas City AL 1981 (part) through 1983.

Huff, George A.—Boston AL 1907.

Huggins, Miller J.—St. Louis NL 1913 through 1917; New York AL 1918 through 1929.

Hughson, George—Buffalo NL 1885.

Hunter, G. William—Texas AL June 28, 1977 through September 30, 1978.

Hurst, Timothy C.—St. Louis NL 1898.

Hutchinson, Frederick C.—Detroit AL 1952 through 1954; St. Louis NL 1956 through 1958; Cincinnati NL 1959 through 1964.

I

Irwin, Arthur A.—Washington NL 1889; Boston AA 1891; Washington NL 1892; Philadelphia NL 1894-95; New York NL 1896; Washington NL 1898-99.

J

Jennings, Hugh A.—Detroit AL 1907 through 1920.

Johnson, Darrell D.—Boston AL 1974 through July 18, 1976; Seattle AL 1977 to 1980 (part); Texas AL 1982 (part).

Johnson, Walter P.—Washington AL 1929 through 1932; Cleveland AL 1933 through 1935.

Jones, Fielder A.—Chicago AL 1904 through 1908; St. Louis AL 1916 through 1918.

Joost, Edwin D.—Philadelphia AL 1954.

Joyce, William M.—New York NL 1896 through 1898.

Jurges, William F.—Boston AL 1959 through 1960.

K

Kasko, Edward M.—Boston AL 1970 through 1973.

Keane, John J.—St. Louis NL 1961 through 1964; New York AL 1965-66.

Kelley, Joseph J.—Cincinnati NL 1902 through 1905; Boston NL 1908.

Kelly, Michael J.—Boston PL 1890; Cincinnati AA 1891.

Kennedy, James C.—Brooklyn AA 1890.

Kennedy, Robert D.—Oakland AL 1968.

Kerins, John A.—Louisville AA 1888.

Kessinger, Donald E.—Chicago AL 1979 through August 2, 1979.

Killefer, William L.—Chicago NL 1921 through 1925; St. Louis AL 1930 through 1933.

King, Clyde E.—San Francisco NL 1969, 1970 (part); Atlanta NL July 25, 1974 through August 29, 1975; New York AL 1982 (part).

Kittredge, Malachi J.—Washington AL 1904.

Kling, John G.—Boston NL 1912.

Knight, Alonzo P.—Philadelphia AA 1883-85.

Kuehl, Karl O.—Montreal NL 1976 through September 3, 1976, second game.

Kuenn, Harvey E.—Milwaukee AL September 28, 1975, 1982 (part) through 1983.

Kuhel, Joseph A.—Washington AL 1948-49.

L

Lachemann, Rene G.—Seattle AL 1981 (part) to 1983 (part).

Lajoie, Napoleon—Cleveland AL 1904 through 1909.

Lake, Frederick L.—Boston AL 1908-09; Boston NL 1910.

Larkin, Henry E.—Cleveland PL 1890.

LaRussa, Anthony—Chicago AL 1979 (part) through 1983.

Lasorda, Thomas C.—Los Angeles NL 1976 (part) through 1983.

Latham, W. Arlington—St. Louis NL 1896.

Lavagetto, Harry A.—Washington AL 1957 through 1960; Minnesota AL 1961.

Leadley, Robert H.—Detroit NL 1888; Cleveland NL 1890-91.

Lemon, James R.—Washington AL 1968.

Lemon, Robert G.—Kansas City AL 1970 (part), 1971-72; Chicago AL 1977 to June 30, 1978; New York AL July 25, 1978 through June 17, 1979, 1981 (part), 1982 (part).

Lillis, Robert P.—Houston NL 1983.

Lipon, John J.—Cleveland AL, July 30, 1971 to end of season.

Lobert, John B.—Philadelphia NL 1942.

Lockman, Carroll W.—Chicago NL July 27, 1972 through July 21, 1974.

Loftus, Thomas J.—Cleveland AA 1888; Cleveland NL 1889; Cincinnati NL 1890-91; Chicago NL 1900-01; Washington AL 1902-03.

Lopat, Edmund W.—Kansas City AL 1963-64.

Lopez, Alfonso R.—Cleveland AL 1951 through 1956; Chicago AL 1957 through 1965, 1968 (part) through May 1, 1969.

Lowe, Robert L.—Detroit AL 1904.

Lucas, Henry V.—St. Louis NL 1885.

Lucas, J. R. C.—St. Louis NL 1877.

Lucchesi, Frank J.—Philadelphia NL 1970 through July 9, 1972; Texas AL July 21, 1975 through June 21, 1977.

Lumley, Harry G.—Brooklyn NL 1909.

Lyons, Theodore A.—Chicago AL 1946 through 1948.

M

Mack, Cornelius (Connie) A.—Pittsburgh NL 1894 through 1896; Philadelphia AL 1901 through 1950.

Manning, James H.—Kansas City AA 1889; Washington AL 1901.

Maranville, Walter J. V.—Chicago NL 1925; Boston NL 1929.

Marion, Martin W.—St. Louis NL 1951; St. Louis AL 1952-53; Chicago AL 1954 through 1956.

Marshall, R. James—Chicago NL 1974 (part) through 1976; Oakland AL 1979.

Martin, Alfred M.—Minnesota AL 1969; Detroit AL 1971 to 1973 (part); Texas AL 1973 (part) to 1975 (part); New York AL 1975 (part) to 1978 (part), 1979 (part), 1983; Oakland AL 1980 through 1982.

Martin, H. B.—St. Louis NL 1894.

Mason, Charles E.—Philadelphia AA 1883 through 1887.

Mathews, Edwin L.—Atlanta NL August 7, 1972 through June 21, 1974.

Mathewson, Christopher—Cincinnati NL 1916 through 1918.

Mattick, Robert J.—Toronto AL 1980 through 1981.

Mauch, Eugene W.—Philadelphia NL 1960 through 1968 (part); Montreal NL 1969 through 1975; Minnesota AL 1976 through August 24, 1980; California AL 1981 (part) through 1982.

McAleer, James R.—Cleveland AL 1901; St. Louis AL 1902 through 1909; Washington AL 1910-11.

McBride, George F.—Washington AL 1921.

McCallister, John—Cleveland AL 1927.

McCarthy, Joseph V.—Chicago NL 1926 through 1930; New York AL 1931 through 1946; Boston AL 1948 through 1950.

McCarthy, Thomas F. M.—St. Louis AA 1890.

McCloskey, John J.—Louisville NL 1895-96; St. Louis NL 1906 through 1908.

McCormick, James—Cleveland NL 1879 through 1881.

McGaha, F. Melvin—Cleveland AL 1962; Kansas City AL 1964-65.

McGraw, John J.—Baltimore NL 1899; Baltimore AL 1901-02; New York NL 1902 through 1932.

McGuire, James T.—Washington NL 1898; Boston AL 1907-08; Cleveland AL 1909 through 1911.

McGunnigle, William H.—Buffalo NL 1879-80; Brooklyn AA 1888-89; Brooklyn NL 1890; Pittsburgh NL 1891; Louisville NL 1896.

McInnis, John P.—Philadelphia NL 1927.

McKechnie, William B.—Pittsburgh NL 1922 through 1926; St. Louis NL 1928-29; Boston NL 1930 through 1937; Cincinnati NL 1938 through 1946.

McKee, James—Milwaukee UA 1884.

McKeon, John A.—Kansas City AL 1973 through July 23, 1975; Oakland AL 1977 through June 9, 1977; May 23, 1978 to end of season.

McKinney, Buck—Louisville AA 1889.

McKnight, Henry D.—Pittsburgh AA 1884.

McManus, Martin J.—Boston AL 1932-33.

McManus, George—St. Louis NL 1877.

McMillan, Roy D.—Milwaukee AL May 28, 29, 1972; New York NL August 6, 1975 to end of season.

McNamara, John F.—Oakland AL September 19, 1969 through 1970; San Diego NL 1974 through May 28, 1977; Cincinnati NL 1979 to 1982 (part); California AL 1983.

McPhee, John A.—Cincinnati NL 1901-02.

McVey, Calvin A.—Cincinnati NL 1878-79.

Means, Harry L.—Louisville AA 1889.

Mele, Sabath A.—Minnesota AL 1961 through 1967.

Metro, Charles—Kansas City AL 1970 (part).

Michael, Eugene R.—New York AL 1981 (part), 1982 (part).

Milan, J. Clyde—Washington AL 1922.

Miller, George F.—St. Louis NL 1894.

Mills, C. Buster—Cincinnati NL 1953.

Meyer, William A.—Pittsburgh NL 1948 through 1952.

Mitchell, Frederick F.—Chicago NL 1917 through 1920; Boston NL 1921 through 1923.

Moore, Terry B.—Philadelphia NL 1954.

Moran, Patrick J.—Philadelphia NL 1915 through 1918; Cincinnati NL 1919 through 1923.

Moriarty, George J.—Detroit AL 1927-28.

Morrill, John F.—Boston NL 1882 through 1888; Washington NL 1889.

Morrow, Robert—Providence NL 1881.

Morton, Charles H.—Toledo AA 1884; Detroit NL 1885; Toledo AA 1890.

Moss, J. Lester—Detroit AL 1979 to June 12, 1979.

Murnane, Timothy H.—Boston UA 1884.

Murray, William J.—Philadelphia NL 1907 through 1909.

Murtaugh, Daniel E.—Pittsburgh NL 1957 through 1964; 1967, 1970-71, September 6, 1973 through 1976.

Mutrie, James J.—New York AA 1883-84; New York NL 1885 through 1891.

Myers, Henry C.—Baltimore AA 1882.

N

Neun, John H.—New York AL 1946; Cincinnati NL 1947-48..

Nichols, Charles A.—St. Louis NL 1904-05.

Nicol, Hugh N.—St. Louis NL 1897.

Nixon, Russell E.—Cincinnati NL 1982 (part) through 1983.

Norman, Willis P.—Detroit AL 1958-59.

O

O'Connor, John J.—St. Louis, AL 1910.

O'Day, Henry F.—Cincinnati NL 1912; Chicago NL 1914.

O'Farrell, Robert A.—St. Louis NL 1927; Cincinnati NL 1934.

O'Leary, Daniel—Cincinnati UA 1884.

O'Neill, Stephen F.—Cleveland AL 1935 through 1937; Detroit AL 1943 through 1948; Boston AL 1950-51; Philadelphia NL 1952 through 1954.

Onslow, John J.—Chicago AL 1949-50.

O'Rourke, James H.—Buffalo NL 1881 through 1884; Washington NL 1893.

Orr, David L.—New York AA 1887.

Ott, Melvin T.—New York NL 1942 through 1948.

Owens, Paul F.—Philadelphia NL 1972 (part), 1983 (part).

Ozark, Daniel L.—Philadelphia NL 1973 through August 30, 1979.

P

Parker, Francis J.—New York NL September 22, 1967 to end of season.

Peckinpaugh, Roger T.—New York AL 1914; Cleveland AL 1928 through 1933, 1941.

Pesky, John M.—Boston AL 1963-64, October 1, 1980 to end of season.

Pfeffer, N. Frederick—Louisville NL 1892.

Phelan, Lewis G.—St. Louis NL 1895.

Phillips, Harold R.—California AL 1969 through 1971.

Phillips, Horace B.—Cincinnati AA 1883; Pittsburgh AA 1884 through 1886; Pittsburgh NL 1887 through 1889.

Popowski, Edward J.—Boston AL September 23, 1969 to end of season; September 30, 1973.

Powers, Patrick T.—Rochester AA 1890; New York NL 1892.

Pratt, Albert G.—Pittsburgh AA 1882-83.

Pratt, Thomas J.—Philadelphia UA 1884.

Price, James L.—New York NL 1884.

Prothro, James T.—Philadelphia NL 1939 through 1941.

Q

Quilici, Frank R.—Minnesota AL July 6, 1972 through 1975.

Quinn, Joseph J.—St. Louis NL 1895; Cleveland NL 1899.

R

Rader, Douglas L.—Texas AL 1983.

Rapp, Vern—St. Louis NL 1977 through April 25, 1978.

Reccius, J. William—Louisville AA 1882-83.

Reccius, Philip—Louisville AA 1882-83.

Rice, Delbert W.—California AL 1972.

Richards, Paul R.—Chicago AL 1951 through 1954; Baltimore AL 1955 through 1961; Chicago AL 1976.

Richardson, Daniel—Washington NL 1892.

Rickey, W. Branch—St. Louis AL 1913 through 1915; St. Louis NL 1919 through 1925.

Rigney, William J.—New York NL 1956-57; San Francisco NL 1958 through 1960; Los Angeles (now California) AL 1961 through 1969; Minnesota AL 1970 through July 5, 1972.

Robinson, Frank—Cleveland AL 1975 to 1977 (part); San Francisco NL 1981 through 1983.

Robinson, Wilbert—Baltimore AL 1902; Brooklyn NL 1914 through 1931.

Robison, M. Stanley—St. Louis NL 1905.

Rodgers, Robert L.—Milwaukee AL 1980 (part), 1981 to 1982 (part).

Rolfe, Robert A.—Detroit AL 1949 through 1952.

Rowe, David E.—Kansas City NL 1886; Kansas City AA 1888.

Rowe, John C.—Buffalo PL 1890.

Rowland, Clarence H.—Chicago AL 1915 through 1918.

Ruel, Herold D.—St. Louis AL 1947.

Runnels, James E.—Boston AL 1966.

Ryan, Cornelius J.—Atlanta NL August 31, 1975 to end of season; Texas AL June 23 through 27, 1977.

S

Sawyer, Edwin M.—Philadelphia NL 1948 through 1952; 1958 through 1960.

Scanlon, Michael B.—Washington UA 1884; Washington NL 1886.

Schalk, Raymond W.—Chicago AL 1927-28.

Scheffing, Robert B.—Chicago NL 1957 through 1959; Detroit AL 1961 to June18, 1963.

Schmelz, Gustavus H.—Columbus AA 1884; St. Louis NL 1886; Cincinnati AA 1887 through 1889; Cleveland NL 1890; Columbus AA 1890-91; Washington NL 1894 through 1897.

Schoendienst, Albert F.—St. Louis NL 1965 through 1976, August 29, 1980 through end of season.

Schultz, Joseph C.—Seattle AL 1969; Detroit AL August 31, September 1, 1973.

Selee, Frank G.—Boston NL 1890 through 1901; Chicago NL 1902 through 1905.

Sewell, J. Luther—St. Louis AL 1941 through 1946; Cincinnati NL 1949 through 1952.

Shannon, Daniel W.—Louisville AA 1899; Washington AA 1891.

Sharsig, William J.—Philadelphia AA 1882 through 1891.

Shawkey, J. Robert—New York AL 1930.

Sheehan, Thomas C.—San Francisco NL 1960.

Shepard, Lawrence W.—Pittsburgh NL 1968, 1969 (part).

Sherry, Norman B.—California AL July 24, 1976, first game through July 10, 1977.

Shettsline, William J.—Philadelphia NL 1896-99 through 1902.

Shotton, Burton E.—Philadelphia NL 1928 through 1933; Brooklyn NL 1947 through 1950.

Silvestri, Kenneth J.—Atlanta NL 1967.

Simmons, Joseph S.—Wilmington UA 1884.

Simmons, Lewis—Philadelphia AA 1886.

Sisler, George H.—St. Louis AL 1924 through 1926.

Sisler, Richard A.—Cincinnati NL 1965.

Skaff, Francis M.—Detroit AL 1966.

Skinner, Robert R.—Philadelphia NL 1968 (part), 1969 (part).

Slattery, John T.—Boston NL 1928.

Smith, E. Mayo—Philadelphia NL 1955 through 1958; Cincinnati NL 1959; Detroit AL 1967 through 1970.

Smith, George H.—New York NL 1902.

Smith, George L.—Syracuse NL 1879.

Smith, Harry T.—Boston NL 1909.

Snyder, Charles N.—Cincinnati AA 1883-84; Washington AA 1891.

Sothoron, Allen S.—St. Louis AL 1933.

Southworth, William H.—St. Louis NL 1929, 1940 through 1945; Boston NL 1946 through 1951.

Spalding, Albert G.—Chicago NL 1876-77.

Speaker, Tristram—Cleveland AL 1919 through 1926.

Spence, Harrison L.—Indianapolis NL 1888.

Stahl, Charles S.—Boston AL 1906.

Stahl, J. Garland—Washington AL 1905-06; Boston AL 1912-13.

Stallings, George T.—Philadelphia NL 1897-98; Detroit AL 1901; New York AL 1909-10; Boston NL 1913 through 1920.

Stanky, Edward R.—St. Louis NL 1952 through 1955 (part); Chicago AL 1966 through 1968 (part); Texas AL June 22, 1977.

Stengel, Charles D.—Brooklyn NL 1934 through 1936; Boston NL 1938 through 1943; New York AL 1949 through 1960; New York NL 1962 through 1965.

Stovall, George T.—Cleveland AL 1911; St. Louis AL 1912-13.

Street, Charles E.—St. Louis NL 1930 through 1933; St. Louis AL 1938.

Strickland, George B.—Cleveland AL 1966.

Sukeforth, Clyde L.—Brooklyn NL April 15, 1947.

Sullivan, Haywood C.—Kansas City AL 1965.

Sullivan, James P.—Columbus AA 1890.

Sullivan, Theodore P.—St. Louis AA 1882-83; St. Louis UA 1884; Kansas City UA 1884; Washington NL 1888.

Sullivan, William J.—Chicago AL 1909.

Swift, Robert V.—Detroit AL 1966.

T

Tanner, Charles W.—Chicago AL 1970 through 1975; Oakland AL 1976; Pittsburgh NL 1977 through 1983.

Taylor, George J.—Brooklyn AA 1884.

Taylor, James W.—St. Louis AL 1946-48 through 1951.

Tebbetts, George R.—Cincinnati NL 1954 through 1958; Milwaukee NL 1961-62; Cleveland AL 1963 through 1966.

Tebeau, Oliver W.—Cleveland PL 1890; Cleveland NL 1891 through 1898; St. Louis NL 1899-1900.

Tenney, Frederick—Boston NL 1905 through 1907, 1911.

Terry, William H.—New York NL 1932 through 1941.

Thomas, Frederick L.—Indianapolis NL 1887.

Tighe, John T.—Detroit AL 1957-58.

Tinker, Joseph B.—Cincinnati NL 1913; Chicago NL 1916.

Torborg, Jeffrey A.—Cleveland AL June 19, 1977 through July 22, 1979.

Torre, Joseph P.—New York NL 1977 (part) through 1981; Atlanta NL 1982 through 1983.

Traynor, Harold J.—Pittsburgh NL 1934 through 1939.

Trott, Samuel W.—Washington AA 1891.

Turner, Robert E. (Ted)—Atlanta NL May 11, 1977.

U

Unglaub, Robert A.—Boston AL 1907.

V

Van Haltren, George E.—Baltimore AA 1891; Baltimore NL 1892.

Vernon, James B.—Washington AL 1961 to June 23, 1963.

Virdon, William C.—Pittsburgh NL 1972 to 1973 (part); New York AL 1974 to 1975 (part); Houston NL 1975 (part) through 1982; Montreal NL 1983.

Vitt, Oscar J.—Cleveland AL 1938 through 1940.

Von der Ahe, Christian F. W.—St. Louis AA 1884; St. Louis NL 1892-95-97.

W

Wagner, Charles F.—Boston AL 1930.

Wagner, John P.—Pittsburgh NL 1917.

Walker, Harry W.—St. Louis NL 1955; Pittsburgh NL 1965 through 1967; Houston NL June 18, 1968 through August 25, 1972.

Wallace, Roderick J.—St. Louis NL 1911-12; Cincinnati NL 1937.

Walsh, Michael F.—Louisville AA 1884.

Walters, William H.—Cincinnati NL 1948-49.

Waltz, John J.—Baltimore NL 1892.

Ward, John M.—Brooklyn PL 1890; Brooklyn NL 1891-92; New York NL 1893-94.

Ware, George—Providence NL 1878.

Watkins, Harvey L.—New York NL 1895.

Watkins, William H.—Indianapolis AA 1884; Detroit NL 1885 through 1888; Kansas City AA 1888-89; St. Louis NL 1893; Pittsburgh NL 1898-99.

Weaver, Earl S.—Baltimore AL 1968 (part) through 1982.

Westrum, Wesley N.—New York NL 1965 through 1967; San Francisco NL June 28, 1974 through 1975.

White, James L.—Cincinnati NL 1879.

White, William H.—Cincinnati AA 1884.

Whitney, James E.—Washington NL 1888.

Wilber, Delbert Q.—Texas AL September 7, 1973.

Wilhelm, Irving K.—Philadelphia NL 1921-22.

Williams, James A.—St. Louis AA 1884; Cleveland AA 1887-88.

Williams, Richard H.—Boston AL 1967 through 1969; Oakland AL 1971 through 1973; California AL 1974 (part) to 1976 (part); Montreal NL 1977 to 1981 (part); San Diego NL 1982 through 1983.

Williams, Theodore S.—Washington AL 1969 through 1971; Texas AL 1972.

Wills, Maurice M.—Seattle AL August 4, 1980 through May 5, 1981.

Wilson, James—Philadelphia NL 1934 through 1938; Chicago NL 1941 through 1944.

Winkles, Bobby B.—California AL 1973 through June 26, 1974; Oakland AL June 10, 1977 to May 23, 1978.

Wolf, William V.—Louisville AA 1889.

Wolverton, Harry S.—New York AL 1912.

Wood, George A.—Philadelphia AA 1891.

Wright, Alfred L. H.—Philadelphia NL 1876.

Wright, George—Providence NL 1879.

Wright, William H.—Boston NL 1876 through 1881; Providence NL 1882-83; Philadelphia NL 1884 through 1893.

Y

Yost, Edward F.—Washington AL May 22, 1963.

Z

Zimmer, Charles L.—Philadelphia NL 1903.

Zimmer, Donald W.—San Diego NL 1972 (part) through 1973; Boston AL 1976 (part) to 1980 (part); Texas AL 1981 to 1982 (part).

OFFICES OF COMMISSIONER

Kenesaw M. Landis, January 12, 1921, until death, November 25, 1944. (Accepted position November 12, 1920.)

Albert B. Chandler, April 24, 1945, until resignation, July 15, 1951.

Ford C. Frick, October 8, 1951 through December 14, 1965. (Elected September 20, 1951.)

William D. Eckert, December 15, 1965 to February 4, 1969. (Elected on November 17, 1965 for seven-year term.)

Bowie K. Kuhn, February 4, 1969, temporary appointment for one year; August 13, 1969, elected for seven-year term; July 17, 1975, elected for seven-year term through August 12, 1983.

NATIONAL LEAGUE PRESIDENTS

Morgan G. Bulkeley, 1876.

William A. Hulbert, 1876 to 1882.

Arthur H. Soden, 1882.

Col. A. G. Mills, 1882 to 1884.

Nicholas E. Young, 1884 to 1902.

Harry C. Pulliam, 1902 until death July 29, 1909.

John A. Heydler, July 30, 1909 to December 15, 1909.

Thomas J. Lynch, December 15, 1909, to December 9, 1913.

John K. Tener, December 9, 1913, until resignation, August 6, 1918.

John A. Heydler, December 10, 1918, until resignation, December 11, 1934.

Ford C. Frick, December 11, 1934, until resignation, October 8, 1951.

Warren C. Giles, October 8, 1951 through December 31, 1969.

Charles S. Feeney, January 1, 1970 through 1983.

AMERICAN LEAGUE PRESIDENTS

Byron Bancroft Johnson, 1901 until resignation, October 17, 1927.

Ernest S. Barnard, October 31, 1927, until death on March 27, 1931.

William Harridge, May 27, 1931, until resignation effective January 31, 1959.

Joseph E. Cronin, elected for seven years, February 1, 1959. (Re-elected on November 17, 1965 for seven-year term.)
Leland S. MacPhail, Jr., January 1, 1974 through 1983.

AMERICAN LEAGUE CLUB PRESIDENTS
BALTIMORE ORIOLES (ST. LOUIS BROWNS PRIOR TO 1953)

Ralph T. Orthwein, 1902-1903; Robert L. Hedges, 1903 to 1915; Philip D. Ball, 1916 to 1933; Louis B. Von Weise, 1934 to 1936; Donald L. Barnes, 1936 to 1945; Richard C. Muckerman, 1945 to 1949; William O. DeWitt, 1949 to 1951; William L. Veeck, Jr., 1951 to 1953; Clarence Miles, 1953 to 1955; James Keelty, Jr., 1955 to 1959; Leland S. MacPhail, Jr., 1959 to December 14, 1965; Jerold C. Hoffberger, December 15, 1965 through 1982; Edward B. Williams, 1983. (Sidney W. Frank 1901, and John J. Mahon, 1902 presidents of earlier Baltimore club.)

BOSTON RED SOX

Charles W. Somers, 1901-02; Henry J. Killilea, 1903-04; John I. Taylor, 1904 to 1911; James R. McAleer, 1912-1913; Joseph J. Lannin, 1913 to 1916; Harry H. Frazee, 1917 to 1923; J. A. Robert Quinn, 1923 to February 25, 1933; Thomas A. Yawkey, February 26, 1933 through July 9, 1976; Jean R. Yawkey, August 17, 1976 through 1983.

CALIFORNIA ANGELS (LOS ANGELES ANGELS PRIOR TO 1966)

Robert O. Reynolds, 1960 to February 22, 1975; Arthur E. Patterson, February 22, 1975 through 1977; Gene Autry, 1978 through 1983.

CHICAGO WHITE SOX

Charles A. Comiskey, 1901 to 1931; J. Louis Comiskey, 1931 to 1939 (none in 1940, Harry Grabiner, vice-president); Mrs. Grace Comiskey, 1941 to 1956; none in 1957—Charles A. Comiskey II and John D. Rigney, co-vice-presidents 1957 to 1959; William L. Veeck, Jr. 1959-60-61; Arthur C. Allyn, 1961 through 1969; John W. Allyn, 1969 through 1975; William L. Veeck, Jr., January 12, 1976 through 1980; Edward M. Einhorn, 1982 through 1983.

CLEVELAND INDIANS

John F. Kilfoyl, 1901 to 1910; Charles W. Somers, 1911 to 1916; James C. Dunn, 1916 to 1922; Ernest S. Barnard, 1922 to 1927; Alva Bradley, 1927 to 1946; William L. Veeck, Jr., 1947 to 1949; Ellis W. Ryan, 1950 to 1952; Myron Wilson, Jr., 1953 to August 19, 1962; Gabriel Paul, November 20, 1962, through February 1972; Nick J. Mileti, March 1972 through 1977; Gabriel Paul, 1978 through 1983.

DETROIT TIGERS

James D. Burns, 1901; Samuel F. Angus, 1902-1903; William H. Yawkey, 1904 to 1907; Frank J. Navin, 1908 to 1935; Walter O. Briggs, Sr., 1935 to 1952; Walter O. Briggs, Jr., 1952 to 1956; Fred A. Knorr, 1957; Harvey Hansen, 1957 to 1959; William O. DeWitt, 1959 through 1960; John E. Fetzer, 1960 through 1978; James A. Campbell, 1979 through 1983.

KANSAS CITY ROYALS

Ewing M. Kauffman, January 11, 1968 through 1981; Joe Burke, 1982 through 1983.

MILWAUKEE BREWERS (SEATTLE PILOTS PRIOR TO 1970)

Allan H. Selig, 1970 through 1983.

MINNESOTA TWINS (WASHINGTON SENATORS PRIOR TO 1961)

Fred Postal, 1901 to 1903; Thomas J. Loftus, 1904; Henry B. Lambert, 1904; Thomas C. Noyes, 1905 to 1912; Benjamin S. Minor, 1912 to 1919; Clark C. Griffith, 1920 to 1955; Calvin R. Griffith, 1955 through 1983.

NEW YORK YANKEES

Joseph W. Gordon, 1903 to 1906; Frank J. Farrell, 1907 to 1914; Jacob Ruppert, 1915 to 1939; Edward G. Barrow, 1939 to February 21, 1945; Leland S. MacPhail, February 21, 1945 through October 6, 1947; Daniel R. Topping, October 7, 1947 to 1953; Daniel R. Topping and Del E. Webb, co-owners, 1954 to 1964; Daniel R. Topping, Sr., 1964 through September 19, 1966; Michael Burke, September 20, 1966 through April 29, 1973; Gabriel Paul, November 1, 1973 through 1977; Albert Rosen, 1978 to July, 1979; George M. Steinbrenner, July, 1979 through 1980; Lou Saban, 1981 through 1982; Eugene J. McHale, 1983.

OAKLAND ATHLETICS
(KANSAS CITY A'S 1955-67, PHILADELPHIA A'S PRIOR TO 1955)

Benjamin F. Shibe, 1901 to 1922; Thomas S. Shibe, 1922 to 1935; John D. Shibe, 1936-37; Connie A. Mack, 1937 to 1954; Arnold M. Johnson, 1955 to March 10, 1960; Charles O. Finley, December 19, 1960 through 1980; Roy Eisenhardt, 1981 through 1983.

SEATTLE MARINERS
Danny Kaye, Lester M. Smith, 1977 through 1978; Daniel F. O'Brien, 1979 through 1983.

SEATTLE PILOTS
Dewey Soriano, 1968-1969; Fred Danz, 1969-1970; Dewey Soriano, 1970.

TEXAS RANGERS (WASHINGTON SENATORS 1961 THROUGH 1971)
Edward R. Quesada, 1960 to 1963; James M. Johnston, 1963 through December 28, 1967; James H. Lemon, Sr., December 29, 1967 through January 27, 1969; Robert E. Short, January 28, 1969 through May 29, 1974; Bradford G. Corbett, May 30, 1974 through March, 1980; Eddie Robinson, April, 1980 to end of season; Eddie Chiles, 1981 through 1983.

TORONTO BLUE JAYS
R. Howard Webster, 1977; Peter Bavasi, 1978 through 1981; R. Howard Webster, 1982 through 1983.

NATIONAL LEAGUE CLUB PRESIDENTS
ATLANTA BRAVES
(MILWAUKEE 1953-65, BOSTON BRAVES PRIOR TO 1953)
N. T. Apolonio, 1876; Arthur H. Soden, 1877 to 1906; George B. Dovey, 1907 to 1909; John S. Dovey, 1909; John P. Harris, 1910; W. Hepburn Russell, 1910-1911; John M. Ward, 1911-1912; James E. Gaffney, 1912 to 1915; Percy D. Haughton, 1916 to 1918; George W. Grant, 1918 to 1922; Christopher Mathewson 1923 to 1925; Emil B. Fuchs, 1925 to 1935; J. A. Robert Quinn, 1935 to 1944; Louis R. Perini, 1945 to 1957; Joseph F. Cairnes, 1957 to 1961; John J. McHale, 1961 through January 11, 1967; William C. Bartholomay, January 12, 1967 through 1972; Daniel J. Donahue, 1973 to 1976; R. E. (Ted) Turner, 1976 through 1983. (J. R. Kaine president of 1878 Milwaukee NL club.)

CHICAGO CUBS
William A. Hulbert, 1876 to 1881; Albert G. Spalding, 1882 to 1891; James A. Hart, 1892 to 1905; Charles W. Murphy, 1906 to 1913; Charles H. Thomas, 1914-15; Charles H. Weeghman, 1916 to 1918; Fred F. Mitchell, 1919; William L. Veeck, 1919 to 1933; William M. Walker, 1934; Philip K. Wrigley, 1934 to 1977; William J. Hagenah, 1977 through 1981; Andrew J. McKenna, 1982 through 1983.

CINCINNATI REDS
J. L. Keck, 1876; J. M. W. Neff, 1878-1879; Justus Horner, 1880; Aaron A. Stern, 1890; John T. Brush, 1891 to 1902; August Herrmann, 1902 to 1927; C. J. McDiarmid, 1927 to 1929; Sidney Weil, 1929 to 1934; Powel Crosley, Jr., 1934 to 1946; Warren C. Giles, 1947 to 1951; Powel Crosley, Jr., 1951 to March 28, 1961; William O. DeWitt, December 23, 1961 through January 9, 1967; Francis L. Dale, January 10, 1967 to 1973; Robert L. Howsam, 1973 through February 28, 1978; Richard Wagner, March 1, 1978 through July 11, 1983; Robert L. Howsam, July 12, 1983 to end of season.

HOUSTON ASTROS
Craig F. Cullman, 1962; Roy Hofheinz, 1963 through 1971; Reuben W. Askanase, 1972, 1973; T. H. Neyland, 1974, 1975; Sidney L. Shienker, 1976; Talbot M. Smith, 1976 through 1980; Albert L. Rosen, 1981 through 1983.

LOS ANGELES DODGERS (BROOKLYN DODGERS PRIOR TO 1958)
Charles H. Byrne, 1890 to 1898; Charles H. Ebbets, 1898 to 1925; Edward J. McKeever, 1925; Wilbert Robinson, 1925 to 1929; Frank B. York, 1930 to 1932; Stephen W. McKeever, 1933 to 1938; Leland S. MacPhail, 1939 to 1942; W. Branch Rickey, 1942 to 1950; Walter F. O'Malley, 1951 through March 15, 1970; Peter O'Malley, March 16, 1970 through 1983.

MONTREAL EXPOS
John J. McHale, 1968 through 1983.

NEW YORK METS
George M. Weiss, 1962 through November 14, 1966; Vaughan P. Devine, November 15, 1966 through December 5, 1967; Joan W. Payson, February 6, 1968 through October 4, 1975; Lorinda de Roulet, 1975 through January 24, 1980; Fred Wilpon, January 25, 1980 through 1983.

PHILADELPHIA PHILLIES
Thomas J. Smith, 1876; Alfred J. Reach, 1883 to 1902; James Potter, 1903-1904; William J. Shettsline, 1905 to 1908; Israel W. Durham, 1909; Horace S. Fogel, 1909 to 1912;

Alfred D. Wiler, 1912; William H. Locke, 1913; William F. Baker, 1913 to 1930; L. Charles Ruch, 1931-32; Gerald P. Nugent, 1932 to 1942; William D. Cox, 1943 to November 22, 1943; Robert R. M. Carpenter, Jr., November 23, 1943 through November 21, 1972; Robert R. M. Carpenter III, November 22, 1972 through 1981; Bill Giles, 1982 through 1983.

PITTSBURGH PIRATES

William A. Nimick, 1887 to 1890; J. Palmer O'Neill, 1891; William C. Temple, 1892; Albert C. Buckenberger, 1893; William W. Kerr, 1894 to 1897; William H. Watkins, 1898; William W. Kerr, 1899; Barney Dreyfuss, 1900 to 1932; William E. Benswanger, 1932 to August 8, 1946; Frank E. McKinney, August 8, 1946 to 1950; John W. Galbreath, 1951 through 1969; Daniel M. Galbreath, 1970 through 1983.

ST. LOUIS CARDINALS

J. B. C. Lucas, 1876-1877; Henry V. Lucas, 1885-1886; Chris Von der Ahe, 1892 to 1897; Benjamin S. Muckenfuss, 1898; Frank De Hass Robison, 1899 to 1906; M. Stanley Robison, 1906 to 1910; E. A. Steininger, 1911-1912; James C. Jones, 1912; Schuyler P. Britton, 1913 to 1916; Mrs. Schuyler P. Britton, 1916; W. Branch Rickey, 1917 to 1919; Samuel Breadon, 1920 to 1947; Robert E. Hannegan, 1947 to 1949; Fred M. Saigh, Jr., 1949 to 1953; August A. Busch, Jr., 1953 to 1973; Richard A. Meyer, 1974; August A. Busch, Jr., 1974 through 1983.

SAN DIEGO PADRES

Emil J. Bavasi, 1968 through 1977; Ray A. Kroc, 1978 to 1979; Ballard Smith, 1980 through 1983.

SAN FRANCISCO GIANTS (NEW YORK GIANTS PRIOR TO 1958)

William H. Cammeyer, 1876; John B. Day, 1883 to 1892; C. C. VanCott, 1893 to 1894; Andrew Freedman, 1895 to 1902; John T. Brush, 1903 to 1912; Harry N. Hempstead, 1912 to 1919; Charles A. Stoneham, 1919 to 1936; Horace C. Stoneham, 1936 to 1976; Robert Lurie & Arthur Herseth, 1976 to 1979; Robert Lurie, 1980 through 1983.

MISCELLANEOUS "FIRSTS" FOR CLUBS

First Shutout Game

N. L.—April 25, 1876, Chicago 4, Louisville 0.
A. L.—May 15, 1901, Washington 4, Boston 0.

First 1-0 Game

N. L.—May 5, 1876, St. Louis 1, Chicago 0.
A. L.—July 27, 1901, Detroit 1, Baltimore 0.

First Tie Game

N. L.—May 25, 1876, Philadelphia 2, Louisville 2 (14 innings), darkness.
A. L.—May 31, 1901, Washington 3, Milwaukee 3 (7 innings), darkness.

First Extra-Inning Game

N. L.—April 29, 1876, Hartford 3, Boston 2 (10 innings).
A. L.—April 30, 1901, Boston 8, Philadelphia 6 (10 innings).

First Extra-Inning Shutout

N. L.—May 25, 1876, Boston 4, Cincinnati 0 (10 innings).
A. L.—August 11, 1902, Philadelphia 1, Detroit 0 (13 innings).

First Extra-Inning 1-0 Shutout

N. L.—June 10, 1876, New York Mutuals 1, Cincinnati 0 (10 innings).
A. L.—August 11, 1902, Philadelphia 1, Detroit 0 (13 innings).

First Extra-Inning Tie Game

N. L.—May 25, 1876, Philadelphia 2, Louisville 2 (14 innings), darkness.
A. L.—August 27, 1901, Milwaukee 5, Baltimore 5 (11 innings), darkness.

First Time Two Games in One Day

N. L.—September 9, 1876, Hartford 14, Cincinnati 6; Hartford 8, Cincinnati 3.
A. L.—May 30, 1901, Baltimore 10, Detroit 7; Detroit 4, Baltimore 1.
    Chicago 8, Boston 3; Chicago 5, Boston 3.
    Milwaukee 5, Washington 2; Milwaukee 14, Washington 3.
    Philadelphia 3, Cleveland 1; Philadelphia 8, Cleveland 2 (8 innings).

First Doubleheader

N. L.—September 25, 1882, Worcester 4, Providence 3; Providence 8, Worcester 6.
A. L.—July 15, 1901, Washington 3, Baltimore 2; Baltimore 7, Washington 3.

First Doubleheader Shutout Victory

N. L.—July 13, 1888, Pittsburgh 4, Boston 0; Pittsburgh 6, Boston 0.
A. L.—September 3, 1901, Cleveland 1, Boston 0; Cleveland 4, Boston 0.

First Forfeited Game

N. L.—August 21, 1876, St. Louis 7, Chicago 6; forfeited to St. Louis.
A. L.—May 2, 1901, Detroit 7, Chicago 5; forfeited to Detroit.

Last Forfeited Game

N. L.—July 18, 1954, second game, Philadelphia 8, St. Louis 1, at St. Louis; forfeited to Philadelphia.
A. L.—July 12, 1979, second game, Detroit 9, Chicago 0, at Chicago; forfeited to Detroit.

First Game Played by

Boston, N. L.—April 22, 1876—Boston 6, Philadelphia Athletics 5 (A).
Philadelphia Athletics, N. L.—April 22, 1876—Boston 6, Philadelphia 5 (H).
New York Mutuals, N. L.—April 25, 1876—Boston 7, New York Mutuals 6 (H).
Chicago, N. L.—April 25, 1876—Chicago 4, Louisville 0 (A).
Cincinnati, N. L.—April 25, 1876—Cincinnati 2, St. Louis 1 (H).
St. Louis, N. L.—April 25, 1876—Cincinnati 2, St. Louis 1 (A).
Philadelphia, N. L.—May 1, 1883—Providence 4, Philadelphia 3 (H).
New York, N. L. (Original Club)—May 1, 1883—New York 7, Boston 5 (H).
Pittsburgh, N. L.—April 30, 1887—Pittsburgh 6, Chicago 2 (H).
Brooklyn, N. L.—April 19, 1890—Boston 15, Brooklyn 9 (A).
Chicago, A. L.—April 24, 1901—Chicago 8, Cleveland 2 (H).
Cleveland, A. L.—April 24, 1901—Chicago 8, Cleveland 2 (A).
Detroit, A. L.—April 25, 1901—Detroit 14, Milwaukee 13 (H).
Baltimore, A. L.—April 26, 1901—Baltimore 10, Boston 6 (H).
Boston, A. L.—April 26, 1901—Baltimore 10, Boston 6 (A).
Philadelphia, A. L.—April 26, 1901—Washington 5, Philadelphia 1 (H).
Washington, A. L. (Original Club)—April 26, 1901—Washington 5, Philadelphia 1 (A).
Milwaukee, A. L.—April 25, 1901—Detroit 14, Milwaukee 13 (A).
St. Louis, A. L.—April 23, 1902—St. Louis 5, Cleveland 2 (H).
New York, A. L.—April 22, 1903—Washington 3, New York 1 (A).
Milwaukee, N. L. since 1900—April 13, 1953—Milwaukee 2, Cincinnati 0 (A).
Baltimore, A. L. (Present Club)—April 13, 1954—Detroit 3, Baltimore 0 (A).
Kansas City, A. L.—April 12, 1955—Kansas City 6, Detroit 2 (H).
Los Angeles, N. L.—April 15, 1958—San Francisco 8, Los Angeles 0 (A).
San Francisco, N. L.—April 15, 1958—San Francisco 8, Los Angeles 0 (H).
Los Angeles, A. L.—April 11, 1961—Los Angeles 7, Baltimore 2 (A).
Minnesota, A. L.—April 11, 1961—Minnesota 6, New York 0 (A).
Washington, A. L. (Second Club)—April 10, 1961—Chicago 4, Washington 3 (H).
Houston, N. L.—April 10, 1962—Houston 11, Chicago 2 (H).
New York, N. L. (Present Club)—April 11, 1962—St. Louis 11, New York 4 (A).
Atlanta, N. L.—April 12, 1966—Pittsburgh 3, Atlanta 2, 13 innings (H).
Oakland, A. L.—April 10, 1968—Baltimore 3, Oakland 1 (A).
San Diego, N. L.—April 8, 1969—San Diego 2, Houston 1 (H).
Seattle, A. L. (Original Club)—April 8, 1969—Seattle 4, California 3 (A).
Montreal, N. L.—April 8, 1969—Montreal 11, New York 10 (A).
Kansas City, A. L. (Present Club)—April 8, 1969—Kansas City 4, Minnesota 3, 12 innings (H).
Milwaukee, A. L. (Present Club)—April 7, 1970—California 12, Milwaukee 0 (H).
Texas, A. L.—April 15, 1972—California 1, Texas 0 (A).
Seattle, A. L. (Present Club)—April 6, 1977—California 7, Seattle 0 (H).
Toronto, A. L.—April 7, 1977—Toronto 9, Chicago 5 (H).

First Game Played

At Sportsman's Park (later Busch Stadium), St. Louis—May 5, 1876, St. Louis N. L. 1, Chicago 0.
    By St. Louis A. L.—April 23, 1902—St. Louis A. L. 5, Cleveland 2.
    By St. Louis N. L. since 1900—July 1, 1920—Pittsburgh N. L. 6, St. Louis 2 (10 innings).
At Shibe Park (later Connie Mack Stadium), Philadelphia—April 12, 1909, Philadelphia A. L. 8, Boston 1.
At Shibe Park (later Connie Mack Stadium), Philadelphia—July 4, 1938, Boston N. L. 10, Philadelphia N. L. 5; Philadelphia N. L. 10, Boston 2.
At Forbes Field, Pittsburgh—June 30, 1909, Chicago N. L. 3, Pittsburgh 2.
At Comiskey Park, Chicago—July 1, 1910, St. Louis A. L. 2, Chicago 0.
At League Park, Cleveland—April 21, 1910, Detroit A. L. 5, Cleveland 0.
At Griffith Stadium, Washington—April 12, 1911, Washington A. L. 8, Boston 5.
At Polo Grounds, New York (first game after fire)—June 28, 1911, New York N. L. 3, Boston 0.
    Formal opening—April 19, 1912, New York N. L. 6, Brooklyn 2.

At Redland Field (later Crosley Field), Cincinnati—April 11, 1912, Cincinnati N. L. 10, Chicago 6.

At Navin Field (later Tiger Stadium), Detroit—April 20, 1912, Detroit A. L. 6, Cleveland 5 (11 innings).

At Fenway Park, Boston—April 20, 1912, Boston 7, New York 6 (11 innings).
Formal opening—May 17, 1912, Chicago A. L. 5, Boston 2.

At Ebbets Field, Brooklyn—April 9, 1913, Philadelphia N. L. 1, Brooklyn 0.

At Wrigley Field, Chicago—April 23, 1914, Chicago F. L. 9, Kansas City 1.
By Chicago N. L.—April 20, 1916—Chicago 7, Cincinnati 6, (11 innings).

At Braves Field, Boston—August 18, 1915—Boston N. L. 3, St. Louis 1.

At Yankee Stadium, New York—April 18, 1923, New York A. L. 4, Boston 1.

At Municipal Stadium, Cleveland—July 31, 1932, Philadelphia A. L. 1, Cleveland 0.

At Milwaukee County Stadium, Milwaukee—April 14, 1953, Milwaukee N. L. 3, St. Louis 2, (10 innings).

At Memorial Stadium, Baltimore—April 15, 1954, Baltimore A. L. 3, Chicago 1.

At Municipal Stadium, Kansas City—April 12, 1955, Kansas City A. L., 6, Detroit 2.

At Seals Stadium, San Francisco—April 15, 1958—San Francisco N. L. 8, Los Angeles 0.

At Memorial Coliseum, Los Angeles—April 18, 1958—Los Angeles N. L. 6, San Francisco 5.

At Candlestick Park, San Francisco—April 12, 1960—San Francisco 3, St. Louis 1.

At Metropolitan Stadium, Minnesota—April 21, 1961—Washington A. L. 5, Minnesota 3.

At Wrigley Field, Los Angeles—April 27, 1961—Minnesota A. L. 4, Los Angeles 2.

At Dodger Stadium, Los Angeles—April 10, 1962—Cincinnati 6, Los Angeles 3.

At Colt Stadium, Houston—April 10, 1962, Houston N. L. 11, Chicago 2.

At District of Columbia Stadium, Washington—April 9, 1962, Washington 4, Detroit 1.

At Shea Stadium, New York—April 17, 1964—Pittsburgh 4, New York 3.

At Astrodome, Houston—April 12, 1965—Philadelphia 2, Houston 0.

At Atlanta Stadium, Atlanta—April 12, 1966, Pittsburgh N. L. 3, Atlanta 2, 13 innings.

At Anaheim Stadium, California—April 19, 1966—Chicago 3, California 1.

At Busch Memorial Stadium, St. Louis—May 12, 1966, St. Louis N. L. 4, Atlanta 3, 12 innings.

At Oakland-Alameda County Coliseum—April 17, 1968, Baltimore 4, Oakland 1.

At San Diego Stadium, San Diego—April 8, 1969, San Diego 2, Houston 1.

At Sicks' Stadium, Seattle—April 11, 1969, Seattle 7, Chicago 0.

At Jarry Park, Montreal—April 14, 1969, Montreal 8, St. Louis 7.

At Riverfront Stadium, Cincinnati, June 30, 1970, Atlanta 8, Cincinnati 2.

At Three Rivers Stadium, Pittsburgh, July 16, 1970, Cincinnati 3, Pittsburgh 2.

At Veterans Stadium, Philadelphia—April 10, 1971, Philadelphia 4, Montreal 1.

At Arlington Stadium, Texas—April 21, 1972, Texas 7, California 6.

At Royals Stadium, Kansas City—April 10, 1973, Kansas City 12, Texas 1.

At Kingdome, Seattle—April 6, 1977, California 7, Seattle 0.

At Exhibition Stadium, Toronto—April 7, 1977, Toronto 9, Chicago 5.

At Olympic Stadium, Montreal—April 15, 1977, Philadelphia 7, Montreal 2.

First Sunday Games

At St. Louis N. L.—April 17, 1892, Cincinnati 5, St. Louis 1.

At Cincinnati—April 24, 1892, Cincinnati 10, St. Louis 2.

At Chicago, N. L.—May 14, 1893, Cincinnati 13, Chicago 12.

At Detroit—April 28, 1901, Detroit 12, Milwaukee 11.

At Chicago, A. L.—April 28, 1901, Chicago 13, Cleveland 1.

At Milwaukee, A. L.—May 5, 1901, Milwaukee 21, Chicago 7.

At St. Louis, A. L.—April 27, 1902, Detroit 6, St. Louis 1.

At Cleveland—May 14, 1911, Cleveland 14, New York 3.

At New York, A. L.—June 17, 1917, St. Louis 2, New York 1.
First legalized Sunday—May 11, 1919, Washington 0, New York 0, 12 innings.

At Brooklyn— (No admission fee)—April 17, 1904, Brooklyn 9, Boston 1.
(Five Sundays in 1904 and five in 1905). First Sunday game with admission fee —July 1, 1917, Brooklyn 3, Philadelphia 2.
First legalized Sunday—May 4, 1919, Brooklyn 6, Boston 2.

At New York, N. L.—August 19, 1917, Cincinnati 5, New York 0.
First legalized Sunday—May 4, 1919, Philadelphia 4, New York 3.

At Washington—May 19, 1918, Washington 1, Cleveland 0, 12 innings.

At Philadelphia A. L.—August 22, 1926, Philadelphia 3, Chicago 2.
First legalized Sunday—April 22, 1934, Washington 4, Philadelphia 3.

At Boston, A. L.—April 28, 1929, Philadelphia 7, Boston 3.

At Boston, N. L.—May 5, 1929, Pittsburgh 7, Boston 2.

At Philadelphia, N. L.—April 29, 1934, Brooklyn 8, Philadelphia 7.

At Pittsburgh—April 29, 1934, Pittsburgh 9, Cincinnati 5.

At Milwaukee N. L.—May 10, 1953, first game, Milwaukee 6, Chicago 2.

At Baltimore—April 18, 1954, Detroit 8, Baltimore 3.

At Kansas City—April 24, 1955, Kansas City 5, Chicago 0.

At Los Angeles, N. L.—April 20, 1958, San Francisco 12, Los Angeles 2.

First Sunday Games—Continued

At San Francisco—April 27, 1958, Chicago 5, San Francisco 4.
At Minnesota—April 23, 1961, Minnesota 1, Washington 0.
At Los Angeles, A. L.—April 30, 1961, Los Angeles 6, Kansas City 4.
At Houston, N. L.—April 22, 1962, Philadelphia 4, Houston 3.
At Atlanta, N. L.—April 24, 1966, first game, Atlanta 5, New York 2.
At Oakland—April 21, 1968, Washington 2, Oakland 0.
At Seattle—April 13, 1969, Chicago 12, Seattle 7.
At San Diego—April 13, 1969, San Francisco 5, San Diego 1.
At Montreal—April 20, 1969, first game, Chicago 6, Montreal 3.
At Texas—April 23, 1972, Texas 5, California 2.
At Toronto—April 10, 1977, Toronto 3, Chicago 1.

First Night Game

At Cincinnati—May 24, 1935, Cincinnati 2, Philadelphia 1.
By Pittsburgh—At Cincinnati—May 31, 1935, Pittsburgh 4, Cincinnati 1.
By Chicago, N. L.—At Cincinnati—July 1, 1935, Chicago 8, Cincinnati 4.
By Brooklyn—At Cincinnati—July 10, 1935, Cincinnati 15, Brooklyn 2.
By Boston, N. L.—At Cincinnati—July 24, 1935, Cincinnati 5, Boston 4.
By St. Louis, N. L.—At Cincinnati—July 31, 1935, Cincinnati 4, St. Louis 3, 10 innings.
At Brooklyn—June 15, 1938, Cincinnati 6, Brooklyn 0.
At Philadelphia, A. L.—May 16, 1939, Cleveland 8, Philadelphia 3, 10 innings.
By Chicago, A. L.—At Philadelphia—May 24, 1939, Chicago 4, Philadelphia 1.
At Philadelphia, N. L.—June 1, 1939, Pittsburgh 5, Philadelphia 2.
By St. Louis, A. L.—At Philadelphia—June 14, 1939, St. Louis 6, Philadelphia 0.
By Detroit—At Philadelphia—June 20, 1939, Detroit 5, Philadelphia 0.
By New York, A. L.—At Philadelphia—June 26, 1939, Philadelphia 3, New York 2.
At Cleveland—June 27, 1939, Cleveland 5, Detroit 0.
By Washington—At Philadelphia—July 6, 1939, Philadelphia 9, Washington 3.
At Chicago, A. L.—August 14, 1939, Chicago 5, St. Louis 2.
By Boston, A. L.—At Cleveland—July 13, 1939, Boston 6, Cleveland 5, 10 innings.
At New York, N. L.—May 24, 1940, New York 8, Boston 1.
By New York, N. L.—May 24, 1940, New York 8, Boston 1.
At St. Louis, A. L.—May 24, 1940, Cleveland 3. St. Louis 2.
At Pittsburgh—June 4, 1940, Pittsburgh 14, Boston 2.
At St. Louis, N. L.—June 4, 1940, Brooklyn 10, St. Louis 1.
At Washington—May 28, 1941, New York 6, Washington 5.
At Boston, N. L.—May 11, 1946, New York 5, Boston 1.
At New York, A. L.—May 28, 1946, Washington 2, New York 1.
At Boston, A. L.—June 13, 1947, Boston 5, Chicago 3.
At Detroit, A. L.—June 15, 1948, Detroit 4, Philadelphia 1.
By Milwaukee, N. L.—At St. Louis—April 20, 1953, St. Louis 9, Milwaukee 4.
At Milwaukee, N. L.—May 8, 1953, Milwaukee 2, Chicago 0.
At Baltimore, A. L.—April 21, 1954, Cleveland 2, Baltimore 1.
At Kansas City, A. L.—April 18, 1955, Cleveland 11, Kansas City 9.
At San Francisco, N. L.—April 16, 1958, Los Angeles 13, San Francisco 1.
At Los Angeles, N. L.—April 22, 1958, Los Angeles 4, Chicago 2.
By Minnesota, A. L.—April 14, 1961, Minnesota 3, Baltimore 2.
At Minnesota, A. L.—May 18, 1961, Kansas City 4, Minnesota 3.
At Los Angeles, A. L.—April 28, 1961, Los Angeles 6, Minnesota 5, 12 innings.
At Houston, N. L.—April 11, 1962, Houston 2, Chicago 0.
At Atlanta, N. L.—April 12, 1966, Pittsburgh 3, Atlanta 2, 13 innings.
At Oakland, A. L.—April 17, 1968, Baltimore 4, Oakland 1.
At San Diego N. L.—April 8, 1969, San Diego 2, Houston 1.
By Seattle A. L.—April 8, 1969, Seattle 4, California 3.
By Montreal N. L.—April 8, 1969, Montreal 11, New York 10.
At Seattle, A. L.—April 12, 1969, Seattle 5, Chicago 1.
At Montreal, N. L.—April 30, 1969, New York 2, Montreal 1.
By Milwaukee A. L.—April 13, 1970, Oakland 2, Milwaukee 1.
At Milwaukee A. L.—May 5, 1970, Boston 6, Milwaukee 0.
At Texas, A. L.—April 21, 1972, Texas 7, California 6.
At Toronto, A. L.—May 2, 1977, Milwaukee 3, Toronto 1.

First Night Opening Game

N. L.—At St. Louis—April 18, 1950, St. Louis 4, Pittsburgh 2.
A. L.—At Philadelphia—April 17, 1951, Washington 6, Philadelphia 1.
N. L.—At New York—April 16, 1952, New York 5, Philadelphia 2.
N. L.—At Philadelphia—April 16, 1957, Brooklyn 7, Philadelphia 6, 12 innings.
N. L.—At Los Angeles—April 14, 1959, St. Louis 6, Los Angeles 2.
A. L.—At Los Angeles—April 17, 1962, Kansas City 5, Los Angeles 3.
N. L.—At Houston—April 16, 1964, Milwaukee 6, Houston 5.
A. L.—At Kansas City—April 21, 1964, Cleveland 5, Kansas City 3.

N. L.—At Atlanta—April 12, 1966, Pittsburgh 3, Atlanta 2, 13 innings.
A. L.—At California—April 19, 1966, Chicago 3, California 1.
N. L.—At Cincinnati—April 22, 1966, Philadelphia 9, Cincinnati 7.
A. L.—At Oakland—April 17, 1968, Baltimore 4, Oakland 1.
N. L.—At San Diego—April 8, 1969, San Diego 2, Houston 1.
A. L.—At Chicago—April 18, 1972, Chicago 14, Texas 0.
A. L.—At New York—April 18, 1972, New York 2, Milwaukee 0.
A. L.—At Texas—April 21, 1972, Texas 7, California 6.
N. L.—At San Francisco—April 21, 1972, Houston 7, San Francisco 3.
A. L.—At Seattle—April 6, 1977, California 7, Seattle 0.

First Ladies Day

N. L.—At Cincinnati, 1876 season.
N. L.—At Philadelphia, 1876 season.
N. L.—At Providence, 1882 season.
N. L.—At New York, June 16, 1883, New York 5, Cleveland 2.
A. L.—At St. Louis, 1912 season.
N. L.—At St. Louis, 1917 season.

First Ladies Night

N. L.—At New York, June 27, 1941, New York 7, Philadelphia 4.
N. L.—At Brooklyn, July 31, 1950, Chicago 8, Brooklyn 5.
A. L.—At Boston, August 17, 1950, Boston 10, Philadelphia 6.

First Day Games Completed With Lights

N. L.—At Boston, April 23, 1950, second game, Philadelphia 6, Boston 5.
A. L.—At New York, August 29, 1950, New York 6, Cleveland 5.

First Time All Games Played at Night

8 (8-club leagues) on August 9, 1946 (4 in N. L.; 4 in A. L.).
12 (12-club leagues) April 25, 1969 (6 in N. L.; 6 in A. L.).

First Time All Games Twilight-Night Doubleheaders

N. L.—On August 25, 1953.

First Time Uniform Numbered

N. L.—Cincinnati, 1883 season.
A. L.—New York, 1929 season (complete).
      (Cleveland vs. Chicago at Cleveland, June 26, 1916 wore numbers on the sleeves of
      their uniforms.)

MISCELLANEOUS INDIVIDUAL "FIRSTS"

First Player Two Clubs, Season

N. L.—Cornelius M. Phelps, New York, Philadelphia, 1876.
A. L.—Harry P. Lockhead, Detroit, Philadelphia, 1901.

First Player Three Clubs, Season

N. L.—August H. Krock, Chicago, Indianapolis, Washington, 1889.
A. L.—Patrick W. Donahue, Boston, Cleveland, Philadelphia, 1910. (See next item:
      Frank Huelsman played with four clubs in 1904).

First Player Four Clubs, Season

N. L.—Thomas J. Dowse, Louisville, Cincinnati, Philadelphia, Washington, 63 games,
      1892.
A. L.—Frank Huelsman, Chicago, Detroit, St. Louis, Washington, 112 games, 1904.

First Pitcher Two Clubs, Season

N. L.—Thomas Healy, Providence, Indianapolis, 1878.
A. L.—Charles Baker, Cleveland, Philadelphia, 1901.

First Pitcher Three Clubs, Season

N. L.—August H. Krock, Chicago, Indianapolis, Washington, 1889.
A. L.—William Henry James, Detroit, Boston, Chicago, 1919.

First Player to Enter Military Service in World War I

Harry M. Gowdy, Boston N. L., June 27, 1917.

First Player to Enter Military Service in World War II

Hugh N. Mulcahy, Philadelphia N. L., March 8, 1941.

Youngest Player, Game

N. L.—15 years, 10 months, 11 days—Joseph H. Nuxhall, Cincinnati, June 10, 1944 (pitcher).

A. L.—16 years, 8 months, 5 days—Carl A. Scheib, Philadelphia, September 6, 1943, second game (pitcher).

Oldest Player, Game

A. L.—59 years, 2 months, 18 days—Leroy Paige, Kansas City, September 25, 1965, (pitched first three innings).

57 years, 10 months, 6 days—Orestes A. Minoso, October 5, 1980 (pinch-hitter).

57 years, 16 days—Nicholas Altrock, Washington, October 1, 1933 (pinch-hitter).

N. L.—52 years, 29 days—James H. O'Rourke, New York, September 22, 1904 (caught complete game).

Youngest Manager to Finish Season

Roger T. Peckinpaugh, New York, A. L., appointed September 16, 1914; 23 years, 7 months, 11 days. Born, February 5, 1891.

Youngest Manager to Start Season

Louis Boudreau, Cleveland, A. L., appointed November 25, 1941; 24 years, 4 months, 8 days when appointed. Born, July 17, 1917.

Oldest to Make Debut as Manager

Thomas C. Sheehan, San Francisco, N. L., appointed June 18, 1960; 66 years, 2 months, 18 days. Born, March 31, 1894.

First Player Facing Pitcher Three Times, Inning

N. L.—Thomas J. Carey, Hartford, May 13, 1876, fourth inning.

A. L.—Theodore S. Williams, Boston, July 4, 1948, seventh inning.

First Player Seven At-Bats in Nine-Inning Game

N. L.—John J. Burdock, Hartford, May 13, 1876.

A. L.—William O. Gilbert, Milwaukee, May 5, 1901.

First Player Eight At-Bats in Nine-Inning Game

N. L.—Roscoe C. Barnes, Chicago, July 22, 1876.

First Player Five Runs in Nine-Inning Game

N. L.—George W. Hall, Philadelphia, June 17, 1876.

A. L.—Michael J. Donlin, Baltimore, June 24, 1901.

First Player Six Runs in Nine-Inning Game

N. L.—James E. Whitney, Boston, June 9, 1883.

A. L.—John Pesky, Boston, May 8, 1946.

First Player Five Hits in Nine-Inning Game

N. L.—Joseph V. Battin, St. Louis, May 13, 1876.
     John J. Burdock, Hartford, May 13, 1876.
     Thomas J. Carey, Hartford, May 13, 1876.

A. L.—Irving Waldron, Milwaukee, April 28, 1901.

First Player Six Hits in Nine-Inning Game

N. L.—David Force, Philadelphia, June 27, 1876 (6 at-bats).

A. L.—Michael J. Donlin, Baltimore, June 24, 1901 (6 at-bats).

First Player Eight Hits in Doubleheader

A. A.—Henry Simon, Syracuse, October 11, 1890. (See next item: Fred Carroll had 9 hits in doubleheader in 1886.)

N. L.—Joseph Quinn, St. Louis, September 30, 1893. (See next item: Wilbert Robinson had 9 hits in doubleheader in 1892.)

A. L.—Charles Hickman, Washington, September 7, 1905.

First Player Nine Hits in Doubleheader

A. A.—Fred H. Carroll, Pittsburgh, July 5, 1886.

N. L.—Wilbert Robinson, Baltimore, June 10, 1892.

A. L.—Ray Morehart, Chicago, August 31, 1926.

First Player Four Long Hits in Nine-Inning Game

N. L.—George W. Hall, Philadelphia, June 14, 1876 (3 triples, 1 home run).

A. L.—Frank Dillon, Detroit, April 25, 1901 (4 doubles).

First Player Five Long Hits in Nine-Inning Game

A. A.—George A. Strief, Philadelphia, June 25, 1885 (4 triples, 1 double).

N. L.—George F. Gore, Chicago, July 9, 1885 (2 triples, 3 doubles).

A. L.—Louis Boudreau, Cleveland, July 14, 1946, first game (4 doubles, 1 home run).

First Player Four Doubles in Nine-Inning Game

N. L.—John O'Rourke, Boston, September 15, 1880.
A. L.—Frank Dillon, Detroit, April 25, 1901.

First Player Three Triples in Nine-Inning Game .

N. L.—George W. Hall, Philadelphia, June 14, 1876.
       Ezra B. Sutton, Philadelphia, June 14, 1876.
A. L.—Elmer H. Flick, Cleveland, July 6, 1902.

First Player Four Triples in Nine-Inning Game

A. A.—George A. Strief, Philadelphia, June 25, 1885.
N. L.—William M. Joyce, New York, May 18, 1897.
A. L.—None.

First Player Hitting Home Run

N. L.—Roscoe C. Barnes, Chicago, May 2, 1876.
       Charles Jones, Cincinnati, May 2, 1876.
A. L.—Erwin T. Beck, Cleveland, April 25, 1901.

First Player Two Homers in Nine-Inning Game

N. L.—George W. Hall, Philadelphia, June 17, 1876.
A. L.—John B. Freeman, Boston, June 1, 1901.

First Player Three Homers in Nine-Inning Game

N. L.—Edward N. Williamson, Chicago, May 30, 1884, p.m. game.
A. L.—Kenneth R. Williams, St. Louis, April 22, 1922.

First Player Four Homers in Nine-Inning Game

N. L.—Robert L. Lowe, Boston, May 30, 1894, p.m. game.
A. L.—H. Louis Gehrig, New York, June 3, 1932.

First Player Two Homers in One Inning

N. L.—Charles Jones, Boston, June 10, 1880, eighth inning.
A. L.—Kenneth R. Williams, St. Louis, August 7, 1922, sixth inning.

First Player Home Run With Bases Filled

N. L.—Roger Connor, Troy, September 10, 1881.
A. L.—Herman W. McFarland, Chicago, May 1, 1901.

First Player Home Run With Bases Filled as Pinch-Hitter

N. L.—Michael J. O'Neill, St. Louis, June 3, 1902, ninth inning.
A. L.—Martin J. Kavanagh, Cleveland, September 24, 1916, fifth inning.

First Player Home Run, Night Game

N. L.—Floyd C. Herman, Cincinnati, July 10, 1935.
A. L.—Frank W. Hayes, Philadelphia, May 16, 1939.

First Player Hitting for Cycle

N. L.—Charles J. Foley, Buffalo, May 25, 1882.
A. L.—Harry H. Davis, Philadelphia, July 10, 1901.

First Player Five Bases on Balls in Nine-Inning Game

A. A.—Henry Larkin, Philadelphia, May 2, 1887.
N. L.—Fred H. Carroll, Pittsburgh, July 4, 1889, a.m. game.
A. L.—Samuel N. Strang, Chicago, April 27, 1902.

First Player Six Bases on Balls in Nine-Inning Game

N. L.—Walter Wilmot, Chicago, August 22, 1891.
A. L.—James E. Foxx, Boston, June 16, 1938.

First Player Two Bases on Balls in One Inning

N. L.—Elmer E. Smith, Pittsburgh, April 22, 1892, first inning.
A. L.—Owen Bush, Detroit, August 27, 1909, fourth inning.

First Player Four Strikeouts in Nine-Inning Game

N. L.—George H. Derby, Detroit, August 6, 1881. (See next item: Oscar Walker had 5
       strikeouts in game in 1879.)
A. L.—J. Emmet Heidrick, St. Louis, May 16, 1902.

First Player Five Strikeouts in Nine-Inning Game

N. L.—Oscar Walker, Buffalo, June 20, 1879.
A. L.—Robert M. Grove, Philadelphia, June 10, 1933, first game.

First Player Two Strikeouts in One Inning

A. L.—William P. Purtell, Chicago, May 10, 1910, sixth inning.
N. L.—Edd J. Roush, Cincinnati, July 22, 1916, sixth inning.

First Pinch-Hitter

N. L.—Michael F. Welch, New York, August 10, 1889 (struck out).
A. L.—John B. McLean, Boston, April 26, 1901 (doubled).

First Hit by Pinch-Hitter

N. L.—John J. Doyle, Cleveland, June 7, 1892 (singled).
A. L.—John B. McLean, Boston, April 26, 1901 (doubled).

First Pitcher to Lose Doubleheader (Two Complete Games)

N. L.—David S. Anderson, Pittsburgh vs. Brooklyn, September 1, 1890; lost 3-2, 8-4
    (pitched 2 games of tripleheader).

First Player to be Intentionally Passed With Bases Filled

A. L.—Napoleon Lajoie, Philadelphia, May 23, 1901, ninth inning.

First Manager to be Removed From Game Twice in One Day by Umpires

N. L.—Melvin T. Ott, New York vs. Pittsburgh, June 9, 1946, doubleheader.
A. L.—Alfred M. Martin, Texas vs. Milwaukee, July 14, 1974, doubleheader.

First Lefthanded Catcher

William A. Harbidge, Hartford, N. L., May 6, 1876.

First Lefthanded Pitcher

Robert Mitchell, Cincinnati, N. L., 1878.

First Bespectacled Pitcher

William H. White, Boston, N. L., 1877.

First Bespectacled Infielder

George Toporcer, St. Louis, N. L., 1921.

First Bespectacled Catcher

Clinton D. Courtney, New York, A. L., 1951.

Individual Season, Career Records

American League

BALTIMORE ORIOLES—(1954 to date)

(Present club only; see St. Louis Browns for club's records prior to franchise transfer in 1954)

Batting

Most years, league, except pitchers	23, Brooks C. Robinson
Most games	163, Brooks C. Robinson, 1961
	163, Brooks C. Robinson, 1964
Most games, league	2896, Brooks C. Robinson
Most at-bats	668, Brooks C. Robinson, 163 games, 1961
Most at-bats, league	10,654, Brooks C. Robinson
Most runs	122, Frank Robinson, 155 games, 1966
Most runs, league	1232, Brooks C. Robinson
Most hits	211, Calvin E. Ripken, 162 games, 1983
Most hits, league	2848, Brooks C. Robinson
Most singles	158, Alonza B. Bumbry, 160 games, 1980
Most singles, league	2030, Brooks C. Robinson
Most doubles	47, Calvin E. Ripken, 162 games, 1983
Most doubles, league	482, Brooks C. Robinson
Most triples	12, Paul L. Blair, 151 games, 1967
Most triples, league	68, Brooks C. Robinson
Most homers, lefthanded batter	46, James E. Gentile, 148 games, 1961
Most homers, righthanded batter	49, Frank Robinson, 155 games, 1966
Most homers, rookie season	27, Eddie C. Murray, 160 games, 1977
Most homers, season at home	27, Frank Robinson, 1966
Most homers, season, on road	30, James, E. Gentile, 1961
Most homers, one month	15, James E. Gentile, August, 1961
Most homers, league, lefthanded batter	303, John W. Powell
Most homers, league, righthander batter	268, Brooks C. Robinson
Most homers with bases filled, season	5, James E. Gentile, 148 games, 1961
Most homers with bases filled, league	7, John W. Powell
Most total bases	367, Frank Robinson, 155 games, 1966
Most total bases, league	4270, Brooks C. Robinson
Most long hits	85, Frank Robinson, 155 games, 1966
Most long hits, league	818, Brooks C. Robinson
Most extra bases on long hits	185, Frank Robinson, 155 games, 1966
Most extra bases on long hits, league	1422, Brooks C. Robinson
Most sacrifice hits	23, Mark H. Belanger, 152 games, 1975
Most sacrifice flies	10, James E. Gentile, 152 games, 1962
	10, Brooks C. Robinson, 162 games, 1962
	10, Brooks C. Robinson, 163 games, 1964
	10, Brooks C. Robinson, 156 games, 1969
Most sacrifice flies, league	114, Brooks C. Robinson
Most stolen bases	57, Luis E. Aparicio, 146 games, 1964
Most stolen bases, league	243, Alonza B. Bumbry
Most caught stealing	18, Donald A. Buford, 144 games, 1969
Most bases on balls	118, Kenneth W. Singleton, 155 games, 1973
Most bases on balls, league	889, John W. Powell
Most strikeouts	125, John W. Powell, 140 games, 1966
Most strikeouts, league	1102, John W. Powell
Fewest strikeouts	19, Richard F. Dauer, 152 games, 1980
Most hit by pitch	20, Robert Grich, 160 games, 1974
Most runs batted in	141, James E. Gentile, 148 games, 1961
Most runs batted in, league	1357, Brooks C. Robinson
Most game-winning RBIs	20, Eddie C. Murray, 151 games, 1982
Highest batting average	.328, Kenneth W. Singleton, 155 games, 1977
Highest batting average, league	.303, Robert C. Nieman
Highest slugging average	.646, James E. Gentile, 148 games, 1961
Highest slugging average, league	.543, Frank Robinson
Most consecutive games batted safely during season	21, Douglas V. DeCinces, 1978

Most consecutive games batted safely, league over two seasons—
22, Douglas V. DeCinces, last 21 in 1978; first 1 in 1979

Most grounded into double play	29, Brooks C. Robinson, 152 games, 1960
Most grounded into double play, league	297, Brooks C. Robinson
Fewest grounded into double play	2, Mark H. Belanger, 152 games, 1975

Pitching

Most years, league	18, James A. Palmer
Most games	76, Felix A. Martinez, 1982

Most games, league ....553, James A. Palmer
Most games started..40, David A. McNally, 1969
40, Miguel Cuellar, 1970
40, David A. McNally, 1970
40, James A. Palmer, 1976
40, Michael K. Flanagan, 1978
Most games started, league...518, James A. Palmer
Most complete games..25, James A. Palmer, 1975
Most complete games, league...211, James A. Palmer
Most games finished...59, Stuart L. Miller, 1963
Most innings...323, James A. Palmer, 1975
Most innings, league ....3929⅔, James A. Palmer
Most games won, season ....25, Steven M. Stone, 1980
Most games won, league...268, James A. Palmer
Most years winning 20 or more games ....8, James A. Palmer
Most games, lost..21, Don J. Larsen, 1954
Most games lost, league..149, James A. Palmer
Highest percentage games won, season ..... .808, David A. McNally (won 21, lost 5 in 1971)
Most consecutive games won, season ....15, David A. McNally, 1969
Most consecutive games won, league over two seasons—
17, David A. McNally, last 2 in 1968; first 15 in 1969
Most consecutive games lost, season ....8, Don J. Larsen, 1954 (twice)
Most saves, season..26, Timothy P. Stoddard, 1980
Most bases on balls...181, Robert L. Turley, 1954
Most bases on balls, league...1294, James A. Palmer
Most strikeouts..202, David A. McNally, 1968
Most strikeouts, league...2208, James A. Palmer
Most strikeouts, nine-inning game ....14, Robert L. Turley, April 21, 1954
14, Clifford Johnson, September 2, 1957, second game
Most shutouts ....10, James A. Palmer, 1975
Most shutouts, league..53, James A. Palmer
Most 1-0 shutouts won ....3, Miguel Cuellar, 1974
3, Ross A. Grimsley, 1974
3, James A. Palmer, 1975, 1978
Most runs..129, J. Dennis Martinez, 1979
Most earned runs..126, Michael K. Flanagan, 1978
Most hits..279, J. Dennis Martinez, 1979
Most wild pitches...14, Milton S. Pappas, 1959
Most hit batsmen ....15, Charles L. Estrada, 1960
Most home runs..35, Robin Roberts, 1963
Most sacrifice hits..20, Miguel Cuellar, 1975
Most sacrifice flies...14, James A. Palmer, 1976
Lowest earned-run average, season ....1.95, David A. McNally, 273 innings, 1968

BOSTON RED SOX—(1901 to date)

Batting

Most years, league, except pitchers.......................................23, Carl M. Yastrzemski
Most games ....163, James E. Rice, 1978
Most games, league...3308, Carl M. Yastrzemski
Most at-bats...677, James E. Rice, 163 games, 1978
Most at-bats, league ....12988, Carl M. Yastrzemski
Most runs...150, Theodore S. Williams, 155 games, 1949
Most runs, league ....1816, Carl M. Yastrzemski
Most hits..222, Tris Speaker, 153 games, 1912
Most hits, league...3419, Carl M. Yastrzemski
Most singles ....172, John Pesky, 155 games, 1947
Most singles, league...2262, Carl M. Yastrzemski
Most doubles...67, Earl W. Webb, 151 games, 1931
Most doubles, league..646, Carl M. Yastrzemski
Most triples ....22, Charles S. Stahl, 157 games, 1904
22, Tris Speaker, 141 games, 1913
Most triples, league...130, Harry B. Hooper
Most homers, righthanded batter......................50, James E. Foxx, 149 games, 1938
Most homers, lefthanded batter ....44, Carl M. Yastrzemski, 161 games, 1967
Most homers, rookie season..................................34, Walter Dropo, 136 games, 1950
Most homers, season, at home, righthanded batter ....35, James E. Foxx, 1938
Most homers, season, at home, lefthanded batter ....28, Fredric M. Lynn, 1979
Most homers, season, on road ....26, Theodore S. Williams, 1957
Most homers, one month ....14, Jack E. Jensen, June, 1958
Most homers, league, righthanded batter ....276, James E. Rice
Most homers, league, lefthanded batter ....521, Theodore S. Williams

Most homers with bases filled ....4, George H. Ruth, 130 games, 1919
Most homers with bases filled, league................................17, Theodore S. Williams
Most total bases...406, James E. Rice, 163 games, 1978
Most total bases, league ....5539, Carl M. Yastrzemski
Most long hits..92, James E. Foxx, 149 games, 1938
Most long hits, league...1157, Carl M. Yastrzemski
Most extra bases on long hits ....201, James E. Foxx, 149 games, 1938
Most extra bases on long hits, league ....2230, Theodore S. Williams
Most sacrifices (S. H. and S. F.) .... 54, John J. Barry, 116 games, 1917
Most sacrifice hits..35, Fred N. Parent, 153 games, 1905
Most sacrifice flies...12, Jack E. Jensen, 152 games, 1955
                                                      12, James E. Piersall, 155 games, 1956
                                                      12, Jack E. Jensen, 148 games, 1959
Most stolen bases...54, Tommy Harper, 147 games, 1973
Most stolen bases, league...300, Harry B. Hooper
Most caught stealing.................................19, Michael W. Menosky, 141 games, 1920
Most bases on balls...............................162, Theodore S. Williams, 156 games, 1947
                                                      162, Theodore S. Williams, 155 games, 1949
Most bases on balls, league...2018, Theodore S. Williams
Most strikeouts ....162, Clell L. Hobson Jr., 159 games, 1977
Most strikeouts, league..1393, Carl M. Yastrzemski
Fewest strikeouts...9, John P. McInnis, 152 games, 1921
Most hit by pitch..13, Carlton E. Fisk, 131 games, 1980
Most runs batted in...175, James E. Foxx, 149 games, 1938
Most runs batted in, league ....1844, Carl M. Yastrzemski
Most game-winning RBIs..15, James E. Rice, 145 games, 1982
Most consecutive games, one or more runs batted in, season—
                                                      12, Theodore S. Williams, (18 RBIs), 1942
                                                      12, Joseph E. Cronin, (19 RBIs), 1939
Highest batting average .... .406, Theodore S. Williams, 143 games, 1941
Highest batting average, league .... .344, Theodore S. Williams
Highest slugging average, lefthanded batter .. .735, Theodore S. Williams, 143 games, 1941
Highest slugging average, righthanded batter ....704, James E. Foxx, 149 games, 1938
Highest slugging average, league.............................. .634, Theodore S. Williams
Most consecutive games batted safely during season .... 34, Dominic P. DiMaggio, 1949
Most grounded into double play, season ....32, Jack E. Jensen, 152 games, 1954
Fewest grounded into double play ....3, Ulysses J. Lupien, 154 games, 1943

Pitching

Most years, league ....11, Ivan M. Delock
Most games ....79, Richard R. Radatz, 1964
Most games, league ....365, Ellis R. Kinder
Most games started..43, Denton T. Young, 1902
Most games started, league ....298, Denton T. Young
Most complete games ....41, Denton T. Young, 1902
Most complete games, league ....275, Denton T. Young
Most games finished ....67, Richard R. Radatz, 1964
Most innings..386, Denton T. Young, 1902
Most innings, league ....2730, Denton T. Young
Most games won, season ....34, Joseph Wood, 1912
Most games won, league, righthander...........................193, Denton T. Young
Most games won, league, lefthander...........................123, Melvin L. Parnell
Most years winning 20 or more games..............................6, Denton T. Young
Most games lost...25, Charles H. Ruffing, 1928
Most games lost, league ....112, Denton T. Young
Highest percentage games won, season .... .882, Robert W. Stanley (15-2 in 1978)
Most consecutive games lost, season ....14, Joseph W. Harris, 1906
Most consecutive games won, season...........................16, Joseph Wood, 1912
Most saves, season ....33, Robert W. Stanley, 1983
Most bases on balls...134, Melvin L. Parnell, 1949
Most bases on balls, league...758, Melvin L. Parnell
Most strikeouts..258, Joseph Wood, 1912
Most strikeouts, league..1363, Denton T. Young
Most strikeouts, nine-inning game   17, William C. Monbouquette, May 12, 1961
Most shutouts..10, Denton T. Young, 1904
                                                      10, Joseph Wood, 1912
Most shutouts, league...39, Denton T. Young
Most 1-0 shutouts won ....5, Leslie A. Bush, 1918
Most runs...162, Charles H. Ruffing, 1929
                                                      162, Jack Russell, 1930
Most earned runs...139, Jack Russell, 1930
Most hits ....337, Denton T. Young, 1902
Most hit batsmen ....20, Howard J. Ehmke, 1923

Most wild pitches ....21, R. Earl Wilson, 1963
Most home runs ....37, R. Earl Wilson, 1964
Most sacrifice hits ....24, Cecil C. Hughson, 1943
Most sacrifice flies ....14, David M. Morehead, 1964
Lowest earned-run average, season ....1.01, Hubert B. Leonard, 222 innings, 1914

CALIFORNIA ANGELS—(1961 to date)
(Club known as Los Angeles Angels until September 2, 1965)
Batting

Most years, league, except pitchers ....11, James L. Fregosi
Most games .... 162, Robert F. Knoop, 1964
                                                                                162, James L. Fregosi, 1966
                                                                                162, Santos C. Alomar, 1970
                                                                                162, Santos C. Alomar, 1971
                                                                                162, Donald E. Baylor, 1979
Most games, league ....1,429, James L. Fregosi
Most at-bats .... 689, Santos C. Alomar, 162 games, 1971
Most at-bats, league .... 5,244, James L. Fregosi
Most runs .... 120, Donald E. Baylor, 162 games, 1979
Most runs, league .... 691, James L. Fregosi
Most hits .... 202, Alexander Johnson, 156 games, 1970
Most hits, league ....1,408, James L. Fregosi
Most singles .... 156, Alexander Johnson, 156 games, 1970
Most singles, league ....1,004, James L. Fregosi
Most doubles .... 42, Douglas V. DeCinces, 153 games, 1982
Most doubles, league .... 219, James L. Fregosi
Most triples .... 13, James L. Fregosi, 159 games, 1968
                                                                         13, John M. Rivers, California, 155 games, 1975
Most triples, league .... 70, James L. Fregosi
Most homers, righthanded batter .... 37, Bobby L. Bonds, 158 games, 1977
Most homers, lefthanded batter .... 39, Reginald M. Jackson, 153 games, 1982
Most homers, season, at home ....21, Don E. Baylor, 1978
                                                                                21, Reginald M. Jackson, 1982
Most homers, season, on road ....24, Leon L. Wagner, 1962
                                                                                24, Leon L. Wagner, 1963
Most homers, one month ....12, Bobby L. Bonds, August, 1977
Most homers, rookie season .... 24, J. Leroy Thomas, 130 games, 1961
Most homers, league, lefthanded batter .... 91, Leon L. Wagner
Most homers, league, righthanded batter .... 141, Donald E. Baylor
Most home runs with bases filled, season .... 3, Joseph O. Rudi, 133 games, 1978
                                                                         3, Joseph O. Rudi, 90 games, 1979
Most home runs with bases filled, league .... 7, Joseph O. Rudi
Most total bases .... 333, Donald E. Baylor, 162 games, 1979
Most total bases, league .... 2,112, James L. Fregosi
Most long hits .... 77, Douglas V. DeCinces, 153 games, 1982
Most long hits, league .... 404, James L. Fregosi
Most extra bases on long hits .... 152, Bobby L. Bonds, 158 games, 1977
Most extra bases on long hits, league .... 704, James L. Fregosi
Most sacrifice hits .... 26, Timothy J. Foli, 150 games, 1982
Most sacrifice flies .... 13, Darnell G. Ford, 142 games, 1979
Most stolen bases .... 70, John M. Rivers, 155 games, 1975
Most stolen bases, league .... 139, Santos C. Alomar
Most caught stealing .... 21, Gerald P. Remy, 147 games, 1975
Most bases on balls .... 96, Albert G. Pearson, 144 games, 1961
Most bases on balls, league .... 558, James L. Fregosi
Most strikeouts .... 156, Reginald M. Jackson, 153 games, 1982
Most strikeouts, league .... 835, James L. Fregosi
Fewest strikeouts .... 36, Albert G. Pearson, 160 games, 1962
Most hit by pitch .... 18, Frederic C. Reichardt, 151 games, 1968
                                                                         18, Donald E. Baylor, 158 games, 1978
Most consecutive games batted safely during season .... 25, Rodney C. Carew, 1982
Most runs batted in .... 139, Donald E. Baylor, 162 games, 1979
Most runs batted in, league .... 546, James L. Fregosi
Most game-winning RBIs .... 21, Donald E. Baylor, 157 games, 1982
Highest batting average .... .339, Rodney C. Carew, 129 games, 1983
Highest batting average, league ....324, Rodney C. Carew
Highest slugging average .... .548, Douglas V. DeCinces, 153 games, 1982
Highest slugging average, league .... .490, Leon L. Wagner
Most grounded into double play .... 26, Lyman W. Bostock, 147 games, 1978
Fewest grounded into double play .... 5, Leon L. Wagner, 160 games, 1962
                                                                         5, Albert G. Pearson, 154 games, 1963

Pitching

Most years pitched	9, Andrew E. Hassler
Most games	72, Alejandro M. Rojas, 1967
Most games, league	304, David E. LaRoche
Most games started	41, L. Nolan Ryan, 1974
Most games started, league	288, L. Nolan Ryan
Most complete games	26, L. Nolan Ryan, 1973
	26, L. Nolan Ryan, 1974
Most complete games, league	156, L. Nolan Ryan
Most games finished	53, Alejandro M. Rojas, 1967
Most innings	333, L. Nolan Ryan, 1974
Most innings, league	2,182, L. Nolan Ryan
Most games won, season	22, Clyde Wright, 1970
	22, L. Nolan Ryan, 1974
Most games won, league	138, L. Nolan Ryan
Highest percentage games won, season	.690, W. Dean Chance (won 20, lost 9 in 1964)
Most consecutive games won, season	10, Kenneth F. McBride, 1962
Most consecutive games lost, season	11, Andrew E. Hassler, 1975
Most saves	25, David E. LaRoche, 1978
Most years winning 20 or more games	2, L. Nolan Ryan
Most games lost, season	19, George S. Brunet, 1967
	19, Clyde Wright, 1973
	19, Frank D. Tanana, 1974
Most games lost, league	121, L. Nolan Ryan
Most bases on balls	204, L. Nolan Ryan, 1977
Most bases on balls, league	1,302, L. Nolan Ryan
Most strikeouts	383, L. Nolan Ryan, 1973
Most strikeouts, league	2,416, L. Nolan Ryan
Most strikeouts, nine-inning game	19, L. Nolan Ryan, August 12, 1974

Most strikeouts, extra-inning game—
19, L. Nolan Ryan, June 14, 1974, pitched first 13 innings of 15-inning game
19, L. Nolan Ryan, August 20, 1974, 11 innings
19, L. Nolan Ryan, June 8, 1977, pitched first 10 innings of 13-inning game

Most shutouts	11, W. Dean Chance, 1964
Most shutouts, league	40, L. Nolan Ryan
Most 1-0 shutouts won	5, W. Dean Chance, 1964
Most runs, season	127, L. Nolan Ryan, 1974
Most earned runs	113, William R. Singer, 1973
Most hits	280, William R. Singer, 1973
Most hit batsmen	21, Thomas A. Murphy, 1969
Most wild pitches	21, L. Nolan Ryan, 1977
Most home runs	32, Thomas A. Murphy, 1970
Most sacrifice hits	22, L. Nolan Ryan, 1977
Most sacrifice flies	14, L. Nolan Ryan, 1978
Lowest earned-run average, season	1.65, W. Dean Chance, 278 innings, 1964

CHICAGO WHITE SOX—(1901 to date)

Batting

Most years, league, except pitchers	20, Lucius B. Appling
Most games	163, Donald A. Buford, 1966
Most games, league	2422, Lucius B. Appling
Most at-bats	649, J. Nelson Fox, 154 games, 1956
Most at-bats, league	8857, Lucius B. Appling
Most runs	135, John A. Mostil, 153 games, 1925
Most runs, league	1319, Lucius B. Appling
Most hits	222, Edward T. Collins, 153 games, 1920
Most hits, league	2749, Lucius B. Appling
Most singles	169, Edward T. Collins, 153 games, 1920
Most singles, league	2162, Lucius B. Appling
Most doubles	45, Floyd A. Robinson, 156 games, 1962
Most doubles, league	440, Lucius B. Appling
Most triples	21, Joseph J. Jackson, 153 games, 1916
Most triples, league	104, John F. Collins
	104, J. Nelson Fox
Most homers, righthanded batter	37, Richard A. Allen, 148 games, 1972
Most homers, lefthanded batter	31, Oscar C. Gamble, 137 games, 1977
Most homers, season, at home, righthanded batter	27, Richard A. Allen, 1972
Most homers, season, at home, lefthanded batter	15, Lawrence E. Doby, 1956
	15, Joseph A. Kuhel, 1940
Most home runs, season, on road	19, W. Edward Robinson, 1951
Most homers, rookie season	35, Ronald D. Kittle, 145 games, 1983

Most homers one month..13, Richard A. Allen, July, 1972
Most homers, league, righthanded batter ....154, William E. Melton
Most homers, league, lefthanded batter...97, Peter T. Ward
Most homers with bases filled, season.................................3, Peter T. Ward, 144 games, 1964
Most homers with bases filled, league ....4, J. Sherman Lollar
                                                                                                                                4, Peter T. Ward
Most total bases ....336, Joseph J. Jackson, 146 games, 1920
Most total bases, league...3528, Lucius B. Appling
Most long hits...74, Joseph J. Jackson, 146 games, 1920
Most long hits, league...587, Lucius B. Appling
Most extra bases on long hits.........................149, Richard A. Allen, 148 games, 1972
Most extra bases on long hits, league ....823, Orestes A. Minoso
Most sacrifices, (S.H. and S.F) .... 44, George D. Weaver, 151 games, 1916
Most sacrifice hits..40, George S. Davis, 151 games, 1905
Most sacrifice flies ....12, Orestes A. Minoso, 1961
Most stolen bases..77, Rudy K. Law, 141 games, 1983
Most stolen bases, league ....368, Edward T. Collins
Most caught stealing...29, Edward T. Collins, 145 games, 1923
Most bases on balls ....127, Luzerne A. Blue, 155 games, 1931
Most bases on balls, league...1302, Lucius B. Appling
Most strikeouts...175, David L. Nicholson, 126 games, 1963
Most strikeouts, league ....595, William E. Melton
Fewest strikeouts ....11, J. Nelson Fox, 155 games, 1958
Most hit by pitch ....23, Orestes A. Minoso, 151 games, 1956
Most runs batted in ....138, Henry J. Bonura, 148 games, 1936
Most runs batted in, league...1116, Lucius B. Appling
Most game-winning RBIs ....22, Harold D. Baines, 156 games, 1983
Most consecutive games, one or more runs batted in, season—
                                                                                         13, Taft S. Wright (22 RBIs), 1941
Highest batting average .... .388, Lucius B. Appling, 138 games, 1936
Highest batting average, league ....340, Joseph J. Jackson
Highest slugging average...................................... .603, Richard A. Allen, 148 games, 1972
Highest slugging average, league .... .518, Henry J. Bonura
Most consecutive games batted safely during season ....27, Lucius B. Appling, 1936
Most grounded into double play........................27, J. Sherman Lollar, 140 games, 1959
Fewest grounded into double play ....3, Ulysses J. Lupien, 154 games, 1948
                                                                                         3, Donald A. Buford, 163 games, 1966
                                                                                         3, Donald A. Buford, 156 games, 1967

Pitching

Most years, league..21, Theodore A. Lyons
Most games, lefthander...88, Wilbur F. Wood, 1968
Most games, righthander ....82, Eddie G. Fisher, 1965
Most games, league...669, Urban C. Faber
Most games started..49, Edward A. Walsh, 1908
                                                                                         49, Wilbur F. Wood, 1972
Most games started, league ....484, Urban C. Faber
                                                                                         484, Theodore A. Lyons
Most complete games ....42, Edward A. Walsh, 1908
Most complete games, league...356, Theodore A. Lyons
Most games finished, lefthander......................................62, Wilbur F. Wood, 1970
Most games finished, righthander ....60, Eddie G. Fisher, 1965
Most innings...464, Edward A. Walsh, 1908
Most innings, league ....4162, Theodore A. Lyons
Most games won, season ....40, Edward A. Walsh, 1908
Most games won, league...260, Theodore A. Lyons
Most years winning 20 or more games...4, Edward A. Walsh
                                                                                         4, Urban C. Faber
                                                                                         4, Wilbur F. Wood
Most games lost...25, Patrick J. Flaherty, 1903
Most games lost, league..230, Theodore A. Lyons
Highest percentage games won, season .. .842, Sandalio Consuegra (won 16, lost 3 in 1954)
Most consecutive games won, season...............................13, D. LaMarr Hoyt, 1983
Most consecutive games lost, season...............................14, Howard K. Judson, 1949
Most saves, season ....30, Edward J. Farmer, 1980
Most bases on balls ....147, L. Vernon Kennedy, 1936
Most bases on balls, league ....1213, Urban C. Faber
Most strikeouts ....269, Edward A. Walsh, 1908
Most strikeouts, league ....1796, W. William Pierce
Most strikeouts, nine-inning game................. 16, Jack Harshman, July 25, 1954, first game
Most shutouts...12, Edward A. Walsh, 1908
Most shutouts, league ....58, Edward A. Walsh
Most 1-0 shutouts won ....5, Ewell A. Russell, 1913

Most runs..182, Richard Kerr, 1921
Most earned runs...162, Richard Kerr, 1921
Most hits...381, Wilbur F. Wood, 1973
Most hit batsmen...16, James Scott, 1909
Most wild pitches..17, Thomas E. John, 1970
Most home runs..33, W. William Pierce, 1958
Most sacrifice hits...21, Wilbur F. Wood, 1972
Most sacrifice flies...12, Wilbur F. Wood, 1974
                                                                            12, C. Barth Johnson, 1976
                                                                            12, Kenneth P. Kravec, 1979
Lowest earned-run average, season.....................1.53, Edward V. Cicotte, 346 innings, 1917

CLEVELAND INDIANS—(1901 to date)

Batting

Most years, league, except pitchers...15, Terrence L. Turner
Most games...163, Leon L. Wagner, 1964
Most games, league...1619, Terrence L. Turner
Most at-bats...653, Michael D. Rocco, 155 games, 1944
Most at-bats, league...6037, Napoleon Lajoie
Most runs...140, H. Earl Averill, 155 games, 1931
Most runs, league...1154, H. Earl Averill
Most hits...233, Joseph J. Jackson, 147 games, 1911
Most hits, league...2051, Napoleon Lajoie
Most singles...172, Charles D. Jamieson, 152 games, 1923
Most singles, league...1516, Napoleon Lajoie
Most doubles...64, George H. Burns, 151 games, 1926
Most doubles, league...486, Tristram Speaker
Most triples...26, Joseph J. Jackson, 152 games, 1912
Most triples, league...121, H. Earl Averill
Most homers, righthanded batter.......................43, Albert L. Rosen, 155 games, 1953
Most homers, lefthanded batter.........................42, Harold A. Trosky, 151 games, 1936
Most homers, rookie season.............................37, Albert L. Rosen, 155 games, 1950
Most homers, season at home.............................30, Harold A. Trosky, 1936
Most homers, season on road...........................22, Rocco D. Colavito, 1959
Most homers one month..13, Harold A. Trosky, July, 1937
                                                                            13, Rocco D. Colavito, August 1958
Most homers, league, lefthanded batter...............................226, H. Earl Averill
Most homers, league, righthanded batter.............................192, Albert L. Rosen
Most homers with bases filled, season................4, Albert L. Rosen, 154 games, 1951
Most homers with bases filled, league..................................9, Albert L. Rosen
Most total bases.....................................405, Harold A. Trosky, 151 games, 1936
Most total bases, league...3201, H. Earl Averill
Most long hits...96, Harold A. Trosky, 151 games, 1936
Most long hits, league...724, H. Earl Averill
Most extra bases on long hits.....................189, Harold A. Trosky, 151 games, 1936
Most extra bases on long hits, league.....................................1904, H. Earl Averill
Most sacrifices (S.H. and S.F.)...................67, Raymond J. Chapman, 156 games, 1917
Most sacrifice hits...46, William J. Bradley, 139 games, 1907
Most sacrifice flies...12, Victor P. Power, 1961
Most stolen bases...............................61, Miguel A. Dilone, 132 games, 1980
Most stolen bases, league...254, Terrence L. Turner
Most caught stealing...............................23, Bobby L. Bonds, 146 games, 1979
Most bases on balls.....................111, D. Michael Hargrove, 160 games, 1980
Most bases on balls, league...726, H. Earl Averill
Most strikeouts.......................................135, Bobby L. Bonds, 146 games, 1979
Most strikeouts league...805, Lawrence E. Doby
Fewest strikeouts..4, Joseph W. Sewell, 155 games, 1925
                                                                            4, Joseph W. Sewell, 152 games, 1929
Most hit by pitch...............................17, Orestes A. Minoso, 148 games, 1959
Most runs batted in.............................162, Harold A. Trosky, 151 games, 1936
Most runs batted in, league...1085, H. Earl Averill
Most game-winning RBIs............................15, Andre Thornton, 161 games, 1982
Most consecutive games, one or more runs batted in, season—
                                                    9, Albert L. Rosen (18 RBI), 1954
Highest batting average..............................408, Joseph J. Jackson, 147 games, 1911
Highest batting average, league..375, Joseph J. Jackson
Highest slugging average................................644, Harold A. Trosky, 151 games, 1936
Highest slugging average, league..551, Harold A. Trosky
Most consecutive games batted safely during season—29; William J. Bradley, 1902
Most grounded into double play.....................27, Albert L. Rosen, 155 games, 1950
Fewest grounded into double play.....................3, Jose D. Cardenal, 157 games, 1968

Pitching

Most years, league..20, Melvin L. Harder
Most games..76, Isidro P. Monge, 1979
Most games, league..582, Melvin L. Harder
Most games started...44, George E. Uhle 1923
Most games started, league ....484, Robert W. Feller
Most complete games...36, Robert W. Feller, 1946
Most complete games, league...279, Robert W. Feller
Most games finished ....54, Daniel R. Spillner, 1982
Most innings ....371, Robert W. Feller, 1946
Most innings, league...3828, Robert W. Feller
Most games won, season ....31, James C. Bagby, 1920
Most games won, league..266, Robert W. Feller
Most years winning 20 or more games...7, Robert G. Lemon
Most games lost...22, H. Peter Dowling, 1901
Most games lost, league..186, Melvin L. Harder
Highest percentage games won, season, 16 or more decisions—
                     .938, John T. Allen (won 15, lost 1 in 1937)
Highest percentage games won, season, righthander, 20 or more decisions—
                     .767, Robert G. Lemon (won 23, lost 7 in 1954)
Highest percentage games won, season, lefthander, 20 or more decisions—
                     .767, Sylveanus A. Gregg (won 23, lost 7 in 1911)
Most consecutive games won, season ....15, John T. Allen, 1937
                                              15, Gaylord J. Perry, 1974
Most consecutive games won, league, over two seasons—
                     17, John T. Allen, last two in 1936; first 15 in 1937
Most consecutive games lost, season ....13, Guy Morton, 1914
Most saves, season ....21, David E. LaRoche, 1976
                                              21, Daniel R. Spillner, 1982
Most bases on balls..208, Robert W. Feller, 1938
Most bases on balls, league ....1764, Robert W. Feller
Most strikeouts..348, Robert W. Feller, 1946
Most strikeouts, nine-inning game ....18, Robert W. Feller, October 2, 1938, first game
Most strikeouts, extra-inning game ....19, Luis C. Tiant, July 3, 1968, 10 innings
Most strikeouts, league..2581, Robert W. Feller
Most shutouts ....10, Robert W. Feller, 1946
                                              10, Robert G. Lemon, 1948
Most shutouts, league ....46, Robert W. Feller
Most 1-0 shutouts won..3, Adrian C. Joss, 1908
                                              3, Stanley Coveleski, 1917
                                              3, James C. Bagby, Jr., 1943
                                              3, Robert W. Feller, 1946
Most runs ....167, George E. Uhle, 1923
Most earned runs ....150, George E. Uhle, 1923
Most hits ....378, George E. Uhle, 1923
Most hit batsmen ....20, Otto Hess, 1906
Most wild pitches ....18, Samuel E. McDowell, 1967
Most home runs ....37, Luis C. Tiant, 1969
Most sacrifice hits...20, Early Wynn, 1951
Most sacrifice flies..12, Early Wynn, 1956
                                              12, Gaylord J. Perry, 1974
Lowest earned-run average, season ....1.60, Luis C. Tiant, 258 innings, 1968

DETROIT TIGERS—(1901 to date)

Batting

Most years, league, except pitchers ....22, Tyrus R. Cobb
                                              22, Albert W. Kaline
Most games..163, Rocco D. Colavito, 1961
Most games, league..2834, Albert W. Kaline
Most at-bats..679, Harvey E. Kuenn, 155 games, 1953
Most at-bats, league...*10,586, Tyrus R. Cobb
Most singles ....169, Tyrus R. Cobb, 146 games, 1911
Most singles, league...2839, Tyrus R. Cobb
Most runs ....147, Tyrus R. Cobb, 146 games, 1911
Most runs, league..*2086, Tyrus R. Cobb
Most hits...248, Tyrus R. Cobb, 146 games, 1911
Most hits, league ....*3902, Tyrus R. Cobb
Most doubles..63, Henry B. Greenberg, 153 games, 1934
Most doubles, league...664, Tyrus R. Cobb
Most triples...26, Samuel Crawford, 157 games, 1914
Most triples, league...287, Tyrus R. Cobb

Most homers, righthanded batter............................58, Henry B. Greenberg, 155 games, 1938
Most homers, lefthanded batter..41, Norman D. Cash, 159 games, 1961
Most home runs, season, at home............................39, Henry B. Greenberg, 1938
Most home runs, season, on road..............................27, Rocco D. Colavito, 1961
Most homers, rookie season..35, Rudolph P. York, 104 games, 1937
Most homers, one month ....18, Rudolph P. York, August, 1937
Most homers, league, righthanded batter ....399, Albert W. Kaline
Most homers, league, lefthanded batter ....373, Norman D. Cash
Most homers with bases filled, season ....4, Rudolph P. York, 135 games, 1938
                                                                                     4, James T. Northrup, 155 games, 1968
Most homers with bases filled, league.....................................10, Rudolph P. York
                                                                                     10, Henry B. Greenberg
Most total bases......................................397, Henry B. Greenberg, 154 games, 1937
Most total bases, league...*5474, Tyrus R. Cobb
Most long hits.......................................103, Henry B. Greenberg, 154 games, 1937
Most long hits, league...*1063, Tyrus R. Cobb
Most extra bases on long hits ....205, Henry B. Greenberg, 155 games, 1938
Most extra bases on long hits, league...1845, Albert W. Kaline
Most sacrifices (S. H. and S. F.) .... 52, Owen Bush, 157 games, 1909
Most sacrifice hits...36, William P. Coughlin, 147 games, 1906
Most sacrifice flies....................................16, Samuel Crawford, 157 games, 1914
Most stolen bases ....96, Tyrus R. Cobb, 156 games, 1915
Most stolen bases, league...865, Tyrus R. Cobb
Most caught stealing..38, Tyrus R. Cobb, 156 games, 1915
Most bases on balls..137, Roy J. Cullenbine, 142 games, 1947
Most bases on balls, league ....1277, Albert W. Kaline
Most strikeouts..141, Jacob Wood, 162 games, 1961
Most strikeouts, league...1081, Norman D. Cash
Fewest strikeouts ....13, Charles L. Gehringer, 154 games, 1936
                                                                        13, Harvey E. Kuenn, 155 games, 1954
Most hit by pitch ....24, William A. Freehan, 155 games, 1968
Most runs batted in ....183, Henry B. Greenberg, 154 games, 1937
Most runs batted in, league...1826, Tyrus R. Cobb
Most game-winning RBIs ....14, Lance M. Parrish, 155 games, 1983
Most consecutive games, one or more runs batted in, season—
                                                            10, William W. Horton (17 RBIs), 1976
Highest batting average... .420, Tyrus R. Cobb, 146 games, 1911
Highest batting average, league .... .368, Tyrus R. Cobb
Highest slugging average .... .683, Henry B. Greenberg, 155 games, 1938
Highest slugging average, league .... .616, Henry B. Greenberg
Most consecutive games batted safely during season ....40, Tyrus R. Cobb, 1911
Most grounded into double play...........................29, James H. Bloodworth, 129 games, 1943
Fewest grounded into double play ....0, Richard J. McAuliffe, 151 games, 1968

Pitching

Most years, league...16, Thomas D. Bridges
Most games, lefthander..69, Frederick J. Scherman, 1971
Most games, righthander..67, Aurelio A. Lopez, 1980
Most games, league ....545, John F. Hiller
Most games started ....45, Michael S. Lolich, 1971
Most games started, league...459, Michael S. Lolich
Most complete games ....42, George Mullin, 1904
Most complete games, league ....336, George Mullin
Most games finished ....60, John F. Hiller, 1973
Most innings...382, George Mullin, 1904
Most innings, league...3398, George Mullin
Most games won ....31, Dennis D. McLain, 1968
Most games won, league ....222, George Dauss
Most games lost, league ....183, George Dauss
Most years winning 20 or more games....................................5, George Mullin
Most games lost..23, George Mullin, 1904
Highest percentage games won, season . .862, William E. Donovan (won 25, lost 4 in 1907)
Most consecutive games won, season ....16, Lynwood T. Rowe, 1934
Most consecutive games lost, season ....10, Michael S. Lolich, 1967
Most saves, season..38, John F. Hiller, 1973
Most bases on balls ....158, Joseph H. Coleman, 1974
Most bases on balls, league...1227, Harold Newhouser
Most strikeouts, lefthander..308, Michael S. Lolich, 1971
Most strikeouts, righthander..280, Dennis D. McLain, 1968
Most strikeouts, league..2679, Michael S. Lolich
Most strikeouts, nine-inning game................................16, Michael S. Lolich, May 23, 1969
                        16, Michael S. Lolich, June 9, 1969 (first 9 inn. of 10-inn. game)
Most shutouts...9, Dennis D. McLain, 1969

Most shutouts, league...39, Michael S. Lolich
Most 1-0 shutouts won ....4, O. Edgar Summers, 1908
Most runs ....160, Joseph H. Coleman, 1974
Most earned runs...142, Michael S. Lolich, 1974
Most hits..336, Michael S. Lolich, 1971
Most hit batsmen ....23, Howard J. Ehmke, 1922
Most wild pitches ....18, John S. Morris, 1983
Most home runs ....42, Dennis D. McLain, 1966
Most sacrifice hits ....28, Earl O. Whitehill, 1931
Most sacrifice flies ....13, John S. Morris, 1980
Lowest earned-run average, season ....1.81, Harold Newhouser, 313 innings, 1945

*Total in dispute. See explanation on Page 3.

KANSAS CITY ATHLETICS (FORMER CLUB)—(1955-1967)

(See Philadelphia Athletics for club's records prior to franchise transfer in 1955)

Batting

Most years, league, except pitchers ....6, Edwin D. Charles
6, William R. Bryan
6, J. Wayne Causey
Most games..162, Norman L. Siebern, 1962
Most games, league ....726, Edwin D. Charles
Most at-bats ....641, Jerry D. Lumpe, 156 games, 1962
Most at-bats, league ....2782, Jerry D. Lumpe
Most runs ....114, Norman L. Siebern, 162 games, 1962
Most runs, league ....361, Jerry D. Lumpe
Most hits..193, Jerry D. Lumpe, 156 games, 1962
Most hits, league ....775, Jerry D. Lumpe
Most doubles ....36, Norman L. Siebern, 153 games, 1961
Most doubles, league..119, Jerry D. Lumpe
Most triples ....15, Gino N. Cimoli, 152 games, 1962
Most triples, league...34, Jerry D. Lumpe
Most homers, righthanded batter......................................38, Robert H. Cerv, 141 games, 1958
Most homers, lefthanded batter ....28, James E. Gentile, 136 games, 1964
Most homers, rookie season ....20, Woodson G. Held, 92 games, 1957
Most homers, season, at home ....22, Rocco D. Colavito, 1964
Most homers, season, on road ....17, Robert H. Cerv, 1958
Most homers, one month ....10, Rocco D. Colavito, May, 1964
Most homers, league ....78, Norman L. Siebern
Most homers with bases filled, season ....2, Roger E. Maris, 99 games, 1958
2, Marvin E. Throneberry, 104 games, 1960
Most homers with bases filled, league ....3, Roger E. Maris
3, Marvin E. Throneberry
Most pinch-hit homers, league...4, George Alusik
4, Robert H. Cerv
Most total bases......................................305, Robert H. Cerv, 141 games, 1958
Most total bases, league ....1065, Edwin D. Charles
Most long hits...67, Rocco D. Colavito, 160 games, 1964
Most extra bases on long hits ....148, Robert H. Cerv, 141 games, 1958
Most sacrifice hits ....11, Richard H. Williams, 130 games, 1959
Most sacrifice flies ....12, Leopoldo J. Posada, 116 games, 1961
Most stolen bases....................................55, Dagoberto B. Campaneris, 147 games, 1967
Most stolen bases, league ....168, Dagoberto B. Campaneris
Most caught stealing ....19, Dagoberto B. Campaneris, 144 games, 1965
Most bases on balls....................................110, Norman L. Siebern, 162 games, 1962
Most bases on balls, league ....343, Norman L. Siebern
Most strikeouts....................................143, Nelson E. Mathews, 157 games, 1964
Fewest strikeouts....................................38, Richard D. Howser, 158 games, 1961
38, Jerry D. Lumpe, 156 games, 1962
Most strikeouts, league ....379, Edwin D. Charles
Most hit by pitch..................................13, Robert G. Del Greco, 132 games, 1962
Most runs batted in..................................117, Norman L. Siebern, 162 games, 1962
Most runs batted in, league...367, Norman L. Siebern
Highest batting average...319, Victor P. Power, 147 games, 1955
Highest slugging average ....592, Robert H. Cerv, 148 games, 1958
Most consecutive games batted safely during season ....22, Hector H. Lopez, 1957
22, Victor P. Power, 1958
Most grounded into double play....................................23, Hector H. Lopez, 151 games, 1958
Fewest grounded into double play ....4, Norman L. Siebern, 153 games, 1961

Pitching

Most years, league ....6, John T. Wyatt
Most games ....81, John T. Wyatt, 1964
Most games, league ....292, John T. Wyatt
Most games started ....35, Buddy Leo Daley, 1960
         35, Edward C. Rakow, 1962
         35, Diego P. Segui, 1964
         35, James A. Hunter, 1967
Most games started, league...98, Raymond E. Herbert
Most complete games..14, Arthur J. Ditmar, 1956
         14, Raymond E. Herbert, 1960
Most complete games, league ....32, Raymond E. Herbert
Most games finished ....57, John T. Wyatt, 1964
         57, Jack D. Aker, 1966
Most innings ....260, James A. Hunter, 1967
Most innings, league...784, Raymond E. Herbert
Most games won, season...16, Buddy Leo Daley, 1959
         16, Buddy Leo Daley, 1960
Most games won, league..39, Buddy Leo Daley
Most games lost, season ....22, Arthur J. Ditmar, 1956
Most games lost, league...48, Raymond E. Herbert
Highest percentage games won, season................923, James E. Nash (won 12, lost 1), 1966
Most consecutive games won, season..9, Buddy Leo Daley, 1960
Most consecutive games lost, season ....11, W. Troy Herriage, 1956
Most bases on balls ....108, Arthur J. Ditmar, 1956
Most bases on balls, league...280, Diego P. Segui
Most strikeouts ....196, James A. Hunter, 1967
Most strikeouts, nine-inning game.......................................12, James E. Nash, July 13, 1967
         12, James E. Nash, July 23, 1967, second game
         12, James A. Hunter, September 12, 1967
Most strikeouts, league ....513, Diego P. Segui
Most shutouts ....5, James A. Hunter, 1967
Most shutouts, league...8, Ned F. Garver
Most 1-0 shutouts won ....2, Alexander R. Kellner, 1955
         2, James A. Hunter, 1967
Most runs ....141, Arthur J. Ditmar, 1956
Most earned runs ....125, Arthur J. Ditmar, 1956
Most hits ....256, Raymond E. Herbert, 1960
Most hit batsmen ....12, John C. Kucks, 1959
Most wild pitches ....13, John T. Wyatt, 1965
Most home runs ....40, Orlando Pena, 1964
Lowest earned-run average, season........................2.80, James A. Hunter, 260 innings, 1967

KANSAS CITY ROYALS—(1969 to date)
Batting

Most years, league, except pitchers...14, Amos J. Otis
Most games ....162, Alfred E. Cowens, 1977
         162, Harold A. McRae, 1977
Most games, league...1891, Amos J. Otis
Most at-bats ....705, Willie J. Wilson, 161 games, 1980
Most at-bats, league ....7050, Amos J. Otis
Most runs ....133, Willie J. Wilson, 161 games, 1980
Most runs, league ....1074, Amos J. Otis
Most hits..230, Willie J. Wilson, 161 games, 1980
Most hits, league...1977, Amos J. Otis
Most singles ....184, Willie J. Wilson, 161 games, 1980
Most singles, league ....1354, Amos J. Otis
Most doubles..54, Harold A. McRae, 162 games, 1977
Most doubles, league ....400, Harold A. McRae
Most triples ....20, George H. Brett, 154 games, 1979
Most triples, league ....100, George H. Brett
Most homers, lefthanded batter ....34, John C. Mayberry, 156 games, 1975
Most homers, righthanded batter ....27, Robert L. Oliver, 160 games, 1970
         27, Harold A. McRae, 159 games, 1982
Most homers, rookie season..13, Robert L. Oliver, 118 games, 1969
Most homers, one month ....12, John C. Mayberry, July, 1975
Most homers, season, at home..14, John C. Mayberry, 1973
Most homers, season, on road..23, John C. Mayberry, 1975
Most homers, league, lefthanded batter ....143, John C. Mayberry
Most homers, league, righthanded batter ....193, Amos J. Otis
Most homers with bases filled, season ....1, held by many players

Most homers with bases filled, league ....2, Robert L. Oliver
2, Octavio R. Rojas
2, Frank White
2, Amos J. Otis
2, Harold A. McRae
Most total bases..363, George H. Brett, 154 games, 1979
Most total bases, league ....3051, Amos J. Otis
Most long hits..86, Harold A. McRae, 162 games, 1977
Most long hits, league..623, Amos J. Otis
Most extra bases on long hits ....151, George H. Brett, 154 games, 1979
Most extra bases on long hits, league..1074, Amos J. Otis
Most sacrifice hits..18, Frank White, 152 games, 1976
Most sacrifice flies..13, Darrell R. Porter, 157 games, 1979
Most stolen bases..83, Willie J. Wilson, 154 games, 1979
Most stolen bases, league..346, Willie J. Wilson
Most caught stealing..16, H. Patrick Kelly, 136 games, 1970
16, Alfred E. Cowens, 152 games, 1976
Most bases on balls ....122, John C. Mayberry, 152 games, 1973
Most strikeouts..138, Jerry L. Martin, 147 games, 1982
Fewest strikeouts..24, George H. Brett, 139 games, 1977
Most hit by pitch..13, Harold A. McRae, 162 games, 1977
Most runs batted in..133, Harold A. McRae, 159 games, 1982
Most runs batted in, league ....992, Amos J. Otis
Most game-winning RBIs ....20, Amos J. Otis, 125 games, 1982
Most consecutive games, batted safely during season—
30, George H. Brett, Kansas City, 1980
Highest batting average .... .390, George H. Brett, 117 games, 1980
Highest batting average, league.. .316, George H. Brett
Highest slugging average .... .664, George H. Brett, 117 games, 1980
Highest slugging average, league... .503, George H. Brett
Most grounded into double play ....26, John D. Wathan, 121 games, 1982
Fewest grounded into double play ....1, Willie J. Wilson, 154 games, 1979

Pitching

Most years, league ....14, Paul W. Splittorff
Most games, lefthander ....67, Thomas H. Burgmeier, 1971
Most games, righthander ....75, Daniel R. Quisenberry, 1980
Most games, league ....417, Paul W. Splittorff
Most games started..40, Dennis P. Leonard, 1978
Most games started, league..389, Paul W. Splittorff
Most complete games ....21, Dennis P. Leonard, 1977
Most complete games, league..98, Dennis P. Leonard
Most games finished..68, Daniel R. Quisenberry, 1980
68, Daniel R. Quisenberry, 1982
Most innings ....295, Dennis P. Leonard, 1978
Most innings, league..2527, Paul W. Splittorff
Most games won, season..22, Steven L. Busby, 1974
Most games won, league..165, Paul W. Splittorff
Most games lost, season ....19, Paul W. Splittorff, 1974
Most games lost, league..140, Paul W. Splittorff
Most years, winning 20 or more games ....3, Dennis P. Leonard
Highest percentage games won, season............800, Lawrence C. Gura (won 16, lost 4) 1978
Most consecutive games won, league—
11, Paul W. Splittorff, August 13, 1977 through April 22, 1978
11, Richard B. Gale, June 17, 1980 through August 23, 1980
Most consecutive games won, season ....11, Richard B. Gale, 1980
Most consecutive games lost, season..8, Richard A. Drago, 1970
8, Wallace E. Bunker, 1970
8, William F. Butler, 1970
Most saves..45, Daniel R. Quisenberry, 1983
Most bases on balls ....105, Steven L. Busby, 1973
Most bases on balls, league..770, Paul W. Splittorff
Most strikeouts ....244, Dennis P. Leonard, 1977
Most strikeouts, league..1208, Dennis P. Leonard
Most strikeouts, nine-inning game ....13, Steven L. Busby, July 10, 1973
13, Dennis P. Leonard, July 8, 1977
13, Dennis P. Leonard, September 23, 1977
Most shutouts won, season ....6, Roger E. Nelson, 1972
Most 1-0 shutouts won, season..2, Richard A. Drago, 1971
2, Roger E. Nelson, 1972
2, Alan J. Fitzmorris, 1974
2, Dennis P. Leonard, 1979
2, Lawrence C. Gura, 1982

Most shutouts, league ....21, Dennis P. Leonard
Most runs..137, Lawrence C. Gura, 1979
                                                                          137, Paul W. Splittorff, 1979
Most earned runs ....118, Dennis P. Leonard, 1980
Most hits ....284, Steven L. Busby, 1974
Most wild pitches ....16, John B. Dal Canton, 1974
Most hit batsmen..13, James W. Colborn, 1977
Most home runs allowed..33, Dennis P. Leonard, 1979
Most sacrifice hits ....18, Lawrence C. Gura, 1978
Most sacrifice flies ....17, Lawrence C. Gura, 1983
Lowest earned run average, season............................2.08, Roger E. Nelson, 173 innings, 1972

MILWAUKEE BREWERS—(1970 to date)

**(Includes only Milwaukee records; see Seattle Pilots for club's records prior
to franchise transfer in 1970)**

Batting

Most years, league, except pitchers...11, Donald W. Money
                                                                          11, Charles W. Moore
Most games ....162, J. Gorman Thomas, 1980
Most games, league ....1389, Robin R. Yount
Most at-bats...666, Paul L. Molitor, 160 games, 1982
Most at-bats, league..5425, Robin R. Yount
Most runs ....136, Paul L. Molitor, 160 games, 1982
Most runs, league ....780, Robin R. Yount
Most hits ....219, Cecil C. Cooper, 153 games, 1980
Most hits, league ....1541, Robin R. Yount
Most singles ....157, Cecil C. Cooper, 153 games, 1980
Most singles, league..1067, Robin R. Yount
Most doubles..49, Robin R. Yount, 143 games, 1980
Most doubles, league ....296, Robin R. Yount
Most triples ....16, Paul L. Molitor, 140 games, 1979
Most triples, league ....65, Robin R. Yount
Most homers, lefthanded batter.............................41, Benjamin A. Oglivie, 156 games, 1980
Most homers, righthanded batter ....45, J. Gorman Thomas, 156 games, 1979
Most homers, season at home..22, J. Gorman Thomas, 1979
Most homers, season on road................................26, Benjamin A. Oglivie, 156 games, 1980
Most homers, rookie season ....16, Darrell R. Porter, 117 games, 1973
Most homers, one month ....12, J. Gorman Thomas, August, 1979
Most homers, league, righthanded batter...202, J. Gorman Thomas
Most homers, league, lefthanded batter ....156, Benjamin A. Oglivie
Most homers with bases filled, season................................2, David L. May, 156 games, 1973
                                                                          2, Sixto Lezcano, 132 games, 1978
                                                                          2, Robin R. Yount, 143 games, 1980
Most homers with bases filled, league..4, Cecil C. Cooper
Most total bases...367, Robin R. Yount, 156 games, 1982
Most total bases, league..2306, Robin R. Yount
Most long hits...87, Robin R. Yount, 156 games, 1982
Most long hits, league ....474, Robin R. Yount
Most extra bases on long hits...................................164, J. Gorman Thomas, 156 games, 1979
Most extra bases on long hits, league..796, J. Gorman Thomas
Most sacrifice hits................................19, Ronald M. Theobald, 126 games, 1971
Most sacrifice flies..10, Robin R. Yount, 156 games, 1982
Most stolen bases ....41, Paul L. Molitor, 160 games, 1982
                                                                          41, Paul L. Molitor, 152 games, 1983
Most stolen bases, league ....189, Paul L. Molitor
Most caught stealing ....16, Tommy Harper, 154 games, 1970
                                                                          16, James E. Wohlford, 129 games, 1977
Most bases on balls...98, J. Gorman Thomas, 156 games, 1979
Most strikeouts..175, J. Gorman Thomas, 156 games, 1979
Fewest strikeouts..42, Cecil C. Cooper, 153 games, 1980
Most hit by pitch................................10, Eliseo C. Rodriguez, 94 games, 1973
Most consecutive games batted safely, during season ....24, David L. May, 1973
Most runs batted in ....126, Cecil C. Cooper, 160 games, 1983
Most runs batted in, league..667, Cecil C. Cooper
Most game-winning RBIs ....17, Cecil C. Cooper, 160 games, 1983
                                                                          17, Ted L. Simmons, 153 games, 1983
Highest batting average .... .352, Cecil C. Cooper, 153 games, 1980
Highest batting average, league.. .316, Cecil C. Cooper
Highest slugging average .... .578, Robin R. Yount, 156 games, 1982
Highest slugging average, league... .505, Cecil C. Cooper
Most grounded into double play ....26, George C. Scott, 158 games, 1975

Fewest grounded into double play....................................3, Tommy Harper, 152 games, 1971

Pitching

Most years, league ....12, James M. Slaton
Most games..83, Kenneth G. Sanders, 1971
Most games, league...364, James M. Slaton
Most games started..38, James M. Slaton, 1973
                        38, James M. Slaton, 1976
Most games started, league..268, James M. Slaton
Most complete games ....23, R. Michael Caldwell, 1978
Most complete games, league ....69, James M. Slaton
Most games finished ....77, Kenneth Sanders, 1971
Most innings..314, James W. Colborn, 1973
Most innings, league ....2025, James M. Slaton
Most games won, season..22, R. Michael Caldwell, 1978
Most games won, league ....117, James M. Slaton
Most games lost, season ....20, Clyde Wright, 1974
Most games lost, league ....121, James M. Slaton
Highest percentage games won, season ..... .750, Peter D. Vuckovich, (won 18, lost 6), 1982
Most years winning 20 or more games..1, James W. Colborn
                        1, R. Michael Caldwell
Most consecutive games won, season...8, R. Michael Caldwell, 1979
                        8, Peter D. Vuckovich, 1981
                        8, Peter D. Vuckovich, 1982
                        8, Bryan E. Haas, 1983
Most consecutive games lost, season ....9, Thomas A. Murphy, 1975
Most saves, season...31, Kenneth G. Sanders, 1971
Most bases on balls...106, Peter S. Broberg, 1975
Most bases on balls, league ....760, James M. Slaton
Most strikeouts..169, Martin W. Pattin, 1971
Most strikeouts, league ....929, James M. Slaton
Most strikeouts, nine-inning game ....14, Bryan E. Haas, April 12, 1978
Most shutouts won, season ....6, R. Michael Caldwell, 1978
Most shutouts, league ....19, James M. Slaton
Most 1-0 shutouts won..1, Held by many pitchers
Most runs..133, James W. Colborn, 1973
Most earned runs ....115, R. Michael Caldwell, 1983
Most hits ....297, James W. Colborn, 1973
Most hit batsmen..16, Peter S. Broberg, 1975
Most wild pitches..14, James M. Slaton, 1974
Most home runs allowed ....35, R. Michael Caldwell, 1983
Most sacrifice hits ....15, James M. Slaton, 1976
Most sacrifice flies ....13, Lary A. Sorensen, 1978
Lowest earned-run average, season...................2.37, R. Michael Caldwell, 293 innings, 1978

MINNESOTA TWINS—(1961 to date)

(Includes only Minnesota records; see Washington Senators for club's records prior to franchise transfer in 1961)

Batting

Most years, league, except pitchers..15, Pedro Oliva
Most games ....164, Cesar L. Tovar, 1967
Most games, league..1939, Harmon C. Killebrew
Most at-bats...672, Pedro Oliva, 161 games, 1964
Most at-bats, league ....6593, Harmon C. Killebrew
Most runs..128, Rodney C. Carew, 155 games, 1977
Most runs, league ....1047, Harmon C. Killebrew
Most hits ....239, Rodney C. Carew, 155 games, 1977
Most hits, league ....2085, Rodney C. Carew
Most singles..180, Rodney C. Carew, 153 games, 1974
Most singles, league...1616, Rodney C. Carew
Most doubles ....45, Zoilo Versalles, 160 games, 1965
Most doubles, league ....329, Pedro Oliva
Most triples ....16, Rodney C. Carew, 155 games, 1977
Most triples, league ....90, Rodney C. Carew
Most homers, righthanded batter ....49, Harmon C. Killebrew, 158 games, 1964
                        49, Harmon C. Killebrew, 162 games, 1969
Most homers, lefthanded batter ....33, Jimmie R. Hall, 156 games, 1963
Most homers, league, righthanded batter ....475, Harmon C. Killebrew
Most homers, league, lefthanded batter ....220, Pedro Oliva
Most homers, season, at home................................29, Harmon C. Killebrew, 1961
                        29, Harmon C. Killebrew, 1969

Most homers, season, on road..28, Harmon C. Killebrew, 1962
Most homers, one month ....14, Harmon C. Killebrew, June, 1964
Most homers, rookie season ....33, Jimmie R. Hall, 156 games, 1963
Most homers with bases filled, season...........................3, W. Robert Allison, 159 games, 1961
                                                       3, Rodney C. Carew, 156 games, 1976
Most homers with bases filled, league ....10, Harmon C. Killebrew
Most total bases...374, Pedro Oliva, 161 games, 1964
Most total bases, league ....3412, Harmon C. Killebrew
Most long hits..84, Pedro Oliva, 161 games, 1964
Most long hits, league ....728, Harmon C. Killebrew
Most extra bases on long hits...........................172, Harmon C. Killebrew, 150 games, 1961
Most extra bases on long hits, league.....................................1699, Harmon C. Killebrew
Most sacrifice hits..25, Robert D. Wilfong, 140 games, 1979
Most sacrifice flies..13, Gary J. Gaetti, 145 games, 1982
Most stolen bases...49, Rodney C. Carew, 156 games, 1976
Most stolen bases, league...271, Rodney C. Carew
Most caught stealing ....22, Rodney C. Carew, 156 games, 1976
Most bases on balls ....145, Harmon C. Killebrew, 162 games, 1969
Most bases on balls, league ....1321, Harmon C. Killebrew
Most strikeouts...145, A. Bobby Darwin, 145 games, 1972
Fewest strikeouts...24, Victor P. Power, 138 games, 1972
Most strikeouts, league ....1314, Harmon C. Killebrew
Most hit by pitch...17, Cesar L. Tovar, 157 games, 1968
Most runs batted in.......................................140, Harmon C. Killebrew, 162 games, 1969
Most runs batted in, league ....1325, Harmon C. Killebrew
Most game-winning RBIs ....15, Thomas A. Brunansky, 151 games, 1983
Most consecutive games, one or more runs batted in, season—
                                                    9, Harmon C. Killebrew (15 RBI), 1961
                                                    9, Garrabrant R. Alyea (17 RBI), 1970
Highest batting average ....388, Rodney C. Carew, 155 games, 1977
Highest batting average, league .... .334, Rodney C. Carew
Highest slugging percentage .... .606, Harmon C. Killebrew, 150 games, 1961
Highest slugging average, league .... .518, Harmon C. Killebrew
Most consecutive games batted safely during season.........31, Kenneth F. Landreaux, 1980
Most grounded into double play...........................28, Harmon C. Killebrew, 157 games, 1970
Fewest grounded into double play ....2, Cesar L. Tovar, 157 games, 1968

Pitching

Most years, league...13, James L. Kaat
Most games, season...90, Michael G. Marshall, 1979
Most games, league...468, James L. Kaat
Most games started...42, James L. Kaat, 1965
Most games started, league ....422, James L. Kaat
Most complete games...25, Rikalbert B. Blyleven, 1973
Most complete games, league..133, James L. Kaat
Most games finished, season..84, Michael G. Marshall, 1979
Most innings ....325, Rikalbert B. Blyleven, 1973
Most innings pitched, league ....2958, James L. Kaat
Most games won, season ....25, James L. Kaat, 1966
Most games won, league...189, James L. Kaat
Most games lost, season...20, Pedro Ramos, 1961
Most games lost, league...152, James L. Kaat
Highest percentage games won, season—
                                   .773, William R. Campbell (won 17, lost 5 in 1976)
Most consecutive games, won, season ....9, Stanley W. Williams, 1970
Most consecutive games, lost, season ....13, Terry L. Felton, 1982
Most saves, season...34, Ronald P. Perranoski, 1970
Most years winning 20 or more games ....2, Camilo A. Pascual
                                                    2, James E. Perry
Most bases on balls...127, James M. Hughes, 1975
Most bases on balls, league ....694, James L. Kaat
Most strikeouts...258, Rikalbert B. Blyleven, 1973
Most strikeouts, league ....1824, James L. Kaat
Most strikeouts, nine-inning game ....15, Camilo A. Pascual, July 19, 1961, first game
                                                  15, George H. Decker, June 26, 1973
                                                  15, Jerry M. Koosman, June 23, 1980
Most shutouts, season...9, Rikalbert B. Blyleven, 1973
Most shutouts, league..24, Rikalbert B. Blyleven
Most 1-0 shutouts won, season...3, Rikalbert B. Blyleven, 1971
Most runs ....141, Frank J. Viola, 1983
Most earned runs ....128, Frank J. Viola, 1983
Most hits ....296, Rikalbert B. Blyleven, 1973
Most hit batsmen..18, James L. Kaat, 1962

Most wild pitches, season ....15, David A. Goltz, 1976
Most home runs...39, Pedro Ramos, 1961
                                                                                  39, James E. Perry, 1971
Most sacrifice hits ....17, W. Dean Chance, 1968
                                                                                  17, Jerry M. Koosman, 1980
Most sacrifice flies ....13, Rikalbert B. Blyleven, 1973
Lowest earned-run average, season.....................2.47, Camilo A. Pascual, 248 innings, 1963

NEW YORK YANKEES—(1903 to date)

Batting

Most years, league, except pitchers...18, Lawrence P. Berra
                                                                                  18, Mickey C. Mantle
Most games ....162, Robert C. Richardson, 1961
                                                                                  162, Roy H. White, 1970
                                                                                  162, C. Christopher Chambliss, 1978
Most games, league ....2401, Mickey C. Mantle
Most at-bats ....692, Robert C. Richardson, 161 games, 1962
Most at-bats, league...8102, Mickey C. Mantle
Most runs ....177, George H. Ruth, 152 games, 1921
Most runs, league...1959, George H. Ruth
Most hits ....231, Earl B. Combs, 152 games, 1927
Most hits, league...2721, H. Louis Gehrig
Most singles...............................166, William H. Keeler, 152 games, 1906
                                                                                  166, Earle B. Combs, 152 games, 1927
Most singles, league...1531, H. Louis Gehrig
Most doubles ....52, H. Louis Gehrig, 155 games, 1927
Most doubles, league ....535, H. Louis Gehrig
Most triples..23, Earle B. Combs, 152 games, 1927
Most triples, league ....162, H. Louis Gehrig
Most homers, righthanded batter ....46, Joseph P. DiMaggio, 151 games, 1937
Most homers, lefthanded batter ....61, Roger E. Maris, 161 games, 1961
                                                                                  60, George H. Ruth, 151 games, 1927
Most homers, rookie season ....29, Joseph P. DiMaggio, 138 games, 1936
Most homers, with bases filled, season ....4, H. Louis Gehrig, 154 games, 1934
                                                                                  4, Thomas D. Henrich, 146 games, 1948
Most homers with bases filled, league...23, H. Louis Gehrig
Most homers, season, at home ....32, George H. Ruth, 1921 (Polo Grounds)
                                                                                  30, H. Louis Gehrig, 1934 (Yankee Stadium)
                                                                                  30, Roger E. Maris, 1961 (Yankee Stadium)
Most homers, season, on road ....32, George H. Ruth, 1927
Most homers, one month, righthanded battergr.............15, Joseph P. DiMaggio, July, 1937
Most homers, one month, lefthanded batter ....17, George H. Ruth, September, 1927
Most homers, league, lefthanded batter ....659, George H. Ruth
Most homers, league, righthanded batter...361, Joseph P. DiMaggio
Most total bases ....457, George H. Ruth, 152 games, 1921
Most total bases, league...5131, George H. Ruth
Most long hits ....119, George H. Ruth, 152 games, 1921
Most long hits, league...1190, H. Louis Gehrig
Most extra bases on long hits ....253, George H. Ruth, 152 games, 1921
Most extra bases on long hits, league ....2613, George H. Ruth
Most sacrifice hits............................42, William H. Keeler, 149 games, 1905
Most sacrifice flies ....17, Roy H. White, 147 games, 1971
Most stolen bases ....74, Fredrick C. Maisel, 149 games, 1914
Most stolen bases, league...248, Harold H. Chase
Most caught stealing.................23, W. Benjamin Chapman, 149 games, 1931
Most bases on balls.............................170, George H. Ruth, 152 games, 1923
Most bases on balls, league..1847, George H. Ruth
Most strikeouts, season.............................137, Bobby L. Bonds, 145 games, 1975
Most strikeouts, league...1710, Mickey C. Mantle
Fewest strikeouts ....3, Joseph W. Sewell, 124 games, 1932
Most hit by pitch ....15, Frank P. J. Crosetti, 157 games, 1938
Most runs batted in............................184, H. Louis Gehrig, 155 games, 1931
Most runs batted in, league..1990, H. Louis Gehrig
Most game-winning RBIs...........................21, David M. Winfield, 152 games, 1983
Most consecutive games one or more runs batted in, season—
                                                                                  11, George H. Ruth, (18 RBIs), 1931
Highest batting average................................ .393, George H. Ruth, 152 games, 1923
Highest batting average, league .... .349, George H. Ruth
Highest slugging average .... .847, George H. Ruth, 142 games, 1920
Highest slugging average, league .... .711, George H. Ruth
Most consecutive games batted safely during season ....56, Joseph P. DiMaggio, 1941

Most grounded into double play..................................30, David M. Winfield, 152 games, 1983
Fewest grounded into double play ....2, Mickey C. Mantle, 153 games, 1961

Pitching

Most years, league...16, Edward C. Ford
Most games, righthander ....65, Pedro Ramos, 1965
                          65, Horace G. Womack, 1967
Most games, righthander, league............................426, Charles H. Ruffing
Most games, lefthander...72, Albert W. Lyle, 1977
Most games, lefthander, league ....498, Edward C. Ford
Most games started..51, John D. Chesbro, 1904
Most games started, league ....438, Edward C. Ford
Most complete games...48, John D. Chesbro, 1904
Most complete games, league ....262, Charles H. Ruffing
Most games finished, righthander ....58, Richard M. Gossage, 1980
Most games finished, lefthander ....60, Albert W. Lyle, 1977
Most innings ....454, John D. Chesbro, 1904
Most innings, league, lefthander................................3171, Edward C. Ford
Most innings, league, righthander ....3168, Charles H. Ruffing
Most games won, season, righthander ....41, John D. Chesbro, 1904
Most games won, season, lefthander ....26, Vernon L. Gomez, 1934
Most games won, league, lefthander...............................236, Edward C. Ford
Most games won, league, righthander ....231, Charles H. Ruffing
Most years winning 20 or more games ....4, J. Robert Shawkey
                         4, Vernon Gomez
                         4, Charles H. Ruffing
Most games lost ....21, Albert C. Orth, 1907
                         21, Samuel P. Jones, 1925
                         21, Joseph Lake, 1908
                         21, Russell Ford, 1912
Most games lost, league ....139, Melvin L. Stottlemyre
Highest percentage games won, season........ .893, Ronald A. Guidry (won 25, lost 3 in 1978)
Most consecutive games won, season.................................14, John D. Chesbro, 1904
                         14, Edward C. Ford, 1961
Most consecutive games lost, season ....9, William Hogg, 1908
                         9, Thaddeus A. Tillotson, 1967
Most saves, season ....35, Albert W. Lyle, 1972
Most bases on balls, lefthander ....179, Thomas J. Byrne, 1949
Most bases on balls, righthander ....177, Robert L. Turley, 1955
Most bases on balls, league ....1090, Vernon Gomez
Most strikeouts ....248, Ronald A. Guidry, 1978
Most strikeouts, league...1956, Edward C. Ford
Most strikeouts, nine-inning game.................................18, Ronald A. Guidry, June 17, 1978
Most shutouts, season ....9, Ronald A. Guidry, 1978
Most shutouts, lefthander, league...45, Edward C. Ford
Most shutouts, righthander, league ....40, Charles H. Ruffing
                         40, Melvin L. Stottlemyre
Most 1-0 shutouts won...2, Held by many pitchers
            Last pitcher: George F. Medich, 1974
Most runs..165, Russell Ford, 1912
Most earned runs...127, Samuel P. Jones, 1925
Most hits...337, John D. Chesbro, 1904
Most hit batsmen...26, John M. Warhop, 1909
Most wild pitches..14, Alphonso E. Downing, 1964
Most home runs..40, Ralph W. Terry, 1962
Most sacrifice hits ....22, Vernon Gomez, 1935
Most sacrifice flies ....15, George F. Medich, 1975
Lowest earned-run average, season................1.64, Spurgeon F. Chandler, 253 innings, 1943

OAKLAND A'S—(1968 to date)

(See Philadelphia Athletics, Kansas City Athletics for club's records prior to franchise transfer in 1968.)

Batting

Most years, league, except pitchers ....10, Joseph O. Rudi
Most games..162, Salvatore L. Bando, 1968
                         162, Salvatore L. Bando, 1969
                         162, Salvatore L. Bando, 1973
Most games, league...1410, Salvatore L. Bando
Most at-bats..642, Dagoberto B. Campaneris, 159 games
Most at-bats, league ....5159, Dagoberto B. Campaneris
Most runs ....123, Reginald M. Jackson, 152 games, 1969

Most runs, league ....725, Salvatore L. Bando
Most hits ....182, Claudell Washington, 148 games, 1975
Most hits, league...1355, Dagoberto B. Campaneris
Most singles...144, Rickey H. Henderson, 158 games, 1980
Most singles, league ....1089, Dagoberto B. Campaneris
Most doubles...39, Joseph O. Rudi, 158 games, 1974
                                                             39, Reginald M. Jackson, 157 games, 1975
Most doubles, league..216, Reginald M. Jackson
Most triples ....12, Philip M. Garner, 159 games, 1976
Most triples, league ....39, Dagoberto B. Campaneris
Most homers league, righthanded batter...192, Salvatore L. Bando
Most homers league, lefthanded batter..253, Reginald M. Jackson
Most homers, season, righthanded batter ....35, Antonio R. Armas, 158 games, 1980
Most homers, season, lefthanded batter ....47, Reginald M. Jackson, 152 games, 1969
Most homers, rookie season ....22, Wayne D. Gross, 146 games, 1977.
Most homers, season at home..26, Reginald M. Jackson, 1969
Most homers, season on road...21, Reginald M. Jackson, 1969
Most homers with bases filled, season...........................3, F. Gene Tenace, 158 games, 1974
Most homers with bases filled, league ....7, Salvatore L. Bando
Most homers, one month ....14, Reginald M. Jackson, June 1969
Most total bases...334, Reginald M. Jackson, 152 games, 1969
Most total bases, league ....2152, Reginald M. Jackson
Most long hits...86, Reginald M. Jackson, 152 games, 1969
Most long hits, league ....491, Reginald M. Jackson
Most extra bases on long hits...................183, Reginald M. Jackson, 152 games, 1969
Most extra bases on long hits, league..1019, Reginald M. Jackson
Most sacrifice hits...22, Dwayne K. Murphy, 159 games, 1980
Most sacrifice flies..13, Salvatore L. Bando, 146 games, 1974
Most stolen bases...130, Rickey H. Henderson, 149 games, 1982
Most stolen bases, league...427, Rickey H. Henderson
Most caught stealing...42, Rickey H. Henderson, 149 games, 1982
Most bases on balls...118, Salvatore L. Bando, 155 games, 1970
Most bases on balls, league ....775, Salvatore L. Bando
Most strikeouts...171, Reginald M. Jackson, 154 games, 1968
Most strikeouts, league ....1083, Reginald M. Jackson
Fewest strikeouts ....31, Felipe R. Alou, 154 games, 1970
Most hit by pitch...20, Donald E. Baylor, 157 games, 1976.
Most runs batted in...118, Reginald M. Jackson, 152 games, 1969
Most runs batted in, league ....789, Salvatore L. Bando
Most game-winning RBIs..........................15, Dwayne K. Murphy, 107 games, 1981
Highest batting average....................................... .319, Rickey H. Henderson, 108 games, 1981
Highest batting average, league .... .291, Rickey H. Henderson
Highest slugging average.................................. .608, Reginald M. Jackson, 152 games, 1969
Highest slugging average, league .... .503, Reginald M. Jackson
Most consecutive games, one or more runs batted in season—
                                                             10, Robert J. Monday, (18 RBIs), 1969
Most consecutive games batted safely during season...............19, Carney R. Lansford, 1983
Most grounded into double play ....25, Danny A. Cater, 152 games, 1969
Fewest grounded into double play...........................3, Reginald M. Jackson, 154 games, 1968

Pitching

Most years, league ....9, Roland G. Fingers
                                                                                                        9, Vida R. Blue
Most games, league ....502, Roland G. Fingers
Most games, righthander...76, Roland G. Fingers, 1974
Most games, lefthander...74, Robert J. Lacey, 1978
Most games started...41, James A. Hunter, 1974
Most games started, league ....270, James A. Hunter
Most complete games...28, J. Rick Langford, 1980
Most complete games, league...96, James A. Hunter
Most games finished ....62, Roland G. Fingers, 1976
Most innings, season...318, James A. Hunter, 1974
Most innings, league ....1946, Vida R. Blue
Most games won, season...25, James A. Hunter, 1974
Most games won, league ....131, James A. Hunter
Most seasons winning 20 or more games...4, James A. Hunter
Most games lost, season...20, Brian P. Kingman, 1980
Most games lost, league ....86, Vida R. Blue
                                                                                                        86, J. Rick Langford
Most consecutive games won, season..13, James A. Hunter, 1973
Most consecutive games lost, season ....14, Matthew L. Keough, 1979
Highest percentage games won, season .... .808, James A. Hunter, (won 21, lost 5), 1973
Most saves, season ....24, James T. Grant, 1970

Most bases on balls..112, Johnny L. Odom, 1969
Most bases on balls, league..617, Vida R. Blue
Most strikeouts...301, Vida R. Blue, 1971
Most strikeouts, league ....1315, Vida R. Blue
Most strikeouts, nine-inning game—
           13, Johnny L. Odom, April 20, 1970, 1st nine inn. of 11-inn. game
                             13, Vida Blue, April 9, 1971, six innings
                                   13, Vida Blue, June 21, 1971
                                   13, Vida Blue, July 23, 1976
Most strikeouts, extra-inning game—
        17, Vida Blue, July 9, 1971, first 11 innings of 20-inning game
Most shutouts won, season..8, Vida Blue, 1971
Most shutouts won, league ....28, Vida R. Blue
Most 1-0 shutouts won, season ....2, Vida Blue, 1971
                                   2, James A. Hunter, 1971
Most runs..144, Matthew L. Keough, 1982
Most earned runs ....133, Matthew L. Keough, 1982
Most hits ....284, Vida R. Blue, 1977
Most hit batsmen ....10, Steven E. McCatty, 1979
                                  10, Michael K. Norris, 1981
Most wild pitches...17, Johnny L. Odom, 1968
Most home runs ....39, James A. Hunter, 1973
Most sacrifice hits ....17, Robert J. Lacey, 1977
Most sacrifice flies ....12, Vida Blue, 1974
                              12, Roland G. Fingers, 1974
                              12, J. Rick Langford, 1980
Lowest earned-run average, season ....1.82, Vida Blue, 312 innings, 1971

PHILADELPHIA ATHLETICS—(1901 through 1954)

(See Kansas City Athletics, Oakland Athletics for club's records since franchise transfer in 1955.)

Batting

Most years, league, except pitchers ....16, Harry H. Davis
Most games ....157, David E. Philley, 1953
Most games, league ....1702, James Dykes
Most at-bats..............................670, Aloysius H. Simmons, 154 games, 1932
Most at-bats, league...6023, James Dykes
Most runs..............................152, Aloysius H. Simmons, 138 games, 1930
Most runs, league...997, Robert L. Johnson
Most hits ....253, Aloysius H. Simmons, 153 games, 1925
Most hits, league ....1827, Aloysius H. Simmons
Most singles.............................174, Aloysius H. Simmons, 153 games, 1925
Most doubles..............................53, Aloysius H. Simmons, 147 games, 1926
Most doubles, league ....365, James Dykes
Most triples ....21, J. Franklin Baker, 154 games, 1912
Most triples, league ....104, Daniel F. Murphy
Most homers, righthanded batter.......................................58, James E. Foxx, 154 games, 1932
Most homers, lefthanded batter ....27, Joseph J. Hauser, 149 games, 1924
Most homers, rookie season ....21, Robert L. Johnson, 142 games, 1933
Most homers, season, at home ....31, James E. Foxx, 1932
Most homers, season, on road ....27, James E. Foxx, 1932
Most homers, one month ....15, Robert L. Johnson, June, 1934
Most homers, league..302, James E. Foxx
Most homers with bases filled, season ....3, James E. Foxx, 154 games, 1932
                              3, James E. Foxx, 150 games, 1934
                    3, Robert L. Johnson, 152 games, 1938
                    3, Gus E. Zernial, 145 games, 1952
Most homers with bases filled, league...9, James E. Foxx
                              9, Samuel B. Chapman
Most total bases ....438, James E. Foxx, 154 games, 1932
Most total bases, league..2998, Aloysius H. Simmons
Most long hits..............................100, James E. Foxx, 154 games, 1932
Most extra bases on long hits ....225, James E. Foxx, 154 games, 1932
Most sacrifices (S. H. and S. F.) .... 43, Roy A. Grover, 141 games, 1917
Most sacrifice hits ....34, Simon Nicholls, 124 games, 1907
Most sacrifice flies, season.........................7, Joseph P. DeMaestri, 146 games, 1954
Most stolen bases..............................81, Edward T. Collins, 153 games, 1910
Most stolen bases, league ....375, Edward T. Collins
Most caught stealing...15, Lawton W. Witt, 154 games, 1921
                    15, Aloysius H. Simmons, 152 games, 1924
                    15, William M. Werber, 134 games, 1938

Most bases on balls...149, Edwin D. Joost, 144 games, 1949
Most strikeouts...110, Edwin D. Joost, 151 games, 1947
Fewest strikeouts..17, Richard W. Siebert, 153 games, 1942
Most hit by pitch...12, Joseph J. Hauser, 146 games, 1923
Most runs batted in...169, James E. Foxx, 154 games, 1932
Most runs batted in, league..................................1178, Aloysius H. Simmons
Most consecutive games, one or more runs batted in, season—
                                    11, Aloysius H. Simmons, (20 RBIs), 1931
Highest batting average...422, Napoleon Lajoie, 131 games, 1901
Highest slugging average...749, James E. Foxx, 154 games, 1932
Most consecutive games batted safely during season.....................29, William Lamar, 1925
Most grounded into double play...........................30, William C. Hitchcock, 115 games, 1950
Fewest grounded into double play...................................5, Edwin D. Joost, 151 games, 1947

Pitching

Most years, league...14, Edward S. Plank
Most games, righthander...56, Edwin A. Rommel, 1923
Most games, lefthander...58, Morris W. Martin, 1953
Most games, league...524, Edward S. Plank
Most games started..46, George E. Waddell, 1904
Most complete games...36, George E. Waddell, 1904
Most games finished, righthander...............................47, Jonas A. Berry, 1944
Most games finished, lefthander..................................41, Morris W. Martin, 1953
Most innings...384, George E. Waddell, 1904
Most games won, season...31, John W. Coombs, 1910
                                    31, Robert M. Grove, 1931
Most games won, league...283, Edward S. Plank
Most years winning 20 or more games.................................7, Edward S. Plank
                                    7, Robert M. Grove
Most games lost..25, Scott Perry, 1920
Most games lost, league..158, Edward S. Plank
Highest percentage games won, season........ .886, Robert M. Grove (won 31, lost 4 in 1931)
Most consecutive games won, season................................16, Robert M. Grove, 1931
Most consecutive games lost, season..............................19, John Nabors, 1916
Most bases on balls..168, Elmer G. Myers, 1916
Most bases on balls, league..879, Edward S. Plank
Most strikeouts...349, George E. Waddell, 1904
Most strikeouts, league..1998, Edward S. Plank
Most strikeouts, nine-inning game.................14, George E. Waddell, July 14, 1903
                            14, George E. Waddell, September 6, 1904, first game
                                    14, George E. Waddell, August 2, 1905
Most strikeouts, extra-inning game......18, John W. Coombs, September 1, 1906, 24 innings
                            18, John W. Coombs, August 4, 1910, 16 innings
Most shutouts..13, John W. Coombs, 1910
Most shutouts, league...60, Edward S. Plank
Most 1-0 shutouts won..4, Henry W. Krause, 1909
Most runs...169, Elmer G. Myers, 1916
Most earned runs...146, George L. Earnshaw, 1930
Most hits...360, John W. Coombs, 1911
Most hit batsmen...31, Charles C. Fraser, 1901
Most wild pitches..16, Stuart M. Flythe, 1936
Most home runs...28, Alexander R. Kellner, 1950
Lowest earned-run average, season...................................1.98, Scott Perry, 332 innings, 1918

ST. LOUIS BROWNS—(1902-1953)

(See Baltimore Orioles for club's records since franchise transfer in 1954)
Batting

Most years, league, except pitchers.. 16, James P. Austin
Most games... 159, Derrill B. Pratt, 1915
Most games, league... 1,647, George H. Sisler
Most at-bats.. 671, John T. Tobin, 150 games, 1921
Most at-bats, league.. 6,667, George H. Sisler
Most runs... 145, Harlond B. Clift, 152 games, 1936
Most runs, league... 1,091, George H. Sisler
Most hits.. 257, George H. Sisler, 154 games, 1920
Most hits, league.. 2,295, George H. Sisler
Most singles... 179, John T. Tobin, 150 games, 1921
Most doubles.. 51, Roy C. Bell, 156 games, 1937
Most doubles, league.. 343, George H. Sisler
Most triples... 20, Henry E. Manush, 154 games, 1928

Most triples, league.. 145, George H. Sisler
Most homers, righthanded batter .... 34, Harlond B. Clift, 149 games, 1938
Most homers, lefthanded batter .... 39, Kenneth R. Williams, 153 games, 1922
Most homers, rookie season .... 24, Walter F. Judnich, 137 games, 1940
Most homers, season, at home.. 32, Kenneth R. Williams, 1922
Most homers, one month .... 15, Harlond B. Clift, August, 1938
Most homers, league.. 185, Kenneth R. Williams
Most homers with bases filled, season .... 2, Held by many players,
Last player: J. Geoffrey Heath, 141 games, 1947
Most homers with bases filled, league .... 5, Kenneth R. Williams.
5, Harlond B. Clift
5, Vernon D. Stephens
Most total bases .... 399, George H. Sisler, 154 games, 1920
Most total bases, league.. 3,201, George H. Sisler
Most long hits .... 86, George H. Sisler, 154 games, 1920
Most extra bases on long hits............................... 173, Kenneth R. Williams, 153 games, 1922
Most sacrifices (S.H. and S.F.) .... 48, Joseph Gedeon, 153 games, 1920
Most sacrifice hits .... 40, Thomas Jones, 144 games, 1906
Most stolen bases... 51, George H. Sisler, 142 games, 1922
Most stolen bases, league.. 351, George H. Sisler
Most caught stealing... 19, George H. Sisler, 142 games, 1922
19, Kenneth R. Williams, 153 games, 1922
Most bases on balls .... 126, Luzerne A. Blue, 151 games, 1929
Most strikeouts .... 120, Gus Williams, 143 games, 1914
Fewest strikeouts... 13, John T. Tobin, 151 games, 1923
Most hit by pitch.. 12, Frank J. O'Rourke, 140 games, 1927
Most runs batted in............................... 155, Kenneth R. Williams, 153 games, 1922
Most runs batted in, league .... 964, George H. Sisler
Highest batting average... .420, George H. Sisler, 142 games, 1922
Highest batting average, league .... .344 George H. Sisler
Highest slugging average.............................. .632, George H. Sisler, 154 games, 1920
Highest slugging average, league.. .558, Kenneth R. Williams
Most consecutive games batted safely during season.................... 41, George H. Sisler, 1922
Most grounded into double play .... 21, Glenn R. McQuillen, 100 games, 1942
Fewest grounded into double play .... 7, Vernon D. Stephens, 150 games, 1947

Pitching

Most years, league.. 10, George F. Blaeholder
10, Barney Pelty
10, John J. Powell
Most games.. 60, Marlin H. Stuart, 1953
Most games, league.. 323, Elam R. VanGilder
Most games started... 40, Louis N. Newsom, 1938
Most complete games.. 36, John Powell, 1902
Most games finished.. 35, Leroy Paige, 1952
Most innings .... 348, Urban J. Shocker, 1922
Most games won, season... 27, Urban J. Shocker, 1922
Most games won, league .... 126, Urban J. Shocker
Most years winning 20 or more games .... 4, Urban J. Shocker
Most games lost... 25, Fred Glade, 1905
Most games lost, league.. 142, John J. Powell
Highest percentage games won, season........ .808, Alvin F. Crowder (won 21, lost 5 in 1928)
Most consecutive games won, season.. Less than 12
Most consecutive games lost, season .... Less than 12
Most bases on balls.. 192, Louis N. Newsom, 1938
Most bases on balls, league... 625, Elam R. VanGilder
Most strikeouts .... 232, George E. Waddell, 1908
Most strikeouts, league.. 884, John J. Powell
Most strikeouts, nine-inning game................................ 16, George E. Waddell, July 29, 1908
Most strikeouts, extra-inning game—
17, George E. Waddell, September 20, 1908, 10 innings
Most shutouts .... 6, Fred Glade, 1904
6, Harry Howell, 1906
Most shutouts, league.. 27, John Powell
Most 1-0 shutouts won .... 3, Fred Glade, 1904
Most runs.. 205, Louis N. Newsom, 1938
Most earned runs.. 186, Louis N. Newsom, 1938
Most hits... 365, Urban J. Shocker, 1922
Most hit batsmen .... 19, Barney Pelty, 1907
Most wild pitches... 11, Carl Weilman, 1914
11, Arthur D. Davenport, 1917
11, John H. Knott, Jr., 1936
Most home runs.. 21, Urban J. Shocker, 1921
Lowest earned-run average, season............................ 2.12, Carl Weilman, 307 innings, 1914

SEATTLE PILOTS—(1969)
Batting

Most games	148, Tommy Harper, 1969
Most at-bats	537, Tommy Harper, 148 games, 1969
Most runs	88, H. Wayne Comer, 147 games, 1969
Most hits	126, Tommy Harper, 148 games, 1969
Most singles	105, Tommy Harper, 148 games, 1969
Most doubles	29, H. Thomas Davis, 123 games, 1969
Most triples	6, J. Michael Hegan, 95 games, 1969
Most homers, lefthanded batter	25, Donald R. Mincher, 140 games, 1969
Most homers, righthanded batter	15, H. Wayne Comer, 147 games, 1969
Most homers, rookie season	3, Steven E. Hovley, 91 games, 1969
	3, Daniel Walton, 23 games, 1969
Most homers, one month	8, Donald R. Mincher, July, 1969
Most homers, season, at home	13, Donald R. Mincher, 1969
Most homers, season, on road	12, Donald R. Mincher, 1969
Most home runs with bases filled	1, Donald R. Mincher, 140 games, 1969
	1, Richard J. Rollins, 58 games, 1969
	1, Frederick L. Talbot, 27 games, 1969
Most total bases	194, Donald R. Mincher, 140 games, 1969
Most long hits	39, Donald R. Mincher, 140 games, 1969
Most extra bases on long hits	89, Donald R. Mincher, 140 games, 1969
Most sacrifice hits	9, Gerald E. McNertney, 128 games, 1969
Most sacrifice flies	5, H. Thomas Davis, 123 games, 1969
Most stolen bases	73, Tommy Harper, 148 games, 1969
Most caught stealing	18, Tommy Harper, 148 games, 1969
Most bases on balls	95, Tommy Harper, 148 games, 1969
Most strikeouts	90, Tommy Harper, 148 games, 1969
Fewest strikeouts	46, H. Thomas Davis, 123 games, 1969
Most hit by pitch	5, Donald R. Mincher, 140 games, 1969
	5, Richard J. Rollins, 58 games, 1969
Most runs batted in	80, H. Thomas Davis, 123 games, 1969
Highest batting average	.271, H. Thomas Davis, 123 games, 1969
Highest slugging average	.454, Donald R. Mincher, 140 games, 1969
Most consecutive games batted safely during season	18, H. Thomas Davis, 1969
Most grounded into double play	17, H. Thomas Davis, 123 games, 1969
Fewest grounded into double play	8, Tommy Harper, 148 games, 1969

Pitching

Most games	66, Diego P. Segui, 1969
Most games started	29, Eugene M. Brabender, 1969
Most complete games	7, Eugene M. Brabender, 1969
Most games finished	38, Diego P. Segui, 1969
Most innings	202, Eugene M. Brabender, 1969
Most games won, season	13, Eugene M. Brabender, 1969
Most games lost, season	14, Eugene M. Brabender, 1969
Highest percentage games won, season	.667, Diego P. Segui (won 12, lost 6), 1969
Most consecutive games won, season	5, Diego P. Segui, 1969
Most consecutive games lost, season	9, John Gelnar, 1969
Most saves, season	12, Diego P. Segui, 1969
Most bases on balls	103, Eugene M. Brabender, 1969
Most strikeouts	139, Eugene M. Brabender, 1969
Most strikeouts, nine-inning game	11, Martin W. Pattin, April 29, 1969
Most shutouts won, season	1, held by 5 pitchers
Most 1-0 shutouts won, season	1, Eugene M. Brabender
	1, Martin W. Pattin
Most runs	111, Eugene M. Brabender, 1969
Most earned runs	99, Martin W. Pattin, 1969
Most hits	193, Eugene M. Brabender, 1969
Most wild pitches	8, James A. Bouton, 1969
Most hit batsmen	13, Eugene M. Brabender, 1969
Most home runs	29, Martin W. Pattin, 1969
Most sacrifice hits	10, Diego P. Segui, 1969
Most sacrifice flies	6, Eugene M. Brabender, 1969
Lowest earned-run average, season	3.36, Diego P. Segui, 142 innings, 1969

SEATTLE MARINERS—(1977 to date)
Batting

Most years, league, except pitchers	7, Julio L. Cruz
Most games	162, Ruppert S. Jones, 1979
	162, Willie W. Horton, 1979

Most games, league .... 742, Julio L. Cruz
Most at-bats .... 646, Willie W. Horton, 162 games, 1979
Most at-bats, league .... 2,667, Julio L. Cruz
Most runs .... 109, Ruppert S. Jones, 162 games, 1979
Most runs, league .... 402, Julio L. Cruz
Most hits .... 180, Willie W. Horton, 162 games, 1979
Most hits, league .... 697, Bruce A. Bochte
Most singles .... 132, G. Craig Reynolds, 148 games, 1978
Most singles, league .... 530, Julio L. Cruz
Most doubles .... 39, Alfred E. Cowens, 146 games, 1982
Most doubles, league .... 134, Bruce A. Bochte
Most triples .... 9, Ruppert S. Jones, 162 games, 1979
Most triples, league .... 20, Ruppert S. Jones
Most homers, righthanded batter .... 29, Willie W. Horton, 162 games, 1979
Most homers, righthanded batter, league .... 47, Leon K. Roberts
Most homers, lefthanded batter .... 24, Ruppert S. Jones, 160 games, 1977
Most homers, lefthanded batter, league .... 64, Daniel T. Meyer
Most homers, rookie season .... 24, Ruppert S. Jones, 160 games, 1977
Most homers, season, at home .... 17, Ruppert S. Jones, 1977
                                                                                            17, Ruppert S. Jones, 1979
Most homers, season, on road .... 15, Willie W. Horton, 1979
Most homers, one month .... 9, Daniel T. Meyer, June, 1979
Most homers with bases filled, season .... 2, G. Robert Stinson, 124 games, 1978
                                                                                    2, Leon K. Roberts, 134 games, 1978
                                                                                    2, Daniel T. Meyer, 144 games, 1979
                                                                                    2, Willie W. Horton, 162 games, 1979
Most homers with bases filled, league .... 3, Leon K. Roberts
Most total bases .... 296, Willie W. Horton, 162 games, 1979
Most total bases, league .... 1031, Bruce A. Bochte
Most long hits .... 67, Alfred E. Cowens, 146 games, 1982
Most long hits, league .... 205, Bruce A. Bochte
Most extra bases on long hits .... 116, Willie W. Horton, 162 games, 1979
Most extra bases on long hits, league .... 334, Bruce A. Bochte
Most sacrifice hits .... 15, G. Craig Reynolds, 135 games, 1977
                                                                                  15, Lawrence W. Milbourne, 106 games, 1980
Most sacrifice flies .... 10, Bruce A. Bochte, 150 games, 1979
Most stolen bases .... 59, Julio L. Cruz, 147 games, 1978
Most stolen bases, league .... 290, Julio L. Cruz
Most caught stealing .... 14, Joe A. Simpson, 105 games, 1982
                                                                                      14, Stephen C. Henderson, 121 games, 1983
Most bases on balls .... 85, Ruppert S. Jones, 162 games, 1979
Most bases on balls, league .... 330, Julio L. Cruz
Most strikeouts .... 120, Ruppert S. Jones, 160 games, 1977
Most strikeouts, league .... 338, Julio L. Cruz
Fewest strikeouts .... 51, Daniel T. Meyer, 159 games, 1977
Most hit by pitch .... 8, Leon K. Roberts, 134 games, 1978
Most runs batted in .... 106, Willie W. Horton, 162 games, 1979
Most runs batted in, league .... 329, Bruce A. Bochte
Most game-winning RBIs .... 13, Thomas M. Paciorek, 104 games, 1981
Highest batting average .... .326, Thomas M. Paciorek, 104 games, 1981
Highest slugging average .... .515, Leon K. Roberts, 134 games, 1978
Most consecutive games batted safely during season .... 21, Daniel T. Meyer, 1979
                                                                                             21, Richard W. Zisk, 1982
Most grounded into double play .... 27, Bruce A. Bochte, 150 games, 1979
Fewest grounded into double play .... 6, Julio L. Cruz, 154 games, 1982

Pitching

Most years .... 5, W. Glenn Abbott
Most games .... 78, Edward J. Vande Berg, 1982
Most games, league .... 205, Shane W. Rawley
Most games started .... 35, Floyd F. Bannister, 1982
Most games started, league .... 132, W. Glenn Abbott
Most complete games .... 13, Michael E. A. Parrott, 1979
Most complete games, league .... 26, W. Glenn Abbott
Most games finished .... 64, William H. Caudill, 1982
Most innings .... 247, Floyd F. Bannister, 1982
Most innings, league .... 821, W. Glenn Abbott
Most games won .... 14, Michael E. A. Parrott, 1979
Most games won, league .... 40, Floyd F. Bannister
Most games lost .... 17, Frederick W. Honeycutt, 1980
                                                                                       17, Robert L. Stoddard, 1983
Most games lost, league .... 59, W. Glenn Abbott
Highest percentage games won, season .... .611, Enrique Romo (won 11, lost 7), 1978

Most consecutive games won, season .... 7, W. Glenn Abbott, 1977
Most consecutive games lost, season .... 16, Michael E. A. Parrott, 1980
Most saves .... 26, William H. Caudill, 1982
                                                                                            26, William H. Caudill, 1983
Most bases on balls .... 98, James L. Beattie, 1980
Most bases on balls, league .... 250, Floyd F. Bannister
Most strikeouts .... 209, Floyd F. Bannister, 1982
Most strikeouts, league .... 564, Floyd F. Bannister
Most strikeouts, game .... 13, Gaylord J. Perry, April 20, 1982
Most shutouts won, season .... 3, Floyd F. Bannister, 1982
Most 1-0 shutouts won, season .... 1, Held by many pitchers
Most runs .... 117, Gaylord J. Perry, 1982
Most earned runs .... 106, Gaylord J. Perry, 1982
Most hits .... 245, Gaylord J. Perry, 1982
Most hit batsmen .... 12, W. Glenn Abbott, 1977
Most wild pitches .... 13, Gaylord J. Perry, 1982
Most home runs allowed .... 32, W. Glenn Abbott, 1977
                                                                                            32, Floyd F. Bannister, 1982
Most sacrifice hits .... 15, Shane W. Rawley, 1980
Most sacrifice flies .... 11, Thomas R. House, 1978
Lowest earned-run average, season .... 3.27, Matthew J. Young, 203⅔ innings, 1983

TEXAS RANGERS—(1972 to date)

Batting

Most years, league, except pitchers ....10, James H. Sundberg
Most games ....163, Albert Oliver, 1980
Most games, league ....1398, James H. Sundberg
Most at-bats ....670, David G. Bell, 162 games, 1979
Most at-bats, league ....4446, James H. Sundberg
Most runs ....102, Elliott T. Wills, 146 games, 1980
Most runs, league ....481, Colbert D. Harrah
Most hits ....210, John M. Rivers, 147 games, 1980
Most hits, league ....1125, James H. Sundberg
Most singles ....165, John M. Rivers, 147 games, 1980
Most singles, league ....856, James H. Sundberg
Most doubles ....43, Albert Oliver, 163 games, 1980
Most doubles, league ....189, James H. Sundberg
Most triples ....7, Victor L. Harris, 152 games, 1973
                                                                7, Leonard S. Randle, 156 games, 1975
                                                                7, Dagoberto B. Campaneris, 150 games, 1977
Most triples, league ....26, James H. Sundberg
Most homers, season, righthanded batter ....30, Jeffrey A. Burroughs, 151 games, 1973
Most homers, season, lefthanded batter ....19, Albert Oliver, 163 games, 1980
Most homers, league, righthanded batter ....106, Colbert D. Harrah
Most homers, league, lefthanded batter ....49, Albert Oliver
Most homers, rookie season ....22, David A. Hostetler, 113 games, 1982
Most homers, season, at home ....14, Bobby L. Bonds, 1978
Most homers, season, on road ....20, Jeffrey A. Burroughs, 1973
Most homers with bases filled, season ....3, Jeffrey A. Burroughs, 151 games, 1973
                                                                3, Larry A. Parrish, 128 games, 1982
Most homers with bases filled, league ....5, Jeffrey A. Burroughs
Most homers, one month ....10, David A. Hostetler, June, 1982
Most total bases ....315, Albert Oliver, 163 games, 1980
Most total bases, league ....1528, James H. Sundberg
Most long hits ....65, Albert Oliver, 163 games, 1980
Most long hits, league ....269, James H. Sundberg
Most extra bases on long hits ....116, Colbert D. Harrah, 159 games, 1977
Most extra bases on long hits, league ....490, Colbert D. Harrah
Most sacrifice hits ....40, Dagoberto B. Campaneris, 150 games, 1977
Most sacrifice flies ....12, Jeffrey A. Burroughs, 152 games, 1974
Most stolen bases ....52, Elliott T. Wills, 157 games, 1978
Most stolen bases, league ....161, Elliott T. Wills
Most caught stealing ....20, Dagoberto B. Campaneris, 150 games, 1977
                                                                20, Bobby L. Bonds, 130 games, 1978
Most bases on balls ....109, Colbert D. Harrah, 159 games, 1977
Most bases on balls, league ....568, James H. Sundberg
Most strikeouts ....155, Jeffrey A. Burroughs, 152 games, 1975
Most strikeouts, league ....690, James H. Sundberg
Most hit by pitch ....10, Colbert D. Harrah, 159 games, 1977
Most runs batted in ....118, Jeffrey A. Burroughs, 152 games, 1974
Most runs batted in, league ....461, Colbert D. Harrah
Most game-winning RBIs ....17, Larry A. Parrish, 145 games, 1983

Most consecutive games one or more runs batted in—
10, Jeffrey A. Burroughs, 1974 (20 RBIs)
Highest batting average .... .333, John M. Rivers, 147 games, 1980
Highest batting average, league.. .319, Albert Oliver
Highest slugging average .... .504, Jeffrey A. Burroughs, 152 games, 1974
Highest slugging average, league .... .465, Albert Oliver
Most consecutive games batted safely, during season ....24, John M. Rivers, 1980
Most grounded into double play..24, David G. Bell, 156 games, 1983
Fewest grounded into double play ....4, John M. Rivers, 147 games, 1980

Pitching

Most years, league ....6, Ferguson A. Jenkins
6, Danny W. Darwin
6, Jonathon T. Matlack
Most games...71, James L. Kern, 1979
Most games, league..206, Steven R. Foucault
Most games started ....41, James B. Bibby, 1974
41, Ferguson A. Jenkins, 1974
Most complete games..29, Ferguson A. Jenkins, 1974
Most games finished, righthander.......................................57, James L. Kern, 1979
Most games finished, lefthander ....53, Albert W. Lyle, 1979
Most innings..328, Ferguson A. Jenkins, 1974
Most innings, league..1410, Ferguson A. Jenkins
Most games won...25, Ferguson A. Jenkins, 1974
Most games won, league ....93, Ferguson A. Jenkins
Most games lost...19, James B. Bibby, 1974
Most games lost, league ....72, Ferguson A. Jenkins
Most years winning 20 or more games........................1, Ferguson A. Jenkins
Highest percentage games won, season..... .692, Ferguson A. Jenkins (won 18, lost 8), 1978
Most consecutive games, won, season ....8, Danny W. Darwin, 1980
Most consecutive games, lost, season ....9, David E. Clyde, 1974
Most saves ....29, James L. Kern, 1979
Most bases on balls ....113, James B. Bibby, 1974
Most bases on balls, league...315, Ferguson A. Jenkins
Most strikeouts..225, Ferguson A. Jenkins, 1974
Most strikeouts, league ....895, Ferguson A. Jenkins
Most strikeouts, nine-inning game.................................14, Rikalbert Blyleven, July 22, 1977
Most strikeouts, extra-inning game.........15, James B. Bibby, August 30, 1973, 10⅔ innings
Most shutouts..6, Ferguson A. Jenkins, 1974
6, Rikalbert Blyleven, 1976
Most shutouts, league...17, Ferguson A. Jenkins
Most 1-0 shutouts won...4, Ferguson A. Jenkins, 1974
4, Rikalbert Blyleven, 1976
Most runs...146, James B. Bibby, 1974
Most earned runs ....139, James B. Bibby, 1974
Most hits ....286, Ferguson A. Jenkins, 1974
Most hit batsmen...13, Peter S. Broberg, 1972
Most wild pitches..14, Peter S. Broberg, 1974
Most home runs ....40, Ferguson A. Jenkins, 1979
Most sacrifice hits ....16, James H. Umbarger, 1976
Most sacrifice flies ....12, Peter S. Broberg, 1972
12, Ferguson A. Jenkins, 1974
Lowest earned-run average..2.17, Michael G. Paul, 162 innings, 1972

TORONTO BLUE JAYS—(1977 to date)

Batting

Most years, league, except pitchers...6, Alvis Woods
6, Otoniel Velez
6, L. Ernest Whitt
Most games...162, Richard A. Bosetti, 1979
162, Alfredo C. Griffin, 1982
162, Alfredo C. Griffin, 1983
Most games, league..733, Alfredo C. Griffin
Most at-bats ....653, Alfredo C. Griffin, 155 games, 1980
Most at-bats, league ....2732, Alfredo C. Griffin
Most runs..104, Lloyd A. Moseby, 151 games, 1983
Most runs, league ....293, Alfredo C. Griffin
Most hits ....185, Damaso D. Garcia, 147 games, 1982
Most hits, league...688, Alfredo C. Griffin
Most singles ....145, Alfredo C. Griffin, 153 games, 1979
145, Damaso D. Garcia, 147 games, 1982

Most singles, league ....522, Alfredo C. Griffin
Most doubles ....35, Richard A. Bosetti, 162 games, 1979
Most doubles, league..109, Alfredo C. Griffin
Most triples...15, Alfredo C. Griffin, 155 games, 1980
Most triples, league ....48, Alfredo C. Griffin
Most homers, lefthanded batter.................................30, John C. Mayberry, 149 games, 1980
Most homers, lefthanded batter, league ....92, John C. Mayberry
Most homers, righthanded batter.............................27, Jesse L. Barfield, 128 games, 1983
Most homers, righthanded batter, league..72, Otoniel Velez
Most homers, rookie, season...18, Jesse L. Barfield, 139 games, 1982
Most homers, one month ....10, Jesse L. Barfield, September, 1983
Most homers, season, at home ....22, Jesse L. Barfield, 1983
Most homers, season, on road ....20, John C. Mayberry, 1980
Most homers with bases filled, season ....2, Roy L. Howell, 138 games, 1979
Most total bases..298, Willie C. Upshaw, 160 games, 1983
Most total bases, league ....920, Alfredo C. Griffin
Most long hits..60, Willie C. Upshaw, 160 games, 1983
Most long hits, league...166, Alfredo C. Griffin
Most extra bases on long hits ....121, Willie C. Upshaw, 160 games, 1983
Most extra bases on long hits, league ....350, John C. Mayberry
Most sacrifice hits..19, Luis Gomez, 153 games, 1978
Most sacrifice flies...7, John C. Mayberry, 152 games, 1978
                                                              7, Richard A. Bosetti, 162 games, 1979
                                                              7, Garth R. Iorg, 129 games, 1982
                                                              7, Willie C. Upshaw, 160 games, 1983
Most stolen bases..54, Damaso D. Garcia, 147 games, 1982
Most stolen bases, league ....111, Damaso D. Garcia
Most caught stealing..23, Alfredo C. Griffin, 155 games, 1980
Most bases on balls...77, John C. Mayberry, 149 games, 1980
Most bases on balls, league...278, Otoniel Velez
Most strikeouts ....110, Jesse L. Barfield, 128 games, 1983
Most strikeouts, league ....337, Roy L. Howell
Fewest strikeouts ....21, Robert M. Bailor, 154 games, 1978
Most hit by pitch..8, John C. Mayberry, 94 games, 1981
                                                              8, Lloyd A. Moseby, 147 games, 1982
Most runs batted in ....104, Willie C. Upshaw, 160 games, 1983
Most runs batted in, league ....272, John C. Mayberry
Most game-winning RBIs ....16, Willie C. Upshaw, 160 games, 1983
Highest batting average .... .315, Lloyd A. Moseby, 151 games, 1983
Highest batting average, league.. .292, Damaso Garcia
Highest slugging average .... .473, John C. Mayberry, 149 games, 1980
Most consecutive games batted safely, season............................21, Damaso D. Garcia, 1983
                                                              21, Lloyd A. Moseby, 1983
Most grounded into double play ....21, Ricardo A. J. Carty, 132 games, 1979
Fewest grounded into double play..................................5, Alfredo C. Griffin, 162 games, 1983

Pitching

Most years ....7, James Clancy
Most games ....61, Theodore J. Garvin, 1980
Most games, league ....196, Theodore J. Garvin
Most games started ....40, James Clancy, 1982
Most games started, league...184, James Clancy
Most complete games...19, David A. Stieb, 1982
Most complete games, league...65, David A. Stieb
Most games finished ....40, Thomas W. Buskey, 1979
Most innings ....288⅓, David A. Stieb, 1982
Most innings, league...1200⅔, James Clancy
Most games won, season, righthander ....17, David A. Stieb, 1982
                                                              17, David A. Stieb, 1983
Most games won, league, righthander...66, James Clancy
Most games won, season, lefthander...10, Theodore J. Garvin, 1977
Most games won, league, lefthander...20, Theodore J. Garvin
Most games lost, season...18, Theodore J. Garvin, 1977
                                                              18, Phillip L. Huffman, 1979
Most games lost, league...81, James Clancy
Most consecutive games won, season...7, Doyle L. Alexander, 1983
                                                              7, Roy L. Jackson, 1983
Most consecutive games lost, season ....10, Theodore J. Garvin, 1977, 1978
                                                              10, Paul T. Mirabella, 1980
Highest percentage games won, season .... .586, David A. Stieb (won 17, lost 12), 1983
Most saves ....11, Dale A. Murray, 1983
Most bases on balls...128, James Clancy, 1980
Most bases on balls, league...499, James Clancy

Most strikeouts..187, David A. Stieb, 1983
Most strikeouts, league ....629, James Clancy
Most strikeouts, game......................................12, Peter D. Vuckovich, June 26, 1977
Most shutouts ....5, David A. Stieb, 1982
Most shutouts, league ....16, David A. Stieb
Most runs ....143, David L. Lemanczyk, 1977
Most earned runs ....119, David L. Lemanczyk, 1977
Most hits...278, David L. Lemanczyk, 1977
Most hit batsmen ....14, David A. Stieb, 1983
Most wild pitches ....20, David L. Lemanczyk, 1977
Most home runs..33, Theodore J. Garvin, 1977
Most sacrifice hits..16, Theodore J. Garvin, 1977
Most sacrifice flies...12, James Clancy, 1983
Lowest earned-run average, season..............................3.18, David A. Stieb, 184 innings, 1980

WASHINGTON SENATORS (ORIGINAL CLUB)—1901-1960

(Includes records only of club prior to transfer of franchise to Minnesota in 1961)

Batting

Most years, league, except pitchers..19, Edgar C. Rice
Most games ....158, Edward C. Foster, 1916
Most games, league ....2307, Edgar C. Rice
Most at-bats..668, John K. Lewis, 156 games, 1937
Most at-bats, league...8934, Edgar C. Rice
Most runs ....127, Joseph E. Cronin, 154 games, 1930
Most runs, league..1467, Edgar C. Rice
Most hits..227, Edgar C. Rice, 152 games, 1925
Most hits, league ....2889, Edgar C. Rice
Most singles ....182, Edgar C. Rice, 152 games, 1925
Most doubles ....51, James B. Vernon, 148 games, 1946
Most doubles, league ....478, Edgar C. Rice
Most triples ....20, Leon A. Goslin, 150 games, 1925
Most triples, league ....183, Edgar C. Rice
Most homers, righthanded batter...................42, Roy E. Sievers, 152 games, 1957
                                                      42, Harmon C. Killebrew, 153 games, 1959
Most homers, lefthanded batter ....20 James B. Vernon, 151 games, 1954
Most homers, rookie season ....30, W. Robert Allison, 150 games, 1959
Most homers, season, at home ....26, Roy E. Sievers, 1957
Most homers, season, on road ....21, Roy E. Sievers, 1958
Most homers, one month...........................15, Harmon C. Killebrew, May, 1959
Most homers, league ....180, Roy E. Sievers
Most home runs with bases filled, season..........................2, held by many players
                                                      last player, Roy E. Sievers, 152 games, 1957
Most homers with bases filled, league..4, Roy E. Sievers
Most total bases ....331, Roy E. Sievers, 152 games, 1957
Most total bases, league ....3832, Edgar C. Rice
Most long hits ....76, Stanley O. Spence, 152 games, 1946
Most extra bases on long hits ....159, Roy E. Sievers, 152 games, 1957
Most sacrifices (S.H. and S.F.) .... 52, Robert S. Ganley, 150 games, 1908
Most sacrifice hits...36, Hunter B. Hill, 103 games, 1905
Most sacrifice flies.............................16, Charles A. Gandil, 145 games, 1914
Most stolen bases...............................88, J. Clyde Milan, 154 games, 1912
Most stolen bases, league..494, J. Clyde Milan
Most caught stealing.............................30, Edgar C. Rice, 153 games, 1920
Most bases on balls ....151, Edward F. Yost, 152 games, 1956
Most strikeouts..............................138, James R. Lemon, 146 games, 1956
Fewest strikeouts..................................9, Edgar C. Rice, 150 games, 1929
Most hit by pitch................................24, Norman A. Elberfeld, 127 games, 1911
Most runs batted in ....129, Leon A. Goslin, 154 games, 1924
Most runs batted in, league..1044, Edgar C. Rice
Highest batting average......................... .379, Leon A. Goslin, 135 games, 1923
Highest batting average, league ....323, Edgar C. Rice
                                                                          .323, Leon A. Goslin
Highest slugging average .... .614, Leon A. Goslin, 135 games, 1928
Most consecutive games batted safely during season ....33, Henry E. Manush, 1933
Most grounded into double play ....25, Samuel J. Dente, 155 games, 1950
Fewest grounded into double play ....5, George W. Case, 154 games, 1940
                                                      5, George W. Case, 153 games, 1941
                                                      5, Stanley O. Spence, 153 games, 1944
                                                      5, Edward F. Yost, 155 games, 1954

Pitching

Most years, league ....21, Walter P. Johnson
Most games..64, Fred Marberry, 1926
Most games, league ....802, Walter P. Johnson
Most games started ....42, Walter P. Johnson, 1910
Most games, started, league..666, Walter P. Johnson
Most complete games..38, Walter P. Johnson, 1910
Most complete games, league ....531, Walter P. Johnson
Most games finished ....47, Fred Marberry, 1926
Most innings..374, Walter P. Johnson, 1910
Most innings, league..5924, Walter P. Johnson
Most games won, season ....36, Walter P. Johnson, 1913
Most games won, league...416, Walter P. Johnson
Most years winning 20 or more games.........................12, Walter P. Johnson
Highest percentage games won, season ..... .837, Walter P. Johnson (won 36, lost 7 in 1913)
Most consecutive games won, season..........................16, Walter P. Johnson, 1912
Most consecutive games lost, season ....19, Robert Groom, 1909
Most games lost..26, John Townsend, 1904
                                                                                        26, Robert B. Groom, 1909
Most games lost, league ....279, Walter P. Johnson
Most bases on balls...146, Louis N. Newsom, 1936
Most bases on balls, league..1353, Walter P. Johnson
Most strikeouts...313, Walter P. Johnson, 1910
Most strikeouts, league ....3508, Walter P. Johnson
Most strikeouts, nine-inning game.........................15, Camilo A. Pascual, April 18, 1960
Most shutouts..12, Walter P. Johnson, 1913
Most 1-0 shutouts won ....5, Walter P. Johnson, 1913 and 1919
Most shutouts, league...113, Walter P. Johnson
Most runs ....172, Albert L. Orth, 1903
Most earned runs ....144, James B. DeShong, 1937
Most hits...328, Emil J. Leonard, 1940
Most hit batsmen ....20, Walter P. Johnson, 1923
Most wild pitches ....21, Walter P. Johnson, 1910
Most home runs...43, Pedro Ramos, 1957
Lowest earned-run average, season ....1.14, Walter P. Johnson, 346 innings, 1913

WASHINGTON SENATORS (SECOND CLUB)—(1961-1971)

(Includes records only of present club established in 1961)

Batting

Most years, league, except pitchers.....................................10, Edwin A. Brinkman
Most games ....161, Frank O. Howard, 1969
                                                                                        161, Frank O. Howard, 1970
Most games, league ....1142, Edwin A. Brinkman
Most at-bats...635, Delbert B. Unser, 156 games, 1968
Most at-bats, league..3845, Edwin A. Brinkman
Most runs ....111, Frank O. Howard, 161 games, 1969
Most runs, league ....516, Frank O. Howard
Most hits..175, Frank O. Howard, 161 games, 1969
Most hits, league ....1071, Frank O. Howard
Most singles..144, Edwin A. Brinkman, 158 games, 1970
Most singles, league ....685, Edwin A. Brinkman
Most doubles..31, Aurelio Rodriguez, 142 games, 1970
Most triples...12, Charles E. Hinton, 150 games, 1963
Most homers, righthanded batter...............................48, Frank O. Howard, 161 games, 1969
Most homers, lefthanded batter.........................30, Michael P. Epstein, 131 games, 1969
Most homers, rookie season..12, Don W. Lock, 71 games, 1962
Most homers, season, at home ....27, Frank O. Howard, 1969
Most homers, season, on road ....26, Frank O. Howard, 1968
Most homers, one month ....15, Frank O. Howard, May, 1968
Most homers, league..237, Frank O. Howard
Most homers with bases filled, league ....3, Michael P. Epstein
Most homers with bases filled, season ....2, Donald W. Zimmer, 121 games, 1964
Most total bases ....340, Frank O. Howard, 161 games, 1969
Most total bases, league ....1968, Frank O. Howard
Most long hits ....75, Frank O. Howard, 158 games, 1968
Most long hits, league..403, Frank O. Howard
Most extra bases on long hits ....166, Frank O. Howard, 158 games, 1968
Most extra bases on long hits, league ....897, Frank O. Howard
Most sacrifice hits ....15, Daniel F. O'Connell, 138 games, 1961
Most sacrifice flies..8, Kenneth L. McMullen, 158 games, 1959

Most stolen bases ....29, Edwin M. Stroud, 129 games, 1970
Most caught stealing...10, Willie Tasby, 141 games, 1961
  10, Charles E. Hinton, 150 games, 1962
  10, Fred L. Valentine, 146 games, 1966
  10, Delbert B. Unser, 153 games, 1969
Most bases on balls...132, Frank O. Howard, 161 games, 1970
Most strikeouts ....155, Frank O. Howard, 149 games, 1967
Fewest strikeouts..41, Edwin A. Brinkman, 158 games, 1970
Most hit by pitch...13, Michael P. Epstein, 123 games, 1968
Most runs batted in ....126, Frank O. Howard, 161 games, 1970
Most runs batted in, league...670, Frank O. Howard
Highest batting average.. .310 Charles E. Hinton, 151 games, 1962
Highest slugging average .... .574, Frank O. Howard, 161 games, 1969
Most consecutive games batted safely during season....19, Kenneth L. McMullen, 1967
Most grounded into double play....................................29, Frank O. Howard, 153 games, 1971
  29, Frank O. Howard, 161 games, 1969
Fewest grounded into double play ....4, Delbert B. Unser, 153 games, 1971

Pitching

Most years, league...9, James Hannan
Most games...74, Ronald L. Kline, 1965
Most games started ....36, Claude W. Osteen, 1964
  36, Joseph H. Coleman, 1969
Most complete games ....13, Claude W. Osteen, 1964
Most games finished..58, Ronald L. Kline, 1965
Most innings ....257, Claude W. Osteen, 1964
Most games won, season...16, Richard A. Bosman, 1970
Most games won, league...49, Richard A. Bosman
Most games lost, season...22, Dennis D. McLain, 1971
Most games lost, league..60, Bennie Daniels
Highest percentage games won, season..........737, Richard A. Bosman (won 14, lost 5) 1969
Most consecutive games won, season.......................................8, Richard A. Bosman, 1969
Most consecutive games lost, season ....10, Bennie Daniels, 1962
Most saves, season ....27, Darold D. Knowles, 1970
Most bases on balls ....100, Joseph H. Coleman, 1969
Most strikeouts ....195, Peter G. Richert, 1966
Most strikeouts, nine-inning game—
  13, James R. Duckworth, September 25, 1965, second game
Most strikeouts, extra-inning game—
  21, Thomas E. Cheney, September 12, 1962, 16 innings
Most shutouts, season...4, Thomas E. Cheney, 1963
  4, Frank L. Bertaina, 1967
  4, Camilo A. Pascual, 1968
  4, Joseph H. Coleman, 1969
Most shutouts, league...7, Thomas E. Cheney
Most 1-0 shutouts won..2, Richard E. Donovan, 1961
  2, David R. Stenhouse, 1962
Most runs ....115, Dennis D. McLain, 1971
Most earned runs...103, Dennis D. McLain, 1971
Most hits..256, Claude W. Osteen, 1964
Most hit batsmen ....12, Joseph H. Coleman, 1968
Most wild pitches ....17, Frank L. Bertaina, 1968
Most home runs ....36, Peter G. Richert, 1966
Most sacrifice hits, allowed ....20, Leslie F. Narum, 1965
Most sacrifice flies, allowed...12, Held by 4 pitchers
Lowest earned-run average, season....................2.19, Richard A. Bosman, 193 innings, 1969

National League

ATLANTA BRAVES—(1966 to date)

(See Boston and Milwaukee for club's records prior to franchise transfer in 1966)
Batting

Most years, league, except pitchers...12, Michael K. Lum
Most games...162, Felix B. Millan, 1969
  162, Dale B. Murphy, 1982
  162, Dale B. Murphy, 1983
Most games, league ....1270, Henry L. Aaron (3076 including Milwaukee)
Most at-bats...668, Ralph A. Garr, 148 games, 1973
Most at-bats, league.............................4548, Henry L. Aaron (11,628 including Milwaukee)
Most runs ....131, Dale B. Murphy, 162 games, 1983

Most runs, league ....818, Henry L. Aaron (2107 including Milwaukee)
Most hits ....219, Ralph A. Garr, 154 games, 1971
Most hits, league ....1334, Henry L. Aaron (3600 including Milwaukee)
Most singles ....180, Ralph A. Garr, 154 games, 1971
Most singles, league ....774, Henry L. Aaron (2171 including Milwaukee)
Most doubles ....37, Henry L. Aaron, 155 games, 1967
                                                       37, Felipe R. Alou, 160 games, 1968
                                37, C. Christopher Chambliss, 158 games, 1980
Most doubles, league ....209, Henry L. Aaron (600 including Milwaukee)
Most triples ....17, Ralph A. Garr, 143 games, 1974
Most triples, league ....40, Ralph A. Garr
Most homers, righthanded batter..............................47, Henry L. Aaron, 139 games, 1971
Most homers, lefthanded batter..............41, Darrell W. Evans, 161 games, 1973
Most homers, season, at home ....31, Henry L. Aaron, 1971
Most homers, season, on road ....23, Henry L. Aaron, 1966
                                        23, Henry L. Aaron, 1969
Most homers, one month..14, J. Robert Horner, July 1980
Most homers, league, righthanded batter—
                                335, Henry L. Aaron, (733 including Milwaukee)
Most homers, league, lefthanded batter ....120, Darrell W. Evans
Most homers, rookie season ....33, Earl C. Williams, 145 games, 1971
Most homers with bases filled, league..............7, Henry L. Aaron (16 including Milwaukee)
Most homers with bases filled, season ....2, held by many players
                         Last player: Dale B. Murphy, 151 games, 1978
Most total bases ....355, Felipe R. Alou, 154 games, 1966
Most total bases, league............................2580, Henry L. Aaron (6591 including Milwaukee)
Most long hits..79, Henry L. Aaron, 155 games, 1967
Most long hits, league ....560, Henry L. Aaron (1429 including Milwaukee)
Most extra bases on long hits ....169, Henry L. Aaron, 139 games, 1971
Most extra bases on long hits, league ....1246, Henry L. Aaron (2991 including Milwaukee)
Most sacrifice hits..20, Rodney C. Gilbreath, 116 games, 1976
                                20, Glenn D. Hubbard, 145 games, 1982
Most sacrifice flies ....9, Darrell W. Evans, 125 games, 1972
                                9, Johnny B. Baker, 159 games, 1973
                                9, J. Robert Horner, 89 games, 1978
Most stolen bases ....39, Brett M. Butler, 151 games, 1983
Most stolen bases, league ....168, Jeron K. Royster
Most caught stealing..23, Brett M. Butler, 151 games, 1983
Most bases on balls..127, James S. Wynn, 148 games, 1976
Most bases on balls, league ....634, Henry L. Aaron (1297 including Milwaukee)
Most strikeouts..145, Dale B. Murphy, 151 games, 1978
Most strikeouts, league ....678, Dale B. Murphy
Fewest strikeouts..35, Felix B. Millan, 162 games, 1969
Most hit by pitch..12, Felipe R. Alou, 154 games, 1966
Most runs batted in..122, Henry L. Aaron, 158 games, 1966
Most runs batted in, league....................897, Henry L. Aaron (2202 including Milwaukee)
Most game-winning RBIs..14, Dale B. Murphy, 162 games, 1982
                              14, Claudell Washington, 150 games, 1982
                              14, Dale B. Murphy, 162 games, 1983
Highest batting average................................ .366, Ricardo A. Carty, 136 games, 1970
Highest batting average, league...317, Ralph A. Garr
Highest slugging average.. .669, Henry L. Aaron, 139 games, 1971
Most consecutive games batted safely during season...................31, Ricardo A. Carty, 1970
Most grounded into double play ....22, Joseph P. Torre, 135 games, 1967
Fewest grounded into double play...5, Brett M. Butler, 151 games, 1983

Pitching

Most years, league..18, Philip H. Niekro
Most games...77, Rick L. Camp, 1980
Most games, league...688, Philip H. Niekro
Most games started..44, Philip H. Niekro, 1979
Most games started, league ....594, Philip H. Niekro
Most complete games ....23, Philip H. Niekro, 1979
Most complete games, league...226, Philip H. Niekro
Most games finished ....56, H. Eugene Garber, 1982
Most innings..342, Philip H. Niekro, 1979
Most innings, league...4529, Philip H. Niekro
Most games won, season ....23, Philip H. Niekro, 1969
Most games won, league...266, Philip H. Niekro
Most years winning, 20 or more games ....3, Philip H. Niekro
Most games lost, season ....20, Philip H. Niekro, 1977, 1979
Most games lost, league...227, Philip H. Niekro

Highest percentage games won, season .... .810, Philip H. Niekro (won 17, lost 4), 1982
Most consecutive games won, season...9, Lee W. Capra, 1974
Most consecutive games lost, season ....9, Thomas W. Boggs, 1981
Most saves, season...30, H. Eugene Garber, 1982
Most bases on balls...164, Philip H. Niekro, 1977
Most bases on balls, league ....1419, Philip H. Niekro
Most strikeouts ....262, Philip H. Niekro, 1977
Most strikeouts, league...2855, Philip H. Niekro
Most strikeouts, nine-inning game........................14, Denver C. Lemaster, August 14, 1966
Most shutouts won, season ....6, Philip H. Niekro, 1974
Most shutouts, league...43, Philip H. Niekro
Most 1-0 shutouts, won, season ....2, Philip H. Niekro, 1969
Most runs...166, Philip H. Niekro, 1977
Most earned runs...148, Philip H. Niekro, 1977
Most hits...315, Philip H. Niekro, 1977
Most hit batsmen...13, Philip H. Niekro, 1978
Most wild pitches...27, Tony L. Cloninger, 1966
Most home runs ....41, Philip H. Niekro, 1979
Most sacrifice hits...19, Philip H. Niekro, 1969
Most sacrifice flies...12, Tony L. Cloninger, 1966
                                                                                            12, Carl W. Morton, 1974
Lowest earned-run average, season ....1.87, Philip H. Niekro, 207 innings, 1967

BOSTON BRAVES—(1876 through 1952)
(See Milwaukee and Atlanta for club's records since franchise transfer in 1953)
Batting

Most years, league, except pitchers ....15, Fred C. Tenney
                                                                                            15, Walter J. Maranville
                                                                                            15, John W. Cooney
Most games...158, Edward J. Konetchy, 1916
Most games, league...1795, Walter J. Maranville
Most at-bats...647, Herman A. Long, 151 games, 1892
Most at-bats, league...6764, Herman A. Long
Most at-bats since 1900 .... 637, Eugene Moore, 151 games, 1936
Most at-bats, league, since 1900 .... 6724, Walter J. Maranville
Most runs...160, Hugh Duffy, 124 games, 1894
Most runs since 1900 .... 125, Thomas F. Holmes, 154 games, 1945
Most runs, league...1294, Herman A. Long
Most hits...236, Hugh Duffy, 124 games, 1894
Most hits, league ....2002, Fred C. Tenney
Most hits since 1900 .... 224, Thomas F. Holmes, 154 games, 1945
Most singles...166, Lance Richbourg, 148 games, 1928
Most doubles...50, Hugh Duffy, 124 games, 1894
Most doubles since 1900 .... 47, Thomas F. Holmes, 154 games, 1945
Most doubles, league ....291, Thomas F. Holmes
Most triples...20, Richard F. Johnston, 124 games, 1887
Most triples since 1900.................................... 18, Raymond R. Powell, 149 games, 1921
Most triples, league...103, Walter J. Maranville
Most homers, righthanded batter ....38, Walter A. Berger, 151 games, 1930
Most homers, lefthanded batter ....28, Thomas F. Holmes, 154 games, 1945
Most home runs, rookie season.................................38, Walter A. Berger, 151 games, 1930
Most homers, season at home, lefthanded batter.....................19, Charles T. Workman, 1945
Most homers, season at home, righthanded batter........................18, Walter A. Berger, 1930
Most homers, season, on road...22, Sidney Gordon, 1950
Most homers with bases filled, season ....4, Sidney Gordon, 134 games, 1950
Most homers with bases filled, league ....6, Walter A. Berger
Most home runs, one month ....11, Walter A. Berger, May, 1930
Most homers, league...199, Walter A. Berger
Most total bases...372, Hugh Duffy, 124 games, 1894
Most total bases since 1900.................................... 367, Thomas F. Holmes, 154 games, 1945
Most total bases, league...2629, Herman A. Long
Most long hits ....81, Hugh Duffy, 124 games, 1894
                                                                                            81, Thomas F. Holmes, 154 games, 1945
Most extra bases on long hits.................................169, Walter A. Berger, 151 games, 1930
Most sacrifices (S.H. and S.F.) .... 37, John P. McInnis, 154 games, 1923
Most sacrifice hits...31, Frederick E. Maguire, 148 games, 1931
Most stolen bases ....93, William R. Hamilton, 131 games, 1896
Most stolen bases since 1900 .... 57, Ralph Meyers, 140 games, 1913
Most stolen bases, league...446, Herman A. Long
Most caught stealing.................................20, William H. Southworth, 141 games, 1921
Most bases on balls ....131, Robert I. Elliott, 151 games, 1948

Most strikeouts...134, Vincent P. DiMaggio, 150 games, 1938
Fewest strikeouts ....9, Thomas F. Holmes, 154 games, 1945
Most hit by pitch..11, Samuel Jethroe, 148 games, 1951
Most runs batted in.........................130, Walter A. Berger, 150 games, 1935
Most runs batted in, league ....746, Walter A. Berger
Highest batting average.................................... .438, Hugh Duffy, 124 games, 1894
Highest batting average since 1900 .... .387, Rogers Hornsby, 140 games, 1928
Highest batting average, league ....338, William R. Hamilton
Highest slugging average .... .632, Rogers Hornsby, 140 games, 1928
Highest batting average, league, since 1900 .... .304, Walter A. Berger
Most consecutive games batted safely during season ....37, Thomas F. Holmes, 1945
Most grounded into double play ....28, Sidney Gordon, 150 games, 1951
Fewest grounded into double play............................4, Vincent P. DiMaggio, 150 games, 1938

Pitching, Since 1900

Most years, league ....12, Charles A. Nichols
Most years, league, since 1900 .... 11, Richard Rudolph
Most games..57, John J. Hutchings, 1945
Most games, league ....517, Charles A. Nichols
Most games started...46, Victor G. Willis, 1902
Most complete games ....45, Victor G. Willis, 1902
Most games finished..................................29, Nelson T. Potter, 1949
Most innings..411, Victor G. Willis, 1902
Most games won, season ....27, Charles Pittinger, 1902
                                                                                    27, Victor G. Willis, 1902
                                                                                    27, Richard Rudolph, 1914
Most games won, league ....328, Charles A. Nichols
Most games won, league, since 1900 .... 122, Richard Rudolph
                                                                                    122, Warren E. Spahn
Most years winning 20 or more games ....4, John F. Sain
                                                                                    4, Warren E. Spahn
Most games lost ....29, Victor G. Willis, 1905
Highest percentage games won, season ... .842, Thomas L. Hughes (won 16, lost 3 in 1916)
Most consecutive games won, season ....12, Richard Rudolph, 1914
Most consecutive games lost, season........................18, Clifton G. Curtis, 1910
Most bases on balls..149, Charles C. Fraser, 1905
Most bases on balls, league................................1118, Charles A. Nichols
Most bases on balls, league, since 1900 .... 678, George A. Tyler
Most strikeouts ....226, Victor G. Willis, 1902
Most strikeouts, league ....1649, Charles A. Nichols
Most strikeouts, league, since 1900 .... 1000, Warren E. Spahn
Most strikeouts, nine-inning game ....13, Victor G. Willis, May 28, 1902
                                                                                    13, Warren E. Spahn, September 13, 1952
Most strikeouts, extra-inning game ....18, Warren E. Spahn, June 14, 1952, 15 innings
Most shutouts, season..7, Charles Pittinger, 1902
                                                                                    7, Irving M. Young, 1905
                                                                                    7, Warren E. Spahn, 1947
                                                                                    7, Warren E. Spahn, 1951
Most shutouts, league..29, Richard Rudolph
Most 1-0 shutouts won ....4, Richard Rudolph, 1916
                                                                                    4, Joseph Oeschger, 1920
Most runs...196, Charles Pittinger, 1903
Most earned runs ....130, John F. Sain, 1949
Most hits...394, Charles Pittinger, 1903
Most hit batsmen..16, Frank X. Pfeffer, 1906
Most wild pitches ....14, Charles Pittinger, 1903
Most home runs...34, John F. Sain, 1950
Lowest earned-run average, season ....1.90, William L. James, 332 innings, 1914

BROOKLYN DODGERS—(1890 through 1957)
(See Los Angeles Dodgers for club's records since franchise transfer in 1958)
Batting

Most years, league, except pitchers.......................................18, Zachariah D. Wheat
Most games...158, Carl A. Furillo, 1951
                                                                                    158, Gilbert R. Hodges, 1951
Most games, league ....2318, Zachariah D. Wheat
Most at-bats...667, Carl A. Furillo, 158 games, 1951
Most at-bats, league..8859, Zachariah D. Wheat
Most runs..143, Hubert Collins, 129 games, 1890
                                                                                    143, Floyd C. Herman, 153 games, 1930

Most runs, league ....1317, Harold H. Reese
Most hits ....241, Floyd C. Herman, 153 games, 1930
Most hits, league ....2804, Zachariah D. Wheat
Most singles ....179, William H. Keeler, 137 games, 1900
Most singles, league ....2038, Zachariah D. Wheat
Most doubles ....52, John H. Frederick, 148 games, 1929
Most doubles, league ....464, Zachariah D. Wheat
Most triples ....27, George Treadway, 122 games, 1894
Most triples, league ....171, Zachariah D. Wheat
Most triples since 1900 ....22, Henry H. Myers, 154 games, 1920
Most homers, righthanded batter ....42, Gilbert R. Hodges, 154 games, 1954
Most homers, lefthanded batter ....43, Edwin D. Snider, 151 games, 1956
Most home runs, rookie season ....25, Adelphia L. Bissonette, 155 games, 1928
Most homers, season, at home, lefthanded batter—
                       25 (Incl. 2 at Jersey City), Edwin D. Snider, 1956
Most homers, season, at home, righthanded batter ....25, Gilbert R. Hodges, 1954
Most homers, season, on road ....24, Gilbert R. Hodges, 1951
Most home runs, one month, lefthanded batter ....15, Edwin D. Snider, Aug., 1953
Most home runs, one month, righthanded batter ....12, Roy Campanella, May, 1953
Most homers, league, righthanded batter ....298, Gilbert R. Hodges
Most homers, league, lefthanded batter ....316, Edwin D. Snider
Most homers with bases filled, season ....2, Held by many players
                   Last player, Gilbert R. Hodges, 150 games, 1957
Most homers, with bases filled, league ....13, Gilbert R. Hodges
Most total bases ....416, Floyd C. Herman, 153 games, 1930
Most total bases, league ....4003, Zachariah D. Wheat
Most long hits ....94, Floyd C. Herman, 153 games, 1930
Most long hits, league ....766, Zachariah D. Wheat
Most extra bases on long hits ....179, Edwin D. Snider, 149 games, 1954
Most extra bases on long hits, league ....1368, Edwin D. Snider
Most sacrifices (S.H. and S.F.) ....39, Jacob E. Daubert, 150 games, 1915
Most sacrifice hits ....32, James P. Casey, 138 games, 1907
Most sacrifice flies ....19, Gilbert R. Hodges, 154 games, 1954
Most stolen bases ....94, John M. Ward, 148 games, 1892
Most stolen bases since 1900 ....67, James T. Sheckard, 139 games, 1903
Most stolen bases, league ....231, Harold H. Reese
Most caught stealing ....16, James H. Johnston, 152 games, 1921
Most bases on balls ....148, Edward R. Stanky, 153 games, 1945
Most strikeouts ....115, Adolph Camilli, 149 games, 1941
Fewest strikeouts ....15, James H. Johnston, 151 games, 1923
Most hit by pitch ....14, Jack R. Robinson, 149 games, 1952
Most runs batted in ....142, Roy Campanella, 144 games, 1953
Most runs batted in, league ....1227, Zachariah D. Wheat
Highest batting average ....393, Floyd C. Herman, 153 games, 1930
Highest batting average, league ....339, Floyd C. Herman
Highest slugging average ....678, Floyd C. Herman, 153 games, 1930
Highest slugging average, league ....560, Edwin D. Snider
Most consecutive games batted safely, season ....29, Zachariah D. Wheat, 1916
Most grounded into double play ....27, Carl A. Furillo, 149 games, 1956
Fewest grounded into double play ....5, Jack R. Robinson, 151 games, 1947
                   5, Harold H. Reese, 155 games, 1949
                   5, James Gilliam, 153 games, 1956

Pitching, Since 1900

Most years, league ....12, Arthur C. Vance
Most games ....62, Clement W. Labine, 1956
Most games, league ....378, Arthur C. Vance
Most games started ....41, Oscar Jones, 1904
Most complete games ....38, Oscar Jones, 1904
Most games finished ....47, Clement W. Labine, 1956
Most innings ....378, Oscar Jones, 1904
Most games won, season ....29, Joseph J. McGinnity, 1900
Most games won, league ....190, Arthur C. Vance
Most years winning 20 or more games ....4, Burleigh A. Grimes
Most games lost ....27, George G. Bell, 1910
Highest percentage games won, season, righthander—
          .889, Frederick L. Fitzsimmons (won 16, lost 2 in 1940)
Highest percentage games won, season, lefthander—
          .880, Elwin C. Roe (won 22, lost 3 in 1951)
Most consecutive games won, season ....15, Arthur C. Vance, 1924
Most consecutive games lost, season ....14, James W. Pastorius, 1908
Most bases on balls ....151, William E. Donovan, 1901
Most bases on balls, league ....764, Arthur C. Vance

Most strikeouts ....262, Arthur C. Vance, 1924
Most strikeouts, league...1915, Arthur C. Vance
Most strikeouts, nine-inning game..............................16, George N. Rucker, July 24, 1909
Most strikeouts, extra-inning game ....17, Arthur C. Vance, July 20, 1925, 10 innings
Most shutouts, season ....7, Burleigh A. Grimes, 1918
7, J. Whitlow Wyatt, 1941
Most shutouts, league ....38, George N. Rucker
Most 1-0 shutouts won ....3, George N. Rucker, 1911
Most runs...188, Harry M. McIntire, 1905
Most earned runs...138, Burleigh A. Grimes, 1925
Most hits ....364, Joseph J. McGinnity, 1900
Most hit batsmen ....41, Joseph J. McGinnity, 1900
Most wild pitches ....15, Lawrence D. Cheney, 1916
Most home runs, lefthander ....34, Elwin C. Roe, 1950
Most home runs, righthander ....35, Donald Newcombe, 1955

CHICAGO CUBS—(1876 to date)

Batting

Most years, league, except pitchers...22, Adrian C. Anson
Most years, league, since 1900.......................................20, Philip J. Cavarretta
Most games...164, Ronald E. Santo, 1965
164, Billy L. Williams, 1965
Most games, league..2,528, Ernest Banks
Most at-bats ....666, William J. Herman, 154 games, 1935
Most at-bats, league..9,421, Ernest Banks
Most runs...156, Rogers Hornsby, 156 games, 1929
Most runs, league..1,712, Adrian C. Anson
Most runs, league, since 1900.................................. 1,306, Billy L. Williams
Most hits......................................229, Rogers Hornsby, 156 games, 1929
Most hits, league..3,081, Adrian C. Anson
Most hits, league, since 1900 .... 2,583, Ernest Banks
Most singles...165, Earl J. Adams, 146 games, 1927
Most singles, league...2,330, Adrian C. Anson
Most singles, league, since 1900 .... 1,692, Stanley C. Hack
Most doubles...57, William J. Herman, 154 games, 1935
57, William J. Herman, 153 games, 1936
Most doubles, league ....530, Adrian C. Anson
Most doubles, league, since 1900 .... 407, Ernest Banks
Most triples...21, Frank M. Schulte, 154 games, 1911
21, Victor S. Saier, 149 games, 1913
Most triples, league ....137, James E. Ryan
Most triples, league, since 1900 .... 117, Frank Schulte
Most homers, lefthanded batter ....42, Billy L. Williams, 161 games, 1970
Most homers, righthanded batter ....56, Lewis R. Wilson, 155 games, 1930
Most homers, season, at home ....33, Lewis R. Wilson, 1930
Most homers, season, on road..23, Lewis R. Wilson, 1930
23, Ernest Banks, 1960
23, David A. Kingman, 1979
Most homers, rookie season...25, Billy L. Williams, 146 games, 1961
Most homers, one month...13, Lewis R. Wilson, August, 1930
13, Ernest Banks, July, 1955
13, Ernest Banks, September, 1957
13, Ernest Banks, August, 1958
Most homers, league, righthanded batter ....512, Ernest Banks
Most homers, league, lefthanded batter.............................392, Billy L. Williams
Most homers with bases filled, season ....5, Ernest Banks, 154 games, 1955
Most homers with bases filled, league ....12, Ernest Banks
Most total bases ....423, Lewis R. Wilson, 155 games, 1930
Most total bases, league..4,706, Ernest Banks
Most long hits..97, Lewis R. Wilson, 155 games, 1930
Most long hits, league ....1,009, Ernest Banks
Most extra bases on long hits............................215, Lewis R. Wilson, 155 games, 1930
Most extra bases on long hits, league..2,123, Ernest Banks
Most sacrifices (S.H. and S.F.) .... 46, James T. Sheckard, 148 games, 1909
Most sacrifice hits...40, James T. Sheckard, 149 games, 1906
Most sacrifice flies ....14, Ronald E. Santo, 1969
Most stolen bases ....100, William A. Lange, 123 games, 1896
Most stolen bases since 1900...........................67, Frank L. Chance, 123 games, 1903
Most stolen bases, league..404, Frank L. Chance
Most caught stealing ....29, Charles J. Hollocher, 152 games, 1922
Most bases on balls...147, James T. Sheckard, 156 games, 1911

Most bases on balls, league..1,092, Stanley C. Hack
Most strikeouts ....143, Byron E. Browne, 120 games, 1966
Most strikeouts, league...1,271, Ronald E. Santo
Fewest strikeouts.................................5, Charles J. Hollocher, 152 games, 1922
Most hit by pitch..................................12, Adolfo E. Philips, 116 games, 1966
Most runs batted in ....190, Lewis R. Wilson, 155 games, 1930
Most runs batted in, league ....1,636, Ernest Banks
Most game-winning RBIs ....15, William J. Buckner, 161 games, 1982
Most consecutive games, one or more runs batted in, season—
                                        17, Oscar R. Grimes (22 RBIs), 1941
Highest batting average..............................388, Michael J. Kelly, 118 games, 1886
                                        .388, William A. Lange, 122 games, 1895
Highest batting average since 1900..........................380, Rogers Hornsby, 156 games, 1929
Highest batting average, league...339, Adrian C. Anson
Highest batting average, league, since 1900....................................336, J. Riggs Stephenson
Highest slugging average...723, Lewis R. Wilson, 155 games, 1930
Most consecutive games batted safely during season.................42, William F. Dahlen, 1894
Most consecutive games batted safely during season, since 1900—
                                        28, Ronald E. Santo, 1966
Most grounded into double play ....25, Ronald E. Santo, 154 games, 1961
Fewest grounded into double play ....0, August J. Galan, 154 games, 1935

Pitching, Since 1900

Most years, league...16, Charles H. Root
Most games ....84, Theodore W. Abernathy, 1965
                                        84, Richard W. Tidrow, 1980
Most games, league...605, Charles H. Root
Most games started...................................42, Ferguson A. Jenkins, 1969
Most games started, league ....339, Charles H. Root
Most complete games ....33, John W. Taylor, 1903
                                        33, Grover C. Alexander, 1920
Most complete games, league ....205, Mordecai P. Brown
Most games finished ....62, Theodore W. Abernathy, 1965
Most innings ....363, Grover C. Alexander, 1920
Most innings, league ....3,138, Charles H. Root
Most games won, season ....29, Mordecai P. Brown, 1908
Most games won, league ....201, Charles H. Root
Most years winning 20 or more games...6, Mordecai P. Brown
                                        6, Ferguson A. Jenkins
Most games lost...22, Thomas J. Hughes, 1901
                                        22, Richard C. Ellsworth, 1966
                                        22, William G. Bonham, 1974
Most games lost, league...156, Charles H. Root
Highest percentage games won, season........... .833, Leonard L. Cole (won 20, lost 4 in 1910)
Most consecutive games won, season...14, Edward M. Reulbach, 1909
Most consecutive games lost, season ....13, Robert L. McCall, 1948
Most saves, season ....37, H. Bruce Sutter, 1979
Most bases on balls...185, Samuel Jones, 1955
Most bases on balls, league ....871, Charles H. Root
Most strikeouts...274, Ferguson A. Jenkins, 1970
Most strikeouts, nine-inning game ....16, John G. Clarkson, August 18, 1886
Most strikeouts, nine-inning game, since 1900—
                                        15, Richard Drott, May 26, 1957, first game
                                        15, Burt C. Hooton, September 15, 1971, second game
Most strikeouts, extra-inning game—
                                        17, John T. Pfiester, May 30, 1906, first game, 15 innings
Most strikeouts, league...2,036, Ferguson A. Jenkins
Most shutouts, season ....9, Mordecai P. Brown, 1906, 1908
                                        9, Orval Overall, 1907, 1909
                                        9, Grover C. Alexander, 1919
                                        9, William C. Lee, 1938
Most shutouts, league...48, Mordecai P. Brown
Most 1-0 shutouts won, season ....3, held by many pitchers
Most runs...174, Guy T. Bush, 1930
Most earned runs..155, Guy T. Bush, 1930
Most hits..335, Grover C. Alexander, 1920
Most hit batsmen...20, James J. Callahan, 1900
Most wild pitches...26, Lawrence D. Cheney, 1914
Most home runs...38, Warren L. Hacker, 1955
Most sacrifice hits...23, William G. Bonham, 1974
Most sacrifice flies...14, Ricky E. Reuschel, 1980
Lowest earned-run average, season....................1.72, Grover Alexander, 235 innings, 1919

CINCINNATI REDS—(1876-1880; 1890 to date)

Batting

Most years, league, except pitchers..17, Johnny L. Bench
Most games ....163, Leonardo A. Cardenas, 1964
                                                                                     163, Peter E. Rose, 1974
Most games, league..2505, Peter E. Rose
Most at-bats...680, Peter E. Rose, 160 games, 1973
Most at-bats, league...10196, Peter E. Rose
Most runs...134, Frank Robinson, 162 games, 1962
Most runs, league ....1657, Peter E. Rose
Most hits...230, Peter E. Rose, 160 games, 1973
Most hits, league...3164, Peter E. Rose
Most singles...181, Peter E. Rose, 160 games, 1973
Most singles, league ....2331, Peter E. Rose
Most doubles ....51, Frank Robinson, 162 games, 1962
                                                                                     51, Peter E. Rose, 159 games, 1978
Most doubles, league...572, Peter E. Rose
Most triples..25, John A. McPhee, 132 games, 1890
Most triples since 1900 .... 23, Samuel Crawford, 140 games, 1902
Most triples, league..153, Edd J. Roush
Most homers, lefthanded batter......................49, Theodore B. Kluszewski, 149 games, 1954
Most homers, righthanded batter................52, George A. Foster, 158 games, 1977
Most homers, league, righthanded batter ....389, Johnny L. Bench
Most homers, league, lefthanded batter ....251, Theodore B. Kluszewski
Most homers, rookie season...........................38, Frank Robinson, 152 games, 1956
Most homers, season, at home, righthanded batter ....30, Johnny L. Bench, 1970
Most homers, season, at home, lefthanded batter ....34, Theodore B. Kluszewski, 1954
Most homers, season, on road ....31, George A. Foster, 1977
Most homers, one month ....14, Frank Robinson, August, 1962
Most homers with bases filled, season ....3, Frank Robinson, 162 games, 1962
                                                                                     3, Lee A. May, 153 games, 1970
                                                                                     3, C. Ray Knight, 162 games, 1980
Most homers with bases filled, league...11, Johnny L. Bench
Most total bases..388, George A. Foster, 158 games, 1977
Most total bases, league...4408, Peter E. Rose
Most long hits...92, Frank Robinson, 162 games, 1962
Most long hits, league ....833, Peter E. Rose
Most extra bases on long hits ....191, George A. Foster, 158 games, 1977
Most extra bases on long hits, league ....1596, Johnny L. Bench
Most sacrifices (S. H. and S. F.) .... 39, Jacob E. Daubert, 140 games, 1919
Most sacrifice hits ....31, Roy D. McMillan, 154 games, 1954
Most sacrifice flies ....13, John E. Temple, 149 games, 1959
Most stolen bases...93, W. Arlie Latham, 135 games, 1891
Most stolen bases since 1900........................ 81, Robert H. Bescher, 153 games, 1911
Most stolen bases, league...406, Joe L. Morgan
Most caught stealing.....................................28, Louis B. Duncan, 151 games, 1922
Most bases on balls.......................................132, Joe L. Morgan, 146 games, 1975
Most bases on balls, league...1085, Peter E. Rose
Most strikeouts...142, Lee A. May, 158 games, 1969
Most strikeouts, league..1278, Johnny L. Bench
Fewest strikeouts ....13, Frank A. McCormick, 154 games, 1941
Most hit by pitch...20, Frank Robinson, 152 games, 1956
Most runs batted in.......................................149, George A. Foster, 158 games, 1977
Most runs batted in, league..1376, Johnny L. Bench
Most game-winning RBIs ....16, George A. Foster, 144 games, 1980
Highest batting average................................. .383, John W. Holliday, 122 games, 1894
Highest batting average since 1900................... .377, J. Bentley Seymour, 149 games, 1905
Highest batting average, league .... .331, Edd J. Roush
Highest slugging average, righthanded batter .... .631, George A. Foster, 158 games, 1977
Highest slugging average, lefthanded batter—
                                 .642, Theodore B. Kluszewski, 149 games, 1954
Most consecutive games batted safely during season........................44, Peter E. Rose, 1978
Most grounded into double play ....30, Ernest N. Lombardi, 129 games, 1938
Fewest grounded into double play ....3, William H. Myers, 151 games, 1939
                                                                                     3, Joe L. Morgan, 146 games, 1975

Pitching, Since 1900

Most years, league..15, Joseph H. Nuxhall
Most games...90, Wayne A. Granger, 1969
Most games, league..531, Pedro Borbon
Most games started..42, Frank Hahn, 1901
Most games started, league .... .356, Eppa Rixey

Most complete games ....41, Frank Hahn, 1901
Most complete games, league ....195, William H. Walters
Most games finished ....62, Thomas H. Hume, 1980
Most innings...375, Frank Hahn, 1901
Most innings, league ....2890, Eppa Rixey
Most games won, season...27, Adolfo Luque, 1923
                                                                             27, William H. Walters, 1939
Most games won, league ....179, Eppa Rixey
Most years winning 20 or more games ....4, Paul M. Derringer
Most games lost..25, Paul M. Derringer, 1933
Most games lost, league...150, Paul M. Derringer
Highest percentage games won, season ..... .875, G. Thomas Seaver (won 14, lost 2 in 1981)
Most consecutive games won, season ....16, Ewell Blackwell, 1947
Most consecutive games lost, season ....12, Henry Thielman, 1902
                                                                             12, Peter J. Schneider, 1914
                                                                             12, Silas K. Johnson, 1933
Most saves, season ....37, Clay P. Carroll, 1972
Most bases on balls...162, John S. Vander Meer, 1943
Most bases on balls, league ....1072, John S. Vander Meer
Most strikeouts ....274, Mario M. Soto, 1982
Most strikeouts, nine-inning game ....16, Frank G. Hahn, May 22, 1901
                                                                             16, James W. Maloney, May 21, 1963
Most strikeouts, extra-inning game ....18, James W. Maloney, June 14, 1965, 11 innings
Most strikeouts, league...1592, James W. Maloney
Most shutouts..7, Jacob Weimer, 1906
                                                                             7, Fred A. Toney, 1917
                                                                             7, Horace O. Eller, 1919
                                                                             7, John E. Billingham, 1973
Most shutouts, league ....32, William H. Walters
Most 1-0 shutouts won..4, Jacob Weimer, 1906
Most runs...158, Frank Hahn, 1901
Most earned runs...145, Herman R. Wehmeier, 1950
Most hits...368, Frank Hahn, 1901
Most hit batsmen ....23, Jacob Weimer, 1907
Most wild pitches ....19, James W. Maloney, 1963
                                                                             19, James W. Maloney, 1965
Most home runs..35, Samuel, J. Ellis, 1966
Most sacrifice hits...17, Joseph R. Jay, 1962
Most sacrifice flies ....12, G. Thomas Seaver, 1978
Lowest earned-run average, season.....................1.81, Walter H. Ruether, 243 innings, 1919

HOUSTON ASTROS—(1962 to date)

Batting

Most years, league, except pitchers...14, Robert J. Watson
Most games ....162, Enos M. Cabell, 1978
Most games, league ....1512, Cesar Cedeno
Most at-bats ....660, Enos M. Cabell, 162 games, 1978
Most at-bats, league...5732, Cesar Cedeno
Most runs...117, James S. Wynn, 145 games, 1972
Most runs, league..890, Cesar Cedeno
Most hits...195, Enos M. Cabell, 162 games, 1978
Most hits, league ....1659, Cesar Cedeno
Most singles..160, Roland T. Jackson, 150 games, 1966
Most singles, league..1098, Cesar Cedeno
Most doubles...44, Daniel J. Staub, 149 games, 1967
Most doubles, league..343, Cesar Cedeno
Most triples ....14, Roger T. Metzger, 154 games, 1973
Most triples, league ....63, Joe L. Morgan
Most homers, righthanded batter..................................37, James S. Wynn, 158 games, 1967
Most homers, league, righthanded batter ....223, James S. Wynn
Most homers, lefthanded batter......................................20, Walter J. Bond, 148 games, 1964
Most homers, league, lefthanded batter ....96, Jose Cruz
Most homers, season, at home...18, Lee A. May, 1974
Most homers, season, on road..22, James S. Wynn, 1967
Most homers, one month ....11, James S. Wynn, June, 1967
                                                                             11, James S. Wynn, May, 1969
Most homers, rookie season ....14, Joe L. Morgan, 157 games, 1965
Most home runs, with bases filled, season—
                              2, Robert T. Aspromonte, 136 games, 1963, 157 games, 1964, 152 games, 1966
                                              2, Robert J. Watson, 97 games, 1970
                                              2, Lee A. May, 148 games, 1973

Most home runs, with bases filled, league ....6, Robert T. Aspromonte
Most homers, pinch-hitter, season ....5, Clifford Johnson, 1974
Most total bases..300, Cesar Cedeno, 139 games, 1972
Most total bases, league...2601, Cesar Cedeno
Most long hits ....69, James S. Wynn, 158 games, 1967
                                        69, Cesar Cedeno, 139 games, 1972
Most long hits, league ....561, Cesar Cedeno
Most extra bases on long hits...........................146, James S. Wynn, 158 games, 1967
Most extra bases on long hits, league.................................961, James S. Wynn
Most sacrifice hits.............................34, G. Craig Reynolds, 146 games, 1979
Most sacrifice flies............................13, C. Ray Knight, 158 games, 1982
Most stolen bases..............................61, Cesar Cedeno, 141 games, 1977
Most stolen bases, league...487, Cesar Cedeno
Most caught stealing ....23, Jose D. Cruz, 157 games, 1977
Most bases on balls ....148, James S. Wynn, 149 games, 1969
Most bases on balls, league...847, James S. Wynn
Most strikeouts.............................145, Lee A. May, 148 games, 1972
Most strikeouts, league ....1088, James S. Wynn
Fewest strikeouts, season ....39, Gregory E. Gross, 156 games, 1974
Most hit by pitch..............................11, Cesar Cedeno, 141 games, 1977
Most runs batted in ....110, Robert J. Watson, 151 games, 1977
Most runs batted in, league...782, Robert J. Watson
Most game-winning RBIs ....18, Richard W. Thon, 154 games, 1983
Highest batting average.................................333, Daniel J. Staub, 149 games, 1967
Highest batting average, league ....297, Robert J. Watson
Highest slugging average ....537, Cesar Cedeno, 139 games, 1972
                                    .537, Cesar Cedeno, 139 games, 1973
Most consecutive games batted safely during season ....23, Arthur H. Howe, 1981
Most grounded into double play ....23, Douglas L. Rader, 156 games, 1970
Fewest grounded into double play ....4, Joe L. Morgan, 157 games, 1965
                                    4, Joe L. Morgan, 160 games, 1971
                                    4, Jose Cruz, 160 games, 1983
                                    4, Philip M. Garner, 154 games, 1983

Pitching

Most years, pitched..13, Lawrence E. Dierker
Most games, lefthander ....64, Joseph C. Sambito, 1980
Most games, righthander..70, Kenneth R. Forsch, 1974
Most games, league ....421, Kenneth R. Forsch
Most games started...40, Jerry Reuss, 1973
Most games started, league..320, Lawrence E. Dierker
Most complete games...............................20, Lawrence E. Dierker, 1969
Most complete games, league..106, Lawrence E. Dierker
Most games finished...............................51, Joseph C. Sambito, 1979
Most innings...............................305, Lawrence E. Dierker, 1969
Most innings, league...2296, Lawrence E. Dierker
Most games won, season ....21, Joseph F. Niekro, 1979
Most games won, league...137, Lawrence E. Dierker
Most years winning, 20 or more games ....2, Joseph F. Niekro
Most games lost, season ....20, Richard J. Farrell, 1962
Most games lost, league...117, Lawrence E. Dierker
Highest percentage games won, season .... .656, Joseph F. Niekro (won 21, lost 11), 1979
Most consecutive games won, season ....9, Joseph F. Niekro, 1979
Most consecutive games lost, season ....11, Richard F. Drott, 1963
Most saves, season.......................................29, Fred E. Gladding, 1969
Most bases on balls...............................151, James R. Richard, 1976
Most bases on balls, league...770, James R. Richard
Most strikeouts ....313, James R. Richard, 1979
Most strikeouts, league...1493, James R. Richard
Most strikeouts, nine-inning game ....18, Donald E. Wilson, July 14, 1968, second game
Most shutouts...6, David A. Roberts, 1973
Most shutouts won, league...25, Lawrence E. Dierker
Most 1-0 shutouts won ....3, Robert J. Bruce, 1964
                                    3. Robert W. Knepper, 1981
Most runs...............................124, Lawrence E. Dierker, 1970
Most earned runs ....116, Lawrence E. Dierker, 1970
                                    116, Jerry Reuss, 1973
Most hits...............................271, Jerry Reuss, 1973
Most hit batsmen ....16, John E. Billingham, 1971
Most wild pitches ....20, Lawrence E. Dierker, 1968
                                    20, James R. Richard, 1975
Most home runs allowed...............................31, Lawrence E. Dierker, 1970
Most sacrifice hits allowed...............................16, Lawrence E. Dierker, 1968
                                    16, Mark Lemongello, 1978

Most sacrifice flies allowed...13, Mark Lemongello, 1978
Lowest earned-run average, season ....2.22, Miguel A. Cuellar, 227 innings, 1966

LOS ANGELES DODGERS—(1958 to date)
(See Brooklyn Dodgers for club's records prior to franchise transfer in 1958)
Batting

Most years, league, except pitchers ....15, William E. Russell
Most games...165, Maurice M. Wills, 1962
Most games, league...1952, William H. Davis
Most at-bats...695, Maurice M. Wills, 165 games, 1962
Most at-bats, league...7495, William H. Davis
Most runs...130, Maurice M. Wills, 165 games, 1962
Most runs, league...1004, William H. Davis
Most hits...230, H. Thomas Davis, 163 games, 1962
Most hits, league...2091, William H. Davis
Most singles...179, Maurice M. Wills, 165 games, 1962
Most singles, league...1509, Maurice M. Wills
Most doubles...47, M. Wesley Parker, 161 games, 1970
Most doubles, league...333, Steven P. Garvey
Most triples...16, William H. Davis, 146 games, 1970
Most triples, league...110, William H. Davis
Most homers, righthanded batter ....33, Steven P. Garvey, 162 games, 1977
Most homers, lefthanded batter.................................27, C. Reginald Smith, 148 games, 1977
Most homers, switch-hitter.............................32, C. Reginald Smith, 148 games, 1977
Most homers, one month...12, Frank O. Howard, July, 1962
Most homers, rookie season ....23, Frank O. Howard, 117 games, 1960
Most homers, league, righthanded batter...228, Ronald C. Cey
Most homers, league, lefthanded batter ....154, William H. Davis
Most homers, season, at home..20, Steven P. Garvey, 1979
Most homers, season, on road ....18, Frank O. Howard, 1962
Most homers with bases filled, season ....2, Frank O. Howard, 117 games, 1960
                                                                                         2, Ronald C. Cey, 153 games, 1977
                                                                                         2, Steven P. Garvey, 162 games, 1977
Most homers with bases filled, league ....5, Ronald C. Cey
Most total bases...356, H. Thomas Davis, 163 games, 1962
Most total bases, league...3094, William H. Davis
Most long hits...66, Steven P. Garvey, 162 games, 1978
Most long hits, league...585, William H. Davis
Most extra bases on long hits.........................133, Pedro Guerrero, 150 games, 1982
Most extra bases on long hits, league...1036, Steven P. Garvey
Most sacrifice hits...21, Charles L. Neal, 151 games, 1959
Most sacrifice flies...13, C. Reginald Smith, 128 games, 1978
Most stolen bases ....104, Maurice M. Wills, 165 games, 1962
Most stolen bases, league...490, Maurice M. Wills
Most caught stealing...31, Maurice M. Wills, 158 games, 1965
Most bases on balls...110, James S. Wynn, 130 games, 1975
Most bases on balls, league ....765, Ronald C. Cey
Most strikeouts ....149, Billy Grabarkewitz, 156 games, 1970
Most strikeouts, league ....838, Ronald C. Cey
Fewest strikeouts...28, James Gilliam, 151 games, 1960
Most hit by pitch...16, Louis B. Johnson, 131 games, 1965
Most runs batted in ....153, H. Thomas Davis, 163 games, 1962
Most runs batted in, league ....992, Steven P. Garvey
Most game-winning RBIs ....18, Pedro Guerrero, 150 games, 1982
Highest batting average, righthanded batter .... .346, H. Thomas Davis, 163 games, 1962
Highest batting average, lefthanded batter .... .328, Wallace W. Moon, 134 games, 1961
Most consecutive games batted safely, during season ....31, William H. Davis, 1969
Highest slugging average, righthanded batter ..... .560, Frank O. Howard, 141 games, 1962
Highest slugging average, lefthanded batter.......... .535, Edwin D. Snider, 126 games, 1959
Highest slugging average, switch-hitter .... .576, C. Reginald Smith, 148 games, 1977
Most grounded into double play.............................25, Steven P. Garvey, 162 games, 1979
Fewest grounded into double play ....3, William H. Davis, 160 games, 1968
                                                                                         3, David E. Lopes, 134 games, 1977

Pitching

Most years, league...15, Donald H. Sutton
Most games, league...534, Donald H. Sutton
Most games, righthander...106, Michael G. Marshall, 1974
Most games, lefthander...72, Ronald P. Perranoski, 1964

Most games, started...42, Donald S. Drysdale, 1963
                                                                        42, Donald S. Drysdale, 1965
Most games, started, league...517, Donald H. Sutton
Most complete games...27, Sanford Koufax, 1965
                                                                        27, Sanford Koufax, 1966
Most complete games, league ....156, Donald S. Drysdale,
                                                                        156, Donald H. Sutton
Most games finished, righthander..83, Michael G. Marshall, 1974
Most games finished, lefthander ....52, Ronald P. Perranoski, 1964
Most innings...336, Sanford Koufax, 1965
Most innings, league..3728, Donald H. Sutton
Most games won, season, righthander...........................25, Donald S. Drysdale, 1962
Most games won, season, lefthander ....27, Sandy Koufax, 1966
Most games won, league, righthander ....230, Donald H. Sutton
Most games won, league, lefthander ....156, Sanford Koufax
Most years winning 20 or more games..3, Sanford Koufax
Most games lost, league..175, Donald H. Sutton
Most games lost, season..18, Claude W. Osteen, 1968
Highest percentage games won, season.... .842, Ronald P. Perranoski (won 16, lost 3), 1963
Most consecutive games won, season ....13, Philip R. Regan, 1966
Most consecutive games lost, season...7, David A. Goltz, 1981
Most saves, season...24, James T. Brewer, 1970
Most bases on balls, season ....108, Stanley W. Williams, 1961
Most bases on balls, league..966, Donald H. Sutton
Most strikeouts, righthander..251, Donald S. Drysdale, 1963
Most strikeouts, lefthander ....382, Sanford Koufax, 1965
Most strikeouts, nine-inning game ....18, Sanford Koufax, August 31, 1959
                                                                        18, Sanford Koufax, April 24, 1962
Most strikeouts, league...2652, Donald H. Sutton
Most shutouts, season ....11, Sanford Koufax, 1963
Most shutouts, league..52, Donald H. Sutton
Most 1-0 shutouts won..4, Donald S. Drysdale, 1968
Most hits..298, Claude W. Osteen, 1967
Most runs...127, Donald H. Sutton, 1970
Most earned runs ....118, Donald H. Sutton, 1970
Most home runs..38, Donald H. Sutton, 1970
Most hit batsmen...20, Donald S. Drysdale, 1961
Most wild pitches...17, Sanford Koufax, 1958
Most sacrifice hits ....27, Fernando Valenzuela, 1983
Most sacrifice flies ....11, Burt C. Hooton, 1979
Lowest earned-run average...1.73, Sanford Koufax, 323 innings, 1966

MILWAUKEE BRAVES—(1953 through 1965)
(See Boston Braves for club's records prior to franchise transfer in 1953)
Batting

Most years, league, except pitchers...13, Edwin L. Mathews
Most games...161, Henry L. Aaron, 1963
Most games, league ....1944, Edwin L. Mathews (2089 including Boston)
Most at-bats..636, William H. Bruton, 149 games, 1955
Most at-bats, league...7080, Henry L. Aaron
Most runs...127, Henry L. Aaron, 156 games, 1962
Most runs, league...1300, Edwin L. Mathews (1380 including Boston)
Most hits ....223, Henry L. Aaron, 154 games, 1959
Most hits, league ....2266, Henry L. Aaron
Most singles...132, Joseph P. Torre, 154 games, 1964
Most doubles...46, Henry L. Aaron, 154 games, 1959
Most doubles, league ....391, Henry L. Aaron
Most triples ....15, William H. Bruton, 147 games, 1956
Most triples, league ....80, Henry L. Aaron
Most homers, lefthanded batter...............................47, Edwin L. Mathews, 157 games, 1953
Most homers, righthanded batter...................................45, Henry L. Aaron, 156 games, 1962
Most home runs, one month, righthanded batter..............15, Joseph W. Adcock, July, 1956
Most home runs, one month, lefthanded batter................13, Edwin L. Mathews, July, 1954
Most homers, rookie season ....22, Ricardo A. Carty, 133 games, 1964
Most homers, season, at home ....23, Joseph W. Adcock, 1956
                                                                        23, Edwin L. Mathews, 1960
Most homers, season, on road ....30, Edwin L. Mathews, 1953
Most homers, league...452, Edwin L. Mathews (477 including Boston)
Most homers with bases filled, season ....3, Delmar W. Crandall, 133 games, 1955
                                                                        3, Henry L. Aaron, 156 games, 1962

Most homers with bases filled, league..9, Henry L. Aaron
Most total bases..400, Henry L. Aaron, 154 games, 1959
Most total bases, league...4011, Henry L. Aaron
Most long hits..92, Henry L. Aaron, 154 games, 1959
Most extra bases on long hits ....188, Edwin L. Mathews, 157 games, 1953
Most sacrifice hits..31, John Logan, 148 games, 1956
Most sacrifice flies ....12, Henry L. Aaron, 153 games, 1960
                                                                   12, Delmar W. Crandall, 142 games, 1960
Most stolen bases...34, William H. Bruton, 142 games, 1954
Most caught stealing ....13, William H. Bruton, 142 games, 1954
Most bases on balls..124, Edwin L. Mathews, 158 games, 1963
Most strikeouts...122, Mack Jones, 122 games, 1965
Fewest strikeouts..33, John Logan, 150 games, 1953
Most hit by pitch..9, Frank J. Torre, 129 games, 1957
                                                                   9, Mack Jones, 122 games, 1965
Most runs batted in ....135, Edwin L. Mathews, 157 games, 1953
Most runs batted in, league...1305, Henry L. Aaron
Highest batting average, lefthanded batter ....306, Edwin L. Mathews, 148 games, 1959
                                                                   .306, Edwin L. Mathews, 152 games, 1961
Highest batting average, righthanded batter ....355, Henry L. Aaron, 154 games, 1959
Highest batting average, league ....320, Henry L. Aaron
Highest slugging average.. .636, Henry L. Aaron, 154 games, 1959
Most consecutive games batted safely during season ....25, Henry L. Aaron, 1956
                                                                   25, Henry L. Aaron, 1962
Most grounded into double play ....26, Joseph P. Torre, 154 games, 1964
Fewest grounded into double play ....4, Edwin L. Mathews, 151 games, 1956
                                                                   4, William H. Bruton, 151 games, 1960

Pitching

Most years, league ....12, Warren E. Spahn
Most games...62, William O. O'Dell, 1965
Most games, started..39, S. Lewis Burdette, 1959
Most complete games...24, Warren E. Spahn, 1953
Most games finished..49, Donald J. McMahon, 1959
Most innings..292, Warren E. Spahn, 1959
Most games won, season, righthander..24, Tony L. Cloninger, 1965
Most games won, season, lefthander ....23, Warren E. Spahn, 1953
                                                                   23, Warren E. Spahn, 1963
Most games won, league..........................234, Warren E. Spahn (356 including Boston)
Most years winning 20 or more games................9, Warren E. Spahn (13 including Boston)
Most games lost, season ....15, S. Lewis Burdette, 1959
                                                                   15, Warren E. Spahn, 1959
Most games lost, league ....138, Warren E. Spahn (229 including Boston)
Highest percentage games won, season ....767, Warren E. Spahn (won 23, lost 7 in 1953)
                                                                   .767, Warren E. Spahn (won 23, lost 7 in 1963)
Most consecutive games won, season ....11, Warren E. Spahn, 1954
Most bases on balls ....121, Robert R. Buhl, 1957
Most strikeouts, season...211, Tony L. Cloninger, 1965
Most strikeouts, nine-inning game........................15, Warren E. Spahn, September 16, 1960
Most shutouts, season...7, Warren E. Spahn, 1963
Most shutouts, league...................................36, Warren E. Spahn (63 including Boston)
Most runs...144, S. Lewis Burdette, 1959
Most earned runs...131, S. Lewis Burdette, 1959
Most hits...312, S. Lewis Burdette, 1959
Most hit batsmen...12, Robert J. Shaw, 1962
Most wild pitches..22, Tony L. Cloninger, 1965
Most home runs...38, S. Lewis Burdette, 1959
Lowest earned-run average, season ....2.10, Warren E. Spahn, 266 innings, 1953

MONTREAL EXPOS—(1969 to date)

Batting

Most years, league, except pitchers..10, Gary E. Carter
Most games ....162, Daniel J. Staub, 1971
                                                                   162, Kenneth W. Singleton, 1973
                                                                   162, Warren L. Cromartie, 1980
Most games, league ....1249, Gary E. Carter
Most at-bats..659, Warren L. Cromartie, 158 games, 1979
Most at-bats, league..4422, Gary E. Carter
Most runs ....133, Timothy Raines, 156 games, 1983
Most runs, league ....625, Andre F. Dawson

Most hits...204, Albert Oliver, 160 games, 1982
Most hits, league ....1190, Gary E. Carter
Most singles ....139, David Cash, 153 games, 1977
Most singles, league..756, Gary E. Carter
Most doubles ....46, Warren L. Cromartie, 158 games, 1979
Most doubles, league ....224, Gary E. Carter
Most triples...13, Rodney D. Scott, 154 games, 1980
Most triples, league ....57, Andre F. Dawson
Most homers, lefthanded batter ....30, Daniel J. Staub, 160 games, 1970
Most homers, righthanded batter ....32, Andre F. Dawson, 159 games, 1983
Most homers, league, righthanded batter ....188, Gary E. Carter
Most homers, league, lefthanded batter...86, Ronald R. Fairly
Most homers, rookie season........................19, Andre F. Dawson, 139 games, 1977
Most homers, one month ....12, Daniel J. Staub, August, 1970
Most homers, season, at home ....22, Gary E. Carter, 1977
Most homers, season on road ....22, Andre F. Dawson, 1983
Most homers, with bases filled, season ....2, Held by many players
Most homers with bases filled, league ....6, Gary E. Carter
Most total bases.....................................341, Andre F. Dawson, 159 games, 1983
Most total bases, league...2022, Gary E. Carter
Most long hits, season ....78, Andre F. Dawson, 159 games, 1983
Most long hits, league ....435, Andre F. Dawson
Most extra bases on long hits ....152, Andre F. Dawson, 159 games, 1983
Most extra bases on long hits, league...............................832, Gary E. Carter
Most sacrifice hits ....23, Larry Lintz, 113 games, 1974
Most sacrifice flies ....18, Andre F. Dawson, 159 games, 1983
Most stolen bases...97, Ronald LeFlore, 139 games, 1980
Most stolen bases, league...246, Timothy Raines
Most caught stealing ....19, Ronald LeFlore, 139 games, 1980
Most bases on balls...........................123, Kenneth W. Singleton, 162 games, 1973
Most bases on balls, league ....502, Robert S. Bailey
Most strikeouts..............................128, Andre F. Dawson, 157 games, 1978
Most strikeouts, league..612, Larry A. Parrish
Fewest strikeouts ....29, David Cash, 159 games, 1978
Most hit by pitch ....50, Ronald K. Hunt, 152 games, 1971
Most runs batted in.........................113, Andre F. Dawson, 159 games, 1983
Most runs batted in, league...688, Gary E. Carter
Most game-winning RBIs................................17, Andre F. Dawson, 151 games, 1980
Highest batting average.. .331, Albert Oliver, 160 games, 1982
Highest batting average, league..................................... .288, Ellis C. Valentine
Highest slugging average, season .... .551, Larry A. Parrish, 153 games, 1979
Most consecutive games batted safely during season............19, Warren L. Cromartie, 1979
                                                    19, Andre F. Dawson, 1980
Most grounded into double play ....27, John A. Bateman, 139 games, 1971
                                                    27, Kenneth W. Singleton, 162 games, 1973
Fewest grounded into double play ....1, Ronald K. Hunt, 152 games, 1971

Pitching

Most years, league ....11, Stephen D. Rogers
Most games ....92, Michael G. Marshall, 1973
Most games, league ....360, Stephen D. Rogers
Most games started...40, Stephen D. Rogers, 1977
Most games started, league..358, Stephen D. Rogers
Most complete games...20, William H. Stoneman, 1971
Most complete games, league ....127, Stephen D. Rogers
Most games finished ....73, Michael G. Marshall, 1973
Most innings..302, Stephen D. Rogers, 1977
Most innings, league..2632, Stephen D. Rogers
Most games won...20, Ross A. Grimsley, 1978
Most games won, league...150, Stephen D. Rogers
Most years winning 20 or more games.......................................1, Ross A. Grimsley
Most games lost ....22, Stephen D. Rogers, 1974
Most games lost, league ....133, Stephen D. Rogers
Highest percentage games, won, season .... .704, Stephen D. Rogers (won 19, lost 8 in 1982)
Most consecutive games won, season...................................8, David W. Palmer, 1979
                                                    8, Charles W. Lea, 1983
Most consecutive games lost, season ....10, Steven Renko, 1972
Most saves ....31, Michael G. Marshall, 1973
Most bases on balls...............................146, William H. Stoneman, 1971
Most bases on balls, league...778, Stephen D. Rogers
Most strikeouts..251, William H. Stoneman, 1971

Most strikeouts, league...1539, Stephen D. Rogers
Most strikeouts, game......................................18, William L. Gullickson, September 10, 1980
Most shutouts won...5, William H. Stoneman, 1969
5, Stephen D. Rogers, 1979, 1983
Most shutouts won, league...37, Stephen D. Rogers
Most 1-0 shutouts won..2, Carl W. Morton, 1970
2, William H. Stoneman, 1972
2, Scott D. Sanderson, 1980
Most runs..139, Stephen D. Rogers, 1974
Most earned runs ....126, Stephen D. Rogers, 1974
Most hits..281, Carl W. Morton, 1970
Most wild pitches..19, Steven Renko, 1974
Most hit batsmen..14, William H. Stoneman, 1970
Most home runs..27, Carl W. Morton, 1970
27, Steven Renko, 1970
Most sacrifice hits...21, Stephen D. Rogers, 1979
Most sacrifice flies...11, Woodrow T. Fryman, 1976
Lowest earned-run average, season.....................2.40, Stephen D. Rogers, 277 innings, 1982

NEW YORK GIANTS—(1883 through 1957)
(See San Francisco Giants for club's records since franchise transfer in 1958)
Batting

Most years, league, except pitchers..22, Melvin T. Ott
Most games..157, Arthur Devlin, 1908
Most games, league ....2730, Melvin T. Ott
Most at-bats...681, Joseph G. Moore, 155 games, 1935
Most at-bats, league..9456, Melvin T. Ott
Most runs..146, Michael J. Tiernan, 122 games, 1889
Most runs, league...1859, Melvin T. Ott
Most runs, since 1900 .... 139, William H. Terry, 154 games, 1930
Most hits...254, William H. Terry, 154 games, 1930
Most hits, league...2876, Melvin T. Ott
Most singles...177, William H. Terry, 154 games, 1930
Most singles, league..1805, Melvin T. Ott
Most doubles...43, William H. Terry, 153 games, 1931
Most doubles, league ....488, Melvin T. Ott
Most triples...26, George S. Davis, 133 games, 1893
Most triples since 1900 .... 25, Lawrence J. Doyle, 141 games, 1911
Most triples, league ....159, Michael J. Tiernan
Most triples, league, since 1900 ....117, Lawrence J. Doyle
Most homers, lefthanded batter ....51, John R. Mize, 154 games, 1947
Most homers, righthanded batter ....51, Willie H. Mays, 152 games, 1955
Most home runs, one month....................................13, W. Walker Cooper, June, 1947
13, John R. Mize, August, 1947
13, Willie H. Mays, July, 1955
Most homers, season, at home...29, John R. Mize, 1947
Most homers, season, on road..29, Willie H. Mays, 1955
Most home runs, rookie season....................................29, Robert B. Thomson, 138 games, 1947
Most home runs, league, lefthanded batter......................................511, Melvin T. Ott
Most home runs, league, righthanded batter ....187, Willie H. Mays
Most homers with bases filled, season ....3, George L. Kelly, 149 games, 1921
3, Sidney Gordon, 142 games, 1948
3, Wesley N. Westrum, 124 games, 1951
Most homers with bases filled, league..7, George L. Kelly
7, Melvin T. Ott
Most total bases ....392, William H. Terry, 154 games, 1930
Most total bases, league...5041, Melvin T. Ott
Most long hits, lefthanded batter................................81, Melvin T. Ott, 150 games, 1929
Most long hits, righthanded batter ....87, Willie H. Mays, 151 games, 1954
Most long hits, league..1071, Melvin T. Ott
Most extra bases on long hits, lefthanded batter.............183, John R. Mize, 154 games, 1947
Most extra bases on long hits, righthanded batter.......197, Willie H. Mays, 152 games, 1955
Most extra bases on long hits, league ....2165, Melvin T. Ott
Most sacrifice hits..36, Arthur Devlin, 143 games, 1907
Most sacrifice flies, season...................................8, Donald F. Mueller, 153 games, 1954
8, Henry C. Thompson, 135 games, 1955
Most stolen bases..111, John M. Ward, 129 games, 1887
Most stolen bases since 1900..62, George J. Burns, 154 games, 1914
Most stolen bases, league ....334, George J. Burns
Most caught stealing..22, George J. Burns, 154 games, 1920

Most bases on balls ....144, Edward R. Stanky, 152 games, 1950
Most strikeouts..93, Wesley N. Westrum, 124 games, 1951
Fewest strikeouts..12, Frank F. Frisch, 151 games, 1923
Most hit by pitch...19, Arthur Fletcher, 151 games, 1917
Most runs batted in ....151, Melvin T. Ott, 150 games, 1929
Most runs batted in, league...1860, Melvin T. Ott
Most consecutive games, one or more runs batted in, season—
                                                         11, Melvin T. Ott (27 RBIs), 1929
Highest batting average .... .401, William H. Terry, 154 games, 1930
Highest batting average, league .... .341, William H. Terry
Highest slugging average, lefthanded batter .... .635, Melvin T. Ott, 150 games, 1929
Highest slugging average, righthanded batter .... .667, Willie H. Mays, 151 games, 1954
Highest slugging average, league.. .593, Willie H. Mays
Most consecutive games batted safely, during season ....33, George S. Davis, 1893
Most consecutive games batted safely during season since 1900—
                                                         24, Fred C. Lindstrom, 1930
                                                         24, Donald F. Mueller, 1955
Most grounded into double play ....26, William F. Jurges, 138 games, 1939
                                                         26, Sidney Gordon, 131 games, 1943
Fewest grounded into double play....................................3, Joseph G. Moore, 152 games, 1936

Pitching, Since 1900

Most years, league..17, Christopher Mathewson
Most games..71, J. Hoyt Wilhelm, 1952
Most games, league ....634, Christopher Mathewson
Most games started ....48, Joseph J. McGinnity, 1903
Most complete games...44, Joseph J. McGinnity, 1903
Most games finished ....52, Ace T. Adams, 1943
Most innings...434, Joseph J. McGinnity, 1903
Most games won, season..37, Christopher Mathewson, 1908
Most games won, league...372, Christopher Mathewson
Most years winning 20 or more games ....13, Christopher Mathewson
Most games lost...27, Luther H. Taylor, 1901
Most games lost, league..188, Christopher Mathewson
Highest percentage games won, season, righthander—
                                       .833, J. Hoyt Wilhelm (won 15, lost 3 in 1952)
Highest percentage games won, season, lefthander—
                                       .813, Carl O. Hubbell (won 26, lost 6 in 1936)
Most consecutive games won, season ....19, Richard W. Marquard, 1912
Most consecutive games lost, season ....12, Richard W. Marquard, 1914
Most bases on balls...128, Charles M. Tesreau, 1914
Most bases on balls, league ....902, Harold H. Schumacher
Most strikeouts...267, Christopher Mathewson, 1903
Most strikeouts, nine-inning game...................16, Christopher Mathewson, October 3, 1904
Most strikeouts, league...2502, Christopher Mathewson
Most shutouts ....12, Christopher Mathewson, 1908
Most shutouts, league...83, Christopher Mathewson
Most 1-0 shutouts won ....5, Carl O. Hubbell, 1933
Most runs ....224, William M. Carrick, 1900
Most earned runs ....117, Fred L. Fitzsimmons, 1932
Most hits..415, William M. Carrick, 1900
Most hit batsmen ....36, Edward R. Doheny, 1899
Most wild pitches ....30, Leon K. Ames, 1905
Most home runs ....36, Lawrence J. Jansen, 1949
Lowest earned-run average, season ....1.66, Carl O. Hubbell, 309 innings, 1933

NEW YORK METS—(1962 to date)
(Includes records only of present franchise established in 1962)
Batting

Most years, league, except pitchers................................. 18, Edward E. Kranepool
Most games... 162, Felix B. Millan, 1975
Most games, league .... 1,853, Edward E. Kranepool
Most at-bats .... 676, Felix B. Millan, 162 games, 1975
Most at-bats, league .... 5,436, Edward E. Kranepool
Most runs .... 107, Tommie L. Agee, 153 games, 1970
Most runs, league... 563, Cleon J. Jones
Most hits.. 191, Felix B. Millan, 162 games, 1975
Most hits, league .... 1,418, Edward E. Kranepool
Most singles .... 155, Felix B. Millan, 153 games, 1973
Most singles, league .... 1,050, Edward E. Kranepool

Most doubles.. 37, Felix B. Millan, 162 games, 1975
37, Joel R. Youngblood, 158 games, 1979
Most doubles, league .... 225, Edward E. Kranepool
Most triples.. 9, Charles L. Neal, 136 games, 1962
9, Stephen C. Henderson, 157 games, 1978
9, Franklin Taveras, 153 games, 1979
9, William H. Wilson, 159 games, 1982
Most triples, league .... 45, Derrel M. Harrelson
Most homers, righthanded batter............................ 37, David A. Kingman, 123 games, 1976
37, David A. Kingman, 149 games, 1982
Most homers, lefthanded batter .... 26, Darryl E. Strawberry, 122 games, 1983
Most homers, season, at home .... 18, Frank J. Thomas, 1962
Most homers, season, on road .... 22, David A. Kingman, 1975
Most homers, rookie season.................................. 26, Darryl E. Strawberry, 122 games, 1983
Most homers, league, lefthanded batter .... 118, Edward E. Kranepool
Most homers, league, righthanded batter... 154, David A. Kingman
Most homers, one month... 13, David A. Kingman, July, 1975
Most homers with bases filled .... 3, John D. Milner, 127 games, 1976
Most homers with bases filled, league.. 5, John D. Milner
Most total bases.. 298, Tommie L. Agee, 153 games, 1970
Most total bases, league .... 2,047, Edward E. Kranepool
Most long hits .... 61, Tommie L. Agee, 153 games, 1970
Most long hits, league .... 368, Edward E. Kranepool
Most extra bases on long hits................................... 132, David A. Kingman, 134 games, 1975
Most extra bases on long hits, league.............................. 629, Edward E. Kranepool
Most sacrifice hits .... 24, Felix B. Millan, 136 games, 1974
Most sacrifice flies .... 9, Daniel J. Staub, 155 games, 1975
9, Guillermo Montanez, 159 games, 1978
9, Joel R. Youngblood, 146 games, 1980
Most stolen bases .... 58, William H. Wilson, 159 games, 1982
Most stolen bases, league .... 143, William H. Wilson
Most caught stealing .... 21, Leonard S. Randle, 136 games, 1977
Most bases on balls.. 95, Derrel M. Harrelson, 157 games, 1970
Most bases on balls, league .... 454, Edward E. Kranepool
Most strikeouts.. 156, Tommie L. Agee, 153 games, 1970
156, David A. Kingman, 149 games, 1982
Fewest strikeouts .... 14, Felix B. Millan, 136 games, 1974
Most strikeouts, league... 697, Cleon J. Jones
Most hit by pitch .... 13, Ronald K. Hunt, 143 games, 1963
Most runs batted in.. 105, Daniel J. Staub, 155 games, 1975
Most runs batted in, league .... 614, Edward E. Kranepool
Most game-winning RBIs .... 12, George A. Foster, 157 games, 1983
Highest batting average .... .340, Cleon J. Jones, 137 games, 1969
Highest batting average, league .... .287, Stephen C. Henderson
Highest slugging average .... .506, David A. Kingman, 123 games, 1976
Most consecutive games batted safely during season .... 23, Cleon J. Jones, 1970
23, Michael L. Vail, 1975
Most grounded into double play .... 26, Cleon J. Jones, 134 games, 1970
Fewest grounded into double play.................................... 4, Lee L. Mazzilli, 159 games, 1977

Pitching

Most years .... 12, Jerry M. Koosman
12, G. Thomas Seaver
Most games... 67, Douglas R. Sisk, 1983
Most games, league .... 401, G. Thomas Seaver
Most complete games.. 21, G. Thomas Seaver, 1971
Most complete games, league .... 171, G. Thomas Seaver
Most games started... 36, John H. Fisher, 1965
36, G. Thomas Seaver, 1970
36, G. Thomas Seaver, 1973
36, G. Thomas Seaver, 1975
Most games started, league... 395, G. Thomas Seaver
Most games finished .... 50, Claude E. Lockwood, 1977
Most innings.. 291, G. Thomas Seaver, 1970
Most innings, league .... 3,045, G. Thomas Seaver
Most games won, season .... 25, G. Thomas Seaver, 1969
Most games, win, league.. 198, G. Thomas Seaver
Most years winning 20 or more games.. 4, G. Thomas Seaver
Most games lost, season .... 24, Roger L. Craig, 1962
24, John H. Fisher, 1965
Most games lost, league .... 137, Jerry M. Koosman
Highest percentage games won, season.......... .781, G. Thomas Seaver, (won 25, lost 7) 1969
Most saves, season.. 27, Frank E. McGraw, 1972

Most consecutive games won, season .... 10, G. Thomas Seaver, 1969
Most consecutive games lost, season... 18, Roger L. Craig, 1963
Most bases on balls.. 116, L. Nolan Ryan, 1971
Most bases on balls, league .... 847, G. Thomas Seaver
Most strikeouts .... 289, G. Thomas Seaver, 1971
Most strikeouts, league .... 2,541, G. Thomas Seaver
Most strikeouts, nine-inning game .... 19, G. Thomas Seaver, April 22, 1970
Most shutouts, season .... 7, Jerry M. Koosman, 1968
7, Jonathan T. Matlack, 1974
Most shutouts, league... 44, G. Thomas Seaver
Most 1-0 shutouts won, season .... 2, nine times, held by 6 pitchers,
Last two pitchers: Jerry M. Koosman, 1976
Jonathan T. Matlack, 1976
Most runs.. 137, James W. Hook, 1962
Most earned runs... 117, Roger L. Craig, 1962
Most hits .... 261, Roger L. Craig, 1962
Most hit batsmen .... 15, L. Nolan Ryan, 1971
Most wild pitches .... 18, Jack E. Hamilton, 1966
Most home runs .... 35, Roger L. Craig, 1962
Most sacrifice flies .... 12, Jerry M. Koosman, 1974
Most sacrifice hits... 21, Michael W. Scott, 1982
Lowest earned-run average, season .... 1.76, G. Thomas Seaver, 286 innings, 1971

PHILADELPHIA PHILLIES—(1883 to date)

Batting

Most years, league, except pitchers ....16, Granville W. Hamner
Most games...163, Peter E. Rose, 1979
Most games, league ....1,794, Richie Ashburn
Most at-bats ....699, David Cash, 162 games, 1975
Most at-bats, league ....7,122, Richie Ashburn
Most runs.....................................196, William R. Hamilton, 131 games, 1894
Most runs since 1900................................158, Charles H. Klein, 156 games, 1930
Most runs, league ....1,365, Edward J. Delahanty
Most runs, league, since 1900 ....1,114, Richie Ashburn
Most hits ....254, Frank J. O'Doul, 154 games, 1929
Most hits, league ....2,217, Richie Ashburn
Most singles..181, Frank J. O'Doul, 154 games, 1929
181, Richie Ashburn, 154 games, 1951
Most singles, league...1,811, Richie Ashburn
Most doubles ....59, Charles H. Klein, 156 games, 1930
Most doubles, league...432, Edward J. Delahanty
Most doubles, league, since 1900 ....337, Sherwood R. Magee
Most triples.......................................26, Samuel L. Thompson, 102 games, 1894
Most triples since 1900...............................17, Elmer H. Flick, 138 games, 1901
17, Sherwood R. Magee, 155 games, 1905
17, Sherwood R. Magee, 154 games, 1910
Most triples, league...151, Edward J. Delahanty
Most triples, league, since 1900 ....127, Sherwood R. Magee
Most homers, lefthanded batter ....43, Charles H. Klein, 149 games, 1929
Most homers, righthanded batter ....48, Michael J. Schmidt, 150 games, 1980
Most homers, rookie season ....30, Guillermo N. Montanez, 158 games, 1971
Most homers, season, at home, lefthanded batter..................29, Charles A. Klein, 1932
Most homers, season, at home, righthanded batter..................25, Michael J. Schmidt, 1980
Most homers, season, on road....................................29, Michael J. Schmidt, 1979
Most homers, one month ....15, Fred Williams, May, 1923
Most homers, league, lefthanded batter ....243, Charles H. Klein
Most homers, league, righthanded batter ....389, Michael J. Schmidt
Most homers with bases filled, season..........4, Vincent P. DiMaggio, 127 games, 1945
Most homers with bases filled, league ....7, Michael J. Schmidt
Most total bases....................................445, Charles H. Klein, 156 games, 1930
Most total bases, league ....3,197, Edward J. Delahanty
Most total bases, league, since 1900 ....3,029, Delmer Ennis
Most long hits ....107, Charles H. Klein, 156 games, 1930
Most long hits, league...667, Edward J. Delahanty
Most long hits, league, since 1900 ....706, Michael J. Schmidt
Most extra bases on long hits.....................195, Charles H. Klein, 156 games, 1930
Most extra bases on long hits, league..1,532, Michael J. Schmidt
Most sacrifice hits...43, William Gleason, 155 games, 1905
Most sacrifice flies ....13, Guillermo N. Montanez, 158 games, 1971
13, Michael J. Schmidt, 150 games, 1980
Most stolen bases ....115, William R. Hamilton, 133 games, 1891

Most stolen bases since 1900..55, Sherwood R. Magee, 154 games, 1906
Most stolen bases, league...437, Edward J. Delahanty
Most stolen bases, league, since 1900 ....387, Sherwood R. Magee
Most caught stealing..15, Fred Williams, 146 games, 1921
Most bases on balls..............................128, Michael J. Schmidt, 154 games, 1983
Most bases on balls, league ....1,086, Michael J. Schmidt
Most strikeouts...180, Michael J. Schmidt, 158 games, 1975
Fewest strikeouts.....................................8, Emil M. Verban, 155 games, 1947
Most strikeouts, league ....1,427, Michael J. Schmidt
Most hit by pitch.................................14, Edward F. Bouchee, 154 games, 1957
Most runs batted in......................170, Charles H. Klein, 154 games, 1930
Most runs batted in, league...1,124, Delmer Ennis
Most game-winning RBIs ....17, Michael J. Schmidt, 150 games, 1980
                                                  17, Gary N. Matthews, 162 games, 1982
Highest batting average........................ .408, Edward J. Delahanty, 145 games, 1899
Highest batting average since 1900 ....398, Frank J. O'Doul, 154 games, 1929
Highest batting average, league .... .362, William R. Hamilton
Highest batting average, league, since 1900...326, Charles H. Klein
Highest slugging average.....................................687, Charles H. Klein, 156 games, 1930
Most consecutive games batted safely during season ....36, William R. Hamilton, 1894
Most consecutive games batted safely during season since 1900—
                                                  26, Charles H. Klein, 1930 (twice)
Most grounded into double play..25, Delmer Ennis, 153 games, 1950
                                                  25, Ted C. Sizemore, 152 games, 1977
Fewest grounded into double play..................................3, Charles H. Klein, 152 games, 1933
                                                  3, Richie Ashburn, 156 games, 1953
                                                  3, Richie Ashburn, 153 games, 1954

Pitching, Since 1900

Most years, league ....14, Robin E. Roberts
Most games...74, C. James Konstanty, 1950
Most games, league ....529, Robin E. Roberts
Most games started ....45, Grover C. Alexander, 1916
Most games started, league...472, Robin E. Roberts
Most complete games...38, Grover C. Alexander, 1916
Most complete games, league ....272, Robin E. Roberts
Most games finished..62, C. James Konstanty, 1950
Most innings...389, Grover C. Alexander, 1916
Most innings, league..3,740, Robin E. Roberts
Most games won, season..33, Grover C. Alexander, 1916
Most games won, league...234, Robin E. Roberts
Most years winning 20 or more games ....6, Grover C. Alexander
                                                  6, Robin E. Roberts
Most games lost, season...24, Charles C. Fraser, 1904
Most games lost, league ....199, Robin E. Roberts
Highest percentage games won, season .... .800, Robin E. Roberts (won 28, lost 7 in 1952)
Most consecutive games won, season.....................................15, Steven N. Carlton, 1972
Most consecutive games lost, season...12, Russell L. Miller, 1928
                                                  12, Hugh N. Mulcahy, 1940
                                                  12, Kenneth L. Reynolds, 1972
Most saves, season...25, Alfred W. Holland, 1983
Most bases on balls ....164, Earl L. Moore, 1911
Most bases on balls, league...1075, Steven N. Carlton
Most strikeouts...310, Steven N. Carlton, 1972
Most strikeouts, nine-inning game...17, Arthur Mahaffey, Jr., April 23, 1961, second game
Most strikeouts, extra-inning game......................18, Christopher J. Short, October 2, 1965,
                                         second game, first 15 innings of 18-inning game
Most strikeouts, league ....2,758, Steven N. Carlton
Most shutouts ....16, Grover C. Alexander, 1916
Most shutouts, league...61, Grover C. Alexander
Most 1-0 shutouts won ....4, Grover C. Alexander, 1916
Most runs..178, Raymond A. Benge, 1930
Most earned runs...147, Robin E. Roberts, 1956
Most hits..348, Claude W. Passeau, 1937
Most hit batsmen..19, Frederick F. Mitchell, 1903
                                                  19, James P. Bunning, 1966
Most wild pitches ....22, Jack E. Hamilton, 1962
Most home runs ....46, Robin E. Roberts, 1956
Most sacrifice hits ....21, Curtis T. Simmons, 1954
                                                  21, Dennis J. Bennett, 1964
                                                  21, James P. Bunning, 1965
                                                  21, Wayne L. Twitchell, 1973
Most sacrifice flies ....15, Randy L. Lerch, 37 games, 1979
Lowest earned-run average, season..................1.22, Grover C. Alexander, 376 innings, 1915

PITTSBURGH PIRATES—(1887 to date)

Batting

Most years, league, except pitchers .... 21, Wilver D. Stargell
Most games.. 163, William S. Mazeroski, 1967
Most games, league .... 2433, Roberto W. Clemente
Most at-bats .... 698, Mateo R. Alou, 162 games, 1969
Most at-bats, league.. 9454, Roberto W. Clemente
Most runs .... 148, Jacob C. Stenzel, 131 games, 1894
Most runs since 1900.................................... 144, Hazen S. Cuyler, 153 games, 1925
Most runs, league .... 1,520, John P. Wagner
Most hits.. 237, Paul G. Waner, 155 games, 1927
Most hits, league.. 3000, Roberto W. Clemente
Most singles .... 198, Lloyd J. Waner, 150 games, 1927
Most singles, league .... 2154, Roberto W. Clemente
Most doubles .... 62, Paul G. Waner, 154 games, 1932
Most doubles, league.. 556, John P. Wagner
556, Paul G. Waner
Most triples .... 36, J. Owen Wilson, 152 games, 1912
Most triples, league.. 231, John P. Wagner
Most homers, righthanded batter .... 54, Ralph M. Kiner, 152 games, 1949
Most home runs, league, righthanded batter.. 301, Ralph M. Kiner
Most homers, lefthanded batter .... 48, Wilver D. Stargell, 141 games, 1971
Most home runs, league, lefthanded batter .... 475, Wilver D. Stargell
Most homers, season, at home .... 31, Ralph M. Kiner, 1948
Most homers, season, on road............................... 27, Wilver D. Stargell, 1971
Most homers, rookie season................................ 23, John C. Rizzo, 143 games, 1938
23, Ralph M. Kiner, 144 games, 1946
Most homers with bases filled, season .... 4, Ralph Kiner, 152 games, 1949
Most home runs with bases filled, league .... 11, Ralph M. Kiner
11, Wilver D. Stargell
Most home runs, one month........................... 16, Ralph M. Kiner, September, 1949
Most total bases .... 366, Hazen S. Cuyler, 153 games, 1925
Most total bases, league.. 4492, Roberto W. Clemente
Most long hits, league .... 953, Wilver D. Stargell
Most long hits, season .... 90, Wilver D. Stargell, 148 games, 1973
Most extra bases on long hits .... 191, Ralph M. Kiner, 152 games, 1949
Most extra bases on long hits, league............................... 1958, Wilver D. Stargell
Most sacrifices (S.H. and S.F.) .... 42, Harold J. Traynor, 144 games, 1928
Most sacrifice hits... 35, Robert S. Ganley, 134 games, 1906
Most sacrifice flies... 13, Bill Madlock, 154 games, 1982
Most stolen bases.. 96, Omar R. Moreno, 162 games, 1980
Most caught stealing .... 33, Omar R. Moreno, 162 games, 1980
Most stolen bases, league... 688, Max G. Carey
Most bases on balls... 137, Ralph M. Kiner, 151 games, 1951
Most bases on balls, league.. 937, Wilver D. Stargell
Most strikeouts....................................... 163, Donn A. Clendenon, 158 games, 1968
Most strikeouts, league .... 1936, Wilver D. Stargell
Fewest strikeouts... 13, Carson L. Bigbee, 150 games, 1922
13, Lloyd J. Waner, 152 games, 1928
Most hit by pitch.. 14, Albert Oliver, 151 games, 1970
Most runs batted in... 131, Paul G. Waner, 155 games, 1927
Most runs batted in, league .... 1540, Wilver D. Stargell
Most game-winning RBIs.................................... 14, Bill Madlock, 154 games, 1982
14, Bill Madlock, 130 games, 1983
Most consecutive games, one or more runs batted in, season—
12, Paul G. Waner (23 RBIs), 1927
Highest batting average .... .385, J. Floyd Vaughan, 137 games, 1935
Highest batting average, league.. .340, Paul G. Waner
Highest slugging average, righthanded batter .... .658, Ralph M. Kiner, 152 games, 1949
Highest slugging average, lefthanded batter .... .607, J. Floyd Vaughan, 137 games, 1935
Most consecutive games batted safely during season, lefthanded batter—
25, Charles J. Grimm, 1923
Most consecutive games batted safely during season, righthanded batter—
26, Daniel F. O'Connell, 1953
Most consecutive games batted safely over two seasons—
30, Charles J. Grimm, 1922 (5), 1923 (25)
Most grounded into double play .... 25, Alfred C. Todd, 133 games, 1938
Fewest grounded into double play .... 4, Omar R. Moreno, 150 games, 1977
4, Franklin Taveras, 157 games, 1978

Pitching, Since 1900

Most years, league .... 18, Charles B. Adams

Most games, lefthanded pitcher .... 76, Rodney G. Scurry, 1982
Most games, righthanded pitcher.. 94, Kenton C. Tekulve, 1979
Most games, league .... 802, El Roy L. Face
Most games started.. 42, Robert B. Friend, 1956
Most games started, league .... 477, Robert B. Friend
Most complete games .... 32, Victor G. Willis, 1906
Most complete games, league .... 263, A. Wilbur Cooper
Most games finished .... 67, Kenton C. Tekulve, 1979
Most innings .... 331, Burleigh A. Grimes, 1928
Most innings, league .... 3,481, Robert B. Friend
Most games won, season .... 28, John D. Chesbro, 1902
Most games won, league .... 202, A. Wilbur Cooper
Most years winning 20 or more games....................................... 4, Charles L. Phillippe
                                                                                                    4, Victor G. Willis
                                                                                                    4, A. Wilbur Cooper
                                                                                                    4, Jesse N. Tannehill
Most games lost .... 21, Murry Dickson, 1952
Most games lost, league.. 218, Robert B. Friend
Highest percentage games won, season .... .947, El Roy L. Face (won 18, lost 1 in 1959)
Most consecutive games won, season .... 17, El Roy L. Face, 1959
Most consecutive games lost, season... 13, Burleigh A. Grimes, 1917
Most saves, season.. 31, Kenton C. Tekulve, 1978
                                                                                           31, Kenton C. Tekulve, 1979
Most bases on balls.. 159, Martin J. O'Toole, 1912
Most bases on balls, league .... 869, Robert B. Friend
Most strikeouts .... 276, Robert A. Veale, 1965
Most strikeouts, game... 16, Robert A. Veale, June 1, 1965
Most strikeouts, league .... 1,682, Robert B. Friend
Most shutouts .... 8, John D. Chesbro, 1902
                                                                                           8, Albert P. Leifield, 1906
                                                                                           8, Albert L. Mamaux, 1915
                                                                                           8, Charles B. Adams, 1920
Most shutouts, league... 46, Charles B. Adams
Most 1-0 shutouts won... 3, Victor G. Willis, 1908
                                                                                           3, Claude R. Hendrix, 1912
                                                                                           3, A. Wilbur Cooper, 1917
                                                                                           3, Edward A. Brandt, 1927
Most runs .... 181, Remy Kremer, 1930
Most earned runs .... 154, Remy Kremer, 1930
Most hits... 366, Remy Kremer, 1930
Most hit batsmen .... 21, John D. Chesbro, 1902
Most wild pitches .... 18, Robert A. Veale, 1964
Most home runs.. 32, Murry M. Dickson, 1951
Most sacrifice hits .... 19, Robert B. Friend, 1956
Most sacrifice flies .... 12, John R. Candelaria, 1980
Lowest earned-run average, season .... 1.87, A. Wilbur Cooper, 246 innings, 1916

ST. LOUIS CARDINALS—(1876-1877; 1885-1886; 1892 to date)

Batting

Most years, league, except pitchers .... 22, Stanley F. Musial
Most games, season .... 162, William D. White, 1963
                                                                                           162, Kenton L. Boyer, 1964
                                                                                           162, Curtis C. Flood, 1964
Most games, league .... 3,026, Stanley F. Musial
Most at-bats.. 689, Louis C. Brock, 159 games, 1967
Most at-bats, league .... 10,972, Stanley F. Musial
Most runs .... 141, Rogers Hornsby, 154 games, 1922
Most runs, league .... 1,949, Stanley F. Musial
Most hits.. 250, Rogers Hornsby, 154 games, 1922
Most hits, league .... 3,630, Stanley F. Musial
Most singles .... 180, Jesse C. Burkett, 142 games, 1901
Most singles, league .... 2,253, Stanley F. Musial
Most doubles .... 64, Joseph M. Medwick, 155 games, 1936
Most doubles, league.. 725, Stanley F. Musial
Most triples .... 33, Perry W. Werden, 124 games, 1893
Most triples since 1900 .... 25, Thomas A. Long, 140 games, 1915
Most triples, league... 177, Stanley F. Musial
Most homers, lefthanded batter .... 43, John R. Mize, 155 games, 1940
Most homers, righthanded batter......'............................ 42, Rogers Hornsby, 154 games, 1922
Most homers, season, at home .... 25, John R. Mize, 1940
Most homers, season, on road.. 23, Stanley F. Musial, 1948

Most homers, one month .... 12, George J. Kurowski, August, 1947
Most homers, rookie season .... 21, Raymond L. Jablonski, 157 games, 1953
Most homers, league, lefthanded batter.. 475, Stanley F. Musial
Most homers, league, righthanded batter.. 255, Kenton L. Boyer
Most homers with bases filled, season .... 3, James L. Bottomley, 153 games, 1925
                                                                              3, Keith Hernandez, 161 games, 1977
Most homers with bases filled, league.. 9, Stanley F. Musial
Most total bases .... 450, Rogers Hornsby, 154 games, 1922
Most total bases, league .... 6,134, Stanley F. Musial
Most long hits, righthanded batter............................ 102, Rogers Hornsby, 154 games, 1922
Most long hits, lefthanded batter............................ 103, Stanley F. Musial, 155 games, 1948
Most long hits, league .... 1,377, Stanley F. Musial
Most extra bases on long hits.................... 200, Rogers Hornsby, 154 games, 1922
Most extra bases on long hits, league .... 2,504, Stanley F. Musial
Most stolen bases.. 118, Louis C. Brock, 153 games, 1974
Most stolen bases, league .... 888, Louis C. Brock
Most caught stealing .... 36, Miller J. Huggins, 148 games, 1914
Most sacrifices (S.H. and S.F.) .... 37, Taylor L. Douthit, 139 games, 1926
Most sacrifice hits.. 36, Harry W. Walker, 148 games, 1943
Most sacrifice flies .... 14, George A. Hendrick, 136 games, 1982
Most bases on balls.. 116, Miller J. Huggins, 151 games, 1910
Most bases on balls, league.. 1,599, Stanley F. Musial
Most intentional bases on balls, season.................... 26, Stanley F. Musial, 135 games, 1958
Most strikeouts.. 134, Louis C. Brock, 156 games, 1966
Most strikeouts, league.. 1,469, Louis C. Brock
Fewest strikeouts.. 10, Frank F. Frisch, 153 games, 1927
Most hit by pitch .... 31, Louis R. Evans, 151 games, 1910
Most runs batted in .... 154, Joseph M. Medwick, 156 games, 1937
Most runs batted in, league.. 1,951, Stanley F. Musial
Most game-winning RBIs .... 21, Keith Hernandez, 160 games, 1982
Most consecutive games, one or more runs batted in . 10, William D. White (15 RBI), 1961
Highest batting average... .424, Rogers Hornsby, 143 games, 1924
Highest batting average, league .... .359, Rogers Hornsby
Highest slugging average, righthanded batter .... .756, Rogers Hornsby, 138 games, 1925
Highest slugging average, lefthanded batter .... .702, Stanley F. Musial, 155 games, 1948
Most consecutive games batted safely during season .... 33, Rogers Hornsby, 1922
Most grounded into double play .... 29, Ted L. Simmons, 161 games, 1973
Fewest grounded into double play .... 2, Louis C. Brock, 155 games, 1965

Pitching, Since 1900

Most years, league .... 18, Jesse J. Haines
Most games, righthander, season... 72, Mark A. Littell, 1978
Most games, lefthander, season... 68, Alan T. Hrabosky, 1976
Most games, league .... 554, Jesse J. Haines
Most games started.. 39, John W. Taylor, 1904
Most games started, league.. 482, Robert Gibson
Most complete games.. 39, John W. Taylor, 1904
Most complete games, league .... 255, Robert Gibson
Most games finished, righthander .... 58, H. Bruce Sutter, 1982
Most games finished, lefthander .... 45, Alan T. Hrabosky, 1976
Most innings.. 352, Grant McGlynn, 1907
Most innings, league.. 3,885, Robert Gibson
Most games won.. 30, Jerome H. Dean, 1934
Most games won, league .... 251, Robert Gibson
Most years winning 20 or more games.. 5, Robert Gibson
Most games lost .... 25, Grant McGlynn, 1907
                                                                              25, Arthur L. Raymond, 1908
Most games lost, league .... 174, Robert Gibson
Highest percentage games won, season .... .811, Jerome H. Dean (won 30, lost 7 in 1934)
Most consecutive games won, season .... 15, Robert Gibson, 1968
Most consecutive games lost, season .... 9, William H. McGee, 1938
                                                                              9, Thomas G. Poholsky, 1951
                                                                              9, Robert H. Forsch, 1978
Most saves.. 36, H. Bruce Sutter, 1982
Most bases on balls.. 181, Robert G. Harmon, 1911
Most bases on balls, league.. 1,336, Robert Gibson
Most strikeouts.. 274, Robert Gibson, 1970
Most strikeouts nine-inning game...................... 19, Steven N. Carlton, September 15, 1969
Most strikeouts, league .... 3,117, Robert Gibson
Most shutouts.. 13, Robert Gibson, 1968
Most shutouts, league.. 56, Robert Gibson
Most 1-0 shutouts won.. 4, Robert Gibson, 1968
Most runs .... 162, Grant McGlynn, 1907

Most earned runs .... 129, William H. Sherdel, 1929
Most hits .... 337, Denton T. Young, 1900
Most hit batsmen .... 17, Gerald L. Staley, 1953
Most wild pitches .... 15, Fred L. Beebe, 1907
                                                                                              15, Fred L. Beebe, 1909
Most home runs.. 39, Murry M. Dickson, 1948
Most sacrifice hits.. 17, David J. LaPoint, 1983
Most sacrifice flies .... 13, Robert H. Forsch, 1979
Lowest earned-run average, season .... 1.12, Robert Gibson, 305 innings, 1968

SAN DIEGO PADRES—(1969 to date)

Batting

Most years, league, except pitchers ....10, Fred L. Kendall
Most games ....162, David M. Winfield, 1980
Most games, league ....1117, David M. Winfield
Most at-bats ....642, Eugene Richards, 158 games, 1980
Most at-bats, league ....3997, David M. Winfield
Most runs ....104, David M. Winfield, 157 games, 1977
Most runs, league ....599, David M. Winfield
Most hits..193, Eugene Richards, 158 games, 1980
Most hits, league ....1134, David, M. Winfield
Most singles ....155, Eugene Richards, 158 games, 1980
Most singles, league...762, David M. Winfield
Most doubles ....42, Terrence E. Kennedy, 153 games, 1982
Most doubles, league ....179, David M. Winfield
Most triples...12, Eugene Richards, 154 games, 1978
Most triples, league...63, Eugene Richards
Most homers, righthanded batter, season ....38, Nathan Colbert, 156 games, 1970
                                                                              38, Nathan Colbert, 151 games, 1972
Most homers, lefthanded batter, season ....23, Willie L. McCovey, 122 games, 1975
Most homers, rookie, season ....8, John M. Grubb, 113 games, 1973
                                                                              8, Michael W. Ivie, 111 games, 1975
Most homers, righthanded batter, league..163, Nathan Colbert
Most homers, lefthanded batter, league ....52, Willie L. McCovey
Most homers, one month ....11, Nathan Colbert, May 1970
                                                                              11, Nathan Colbert, July 1972
                                                                              11, Nathan Colbert, August 1972
Most homers, season, at home ....16, Nathan Colbert, 1970
                                                                              16, Nathan Colbert, 1972
                                                                              16, David M. Winfield, 1979
Most homers season, on road ....22, Nathan Colbert, 1970
                                                                              22, Nathan Colbert, 1972
Most homers with bases filled, season ....2, Nathan Colbert, 151 games, 1972
                                                                              2, David M. Winfield, 137 games, 1976
                                                                              2, David A. Kingman, 56 games, 1977
Most homers with bases filled, league..5, Nathan Colbert
Most total bases ....333, David M. Winfield, 159 games, 1979
Most total bases, league...1853, David M. Winfield
Most long hits...71, David M. Winfield 159 games, 1979
Most long hits, league...372, David M. Winfield
Most extra bases on long hits ....149, David M. Winfield, 159 games, 1979
Most extra bases on long hits, league ....719, David M. Winfield
Most sacrifice hits...28, Osborne E. Smith, 159 games, 1978
Most sacrifice flies...9, Terrence E. Kennedy, 149 games, 1983
Most stolen bases, season...66, Alan A. Wiggins, 144 games, 1983
Most stolen bases, league...242, Eugene Richards
Most caught stealing...20, Eugene Richards, 132 games, 1982
Most bases on balls...125, F. Gene Tenace, 147 games, 1977
Most bases on balls, league...463, David M. Winfield
Most strikeouts...150, Nathan Colbert, 156 games, 1970
Most strikeouts, league...856, Nathan Colbert
Fewest strikeouts...34, Enzo O. Hernandez, 143 games, 1971
Most hit by pitch...13, F. Gene Tenace, 147 games, 1977
Most runs batted in ....118, David M. Winfield, 159 games, 1979
Most runs batted in, league...626, David M. Winfield
Most game-winning RBIs ....15, Terrence E. Kennedy, 153 games, 1982
Highest batting average...318, Clarence E. Gaston, 146 games, 1970
Highest batting average, league ....291, Eugene Richards
Highest slugging average ....558, David M. Winfield, 159 games, 1979
Most consecutive games batted safely during season...............25, Anthony W. Gwynn, 1983
Most grounded into double plays, season.......................20, Fred L. Kendall, 146 games, 1976

Fewest grounded into double play ....7, David W. Campbell, 154 games, 1970
7, Eugene Richards, 150 games, 1979
7, F. Gene Tenace, 151 games, 1979
7, Terrence E. Kennedy, 153 games, 1982

Pitching

Most years...8, Randall L. Jones
Most games, season...78, Roland G. Fingers, 1977
Most games, league ....265, Roland G. Fingers
Most games started ....40, Randall L. Jones, 1976
Most games started, league ....253, Randall L. Jones
Most complete games...25, Randall L. Jones, 1976
Most complete games, league..71, Randall L. Jones
Most games finished ....69, Roland G. Fingers, 1977
Most innings...315, Randall L. Jones, 1976
Most innings, league..1765, Randall L. Jones
Most games won ....22, Randall L. Jones, 1976
Most games won, league...92, Randall L. Jones
Most years winning 20 or more games ....2, Randall L. Jones
Most games lost ....22, Randall L. Jones, 1974
Most games lost, league...105, Randall L. Jones
Highest percentage games won, season........ .778, Gaylord J. Perry (won 21, lost 6 in 1978)
Most saves, season ....37, Roland G. Fingers, 1978
Most consecutive games won, season ....10, Clarence E. Metzger, 1976
Most consecutive games lost, season...11, Gary D. Ross, 1969
Most bases on balls...122, Stephen R. Arlin, 1972
Most bases on balls, league ....505, Clayton L. Kirby
Most strikeouts ....231, Clayton L. Kirby, 1971
Most strikeouts, league..802, Clayton L. Kirby
Most strikeouts nine-inning game....................15, Fredie H. Norman, September, 15, 1972
Most shutouts won...6, Fredie H. Norman, 1972
6, Randall L. Jones, 1975
Most shutouts won, league ....18, Randall L. Jones
Most 1-0 shutouts won, season ....2, Joseph F. Niekro, 1969
2, Randall L. Jones, 1978
Most runs, allowed...126, Patrick E. Dobson, 1970
126, William B. Greif, 1974
Most earned runs..117, William B. Greif, 1974
Most hits...274, Randall L. Jones, 1976
Most wild pitches...15, Stephen R. Arlin, 1972
Most hit batsmen..14, William B. Greif, 1974
Most homers...30, Clayton L. Kirby, 1973
Most sacrifice hits...23, Randall L. Jones, 1979
Most sacrifice flies..12, David A. Roberts, 1971
Lowest earned-run average, season ....2.10, David A. Roberts, 270 innings, 1971

SAN FRANCISCO GIANTS—(1958 to date)
(See New York Giants for club's records prior to franchise transfer in 1958)

Batting

Most years, league, except pitchers...19, Willie L. McCovey
Most games..164, Jose A. Pagan, 1962
Most games, league ....2256, Willie L. McCovey
Most at-bats ....663, Bobby L. Bonds, 157 games, 1970
Most at-bats, league ....7578, Willie H. Mays
Most runs...134, Bobby L. Bonds, 157 games, 1970
Most runs, league ....1480, Willie H. Mays
Most hits...208, Willie H. Mays, 152 games, 1958
Most hits, league..2284, Willie H. Mays
Most singles.............................146, Rigoberto P. Fuentes, 160 games, 1973
Most singles, league ....1373, Willie H. Mays
Most doubles...46, Jack A. Clark, 156 games, 1978
Most doubles, league..376, Willie H. Mays
Most triples ....12, Willie H. Mays, 153 games, 1960
Most triples, league ....76, Willie H. Mays
Most homers, righthanded batter ....52, Willie H. Mays, 157 games, 1965
Most homers, lefthanded batter.....................45, Willie L. McCovey, 149 games, 1969
Most homers, one month, righthanded batter ....17, Willie H. Mays, August, 1965
Most homers, one month, lefthanded batter ....13, Willie L. McCovey, July, 1963
Most homers, season, at home ....28, Willie H. Mays, 1962
Most homers, season, on road..28, Willie H. Mays, 1965

Most homers, rookie season...31, James R. Hart, 153 games, 1964
Most homers, league, righthanded batter...459, Willie H. Mays
Most homers, league, lefthanded batter ....469, Willie L. McCovey
Most homers with bases filled, season ....3, Willie L. McCovey, 135 games, 1967
Most homers with bases filled, league...16, Willie L. McCovey
Most total bases...382, Willie H. Mays, 162 games, 1962
Most total bases, league ....4189, Willie H. Mays
Most long hits ....90, Willie H. Mays, 162 games, 1962
Most long hits, league ....911, Willie H. Mays
Most extra bases on long hits ....193, Willie H. Mays, 162 games, 1962
Most extra bases on long hits, league...1905, Willie H. Mays
Most sacrifice hits ....17, James H. Davenport, 134 games, 1958
17, Rigoberto P. Fuentes, 160 games, 1973
17, Terry B. Whitfield, 149 games, 1978
Most sacrifice flies...12, Bobby R. Murcer, 147 games, 1975
Most stolen bases ....58, William A. North, 142 games, 1979
Most stolen bases, league...263, Bobby L. Bonds
Most caught stealing...24, William A. North, 142 games, 1979
Most bases on balls..137, Willie L. McCovey, 152 games, 1970
Most intentional bases on balls ....45, Willie L. McCovey, 149 games, 1969
Most bases on balls, league...1168, Willie L. McCovey
Most strikeouts...189, Bobby L. Bonds, 157 games, 1970
Most strikeouts, league..1351, Willie L. McCovey
Fewest strikeouts, season ....48, Kenneth J. Reitz, 155 games, 1976
Most hit by pitch ....26, Ronald K. Hunt, 117 games, 1970
Most runs batted in ....142, Orlando M. Cepeda, 152 games, 1961
Most runs batted in, league...1388, Willie L. McCovey
Most game-winning RBIs....................................21, Jack A. Clark, 157 games, 1982
Highest batting average ....347, Willie H. Mays, 152 games, 1958
Highest slugging average .... .656, Willie L. McCovey, 149 games, 1969
Most consecutive games batted safely, during season ....26, Jack A. Clark, 1978
Most grounded into double play, season............................25, Bill Madlock, 140 games, 1977
Fewest grounded into double play.................................4, Felipe R. Alou, 154 games, 1962
4, Bobby L. Bonds, 150 games, 1974

Pitching

Most years, league...14, Juan A. Marichal
Most games ....78, Gregory B. Minton, 1982
Most games, league...570, Gary R. Lavelle
Most games started ....42, John S. Sanford, 1963
Most games started, league..446, Juan A. Marichal
Most complete games ....30, Juan A. Marichal, 1968
Most complete games, league...244, Juan A. Marichal
Most games finished ....66, Gregory B. Minton, 1982
Most innings ....329, Gaylord J. Perry, 1970
Most innings, league ....3443, Juan A. Marichal
Most games won, season......................................26, Juan A. Marichal, 1968
Most games won, league ....238, Juan A. Marichal
Most games lost, league..140, Juan A. Marichal
Most years winning 20 or more games..6, Juan A. Marichal
Most games lost, season...18, Raymond M. Sadecki, 1968
Highest percentage games won, season .... .806, Juan A. Marichal (won 25, lost 6, 1966)
Most consecutive games, won, season................................16, John S. Sanford, 1962
Most consecutive games lost, season ....8, Ronald R. Bryant, 1974
Most saves, season..30, Gregory B. Minton, 1982
Most bases on balls...124, John F. D'Acquisto, 1974
Most bases on balls, league...690, Juan A. Marichal
Most strikeouts ....248, Juan A. Marichal, 1963
Most strikeouts, league..2281, Juan A. Marichal
Most strikeouts, nine-inning game................................... 15, Gaylord J. Perry, July 22, 1966
Most shutouts, season ....10, Juan A. Marichal, 1965
Most 1-0 shutouts won, season..2, Michael F. McCormick, 1960
2, Juan A. Marichal, 1963
2, Gaylord J. Perry, 1968
2, Raymond M. Sadecki, 1968
2, Juan A. Marichal, 1971
2, Robert W. Knepper, 1978
2, John D. Curtis, 1979
Most shutouts, league ....52, Juan A. Marichal
Most runs...143, Vida R. Blue, 1979
Most earned runs...132, Vida R. Blue, 1979
Most hits ....295, Juan A. Marichal, 1968
Most hit batsmen...11, Gaylord J. Perry, 1969

Most wild pitches ....18, Richard P. Robertson, 1970
Most home runs ....34, Juan A. Marichal, 1962
Most sacrifice hits ....18, Michael F. McCormick, 1959
                                                                                    18, Ronald R. Bryant, 1974
Most sacrifice flies..13, Gaylord J. Perry, 1971
Lowest earned-run average, season ....1.98, Bobby D. Bolin, 177 innings, 1968

Club Season, Game Records

LAST YEAR WON LEAGUE CHAMPIONSHIP AND LAST YEAR LOWEST PERCENTAGE GAMES WON

American League

	League Championship	Lowest Percentage Games Won
Baltimore	1983	
Boston	1975	1932
California		1974
Chicago	1959	1976
Cleveland	1954	1971
Detroit	1968	1975
Kansas City (present club)	1980	
Kansas City (former club)		1967
Milwaukee (present club)	1982	
Minnesota	1965	1982
New York	1981	1966
Oakland	1974	
Philadelphia	1931	1954
St. Louis	1944	1953
Seattle		1983
Texas		1973
Toronto		1981
Washington (second club)		1968
Washington (original club)	1933	1959

National League

	League Championship	Lowest Percentage Games Won
Atlanta		1977
Boston	1948	1935
Brooklyn	1956	1905
Chicago	1945	1981
Cincinnati	1976	1982
Houston		1975
Los Angeles	1981	
Milwaukee	1958	
Montreal		1976
New York (present club)	1973	1983
New York (former club)	1954	1946
Philadelphia	1983	1972
Pittsburgh	1979	(tied) 1957
San Diego		1974
St. Louis	1982	1918
San Francisco	1962	

American League

BALTIMORE ORIOLES—(1954 to date)

(Present franchise only; see St. Louis Browns for club's records prior to franchise transfer in 1954)

Most players	54 in 1955
Fewest players	30 in 1969
Most games	163 in 1961, 1964, 1982
Most at-bats	5585 in 1980 (162 games)
Most runs	805 in 1980 (162 games)
Fewest runs	483 in 1954 (154 games)
Most opponents' runs	754 in 1955 (156 games)
Most hits	1523 in 1980 (162 games)
Fewest hits	1153 in 1972 (154 games)
Most singles	1080 in 1980 (162 games)
Most doubles	283 in 1983 (162 games)
Most triples	49 in 1954 (154 games)
Most homers	181 in 1979 (159 games)
Most home runs with bases filled	8 in 1979, 1982, 1983.
Most home runs by pinch-hitters	11 in 1982
Most long hits	478 in 1983 (162 games)
Most extra bases on long hits	850 in 1982 (163 games)
Most total bases	2333 in 1983 (162 games)
Most sacrifice hits	110 in 1957 (154 games)
Most sacrifice flies	59 in 1969 (162 games)
Most stolen bases	150 in 1976 (162 games)
Most caught stealing	64 in 1973 (162 games)
Most bases on balls	717 in 1970 (162 games)
Most strikeouts	1019 in 1964 (163 games)
	1019 in 1968 (162 games)
Fewest strikeouts	634 in 1954 (154 games)
Most hit by pitch	58 in 1974 (162 games)
Fewest hit by pitch	19 in 1955 (156 games)
Most runs batted in	751 in 1980 (162 games)
Most game-winning RBIs	95 in 1980 (162 games)
	95 in 1983 (162 games)
Highest batting average	.273 in 1980 (162 games)
Lowest batting average	.225 in 1968 (162 games)
Highest slugging average	.421 in 1983 (162 games)
Lowest slugging average	.320 in 1955 (156 games)
Most grounded into double play	158 in 1980 (162 games)
Fewest grounded into double play	102 in 1968 (162 games)
Most left on bases	1262 in 1970 (162 games)
Fewest left on bases	1043 in 1972 (154 games)
Most .300 hitters	3 in 1980
Most putouts	4436 in 1970 (162 games)
Fewest putouts	4082 in 1956 (156 games)
Most assists	1974 in 1975 (159 games)
Fewest assists	1516 in 1958 (154 games)
Most chances accepted	6344 in 1974 (162 games)
Fewest chances accepted	5625 in 1958 (154 games)
Most errors	167 in 1955 (156 games)
Fewest errors	95 in 1964 (163 games)
	95 in 1980 (162 games)
Most errorless games	92 in 1980 (162 games)
Most consecutive errorless games	10 in 1962
Most double plays	189 in 1977 (161 games)
Fewest double plays	131 in 1968 (162 games)
Most passed balls	49 in 1959 (155 games)
Fewest passed balls	5 in 1956 (154 games)
	5 in 1975 (159 games)
	5 in 1983 (162 games)
Highest fielding average	.985 in 1964 (163 games)
	.985 in 1980 (162 games)
Lowest fielding average	.972 in 1955 (156 games)
Most games won	109 in 1969
Most games lost	100 in 1954
Highest percentage games won	.673 in 1969 (won 109, lost 53)
Lowest percentage games won	.351 in 1954 (won 54, lost 100)
Games won, league	2610 in 30 years
Games lost, league	2111 in 30 years

Most shutouts won, season.. 21 in 1961
Most shutouts lost, season... 22 in 1955
Most 1-0 games won .... 8 in 1974
Most 1-0 games lost .... 5 in 1973
Most consecutive games won, season .... 14 in 1973
Most consecutive games lost, season .... 14 in 1954
Most times league champions... 6
Most times lowest percentage games won, season 0
Most runs, game.. Baltimore 19, Cleveland 6, August 28, 1957
Most runs, game, by opponent....................................Toronto 24, Baltimore 10, June 26, 1978
Most runs, shutout game.. Baltimore 17, Chicago 0, July 27, 1969
Most runs, shutout game by opponent .... New York 16, Baltimore 0, April 30, 1960
Most runs doubleheader shutout ....13, Baltimore vs. Washington, July 9, 1959
Most runs, inning ....10, Baltimore vs. New York, July 8, 1969, first game, fourth inning
                     10, Baltimore vs. Oakland, April 29, 1979, seventh inning
Longest 1-0 game won.................17 innings, Baltimore 1, Milwaukee 0, September 27, 1974
Longest 1-0 game lost...........15 innings, Cleveland 1, Baltimore 0, May 14, 1961, first game
Most hits, nine-inning game ....26, Baltimore vs. California, August 28, 1980
Most home runs, game ....7, Baltimore vs. Boston, May 17, 1967
Most consecutive games, one or more home runs ....13 (26 homers, 1982)
Most home runs in consecutive games in which home runs were made—
                                               26 (13 games, 1982)
Most total bases, game ....39, Baltimore vs. Chicago, July 27, 1969

BOSTON RED SOX—(1901 to date)

Most players..	48 in 1952	
Fewest players	18 in 1904	
Most games	163 in 1961,	1978
Most at-bats...	5603 in 1980	(160 games)
Most runs...	1027 in 1950	(154 games)
Fewest runs...	462 in 1906	(155 games)
Most opponents' runs..	921 in 1925	(152 games)
Most hits	1665 in 1950	(154 games)
Fewest hits	1175 in 1905	(153 games)
Most singles...	1156 in 1950	(154 games)
Most doubles...	310 in 1979	(160 games)
Most triples	112 in 1903	(141 games)
Most homers..	213 in 1977	(161 games)
Most home runs with bases filled	9 in 1941, 1950	
Most home runs by pinch-hitters, season........................	6 in 1953	
Most long hits...	538 in 1979	(160 games)
Most extra bases on long hits	1009 in 1977	(161 games)
Most total bases..	2560 in 1977	(161 games)
Most sacrifices (S. H. and S. F.)	310 in 1917	(157 games)
Most sacrifice hits...	142 in 1906	(155 games)
Most sacrifice flies	59 in 1976	(162 games)
	59 in 1977	(161 games)
	59 in 1979	(160 games)
Most stolen bases..	215 in 1909	(151 games)
Most caught stealing	111 in 1920	(154 games)
Most bases on balls..	835 in 1949	(155 games)
Most strikeouts..	1020 in 1966	(162 games)
	1020 in 1967	(162 games)
Fewest strikeouts..	329 in 1921	(154 games)
Most hit by pitch	46 in 1920	(154 games)
	46 in 1924	(156 games)
Fewest hit by pitch	11 in 1934	(153 games)
Most runs batted in	974 in 1950	(154 games)
Most game-winning RBIs	84 in 1982	(162 games)
Highest batting average	.302 in 1950	(154 games)
Lowest batting average	.234 in 1905	(153 games)
	.234 in 1907	(155 games)
Highest slugging average	.465 in 1977	(161 games)
Lowest slugging average..	.318 in 1916	(156 games)
	.318 in 1917	(157 games)
Most grounded into double play	171 in 1982	(162 games)
	171 in 1983	(162 games)
Fewest grounded into double play	94 in 1942	(152 games)
Most left on bases..	1304 in 1948	(155 games)
Fewest left on bases...	1015 in 1929	(155 games)
Most .300 hitters	9 in 1950	

Most putouts	4418 in 1978 (163 games)
Fewest putouts	3949 in 1938 (150 games)
Most assists	2195 in 1907 (155 games)
Fewest assists	1555 in 1964 (162 games)
Most chances accepted	6425 in 1907 (155 games)
Fewest chances accepted	5667 in 1938 (150 games)
Most errors	373 in 1901 (137 games)
Fewest errors	111 in 1950 (154 games)
Most errorless games	86 in 1971 (162 games)
Most consecutive errorless games	9 in 1951, 1961
Most double plays	207 in 1949 (155 games)
Fewest double plays	74 in 1913 (151 games)
Most passed balls	24 in 1913 (151 games)
Fewest passed balls	3 in 1933 (149 games)
	3 in 1975 (160 games)
Highest fielding average	.981 in 1948 (155 games)
	.981 in 1950 (154 games)
	.981 in 1971 (162 games)
	.981 in 1982 (162 games)
Lowest fielding average	.943 in 1901 (137 games)
Most games won	105 in 1912
Most games lost	111 in 1932
Highest percentage games won	.691 in 1912 (won 105, lost 47)
Lowest percentage games won	.279 in 1932 (won 43, lost 111)
Games won, league	6484 in 83 years
Games lost, league	6261 in 83 years
Most shutouts won, season	26 in 1918
Most shutouts lost, season	28 in 1906
Most 1-0 games won	8 in 1918
Most 1-0 games lost	7 in 1909, 1914
Most consecutive games won, season	15 in 1946
Most consecutive games lost, season	20 in 1906
Most times league champions	9
Most times lowest percentage games, won	10

Most runs, game .... Boston 29, St. Louis 4, June 8, 1950
Most runs, game, by opponent .... Cleveland 27, Boston 3, July 7, 1923, first game
Most runs, shutout game .... Boston 19, Philadelphia 0, April 30, 1950, first game
Most runs, shutout game by opponent .... Cleveland 19, Boston 0, May 18, 1955
Most runs, doubleheader shutout ....16, Boston vs. Cleveland, August 21, 1920
Most runs, inning ....17, Boston vs. Detroit, June 18, 1953, seventh inning
Longest 1-0 game won ....15 innings, Boston 1, Detroit 0, May 11, 1904
Longest 1-0 game lost ....15 innings, Washington 1, Boston 0, July 3, 1915
Most hits, game ....28, Boston vs. St. Louis, June 8, 1950
Most home runs, game ....8, Boston vs. Toronto, July 4, 1977
Most consecutive games, one or more home runs ....13 (21 homers), 1962
                                                                          13 (26 homers), 1963
Most home runs in consecutive games in which home runs were made—
                                                                       33 (10 games), 1977
Most total bases, game ....60, Boston vs. St. Louis, June 8, 1950

CALIFORNIA ANGELS—(1961 to date)
(Club known as Los Angeles Angels until September 2, 1965)

Most players	48 in 1975 (161 games)
Fewest players	33 in 1963 (161 games)
Most games	163 in 1969
	163 in 1974
Most at-bats	5640 in 1983 (162 games)
Most runs	866 in 1979 (162 games)
Fewest runs	454 in 1972 (155 games)
Most opponents' runs	797 in 1980 (160 games)
Most hits	1563 in 1979 (162 games)
Fewest hits	1209 in 1968 (162 games)
Most singles	1114 in 1979 (162 games)
Most doubles	268 in 1982 (162 games)
Most triples	54 in 1966 (162 games)
Most homers	189 in 1961 (162 games)
Most home runs with bases filled	8 in 1979, 1983
Most home runs by pinch-hitters, season	5 in 1962
Most total bases	2396 in 1982 (162 games)
Most long hits	480 in 1982 (162 games)
Most extra bases on long hits	878 in 1982 (162 games)

Most sacrifice hits	114 in 1982 (162 games)
Most sacrifice flies	56 in 1978 (162 games)
	56 in 1979 (162 games)
	56 in 1982 (162 games)
Most stolen bases	220 in 1975 (161 games)
Most caught stealing	108 in 1975 (161 games)
Most bases on balls	681 in 1961 (162 games)
Most strikeouts	1080 in 1968 (162 games)
Fewest strikeouts	682 in 1978 (162 games)
Most hit by pitch	67 in 1978 (162 games)
Fewest hit by pitch	22 in 1965 (162 games)
Most runs batted in	808 in 1979 (162 games)
Most game-winning RBIs	85 in 1982 (162 games)
Highest batting average	.282 in 1979 (162 games)
Lowest batting average	.227 in 1968 (162 games)
Highest slugging average	.433 in 1982 (162 games)
Lowest slugging average	.318 in 1968 (162 games)
	.318 in 1976 (162 games)
Most grounded into double play	145 in 1964 (162 games)
Fewest grounded into double play	98 in 1975 (161 games)
Most left on bases	1180 in 1982 (162 games)
Fewest left on bases	1044 in 1972 (155 games)
Most .300 hitters	2 in 1963, 1964, 1979, 1982
Most putouts	4443 in 1971 (162 games)
Fewest putouts	4133 in 1972 (155 games)
Most assists	2077 in 1983 (162 games)
Fewest assists	1576 in 1980 (160 games)
Most chances accepted	6499 in 1983 (162 games)
Fewest chances	5740 in 1972 (155 games)
Most errors	192 in 1961 (162 games)
Fewest errors	108 in 1982 (162 games)
Most errorless games	88 in 1967 (161 games)
Most consecutive errorless games	8 in 1972
Most double plays	190 in 1983 (162 games)
Fewest double plays	135 in 1967 (161 games)
	135 in 1972 (155 games)
	135 in 1978 (162 games)
Most passed balls	30 in 1969 (163 games)
Fewest passed balls	4 in 1982 (162 games)
Highest fielding average	.983 in 1982 (162 games)
Lowest fielding average	.969 in 1961 (162 games)
Most games won	93 in 1982
Most games lost	95 in 1968, 1980
Games won, league	1745 in 23 years
Games lost, league	1916 in 23 years
Highest percentage games won, season	.574 in 1982 (won 93, lost 69)
Lowest percentage games won, season	.406 in 1980 (won 65, lost 95)
Most shutouts won, season	28 in 1964
Most shutouts lost, season	23 in 1971
Most 1-0 games won, season	10 in 1964
Most 1-0 games lost, season	5 in 1968

Most runs, inning .... 13, California vs. Texas, September 14, 1978, ninth inning
Most runs, game .... California 24, Toronto 2, August 25, 1979
Most runs, game, by opponent ..Kansas City 17, Los Angeles 3, August 31, 1961, first game
      Chicago 17, California 2, May 31, 1978
Most hits, game .... 26, California vs. Toronto, August 25, 1979
      26, California vs. Boston, June 20, 1980
Most home runs, game .... 6, California vs. Boston June 20, 1980
Most runs, shutout game .... Los Angeles 17, Washington 0, August 23, 1963
      California 17, Minnesota 0, April 23, 1980

Most runs, shutout game, by opponent—
      Washington 13, Los Angeles 0, June 2, 1965, first game
      Chicago 13, California 0, May 22, 1971
      Kansas City 13, California 0, June 18, 1975
Most runs, doubleheader shutout .... 7, Los Angeles vs. Kansas City, June 26, 1964
Longest 1-0 game won .... 15 innings, Los Angeles 1, Chicago 0, April 13, 1963
Longest 1-0 game lost .... 20 innings, Oakland 1, California 0, July 9, 1971
Longest shutout game won .... 16 innings, California 3, Chicago 0, September 22, 1975
Most consecutive games won, season .... 11 in 1964
Most consecutive games lost, season .... 11 in 1974
Most times league champions .... None
Most times lowest percentage games won, season 1
Most consecutive games, one or more home runs .... 18 (30 homers), 1982

Most home runs in consecutive games in which home runs were made—
30 (18 games), 1982
Most total bases, game..52, California vs. Boston, June 20, 1980

CHICAGO WHITE SOX—(1901 to date)

Most players	50 in 1932
Fewest players	19 in 1905
Most games	163 in 1961, 1966, 1974
Most at-bats	5633 in 1977 (162 games)
Most runs	920 in 1936 (153 games)
Most opponents' runs	946 in 1934 (153 games)
Fewest runs	447 in 1910 (156 games)
Most hits	1597 in 1936 (153 games)
Fewest hits	1061 in 1910 (156 games)
Most singles	1199 in 1936 (153 games)
Most doubles	314 in 1926 (155 games)
Most triples	102 in 1915 (155 games)
Most homers	192 in 1977 (162 games)
Most home runs with bases filled	7 in 1961
Most home runs by pinch-hitters, season	6 in 1953, 1961
Most total bases	2502 in 1977 (162 games)
Most long hits	498 in 1977 (162 games)
Most extra bases on long hits	934 in 1977 (162 games)
Most sacrifices (S. H. and S. F.)	270 in 1915 (154 games)
Most sacrifice hits	207 in 1906 (154 games)
Most sacrifice flies	63 in 1977 (162 games)
Most stolen bases	275 in 1901 (138 games)
Most caught stealing	119 in 1923 (156 games)
Most bases on balls	702 in 1949 (154 games)
Most strikeouts	991 in 1972 (154 games)
Fewest strikeouts	355 in 1920 (154 games)
Most hit by pitch	75 in 1956 (154 games)
Fewest hit by pitch	10 in 1940 (155 games)
Highest batting average	.295 in 1920 (154 games)
Lowest batting average	.212 in 1910 (156 games)
Most runs batted in	862 in 1936 (153 games)
Most game-winning RBIs	95 in 1983 (162 games)
Highest slugging average	.444 in 1977 (162 games)
Lowest slugging average	.261 in 1910 (156 games)
Most grounded into double play	156 in 1950 (156 games)
	156 in 1974 (163 games)
Fewest grounded into double play	94 in 1966 (163 games)
Most left on bases	1279 in 1936 (153 games)
Fewest left on bases	1014 in 1967 (162 games)
Most .300 hitters	8 in 1924
Most putouts	4471 in 1967 (162 games)
Fewest putouts	3943 in 1942 (148 games)
Most assists	2446 in 1907 (157 games)
Fewest assists	1622 in 1977 (162 games)
Most chances accepted	6655 in 1907 (157 games)
Fewest chances accepted	5670 in 1942 (148 games)
Most errors	358 in 1901 (137 games)
Fewest errors	107 in 1957 (155 games)
Most errorless games	89 in 1962 (162 games)
Most consecutive errorless games	9 in 1955, 1964
Most double plays	188 in 1974 (163 games)
Fewest double plays	94 in 1915 (155 games)
Most passed balls	45 in 1965 (162 games)
Fewest passed balls	3 in 1922 (155 games)
Highest fielding average	.982 in 1954 (155 games)
	.982 in 1957 (155 games)
	.982 in 1960 (154 games)
	.982 in 1962 (162 games)
Lowest fielding average	.938 in 1901 (137 games)
Most games won	100 in 1917
Most games lost	106 in 1970
Highest percentage games won	.649 in 1917 (won 100, lost 54)
Lowest percentage games won	.325 in 1932 (won 49, lost 102)
Games won, league	6419 in 83 years
Games lost, league	6318 in 83 years
Most shutouts won, season	30 in 1906
Most shutouts lost, season	24 in 1910

Most 1-0 games won .... 9 in 1909
9 in 1967
Most 1-0 games lost .... 9 in 1968
Most consecutive games won, season .... 19 in 1906
Most consecutive games lost, season .... 13 in 1924
Most times league champion 5
Most times lowest percentage games won, season 6
Most runs, game .... Chicago 29, Kansas City 6, April 23, 1955
Most runs game, by opponent ....New York 22, Chicago 5, July 26, 1931, second game
Most runs, shutout game ....Chicago 17, Washington 0, September 19, 1925, second game
Most runs, shutout game, by opponent....................... Baltimore 17, Chicago 0, July 27, 1969
Most runs, doubleheader shutout ....17, Chicago vs. Detroit, September 6, 1905
Most runs, inning ....13, Chicago vs. Washington, Sept. 26, 1943, first game, fourth inning
Most home runs, game ....7, Chicago vs. Kansas City, April 23, 1955
Longest 1-0 game won...........17 innings, Chicago 1, Cleveland 0, Sept. 13, 1967, night game
Longest 1-0 game lost ....18 innings, Washington 1, Chicago 0, May 15, 1918
Washington 1, Chicago 0, June 8, 1947, first game
Most consecutive games, one or more home runs ....12 (20 homers), 1983
Most home runs in consecutive games in which home runs were made—
20 (10 games), 1977
20 (12 games), 1983
Most hits, game..29, Chicago vs. Kansas City, April 23, 1955
Most total bases, game ....55, Chicago vs. Kansas City, April 23, 1955

CLEVELAND INDIANS—(1901 to date)

Most players.. 48 in 1912, 1946
Fewest players .... 24 in 1904
Most games .... 164 in 1964
Most at-bats... 5646 in 1936 (157 games)
Most runs... 925 in 1921 (154 games)
Fewest runs.. 472 in 1972 (156 games)
Most opponents' runs... 915 in 1930 (154 games)
Most hits.. 1715 in 1936 (157 games)
Fewest hits... 1210 in 1915 (154 games)
Most singles... 1218 in 1925 (155 games)
Most doubles.. 358 in 1930 (154 games)
Most triples .... 95 in 1920 (154 games)
Most homers... 183 in 1970 (162 games)
Most home runs with bases filled .... 8 in 1979
Most home runs by pinch-hitters, season.................... 9 in 1965, 1970
Most total bases.. 2605 in 1936 (157 games)
Most long hits.. 562 in 1936 (157 games)
Most extra bases on long hits .... 890 in 1936 (157 games)
Most sacrifices (S. H. and S. F.) .... 262 in 1917 (156 games)
Most sacrifice hits.. 195 in 1906 (157 games)
Most sacrifice flies .... 74 in 1980 (160 games)
Most stolen bases... 211 in 1917 (156 games)
Most caught stealing .... 92 in 1920 (154 games)
Most bases on balls... 723 in 1955 (154 games)
Most strikeouts... 1063 in 1964 (164 games)
Fewest strikeouts.. 331 in 1922 (155 games)
331 in 1926 (154 games)
Most hit by pitch .... 54 in 1962 (162 games)
Fewest hit by pitch .... 11 in 1943 (153 games)
11 in 1976 (162 games)
Most runs batted in.. 852 in 1936 (157 games)
Most game-winning RBIs .... 72 in 1980 (160 games)
Highest batting average .... .308 in 1921 (154 games)
Lowest batting average .... .234 in 1968 (162 games)
.234 in 1972 (156 games)
Highest slugging average .... .461 in 1936 (157 games)
Lowest slugging average .... .305 in 1910 (161 games)
Most grounded into double play .... 165 in 1980 (160 games)
Fewest grounded into double play .... 94 in 1941 (155 games)
Most left on bases.. 1258 in 1982 (162 games)
Fewest left on bases.. 995 in 1959 (154 games)
Most .300 hitters .... 9 in 1921
Most putouts... 4463 in 1964 (164 games)
Fewest putouts.. 3907 in 1945 (147 games)
Most assists .... 2206 in 1907 (158 games)
Fewest assists.. 1468 in 1968 (162 games)

Most chances accepted	6563 in 1910	(161 games)
Fewest chances accepted	5470 in 1945	(147 games)
Most errors	336 in 1901	(138 games)
Fewest errors	103 in 1949	(154 games)
Most errorless games	85 in 1971	(162 games)
Most consecutive errorless games	11 in 1967	
Most double plays	197 in 1953	(155 games)
Fewest double plays	77 in 1915	(154 games)
Most passed balls	35 in 1958	(153 games)
Fewest passed balls	3 in 1943	(153 games)
Highest fielding average	.983 in 1947	(157 games)
	.983 in 1949	(154 games)
	.983 in 1980	(160 games)
Lowest fielding average	.941 in 1901	(138 games)
Most games won	111 in 1954	
Most games lost	102 in 1914	
	102 in 1971	
Highest percentage games won	.721 in 1954	(won 111, lost 43)
Lowest percentage games won	.333 in 1914	(won 51, lost 102)
Games won, league	6552 in 83 years	
Games lost, league	6201 in 83 years	
Most shutouts won, season	27 in 1906	
Most shutouts lost, season	24 in 1914	
Most 1-0 games won	6 in 1905, 1908, 1968	
Most 1-0 games lost	7 in 1918, 1955	
Most consecutive games, won, season	13 in 1942, 1951	
Most consecutive games lost, season	12 in 1931	
Most times league champions	3	
Most time lowest percentage games, won	3	

Most runs, game .... Cleveland 27, Boston 3, July 7, 1923, first game
Most runs, game, by opponent....Detroit 21, Cleveland 0, September 15, 1901, eight games
New York 21, Cleveland 3, July 14, 1904
New York 21, Cleveland 7, September 25, 1921
Philadelphia 21, Cleveland 3, July 25, 1929
Most runs, shutout game .... Cleveland 19, Boston 0, May 18, 1955
Most runs, shutout game, by opponent—
Detroit 21, Cleveland 0, September 15, 1901, eight innings
Most runs, doubleheader shutout ....23, Cleveland vs. Boston, June 23, 1931
Longest 1-0 game won ....15 innings, Cleveland 1, Baltimore 0, May 14, 1961, first game
Longest 1-0 game lost........................17 innings, Chicago 1, Cleveland 0, September 13, 1967
Most runs, inning..14, Cleveland vs. Philadelphia, June 18, 1950, second game, first inning
Most hits, game ....29, Cleveland vs. St. Louis, August 12, 1948, second game
Most home runs, game ....7, Cleveland vs. Detroit, July 17, 1966, second game
Most consecutive games, one or more home runs ....16 (25 homers), 1963
Most home runs in consecutive games in which home runs were made—
28 (9 games), 1962
Most total bases, game..43, Cleveland vs. Boston, May 25, 1934
43, Cleveland vs. Detroit, July 17, 1966, second game
Most total bases, extra-inning game—
45, Cleveland vs. Philadelphia, July 10, 1932, 18 innings

DETROIT TIGERS—(1901 to date)

Most players	53 in 1912	
Fewest players	24 in 1906, 1907	
Most games	164 in 1968	
Most at-bats	5648 in 1980	(163 games)
Most runs	958 in 1934	(154 games)
Most opponents' runs	928 in 1929	(155 games)
Fewest runs	499 in 1904	(162 games)
Most hits	1724 in 1921	(154 games)
Fewest hits	1204 in 1905	(154 games)
Most singles	1298 in 1921	(154 games)
Most doubles	349 in 1934	(154 games)
Most triples	102 in 1913	(153 games)
Most homers	209 in 1962	(161 games)
Most home runs with bases filled	10 in 1938	
Most home runs by pinch-hitters, season	8 in 1971	
Most total bases	2534 in 1929	(155 games)
Most long hits	546 in 1929	(155 games)
Most extra bases on long hits	890 in 1962	(161 games)
Most sacrifices (S. H. and S. F.)	256 in 1923	(155 games)

Most sacrifice hits	182 in 1906	(151 games)
Most sacrifice flies	59 in 1983	(162 games)
Most stolen bases	281 in 1909	(158 games)
Most caught stealing	92 in 1921	(154 games)
Most bases on balls	762 in 1947	(158 games)
Most strikeouts	994 in 1967	(163 games)
Fewest strikeouts	376 in 1921	(154 games)
Most hit by pitch	61 in 1968	(164 games)
Fewest hit by pitch	9 in 1945	(155 games)
Most runs batted in	873 in 1937	(155 games)
Most game-winning RBIs	89 in 1983	(162 games)
Highest batting average	.316 in 1921	(154 games)
Lowest batting average	.230 in 1904	(162 games)
Highest slugging average	.453 in 1929	(155 games)
Lowest slugging average	.321 in 1918	(128 games)
Most grounded into double play	164 in 1949	(154 games)
Fewest grounded into double play	99 in 1982	(162 games)
Most left on base	1266 in 1924	(156 games)
Fewest left on base	1025 in 1972	(156 games)
Most .300 hitters	8 in 1922, 1924, 1934	
Most putouts	4469 in 1968	(164 games)
Fewest putouts	4006 in 1906	(151 games)
Most assists	2272 in 1914	(157 games)
Fewest assists, season	1443 in 1962	(161 games)
Most chances accepted	6504 in 1914	(157 games)
Fewest chances accepted	5594 in 1959	(154 games)
Most errors	425 in 1901	(136 games)
Most errorless games	84 in 1964	(163 games)
	84 in 1968	(164 games)
	84 in 1972	(156 games)
	84 in 1973	(162 games)
Fewest errors	96 in 1972	(156 games)
Most consecutive errorless games	12 in 1963	
Most double plays	194 in 1950	(157 games)
Fewest double plays	94 in 1912	(152 games)
	94 in 1917	(154 games)
Most passed balls	28 in 1912	(154 games)
Fewest passed balls	4 in 1924	(156 games)
Highest fielding average	.984 in 1972	(156 games)
Lowest fielding average	.922 in 1901	(136 games)
Most games won	103 in 1968	
Most games lost	104 in 1952	
Highest percentage games won	.656 in 1934 (won 101, lost 53)	
Lowest percentage games won	.325 in 1952 (won 50, lost 104)	
Games won, league	6613 in 83 years	
Games lost, league	6162 in 83 years	
Most shutouts won, season	20 in 1917, 1944, 1969	
Most shutouts lost, season	22 in 1904	
Most 1-0 games won	9 in 1908	
Most 1-0 games lost	7 in 1903, 1943	
Most consecutive games won, season	14 in 1909, 1934	
Most consecutive games lost, season	19 in 1975	
Most times league champions	8	
Most times lowest percentage games won, season	2	

Most runs, game........................... Detroit 21, Cleveland 0, September 15, 1901, eight innings
Detroit 21, Philadelphia 2, July 17, 1908
Detroit 21, St. Louis 8, July 25, 1920
Detroit 21, Chicago 6, July 1, 1936
Most runs, game, by opponent .... Philadelphia 24, Detroit 2, May 18, 1912
Most runs, shutout game .... Detroit 21, Cleveland 0, September 15, 1901, eight innings
Most runs, shutout game, by opponent .... St. Louis 16, Detroit 0, September 9, 1922
Most runs, doubleheader shutout .... 26, Detroit vs. St. Louis, September 22, 1936
Most runs, inning .... 13, Detroit vs. New York, June 17, 1925, sixth inning
Longest 1-0 game won .... 12 innings, Detroit 1, St. Louis 0, September 8, 1917
Detroit 1, Cleveland 0, June 26, 1919
Detroit 1, Chicago 0, September 10, 1950, first game
Longest 1-0 game lost .... 16 innings, Chicago 1, Detroit 0, August 14, 1954
Most hits, game .... 28, Detroit vs. New York, September 29, 1928
Most home runs, game .... 6, Detroit vs. St. Louis, August 14, 1937, second game
6, Detroit vs. Philadelphia, June 11, 1954, first game
6, Detroit vs. Kansas City, July 20, 1962
6, Detroit vs. California, July 4, 1968
6, Detroit vs. Oakland, August 17, 1969
6, Detroit vs. Boston, August 9, 1971

Most consecutive games, one or more home runs ....17 (26 homers), 1940
Most home runs in consecutive games in which home runs were made—
                                                                                   31 (15 games), 1970
Most total bases....................................45, Detroit vs. St. Louis, August 14, 1937, second game

KANSAS CITY A's—(1955 through 1967)
(See Philadelphia Athletics for club's records prior to franchise transfer in 1955)

Most players ....52 in 1955 (155 games), 1961 (162 games)
Fewest players	38 in 1957 (154 games)
Most games	163 in 1964
Most at-bats...	5576 in 1962 (162 games)
Most runs	745 in 1962 (162 games)
Most opponents' runs.......................................	911 in 1955 (155 games)
Most hits	1467 in 1962 (162 games)
Most singles..	1073 in 1962 (162 games)
Most doubles	231 in 1959 (154 games)
Most triples	59 in 1965 (162 games)
Most homers..	166 in 1957 (154 games)
	166 in 1964 (163 games)
Most home runs with bases filled	4 in 1958, 1959, 1960
Most home runs by pinch-hitters, season....................	7 in 1964
Most total bases...	2151 in 1962 (162 games)
Most long hits..	411 in 1964 (163 games)
Most extra bases on long hits	773 in 1957 (154 games)
Most sacrifice hits	89 in 1961 (162 games)
Most sacrifice flies	50 in 1962 (162 games)
Fewest sacrifice flies	25 in 1964 (163 games)
Most stolen bases...	132 in 1966 (160 games)
	132 in 1967 (161 games)
Most caught stealing	59 in 1967 (161 games)
Fewest caught stealing	11 in 1960 (155 games)
Most bases on balls..	580 in 1961 (162 games)
Most strikeouts..	1104 in 1964 (163 games)
Most hit by pitch	42 in 1962 (162 games)
	42 in 1964 (163 games)
	42 in 1967 (161 games)
Fewest hit by pitch	12 in 1960 (155 games)
Most runs batted in	691 in 1962 (162 games)
Highest batting average	.263 in 1959 (154 games)
	.263 in 1962 (162 games)
Lowest batting average.......................................	.233 in 1967 (161 games)
Highest slugging average	.394 in 1957 (154 games)
Lowest slugging average......................................	.330 in 1967 (161 games)
Most grounded into double play	154 in 1960 (155 games)
Fewest grounded into double play	79 in 1967 (161 games)
Most left on bases..	1224 in 1962 (162 games)
Fewest left on bases...	925 in 1957 (154 games)
Most .300 hitters	4 in 1955
Most putouts	4374 in 1963 (162 games)
Most assists	1782 in 1956 (154 games)
Fewest assists	1532 in 1967 (161 games)
Most chances accepted	6103 in 1963 (162 games)
Fewest chances accepted.....................................	5750 in 1959 (154 games)
Most errors...	175 in 1961 (162 games)
Most errorless games..	78 in 1963 (162 games)
Fewest errors..	125 in 1957 (154 games)
	125 in 1958 (156 games)
Most consecutive errorless games.........................	8 in 1960, 1964
Most double plays	187 in 1956 (154 games)
Most passed balls	34 in 1958 (156 games)
Highest fielding average......................................	.980 in 1963 (162 games)
Lowest fielding average.......................................	.972 in 1961 (162 games)
Most games won...	74 in 1966
Most games lost...	105 in 1964
Highest percentage games won..............................474 in 1958 (won 73, lost 81)
Lowest percentage games won...........................338 in 1956 (won 52, lost 102)
Games won, league	829 in 13 years
Games lost, league	1224 in 13 years
Most shutouts won, season..................................	11 in 1963
	11 in 1966
Most shutouts lost, season...................................	19 in 1967

Most 1-0 games won, season.. 4 in 1966
Most 1-0 games lost, season.. 5 in 1967
Most consecutive games won, season .... 11 in 1959
Most consecutive games lost, season .... 13 in 1959
Most times league champions.. 0
Most times lowest percentage games won, season............................6 (tied in 1961)
Most runs, game.................................... Kansas City 20, Minnesota 2, April 25, 1961
Most runs, game, by opponent .... Chicago 29, Kansas City 6, April 23, 1955
Most runs, shutout game.. Kansas City 16, Chicago 0, May 23, 1959
Most runs, shutout game, by opponent .... Detroit 16, Kansas City 0, April 17, 1955
                                                             Boston 16, Kansas City 0, August 26, 1957
Most runs, doubleheader shutout ....9, Kansas City vs. Detroit 0, July 9, 1959
Most runs, inning ....13, Kansas City vs. Chicago, April 21, 1956, second inning
Longest 1-0 game won ....11 innings, Kansas City 1, Cleveland 0, September 15, 1966
Longest 1-0 game lost .... None over nine innings
Most hits, nine-inning game ....21, Kansas City vs. Washington, June 13, 1956
                                                21, Kansas City vs. Chicago, May 23, 1959
                                      21, Kansas City vs. Cleveland May 5, 1962, first game
Most hits, extra-inning game ....26, Kansas City vs. New York, July 27, 1956, 14 innings
Most home runs, game...5, Kansas City vs. Cleveland, April 18, 1955
                                                5, Kansas City vs. Cleveland, April 24, 1957
                                      5, Kansas City vs. Baltimore, September 9, 1958
Most consecutive games, one or more home runs ....11 (13 homers), 1964
Most home runs in consecutive games in which home runs were made..15 (9 games), 1957
Most total bases, game...............................34, Kansas City vs. Washington, June 13, 1956
                                                34, Kansas City vs. Chicago, May 23, 1959
                                      34, Kansas City vs. Cleveland, May 5, 1962, first game
Most total bases, extra-inning game—
                                      36, Kansas City vs. New York, July 27, 1956, 14 innings

KANSAS CITY ROYALS—(1969 to date)

Most players..	39 in 1969 (163 games)
	39 in 1973 (162 games)
	39 in 1982 (162 games)
Fewest players	32 in 1975 (162 games)
Most games	163 in 1969, 1983
Most at-bats..	5714 in 1980 (162 games)
Most runs..	851 in 1979 (162 games)
Fewest runs..	580 in 1972 (154 games)
Most opponents runs...................................	816 in 1979 (162 games)
Fewest opponents runs................................	566 in 1971 (161 games)
Most hits	1633 in 1980 (162 games)
Fewest hits	1311 in 1969 (163 games)
Most singles...	1193 in 1980 (162 games)
Most doubles..	305 in 1978 (162 games)
Most triples	79 in 1979 (162 games)
Most homers...	146 in 1977 (162 games)
Most home runs with bases filled	3 in 1972
	3 in 1974
	3 in 1982
Most home runs by pinch-hitters, season....	4 in 1971
Most total bases...	2440 in 1977 (162 games)
Most long hits...	522 in 1977 (162 games)
Most extra bases on long hits	891 in 1977 (162 games)
Most sacrifice hits	72 in 1972 (154 games)
Most sacrifice flies	76 in 1979 (162 games)
Most stolen bases...	218 in 1976 (162 games)
Most caught stealing	87 in 1977 (162 games)
Most bases on balls.......................................	644 in 1973 (162 games)
Most strikeouts...	958 in 1970 (162 games)
Fewest strikeouts...	644 in 1978 (162 games)
Most hit by pitch	45 in 1977 (162 games)
Fewest hit by pitch	23 in 1983 (163 games)
Most runs batted in......................................	791 in 1979 (162 games)
Most game-winning RBIs	92 in 1981 (162 games)
Highest batting average...............................	.286 in 1980 (162 games)
Lowest batting average	.240 in 1969 (162 games)
Most .300 hitters...	3 in 1980, 1982
Highest slugging average	.436 in 1977 (162 games)
Lowest slugging average...............................	.338 in 1969 (163 games)
Most grounded into double play	147 in 1980 (162 games)

Fewest grounded into double play .... 95 in 1978 (162 games)
Most left on bases... 1209 in 1980 (162 games)
Fewest left on bases... 1063 in 1983 (163 games)
Most putouts .... 4417 in 1976 (162 games)
Fewest putouts, season .... 4144 in 1972 (154 games)
Most assists .... 1912 in 1973 (162 games)
Fewest assists, season.. 1659 in 1969 (163 games)
Most chances accepted .... 6290 in 1974 (162 games)
Fewest chances accepted, season .... 5906 in 1972 (154 games)
Most errors... 167 in 1973 (162 games)
Fewest errors... 116 in 1972 (154 games)
Most errorless games.. 74 in 1974 (161 games)
Most consecutive errorless games....................................... 8 in 1971
Most double plays .... 192 in 1973 (162 games)
Fewest double plays .... 114 in 1969 (163 games)
Most passed balls.. 29 in 1974 (162 games)
Fewest passed balls .... 4 in 1983 (163 games)
Highest fielding average... .981 in 1972 (154 games)
Lowest fielding average.. .974 in 1973 (162 games)
                                                                                                     .974 in 1983 (163 games)
Most games won... 102 in 1977
Most games lost... 97 in 1970
Highest percentage games won, season .... .630 in 1977 (won 102 lost 60)
Lowest percentage games won, season .... .401 in 1970 (won 65, lost 97)
Games won, league .... 1236 in 15 years
Games lost, league .... 1126 in 15 years
Most shutouts won, season... 16 in 1972
Most shutouts lost, season... 18 in 1971
Most 1-0 shutouts won, season .... 5 in 1972
Most 1-0 shutouts lost, season .... 4 in 1971
Most consecutive games won, season .... 16 in 1977
Most consecutive games lost, season .... 8 in 1971, 1980
Most times league champions.. 1
Most times lowest percentage games won, season 0
Most runs inning ....11, Kansas City vs. Toronto, August 6, 1979, seventh inning
Most runs, game .... Kansas City 23, Minnesota 6, April 6, 1974
Most runs game, by opponent.............................. California 19, Kansas City 8, July 28, 1973
Most runs shutout game .... Kansas City 13, California 0, June 18, 1975
Most runs shutout game, by opponent.........Oakland 13, Kansas City 0, September 10, 1973
Most runs, doubleheader shutout... No performance
Longest 1-0 game won ....15 innings, Kansas City 1, Minnesota 0, May 23, 1981
Longest 1-0 game lost—
                           13 innings, Milwaukee 1, Kansas City 0, August 23, 1974, second game
Most hits, game...24, Kansas City vs. Detroit, June 15, 1976
Most home runs, game..............5, Kansas City vs. California, September 7, 1975, 11 innings
                                             5, Kansas City vs. Seattle, September 8, 1977
Most consecutive games, one or more home runs ....10 (10 homers), 1975
Most home runs in consecutive games in which home runs were made—
                                                                                    17 (9 games), 1982
Most total bases, game ....36, Kansas City vs. Detroit, June 15, 1976
                                             36, Kansas City vs. Chicago, May 13, 1979
                                             36, Kansas City vs. Milwaukee, May 11, 1982

MILWAUKEE BREWERS—(1970 to date)

Most players.. 45 in 1970 (163 games)
Fewest players .... 31 in 1979 (161 games)
Most games .... 163 in 1970, 1982
Most at-bats.. 5733 in 1982 (163 games)
Most runs... 891 in 1982 (163 games)
Fewest runs... 494 in 1972 (156 games)
Most opponents' runs.. 792 in 1975 (162 games)
Fewest opponents' runs... 595 in 1972 (156 games)
Most hits .... 1599 in 1982 (163 games)
Fewest hits .... 1188 in 1971 (161 games)
Most singles... 1065 in 1982 (163 games)
Most doubles .... 298 in 1980 (162 games)
Most triples .... 57 in 1983 (162 games)
Most homers... 216 in 1982 (163 games)
Most home runs with bases filled .... 8 in 1980
Most home runs by pinch-hitters .... 5 in 1970

Most long hits	537 in 1980	(162 games)
Most extra bases on long hits	1007 in 1982	(163 games)
Most total bases	2606 in 1982	(163 games)
Most sacrifice hits	115 in 1970	(163 games)
Most sacrifice flies	57 in 1983	(162 games)
Most stolen bases	131 in 1980	(162 games)
Most caught stealing	75 in 1974	(162 games)
Most bases on balls	592 in 1970	(163 games)
Fewest bases on balls	443 in 1977	(162 games)
Most strikeouts	985 in 1970	(163 games)
Fewest strikeouts	714 in 1982	(163 games)
Most hit by pitch	42 in 1973	(162 games)
Fewest hit by pitch	18 in 1982	(163 games)
Most runs batted in	843 in 1982	(163 games)
Most game-winning RBIs	87 in 1982	(163 games)
Highest batting average	.280 in 1979	(161 games)
Lowest batting average	.229 in 1971	(156 games)
Most .300 batters	3 in 1979, 1980, 1982	
Highest slugging average	.455 in 1982	(163 games)
Lowest slugging average	.328 in 1972	(156 games)
Most grounded into double play	144 in 1972	(156 games)
Fewest grounded into double play	94 in 1978	(162 games)
Most left on bases	1162 in 1970	(163 games)
	1162 in 1978	(162 games)
Fewest left on bases	1031 in 1972	(156 games)
Most putouts	4402 in 1982	(163 games)
Fewest putouts	4175 in 1972	(156 games)
Most assists	1976 in 1978	(162 games)
Most chances accepted	6284 in 1978	(162 games)
Fewest chances accepted	5784 in 1972	(156 games)
Most errors	180 in 1975	(162 games)
Fewest errors	112 in 1983	(162 games)
Most errorless games	78 in 1971	(161 games)
Most consecutive errorless games	10 in 1970, 1979	
Most double plays	189 in 1980	(162 games)
Fewest double plays	142 in 1970	(163 games)
Most passed balls	20 in 1975	(162 games)
Fewest passed balls	4 in 1978	(162 games)
Highest fielding average	.982 in 1983	(162 games)
Lowest fielding average, season	.971 in 1975	(162 games)
Most games won	95 in 1979	
	95 in 1982	
Most games lost, season	97 in 1970	
Games won, league	1068 in 14 years	
Games lost, league	1138 in 14 years	
Highest percentage games won, season	.590 in 1979 (won 95, lost 66)	
Lowest percentage games won, season	.401 in 1970 (won 65, lost 97)	
Most shutouts won, season	23 in 1971	
Most shutouts lost, season	20 in 1972	
Most 1-0 games won, season	5 in 1971	
Most 1-0 games lost, season	4 in 1974	
Most consecutive games won, season	10 in 1973, 1978, 1979	
Most consecutive games lost, season	10 in 1983	
Most times league champions	1	
Most times lowest percentage games won, season	0	

Most runs, game ....Milwaukee 19, Boston 8, May, 31, 1980
Most runs, game, by opponent .... Boston 20, Milwaukee 6, September 6, 1975
Most runs, shutout game .... Milwaukee 14, New York 0, September 17, 1982
                                                                      Milwaukee 14, Boston 0, April 18, 1983
Most runs, shutout game by opponent ....Chicago 14, Milwaukee 0, September 4, 1973
Most runs, doubleheader shutout.. No performance
Most runs, inning ....9, Milwaukee vs. Boston, April 12, 1980, second inning
                                9, Milwaukee vs. New York, September 19, 1982, eighth inning
Longest 1-0 game won ....14 innings, Milwaukee 1, California 0, August 24, 1983
Longest 1-0 game lost................17 innings, Baltimore 1, Milwaukee 0, September 27, 1974
Most hits, game..22, Milwaukee vs. Boston, May 31, 1980
                                22, Milwaukee vs. Boston, April 18, 1983
Most home runs, game.............................. 7, Milwaukee vs. Cleveland, April 29, 1980
Most consecutive games, one or more home runs ....15 games (35 homers) 1982
Most home runs in consecutive games in which home runs were made—
                                                                      35 (15 games), 1982
Most total bases, game... 36, Milwaukee vs. Cleveland, April 29, 1980
                                36, Milwaukee vs. Boston, May 31, 1980

MINNESOTA TWINS—(1961 to date)

(See Washington Senators for club's records prior to franchise transfer in 1961)

Most players	44 in 1964 (163 games)
Fewest players	31 in 1976 (162 games)
Most games	164 in 1967
Fewest games	154 in 1972
Most at-bats	5677 in 1969 (162 games)
Most runs	867 in 1977 (161 games)
Most opponents' runs	819 in 1982 (162 games)
Fewest opponents' runs	535 in 1972 (154 games)
Most hits	1588 in 1977 (161 games)
Fewest hits	1274 in 1968 (162 games)
Most singles	1192 in 1974 (163 games)
Most doubles	280 in 1983 (162 games)
Most triples	60 in 1977 (161 games)
Most homers	225 in 1963 (161 games)
Most home runs with bases filled	8 in 1961
Most home runs by pinch-hitters	7 in 1964, 1967
Most total bases	2395 in 1964 (163 games)
Most long hits	494 in 1964 (163 games)
Most extra bases on long hits	982 in 1964 (163 games)
Most sacrifice hits	142 in 1979 (162 games)
Most sacrifice flies	59 in 1965 (162 games)
Most stolen bases	146 in 1976 (162 games)
Most caught stealing	75 in 1976 (162 games)
Most bases on balls	649 in 1962 (163 games)
Most strikeouts	1019 in 1964 (163 games)
Fewest strikeouts	684 in 1978 (162 games)
Most hit by pitch	49 in 1968 (162 games)
Fewest hit by pitch	21 in 1980 (161 games)
Most runs batted in	804 in 1977 (161 games)
Most game-winning RBIs	75 in 1980 (161 games)
Highest batting average	.282 in 1977 (161 games)
Lowest batting average	.237 in 1968 (162 games)
Highest slugging average	.430 in 1963 (161 games)
Lowest slugging average	.344 in 1972 (154 games)
Most grounded into double play	159 in 1974 (163 games)
Fewest grounded into double play	93 in 1965 (162 games)
Most left on bases	1263 in 1974 (163 games)
Fewest left on bases	1079 in 1966 (162 games)
Most .300 hitters	3 in 1969, 1970, 1977
Most putouts	4493 in 1969 (162 games)
Fewest putouts	4198 in 1972 (154 games)
Most assists	2007 in 1979 (162 games)
Fewest assists	1559 in 1982 (162 games)
Most chances accepted	6349 in 1969 (162 games)
Fewest chances accepted	5854 in 1971 (160 games)
Most double plays	203 in 1979 (162 games)
Fewest double plays	117 in 1968 (162 games)
Most errors	174 in 1961 (161 games)
Fewest errors	108 in 1982 (162 games)
Most errorless games	79 in 1973 (162 games)
Most consecutive errorless games	8 in 1962, 1965, 1970
Most passed balls	19 in 1973 (162 games)
Fewest passed balls	4 in 1979 (162 games)
Highest fielding average	.982 in 1982 (162 games)
Lowest fielding average	.972 in 1961 (161 games)
Most games won	102 in 1965
Most games lost	102 in 1982
Highest percentage games won, season	.630, in 1965 (won 102, lost 60)
Lowest percentage games won, season	.370, in 1982 (won 60, lost 102)
Games won, league	1849 in 23 years
Games lost, league	1806 in 23 years
Most shutouts won, season	18 in 1967
	18 in 1973
Most shutouts lost, season	14 in 1964
	14 in 1972
Most 1-0 games won, season	5 in 1966
Most 1-0 games lost, season	5 in 1974
Most consecutive games won, season	12 in 1980
Most consecutive games lost, season	14 in 1982
Most times league champions	1
Most times lowest percentage games won, season	1

Most runs, game ....Minnesota 20, Oakland 11, April 27, 1980
Most runs, game, by opponent .... Kansas City 23, Minnesota 6, April 6, 1974
Most runs, shutout game ....15, Minnesota vs. Seattle, July 10, 1977
Most runs, shutout game, by opponent ....California 17, Minnesota 0, April 23, 1980
Most runs, doubleheader shutout ....14, Minnesota vs. Cleveland, July 24, 1963
Most runs, inning..............................11, Minnesota vs. Cleveland, July 18, 1962, first inning
                                              11, Minnesota vs. Oakland, June 21, 1969, tenth inning
                                              11, Minnesota vs. Cleveland, August 5, 1977, fourth inning
Longest 1-0 game won ....11 innings, Minnesota 1, Milwaukee 0, August 27, 1975
                                              11 innings, Minnesota 1, New York 0, May 10, 1980
Longest 1-0 game lost ....15 innings, Kansas City 1, Minnesota 0, May 23,1981
Most hits, game ....24, Minnesota vs. Boston, May 25, 1977
Most home runs, game ....8, Minnesota vs. Washington, August 29, 1963, first game
Most consecutive games, one or more home runs ....16 (28 homers), 1979
Most home runs in consecutive games in which home runs were made—
                                                                                      28 (16 games), 1979
Most total bases, game ....47, Minnesota vs. Washington, August 29, 1963, first game

NEW YORK YANKEES—(1903 to date)

Most players..	47 in 1979, 1982
Fewest players	25 in 1923, 1927
Most games	164 in 1964, 1968
Most at-bats...	5705 in 1964 (164 games)
Most runs..	1067 in 1931 (155 games)
Fewest runs..	459 in 1908 (155 games)
Most opponents' runs..	898 in 1930 (154 games)
Most hits	1683 in 1930 (154 games)
Fewest hits..	1137 in 1968 (164 games)
Most singles...	1157 in 1931 (155 games)
Most doubles	315 in 1936 (155 games)
Most triples..	110 in 1930 (154 games)
Most homers...	240 in 1961 (163 games)
Most home runs by pinch-hitters, season....................................	10 in 1961
Most home runs with bases filled	7 in 1948
	7 in 1980
Most long hits..	580 in 1936 (155 games)
Most extra bases on long hits	1027 in 1936 (155 games)
Most total bases..	2703 in 1936 (155 games)
Most sacrifices (S. H. and S. F.)	218 in 1922 (154 games)
	218 in 1926 (155 games)
Most sacrifice hits	178 in 1906 (155 games)
Most sacrifice flies	72 in 1974 (162 games)
Most stolen bases..	289 in 1910 (156 games)
Most caught stealing	82 in 1920 (154 games)
Most bases on balls...	766 in 1932 (156 games)
Most strikeouts..	1043 in 1967 (163 games)
Fewest strikeouts...	420 in 1924 (153 games)
Most hit by pitch	46 in 1955 (154 games)
Fewest hit by pitch	14 in 1969 (162 games)
Most runs batted in	995 in 1936 (155 games)
Most game-winning RBIs	96 in 1980 (162 games)
Highest batting average..	.309 in 1930 (154 games)
Lowest batting average...	.214 in 1968 (164 games)
Highest slugging average..	.489 in 1927 (155 games)
Lowest slugging average..	.287 in 1914 (157 games)
Most grounded into double play	152 in 1982 (162 games)
Fewest grounded into double play	91 in 1963 (161 games)
Most left on bases...	1239 in 1934 (154 games)
Fewest left on bases..	1010 in 1920 (154 games)
Most .300 hitters	9 in 1930
Most putouts..	4520 in 1964 (164 games)
Fewest putouts...	3993 in 1935 (149 games)
Most assists	2086 in 1904 (155 games)
Fewest assists..	1493 in 1948 (154 games)
Most chances accepted	6377 in 1968 (164 games)
Fewest chances accepted...	5551 in 1935 (149 games)
Most errors...	386 in 1912 (153 games)
Fewest errors..	109 in 1947 (155 games)
	109 in 1964 (164 games)
Most errorless games...	91 in 1964 (164 games)
Most consecutive errorless games..	10 in 1977

Most double plays	214 in 1956 (154 games)
Fewest double plays	81 in 1912 (153 games)
Most passed balls	32 in 1913 (153 games)
Fewest passed balls	0 in 1931 (155 games)
Highest fielding average	.983 in 1964 (164 games)
Lowest fielding average	.939 in 1912 (153 games)
Most games won	110 in 1927
Most games lost	103 in 1908
Highest percentage games won	.714 in 1927 (won 110, lost 44)
Lowest percentage games won	.329 in 1912 (won 50, lost 102)
Games won, league	7119 in 81 years
Games lost, league	5341 in 81 years
Most shutouts won, season	24 in 1951
Most shutouts lost, season	27 in 1914
Most 1-0 games won	6 in 1908, 1968
Most 1-0 games lost	9 in 1914
Most consecutive games won, season	19 in 1947
Most consecutive games lost, season	13 in 1913
Most times league champions	33
Most times lowest percentage games won, season	3

Most runs, game .... New York 25, Philadelphia 2, May 24, 1936
Most runs, game, by opponent, on road...Cleveland 24, New York 6, July 29, 1928
Most runs, game, by opponent, at home .... Detroit 19, New York 1, June 17, 1925
          Toronto 19, New York 3, September 10, 1977
Most runs, shutout game—
          New York 21, Philadelphia 0, August 13, 1939, 2nd game, eight innings
Most runs, shutout game, by opponent .... Chicago 15, New York 0, July 15, 1907
          Chicago 15, New York 0, May 4, 1950
Most runs, doubleheader shutout ....24, New York vs. Philadelphia, September 4, 1944
Most runs, inning ....14, New York vs. Washington, July 6, 1920, fifth inning
Longest 1-0 game won ......15 innings, New York 1, Philadelphia 0, July 4, 1925, first game
Longest 1-0 game lost ....13 innings, Chicago 1, New York 0, July 25, 1914
Most hits, game ....30, New York vs. Boston, September 28, 1923
Most home runs, game...8, New York vs. Philadelphia, June 28, 1939, first game
Most consecutive games, one or more home runs ....25 (40 homers), 1941
Most home runs in consecutive games in which home runs were made—
          40 (25 games), 1941
Most total bases, game...53, New York vs. Philadelphia, June 28, 1939, first game

OAKLAND A's—(1968 to date)
(See Philadelphia and Kansas City for club's records prior to franchise transfer in 1968)

Most players	47 in 1972 (155 games)
Fewest players	34 in 1968 (163 games)
	34 in 1980 (162 games)
Most games	163 in 1968
Most at-bats	5614 in 1969 (162 games)
Most runs	758 in 1973 (162 games)
	758 in 1975 (162 games)
Fewest runs	532 in 1978 (162 games)
Most opponents' runs	860 in 1979 (162 games)
Fewest opponents' runs	457 in 1972 (155 games)
Most hits	1459 in 1977 (161 games)
Fewest hits	1248 in 1972 (155 games)
Most singles	1061 in 1983 (162 games)
Most doubles	237 in 1983 (162 games)
Most triples	40 in 1968 (163 games)
Most homers	171 in 1970 (162 games)
Most home runs with bases filled	7 in 1974
Most home runs by pinch-hitters, season	8 in 1970
Most long hits	404 in 1975 (162 games)
Most extra bases on long hits	769 in 1970 (162 games)
Most total bases	2144 in 1973 (162 games)
Most sacrifice hits	108 in 1978 (162 games)
Most sacrifice flies	62 in 1983 (162 games)
Most stolen bases	341 in 1976 (161 games)
Most caught stealing	123 in 1976 (161 games)
Most bases on balls	617 in 1969 (162 games)
Most strikeouts	1022 in 1968 (163 games)
Fewest strikeouts	751 in 1979 (162 games)
Most hit by pitch	63 in 1969 (162 games)

Fewest hit by pitch	19 in 1980	(162 games)
Most runs batted in	714 in 1973	(162 games)
Most game-winning RBIs	79 in 1980	(162 games)
Highest batting average	.262 in 1983	(162 games)
Lowest batting average	.236 in 1982	(162 games)
Highest slugging average	.392 in 1970	(162 games)
	.392 in 1971	(161 games)
Lowest slugging average	.343 in 1968	(163 games)
Most grounded into double play	131 in 1979	(162 games)
Fewest grounded into double play	87 in 1968	(163 games)
Most left on bases	1244 in 1969	(162 games)
Fewest left on bases	1030 in 1979	(162 games)
Most putouts	4442 in 1969	(162 games)
Fewest putouts	4288 in 1979	(162 games)
Most assists	1821 in 1976	(161 games)
Fewest assists	1626 in 1978	(162 games)
Most chances accepted	6230 in 1969	(162 games)
Fewest chances accepted	5926 in 1978	(162 games)
Most errors	190 in 1977	(161 games)
Fewest errors	117 in 1971	(161 games)
Most errorless games	78 in 1969	(162 games)
Most consecutive errorless games	9 in 1975	
Most double plays	170 in 1973	(162 games)
Fewest double plays	115 in 1980	(162 games)
Most passed balls	26 in 1969	(162 games)
Fewest passed balls	8 in 1982	(162 games)
Highest fielding average	.981 in 1971	(161 games)
Lowest fielding average	.970 in 1977	(161 games)
Most games won, season	101 in 1971	
Most games lost, season	108 in 1979	
Games won, league	1297 in 16 years	
Games lost, league	1232 in 16 years	
Highest percentage games won, season	.627 in 1971 (won 101, lost 60)	
Lowest percentage games won, season	.333 in 1979 (won 54, lost 108)	
Most shutouts won, season	23 in 1972	
Most shutouts lost, season	19 in 1978	
Most 1-0 games won, season	5 in 1971	
Most 1-0 games lost, season	5 in 1971	
	5 in 1978	
Most consecutive games, won, season	11 in 1981	
Most consecutive games, lost, season	14 in 1977	
Most times, league champions	3	
Most times lowest percentage games won, season	0	

Most runs, game .... Oakland 21, Boston 7, June 14, 1969
Most runs, game, by opponents .... Minnesota 20, Oakland 11, April 27, 1980
Most runs, shutout game ....Oakland 13, Kansas City 0, September 10, 1973
Most runs, shutout game, by opponent .... Detroit 15, Oakland 0, May 14, 1978
Most runs, doubleheader shutout ....10, Oakland vs. Kansas City, September 9, 1974
Most runs, inning ....10, Oakland vs. Milwaukee, May 9, 1972, first game, fourth inning
Longest 1-0 game won ....20 innings, Oakland 1, California 0, July 9, 1971
Longest 1-0 game lost ....13 innings, Detroit 1, Oakland 0, May 25, 1973
Most hits, nine-inning game ....25, Oakland vs. Boston, June 14, 1969
Most hits, extra-inning game ....29, Oakland vs. Texas, July 1, 1979, 15 innings
Most home runs, game...6, Oakland vs. Cleveland, July 18, 1980
Most consecutive games, one or more home runs ....13 (26 homers), 1971
Most home runs in consecutive games in which home runs were made—
                                                                26 (13 games), 1971
Most total bases, game..38, Oakland vs. Boston, June 14, 1969

PHILADELPHIA ATHLETICS—(1901 through 1954)
(See Kansas City Athletics for club's records since franchise transfer in 1955)

Most players	56 in 1915	
Fewest players	19 in 1905	
Most games	158 in 1914	
Most at-bats	5537 in 1932	(154 games)
Most runs	981 in 1932	(154 games)
Fewest runs	447 in 1916	(154 games)
Most hits	1659 in 1925	(153 games)
Fewest hits	1132 in 1908	(157 games)
Most singles	1206 in 1925	(153 games)
Most doubles	323 in 1928	(153 games)

Most triples	108 in 1912 (153 games)
Most homers..	173 in 1932 (154 games)
Most home runs by pinch-hitters, season................................	6 in 1952 (155 games)
Most home runs with bases filled	8 in 1932
Most long hits..	527 in 1932 (154 games)
Most extra bases on long hits	924 in 1932 (154 games)
Most total bases..	2530 in 1932 (154 games)
Most sacrifices, (S. H. and S. F.)	239 in 1926 (150 games)
Most sacrifice hits	147 in 1906 (149 games)
Most sacrifice flies	31 in 1954 (156 games)
Most stolen bases..	259 in 1912 (153 games)
Most bases on balls...	783 in 1949 (154 games)
Most strikeouts..	667 in 1954 (156 games)
Fewest strikeouts..	326 in 1927 (155 games)
Most hit by pitch	46 in 1920 (156 games)
Fewest hit by pitch	5 in 1937 (154 games)
Most runs batted in..	923 in 1932 (154 games)
Highest batting average	.307 in 1925 (153 games)
Lowest batting average	.223 in 1908 (157 games)
Highest slugging average	.457 in 1932 (154 games)
Lowest slugging average	.308 in 1918 (130 games)
Most grounded into double play	170 in 1950 (154 games)
Fewest grounded into double play	105 in 1945 (153 games)
Most left on bases	1235 in 1949 (154 games)
Fewest left on bases	999 in 1924 (152 games)
Most .300 hitters	11 in 1927
Most putouts	4231 in 1910 (155 games)
Fewest putouts	3953 in 1906 (149 games)
Most assists	2172 in 1920 (156 games)
Fewest assists	1591 in 1946 (155 games)
Most chances accepted	6297 in 1920 (156 games)
Fewest chances accepted	5610 in 1938 (154 games)
Most errors..	317 in 1901 (136 games)
Fewest errors...	113 in 1948 (154 games)
Most consecutive errorless games..	7 in 1951
Most double plays	217 in 1949 (154 games)
Fewest double plays	102 in 1917 (154 games)
Most passed balls..	25 in 1914 (158 games)
Fewest passed balls	5 in 1947 (156 games)
Highest fielding average..	.981 in 1948 (154 games)
Lowest fielding average..	.936 in 1901 (136 games)
Most games won..	107 in 1931
Most games lost...	117 in 1916
Highest percentage games won...	.704 in 1931 (won 107, lost 45)
Lowest percentage games won..	.235 in 1916 (won 36, lost 117)
Games won, league	3886 in 54 years
Games lost, league	4248 in 54 years
Most shutouts won, season..	27 in 1909
	also 1 tie, 26 in 1908
Most shutouts lost, season..	
Most 1-0 games won	9 in 1909
Most 1-0 games lost	7 in 1908, 1909
Most consecutive games won, season	17 in 1931
Most consecutive games lost, season	20 in 1916, 1943
Most times league champions...	9
Most times lowest percentage games won, season	18

Most runs, game... Philadelphia 24, Detroit 2, May 18, 1912
Philadelphia 24, Boston 6, May 1, 1929
Most runs, game, by opponent .... Cleveland 25, Philadelphia 7, May 11, 1930
New York 25, Philadelphia 2, May 24, 1936
Most runs, shutout game .... Philadelphia 16, Chicago 0, July 25, 1928, first game
Philadelphia 16, Chicago 0, August 29, 1937, first game
Most runs, shutout game, by opponent—
New York 21, Philadelphia 0, August 13, 1939, second game, eight innings
Most runs, doubleheader shutout ....17, Philadelphia vs. Detroit, August 13, 1902
Most runs, inning ....13, Philadelphia vs. Cleveland, June 15, 1925, eighth inning
Most hits, game..29, Philadelphia vs. Boston, May 1, 1929
Longest 1-0 game won.........................13 innings, Philadelphia 1, Detroit 0, August 11, 1902
13 innings, Philadelphia 1, Boston 0, September 10, 1904
13 innings, Philadelphia 1, Chicago 0, May 16, 1909
13 innings, Philadelphia 1, Cleveland 0, May 14, 1914
Longest 1-0 game, lost ....16 innings, St. Louis 1, Philadelphia 0, June 5, 1942
Most home runs, game ....7, Philadelphia vs. Detroit, June 3, 1921

Most consecutive games, one or more home runs ....12 (20 homers), 1951
Most total bases, game...44, Philadelphia vs. Boston, May 1, 1929

ST. LOUIS BROWNS—(1902 through 1953)
(See Baltimore Orioles for club's records since franchise transfer in 1954)

Most players...	52 in 1951
Fewest players	19 in 1906
Most games	159 in 1914, 1915
Most at-bats..	5510 in 1937 (157 games)
Most runs..	897 in 1925 (154 games)
Fewest runs..	441 in 1909 (154 games)
Most hits	1693 in 1922 (154 games)
Fewest hits	1092 in 1910 (158 games)
Most singles..	1239 in 1920 (154 games)
Most doubles..	327 in 1937 (156 games)
Most triples	106 in 1921 (154 games)
Most homers...	118 in 1940 (156 games)
Most home runs with bases filled	5 in 1950
Most home runs by pinch-hitters, season...........................	4 in 1951
Most total bases...	2463 in 1922 (154 games)
Most long hits..	482 in 1922 (154 games)
	482 in 1925 (154 games)
Most extra bases on long hits	770 in 1922 (154 games)
	770 in 1925 (154 games)
Most sacrifices, (S. H. and S. F.)	214 in 1928 (154 games)
Most sacrifices hits	163 in 1906 (154 games)
Most stolen bases...	234 in 1916 (158 games)
Most bases on balls..	775 in 1941 (157 games)
Most strikeouts...	863 in 1914 (159 games)
Fewest strikeouts...	339 in 1920 (154 games)
Most hit by pitch	43 in 1927 (155 games)
Fewest hit by pitch	12 in 1931 (154 games)
Most runs batted in	761 in 1936 (155 games)
Highest batting average	.313 in 1922 (154 games)
Lowest batting average	.216 in 1910 (158 games)
Highest slugging average...	.455 in 1922 (154 games)
Lowest slugging average...	.273 in 1910 (158 games)
Most grounded into double play	151 in 1951 (154 games)
Fewest grounded into double play	93 in 1944 (154 games)
Most left on bases..	1334 in 1941 (157 games)
Fewest left on bases..	1055 in 1951 (154 games)
Most .300 hitters	8 in 1922
Most putouts	4328 in 1916 (158 games)
Fewest putouts...	3993 in 1911 (152 games)
Most assists...	2189 in 1910 (156 games)
Fewest assists	1584 in 1938 (156 games)
Most chances accepted	6516 in 1916 (158 games)
Fewest chances accepted..	5618 in 1938 (156 games)
Most errors...	378 in 1910 (158 games)
Fewest errors...	134 in 1947 (154 games)
Most consecutive errorless games..	8 in 1928
Most double plays	190 in 1948 (155 games)
Fewest double plays	116 in 1914 (159 games)
Most passed balls...	30 in 1914 (159 games)
	30 in 1915 (159 games)
Fewest passed balls	4 in 1930 (154 games)
	4 in 1933 (154 games)
Highest fielding average...	.977 in 1947 (154 games)
Lowest fielding average...	.943 in 1910 (158 games)
Most games won...	93 in 1922
Most games lost..	111 in 1939
Highest percentage games won...	.604 in 1922 (won 93, lost 61)
Lowest percentage games won...	.279 in 1939 (won 43, lost 111)
Games won, league...	3416 in 52 years
Games lost, league	4465 in 52 years
Most shutouts won, season..	21 in 1909
Most shutouts lost, season...	25 in 1904
	25 in 1906
	25 in 1910
Most 1-0 games won	6 in 1909
Most 1-0 games lost	7 in 1907
Most consecutive games won, season	14 in 1916
Most consecutive games lost, season	14 in 1911, 1953

Most times league champions... 1
Most times lowest percentage games won, season 10
Most runs, game .... St. Louis 20, Detroit 9, August 18, 1951
Most runs, game by opponent................................ Boston 29, St. Louis 4, June 8, 1950
Most runs, shutout game .... St. Louis 16, Detroit 0, September 9, 1922
Most runs, shutout game, by opponent........................ Detroit 18, St. Louis 0, April 29, 1935
Most runs, doubleheader shutout ....5, St. Louis vs. Philadelphia, September 23, 1906
Most runs, inning ....11, St. Louis vs. Philadelphia, July 21, 1949, first game, sixth inning
                                     11, St. Louis vs. Detroit, August 18, 1951, seventh inning
Longest 1-0 game won ....16 innings, St. Louis 1, Philadelphia 0, June 5, 1942
Longest 1-0 game lost .....15 innings, Washington 1, St. Louis 0, August 14, 1903, first game
                                     Washington 1, St. Louis 0, July 25, 1918
Most hits, game..24, St. Louis vs. Philadelphia, September 17, 1920
                                     24, St. Louis vs. Washington, June 14, 1932
Most home runs, game......................................5, St. Louis vs. New York, September 16, 1940
Most consecutive games, one or more home runs ....11 (20 homers), 1922
Most home runs in consecutive games in which home runs were made—
                                     20 (11 games), 1922
Most total bases, game..40, St. Louis vs. Chicago, May 31, 1925

SEATTLE PILOTS—(1969)

Most players... 53 in 1969 (163 games)
Most games .... 163 in 1969
Most at-bats... 5444 in 1969 (163 games)
Most runs... 639 in 1969 (163 games)
Most opponents' runs... 799 in 1969 (163 games)
Most hits .... 1276 in 1969 (163 games)
Most singles .... 945 in 1969 (163 games)
Most doubles .... 179 in 1969 (163 games)
Most triples .... 27 in 1969 (163 games)
Most homers.. 125 in 1969 (163 games)
Most home runs with bases filled .... 3 in 1969
Most home runs by pinch-hitters, season.............................. 3 in 1969
Most total bases.. 1884 in 1969 (163 games)
Most long hits.. 331 in 1969 (163 games)
Most extra bases on long hits .... 608 in 1969 (163 games)
Most sacrifice hits .... 72 in 1969 (163 games)
Most sacrifice flies .... 29 in 1969 (163 games)
Most stolen bases.. 167 in 1969 (163 games)
Most caught stealing .... 59 in 1969 (163 games)
Most bases on balls... 626 in 1969 (163 games)
Most strikeouts... 1015 in 1969 (163 games)
Most hit by pitch .... 34 in 1969 (163 games)
Most runs batted in .... 583 in 1969 (163 games)
Highest batting average .... .234 in 1969 (163 games)
Highest slugging average .... .346 in 1969 (163 games)
Most grounded into double play .... 111 in 1969 (163 games)
Most left on bases... 1130 in 1969 (163 games)
Most putouts .... 4391 in 1969 (163 games)
Most assists .... 1763 in 1969 (163 games)
Most chances accepted .... 6154 in 1969 (163 games)
Most errors.. 167 in 1969 (163 games)
Most errorless games.. 65 in 1969 (163 games)
Most consecutive errorless games... 4 in 1969
Most double plays .... 149 in 1969 (163 games)
Most passed balls... 21 in 1969 (163 games)
Highest fielding average... .974 in 1969 (163 games)
Most games won... 64 in 1969
Most games lost... 98 in 1969
Highest percentage games won, season .... .395 in 1969 (won 64, lost 98)
Most consecutive games won, season .... 5 in 1969
Most consecutive games lost, season .... 10 in 1969
Most shutouts won, season... 6 in 1969
Most shutouts lost, season.. 6 in 1969
Most 1-0 games won, season.. 2 in 1969
Most 1-0 games lost, season.. 0 in 1969
Most times league champions.. 0
Most times lowest percentage games won, season 0
Most runs, inning ....6, Seattle vs. Boston, May 16, 1969, eleventh inning
Most runs, game..Seattle 16, Washington 13, May 10, 1969
Most runs, game, by opponent ....Baltimore 15, Seattle 3, August 16, 1969
Most runs shutout game ....Seattle 8, California 0, July 9, 1969, first game

Most runs shutout game by opponent ....Baltimore 10, Seattle 0, June 7, 1969
Most runs doubleheader shutout.. No performance
Longest 1-0 game won ....9 innings, Seattle 1, California 0, April 29, 1969
                                                                         Seattle 1, Kansas City 0, June 21, 1969
Longest 1-0 game lost .... None
Most hits, game ....16, Seattle vs. Oakland, September 10, 1969
Most hits, extra-inning game ....20, Seattle vs. Minnesota, July 19, 1969, 18 innings
Most home runs, game ....4, Seattle vs. Boston, May 16, 1969, 11 innings
Most home runs in consecutive games in which home runs were made....8 (5 games), 1969
Most consecutive games one or more home runs ....5 (8 homers), 1969
Most total bases game ....31, Seattle vs. Boston, May 16, 1969, 11 innings

SEATTLE MARINERS—(1977 to date)

Most players	43 in 1977	(162 games)
Fewest players	34 in 1978	(160 games)
	34 in 1980	(163 games)
Most games	163 in 1980	
Fewest games	160 in 1978	
Most at-bats	5626 in 1982	(162 games)
Fewest at-bats	5336 in 1983	(162 games)
Most runs	711 in 1979	(162 games)
Fewest runs	558 in 1983	(162 games)
Most opponent's runs	855 in 1977	(162 games)
Fewest opponent's runs	712 in 1982	(162 games)
Most hits	1490 in 1979	(162 games)
Fewest hits	1280 in 1983	(162 games)
Most singles	1056 in 1979	(162 games)
Most doubles	259 in 1982	(162 games)
Most triples	52 in 1979	(162 games)
Most homers	133 in 1977	(162 games)
Most home runs with bases filled	7 in 1978	(160 games)
Most home runs by pinch hitters, season	4 in 1978	(160 games)
	4 in 1979	(162 games)
	4 in 1980	(163 games)
Most total bases	2240 in 1979	(162 games)
Most long hits	434 in 1979	(162 games)
Most extra bases on long hits	750 in 1979	(162 games)
Most sacrifice hits	106 in 1980	(163 games)
Most sacrifice flies	54 in 1979	(162 games)
Most stolen bases	144 in 1983	(162 games)
Most caught stealing	82 in 1982	(162 games)
Most bases on balls	522 in 1978	(160 games)
Most strikeouts	840 in 1983	(162 games)
Fewest strikeouts	702 in 1978	(160 games)
Most hit by pitch	35 in 1977	(162 games)
Most runs batted in	676 in 1979	(162 games)
Most game-winning RBIs	68 in 1982	(162 games)
Highest batting average	.269 in 1979	(162 games)
Lowest batting average	.240 in 1983	(162 games)
Highest slugging average	.404 in 1979	(162 games)
Lowest slugging average	.356 in 1980	(163 games)
Most grounded into double play	158 in 1979	(162 games)
Fewest grounded into double play	112 in 1978	(160 games)
Most left on bases	1145 in 1979	(162 games)
Fewest left on bases	1034 in 1983	(162 games)
Most .300 hitters	1 in 1978, 1979, 1980	
Most putouts	4429 in 1982	(162 games)
Fewest putouts	4255 in 1983	(162 games)
Most assists	1930 in 1980	(163 games)
Fewest assists	1773 in 1982	(162 games)
Most chances accepted	6302 in 1980	(163 games)
Fewest chances accepted	6106 in 1977	(162 games)
Most errors	149 in 1980	(163 games)
Most errorless games	74 in 1978	(160 games)
Fewest errors	136 in 1983	(162 games)
Most consecutive errorless games	10 in 1979	
Most double plays	189 in 1980	(163 games)
Fewest double plays	158 in 1982	(162 games)
Most passed balls	16 in 1983	(162 games)
Fewest passed balls	6 in 1978	(160 games)

Highest fielding average	.978 in 1978 (160 games)
	.978 in 1979 (162 games)
	.978 in 1982 (162 games)
	.978 in 1983 (162 games)
Lowest fielding average	.976 in 1977 (162 games)
Most games won	76 in 1982
Most games lost	104 in 1978
Games won, league	426 in 7 years
Games lost, league	653 in 7 years
Highest percentage games won	.469 in 1982 (won 76, lost 86)
Lowest percentage games won	.350 in 1978 (won 56, lost 104)
Most shutouts won, season	11 in 1982
Most shutouts lost, season	15 in 1978, 1983
Most 1-0 games won, season	3 in 1979
Most 1-0 games lost, season	4 in 1980
Most consecutive games won, season	6 in 1980
Most consecutive games lost, season	12 in 1980
Most times league champions	0
Most times lowest percentage games won, season	3
Most runs, game	Seattle 16, New York 1, July 11, 1979
Most runs, game, by opponent	Toronto 19, Seattle 7, June 26, 1983
Most runs, shutout game	Seattle 9, Cleveland 0, July 24, 1982
Most runs, shutout game, by opponent	Minnesota 15, Seattle 0, July 10, 1977
Most runs, inning	9, Seattle vs. California, April 6, 1979, second inning
	9, Seattle vs. New York, July 11, 1979, first inning
	9, Seattle vs. Chicago, September 15, 1980, third inning
Longest 1-0 game won	None over nine innings
Longest 1-0 game lost	None over nine innings
Most hits, nine-inning game	20, Seattle vs. Cleveland, August 30, 1981
Most hits, extra-inning game	24, Seattle vs. Boston, September 3, 1981, 20 innings
Most home runs, game	6, Seattle vs. Detroit, June 4, 1979
Most consecutive games, one or more home runs	8 (12 homers), 1977
Most home runs in consecutive games in which home runs were made—	
	12 (8 games), 1977
Most total bases, game	34, Seattle vs. Detroit, June 4, 1979

TEXAS RANGERS—(1972 to date)

(Includes only Texas records: See Washington Senators, Second Club for club's records prior to franchise transfer in 1972)

Most players	42 in 1973 (162 games)
	42 in 1977 (162 games)
Fewest players	36 in 1976 (162 games)
Most games	163 in 1980, 1983
Fewest games	154 in 1972
Most at-bats	5690 in 1980 (163 games)
Most runs	767 in 1977 (162 games)
Most opponents' runs	844 in 1973 (162 games)
Most hits	1616 in 1980 (163 games)
Most singles	1202 in 1980 (163 games)
Most doubles	265 in 1977 (162 games)
Most triples	39 in 1974 (161 games)
	39 in 1977 (162 games)
Most homers	140 in 1979 (162 games)
Most home runs with bases filled	5 in 1975, 1980
Most home runs by pinch-hitters	7 in 1980
Most long hits	439 in 1977 (162 games)
Most extra bases on long hits	748 in 1977 (162 games)
Most total bases	2305 in 1980 (163 games)
Most sacrifice hits	116 in 1977 (162 games)
Most sacrifice flies	59 in 1979 (162 games)
Most stolen bases	196 in 1978 (162 games)
Most caught stealing	91 in 1978 (162 games)
Most bases on balls	624 in 1978 (162 games)
Most strikeouts	926 in 1972 (154 games)
Most hit by pitch	39 in 1977 (162 games)
Most runs batted in	720 in 1980 (163 games)
Most game-winning RBIs	74 in 1980 (163 games)
Highest batting average	.284 in 1980 (163 games)
Highest slugging average	.409 in 1979 (162 games)
Most grounded into double play	156 in 1980 (163 games)
Most left on bases	1215 in 1976 (162 games)
Fewest left on bases	1082 in 1982 (162 games)

Most .300 hitters .... 3 in 1980
Most putouts .... 4417 in 1977 (162 games)
Most assists .... 1980 in 1975 (162 games)
Fewest assists .... 1704 in 1973 (162 games)
Most chances accepted .... 6377 in 1975 (162 games)
Most errors .... 191 in 1975 (162 games)
Fewest errors .... 112 in 1983 (163 games)
Most errorless games .... 79 in 1977 (162 games)
Most consecutive errorless games .... 7 in 1977 (162 games)
Most double plays .... 173 in 1975 (162 games)
Most passed balls .... 21 in 1980 (163 games)
Fewest passed balls .... 5 in 1977 (162 games)
Highest fielding average .... .983 in 1983 (163 games)
Lowest fielding average .... .971 in 1975 (162 games)
Most games won .... 94 in 1977
Most games lost .... 105 in 1973
Highest percentage games won, season .... .580 in 1977 (won 94, lost 68)
Lowest percentage games won, season .... .351 in 1972 (won 54, lost 100)
Games won, league .... 888 in 12 years
Games lost, league .... 988 in 12 years
Most shutouts won, season .... 17 in 1977
Most shutouts lost, season .... 27 in 1972
Most 1-0 games won, season .... 5 in 1974, 1975, 1976
Most 1-0 games lost, season .... 7 in 1976
Most consecutive games, won, season .... 8 in 1976, 1979
Most consecutive games lost, season .... 15 in 1972
Most times league champions 0
Most times lowest percentage games won, season 2
Most runs, game .... Texas 16, Minnesota 2, May 27, 1972
                                    Texas 16, Detroit 9, August 8, 1979, first game
                                    Texas 16, Boston 8, April 22, 1981
                                    Texas 16, Oakland 4, July 3, 1983, 15 innings
Most runs, inning .... 12, Texas vs. Oakland, July 3, 1983, fifteenth inning
Most runs, game by opponent .... Oakland 17, Texas 2, May 10, 1973
Most runs, shutout game .... Texas 14, Oakland 0, July 26, 1977
Most runs, shutout game by opponent .... Chicago 14, Texas 0, April 18, 1972
                                    Chicago 14, Texas 0, September 4, 1973
Most runs, doubleheader shutout .... No performance
Longest 1-0 game won .... 14 innings, Texas 1, Boston 0, April 17, 1983
Longest 1-0 games lost .... 11 innings, Chicago 1, Texas 0, June 2, 1976
Most hits, nine-inning game .... 20, Texas vs. California, June 28, 1979
Most hits, extra-inning game .... 22, Texas vs. Baltimore, May 14, 1983, 11 innings
Most home runs, game .... 5, Texas vs. New York, August 27, 1977
                                    5, Texas vs. Boston, July 13, 1978
                                    5, Texas vs. Minnesota, May 23, 1979
Most consecutive games, one or more home runs .... 9 (18 homers) 1975
Most home runs in consecutive games in which home runs were made—
                                    18 (9 games) 1975
Most total bases, game .... 33, Texas vs. California, June 21, 1974, first game

TORONTO BLUE JAYS—(1977 to date)

Most players .... 40 in 1979 (162 games)
Fewest players .... 33 in 1983 (162 games)
Most games .... 162 in 1979, 1980, 1982, 1983
Most at-bats .... 5581 in 1983 (162 games)
Fewest at-bats .... 5418 in 1977 (161 games)
Most runs .... 795 in 1983 (162 games)
Fewest runs .... 590 in 1978 (161 games)
Most opponent's runs .... 862 in 1979 (162 games)
Fewest opponent's runs .... 701 in 1982 (162 games)
Most hits .... 1546 in 1983 (162 games)
Fewest hits .... 1358 in 1978 (161 games)
Most singles .... 1052 in 1983 (162 games)
Most doubles .... 269 in 1983 (162 games)
Most triples .... 58 in 1983 (162 games)
Most homers .... 167 in 1983 (162 games)
Most home runs with bases filled .... 3 in 1979 (162 games)
                                    3 in 1983 (162 games)
Most home runs by pinch-hitters .... 5 in 1977 (161 games)
                                    5 in 1983 (162 games)
Most total bases .... 2432 in 1983 (162 games)

Most long hits	494 in 1983 (162 games)
Most extra bases on long hits	886 in 1983 (162 games)
Most sacrifice hits	81 in 1977 (161 games)
Most sacrifice flies	54 in 1983 (162 games)
Most stolen bases	128 in 1983 (162 games)
Most caught stealing	81 in 1982 (162 games)
Most bases on balls	510 in 1983 (162 games)
Fewest bases on balls	415 in 1982 (162 games)
Most strikeouts	819 in 1977 (161 games)
Fewest strikeouts	645 in 1978 (160 games)
Most hit by pitch	36 in 1979 (162 games)
Most runs batted in	748 in 1983 (162 games)
Most game-winning RBIs	85 in 1983 (162 games)
Highest batting average	.277 in 1983 (162 games)
Lowest batting average	.250 in 1978 (161 games)
Highest slugging average	.436 in 1983 (162 games)
Lowest slugging average	.359 in 1978 (161 games)
Most grounded into double play	156 in 1977 (161 games)
Fewest grounded into double play	107 in 1982 (162 games)
Most left on bases	1106 in 1983 (162 games)
Fewest left on bases	1064 in 1979 (162 games)
Most .300 hitters	3 in 1983
Most putouts	4398 in 1980 (162 games)
Fewest putouts	4251 in 1979 (162 games)
Most assists	1939 in 1980 (162 games)
Fewest assists	1763 in 1978 (161 games)
Most chances accepted	6337 in 1980 (162 games)
Fewest chances accepted	6051 in 1978 (161 games)
Most errors	164 in 1977 (161 games)
Most errorless games	70 in 1980 (162 games)
Fewest errors	115 in 1983 (162 games)
Most consecutive errorless games	7 in 1982 (162 games)
	7 in 1983 (162 games)
Most double plays	206 in 1980 (162 games)
Fewest double plays	133 in 1977 (161 games)
Most passed balls	16 in 1978 (161 games)
Fewest passed balls	6 in 1983 (162 games)
Highest fielding average	.981 in 1983 (162 games)
Lowest fielding average	.974 in 1977 (161 games)
Most games won	89 in 1983
Most games lost	109 in 1979
Highest percentage games won	.549 in 1983 (won 89, lost 73)
Lowest percentage games won	.327 in 1979 (won 53, lost 109)
Games won, league	437 in 7 years
Games lost, league	639 in 7 years
Most shutouts won, season	13 in 1982
Most shutouts lost, season	20 in 1981
Most 1-0 games won, season	5 in 1980
Most 1-0 games lost, season	3 in 1979
Most consecutive games won, season	6 in 1980
	6 in 1982 (Twice)
Most consecutive games lost, season	12 in 1981
Most times league champions	0
Most times lowest percentage games won, season	3

Most runs, game............................ Toronto 24, Baltimore 10, June 26, 1978
Most runs, game, by opponent................................. California 24, Toronto 2, August 25, 1979
Most runs, shutout game... Toronto 8, Chicago 0, August 9, 1978
Toronto 8, Chicago 0, May 1, 1983
Toronto 8, Chicago 0, July 14, 1983
Toronto 8, New York 0, August 9, 1983
Toronto 8, Minnesota 0, September 30, 1983
Most runs, shutout game, by opponent—
New York 15, Toronto 0, September 25, 1977, first game
Most runs, inning .... 9, Toronto vs. California, May 15, 1978, seventh inning
9, Toronto vs. Baltimore, June 26, 1978, second inning
Longest 1-0 game won ....11 innings, Toronto 1, Oakland 0, May 16, 1980
Longest 1-0 game lost ....None over nine innings
Most hits, game .... 24, Toronto vs. Baltimore, June 26, 1978
Most home runs, game........................5, Toronto vs. Minnesota, September 17, 1983
Most consecutive games, one or more home runs ....9 (14 homers), 1983
Most home runs in consecutive games in which home runs were made—
16 (8 games), 1983
Most total bases, game..41, Toronto vs. Baltimore, June 26, 1978

WASHINGTON SENATORS (Original Club)—(1901 through 1960)
(Includes records only of club until franchise transfer to Minnesota in 1961)

Most players	44 in 1909
Fewest players	25 in 1908, 1917
Most games	159 in 1916
Most at-bats	5592 in 1935 (154 games)
Most runs	892 in 1930 (154 games)
Fewest runs	380 in 1909 (156 games)
Most hits	1620 in 1930 (154 games)
Fewest hits	1112 in 1909 (156 games)
Most singles	1209 in 1935 (154 games)
Most doubles	308 in 1931 (156 games)
Most triples	100 in 1932 (154 games)
Most homers	163 in 1959 (154 games)
Most home runs with bases filled, season	8 in 1938
Most home runs by pinch-hitter, season	4 in 1955, 1960
Most total bases	2287 in 1930 (154 games)
Most long hits	464 in 1932 (154 games)
Most extra bases on long hits	732 in 1960 (154 games)
Most sacrifices (S. H. and S. F.)	232 in 1923 (155 games)
	232 in 1924 (156 games)
Most sacrifice hits	135 in 1906 (151 games)
Most sacrifice flies	42 in 1954 (155 games)
Most stolen bases	291 in 1913 (155 games)
Most bases on balls	690 in 1956 (155 games)
Most strikeouts	883 in 1960 (154 games)
Fewest strikeouts	359 in 1927 (157 games)
Most hit by pitch	80 in 1911 (154 games)
Fewest hit by pitch	8 in 1947 (154 games)
Most runs batted in	822 in 1936 (153 games)
Highest batting average	.303 in 1925 (152 games)
Lowest batting average	.223 in 1909 (156 games)
Highest slugging average	.426 in 1930 (154 games)
Lowest slugging average	.287 in 1910 (157 games)
Most grounded into double play	145 in 1951 (154 games)
Fewest grounded into double play	94 in 1943 (153 games)
Most left on bases	1305 in 1935 (154 games)
Fewest left on bases	998 in 1959 (154 games)
Most .300 hitters	9 in 1925
Most putouts	4291 in 1916 (159 games)
Fewest putouts	3944 in 1906 (151 games)
Most assists	2232 in 1911 (154 games)
Fewest assists	1587 in 1951 (154 games)
Most chances accepted	6363 in 1910 (157 games)
Fewest chances accepted	5672 in 1953 (152 games)
Most errors	325 in 1901 (134 games)
Fewest errors	118 in 1958 (156 games)
Most consecutive errorless games	9 in 1952
Most double plays	186 in 1935 (154 games)
Fewest double plays	93 in 1912 (154 games)
Most passed balls	40 in 1945 (156 games)
Fewest passed balls	3 in 1927 (157 games)
Highest fielding average	.980 in 1958 (156 games)
Lowest fielding average	.936 in 1902 (138 games)
Most games won	99 in 1933
Most games lost	113 in 1904
Highest percentage games won	.651 in 1933 (won 99, lost 53)
Lowest percentage games won	.252 in 1904 (won 38, lost 113)
Games won, league	4223 in 60 years
Games lost, league	4864 in 60 years
Most shutouts won, season	25 in 1914
Most shutouts lost, season	29 in 1909
Most 1-0 games won	11 in 1914
Most 1-0 games lost	7 in 1915
Most consecutive games won, season	17 in 1912
Most consecutive games lost, season	18 in 1948
	18 in 1959
Most times league champions	3
Most times lowest percentage games won, season	10
Most runs, game	Washington 21, Detroit 5, August 5, 1929
Most runs, game, by opponent	Boston 24, Washington 4, September 27, 1940

Most runs, shutout game—
Washington 14, Boston 0, September 11, 1905, second game, 7 innings
Washington 14, Chicago 0, September 3, 1942, second game
Most runs, shutout game, by opponent .... New York 17, Washington 0, April 24, 1909
New York 17, Washington 0, July 6, 1920
Chicago 17, Washington 0, September 19, 1925, second game
Most runs, doubleheader shutout .... 13, Washington vs. Cleveland, August 20, 1945
Most runs, inning .... 12, Washington vs. St. Louis, July 10, 1926, eighth inning
Longest 1-0 game won .... 18 innings, Washington 1, Chicago 0, May 15, 1918
18 innings, Washington 1, Chicago 0, June 8, 1947, first game
Longest 1-0 game lost .... 13 innings, Boston 1, Washington 0, August 15, 1916
13 innings, Chicago 1, Washington 0, July 29, 1918
Most hits, game .... 24, Washington vs. Detroit, July 9, 1903
24, Washington vs. Cleveland, July 18, 1925
Most home runs, nine-inning game .... 5, Washington vs. Detroit, May 2, 1959
Most home runs, 10-inning game .... 7, Washington vs. Chicago, May 3, 1949
Most consecutive games, one or more home runs .... 8 (14 homers), 1959
Most home runs in consecutive games in which home runs were made—
17 (7 games), 1959
Most total bases, game .... 41, Washington vs. Detroit, July 9, 1904

WASHINGTON SENATORS (Second Club)—(1961 through 1971)
(Includes records only of franchise established in 1961)

Most players	43 in 1963 (162 games)
Fewest players	36 in 1969 (162 games)
Most games ....162 in 1962, 1963, 1964, 1966, 1969, 1970
Fewest games	159 in 1966, 1971
Most at-bats	5484 in 1962 (162 games)
Most runs	694 in 1969 (162 games)
Fewest runs	524 in 1968 (161 games)
Most opponents' runs	812 in 1963 (162 games)
Most hits	1370 in 1962 (162 games)
Most singles	1006 in 1969 (162 games)
Most doubles	217 in 1961 (161 games)
Most triples	44 in 1961 (161 games)
Most homers	148 in 1969 (162 games)
Most home runs with bases filled	4 in 1961
	4 in 1963
	4 in 1967
Most home runs by pinch-hitters	8 in 1965, 1966
Most total bases	2060 in 1969 (162 games)
Most long hits	380 in 1961 (161 games)
Most extra bases on long hits	695 in 1969 (162 games)
Most sacrifice hits	84 in 1966 (159 games)
Most sacrifice flies	44 in 1961 (161 games)
Most stolen bases	99 in 1962 (162 games)
Most caught stealing	53 in 1962 (162 games)
Most bases on balls...	635 in 1970 (162 games)
Most strikeouts..	1125 in 1965 (162 games)
Fewest strikeouts..	789 in 1962 (162 games)
Most hit by pitch	46 in 1970 (162 games)
Fewest hit by pitch	15 in 1962 (162 games)
Most runs batted in	640 in 1969 (162 games)
Highest batting average	.251 in 1969 (162 games)
Lowest batting average	.223 in 1967 (161 games)
Highest slugging average	.378 in 1969 (162 games)
Lowest slugging average	.326 in 1967 (161 games)
	.326 in 1971 (159 games)
Most grounded into double play	158 in 1969 (162 games)
Fewest grounded into double play	111 in 1963 (162 games)
Most left on bases...	1196 in 1970 (162 games)
Fewest left on bases..	1054 in 1966 (159 games)
Most .300 hitters	1 in 1961, 1962
Most putouts	4420 in 1967 (161 games)
Fewest putouts	4256 in 1971 (159 games)
Most assists	1946 in 1970 (162 games)
Fewest assists	1647 in 1965 (162 games)
Most chances accepted...	6319 in 1970 (162 games)
Fewest chances accepted..	5954 in 1965 (162 games)
Most errors..	182 in 1963 (162 games)
Fewest errors...	116 in 1970 (162 games)

Most errorless games	83 in 1964 (162 games)
Most consecutive errorless games	6 in 1970
Most double plays	173 in 1970 (162 games)
Fewest double plays	139 in 1966 (159 games)
Most passed balls	23 in 1961 (161 games)
	23 in 1971 (159 games)
Fewest passed balls	12 in 1970 (162 games)
Highest fielding average	.982 in 1970 (162 games)
Lowest fielding average	.971 in 1963 (162 games)
Most games won	86 in 1969
Most games lost	106 in 1963
Games won, league	740 in 11 years
Games lost, league	1032 in 11 years
Highest percentage games won, season	.531 in 1969 (won 86, lost 76)
Lowest percentage games won, season	.346 in 1963 (won 56, lost 106)
Most shutouts won, season	14 in 1967
Most shutouts lost, season	22 in 1964
Most 1-0 games won, season	4 in 1962, 1967, 1968
Most 1-0 games lost, season	5 in 1963, 1971
Most consecutive games won, season	8 in 1967
Most consecutive games lost, season	14 in 1961
	14 in 1970
Most times league champions	0
Most times lowest percentage games won, season	4 (tied in 1961)
Most runs, game	Washington 15, Detroit 9, May 18, 1965
	Washington 15, Cleveland 6, July 5, 1971
Most runs, game, by opponent	Los Angeles 17, Washington 0, August 23, 1963
Most runs, shutout game	Washington 13, Los Angeles 0, June 2, 1965, first game
Most runs, shutout game, by opponent	Los Angeles 17, Washington 0, August 23, 1963
Most runs, doubleheader shutout	No performance
Most runs, inning	9, Washington vs. New York, April 12, 1967, second inning
	9, Washington vs. Detroit, June 22, 1969, second game, fourth inning
Longest 1-0 game won	10 innings, Washington 1, Chicago 0, June 9, 1961, first game
	10 innings, Washington 1, Chicago 0, September 19, 1964
Longest 1-0 game lost	10 innings, Chicago 1, Washington 0, September 9, 1966
Most hits, game	20, Washington vs. Boston, July 27, 1962, second game
Most home runs, game	5, Washington vs. Detroit, May 20, 1965
	5, Washington vs. Chicago, May 16, 1969
	5, Washington vs. Chicago, June 13, 1970
Most consecutive games, one or more home runs	10 (16 homers), 1970
Most home runs in consecutive games in which home runs were made—	
	16 (10 games), 1970
Most total bases, game	32, Washington vs. Boston, July 27, 1962, second game
	32, Washington vs. Chicago, June 13, 1970

National League

ATLANTA BRAVES—(1966 to date)
(See Boston and Milwaukee for club's records prior to franchise transfer in 1966)

Most players	44 in 1966 (163 games)
Fewest players	32 in 1980 (161 games)
Most games	163 in 1966, 1968, 1974
Most at-bats	5631 in 1973 (162 games)
Most runs	799 in 1973 (162 games)
Fewest runs	514 in 1968 (163 games)
Most opponents' runs	895 in 1977 (162 games)
Most hits	1497 in 1973 (162 games)
Fewest hits	1307 in 1967 (162 games)
Most singles	1109 in 1968 (163 games)
Most doubles	226 in 1980 (161 games)
Most triples	45 in 1983 (162 games)
Most homers	207 in 1966 (163 games)
Most home runs with bases filled	7 in 1977
Most home runs by pinch-hitters, season	8 in 1977
Most total bases	2402 in 1973 (162 games)
Most long hits	459 in 1966 (163 games)
	459 in 1974 (163 games)

Most extra bases on long hits	905 in 1966 (163 games)
	905 in 1973 (162 games)
Most sacrifice hits	109 in 1974 (163 games)
Most sacrifice flies	47 in 1976 (162 games)
	47 in 1978 (162 games)
Most stolen bases	151 in 1982 (162 games)
Most caught stealing	88 in 1983 (162 games)
Most bases on balls	608 in 1973 (162 games)
Fewest bases on balls	414 in 1968 (163 games)
Most strikeouts	947 in 1967 (163 games)
Fewest strikeouts	665 in 1969 (162 games)
Most hit by pitch	40 in 1966 (163 games)
Fewest hit by pitch	17 in 1977 (162 games)
	17 in 1983 (162 games)
Most runs batted in	758 in 1973 (162 games)
Most game-winning RBIs	82 in 1982 (162 games)
	82 in 1983 (162 games)
Highest batting average	.272 in 1983 (162 games)
Lowest batting average	.240 in 1967 (162 games)
Highest slugging average	.427 in 1973 (162 games)
Lowest slugging average	.334 in 1976 (162 games)
Most grounded into double play	145 in 1968 (163 games)
Fewest grounded into double play	102 in 1982 (162 games)
Most left on bases	1213 in 1974 (163 games)
Fewest left on bases	1054 in 1980 (161 games)
Most .300 hitters	3 in 1966
	3 in 1970
Most putouts	4424 in 1971 (162 games)
Fewest putouts	4223 in 1979 (160 games)
Most assists	1950 in 1980 (161 games)
Fewest assists	1633 in 1972 (155 games)
Most chances accepted	6311 in 1982 (162 games)
Fewest chances accepted	5764 in 1972 (155 games)
Most errors	183 in 1979 (160 games)
Fewest errors	115 in 1969 (162 games)
Most errorless games	78 in 1968 (163 games)
Most consecutive errorless games	6 in 1967
Most double plays	186 in 1982 (162 games)
Fewest double plays	114 in 1969 (162 games)
Most passed balls	42 in 1967 (162 games)
Fewest passed balls	6 in 1983 (162 games)
Highest fielding average	.981 in 1969 (162 games)
Lowest fielding average	.970 in 1979 (160 games)
Most games won	93 in 1969
Most games lost	101 in 1977
Games won, league	1369 in 18 years
Games lost, league	1478 in 18 years
Highest percentage games won	.574 in 1969 (won 93, lost 69)
Lowest percentage games won	.377 in 1977 (won 61, lost 101)
Most shutouts won, season	21 in 1974
Most shutouts lost, season	24 in 1978
Most 1-0 shutouts won, season	7 in 1974
Most 1-0 shutouts lost, season	3 in 1968
	3 in 1974
Most consecutive games won, season	13 in 1982
Most consecutive games lost, season	17 in 1977
Most times league champions	0
Most times lowest percentage games won	1
Most runs, game	Atlanta 18, Pittsburgh 3, June 13, 1973
Most runs, game, by opponent	Cincinnati 23, Atlanta 9, April 25, 1977
Most runs shutout game	Atlanta 14, Houston 0, July 2, 1980
Most runs shutout game by opponent	Montreal 19, Atlanta 0, July 30, 1978
Most runs doubleheader shutout	No performance
Most hits game	22, Atlanta vs. New York, June 16, 1966
Most runs inning	13, Atlanta vs. Houston, September 20, 1972, second inning
Longest 1-0 game won	12 innings, Atlanta 1, Los Angeles 0, September 17, 1976, first game
Longest 1-0 game lost	13 innings, Los Angeles 1, Atlanta 0, May 18, 1974
Most home runs, game	7, Atlanta vs. Chicago, August 3, 1967
Most consecutive games, one or more home runs	20 (36 homers), 1973
Most home runs in consecutive games in which home runs were made—	36 (20 games), 1973
Most total bases, game	39, Atlanta vs. San Francisco, July 3, 1966

BOSTON BRAVES—(1876 through 1952)
(See Milwaukee and Atlanta for club's records since franchise transfer in 1953)

Most players	48 in 1946
Fewest players	23 in 1905
Most games	158 in 1914, 1916
Most at-bats	5506 in 1932 (155 games)
Most runs	1221 in 1894 (133 games)
Most runs, since 1900	785 in 1950 (156 games)
Fewest runs	408 in 1906 (152 games)
Most hits	1567 in 1925 (153 games)
Fewest hits	1115 in 1906 (152 games)
Most singles	196 in 1925 (153 games)
Most doubles	272 in 1948 (154 games)
Most triples	100 in 1921 (153 games)
Most home runs	148 in 1950 (156 games)
Most home runs with bases filled	7 in 1950
Most total bases	2173 in 1950 (156 games)
Most long hits	430 in 1950 (156 games)
Most extra bases on long hits	762 in 1950 (156 games)
Most sacrifices, (S. H. and S. F.)	221 in 1914 (158 games)
Most sacrifice hits	140 in 1948 (154 games)
Most stolen bases	190 in 1909 (155 games)
Most bases on balls	684 in 1949 (157 games)
Most strikeouts	711 in 1952 (155 games)
Fewest strikeouts	348 in 1926 (153 games)
Most hit by pitch	45 in 1917 (157 games)
Fewest hit by pitch	13 in 1941 (156 games)
Most runs batted in	726 in 1950 (156 games)
Highest batting average	.292 in 1925 (153 games)
Lowest batting average	.223 in 1909 (155 games)
Highest slugging average	.405 in 1950 (156 games)
Lowest slugging average	.274 in 1909 (155 games)
Most grounded into double play	146 in 1936 (157 games)
Fewest grounded into double play	93 in 1944 (155 games)
Most left on bases	1255 in 1948 (154 games)
Fewest left on bases	1003 in 1933 (156 games)
Most .300 hitters	8 in 1931
Most putouts	4262 in 1914 (158 games)
Fewest putouts	3975 in 1906 (152 games)
Most assists	2225 in 1908 (156 games)
Fewest assists	1665 in 1946 (154 games)
Most chances accepted	6424 in 1914 (158 games)
Fewest chances accepted	5750 in 1935 (153 games)
Most errors	353 in 1904 (155 games)
Fewest errors	138 in 1933 (156 games)
Most consecutive errorless games, season	5 in 1933 (twice)
Most double plays	178 in 1939 (152 games)
Fewest double plays	101 in 1935 (153 games)
Most passed balls	167 in 1883 (98 games)
Most passed balls since 1900	42 in 1905 (156 games)
Fewest passed balls	2 in 1943 (153 games)
Highest fielding average	.978 in 1933 (156 games)
Lowest fielding average	.945 in 1904 (155 games)
Most games won	102 in 1898
Most games won since 1900	94 in 1914
Most games lost	115 in 1935
Highest percentage games won	.705 in 1897 (won 93, lost 39)
Highest percentage games won since 1900	.614 in 1914 (won 94, lost 59)
Lowest percentage games won	.248 in 1935 (won 38, lost 115)
Games won, league	5118 in 77 years
Games lost, league	5598 in 77 years
Most shutouts won, season	21 in 1916
Most shutouts lost, season	28 in 1906
Most 1-0 games, won	9 in 1916
Most 1-0 games, lost	6 in 1906, 1933
Most consecutive games won, season	17 in 1897
Most consecutive games won, season, since 1900	8 in 1948
Most consecutive games lost, season	19 in 1906
Most times league champions	10
Most times lowest percentage games won, season	9
Most runs, game	Boston 30, Detroit 8, June 9, 1883

Most runs, game, since 1900 ....Boston 20, Philadelphia 4, June 25, 1900
Boston 20, Philadelphia 7, October 6, 1910
Boston 20, St. Louis 1, September 18, 1915, first game
Boston 20, St. Louis 3, August 25, 1936, first game
Most runs, game, by opponent......................................Pittsburgh 27, Boston 11, June 6, 1894
Most runs, game, by opponent, since 1900 ....Cincinnati 26, Boston 3, June 4, 1911
Most runs, shutout game.. Boston 18, Buffalo 0, October 3, 1885
Most runs, shutout game, since 1900 ....Boston 16, Brooklyn 0, May 7, 1918
Boston 16, Pittsburgh 9, September 12, 1952, second game
Most runs, shutout game, by opponent ....Chicago 17, Boston 0, September 16, 1884
Most runs, shutout game, by opponent, since 1900.....New York 15, Boston 0, April 15, 1905
Cincinnati 15, Boston 0, May 19, 1906
Philadelphia 15, Boston 0, July 3, 1928
New York 15, Boston 0, May 29, 1936
New York 15, Boston 0, July 4, 1934, second game
St. Louis 15, Boston 0, August 18, 1934
St. Louis 15, Boston 0, May 7, 1950
Most runs, doubleheader shutout ....8, Boston vs. Cincinnati, August 7, 1916
8, Boston vs. Brooklyn, June 30, 1937
8, Boston vs. Cincinnati, August 3, 1941
Most runs, inning ....16, Boston vs. Baltimore, June 18, 1894, a.m. game, first inning
Most runs, inning, since 1900.....................13, Boston vs. St. Louis, July 25, 1900, first inning
Longest 1-0 game won—
13 innings, 5 times; last time Boston 1, Pittsburgh 0, May 11, 1921
Longest 1-0 game lost.............................17 innings, Chicago 1, Boston 0, September 21, 1901
Most hits, game...................................30, Boston vs. St. Louis, September 3, 1896, first game
Most hits, game, since 1900 .... 25, Boston vs. St. Louis, August 25, 1936, first game
Most home runs, game ....5, Boston vs. Cincinnati, May 30, 1894, p.m. game
5, Boston vs. Chicago, May 13, 1942
5, Boston vs. Cincinnati, May 6, 1950
Most total bases, game ....46, Boston vs. Detroit, June 9, 1883
46, Boston vs. Cleveland, July 5, 1894
Most total bases, game, since 1900 .... 37, Boston vs. Philadelphia, July 6, 1934
37, Boston vs. Cincinnati, May 6, 1950

BROOKLYN DODGERS—(1890-1957)

(See Los Angeles Dodgers for club's records since franchise transfer in 1958)

Most players..	53 in 1944
Fewest players	23 in 1905
Most games..	158 in 1951
Most at-bats..	5574 in 1936 (156 games)
Most runs...	995 in 1953 (155 games)
Fewest runs...	375 in 1908 (154 games)
Most hits	1654 in 1930 (154 games)
Fewest hits..	1044 in 1908 (154 games)
Most singles..	1223 in 1925 (153 games)
Most doubles	303 in 1930 (153 games)
Most triples	99 in 1920 (155 games)
Most homers..	208 in 1953 (155 games)
Most home runs with bases filled	8 in 1952
Most home runs by pinch-hitters, season........................	7 in 1932
Most long hits...	541 in 1953 (155 games)
Most extra bases on long hits	1016 in 1953 (155 games)
Most total bases..	2545 in 1953 (155 games)
Most sacrifices (S. H. and S. F.)	203 in 1916 (156 games)
Most sacrifice hits..	197 in 1907 (153 games)
Most sacrifice flies	59 in 1954 (154 games)
Most stolen bases..	205 in 1904 (154 games)
Most caught stealing...	73 in 1921 (152 games)
Most bases on balls...	732 in 1947 (155 games)
Most strikeouts...	848 in 1957 (154 games)
Fewest strikeouts...	318 in 1922 (155 games)
Most hit by pitch	44 in 1951 (158 games)
Fewest hit by pitch	14 in 1942 (155 games)
	14 in 1944 (155 games)
Most runs batted in..	887 in 1953 (155 games)
Fewest runs batted in..	499 in 1927 (154 games)
Highest batting average	.304 in 1930 (154 games)
Lowest batting average	.213 in 1908 (154 games)
Highest slugging average	.474 in 1953 (155 games)
Lowest slugging average...	.277 in 1908 (154 games)

Most grounded into double play	151 in 1952 (155 games)
Fewest grounded into double play	86 in 1947 (155 games)
Most left on bases	1278 in 1947 (155 games)
Fewest left on bases	1012 in 1921 (152 games)
Most .300 hitters	6 in 1900, 1922, 1925, 1930, 1943, 1953
Most putouts	4295 in 1940 (156 games)
Fewest putouts	3911 in 1909 (155 games)
Most assists	2132 in 1921 (152 games)
Fewest assists	1574 in 1944 (155 games)
Most chances accepted	6334 in 1920 (155 games)
Fewest chances accepted	5672 in 1944 (155 games)
Most errors	408 in 1905 (155 games)
Fewest errors	106 in 1952 (155 games)
Most consecutive errorless games	10 in 1942
Most double plays	192 in 1951 (158 games)
Fewest double plays	95 in 1926 (155 games)
Most passed balls	21 in 1905 (155 games)
Fewest passed balls	4 in 1933 (157 games)
	4 in 1951 (158 games)
	4 in 1953 (155 games)
	4 in 1954 (154 games)
Highest fielding average	.982 in 1952 (155 games)
Lowest fielding average	.937 in 1905 (155 games)
Most games won	105 in 1953
Most games lost	104 in 1905
Highest percentage games won	.682 in 1953 (won 105, lost 49)
Lowest percentage games won	.316 in 1905 (won 48, lost 104)
Games won, league	5214 in 68 years
Games lost, league	4926 in 68 years
Most shutouts won, season	22 in 1906, 1916
Most shutouts lost, season	26 in 1907
Most 1-0 games won	7 in 1907
	7 in 1909
Most 1-0 games lost	9 in 1910, 1913
Most consecutive games won, season	15 in 1924
Most consecutive games lost, season	16 in 1944
Most times league champions	12
Most times lowest percentage games won, season	1

Most runs, game .... Brooklyn 25, Pittsburgh 6, May 20, 1896
Brooklyn 25, Cincinnati 6, September 23, 1901
Most runs, game, by opponent .... Chicago 28, Brooklyn 5, August 25, 1891
Most runs, game, by opponent, since 1900—
New York 26, Brooklyn 8, April 30, 1944, first game
Most runs, shutout game ....Brooklyn 15, Philadelphia 0, August 16, 1952, 6⅓ innings
Most runs, shutout game, by opponent—
St. Louis 17, Brooklyn 0, August 24, 1924, second game
Most runs doubleheader shutout ....18, Brooklyn vs. Philadelphia, September 3, 1906
Most runs, inning..................................15, Brooklyn vs. Cincinnati, May 21, 1952, first inning
Longest 1-0 game won ....13 innings, Brooklyn 1, St. Louis 0, August 21, 1909
13 innings, Brooklyn 1, Boston 0, May 29, 1938
Longest 1-0 game lost ....15 innings, Cincinnati 1, Brooklyn 0, June 11, 1915
Most hits, game ....28, Brooklyn vs. Pittsburgh, June 23, 1930
Most home runs, game ....6, Brooklyn vs. Milwaukee, June 1, 1955
Most consecutive games, one or more home runs....................................24 (39 homers), 1953
Most home runs in consecutive games in which home runs were made, since 1900—
39 (24 games), 1953
Most total bases, game ....46, Brooklyn vs. Philadelphia, September 23, 1939, first game

CHICAGO CUBS—(1876 to date)

Most players	49 in 1966
Fewest players	20 in 1905
Most games	164 in 1965
Most at-bats	5619 in 1980 (162 games)
Most runs	998 in 1930 (156 games)
Most opponents' runs	870 in 1930 (156 games)
Fewest runs	530 in 1906 (154 games)
Most hits	1722 in 1930 (156 games)
Fewest hits	1224 in 1907 (155 games)
Most singles	1226 in 1921 (153 games)
Most doubles	340 in 1931 (156 games)
Most triples	101 in 1911 (157 games)
Most homers	182 in 1958 (154 games)

Most homers with bases filled	9 in 1929	
Most home runs by pinch-hitters, season	8 in 1958	
Most total bases	2684 in 1930	(156 games)
Most long hits	548 in 1930	(156 games)
Most extra bases on long hits	962 in 1930	(156 games)
Most sacrifices, (S.H. and S.F.)	270 in 1908	(158 games)
Most sacrifice hits	231 in 1906	(154 games)
Most sacrifice flies	66 in 1975	(162 games)
Most stolen bases	283 in 1906	(154 games)
Most caught stealing	149 in 1924	(154 games)
Most bases on balls	650 in 1975	(162 games)
Most strikeouts	1049 in 1963	(162 games)
Fewest strikeouts	374 in 1921	(153 games)
Most hit by pitch	47 in 1966	(162 games)
Fewest hit by pitch	13 in 1956	(157 games)
Most runs batted in	940 in 1930	(156 games)
Most game-winning RBIs	70 in 1982	(162 games)
Highest batting average	.309 in 1930	(156 games)
Lowest batting average	.238 in 1963	(162 games)
	.238 in 1965	(164 games)
Highest slugging average	.481 in 1930	(156 games)
Lowest slugging average	.311 in 1907	(155 games)
Most grounded into double play	157 in 1938	(154 games)
Fewest grounded into double play	93 in 1945	(155 games)
Most left on bases	1262 in 1975	(162 games)
Fewest left on bases	964 in 1924	(154 games)
Most .300 hitters	8 in 1921	
Most putouts	4437 in 1980	(162 games)
Fewest putouts	4024 in 1909	(155 games)
Most assists	2155 in 1916	(156 games)
Fewest assists	1607 in 1956	(157 games)
Most chances accepted	6508 in 1977	(162 games)
Fewest chances accepted	5706 in 1953	(155 games)
Most errors	310 in 1914	(156 games)
Fewest errors	119 in 1968	(163 games)
Most errorless games	83 in 1968	(163 games)
Most consecutive errorless games	8 in 1978	
Most double plays	176 in 1928	(154 games)
Fewest double plays	110 in 1982	(162 games)
Most passed balls	35 in 1961	(156 games)
Fewest passed balls	4 in 1967	(162 games)
Highest fielding average	.982 in 1983	(162 games)
Lowest fielding average	.951 in 1914	(156 games)
Most games won	116 in 1906	
Most games lost	103 in 1962	
	103 in 1966	
Highest percentage games won	.798 in 1880 (won 67, lost 17)	
Highest percentage games won since 1900	.763 in 1906 (won 116, lost 36)	
Lowest percentage games won	.364 in 1962 (won 59, lost 103)	
	.364 in 1966 (won 59, lost 103)	
Games won, league	8131 in 108 years	
Games lost, league	7499 in 108 years	
Most shutouts won, season	32 in 1907, 1909	
Most shutouts lost, season	22 in 1915	
	22 in 1968	
Most 1-0 games won	9 in 1906	
Most 1-0 games lost	10 in 1916	
Most consecutive games won, season	21 in 1880, 1935	
Most consecutive games lost, season	13 in 1944, 1982	
Most times league champions	16	
Most times lowest percentage games won, season	12	

Most runs, game	Chicago 36, Louisville 7, June 29, 1897
Most runs, game, since 1900	Chicago 26, Philadelphia 23, August 25, 1922
Most runs, games, by opponent, since 1900	Chicago 26, Philadelphia 23, August 25, 1922
	Cincinnati 23, Chicago 4, July 6, 1949
	Philadelphia 23, Chicago 22, May 17, 1979, 10 innings
Most runs, shutout game	Chicago 24, Boston 0, July 1, 1885
Most runs, shutout game, since 1900	Chicago 19, New York 0, June 7, 1906
	Chicago 19, San Diego 0, May 13, 1969
Most runs, shutout game, by opponent	Pittsburgh 22, Chicago 0, September 16, 1975
Most runs, doubleheader shutout	12, Chicago vs. St. Louis, July 11, 1965
Most runs, inning	18, Chicago vs. Detroit, Sept. 6, 1883, seventh inning
Most runs, inning, since 1900	14, Chicago vs. Philadelphia, August 25, 1922, fourth inning

Longest 1-0 game won ....17 innings, Chicago 1, Boston 0, September 21, 1901
Longest 1-0 game lost ....17 innings, Houston 1, Chicago 0, August 23, 1980
Most hits, game ....32, Chicago vs. Buffalo, July 3, 1883
                                                                                   32, Chicago vs. Louisville, June 29, 1897
Most hits, game, since 1900...28, Chicago vs. Boston, July 3, 1945
Most home runs, game ....7, Chicago vs. New York, June 11, 1967, second game
                                                                   7, Chicago vs. San Diego, August 19, 1970
                                                                   7, Chicago vs. San Diego, May 17, 1977
Most consecutive games, one or more home runs ....14 (29 homers), 1884
                                                                                   14 (27 homers), 1961
Most home runs in consecutive games in which home runs were made—
                                                                                   29 (14 games), 1884
Most home runs in consecutive games in which home runs were made, since
     1900... 28 (13 games), 1954
Most total bases, game...54, Chicago vs. Brooklyn, August 25, 1891
Most total bases, game, since 1900 ..45, Chicago vs. New York, June 11, 1967, second game
Most total bases, extra-inning game, since 1900—
                                                          49, Chicago vs. Philadelphia, May 17, 1979, 10 innings

CINCINNATI REDS—(1876-1880; 1890 to date)

Most players..	45 in 1913
Fewest players	21 in 1904
Most games...163 in 1964, 1968, 1969, 1974, 1980	
Most at-bats..	5767 in 1968 (163 games)
Most runs..	857 in 1976 (162 games)
Most opponents' runs..	857 in 1930 (154 games)
Fewest opponents' runs..	528 in 1940 (155 games)
Fewest runs...	488 in 1908 (155 games)
Most hits...	1599 in 1976 (162 games)
Fewest hits...	1108 in 1908 (155 games)
Most singles...	1191 in 1922 (156 games)
Most doubles..	281 in 1968 (163 games)
Most triples	120 in 1926 (157 games)
Most homers...	221 in 1956 (155 games)
Most home runs with bases filled	7 in 1974, 1980
Most home runs by pinch-hitters, season............................	12 in 1957 (154 games)
Most long hits..	512 in 1965 (162 games)
Most extra bases on long hits	939 in 1965 (162 games)
Most total bases..	2483 in 1965 (162 games)
Most sacrifices (S. H. and S. F.)	239 in 1926 (157 games)
Most sacrifice hits..	195 in 1907 (156 games)
Most sacrifice flies	60 in 1976 (162 games)
Most stolen bases..	310 in 1910 (156 games)
Most caught stealing	136 in 1922 (156 games)
Most bases on balls..	693 in 1974 (163 games)
Most strikeouts...	1042 in 1969 (163 games)
Fewest strikeouts...	308 in 1921 (153 games)
Most hit by pitch	51 in 1956 (155 games)
Fewest hit by pitch	11 in 1951 (155 games)
Most runs batted in	802 in 1976 (162 games)
Most game-winning RBIs	84 in 1980 (163 games)
Highest batting average	.296 in 1922 (156 games)
Lowest batting average	.227 in 1908 (155 games)
Highest slugging average	.441 in 1956 (155 games)
Lowest slugging average	.304 in 1906 (155 games)
Most grounded into double play	143 in 1982 (162 games)
Fewest grounded into double play	93 in 1935 (154 games)
Most left on bases..	1328 in 1976 (162 games)
Fewest left on bases..	997 in 1921 (153 games)
Most .300 hitters	8 in 1926
Most putouts..	4471 in 1968 (163 games)
Fewest putouts..	4006 in 1930 (154 games)
Most assists	2151 in 1905 (155 games)
Fewest assists...	1534 in 1966 (160 games)
Most chances accepted..	6399 in 1915 (160 games)
Fewest chances accepted..	5655 in 1950 (153 games)
Most errors..	314 in 1914 (157 games)
Fewest errors..	95 in 1977 (162 games)
Most errorless games..	94 in 1977 (162 games)
Most consecutive errorless games.......................................	15 in 1975 (162 games)

Most double plays	194 in 1928	(153 games)
	194 in 1931	(154 games)
	194 in 1954	(154 games)
Fewest double plays	120 in 1978	(161 games)
Most passed balls	39 in 1914	(157 games)
Fewest passed balls	3 in 1975	(162 games)
Highest fielding average	.984 in 1971	(162 games)
	.984 in 1975	(162 games)
	.984 in 1976	(162 games)
	.984 in 1977	(162 games)
Lowest fielding average	.952 in 1914	(157 games)
Most games won	108 in 1975	
Most games lost	101 in 1982	
Highest percentage games won	.686 in 1919 (won 96, lost 44)	
Lowest percentage games won	.138 in 1876 (won 9, lost 56)	
Lowest percentage games won since 1900	.344 in 1934 (won 52, lost 99)	
Games won, league, 1890 to date	7224 in 94 years	
Games lost, league, 1890 to date	7058 in 94 years	
Most shutouts won, season	23 in 1919	
Most shutouts lost, season	24 in 1908	
Most 1-0 games won, season	7 in 1910, 1943, 1963	
Most 1-0 games lost, season	7 in 1907, 1916	
Most consecutive games won, season	14 in 1899	
Most consecutive games won, season, since 1900	12 in 1939, 1957	
Most consecutive games lost, season	19 in 1914	
Most times league champions	8	
Most times lowest percentage games won, season	11 (tied in 1916)	
Most runs, game	Cincinnati 30, Louisville 12, June 18, 1893	
Most runs, game, since 1900	Cincinnati 26, Boston 3, June 4, 1911	
Most runs, game, by opponent	Philadelphia 26, Cincinnati 6, July 26, 1892	
Most runs, game, by opponent, since 1900	New York 25, Cincinnati 13, June 9, 1901	
	Brooklyn 25, Cincinnati 6, September 23, 1901	
Most runs, shutout game	Cincinnati 18, Los Angeles 0, August 8, 1965	

Most runs, shutout game, by opponent—
               Philadelphia 18, Cincinnati 0, August 10, 1930, first game
               Philadelphia 18, Cincinnati 0, July 14, 1934, first game
               St. Louis 18, Cincinnati 0, June 10, 1944

Most runs, doubleheader shutout	14, Cincinnati vs. St. Louis, September 1, 1924
	14, Cincinnati vs. Los Angeles, August 16, 1961
Most runs, inning	14, Cincinnati vs. Louisville, June 18, 1893, first inning
Most runs, inning, since 1900	12, Cincinnati vs. New York, May 4, 1942, fourth inning
	12, Cincinnati vs. Atlanta, April 25, 1977, fifth inning
Longest 1-0 game won	15 innings, Cincinnati 1, New York 0, July 16, 1933, first game
	15 innings, Cincinnati 1, Brooklyn 0, June 11, 1915
Longest 1-0 game lost	21 innings, San Francisco 1, Cincinnati 0, September 1, 1967
Most hits, game	32, Cincinnati vs. Louisville, June 18, 1893
Most hits, game, since 1900	28, Cincinnati vs. Philadelphia, May 13, 1902
Most home runs, game	8, Cincinnati vs. Milwaukee, August 18, 1956
Most consecutive games, one or more home runs	21 (41 homers), 1956

Most home runs in consecutive games in which home runs were made—
               41 (21 games), 1956—

Most total bases, game	55, Cincinnati vs. Louisville, June 18, 1893
Most total bases, game, since 1900	48, Cincinnati vs. Chicago, June 1, 1957

HOUSTON ASTROS—(1962 to date)

Most players	48 in 1965	(162 games)
Fewest players	32 in 1972	(153 games)
Most games	163 in 1966, 1980	
Most at-bats	5574 in 1970	(162 games)
Most runs	744 in 1970	(162 games)
Fewest runs	464 in 1963	(162 games)
Most opponents' runs	763 in 1970	(162 games)
Most hits	1455 in 1980	(163 games)
Fewest hits	1184 in 1963	(162 games)
Most singles	1090 in 1976	(162 games)
Most doubles	263 in 1977	(162 games)
Most triples	67 in 1980	(163 games)
Most homers	134 in 1972	(153 games)
	134 in 1973	(162 games)
Most home runs with bases filled	5 in 1970	
	5 in 1973	
Most home runs by pinch-hitters, season	7 in 1974	

Most total bases	2177 in 1970 (162 games)
Most long hits	437 in 1977 (162 games)
Most extra bases on long hits	731 in 1970 (162 games)
Most sacrifice hits	109 in 1979 (162 games)
Most sacrifice flies	51 in 1972 (153 games)
Most stolen bases	194 in 1980 (163 games)
Most caught stealing	95 in 1979 (162 games)
	95 in 1983 (162 games)
Most bases on balls	699 in 1969 (162 games)
Most strikeouts	988 in 1968 (162 games)
Fewest strikeouts	719 in 1976 (162 games)
Most hit by pitch	49 in 1964 (162 games)
Fewest hit by pitch	13 in 1980 (163 games)
Most runs batted in	694 in 1970 (162 games)
Most game-winning RBIs	80 in 1980 (163 games)
Highest batting average	.263 in 1974 (162 games)
Lowest batting average	.220 in 1963 (162 games)
Most .300 hitters	3 in 1970
Highest slugging average	.393 in 1972 (153 games)
Lowest slugging average	.301 in 1963 (162 games)
Most grounded into double play	144 in 1970 (162 games)
Fewest grounded into double play	76 in 1983 (162 games)
Most left on bases	1212 in 1969 (162 games)
Fewest left on bases	1040 in 1964 (162 games)
Most putouts	4448 in 1980 (163 games)
Fewest putouts	4284 in 1964 (162 games)
Most assists	1880 in 1975 (162 games)
Fewest assists	1617 in 1978 (162 games)
Most chances accepted	6255 in 1975 (162 games)
Fewest chances accepted	5827 in 1972 (153 games)
Most errors	174 in 1966 (163 games)
Fewest errors	106 in 1971 (162 games)
Most errorless games	85 in 1973 (162 games)
	85 in 1974 (162 games)
Most consecutive errorless games	11 in 1973
Most double plays	166 in 1975 (162 games)
Fewest double plays	100 in 1963 (162 games)
Most passed balls	35 in 1983 (162 games)
Fewest passed balls	12 in 1970 (162 games)
Highest fielding average	.983 in 1971 (162 games)
Lowest fielding average	.972 in 1966 (163 games)
Most games won	93 in 1980
Most games lost	97 in 1965
	97 in 1975
Highest percentage games won, season	.571 in 1980 (won 93, lost 70)
Lowest percentage games won, season	.398 in 1975 (won 64, lost 97)
Games won, league	1664 in 22 years
Games lost, league	1837 in 22 years
Most shutouts won, season	19 in 1979, 1981
Most shutouts lost, season	23 in 1963
Most 1-0 games won, season	9 in 1976
Most 1-0 games lost, season	6 in 1964, 1969
Most consecutive games won, season	10 in 1965
	10 in 1969 (twice)
	10 in 1980
Most consecutive games lost, season	10 in 1963
	10 in 1967 (twice)
	10 in 1974
Most times league champions	0
Most times lowest percentage games won, season	2
Longest 1-0 game won	24 innings, Houston 1, New York 0, April 15, 1968
Longest 1-0 game lost	13 innings, Cincinnati 1, Houston 0, August 6, 1962
Most runs, inning	12, Houston vs. Philadelphia, May 31, 1975, eighth inning
Most runs, inning by opponent—	
	13, Atlanta vs. Houston, September 20, 1972, second inning
Most runs, game	Houston 18, San Francisco 4, July 7, 1971
	Houston 18, Chicago 2, April 29, 1974
Most runs, game, by opponent	St. Louis 19, Houston 8, September 30, 1965
	Montreal 19, Houston 3, June 17, 1979
Most home runs, game	5, Houston vs. Atlanta, April 12, 1970
	5, Houston vs. San Diego, June 26, 1972
	5, Houston vs. San Diego, June 21, 1973
	5, Houston vs. Cincinnati, September 12, 1977

Most consecutive games, one or more home runs ....10 (15 homers), 1973
Most home runs in consecutive games in which home runs were made—
                                                                                        15 (10 games), 1973
Most runs, shutout game...Houston 13, Cincinnati 0, June 4, 1983
Most runs, shutout game, by opponent ....Philadelphia 16, Houston 0, September 10, 1963
Most runs, doubleheader shutout...No performance
Most hits, game...25, Houston vs. Atlanta, May 30, 1976, second game
Most hits, extra-inning game—
                        25, Houston vs. Cincinnati, July 2, 1976, first game, 14 innings
Most total bases, game...36, Houston vs. Montreal, August 17, 1972

LOS ANGELES DODGERS—(1958 to date)
(See Brooklyn Dodgers for club's records prior to franchise transfer in 1958)

Most players	43 in 1958
Fewest players	30 in 1962
Most games	165 in 1962
Most at-bats	5642 in 1982 (162 games)
Most runs	842 in 1962 (165 games)
Fewest runs	470 in 1968 (162 games)
Most opponents' runs	761 in 1958 (154 games)
Fewest opponents' runs	490 in 1966 (162 games)
Most hits	1515 in 1970 (161 games)
Fewest hits	1234 in 1968 (162 games)
Most singles	1128 in 1970 (161 games)
Most doubles	251 in 1978 (162 games)
Most triples	67 in 1970 (161 games)
Most homers	191 in 1977 (162 games)
Most home runs with bases filled	6 in 1960, 1977, 1979
Most home runs by pinch-hitters, season	8 in 1983
Most long hits	442 in 1977 (162 games)
Most extra bases on long hits	852 in 1977 (162 games)
Most total bases	2336 in 1977 (162 games)
Most sacrifice hits	120 in 1964 (164 games)
Most sacrifice flies	64 in 1974 (162 games)
Most stolen bases	198 in 1962 (165 games)
Most caught stealing	77 in 1965 (162 games)
Most bases on balls	611 in 1975 (162 games)
Most strikeouts	980 in 1968 (162 games)
Fewest strikeouts	744 in 1976 (162 games)
Most hit by pitch	52 in 1968 (162 games)
Fewest hit by pitch	18 in 1968 (162 games)
Most runs batted in	781 in 1962 (165 games)
Most game-winning RBIs	86 in 1980 (163 games)
	86 in 1982 (162 games)
Highest batting average	.272 in 1974 (162 games)
Lowest batting average	.230 in 1968 (162 games)
Highest slugging average	.418 in 1977 (162 games)
Lowest slugging average	.319 in 1968 (162 games)
Most left on bases	1223 in 1982 (162 games)
Fewest left on bases	1012 in 1958 (154 games)
Most grounded into double play	145 in 1979 (162 games)
Fewest grounded into double play	79 in 1965 (162 games)
Most .300 hitters	4 in 1970
Most putouts	4473 in 1973 (162 games)
Fewest putouts	4105 in 1958 (154 games)
Most assists	1946 in 1982 (162 games)
Fewest assists	1573 in 1961 (154 games)
Most errors	193 in 1962 (165 games)
Fewest errors	114 in 1959 (156 games)
Most errorless games	90 in 1979 (162 games)
Most consecutive errorless games	11 in 1979
Most chances accepted	6411 in 1982 (162 games)
Fewest chances accepted	5708 in 1961 (154 games)
Most double plays	198 in 1959 (156 games)
Fewest double plays	106 in 1975 (162 games)
Most passed balls	24 in 1973 (162 games)
Fewest passed balls	6 in 1958 (154 games)
Highest fielding average	.981 in 1959 (156 games)
	.981 in 1973 (162 games)
	.981 in 1977 (162 games)
	.981 in 1979 (162 games)
	.981 in 1980 (163 games)

Lowest fielding average.. .970 in 1962 (165 games)
Most games won.. 102 in 1962
                                                                                                                       102 in 1974
                                                                                                                         89 in 1967
Most games lost ....
Highest percentage games won...630 in 1974 (won 102, lost 60)
Lowest percentage games won...451 in 1967 (won 73, lost 89)
Games won, league .... 2281 in 26 years
Games lost, league .... 1844 in 26 years
Most shutouts won, season... 24 in 1963
Most shutouts lost, season.. 23 in 1968
Most 1-0 games won, season.. 7 in 1963
Most 1-0 games lost, season.. 6 in 1964
                                                                                                                           6 in 1968
Most consecutive games won, season .... 13 in 1962
                                                                                                                         13 in 1965
Most consecutive games lost, season .... 10 in 1961
Most times league champions 8
Most times lowest percentage games won, season 0
Most runs, game................................ Los Angeles 19, San Diego 0, June 28, 1969
                                             Los Angeles 19, San Francisco 3, May 26, 1970
Most runs game, by opponent .... Chicago 20, Los Angeles 3, May 20, 1967
Most runs, shutout game ....Los Angeles 19, San Diego 0, June 28, 1969
Most runs shutout game by opponent ....Cincinnati 18, Los Angeles 0, August 8, 1965
Most runs doubleheader shutout................. 16, Los Angeles vs. Atlanta, September 19, 1971
Most runs inning .... 10, Los Angeles vs. San Diego, June 28, 1969, third inning
                          10, Los Angeles vs. San Francisco, July 4, 1971, eighth inning
                          10, Los Angeles vs. San Diego, September 13, 1977, second inning
Longest 1-0 game won ....15 innings, Los Angeles 1, New York 0, April 24, 1970
Longest 1-0 game lost .... 16 innings, Houston 1, Los Angeles 0, April 21, 1976
Most hits, game...24, Los Angeles vs. Chicago, August 20, 1974
Most home runs, game ....7, Los Angeles vs. Chicago, May 5, 1976
                                                     7, Los Angeles vs. Cincinnati, May 25, 1979
Most consecutive games, one or more home runs ....15 (23 homers), 1977
Most home runs in consecutive games in which home runs were made—
                                                                      23 (15 games), 1977
                                                                      23 (13 games), 1979
Most total bases, game ....48, Los Angeles vs. Chicago, August 20, 1974

MILWAUKEE BRAVES—(1953 through 1965)
(See Boston Braves for club's records prior to franchise transfer in 1953)

Most players... 42 in 1964 (162 games)
Fewest players .... 31 in 1953 (157 games)
                                                                                                                         31 in 1954 (154 games)
Most games .... 163 in 1963
Most at-bats.. 5591 in 1964 (162 games)
Most runs.. 803 in 1964 (162 games)
Fewest runs.. 670 in 1954 (154 games)
Most opponents' runs... 744 in 1964 (162 games)
Fewest opponents' runs... 541 in 1968 (154 games)
Most hits .... 1522 in 1964 (162 games)
Most singles.. 1057 in 1964 (162 games)
Most doubles .... 274 in 1964 (162 games)
Most triples .... 62 in 1957 (155 games)
Most homers.. 199 in 1957 (155 games)
Most home runs with bases filled .... 8 in 1962
Most home runs by pinch-hitters, season.................................... 7 in 1965
Most total bases... 2411 in 1957 (155 games)
Most long hits... 482 in 1957 (155 games)
Most extra bases on long hits .... 942 in 1957 (155 games)
Most sacrifice hits .... 142 in 1956 (155 games)
Most sacrifice flies .... 60 in 1960 (154 games)
Most stolen bases... 75 in 1963 (163 games)
Most caught stealing .... 52 in 1963 (163 games)
Most bases on balls.. 581 in 1962 (162 games)
Most strikeouts... 976 in 1965 (162 games)
Fewest strikeouts... 619 in 1954 (154 games)
Most hit by pitcher .... 38 in 1964 (162 games)
Most runs batted in .... 755 in 1964 (162 games)
Highest batting average .... .272 in 1964 (162 games)
Highest slugging average .... .442 in 1957 (155 games)
Most grounded into double play .... 134 in 1964 (162 games)

Fewest grounded into double play .... 99 in 1956 (155 games)
Most left on bases.. 1138 in 1962 (162 games)
1138 in 1963 (163 games)
Most .300 hitters .... 5 in 1964
Most players 100 or more runs... 3 in 1955, 1960
Most players 100 or more runs batted in ....2 in 1955, 1959, 1960, 1961
Most putouts .... 4416 in 1963 (163 games)
Most assists .... 1848 in 1961 (155 games)
1848 in 1963 (163 games)
Most chances accepted .... 6264 in 1963 (163 games)
Most errors.. 152 in 1955 (154 games)
Fewest errors.. 111 in 1961 (155 games)
Most consecutive errorless games....................................... 7 in 1954, 1956, 1964
Most double plays .... 173 in 1957 (155 games)
Most passed balls .... 28 in 1965 (162 games)
Fewest passed balls.............................5 in 1956 (155 games, 1959 (157 games)
Highest fielding average.. .982 in 1961 (155 games)
Most games won .... 95 in 1957
Most games lost... 78 in 1963
Highest percentage games won... .617 in 1957 (won 95, lost 59)
Lowest percentage games won... .519 in 1963 (won 84, lost 78)
Games won, league .... 1146 in 13 years
Games lost, league .... 890 in 13 years
Most shutouts won, season.. 18 in 1959, 1963
Most shutouts lost, season.. 13 in 1963
Most 1-0 games won, season.. 4 in 1963
Most consecutive games won, season .... 11 in 1956
Most consecutive games lost, season .... 8 in 1961
Most times league champions 2
Most times lowest percentage games won, season 0
Most runs, game .... Milwaukee 23, Chicago 10, September 2, 1957, first game
Most runs, shutout game.................... Milwaukee 15, Cincinnati 0, May 13, 1956, first game
Most runs, shutout game, by opponent—
Philadelphia 10, Milwaukee 0, July 21, 1953, first game
Most runs, doubleheader shutout.. No performance
Most runs, inning ...10, Milwaukee vs. Pittsburgh, June 12, 1953, second game, first inning
Longest 1-0 game won ....13 innings, Milwaukee 1, Pittsburgh 0, May 26, 1959
Longest 1-0 game lost........................16 innings, San Francisco 1, Milwaukee 0, July 2, 1963
Most hits, game............................26, Milwaukee vs. Chicago, September 2, 1957, first game
Most home runs, game..................8, Milwaukee vs. Pittsburgh, August 30, 1953, first game
Most consecutive games, one or more home runs....................22 (39 homers), 1956
Most home runs in consecutive games in which home runs were made—
39 (22 games), 1956
Most total bases, game................47, Milwaukee vs. Pittsburgh, August 30, 1953, first game

MONTREAL EXPOS—(1969 to date)

Most players... 47 in 1976 (162 games)
Fewest players .... 30 in 1972 (156 games)
Most games... 163 in 1983
Most at-bats... 5675 in 1977 (162 games)
Most runs... 701 in 1979 (160 games)
Fewest runs... 513 in 1972 (156 games)
Most opponents' runs... 807 in 1970 (162 games)
Fewest opponents' runs.. 581 in 1979 (160 games)
Most hits .... 1482 in 1983 (163 games)
Fewest hits .... 1205 in 1972 (156 games)
Most singles... 1042 in 1983 (163 games)
Most doubles .... 297 in 1983 (163 games)
Most triples .... 61 in 1980 (162 games)
Most homers... 143 in 1979 (160 games)
Most home runs with bases filled .... 5 in 1970
5 in 1973
5 in 1974
5 in 1983
Most home runs by pinch-hitters, season.................... 9 in 1973
Most total bases.. 2282 in 1977 (162 games)
Most long hits.. 482 in 1977 (162 games)
Most extra bases on long hits .... 808 in 1977 (162 games)
Most sacrifice hits.. 115 in 1973 (162 games)
Most sacrifice flies .... 57 in 1983 (163 games)
Most stolen bases.. 237 in 1980 (162 games)

Most caught stealing	82 in 1980 (162 games)
Most bases on balls	695 in 1973 (162 games)
Most strikeouts	972 in 1970 (162 games)
Fewest strikeouts	733 in 1983 (163 games)
Most hit by pitch	78 in 1971 (162 games)
Fewest hit by pitch	16 in 1976 (162 games)
Most runs batted in	656 in 1982 (162 games)
Most game-winning RBIs	83 in 1980 (162 games)
Highest batting average	.264 in 1979 (160 games)
	.264 in 1983 (163 games)
Lowest batting average	.234 in 1972 (156 games)
Highest slugging average	.408 in 1979 (160 games)
Lowest slugging average	.325 in 1972 (156 games)
Most grounded into double play	144 in 1973 (162 games)
Fewest grounded into double play	96 in 1972 (156 games)
Most left on bases	1232 in 1973 (162 games)
Fewest left on bases	1026 in 1979 (160 games)
Most .300 hitters	2 in 1973, 1982
Most putouts	4443 in 1977 (162 games)
Fewest putouts	4204 in 1972 (156 games)
Most assists	1956 in 1976 (162 games)
Fewest assists	1630 in 1982 (162 games)
Most chances accepted	6393 in 1975 (162 games)
Fewest chances accepted	5993 in 1972 (162 games)
Most errors	184 in 1969 (162 games)
Fewest errors	116 in 1983 (163 games)
Most errorless games	79 in 1982 (162 games)
Most consecutive errorless games, season	10 in 1977
Most double plays	193 in 1970 (162 games)
Fewest double plays	117 in 1982 (162 games)
Most passed balls	24 in 1973 (162 games)
Fewest passed balls	3 in 1978 (162 games)
Highest fielding average	.981 in 1983 (163 games)
Lowest fielding average	.971 in 1969 (162 games)
Most games won	95 in 1979
Most games lost	110 in 1969
Highest percentage games won, season	.594 in 1979 (won 95, lost 65)
Lowest percentage games won, season	.321 in 1969 (won 52, lost 110)
Games won, league	1118 in 15 years
Games lost, league	1248 in 15 years
Most shutouts won, season	18 in 1979
Most shutouts lost, season	20 in 1972
Most 1-0 shutouts won, season	4 in 1972
Most 1-0 shutouts lost, season	5 in 1982
Most consecutive games won, season	10 in 1979
	10 in 1980
Most consecutive games lost, season	20 in 1969
Most times league champions	0
Most times lowest percentage games won, season	2 (tied in 1969)

Most runs, inning ....11, Montreal vs. Atlanta, June 6, 1979, fourth inning
Most runs, game... Montreal 19, New York 8, July 3, 1973
Montreal 19, Chicago 3, July 4, 1977, first game
Montreal 19, Cincinnati 5, May 7, 1978, first game
Montreal 19, Atlanta 0, July 30, 1978
Montreal 19, Houston 3, June 17, 1979
Most runs game by opponent.....................Houston 17, Montreal 5, August 17, 1972
Most runs shutout game..Montreal 19, Atlanta 0, July 30, 1978
Most runs shutout game, by opponent ....St. Louis 16, Montreal 0, August 11, 1980
Most runs doubleheader shutout.........................14, Montreal vs. New York, August 5, 1975
Longest 1-0 game, won ....17 innings, Montreal 1, Philadelphia 0, September 21, 1981
Longest 1-0 game, lost.....................12 innings, Cincinnati 1, Montreal 0, September 1, 1972
Most hits, game..28, Montreal vs. Atlanta, July 30, 1978
Most home runs, game................................8, Montreal vs. Atlanta, July 30, 1978
Most consecutive games, one or more home runs ....10 (22 homers), 1969
Most home runs in consecutive games in which home runs were made—
22 (10 games), 1969
Most total bases, game ....58, Montreal vs. Atlanta, July 30, 1978

NEW YORK GIANTS—(1883 through 1957)

(See San Francisco Giants for club's records since franchise transfer in 1958)

Most players	49 in 1946
Fewest players	21 in 1905

Most games	158 in 1904, 1909, 1917
Most at-bats	5623 in 1935 (156 games)
Most runs	959 in 1930 (154 games)
Fewest runs	540 in 1956 (154 games)
Most opponents runs	814 in 1930 (154 games)
Most hits	1769 in 1930 (154 games)
Fewest hits	1217 in 1906 (152 games)
Most singles	1279 in 1930 (154 games)
Most doubles	276 in 1928 (155 games)
Most triples	105 in 1911 (154 games)
Most homers	221 in 1947 (155 games)
Most home runs with bases filled	7 in 1951, also 1954
Most home runs by pinch-hitters, season	10 in 1954
Most total bases	2628 in 1930 (154 games)
Most long hits	490 in 1930 (154 games)
Most extra bases on long hits	979 in 1947 (155 games)
Most sacrifices (S. H. and S. F.)	250 in 1908 (157 games)
Most sacrifice hits	166 in 1904 (158 games)
Most sacrifice flies	52 in 1954 (154 games)
Most stolen bases	347 in 1911 (154 games)
Most caught stealing	114 in 1921 (153 games)
Most bases on balls	671 in 1951 (157 games)
Most strikeouts	672 in 1952 (154 games)
Fewest strikeouts	376 in 1928 (155 games)
Most hit by pitch	52 in 1917 (158 games)
Fewest hit by pitch	15 in 1933 (156 games)
Most runs batted in	880 in 1930 (154 games)
Highest batting average	.319 in 1930 (154 games)
Lowest batting average	.243 in 1909 (158 games)
Highest slugging average	.473 in 1930 (154 games)
Lowest slugging average	.302 in 1906 (152 games)
Most grounded into double play	153 in 1939 (151 games)
Fewest grounded into double play	96 in 1952 (154 games)
Most left on bases	1214 in 1935 (156 games)
Fewest left on bases	975 in 1926 (151 games)
Most .300 hitters	8 in 1921
	8 in 1922
	8 in 1924
	8 in 1930
	8 in 1931
Most putouts	4306 in 1909 (158 games)
Fewest putouts	3964 in 1939 (151 games)
Most assists	2240 in 1920 (155 games)
Fewest assists	1660 in 1956 (154 games)
Most chances accepted	6472 in 1920 (155 games)
Fewest chances accepted	5794 in 1956 (154 games)
Most errors	307 in 1909 (158 games)
Fewest errors	137 in 1950 (154 games)
Most consecutive errorless games	8 in 1950
Most double plays	181 in 1950 (154 games)
Fewest double plays	112 in 1945 (154 games)
Most passed balls	26 in 1906 (152 games)
Fewest passed balls	4 in 1928 (155 games)
Highest fielding average	.977 in 1940 (152 games)
	.977 in 1942 (154 games)
	.977 in 1950 (154 games)
Lowest fielding average	.954 in 1909 (158 games)
Most games won	106 in 1904
Most games lost	98 in 1943
Highest percentage games won	.759 in 1885 (won 85, lost 27)
Highest percentage games won, since 1900	.693 in 1904 (won 106, lost 47)
Lowest percentage games won	.353 in 1902 (won 48, lost 88)
Games won, league	6067 in 75 years
Games lost, league	4898 in 75 years
Most shutouts won, season	25 in 1908
Most shutouts lost, season	20 in 1915
Most 1-0 games won	6 in 1907
	6 in 1933
Most 1-0 games lost	8 in 1907
Most consecutive games won, season	26 in 1916
Most consecutive games lost, season	13 in 1902, 1944
Most times league champions	17
Most times lowest percentage games won, season	5

Most runs, game.. New York 29, Philadelphia 1, June 15, 1887
Most times finished second.. 15
Most runs, game, since 1900.................New York 26, Brooklyn 8, April 30, 1944, first game
Most runs, game, by opponent .... Hartford 28, New York 3, May 13, 1876
Most runs, game, by opponent, since 1900 ....St. Louis 21, New York 5, August 2, 1948
Most runs, shutout game .... New York 24, Buffalo 0, May 27, 1885
Most runs, shutout game, since 1900 ....New York 16, Brooklyn 0, July 3, 1949
Most runs, shutout game, by opponent........................ Chicago 19, New York 0, June 7, 1906
Most runs, doubleheader shutout.........................19, New York vs. Cincinnati, July 31, 1949
Most runs, inning ....13, New York vs. Philadelphia, September 8, 1883, third inning
　　　　　　　　　　13, New York vs. Cleveland, July 19, 1890, first game, second inning
　　　　　　　　　　13, New York vs. St. Louis, May 13, 1911, first inning
Longest 1-0 game won .... 18 innings, New York 1, St. Louis 0, July 2, 1933, first game
Longest 1-0 game lost ....15 innings, Cincinnati 1, New York 0, July 16, 1933, first game
Most hits, game ....31, New York vs. Cincinnati, June 9, 1901
Most home runs, game..7, New York vs. Indianapolis, May 9, 1888
　　　　　　　　　　　　　　　　　　　7, New York vs. Cincinnati, June 6, 1939
　　　　　　　　　　7, New York vs. Philadelphia, August 13, 1939, first game
　　　　　　　　　　　　　　7, New York vs. Cincinnati, June 24, 1950
　　　　　　　　　　7, New York vs. Pittsburgh, July 8, 1956, first game
Most consecutive games, one or more home runs ....19 (33 homers), 1947
Most home runs in consecutive games in which home runs were made—
　　　　　　　　　　　　　　　　　　　37 (16 games) 1947
Most total bases, game...................47, New York vs. Philadelphia, July 11, 1931, first game

NEW YORK METS—(1962 to date)
(Includes records only of present franchise established in 1962)

Most players..	54 in 1967　(162 games)
Fewest players	34 in 1968　(163 games)
	34 in 1970　(162 games)
	34 in 1971　(162 games)
	34 in 1972　(156 games)
Most games	164 in 1965
Fewest games..	156 in 1972
Most at-bats..	5591 in 1979　(163 games)
Most runs..	695 in 1970　(162 games)
Fewest runs..	473 in 1968　(163 games)
Most opponents' runs...	948 in 1962　(161 games)
Most hits..	1430 in 1975　(162 games)
Fewest hits..	1154 in 1972　(156 games)
Most singles..	1087 in 1980　(162 games)
Most doubles	255 in 1979　(163 games)
Most triples	47 in 1978　(162 games)
Most homers..	139 in 1962　(161 games)
Most home runs with bases filled	5 in 1973
Most home runs by pinch-hitters	12 in 1983
Most total bases..	2018 in 1975　(162 games)
Most long hits..	373 in 1970　(162 games)
Most extra bases on long hits	663 in 1962　(161 games)
Most sacrifice hits..	108 in 1973　(161 games)
Most sacrifice flies	55 in 1978　(162 games)
Most stolen bases..	158 in 1980　(162 games)
Most caught stealing	99 in 1980　(162 games)
Most bases on balls..	684 in 1970　(162 games)
Most strikeouts..	1203 in 1968　(163 games)
Fewest strikeouts..	735 in 1974　(162 games)
Most hit by pitch..	48 in 1964　(163 games)
Fewest hit by pitch	23 in 1973　(161 games)
Most runs batted in..	640 in 1970　(162 games)
Most game-winning RBIs	63 in 1983　(162 games)
Highest batting average	.257 in 1980　(162 games)
Lowest batting average	.219 in 1963　(162 games)
Highest slugging average	.370 in 1970　(162 games)
Lowest slugging average..	.315 in 1963　(162 games)
	.315 in 1968　(163 games)
Most grounded into double play	148 in 1974　(162 games)
Fewest grounded into double play	104 in 1968　(163 games)
Most left on bases..	1228 in 1974　(162 games)
Fewest left on bases..	1032 in 1965　(164 games)
Most .300 hitters..	3 in 1964
Most putouts	4450 in 1968　(163 games)

Fewest putouts	4244 in 1972	(156 games)
Most assists	1995 in 1966	(161 games)
Fewest assists	1539 in 1972	(156 games)
Most chances accepted	6309 in 1965	(164 games)
Fewest chances accepted	5783 in 1972	(156 games)
Most errors	210 in 1962	(161 games)
	210 in 1963	(162 games)
Fewest errors	114 in 1971	(162 games)
Most errorless games	82 in 1969	(162 games)
Most consecutive errorless games, season	9 in 1977	
Most double plays	171 in 1966	(161 games)
	171 in 1983	(162 games)
Fewest double plays	116 in 1976	(162 games)
Most passed balls	32 in 1964	(163 games)
Fewest passed balls	2 in 1980	(162 games)
Highest fielding average	.981 in 1971	(162 games)
Lowest fielding average	.967 in 1962	(161 games)
	.967 in 1963	(162 games)
Most games won	100 in 1969	
Most games lost	120 in 1962	
Games won, league	1498 in 22	years
Games lost, league	1997 in 22	years
Highest percentage games won, season	.617 in 1969	(won 100, lost 62)
Lowest percentage games won, season	.250 in 1962	(won 40, lost 120)
Most shutouts won, season	28 in 1969	
Most shutouts lost, season	30 in 1963	
Most 1-0 games won, season	9 in 1969	
Most 1-0 games lost, season	8 in 1963	
Most consecutive games won, season	11 in 1969	
	11 in 1972	
Most consecutive games lost, season	17 in 1962	
Most times league champions	2	
Most times lowest percentage games won, season	8	

Most runs, inning............................10, New York vs. Cincinnati, June 12, 1979, sixth inning
Most runs, inning, by opponent.......11, St. Louis vs. New York, July 18, 1964, eighth inning
                              11, Houston vs. New York, July 30, 1969, first game, ninth inning
Most runs, game.. New York 20, Atlanta 6, August 7, 1971
Most runs, game, by opponent.....................................Montreal 19, New York 8, July 3, 1973
Most runs, shutout game.......................... New York 14, Chicago 0, July 29, 1965, first game
Most runs, shutout game, by opponent—
                              Chicago 12, New York 0, May 30, 1963, first game
                              Pittsburgh 12, New York 0, May 30, 1965, second game
                              Pittsburgh 12, New York 0, July 1, 1966
                              Chicago 12, New York 0, September 14, 1974
Most runs, doubleheader shutout................2, New York vs. Pittsburgh, September 12, 1969
Longest 1-0 game won............................15 innings, New York 1, Los Angeles 0, June 4, 1969
Longest 1-0 game lost................................24 innings, Houston 1, New York 0, April 15, 1968
Most hits, game...23, New York vs. Chicago, May 26, 1964
Most home runs, game ....5, New York vs. Philadelphia, April 28, 1962
                              5, New York vs. Cincinnati, August 3, 1962
                              5, New York vs. St. Louis, October 3, 1964
                              5, New York vs. Montreal, May 19, 1970
Most consecutive games, one or more home runs ....10 (14 homers), 1970
                              10 (15 homers) 1975
Most home runs in consecutive games in which home runs were made .17 (6 games), 1962
Most total bases, game..33, New York vs. Chicago, May 26, 1964
                              33, New York vs. St. Louis, October 3, 1964

PHILADELPHIA PHILLIES—(1883 to date)

Most players	49 in 1946	
Fewest players	23 in 1915	
Most games	163 in 1979, 1983	
Most at-bats	5667 in 1930	(156 games)
Most runs	944 in 1930	(156 games)
Fewest runs	394 in 1942	(151 games)
Most opponents' runs	1199 in 1930	(156 games)
Most hits	1783 in 1930	(156 games)
Fewest hits	1113 in 1907	(149 games)
Most singles	1338 in 1894	(132 games)
Most singles since 1900	1268 in 1930	(156 games)

Most doubles	345 in 1930 (156 games)
Most triples	148 in 1894 (132 games)
Most triples since 1900	82 in 1905 (155 games)
Most homers	186 in 1977 (162 games)
Most home runs by pinch-hitters, season	11 in 1958
Most home runs with bases filled	7 in 1925, 1929, 1976
Most total bases	2594 in 1930 (156 games)
Most long hits	519 in 1932 (154 games)
Most extra bases on long hits	936 in 1977 (162 games)
Most sacrifices, (S. H. and S. F.)	239 in 1909 (154 games)
Most sacrifice hits	174 in 1905 (155 games)
Most sacrifice flies	74 in 1977 (162 games)
Most stolen bases	200 in 1908 (155 games)
Most caught stealing	80 in 1921 (153 games)
Most bases on balls	652 in 1955 (154 games)
Most strikeouts	1130 in 1969 (162 games)
Fewest strikeouts	452 in 1924 (152 games)
Most hit by pitch	53 in 1962 (161 games)
Fewest hit by pitch	9 in 1939 (152 games)
Most runs batted in	884 in 1930 (156 games)
Most game-winning RBIs	86 in 1980 (162 games)
Highest batting average	.343 in 1894 (132 games)
Highest batting average since 1900	.315 in 1930 (156 games)
Lowest batting average	.232 in 1942 (151 games)
Highest slugging average	.467 in 1929 (154 games)
Lowest slugging average	.305 in 1907 (149 games)
Most grounded into double play	144 in 1950 (157 games)
Fewest grounded into double play	91 in 1935 (156 games)
	91 in 1973 (162 games)
Most left on bases	1272 in 1975 (162 games)
Fewest left on bases	991 in 1920 (153 games)
Most .300 hitters	10 in 1925
Most putouts	4440 in 1980 (162 games)
Fewest putouts	3887 in 1907 (149 games)
Most assists	2176 in 1921 (154 games)
Fewest assists	1437 in 1957 (156 games)
Most chances accepted	6440 in 1913 (159 games)
Fewest chances accepted	5545 in 1955 (154 games)
Most errors	403 in 1904 (155 games)
Fewest errors	104 in 1978 (162 games)
Most errorless games	89 in 1966 (162 games)
Most consecutive errorless games, season	11 in 1967
Most double plays	179 in 1961 (155 games)
	179 in 1973 (162 games)
Fewest double plays	117 in 1955 (154 games)
	117 in 1957 (156 games)
	117 in 1983 (163 games)
Most passed balls	27 in 1947 (155 games)
	27 in 1971 (162 games)
Fewest passed balls	3 in 1952 (154 games)
	3 in 1956 (154 games)
Highest fielding average	.983 in 1978 (162 games)
	.983 in 1979 (163 games)
Lowest fielding average	.936 in 1904 (155 games)
Most games won	101 in 1976, 1977
Most games lost	111 in 1941
Highest percentage games won	.623 in 1886 (won 71, lost 43)
	.623 in 1976 (won 101, lost 61)
	.623 in 1977 (won 101, lost 61)
Lowest percentage games won	.173 in 1883 (won 17, lost 81)
Lowest percentage games won since 1900	.279 in 1941 (won 43, lost 111)
Games won, league	7002 in 101 years
Games lost, league	8060 in 101 years
Most shutouts won, season	24 in 1916
Most shutouts lost, season	23 in 1908, 1909
Most 1-0 games won	7 in 1913
Most 1-0 games lost	10 in 1967
Most consecutive games won, season	16 in 1887, 1890, 1892
Most consecutive games won, season, since 1900	13 in 1977
Most consecutive games lost, season	23 in 1961
Most times league champions	4
Most times lowest percentage games won, season	24 (tied in 1947)
Most runs, game	Philadelphia 29, Louisville 4, August 17, 1894

Most runs, game, since 1900...............Philadelphia 23, Pittsburgh 8, July 13, 1900, 8 innings
Chicago 26, Philadelphia 23, August 25, 1922
Philadelphia 23, Chicago 22, May 17, 1979, 10 innings
Longest 1-0 game won..........15 innings, Philadelphia 1, Boston 0, June 22, 1944, first game
15 innings, Philadelphia 1, Boston 0, August 7, 1951, second game
15 innings, Philadelphia 1, Chicago 0, June 19, 1955, first game
Longest 1-0 game lost..................17 innings, Montreal 1, Philadelphia 0, September 21,1981
Most runs, game, by opponent .... Boston 29, Philadelphia 4, June 20, 1883
New York 29, Philadelphia 1, June 15, 1887
Most runs, game, by opponent, since 1900—
St. Louis 28, Philadelphia 6, July 6, 1929, second game
Most runs, shutout game .... Philadelphia 24, Indianapolis 0, June 28, 1887
Most runs, shutout game, since 1900—Philadelphia 18, Pittsburgh 0, July 11, 1910
Philadelphia 18, Cincinnati 0, August 10, 1930, first game
Most runs, shutout game, by opponent ....Providence 28, Philadelphia 0, August 21, 1883
Most runs, shutout game, by opponent, since 1900—
Chicago 16, Philadelphia 0, May 4, 1929, first game
Most runs doubleheader shutout ....18, Philadelphia vs. Brooklyn, September 26, 1912
Most runs, inning—12, Philadelphia vs. New York, October 2, 1897, second inning
12, Philadelphia vs. Chicago, July 21, 1923, first game, sixth inning
Most hits, game...36, Philadelphia vs. Louisville, August 17, 1894
Most hits, game, since 1900 .... 26, Philadelphia vs. Cincinnati, August 25, 1922
Most home runs, game ....6, Philadelphia vs. St. Louis, May 11, 1923
6, Philadelphia vs. Pittsburgh, August 28, 1948, second game
6, Philadelphia vs. Cincinnati, June 2, 1949
6, Philadelphia vs. San Francisco, April 27, 1965, night game
6, Philadelphia vs. Chicago, October 3, 1972
6, Philadelphia vs. Chicago, April 17, 1976, 10 innings
6, Philadelphia vs. Chicago, August 12, 1977
Most consecutive games, one or more home runs ....13 (16 homers), 1964
Most home runs in consecutive games in which home runs were hit.....18 (10 games), 1929
Most total bases, game ....49, Philadelphia vs. Louisville, August 17, 1894
Most total bases, game, since 1900..................43, Philadelphia vs. Cincinnati, May 15, 1911
Most total bases, extra-inning game, since 1900—
48, Philadelphia vs. Pittsburgh, July 23, 1930, second game, 13 innings
48, Philadelphia vs. Chicago, May 17, 1979, 10 innings

PITTSBURGH PIRATES—(1887 to date)

Most players..	45 in 1916, 1951, 1952
Fewest players	25 in 1938
Most games..	163 in 1965, 1967, 1968, 1979
Most at-bats...	5724 in 1967 (163 games)
Most runs...	912 in 1925 (153 games)
Fewest runs...	464 in 1917 (157 games)
Most opponents' runs..	928 in 1930 (154 games)
Most hits..	1698 in 1922 (155 games)
Fewest hits..	1197 in 1914 (158 games)
Most singles..	1297 in 1922 (155 games)
Most doubles	316 in 1925 (153 games)
Most triples...	129 in 1912 (152 games)
Most homers..	158 in 1966 (162 games)
Most home runs with bases filled	7 in 1978
Most home runs by pinch-hitters, season..............	8 in 1944
Most total bases...	2430 in 1966 (162 games)
Most long hits...	498 in 1925 (153 games)
Most extra bases on long hits	812 in 1979 (163 games)
Most sacrifices, (S. H. and S. F.)	214 in 1927 (156 games)
Most sacrifice hits...	190 in 1906 (154 games)
Most sacrifice flies	67 in 1982 (162 games)
Most stolen bases..	264 in 1907 (157 games)
Most caught stealing	120 in 1977 (162 games)
Most bases on balls...	607 in 1947 (156 games)
Most strikeouts...	1011 in 1966 (162 games)
Fewest strikeouts...	326 in 1922 (155 games)
Most hit by pitch	46 in 1917 (157 games)
	46 in 1969 (162 games)
Fewest hit by pitch	11 in 1937 (154 games)
Most runs batted in	844 in 1930 (154 games)
Most game-winning RBIs	80 in 1980 (162 games)
	80 in 1982 (162 games)
Highest batting average	.309 in 1928 (152 games)
Lowest batting average	.233 in 1914 (158 games)

Highest slugging average	.449 in 1930 (154 games)
Lowest slugging average	.298 in 1917 (157 games)
Most grounded into double play	142 in 1950 (154 games)
Fewest grounded into double play	95 in 1978 (161 games)
Most left on bases	1241 in 1936 (156 games)
Fewest left on bases	992 in 1924 (153 games)
Most .300 hitters	9 in 1928
Most putouts	4480 in 1979 (163 games)
Fewest putouts	3983 in 1934 (151 games)
Most assists	2089 in 1905 (155 games)
Fewest assists	1584 in 1934 (151 games)
Most chances accepted	6462 in 1968 (163 games)
Fewest chances accepted	5567 in 1934 (151 games)
Most errors	291 in 1904 (156 games)
Fewest errors	115 in 1983 (162 games)
Most errorless games	81 in 1968 (163 games)
Most consecutive errorless games	8 in 1958, 1963
Most double plays	215 in 1966 (162 games)
Fewest double plays	94 in 1935 (153 games)
Most passed balls	32 in 1953 (154 games)
Fewest passed balls	3 in 1941 (156 games)
	3 in 1943 (157 games)
Highest fielding average	.982 in 1983 (162 games)
Lowest fielding average	.955 in 1904 (156 games)
Most games won	110 in 1909
Most games lost	113 in 1890
Most games lost since 1900	112 in 1952
Highest percentage games won	.741 in 1902 (won 103, lost 36)
Lowest percentage games won	.169 in 1890 (won 23, lost 113)
Lowest percentage games won since 1900	.273 in 1952 (won 42, lost 112)
Games won, league	7627 in 97 years
Games lost, league	7034 in 97 years
Most shutouts won, season	26 in 1906
Most shutouts lost, season	27 in 1916
Most 1-0 games won	10 in 1908
Most 1-0 games lost	10 in 1914
Most consecutive games won, season	16 in 1909
Most consecutive games lost, season	23 in 1890
Most consecutive games lost, since 1900	12 in 1939
Most times league champions	9
Most times lowest percentage games won, season	10 (tied in 1947, 1957)
Most runs, game	Pittsburgh 27, Boston 11, June 6, 1894
Most runs, game, since 1900	Pittsburgh 24, St. Louis 6, June 22, 1925
Most runs, game, by opponent	Boston 28, Pittsburgh 14, August 27, 1887

Most runs, game, by opponent, since 1900—
Philadelphia 23, Pittsburgh 8, July 13, 1900, 8 innings
Brooklyn 23, Pittsburgh 6, July 10, 1943

Most runs, shutout game	Pittsburgh 22, Chicago 0, September 16, 1975
Most runs, shutout game, by opponent	Philadelphia 18, Pittsburgh 0, July 11, 1910
Most runs, doubleheader shutout	15, Pittsburgh vs. Philadelphia, August 7, 1915
Most runs, inning	12, Pittsburgh vs. St. Louis, April 22, 1892, first inning
	12, Pittsburgh vs. Boston, June 6, 1894, third inning

Most runs, inning, since 1900—
11, Pittsburgh vs. St. Louis, September 7, 1942, first game, sixth inning

Longest 1-0 game won	18 innings, Pittsburgh 1, San Diego 0, June 7, 1972, second game
Longest 1-0 game lost	14 innings, Cincinnati 1, Pittsburgh 0, June 18, 1943
Most hits, game	27, Pittsburgh vs. Philadelphia, August 8, 1922, first game
Most home runs, game	7, Pittsburgh vs. Boston, June 8, 1894
	7, Pittsburgh vs. St. Louis, August 16, 1947
Most consecutive games, one or more home runs	12 (26 homers) 1966
Most home runs in consecutive games in which home runs were hit	26 (12 games) 1966
Most total bases, game	47, Pittsburgh vs. Atlanta, August 1, 1970

ST. LOUIS CARDINALS—(1876-77; 1885-86; 1892 to date)

Most players	49 in 1959
Fewest players	25 in 1904
Most games	163 in 1962, 1971, 1975, 1979
Most at-bats	5734 in 1979 (163 games)
Most runs	1004 in 1930 (154 games)
Most opponents' runs	806 in 1929 (154 games)
Fewest runs	372 in 1908 (154 games)
Most hits	1732 in 1930 (154 games)

Fewest hits	1105 in 1908	(154 games)
Most singles	1223 in 1920	(155 games)
Most doubles	373 in 1939	(154 games)
Most triples	96 in 1920	(155 games)
Most homers	143 in 1955	(154 games)
Most home runs, with bases filled	7 in 1961	
Most home runs by pinch-hitters, season	7 in 1946, 1960	
Most total bases	2595 in 1930	(154 games)
Most long hits	566 in 1930	(154 games)
Most extra bases on long hits	863 in 1930	(154 games)
Most sacrifices (S. H. and S. F.)	212 in 1926	(156 games)
Most sacrifice hits	172 in 1943	(147 games)
Most sacrifice flies	66 in 1954	(154 games)
Most stolen bases	207 in 1983	(162 games)
Most caught stealing	112 in 1977	(162 games)
Most bases on balls	655 in 1910	(153 games)
Most strikeouts	977 in 1966	(162 games)
Fewest strikeouts	414 in 1925	(153 games)
Most hit by pitch	78 in 1910	(153 games)
Fewest hit by pitch	15 in 1925	(153 games)
Most runs batted in	942 in 1930	(154 games)
Most game-winning RBIs	87 in 1982	(162 games)
Highest batting average	.314 in 1930	(154 games)
Lowest batting average	.223 in 1908	(154 games)
Highest slugging average	.471 in 1930	(154 games)
Lowest slugging average	.288 in 1908	(154 games)
Most grounded into double play	166 in 1958	(154 games)
Fewest grounded into double play	75 in 1945	(155 games)
Most left on bases	1251 in 1939	(155 games)
Fewest left on bases	968 in 1924	(154 games)
Most .300 hitters	11 in 1930	
Most putouts	4460 in 1979	(163 games)
Fewest putouts	3952 in 1906	(154 games)
Most assists	2293 in 1917	(154 games)
Fewest assists	1595 in 1935	(154 games)
Most chances accepted	6459 in 1917	(154 games)
Fewest chances accepted	5752 in 1935	(154 games)
Most errors	348 in 1908	(154 games)
Fewest errors	112 in 1944	(157 games)
Most errorless games	82 in 1980	(162 games)
Most consecutive errorless games	11 in 1980	
Most double plays	192 in 1974	(161 games)
Fewest double plays	122 in 1922	(154 games)
Most passed balls	38 in 1906	(154 games)
Fewest passed balls	4 in 1925	(153 games)
Highest fielding average	.982 in 1944	(157 games)
Lowest fielding average	.946 in 1908	(154 games)
Most games won	106 in 1942	
Most games lost	111 in 1898	
Most games lost since 1900	105 in 1908	

Highest percentage games won	.703 in 1876 (won 45, lost 19)
Highest percentage games won since 1900	.688 in 1942 (won 106, lost 48)
Lowest percentage games won	.221 in 1897 (won 29, lost 102)
Lowest percentage games won since 1900	.314 in 1903 (won 43, lost 94)
Games won, league	7047 in 92 years
Games lost, league	6960 in 92 years
Most shutouts won, season	30 in 1968
Most shutouts lost, season	33 in 1908
Most 1-0 games won	8 in 1907
	8 in 1968
Most 1-0 games lost	8 in 1918
Most consecutive games won, season	14 in 1935
Most consecutive games lost, season	15 in 1909
Most times league champions	13
Most times lowest percentage games won, season	10 (tied in 1916)
Most runs, game	St. Louis 28, Philadelphia 6, July 6, 1929, second game
Most runs, game, by opponent	Boston 28, St. Louis 7, September 3, 1896, first game
Most runs, game, by opponent, since 1900	Pittsburgh 24, St. Louis 6, June 22, 1925
Most runs, inning	12, St. Louis vs. Philadelphia, Sept. 16, 1926, first game, third inning
Most runs, shutout game	St. Louis 18, Cincinnati 0, June 10, 1944
Most runs, shutout game, by opponent	Pittsburgh 19, St. Louis 0, August 3, 1961
Most runs doubleheader shutout	16, St. Louis vs. Brooklyn, September 21, 1934
Most hits, game	30, St. Louis vs. New York, June 1, 1895

Longest 1-0 game, won.....................................14 innings, St. Louis 1, Boston 0, June 15, 1939
Longest 1-0 game, lost..............18 innings, New York 1, St. Louis 0, July 2, 1933, first game
Most hits, since 1900 ....28, St. Louis vs. Philadelphia, July 6, 1929, second game
Most home runs, game...7, St. Louis vs. Brooklyn, May 7, 1940
Most consecutive games, one or more home runs ....12 (18 homers), 1955
Most home runs in consecutive games in which home runs were made—
                                               18 (12 games), 1955
Most total bases, game ....49, St. Louis vs. Brooklyn, May 7, 1940

SAN DIEGO PADRES—(1969 to date)

Most players........	42 in 1969 (162 games)
Fewest players	32 in 1973 (162 games)
Most games........	163 in 1980, 1983
Fewest games........	153 in 1972
Most at-bats........	5602 in 1977 (162 games)
Most runs........	692 in 1977 (162 games)
Fewest runs........	468 in 1969 (162 games)
Most opponents' runs........	834 in 1977 (162 games)
Most hits	1435 in 1982 (162 games)
Fewest hits	1181 in 1972 (153 games)
Most singles........	1105 in 1980 (163 games)
Most doubles	245 in 1977 (162 games)
Most triples	53 in 1979 (161 games)
Most homers........	172 in 1970 (162 games)
Most home runs with bases filled	4 in 1969, 1977, 1983
Most home runs by pinch-hitters, season........	5 in 1972
Most total bases........	2149 in 1970 (162 games)
Most long hits........	416 in 1970 (162 games)
Most extra bases on long hits	796 in 1970 (162 games)
Most sacrifice hits	133 in 1975 (162 games)
Most sacrifice flies	47 in 1982 (162 games)
Most stolen bases........	239 in 1980 (163 games)
Most caught stealing	77 in 1982 (162 games)
Most bases on balls........	602 in 1977 (162 games)
Most strikeouts........	1164 in 1970 (162 games)
Fewest strikeouts........	716 in 1976 (162 games)
Most hit by pitch	39 in 1970 (162 games)
Fewest hit by pitch	15 in 1973 (153 games)
Most runs batted in	652 in 1977 (162 games)
Most game-winning RBIs	76 in 1983 (163 games)
Most .300 hitters	2 in 1978
Highest batting average	.257 in 1982 (162 games)
Lowest batting average	.225 in 1969 (162 games)
Highest slugging average	.391 in 1970 (162 games)
Lowest slugging average	.329 in 1969 (162 games)
Most grounded into double play	134 in 1971 (161 games)
Fewest grounded into double play	81 in 1978 (162 games)
Most left on bases........	1239 in 1980 (163 games)
Fewest left on bases........	1006 in 1972 (153 games)
Most putouts	4428 in 1982 (162 games)
Fewest putouts........	4211 in 1972 (153 games)
Most assists	2012 in 1980 (163 games)
Fewest assists	1621 in 1972 (153 games)
Most chances accepted	6411 in 1980 (163 games)
Fewest chances accepted	5832 in 1972 (153 games)
Most errors........	189 in 1977 (162 games)
Fewest errors........	132 in 1980 (163 games)
Most errorless games........	75 in 1980 (163 games)
Most consecutive errorless games........	7 in 1973
Most double plays	171 in 1978 (162 games)
Fewest double plays	126 in 1974 (162 games)
Most passed balls........	21 in 1969 (162 games)
	21 in 1977 (162 games)
Fewest passed balls	3 in 1970 (162 games)
	3 in 1974 (162 games)
Highest fielding average........	.980 in 1980 (163 games)
Lowest field average average	.971 in 1975 (162 games)
	.971 in 1977 (162 games)
Most games won........	84 in 1978
Most games lost........	110 in 1969
Games won, league........	995 in 15 years
Games lost, league	1372 in 15 years

Highest percentage games won, season .... .519 in 1978 (won 84, lost 78)
Lowest percentage games won, season .... .321 in 1969 (won 52, lost 110)
Most shutouts won, season.. 17 in 1972
Most shutouts lost, season.. 23 in 1969
                                                                                                  23 in 1976
Most 1-0 shutouts won, season .... 5 in 1972
Most 1-0 shutouts lost, season .... 4 in 1972, 1978
Most consecutive games won, season .... 11 in 1982
Most consecutive games lost, season .... 11 in 1969
Most times league champions... 0
Most times lowest percentage games won, season..........................5 (tied in 1969)
Most runs, inning ....9, San Diego vs. Cincinnati, May 3, 1969, first inning
Most runs, nine-inning game .... San Diego 16, Philadelphia 2, July 26, 1970
                                                                   San Diego 16, San Francisco 13, April 5, 1983
Most runs, extra-inning game .....San Diego 17, San Francisco 16, May 23, 1970, 15 innings
Most runs, game, by opponent .... Chicago 23, San Diego 6, May 17, 1977
Most runs, shutout game.............................. San Diego 12, San Francisco 0, October 3, 1980
Most runs, shutout game, by opponent...................... Chicago 19, San Diego 0, May 13, 1969
                                                                  Los Angeles 19, San Diego 0, June 28, 1969
Most runs, doubleheader shutout... No performance
Longest 1-0 game won—
                          14 innings, San Diego 1, Cincinnati 0, August 4, 1974, second game
Longest 1-0 game lost ......18 innings, Pittsburgh 1, San Diego 0, June 7, 1972, second game
Most hits, game ....24, San Diego vs. San Francisco, April 19, 1982
Most home runs, nine-inning game ....4, San Diego vs. Philadelphia, May 5, 1970
                                                                  4, San Diego vs. Atlanta, July 3, 1970, second game
                                                                  4, San Diego vs. Philadelphia, July 26, 1970
                                                                  4, San Diego vs. Los Angeles, April 11, 1971
                                                                  4, San Diego vs. Cincinnati, September 26, 1973
                                                                  4, San Diego vs. Atlanta, April 18, 1977
                                                                  4, San Diego vs. Chicago, August 5, 1977
Most home runs, extra-inning game—
                          5, San Diego vs. San Francisco, May 23, 1970, 15 innings
Most consecutive games, one or more home runs ....10 (15 homers), 1970
Most home runs in consecutive games in which home runs were made—
                                                                                          18 (8 games), 1970
Most total bases, nine-inning game......................33, San Diego vs. Pittsburgh, June 2, 1970
Most total bases, extra-inning game—
                          39, San Diego vs. San Francisco, May 23, 1970, 15 innings

SAN FRANCISCO GIANTS—(1958 to date)

(See New York Giants for club's records prior to franchise transfer in 1958)

Most players...	41 in 1983	(162 games)
Fewest players...	31 in 1968	(163 games)
Most games...	165 in 1962	
Most at-bats...	5588 in 1962	(165 games)
Most runs...	878 in 1962	(165 games)
Fewest runs..	573 in 1980	(161 games)
Most opponents' runs..	826 in 1970	(162 games)
Most hits..	1552 in 1962	(165 games)
Fewest hits...	1281 in 1972	(155 games)
Most singles...	1081 in 1962	(165 games)
Most doubles..	257 in 1970	(162 games)
Most triples..	62 in 1960	(156 games)
Most homers...	204 in 1962	(165 games)
Most home runs with bases filled	7 in 1970	
Most home runs by pinch-hitters, season...................	11 in 1977	
Most long hits..	471 in 1962	(165 games)
Most extra bases on long hits	911 in 1962	(165 games)
Most total bases..	2463 in 1962	(165 games)
Most sacrifice hits...	127 in 1978	(162 games)
Most sacrifice flies	54 in 1980	(161 games)
Most stolen bases..	140 in 1979	(162 games)
	140 in 1983	(162 games)
Most caught stealing	78 in 1983	(162 games)
Most bases on balls..	729 in 1970	(162 games)
Most strikeouts..	1054 in 1969	(162 games)
Fewest strikeouts...	764 in 1961	(155 games)
Most hit by pitch	66 in 1969	(162 games)
Fewest hit by pitch..	14 in 1969	(161 games)
Most runs batted in...	807 in 1962	(165 games)
Most game-winning RBIs	82 in 1982	(162 games)

Highest batting average	.278 in 1962	(165 games)
Lowest batting average	.239 in 1968	(163 games)
Highest slugging average	.441 in 1962	(165 games)
Lowest slugging average	.341 in 1968	(163 games)
Most left on bases	1280 in 1969	(162 games)
Fewest left on bases	983 in 1961	(155 games)
Most grounded into double play	149 in 1965	(163 games)
Fewest grounded into double play	96 in 1959	(154 games)
Most .300 hitters	4 in 1962	
Most putouts	4429 in 1966	(161 games)
Fewest putouts	4129 in 1959	(154 games)
Most assists	1940 in 1976	(162 games)
Fewest assists	1513 in 1961	(155 games)
Most errors	186 in 1976	(162 games)
Fewest errors	133 in 1961	(155 games)
Most errorless games	74 in 1965	(163 games)
	74 in 1967	(162 games)
Most consecutive errorless games	8 in 1962	
Most chances accepted	6349 in 1969	(162 games)
Fewest chances accepted	5677 in 1961	(155 games)
Most double plays	164 in 1975	(161 games)
Fewest double plays	109 in 1983	(162 games)
Most passed balls	30 in 1970	(162 games)
Fewest passed balls	6 in 1978	(162 games)
Highest fielding average	.979 in 1967	(162 games)
Lowest fielding average	.971 in 1976	(162 games)
Most games won	103 in 1962	
Most games lost	91 in 1979	
Highest percentage games won	.624 in 1962 (won 103, lost 62)	
Lowest percentage games won	.438 in 1979 (won 71, lost 91)	
Games won, league	2156 in 26 years	
Games lost, league	1966 in 26 years	
Most shutouts won, season	20 in 1968	
Most shutouts lost, season	17 in 1968	
	17 in 1976	
Most 1-0 games won, season	6 in 1968	
Most 1-0 games lost, season	4 in 1972, 1978	
Most consecutive games won, season	14 in 1965	
Most consecutive games lost, season	8 in 1977, 1979	
Most times league champions	1	
Most times lowest percentage games won, season	0	

Most runs, inning............................13, San Francisco vs. St. Louis, May 7, 1966, third inning
Most runs, game..........San Francisco 19, Philadelphia 2, September 12, 1958, second game
San Francisco 19, Chicago 3, July 4, 1961, first game
San Francisco 19, Los Angeles 8, April 16, 1962
Most runs, game, by opponent ....20, August 13, 1959; Chicago 20, San Francisco 9
Most runs, shutout game .... San Francisco 14, Cincinnati 0, August 23, 1961
Most runs, shutout game, by opponent ....Chicago 15, San Francisco 0, August 22, 1970
Most runs, doubleheader shutout......................13, San Francisco vs. Chicago, April 29, 1962
Longest 1-0 game won ....21 innings, San Francisco 1, Cincinnati 0, September 1, 1967
Longest 1-0 game lost ....14 innings, New York 1, San Francisco 0, August 19, 1969
Most hits, game ....26, San Francisco vs. Los Angeles, May 13, 1958
Most home runs, game ....8, San Francisco vs. Milwaukee, April 30, 1961
Most consecutive games, one or more home runs ....16 (22 homers), 1962
16 (30 homers), 1963
Most home runs in consecutive games in which home runs were made—
30 (16 games), 1963
Most total bases, game..................................50, San Francisco vs. Los Angeles, May 13, 1958

Attendance Records

AMERICAN LEAGUE

Club	Single Day Game	Doubleheader	Night Game
Baltimore	51,956 (April 5, 1982)	51,883 (Oct. 1, 1982)	51,649 (Aug. 16, 1980)
Boston	36,388 (Apr. 22, 1978)	41,766 (Aug. 12, 1934)	36,228 (June 28, 1949)
California	62,020 (Oct. 3, 1982)	41,723 (Aug. 5, 1978)	63,073 (Apr. 23, 1983)
Chicago	51,560 (April 14, 1981)	55,555 (May 20, 1973)	53,940 (June 8, 1951)
Cleveland	74,420 (April 7, 1973)	84,587 (Sept. 12, 1954)	78,382 (Aug. 20, 1948)
Detroit	57,888 (Sept. 26, 1948)	58,369 (July 20, 1947)	56,586 (Aug. 9, 1948)
•Kansas City	41,329 (Sept. 21, 1980)	42,039 (Aug. 8, 1983)	41,860 (July 26, 1980)
‡Kansas City	34,065 (Aug. 27, 1961)	35,147 (Aug. 18, 1962)	33,471 (April 29, 1955)
Milwaukee	55,120 (April 12, 1977)	54,630 (July 6, 1979)	55,716 (July 3, 1982)
Minnesota	46,463 (June 26, 1977)	43,419 (July 16, 1967)	52,279 (April 6, 1982)
New York	73,205 (April 19, 1931)	81,841 (May 30, 1938)	74,747 (May 26, 1947)
Oakland	48,758 (June 6, 1970)	48,592 (May 3, 1981)	49,300 (Aug. 25, 1980)
Philadelphia	37,534 (May 16, 1937)	38,800 (July 13, 1931)	37,383 (June 27, 1947)
St. Louis	34,625 (Oct. 1, 1944)	31,932 (June 27, 1928)	22,847 (May 24, 1940)
*Seattle	23,657 (Aug. 3, 1969)	18,147 (June 20, 1969)	20,490 (May 28, 1969)
xSeattle	47,353 (May 15, 1977)	25,344 (July 24, 1977)	57,762 (April 6, 1977)
Texas	40,078 (April 8, 1978)	42,163 (July 10, 1982)	43,709 (July 23, 1983)
Toronto	44,649 (April 7, 1977)	45,102 (Aug. 2, 1983)	39,347 (June 28, 1979)
§Washington	31,728 (April 19, 1948)	35,563 (July 4, 1936)	30,701 (June 17, 1947)
†Washington	45,125 (April 7, 1969)	40,359 (June 14, 1964)	30,421 (July 31, 1962)

†Washington second club. §Washington original club (now Minnesota). ‡Former Kansas City club (now Oakland). •Present Kansas City club. *Original Seattle club (now Milwaukee). xPresent Seattle club.

NATIONAL LEAGUE

Club	Single Day Game	Doubleheader	Night Game
Atlanta	51,275 (June 26, 1966)	50,597 (July 4, 1972)	53,775 (April 8, 1974)
Boston	41,527 (Aug. 8, 1948)	47,123 (May 22, 1932)	39,549 (Aug. 5, 1946)
Brooklyn	37,512 (Aug. 30, 1947)	41,209 (May 30, 1934)	35,583 (Sept. 24, 1949)
Chicago	46,572 (May 18, 1947)	46,965 (May 31, 1948)	No lights
Cincinnati	53,390 (April 11, 1976)	53,328 (July 9, 1976)	53,790 (Sept. 17, 1983)
Houston	49,442 (Sept. 5, 1965)	45,115 (Aug. 4, 1979)	50,908 (June 22, 1966)
Los Angeles	78,672 (April 18, 1958)	72,140 (Aug. 16, 1961)	67,550 (April 12, 1960)
Milwaukee	48,642 (Sept. 27, 1959)	47,604 (Sept. 3, 1956)	46,944 (Aug. 27, 1954)
Montreal	57,694 (Aug. 15, 1982)	59,282 (Sept. 16, 1979)	57,121 (Oct. 3, 1980)
‡New York	54,922 (April 20, 1941)	60,747 (May 31, 1937)	51,790 (May 27, 1947)
§New York	56,738 (June 23, 1968)	57,175 (June 13, 1965)	56,658 (May 13, 1966)
Philadelphia	60,120 (May 6, 1973)	63,346 (Aug. 10, 1979)	63,501 (July 5, 1982)
Pittsburgh	51,726 (June 6, 1976)	49,341 (July 16, 1972)	48,846 (July 16, 1970)
St. Louis	50,548 (Sept. 14, 1975)	49,743 (June 23, 1968)	50,340 (July 2, 1977)
San Diego	44,227 (May 2, 1982)	43,473 (June 13, 1976)	50,569 (April 24, 1976)
San Fran.	56,196 (April 10, 1979)	53,178 (July 31, 1983)	55,920 (June 20, 1978)

52,608 admitted free, August 10, 1981, Atlanta at San Diego.
‡Former New York club (now San Francisco). §Present New York club.

AMERICAN LEAGUE ALL-TIME CLUB SEASON RECORD

Club	Home	Year	Finished	Road	Year	Finished
Baltimore	2,042,071	1983	First (E)	1,854,401	1983	First (E)
Boston	2,353,114	1979	Third (E)	2,183,113	1978	Second (E)
California	2,807,360	1982	First (W)	1,897,660	1982	First (W)
Chicago	2,132,821	1983	First (W)	1,657,869	1982	Third (W)
Cleveland	2,620,627	1948	First	1,762,564	1948	First
Detroit	2,031,847	1968	First	1,793,315	1983	Second (E)
Kansas City‡	2,288,714	1980	First (W)	1,628,236	1979	Second (W)
Kansas City§	1,393,054	1955	Sixth	938,214	1967	Tenth
Milwaukee	2,397,131	1983	Fifth (E)	1,885,884	1983	Fifth (E)
Minnesota	1,483,547	1967	Second	1,502,733	1983	xFifth (W)
New York	2,627,417	1980	First (E)	2,460,645	1980	First (E)
Oakland	1,735,489	1982	Fifth (W)	1,709,054	1982	Fifth (W)
Philadelphia	945,076	1948	Fourth	1,562,360	1948	Fourth
St. Louis	712,918	1922	Second	1,170,349	1948	Sixth
Seattle y	677,944	1969	Sixth (W)	889,578	1969	Sixth (W)
Seattle z	1,338,511	1977	Sixth (W)	1,492,526	1983	Seventh (W)
Texas	1,519,671	1979	Third (W)	1,587,236	1979	Third (W)
Toronto	1,930,415	1983	Fourth (E)	1,713,302	1983	Fourth (E)
Washington*	1,027,216	1946	Fourth	1,055,171	1948	Seventh
Washington†	918,106	1969	Fourth (E)	1,042,638	1968	Tenth

American League Attendance, Season...11,150,099 in 1948 (8-club league)
11,336,923 in 1967 (10-club league)
14,657,802 in 1976 (12-club league)
23,991,053 in 1983 (14-club league)

*Original Washington club (now Minnesota). †Second Washington club (now Texas). ‡Present Kansas City club. §Former Kansas City club (now Oakland). xTied for position. yOriginal Seattle club (now Milwaukee). zPresent Seattle club.

NATIONAL LEAGUE ALL-TIME CLUB SEASON RECORD

Club	Home	Year	Finished	Road	Year	Finished
Atlanta	2,119,935	1983	Second (W)	1,985,595	1982	First (W)
Boston	1,455,439	1948	First	1,308,175	1947	Third
Brooklyn	1,807,526	1947	First	1,863,542	1947	First
Chicago	1,674,993	1969	Second (E)	1,827,275	1982	Fifth (E)
Cincinnati	2,629,708	1976	First (W)	2,320,693	1978	Second (W)
Houston	2,278,217	1980	First (W)	1,838,719	1980	First (W)
Los Angeles	3,608,881	1982	Second (W)	2,250,191	1982	Second (W)
Milwaukee	2,215,404	1957	First	1,633,569	1959	Second
Montreal	2,320,651	1983	Third (E)	1,713,662	1979	Second (E)
New York*	1,600,793	1947	Fourth	1,228,330	1949	Fifth
New York†	2,697,749	1970	Third (E)	1,673,050	1970	Third (E)
Philadelphia	2,775,011	1979	Fourth (E)	1,912,647	1979	Fourth (E)
Pittsburgh	1,705,828	1960	First	2,197,247	1980	Third (E)
St. Louis	2,317,914	1983	Fourth (E)	1,914,537	1983	Fourth (E)
San Diego	1,670,107	1978	Fourth (W)	1,740,929	1982	Fourth (W)
San Francisco	1,795,356	1960	Fifth	2,207,530	1966	Second

National League Attendance, Season...10,684,963 in 1960 (8-club league)
15,015,471 in 1966 (10-club league)
21,549,285 in 1983 (12-club league)

*Former New York club (now San Francisco). †Present New York club.

OPENING DAY AT HOME

American League				National League		
Club	Attendance	Year		Club	Attendance	Year
Baltimore	52,034	1982		Atlanta	*53,775	1974
Boston	35,343	1969		Boston	25,000	1935
California	*38,076	1981		Brooklyn	34,530	1949
Chicago	51,560	1981		Chicago	45,777	1978
Cleveland	74,420	1973		Cincinnati	52,949	1976
Detroit	54,089	1971		Houston	*42,652	1965
Kansas City§	31,895	1955		Los Angeles	78,672	1958
Kansas City‡	*40,700	1981		Milwaukee	43,640	1955
Milwaukee	55,120	1977		Montreal	57,592	1977
Minnesota	*52,279	1982		New York z	54,393	1936
New York	55,579	1983		New York‡	52,812	1966
Oakland	*48,348	1982		Philadelphia	*60,404	1981
Philadelphia	32,825	1927		Pittsburgh	51,695	1973
St. Louis	19,561	1923		St. Louis	*47,568	1970
Seattle†	14,993	1969		San Diego	*46,375	1977
Seattle‡	*57,762	1977		San Francisco	56,196	1979
Texas	40,078	1978				
Toronto	44,649	1977				
Washington x	31,728	1948				
Washington y	45,125	1969				

*Night game. §Former club (now Oakland). ‡Present club. †Former club (now Milwaukee). xOriginal club (now Minnesota). ySecond club (now Texas). zFormer club (now San Francisco).

Index to Contents

THE LEADERS YEAR-BY-YEAR

ALL-TIME GREAT INDIVIDUAL CAREER RECORDS
AND PERFORMANCES

ALL-TIME GREAT INDIVIDUAL CAREER RECORDS
AND PERFORMANCES—Continued

INDIVIDUAL BATTING RECORDS

INDIVIDUAL BATTING RECORDS—Continued

INDIVIDUAL BATTING RECORDS—Continued

INDIVIDUAL BASE-RUNNING RECORDS

INDIVIDUAL PITCHING RECORDS

INDIVIDUAL FIELDING RECORDS

INDIVIDUAL SERVICE RECORDS

INDIVIDUAL SERVICE RECORDS—Continued

CLUB (AS A TEAM) BATTING—
SEASON RECORDS

CLUB (AS A TEAM) BATTING—INNING, GAME,
DOUBLEHEADER

CLUB (AS A TEAM) BASE-RUNNING RECORDS

CLUB (AS A TEAM) PITCHING RECORDS

CLUB FIELDING RECORDS—ALL-TIME, BY INDIVIDUALS

CLUB FIELDING (AS A TEAM)

CLUB RECORDS FOR LEAGUE AND SEASON

NOTES

NOTES

NOTES

NOTES

NOTES